Cover Image:
Japanese, lacquered manuscript box
with tray (detail), 19th Century.

The Metropolitan Museum of Art,
bequest of Benjamin Altman, 1913
(14.40.883a–c)

ADVENTURES
in Reading

ATHENA EDITION

HOLT, RINEHART AND WINSTON
Harcourt Brace & Company

Austin • **New York** • Orlando • Atlanta • San Francisco • Boston • Dallas • Toronto • London

Staff Credits

EDITORIAL
Project Director: Fannie Safier
Editorial Coordinator: Katie Vignery
Editorial Staff: Lynda Abbott, Sally Ahearn, Judith Austin-Mills, Laura Baci, Amanda Beard, Richard Blake, Susan Britt, Robert Carranza, Daniela Guggenheim, Scott Hall, Bobbi Hernandez, Constance D. Israel, Susan Lynch, Mary Malone, Jennifer Osborne, Marie Hoffman Price, Sara Schroeder, Amy D.D. Simpson, Atietie O. Tonwe
Editorial Support: Carla M. Beer, Ruth Hooker, Margaret Guerrero
Editorial Permissions: Carrie Jones
Software Development: Armin Gutzmer, Lydia Doty

DESIGN AND PHOTO RESEARCH
Design: Pun Nio, *Senior Art Director;* Richard Metzger, *Design Supervisor;* Diane Motz, *Senior Designer;* Debora Diane Hildreth, *Designer*
Photo: Debra Saleny, *Photo Research Manager;* V. Sing Griffin Bitzer, Yvonne Gerin, Ann Gillespie, Jeannie Taylor, *Photo Researchers*

PRODUCTION
Beth Prevelige, *Senior Production Manager;* Simira Davis, *Production Assistant;* Sergio Durante, *Secretary;* George Prevelige; *Production Manager;* Rose Degollado, *Production Coordinator*
Electronic Publishing: Carol Martin, *Electronic Publishing Manager;* Kristy Sprott, *Electronic Publishing Supervisor;* Debra Schorn, *Electronic Publishing Senior Coordinator;* Lana Castle, Denise Haney, David Hernandez, Maria Homic, Barbara Hudgens, Mercedes Newman, Monica Shomos, *Electronic Publishing Staff*

Cover Design: Design 5

Curriculum AND Writing

Ken Holmes
Lincoln High School
East St. Louis, Illinois

Carroll Moulton
Formerly of Duke University
Durham, North Carolina

Contributors AND Critical Readers

Christine O'Donnell Allen
Bonanza High School
Las Vegas, Nevada

Cheryl Bromley Jones
Sandwich High School
Sandwich, Massachusetts

Joseph Claro
St. Francis Preparatory School
Fresh Meadows, New York

Grace N. Lomba
Alfred Lawless High School
New Orleans, Louisiana

Jane E. Davis
Milton High School
Alpharetta, Georgia

Linda E. Sanders
Jenks High School
Jenks, Oklahoma

Neil F. Hurdle
Milford Mill Academy
Baltimore, Maryland

Acknowledgments

For permission to reprint copyrighted material, grateful acknowledgment is made to the following sources:

Margaret Walker Alexander: "Lineage" from *This Is My Century: New and Collected Poems* by Margaret Walker Alexander. Copyright 1942 by Yale University Press; copyright renewed © 1970 by Margaret Walker Alexander. Published by the University of Georgia Press, 1989.

Samuel Allen: "To Satch" by Samuel Allen from *I Am the Darker Brother: An Anthology of Modern Poems by Black Americans,* edited by Arnold Adoff. Copyright © 1968 by Samuel W. Allen.

American-Scandinavian Foundation: "The Eclipse" by Selma Lagerlöf, translated by Velma Swanston Howard from *American-Scandinavian Review,* December 1922.

Arte Público Press, University of Houston: "Bribe" from *Chants* by Pat Mora. Copyright © 1983 by Pat Mora.

Toni Cade Bambara: "My Delicate Heart Condition" by Toni Cade Bambara. Copyright © 1965 and renewed © 1993 by Toni Cade Bambara.

Elizabeth Barnett, Literary Executor: "The Fawn" from *Collected Poems* by Edna St. Vincent Millay. Copyright © 1934, 1962 by Edna St. Vincent Millay and Norma Millay Ellis. Published by HarperCollins.

Susan Bergholz Literary Services, New York: "Straw into Gold: The Metamorphosis of the Everyday" by Sandra Cisneros. Copyright © 1987 by Sandra Cisneros. First published under the title "A Writer's Voyage" in *The Texas Observer,* September 1987.

BOA Editions, Ltd., 92 Park Avenue, Brockport, NY 14420: "if something should happen" from *good woman: poems and a memoir 1969–1980* by Lucille Clifton. Copyright © 1987 by Lucille Clifton.

The Estate of Heinrich Böll, c/o of Joan Daves Agency as agent for the proprietor: "The Balek Scales" by Heinrich Böll from *18 Stories of Heinrich Böll,* translated by Leila Vennewitz. Copyright © 1966 by Heinrich Böll.

Brandt & Brandt Literary Agents, Inc.: "The Most Dangerous Game" by Richard Connell. Copyright 1924 by Richard Connell; copyright renewed © 1952 by Louise Fox Connell. "Mozart and the Gray Steward" from *The Angel That Troubled the Waters* by Thornton Wilder. Copyright © 1928 by Coward-McCann, Inc.; copyright renewed © 1956 by Thornton Wilder. ALL RIGHTS RESERVED. Caution: *Mozart and the Gray Steward* is the sole property of the author and is fully protected by copyright. It may not be acted by professionals or amateurs without formal permission and the payment of a royalty. All rights including but not limited to professional, amateur, stock, radio and television, broadcasting, motion picture, recitation, lecturing, public reading, and the rights of translation into foreign languages are reserved. All inquiries should be addressed to Robert A. Freedman Dramatic Agency, Inc., 1501 Broadway, Suite 2310, New York, NY 10036.

José Antonio Burciaga: Adaptation of "La Puerta" by José Antonio Burciaga. Copyright © 1992 by José Antonio Burciaga. Comment on "La Puerta" by José Antonio Burciaga. Copyright © 1996 by José Antonio Burciaga.

Capra Press: "A Taste of Snow" from *Beyond Manzanar* by Jeanne Wakatsuki Houston. Copyright © 1985 by Jeanne Wakatsuki Houston.

Judith Ortiz Cofer: "Learning to Walk Alone" from *Penelope's Journal* by Judith Ortiz Cofer. Copyright © 1988 by Judith Ortiz Cofer. First published in *The Kenyon Review,* October 4, 1988. Comment on "Learning to Walk Alone" by Judith Ortiz Cofer. Copyright © 1996 by Judith Ortiz Cofer.

Bill Cooper Associates, Inc.: "The Fifty-First Dragon" adapted from *The Collected Edition of Heywood Hale Broun.* Copyright 1921 and renewed 1941 by Heywood Hale Broun.

Carl Cowl, Administrator for the Archives of Claude McKay: "A Song of the Moon" from *Selected Poems of Claude McKay.* Copyright © 1979 by Harcourt Brace & Company.

Doubleday, a division of Bantam Doubleday Dell Publishing Group, Inc.: "The Meadow Mouse" from *The Collected Poems of Theodore Roethke.* Copyright © 1963 by Beatrice Roethke, Administratrix of the Estate of Theodore Roethke.

The Ecco Press: "Illuminations" from *Descending Figure* by Louise Glück. Copyright © 1980 by Louise Glück. Published by The Ecco Press in 1980.

Farrar, Straus & Giroux, Inc.: "Medusa" from *The Blue Estuaries* by Louise Bogan. Copyright © 1968 by Louise Bogan. "A Summer's Reading" from *The Magic Barrel* by Bernard Malamud. Copyright © 1958 and renewed © 1986 by Bernard Malamud.

Harcourt Brace & Company: Abridgment of "Great Expectations" by Charles Dickens from *Adventures in Reading,* Laureate Edition, Volume 4, by Evan Lodge, Marjorie Braymer, and Herbert Potell. Copyright © 1963 by Harcourt Brace & Company; copyright renewed © 1991 by Deborah Jean Lodge, Alice Lodge, Jeanne M. Shutes, Jessica Sand, Lydia Winderman, Florence E. Potell and Mary Rives Bowman. "Art Review" from *Afternoon of a Pawnbroker and Other Poems* by Kenneth Fearing. Copyright 1943 by Kenneth Fearing; copyright renewed © 1971 by Bruce Fearing. "The Necklace" by Guy de Maupassant, translated by Newbury LeB. Morse from *Adventures in Reading,* Laureate Edition, Volume 1, by Evan Lodge and Marjorie Braymer. Copyright © 1963 by Harcourt Brace & Company; copyright renewed © 1991 by Deborah Jean Lodge, Alice Lodge, Jeanne M. Shutes, Jessica Sand, Lydia Winderman, Florence E. Potell and Mary Rives Bowman. Notes to *Romeo and Juliet* by William Shakespeare from *Adventures in Reading,* Laureate Edition, Volume 3, by Evan Lodge and Marjorie Braymer. Copyright © 1963 by Harcourt Brace & Company; copyright renewed © 1991 by Deborah Jean Lodge, Alice Lodge, Jeanne M. Shutes, Jessica Sand, Lydia Winderman, Florence E. Potell and Mary Rives Bowman. "The Pacing Goose" from *The Friendly Persuasion* by Jessamyn West. Copyright 1945 and renewed © 1973 by Jessamyn West.

HarperCollins Publishers, Inc.: "By Any Other Name" from *Gifts of Passage* by Santha Rama Rau. Copyright © 1951 by Vasanthi Rama Rau Bowers. "Security" from *One Man's Meat* by E. B. White. Copyright 1938 and renewed © 1966 by E. B. White.

Hirt Music Inc.: "The Gamut" from *The Poetry of Maya Angelou.* Copyright © 1969 by Hirt Music Inc.

Henry Holt and Company, Inc.: "At Woodward's Gardens," "Desert Places," and "It Bids Pretty Fair" from *The Poetry of Robert Frost,* edited by Edward Connery Lathem. Copyright 1936 by Robert Frost; copyright renewed © 1964, 1975 by Lesley Frost Ballantine; copyright 1947, © 1968, 1969 by Henry Holt and Company, Inc. "Loveliest of trees, the cherry now" from "A Shropshire Lad"–Authorised Edition–from *The Collected Poems of A. E. Housman.* Copyright 1939, 1940, © 1965 by Henry Holt and Company, Inc.; copyright © 1967, 1968 by Robert E. Symons.

Houghton Mifflin Company: Pronunciation key from *The American Heritage Dictionary of the English Language.* Copyright © 1981 by Houghton Mifflin Company. *Houghton Mifflin Company:* From *Silent Spring* by Rachel Carson. Copyright © 1962 by Rachel L. Carson. "The Pond" from *The Complete Poetical Works of Amy Lowell.* Copyright © 1955 by Houghton Mifflin Company; copyright renewed © 1983 by Houghton Mifflin Company, Brinton P. Roberts, Esquire and G. D'Andelot Belin, Esquire. All rights reserved.

Jeanne Wakatsuki Houston: Comment on "A Taste of Snow" by Jeanne Wakatsuki Houston. Copyright © 1996 by Jeanne Wakatsuki Houston.

James Hurst: "The Scarlet Ibis" by James Hurst from *The Atlantic Monthly,* July 1960. Copyright © 1960 and renewed © 1988 by James Hurst.

International Creative Management, Inc.: "The Portable Phonograph" from *The Watchful Gods and Other Stories* by Walter Van Tilburg Clark.

v

Contents

**SHORT
STORIES**

NONFICTION

POETRY

Types of Poetry

DRAMA

AN EPIC POEM
THE ODYSSEY

THE NOVEL

WRITING ABOUT LITERATURE

SHORT STORIES

Stories can be found anywhere and everywhere. Think of the number of different stories that might be inspired by the painting shown on these pages. Examine the painting closely. Use your imagination to write a story. Some of the following suggestions may help you freewrite your first thoughts.

1. Sit on the settee with this woman and speak with her. What is her story? What is her mood?
2. Become this woman yourself and tell her tale. What was her past? What is her present? What is her future? Does this day have any special meaning?
3. Open the book on this woman's lap. Is it her diary? What has she written? Take a look and see what it says. Maybe this is not her own diary. To whom does it belong then? Has she read something that has hurt her? surprised her?

Have members of the class share their varied stories. As you listen to other students' stories, note what works well. Save your draft until you have read some of the stories in this unit. You may wish to return to your draft and rewrite your story, applying the techniques and strategies you have learned from other writers.

Madame Monet on the Couch by Claude Monet (1840–1926). Oil on canvas.
Musée D'Orsay

*I*t is customary to begin the study of short stories with the element of plot. Plot is the organized pattern of events in a story. Sometimes the plot is relatively simple and straightforward, as in "The Most Dangerous Game." Sometimes the plot is more complicated; there may be more than one action to follow. Occasionally, a plot is constructed to lead to an ingenious surprise at the end, such as the famous surprise ending of "The Gift of the Magi."

In some stories, plot is the most important element. Readers keep reading to find out what will happen next. But in most stories, the characters are of primary importance. Generally, a story focuses on a main character. Although "Secrets" tells us about the different members of a family, it is Jean who is at the center of the action.

Another element is point of view. Point of view is like the camera in a movie, the lens through which you, the reader, view the action. "Rules of the Game" is told from a first-person point of view, by the central character in the story. Other stories are told from the third-person point of view, as if the action were seen by an objective observer who merely records what happens. Still other stories are told by an omniscient (all-knowing) narrator, who tells not only what happens but what the characters think and feel.

Just as every story has a point of view, so every story has a setting, the time and place of the action. Some settings are strange and exotic, such as Ship-Trap Island in "The Most Dangerous Game." Some settings are familiar, such as the neighborhood in "A Summer's Reading."

Finally, many short stories do more than entertain readers. They also express a theme, an idea about life. Occasionally, a theme is expressed directly through the author's comments, but generally theme is not directly stated—it must be inferred from other elements in the story.

Readers who enter imaginatively into a short story read actively, asking questions as they read and noting their own reactions to characters and events. The better you understand how such elements as plot, character, setting, point of view, and theme work together, the better you will understand and appreciate the author's intent and meaning.

Guidelines for Close Reading

1. Read actively for both pleasure and insight. Ask yourself questions as you read. Short stories provide us with entertainment, and they can also provide us with greater understanding of ourselves and others. Keep both aims in mind as you read.

2. Ask questions about unfamiliar words and references. If you are unable to get the meaning of a word from its context, look it up in a standard dictionary or other reference work.

3. Make predictions as you read. Ask yourself, "What will happen next?" Become aware of your response to the plot as it unfolds.

4. Draw conclusions about the characters by asking how they are presented and how they develop. Be aware of details that reveal characters and their values indirectly. Authors often do not tell us things directly but allow us to draw inferences from evidence in their stories.

5. Look for clues that tell you what the setting is. As you read, be aware of how the setting affects characters and plot.

6. Note from which point of view the story is told. Ask yourself why the author chooses a narrator who takes part in the action or an outside observer.

7. Ask yourself about the central idea or theme—the underlying meaning of the work. In reading a story, ask what it shows about human nature. State this central idea in a sentence. For example: People who live in harmony with the natural world accept its difficulties as well as its blessings.

Here is a brief story that has been read carefully by one reader. The comments in the margin show how this reader has responded to the story. If you like, make notes of your own on a separate sheet of paper, covering up the printed notes as you read. You may wish to compare your responses with these printed comments at a later point.

ONE READER'S RESPONSE

What kind of eclipse? solar? lunar? Or is there another meaning? Why this title?

I think this must be somewhere in Scandinavia because of the names.

This is not a good land for farming—it's rocky and there's not enough sunlight.

Moving the soil reminds me of how my father transported rich soil to a new home where the soil wasn't good for gardening.

These women work very hard for their crop of potatoes. They are lonely during the day.

References to America sound like a yearning for a better life elsewhere.

The Eclipse

SELMA LAGERLÖF

Translated by Velma Swanston Howard

There were Stina of Ridgecôte and Lina of Birdsong and Kajsa of Littlemarsh and Maja of Skypeak and Beda of Finn-darkness and Elin, the new wife on the old soldier's place, and two or three other peasant women besides—all of them lived at the far end of the parish, below Storhöjden, in a region so wild and rocky none of the big farm owners had bothered to lay hands on it.

One had her cabin set up on a shelf of rock, another had hers put up at the edge of a bog, while a third had one that stood at the crest of a hill so steep it was a toilsome climb getting to it. If by chance any of the others had a cottage built on more favorable ground, you may be sure it lay so close to the mountain as to shut out the sun from autumn fair time clear up to Annunciation Day.[1]

They each cultivated a little potato patch close by the cabin, though under serious difficulties. To be sure, there were many kinds of soil there at the foot of the mountain, but it was hard work to make the patches of land yield anything. In some places they had to clear away so much stone from their fields, it would have built a cow-house on a manorial estate;[2] in some they had dug ditches as deep as graves, and in others they had brought their earth in sacks and spread it on the bare rocks. Where the soil was not so poor, they were forever fighting the tough thistle and pigweed which sprang up in such profusion you would have thought the whole potato land had been prepared for their benefit.

All the livelong day the women were alone in their cabins; for even where one had a husband and children, the man went off to his work every morning and the children went to school. A few among the older women had grown sons and daughters, but they had gone to America. And some there were with little

---

1. **Annunciation Day:** March 25, the day commemorating the appearance of the angel Gabriel to Mary (Luke 1:26–38).
2. **manorial** (mă-nôr′ē-əl) **estate:** The manor was the main house or mansion located on a large, landed estate.

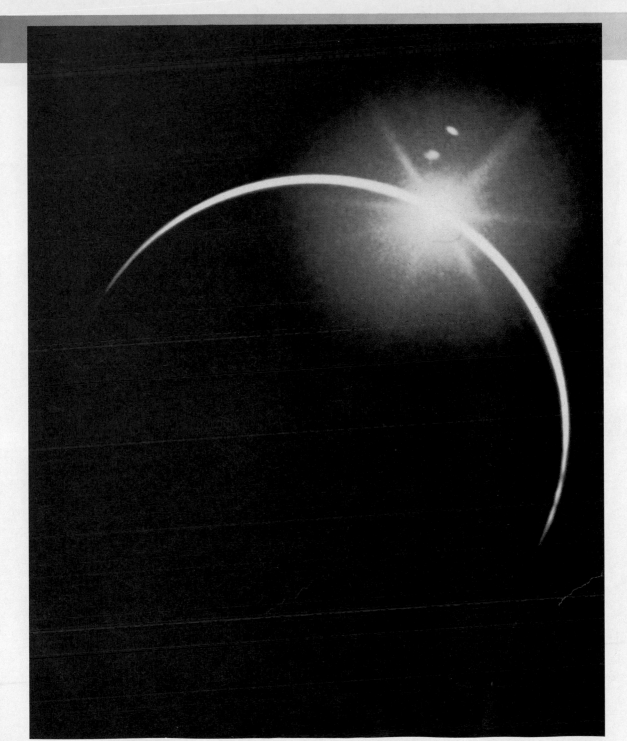

Earth eclipsing the sun. Photograph taken aboard *Apollo 12*.

The Potato Harvest by Arkadi Plastov.

children, who were always around, of course; but these could hardly be regarded as company.

Being so much alone, it was really necessary that they should meet sometimes over the coffee cups. Not that they got on so very well together, nor had any great love for each other; but some liked to keep posted on what the others were doing, and some grew despondent living like that, in the shadow of the mountain, unless they met people now and then. And there were those, too, who needed to unburden their hearts, and talk about the last letter from America, and those who were naturally talkative and jocular,[3] and who longed for opportunity to make use of these happy God-given talents.

Nor was it any trouble at all to prepare for a little party.

3. **jocular** (jŏk′yə-lər): given to joking.

Coffeepot and coffee cups they all had of course, and cream could be got at the manor, if one had no cow of one's own to milk; fancy biscuits and small cakes one could, at a pinch, get the dairyman's driver to fetch from the municipal[4] bakery, and country merchants who sold coffee and sugar were to be found everywhere. So, to get up a coffee party was the easiest thing imaginable. The difficulty lay in finding an occasion.

For Stina of Ridgecôte, Lina of Birdsong, Kajsa of Little-marsh, Maja of Skypeak, Beda of Finn-darkness, and Elin, the new wife at the old soldier's, were all agreed that it would never do for them to celebrate in the midst of the common everyday life. Were they to be that wasteful of the precious hours which never return, they might get a bad name. And to hold coffee parties on Sundays or great Holy Days was out of the question; for then the married women had husband and children at home, which was quite company enough. As for the rest—some liked to attend church, some wished to visit relatives, while a few preferred to spend the day at home, in perfect peace and stillness, that they might really feel it was a Holy Day.

Therefore they were all the more eager to take advantage of every possible opportunity. Most of them gave parties on their name days,[5] though some celebrated the great event when the wee little one cut its first tooth, or when it took its first steps. For those who received money-letters from America, that was always a convenient excuse, and it was also in order to invite all the women of the neighborhood to come and help tack a quilt or stretch a web just off the loom.

All the same, there were not nearly as many occasions to meet as were needed. One year one of the women was at her wits' end. It was her turn to give a party, and she had no objection to carrying out what was expected of her; but she could not seem to hit upon anything to celebrate. Her own name day she could not celebrate, being named Beda, as Beda had been stricken out of the almanac. Nor could she celebrate that of any member of her family, for all her dear ones were resting in the churchyard. She was very old, and the quilt she slept under would probably outlast her. She had a cat of which she was very

These coffee parties remind me of what my mother and her neighbors used to do sometimes after the children left for school.

My mother's friends would meet often to make curtains or wallpaper just as these women meet to make a quilt. One woman was always in charge of refreshments.

---

4. **municipal** (myo͞o-nĭs′ə-pəl): city.
5. **name days:** The name day is the feast day of the saint after whom a person is named or the day of baptism.

fond. Truth to tell, it drank coffee just as well as she did; but she could hardly bring herself to hold a party for a cat!

Pondering, she searched her almanac again and again, for there she felt she must surely find the solution of her problem.

She began at the beginning, with "The Royal House" and "Signs and Forecasts," and read on, right through to "Markets and Postal Transmittances for 1912," without finding anything.

As she was reading the book for the seventh time, her glance rested on "Eclipses." She noted that that year, which was the year of our Lord nineteen-hundred twelve, on April seventeenth there would be a solar eclipse. It would begin at twenty minutes past high noon and end at 2:40 o'clock, and would cover nine-tenths of the sun's disk.

This she had read before, many times, without attaching any significance to it; but now, all at once, it became dazzlingly clear to her.

"Now I have it!" she exclaimed.

But it was only for a second or two that she felt confident; and then she put the thought away, fearing that the other women would just laugh at her.

The next few days, however, the idea that had come to her when reading her almanac kept recurring to her mind, until at last she began to wonder whether she hadn't better venture.[6] For when she thought about it, what friend had she in all the world she loved better than the Sun? Where her hut lay not a ray of sunlight penetrated her room the whole winter long. She counted the days until the Sun would come back to her in the spring. The Sun was the only one she longed for, the one who was always friendly and gracious to her and of whom she could never see enough.

She looked her years, and felt them, too. Her hands shook as if she were in a perpetual chill and when she saw herself in the looking glass, she appeared so pale and washed out, as if she had been lying out to bleach. It was only when she stood in a strong, warm, down-pouring sunshine that she felt like a live human being and not a walking corpse.

The more she thought about it, the more she felt there was no day in the whole year she would rather celebrate than the one

6. **venture** (vĕn'chər): dare, take a chance, or risk something.

when her friend the Sun battled against darkness, and after a glorious conquest, came forth with new splendor and majesty.

The seventeenth of April was not far away, but there was ample time to make ready for a party. So, on the day of the eclipse Stina, Lina, Kajsa, Maja, and the other women all sat drinking coffee with Beda at Finn-darkness. They drank their second and third cups, and chatted about everything imaginable. For one thing, they said they couldn't for the life of them understand why Beda should be giving a party.

Meanwhile, the eclipse was under way. But they took little notice of it. Only for a moment, when the sky turned blackish gray, when all nature seemed under a leaden pall,[7] and there came driving a howling wind with sounds as of the Trumpet of Doom and the lamentations of Judgment Day[8]—only then did they pause and feel a bit awed. But here they each had a fresh cup of coffee, and the feeling soon passed.

When all was over, and the Sun stood out in the heavens so beamingly happy—it seemed to them it had not shone with such brilliancy and power the whole year—they saw old Beda go over to the window, and stand with folded hands. Looking out toward the sunlit slope, she sang in her quavering[9] voice:

> *Thy shining sun goes up again,*
> *I thank Thee, O my Lord!*
> *With new-found courage, strength and hope,*
> *I raise a song of joy.*

Thin and transparent, old Beda stood there in the light of the window, and as she sang the sunbeams danced about her, as if wanting to give her, also, of their life and strength and color.

When she had finished the old hymn-verse she turned and looked at her guests, as if in apology.

"You see," she said, "I haven't any better friend than the Sun, and I wanted to give her a party on the day of her eclipse. I felt that we should come together to greet her, when she came out of her darkness."

7. **leaden pall:** gloomy atmosphere. A *pall* is a dark covering.
8. **Trumpet...Day:** the day of God's final judgment; doomsday.
9. **quavering:** trembling.

Is something bad going to happen because of the "blackish gray" sky?

I think an eclipse is a good idea for a party.

I can understand why these women love the sun and think of it as a friend.

Now they understood what old Beda meant, and their hearts were touched. They began to speak well of the Sun. "She was kind to rich and poor alike, and when she came peeping into the hut on a winter's day, she was as comforting as a glowing fire on the hearth. Just the sight of her smiling face made life worth living, whatever the troubles one had to bear."

The women went back to their homes after the party, happy and content. They somehow felt richer and more secure in the thought that they had a good, faithful friend in the Sun.

A coffee party, c. 1880.

Photograph by Bannister, Norwegian-American Historical Association

Looking at Yourself as a Reader

Compare your own responses with the marginal comments. Using the guidelines on page 3, evaluate the reader's responses. Do you agree or disagree with any of these responses?

Develop your own impression of the story in one of the following ways:

1. Write a letter to Beda, telling her what you think of her idea for a party. Be sure to include information from the story. When you have finished, share your letter with a partner or small group. Compare letters. What do you learn from others' responses to the story?

2. Write a statement that best expresses the overall purpose or main idea of the story. List several pieces of evidence to support your statement. Share your ideas with a small group or with the class. What similarities and differences are there in other readers' responses? After listening to various interpretations of the story's meaning, do you still support your statement or will you create a new one?

The Most Dangerous Game

RICHARD CONNELL

*From the time of its publication, in 1924, this story has been greatly admired
for its original plot and skillful use of suspense. As you read, try to determine
what meaning the title has. Does it have more than one meaning?*

"Off there to the right—somewhere—is a large
island," said Whitney. "It's rather a mystery——"

"What island is it?" Rainsford asked.

"The old charts call it 'Ship-Trap Island,'"
Whitney replied. "A suggestive name, isn't it?
Sailors have a curious dread of the place. I
don't know why. Some superstition——"

"Can't see it," remarked Rainsford, trying to
peer through the dank tropical night that was
palpable as it pressed its thick warm blackness
in upon the yacht.

"You've good eyes," said Whitney, with a
laugh, "and I've seen you pick off a moose
moving in the brown fall bush at four hundred
yards, but even you can't see four miles or so
through a moonless Caribbean night."

"Nor four yards," admitted Rainsford.
"Ugh! It's like moist black velvet."

"It will be light in Rio," promised Whitney.
"We should make it in a few days. I hope the
jaguar guns have come from Purdey's.[1] We
should have some good hunting up the Amazon. Great sport, hunting."

"The best sport in the world," agreed
Rainsford.

"For the hunter," amended Whitney. "Not
for the jaguar."

"Don't talk rot, Whitney," said Rainsford.
"You're a big-game hunter, not a philosopher.
Who cares how a jaguar feels?"

"Perhaps the jaguar does," observed
Whitney.

"Bah! They've no understanding."

"Even so, I rather think they understand one

---

1. **Purdey:** a famous English manufacturer of hunting rifles and shotguns.

thing—fear. The fear of pain and the fear of death."

"Nonsense," laughed Rainsford. "This hot weather is making you soft, Whitney. Be a realist. The world is made up of two classes—the hunters and the huntees. Luckily, you and I are hunters. Do you think we've passed that island yet?"

"I can't tell in the dark. I hope so."

"Why?" asked Rainsford.

"The place has a reputation—a bad one."

"Cannibals?" suggested Rainsford.

"Hardly. Even cannibals wouldn't live in such a Godforsaken place. But it's gotten into sailor lore, somehow. Didn't you notice that the crew's nerves seemed a bit jumpy today?"

"They were a bit strange, now you mention it. Even Captain Nielsen——"

"Yes, even that tough-minded old Swede, who'd go up to the devil himself and ask him for a light. Those fishy blue eyes held a look I never saw there before. All I could get out of him was: 'This place has an evil name among seafaring men, sir.' Then he said to me, very gravely: 'Don't you feel anything?'—as if the air about us was actually poisonous. Now, you mustn't laugh when I tell you this—I did feel something like a sudden chill.

"There was no breeze. The sea was as flat as a plate-glass window. We were drawing near the island then. What I felt was a—a mental chill; a sort of sudden dread."

"Pure imagination," said Rainsford. "One superstitious sailor can taint the whole ship's company with his fear."

"Maybe. But sometimes I think sailors have an extra sense that tells them when they are in danger. Sometimes I think evil is a tangible thing—with wavelengths, just as sound and light have. An evil place can, so to speak, broadcast vibrations of evil. Anyhow, I'm glad we're getting out of this zone. Well, I think I'll turn in now, Rainsford."

"I'm not sleepy," said Rainsford. "I'm going to smoke another pipe up on the afterdeck."

"Good night, then, Rainsford. See you at breakfast."

"Right. Good night, Whitney."

There was no sound in the night as Rainsford sat there, but the muffled throb of the engine that drove the yacht swiftly through the darkness, and the swish and ripple of the wash of the propeller.

Rainsford, reclining in a steamer chair, indolently puffed on his favorite brier. The sensuous drowsiness of the night was on him. "It's so dark," he thought, "that I could sleep without closing my eyes; the night would be my eyelids——"

An abrupt sound startled him. Off to the right he heard it, and his ears, expert in such matters, could not be mistaken. Again he heard the sound, and again. Somewhere, off in the blackness, someone had fired a gun three times.

Rainsford sprang up and moved quickly to the rail, mystified. He strained his eyes in the direction from which the reports had come, but it was like trying to see through a blanket. He leaped upon the rail and balanced himself there, to get greater elevation; his pipe, striking a rope, was knocked from his mouth. He lunged for it; a short, hoarse cry came from his lips as he realized he had reached too far and had lost his balance. The cry was pinched off short as the blood-warm waters of the Caribbean Sea closed over his head.

He struggled up to the surface and tried to cry out, but the wash from the speeding yacht slapped him in the face and the salt water in his open mouth made him gag and strangle. Desperately he struck out with strong strokes after the receding lights of the yacht, but he stopped before he had swum fifty feet. A certain coolheadedness had come to him; it was not the first time he had been in a tight place. There was a chance that his cries could be heard by someone aboard the yacht, but that chance was slender, and grew more slender as the yacht raced on. He wrestled himself out of his clothes, and shouted with all his power. The lights of the yacht became faint and ever-vanishing fireflies; then they were blotted out entirely by the night.

Rainsford remembered the shots. They had come from the right, and doggedly he swam in that direction, swimming with slow, deliberate strokes, conserving his strength. For a seemingly endless time he fought the sea. He began to count his strokes; he could do possibly a hundred more and then——

Rainsford heard a sound. It came out of the darkness, a high screaming sound, the sound of an animal in an extremity of anguish and terror.

He did not recognize the animal that made the sound; he did not try to; with fresh vitality he swam toward the sound. He heard it again; then it was cut short by another noise, crisp, staccato.

"Pistol shot," muttered Rainsford, swimming on.

Ten minutes of determined effort brought another sound to his ears—the most welcome he had ever heard—the muttering and growling of the sea breaking on a rocky shore. He was almost on the rocks before he saw them; on a night less calm he would have been shattered against them. With his remaining strength he dragged himself from the swirling waters. Jagged crags appeared to jut up into the opaqueness; he forced himself upward, hand over hand. Gasping, his hands raw, he reached a flat place at the top. Dense jungle came down to the very edge of the cliffs. What perils that tangle of trees and underbrush might hold for him did not concern Rainsford

just then. All he knew was that he was safe from his enemy, the sea, and that utter weariness was on him. He flung himself down at the jungle edge and tumbled headlong into the deepest sleep of his life.

When he opened his eyes he knew from the position of the sun that it was late in the afternoon. Sleep had given him new vigor; a sharp hunger was picking at him. He looked about him, almost cheerfully.

"Where there are pistol shots, there are men. Where there are men, there is food," he thought. But what kind of men, he wondered, in so forbidding a place? An unbroken front of snarled and ragged jungle fringed the shore.

He saw no sign of a trail through the closely knit web of weeds and trees; it was easier to go along the shore, and Rainsford floundered along by the water. Not far from where he had landed, he stopped.

Some wounded thing, by the evidence a large animal, had thrashed about in the underbrush; the jungle weeds were crushed down and the moss was lacerated; one patch of weeds was stained crimson. A small, glittering object not far away caught Rainsford's eye and he picked it up. It was an empty cartridge.

"A twenty-two," he remarked. "That's odd. It must have been a fairly large animal too. The hunter had his nerve to tackle it with a light gun. It's clear that the brute put up a fight. I suppose the first three shots I heard was when the hunter flushed his quarry[2] and wounded it. The last shot was when he trailed it here and finished it."

He examined the ground closely and found what he had hoped to find—the print of hunting boots. They pointed along the cliff in the direction he had been going. Eagerly he hurried along, now slipping on a rotten log or a

2. **flushed his quarry:** forced the game that was being hunted into the open.

loose stone, but making headway; night was beginning to settle down on the island.

Bleak darkness was blacking out the sea and jungle when Rainsford sighted the lights. He came upon them as he turned a crook in the coastline, and his first thought was that he had come upon a village, for there were many lights. But as he forged along he saw to his great astonishment that all the lights were in one enormous building—a lofty structure with pointed towers plunging upward into the gloom. His eyes made out the shadowy outlines of a palatial château;[3] it was set on a high bluff, and on three sides of it cliffs dived down to where the sea licked greedy lips in the shadows.

"Mirage," thought Rainsford. But it was no mirage, he found, when he opened the tall spiked iron gate. The stone steps were real enough; the massive door with a leering gargoyle[4] for a knocker was real enough; yet about it all hung an air of unreality.

He lifted the knocker, and it creaked up stiffly, as if it had never before been used. He let it fall, and it startled him with its booming loudness. He thought he heard steps within; the door remained closed. Again Rainsford lifted the heavy knocker, and let it fall. The door opened then, opened as suddenly as if it were on a spring, and Rainsford stood blinking in the river of glaring gold light that poured out. The first thing Rainsford's eyes discerned was the largest man Rainsford had ever seen—a gigantic creature, solidly made and black-bearded to the waist. In his hand the man held a long-barreled revolver, and he was pointing it straight at Rainsford's heart.

Out of the snarl of beard two small eyes regarded Rainsford.

"Don't be alarmed," said Rainsford, with a smile which he hoped was disarming. "I'm no robber. I fell off a yacht. My name is Sanger Rainsford of New York City."

The menacing look in his eyes did not change. The revolver pointed as rigidly as if the giant were a statue. He gave no sign that he understood Rainsford's words, or that he had even heard them. He was dressed in uniform, a black uniform trimmed with gray astrakhan.[5]

"I'm Sanger Rainsford of New York," Rainsford began again. "I fell off a yacht. I am hungry."

The man's only answer was to raise with his thumb the hammer of his revolver. Then Rainsford saw the man's free hand go to his forehead in a military salute, and he saw him click his heels together and stand at attention. Another man was coming down the broad marble steps, an erect, slender man in evening clothes. He advanced to Rainsford and held out his hand.

In a cultivated voice marked by a slight accent that gave it added precision and deliberateness, he said: "It is a very great pleasure and honor to welcome Mr. Sanger Rainsford, the celebrated hunter, to my home."

Automatically Rainsford shook the man's hand.

"I've read your book about hunting snow leopards in Tibet, you see," explained the man. "I am General Zaroff."

Rainsford's first impression was that the man was singularly handsome; his second was that there was an original, almost bizarre quality about the general's face. He was a tall man past middle age, for his hair was a vivid white; but his thick eyebrows and pointed military mustache were as black as the night from which Rainsford had come. His eyes, too, were black

3. **château** (shă-tō′): castle or large country house.
4. **gargoyle** (gär′goil′): a grotesque carved figure, usually of an animal or mythical creature.

5. **astrakhan** (ăs′trə-kăn′): the curled fur of young lambs.

Scenes on pages 16, 23, and 26–27 are from a film version of "The Most Dangerous Game."

and very bright. He had high cheekbones, a sharp-cut nose, a spare, dark face, the face of a man used to giving orders, the face of an aristocrat. Turning to the giant in uniform, the general made a sign. The giant put away his pistol, saluted, withdrew.

"Ivan is an incredibly strong fellow," remarked the general, "but he has the misfortune to be deaf and dumb. A simple fellow, but, I'm afraid, like all his race, a bit of a savage."

"Is he Russian?"

"He is a Cossack,"[6] said the general, and his

smile showed red lips and pointed teeth. "So am I."

"Come," he said, "we shouldn't be chatting here. We can talk later. Now you want clothes, food, rest. You shall have them. This is a most restful spot."

Ivan had reappeared, and the general spoke to him with lips that moved but gave forth no sound.

"Follow Ivan, if you please, Mr. Rainsford," said the general. "I was about to have my dinner when you came. I'll wait for you. You'll find that my clothes will fit you, I think."

It was to a huge, beam-ceilinged bedroom with a canopied bed big enough for six men that Rainsford followed the silent giant. Ivan

6. **Cossack:** Cossacks are a people of southern European Russia noted for their horsemanship and their courage and fierceness in battle.

laid out an evening suit, and Rainsford, as he put it on, noticed that it came from a London tailor who ordinarily cut and sewed for none below the rank of duke.

The dining room to which Ivan conducted him was in many ways remarkable. There was a medieval magnificence about it; it suggested a baronial hall of feudal times with its oaken panels, its high ceiling, its vast refectory table where twoscore men could sit down to eat. About the hall were the mounted heads of many animals—lions, tigers, elephants, moose, bears; larger or more perfect specimens Rainsford had never seen. At the great table the general was sitting, alone.

"You'll have a cocktail, Mr. Rainsford," he suggested. The cocktail was surpassingly good; and, Rainsford noted, the table appointments were of the finest—the linen, the crystal, the silver, the china.

They were eating borsch, the rich, red soup with sour cream so dear to Russian palates. Half apologetically General Zaroff said: "We do our best to preserve the amenities of civilization here. Please forgive any lapses. We are well off the beaten track, you know. Do you think the champagne has suffered from its long ocean trip?"

"Not in the least," declared Rainsford. He was finding the general a most thoughtful and affable host, a true cosmopolite. But there was one small trait of the general's that made Rainsford uncomfortable. Whenever he looked up from his plate he found the general studying him, appraising him narrowly.

"Perhaps," said General Zaroff, "you were surprised that I recognized your name. You see, I read all books on hunting published in English, French, and Russian. I have but one passion in my life, Mr. Rainsford, and it is the hunt."

"You have some wonderful heads here," said Rainsford as he ate a particularly well-cooked filet mignon. "That Cape buffalo is the largest I ever saw."

"Oh, that fellow. Yes, he was a monster."

"Did he charge you?"

"Hurled me against a tree," said the general. "Fractured my skull. But I got the brute."

"I've always thought," said Rainsford, "that the Cape buffalo is the most dangerous of all big game."

For a moment the general did not reply; he was smiling his curious red-lipped smile. Then he said slowly: "No. You are wrong, sir. The Cape buffalo is not the most dangerous big game." He sipped his wine. "Here in my preserve on this island," he said in the same slow tone, "I hunt more dangerous game."

Rainsford expressed his surprise. "Is there big game on this island?"

The general nodded. "The biggest."

"Really?"

"Oh, it isn't here naturally, of course. I have to stock the island."

"What have you imported, general?" Rainsford asked. "Tigers?"

The general smiled. "No," he said. "Hunting tigers ceased to interest me some years ago. I exhausted their possibilities, you see. No thrill left in tigers, no real danger. I live for danger, Mr. Rainsford."

The general took from his pocket a gold cigarette case and offered his guest a long black cigarette with a silver tip; it was perfumed and gave off a smell like incense.

"We will have some capital hunting, you and I," said the general. "I shall be most glad to have your society."

"But what game——" began Rainsford.

"I'll tell you," said the general. "You will be amused, I know. I think I may say, in all modesty, that I have done a rare thing. I have invented a new sensation. May I pour you another glass of port, Mr. Rainsford?"

"Thank you, general."

The general filled both glasses, and said: "God makes some men poets. Some He makes kings, some beggars. Me He made a hunter. My hand was made for the trigger, my father said. He was a very rich man with a quarter of a million acres in the Crimea, and he was an ardent sportsman. When I was only five years old he gave me a little gun, specially made in Moscow for me, to shoot sparrows with. When I shot some of his prize turkeys with it, he did not punish me; he complimented me on my marksmanship. I killed my first bear in the Caucasus when I was ten. My whole life has been one prolonged hunt. I went into the army—it was expected of noblemen's sons—and for a time commanded a division of Cossack cavalry, but my real interest was always the hunt. I have hunted every kind of game in every land. It would be impossible for me to tell you how many animals I have killed."

The general puffed at his cigarette.

"After the debacle[7] in Russia I left the country, for it was imprudent for an officer of the Czar to stay there. Many noble Russians lost everything. I, luckily, had invested heavily in American securities, so I shall never have to open a tearoom in Monte Carlo or drive a taxi in Paris. Naturally, I continued to hunt—grizzlies in your Rockies, crocodiles in the Ganges, rhinoceroses in East Africa. It was in Africa that the Cape buffalo hit me and laid me up for six months. As soon as I recovered I started for the Amazon to hunt jaguars, for I had heard they were unusually cunning. They weren't." The Cossack sighed. "They were no match at all for a hunter with his wits about him, and a high-powered rifle. I was bitterly disappointed. I was lying in my tent with a splitting headache one night when a terrible thought pushed its way into my mind. Hunting was beginning to bore me! And hunting, remember, had been my life. I have heard that in America businessmen often go to pieces when they give up the business that has been their life."

"Yes, that's so," said Rainsford.

The general smiled. "I had no wish to go to pieces," he said. "I must do something. Now, mine is an analytical mind, Mr. Rainsford. Doubtless that is why I enjoy the problems of the chase."

"No doubt, General Zaroff."

"So," continued the general, "I asked myself why the hunt no longer fascinated me. You are much younger than I am, Mr. Rainsford, and have not hunted as much, but you perhaps can guess the answer."

"What was it?"

"Simply this: hunting had ceased to be what you call 'a sporting proposition.' It had become too easy. I always got my quarry. Always. There is no greater bore than perfection."

The general lit a fresh cigarette.

"No animal had a chance with me any more. That is no boast; it is a mathematical certainty. The animal had nothing but his legs and his instinct. Instinct is no match for reason. When I thought of this it was a tragic moment for me, I can tell you."

Rainsford leaned across the table, absorbed in what his host was saying.

"It came to me as an inspiration what I must do," the general went on.

"And that was?"

The general smiled the quiet smile of one who has faced an obstacle and surmounted it with success. "I had to invent a new animal to hunt," he said.

"A new animal? You're joking."

"Not at all," said the general. "I never joke about hunting. I needed a new animal. I found one. So I bought this island, built this house,

7. **debacle** (dĭ-bä′kəl): collapse; here, referring to the overthrow of the empire of the czars in 1917.

and here I do my hunting. The island is perfect for my purposes—there are jungles with a maze of trails in them, hills, swamps——"

"But the animal, General Zaroff?"

"Oh," said the general, "it supplies me with the most exciting hunting in the world. No other hunting compares with it for an instant. Every day I hunt, and I never grow bored now, for I have a quarry with which I can match my wits."

Rainsford's bewilderment showed in his face.

"I wanted the ideal animal to hunt," explained the general. "So, I said: 'What are the attributes of an ideal quarry?' And the answer was, of course: 'It must have courage, cunning, and, above all, it must be able to reason.'"

"But no animal can reason," objected Rainsford.

"My dear fellow," said the general, "there is one that can."

"But you can't mean——" gasped Rainsford.

"And why not?"

"I can't believe you are serious, General Zaroff. This is a grisly joke."

"Why should I not be serious? I am speaking of hunting."

"Hunting? General Zaroff, what you speak of is murder."

The general laughed with entire good nature. He regarded Rainsford quizzically. "I refuse to believe that so modern and civilized a young man as you seem to be harbors romantic ideas about the value of human life. Surely your experiences in the war——"

"Did not make me condone cold-blooded murder," finished Rainsford stiffly.

Laughter shook the general. "How extraordinarily droll you are!" he said. "One does not expect nowadays to find a young man of the educated class, even in America, with such a naive, and, if I may say so, mid-Victorian point of view. It's like finding a snuffbox in a limousine. Ah, well, doubtless you had Puritan ancestors. So many Americans appear to have had. I'll wager you'll forget your notions when you go hunting with me. You've a genuine new thrill in store for you, Mr. Rainsford."

"Thank you, I'm a hunter, not a murderer."

"Dear me," said the general, quite unruffled. "Again that unpleasant word. But I think I can show you that your scruples are quite ill-founded."

"Yes?"

"Life is for the strong, to be lived by the strong, and, if need be, taken by the strong. The weak of the world were put here to give the strong pleasure. I am strong. Why should I not use my gift? If I wish to hunt, why should I not? I hunt the scum of the earth—sailors from tramp ships—lascars, blacks, Chinese, whites, mongrels—a thoroughbred horse or hound is worth more than a score of them."

"But they are men," said Rainsford hotly.

"Precisely," said the general. "That is why I use them. It gives me pleasure. They can reason, after a fashion. So they are dangerous."

"But where do you get them?"

The general's left eyelid fluttered down in a wink. "This island is called Ship-Trap," he answered. "Sometimes an angry god of the high seas sends them to me. Sometimes, when Providence is not so kind, I help Providence a bit. Come to the window with me."

Rainsford went to the window and looked out toward the sea.

"Watch! Out there!" exclaimed the general, pointing into the night. Rainsford's eyes saw only blackness, and then, as the general pressed a button, far out to sea Rainsford saw the flash of lights.

The general chuckled. "They indicate a channel," he said, "where there's none: giant rocks with razor edges crouch like a sea monster with wide-open jaws. They can crush a ship as easily as I crush this nut." He dropped a walnut on the hardwood floor and brought his heel grinding down on it. "Oh, yes," he said, casually, as if in answer to a question, "I have electricity. We try to be civilized here."

"Civilized? And you shoot down men?"

A trace of anger was in the general's black eyes, but it was there for but a second, and he said, in his most pleasant manner: "Dear me, what a righteous young man you are! I assure you I do not do the thing you suggest. That would be barbarous. I treat these visitors with every consideration. They get plenty of good food and exercise. They get into splendid physical condition. You shall see for yourself tomorrow."

"What do you mean?"

"We'll visit my training school," smiled the general. "It's in the cellar. I have about a dozen pupils down there now. They're from the Spanish bark *San Lucar* that had the bad luck to go on the rocks out there. A very inferior lot, I regret to say. Poor specimens and more accustomed to the deck than to the jungle."

He raised his hand, and Ivan, who served as waiter, brought thick Turkish coffee. Rainsford, with an effort, held his tongue in check.

"It's a game, you see," pursued the general blandly. "I suggest to one of them that we go hunting. I give him a supply of food and an excellent hunting knife. I give him three hours' start. I am to follow, armed only with a pistol of the smallest caliber and range. If my quarry eludes me for three whole days, he wins the game. If I find him"—the general smiled—"he loses."

"Suppose he refuses to be hunted?"

"Oh," said the general, "I give him his option, of course. He need not play that game if he doesn't wish to. If he does not wish to hunt, I turn him over to Ivan. Ivan once had the honor of serving as official knouter[8] to the Great White Czar, and he has his own ideas of sport. Invariably, Mr. Rainsford, invariably they choose the hunt."

"And if they win?"

The smile on the general's face widened. "To date I have not lost," he said.

Then he added, hastily: "I don't wish you to think me a braggart, Mr. Rainsford. Many of them afford only the most elementary sort of problem. Occasionally I strike a tartar. One almost did win. I eventually had to use the dogs."

"The dogs?"

"This way, please. I'll show you."

The general steered Rainsford to a window. The lights from the windows sent a flickering illumination that made grotesque patterns on the courtyard below, and Rainsford could see moving about there a dozen or so huge black shapes; as they turned toward him, their eyes glittered greenly.

"A rather good lot, I think," observed the general. "They are let out at seven every night. If anyone should try to get into my house—or out of it—something extremely regrettable would occur to him." He hummed a snatch of song from the Folies Bergère.

"And now," said the general, "I want to show you my new collection of heads. Will you come with me to the library?"

"I hope," said Rainsford, "that you will excuse me tonight, General Zaroff. I'm really not feeling at all well."

"Ah, indeed?" the general inquired solicitously. "Well, I suppose that's only natural, after your long swim. You need a good, restful night's sleep. Tomorrow you'll feel like a new man, I'll wager. Then we'll hunt, eh? I've one rather promising prospect——"

Rainsford was hurrying from the room.

8. **knouter** (nout'ər): A knout is a leather whip that was used in Russia to punish criminals.

"Sorry you can't go with me tonight," called the general. "I expect rather fair sport—a big, strong fellow. He looks resourceful——Well, good night, Mr. Rainsford; I hope you have a good night's rest."

The bed was good, and the pajamas of the softest silk, and he was tired in every fiber of his being, but nevertheless Rainsford could not quiet his brain with the opiate of sleep. He lay, eyes wide open. Once he thought he heard stealthy steps in the corridor outside his room. He sought to throw open the door; it would not open. He went to the window and looked out. His room was high up in one of the towers. The lights of the château were out now, and it was dark and silent, but there was a fragment of sallow moon, and by its wan light he could see, dimly, the courtyard; there, weaving in and out in the pattern of shadow, were black, noiseless forms; the hounds heard him at the window and looked up, expectantly, with their green eyes. Rainsford went back to the bed and lay down. By many methods he tried to put himself to sleep, He had achieved a doze when, just as morning began to come, he heard, far off in the jungle, the faint report of a pistol.

General Zaroff did not appear until luncheon. He was dressed faultlessly in the tweeds of a country squire. He was solicitous about the state of Rainsford's health.

"As for me," sighed the general, "I do not feel so well. I am worried, Mr. Rainsford. Last night I detected traces of my old complaint."

To Rainsford's questioning glance the general said: "Ennui. Boredom."

Then, taking a second helping of crêpes suzette, the general explained: "The hunting was not good last night. The fellow lost his head. He made a straight trail that offered no problems at all. That's the trouble with these sailors; they have dull brains to begin with, and they do not know how to get about in the woods. They do excessively stupid and obvious things. It's most annoying. Will you have another glass of Chablis, Mr. Rainsford?"

"General," said Rainsford firmly, "I wish to leave this island at once."

The general raised his thickets of eyebrows; he seemed hurt. "But, my dear fellow," the general protested, "you've only just come. You've had no hunting——"

"I wish to go today," said Rainsford. He saw the dead black eyes of the general on him, studying him. General Zaroff's face suddenly brightened.

He filled Rainsford's glass with venerable Chablis from a dusty bottle.

"Tonight," said the general, "we will hunt—you and I."

Rainsford shook his head. "No, general," he said. "I will not hunt."

The general shrugged his shoulders and delicately ate a hothouse grape. "As you wish, my friend," he said. "The choice rests entirely with you. But may I not venture to suggest that you will find my idea of sport more diverting than Ivan's?"

He nodded toward the corner to where the giant stood, scowling, his thick arms crossed on his hogshead of chest.

"You don't mean——" cried Rainsford.

"My dear fellow," said the general, "have I not told you I always mean what I say about hunting? This is really an inspiration. I drink to a foeman worthy of my steel—at last."

The general raised his glass, but Rainsford sat staring at him.

"You'll find this game worth playing," the general said enthusiastically. "Your brain against mine. Your woodcraft against mine. Your strength and stamina against mine. Outdoor chess! And the stake is not without value, eh?"

"And if I win——" began Rainsford huskily.

"I'll cheerfully acknowledge myself defeated if I do not find you by midnight of the third day," said General Zaroff. "My sloop will place you on the mainland near a town."

The general read what Rainsford was thinking.

"Oh, you can trust me," said the Cossack. "I will give you my word as a gentleman and a sportsman. Of course you, in turn, must agree to say nothing of your visit here."

"I'll agree to nothing of the kind," said Rainsford.

"Oh," said the general, "in that case——But why discuss that now? Three days hence we can discuss it over a bottle of Veuve Cliquot, unless——"

The general sipped his wine.

Then a businesslike air animated him. "Ivan," he said to Rainsford, "will supply you with hunting clothes, food, a knife. I suggest you wear moccasins; they leave a poorer trail. I suggest too that you avoid a big swamp in the southeast corner of the island. We call it Death Swamp. There's quicksand there. One foolish fellow tried it. The deplorable part of it was that Lazarus followed him. You can imagine my feelings, Mr. Rainsford. I loved Lazarus; he was the finest hound in my pack. Well, I must beg you to excuse me now. I always take a siesta after lunch. You'll hardly have time for a nap, I fear. You'll want to start, no doubt. I shall not follow till dusk. Hunting at night is so much more exciting than by day, don't you think? Au revoir,[9] Mr. Rainsford, au revoir."

General Zaroff, with a deep, courtly bow, strolled from the room.

From another door came Ivan. Under one arm he carried khaki hunting clothes, a haversack of food, a leather sheath containing a long-bladed hunting knife; his right hand

9. **Au revoir** (ō rə-vwar'): French for "until we meet again."

rested on a cocked revolver thrust in the crimson sash about his waist. . . .

Rainsford had fought his way through the bush for two hours. "I must keep my nerve. I must keep my nerve," he said through tight teeth.

He had not been entirely clearheaded when the château gates snapped shut behind him. His whole idea at first was to put distance between himself and General Zaroff, and, to this end, he had plunged along, spurred on by the sharp rowels of something very like panic. Now he had got a grip on himself, had stopped, and was taking stock of himself and the situation.

He saw that straight flight was futile; inevitably it would bring him face to face with the sea. He was in a picture with a frame of water, and his operations, clearly, must take place within that frame.

"I'll give him a trail to follow," muttered Rainsford, and he struck off from the rude paths he had been following into the trackless wilderness. He executed a series of intricate loops; he doubled on his trail again and again, recalling all the lore of the fox hunt, and all the dodges of the fox. Night found him leg-weary, with hands and face lashed by the branches, on a thickly wooded ridge. He knew it would be insane to blunder on through the dark, even if he had the strength. His need for rest was imperative and he thought: "I have played the fox, now I must play the cat of the fable." A big tree with a thick trunk and outspread branches was nearby, and, taking care to leave not the slightest mark, he climbed up into the crotch, and stretching out on one of the broad limbs, after a fashion, rested. Rest brought him new confidence and almost a feeling of security. Even so zealous a hunter as General Zaroff could not trace him there, he told himself; only the devil himself could follow that complicated trail through the jungle after dark. But, perhaps, the general was a devil——

An apprehensive night crawled slowly by like a wounded snake, and sleep did not visit Rainsford, although the silence of a dead world was on the jungle. Toward morning when a dingy gray was varnishing the sky, the cry of some startled bird focused Rainsford's attention in that direction. Something was coming through the bush, coming slowly, carefully, coming by the same winding way Rainsford had come. He flattened himself down on the limb, and through a screen of leaves almost as thick as tapestry, he watched.

The thing that was approaching was a man.

It was General Zaroff. He made his way along with his eyes fixed in utmost concentration on the ground before him. He paused, almost beneath the tree, dropped to his knees and studied the ground. Rainsford's impulse was to hurl himself down like a panther, but he saw that the general's right hand held something metallic—a small automatic pistol.

The hunter shook his head several times, as if he were puzzled. Then he straightened up and took from his case one of his black cigarettes; its pungent incenselike smoke floated up to Rainsford's nostrils.

Rainsford held his breath. The general's eyes had left the ground and were traveling inch by inch up the tree. Rainsford froze there, every muscle tensed for a spring. But the sharp eyes of the hunter stopped before they reached the limb where Rainsford lay; a smile spread over his brown face. Very deliberately he blew a smoke ring into the air; then he turned his back on the tree and walked carelessly away, back along the trail he had come. The swish of the underbrush against his hunting boots grew fainter and fainter.

The pent-up air burst hotly from Rainsford's lungs. His first thought made him feel sick and numb. The general could follow a trail through the woods at night; he could follow an extremely difficult trail; he must have uncanny powers; only by the merest chance had the Cossack failed to see his quarry.

Rainsford's second thought was even more terrible. It sent a shudder of cold horror through his whole being. Why had the general smiled? Why had he turned back?

Rainsford did not want to believe what his reason told him was true, but the truth was as evident as the sun that had by now pushed through the morning mists. The general was playing with him! The general was saving him for another day's sport! The Cossack was the cat; he was the mouse. Then it was that Rainsford knew the full meaning of terror.

"I will not lose my nerve. I will not."

He slid down from the tree, and struck off again into the woods. His face was set and he forced the machinery of his mind to function. Three hundred yards from his hiding place he stopped where a huge dead tree leaned precariously on a smaller, living one. Throwing off his sack of food, Rainsford took his knife from its sheath and began to work with all his energy.

The job was finished at last, and he threw himself down behind a fallen log a hundred feet away. He did not have to wait long. The cat was coming again to play with the mouse.

Following the trail with the sureness of a bloodhound came General Zaroff. Nothing escaped those searching black eyes, no crushed blade of grass, no bent twig, no mark, no matter how faint, in the moss. So intent was the Cossack on his stalking that he was upon the thing Rainsford had made before he saw it. His foot touched the protruding bough that was the trigger. Even as he touched it, the general sensed his danger and leaped back with the agility of an ape. But he was not quite quick enough; the dead tree, delicately adjusted to rest on the cut living one, crashed down and struck the general a glancing blow on the shoulder as it fell; but for his alertness, he must have been smashed beneath it. He staggered, but he did not fall; nor did he drop his revolver. He stood there, rubbing his injured shoulder, and Rainsford, with fear again gripping his heart, heard the general's mocking laugh ring through the jungle.

"Rainsford," called the general, "if you are within sound of my voice, as I suppose you are, let me congratulate you. Not many men know how to make a Malay man-catcher. Luckily, for me, I too have hunted in Malacca. You are proving interesting, Mr. Rainsford. I am going now to have my wound dressed; it's only a slight one. But I shall be back. I shall be back."

When the general, nursing his bruised shoulder, had gone, Rainsford took up his flight again. It was flight now, a desperate, hopeless flight, that carried him on for some hours. Dusk came, then darkness, and still he pressed on. The ground grew softer under his moccasins; the vegetation grew ranker, denser; insects bit him savagely. Then, as he stepped forward, his foot sank into the ooze. He tried to wrench it back, but the muck sucked viciously at his foot as if it were a giant leech.

With a violent effort, he tore his foot loose. He knew where he was now. Death Swamp and its quicksand.

His hands were tight closed as if his nerve were something tangible that someone in the darkness was trying to tear from his grip. The softness of the earth had given him an idea. He stepped back from the quicksand a dozen feet or so and, like some huge prehistoric beaver, he began to dig.

Rainsford had dug himself in in France when a second's delay meant death. That had been a placid pastime compared to his digging now. The pit grew deeper; when it was above his shoulders, he climbed out and from some hard saplings cut stakes and sharpened them to a fine point. These stakes he planted in the bottom of the pit with the points sticking up. With flying fingers he wove a rough carpet of weeds and branches and with it he covered the mouth of the pit. Then, wet with sweat and aching with tiredness, he crouched behind the stump of a lightning-charred tree.

He knew his pursuer was coming; he heard the padding sound of feet on the soft earth, and the night breeze brought him the perfume of the general's cigarette. It seemed to Rainsford that the general was coming with unusual swiftness; he was not feeling his way along, foot by foot. Rainsford, crouching there, could not see the general, nor could he see the pit. He lived a year in a minute. Then he felt an impulse to cry aloud with joy, for he heard the sharp crackle of the breaking branches as the cover of the pit gave way; he heard the sharp scream of pain as the pointed stakes found their mark. He leaped up from his place of concealment. Then he cowered back. Three feet from the pit a man was standing, with an electric torch in his hand.

"You've done well, Rainsford," the voice of the general called. "Your Burmese tiger pit has claimed one of my best dogs. Again you score. I think, Mr. Rainsford, I'll see what you can do against my whole pack. I'm going home for a rest now. Thank you for a most amusing evening."

At daybreak Rainsford, lying near the swamp, was awakened by a sound that made him know that he had new things to learn about fear. It was a distant sound, faint and wavering, but he knew it. It was the baying of a pack of hounds.

Rainsford knew he could do one of two things. He could stay where he was and wait. That was suicide. He could flee. That was postponing the inevitable. For a moment he stood there, thinking. An idea that held a wild chance came to him, and tightening his belt, he headed away from the swamp.

The baying of the hounds drew nearer, then still nearer, nearer, ever nearer. On a ridge Rainsford climbed a tree. Down a watercourse, not a quarter of a mile away, he could see the bush moving. Straining his eyes, he saw the lean figure of General Zaroff; just ahead of him Rainsford made out another figure whose wide shoulders surged through the tall jungle weeds; it was the giant Ivan, and he seemed pulled forward by some unseen force; Rainsford knew that Ivan must be holding the pack in leash.

They would be on him any minute now. His mind worked frantically. He thought of a native trick he had learned in Uganda. He slid down the tree. He caught hold of a springy young sapling and to it he fastened his hunting knife, with the blade pointing down the trail; with a bit of wild grapevine he tied back the sapling. Then he ran for his life. The hounds raised their voices as they hit the fresh scent. Rainsford knew now how an animal at bay feels.

He had to stop to get his breath. The baying

of the hounds stopped abruptly, and Rainsford's heart stopped too. They must have reached the knife.

He shinnied excitedly up a tree and looked back. His pursuers had stopped. But the hope that was in Rainsford's brain when he climbed died, for he saw in the shallow valley that General Zaroff was still on his feet. But Ivan was not. The knife, driven by the recoil of the springing tree, had not wholly failed.

Rainsford had hardly tumbled to the ground when the pack took up the cry again.

"Nerve, nerve, nerve!" he panted, as he dashed along. A blue gap showed between the trees dead ahead. Ever nearer drew the hounds. Rainsford forced himself on toward that gap. He reached it. It was the shore of the sea. Across a cove he could see the gloomy gray stone of the château. Twenty feet below him the sea rumbled and hissed. Rainsford hesitated. He heard the hounds. Then he leaped far out into the sea. . . .

When the general and his pack reached the place by the sea, the Cossack stopped. For some minutes he stood regarding the blue-green expanse of water. He shrugged his shoulders. Then he sat down, took a drink of brandy from a silver flask, lit a perfumed cigarette, and hummed a bit from *Madame Butterfly*.[10]

General Zaroff had an exceedingly good dinner in his great paneled dining hall that evening. With it he had a bottle of Pol Roger and half a bottle of Chambertin. Two slight annoyances kept him from perfect enjoyment. One was the thought that it would be difficult to replace Ivan; the other was that his quarry had escaped him; of course the American hadn't played the game—so thought the general as he tasted his after-dinner liqueur. In his library he read, to soothe himself, from the

works of Marcus Aurelius.[11] At ten he went up to his bedroom. He was deliciously tired, he said to himself, as he locked himself in. There was a little moonlight, so, before turning on his light, he went to the window and looked down at the courtyard. He could see the great

10. *Madame Butterfly:* an opera by Giacomo Puccini.

11. **Marcus Aurelius:** Roman emperor (161–180), whose book, *Meditations,* is considered a classic of philosophy.

hounds, and he called: "Better luck another time," to them. Then he switched on the light.

A man, who had been hiding in the curtains of the bed, was standing there.

"Rainsford!" screamed the general. "How did you get here?"

"Swam," said Rainsford. "I found it quicker than walking through the jungle."

The general sucked in his breath and smiled. "I congratulate you," he said. "You have won the game."

Rainsford did not smile. "I am still a beast at bay," he said, in a low, hoarse voice. "Get ready, General Zaroff."

The general made one of his deepest bows.

"I see," he said. "Splendid! One of us is to furnish a repast for the hounds. The other will sleep in this very excellent bed. On guard, Rainsford. . . ."

He had never slept in a better bed, Rainsford decided.

Reading Check

1. What is the name of Zaroff's island?
2. Which animal does Rainsford consider to be the most dangerous game?
3. What weapon does Rainsford carry during the hunt?
4. What is the first trap Rainsford plans for Zaroff?
5. How does Rainsford escape from Zaroff and his hounds?

For Study and Discussion

Analyzing and Interpreting the Story

1. "The Most Dangerous Game" tells of a struggle between Sanger Rainsford and General Zaroff. **a.** Who are these two men, and what have they in common? **b.** Why would their struggle be less interesting if Rainsford were a doctor, for example, rather than a hunter?

2. Two parts of the story provide clues for the struggle that is to come: the discussion on ship between Rainsford and Whitney; and Rainsford's observations—what he sees and hears—as he swims to the island and as he walks to Zaroff's château. How do these episodes hint at the coming struggle?

3. The discussions about hunting between Rainsford and Zaroff are important for two reasons: (a) they provide information about the two men and about the coming struggle; and (b) they provide a contrast between them. **a.** What information is provided? **b.** What is the contrast?

4. Tell about the hunt itself. **a.** What incidents make you anxious for Rainsford's safety? **b.** What incidents show that he is a worthy foe?

5. Near the end of the story, Rainsford is forced to take a desperate chance. **a.** What is it? **b.** Why do you think the author suddenly leaves Rainsford at this point and begins to tell the story through Zaroff's eyes?

6. The conversation between Rainsford and Whitney at the opening of the story reveals Rainsford's attitude toward hunting. Do you think his attitude changes in the course of the story? Give evidence to support your answer.

Literary Elements

Conflict

Conflict is an important element in stories, novels, and plays. A conflict is a struggle between opposing forces or points of view. A conflict may take place between two individuals, between an individual and an animal, or between an individual and some natural force. Conflicts in which individuals struggle against something outside themselves are known as **external conflicts**. A conflict that takes place within an individual is called **internal conflict**.

The most obvious conflict in "The Most Dangerous Game" is between Rainsford and Zaroff. Are there other external conflicts? Is there also an internal conflict?

Suspense and Foreshadowing

Skillful writers can build interest in a story through **suspense**, the quality that makes readers eager to know what happens next. Notice how the author creates suspense about Rainsford's fate in this episode of the story:

Rainsford held his breath. The general's eyes had left the ground and were traveling inch by inch up the tree. Rainsford froze there, every muscle tensed for a spring. But the sharp eyes of the hunter stopped before they reached the limb where Rainsford lay; a smile spread over his brown face. Very deliberately he blew a smoke ring into the air; then he turned his back on the tree and walked carelessly away, back along the trail he had come. The swish of the underbrush against his hunting boots grew fainter and fainter.

To build up suspense, an author often plants clues early in the story that hint at what will come later. The planting of such clues is called **foreshadowing**. How is the major action of the story foreshadowed in the conversation between Rainsford and Whitney? In Rainsford's arrival at the island? How does this foreshadowing help create suspense?

Language and Vocabulary

Finding Meaning from Context

Sometimes you may be able to derive the definition of an unfamiliar word (or a familiar word used in an unfamiliar way) by using **context clues**—clues supplied by other words within the sentence or paragraph:

. . . Rainsford noted, the table *appointments* were of the finest—the linen, the crystal, the silver, the china.

The word *appointments*, meaning "equipment" or "furnishings" is made clear by the context.

Use context clues to determine the meaning of the italicized words in these sentences from the story. Check your answers in the glossary at the back of this book or in a dictionary.

Whenever he looked up from his plate he found the general studying him, *appraising* him narrowly.

His hands were tight closed as if his nerve were something *tangible* that someone in the darkness was trying to tear from his grip.

"One of us is to furnish a *repast* for the hounds."

Writing About Literature

Analyzing a Title

The title of a literary work often is an important clue to what is in store for the reader. Consider the word *game* in the title of Connell's story. What different meanings could it have? In a paragraph, tell what you think is the best interpretation of the title.

Prewriting Suggestions: Consult a dictionary to determine if the word *game* has any additional meanings relevant to the story.

Choose those meanings that are best.

List specific evidence in the story (details, dialogue, description) to support your choices.

For additional help in planning and writing this paper, see the section called *Writing About Literature* in this textbook.

Focus on Narrative Writing

Beginning a Story

Like all good storytellers, Richard Connell captures his readers' interest right at the beginning of "The Most Dangerous Game." Besides introducing one of the main characters and the setting, the dialogue between Rainsford and Whitney also creates **conflict** and **suspense** (see page 29).

Try using Connell's dialogue as a model for beginning a story of your own. To find a plot line for your story, brainstorm some "What if?" scenarios with a small group of classmates. For example, "What if I were invisible?" or "What if I discovered a way to reverse the aging process?" Create two characters and write a short dialogue between them as the opening for your story. Try to hook the reader by using conflict and suspense.

When you have finished writing, rejoin your small group and get your classmates' opinion of your dialogue. Save your writing.

About the Author

Richard Connell   (1893–1949)

Richard Connell began his writing career at an early age. He once said, "My first writing was done for the newspaper my father edited in Poughkeepsie, New York. I covered baseball games. I was ten years old and got ten cents a game."

Connell attended Harvard College, where he was an editor on the *Daily Crimson* and the *Lampoon,* Harvard's humor magazine. After college, he worked in New York City, first for a newspaper and then for an advertising firm. In 1919 he decided to make his living as a freelance writer. He once estimated that he had sold about three hundred short stories to American and English magazines. He also wrote several novels and many screenplays. "The Most Dangerous Game" is his best known story. It has appeared in numerous anthologies and has been adapted for the movies and television.

The Lady, or the Tiger?

FRANK R. STOCKTON

The title of this story poses a question. How will you answer it?

In the very olden time there lived a semibarbaric king, whose ideas, though somewhat polished and sharpened by the progressiveness of distant Latin neighbors, were still large, florid, and untrammeled,[1] as became the half of him which was barbaric. He was a man of exuberant fancy, and, withal,[2] of an authority so irresistible that, at his will, he turned his varied fancies into facts. He was greatly given to self-communing; and when he and himself agreed upon anything, the thing was done. When every member of his domestic and political systems moved smoothly in its appointed course, his nature was bland and genial; but whenever there was a little hitch, and some of his orbs got out of their orbits, he was blander and more genial still, for nothing pleased him so much as to make the crooked straight, and crush down uneven places.

Among the borrowed notions by which his barbarism had become semified[3] was that of the public arena, in which, by exhibitions of manly and beastly valor, the minds of his subjects were refined and cultured.

But even here the exuberant and barbaric fancy asserted itself. The arena of the king was built not to give the people an opportunity of hearing the rhapsodies of dying gladiators, nor to enable them to view the inevitable conclusion of a conflict between religious opinions and hungry jaws, but for purposes far better adapted to widen and develop the mental energies of the people. This vast amphitheater,[4] with its encircling galleries, its mysterious vaults, and its unseen passages, was an agent of poetic justice, in which crime was punished, or virtue rewarded, by the decrees of an impartial and incorruptible chance.

When a subject was accused of a crime of sufficient importance to interest the king, public notice was given that on an appointed day the fate of the accused person would be decided in the king's arena—a structure which well deserved its name; for, although its form and plan were borrowed from afar, its purpose emanated solely from the brain of this man,

---

1. **untrammeled** (ŭn-trăm′əld): not hindered or restrained.
2. **withal** (wĭth-ôl′): besides.
3. **semified:** reduced in half or made partial.

4. **amphitheater** (ăm′fə-thē′ə-tər): an open arena with rising tiers of seats.

Detail from *Italian Woman Spinning* (1846) by Felix-Joseph Barrias (1822–1907). Oil on canvas.

Ackland Art Museum, the University of North Carolina at Chapel Hill, Ackland Fund

who, every barleycorn a king, knew no tradition to which he owed more allegiance than pleased his fancy, and who ingrafted on every adopted form of human thought and action the rich growth of his barbaric idealism.

When all the people had assembled in the galleries, and the king, surrounded by his court, sat high up on his throne of royal state on one side of the arena, he gave a signal, a door beneath him opened, and the accused subject stepped out into the amphitheater. Directly opposite him, on the other side of the enclosed space, were two doors, exactly alike and side by side. It was the duty and the privilege of the person on trial to walk directly to these doors and open one of them. He could open either door he pleased: he was subject to no guidance or influence but that of the aforementioned impartial and incorruptible chance. If he opened the one, there came out of it a hungry tiger, the fiercest and most cruel that could be procured, which immediately sprang

Tiger: Woodward's Gardens, San Francisco (1873), by Samuel Marsden Brookes. Oil on canvas, 30 x 25 in.

upon him and tore him to pieces, as a punishment for his guilt. The moment that the case of the criminal was thus decided, doleful iron bells were clanged, great wails went up from the hired mourners posted on the outer rim of the arena, and the vast audience, with bowed heads and downcast hearts, wended slowly their homeward way, mourning greatly that one so young and fair, or so old and respected, should have merited so dire a fate.

But if the accused person opened the other door, there came forth from it a lady, the most suitable to his years and station that his Majesty could select among his fair subjects; and to this lady he was immediately married, as a reward of his innocence. It mattered not that he might already possess a wife and family, or that his affections might be engaged upon an object of his own selection: the king allowed no such subordinate arrangements to interfere with his great scheme of retribution and reward. The exercises, as in the other instance, took place

The Lady, or the Tiger?   **33**

immediately, and in the arena. Another door opened beneath the king, and a priest, followed by a band of choristers, and dancing maidens blowing joyous airs on golden horns and treading an epithalamic measure,[5] advanced to where the pair stood side by side; and the wedding was promptly and cheerily solemnized. Then the gay brass bells rang forth their merry peals, the people shouted glad hurrahs, and the innocent man, preceded by children strewing flowers on his path, led his bride to his home.

This was the king's semibarbaric method of administering justice. Its perfect fairness is obvious. The criminal could not know out of which door would come the lady: he opened either he pleased, without having the slightest idea whether, in the next instant, he was to be devoured or married. On some occasions the tiger came out of one door, and on some out of the other. The decisions of this tribunal were not only fair, they were positively determinate:[6] the accused person was instantly punished if he found himself guilty; and if innocent, he was rewarded on the spot, whether he liked it or not. There was no escape from the judgments of the king's arena.

The institution was a very popular one. When the people gathered together on one of the great trial days, they never knew whether they were to witness a bloody slaughter or a hilarious wedding. This element of uncertainty lent an interest to the occasion which it could not otherwise have attained. Thus the masses were entertained and pleased, and the thinking part of the community could bring no charge of unfairness against this plan; for did not the accused person have the whole matter in his own hands?

This semibarbaric king had a daughter as

blooming as his most florid fancies, and with a soul as fervent and imperious as his own. As is usual in such cases, she was the apple of his eye, and was loved by him above all humanity. Among his courtiers was a young man of that fineness of blood and lowness of station common to the conventional heroes of romance who love royal maidens. This royal maiden was well satisfied with her lover, for he was handsome and brave to a degree unsurpassed in all this kingdom; and she loved him with an ardor that had enough of barbarism in it to make it exceedingly warm and strong. This love affair moved on happily for many months, until one day the king happened to discover its existence. He did not hesitate nor waver in regard to his duty in the premises. The youth was immediately cast into prison, and a day was appointed for his trial in the king's arena. This, of course, was an especially important occasion; and his Majesty, as well as all the people, was greatly interested in the workings and development of this trial. Never before had such a case occurred; never before had a subject dared to love the daughter of a king. In after years such things became commonplace enough; but then they were, in no slight degree, novel and startling.

The tiger cages of the kingdom were searched for the most savage and relentless beasts, from which the fiercest monster might be selected for the arena; and the ranks of maiden youth and beauty throughout the land were carefully surveyed by competent judges, in order that the young man might have a fitting bride in case fate did not determine for him a different destiny. Of course everybody knew that the deed with which the accused was charged had been done. He had loved the princess, and neither he, she, nor anyone else thought of denying the fact; but the king would not think of allowing any fact of this kind to interfere with the workings of the tri-

5. **treading an epithalamic** (ĕp'ə-thə-lă'mĭk) **measure:** performing a wedding dance.
6. **determinate** (dĭ-tûr'mə-nĭt): final.

bunal, in which he took such a great delight and satisfaction. No matter how the affair turned out, the youth would be disposed of; and the king would take an aesthetic[7] pleasure in watching the course of events, which would determine whether or not the young man had done wrong in allowing himself to love the princess.

The appointed day arrived. From far and near the people gathered, and thronged the great galleries of the arena; and crowds, unable to gain admittance, massed themselves against its outside walls. The king and his court were in their places, opposite the twin doors—those fateful portals, so terrible in their similarity.

All was ready. The signal was given. A door beneath the royal party opened, and the lover of the princess walked into the arena. Tall, beautiful, fair, his appearance was greeted with a low hum of admiration and anxiety. Half the audience had not known so grand a youth had lived among them. No wonder the princess loved him! What a terrible thing for him to be there!

As the youth advanced into the arena, he turned, as the custom was, to bow to the king: but he did not think at all of that royal personage; his eyes were fixed upon the princess, who sat to the right of her father. Had it not been for the moiety[8] of barbarism in her nature it is probable that lady would not have been there; but her intense and fervid soul would not allow her to be absent on an occasion in which she was so terribly interested. From the moment that the decree had gone forth that her lover should decide his fate in the king's arena, she had thought of nothing, night or day, but this great event and the various subjects connected with it. Possessed of more power, influence,

and force of character than anyone who had ever before been interested in such a case, she had done what no other person had done—she had possessed herself of the secret of the doors. She knew in which of the two rooms that lay behind those doors stood the cage of the tiger, with its open front, and in which waited the lady. Through these thick doors, heavily curtained with skins on the inside, it was impossible that any noise or suggestion should come from within to the person who should approach to raise the latch of one of them; but gold, and the power of a woman's will, had brought the secret to the princess.

And not only did she know in which room stood the lady ready to emerge, all blushing and radiant, should her door be opened, but she knew who the lady was. It was one of the fairest and loveliest of the damsels of the court who had been selected as the reward of the accused youth, should he be proved innocent of the crime of aspiring to one so far above him; and the princess hated her. Often had she seen, or imagined that she had seen, this fair creature throwing glances of admiration upon the person of her lover, and sometimes she thought these glances were perceived and even returned. Now and then she had seen them talking together; it was but for a moment or two, but much can be said in a brief space; it may have been on most unimportant topics, but how could she know that? The girl was lovely, but she had dared to raise her eyes to the loved one of the princess; and, with all the intensity of the savage blood transmitted to her through long lines of wholly barbaric ancestors, she hated the woman who blushed and trembled behind that silent door.

When her lover turned and looked at her, and his eye met hers as she sat there paler and whiter than anyone in the vast ocean of anxious faces about her, he saw, by that power of quick perception which is given to those whose

7. **aesthetic** (ĕs-thĕt′ĭk): sensitive to beauty.
8. **moiety** (moi′ə-tē): share.

souls are one, that she knew behind which door crouched the tiger, and behind which stood the lady. He had expected her to know it. He understood her nature, and his soul was assured that she would never rest until she had made plain to herself this thing, hidden to all other lookers-on, even to the king. The only hope for the youth in which there was any element of certainty was based upon the success of the princess in discovering this mystery; and the moment he looked upon her, he saw she had succeeded, as in his soul he knew she would succeed.

Then it was that his quick and anxious glance asked the question, "Which?" It was as plain to her as if he shouted it from where he stood. There was not an instant to be lost. The question was asked in a flash; it must be answered in another.

Her right arm lay on the cushioned parapet before her. She raised her hand, and made a slight, quick movement toward the right. No one but her lover saw her. Every eye was fixed on the man in the arena.

He turned, and with a firm and rapid step he walked across the empty space. Every heart stopped beating, every breath was held, every eye was fixed immovably upon that man. Without the slightest hesitation, he went to the door on the right and opened it.

Now, the point of the story is this: Did the tiger come out of that door, or did the lady?

The more we reflect upon this question the harder it is to answer. It involves a study of the human heart which leads us through devious mazes of passion, out of which it is difficult to find our way. Think of it, fair reader, not as if the decision of the question depended upon yourself, but upon that hot-blooded, semibarbaric princess, her soul at a white heat beneath the combined fires of despair and jealousy. She had lost him, but who should have him?

How often, in her waking hours and in her dreams, had she started in wild horror and covered her face with her hands as she thought of her lover opening the door on the other side of which waited the cruel fangs of the tiger!

But how much oftener had she seen him at the other door! How in her grievous reveries had she gnashed her teeth and torn her hair when she saw his start of rapturous delight as he opened the door of the lady! How her soul had burned in agony when she had seen him rush to meet that woman, with her flushing cheek and sparkling eye of triumph; when she had seen him lead her forth, his whole frame kindled with the joy of recovered life; when she had heard the glad shouts from the multitude, and the wild ringing of the happy bells; when she had seen the priest, with his joyous followers, advance to the couple, and make them man and wife before her very eyes; and when she had seen them walk away together upon their path of flowers, followed by the tremendous shouts of the hilarious multitude, in which her one despairing shriek was lost and drowned!

Would it not be better for him to die at once, and go to wait for her in the blessed regions of semibarbaric futurity?

And yet, that awful tiger, those shrieks, that blood!

Her decision had been indicated in an instant, but it had been made after days and nights of anguished deliberation. She had known she would be asked, she had decided what she would answer, and, without the slightest hesitation, she had moved her hand to the right.

The question of her decision is one not to be lightly considered, and it is not for me to presume to set myself up as the one person able to answer it. And so I leave it with all of you: Which came out of the opened door—the lady, or the tiger?

Reading Check

1. For what purpose did the king use his arena?
2. How was a subject's guilt determined?
3. Why was the young courtier thrown into prison?
4. How did the princess learn the secret of the doors?

For Study and Discussion

Analyzing and Interpreting the Story

1. The author challenges you to guess the outcome of the story. From what you know of the princess, which do you think she would point to: the lady or the tiger? Give reasons to support your answer.

2. At one point you are told that the solution to the question lies in understanding the nature of the princess: "Think of it, fair reader, not as if the decision of the question depended upon yourself, but upon that hot-blooded, semibarbaric princess, . . ." Does the answer lie within the story or within the individual reader?

Literary Elements

Plot

Plot is the sequence of events or actions in a story. Plot includes the following: whatever the characters do; whatever they say; whatever they think; and whatever happens to them.

Often before the plot proper begins, a section of **exposition** is provided. The exposition is an introduction; it presents information that helps readers understand the situation of the story. In "The Lady, or the Tiger?" the exposition is given in the first eight paragraphs. What information is presented?

The action of a story generally evolves out of **conflict**. What external and internal conflicts are presented in "The Lady, or the Tiger?" Which do you consider the central conflict?

Complications are introduced that make it difficult to settle the conflict. What complications does Stockton introduce into his story? How do they add interest?

As the story becomes more complicated, it moves to a **climax**. A climax is the point of highest intensity in the story, the point that determines the outcome of the action. What is the climax of this story?

The final part of a story is its **resolution**. A resolution moves down from the high point of the climax and usually settles the conflict or conflicts. How does Stockton handle the resolution in this story?

The plots of many stories follow this pattern: exposition, conflict, complications, climax, resolution. If you have already read "The Most Dangerous Game," identify these elements in that story.

Irony

There are several kinds of **irony**. All of them depend upon a contrast between appearance and reality. A common kind is **verbal irony**. Verbal irony is a way of saying or writing one thing and meaning the direct opposite. For example, imagine you are tramping through five feet of snow. The temperature is below freezing, and a twenty-mile-an-hour wind is scraping at your cheeks. You say to a friend, "What a lovely day!" By using verbal irony, you give emphasis to your real meaning: What a terrible day!

Writers often describe unpleasant characters or ideas ironically. By pretending to accept these characters or ideas at face value, writers force us to realize how bad they really are. Stockton calls the king's system "poetic justice," but he expects his readers to understand that his meaning is quite the opposite. In order to understand a writer's irony, we must first decide what the facts really are. If the way things seem to us is very different from the way the writer describes them, then the chances are that the writer is using verbal irony.

Explain why each of the following statements in "The Lady, or the Tiger?" is ironic. If the irony is not clear, reread each statement in its context in the selection.

[In] the public arena . . . the minds of his subjects were *refined and cultured.* (page 31)

This was the king's semibarbaric method of administering justice. *Its perfect fairness is obvious.* (page 34)

Find other ironic statements in the story. Point out the contrast between the apparent meaning and the intended meaning.

Language and Vocabulary

Distinguishing Meanings

Frank Stockton uses the words *bland* and *genial* to describe the king. Although these words are close in meaning, there is a distinction to be made between them. The word *bland* means "mild or pleasant": *genial* means "warm and friendly." One could be *bland* without also being *genial*.

Stockton refers to the king's "poetic justice" as "impartial and incorruptible chance." What is the distinction between *impartial* and *incorruptible*? Use a dictionary to determine the exact meanings of these words and the italicized words in the following sentences:

He did not *hesitate* nor *waver* in regard to his duty . . .

In after years such things became commonplace enough; but then they were, in no slight degree, *novel* and *startling.*

. . . but her *intense* and *fervid* soul would not allow her to be absent on an occasion in which she was so terribly interested.

Writing About Literature

Reacting to a Story

"The Lady, or the Tiger?" is considered a classic of the short-story form. It became an immediate favorite when it appeared in 1882, and it has stood the test of time. What do you think is the reason for the story's continued appeal? Write a paragraph discussing your own reaction to the story.

Creative Writing

Writing an Ending to the Story

Frank Stockton leaves it up to you, the reader, to decide what finally happens. Write your own version of the ending, telling what happens when the young man opens the door. To make your ending effective, you might want to show the princess' reaction as the door opens. Or, you might want to show the young man's reaction to what he finds.

About the Author

Frank R. Stockton   (1834–1902)

Frank R. Stockton was born in Philadelphia. His parents thought that he might become a doctor, but he became a wood engraver instead. By 1867 he began to devote more and more time to writing and less to engraving. First he contributed children's stories to the *Riverside Magazine for Young People.* Then he began to contribute many stories to adult magazines. Stockton's most famous story, "The Lady, or the Tiger?" appeared in 1882 in the *Century* magazine. It caused a great sensation. Debates were held all over the country to decide the ending.

War

JACK LONDON

As you read, ask yourself why London does not identify this war or the causes for which the soldiers are fighting.

I

He was a young man, not more than twenty-four or -five, and he might have sat his horse with the careless grace of his youth had he not been so catlike and tense. His black eyes roved everywhere, catching the movements of twigs and branches where small birds hopped, questing ever onward through the changing vistas of trees and brush, and returning always to the clumps of undergrowth on either side. And as he watched, so did he listen, though he rode on in silence, save for the boom of heavy guns from far to the west. This had been sounding monotonously in his ears for hours, and only its cessation[1] would have aroused his notice. For he had business closer to hand. Across his saddlebow was balanced a carbine.

So tensely was he strung that a bunch of quail, exploding into flight from under his horse's nose, startled him to such an extent that automatically, instantly, he had reined in and fetched the carbine halfway to his shoulder. He grinned sheepishly, recovered himself, and rode on. So tense was he, so bent upon the work he had to do, that the sweat stung his eyes unwiped, and unheeded rolled down his nose and spattered his saddle pommel. The band of his cavalryman's hat was fresh-stained with sweat. The roan horse under him was likewise wet. It was high noon of a breathless day of heat. Even the birds and squirrels did not dare the sun, but sheltered in shady hiding places among the trees.

Man and horse were littered with leaves and dusted with yellow pollen, for the open was ventured no more than was compulsory. They kept to the brush and trees, and invariably the man halted and peered out before crossing a dry glade or naked stretch of upland pasturage. He worked always to the north, though his way was devious,[2] and it was from the north that he seemed most to apprehend[3] that for which he was looking. He was no coward, but his courage was only that of the average civilized man, and he was looking to live, not die.

1. **cessation** (sĕ-sā′shən): stopping, ceasing.

2. **devious** (dē′vē-əs): roundabout, not straight.
3. **apprehend** (ăp′rĭ-hĕnd′): fear, be afraid of.

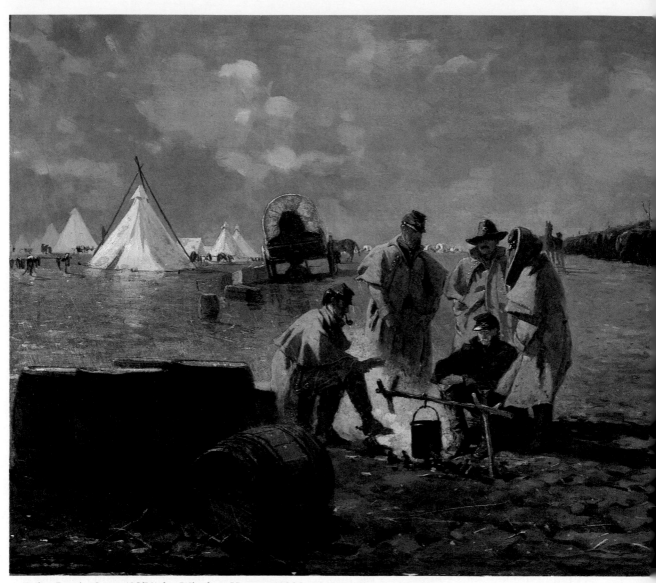

A Rainy Day in Camp (1871) by Winslow Homer (1836–1910). Oil on canvas.

Up a small hillside he followed a cowpath through such dense scrub that he was forced to dismount and lead his horse. But when the path swung around to the west, he abandoned it and headed to the north again along the oak-covered top of the ridge.

The ridge ended in a steep descent—so steep that he zigzagged back and forth across the face of the slope, sliding and stumbling among the dead leaves and matted vines and keeping a watchful eye on the horse above that threatened to fall down upon him. The sweat ran from him, and the pollen dust, settling pungently[4] in mouth and nostrils, increased

4. **pungently** (pŭn′jənt-lē): in a way producing sharp sensations of taste and smell.

extent. Here the character of the woods changed, and he was able to remount. Instead of the twisted hillside oaks, tall, straight trees, big-trunked and prosperous, rose from the damp, fat soil. Only here and there were thickets, easily avoided, while he encountered winding, parklike glades where the cattle had pastured in the days before war had run them off.

His progress was more rapid now, as he came down into the valley, and at the end of half an hour he halted at an ancient rail fence on the edge of a clearing. He did not like the openness of it, yet his path lay across to the fringe of trees that marked the banks of the stream. It was a mere quarter of a mile across that open, but the thought of venturing out in it was repugnant.[6] A rifle, a score of them, a thousand, might lurk in that fringe by the stream.

Twice he essayed[7] to start, and twice he paused. He was appalled by his own loneliness. The pulse of war that beat from the west suggested the companionship of battling thousands; here was naught but silence, and himself, and possible death-dealing bullets from a myriad[8] ambushes. And yet his task was to find what he feared to find. He must go on, and on, till somewhere, sometime, he encountered another man, or other men, from the other side, scouting, as he was scouting, to make report, as he must make report, of having come in touch.

Changing his mind, he skirted inside the woods for a distance, and again peeped forth. This time, in the middle of the clearing, he saw a small farmhouse. There were no signs of life. No smoke curled from the chimney, not a barnyard fowl clucked and strutted. The

The Metropolitan Museum of Art, gift of Mrs. William F. Milton

his thirst. Try as he would, nevertheless the descent was noisy, and frequently he stopped, panting in the dry heat and listening for any warning from beneath.

At the bottom he came out on a flat,[5] so densely forested that he could not make out its

5. **flat:** a level surface.

6. **repugnant** (rĭ-pŭg′nənt): hateful.
7. **essayed:** tried; attempted.
8. **myriad** (mĭr′ē-əd): a countless number of.

kitchen door stood open, and he gazed so long and hard into the black aperture[9] that it seemed almost that a farmer's wife must emerge at any moment.

He licked the pollen and dust from his dry lips, stiffened himself, mind and body, and rode out into the blazing sunshine. Nothing stirred. He went on past the house, and approached the wall of trees and bushes by the river's bank. One thought persisted maddeningly. It was of the crash into his body of a high-velocity bullet. It made him feel very fragile and defenseless, and he crouched lower in the saddle.

Tethering his horse in the edge of the wood, he continued a hundred yards on foot till he came to the stream. Twenty feet wide it was, without perceptible current, cool and inviting, and he was very thirsty. But he waited inside his screen of leafage, his eyes fixed on the screen on the opposite side. To make the wait endurable, he sat down, his carbine resting on his knees. The minutes passed, and slowly his tenseness relaxed. At last he decided there was no danger; but just as he prepared to part the bushes and bend down to the water, a movement among the opposite bushes caught his eye.

It might be a bird. But he waited. Again there was an agitation[10] of the bushes, and then, so suddenly that it almost startled a cry from him, the bushes parted and a face peered out. It was a face covered with several weeks' growth of ginger-colored beard. The eyes were blue and wide apart, with laughter-wrinkles in the corners that showed despite the tired and anxious expression of the whole face.

All this he could see with microscopic clearness, for the distance was no more than twenty feet. And all this he saw in such brief time that he saw it as he lifted his carbine to his shoulder.

9. **aperture** (ăp'ər-chŏor'): opening.
10. **agitation** (ă'jĭ-tā'shən): disturbance.

He glanced along the sights, and knew that he was gazing upon a man who was as good as dead. It was impossible to miss at such point-blank range.

But he did not shoot. Slowly he lowered the carbine and watched. A hand, clutching a water bottle, became visible, and the ginger beard bent downward to fill the bottle. He could hear the gurgle of the water. Then arm and bottle and ginger beard disappeared behind the closing bushes. A long time he waited, when, with thirst unslaked,[11] he crept back to his horse, rode slowly across the sunwashed clearing, and passed into the shelter of the woods beyond.

II

Another day, hot and breathless. A deserted farmhouse, large, with many outbuildings and an orchard, standing in a clearing. From the woods, on a roan horse, carbine across pommel, rode the young man with the quick black eyes. He breathed with relief as he gained the house. That a fight had taken place here earlier in the season was evident. Clips and empty cartridges, tarnished with verdigris,[12] lay on the ground, which, while wet, had been torn up by the hoofs of horses. Hard by the kitchen garden were graves, tagged and numbered. From the oak tree by the kitchen door, in tattered, weather-beaten garments, hung the bodies of two men. The faces, shriveled and defaced, bore no likeness to the faces of men. The roan horse snorted beneath them, and the rider caressed and soothed it and tied it farther away.

Entering the house, he found the interior a wreck. He trod on empty cartridges as he walked from room to room to reconnoiter[13]

11. **unslaked** (ŭn-slākd'): unsatisfied.
12. **verdigris** (vûr'də-grēs): a greenish coating that forms, like rust, on certain metals.
13. **reconnoiter** (rē'kə-noi'tər): make a survey.

from the windows. Men had camped and slept everywhere, and on the floor of one room he came upon stains unmistakable where the wounded had been laid down.

Again outside, he led the horse around behind the barn and invaded the orchard. A dozen trees were burdened with ripe apples. He filled his pockets, eating while he picked. Then a thought came to him, and he glanced at the sun, calculating the time of his return to camp. He pulled off his shirt, tying the sleeves and making a bag. This he proceeded to fill with apples.

As he was about to mount his horse, the animal suddenly pricked up its ears. The man, too, listened, and heard, faintly, the thud of hoofs on soft earth. He crept to the corner of the barn and peered out. A dozen mounted men, strung out loosely, approaching from the opposite side of the clearing, were only a matter of a hundred yards or so away. They rode on to the house. Some dismounted, while others remained in the saddle as an earnest[14] that their stay would be short. They seemed to be holding a council, for he could hear them talking excitedly in the detested tongue of the alien invader. The time passed, but they seemed unable to reach a decision. He put the carbine away in its boot, mounted, and waited impatiently, balancing the shirt of apples on the pommel.

He heard footsteps approaching, and drove his spurs so fiercely into the roan as to force a surprised groan from the animal as it leaped forward. At the corner of the barn he saw the intruder, a mere boy of nineteen or twenty for all of his uniform, jump back to escape being run down. At the same moment the roan swerved, and its rider caught a glimpse of the aroused men by the house. Some were springing from their horses, and he could see the ri-

fles going to their shoulders. He passed the kitchen door and the dried corpses swinging in the shade, compelling his foes to run around the front of the house. A rifle cracked, and a second, but he was going fast, leaning forward, low in the saddle, one hand clutching the shirt of apples, the other guiding the horse.

The top bar of the fence was four feet high, but he knew his roan and leaped it at full career[15] to the accompaniment of several scattered shots. Eight hundred yards straight away were the woods, and the roan was covering the distance with mighty strides. Every man was now firing. They were pumping their guns so rapidly that he no longer heard individual shots. A bullet went through his hat, but he was unaware, though he did know when another tore through the apples on the pommel. And he winced and ducked even lower when a third bullet, fired low, struck a stone between his horse's legs and ricocheted off through the air, buzzing and humming like some incredible insect.

The shots died down as the magazines were emptied, until, quickly, there was no more shooting. The young man was elated. Through that astonishing fusillade he had come unscathed. He glanced back. Yes, they had emptied their magazines. He could see several reloading. Others were running back behind the house for their horses. As he looked, two, already mounted, came back into view around the corner, riding hard. And at the same moment, he saw the man with the unmistakable ginger beard kneel down on the ground, level his gun, and coolly take his time for the long shot.

The young man threw his spurs into the horse, crouched very low, and swerved in his flight in order to distract the other's aim. And still the shot did not come. With each jump of

14. **earnest:** a pledge; an assurance.

15. **at full career:** at full speed.

the horse, the woods sprang nearer. They were only two hundred yards away, and still the shot was delayed.

And then he heard it, the last thing he was to hear, for he was dead ere he hit the ground in the long crashing fall from the saddle. And they, watching at the house, saw him fall, saw his body bounce when it struck the earth, and saw the burst of red-cheeked apples that rolled about him. They laughed at the unexpected eruption of apples, and clapped their hands in applause of the long shot by the man with the ginger beard.

Reading Check

1. At the opening of the story, in what direction is the young cavalryman moving?
2. What does he see at the edge of the stream?
3. What evidence does he find that a battle has been fought at the deserted farmhouse?
4. Why is he forced to try a desperate escape?

For Study and Discussion

Analyzing and Interpreting the Story

1a. What is the young cavalryman's quest? **b.** In what way is his task more fearful than being in the midst of battle?

2. Why do you think the soldier decides not to shoot the man with the ginger-colored beard?

3. The young cavalryman is killed by the very man he spared earlier in the story. What does this ironic ending suggest about the nature of war?

4. Why do you suppose London does not identify his young soldier by name?

Literary Elements

Irony of Situation

Irony of situation occurs when a character's actions bring about unexpected results. The young cavalryman in London's story spares the life of the man he sees at the stream. Ironically, he is killed by that very man.

Irony is a powerful element in literature because it enables an author to suggest a great deal without commenting directly on characters and actions. How does the irony in London's story give the events universal significance?

Language and Vocabulary

Recognizing Word Origins

When we hear the word *magazine,* we usually think of a periodical like *Time* or *Family Circle,* which contains various articles and photographs. But *magazine* is also a military term meaning "a place to store ammunition or explosives." In this story, it refers to a clip or a small metal container for cartridges, which is inserted into a rifle.

What can you find out about the origins and meanings of these terms?

carbine	cavalry	fusillade
cartridge	clip	

Which of these words also have meanings *not* directly associated with the military?

Focus on Narrative Writing

Using Chronological Order

Most narratives follow **chronological** or **time order.** Jack London tells "War," for example, in the order that the events happened. This order is critical for the powerful irony of the tale's outcome. If the reader was told in advance that the young cavalryman would be killed by the man with the ginger beard, the story's events would still be ironic, but the irony would be much less forceful.

Notice that London often uses **transitional words and phrases** to help the reader follow the time order of events. Some examples of transitions are *slowly, at last,* and *just as* in the second full paragraph on page 42. Other useful transitions are the following:

after	finally	suddenly
at once	first	then
before	meanwhile	when
eventually	next	

Write a paragraph or two telling about a recent occasion when you were pleasantly surprised, either at home or at school. Use time order and transitions to show the sequence of events. Save your writing.

About the Author

Jack London   (1876–1916)

Born in poverty in San Francisco, Jack London worked for ten cents an hour in a cannery as soon as he graduated from grammar school. By the time he published his first book at the age of twenty-four, he had been a hobo, a longshoreman, an oyster pirate, a seaman, and a gold prospector in Alaska. He had also been in jail twice—once for vagrancy in New York and once for speaking at a socialist meeting in California. London's participation in the gold rush to the Klondike in 1896 paid off—not in gold, but in material for stories. London soon became one of the most highly paid writers in the United States. Disciplined to write a thousand words a day, he turned out popular adventure fiction, such as the famous story "To Build a Fire" and the best-selling novel *The Call of the Wild.* London's fiction was realistic and often portrayed people locked in a grim struggle for survival.

The Musgrave Ritual

SIR ARTHUR CONAN DOYLE

In this story from The Memoirs of Sherlock Holmes, *Holmes recalls one of his earliest cases, involving a strange ceremony. Note how he uses his famous powers of deductive reasoning to unravel the mystery.*

An anomaly[1] which often struck me in the character of my friend Sherlock Holmes was that, although in his methods of thought he was the neatest and most methodical of mankind, and although also he affected a certain quiet primness of dress, he was none the less in his personal habits one of the most untidy men that ever drove a fellow lodger to distraction. Not that I am in the least conventional in that respect myself. The rough-and-tumble work in Afghanistan,[2] coming on the top of natural Bohemianism[3] of disposition, has made me rather more lax than befits a medical man. But with me there is a limit, and when I find a man who keeps his cigars in the coal scuttle, his tobacco in the toe end of a Persian slipper, and his unanswered correspondence transfixed by a jackknife into the very center of his wooden mantelpiece, then I begin to give myself virtuous airs. I have always held, too, that pistol practice should be distinctly an open-air pas-

time; and when Holmes, in one of his queer humors, would sit in an armchair with his hair-trigger and a hundred Boxer cartridges and proceed to adorn the opposite wall with a patriotic V. R.[4] done in bullet-pocks, I felt strongly that neither the atmosphere nor the appearance of our room was improved by it.

Our chambers were always full of chemicals and of criminal relics which had a way of wandering into unlikely positions, and of turning up in the butter dish or in even less desirable places. But his papers were my great crux. He had a horror of destroying documents, especially those which were connected with his past cases, and yet it was only once in every year or two that he would muster energy to docket and arrange them; for, as I have mentioned somewhere in these incoherent memoirs, the outbursts of passionate energy when he performed the remarkable feats with which his name is associated were followed by reactions of lethargy during which he would lie about with his violin and his books, hardly moving

---

1. **anomaly** (ə-nŏm′ə-lē): unusual or irregular quality or characteristic.
2. **Afghanistan:** Before his association with Holmes, Watson had served in the British army.
3. **Bohemianism** (bō-hē′mē-ən-ĭsm′): unconventional behavior.

4. **V. R.:** The initials stand for *Victoria Regina* (*Queen Victoria*). Victoria reigned in England from 1837 to 1901.

save from the sofa to the table. Thus month after month his papers accumulated until every corner of the room was stacked with bundles of manuscript which were on no account to be burned, and which could not be put away save by their owner. One winter's night, as we sat together by the fire, I ventured to suggest to him that, as he had finished pasting extracts into his commonplace book,[5] he might employ the next two hours in making our room a little more habitable. He could not deny the justice of my request, so with a rather rueful face he went off to his bedroom, from which he returned presently pulling a large tin box behind him. This he placed in the middle of the floor, and, squatting down upon a stool in front of it, he threw back the lid. I could see that it was already a third full of bundles of paper tied up with red tape into separate packages.

"There are cases enough here, Watson," said he, looking at me with mischievous eyes. "I think that if you knew all that I had in this box you would ask me to pull some out instead of putting others in."

"These are the records of your early work, then?" I asked. "I have often wished that I had notes of those cases."

"Yes, my boy, these were all done prematurely before my biographer had come to glorify me." He lifted bundle after bundle in a tender, caressing sort of way. "They are not all successes, Watson," said he. "But there are some pretty little problems among them. Here's the record of the Tarleton murders, and the case of Vamberry, the wine merchant, and the adventure of the old Russian woman, and the singular affair of the aluminum crutch, as well as a full account of Ricoletti of the clubfoot, and his abominable wife. And

here—ah, now, this really is something a little *recherché*."[6]

He dived his arm down to the bottom of the chest and brought up a small wooden box with a sliding lid such as children's toys are kept in. From within he produced a crumpled piece of paper, an old-fashioned brass key, a peg of wood with a ball of string attached to it, and three rusty old discs of metal.

"Well, my boy, what do you make of this lot?" he asked, smiling at my expression.

"It is a curious collection."

"Very curious, and the story that hangs round it will strike you as being more curious still."

"These relics have a history, then?"

"So much so that they *are* history."

"What do you mean by that?"

Sherlock Holmes picked them up one by one and laid them along the edge of the table. Then he reseated himself in his chair and looked them over with a gleam of satisfaction in his eyes.

"These," said he, "are all that I have left to remind me of the adventure of the Musgrave Ritual."

I had heard him mention the case more than once, though I had never been able to gather the details. "I should be so glad," said I, "if you would give me an account of it."

"And leave the litter as it is?" he cried mischievously. "Your tidiness won't bear much strain, after all, Watson. But I should be glad that you should add this case to your annals, for there are points in it which make it quite unique in the criminal records of this or, I believe, of any other country. A collection of my trifling achievements would certainly be incomplete which contained no account of this very singular business.

"You may remember how the affair of the

---

5. **commonplace book:** a journal containing passages for reference and personal comments.

6. *recherché* (rə-shâr′shā′): uncommon; choice.

All drawings for "The Musgrave Ritual" were originally done by Sidney Paget for the *Strand* magazine (1901–1905).

Gloria Scott,[7] and my conversation with the unhappy man whose fate I told you of, first turned my attention in the direction of the profession which has become my life's work. You see me now when my name has become known far and wide, and when I am generally recognized both by the public and by the official force as being a final court of appeal in doubtful cases. Even when you knew me first, at the time of the affair which you have commemorated in 'A Study in Scarlet,' I had already established a considerable, though not a

very lucrative, connection. You can hardly realize, then, how difficult I found it at first, and how long I had to wait before I succeeded in making any headway.

"When I first came up to London I had rooms in Montague Street, just round the corner from the British Museum, and there I waited, filling in my too abundant leisure time by studying all those branches of science which might make me more efficient. Now and again cases came in my way, principally through the introduction of old fellow students, for during my last years at the university there was a good deal of talk there about myself and my meth-

7. ***Gloria Scott:*** a ship that figures in Holmes's first case.

ods. The third of these cases was that of the Musgrave Ritual, and it is to the interest which was aroused by that singular chain of events, and the large issues which proved to be at stake, that I trace my first stride towards the position which I now hold.

"Reginald Musgrave had been in the same college as myself, and I had some slight acquaintance with him. He was not generally popular among the undergraduates, though it always seemed to me that what was set down as pride was really an attempt to cover extreme natural diffidence. In appearance he was a man of an exceedingly aristocratic type, thin, high-nosed, and large-eyed, with languid and yet courtly manners. He was indeed a scion of one of the very oldest families in the kingdom, though his branch was a cadet one[8] which had separated from the northern Musgraves some time in the sixteenth century and had established itself in western Sussex, where the Manor House of Hurlstone is perhaps the oldest inhabited building in the county. Something of his birthplace seemed to cling to the man, and I never looked at his pale, keen face or the poise of his head without associating him with gray archways and mullioned windows[9] and all the venerable wreckage of a feudal keep.[10] Once or twice we drifted into talk, and I can remember that more than once he expressed a keen interest in my methods of observation and inference.

"For four years I had seen nothing of him until one morning he walked into my room in Montague Street. He had changed little, was dressed like a young man of fashion—he was always a bit of a dandy—and preserved the same quiet, suave manner which had formerly distinguished him.

8. **cadet one:** a younger branch of the family.
9. **mullioned** (mŭl′yənd) **windows:** windows with vertical strips dividing the panes.
10. **feudal keep:** a medieval fortress.

" 'How has all gone with you, Musgrave?' I asked after we had cordially shaken hands.

" 'You probably heard of my poor father's death,' said he; 'he was carried off about two years ago. Since then I have of course had the Hurlstone estate to manage, and as I am member for my district[11] as well, my life has been a busy one. But I understand, Holmes, that you are turning to practical ends those powers with which you used to amaze us?'

" 'Yes,' said I, 'I have taken to living by my wits.'

" 'I am delighted to hear it, for your advice at present would be exceedingly valuable to me. We have had some very strange doings at Hurlstone, and the police have been able to throw no light upon the matter. It is really the most extraordinary and inexplicable business.'

"You can imagine with what eagerness I listened to him, Watson, for the very chance for which I had been panting during all those months of inaction seemed to have come within my reach. In my inmost heart I believed that I could succeed where others failed, and now I had the opportunity to test myself.

" 'Pray let me have the details,' I cried.

"Reginald Musgrave sat down opposite to me and lit the cigarette which I had pushed towards him.

" 'You must know,' said he, 'that though I am a bachelor, I have to keep up a considerable staff of servants at Hurlstone, for it is a rambling old place and takes a good deal of looking after. I preserve,[12] too, and in the pheasant months I usually have a house party, so that it would not do to be short-handed. Altogether there are eight maids, the cook, the butler, two footmen, and a boy. The garden and the stables of course have a separate staff.

11. **member . . . district:** a representative in Parliament.
12. **preserve:** here, maintain game for hunting.

"'Of these servants the one who had been longest in our service was Brunton, the butler. He was a young schoolmaster out of place when he was first taken up by my father, but he was a man of great energy and character, and he soon became quite invaluable in the household. He was a well-grown, handsome man, with a splendid forehead, and though he has been with us for twenty years he cannot be more than forty now. With his personal advantages and his extraordinary gifts—for he can speak several languages and play nearly every musical instrument—it is wonderful that he should have been satisfied so long in such a position, but I suppose that he was comfortable and lacked energy to make any change. The butler of Hurlstone is always a thing that is remembered by all who visit us.

"'But this paragon has one fault. He is a bit of a Don Juan,[13] and you can imagine that for a man like him it is not a very difficult part to play in a quiet country district. When he was married it was all right, but since he has been a widower we have had no end of trouble with him. A few months ago we were in hopes that he was about to settle down again, for he became engaged to Rachel Howells, our second housemaid; but he has thrown her over since then and taken up with Janet Tregellis, the daughter of the head gamekeeper. Rachel—who is a very good girl, but of an excitable Welsh temperament—had a sharp touch of brain fever and goes about the house now—or did until yesterday—like a black-eyed shadow of her former self. That was our first drama at Hurlstone; but a second one came to drive it from our minds, and it was prefaced by the disgrace and dismissal of butler Brunton.

"'This was how it came about. I have said that the man was intelligent, and this very intelligence has caused his ruin, for it seems to

have led to an insatiable curiosity about things which did not in the least concern him. I had no idea of the lengths to which this would carry him until the merest accident opened my eyes to it.

"'I have said that the house is a rambling one. One day last week—on Thursday night, to be more exact—I found that I could not sleep, having foolishly taken a cup of strong *café noir*[14] after my dinner. After struggling against it until two in the morning, I felt that it was quite hopeless, so I rose and lit the candle with the intention of continuing a novel which I was reading. The book, however, had been left in the billiard room, so I pulled on my dressing gown and started off to get it.

"'In order to reach the billiard room I had to descend a flight of stairs and then to cross the head of a passage which led to the library and the gun room. You can imagine my surprise when, as I looked down this corridor, I saw a glimmer of light coming from the open door of the library. I had myself extinguished the lamp and closed the door before coming to bed. Naturally my first thought was of burglars. The corridors at Hurlstone have their walls largely decorated with trophies of old weapons. From one of these I picked a battle-axe, and then, leaving my candle behind me, I crept on tiptoe down the passage and peeped in at the open door.

"'Brunton, the butler, was in the library. He was sitting, fully dressed, in an easy chair, with a slip of paper which looked like a map upon his knee, and his forehead sunk forward upon his hand in deep thought. I stood dumb with astonishment, watching him from the darkness. A small taper on the edge of the table shed a feeble light which sufficed to show me that he was fully dressed. Suddenly, as I looked, he rose from his chair, and, walking

13. **Don Juan** (dŏn′wän′): a legendary Spanish nobleman obsessed with the pursuit of women.

14. *café noir* (kă-fā′ nwär′): black coffee.

over to a bureau at the side, he unlocked it and drew out one of the drawers. From this he took a paper, and, returning to his seat, he flattened it out beside the taper on the edge of the table and began to study it with minute attention.

My indignation at this calm examination of our family documents overcame me so far that I took a step forward, and Brunton, looking up, saw me standing in the doorway. He sprang to his feet, his face turned livid with fear, and he thrust into his breast the chartlike paper which he had been originally studying.

"'"So!" said I. "This is how you repay the trust which we have reposed in you. You will leave my service tomorrow."

"'He bowed with the look of a man who is utterly crushed and slunk past me without a word. The taper was still on the table, and by its light I glanced to see what the paper was which Brunton had taken from the bureau. To my surprise it was nothing of any importance at all, but simply a copy of the questions and answers in the singular old observance called the Musgrave Ritual. It is a sort of ceremony peculiar to our family, which each Musgrave for centuries past has gone through on his coming of age—a thing of private interest, and perhaps of some little importance to the archæologist, like our own blazonings and charges,[15] but of no practical use whatever.'

"'We had better come back to the paper afterwards,' said I.

"'If you think it really necessary,' he answered with some hesitation. 'To continue my statement, however: I relocked the bureau, using the key which Brunton had left, and I had turned to go when I was surprised to find that the butler had returned, and was standing before me.

"'"Mr. Musgrave, sir," he cried in a voice which was hoarse with emotion, "I can't bear disgrace, sir. I've always been proud above my station in life, and disgrace would kill me. My blood will be on your head, sir—it will, indeed—if you drive me to despair. If you cannot keep me after what has passed, then for

15. **blazonings and charges:** descriptions of coats of arms and heraldic emblems.

God's sake let me give you notice and leave in a month, as if of my own free will. I could stand that, Mr. Musgrave, but not to be cast out before all the folk that I know so well."

"'"You don't deserve much consideration, Brunton," I answered. "Your conduct has been most infamous. However, as you have been a long time in the family, I have no wish to bring public disgrace upon you. A month, however, is too long. Take yourself away in a week, and give what reason you like for going."

"'"Only a week, sir?" he cried in a despairing voice. "A fortnight[16]—say at least a fortnight!"

"'"A week," I repeated, "and you may consider yourself to have been very leniently dealt with."

"'He crept away, his face sunk upon his breast, like a broken man, while I put out the light and returned to my room.

"'For two days after this Brunton was most assiduous in his attention to his duties. I made no allusion to what had passed and waited with some curiosity to see how he would cover his disgrace. On the third morning, however, he did not appear, as was his custom, after breakfast to receive my instructions for the day. As I left the dining room I happened to meet Rachel Howells, the maid. I have told you that she had only recently recovered from an illness and was looking so wretchedly pale and wan that I remonstrated[17] with her for being at work.

"'"You should be in bed," I said. "Come back to your duties when you are stronger."

"'She looked at me with so strange an expression that I began to suspect that her brain was affected.

"'"I am strong enough, Mr. Musgrave," said she.

"'"We will see what the doctor says," I answered. "You must stop work now, and when you go downstairs just say that I wish to see Brunton."

"'"The butler is gone," said she.

"'"Gone! Gone where?"

"'"He is gone. No one has seen him. He is not in his room. Oh, yes, he is gone, he is gone!" She fell back against the wall with shriek after shriek of laughter, while I, horrified at this sudden hysterical attack, rushed to the bell to summon help. The girl was taken to her room, still screaming and sobbing, while I made inquiries about Brunton. There was no doubt about it that he had disappeared. His bed had not been slept in, he had been seen by no one since he had retired to his room the night before, and yet it was difficult to see how he could have left the house, as both windows and doors were found to be fastened in the morning. His clothes, his watch, and even his money were in his room, but the black suit which he usually wore was missing. His slippers, too, were gone, but his boots[18] were left behind. Where then could butler Brunton have gone in the night, and what could have become of him now?

"'Of course we searched the house from cellar to garret, but there was no trace of him. It is, as I have said, a labyrinth of an old house, especially the original wing, which is now practically uninhabited; but we ransacked every room and cellar without discovering the least sign of the missing man. It was incredible to me that he could have gone away leaving all his property behind him, and yet where could he be? I called in the local police, but without success. Rain had fallen on the night before, and we examined the lawn and the paths all round the house, but in vain. Matters were in this state, when a new development quite drew our

16. **fortnight:** two weeks.
17. **remonstrated** (rĭ′mŏn-strāt′əd): argued or made protest.

18. **boots:** shoes.

attention away from the original mystery.

"'For two days Rachel Howells had been so ill, sometimes delirious, sometimes hysterical, that a nurse had been employed to sit up with her at night. On the third night after Brunton's disappearance, the nurse, finding her patient sleeping nicely, had dropped into a nap in the armchair, when she woke in the early morning to find the bed empty, the window open, and no signs of the invalid. I was instantly aroused, and, with the two footmen, started off at once in search of the missing girl. It was not difficult to tell the direction which she had taken, for, starting from under her window, we could follow her footmarks easily across the lawn to the edge of the mere,[19] where they vanished close to the gravel path which leads out of the grounds. The lake there is eight feet deep, and you can imagine our feelings when we saw that the trail of the poor demented girl came to an end at the edge of it.

"'Of course, we had the drags at once and set to work to recover the remains, but no trace of the body could we find. On the other hand, we brought to the surface an object of a most unexpected kind. It was a linen bag which contained within it a mass of old rusted and discolored metal and several dull-colored pieces of pebble or glass. This strange find was all that we could get from the mere, and, although we made every possible search and inquiry yesterday, we know nothing of the fate either of Rachel Howells or of Richard Brunton. The county police are at their wits' end, and I have come up to you as a last resource.'

"You can imagine, Watson, with what eagerness I listened to this extraordinary sequence of events, and endeavored to piece them together, and to devise some common thread upon which they might all hang. The butler was gone. The maid was gone. The maid had loved the butler, but had afterwards had cause to hate him. She was of Welsh blood, fiery and passionate. She had been terribly excited immediately after his disappearance. She had flung into the lake a bag containing some curious contents. These were all factors which had to be taken into consideration, and yet none of them got quite to the heart of the matter. What was the starting point of this chain of events? There lay the end of this tangled line.

"'I must see that paper, Musgrave,' said I, 'which this butler of yours thought it worth his while to consult, even at the risk of the loss of his place.'

"'It is rather an absurd business, this ritual of ours,' he answered. 'But it has at least the saving grace of antiquity to excuse it. I have a copy of the questions and answers here if you care to run your eye over them.'

"He handed me the very paper which I have here, Watson, and this is the strange catechism[20] to which each Musgrave had to submit when he came to man's estate. I will read you the questions and answers as they stand.

"'Whose was it?'

"'His who is gone.'

"'Who shall have it?'

"'He who will come.'

"'Where was the sun?'

"'Over the oak.'

"'Where was the shadow?'

"'Under the elm.'

"'How was it stepped?'

"'North by ten and by ten, east by five and by five, south by two and by two, west by one and by one, and so under.'

"'What shall we give for it?'

"'All that is ours.'

"'Why should we give it?'

"'For the sake of the trust.'

"'The original has no date, but is in the

---

19. **mere:** pond, lake.

20. **catechism** (kăt'ə-kĭz'əm): a series of questions and answers, used for instruction.

spelling of the middle of the seventeenth century,' remarked Musgrave. 'I am afraid, however, that it can be of little help to you in solving this mystery.'

" 'At least,' said I, 'it gives us another mystery, and one which is even more interesting than the first. It may be that the solution of the one may prove to be the solution of the other. You will excuse me, Musgrave, if I say that your butler appears to me to have been a very clever man, and to have had a clearer insight than ten generations of his masters.'

" 'I hardly follow you,' said Musgrave. 'The paper seems to me to be of no practical importance.'

" 'But to me it seems immensely practical, and I fancy that Brunton took the same view. He had probably seen it before that night on which you caught him.'

" 'It is very possible. We took no pains to hide it.'

" 'He simply wished, I should imagine, to refresh his memory upon that last occasion. He had, as I understand, some sort of map or chart which he was comparing with the manuscript, and which he thrust into his pocket when you appeared.'

" 'That is true. But what could he have to do with this old family custom of ours, and what does this rigmarole[21] mean?'

" 'I don't think that we should have much difficulty in determining that,' said I; 'with your permission we will take the first train down to Sussex and go a little more deeply into the matter upon the spot.'

"The same afternoon saw us both at Hurlstone. Possibly you have seen pictures and read descriptions of the famous old building, so I will confine my account of it to saying that it is built in the shape of an L, the long arm being the more modern portion, and the

21. **rigmarole** (rĭg′mə-rōl): nonsense.

shorter the ancient nucleus from which the other has developed. Over the low, heavy-lintelled door, in the center of this old part, is chiseled the date, 1607, but experts are agreed that the beams and stonework are really much older than this. The enormously thick walls and tiny windows of this part had in the last century driven the family into building the new wing, and the old one was used now as a storehouse and a cellar, when it was used at all. A splendid park with fine old timber surrounds the house, and the lake, to which my client had referred, lay close to the avenue, about two hundred yards from the building.

"I was already firmly convinced, Watson, that there were not three separate mysteries here, but one only, and that if I could read the Musgrave Ritual aright I should hold in my hand the clue which would lead me to the truth concerning both the butler Brunton and the maid Howells. To that then I turned all my energies. Why should this servant be so anxious to master this old formula? Evidently because he saw something in it which had escaped all those generations of country squires, and from which he expected some personal advantage. What was it then, and how had it affected his fate?

"It was perfectly obvious to me, on reading the Ritual, that the measurements must refer to some spot to which the rest of the document alluded, and that if we could find that spot we should be in a fair way towards finding what the secret was which the old Musgraves had thought it necessary to embalm in so curious a fashion. There were two guides given us to start with, an oak and an elm. As to the oak there could be no question at all. Right in front of the house, upon the lefthand side of the drive, there stood a patriarch among oaks, one of the most magnificent trees that I have ever seen.

" 'That was there when your Ritual was

drawn up,' said I as we drove past it.

"'It was there at the Norman Conquest[22] in all probability,' he answered. 'It has a girth of twenty-three feet.'

22. **Norman Conquest:** an important event in English history. In 1066, William the Conqueror and the Normans, from Normandy in France, invaded and conquered England.

"Here was one of my fixed points secured.

"'Have you any old elms?' I asked.

"'There used to be a very old one over yonder, but it was struck by lightning ten years ago, and we cut down the stump.'

"'You can see where it used to be?'

"'Oh, yes.'

"'There are no other elms?'

" 'No old ones, but plenty of beeches.'

" 'I should like to see where it grew.'

"We had driven up in a dogcart,[23] and my client led me away at once, without our entering the house, to the scar on the lawn where the elm had stood. It was nearly midway between the oak and the house. My investigation seemed to be progressing.

" 'I suppose it is impossible to find out how high the elm was?' I asked.

" 'I can give you it at once. It was sixty-four feet.'

" 'How do you come to know it?' I asked in surprise.

" 'When my old tutor used to give me an exercise in trigonometry,[24] it always took the shape of measuring heights. When I was a lad I worked out every tree and building in the estate.'

"This was an unexpected piece of luck. My data were coming more quickly than I could have reasonably hoped.

" 'Tell me,' I asked, 'did your butler ever ask you such a question?'

"Reginald Musgrave looked at me in astonishment. 'Now that you call it to my mind,' he answered, 'Brunton *did* ask me about the height of the tree some months ago in connection with some little argument with the groom.'

"This was excellent news, Watson, for it showed me that I was on the right road. I looked up at the sun. It was low in the heavens, and I calculated that in less than an hour it would lie just above the topmost branches of the old oak. One condition mentioned in the Ritual would then be fulfilled. And the shadow of the elm must mean the farther end of the shadow, otherwise the trunk would have been

chosen as the guide. I had, then, to find where the far end of the shadow would fall when the sun was just clear of the oak."

"That must have been difficult, Holmes, when the elm was no longer there."

"Well, at least I knew that if Brunton could do it, I could also. Besides, there was no real difficulty. I went with Musgrave to his study and whittled myself this peg, to which I tied this long string with a knot at each yard. Then I took two lengths of a fishing rod, which came to just six feet, and I went back with my client to where the elm had been. The sun was just grazing the top of the oak. I fastened the rod on end, marked out the direction of the shadow, and measured it. It was nine feet in length.

"Of course the calculation now was a simple one. If a rod of six feet threw a shadow of nine, a tree of sixty-four feet would throw one of ninety-six, and the line of the one would of course be the line of the other. I measured out the distance, which brought me almost to the wall of the house, and I thrust a peg into the spot. You can imagine my exultation, Watson, when within two inches of my peg I saw a conical depression in the ground. I knew that it was the mark made by Brunton in his measurements, and that I was still upon his trail.

"From this starting point I proceeded to step, having first taken the cardinal points[25] by my pocket-compass. Ten steps with each foot took me along parallel with the wall of the house, and again I marked my spot with a peg. Then I carefully paced off five to the east and two to the south. It brought me to the very threshold of the old door. Two steps to the west meant now that I was to go two paces down the stone-flagged passage, and this was the place indicated by the Ritual.

"Never have I felt such a cold chill of disap-

23. **dogcart:** a small cart drawn by one horse.
24. **trigonometry** (trĭg′ə-nŏm′ə-trē): a branch of mathematics applied in finding unknown sides and angles of triangles.

25. **cardinal points:** the points of the compass: north, south, east, and west.

pointment, Watson. For a moment it seemed to me that there must be some radical mistake in my calculations. The setting sun shone full upon the passage floor, and I could see that the old, footworn gray stones with which it was paved were firmly cemented together, and had certainly not been moved for many a long year. Brunton had not been at work here. I tapped upon the floor, but it sounded the same all over, and there was no sign of any crack or crevice. But, fortunately, Musgrave, who had begun to appreciate the meaning of my proceedings, and who was now as excited as myself, took out his manuscript to check my calculations.

"'And under,' he cried. 'You have omitted the "and under."'

"I had thought that it meant that we were to dig, but now, of course, I saw at once that I was wrong. 'There is a cellar under this then?' I cried.

"'Yes, and as old as the house. Down here, through this door.'

"We went down a winding stone stair, and my companion, striking a match, lit a large lantern which stood on a barrel in the corner. In an instant it was obvious that we had at last come upon the true place, and that we had not been the only people to visit the spot recently.

"It had been used for the storage of wood, but the billets,[26] which had evidently been littered over the floor, were now piled at the sides, so as to leave a clear space in the middle. In this space lay a large and heavy flagstone with a rusted iron ring in the center to which a thick shepherd's-check muffler was attached.

"'By Jove!' cried my client. 'That's Brunton's muffler. I have seen it on him and could swear to it. What has the villain been doing here?'

"At my suggestion a couple of the county po-lice were summoned to be present, and I then endeavored to raise the stone by pulling on the cravat.[27] I could only move it slightly, and it was with the aid of one of the constables that I succeeded at last in carrying it to one side. A black hole yawned beneath into which we all peered, while Musgrave, kneeling at the side, pushed down the lantern.

"A small chamber about seven feet deep and four feet square lay open to us. At one side of this was a squat, brass-bound wooden box, the lid of which was hinged upward, with this curious old-fashioned key projecting from the lock. It was furred outside by a thick layer of dust, and damp and worms had eaten through the wood, so that a crop of livid fungi was growing on the inside of it. Several discs of metal, old coins apparently, such as I hold here, were scattered over the bottom of the box, but it contained nothing else.

"At the moment, however, we had no thought for the old chest, for our eyes were riveted upon that which crouched beside it. It was the figure of a man, clad in a suit of black, who squatted down upon his hams with his forehead sunk upon the edge of the box and his two arms thrown out on each side of it. The attitude had drawn all the stagnant blood to the face, and no man could have recognized that distorted liver-colored countenance; but his height, his dress, and his hair were all sufficient to show my client, when we had drawn the body up, that it was indeed his missing butler. He had been dead some days, but there was no wound or bruise upon his person to show how he had met his dreadful end. When his body had been carried from the cellar we found ourselves still confronted with a problem which was almost as formidable as that with which we had started.

"I confess that so far, Watson, I had been

---

26. **billets:** firewood cut in short, thick pieces.

27. **cravat** (krə-văt'): scarf.

disappointed in my investigation. I had reckoned upon solving the matter when once I had found the place referred to in the Ritual; but now I was there, and was apparently as far as ever from knowing what it was which the family had concealed with such elaborate precautions. It is true that I had thrown a light upon the fate of Brunton, but now I had to ascertain how that fate had come upon him, and what part had been played in the matter by the

woman who had disappeared. I sat down upon a keg in the corner and thought the whole matter carefully over.

"You know my methods in such cases, Watson. I put myself in the man's place, and, having first gauged his intelligence, I try to imagine how I should myself have proceeded under the same circumstances. In this case the matter was simplified by Brunton's intelligence being quite first-rate, so that it was unnecessary to make any allowance for the personal equation,[28] as the astronomers have dubbed it. He knew that something valuable was concealed. He had spotted the place. He found that the stone which covered it was just too heavy for a man to move unaided. What would he do next? He could not get help from outside, even if he had someone whom he could trust, without the unbarring of doors and considerable risk of detection. It was better, if he could, to have his helpmate inside the house. But whom could he ask? This girl had been devoted to him. A man always finds it hard to realize that he may have finally lost a woman's love, however badly he may have treated her. He would try by a few attentions to make his peace with the girl Howells, and then would engage her as his accomplice. Together they would come at night to the cellar, and their united force would suffice to raise the stone. So far I could follow their actions as if I had actually seen them.

"But for two of them, and one a woman, it must have been heavy work, the raising of that stone. A burly Sussex policeman and I had found it no light job. What would they do to assist them? Probably what I should have done myself. I rose and examined carefully the different billets of wood which were scattered round the floor. Almost at once I came upon

28. **allowance . . . personal equation:** taking into account variations in an individual's observation, judgment, and reasoning.

what I expected. One piece, about three feet in length, had a very marked indentation at one end, while several were flattened at the sides as if they had been compressed by some considerable weight. Evidently, as they had dragged the stone up, they had thrust the chunks of wood into the chink until at last when the opening was large enough to crawl through, they would hold it open by a billet placed lengthwise, which might very well become indented at the lower end, since the whole weight of the stone would press it down on to the edge of this other slab. So far I was still on safe ground.

"And now how was I to proceed to reconstruct this midnight drama? Clearly, only one could fit into the hole, and that one was Brunton. The girl must have waited above. Brunton then unlocked the box, handed up the contents presumably—since they were not to be found—and then—and then what happened?

"What smoldering fire of vengeance had suddenly sprung into flame in this passionate Celtic woman's soul when she saw the man who had wronged her—wronged her, perhaps, far more than we suspected—in her power? Was it a chance that the wood had slipped and that the stone had shut Brunton into what had become his sepulcher? Had she only been guilty of silence as to his fate? Or had some sudden blow from her hand dashed the support away and sent the slab crashing down into its place? Be that as it might, I seemed to see that woman's figure still clutching at her treasure trove and flying wildly up the winding stair, with her ears ringing perhaps with the muffled screams from behind her and with the drumming of frenzied hands against the slab of stone which was choking her faithless lover's life out.

"Here was the secret of her blanched face, her shaken nerves, her peals of hysterical laughter on the next morning. But what had been in the box? What had she done with that? Of course, it must have been the old metal and pebbles which my client had dragged from the mere. She had thrown them in there at the first opportunity to remove the last trace of her crime.

"For twenty minutes I had sat motionless, thinking the matter out. Musgrave still stood with a very pale face, swinging his lantern and peering down into the hole.

"'These are coins of Charles the First,'[29] said he, holding out the few which had been in the box; 'you see we were right in fixing our date for the Ritual.'

"'We may find something else of Charles the First,' I cried, as the probable meaning of the first two questions of the Ritual broke suddenly upon me. 'Let me see the contents of the bag which you fished from the mere.'

"We ascended to his study, and he laid the débris before me. I could understand his regarding it as of small importance when I looked at it, for the metal was almost black and the stones lusterless and dull. I rubbed one of them on my sleeve, however, and it glowed afterwards like a spark in the dark hollow of my hand. The metal work was in the form of a double ring, but it had been bent and twisted out of its original shape.

"'You must bear in mind,' said I, 'that the royal party made head[30] in England even after the death of the king, and that when they at last fled they probably left many of their most precious possessions buried behind them, with the intention of returning for them in more peaceful times.'

"'My ancestor, Sir Ralph Musgrave, was a prominent Cavalier[31] and the right-hand man

---

29. **Charles the First:** Charles Stuart, king of England, Scotland, and Ireland from 1625 to 1649. He was beheaded after the English Civil War, in which the Parliamentary forces defeated the Royalists.
30. **made head:** advanced.
31. **Cavalier** (kăv′ə-lîr′): a supporter of Charles Stuart.

of Charles the Second[32] in his wanderings,' said my friend.

"'Ah, indeed!' I answered. 'Well now, I think that really should give us the last link that we wanted. I must congratulate you on coming into the possession, though in rather a tragic manner, of a relic which is of great intrinsic value, but of even greater importance as a historical curiosity.'

"'What is it, then?' he gasped in astonishment.

"'It is nothing less than the ancient crown of the kings of England.'

"'The crown!'

"'Precisely. Consider what the Ritual says How does it run? "Whose was it?" "His who is gone." That was after the execution of Charles. Then, "Who shall have it?" "He who will come." That was Charles the Second, whose advent was already foreseen. There can, I think, be no doubt that this battered and shapeless diadem once encircled the brows of the royal Stuarts.'

"'And how came it in the pond?'

"'Ah, that is a question that will take some time to answer.' And with that I sketched out to him the whole long chain of surmise and of proof which I had constructed. The twilight had closed in and the moon was shining brightly in the sky before my narrative was finished.

"'And how was it then that Charles did not get his crown when he returned?' asked Musgrave, pushing back the relic into its linen bag.

"'Ah, there you lay your finger upon the one point which we shall probably never be able to clear up. It is likely that the Musgrave who held the secret died in the interval, and by some oversight left this guide to his descendant without explaining the meaning of it. From that day to this it has been handed down from father to son, until at last it came within reach of a man who tore its secret out of it and lost his life in the venture.'

"And that's the story of the Musgrave Ritual, Watson. They have the crown down at Hurlstone—though they had some legal bother and a considerable sum to pay before they were allowed to retain it. I am sure that if you mentioned my name they would be happy to show it to you. Of the woman nothing was ever heard, and the probability is that she got away out of England and carried herself and the memory of her crime to some land beyond the seas."

32. **Charles the Second:** the son of Charles the First. He lived in exile until he was called back to England and the monarchy was restored in 1660.

Reading Check

1. What does Dr. Watson consider Holmes's most annoying habit?
2. What is contained in the wooden box Holmes shows Watson?
3. How does Holmes know Reginald Musgrave?
4. Why was Brunton dismissed?
5. Who tells Musgrave that Brunton is gone?
6. What do the servants find when they drag the lake?
7. How does Musgrave happen to know the height of the old tree that once stood on the lawn?
8. What does Holmes use in order to calculate the length of the shadow thrown by the elm?
9. What clue in the Musgrave Ritual does Holmes misread?
10. What is the treasure Brunton was after?

Analyzing and Interpreting the Story

1. At the opening of the story, Watson speaks about an *anomaly* in Holmes's character. **a.** What aspects of Holmes's character does he find it difficult to reconcile? **b.** Do you think these contrasting qualities make Holmes a more believable or less believable figure?

2. Holmes arrives at his conclusions by the process of deductive reasoning. He first gathers his evidence and then draws inferences logically from this evidence. Trace the steps by which he arrives at the precise location indicated in the Ritual.

3a. According to Holmes, what are his methods in solving problems? **b.** How does he reconstruct the drama that must have taken place in the cellar?

4. After Holmes solves the case of the Musgrave Ritual, what questions still remain unanswered?

5. "The Musgrave Ritual," like the other adventures of Sherlock Holmes, is a special kind of story—the **detective story**, in which the main action consists of solving some mystery. Since the detective story challenges us to match our wits against those of the sleuth, evidence is not withheld. We are in possession of all the facts, but we do not possess Holmes's brilliant powers of deductive reasoning that enable him to draw the right conclusions from these facts. **a.** What do you consider the most impressive example of Holmes's reasoning in this story? **b.** What is the climax of the story?

6. Sherlock Holmes is one of the most famous characters in all of literature. He appears regularly on stage, on screen, and on television in various adaptations of Arthur Conan Doyle's stories. What do you think is the reason for his immense popularity?

Literary Elements

The Story Within a Story

Sometimes an author chooses to tell a story within the **framework** of another story. In its simplest form, the framework can introduce a group of people discussing a particular topic. One of the group will then say, "Oh, yes. That reminds me of something that happened several years ago." And so, the inner story begins. In such a story, the inner story is usually much more important than the framework.

In other stories the framework plays a much more important role. "The Musgrave Ritual," for example, tells two stories that are important. In the framework story, Watson introduces us to Sherlock Holmes, and we listen in on their conversation about Holmes's career. The inner story, about the facts in the case of the Musgrave Ritual, is related by Holmes. The framework story and the story within a story reinforce one another, and each story adds meaning to the other.

In what way are the framework story and the inner story related? How do both cast light on the character and achievements of Sherlock Holmes?

Language and Vocabulary

Finding Appropriate Meanings

Many words in our language have several different meanings. If you consult a college dictionary, you will find more than one entry for the word *affect*. As a verb, *affect* can have the meaning "to influence," as in this sentence: "Prolonged stress *affects* one's health." The verb *affect* can have the meaning "to move the emotions," as in this sentence: "Lincoln's speech at Gettysburg *affected* his audience profoundly." Still another meaning of *affect* is "to pretend or feign," as in this sentence: "She *af-*

fected an aloof manner in order to hide her shyness." *Affect* can also have the meaning "to have a preference for," as in this sentence: "He *affects* English tweeds." What meaning does Watson have in mind when he says that Holmes "*affected* a certain quiet primness of dress"?

Check the different meanings of the word *singular* in a dictionary. What specific meaning does it have in this sentence: "A collection of my trifling achievements would certainly be incomplete which contained no account of this very *singular* business"?

What are the various meanings of *distraction*? What meaning does it have in Watson's complaint that Holmes was "one of the most untidy men that ever drove a fellow lodger to *distraction*"?

Writing About Literature

Classifying Stories

Laurence Perrine, a noted critic, has identified two broad categories of literature that he calls literature of escape and literature of interpretation. *Escape literature* exists primarily for our pleasure, to entertain us by taking us away from everyday reality. By contrast, *interpretive literature* exists to expand our awareness and understanding of life, to give us insight into our own behavior and the behavior of others.

Consider the stories you have read thus far in this unit. Into which category would you place each one? Do any of the stories fit both categories? In a paragraph give reasons for your answers.

Investigating a Topic

Sherlock Holmes is so popular a character that readers have formed groups that meet to share their encyclopedic knowledge of the adventures of Holmes and Dr. Watson. Locate an article or a book on Sherlock Holmes and report briefly on the significance of each of the following in Holmes's career:

221B Baker Street
Professor Moriarty
Mrs. Hudson
Inspector Lestrade
Irene Adler

About the Author

Sir Arthur Conan Doyle (1859–1930)

Arthur Conan Doyle once said that the character of Sherlock Holmes was suggested by his memories of an actual doctor at the Edinburgh Infirmary, where Conan Doyle studied medicine. In all, Conan Doyle produced four full-length novels and fifty-six stories about Sherlock Holmes. Holmes first appeared in print in *A Study in Scarlet*, in 1887. At one point, Conan Doyle became tired of his creation and tried to kill him off in "The Final Problem." Readers, however, would not allow Holmes to die and Conan Doyle had to bring him back in *The Return of Sherlock Holmes*.

CHARACTER

The Secret Life of Walter Mitty

JAMES THURBER

This is one of the most popular short stories ever written. During World War II American fliers formed "Walter Mitty" clubs, and the phrase "pocketa-pocketa" became familiar on many airfields. As you read, ask yourself what is the reason for the title character's wide appeal.

"We're going through!" The Commander's voice was like thin ice breaking. He wore his full-dress uniform, with the heavily braided white cap pulled down rakishly over one cold gray eye. "We can't make it, sir. It's spoiling for a hurricane, if you ask me." "I'm not asking you, Lieutenant Berg," said the Commander. "Throw on the power lights! Rev her up to 8,500! We're going through!" The pounding of the cylinders increased: ta-pocketa-pocketa-pocketa-*pocketa-pocketa*. The Commander stared at the ice forming on the pilot window. He walked over and twisted a row of complicated dials. "Switch on No. 8 auxiliary!" he shouted. "Switch on No. 8 auxiliary!" repeated Lieutenant Berg. "Full strength in No. 3 turret!" shouted the Commander. "Full strength in No. 3 turret!" The crew, bending to their various tasks in the huge, hurtling eight-engined Navy hydroplane, looked at each other and grinned. "The Old Man'll get us through," they said to one another. "The Old Man ain't afraid of Hell!" . . .

"Not so fast! You're driving too fast!" said Mrs. Mitty. "What are you driving so fast for?"

"Hmm?" said Walter Mitty. He looked at his wife, in the seat beside him, with shocked astonishment. She seemed grossly unfamiliar, like a strange woman who had yelled at him in a crowd. "You were up to fifty-five," she said. "You know I don't like to go more than forty. You were up to fifty-five." Walter Mitty drove on toward Waterbury in silence, the roaring of the SN202 through the worst storm in twenty years of Navy flying fading in the remote, intimate airways of his mind. "You're tensed up again," said Mrs. Mitty. "It's one of your days. I wish you'd let Dr. Renshaw look you over."

Walter Mitty stopped the car in front of the building where his wife went to have her hair

A scene from a film version of "The Secret Life of Walter Mitty."

done. "Remember to get those overshoes while I'm having my hair done," she said. "I don't need overshoes," said Mitty. She put her mirror back into her bag. "We've been all through that," she said, getting out of the car. "You're not a young man any longer." He raced the engine a little. "Why don't you wear your gloves? Have you lost your gloves?" Walter Mitty reached in a pocket and brought out the gloves. He put them on, but after she had turned and gone into the building and he had driven on to a red light, he took them off again. "Pick it up, brother!" snapped a cop as the light changed, and Mitty hastily pulled on his gloves and lurched ahead. He drove around the streets aimlessly for a time, and then he drove past the hospital on his way to the parking lot.

. . . "It's the millionaire banker, Wellington McMillan," said the pretty nurse. "Yes?" said Walter Mitty, removing his gloves slowly. "Who has the case?" "Dr. Renshaw and Dr. Benbow, but there are two specialists here, Dr. Remington from New York and Dr. Pritchard-Mitford from London. He flew over!" A door opened down a long cool corridor and Dr. Renshaw came out. He looked distraught and haggard. "Hello, Mitty," he said. "We're having the devil's own time with McMillan, the millionaire banker and close personal friend of Roosevelt. Obstreosis of the ductal tract. Tertiary. Wish you'd take a look at him." "Glad to," said Mitty.

In the operating room there were whispered introductions: "Dr. Remington, Dr. Mitty. Dr. Pritchard-Mitford, Dr. Mitty." "I've read your book on streptothricosis," said Pritchard-Mitford, shaking hands. "A brilliant performance, sir." "Thank you," said Walter Mitty. "Didn't know you were in the States, Mitty," grumbled Remington. "Coals to Newcastle,[1]

1. **Coals to Newcastle:** a saying used to indicate unnecessary labor. Newcastle, a city in England, is famous for its production of coal.

bringing Mitford and me up here for a tertiary." "You are very kind," said Mitty. A huge, complicated machine, connected to the operating table, with many tubes and wires, began at this moment to go pocketa-pocketa-pocketa. "The new anesthetizer is giving way!" shouted an intern. "There is no one in the East who knows how to fix it!" "Quiet, man!" said Mitty, in a low, cool voice. He sprang to the machine, which was now going pocketa-pocketa-queep-pocketa-queep. He began fingering delicately a row of glistening dials. "Give me a fountain pen!" he snapped. Someone handed him a fountain pen. He pulled a faulty piston out of the machine and inserted the pen in its place. "That will hold for ten minutes," he said. "Get on with the operation." A nurse hurried over and whispered to Renshaw, and Mitty saw the man turn pale. "Coreopsis has set in," said Renshaw nervously. "If you would take over, Mitty?" Mitty looked at him and at the craven figure of Benbow, who drank, and at the grave, uncertain faces of the two great specialists. "If you wish," he said. They slipped a white gown on him; he adjusted a mask and drew on thin gloves; nurses handed him shining . . .

"Back it up, Mac! Look out for that Buick!" Walter Mitty jammed on the brakes. "Wrong lane, Mac," said the parking-lot attendant, looking at Mitty closely. "Gee. Yeh," muttered Mitty. He began cautiously to back out of the lane marked "Exit Only." "Leave her sit there," said the attendant. "I'll put her away." Mitty got out of the car. "Hey, better leave the key." "Oh," said Mitty, handing the man the ignition key. The attendant vaulted into the car, backed it up with insolent skill, and put it where it belonged.

They're so cocky, thought Walter Mitty, walking along Main Street; they think they know everything. Once he had tried to take his chains off, outside New Milford, and he had got them wound around the axles. A man had had to come out in a wrecking car and unwind them, a young, grinning garageman. Since then Mrs. Mitty always made him drive to a garage to have the chains taken off. The next time, he thought, I'll wear my right arm in a sling; they won't grin at me then. I'll have my right arm in a sling and they'll see I couldn't possibly take the chains off myself. He kicked at the slush on the sidewalk. "Overshoes," he said to himself, and he began looking for a shoe store.

When he came out into the street again, with the overshoes in a box under his arm, Walter Mitty began to wonder what the other thing was his wife had told him to get. She had told him twice before they set out from their house for Waterbury. In a way he hated these weekly trips to town—he was always getting something wrong. Kleenex, he thought, Squibb's, razor blades? No. Toothpaste, toothbrush, bicarbonate, carborundum, initiative and referendum?[2] He gave it up. But she would remember it. "Where's the what's-its-name?" she would ask. "Don't tell me you forgot the what's-its-name." A newsboy went by shouting something about the Waterbury trial.

. . . "Perhaps this will refresh your memory." The District Attorney suddenly thrust a heavy automatic at the quiet figure on the witness stand. "Have you ever seen this before?" Walter Mitty took the gun and examined it expertly. "This is my Webley-Vickers 50.80," he said calmly. An excited buzz ran around the courtroom. The Judge rapped for order. "You are a crack shot with any sort of firearms, I believe?" said the District Attorney, insinuatingly. "Objection!" shouted Mitty's attorney. "We

2. **carborundum, initiative and referendum:** Carborundum is a hard, abrasive material. Initiative refers to the right of citizens to introduce new legislation. Referendum refers to the right of citizens to vote directly on laws. The association in Mitty's mind is one of sound, not of sense.

have shown that the defendant could not have fired the shot. We have shown that he wore his right arm in a sling on the night of the fourteenth of July," Walter Mitty raised his hand briefly and the bickering attorneys were stilled. "With any known make of gun," he said evenly, "I could have killed Gregory Fitzhurst at three hundred feet *with my left hand.*" Pandemonium broke loose in the courtroom. A woman's scream rose above the bedlam and suddenly a lovely, dark-haired girl was in Walter Mitty's arms. The District Attorney struck at her savagely. Without rising from his chair, Mitty let the man have it on the point of the chin. "You miserable cur!" . . .

"Puppy biscuit," said Walter Mitty. He stopped walking and the buildings of Waterbury rose up out of the misty courtroom and surrounded him again. A woman who was passing laughed. "He said 'Puppy biscuit,'" she said to her companion. "That man said 'Puppy biscuit' to himself." Walter Mitty hurried on. He went into an A & P, not the first one he came to but a smaller one farther up the street. "I want some biscuit for small, young dogs," he said to the clerk. "Any special brand, sir?" The greatest pistol shot in the world thought a moment. "It says 'Puppies Bark for It' on the box," said Walter Mitty.

His wife would be through at the hairdresser's in fifteen minutes, Mitty saw in looking at his watch, unless they had trouble drying it; sometimes they had trouble drying it. She didn't like to get to the hotel first; she would want him to be there waiting for her as usual. He found a big leather chair in the lobby, facing a window, and he put the overshoes and the puppy biscuit on the floor beside it. He picked up an old copy of *Liberty* and sank down into the chair. "Can Germany Conquer the World Through the Air?" Walter Mitty looked at the pictures of bombing planes and of ruined streets.

. . . "The cannonading has got the wind up in young Raleigh, sir," said the sergeant. Captain Mitty looked up at him through tousled hair. "Get him to bed," he said wearily, "with the others. I'll fly alone." "But you can't, sir," said the sergeant anxiously. "It takes two men to handle that bomber and the Archies[3] are pounding hell out of the air. Von Richtman's circus[4] is between here and Saulier." "Somebody's got to get that ammunition dump," said Mitty. "I'm going over. Spot of brandy?" He poured a drink for the sergeant and one for himself. War thundered and whined around the dugout and battered at the door. There was a rending of wood and splinters flew through the room. "A bit of a near thing," said Captain Mitty carelessly. "The box barrage is closing in," said the sergeant. "We only live once, Sergeant," said Mitty, with his faint, fleeting smile. "Or do we?" He poured another brandy and tossed it off. "I never see a man could hold his brandy like you, sir," said the sergeant. "Begging your pardon, sir." Captain Mitty stood up and strapped on his huge Webley-Vickers automatic. "It's forty kilometers through hell, sir," said the sergeant. Mitty finished one last brandy. "After all," he said softly, "what isn't?" The pounding of the cannon increased; there was the rat-tat-tatting of machine guns, and from somewhere came the menacing pocketa-pocketa-pocketa of the new flame-throwers. Walter Mitty walked to the door of the dugout humming "Auprès de Ma Blonde."[5] He turned and waved to the sergeant. "Cheerio!" he said. . . .

Something struck his shoulder. "I've been looking all over this hotel for you," said Mrs. Mitty. "Why do you have to hide in this old chair? How did you expect me to find you?"

3. **Archies:** allied troops' name for the antiaircraft guns in World War I.
4. **circus:** here, a squadron of planes flying in close formation.
5. **"Auprès de Ma Blonde":** popular French song.

"Things close in," said Walter Mitty vaguely. "What?" Mrs. Mitty said. "Did you get the what's-its-name? The puppy biscuit? What's in that box?" "Overshoes," said Mitty. "Couldn't you have put them on in the store?" "I was thinking," said Walter Mitty. "Does it ever occur to you that I am sometimes thinking?" She looked at him. "I'm going to take your temperature when I get you home," she said.

They went out through the revolving doors that made a faintly derisive whistling sound when you pushed them. It was two blocks to the parking lot. At the drugstore on the corner she said, "Wait here for me. I forgot something. I won't be a minute." She was more than a minute. Walter Mitty lighted a cigarette. It began to rain, rain with sleet in it. He stood up against the wall of the drugstore, smoking. . . . He put his shoulders back and his heels together. "To hell with the handkerchief," said Walter Mitty scornfully. He took one last drag on his cigarette and snapped it away. Then, with that faint, fleeting smile playing about his lips, he faced the firing squad; erect and motionless, proud and disdainful, Walter Mitty the Undefeated, inscrutable[6] to the last.

6. **inscrutable:** unknowable, mysterious.

Reading Check

1. Who is the "Old Man" in Mitty's first fantasy?
2. Where does Mitty drop off his wife?
3. In the hospital fantasy, how does Dr. Mitty repair the broken machine?
4. What causes the woman who passes Mitty in the street to begin laughing?
5. Why does Mitty's wife decide that she must take his temperature when they get home?

For Study and Discussion

Analyzing and Interpreting the Story

1. Contrast Walter Mitty's real life with his secret life. Why does he feel the need to escape from real life?

2. Each of Mitty's daydreams is sparked by some detail of everyday life. For example, Mitty drives past a hospital and imagines himself a famous doctor. Explain how his other daydreams grow out of actual events.

3. What kind of person is Mrs. Mitty?

4. The final incident of the story shows Walter Mitty dreaming of himself before a firing squad. **a.** How is this incident symbolic of his view of himself? **b.** Is this final daydream of Walter Mitty's an adequate summing-up of the total effect of the story? Why or why not?

5. Readers have found "The Secret Life of Walter Mitty" both funny and sad. How is it funny and how is it sad?

Literary Elements

Direct and Indirect Characterization

A writer can develop and reveal character in a number of ways: (1) through a physical description of the character; (2) through the character's actions; (3) through the character's thoughts, feelings, and speeches; (4) through the comments and reactions of other characters; (5) through direct statements giving the writer's opinion of the character. The first four methods are **indirect** methods of characterization; they *show* or *dramatize* character. The last method is **direct** characterization; it *tells* rather than dramatizes. Within a single passage, an author may use both direct and indirect methods of characterization.

James Thurber uses three of these methods of characterization to develop Walter Mitty.

Tell which methods he uses and give examples of their use.

Dramatic Irony

Irony contrasts what is real with what only seems to be real. A writer may say one thing and mean quite another. This kind of irony, which was discussed on page 37, is called **verbal irony**. Another kind of irony is **dramatic irony**. In dramatic irony, the contrast depends upon the difference between what a character believes and what readers know is true. For example, Mitty has a fantasy about being a flying ace, but the reader knows from Mitty's inept behavior in the parking lot that he has trouble just parking his car.

Find other examples of dramatic irony in "The Secret Life of Walter Mitty." How do the ironic contrasts in this story deepen your understanding of Mitty as a character?

Language and Vocabulary

Recognizing Jargon

Jargon usually refers to the special language of a group of people, especially people in the same job. Engineers have their jargon, as do doctors, lawyers, and carpenters. Often, such language is necessary to communicate complex or technical ideas. But sometimes, special language is used simply to impress outsiders, to show that writers or speakers know more than their readers or listeners. Language used for this purpose fits another definition of jargon— "incomprehensible speech."

"The Secret Life of Walter Mitty" pokes fun at the jargon of several groups. Find examples of the jargon of doctors. Can you find other examples of jargon? What are they?

Writing About Literature

Analyzing the Use of Dramatic Irony

Write a paper analyzing the use of dramatic irony in "The Secret Life of Walter Mitty." If you wish, you may follow this plan.

1. Make two lists, one for the way Mitty views himself in his fantasies, and one for the way he really is. Here is an example:

In fantasy	*In reality*
Page 63	
Mitty daydreams about flying fearlessly through a storm.	He always drives at moderate speed, below 55.

Add at least one example for each fantasy.

2. Compose a topic sentence that draws together the evidence.

3. Develop the topic sentence. One way to develop it is to divide the evidence you have gathered. In one paragraph, focus on the character of the daydreamer. In another paragraph, focus on the character in real life. Fill in supporting evidence for each subordinate idea.

4. Write a concluding sentence that summarizes the effect of the irony.

This is what your outline for the essay might look like:

In "The Secret Life of Walter Mitty," James Thurber uses dramatic irony to contrast the bold hero Mitty dreams of being with the meek person he is in real life.

In his daydreams, Mitty is a brave, unconquerable figure who is equal to any challenge and who wins everyone's admiration.

1.
2.
3.

In actuality, Mitty is a timid man who is unable to cope with the everyday world and who is treated with contempt by others.

1.

2.

3.

The irony in the story deepens the reader's understanding of Mitty as both a humorous and a serious character.

Focus on Narrative Writing

Writing a Story Treatment

In Hollywood a **story treatment** is a preliminary outline for a film or a television show. A treatment lays out the key scenes, characters, and settings.

Write a story treatment about another character who lives a double life—an everyday life and a secret life. At least one scene in your story should show the reader why your character needs a secret life. Keep in mind that *showing*— or indirect characterization—is usually more effective than *telling* your readers directly about a character. You may write your treatment either as an outline or as a short narrative. Save your writing.

About the Author

James Thurber   (1894–1961)

James Thurber, one of America's most highly regarded humorists, achieved success as both a writer and a cartoonist. Part of his success lies in his gift for being funny and serious at the same time. His writings and drawings are populated by men and women who attempt to cope with one another and with modern life, and by puzzled, compassionate dogs who quietly observe the human scene.

Thurber grew up in Columbus, Ohio, and attended Ohio State University. Later he wrote about these early years in the wildly funny *My Life and Hard Times*. After working on newspapers in Columbus, Paris, and New York, he joined the staff of *The New Yorker* magazine. He was associated with *The New Yorker* for the rest of his life, first as an editor, then as a writer. He created essays, stories, and cartoons for the magazine and became one of its best-known contributors. Much of his work is collected in books with titles that reveal his ironic attitude toward the world at large: for example, *My World and Welcome to It*, *The Middle-Aged Man on the Flying Trapeze*, and *The Beast in Me and Other Animals*. He also collaborated on a play with Elliot Nugent, an old college friend. *The Male Animal* was a considerable success when first produced and is still occasionally revived. Some of his best satire appears in *Fables for Our Time* and *Further Fables for Our Time*. Thurber also wrote several children's books that are regarded as classics, among them *The White Deer* and *The Thirteen Clocks*.

Secrets

JUDY TROY

In order for characters in a short story to be credible, there must be motivation for their actions or for changes in their way of thinking. Read until you reach the paragraph ending "…cars on the highway" on page 71. Then stop and write a sentence or two about what changes, if any, you think Jean will make in her way of thinking. Check your predictions after you complete the story to see how close you came.

My father died in 1966, from a fall at a construction site where he was working, in Jacksonville, Florida. I was thirteen, and my brothers, Eddie and Lee, were eleven and eight. We had just moved from an apartment into a small house near Interstate 95, but our real home was South Bend, Indiana. We had only been in Florida for eight months. Both sets of grandparents wanted us to return to Indiana.

"They think I'm helpless," my mother said, "which makes me angry."

We were in the car on a Sunday night, two weeks after my father's funeral, driving home from the beach. My mother was working as a secretary at my brothers' elementary school, and her friends from work had invited us to a cookout. My mother said the cookout was to cheer us up. But, once her friends had got the fire going, they talked about how sad they felt for us. "What kind of food did your father like?" my mother's friend Grace Nolan asked us.

"Meat," Eddie said, "and not many kinds of vegetables."

Grace Nolan started to cry.

"Well, he liked potatoes, too," Lee told her.

"So," my mother said to us now, in the car, "I told your grandparents we'd be staying here."

"Good," Eddie said, from the back seat. Of the three of us—Eddie and Lee and me—he was the one who had made the most friends.

"I'm not sure I want to stay," I told my mother. "Or if Lee does." Lee was asleep, next to Eddie, with his head and shoulders on the seat and the rest of him limp on the floor.

"Lee wants to stay, Jean," my mother said. "I already know that." She pulled up in front of our house. It was ten o'clock, and we had forgotten to leave on any lights.

"Wake up, Lee," my mother said. She got out of the car and opened the back door and gently shook him. Sometimes he slept so soundly that it was impossible to wake him up. He opened his eyes for a moment and looked at the dark house.

"Why isn't Dad home yet?" he asked. My mother picked him up and carried him inside. He and Eddie were small for their ages, whereas I was tall and too heavy. I watched my mother put Lee into bed. Eddie lay down on his own bed, against the opposite wall, and fell asleep with his clothes on.

My mother and I went into the kitchen. Spread out over the table were letters from the construction company my father had worked for, and forms from its insurance company. We were supposed to receive twenty-five thousand dollars, and my mother was planning to use this money to buy the house we were in, which would allow us to live on the salary she made. The problem was that there had been people around, when the accident happened, who said that the fall had been my father's own fault, and not the fault of the construction company. So there was a chance the insurance company might not pay us. My mother was worried about this, and now she sat down at the table and began to fill out the forms.

I went into my room, next to the kitchen, which was really meant to be a small utility room. My father had painted it yellow and put in carpeting for me. I changed into my nightgown and got into bed. Every night since my father died, I had been unable to fall asleep. During the day I didn't cry, and it didn't upset me to hear about things my father had said or done. But as soon as I was almost asleep, memories would come into my mind that made our situation seem real to me. I stayed awake all night, it seemed to me, listening to my mother in the kitchen and to the distant noise of the cars on the highway.

In the morning, my mother made me get up and get ready for school. My brothers and I had stayed home for a week after my father died, and then my mother allowed me to stay home for an additional week. I told her I didn't want to talk to people at school yet, but the truth was also that I had got used to staying home—to being able to wear my nightgown all day if I wanted to, or lie in bed all morning, reading a book. I didn't want to go back to living my life, because my life had started to seem like too much trouble. Each small thing, like brushing my teeth or putting on knee-socks, now made me tired. I felt I had to do fewer things each

morning, in order to save energy for some more important thing I might have to do in the afternoon.

After I ate breakfast, I walked to the end of our block and waited for the bus with Nancy Dyer, who was in my class. It was November, and she was wearing a blue corduroy jumper her mother had made. She had brought over my assignments, for the two weeks I had been home, and on the bus we went over them. I made corrections according to the answers she remembered from class. "You did real well," she said when we were finished. "But then, you're smarter than I am to begin with."

"That's not true," I told her. "I just do more homework."

"That's what I mean," she said. She had her eyes on her boyfriend, who was getting on the bus. He was a thin boy, with black hair. He sat in front of us. He ignored her and took out a piece of notebook paper and shot spitballs at a red-haired boy across the aisle.

"He's mad at me all the time now," Nancy whispered. "I don't know why."

She had tears in her eyes, and I looked away and watched the trees flashing past in the window. In the reflection, I could see that three people on the bus were looking at me—the red-haired boy, and two girls in the seat in front of him. When I first got on the bus, one of these girls had said, "There was an announcement in school about your dad."

"I know," I said. "Nancy told me."

"I can't believe that happened to you," she said, and whispered something that I couldn't hear to the other girl. Now, as I turned away from the window and looked across the aisle, the red-haired boy smiled at me and was about to say something when he was hit in the forehead by a spitball.

When we got to school, I went to my locker to put away my sweater, and then I went to science and algebra and history. In each class, the teacher took me aside and talked to me about my father, and two or three other people spoke to me about him as well. The boys, especially, wanted to know exactly what had happened. "Did he step off the beam by accident," one boy asked, "or was there something he tripped over?"

"I think he tripped," I told him.

"Wow," the boy said. "I can just picture that."

During lunch, the group of girls I sat with stopped talking to each other when I walked up. "You can sit here, in the middle," Roberta Price said. Everyone moved over, and Carla Norris unwrapped my straw and put it in my milk. "We wondered when you were coming back," Roberta said. "The principal thought maybe last week."

"I decided to wait until today," I told her. We began to eat. Most of us had bought hot lunches. We all had mothers who were either too busy in the mornings to make us sandwiches or who felt we were old enough now to make them ourselves. Carla was the one exception. Her mother not only made her a sandwich but put a note in with her lunch every day.

"Here it is," Carla said. She unfolded a small piece of yellow paper. "Good luck on your geography quiz," she read out loud. "Your father and I are very proud of you." She and everybody else at the table looked down at their food.

"That's better than the one where she told you to wash off your mascara," I said, after a silence.

"It sure is," Roberta said quickly. "That one was sickening."

I had English class afterward, during fourth period. My English teacher, Mr. Thompson, was sitting at his desk when I walked in. I went to my seat and listened to a boy standing next to Mr. Thompson's desk talk to him about com-mas. "I don't think we need them," the boy said. "Periods are good enough."

Other people were coming into the room, and Mr. Thompson went up to the blackboard and wrote down a sentence from *A Separate Peace*.[1] The sentence was, "Perhaps I was stopped by that level of feeling, deeper than thought, which contains the truth." After the bell rang, he stepped back from the board and asked, "What, exactly, does this sentence mean?"

Four people he called on said they didn't know. The fifth person said, "I think it means a feeling you keep to yourself."

"Why wouldn't you want anyone to know?" Mr. Thompson asked.

"Because it's a secret," someone else said.

"Maybe it's a secret you keep from yourself," a girl in the back row said. "Maybe people don't want to know their own secrets."

"That doesn't make sense," a boy said.

"A lot of things don't make sense," Mr. Thompson told him, "but they're still true." He gave us an assignment, which we were to do in class, and then he sat on the radiator and watched us work. "Don't forget to use commas," he told us.

After class, I went downstairs to the girls' locker room to change my clothes for gym. Our teacher was already there, marking off our names as we walked in. She talked to me about my father, and then a girl I knew from another class said, "I don't know what I would do if my father died, even though I hate him."

We all went out to the basketball court and shot baskets from the free-throw line. After gym, I went to the library for study hall, and then I met Nancy in front of my locker, and we walked out to the school bus. Her boyfriend, who got on the bus a few minutes after we did,

1. *A Separate Peace:* a novel by John Knowles, set in a New England prep school during the 1940s.

Girl Arranging Her Hair (1886) by Mary Cassatt (1844–1926).

sat down four rows ahead of us. He spent the whole bus ride talking loudly to a small, blond girl.

"Sometimes people try to hurt you just to see if they can do it," Nancy said.

"You don't know that for sure," I told her.

"Yes, I do," she said. "I've done it to people myself."

We got off at our block and stood for a moment at the corner before we each went home. The air was so still that the traffic from the highway seemed louder than usual. "I guess I don't need to talk to you about feeling sad," Nancy said. "I forgot for a minute."

"It's different with me," I told her. "It's not something you feel every second."

I walked across the neighbors' yard and into our own; I put Lee's bike in the shed and went into the house through the kitchen door. My mother was standing in Lee's doorway, and I heard Lee say, "I got an A in spelling. Dad gave me fifty cents last time."

My mother gave Lee two quarters, and then she walked past me into the kitchen, opened the kitchen door, and sat outside on our steps. I went out and sat beside her. "Did Dad really give Lee fifty cents?" she asked me.

"I thought it was a quarter," I told her, "but I might be remembering it wrong." She held my hand, and we watched a squirrel race around the shed.

"Would you give me a hug, honey?" she asked. I put my arms around her. In the past year, I had grown a lot, and now I was bigger than she was; when I hugged her, I was able to put my arms all the way around her.

"I wish I'd stop growing," I told her.

"You'll be tall, like Dad was," she said. "Someday you'll appreciate it." She stood up and walked down into the yard. She was still dressed in her work clothes—a skirt and blouse and high heels—and her shoes were invisible in the long grass. No one had mowed the yard since my father had died. "The lawn will have to be Eddie's job now," my mother said. "You and Lee can do the raking." She looked up toward the clatter of a woodpecker in our sweet-gum tree. "I'll find a gas station that will change the oil in the car, and then I'll teach myself to do the other things Dad did."

"That seems like a lot," I told her.

"I know it does, honey." She sat back down beside me and pulled up weeds that were growing out of the cracks in the steps. I looked around at the yard and the house—at the patches of bare ground under the trees, the peeling paint around the windows, and all the small holes in the screens—and thought that it would take an army of men to fix everything that was broken.

My mother and I went inside to peel potatoes. At six o'clock, when Eddie came home from playing football with his friends, we all had supper in the kitchen.

"I made a touchdown today," Eddie said.

"Well, good for you," my mother said. "I wish I could have seen it." She had eaten quickly, and she put her plate in the sink and drank a cup of instant coffee while she watched us finish.

Afterward, I cleared the table and washed the dishes. I forgot that it was Eddie's turn, and he didn't remind me until I was done. He and Lee were sitting on the floor in the living room, with Lee's toy soldiers all around them. They were watching television with my mother. I came into the room and said, "I don't feel like watching TV."

"Who cares?" Eddie asked.

"We all care," my mother said sharply. "We're a family, even without Dad. We care what happens to each other." The way she spoke and the look on her face reminded me of my father, of the times he'd lost his temper with us. Eddie and Lee looked surprised, and then, a second later, there were tears on their faces.

I was crying, too, because my mother had started to cry. But I wasn't upset about what Eddie had said or because my mother had got angry. I startled myself by feeling almost glad. It seemed to me that all of a sudden our lives were ordinary again, except that my father wasn't there, and I felt like I was paying attention after being lost in a daydream, or like I was opening my eyes after seeing how long I could keep them closed. When my mother started to speak, I hoped she wouldn't say something nice that would cancel out her angry words. But what she said was, "Okay. Pick up these toys. Then we're going to turn off the television and go to bed."

It was only seven-thirty, but we went into our rooms. I didn't bother to put on my nightgown.

I took off my clothes and got into bed in my underwear, and, even though it was early, I didn't have my same trouble falling asleep. I knew now that my father was dead and that we would live our lives without him, and I fell asleep right away, so that for a while I could not know these things.

Reading Check

1. Why does Eddie want to stay in Florida?
2. Why is Jean's mother worried about the insurance payments?
3. Why is Jean unable to fall asleep?
4. When does Jean return to school?
5. What causes Jean's mother to become angry at Eddie?

For Study and Discussion

Analyzing and Interpreting the Story

1. This story deals with the way different members of a family react to a father's death. What do the mother's actions and words reveal about her character?

2a. What impression do you get of Jean from her relationship with her mother and brothers? b. What do you learn about her during her day at school?

3. The sentence the teacher writes on the blackboard states that feelings can be deeper and truer than thoughts. How does this sentence give you insight into Jean's conflict?

4a. What causes Jean to re-examine her feelings? b. What truth finally comes to her?

5. During class one student suggests that people don't want to know their own secrets. a. Does this interpretation make sense to you? b. Do you agree or disagree with this idea?

Literary Elements

Static and Dynamic Characters

Characters in fiction are often described as **static** or **dynamic.** Static characters remain the same throughout a selection. Dynamic characters change in some important way.

Jean undergoes an important change at the end of the story. How does insight into her own character cause her to change? Consider this statement: "It seemed to me that all of a sudden our lives were ordinary again." Does the change mean that Jean will no longer think about her father's death?

Is Walter Mitty in "The Secret Life of Walter Mitty" a static or dynamic character? How would you classify Sanger Rainsford in "The Most Dangerous Game"?

Focus on Narrative Writing

Writing Dialogue

Dialogue is the conversation of the characters in a story. Good dialogue reveals the characters' personalities and also helps to move the story's plot along. The diagram below shows some guidelines for writing dialogue.

Skim some recent issues of newspapers or magazines for a short item about a celebrity. Try telling the story through dialogue. (You may have to make up another character or two.) Get together with a small group of classmates. Offer to review each other's dialogues.

About the Author

Judy Troy (1951–   )

Judy Troy grew up in northwest Indiana. She now lives in Auburn, Alabama, with her husband, and teaches at Auburn University. Her work has appeared in *The New Yorker, Witness,* and *Antaeus.* "Secrets" is included in her collection of stories, *Mourning Doves* (1993).

The Author Comments on Her Story

I have always liked stories that sound like autobiography, but I write better about made-up characters than I do about myself and my own childhood. I wrote "Secrets," therefore, as a kind of invented autobiography—I imitated the form and style but made up the characters and their situation. What's important in writing is not that you tell the factual truth but that you tell the emotional truth. You have to be sure that your characters respond and feel just as they would if they were real people, and it's impossible to do that unless there is a part of you in your characters. There is a lot of me in Jean, and since she is my invention, there is now a lot of Jean in me. But we are not the same people, and we didn't have the same experiences. In terms of the setting of the story, I, myself, am from Indiana, though not from South Bend, and I've only driven through Jacksonville, Florida. I write best about places I hardly know; that way, I'm still curious about them. They seem mysterious and interesting to me, and I like to imagine who lives there and what their lives are like. That's how Jean and her family came into being.

Rules of the Game

AMY TAN

Chess is a board game involving two players, each of whom has sixteen pieces that follow specific rules of movement. The adversaries make alternate moves until one wins the game by "checkmating" the opponent's king. As you read, note the "moves" made by the adversaries in the story, Waverly and her mother. Is there a clear winner or is the game stalemated?

I was six when my mother taught me the art of invisible strength. It was a strategy for winning arguments, respect from others, and eventually, though neither of us knew it at the time, chess games.

"Bite back your tongue," scolded my mother when I cried loudly, yanking her hand toward the store that sold bags of salted plums. At home, she said, "Wise guy, he not go against wind. In Chinese we say, Come from South, blow with wind—poom!—North will follow. Strongest wind cannot be seen."

The next week I bit back my tongue as we entered the store with the forbidden candies. When my mother finished her shopping, she quietly plucked a small bag of plums from the rack and put it on the counter with the rest of the items.

My mother imparted her daily truths so she could help my older brothers and me rise above our circumstances. We lived in San Francisco's Chinatown. Like most of the other Chinese children who played in the back alleys of restaurants and curio shops, I didn't think we were poor. My bowl was always full, three five-course meals every day, beginning with a soup full of mysterious things I didn't want to know the names of.

We lived on Waverly Place, in a warm, clean, two-bedroom flat[1] that sat above a small Chinese bakery specializing in steamed pastries and dim sum.[2] In the early morning, when the alley was still quiet, I could smell fragrant red beans as they were cooked down to a pasty sweetness. By daybreak, our flat was heavy with

1. **flat:** an apartment on one floor of a building.
2. **dim sum** (dĭm' sŏŏm', sŭm'): a general term in Chinese for a kind of dumpling served as an appetizer.

An overhead shot of a marble chessboard with antique chess pieces.

the odor of fried sesame balls and sweet curried chicken crescents. From my bed, I would listen as my father got ready for work, then locked the door behind him, one-two-three clicks.

At the end of our two-block alley was a small sandlot playground with swings and slides well-shined down the middle with use. The play area was bordered by wood-slat benches where old-country people sat cracking roasted watermelon seeds with their golden teeth and scattering the husks to an impatient gathering of gurgling pigeons. The best playground, however, was the dark alley itself. It was crammed with daily mysteries and adventures. My brothers and I would peer into the medicinal herb shop, watching old Li dole out onto a stiff sheet of white paper the right amount of insect shells, saffron-colored seeds, and pungent leaves for his ailing customers. It was said that he once cured a woman dying of an ancestral curse that had eluded the best of American doctors. Next to the pharmacy was a printer who specialized in gold-embossed wedding invitations and festive red banners.

Farther down the street was Ping Yuen Fish Market. The front window displayed a tank crowded with doomed fish and turtles struggling to gain footing on the slimy green-tiled sides. A hand-written sign informed tourists, "Within this store, is all for food, not for pet." Inside, the butchers with their bloodstained white smocks deftly gutted the fish while customers cried out their orders and shouted, "Give me your freshest," to which the butchers always protested, "All are freshest." On less crowded market days, we would inspect the crates of live frogs and crabs which we were warned not to poke, boxes of dried cuttlefish, and row upon row of iced prawns, squid, and slippery fish. The sanddabs made me shiver each time; their eyes lay on one flattened side

and reminded me of my mother's story of a careless girl who ran into a crowded street and was crushed by a cab. "Was smash flat," reported my mother.

At the corner of the alley was Hong Sing's, a four-table café with a recessed stairwell in front that led to a door marked "Tradesmen." My brothers and I believed the bad people emerged from this door at night. Tourists never went to Hong Sing's, since the menu was printed only in Chinese. A Caucasian man with a big camera once posed me and my playmates in front of the restaurant. He had us move to the side of the picture window so the photo would capture the roasted duck with its head dangling from a juice-covered rope. After he took the picture, I told him he should go into Hong Sing's and eat dinner. When he smiled and asked me what they served, I shouted, "Guts and duck's feet and octopus gizzards!" Then I ran off with my friends, shrieking with laughter as we scampered across the alley and hid in the entryway grotto of the China Gem Company, my heart pounding with hope that he would chase us.

My mother named me after the street that we lived on: Waverly Place Jong, my official name for important American documents. But my family called me Meimei, "Little Sister." I was the youngest, the only daughter. Each morning before school, my mother would twist and yank on my thick black hair until she had formed two tightly wound pigtails. One day, as she struggled to weave a hard-toothed comb through my disobedient hair, I had a sly thought.

I asked her, "Ma, what is Chinese torture?" My mother shook her head. A bobby pin was wedged between her lips. She wetted her palm and smoothed the hair above my ear, then pushed the pin in so that it nicked sharply against my scalp.

"Who say this word?" she asked without a

trace of knowing how wicked I was being. I shrugged my shoulders and said, "Some boy in my class said Chinese people do Chinese torture."

"Chinese people do many things," she said simply. "Chinese people do business, do medicine, do painting. Not lazy like American people. We do torture. Best torture."

My older brother Vincent was the one who actually got the chess set. We had gone to the annual Christmas party held at the First Chinese Baptist Church at the end of the alley. The missionary ladies had put together a Santa bag of gifts donated by members of another church. None of the gifts had names on them. There were separate sacks for boys and girls of different ages.

One of the Chinese parishioners had donned a Santa Claus costume and a stiff paper beard with cotton balls glued to it. I think the only children who thought he was the real thing were too young to know that Santa Claus was not Chinese. When my turn came up, the Santa man asked me how old I was. I thought it was a trick question; I was seven according to the American formula and eight by the Chinese calendar. I said I was born on March 17, 1951. That seemed to satisfy him. He then solemnly asked if I had been a very, very good girl this year and did I believe in Jesus Christ and obey my parents. I knew the only answer to that. I nodded back with equal solemnity.

Having watched the other children opening their gifts, I already knew that the big gifts were not necessarily the nicest ones. One girl my age got a large coloring book of biblical characters, while a less greedy girl who selected a smaller box received a glass vial of lavender toilet water. The sound of the box was also important. A ten-year-old boy had chosen a box that jangled when he shook it. It was a tin globe

of the world with a slit for inserting money. He must have thought it was full of dimes and nickels, because when he saw that it had just ten pennies, his face fell with such undisguised disappointment that his mother slapped the side of his head and led him out of the church hall, apologizing to the crowd for her son who had such bad manners he couldn't appreciate such a fine gift.

As I peered into the sack, I quickly fingered the remaining presents, testing their weight, imagining what they contained. I chose a heavy, compact one that was wrapped in shiny silver foil and a red satin ribbon. It was a twelve-pack of Life Savers and I spent the rest of the party arranging and rearranging the candy tubes in the order of my favorites. My brother Winston chose wisely as well. His present turned out to be a box of intricate plastic parts; the instructions on the box proclaimed that when they were properly assembled he would have an authentic miniature replica of a World War II submarine.

Vincent got the chess set, which would have been a very decent present to get at a church Christmas party, except it was obviously used and, as we discovered later, it was missing a black pawn and a white knight. My mother graciously thanked the unknown benefactor, saying, "Too good. Cost too much." At which point, an old lady with fine white, wispy hair nodded toward our family and said with a whistling whisper, "Merry, merry Christmas."

When we got home, my mother told Vincent to throw the chess set away. "She not want it. We not want it," she said, tossing her head stiffly to the side with a tight, proud smile. My brothers had deaf ears. They were already lining up the chess pieces and reading from the dog-eared instruction book.

I watched Vincent and Winston play during

Christmas week. The chess board seemed to hold elaborate secrets waiting to be untangled. The chessmen were more powerful than Old Li's magic herbs that cured ancestral curses. And my brothers wore such serious faces that I was sure something was at stake that was greater than avoiding the tradesmen's door to Hong Sing's.

"Let me! Let me!" I begged between games when one brother or the other would sit back with a deep sigh of relief and victory, the other annoyed, unable to let go of the outcome. Vincent at first refused to let me play, but when I offered my Life Savers as replacements for the buttons that filled in for the missing pieces, he relented. He chose the flavors: wild cherry for the black pawn and peppermint for the white knight. Winner could eat both.

As our mother sprinkled flour and rolled out small doughy circles for the steamed dumplings that would be our dinner that night, Vincent explained the rules, pointing to each piece. "You have sixteen pieces and so do I. One king and queen, two bishops, two knights, two castles, and eight pawns. The pawns can only move forward one step, except on the first move. Then they can move two. But they can only take men by moving crossways like this, except in the beginning, when you can move ahead and take another pawn."

"Why?" I asked as I moved my pawn. "Why can't they move more steps?"

"Because they're pawns," he said.

"But why do they go crossways to take other men. Why aren't there any women and children?"

"Why is the sky blue? Why must you always ask stupid questions?" asked Vincent. "This is a game. These are the rules. I didn't make them up. See. Here. In the book." He jabbed a page with a pawn in his hand. "Pawn. P-A-W-N. Pawn. Read it yourself."

My mother patted the flour off her hands. "Let me see book," she said quietly. She scanned the pages quickly, not reading the foreign English symbols, seeming to search deliberately for nothing in particular.

"This American rules," she concluded at last. "Every time people come out from foreign country, must know rules. You not know, judge say, Too bad, go back. They not telling you why so you can use their way go forward. They say, Don't know why, you find out yourself. But they knowing all the time. Better you take it, find out why yourself." She tossed her head back with a satisfied smile.

I found out about all the whys later. I read the rules and looked up all the big words in a dictionary. I borrowed books from the Chinatown library. I studied each chess piece, trying to absorb the power each contained.

I learned about opening moves[3] and why it's important to control the center early on; the shortest distance between two points is straight down the middle. I learned about the middle game and why tactics between two adversaries are like clashing ideas; the one who plays better had the clearest plans for both attacking and getting out of traps. I learned why it is essential in the endgame to have foresight, a mathematical understanding of all possible moves, and patience; all weaknesses and advantages become evident to a strong adversary and are obscured to a tiring opponent. I discovered that for the whole game one must gather invisible strengths and see the endgame before the game begins.

I also found out why I should never reveal "why" to others. A little knowledge withheld is a great advantage one should store for future

---

3. **opening moves:** One opening move is the *gambit,* in which a pawn or other piece is sacrificed in order to gain some advantage in position. For a description of the narrator's strategy, see page 82.

Checking the opponent's king so that defense is impossible.

use. That is the power of chess. It is a game of secrets in which one must show and never tell.

I loved the secrets I found within the sixty-four black and white squares. I carefully drew a handmade chessboard and pinned it to the wall next to my bed, where at night I would stare for hours at imaginary battles. Soon I no longer lost any games or Life Savers, but I lost my adversaries. Winston and Vincent decided they were more interested in roaming the streets after school in their Hopalong Cassidy[4] cowboy hats.

On a cold spring afternoon, while walking home from school, I detoured through the playground at the end of our alley. I saw a group of old men, two seated across a folding table playing a game of chess, others smoking pipes, eating peanuts, and watching. I ran home and grabbed Vincent's chess set, which was bound in a cardboard box with rubber bands. I also carefully selected two prized rolls of Life Savers. I came back to the park and approached a man who was observing the game.

"Want to play?" I asked him. His face widened with surprise and he grinned as he looked at the box under my arm.

"Little sister, been a long time since I play with dolls," he said, smiling benevolently. I

4. **Hopalong Cassidy:** a popular character in Western films, portrayed by the actor William Boyd (1895–1972).

quickly put the box down next to him on the bench and displayed my retort.

Lau Po, as he allowed me to call him, turned out to be a much better player than my brothers. I lost many games and many Life Savers. But over the weeks, with each diminishing roll of candies, I added new secrets. Lau Po gave me the names. The Double Attack from the East and West Shores. Throwing Stones on the Drowning Man. The Sudden Meeting of the Clan. The Surprise from the Sleeping Guard. The Humble Servant Who Kills the King. Sand in the Eyes of Advancing Forces. A Double Killing Without Blood.

There were also the fine points of chess etiquette.[5] Keep captured men in neat rows, as well-tended prisoners. Never announce "Check" with vanity, lest someone with an unseen sword slit your throat. Never hurl pieces into the sandbox after you have lost a game, because then you must find them again, by yourself, after apologizing to all around you. By the end of the summer, Lau Po had taught me all he knew, and I had become a better chess player.

A small weekend crowd of Chinese people and tourists would gather as I played and defeated my opponents one by one. My mother would join the crowds during these outdoor exhibition games. She sat proudly on the bench, telling my admirers with proper Chinese humility, "Is luck."

A man who watched me play in the park suggested that my mother allow me to play in local chess tournaments. My mother smiled graciously, an answer that meant nothing. I desperately wanted to go, but I bit back my tongue. I knew she would not let me play among strangers. So as we walked home I said in a small voice that I didn't want to play in the local

Chinese Art: Birds.

tournament. They would have American rules. If I lost, I would bring shame on my family.

"Is shame you fall down nobody push you," said my mother.

During my first tournament, my mother sat with me in the front row as I waited for my turn. I frequently bounced my legs to unstick them from the cold metal seat of the folding chair. When my name was called, I leapt up. My mother unwrapped something in her lap. It was her *chang*, a small tablet of red jade which held the sun's fire. "Is luck," she whispered, and tucked it into my dress pocket. I turned to my opponent, a fifteen-year-old boy from Oakland. He looked at me, wrinkling his nose.

As I began to play, the boy disappeared, the color ran out of the room, and I saw only my white pieces and his black ones waiting on the other side. A light wind began blowing past my ears. It whispered secrets only I could hear.

"Blow from the South," it murmured. "The wind leaves no trail." I saw a clear path, the traps to avoid. The crowd rustled. "Shhh! Shhh!" said the corners of the room. The wind

5. **chess etiquette** (ĕt′ĭ-kĕt′, kĭt): the code of behavior and courtesy observed by players, such as doing nothing to distract an opponent.

blew stronger. "Throw sand from the East to distract him." The knight came forward ready for the sacrifice. The wind hissed, louder and louder. "Blow, blow, blow. He cannot see. He is blind now. Make him lean away from the wind so he is easier to knock down."

"Check," I said, as the wind roared with laughter. The wind died down to little puffs, my own breath.

My mother placed my first trophy next to a new plastic chess set that the neighborhood Tao society[6] had given to me. As she wiped each piece with a soft cloth, she said, "Next time win more, lose less."

"Ma, it's not how many pieces you lose," I said. "Sometimes you need to lose pieces to get ahead."

"Better to lose less, see if you really need."

At the next tournament, I won again, but it was my mother who wore the triumphant grin.

"Lost eight piece this time. Last time was eleven. What I tell you? Better off lose less!" I was annoyed, but I couldn't say anything.

I attended more tournaments, each one farther away from home. I won all games, in all divisions. The Chinese bakery downstairs from our flat displayed my growing collection of trophies in its window, amidst the dust-covered cakes that were never picked up. The day after I won an important regional tournament, the window encased a fresh sheet cake with whipped-cream frosting and red script saying, "Congratulations, Waverly Jong, Chinatown Chess Champion." Soon after that, a flower shop, headstone engraver, and funeral parlor offered to sponsor me in national tournaments. That's when my mother decided I no longer had to do the dishes. Winston and Vincent had to do my chores.

"Why does she get to play and we do all the work," complained Vincent.

"Is new American rules," said my mother. "Meimei play, squeeze all her brains out for win chess. You play, worth squeeze towel."

By my ninth birthday, I was a national chess champion. I was still some 429 points away from grand-master status,[7] but I was touted as the Great American Hope, a child prodigy and a girl to boot. They ran a photo of me in *Life* magazine next to a quote in which Bobby Fischer[8] said, "There will never be a woman grand master." "Your move, Bobby," said the caption.

The day they took the magazine picture I wore neatly plaited braids clipped with plastic barrettes trimmed with rhinestones. I was playing in a large high school auditorium that echoed with phlegmy coughs and the squeaky rubber knobs of chair legs sliding across freshly waxed wooden floors. Seated across from me was an American man, about the same age as Lau Po, maybe fifty. I remember that his sweaty brow seemed to weep at my every move. He wore a dark, malodorous suit. One of his pockets was stuffed with a great white kerchief on which he wiped his palm before sweeping his hand over the chosen chess piece with great flourish.

In my crisp pink-and-white dress with scratchy lace at the neck, one of two my mother had sewn for these special occasions, I would clasp my hands under my chin, the delicate points of my elbows poised lightly on the table in the manner my mother had shown me for posing for the press. I would swing my patent leather shoes back and forth like an impatient child riding on a school bus. Then I would

6. **Tao society:** a group that meets to study Taoism (tou'ĭz'əm), a philosophy and system of religion based on the teachings of Lao-tse.

7. **grand-master status:** The title *International Grand Master* is awarded to the world's strongest players.
8. **Bobby Fischer:** Robert James Fischer was American chess champion eight times from 1958 to 1967, and world champion from 1972 to 1975. He received the title of International Grand Master in 1958.

pause, suck in my lips, twirl my chosen piece in midair as if undecided, and then firmly plant it in its new threatening place, with a triumphant smile thrown back at my opponent for good measure.

I no longer played in the alley of Waverly Place. I never visited the playground where the pigeons and old men gathered. I went to school, then directly home to learn new chess secrets, cleverly concealed advantages, more escape routes.

But I found it difficult to concentrate at home. My mother had a habit of standing over me while I plotted out my games. I think she thought of herself as my protective ally. Her lips would be sealed tight, and after each move I made, a soft "Hmmmmph" would escape from her nose.

"Ma, I can't practice when you stand there like that," I said one day. She retreated to the kitchen and made loud noises with the pots and pans. When the crashing stopped, I could see out of the corner of my eye that she was standing in the doorway. "Hmmmmph!" Only this one came out of her tight throat.

My parents made many concessions to allow me to practice. One time I complained that the bedroom I shared was so noisy that I couldn't think. Thereafter, my brothers slept in a bed in the living room facing the street. I said I couldn't finish my rice; my head didn't work right when my stomach was too full. I left the table with half-finished bowls and nobody complained. But there was one duty I couldn't avoid. I had to accompany my mother on Saturday market days when I had no tournament to play. My mother would proudly walk with me, visiting many shops, buying very little. "This my daughter Wave-ly Jong," she said to whoever looked her way.

One day, after we left a shop I said under my breath, "I wish you wouldn't do that, telling everybody I'm your daughter." My mother stopped walking. Crowds of people with heavy bags pushed past us on the sidewalk, bumping into first one shoulder, then another.

"Aiii-ya. So shame be with mother?" She grasped my hand even tighter as she glared at me.

I looked down. "It's not that, it's just so obvious. It's just so embarrassing."

"Embarrass you be my daughter?" Her voice was cracking with anger.

"That's not what I meant. That's not what I said."

"What you say?"

I knew it was a mistake to say anything more, but I heard my voice speaking. "Why do you have to use me to show off? If you want to show off, then why don't you learn to play chess."

My mother's eyes turned into dangerous black slits. She had no words for me, just sharp silence.

I felt the wind rushing around my hot ears. I jerked my hand out of my mother's tight grasp and spun around, knocking into an old woman. Her bag of groceries spilled to the ground.

"Aii-ya! Stupid girl!" my mother and the woman cried. Oranges and tin cans careened down the sidewalk. As my mother stooped to help the old woman pick up the escaping food, I took off.

I raced down the street, dashing between people, not looking back as my mother screamed shrilly, "Meimei! Meimei!" I fled down an alley, past dark curtained shops and merchants washing the grime off their windows. I sped into the sunlight, into a large street crowded with tourists examining trinkets and souvenirs. I ducked into another dark alley, down another street, up another alley. I ran until it hurt and I realized I had nowhere to go, that I was not running from anything. The alleys contained no escape routes.

My breath came out like angry smoke. It was

cold. I sat down on an upturned plastic pail next to a stack of empty boxes, cupping my chin with my hands, thinking hard. I imagined my mother, first walking briskly down one street or another looking for me, then giving up and returning home to await my arrival. After two hours, I stood up on creaking legs and slowly walked home.

The alley was quiet and I could see the yellow lights shining from our flat like two tiger's eyes in the night. I climbed the sixteen steps to the door, advancing quietly up each so as not to make any warning sounds. I turned the knob; the door was locked. I heard a chair moving, quick steps, the locks turning—click! click! click!—and then the door opened.

"About time you got home," said Vincent.

"Boy, are you in trouble."

He slid back to the dinner table. On a platter were the remains of a large fish, its fleshy head still connected to bones swimming upstream in vain escape. Standing there waiting for my punishment, I heard my mother speak in a dry voice.

"We not concerning this girl. This girl not have concerning for us."

Nobody looked at me. Bone chopsticks clinked against the insides of bowls being emptied into hungry mouths.

I walked into my room, closed the door, and lay down on my bed. The room was dark, the ceiling filled with shadows from the dinnertime lights of neighboring flats.

In my head, I saw a chessboard with sixty-

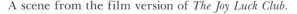

A scene from the film version of *The Joy Luck Club.*

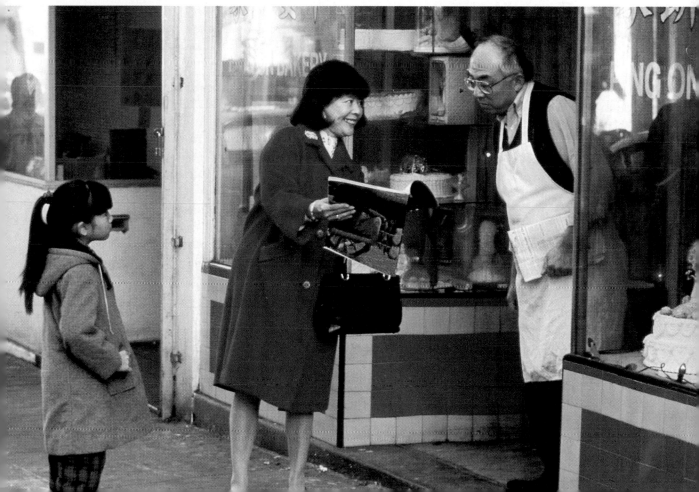

four black and white squares. Opposite me was my opponent, two angry black slits. She wore a triumphant smile. "Strongest wind cannot be seen," she said.

Her black men advanced across the plane, slowly marching to each successive level as a single unit. My white pieces screamed as they scurried and fell off the board one by one. As her men drew closer to my edge, I felt myself growing light. I rose up into the air and flew out the window. Higher and higher, above the alley, over the tops of tiled roofs, where I was gathered up by the wind and pushed up toward the night sky until everything below me disappeared and I was alone.

I closed my eyes and pondered my next move.

Reading Check

1. What name is used for Waverly by her family?
2. Who receives the chess set at the Christmas party?
3. What does Waverly learn from Lau Po?
4. List some of the rules of chess etiquette.
5. Why does Waverly run from her mother?

For Study and Discussion

Analyzing and Interpreting the Story

1. At the beginning of the story, Waverly says that her mother taught her "the art of invisible strength." What does she mean?

2. There are several conflicts in the story. Waverly's mother believes that Chinese ways are better than American ways. Waverly challenges the male-dominated world of chess. But the most important conflict is between Waverly and her mother. Describe that conflict with specific references to events in the story.

3. A static character remains the same while a dynamic character changes in some significant way. Does Waverly simply change her ideas or does she change in some deeper way? Explain.

4. This story could be divided into parts as a chess game is divided: opening game, middle game, and end game. Reread the story and find where each part begins and ends. Indicate the change that Waverly undergoes in each part.

5. Is the central conflict between Waverly and her mother resolved? Explain your answer.

6. Consider the title of the story. Do the rules apply only to chess, or might they have another meaning?

Literary Elements

Complex Characterization

Perhaps you have known people who at first seemed cold and aloof, perhaps even snobbish. After you got to know them better, you found they were actually warm and friendly. Their coolness was a mask for their shyness. Thus, as you learned more about them, your attitude toward them changed.

You sometimes go through this same process of changing your opinion as you read a story or a novel. At the beginning a character seems one kind of person. As you continue to read, you learn more about the character and your first impressions are modified. The writer has deliberately controlled your reaction by giving certain information at the beginning of the story and other information later on.

What do each of the following incidents in "Rules of the Game" reveal about Waverly and her mother?

The terms **flat** and **round** are sometimes used in distinguishing characters. A **flat character** is one-sided and often represents a stereotype. A **round character,** like Waverly, is presented in depth from many angles.

Writing About Literature

Exploring a Character's Nature

In "Rules of the Game," Waverly seems at first to be simply an inquisitive girl who is interested in chess, but by the end of the story, you see her emerging as a complex character in open conflict with her mother. As you learn more about Waverly, you become an active participant in the story. Just as Waverly's awareness of the changing relationship with her mother increases, so does your understanding of Waverly's character grow. You come to know and appreciate a complex, many-sided character who has demonstrated the capacity to change. Write an essay tracing Waverly's development. Refer to both direct and indirect methods of characterization used in the story.

About the Author

Amy Tan (1952   )

Amy Tan, an American-born daughter of Chinese immigrants, had not planned on becoming a writer of fiction. After receiving her B.A. and M.A. from San Jose State University, she freelanced as a technical writer, sometimes working ninety hours a week to build a successful business. Writing fiction and playing the piano served as an escape from her work. Hoping to develop an understanding between herself and her mother, Tan began writing stories about their relationship. The result was a collection of sixteen stories that became *The Joy Luck Club* (1989), from which "Rules of the Game" is taken. Tan's recent publications include a novel, *The Kitchen God's Wife* (1991), and a book for children, *The Moon Lady* (1992).

A Mother in Mannville

MARJORIE KINNAN RAWLINGS

You have seen that characters in stories can be complex and that your reactions to them may change as you come to understand them. What do you come to know about the narrator in this story? Does she understand the boy Jerry as well as you, the reader, do?

The orphanage is high in the Carolina mountains. Sometimes in winter the snowdrifts are so deep that the institution is cut off from the village below, from all the world. Fog hides the mountain peaks, the snow swirls down the valleys, and a wind blows so bitterly that the orphanage boys who take the milk twice daily to the baby cottage reach the door with fingers stiff in an agony of numbness.

"Or when we carry trays from the cookhouse for the ones that are sick," Jerry said, "we get our faces frostbit, because we can't put our hands over them. I have gloves," he added. "Some of the boys don't have any."

He liked the late spring, he said. The rhododendron was in bloom, a carpet of color, across the mountainsides, soft as the May winds that stirred the hemlocks. He called it laurel.

"It's pretty when the laurel blooms," he said. "Some of it's pink and some of it's white."

I was there in the autumn. I wanted quiet, isolation, to do some troublesome writing. I wanted mountain air to blow out the malaria from too long a time in the subtropics. I was homesick, too, for the flaming of maples in Oc-

tober, and for corn shocks and pumpkins and black-walnut trees and the lift of hills. I found them all, living in a cabin that belonged to the orphanage, half a mile beyond the orphanage farm. When I took the cabin, I asked for a boy or man to come and chop wood for the fireplace. The first few days were warm, I found what wood I needed about the cabin, no one came, and I forgot the order.

I looked up from my typewriter one late afternoon, a little startled. A boy stood at the door, and my pointer dog, my companion, was at his side and had not barked to warn me. The boy was probably twelve years old, but undersized. He wore overalls and a torn shirt, and was barefooted.

He said, "I can chop some wood today."

I said, "But I have a boy coming from the orphanage."

"I'm the boy."

"You? But you're small."

"Size don't matter, chopping wood," he said. "Some of the big boys don't chop good. I've been chopping wood at the orphanage a long time."

I visualized mangled and inadequate branches for my fires. I was well into my work and not inclined to conversation. I was a little blunt.

"Very well. There's the ax. Go ahead and see what you can do."

I went back to work, closing the door. At first the sound of the boy dragging brush annoyed me. Then he began to chop. The blows were rhythmic and steady, and shortly I had forgotten him, the sound no more of an interruption than a consistent rain. I suppose an hour and a half passed, for when I stopped and stretched, and heard the boy's steps on the cabin stoop, the sun was dropping behind the farthest mountain, and the valleys were purple with something deeper than the asters.

The boy said, "I have to go to supper now. I can come again tomorrow evening."

I said, "I'll pay you now for what you've done," thinking I should probably have to insist on an older boy. "Ten cents an hour?"

"Anything is all right."

We went together back of the cabin. An astonishing amount of solid wood had been cut. There were cherry logs and heavy roots of rhododendron, and blocks from the waste pine and oak left from the building of the cabin.

"But you've done as much as a man," I said. "This is a splendid pile."

I looked at him, actually, for the first time. His hair was the color of the corn shocks and his eyes, very direct, were like the mountain sky when rain is pending—gray, with a shadowing of that miraculous blue. As I spoke, a light came over him, as though the setting sun had touched him with the same suffused glory with which it touched the mountains. I gave him a quarter.

"You may come tomorrow," I said, "and thank you very much."

He looked at me, and at the coin, and

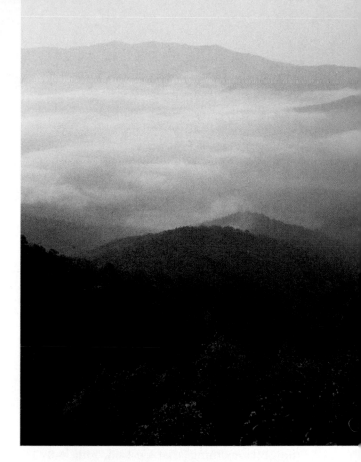

seemed to want to speak, but could not, and turned away.

"I'll split kindling tomorrow," he said over his thin ragged shoulder. "You'll need kindling and medium wood and logs and backlogs."

At daylight I was half wakened by the sound of chopping. Again it was so even in texture that I went back to sleep. When I left my bed in the cool morning, the boy had come and gone, and a stack of kindling was neat against the cabin wall. He came after school in the afternoon and worked until time to return to the orphanage. His name was Jerry; he was twelve years old, and he had been at the orphanage since he was four. I could picture him at four, with the same grave gray-blue eyes and the same—independence? No, the word that comes to me is "integrity."

The word means something very special to

me, and the quality for which I use it is a rare one. My father had it—there is another of whom I am almost sure—but almost no man of my acquaintance possesses it with the clarity, the purity, the simplicity of a mountain stream. But the boy Jerry had it. It is bedded on courage, but it is more than brave. It is honest, but it is more than honesty. The ax handle broke one day. Jerry said the woodshop at the orphanage would repair it. I brought money to pay for the job and he refused it.

"I'll pay for it," he said. "I broke it. I brought the ax down careless."

"But no one hits accurately every time," I told him. "The fault was in the wood of the handle. I'll see the man from whom I bought it."

It was only then that he would take the money. He was standing back of his own carelessness. He was a free-will agent and he chose to do careful work, and if he failed, he took the responsibility without subterfuge.[1]

And he did for me the unnecessary thing, the gracious thing, that we find done only by the great of heart. Things no training can teach, for they are done on the instant, with no predicated[2] experience. He found a cubbyhole beside the fireplace that I had not noticed. There, of his own accord, he put kindling and "medium" wood, so that I might always have dry fire material ready in case of sudden wet weather. A stone was loose in the rough walk to the cabin. He dug a deeper hole and steadied it, although he came, himself, by a short cut over the bank. I found that when I tried to return his thoughtfulness with such things as candy and apples, he was wordless. "Thank you" was, perhaps, an expression for which he had had no use, for his courtesy was instinctive. He only looked at the gift and at me, and a curtain lifted, so that I saw deep into the clear

well of his eyes, and gratitude was there, and affection, soft over the firm granite of his character.

He made simple excuses to come and sit with me. I could no more have turned him away than if he had been physically hungry. I suggested once that the best time for us to visit was just before supper, when I left off my writing. After that, he waited always until my typewriter had been some time quiet. One day I worked until nearly dark. I went outside the cabin, having forgotten him. I saw him going up over the hill in the twilight toward the orphanage. When I sat down on my stoop, a place was warm from his body where he had been sitting.

He became intimate, of course, with my pointer, Pat. There is a strange communion between a boy and a dog. Perhaps they possess the same singleness of spirit, the same kind of wisdom. It is difficult to explain, but it exists. When I went across the state for a weekend, I left the dog in Jerry's charge. I gave him the dog whistle and the key to the cabin, and left sufficient food. He was to come two or three times a day and let out the dog, feed and exercise him. I should return Sunday night, and Jerry would take out the dog for the last time Sunday afternoon and then leave the key under an agreed hiding place.

My return was belated and fog filled the mountain passes so treacherously that I dared not drive at night. The fog held the next morning, and it was Monday noon before I reached the cabin. The dog had been fed and cared for that morning. Jerry came early in the afternoon, anxious.

"The superintendent said nobody would drive in the fog," he said. "I came just before bedtime last night and you hadn't come. So I brought Pat some of my breakfast this morning. I wouldn't have let anything happen to him."

---

1. **subterfuge** (sŭb′tər-fyōōj′): deception.
2. **predicated** (prĕd′ə-kāt′əd): established.

"I was sure of that. I didn't worry."

"When I heard about the fog, I thought you'd know."

He was needed for work at the orphanage and he had to return at once. I gave him a dollar in payment, and he looked at it and went away. But that night he came in the darkness and knocked at the door.

"Come in, Jerry," I said, "if you're allowed to be away this late."

"I told maybe a story," he said. "I told them I thought you would want to see me."

"That's true," I assured him, and I saw his relief. "I want to hear about how you managed with the dog."

He sat by the fire with me, with no other light, and told me of their two days together. The dog lay close to him, and found a comfort there that I did not have for him. And it seemed to me that being with my dog, and caring for him, had brought the boy and me, too, together, so that he felt that he belonged to me as well as to the animal.

"He stayed right with me," he told me, "except when he ran in the laurel. He likes the laurel. I took him up over the hill and we both ran fast. There was a place where the grass was high and I lay down in it and hid. I could hear Pat hunting for me. He found my trail and he barked. When he found me, he acted crazy, and he ran around and around me, in circles."

We watched the flames.

"That's an apple log," he said. "It burns the prettiest of any wood."

We were very close.

He was suddenly impelled to speak of things he had not spoken of before, nor had I cared to ask him.

"You look a little bit like my mother," he said. "Especially in the dark, by the fire."

"But you were only four, Jerry, when you came here. You have remembered how she looked, all these years?"

"My mother lives in Mannville," he said.

For a moment, finding that he had a mother shocked me as greatly as anything in my life has ever done, and I did not know why it disturbed me. Then I understood my distress. I was filled with a passionate resentment that any woman should go away and leave her son. A fresh anger added itself. A son like this one—The orphanage was a wholesome place, the executives were kind, good people, the food was more than adequate, the boys were healthy, a ragged shirt was no hardship, nor the doing of clean labor. Granted, perhaps, that the boy felt no lack, what blood fed the bowels[3] of a woman who did not yearn over this child's lean body that had come in parturition[4] out of her own? At four he would have looked the same as now. Nothing, I thought, nothing in life could change those eyes. His quality must be apparent to an idiot, a fool. I burned with questions I could not ask. In any, I was afraid, there would be pain.

"Have you seen her, Jerry—lately?"

"I see her every summer. She sends for me."

I wanted to cry out, "Why are you not with her? How can she let you go away again?"

He said, "She comes up here from Mannville whenever she can. She doesn't have a job now."

His face shone in the firelight.

"She wanted to give me a puppy, but they can't let any one boy keep a puppy. You remember the suit I had on last Sunday?" He was plainly proud. "She sent me that for Christmas. The Christmas before that"—he drew a long breath, savoring the memory—"she sent me a pair of skates."

"Roller skates?"

My mind was busy, making pictures of her, trying to understand her. She had not, then, entirely deserted or forgotten him. But why, then—I thought, "I must not condemn her without knowing."

"Roller skates. I let the other boys use them. They're always borrowing them. But they're careful of them."

What circumstances other than poverty—

"I'm going to take the dollar you gave me for taking care of Pat," he said, "and buy her a pair of gloves."

I could only say, "That will be nice. Do you know her size?"

"I think it's 8½," he said.

He looked at my hands.

"Do you wear 8½?" he asked.

"No. I wear a smaller size, a 6."

"Oh! Then I guess her hands are bigger than yours."

I hated her. Poverty or no, there was other food than bread, and the soul could starve as quickly as the body. He was taking his dollar to buy gloves for her big stupid hands, and she lived away from him, in Mannville, and contented herself with sending him skates.

"She likes white gloves," he said. "Do you think I can get them for a dollar?"

"I think so," I said.

I decided that I should not leave the mountains without seeing her and knowing for myself why she had done this thing.

The human mind scatters its interests as though made of thistledown, and every wind stirs and moves it. I finished my work. It did not please me, and I gave my thoughts to another field. I should need some Mexican material.

I made arrangements to close my Florida place. Mexico immediately, and doing the writing there, if conditions were favorable. Then, Alaska with my brother. After that, heaven knew what or where.

I did not take time to go to Mannville to see Jerry's mother, nor even to talk with the orphanage officials about her. I was a trifle abstracted about the boy, because of my work and plans. And after my first fury at her—we did not speak of her again—his having a mother, any sort at all, not far away, in Mannville, relieved me of the ache I had about him. He did not question the anomalous[5] relation. He was not lonely. It was none of my concern.

He came every day and cut my wood and did

3. **bowels:** an archaic meaning. The bowels were once believed to be the seat of pity.
4. **parturition** (pär′tyŏŏ-rĭsh′ən, pär′chŏŏ-, pär′tŏŏ-): childbirth.

5. **anomalous** (ə-nŏm′ə-ləs): irregular; abnormal.

small helpful favors and stayed to talk. The days had become cold, and often I let him come inside the cabin. He would lie on the floor in front of the fire, with one arm across the pointer, and they would both doze and wait quietly for me. Other days they ran with a common ecstasy through the laurel, and since the asters were not gone, he brought me back vermilion maple leaves, and chestnut boughs dripping with imperial yellow. I was ready to go.

I said to him, "You have been my friend, Jerry. I shall often think of you and miss you. Pat will miss you too. I am leaving tomorrow."

He did not answer. When he went away, I remember that a new moon hung over the mountains, and I watched him go in silence up the hill. I expected him the next day, but he did not come. The details of packing my personal belongings, loading my car, arranging the bed over the seat, where the dog would ride, occupied me until late in the day. I closed the cabin and started the car, noticing that the sun was in the west and I should do well to be out of the mountains by nightfall. I stopped by the orphanage and left the cabin key and money for my light bill with Miss Clark.

"And will you call Jerry for me to say goodbye to him?"

"I don't know where he is," she said. "I'm afraid he's not well. He didn't eat his dinner this noon. One of the other boys saw him going over the hill into the laurel. He was supposed to fire the boiler this afternoon. It's not like him; he's unusually reliable."

I was almost relieved, for I knew I should never see him again, and it would be easier not to say goodbye to him.

I said, "I wanted to talk with you about his mother—why he's here—but I'm in more of a hurry than I expected to be. It's out of the question for me to see her now too. But here's

some money I'd like to leave with you to buy things for him at Christmas and on his birthday. It will be better than for me to try to send him things. I could so easily duplicate—skates, for instance."

She blinked her honest spinster's eyes.

"There's not much use for skates here," she said.

Her stupidity annoyed me.

"What I mean," I said, "is that I don't want to duplicate things his mother sends him. I might have chosen skates if I didn't know she had already given them to him."

She stared at me.

"I don't understand," she said. "He has no mother. He has no skates."

Reading Check

1. At what season does the story open?
2. Why does the narrator go to a cabin in the Carolina mountains?
3. Why does Jerry come to the narrator's cabin?
4. What does Jerry say he will do with the money he has earned for taking care of the dog?
5. How does the narrator find out that Jerry has lied about his mother?

For Study and Discussion

Analyzing and Interpreting the Story

1a. What is the narrator's first impression of Jerry? **b.** How does the narrator's attitude toward Jerry change during the course of the story?

2a. In what way is the relationship that develops between Jerry and the narrator a mother-son relationship? **b.** How does the narrator fail to understand Jerry's feelings?

3. The narrator says that Jerry had integrity. Yet he tells a lie. **a.** What causes Jerry to lie about his mother? **b.** Why do you think the narrator does not suspect that Jerry is lying?

4. After deciding to see Jerry's mother, the narrator decides against it: "It was none of my concern." How would you describe the conflict within her?

5. Which of the narrator's words indicate that she feels guilty as she remembers her relationship with Jerry?

6. The narrator judges Jerry's mother harshly for living in Mannville, apart from her son, and sending him gifts. **a.** What is ironic about her own behavior at the end of the story? **b.** Do you find her reaction to Jerry sensitive or insensitive? Explain your answer.

Language and Vocabulary

Recognizing Related Words

Etymology (ĕt′ə-mŏl′ə-jē) is the study of the origin and development of words. The history of a word can often be found at the beginning of a dictionary entry. Etymologies often reveal how words are related in meaning.

The word *integrity* comes from a Latin word meaning "whole" or "entire." Can you see a connection between the current usage of the word and its etymological meaning?

Some other words in our language come from the same source as *integrity*. In a dictionary, check the etymologies of *integer, integral,* and *integrate.* How is each word related to *integrity?*

Writing About Literature

Analyzing Methods of Characterization

As you have learned, an author reveals what a character is like through methods of direct and indirect characterization (see page 67). Show how Rawlings presents and develops the character of Jerry, referring to specific details in the story.

About the Author

Marjorie Kinnan Rawlings (1896–1953)

Marjorie Kinnan Rawlings was born in Washington, D.C. She attended the University of Wisconsin and worked as a journalist. In 1928 she bought an orange grove at Cross Creek in Florida and settled there. The swamplands and back country of Florida became the setting for many of her stories. She won the Pulitzer Prize in 1939 for *The Yearling,* a story of a boy and his pet fawn. Her other books include a collection of short stories, *When the Whippoorwill,* and a collection of remembrances, *Cross Creek.*

The Cask of Amontillado°

EDGAR ALLAN POE

The person telling a story—the narrator—*may be a character who observes or participates in the action. Note how Poe achieves* dramatic irony *in this story by having his narrator, Montresor, tell us directly what he sees, thinks, and feels. What differences are there between what Montresor perceives and what you, the reader, perceive?*

The thousand injuries of Fortunato I had borne as I best could; but when he ventured upon insult, I vowed revenge. You, who so well know the nature of my soul, will not suppose, however, that I gave utterance to a threat. *At length* I would be avenged; this was a point definitively settled—but the very definitiveness with which it was resolved precluded the idea of risk. I must not only punish, but punish with impunity. A wrong is unredressed when retribution overtakes its redresser. It is equally unredressed when the avenger fails to make himself felt as such to him who has done the wrong.

It must be understood that neither by word nor deed had I given Fortunato cause to doubt my good will. I continued, as was my wont, to smile in his face, and he did not perceive that my smile *now* was at the thought of his immolation.[1]

He had a weak point—this Fortunato—although in other regards he was a man to be respected and even feared. He prided himself on his connoisseurship in wine. Few Italians have the true virtuoso spirit.[2] For the most part their enthusiasm is adopted to suit the time and opportunity—to practice imposture upon the British and Austrian millionaires. In painting and gemmary[3] Fortunato, like his countrymen, was a quack—but in the matter of old wines he was sincere. In this respect I did not differ from him materially: I was skillful in the

° **Amontillado** (ə-män′tə-lä′dō): a variety of sherry.

1. **immolation** (ĭm′ə-lā′shən): sacrifice.
2. **virtuoso spirit:** deep interest in and knowledge of the arts.
3. **gemmary** (jĕm′ə-rē′): knowledge of precious stones.

The Cask of Amontillado　**95**

Italian vintages myself, and bought largely whenever I could.

It was about dusk, one evening during the supreme madness of the carnival season,[4] that I encountered my friend. He accosted me with excessive warmth, for he had been drinking much. The man wore motley.[5] He had on a tight-fitting parti-striped dress, and his head was surmounted by the conical cap and bells. I was so pleased to see him that I thought I should never have done wringing his hand.

I said to him: "My dear Fortunato, you are luckily met. How remarkably well you are looking today! But I have received a pipe[6] of what passes for Amontillado, and I have my doubts."

"How?" said he. "Amontillado? A pipe? Impossible! And in the middle of the carnival!"

"I have my doubts," I replied; "and I was silly enough to pay the full Amontillado price without consulting you in the matter. You were not to be found, and I was fearful of losing a bargain."

"Amontillado!"

"I have my doubts."

"Amontillado!"

"And I must satisfy them."

"Amontillado!"

"As you are engaged, I am on my way to Luchesi. If anyone has a critical turn, it is he. He will tell me——"

"Luchesi cannot tell Amontillado from sherry."[7]

"And yet some fools will have it that his taste is a match for your own."

"Come, let us go."

"Whither?"

"To your vaults."

"My friend, no; I will not impose upon your good nature. I perceive you have an engagement. Luchesi——"

"I have no engagement—come."

"My friend, no. It is not the engagement, but the severe cold with which I perceive you are afflicted. The vaults are insufferably damp. They are incrusted with niter."[8]

"Let us go, nevertheless. The cold is merely nothing. Amontillado! You have been imposed upon. And as for Luchesi, he cannot distinguish sherry from Amontillado."

Thus speaking, Fortunato possessed himself of my arm. Putting on a mask of black silk, and drawing a *roquelaure*[9] closely about my person, I suffered him to hurry me to my palazzo.[10]

There were no attendants at home; they had absconded to make merry in honor of the time. I had told them that I should not return until the morning, and had given them explicit orders not to stir from the house. These orders were sufficient, I well knew, to insure their immediate disappearance, one and all, as soon as my back was turned.

I took from their sconces two flambeaux,[11] and giving one to Fortunato, bowed him through several suites of rooms to the archway that led into the vaults. I passed down a long and winding staircase, requesting him to be cautious as he followed. We came at length to the foot of the descent and stood together on the damp ground of the catacombs of the Montresors.

The gait of my friend was unsteady, and the bells upon his cap jingled as he strode.

"The pipe?" said he.

"It is farther on," said I; "but observe the white webwork which gleams from these cavern walls."

---

4. **carnival season:** the period of celebration before Lent, such as the Mardi Gras festival in New Orleans.
5. **motley:** the varicolored costume of a jester.
6. **pipe:** a large cask.
7. **sherry:** Fortunato is probably using "sherry" for the sweet variety of sherry. Amontillado is a dry variety.

8. **niter** (nī′tər): white or gray salt deposit.
9. *roquelaure* (rŏk′ə-lôr): a short cloak.
10. **palazzo** (pə-lät′sō): a palace or very luxurious house.
11. **flambeaux** (flăm′bōz′): lighted torches.

He turned toward me, and looked into my eyes with two filmy orbs that distilled the rheum of intoxication.

"Niter?" he asked at length.

"Niter," I replied. "How long have you had that cough?"

"Ugh! ugh! ugh!—ugh! ugh! ugh!—ugh! ugh! ugh!—ugh! ugh! ugh!—ugh! ugh! ugh!"

My poor friend found it impossible to reply for many minutes.

"It is nothing," he said, at last.

"Come," I said, with decision, "we will go back; your health is precious. You are rich, respected, admired, beloved; you are happy, as once I was. You are a man to be missed. For me it is no matter. We will go back; you will be ill, and I cannot be responsible. Besides, there is Luchesi——"

"Enough," he said; "the cough is a mere nothing; it will not kill me. I shall not die of a cough."

"True—true," I replied; "and, indeed, I had no intention of alarming you unnecessarily; but you should use all proper caution. A draft of this Medoc will defend us from the damps."

Here I knocked off the neck of a bottle which I drew from a long row of its fellows that lay upon the mold.

"Drink," I said, presenting him the wine.

He raised it to his lips with a leer. He paused and nodded to me familiarly, while his bells jingled.

"I drink," he said, "to the buried that repose around us."

"And I to your long life."

He again took my arm, and we proceeded.

"These vaults," he said, "are extensive."

"The Montresors," I replied, "were a great and numerous family."

"I forget your arms."[12]

"A huge human foot d'or, in a field azure; the foot crushes a serpent rampant[13] whose fangs are embedded in the heel."

"And the motto?"

"*Nemo me impune lacessit.*"[14]

"Good!" he said.

The wine sparkled in his eyes and the bells jingled. My own fancy grew warm with the Medoc. We had passed through walls of piled bones, with casks and puncheons[15] intermingling, into the inmost recesses of the catacombs. I paused again, and this time I made bold to seize Fortunato by an arm above the elbow.

"The niter!" I said; "see, it increases. It hangs like moss upon the vaults. We are below the river's bed. The drops of moisture trickle among the bones. Come, we will go back ere it is too late. Your cough——"

"It is nothing," he said; "let us go on. But first, another draft of the Medoc."

I broke and reached him a flagon of De Grâve. He emptied it at a breath. His eyes flashed with a fierce light. He laughed and threw the bottle upwards with a gesticulation I did not understand.

I looked at him in surprise. He repeated the movement—a grotesque one.

"You do not comprehend?" he said.

"Not I," I replied.

"Then you are not of the brotherhood."

"How?"

"You are not of the masons."[16]

"Yes, yes," I said; "yes, yes."

"You? Impossible! A mason?"

12. **arms:** coat of arms, an insignia with several figures and a family motto.

13. **foot d'or . . . rampant:** The Montresor coat of arms shows a huge golden foot against a blue background, crushing a serpent that is rearing up.

14. *Nemo . . . lacessit:* Latin for "No one assails me with impunity." In other words: "No one can attack me without being punished."

15. **puncheons** (pŭn'chənz): large casks for beer or wine.

16. **masons:** the Freemasons, a secret fraternal order; also, bricklayers.

"A mason," I replied.

"A sign," he said.

"It is this," I answered, producing a trowel from beneath the folds of my *roquelaure*.

"You jest," he exclaimed, recoiling a few paces. "But let us proceed to the Amontillado."

"Be it so," I said, replacing the tool beneath the cloak, and again offering him my arm. He leaned upon it heavily. We continued our route in search of the Amontillado. We passed through a range of low arches, descended, passed on, and, descending again, arrived at a deep crypt, in which the foulness of the air caused our flambeaux rather to glow than flame.

At the most remote end of the crypt there appeared another less spacious. Its walls had been lined with human remains, piled to the vault overhead, in the fashion of the great catacombs of Paris. Three sides of this interior crypt were still ornamented in this manner. From the fourth the bones had been thrown down, and lay promiscuously upon the earth, forming at one point a mound of some size. Within the wall thus exposed by the displacing of the bones, we perceived a still interior recess, in depth about four feet, in width three, in height six or seven. It seemed to have been constructed for no especial use within itself, but formed merely the interval between two of the colossal supports of the roof of the catacombs, and was backed by one of their circumscribing walls of solid granite.

It was in vain that Fortunato, uplifting his dull torch, endeavored to pry into the depth of the recess. Its termination the feeble light did not enable us to see.

"Proceed," I said; "herein is the Amontillado. As for Luchesi——"

"He is an ignoramus," interrupted my friend, as he stepped unsteadily forward, while I followed immediately at his heels. In an instant he had reached the extremity of the niche, and finding his progress arrested by the rock, stood stupidly bewildered. A moment more and I had fettered him to the granite. In its surface were two iron staples, distant from each other about two feet, horizontally. From one of these depended a short chain, from the other a padlock. Throwing the links about his waist, it was but the work of a few seconds to secure it. He was too much astounded to resist. Withdrawing the key I stepped back from the recess.

"Pass your hand," I said, "over the wall; you cannot help feeling the niter. Indeed it is *very* damp. Once more let me *implore* you to return. No? Then I must positively leave you. But I must first render you all the little attentions in my power."

"The Amontillado!" ejaculated my friend, not yet recovered from his astonishment.

"True," I replied; "the Amontillado."

As I said these words I busied myself among the pile of bones of which I have before spoken. Throwing them aside, I soon uncovered a quantity of building stone and mortar. With these materials and with the aid of my trowel, I began vigorously to wall up the entrance of the niche.

I had scarcely laid the first tier of the masonry when I discovered that the intoxication of Fortunato had in a great measure worn off. The earliest indication I had of this was a low moaning cry from the depth of the recess. It was *not* the cry of a drunken man. There was then a long and obstinate silence. I laid the second tier, and the third, and the fourth; and then I heard the furious vibrations of the chain. The noise lasted for several minutes, during which, that I might hearken to it with the more satisfaction, I ceased my labors and sat down upon the bones. When at last the clanking subsided, I resumed the trowel, and finished without interruption the fifth, the

Illustration from *Illustrated London News* (1935).

sixth, and the seventh tier. The wall was now nearly upon a level with my breast. I again paused, and holding the flambeaux over the masonwork, threw a few feeble rays upon the figure within.

A succession of loud and shrill screams, bursting suddenly from the throat of the chained form, seemed to thrust me violently back. For a brief moment I hesitated—I trembled. Unsheathing my rapier,[17] I began to grope with it about the recess; but the thought of an instant reassured me. I placed my hand upon the solid fabric of the catacombs, and felt satisfied. I reapproached the wall. I replied to the yells of him who clamored. I reechoed—I aided—I surpassed them in volume and in strength. I did this, and the clamorer grew still.

It was now midnight, and my task was drawing to a close. I had completed the eighth, the ninth, and the tenth tier. I had finished a portion of the last and the eleventh; there remained but a single stone to be fitted and plastered in. I struggled with its weight; I placed it partially in its destined position. But now there came from out the niche a low laugh that erected the hairs upon my head. It was succeeded by a sad voice, which I had difficulty in recognizing as that of the noble Fortunato. The voice said—

"Ha! ha! ha!—he! he!—a very good joke indeed—an excellent jest. We will have many a rich laugh about it at the palazzo—he! he! he! —over our wine—he! he! he!"

"The Amontillado!" I said.

"He! he! he!—he! he! he!—yes, the Amontillado. But is it not getting late? Will not they be awaiting us at the palazzo—the Lady Fortunato and the rest? Let us be gone."

"Yes," I said, "let us be gone."

"*For the love of God, Montresor!*"

"Yes," I said, "for the love of God!"

17. **rapier** (rā′pē-ər): a long two-edged sword.

But to these words I hearkened in vain for a reply. I grew impatient. I called aloud:

"Fortunato!"

No answer. I called again:

"Fortunato!"

No answer still. I thrust a torch through the remaining aperture and let it fall within. There came forth in return only a jingling of the bells. My heart grew sick—on account of the dampness of the catacombs. I hastened to make an end of my labor. I forced the last stone into its position; I plastered it up. Against the new masonry I reerected the old rampart of bones. For the half of a century no mortal has disturbed them. *In pace requiescat!*[18]

18. *In . . . requiescat!:* Latin for "May he rest in peace!"

Reading Check

1. According to Montresor, what is Fortunato's weak point?
2. Why are there no attendants at the narrator's palazzo?
3. Where does Montresor lead Fortunato?
4. What does Montresor produce to indicate ironically that he is a member of the Freemasons?
5. Why is Fortunato unable to resist when Montresor chains him to the granite wall?

For Study and Discussion

Analyzing and Interpreting the Story

1. In the opening paragraph Montresor speaks of carrying out his revenge with "impunity"—with freedom from risk or punishment. Give a step-by-step account of his plan.

2. The story takes place during the carnival season. During such a season there are many parties and costume balls. People often appear in the streets in costume, as Fortunato does. Why is it appropriate for Fortunato to wear a jester's costume?

3. Montresor speaks of bearing the "thousand injuries of Fortunato." **a.** From what you learn of Fortunato through his words and actions, do you think he has deliberately injured Montresor? Explain. (For example, if he had, he would be cautious in his dealings with Montresor. Is he?) **b.** What does the mention of the "thousand injuries" tell you about Montresor?

4a. Montresor ironically gives Fortunato hints of his intentions. Find examples. **b.** How does Fortunato react to these hints?

5. The last part of the story, after Montresor has chained Fortunato to the granite wall, is told in considerable detail to arouse the reader's horror. **a.** Point out some of the details. **b.** How does Montresor's matter-of-fact account of these details heighten the effect of horror?

6. Dramatic irony results when the reader knows something that a character does not know. Montresor is proud of his revenge and considers it an act of justice. Do you think the author meant you to share Montresor's attitude? Give details in the story to support your answer.

Literary Elements

Point of View

Point of View is the angle or position from which a story is told. Just as a movie camera remains at a distance to take in a large scene or moves in to concentrate on one face, so the point of view in a story determines the distance between readers and characters. A story can be told by an outside observer, by a single character, or by several characters within a story.

Edgar Allan Poe chose to tell "The Cask of Amontillado" from the inside, through the words of its principal character. This point of view, in which the narrator speaks in his own person as "I," is called the **first-person point of view**. Poe never steps outside of his narrator to tell you what he, the author, thinks about the characters or actions. Yet he does leave clues to indicate how his readers should regard Montresor. You probably concluded that Montresor is not a reliable narrator and that you should not take his word for the "thousand injuries" he had endured or for the justice of his revenge.

Why do you think Poe decided to limit the point of view so that you see the events through Montresor's eyes and mind? To answer this question, imagine that "The Cask of Amontillado" had been told by an outside observer, as in a police report or in a newspaper story. Would the story be as horrible or as shocking? Explain.

Language and Vocabulary

Analyzing Word Structure

In the opening paragraph of the story, the narrator says, "I must not only *punish*, but punish with *impunity*." Both italicized words have the same ancestor, the word *poena* meaning "penalty or punishment." The syllable *im-* has the meaning "not" or "without." *Impunity* means "without penalty or punishment." Montresor intends to punish Fortunato and to get away without any harm to himself.

Many words in our language are composed of separate word elements. A **prefix** is a syllable joined to the beginning of a word or a word base to create a new word. The prefix *pre-* means "before." When it is joined to the word *school*, we get a new word, *preschool*, which literally means "before school," or that period of a child's life before school age.

A **suffix** is a syllable added at the end of a word or word base to form a new word. The suffix *-able* means "capable of, having qualities of, or tending to." The word *readable* literally means "capable of being read." In actual usage, it means "easy to read" or "legible."

The following exercise deals with several useful prefixes and suffixes.

Prefixes

The prefix *re-* means "back" or "again." Determine the meanings of these words: *resolve, redress, recess, recoil, resist, resume, reassure.* Check your answers in a dictionary.

The prefix *sur-* means "over, above, beyond." Determine the meaning of *surmount* and *surpass.*

The prefix *sub-*, sometimes spelled *suc-, suf-, sug-, sum-, sup-, sur-,* or *sus-*, means "under, beneath, below, or lower in rank." Look up these words in a dictionary, and determine what the prefix means in each one: *support, subside, suppose.*

Suffixes

The suffix *-ance* means "the act of" or "the state of being." What does *utterance* mean?

The suffix *-ness* means "condition, quality, or state of being." What does *definiteness* mean?

The suffix *-ship* means "condition, quality, state of being" or "ability or skill in." What is the meaning of *connoisseurship*?

The suffix *-ive* means "of, relating to, belonging to, having the nature of, having the quality of," or "tending to, given to." What is the meaning of *excessive*?

Writing About Literature

Analyzing the Narrator

"The Cask of Amontillado" is generally considered to be one of Poe's masterpieces because of the skill with which he handles the elements of horror and irony. Montresor's bizarre act of revenge is without doubt the act of an insane person, yet his plan and its execution are clever, and his comments reveal a kind of diabolic humor. Write an essay in which you give your impression of Montresor. Although his crime is appalling, how does Poe create an interest in the way his mind works?

Creative Writing

Writing a Radio Play

"The Cask of Amontillado" has several times been adapted and performed as a radio play. Make your own adaptation for the medium of radio, providing narration, dialogue, and sound effects. Remember that a radio play appeals to the imagination through the mind's eye. Sound effects and pauses can be as effective as words in stirring your listeners' emotions. You may present your play already taped or perform it "live," making use of a narrator and a sound-effects technician.

Focus on Narrative Writing

Focusing on the Climax

The **climax** of a narrative is the point of greatest emotional intensity, interest, or suspense. The climax settles the main conflict in a story, one way or the other.

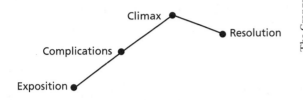

In Poe's story, the climax occurs when Montresor turns a deaf ear to his victim Fortunato's pleas for mercy.

Choose an event—either real or imaginary—that you think could serve as the climax for a story. Make sure that this event could be a genuine turning point: for example, the winning touchdown in a football game, the final burst of speed in a race, a bitter argument with a friend, or a breakthrough in learning to play a musical instrument. Freewrite about the event for five minutes, adding plot details, characters, and setting. Talk over your story ideas with a small group of classmates, and save your writing.

About the Author

Edgar Allan Poe (1809 1849)

The son of actors, Edgar Allan Poe was orphaned at the age of two. He was taken in by a childless couple, Mr. and Mrs. John Allan of Richmond, Virginia. The Allans gave Poe a gentleman's education but never formally adopted him. Poe entered the University of Virginia and soon ran up large debts, which the Allans refused to pay. Poe left the University before his first academic year ended. Under an assumed name, he enlisted in the army and rose to the rank of sergeant major. After two years he entered West Point, but chafing under the restraints of military discipline, he deliberately provoked a court-martial and was expelled from the Academy. Thereafter, the Allans would no longer help him.

The rest of Poe's life was a struggle to support himself through writing and editing. His marriage to Virginia Clemm, his thirteen-year-old cousin, added to his financial burdens. She died of tuberculosis when she was twenty-five. Poe worked as an editor on several magazines, but the work was taxing and the pay small.

Today Poe is equally famous for his short stories and his poetry. Among his best-known poems are "The Raven," "Ulalume," "Annabel Lee," and "The Bells." Among his most famous short stories are "The Black Cat," "The Fall of the House of Usher," "The Pit and the Pendulum," and "The Murders in the Rue Morgue." Poe believed that a short story should be planned and written so that every word, every detail contributes toward a single, powerful impression.

My Delicate Heart Condition

TONI CADE BAMBARA

The narrator of this story has an individual way of speaking and of describing other people. What impression do you form of her character? Do you consider her a reliable observer?

My cousin Joanne has not been allowed to hang out with me for some time because she went and told Aunt Hazel that I scare her to death whenever she sleeps over at our house or I spend the weekend at hers. The truth is I sometimes like to tell stories about blood-thirsty vampires or ugly monsters that lurk in clothes closets or giant beetles that eat their way through the shower curtain, like I used to do at camp to entertain the kids in my bunk. But Joanne always cries and that makes the stories even weirder, like background music her crying. And too—I'm not going to lie about it—I get spookier on purpose until all the little crybabies are stuffing themselves under their pillows and throwing their sneakers at me and making such a racket that Mary the counselor has to come in and shine her flashlight around the bunkhouse. I play like I'm asleep. The rest of them are too busy blubbering and finding their way out from under the blankets to tell Mary that it's me. Besides, once they get a load

of her standing against the moonlight in that long white robe of hers looking like a ghost, they just start up again and pretty soon the whole camp is awake. Anyway, that's what I do for fun. So Joanne hasn't been around. And this year I'll have to go to the circus by myself and to camp without her. My mother said on the phone to Aunt Hazel—"Good, keep Jo over there and maybe Harriet'll behave herself if she's got no one to show off to." For all the years my mother's known me, she still doesn't understand that my behaving has got nothing to do with who I hang out with. A private thing between me and me or maybe between me and the Fly family since they were the ones that first got me to sit through monster movies and withstand all the terror I could take.

For four summers now, me and the Fly family have had this thing going. A battle of nerves, you might say. Each year they raise the rope closer and closer to the very top of the tent—I hear they're going to perform outdoors this year and be even higher—and they stretch the rope further across the rings where the clowns and the pony riders perform. Each year they get bolder and more daring with their rope dancing and the swinging by the legs and flinging themselves into empty space making everyone throw up their hands and gasp for air until Mr. Fly at the very last possible second swings out on his bar to catch them up by the tips of their heels. Everyone just dies and clutches at their hearts. Everybody but me. I sit there calmly. I've trained myself. Joanne used to die and duck her head under the benches and stay there till it was all over.

Last summer they really got bold. On the final performance just before the fair closed, and some revival-type tent show comes in and all the kids go off to camp, the Fly family performed without a net. I figured they'd be up to something so I made sure my stomach was like steel. I did ten push-ups before breakfast, twenty sit-ups before lunch, skipped dinner altogether. My brother Teddy kidded me all day—"Harriet's trying out for the Olympics." I passed up the ice man on the corner and the pizza and sausage stand by the schoolyard and the cotton candy and jelly-apple lady and the pickle and penny-candy boy, in fact I passed up all the stands that lead from the street down the little roadway to the fair grounds that used to be a swamp when we first moved from Baltimore to Jamaica, Long Island. It wasn't easy,

I'm not going to lie, but I was taking no chances. Between the balloon man and the wheel of fortune was the usual clump of ladies from church who came night after night to try to win the giant punch bowl set on the top shelf above the wheel, but had to settle night after night for a jar of gumdrops or salt-and-pepper shakers or some other little thing from the bottom shelf. And from the wheel of fortune to the tent was at least a million stands selling B.B. bats and jawbreakers and gingerbread and sweet potato pie and frozen custard and—like I said it wasn't easy. A million ways to tempt you, to unsettle your stomach, and make you lose the battle to the Fly family.

I sat there almost enjoying the silly clowns who came tumbling out of a steamer trunk no bigger than the one we have in the basement where my mother keeps my old report cards and photographs and letters and things. And I almost enjoyed the fire-eater and the knife-thrower, but I was so close up I could see how there wasn't any real thrill. I almost enjoyed the fat-leg girls who rode the ponies two at a time and standing up, but their costumes weren't very pretty—just an ordinary polo shirt like you get if you run in the PAL meets and short skirts you can wear on either side like the big girls wear at the roller rink. And I almost enjoyed the jugglers except that my Uncle Bubba can juggle the dinner plates better any day of the week so long as Aunt Hazel isn't there to stop him. I was impatient and started yawning. Finally all the clowns hitched up their baggy pants and tumbled over each other out of the ring and into the dark, the jugglers caught all the things that were up in the air and yawning just like me went off to the side. The pony girls brought their horses to a sudden stop that raised a lot of dust, then jumped down into the dirt and bowed. Then the ringmaster stepped into the circle of light and tipped his hat which was a little raggedy

from where I was sitting and said—"And now, Ladieeez and Gentlemen, what you've alll been waiting forrr, the Main aTTRACtion, the FLY FAMILEEE." And everyone jumped up to shout like crazy as they came running out on their toes to stand in the light and then climb the ropes. I took a deep breath and folded my arms over my chest and a kid next to me went into hiding, acting like she was going to tie her shoelaces.

There used to be four of them—the father, a big guy with a bald head and bushy mustache and shoulders and arms like King Kong; a tall lanky mother whom you'd never guess could even climb into a high chair or catch anything heavier than a Ping-Pong ball to look at her; the oldest son who looked like his father except he had hair on his head but none on his face and a big face it was, so that no matter how high up he got you could always tell whether he was smiling or frowning or counting; the younger boy about thirteen, maybe, had a vacant stare like he was a million miles away feeding his turtles or something, anything but walking along a tightrope or flying through the air with his family. I had always liked to watch him because he was as cool as I was. But last summer the little girl got into the act. My grandmother says she's probably a midget cause no self-respecting mother would allow her child to be up there acting like a bird. "Just a baby," she'd say, "Can't be more than six years old. Should be home in bed. Must be a midget." My grandfather would give me a look when she started in and we'd smile at her together.

They almost got to me that last performance, dodging around with new routines and two at a time so that you didn't know which one Mr. Fly was going to save at the last minute. But he'd fly out and catch the little boy and swing over to the opposite stand where the big boy was flying out to catch them both by the wrists and the poor woman would be left kind of dangling there, suspended, then she'd do this double flip which would kill off everyone in the tent except me, of course, and swing out on the very bar she was on in the first place. And then they'd mess around two or three flying at once just to confuse you until the big drum roll started and out steps the little girl in a party dress and huge blindfold wrapped around her little head and a pink umbrella like they sell down in Chinatown. And I almost—I won't lie about it—I almost let my heart thump me off the bench. I almost thought I too had to tie my shoelaces. But I sat there. Stubborn. And the kid starts bouncing up and down on the rope like she was about to take off and tear through the canvas roof. Then out swings her little brother and before you know it, Fly Jr. like a great eagle with his arms flapping grabs up the kid, her eyeband in his teeth and swoops her off to the bar that's already got Mrs. Mr. and Big Bro on it and surely there's no room for him. And everyone's standing on their feet clutching at their faces. Everyone but me. Cause I know from the getgo that Mr. and Mrs. are going to leave the bar to give Jr. room and fly over to the other side. Which is exactly what they do. The lady in front of me, Mrs. Perez, who does all the sewing in our neighborhood, gets up and starts shaking her hands like ladies do to get the fingernail polish dry and she says to me with her eyes jammed shut "I must go finish the wedding gowns. Tell me later who died." And she scoots through the aisle, falling all over everybody with her eyes still shut and never looks up. And Mrs. Caine

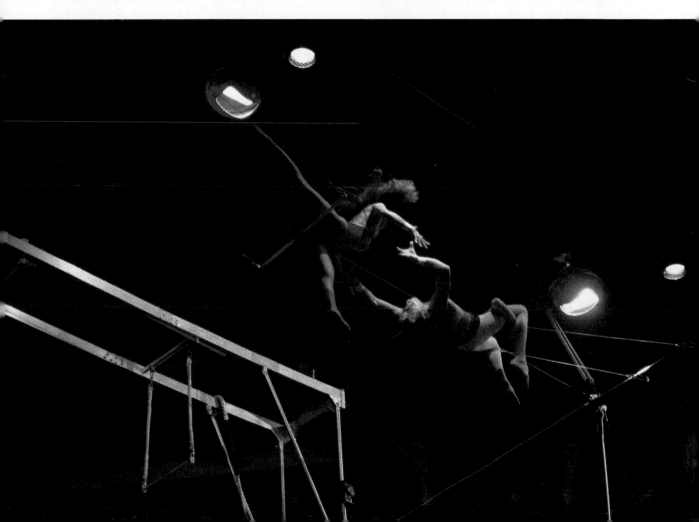

taps me on the back and leans over and says, "Some people just can't take it." And I smile at her and at her twins who're sitting there with their mouths open. I fold my arms over my chest and just dare the Fly family to do their very worst.

The minute I got to camp, I ran up to the main house where all the counselors gather to say hello to the parents and talk with the directors. I had to tell Mary the latest doings with the Fly family. But she put a finger to her mouth like she sometimes does to shush me. "Let's not have any scary stuff this summer, Harriet," she said, looking over my shoulder at a new kid. This new kid, Willie, was from my old neighborhood in Baltimore so we got friendly right off. Then he told me that he had a romantic heart so I quite naturally took him under my wing and decided not to give him a heart attack with any ghost tales. Mary said he meant "rheumatic" heart,[1] but I don't see any difference. So I told Mary to move him out of George's tent and give him a nicer counselor who'd respect his romantic heart. George used to be my play boyfriend when I first came to camp as a little kid and didn't know any better. But he's not a nice person. He makes up funny nicknames for people which aren't funny at all. Like calling Eddie Michaels the Watermelon Kid or David Farmer Charcoal Plenty which I really do not appreciate and especially from a counselor. And once he asked Joanne, who was the table monitor, to go fetch a pail of milk from the kitchen. And the minute she got up, he started hatching a plot, trying to get the kids to hide her peanut butter sandwich and put spiders in her soup. I had to remind everyone at the table that Joanne was my first cousin by blood, and I would be forced to waste the first

1. **rheumatic** (rōō-măt'ĭk): **heart:** caused by rheumatic fever in childhood, which often damages the valves of the heart.

bum that laid a hand on her plate. And ole George says, "Oh don't be a dumbhead, Harriet. Jo's so stupid she won't even notice." And I told him right then and there that I was not his play girlfriend anymore and would rather marry the wolfman than grow up and be his wife. And just in case he didn't get the message, that night around campfire when we were all playing Little Sally Walker sittin' in a saucer and it was my turn to shake it to the east and to shake it to the west and to shake it to the very one that I loved the best—I shook straight for Mr. Nelson the lifeguard, who was not only the ugliest person in camp but the arch enemy of ole George.

And that very first day of camp last summer when Willie came running up to me to get in line for lunch, here comes George talking some simple stuff about "What a beautiful head you have, Willie. A long, smooth, stream-lined head. A sure sign of superior gifts. Definitely genius proportions." And poor Willie went for it, grinning and carrying on and touching his head, which if you want to know the truth is a bullet head and that's all there is to it. And he's turning to me every which way, like he's modeling his head in a fashion show. And the minute his back is turned, ole George makes a face about Willie's head and all the kids in the line bust out laughing. So I had to beat up a few right then and there and finish off the rest later in the shower for being so stupid, laughing at a kid with a romantic heart.

One night in the last week of August when the big campfire party is held, it was very dark and the moon was all smoky, and I just couldn't help myself and started in with a story about the great caterpillar who was going to prowl through the tents and nibble off everybody's toes. And Willie started this whimpering in the back of his throat so I had to switch the story real quick to something cheerful. But before I could do that, ole George picked up my story and added a wicked witch who put spells on city kids who come to camp, and a hunchback dwarf that chopped up tents and bunk beds, and a one-eyed phantom giant who gobbled up the hearts of underprivileged kids. And every time he got to the part where the phantom ripped out a heart, poor Willie would get louder and louder until finally he started rolling around in the grass and screaming and all the kids went crazy and scattered behind the rocks almost kicking the fire completely out as they dashed off into the darkness yelling bloody murder. And the counselors could hardly round us all up—me, too, I'm not going to lie about it. Their little circles of flashlight bobbing in and out of the bushes along the patches of pine, bumping into each other as they scrambled for us kids. And poor Willie rolling around something awful, so they took him to the infirmary.

I was sneaking some gingersnaps in to him later that night when I heard Mary and another senior counselor fussing at ole George in the hallway.

"You've been picking on that kid ever since he got here, George. But tonight was the limit——"

"I wasn't picking on him, I was just trying to tell a story——"

"All that talk about hearts, gobblin' up hearts, and underpriv——"

"Yeh, you were directing it all at the little kid. You should be——"

"I wasn't talking about him. They're all underprivileged kids, after all. I mean all the kids are underprivileged."

I huddled back into the shadows and almost banged into Willie's iron bed. I was hoping he'd open his eyes and wink at me and tell me he was just fooling. That it wasn't so bad to have an underprivileged heart. But he just slept. "I'm an underprivileged kid too," I thought to myself. I knew it was a special camp, but I'd never realized. No wonder Aunt Hazel screamed so about my scary stories and my mother flicked off the TV when the monsters came on and Mary was always shushing me. We all had bad hearts. I crawled into the supply cabinet to wait for Willie to wake up so I could ask him about it all. I ate all the gingersnaps but I didn't feel any better. You have a romantic heart, I whispered to myself settling down among the bandages. You will have to be very careful.

It didn't make any difference to Aunt Hazel that I had changed, that I no longer told scary stories or dragged my schoolmates to the latest creature movie, or raced my friends to the edge of the roof, or held my breath, or ran under the train rail when the train was already in sight. As far as she was concerned, I was still the same ole spooky kid I'd always been. So Joanne was kept at home. My mother noticed the difference, but she said over the phone to my grandmother, "She's acting very ladylike these days, growing up." I didn't tell her about my secret, that I knew about my heart. And I was kind of glad Joanne wasn't around 'cause I would have blabbed it all to her and scared her to death. When school starts again, I decided, I'll ask my teacher how to outgrow my underprivileged heart. I'll train myself, just like I did with the Fly family.

"Well, I guess you'll want some change to go to the fair again, hunh?" my mother said coming into my room dumping things in her pocketbook.

"No," I said. "I'm too grown up for circuses."

She put the money on the dresser anyway. I was lying, of course. I was thinking what a terrible strain it would be for Mrs. Perez and everybody else if while sitting there, with the

Fly family zooming around in the open air a million miles above the ground, little Harriet Watkins should drop dead with a fatal heart attack behind them.

"I lost," I said out loud.

"Lost what?"

"The battle with the Fly family."

She just stood there a long time looking at me, trying to figure me out, the way mothers are always doing but should know better. Then she kissed me goodbye and left for work.

Reading Check

1. Why have Harriet and her cousin Joanne been kept apart?
2. Who are the members of the Fly family?
3. Who is the new camper Harriet befriends?
4. Why is Willie taken to the infirmary?
5. How does Harriet's mother interpret the change in her behavior?

For Study and Discussion

Analyzing and Interpreting the Story

1. The narrator, Harriet Watkins, tells us that she has a reputation for being a "spooky kid" who tells scary stories and who likes to take risks. What evidence is there that her reputation is well deserved?

2. According to Harriet, she has learned to master her fear in a "battle of nerves" with the Fly family. **a.** Before leaving for camp, how does she prepare herself for the final performance of the Fly family? **b.** How does she react to their new routines?

3. When Harriet arrives at summer camp, she finds a new camper, Willie, who tells her that he has a "romantic" heart. **a.** Why is it significant that Harriet does not see any difference between the words *romantic* and *rheumatic*? **b.** How does Harriet take Willie "under her wing"?

4a. How do you know that Harriet dislikes George? **b.** What impression do you form of him from his treatment of Willie and from his stories about a "phantom giant who gobbled up the hearts of underprivileged kids"?

5a. When Harriet overhears George talking about "underprivileged kids," what conclusion does she draw? **b.** Why does she now believe that she, too, has a "bad heart"?

6. Toward the end of the story, Harriet says she will ask her teacher "how to outgrow my underprivileged heart." In what way is this statement both humorous and sad?

7. The reader of a story often grasps many things that the narrator is unaware of. This is particularly true when the narrator is a child, like Harriet. **a.** Which of Harriet's perceptions seem to be accurate? **b.** What does she fail to understand?

8. What insight does this story give into the way children develop perceptions about themselves?

Language and Vocabulary

Recognizing Characteristics of Speech

In literature characters are defined not only by *what* they say but by *how* they say it. Harriet's individual manner of speaking is characterized by slang, vivid comparisons, and exaggeration.

Harriet says she is not allowed to "hang out" with her cousin Joanne. The phrase "hang out" is slang for "spend time." Harriet also uses "cool" and "can't take it" in their slang meanings. What do these words mean?

Harriet uses both vivid comparisons and exaggeration when she says that the father of the Fly family has arms "like King Kong," and when she describes "Fly Jr. like a great eagle with his arms flapping." She tells George that she would rather marry "the wolfman" than grow up and be married to him.

What other examples can you find of Harriet's colorful speech?

Focus on Narrative Writing

Telling an Anecdote

An **anecdote** is a mini-story about an interesting or humorous incident. Although we may not all be as gifted at storytelling as Harriet Watkins in Toni Cade Bambara's story, most of us tell anecdotes every day to our family and friends—sometimes without even realizing it.

Jot down some notes for an anecdote from your own experience. The diagram below shows three helpful guidelines for preparing anecdotes:

Get together with a small group of classmates and trade anecdotes, delivering them orally. After each person in the group tells an anecdote, allow time for a brief discussion period. In the discussion, offer your classmates suggestions about ways to make their anecdotes funnier, clearer, or more interesting. Save your notes.

About the Author

Toni Cade Bambara (1939–1995)

Toni Cade Bambara (bäm–bä′rä) grew up in New York City and Jersey City. She began writing when she was still a child. She took the name Bambara from a signature she found in a sketchbook in a trunk belonging to her great-grandmother. Bambara was known for the poetic quality of her prose and for her accurate rendering of African American street talk. The writer Anne Tyler said of Bambara's characters: "Everything these people say, you feel, ordinary, real-life people are saying right now on any street corner. It's only that the rest of us didn't realize it was sheer poetry they were speaking." Bambara's books include *Tales and Stories for Black Folks* (1971); *Gorilla, My Love* (1972); *The Sea Birds Are Still Alive* (1977); and *The Salt Eaters* (1980).

Before the End of Summer

GRANT MOSS, JR.

The events in this story are told in the third person, from the point of view of one character, so that the reader is made aware of what Bennie observes, thinks, and feels. In what way is this point of view different from the first-person point of view?

When Dr. Frazier came, Bennie's grandmother told him to run down to the spring and wade in the stream that flowed from it across the pasture field to Mr. Charley Miller's pond, or play under the big oak tree that stood between her field and Mr. Charley Miller's. He started along the path, but when he was about midway to the spring he stopped. He had waded in the stream and caught minnows all that morning. He had played under the oak tree all yesterday afternoon. He had asked his grandmother to let him walk the mile and a half down the road to James and Robert Lee Stewart's to play, but she had not let him go. There was nothing he wanted to do alone. He wanted someone to play with. He turned and went back and crept under the window of his grandmother's room. Their voices floated low and quiet out into the cool shade that lay over the house.

"How long will it be?" he heard his grandmother say.

"Before the end of summer."

"Are you sure?"

"Yes. You should have sent for me long ago."

"I've passed my threescore and ten years. I'm eighty-four."

What did they mean? Perhaps he ought not to be listening.

"How will it come? Tell me, Doctor. I can stand it."

"There will be sharp, quick pains like the ones you've been having. Your heart cannot stand many more attacks. It grows weaker with each one, even though you're able to go about your work as you did before the attack came. I'm going to leave you a prescription for some pills that will kill the pain almost instantly. But that's about all they will do. When an attack comes, take two with a glass of water. They'll make you drop off to sleep. One time you won't wake up."

Now Bennie understood. But he could not turn and run away.

There was a brief silence. Then his grandmother said, "Don't tell Birdie nor anybody else."

"But you can't stay here alone with the child all day long. Why, he's only ten years old."

"I know. . . . Doctor, there ain't anyone to come stay with me. Birdie must go to the Fieldses' to work. You know it's just Birdie, the boy, and me. I got no close kin. My husband, my three sons, and my other daughter's been

Farm Boy (1941) by Charles Alston. Oil on canvas.   Atlanta University Collection of Afro-American Art dead for years now. You see, I know death, Doctor, I know it well. I'm just not use to it."

"No one is," Dr. Frazier said.

"Here's what I want to do. I'll go on just like before. There ain't nothin' else for me to do. When an attack comes, I'll take the two pills and I'll send Bennie runnin' down the road for May Mathis. She'll come. May will come. I know nobody I'd rather have set beside me than May. I knowed her all my life. Me and her done talked about this thing many times. It's July now. July the seventh. Then August— then September. But here I go runnin' on and on. Let me get your money. You've got to be paid. You've got to live."

"Please," Dr. Frazier said.

"No harm meant."

In a moment, Bennie heard them walking out onto the porch through the door of her room. Then he could see them as they crossed the yard to the gate, where Dr. Frazier's horse and buggy stood. He was a little man, with a skin that was almost black. He climbed into his buggy and started up the road toward the town, which was three miles away, and she stood and looked after him. Her back was to the house. People said that Bennie's grandmother had Indian blood in her veins, for she had high cheekbones and her nose was long and straight, but her mouth was big. Her eyes seemed as though they were buried way back in her head, in a mass of wrinkles. They danced and twinkled whenever they looked at him. She was a big woman, and she wore long full skirts that came all the way to the ground.

She closed the gate and started back to the house, and it came to Bennie that he was alone with her, and that she was going to die soon. He turned and ran noiselessly across the backyard, through the back gate, and down the path to the spring.

When he reached the spring, he kept run-ning. He ran across the pasture field and up the hill to the barbed-wire fence that divided his grandmother's land from Mr. Charley Miller's. He threw himself to the ground and rolled under the fence, picked himself up on the other side, and ran through Mr. Charley Miller's field of alfalfa and into the woods, until at last he fell exhausted in the cool damp grass of a shaded clearing.

His grandmother was going to die. She might even be dead now. She was going to lie cold and still, in a long black casket that would be put into a hearse that would take her to church in town. The Reverend Isaiah Jones would preach her funeral. People would cry, because people liked his grandmother. His mother would cry. He would cry. And now he was crying, and he could not stop crying.

But at last he did, and he sat up and took from his pocket the clean white rag that his grandmother had given him to use as a hand-kerchief and dried his eyes. He must get up and go back to the house. He would have to be alone with his grandmother until his mother came home from the Fieldses' after she had cooked their supper. And he must tell no one what he had heard Dr. Frazier say to his grand-mother.

He found her sitting in her big rocking chair, her hands clasped in her lap. "You been gone a long time," she said. "The water buck-et's empty. Take it and go fill it at the spring. Time for me to be gettin' up from here and cookin' supper."

When he got back from the spring, he found her laying a fire in the kitchen stove.

It was nearly dark when he saw his mother coming, and he ran to meet her. She looked at him closely and said, "Bennie, why on earth did you run so fast?"

He could only say breathlessly, "I don't know." He added quickly, "What did you bring me?" Sometimes she brought him a piece of cake or pie, or the leg of chicken from the Fieldses'. Today she did not have anything.

It was a long time before he went to sleep that night.

The next day, he stayed outdoors and only went into the house when his grandmother called him to do something for her. She did not notice.

On Sunday, his mother did not go to the Fieldses'. In the morning, they went to church. That afternoon, Mr. Joe Bailey drove up to the house in his horse and buggy to take Bennie's mother for a buggy ride. She had put on her pretty blue-flowered dress and her big wide-brimmed black straw hat with the red roses around its crown and the black ribbon that fell over the brim and down her back. She looked very pretty and as pleased as she could be. Bennie wanted to go riding with them. Once, he had asked Mr. Joe if he could go along, and Mr. Joe had grinned and said yes, but Bennie's mother had not been pleased at all, for some reason. This Sunday, after they had gone, his grandmother let him walk the mile and a half down the road to play with James and Robert Lee Stewart.

He knew that his grandmother was preparing to die. He came upon her kneeling in prayer beside her bed and its high headboard that almost touched the ceiling. As she sat in her rocking chair, she said the Twenty-third Psalm. He knew only the first verse: "The Lord is my shepherd; I shall not want."

Now he felt toward his grandmother the way he felt toward certain people, only more so. There was a feeling that made people seem strange—a feeling that came from them to you—that made you stand away from them. There was Miss Sally Cannon, his teacher. You did not go close to Miss Sally. She made you sit still and always keep your reader or your spelling book open on your desk, or do your arithmetic problems. If she caught you whispering or talking, she called you up to the front of the room and gave you several stinging lashes on your leg or across your back with one of the long switches that always lay across her desk. You did not go close to Miss Sally unless you had to. You did not go close to Dr. Frazier or the Reverend Isaiah Jones. Teachers, doctors, and preachers were special people.

You did not go close to white people, either. Sometimes when he and his grandmother went to town, they would stop at the Fieldses'. They would walk up the long green yard and go around the big red brick house, with its tall white columns, to the kitchen, where his mother was; it always seemed a nice place to be, even on a hot summer day. His mother and his grandmother would chuckle over something that Miss Marion Fields or Mr. Ridley Fields had done. They would stop smiling the minute Miss Marion came into the room, and they would become like people waiting in the vestibule of a church for the prayer to be finished so they could go in. He knew that he acted the same way.

Miss Marion had light-brown hair and light-brown eyes. His grandmother said that she was like a sparrow, for she was a tiny woman. She always wore a dress that was pretty enough to wear to church. The last time he was at the Fieldses', Miss Marion came into the kitchen. After she had spoken to his grandmother, she turned to him. He was sitting in a chair near the window, and he felt himself stiffen both inside and outside. She said, "I declare, Birdie, Bennie's the prettiest colored child I ever did see. Lashes long as a girl's. Is he a good boy, Hannah?"

"He's a quiet child," his grandmother said. "Sometimes I think he's too quiet, but he's a good child—at least when I got my eyes on him." They all laughed.

"I'm sure Bennie's good," Miss Marion said. "Be a good boy, Bennie. Eat plenty and grow strong, and when you're big enough to work, Mr. Ridley will be glad to give you work here on his place. We're so glad to have your mother here with us. Now, be good, won't you?"

"Yes, Ma'am," he answered.

"Birdie, give him a piece of that lemon pie you baked for supper. Well, Hannah, it's been nice talking with you again. Always stop on your way to town."

Two weeks to the day after Dr. Frazier's visit, Miss May Mathis came to see his grandmother. She was much shorter than his grandmother—a plump woman, who always wore long black-and-white checked gingham dresses that fell straight down from her high full breasts to her knees and then flared outward. Her chin was sharp, with folds of flesh around it. Her nose was wide and flat. She had small, snapping black eyes. Her skin was like cream that had been kept too long and into which hundreds of tiny black specks had fallen.

As she came into the yard, she asked Bennie if his grandmother was at home. She said she would sit on the porch, where it was cool. He ran into the house to tell his grandmother that she was there.

His grandmother put away her sewing and went out on the porch. "May, I'm glad you come. I've been lookin' for you," she said.

"I'd been here sooner, but my stomach's been givin' me trouble lately. Sometimes I think my time ain't long."

"Hush—hush! You'll live to see me put under the ground."

"Well, the day before yesterday I spent half the day in bed. I thought I'd have to send John for you," Miss May answered, and she went into a long account of the illness that troubled her.

Bennie got up from the edge of the porch and ran around the house. The two old women paid no attention to his going. He knew what his grandmother would say to Miss May. She would tell Miss May how she wanted to be dressed for burial. She would name the song she wanted to be sung over her. He had heard the same conversation many times. Now it was different. What they were talking about would soon "come to pass," as his grandmother would say. Miss May did not know, but he knew.

He went out of the back gate and down the path to the spring. He waded in the stream awhile, catching minnows in his hands and then letting them go. He went across the pasture field. He broke off a persimmon bush to use as a switch, and he chased his grandmother's cow about the pasture a bit. But the cow was old and soon grew tired of moving when he hit her with the switch. Then he went to the big oak tree that stood between the fields and sat down. He stayed there until he saw Miss May Mathis going out of the front gate.

The July days went slowly by, one much like another. It grew hotter and hotter.

One day when he walked into the house after playing a long time in the stream and the pasture field, he found his grandmother quietly sleeping in her big rocking chair. He saw a bottle full of big white pills on the dresser. It had not been there when he left the house. An empty glass stood beside the pills. He felt too frightened to move. Her breast was rising and falling evenly. She stirred and then opened her eyes.

She seemed dazed and not to see him for a moment. Then her lips curved into a queer smile, and a twinkle came into her eyes. "Must have dropped off to sleep like a baby," she said. "Run outdoors and play. I'll set here awhile, and then I'll get up and start supper."

Later on, she called him and asked if he

could make out with milk and cold food from dinner. She left the milking for his mother to do when she came home from the Fieldses'. But the next morning his grandmother was all right, and he thought she was not going to die that summer, after all.

One morning, a little after his mother had gone to the Fieldses', Mr. John Mathis drove up. He turned his horse and buggy around to face the way he had come. Then he walked up the path to the house. He was a tall, rawboned man with a bullet-shaped head, and he looked exactly like what he was—a deacon in a church.

"What is it, John?" Bennie's grandmother asked.

"It's May. She was sick all day yesterday. Last night I had to get the doctor for her. Jennie Stewart's there now."

"I'll be ready to go in a minute," his grandmother said.

On the way to the Mathises', Bennie sat on the back of the buggy. His grandmother and Mr. John said only a few words. When they reached the house, his grandmother told him to keep very quiet and to be good, and she went inside at once. There were people on the porch, and people continued to come and go. It was midafternoon, and still his grandmother had not come from within the house. A Ford car drove up to the gate. In it were Philomena Jones and her mother. Philomena was a year younger than Bennie. She had a sharp little yellow face, big black eyes that went everywhere, and she wore her hair in two long plaits. "Come on," she said, "and let's play something." When they were out of hearing of the grown-up people, she said, "Miss May going to die."

"How do you know?"

"I heard my mama say she was. She's old. When you're old you have to die."

Next, Philomena said, "Your mama's tryin'

to catch Mr. Joe Bailey for a husband. Mama said it's time she's getting another husband if she's ever going to get one."

"You stop talkin'!" Bennie told her.

"She said you pa's been dead nine years now and if your mama don't hurry and take Mr. Joe Bailey—that is, if she can get him—she may never get a chance to marry again."

"If you don't stop talkin', I'll hit you!"

"No, you won't. I'm not scared of you, even if you are a boy, and I'll say what I want to. Mama said, 'Birdie Wilson's in her forties, if she a day, and if a woman lets herself get into her forties without marryin', her chance are mighty slim after that.' I'm goin' to marry when I'm twenty."

"Nobody'd want you. You talk too much."

"I don't, either."

"I won't play with you. I'm goin' back to the porch," he said.

Philomena stayed in the yard a little longer. She carried on an imaginary conversation with a person who seemed as eager to talk as she. After a while, she ran back to the porch and sat down and gave her attention to what the grown-up people were saying, now and then putting in a word herself.

Then his grandmother came out from the house. People stopped talking at the sight of her face. "May's gone," she said.

The people on the porch bowed their heads, and their faces became as though they were already at Miss May Mathis's funeral.

His grandmother looked very tired. After a moment she said, "The Lord giveth and the Lord taketh. Blessed be the name of the Lord." There was a silence. Then she spoke again. "I thought May would do for me what I have to do for her now." She turned and went back into the house. Some of the women rose and followed her.

The people who remained on the porch spoke in low voices. Someone wondered when the funeral would be. Someone wondered if Miss May's sister Ethel, who lived in St. Louis, would come. Someone hoped it would not rain the day of the funeral.

Then Mr. John Mathis and Bennie's grandmother came out on the porch. Mr. John said, "Hannah, you done all you could do. May couldn't have had a better friend. You're tired now. I'll send you home."

At home, his grandmother seemed not to notice him. Her eyes seemed to be taking a great sad rest. She sent him to the spring to get water to cook supper.

As he walked down the path, he thought about his grandmother. He felt more sorry for her than he felt fear of her. Miss May Mathis was dead; he could not run and get her now.

On Sunday afternoon at two o'clock at the Baptist Church, Miss May Mathis's funeral service was held. There was a procession of buggies, surreys, and even a few automobiles from the house to the church. Mr. Joe Bailey came and took Bennie's mother, his grandmother, and him to church. The funeral was a long one. He sat beside his grandmother and listened to the prayers, the songs, and the sermon, all the time dreading the moment when the flowers would be taken from the gray casket, the casket would be opened, and the people would file by to see the body for the last time.

The Reverend Isaiah Jones described Heaven as a land flowing with milk and honey, a place where people ate fruit from the tree of life, wore golden slippers, long white robes, and starry crowns, and rested forever. The Reverend Isaiah Jones was certain that Miss May Mathis was there, resting in the arms of Jesus, done with the sins and sorrows of this world. Bennie wondered why Mr. John covered his face with his hands, and why Miss May's sister Ethel, who had come all the way from St. Louis, cried out, and why people

cried, if Miss May was so happy in this land. It seemed that they would be glad for her, so glad they would not cry. Or did they cry because they were glad? He could not understand. The Reverend Jones said that they would see Miss May on the Resurrection morning. Bennie could not understand this, either.

At last the gray casket was opened, and people began to file by it. And at last he was close. His mother went by, and then Mr. Joe. Now his grandmother. The line of people stopped, waiting expectantly. His grandmother stood and looked down on Miss May for a long time. She did not cry out. She simply stood there and looked down, and finally she moved on. Now he was next. Miss May Mathis looked as though she had simply combed her hair and piled it on top of her head, put on her best black silk dress, pinned her big old brooch to its lace collar, picked up a white handkerchief with one hand, and then decided that instead of going to church she would sleep a little while. As he looked down on her, he was not as afraid as he'd thought he would be.

Outside the church, as the procession was forming to go to the graveyard, Dr. Frazier came up to his grandmother and asked how she was.

"As well as could be expected, Doctor," his grandmother said. And then, in a low voice, "I've had only one."

"You got through it all right."

"Yes."

"And this?"

"I've managed to get through it."

"You will be careful."

"Yes."

"Now?"

"He'll have to go to the Stewarts'."

They did not know that he understood what they were talking about, even if none of the other people around them did. He heard two women whispering. One said to the other, "It's wonderful the way Aunt Hannah took it." He felt very proud of his grandmother.

Now his grandmother's footsteps were slower as she moved about the house and yard. He kept the garden and the flower beds along the yard fences weeded, the stove box full of wood, the water bucket full all the time, without her having to ask him to do these things for her. He overheard her say to his mother, "Child does everything without being told. It ain't natural."

"Reckon he's not well?" his mother asked anxiously.

"Don't think so. He eats well. Maybe the trouble is the child don't have nobody to play with every day. He'll be all right when fall comes and school starts."

August came, and it grew hotter. The sun climbed up the sky in the morning and down the sky in the evening like a tired old man with a great load on his back going up and down a hill. Then one hot mid-August day dawned far hotter and sultrier than the one just past. It grew still hotter during the early part of the morning, but by midday there was a change, for there was a breeze, and in the west a few dark clouds gathered in the sky. His grandmother said, "I believe the rain will come at last."

About three o'clock, the wind rose suddenly. It bent the top of the big oak tree that stood in the yard. There were low rumbles of thunder.

"Bennie, Bennie, come! Let's get the chickens up!" his grandmother called to him.

By the time the chickens were safe in the henhouse and chicken coops, it was time to go into the house and put the windows down. The wind lifted the curtains almost to the ceiling. They got the windows down. His grandmother went into the kitchen. He went out on the porch. He wanted to watch the clouds, for he had never seen any bigger or blacker or quite so low to the earth—he was sure they must be touching the ground somewhere. He wanted to see what the wind did to the trees, the corn, and the grass.

At last the rain fell, first in great drops that were blown onto the edge of the porch by the wind and felt cool and good as they touched his face. They made him want to run out into the yard. Then the rain came so quickly and so heavily, and with it so much wind, that it came up on the porch and almost pushed him back into the house. The thunder roared and there were flashes of lightning.

"Bennie, Bennie, where are you?" his grandmother called, and when he went inside she said, "Set down—set down in the big chair there or come into my room if you want to. I'm goin' to just set in my rocker."

"I'll stay here," he said, and he went to the big chair near the fireplace and sat down.

"There—there—just set there. I'll leave the door open."

He tried to keep from thinking what might happen if his grandmother had one of her spells, but he could not. He went to the fire-

Detail from *Mending Socks* (1924) by Archibald John Motley, Jr. Oil on canvas.

place. The back of the fireplace was wet; water stood on it in drops that looked like tears on a face. He stood and looked at it awhile, then he sat down in the big chair. There was nothing else to do but to sit there.

He heard her cry out. The cry was sharp and quick. Then it was cut off.

She called him. "Bennie! Bennie!" Her voice was thick.

He could not move.

"Bennie!"

He went into the room where she was.

She sat on the side of her bed. She was breathing hard, and in one hand she had the bottle of white pills. "Get me a glass of water. One of my spells done come over me."

He went into the kitchen and got a glass from the kitchen safe and filled it with water from the bucket that sat on the side table. Then he went back to her and gave her the water.

She took it and put two pills in her mouth and gulped them down with the water. She was breathing hard. "Pull off my shoes," she said.

As he was unlacing the high-top shoes she always wore, she gave a little cry. He felt her body tremble. "Just a bit of pain. Don't worry. I'm all right," she said. "It's gone," she added a moment later.

When he got her shoes off, he lifted her legs onto the bed, and she lay back and closed her eyes. "Go into the front room," she said, "and close the door behind you and stay there until the storm is past. I'm goin' to drop off to sleep—and if I'm still asleep when the storm is over, just let me sleep until your mama comes. Don't come in here. Don't try to wake me. 'Twon't do me no harm to take me a long good sleep."

He could not move. He could only stand and stare at her.

"Hear me? Go on, I tell you. Go on—don't, I'll get up from here and skin you alive."

He crept from the room, closing the door after him.

He went to the big chair and sat down. He must not cry. Crying could not help him. There was nothing to do but to sit there until the storm was past.

The rain and the wind came steadily now. He sat back in the big chair. He wondered about his mother. Was she safe at the Fieldses'? He wondered if the water had flowed into the henhouse and under the chicken coops, where the little chickens were. If it had, some of the little chickens might get drowned. The storm lasted so long that it began to seem to him that it had always been there.

At last he became aware that the room was growing lighter and the rain was not so hard. The thunder and lightning were gone. Then, almost as suddenly as it had begun, the storm was over.

He got up and went out on the porch. Everything was clean. Everything looked new. There were little pools of water everywhere, and it was cool. There were a few clouds in the sky, but they were white and light gray. He looked across the field toward Mr. Charley Miller's, and he opened his eyes wide when he saw that the storm had blown down the big oak tree. He started to run back into the house to tell his grandmother that the storm had blown the tree down, and then he stopped. After a minute, he stepped down from the porch. The wet grass felt good on his bare feet.

He felt his grandmother in the doorway even before he heard her call. He turned and looked at her. She had put on her shoes and the long apron she always wore. She came out on the porch, and he decided that she looked as though her sleep had done her good.

He remembered the tree, and he cried, "Look—look, Grannie! The storm blowed down the tree between your field and Mr. Charley Miller's."

"That tree was there when me and your grandpa came here years and years ago," she said. "The Lord saw fit to let it be blowed down in this storm. I—I——" She broke off and went back into the house.

He ran into the house and said to her, "I'm going down to the spring. I bet the stream's deep as a creek."

"Don't you get drowned like old Pharaoh's army," she said.

The storm drove away the heat, for the days were now filled with cool winds that came and rattled the cornstalks and the leaves on the oak tree in the yard. There were showers. The nights were long and cool; the wind came into the rooms, gently pushing aside the neat white curtains to do so.

One morning when he went into the kitchen to get hot water and soap to take to the back porch to wash his face and hands, he found his mother and grandmother busy talking. They stopped the moment they saw him. His mother's face seemed flushed and uncomfortable, but her eyes were very bright.

"Done forgot how to say good mornin' to a body?" his grandmother said.

"Good mornin', Grannie. Good mornin', Mama."

"That's more like it."

"Good mornin', Bennie," his mother said. She looked at him, and he had a feeling that she was going to come to him and take him in her arms the way she used to do when he was a little boy. But she did not.

His grandmother laughed. "Well, son, Mr. Joe Bailey went and popped the question to your mama last night."

His mother blushed. He did not know what to say to either of them. He just stood and looked at them.

"What you goin' to say to that?" his mother said.

All he could think to say was "It's all right."

His grandmother laughed again, and his mother smiled at him the way she did when he ran down the road to meet her and asked her to let him carry the packages that she had.

"When will they be married?" he asked.

"Soon," his mother said.

"Where will they live—here?"

"That ain't been settled yet," his grandmother said. "Nothin' been settled. They just got engaged last night while they were settin' in the front room and you was sleepin' in your bed. Things can be settled later." She gave a sigh that his mother did not hear. But he heard it.

He poured water from the teakettle into the wash pan and took the pan out on the back porch and washed and dried his hands. He looked across the fields and hills. The sun had not come up yet, but the morning lay clear and soft and quiet as far as his eyes could see.

His mother was going to marry Mr. Joe Bailey. He did mind a little. He knew that was what she wanted. He liked Mr. Joe. When Mr. Joe smiled at him, he always had to smile back at him; something seemed to make him do so.

After his mother had gone to the Fieldses', he and his grandmother sat down to breakfast at the table in the kitchen. His grandmother never ate a meal without saying grace. Usually she gave thanks just for the food that they were about to eat. This morning she asked the Lord to bless his mama, Mr. Joe, and him, and she thanked the Lord for answering all her prayers.

As they ate, she talked to him. She spoke as though she were talking to herself, expecting no answer from him, but he knew that she meant for him to listen to her words, and he knew why she was talking to him. "Joe Bailey will make your mama a good husband and you a good father to take the place of your father who you never knew. The Lord took your father when your father was still young, but that was the Lord's will. Joe Bailey will be good to you, for he is a good man. Mind him. Don't make trouble between him and your mama. Hear me?"

"Yes, Ma'am."

"Don't you worry about where you'll stay. You'll be with your mama. Hear me?"

"Yes'm."

She sat silent for a moment, and then she added, "Well, no matter if your mama is going to marry Mr. Joe Bailey. We got to work today just like we always has. No matter what comes, we have to do the little things that our hands find to do. Soon as you finish eatin', go to the spring and get water and fill the pot and the tubs."

August drew toward its close, but the soft cool days stayed on, and they were calm and peaceful. His grandmother cooked the meals, and washed and ironed their own clothes and those that his mother brought home from the Fieldses' and Mr. Charley Miller's. Sometimes Bennie wondered if she had put from her mind the things that Dr. Frazier had said to her that day he listened under the window. Sometimes it seemed to him that he had never crept close to the window and listened to her and Dr. Frazier. The summer seemed just like last summer and the summer before that.

One day near the end of the month, Mr. John Mathis stopped by the house on his way to town. He was on horseback, riding a big black horse whose sides glistened. He hailed Bennie's grandmother, and she came out on the porch to pass the time of day with him.

"Ever see such a fine summer day, John?" she said.

"It's not a summer day, Hannah. It's a fall day. It's going to be an early fall this year."

"Think so?" his grandmother asked. Her face changed, but Mr. John did not notice.

"I can feel it. I can feel it in the air. The smell of fall is here already." Then they fell to talking about the church and people they knew.

She stood on the porch and watched Mr. John ride up the road on his big black horse. Often that day, she came out on the porch and stood and looked across the fields and hills.

When Bennie went outside for the first time the next morning and looked around him, he did not see a single cloud in the sky. The quiet that lay about him felt like a nice clean sheet you pull over your head before you go to sleep at night that shuts out everything to make a space both warm and cool just for you. The day grew warm. A little after midday, clouds began to float across the sky, but for the most part it remained clear and very blue. He played in the yard under the oak tree, and then he went down to the spring and played. In the afternoon, he rolled his hoop up and down the road in front of the house. He grew tired of this and went and sat under the tree.

He was still sitting under the tree when his grandmother cried out. She gave a sharp sudden cry, like the cry people make when they've been stung by a bee or a wasp. He got to his feet. Then he heard her call. "Bennie! Bennie!"

He ran into the house and into her room.

She sat in her big rocking chair, leaning forward a little, her hands clutching the arms of the chair. She was breathing hard. He had never seen her eyes as they were now. "Water—the pills—in the dresser."

He ran into the kitchen and got a glass of water and ran back to the room and gave it to her and then went to the dresser and got the bottle of pills. He unscrewed the top and took out two of them and gave them to her.

She put the pills in her mouth and gulped

them down with water. Then she leaned back and closed her eyes. At last she breathed easier, and in a few moments she opened her eyes. "Run and get—get Miss—No, go get your mama. Hurry! Your grandmother is very sick."

It was a long way to the Fieldses'—even longer than to the Stewarts'! He stood still and looked at her. She was a big woman, and the chair was a big chair. Now she seemed smaller—lost in the chair.

"Hurry—hurry, child."

"Grannie, I'll stay with you until you go to sleep, if you want me to," he heard himself say.

"No! No! Hurry!"

"I heard you and Dr. Frazier talking that day."

"Child! Child! You knew all the time?"

"Yes, Grannie."

"When I drop off to sleep, I won't wake up. Your grandmother won't wake up here."

"I know."

"You're not afraid?"

He shook his head.

She seemed to be thinking hard, and at last she said, "Set down, child. Set down beside me."

He pulled up the straight chair and sat down facing her.

"Seems like I don't know what to say to you, Bennie. Be a good boy. Seems like I can't think any more. Everything leavin' me—leavin' me."

"I'll set here until you go to sleep, and then I'll go and get Mama."

"That's a good boy," she said, and she closed her eyes.

He sat still and quiet until her breath came softly and he knew that she was asleep. It was not long. Then he got up and walked from the room and out of the house.

He did not look back, and he did not run until he was a good way down the road. Then suddenly he began to run, and he ran as fast as he could.

Reading Check

1. How does Bennie learn that his grandmother will die before the end of summer?
2. Whose funeral does Bennie attend with his grandmother?
3. What news do his mother and grandmother give him?
4. What does Bennie say when his grandmother tells him to leave as she is dying?
5. What does Bennie do after his grandmother goes to sleep?

For Study and Discussion

Analyzing and Interpreting the Story

1. At the beginning of the story, Bennie learns that his grandmother is expected to die before the end of summer. At the end of the story, Bennie witnesses her death. **a.** Compare his reactions in the opening and closing scenes of the story. **b.** What change would you say has taken place in his understanding of death?

2. Throughout the story Bennie is reminded of his grandmother's impending death. How does Miss May's funeral prepare Bennie to face the death of someone he loves?

3. This story is told from the point of view of a ten-year-old. **a.** How does the author convince you that Bennie's perceptions are those of a child? **b.** What aspects of the adult world are beyond Bennie's grasp?

Literary Elements

Limited Third-Person Point of View

A writer may sometimes tell a story in the third person from the point of view of a character in the story. "Before the End of Summer" is told from the point of view of Bennie.

Because Bennie is only ten years old, there are many things he does not understand. At the funeral service of May Mathis, he is confused by the mourners' grief when they are told that Miss May is in heaven:

> Bennie wondered why Mr. John covered his face with his hands, and why Miss May's sister Ethel, who had come all the way from St. Louis, cried out, and why people cried, if Miss May was so happy in this land. It seemed that they would be glad for her, so glad they would not cry. Or did they cry because they were glad? He could not understand.

The language of the story is also carefully controlled so that Bennie's thoughts are conveyed realistically:

> He went to the big chair and sat down. He must not cry. Crying could not help him. There was nothing to do but to sit there until the storm was past.
>
> The rain and the wind came steadily now. He sat back in the big chair. He wondered about his mother. Was she safe at the Fieldses'? He wondered if the water had flowed into the henhouse and under the chicken coops, where the little chickens were. If it had, some of the little chickens might get drowned. The storm lasted so long that it began to seem to him that it had always been there.

In this story the author has chosen to use the **limited third-person point of view**. You know only what Bennie sees and feels. You are not told what the other characters are thinking and feeling. Why do you think the author chose to tell the story in this way? Would the story have been as effective if it had been told from the point of view of an adult? Explain.

Writing About Literature

Tracing a Character's Thoughts and Feelings

Bennie does not describe himself. However, we know more about him than we do about any other character in the story. Because the story is told from Bennie's point of view, we know his thoughts and feelings about things that happen, sometimes through his actions rather than through his words. Write a paper in which you trace Bennie's reactions to his grandmother's impending death. Use details from the story, and be sure to use quotation marks for any direct quotations from the story.

About the Author

Grant Moss, Jr. (1910–   )

Grant Moss, Jr., grew up in Winchester, Tennessee. He attended Knoxville College, and he served in the army during World War II. After the war he earned a Master of Arts degree at Columbia University. He has had stories published in *Opportunity*, *The New Yorker*, and *Essence* magazines. After teaching English for twenty-two years at Grambling College in Louisiana, he retired and moved back to his boyhood home town in Tennessee.

The Pacing Goose

JESSAMYN WEST

*The characters in this story are Quakers living in Indiana around the time of
the Civil War. In their dialogue, the author reproduces characteristics of
Quaker and regional speech.*

Jess sat in the kitchen at the long table by the
west window where in winter he kept his grafting tools: the thin-bladed knife, the paper
sweet with the smell of beeswax and the resin,
the boxes of roots and scions.[1] Jess was a nurs-
eryman and spring meant for him not only
spirits' flowering—but the earth's. A week
more of moderating weather and he'd be out,
still in gum boots, but touching an earth that
had thawed, whose riches were once again
fluid enough to be sucked upward, toward
those burgeonings which by summer would
have swelled into Early Harvests, Permains,
and Sweet Bows.[2]

Spring's a various season, Jess thought, no
two years the same: comes in with rains, mud
deep enough to swallow horse and rider;
comes in cold, snow falling so fast it weaves a
web; comes in with a warm wind blowing about
thy ears and bringing a smell of something
flowering, not here, but southaways, across the
Ohio, maybe, in Kentucky. Nothing here now
but a smell of melting snow—which is no smell
at all, but a kind of prickle in the nose, like a
bygone sneeze. Comes in so various, winter put
by and always so welcome.

"And us each spring so much the same."

"Thee speaking to me, Jess?"

"Nothing thee'd understand, Eliza."

Spring made Jess discontented with the
human race—and with women, if anything,
more than men. It looked as if spring put them
all in the shade: the season so resourceful and
they each year meeting it with nothing
changed from last year, digging up roots from
the same sassafras thicket, licking sulfur and
molasses[3] from the big-bowled spoon.

Behind him the table was set for supper,
plates neatly turned to cover the bone-handled
knives and forks, spoon vase aglitter with steel
well burnished by brick dust, dishes of jam
with more light to them than the sun, which
was dwindling away, peaked and overcast, outside his window.

"Spring opening up," he said, "and nobody
in this house so much as putting down a line of
poetry."

Eliza, who was lifting dried-peach pies from
a hot oven, said nothing. She set the four of
them in a neat row on the edge of her kitchen
cabinet to cool, and slid her pans of cornbread
into the oven. Then she turned to Jess, her

---

1. **scions** (sī′ənz): plant shoots prepared for grafting.
2. **Early . . . Bows:** varieties of apples.

3. **sulfur and molasses:** an old-time "spring tonic."

Detail from *Quaker Meeting* (variant of a painting entitled *Gracechurch Street Meeting, Society of Friends, London*), British, last quarter of 18th century or first quarter of 19th century. Oil on canvas, 25¼ x 30 in. (64 x 76.2 cm.)

cheeks red with heat, and her black eyes warm with what she had to say. "Thee'd maybe relish a nice little rhyme for thy supper, Jess Birdwell."

Jess sighed, then sniffed the pies, so rich with ripe peach flavor that the kitchen smelled like a summer orchard, nothing lacking but the sound of bees. "Now, Eliza," he said, "thee knows I wouldn't have thee anyways altered. Thee . . ."

"Thee," Eliza interrupted him, "is like all men. Thee wants to have thy poetry and eat it too."

Jess wondered how what he'd felt about spring, a season with the Lord's thumbprint fresh on it, could've led to anything so unspringlike as an argument about a batch of dried-peach pies.

"Eliza," he said firmly, "I didn't mean thee. Though it's crossed my mind sometimes as strange that none of the boys have ever turned, this time of year, to rhyming."

"Josh writes poems," Eliza said.

"Thee ever read what Josh writes, Eliza?" Eliza nodded.

Ah, well, Jess thought, no use at this late date to tell her what's the difference.

Eliza looked her husband over carefully. "Jess Birdwell," she said, "thee's full of humors. Thy blood needs thinning. I'll boil thee up a good cup of sassafras tea."

Jess turned away from the green and gold sunset and the patches of snow it was gilding and fairly faced the dried-peach pies and Eliza, who was dropping dumplings into a pot of beans.

"That's just it, Eliza," he said. "That's just the rub."

Eliza gave him no encouragement, but he went on anyway. "Earth alters, season to season, spring comes in never two times the same, only us pounding on steady as pump bolts and not freshened by so much as a grass blade."

"Jess, thee's got spring fever."

"I could reckon time and temperature, each spring, by the way thee starts honing[4] for geese. 'Jess, don't thee think we might have a

4. **honing:** yearning.

few geese?' It's a tardy spring," Jess said. "Snow still on the ground and not a word yet from thee about geese."

Eliza pulled a chair out from the table and sat. "Jess, why's thee always been so set against geese?"

"I'm not set against geese. It's geese that's set against farming. They can mow down a half-acre of sprouting corn while thee's trying to head them off—and in two minutes they'll level a row of pie plant it's taken two years to get started. No, Eliza, it's the geese that's against me."

"If thee had tight fences . . ." Eliza said.

"Eliza, I got tight fences, but the goose's never been hatched that'll admit fences exist. And an old gander'd just as soon go through a fence as hiss—and if he can't find a hole or crack in a fence he'll lift the latch."

"Jess," said Eliza flatly, "thee don't like geese."

"Well," said Jess, "I wouldn't go so far's to say I didn't like them, but I will say that if there's any meaner, dirtier animal, or one that glories in it more, I don't know it. And a thing I've never been able to understand about thee, Eliza, is what thee sees in the shifty-eyed birds."

"Geese," said Eliza, with a dreaminess unusual to her, "march along so lordly like . . . they're pretty as swans floating down a branch . . . in fall they stretch out their necks and honk to geese passing overhead as if they's wild. My father never had any trouble raising geese and I've heard him say many a time that there's no better food for a brisk morning than a fried goose egg."

Jess knew, with spring his topic, he'd ought to pass over Eliza's father and his fried goose egg but he couldn't help saying, "A fried goose egg always had a kind of bloated look to me, Eliza"—but then he went on fast. "The season's shaping up," he said. "I can see thee's all primed to say, 'Jess, let's get a setting of goose eggs.'"

Eliza went over to the bean kettle and began to lift out dumplings. "It's a forwarder season than thee thinks, Jess," she said. "I got a setting under a hen now."

Jess looked at his wife. He didn't know what had made him want spring's variety in a human being—nor Eliza's substituting doing for asking. And speaking of it just now, as he had, made opposition kind of ticklish.

"When'd thee set them?" he asked finally.

"Yesterday," said Eliza.

"Where'd thee get the eggs?"

"Overbys'," said Eliza. The Overbys were their neighbors to the south.

"Well, they got enough for a surety," Jess said, "to give a few away."

"The Overbys don't give anything away, as thee knows. I paid for them. With my own money," Eliza added.

"How many?" Jess asked.

"Eight," Eliza said.

Jess turned back to his window. The sun had set, leaving a sad green sky and desolate black and white earth. "Five acres of corn gone," he calculated.

"Thee said," Eliza reminded him, "that what thee wanted was a little variety in me. 'Steady as a pump bolt,' were thy words."

"I know I did," Jess admitted glumly. "I talk too much."

"Draw up thy chair," Eliza said placidly, not contradicting him; "here's Enoch and the boys."

Next morning after breakfast Jess and Enoch left the kitchen together. The sun was the warmest the year had yet produced and the farm roofs were steaming; south branch, swollen by melting snow, was running so full the soft lap of its eddies could be heard in the barnyard; a rooster tossed his voice into the bright air, loud and clear as if aiming to be heard by every fowl in Jennings County.

"Enoch," said Jess to his hired man, "what's thy feeling about geese?"

Enoch was instantly equipped, for the most part, with feelings on every subject. Geese was a homelier topic than he'd choose himself to enlarge upon, not one that could be much embellished nor one on which Mr. Emerson,[5] so far's he could recall, had ever expressed an opinion. "In the fall of the year," he said, "long about November or December, there's nothing tastier on the table than roast goose."

"Goose on the table's not what I mean," Jess said. "I was speaking of goose on the hoof. Goose nipping off a stand of corn, Enoch, goose roistering round, honking and hissing so's thee can't hear thyself think, goose eyeing thee like a snake on stilts."

Enoch gazed at his employer for a few seconds. "Mr. Birdwell," he said, "I think that if they's an ornery bird, it's a goose. Ornery and undependable."

"I'm glad we's so like-minded about them," Jess said. "Otherwise, I'd not like to ask thee to do this little job." He pulled a long darning needle from beneath the lapel of his coat.

Enoch eyed it with some mistrust. "I can't say's I've been handy with a needle, Mr. Birdwell."

"Thee'll be handy enough for this," Jess said with hearty conviction. "To come to it, Enoch, Eliza's set eight goose eggs. Next year with any luck she'd have two dozen. And so on. More and more. Feeling the way thee does, Enoch, about geese, it's no more'n fair to give thee a chance to put a stop to this before it goes too far. One little puncture in each egg with this and the goose project's nipped in the bud and Eliza none the wiser."

"I'm mighty awkward with my hands," said Enoch, "doing fine work. Ticklish job like this I might drop an egg and break it."

"Enoch," said Jess, "thee's not developing a weakness for geese, is thee?"

"It ain't the geese," said Enoch frankly, "it's your wife. She's been mighty clever[6] to me and if she's got her heart set on geese, it'd go against the grain to disappoint her. Whyn't you do it, Mr. Birdwell?"

"Same reason," said Jess, "only more of them—and if Eliza ever asks if I tampered with that setting of eggs I figure on being able to say no." Jess held the needle nearer Enoch, who looked at it but still made no motion to take it.

"Likely no need to do a thing," Enoch said. "Two to one those eggs'll never hatch anyways. Overbys're such a fox-eared tribe they more'n likely sold her bad eggs to begin with."

"Thee's knowed about this," Jess asked, "all along?"

"Yes," Enoch said.

"Here's the needle," Jess said.

"You look at this," Enoch inquired, "not so much as a favor asked as a part of the day's work with orders from you?"

"Yes," Jess said, "that's about the way I look at it."

Enoch took the needle, held it somewhat gingerly, and with the sun glinting across its length walked slowly toward the chicken house.

It takes thirty days for a goose egg to hatch, and the time, with spring work to be done, went fast. The hen Eliza had picked was a good one and kept her mind strictly on her setting. Eliza kept her mind on the hen, and Jess and Enoch found their minds oftener than they liked on Eliza and her hoped-for geese.

At breakfast on the day the geese were due to break their shells Jess said, "If I's thee, Eliza,

---

5. **Mr. Emerson:** Ralph Waldo Emerson, American essayist and poet (1803–1882).

6. **clever:** kind (a local use of the word).

I wouldn't bank too much on them geese. I heard Enoch say a while back he wouldn't be surprised if not an egg hatched. Thought the eggs were likely no good."

Enoch was busy pouring coffee into a saucer, then busy cooling it, but Eliza waited until he was through. "Did thee say that, Enoch?"

Enoch looked at Jess. "Yes," he said, "I kind of recollect something of the sort."

"What made thee think so, Enoch?"

"Why," said Jess, for Enoch was busy with his coffee again, "it was the Overbys. Enoch's got a feeling they's kind of unreliable. Fox-eared, I think thee said, Enoch, didn't thee?"

Enoch's work took him outside almost at once and Jess himself said, "If thee'll just give me a little packet of food, Eliza, I won't trouble thee for anything at noon. I'm going to be over'n the south forty and it'll save time coming and going."

Eliza was surprised, for Jess'd usually come twice as far for a hot dinner at midday, but she made him fried-ham sandwiches and put them and some cold apple turnovers in a bag.

"It's a pity thee has to miss thy dinner," she told him, but Jess only said, "Press of work, press of work," and hurriedly departed.

Jess came home that evening through the spring twilight, somewhat late, and found a number of things to do at the barn before he went up to the house. When he entered the kitchen nothing seemed amiss—lamps ruddy, table set, stove humming, and beside the stove a small box over which Eliza was bending. Jess stopped to look—and listen; from inside the box was coming a kind of birdlike peeping, soft and not unpleasant. Reluctantly he walked to Eliza's side. There, eating minced boiled egg, and between bites lifting its beak to Eliza, it seemed, and making those chirping sounds he'd heard, was a gray-gold gosling.

Eliza looked up pleasantly. "Enoch was right," she said. "The eggs were bad. Only one hatched. I plan to call it Samantha," she told Jess. "It's a name I've always been partial to."

"Samantha," said Jess without any enthusiasm whatever for either name or gosling. "How's thee know it's a she?"

"I don't," said Eliza, "but if it's a gander it's a name easily changed to Sam."

Enoch came in just then with a load of wood for the kitchen woodbox. "Enoch," asked Jess, "has thee seen Samantha—or Sam?"

Enoch mumbled but Jess understood him to say he had.

"It was my understanding, Enoch, that thy opinion was that all those eggs were bad."

"Well, Mr. Birdwell," said Enoch, "a man could make a mistake. He could count wrong."

"A man ought to be able to count to eight without going astray," said Jess.

Eliza was paying no attention to either of them; she was making little tweeting sounds herself, bending over the chirping gosling. "Does thee know," she asked Jess, "that this is the first pet I ever had in my life?"

"Thee's got Ebony," Jess said.

"I don't mean a caged pet," Eliza said, "but one to walk beside thee. I'm reconciled the others didn't hatch. With eight I'd've had to raise geese for the table. With one only I can make Samantha a pure pet."

A pure pet was what she made of her: Samantha ate what the family ate, with the exception of articles which Eliza thought might be indigestible and would risk on humans but not on her goose. Cake, pie, corn on the cob, there was nothing too good for Samantha. From a big-footed, gold-downed gosling she swelled, almost at once, like a slack sail which gets a sudden breeze, into a full-rounded convexity.

"Emphasis on the vexity," Jess said when he

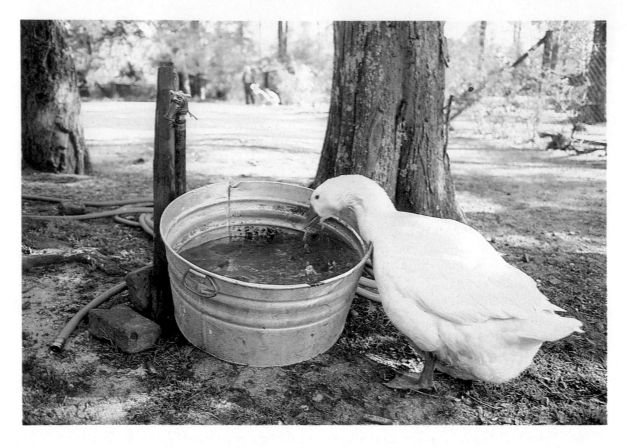

thought of this. Samantha was everything he'd disliked in the general run of geese, with added traits peculiar to herself, which vexed him. Because she was fed at the doorstep, she was always underfoot. No shout, however loud, would move her before she's ready to move. If she's talked to too strong she'd flail you with her wings and pinch the calf of your leg until for some days it would look to be mortifying. She'd take food out of children's hands, and the pansies Jess had planted in a circle at the base of the Juneberry tree she sheared so close that there was not a naked stem left to show for all his work. And when not being crossed in any way, Jess simply looking at her and meditating, trying to fathom Samantha's fascination for Eliza, the goose would suddenly extend her snakelike neck, and almost touching Jess, hiss with such a hint of icy disapprobation that Jess would involuntarily recoil.

But she was Eliza's pure pet, no two ways about that, and would lift her head for Eliza to scratch, and walk beside her with the lordly roll of the known elect.[7]

"There was some goddess," Enoch remembered, "who always had a big bird with her." Jess supposed Enoch was thinking of Juno and her peacock, but the reference didn't convince him that a goose was a suitable companion for any goddess—let alone Eliza, and he couldn't honestly feel much regret when one evening toward the end of November Eliza told him

---

7. **elect:** according to Calvinist doctrine, those who have been selected by God for salvation.

Samantha was missing. "She'll turn up," Jess said. "That bird's too ornery to die young."

Eliza said nothing, but next evening she proved Jess was right. "Samantha's over at Overbys'," she said.

"Well, did thee fetch her home?" Jess asked.

"No," said Eliza with righteous indignation, "they wouldn't let me. They said they had forty geese—and forty's what they got now, and they don't think Samantha's there. They provoked me so, Jess, I told them they'd sold me seven bad eggs and now they try to take the eighth away from me."

Jess felt a little abashed at this, but he asked, "How can thee be so sure Samantha's there? She might've been carried off by a varmint."

Eliza was scornful. "Thee forgets I hand-raised Samantha from a gosling. I'd know her among four hundred—let alone forty."

"Whyn't thee buy her back then," Jess asked, "if that's the only way?"

"After what I said about their eggs," Eliza answered sadly, "the Overbys say they don't want any more dealings with me."

Eliza mourned so for the lost Samantha that first Enoch and then Jess went over to the Overbys' but no one there would admit the presence of a visiting goose—forty they had, and forty you could see by counting was what they had now. Short of force there didn't seem any way of getting Samantha home again.

When Eliza heard the Overbys were going to sell geese for Christmas eating she was frantic. "Jess," she said, "I just can't bear to think of Samantha, plucked naked and resting on a table waiting to be carved. She used to sing as sweet as any bird when she was little, and she'd walk by my side taking the air. She's the only goose I ever heard of," Eliza remembered mournfully, "who'd drink tea."

In Jess's opinion a goose'd eat anything at either end of the scale, but he didn't suppose this was a suitable time to mention it to Eliza. "Eliza," he said, "short of me and Enoch's going over there and using force on old man Overby—or sneaking over at night and breaking into their chicken pen, I don't know how in the world we're going to get Samantha back for thee."

"We could sue," said Eliza.

"Thee mean go to law?" Jess asked, astounded. Quakers stayed out of courts, believing in amicable settlements without recourse to law.

"Yes," said Eliza. "I'd do it for Samantha. I'd think it my duty. Going to law'd be a misery for us . . . but not so lasting a misery as being roasted would be for Samantha."

Jess couldn't deny this, but he said, "I'd have to think it over. I've never been to law yet in my life and suing for a gone goose don't seem to me a very likely place to start."

Next morning Eliza served a good but silent breakfast, not sitting herself to eat with the rest of her family.

"Thee feeling dauncy,[8] Eliza?" Jess asked.

"I just can't eat," she said, "for thinking of Samantha."

Labe and Mattie had tears in their eyes. Little Jess was mournfully bellowing. Enoch looked mighty glum. Jess felt ashamed to be swallowing victuals in the midst of so much sorrow. Eliza stood at the end of the stove where the gosling's box had rested for the first few weeks of its life, looking down, as if remembering how it had sung and lifted its beak to her.

Jess couldn't stand it. "Eliza," he said, "if thee wants to go through with it I'll go to Vernon and fee a lawyer for thee. Thee'll have to go to court, be on the witness stand—and even then I misdoubt thee'll ever get thy goose back. Does thee still want me to do it?"

8. **dauncy:** ill.

Eliza came to the table and stood with her hand on Jess's shoulder. "Yes, Jess," she said, "I want thee to do it."

Jess went to Vernon, fee'd a lawyer, had a restraining order put on the Overbys so they couldn't sell or kill the goose Eliza said was Samantha, and awaited with misgivings the day of the trial. It came in mid-December.

Eliza, Jess and Enoch rode to the trial through a fall of light, fresh snow. Brilliant sunlight, crisp air, glittering snow, and Rome's[9] spirited stepping made the occasion, in spite of its purpose, seem festive. Eliza made it seem festive. Jess, who did not forget its purpose, regarded her with some wonder. He couldn't say what it was about her—dress and bonnet appeared to be simply her First Day[10] best—but she had a holiday air.

He considered it his duty to warn her. "Eliza," he said, "thee understands thee's not going to Meeting?[11] They're not going to sit silent while thee tells them how much thee loves Samantha and how she sang when young and drank tea. Old man Overby'll have his say and he's got a lawyer hired for no other purpose than to trip thee up."

Eliza was unimpressed. "What's our lawyer fee'd for, Jess?" she asked.

Jess took another tack. "Eliza," he told her, "I don't figger thee's got a chance in a thousand to get Samantha back."

"This is a court of justice, isn't it?" Eliza asked.

"Yes," Jess said.

"Then there's no need for thee to fash[12] thyself, Jess Birdwell. I'll get Samantha back."

Not getting Samantha back wasn't what fashed Jess—he reckoned he could bear up under that mighty well. What fashed him was the whole shooting match. . . . In some few cases, matters of life and death, going to court might be necessary, and he could imagine such. But a suit over a goose named Samantha wasn't one of them. And poor Eliza. Law to her was all Greek and turkey tracks . . . and here she was bound for court as chipper as if she was Chief Justice Taney[13] himself. Jess sighed and shook his head. Getting shut of Samantha would be no hardship for him, but he was downcast for Eliza's sake and the way she'd have to turn homeward empty-handed.

In the courtroom hard, clear light reflected upward from the snow fell onto what Jess thought were hard faces: courthouse hangers-on; farmers whose slackening work made the diversion of a trial an inviting possibility; lovers of oddity who figured a tilt between a Quaker female, preacher to boot, and an old sinner like Milt Overby over the ownership of a goose ought to produce some enlivening quirks. They stared at Eliza, exchanged salutes with Milt Overby and inspected Samantha, who in her crate awaited the court's decision.

The two lawyers Jess considered to be on a par. Nothing fancy, either one . . . old roadsters both, gone gray in service and with a knowledge of their business. The circuit judge was something else, unaccountably young, jug-eared and dressed more sprightly than a groom for his own wedding. A city whippersnapper, born and trained north of the Mississinewa,[14] and now, in Jess's opinion, setting a squeamish foot in backwoods provinces, and irked to find himself trying so trifling a case. Didn't know a goose from a guinea hen, like as not, and would consider tossing a coin a more suitable manner of settling such a

---

9. **Rome:** Rome Beauty, the Birdwells' carriage horse.
10. **First Day:** Quaker name for Sunday.
11. **Meeting:** Quaker church meeting.
12. **fash:** worry.

13. **Taney** (tā′nē): Roger B. Taney, a Chief Justice of the Supreme Court (1836–1864).
14. **Mississinewa** (mĭs-ĭs-sĭn′ĭ-wä): a small river flowing into the Wabash River in Indiana.

matter—just as near right in the end—and his valuable time saved.

Eliza, Jess saw, was of no such opinion. She, too, was scanning the young judge, and Jess, who knew her, saw from the look on her face that she was taken by him. A neat, thin, pious boy—far from home—he looked, no doubt, to her; a young man who could do with better cooking and more regular eating.

The young man rapped the court to order. Spitting and shuffling slackened and in a high, precise voice he read, "Birdwell versus Overby. Charge, petty larceny. Appropriation and willful withholding of goose named Samantha." The name Samantha seemed to somewhat choke him, but he got it out.

"Ready for Birdwell," said Mr. Abel Samp, Eliza's lawyer.

"Ready for Overby," said the defendant's lawyer.

Eliza was the first witness on the stand. Jess sometimes forgot what a good-looking woman Eliza was, but the interest shown on lifted faces all about him refreshed his memory.

"Swear the plaintiff in," the judge said.

Eliza, in her sweet voice, spoke directly to the judge. "I don't swear," she said.

The judge explained that profanity was not asked for. "I understood," said Eliza, "that thee wasn't asking for profanity. No one would think that of thee. But we Quakers do not take oaths in court. We affirm."

"Permit Mrs. Birdwell to affirm," said the judge. Eliza affirmed.

Mr. Samp then proceeded to question Eliza as to Samantha's birth and habits.

"Judge," Eliza began.

"Address the judge," Mr. Samp said, "as Your Honor."

"We Quakers," Eliza told the judge, gently, "do not make use of such titles. What is thy name? I think thee'll go far in our state and thy name's one I'd like to know."

The judge appeared somewhat distraught, undecided as to whether to make the tone of the court brisk and legal (if possible) or to follow Eliza's lead of urbane sociability.

"Pomeroy," he said and made a slight bow in Eliza's direction.

Eliza returned the bow, deeper and with more grace. "Friend Pomeroy," she said, "it is indeed a pleasure to know thee."

Samantha's story as Eliza told it to Friend Pomeroy was surprisingly terse. Affecting, and losing nothing by Eliza's telling, but to the point.

"Mrs. Birdwell," said Samp, "how long have you had an acquaintanceship with geese and their habits?"

"Since I was a child," Eliza said. "My father was a great fancier of geese."

"And you think you could identify this goose Samantha, which you admit in looks was similar to the defendant's?"

"I could," Eliza said with much authority.

Mr. Samp, to Jess's surprise, left the matter there. "Take the witness," he said to Overby's lawyer—but the counsel for the defendant was in no hurry to cross-examine Eliza. Instead he put his client on the stand.

"Farewell, Samantha," Jess said to Enoch.

"You relieved?" Enoch asked.

"Putting Eliza first," Jess said, "as I do, no."

Milt Overby, whose natural truculence was somewhat stimulated by a nip he'd had to offset snappy weather, bellowed his way through his testimony. At one juncture he set the judge aright when he asked some elementary questions concerning the habits and configurations of geese. "Where in tarnation you from?" he snorted. "What they mean sending us judges down here who don't know Toulouse from Wyandotte,[15] or goose from gander?"

The young judge used voice and gavel to

15. **Toulouse** (tōō-lōōz´) . . . **Wyandotte** (wī´ən-dŏt): breeds of fowl.

Detail from *Quaker Meeting* (variant of a painting entitled *Gracechurch Street Meeting, Society of Friends, London*), British, last quarter of 18th century or first quarter of 19th century. Oil on canvas, 25¼ x 30 in. (64 x 76.2 cm.)

quiet the guffawing which filled the courtroom and the trial proceeded. A number of witnesses for both sides were brought to the stand and while it was shown that Overbys had maybe eaten a goose or two and neglected out of pure fondness for the creatures to count them as among the departed, still nobody had been able to positively identify Samantha.

Mr. Overby's lawyer seemed somewhat loath to cross-examine Eliza, but he put her on the stand. She'd said she knew geese and her testimony had been direct and positive. "Mrs. Birdwell," he said, "how can you be so sure your goose was with my client's geese?"

Eliza's black eyes rested confidingly upon the judge. "Friend Pomeroy," she said, "I raised Samantha from a gosling."

Jess sighed. "Here it comes," he said, "how

that goose could sing and drink tea."

Eliza continued, "And there's one thing about her that always set her apart from every other goose."

"Yes, Mrs. Birdwell," said Judge Pomeroy, who was inclined to forget, with Eliza on the stand, that he was in a courtroom.

"Samantha," said Eliza, with much earnestness, "from the day she was born had a gait unlike any other goose I ever saw and one that set her apart from all her Overby connections. I picked her out at once when I went over there, because of it. Thee couldn't've missed it, Friend Pomeroy."

"Yes, Mrs. Birdwell," said the judge with interest in his voice.

"Samantha," said Eliza, "was a born pacer. Thee knows what a pacer is?"

"Certainly," said Judge Pomeroy. "A pacer," he repeated with no surprise—and with obvious pleasure that Eliza'd hit upon so clear and differentiating an aspect of her goose and one that made identification possible.

A titter was mounting through the courtroom—Judge Pomeroy lifted his head. He had no desire to be further instructed as to the history, habits, and breeds of geese, and he liked to see a trial settled by some such little and too often overlooked subtlety. Judge Pomeroy brought down his gavel. "The court awards decision in favor of the plaintiff. Case dismissed." While the silence that followed on his words still prevailed Judge Pomeroy stepped briskly and with obvious pleasure out through the rear door.

Jess was also brisk about departure. No use lingering until Friend Pomeroy had been more thoroughly informed as to gaits in general and geese in particular. Midafternoon's a quiet time in any season. In winter with snow on the ground, no leaves to rustle and bare limbs rigid as rock against a cloudless sky, the hush is deepest of all. Nothing broke that hush in the surrey,[16] except the squeak of leather and snow, the muffled footfalls of Rome Beauty. Jess and Eliza, on the front seat, rode without speaking. Enoch, in the back, seemed to meditate. Even Samantha in her crate at Enoch's feet was silent.

Maple Grove Nursery was in sight before Jess spoke. "Eliza," he said, "would thee mind telling me—did thee ever see a trotting goose?"

Enoch ceased to meditate and listened. He had been wondering about this himself.

"Certainly not," said Eliza. "Thee knows as well as I, Jess Birdwell, an animal can't trot without hind feet and forefeet."

"So far, Eliza," Jess said, "we see eye to eye. Now maybe thee'd tell me—did thee ever see a goose that didn't pace?"

Eliza was truly amazed, it seemed. "Why, Jess," she said, "an ordinary goose just walks—but Samantha paces."

Jess was silent for a spell. "What'd thee say the difference is?"

"It's the swing, Jess Birdwell," said Eliza, "same as in a horse that nature's formed for a pacer . . . it's the natural bent, the way the spirit leads the beast to set his feet down. Samantha's a natural pacer."

That seemed as far as they'd likely get on the subject and Jess joined Enoch in meditation. In the barnyard, before she went up to the house, Eliza said, like an old hand at the business, "Attending court whettens the appetite. It's a little early but I thought if thee'd relish it"—and she looked at Jess and Enoch, never sparing a glance for Samantha, as if her menfolk's welfare was her sole concern—"I'd stir us up a bite to eat. Hot tea and fresh sweetcakes, say. Might fry a little sausage and open some cherry preserves. If thee'd relish it," she repeated.

Jess wasn't taken in, but he'd relish it, and so would Enoch, and they both said so. They hustled with the unhitching so they could uncrate Samantha and note her progress with eyes newly instructed as to what made a pacer. Jess dumped her in the snow, and Enoch tapped her with his hat. Samantha made for the back door.

"By sugar," said Jess, "Eliza's right. She paces." Samantha had the smooth roll of a racker[17]—there were no two ways about it. At heart she was a pacer, and what two legs could do in that line, Samantha accomplished.

"With four legs," Enoch said, "you could enter her in any county fair—rack on," he

16. **surrey:** a light carriage.

17. **racker:** a horse that paces.

cried with enthusiasm. As they followed Samantha to the house, Enoch, for whom any event existed chiefly in its after aspects as a cud for rumination, asked, "How you feel in respect of court trials, now, Mr. Birdwell?"

"I'm still against them," Jess said, "though they's three things this trial's taught me I might never otherwise have learned. Two's about women."

Enoch revered all knowledge and he had a notion that information on this subject might have a more than transcendental[18] value. "What's the two things you learned about women, Mr. Birdwell?"

"Well, Enoch, I learned first, dependability's woman's greatest virtue. Steady as a pump bolt, day in, day out. When thee finds a woman like that, Enoch, don't try to change her. Not even in spring."

"No, sir," said Enoch, "I won't."

"Second, when it's a case of woman and the law—thee don't need to waste any worry on the woman."

"No, sir," said Enoch again.

When they reached the back steps, Enoch asked, "I understood you to say you'd learned three things, Mr. Birdwell. What's the third about?"

"Hired men," said Jess.

Enoch was taken aback, but he'd asked for it. "Yes, Mr. Birdwell," he said.

"Never hire one," Jess told him, "till thee finds out first if he can count to eight. Save thyself a lot of trouble that way, Enoch."

"How's I to know the eighth'd turn out to be Samantha?" Enoch asked.

Samantha herself, who was waiting at the doorstep for an expected tidbit, reached out and, unhampered by either boots or work pants, nipped Enoch firmly through his thin Sunday best.

18. **transcendental:** here, abstract.

SHORT STORIES

"Thee say something, Enoch?" Jess asked.

Enoch had but he didn't repeat it. Instead he said, "Pacer or no pacer, that's Samantha," and the two of them stepped out of the snow into the warm kitchen, scented with baking sweetcakes and frying sausage.

Reading Check

1. Why does only one of the goose eggs hatch?
2. Why do the Overbys refuse to sell Samantha back to Eliza?
3. Why does Eliza decide to bring suit against the Overbys?
4. What does Jess think will be the result of the trial?
5. How does Eliza claim she can identify Samantha?

For Study and Discussion

Analyzing and Interpreting the Story

1. When the story opens, Jess is feeling discontented. **a.** How is his discontent linked to the season of the year? **b.** Why does Eliza's announcement about the goose eggs come as a surprise?

2a. Explain how the conflict between Jess and Eliza over Samantha is a result of their different personalities. **b.** Despite the conflict Jess and Eliza continue to live in harmony. What evidence is there, in their speech and action, of mutual love and esteem?

3. "The Pacing Goose" appears in a collection of stories about the Birdwells called *The Friendly Persuasion*. The title refers to Jess and Eliza being Quakers, since Quakers prefer to be known as the Society of Friends. Quakers believe in the importance of acting in accord-

136 SHORT STORIES

ance with the dictates of individual conscience. Why is Eliza's going to court a particularly significant act?

4. Jess is clearly surprised by the events in the courtroom. **a.** What does he think will happen? **b.** How does he underestimate Eliza's character?

5a. Jess claims to have learned three things from the trial. What are they? **b.** In what way has his admiration for his wife deepened?

Literary Elements

The Omniscient Point of View

A story is sometimes told from the point of view of an outside observer who has complete knowledge of all the characters and who can therefore reveal not only their actions, their words, and their physical characteristics, but also their unspoken thoughts and feelings. Such an observer is *omniscient,* or "all-knowing," and the story is said to be told from the **omniscient point of view.**

This point of view allows readers to explore the internal as well as the external lives of characters. In "The Pacing Goose," for example, the conflict between Jess and Eliza is often expressed through thoughts:

Spring made Jess discontented with the human race—and with women, if anything, more than men. It looked as if spring put them all in the shade: the season so resourceful and they each year meeting it with nothing changed from last year . . . (page 125).

Ah, well, Jess thought, no use at this late date to tell her what's the difference (page 126).

Eliza kept her mind on the hen, and Jess and Enoch found their minds oftener than they liked on Eliza and her hoped-for geese (page 128).

Samantha was everything he'd disliked in the general run of geese, with added traits peculiar to herself, which vexed him (page 130).

Find passages where the author makes known the thoughts and feelings of Enoch, Overby, and Judge Pomeroy.

This technique gives Jessamyn West considerable freedom. It allows her to tell more than any individual character in the story could tell about the action.

Language and Vocabulary

Understanding Dialect

Dialects within a single language vary greatly in matters of pronunciation, sentence structure, and vocabulary, and writers make use of these differences in the realistic portrayal of character. Mark Twain, for example, uses the dialect of the Mississippi Valley.

"The Pacing Goose" is set on a farm in Indiana during the Civil War, and Jessamyn West has reproduced characteristics of Quaker and regional speech. Look up each of the italicized words in the following list and tell what it means:

Thee speaking to me, Jess?
She might've been carried off by a *varmint.*
Nothing fancy, either one . . . old *roadsters* both . . .
Where in *tarnation* you from?
Attending court *whettens* the appetite.

Writing About Literature

Discussing a Change in Attitude

At the opening of the story, Jess is discontented because he wants to see spring's variety in human beings. He complains that Eliza is "as steady as a pump bolt." At the end of the story, he tells Enoch that "dependability's woman's greatest virtue." In a paragraph tell what has happened to change his attitude.

Focus on Narrative Writing

Experimenting with Point of View

The **point of view** of a story is the vantage point from which readers or listeners see the events and characters. There are three basic points of view to choose from when you tell a story.

First-person: One of the characters in the story tells it in his or her own words. This point of view uses the first-person pronouns *I, me, my, we, our,* and so on.

Third-person limited: The writer tells the story from the point of view of one character.

Third-person omniscient: An outside observer with complete knowledge of all the characters tells the story.

Experiment with point of view by writing an opening paragraph for the same story in two different ways. For example, you might want to retell a familiar children's story, such as "Cinderella" or "Little Red Riding Hood." In your first version, use first-person point of view. In the second, use third-person point of view. Exchange papers with a peer reader and make comments on each other's writing. Which version seems more effective? Save your paragraphs.

About the Author

Jessamyn West (1907–1984)

Jessamyn West was born in Indiana but grew up in California. She studied at Whittier College, where she married a classmate. She continued her studies in England, then returned to the United States to attend the University of California. When she was confined to bed with tuberculosis, she began to write. Her first book was *The Friendly Persuasion,* a group of stories about a Quaker family (much like her mother's people), who lived on a farm in Indiana during the Civil War. The book was praised for its humor, its richness of language, and its fine sense of daily life. Some years later, she published another collection of stories about the Birdwell family, *Except for Me and Thee: a Companion to The Friendly Persuasion.* In addition, West wrote *Cress Delahanty,* a collection of stories about a teenage girl, and two other short-story collections: *Love, Death, and the Ladies' Drill Team* and *Crimson Ramblers of the World, Farewell.* She produced several novels, including *The Witch Diggers* and *The Massacre at Fall Creek;* and two autobiographical works: *Hide and Seek: A Continuing Journey* and *To See the Dream,* an account of her trip to Los Angeles to work on the script for the film version of *The Friendly Persuasion.*

The Portable Phonograph

WALTER VAN TILBURG CLARK

Many stories have been written about the collapse of civilization as we know it, but few have ever achieved the impact of this story. How does the author prepare you for the final, devastating scene?

The red sunset, with narrow, black cloud strips like threats across it, lay on the curved horizon of the prairie. The air was still and cold, and in it settled the mute darkness and greater cold of night. High in the air there was wind, for through the veil of the dusk the clouds could be seen gliding rapidly south and changing shapes. A sensation of torment, of two-sided, unpredictable nature, arose from the stillness of the earth air beneath the violence of the upper air. Out of the sunset, through the dead, matted grass and isolated weed stalks of the prairie, crept the narrow and deeply rutted remains of a road. In the road, in places, there were crusts of shallow, brittle ice. There were little islands of an old oiled pavement in the road too, but most of it was mud, now frozen rigid. The frozen mud still bore the toothed impress of great tanks, and a wanderer on the neighboring undulations might have stumbled, in this light, into large, partially filled-in and weed-grown cavities, their banks channeled and beginning to spread into badlands.[1] These pits were such as might have been made by falling meteors, but they were not. They were the scars of gigantic bombs, their rawness already made a little natural by rain, seed and time. Along the road there were rakish remnants of fence. There was also, just visible, one portion of tangled and multiple barbed wire still erect, behind which was a shelving ditch with small caves, now very quiet and empty, at

1. **badlands:** sections of barren land where erosion has cut the soil into ridges and peaks.

intervals in its back wall. Otherwise there was no structure or remnant of a structure visible over the dome of the darkling[2] earth, but only, in sheltered hollows, the darker shadows of young trees trying again.

Under the wuthering[3] arch of the high wind a V of wild geese fled south. The rush of their pinions sounded briefly, and the faint, plaintive notes of their expeditionary talk. Then they left a still greater vacancy. There was the smell and expectation of snow, as there is likely to be when the wild geese fly south. From the remote distance, toward the red sky, came faintly the protracted howl and quick yap-yap of a prairie wolf.

North of the road, perhaps a hundred yards, lay the parallel and deeply intrenched course of a small creek, lined with leafless alders and willows. The creek was already silent under ice. Into the bank above it was dug a sort of cell, with a single opening, like the mouth of a mine tunnel. Within the cell there was a little red of fire, which showed dully through the opening, like a reflection or a deception of the imagination. The light came from the chary burning of four blocks of poorly aged peat, which gave off a petty warmth and much acrid smoke. But the precious remnants of wood, old fence posts and timbers from the long-deserted dugouts, had to be saved for the real cold, for the time when a man's breath blew white, the moisture in his nostrils stiffened at once when he stepped out, and the expansive blizzards paraded for days over the vast open, swirling and settling and thickening, till the dawn of the cleared day when the sky was a thin blue-green and the terrible cold, in which a man could not live for three hours unwarmed, lay over the uniformly drifted swell of the plain.

Around the smoldering peat four men were

The Granger Collection, New York

seated cross-legged. Behind them, traversed by their shadows, was the earth bench, with two old and dirty army blankets, where the owner of the cell slept. In a niche in the opposite wall were a few tin utensils which caught the glint of the coals. The host was rewrapping in a piece of daubed burlap, four fine, leather-bound books. He worked slowly and very carefully, and at last tied the bundle securely with a piece of grass-woven cord. The other three looked intently upon the process, as if a great

2. **darkling:** dark; dim.
3. **wuthering:** rushing, blustering.

significance lay in it. As the host tied the cord, he spoke. He was an old man, his long, matted beard and hair gray to nearly white. The shadows made his brows and cheekbones appear gnarled, his eyes and cheeks deeply sunken. His big hands, rough with frost and swollen by rheumatism, were awkward but gentle at their task. He was like a prehistoric priest performing a fateful ceremonial rite. Also his voice had in it a suitable quality of deep, reverent despair, yet perhaps, at the moment, a sharpness of selfish satisfaction.

"When I perceived what was happening," he said, "I told myself, 'It is the end. I cannot take much; I will take these.'

"Perhaps I was impractical," he continued. "But for myself, I do not regret, and what do we know of those who will come after us? We are the doddering remnant of a race of mechanical fools. I have saved what I love; the soul of what was good in us here; perhaps the new ones will make a strong enough beginning not to fall behind when they become clever."

He rose with slow pain and placed the wrapped volumes in the niche with his utensils. The others watched him with the same ritualistic gaze.

"Shakespeare, the Bible, *Moby Dick, The Divine Comedy*,"[4] one of them said softly. "You might have done worse; much worse."

"You will have a little soul left until you die," said another harshly. "That is more than is true of us. My brain becomes thick, like my hands." He held the big, battered hands, with their black nails, in the glow to be seen.

"I want paper to write on," he said. "And there is none."

The fourth man said nothing. He sat in the shadow farthest from the fire, and sometimes his body jerked in its rags from the cold. Although he was still young, he was sick, and coughed often. Writing implied a greater future than he now felt able to consider.

The old man seated himself laboriously, and reached out, groaning at the movement, to put another block of peat on the fire. With bowed heads and averted eyes, his three guests acknowledged his magnanimity.

"We thank you, Doctor Jenkins, for the reading," said the man who had named the books.

They seemed then to be waiting for something. Doctor Jenkins understood, but was loath to comply. In an ordinary moment he would have said nothing. But the words of *The Tempest*,[5] which he had been reading, and the religious attention of the three, made this an unusual occasion.

"You wish to hear the phonograph," he said grudgingly.

The two middle-aged men stared into the fire, unable to formulate and expose the enormity of their desire.

The young man, however, said anxiously, between suppressed coughs, "Oh, please," like an excited child.

The old man rose again in his difficult way, and went to the back of the cell. He returned and placed tenderly upon the packed floor, where the firelight might fall upon it, an old, portable phonograph in a black case. He smoothed the top with his hand, and then opened it. The lovely green-felt-covered disk became visible.

"I have been using thorns as needles," he said. "But tonight, because we have a musician among us"—he bent his head to the young man, almost invisible in the shadow—"I will use a steel needle. There are only three left."

The two middle-aged men stared at him in speechless adoration. The one with the big

4. *Moby Dick:* a classic American novel by Herman Melville (1819–1891); *The Divine Comedy:* a great epic poem by Dante Alighieri (1265–1321).

5. *The Tempest:* Shakespeare's last great comedy.

hands, who wanted to write, moved his lips, but the whisper was not audible.

"Oh, don't," cried the young man, as if he were hurt. "The thorns will do beautifully."

"No," the old man said. "I have become accustomed to the thorns, but they are not really good. For you, my young friend, we will have good music tonight.

"After all," he added generously, and beginning to wind the phonograph, which creaked, "they can't last forever."

"No, nor we," the man who needed to write said harshly. "The needle, by all means."

"Oh, thanks," said the young man. "Thanks," he said again, in a low, excited voice, and then stifled his coughing with a bowed head.

"The records, though," said the old man when he had finished winding, "are a different matter. Already they are very worn. I do not play them more than once a week. One, once a week, that is what I allow myself.

"More than a week I cannot stand it; not to hear them," he apologized.

"No, how could you?" cried the young man. "And with them here like this."

"A man can stand anything," said the man who wanted to write, in his harsh, antagonistic voice.

"Please, the music," said the young man.

"Only the one," said the old man. "In the long run we will remember more that way."

He had a dozen records with luxuriant gold and red seals. Even in that light the others could see that the threads of the records were becoming worn. Slowly he read out the titles, and the tremendous, dead names of the composers and the artists and the orchestras. The three worked upon the names in their minds, carefully. It was difficult to select from such a wealth what they would at once most like to remember. Finally the man who wanted to write named Gershwin's "New York."

"Oh, no," cried the sick young man, and then could say nothing more because he had to cough. The others understood him, and the harsh man withdrew his selection and waited for the musician to choose.

The musician begged Doctor Jenkins to read the titles again, very slowly, so that he could remember the sounds. While they were read, he lay back against the wall, his eyes closed, his thin, horny hand pulling at his light beard, and listened to the voices and the orchestras and the single instruments in his mind.

When the reading was done he spoke despairingly. "I have forgotten," he complained. "I cannot hear them clearly.

"There are things missing," he explained.

"I know," said Doctor Jenkins. "I thought that I knew all of Shelley[6] by heart. I should have brought Shelley."

"That's more soul than we can use," said the harsh man. "*Moby Dick* is better.

"By God, we can understand that," he emphasized.

The doctor nodded.

"Still," said the man who had admired the books, "we need the absolute if we are to keep a grasp on anything.

"Anything but these sticks and peat clods and rabbit snares," he said bitterly.

"Shelley desired an ultimate absolute," said the harsh man. "It's too much," he said. "It's no good; no earthly good."

The musician selected a Debussy[7] nocturne. The others considered and approved. They rose to their knees to watch the doctor prepare for the playing, so that they appeared to be actually in an attitude of worship. The peat glow showed the thinness of their bearded faces,

6. **Shelley:** Percy Bysshe Shelley (1792–1822), an English poet known for his devotion to ideals and philosophical speculation.
7. **Debussy:** Claude Debussy (də-byoo͞′sē), a French composer (1862–1918).

and the deep lines in them, and revealed the condition of their garments. The other two continued to kneel as the old man carefully lowered the needle onto the spinning disk, but the musician suddenly drew back against the wall again, with his knees up, and buried his face in his hands.

At the first notes of the piano the listeners were startled. They stared at each other. Even the musician lifted his head in amazement, but then quickly bowed it again, strainingly, as if he were suffering from a pain he might not be able to endure. They were all listening deeply, without movement. The wet, blue-green notes tinkled forth from the old machine, and were individual, delectable presences in the cell. The individual, delectable presences swept into a sudden tide of unbearably beautiful dissonance, and then continued fully the swelling and ebbing of that tide, the dissonant inpourings, and the resolutions, and the diminishments, and the little, quiet wavelets of interlude lapping between. Every sound was piercing and singularly sweet. In all the men except the musician, there occurred rapid sequences of tragically heightened recollection. He heard nothing but what was there. At the final, whispering disappearance, but moving quietly, so that the others would not hear him and look at him, he let his head fall back in agony, as if it were drawn there by the hair, and clenched the fingers of one hand over his teeth. He sat that way while the others were silent, and until they began to breathe again normally. His drawn-up legs were trembling violently.

Quickly Doctor Jenkins lifted the needle off, to save it, and not to spoil the recollection with scraping. When he had stopped the whirling of the sacred disk, he courteously left the phonograph open and by the fire, in sight.

The others, however, understood. The musician rose last, but then abruptly, and went quickly out at the door without saying anything. The others stopped at the door and gave their thanks in low voices. The doctor nodded magnificently.

"Come again," he invited, "in a week. We will have the 'New York.'"

When the two had gone together, out toward the rimed[8] road, he stood in the entrance, peering and listening. At first there was only the resonant boom of the wind overhead, and then, far over the dome of the dead, dark plain, the wolf cry lamenting. In the rifts of clouds the doctor saw four stars flying. It impressed the doctor that one of them had just been obscured by the beginning of a flying cloud at the very moment he heard what he had been listening for, a sound of suppressed coughing. It was not near by, however. He believed that down against the pale alders he could see the moving shadow.

With nervous hands he lowered the piece of canvas which served as his door, and pegged it at the bottom. Then quickly and quietly, looking at the piece of canvas frequently, he slipped the records into the case, snapped the lid shut, and carried the phonograph to his couch. There, pausing often to stare at the canvas and listen, he dug earth from the wall and disclosed a piece of board. Behind this there was a deep hole in the wall, into which he put the phonograph. After a moment's consideration, he went over and reached down his bundle of books and inserted it also. Then, guardedly, he once more sealed up the hole with the board and the earth. He also changed his blankets, and the grass-stuffed sack which served as a pillow, so that he could lie facing the entrance. After carefully placing two more blocks of peat on the fire, he stood for a long time watching the stretched canvas, but it seemed to billow naturally with the first gusts

8. **rimed:** frosty.

of a lowering wind. At last he prayed, and got in under his blankets, and closed his smoke-smarting eyes. On the inside of the bed, next the wall, he could feel with his hand, the comfortable piece of lead pipe.

Reading Check

1. What do the men use for fuel?
2. What has Dr. Jenkins managed to salvage?
3. Why has Dr. Jenkins been using thorns for his phonograph?
4. How often does he play the records?
5. How does he protect his phonograph?

For Study and Discussion

Analyzing and Interpreting the Story

1. The first three paragraphs focus on the **setting** of the story. **a.** Judging from details in the description, what event has occurred? **b.** Which words and phrases contribute to an ominous, or threatening, mood? **c.** What evidence is there that the earth is beginning to heal?

2. We learn that Dr. Jenkins has managed to salvage a few great works of civilization. **a.** How is he "like a prehistoric priest performing a fateful ceremonial rite"? **b.** What are the objects that his guests revere?

3. Dr. Jenkins says, "We are the doddering remnant of a race of mechanical fools." What does this statement reveal about his values?

4. The men in the story do not seem concerned about food or shelter or other physical comforts. **a.** What do they fear losing?

b. How is the fear implied in this statement: "You will have a little soul left until you die"?

5. A **symbol** is something that has meaning in itself and that also stands for something else. **a.** How is the phonograph in this story a symbol? **b.** How does it bring out "the soul of what was good in us"?

6. Consider Dr. Jenkins' actions after the guests leave. **a.** Why does he take such precautions? **b.** Do you believe that the threat is real?

7a. What is ironic about the ending of the story? **b.** What point is Clark trying to make? **c.** Which statement in the story comes closest to expressing this point?

Literary Elements

Setting

The element of **setting** is the physical background of a story—its time and place. Sometimes an entire story is dependent upon setting. Think, for example, of "The Most Dangerous Game" (page 12), where the conflict of Rainsford and Zaroff is confined to Ship-Trap Island. In a story such as "The Musgrave Ritual" (page 46), the setting is an integral part of the plot. Setting can also lend atmosphere, as the underground crypt does in "The Cask of Amontillado" (page 95).

Sometimes setting in a story can be **symbolic,** representing some idea larger or more significant than itself. Walter Van Tilburg Clark projects us into a nightmare world that has been ravaged by a terrible war. The winter landscape has been scarred by bombs and tanks. The human beings who have survived this holocaust now live in dugouts with scarcely any shelter from the elements. Do you think this setting has a symbolic meaning? What ideas does it convey?

Language and Vocabulary

Distinguishing Denotative from Connotative Meanings

In addition to their literal, or **denotative,** meanings, words may have suggested, or **connotative,** meanings. The word *sunset,* for example, denotes the disappearance of the sun below the horizon at the end of each day. The word *sunset* also evokes certain associations. Some people connect the sunset with thoughts of great natural splendor; others may think of it as the waning or death of the day.

In the opening passage of "The Portable Phonograph," Walter Van Tilburg Clark chooses words and phrases that have powerful connotations. What are the dictionary definitions of the following italicized words? What additional feelings or qualities do they connote?

> . . . through the dead, matted grass and *isolated* weed stalks of the prairie . . .
>
> They were the *scars* of gigantic bombs . . .
>
> Along the road there were *rakish* remnants of fence.
>
> . . . faint, *plaintive* notes . . .

Writing About Literature

Discussing the Role of Setting

Choose one of the stories you have read in this unit and consider how setting functions in the story. Here are some questions to guide you:

1. Is the setting chiefly important to the plot? In other words, is the physical background of the story essential to the action?

2. Does the setting provide atmosphere? What kind of mood does it evoke?

3. Does setting contribute to understanding of characters? Does it help explain personalities or indicate characters' motivations? Would the characters fit as well in another physical setting?

Discuss your findings in a brief essay.

About the Author

Walter Van Tilburg Clark   (1909–1971)

Walter Van Tilburg Clark was born in East Oreland, Maine. He taught English and sports in New York State high schools before becoming a professor at the University of Montana, San Francisco State College (which is now California State University), and the University of Nevada. He also served as guest lecturer at universities across the country. Clark wrote stories and novels about the American West. His stories portray the emotions of fear and insecurity in characters who are often in conflict with nature. Two of his most famous novels, *The Ox-Bow Incident* and *The Track of the Cat,* were made into motion pictures, and his stories have been translated into more than twenty languages. Clark loved the wide-open spaces of the Pacific Northwest, and he was interested in preserving the earth's natural resources and wildlife.

A Summer's Reading

BERNARD MALAMUD

Some stories, like "The Most Dangerous Game," take you to strange, remote settings. Other stories, like this one, have realistic, recognizable settings. Note how carefully Malamud creates a sense of the neighborhood and its people.

George Stoyonovich was a neighborhood boy who had quit high school on an impulse when he was sixteen, run out of patience, and though he was ashamed every time he went looking for a job, when people asked him if he had finished and he had to say no, he never went back to school. This summer was a hard time for jobs and he had none. Having so much time on his hands, George thought of going to summer school, but the kids in his classes would be too young. He also considered registering in a night high school, only he didn't like the idea of the teachers always telling him what to do. He felt they had not respected him. The result was he stayed off the streets and in his room most of the day. He was close to twenty and had needs with the neighborhood girls, but no money to spend, and he couldn't get more than an occasional few cents because his father was poor, and his sister Sophie, who resembled George, a tall bony girl of twenty-three, earned very little and what she had she kept for herself. Their mother was dead, and Sophie had to take care of the house.

Very early in the morning George's father got up to go to work in a fish market. Sophie left at about eight for her long ride in the subway to a cafeteria in the Bronx.[1] George had his coffee by himself, then hung around in the house. When the house, a five-room railroad flat[2] above a butcher store, got on his nerves he cleaned it up—mopped the floors with a wet mop and put things away. But most of the time he sat in his room. In the afternoons he listened to the ball game. Otherwise he had a couple of old copies of the *World Almanac* he had bought long ago, and he liked to read in them and also the magazines and newspapers that Sophie brought home, that had been left on the tables in the cafeteria. They were mostly picture magazines about movie stars and sports figures, also usually the *News* and *Mirror*.[3] Sophie herself read whatever fell into her hands, although she sometimes read good books.

1. **Bronx:** a borough of New York City.
2. **railroad flat:** an apartment of rooms in a line. Each room is entered from another.
3. *News* **and** *Mirror:* daily newspapers. The *Mirror* no longer exists.

She once asked George what he did in his room all day and he said he read a lot too.

"Of what besides what I bring home? Do you ever read any worthwhile books?"

"Some," George answered, although he really didn't. He had tried to read a book or two that Sophie had in the house but found he was in no mood for them. Lately he couldn't stand made-up stories, they got on his nerves. He wished he had some hobby to work at—as a kid he was good in carpentry, but where could he work at it? Sometimes during the day he went for walks, but mostly he did his walking after the hot sun had gone down and it was cooler in the streets.

In the evening after supper George left the house and wandered in the neighborhood. During the sultry days some of the storekeepers and their wives sat in chairs on the thick, broken sidewalks in front of their shops, fanning themselves, and George walked past them and the guys hanging out on the candy-store corner. A couple of them he had known his whole life, but nobody recognized each other. He had no place special to go, but generally, saving it till the last, he left the neighborhood and walked for blocks till he came to a darkly lit little park with benches and trees and an iron railing, giving it a feeling of privacy. He sat on a bench here, watching the leafy trees and the flowers blooming on the inside of the railing, thinking of a better life for himself. He thought of the jobs he had had since he had quit school—delivery boy, stock clerk, runner, lately working in a factory—and he was dissatisfied with all of them. He felt he would someday like to have a good job and live in a private house with a porch, on a street with trees. He wanted to have some dough in his pocket to buy things with, and a girl to go with, so as not to be so lonely, especially on Saturday nights. He wanted people to like and respect him. He thought about these things often but mostly when he was alone at night. Around midnight he got up and drifted back to his hot and stony neighborhood.

One time while on his walk George met Mr. Cattanzara coming home very late from work. He wondered if he was drunk but then could tell he wasn't. Mr. Cattanzara, a stocky, bald-headed man who worked in a change booth on an IRT station,[4] lived on the next block after George's, above a shoe repair store. Nights, during the hot weather, he sat on his stoop[5] in an undershirt, reading the *New York Times* in the light of the shoemaker's window. He read it from the first page to the last, then went up to sleep. And all the time he was reading the paper, his wife, a fat woman with a white face, leaned out of the window, gazing into the street, her thick white arms folded under her loose breast, on the window ledge.

Once in a while Mr. Cattanzara came home drunk, but it was a quiet drunk. He never made any trouble, only walked stiffly up the street and slowly climbed the stairs into the hall. Though drunk, he looked the same as always, except for his tight walk, the quietness, and that his eyes were wet. George liked Mr. Cattanzara because he remembered him giving him nickels to buy lemon ice with when he was a squirt. Mr. Cattanzara was a different type than those in the neighborhood. He asked different questions than the others when he met you, and he seemed to know what went on in all the newspapers. He read them, as his fat sick wife watched from the window.

"What are you doing with yourself this summer, George?" Mr. Cattanzara asked. "I see you walkin' around at nights."

George felt embarrassed. "I like to walk."

"What are you doin' in the day now?"

"Nothing much just right now. I'm waiting

4. **IRT station:** The IRT is one of the public-transportation systems in New York City.
5. **stoop:** staircase leading to the entrance of a building.

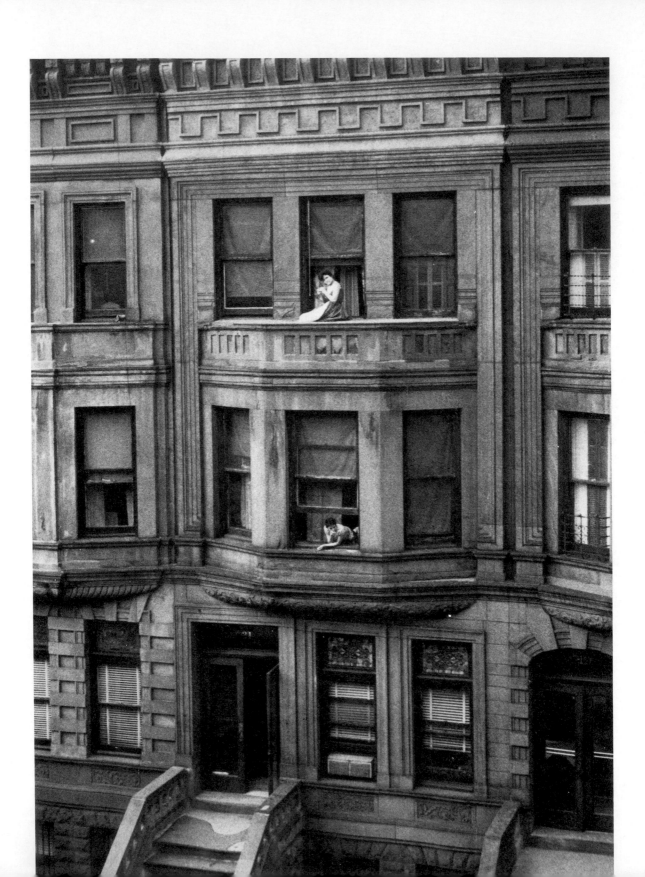

for a job." Since it shamed him to admit he wasn't working, George said, "I'm staying home—but I'm reading a lot to pick up my education."

Mr. Cattanzara looked interested. He mopped his hot face with a red handkerchief.

"What are you readin'?"

George hesitated, then said, "I got a list of books in the library once, and now I'm gonna read them this summer." He felt strange and a little unhappy saying this, but he wanted Mr. Cattanzara to respect him.

"How many books are there on it?"

"I never counted them. Maybe around a hundred."

Mr. Cattanzara whistled through his teeth.

"I figure if I did that," George went on earnestly, "it would help me in my education. I don't mean the kind they give you in high school. I want to know different things than they learn there, if you know what I mean."

The change maker nodded. "Still and all, one hundred books is a pretty big load for one summer."

"It might take longer."

"After you're finished with some, maybe you and I can shoot the breeze about them?" said Mr. Cattanzara.

"When I'm finished," George answered.

Mr. Cattanzara went home and George continued on his walk. After that, though he had the urge to, George did nothing different from usual. He still took his walks at night, ending up in the little park. But one evening the shoemaker on the next block stopped George to say he was a good boy, and George figured that Mr. Cattanzara had told him all about the books he was reading. From the shoemaker it must have gone down the street, because George saw a couple of people smiling kindly at him, though nobody spoke to him personally. He felt a little better around the neighborhood and liked it more, though not so much he would want to live in it forever. He had never exactly disliked the people in it, yet he had never liked them very much either. It was the fault of the neighborhood. To his surprise, George found out that his father and Sophie knew about his reading too. His father was too shy to say anything about it—he was never much of a talker in his whole life—but Sophie was softer to George, and she showed him in other ways she was proud of him.

As the summer went on George felt in a good mood about things. He cleaned the house every day, as a favor to Sophie, and he enjoyed the ball games more. Sophie gave him a buck a week allowance, and though it still wasn't enough and he had to use it carefully, it was a helluva lot better than just having two bits now and then. What he bought with the money—cigarettes mostly, an occasional beer or movie ticket—he got a big kick out of. Life wasn't so bad if you knew how to appreciate it. Occasionally he bought a paperback book from the newsstand, but he never got around to reading it, though he was glad to have a couple of books in his room. But he read thoroughly Sophie's magazines and newspapers. And at night was the most enjoyable time, because when he passed the storekeepers sitting outside their stores, he could tell they regarded him highly. He walked erect, and though he did not say much to them, or they to him, he could feel approval on all sides. A couple of nights he felt so good that he skipped the park at the end of the evening. He just wandered in the neighborhood, where people had known him from the time he was a kid playing punchball whenever there was a game of it going; he wandered there, then came home and got undressed for bed, feeling fine.

For a few weeks he had talked only once with Mr. Cattanzara, and though the change maker had said nothing more about the books, asked no questions, his silence made George a little uneasy. For a while George didn't pass in front of Mr. Cattanzara's house any more, until one night, forgetting himself, he approached it from a different direction than he usually did when he did. It was already past midnight. The street, except for one or two people, was deserted, and George was surprised when he saw Mr. Cattanzara still reading his newspaper by the light of the streetlamp overhead. His impulse was to stop at the stoop and talk to him. He wasn't sure what he wanted to say, though he felt the words would come when he began to talk; but the more he thought about it, the more the idea scared him, and he decided he'd better not. He even considered beating it home by another street, but he was too near Mr. Cattanzara, and the change maker might see him as he ran, and get annoyed. So George unobtrusively crossed the street, trying to make it seem as if he had to look in a store window on the other side, which he did, and then went on, uncomfortable at what he was doing. He feared Mr. Cattanzara would glance up from his paper and call him a dirty rat for walking on the other side of the street, but all he did was sit there, sweating through his undershirt, his bald head shining in the dim light as he read his *Times,* and upstairs his fat wife leaned out of the window, seeming to read the paper along with him. George thought she would spy him and yell out to Mr. Cattanzara, but she never moved her eyes off her husband.

George made up his mind to stay away from the change maker until he had got some of his softback books read, but when he started them and saw they were mostly storybooks, he lost his interest and didn't bother to finish them. He lost his interest in reading other things too. Sophie's magazines and newspapers went unread. She saw them piling up on a chair in his room and asked why he was no longer looking

at them, and George told her it was because of all the other reading he had to do. Sophie said she had guessed that was it. So for most of the day, George had the radio on, turning to music when he was sick of the human voice. He kept the house fairly neat, and Sophie said nothing on the days when he neglected it. She was still kind and gave him his extra buck, though things weren't so good for him as they had been before.

But they were good enough, considering. Also his night walks invariably picked him up, no matter how bad the day was. Then one night George saw Mr. Cattanzara coming down the street toward him. George was about to turn and run but he recognized from Mr. Cattanzara's walk that he was drunk, and if so, probably he would not even bother to notice him. So George kept on walking straight ahead until he came abreast of Mr. Cattanzara and though he felt wound up enough to pop into the sky, he was not surprised when Mr. Cattanzara passed him without a word, walking slowly, his face and body stiff. George drew a breath in relief at his narrow escape, when he heard his name called, and there stood Mr. Cattanzara at his elbow, smelling like the inside of a beer barrel. His eyes were sad as he gazed at George, and George felt so intensely uncomfortable he was tempted to shove the drunk aside and continue on his walk.

But he couldn't act that way to him, and, besides, Mr. Cattanzara took a nickel out of his pants pocket and handed it to him.

"Go buy yourself a lemon ice, Georgie."

"It's not that time any more, Mr. Cattanzara," George said, "I am a big guy now."

"No, you ain't," said Mr. Cattanzara, to which George made no reply he could think of.

"How are all your books comin' along now?" Mr. Cattanzara asked. Though he tried to stand steady, he swayed a little.

"Fine, I guess," said George, feeling the red crawling up his face.

"You ain't sure?" The change maker smiled slyly, a way George had never seen him smile.

"Sure I'm sure. They're fine."

Though his head swayed in little arcs, Mr. Cattanzara's eyes were steady. He had small blue eyes which could hurt if you looked at them too long.

"George," he said, "name me one book on that list that you read this summer, and I will drink to your health."

"I don't want anybody drinking to me."

"Name me one so I can ask you a question on it. Who can tell, if it's a good book maybe I might wanna read it myself."

George knew he looked passable on the outside, but inside he was crumbling apart.

Unable to reply, he shut his eyes, but when— years later—he opened them, he saw that Mr. Cattanzara had, out of pity, gone away, but in his ears he still heard the words he had said when he left: "George, don't do what I did."

The next night he was afraid to leave his room, and though Sophie argued with him he wouldn't open the door.

"What are you doing in there?" she asked.

"Nothing."

"Aren't you reading?"

"No."

She was silent a minute, then asked, "Where do you keep the books you read? I never see any in your room outside of a few cheap trashy ones."

He wouldn't tell her.

"In that case you're not worth a buck of my hard-earned money. Why should I break my back for you? Go on out, you bum, and get a job."

He stayed in his room for almost a week, except to sneak into the kitchen when nobody was home. Sophie railed at him, then begged him to come out, and his old father wept, but George wouldn't budge, though the weather was terrible and his small room stifling. He found it very hard to breathe, each breath was like drawing a flame into his lungs.

One night, unable to stand the heat anymore, he burst into the street at one A.M., a shadow of himself. He hoped to sneak to the park without being seen, but there were people all over the block, wilted and listless, waiting for a breeze. George lowered his eyes and walked, in disgrace, away from them, but before long he discovered they were still friendly to him. He figured Mr. Cattanzara hadn't told on him. Maybe when he woke up out of his drunk the next morning, he had forgotten all about meeting George. George felt his confidence slowly come back to him.

That same night a man on a street corner asked him if it was true that he had finished reading so many books, and George admitted he had. The man said it was a wonderful thing for a boy his age to read so much.

"Yeah," George said, but he felt relieved. He hoped nobody would mention the books anymore, and when, after a couple of days, he accidentally met Mr. Cattanzara again, *he* didn't, though George had the idea he was the one who had started the rumor that he had finished all the books.

One evening in the fall, George ran out of his house to the library, where he hadn't been in years. There were books all over the place, wherever he looked, and though he was struggling to control an inward trembling, he easily counted off a hundred, then sat down at a table to read.

Reading Check

1. Why does George decide against going back to school?
2. Whom does George live with?
3. How does George spend the day?
4. Where does George like to walk in the evenings?
5. How do the people in the neighborhood learn about George's ambitious reading project?

For Study and Discussion

Analyzing and Interpreting the Story

1a. What is George's problem at the opening of the story? **b.** How much of George's difficulty is caused by circumstances and how much by his own character?

2. This story takes place in New York City during the summer. **a.** What impression do you have of George's neighborhood and his neighbors? **b.** Why is it significant that this story takes place in the summer rather than, say, in the spring?

3a. Why does George lie to Mr. Cattanzara about the books he is reading? **b.** How does this lie affect George's status in the neighborhood? **c.** How does his attitude toward the neighborhood change?

4a. How is George made to face the consequences of his lie? **b.** What does Mr. Cattanzara mean when he says "George, don't do what I did"?

5a. What do you think finally drives George to the library? **b.** Do you believe this action marks a change in his life? Why or why not? **c.** Why is it significant that the story ends in the fall?

Literary Elements

Verisimilitude

A short story is often given a setting that is true to a specific time and place. This appearance of reality in fiction is known as **verisimilitude** (věr′ə-sĭm-ĭl′ə-to͞od′, -tyo͞od′). We know from specific references to daily newspapers and to public-transportation systems, as well as other details, that "A Summer's Reading" takes place in New York City within recent times. What other details in Malamud's story re-create a modern urban setting?

Language and Vocabulary

Distinguishing Informal English from Slang

Standard English can be formal or informal. **Informal standard English** is the language used most of the time in writing and speaking. **Formal standard English** is more elegant and elaborate. It is used in scholarly books, research papers, technical writing, and on formal occasions in public speaking.

Slang lies outside of standard usage and is generally used in very informal situations. Slang tends to be colorful, humorous, and fresh. Sometimes slang is made up or invented. Sometimes slang is the result of giving a new meaning to an established word or phrase: "in the doghouse." A slang expression may pass quickly from the language or it may become part of standard usage.

In this sentence from "A Summer's Reading," the italicized phrase is an example of informal standard English:

George had his coffee by himself, then *hung around* in the house.

In a formal context, instead of "hang around" you might use "loiter" or "linger indolently."

The phrase *hang out* is slang:

> . . . George walked past them and the guys *hanging out* on the candy-store corner.

In standard English you might use "spending time" or "frequenting."

Dictionaries often identify informal and nonstandard usage of words. Using your dictionary, find out if each of the italicized expressions listed here is classified as informal standard English or slang. Tell what each one means.

> He wanted to have some *dough* in his pocket to buy things with . . .

> George liked Mr. Cattanzara because he remembered him giving him nickels to buy lemon ice with when he was a *squirt.*

> . . . it was a . . . lot better than just having *two bits* now and then.

> He even considered *beating it* home by another street . . .

Focus on Narrative Writing

Listing Details of Setting

Specific references in Malamud's story help us visualize George's neighborhood. Suppose that you were writing a story about your own neighborhood. Which details of **setting** do you think would best contribute to your story's verisimilitude? Make a list of five to eight specific details that would create an appearance of reality in your story. Then get together with a partner and compare your lists. Save your notes.

About the Author

Bernard Malamud (1914–1986)

Bernard Malamud was born in Brooklyn, New York. He attended the City College of New York and Columbia University. In 1952 his first novel, *The Natural,* was published. His second novel, *The Assistant,* appeared in 1957. "A Summer's Reading" is from a collection of stories called *The Magic Barrel,* which received the National Book Award for fiction in 1959. Malamud's other works include *A New Life* (1961), *Idiots First* (1963), *The Fixer* (1966), which received both a National Book Award and the Pulitzer Prize for fiction, *Pictures of Fidelman* (1969), and *The Tenants* (1971).

The Scarlet Ibis°

JAMES HURST

The two elements of setting—time and place—are important in this story. How does the rural setting contribute to what happens in the story? What is the importance of the year, 1918, to the story?

It was in the clove of seasons, summer was dead but autumn had not yet been born, that the ibis lit in the bleeding tree. The flower garden was stained with rotting brown magnolia petals and ironweeds grew rank amid the purple phlox. The five o'clocks by the chimney still marked time, but the oriole nest in the elm was untenanted and rocked back and forth like an empty cradle. The last graveyard flowers were blooming, and their smell drifted across the cotton field and through every room of our house, speaking softly the names of our dead.

It's strange that all this is still so clear to me, now that that summer has long since fled and time has had its way. A grindstone stands where the bleeding tree stood, just outside the kitchen door, and now if an oriole sings in the elm, its song seems to die up in the leaves, a silvery dust. The flower garden is prim, the house a gleaming white, and the pale fence across the yard stands straight and spruce. But sometimes (like right now), as I sit in the cool, green-draped parlor, the grindstone begins to turn, and time with all its changes is ground away—and I remember Doodle.

Doodle was just about the craziest brother a boy ever had. Of course, he wasn't a crazy crazy like old Miss Leedie, who was in love with President Wilson and wrote him a letter every day, but was a nice crazy, like someone you meet in your dreams. He was born when I was six and was, from the outset, a disappointment. He seemed all head, with a tiny body which was red and shriveled like an old man's. Everybody thought he was going to die—everybody except Aunt Nicey, who had delivered him. She said he would live because he was born in a caul and cauls were made from Jesus' nightgown. Daddy had Mr. Heath, the carpenter, build a little mahogany coffin for him. But he didn't die, and when he was three months old Mama and Daddy decided they might as well name him. They named him William Armstrong, which was like tying a big tail on a small kite. Such a name sounds good only on a tombstone.

I thought myself pretty smart at many things, like holding my breath, running, jumping, or climbing the vines in Old Woman Swamp, and I wanted more than anything else someone to race to Horsehead Landing, someone to box with, and someone to perch with in the top fork of the great pine behind the barn,

° **Ibis** (ī'bĭs): a wading bird with a long bill.

The Reserve in Summer by Alice Ravenel Huger Smith. Watercolor.

where across the fields and swamps you could see the sea. I wanted a brother. But Mama, crying, told me that even if William Armstrong lived, he would never do these things with me. He might not, she sobbed, even be "all there." He might, as long as he lived, lie on the rubber sheet in the center of the bed in the front bedroom, where the white marquisette[1] curtains billowed out in the afternoon sea breeze, rustling like palmetto fronds.

It was bad enough having an invalid brother, but having one who possibly was not all there was unbearable, so I began to make plans to kill him by smothering him with a pillow. However, one afternoon as I watched him, my head poked between the iron posts of the foot of the bed, he looked straight at me and grinned. I skipped through the rooms, down the echoing halls, shouting, "Mama, he smiled. He's all there! He's all there!" and he was.

When he was two, if you laid him on his stomach, he began to try to move himself, straining terribly. The doctor said that with his weak heart this strain would probably kill him, but it didn't. Trembling, he'd push himself up, turning first red, then a soft purple, and finally collapse back onto the bed like an old worn-out doll. I can still see Mama watching him, her hand pressed tight across her mouth, her eyes wide and unblinking. But he learned to crawl (it was his third winter), and we brought him out of the front bedroom, putting him on the rug before the fireplace. For the first time he became one of us.

As long as he lay all the time in bed, we called him William Armstrong, even though it was formal and sounded as if we were referring to one of our ancestors, but with his creeping around on the deerskin rug and beginning to talk, something had to be done about his

1. **marquisette** (mär′kĭ-zĕt′, mär′kwĭ-): a sheer fabric used for curtains.

name. It was I who renamed him. When he crawled, he crawled backward, as if he were in reverse and couldn't change gears. If you called him, he'd turn around as if he were going in the other direction, then he'd back right up to you to be picked up. Crawling backward made him look like a doodlebug, so I began to call him Doodle, and in time even Mama and Daddy thought it was a better name than William Armstrong. Only Aunt Nicey disagreed. She said caul babies should be treated with special respect since they might turn out to be saints. Renaming my brother was perhaps the kindest thing I ever did for him, because nobody expects much from someone called Doodle.

Although Doodle learned to crawl, he showed no signs of walking, but he wasn't idle. He talked so much that we all quit listening to what he said. It was about this time that Daddy built him a go-cart and I had to pull him around. At first I just paraded him up and down the piazza, but then he started crying to be taken out into the yard and it ended up by my having to lug him wherever I went. If I so much as picked up my cap, he'd start crying to go with me and Mama would call from wherever she was, "Take Doodle with you."

He was a burden in many ways. The doctor had said that he mustn't get too excited, too hot, too cold, or too tired and that he must always be treated gently. A long list of don'ts went with him, all of which I ignored once we got out of the house. To discourage his coming with me, I'd run with him across the ends of the cotton rows and careen him around corners on two wheels. Sometimes I accidentally turned him over, but he never told Mama. His skin was very sensitive, and he had to wear a big straw hat whenever he went out. When the going got rough and he had to cling to the sides of the go-cart, the hat slipped all the way down over his ears. He was a sight. Finally, I could see I was licked. Doodle was my brother and he was going to cling to me forever, no matter what I did, so I dragged him across the burning cotton field to share with him the only beauty I knew, Old Woman Swamp. I pulled the go-cart through the sawtooth fern, down into the green dimness where the palmetto fronds whispered by the stream. I lifted him out and set him down in the soft rubber grass beside a tall pine. His eyes were round with wonder as he gazed about him, and his little hands began to stroke the rubber grass. Then he began to cry.

"For heaven's sake, what's the matter?" I asked, annoyed.

"It's so pretty," he said. "So pretty, pretty, pretty."

After that day Doodle and I often went down into Old Woman Swamp. I would gather wildflowers, wild violets, honeysuckle, yellow jasmine, snakeflowers, and water lilies, and with wire grass we'd weave them into necklaces and crowns. We'd bedeck ourselves with our handiwork and loll about thus beautified, beyond the touch of the everyday world. Then when the slanted rays of the sun burned orange in the tops of the pines, we'd drop our jewels into the stream and watch them float away toward the sea.

There is within me (and with sadness I have watched it in others) a knot of cruelty borne by the stream of love, much as our blood sometimes bears the seed of our destruction, and at times I was mean to Doodle. One day I took him up to the barn loft and showed him his casket, telling him how we all had believed he would die. It was covered with a film of Paris green[2] sprinkled to kill the rats, and screech owls had built a nest inside it.

Doodle studied the mahogany box for a long time, then said, "It's not mine."

2. **Paris green:** a poisonous powder used as a preservative and as an insecticide.

"It is," I said. "And before I'll help you down from the loft, you're going to have to touch it."

"I won't touch it," he said sullenly.

"Then I'll leave you here by yourself," I threatened, and made as if I were going down.

Doodle was frightened of being left. "Don't go leave me, Brother," he cried, and he leaned toward the coffin. His hand, trembling, reached out, and when he touched the casket he screamed. A screech owl flapped out of the box into our faces, scaring us and covering us with Paris green. Doodle was paralyzed, so I put him on my shoulder and carried him down the ladder, and even when we were outside in the bright sunshine, he clung to me, crying, "Don't leave me. Don't leave me."

When Doodle was five years old, I was embarrassed at having a brother of that age who couldn't walk, so I set out to teach him. We were down in Old Woman Swamp and it was spring and the sick-sweet smell of bay flowers hung everywhere like a mournful song. "I'm going to teach you to walk, Doodle," I said.

He was sitting comfortably on the soft grass, leaning back against the pine. "Why?" he asked.

I hadn't expected such an answer. "So I won't have to haul you around all the time."

"I can't walk, Brother," he said.

"Who says so?" I demanded.

"Mama, the doctor—everybody."

"Oh, you can walk," I said, and I took him by the arms and stood him up. He collapsed onto the grass like a half-empty flour sack. It was as if he had no bones in his little legs.

"Don't hurt me, Brother," he warned.

"Shut up. I'm not going to hurt you. I'm going to teach you to walk." I heaved him up again, and again he collapsed.

This time he did not lift his face up out of

the rubber grass. "I just can't do it. Let's make honeysuckle wreaths."

"Oh yes you can, Doodle," I said. "All you got to do is try. Now come on," and I hauled him up once more.

It seemed so hopeless from the beginning that it's a miracle I didn't give up. But all of us must have something or someone to be proud of, and Doodle had become mine. I did not know then that pride is a wonderful, terrible thing, a seed that bears two vines, life and death. Every day that summer we went to the pine beside the stream of Old Woman Swamp, and I put him on his feet at least a hundred times each afternoon. Occasionally I too became discouraged because it didn't seem as if he was trying, and I would say, "Doodle, don't you *want* to learn to walk?"

He'd nod his head, and I'd say, "Well, if you don't keep trying, you'll never learn." Then I'd paint for him a picture of us as old men, white-haired, him with a long white beard and me still pulling him around in the go-cart. This never failed to make him try again.

Finally one day, after many weeks of practicing, he stood alone for a few seconds. When he fell, I grabbed him in my arms and hugged him, our laughter pealing through the swamp like a ringing bell. Now we knew it could be done. Hope no longer hid in the dark palmetto thicket but perched like a cardinal in the lacy toothbrush tree, brilliantly visible. "Yes, yes," I cried, and he cried it too, and the grass beneath us was soft and the smell of the swamp was sweet.

With success so imminent, we decided not to tell anyone until he could actually walk. Each day, barring rain, we sneaked into Old Woman Swamp, and by cotton-picking time Doodle was ready to show what he could do. He still wasn't able to walk far, but we could wait no longer. Keeping a nice secret is very hard to do, like holding your breath. We chose to re-

veal all on October eighth, Doodle's sixth birthday, and for weeks ahead we mooned around the house, promising everybody a most spectacular surprise. Aunt Nicey said that, after so much talk, if we produced anything less tremendous than the Resurrection, she was going to be disappointed.

At breakfast on our chosen day, when Mama, Daddy, and Aunt Nicey were in the dining room, I brought Doodle to the door in the go-cart just as usual and had them turn their backs, making them cross their hearts and hope to die if they peeked. I helped Doodle up, and when he was standing alone I let them look. There wasn't a sound as Doodle walked slowly across the room and sat down at his place at the table. Then Mama began to cry and ran over to him, hugging him and kissing him. Daddy hugged him too, so I went to Aunt Nicey, who was thanks-praying in the doorway, and began to waltz her around. We danced together quite well until she came down on my big toe with her brogans,[3] hurting me so badly I thought I was crippled for life.

Doodle told them it was I who had taught him to walk, so everyone wanted to hug me, and I began to cry.

"What are you crying for?" asked Daddy, but I couldn't answer. They did not know that I did it for myself; that pride, whose slave I was, spoke to me louder than all their voices, and that Doodle walked only because I was ashamed of having a crippled brother.

Within a few months Doodle had learned to walk well and his go-cart was put up in the barn loft (it's still there) beside his little mahogany coffin. Now, when we roamed off together, resting often, we never turned back until our destination had been reached, and to help pass the time, we took up lying. From the beginning Doodle was a terrible liar and he got

---

3. **brogans** (brō′gənz): ankle-high work shoes.

me in the habit. Had anyone stopped to listen to us, we would have been sent off to Dix Hill.

My lies were scary, involved, and usually pointless, but Doodle's were twice as crazy. People in his stories all had wings and flew wherever they wanted to go. His favorite lie was about a boy named Peter who had a pet peacock with a ten-foot tail. Peter wore a golden robe that glittered so brightly that when he walked through the sunflowers they turned away from the sun to face him. When Peter was ready to go to sleep, the peacock spread his magnificent tail, enfolding the boy gently like a closing go-to-sleep flower, burying him in the gloriously iridescent,[4] rustling vortex.[5] Yes, I must admit it. Doodle could beat me lying.

Doodle and I spent lots of time thinking about our future. We decided that when we were grown we'd live in Old Woman Swamp and pick dog-tongue for a living. Beside the stream, he planned, we'd build us a house of whispering leaves and the swamp birds would be our chickens. All day long (when we weren't gathering dog-tongue) we'd swing through the cypresses on the rope vines, and if it rained we'd huddle beneath an umbrella tree and play stickfrog. Mama and Daddy could come and live with us if they wanted to. He even came up with the idea that he could marry Mama and I could marry Daddy. Of course, I was old enough to know this wouldn't work out, but the picture he painted was so beautiful and serene that all I could do was whisper Yes, yes.

Once I had succeeded in teaching Doodle to walk, I began to believe in my own infallibility and I prepared a terrific development program for him, unknown to Mama and Daddy,

of course. I would teach him to run, to swim, to climb trees, and to fight. He, too, now believed in my infallibility, so we set the deadline for these accomplishments less than a year away, when, it had been decided, Doodle could start to school.

That winter we didn't make much progress, for I was in school and Doodle suffered from one bad cold after another. But when spring came, rich and warm, we raised our sights again. Success lay at the end of summer like a pot of gold, and our campaign got off to a good start. On hot days, Doodle and I went down to Horsehead Landing and I gave him swimming lessons or showed him how to row a boat. Sometimes we descended into the cool greenness of Old Woman Swamp and climbed the rope vines or boxed scientifically beneath the pine where he had learned to walk. Promise hung about us like the leaves, and wherever we looked, ferns unfurled and birds broke into song.

That summer, the summer of 1918, was blighted. In May and June there was no rain and the crops withered, curled up, then died under the thirsty sun. One morning in July a hurricane came out of the east, tipping over the oaks in the yard and splitting the limbs of the elm trees. That afternoon it roared back out of the west, blew the fallen oaks around, snapping their roots and tearing them out of the earth like a hawk at the entrails of a chicken. Cotton bolls were wrenched from the stalks and lay like green walnuts in the valleys between the rows, while the cornfield leaned over uniformly so that the tassels touched the ground. Doodle and I followed Daddy out into the cotton field, where he stood, shoulders sagging, surveying the ruin. When his chin sank down onto his chest, we were frightened, and Doodle slipped his hand into mine. Suddenly Daddy straightened his shoulders, raised a giant knuckly fist, and with a voice that seemed

---

4. **iridescent** (ĭr′ə-dĕs′ənt): rainbowlike.
5. **vortex:** something that draws everything into its center like a whirlpool.

to rumble out of the earth itself began cursing heaven, hell, the weather, and the Republican Party. Doodle and I, prodding each other and giggling, went back to the house, knowing that everything would be all right.

And during that summer, strange names were heard through the house: Château Thierry, Amiens, Soissons, and in her blessing at the supper table, Mama once said, "And bless the Pearsons, whose boy Joe was lost at Belleau Wood."[6]

So we came to that clove of seasons. School was only a few weeks away, and Doodle was far behind schedule. He could barely clear the ground when climbing up the rope vines and his swimming was certainly not passable. We decided to double our efforts, to make that last drive and reach our pot of gold. I made him swim until he turned blue and row until he couldn't lift an oar. Wherever we went, I purposely walked fast, and although he kept up, his face turned red and his eyes became glazed. Once, he could go no further, so he collapsed on the ground and began to cry.

"Aw, come on, Doodle," I urged. "You can do it. Do you want to be different from everybody else when you start school?"

"Does it make any difference?"

"It certainly does," I said. "Now, come on," and I helped him up.

As we slipped through dog days, Doodle began to look feverish, and Mama felt his forehead, asking him if he felt ill. At night he didn't sleep well, and sometimes he had nightmares, crying out until I touched him and said, "Wake up, Doodle. Wake up."

It was Saturday noon, just a few days before school was to start. I should have already admitted defeat, but my pride wouldn't let me. The excitement of our program had now been gone for weeks, but still we kept on with a tired doggedness. It was too late to turn back, for we had both wandered too far into a net of expectations and had left no crumbs behind.

Daddy, Mama, Doodle, and I were seated at the dining-room table having lunch. It was a hot day, with all the windows and doors open in case a breeze should come. In the kitchen Aunt Nicey was humming softly. After a long silence, Daddy spoke. "It's so calm, I wouldn't be surprised if we had a storm this afternoon."

"I haven't heard a rain frog," said Mama, who believed in signs, as she served the bread around the table.

"I did," declared Doodle. "Down in the swamp."

"He didn't," I said contrarily.

"You did, eh?" said Daddy, ignoring my denial.

"I certainly did," Doodle reiterated, scowling at me over the top of his iced-tea glass, and we were quiet again.

Suddenly, from out in the yard, came a strange croaking noise. Doodle stopped eating, with a piece of bread poised ready for his mouth, his eyes popped round like two blue buttons. "What's that?" he whispered.

I jumped up, knocking over my chair, and had reached the door when Mama called, "Pick up the chair, sit down again, and say excuse me."

By the time I had done this, Doodle had excused himself and had slipped out into the yard. He was looking up into the bleeding tree. "It's a great big red bird!" he called.

The bird croaked loudly again, and Mama and Daddy came out into the yard. We shaded our eyes with our hands against the hazy glare of the sun and peered up through the still leaves. On the topmost branch a bird the size of a chicken, with scarlet feathers and long legs, was perched precariously. Its wings hung

6. **Château Thierry** (shá-tō′ tyĕ-rē′), **Amiens** (a-myaN′), **Soissons** (swa-sôN′) . . . **Belleau** (bĕl-ō′) **Wood:** places in France where battles took place during World War I.

down loosely, and as we watched, a feather dropped away and floated slowly down through the green leaves.

"It's not even frightened of us," Mama said.

"It looks tired," Daddy added. "Or maybe sick."

Doodle's hands were clasped at his throat, and I had never seen him stand still so long. "What is it?" he asked.

Daddy shook his head. "I don't know, maybe it's——"

At that moment the bird began to flutter, but the wings were uncoordinated, and amid much flapping and a spray of flying feathers, it tumbled down, bumping through the limbs of the bleeding tree and landing at our feet with a thud. Its long, graceful neck jerked twice into an S, then straightened out, and the bird was still. A white veil came over the eyes and the long white beak unhinged. Its legs were crossed and its clawlike feet were delicately

curved at rest. Even death did not mar its grace, for it lay on the earth like a broken vase of red flowers, and we stood around it, awed by its exotic beauty.

"It's dead," Mama said.

"What is it?" Doodle repeated.

"Go bring me the bird book," said Daddy.

I ran into the house and brought back the bird book. As we watched, Daddy thumbed through its pages. "It's a scarlet ibis," he said, pointing to a picture. "It lives in the tropics— South America to Florida. A storm must have brought it here."

Sadly, we all looked back at the bird. A scarlet ibis! How many miles it had traveled to die like this, in *our* yard, beneath the bleeding tree.

"Let's finish lunch," Mama said, nudging us back toward the dining room.

"I'm not hungry," said Doodle, and he knelt down beside the ibis.

"We've got peach cobbler for dessert," Mama tempted from the doorway.

Doodle remained kneeling. "I'm going to bury him."

"Don't you dare touch him," Mama warned. "There's no telling what disease he might have had."

"All right," said Doodle. "I won't."

Daddy, Mama, and I went back to the dining-room table, but we watched Doodle through the open door. He took out a piece of string from his pocket and, without touching the ibis, looped one end around its neck. Slowly, while singing softly "Shall We Gather at the River," he carried the bird around to the front yard and dug a hole in the flower garden, next to the petunia bed. Now we were watching him through the front window, but he didn't know it. His awkwardness at digging the hole with a shovel whose handle was twice as long as he was made us laugh, and we covered our mouths with our hands so he wouldn't hear.

When Doodle came into the dining room, he found us seriously eating our cobbler. He was pale and lingered just inside the screen door. "Did you get the scarlet ibis buried?" asked Daddy.

Doodle didn't speak but nodded his head.

"Go wash your hands, and then you can have some peach cobbler," said Mama.

"I'm not hungry," he said.

"Dead birds is bad luck," said Aunt Nicey, poking her head from the kitchen door. "Specially *red* dead birds!"

As soon as I had finished eating, Doodle and I hurried off to Horsehead Landing. Time was short, and Doodle still had a long way to go if he was going to keep up with the other boys when he started school. The sun, gilded with the yellow cast of autumn, still burned fiercely, but the dark green woods through which we passed were shady and cool. When we reached the landing, Doodle said he was too tired to swim, so we got into a skiff and floated down the creek with the tide. Far off in the marsh a rail was scolding, and over on the beach locusts were singing in the myrtle trees. Doodle did not speak and kept his head turned away, letting one hand trail limply in the water.

After we had drifted a long way, I put the oars in place and made Doodle row back against the tide. Black clouds began to gather in the southwest, and he kept watching them, trying to pull the oars a little faster. When we reached Horsehead Landing, lightning was playing across half the sky and thunder roared out, hiding even the sound of the sea. The sun disappeared and darkness descended, almost like night. Flocks of marsh crows flew by, heading inland to their roosting trees, and two egrets, squawking, arose from the oyster-rock shallows and careened away.

Doodle was both tired and frightened, and when he stepped from the skiff he collapsed onto the mud, sending an armada of fiddler crabs rustling off into the marsh grass. I helped him up, and as he wiped the mud off his trousers, he smiled at me ashamedly. He had failed and we both knew it, so we started back home, racing the storm. We never spoke (What are the words that can solder cracked pride?), but I knew he was watching me, watching for a sign of mercy. The lightning was near now, and from fear he walked so close behind me he kept stepping on my heels. The faster I walked, the faster he walked, so I began to run. The rain was coming, roaring through the pines, and then, like a bursting Roman candle, a gum tree ahead of us was shattered by a bolt of lightning. When the deafening peal of thunder had died, and in the moment before the rain arrived, I heard Doodle, who had fallen behind, cry out, "Brother, Brother, don't leave me! Don't leave me!"

The knowledge that Doodle's and my plans had come to naught was bitter, and that streak of cruelty within me awakened. I ran as fast as I could, leaving him far behind with a wall of rain dividing us. The drops stung my face like nettles, and the wind flared the wet, glistening leaves of the bordering trees. Soon I could hear his voice no more.

I hadn't run too far before I became tired, and the flood of childish spite evanesced[7] as well. I stopped and waited for Doodle. The sound of rain was everywhere, but the wind had died and it fell straight down in parallel paths like ropes hanging from the sky. As I waited, I peered through the downpour, but no one came. Finally I went back and found him huddled beneath a red nightshade bush beside the road. He was sitting on the ground, his face buried in his arms, which were resting on his drawn-up knees. "Let's go, Doodle," I said.

He didn't answer, so I placed my hand on his

---

7. **evanesced** (ĕvʹə-nĕsdʹ): vanished.

forehead and lifted his head. Limply, he fell backwards onto the earth. He had been bleeding from the mouth, and his neck and the front of his shirt were stained a brilliant red.

"Doodle! Doodle!" I cried, shaking him, but there was no answer but the ropy rain. He lay very awkwardly, with his head thrown far back, making his vermilion neck appear unusually long and slim. His little legs, bent sharply at the knees, had never before seemed so fragile, so thin.

I began to weep, and the tear-blurred vision in red before me looked very familiar. "Doodle!" I screamed above the pounding storm and threw my body to the earth above his. For a long long time, it seemed forever, I lay there crying, sheltering my fallen scarlet ibis from the heresy of rain.

Reading Check

1. Why isn't Doodle given a name immediately after his birth?
2. How does the narrator discover that the baby is "all there"?
3. What prompts the narrator to rename his brother "Doodle"?
4. What secret is revealed on Doodle's sixth birthday?
5. What does Doodle do with the scarlet ibis?

For Study and Discussion

Analyzing and Interpreting the Story

1. The narrator in this story is presumably an adult recalling certain events in his childhood. What changes noted in the opening paragraphs indicate that a considerable amount of time has passed?

2. The narrator says that his brother, Doodle, was "a nice crazy, like someone you meet in your dreams." **a.** What special gifts did Doodle have? **b.** What were some of the special things the brothers did together?

3. The narrator speaks of having "a knot of cruelty borne by the stream of love." **a.** What does he mean? **b.** How does the cruelty manifest itself in his treatment of Doodle? **c.** How does he show his love for Doodle?

4. We are told that the summer of 1918 was "blighted." How do the events of that summer foreshadow Doodle's death?

5. The scarlet ibis in this story is a **symbol.** It stands for itself but also suggests a wider meaning. **a.** In what way does Doodle resemble the scarlet ibis? **b.** How do you know that he identifies with the bird?

6. This story takes place in an area near the sea that is lush with vegetation. **a.** How does the narrator make us aware of the growth and death of plant life? **b.** What is the symbolic significance of Doodle's death at the end of the summer?

7. Doodle shows a great deal of courage and strength of purpose in trying to overcome his limitations. How does this determination of spirit make his story heartening as well as sad?

Literary Elements

Figurative Language

When writers choose to state a fact or an idea directly, they use **literal language.** Quite often, however, writers decide that an indirect statement is more effective than a direct statement. They then use **figurative language.** Compare these statements:

He collapsed onto the grass weakly.

He collapsed onto the grass like a half-empty flour sack.

The second sentence is an example of figurative language. It makes us think of a person in terms of something that is shapeless and lifeless.

Writers frequently use figurative language to give emphasis to ideas and to make their style vivid. One kind of figurative language is the **simile**. A simile expresses a comparison between two unlike things. A word such as *like* or *as* is used to suggest the similarity.

Explain the comparisons expressed in each of these similes:

> . . . the oriole nest in the elm was untenanted and rocked back and forth *like an empty cradle.*

> Trembling, he'd push himself up, . . . and finally collapse back onto the bed *like an old worn-out doll.*

> When he crawled, he crawled backward, *as if he were in reverse and couldn't change gears.*

> . . . his eyes popped round *like two blue buttons.*

> . . . it lay on the earth *like a broken vase of* red flowers . . .

Metaphor is another kind of figurative language. Like simile, metaphor compares two things that are basically different. However, a metaphor does not use connecting words to express the comparison. A metaphor identifies the two things—that is, it says that one thing *is* another:

> Doodle . . . collapsed onto the mud, sending an armada of fiddler crabs rustling off into the marsh grass.

An *armada* is a fleet of warships, like the Spanish Armada that was sent against England in 1588. The author does not say that the crabs looked like an armada; he identifies the two things directly.

Explain the metaphor in the opening sentence of the story:

> It was in the clove of seasons, summer was dead but autumn had not yet been born . . .

Language and Vocabulary

Finding Meaning from Context

The **context** of a word refers to the words that surround it and to the total situation in which it is used. You often can use context clues to determine the meaning of an unfamiliar word. For example, the following sentence provides clues to the meaning of *careen:*

> To discourage his coming with me, I'd run with him across the ends of the cotton rows and *careen* him around corners on two wheels.

You can visualize the go-cart moving from side to side in an uncontrolled manner and leaning sideways on two of its four wheels as it rounds a corner.

Use context clues to define the italicized words in the following passages from the story. Then check your answers in the glossary or in a dictionary.

> We'd *bedeck* ourselves with our handiwork and loll about thus beautified, beyond the touch of the everyday world.

> With success so *imminent,* we decided not to tell anyone until he could actually walk.

> Once I had succeeded in teaching Doodle to walk, I began to believe in my own *infallibility,* and I prepared a terrific program for him . . .

> The excitement of our program had now been gone for weeks, but still we kept on with a tired *doggedness.*

Writing About Literature

Analyzing the Function of Setting

Setting is an important element in "The Scarlet Ibis." Write a brief essay in which you analyze its importance to the plot and to characterization. Here are some questions to guide you in your analysis:

1. Where and when does the story take place?

2. How much time is covered?

3. Which places or scenes are of particular importance?

4. How does nature itself mirror the hopes and dreams of the characters as well as their disappointments?

5. How are the happy times of the brothers reflected in descriptions of background?

6. What is the relationship between the storms and the events in the characters' lives?

Focus on Narrative Writing

Using Sensory Images

Sensory images are details that appeal to one of the five senses: sight, hearing, smell, taste, and touch. In the first paragraph of "The Scarlet Ibis," for example, James Hurst uses images appealing to sight, smell, and hearing in order to describe the setting, or time and place of the story (see page 154). As this passage shows, sensory images can help to make a narrative vivid and interesting.

Skim some recent issues of newspapers or magazines for an interesting article on fashion, travel, or entertainment. Read the article carefully, and fill in a chart like the following one that shows all the sensory images the writer uses. Save your notes.

Sensory Images				
Sight	Sound	Touch	Smell	Taste
————	————	————	————	————
————	————	————	————	————
————	————	————	————	————

About the Author

James Hurst (1922–   )

James Hurst grew up in North Carolina on a farm by the sea. After studying at North Carolina State College, he served in the army during World War II. When the war ended he studied singing at the Juilliard School of Music, then continued his musical studies in Rome, Italy, where he lived for three years. Back in New York in 1951, he began a thirty-four year career in the International Department of a large bank. For a decade, in the fifties and early sixties, he also wrote, publishing several short stories and a play. His most famous short story, "The Scarlet Ibis," first appeared in *The Atlantic Monthly* in July 1960, winning their "Atlantic First" award for that year. This beautiful and moving story has been widely reprinted in high-school and college literature books as well as in short-story collections. Hurst is now retired and has moved back to North Carolina, where he lives in a small eighteenth-century town not far from the place of his birth.

La Puerta°

JOSÉ ANTONIO BURCIAGA°

Speech is as much a part of setting as details of dress, customs, and scenery. Language can help give a reader the flavor of a certain locale. This story contains Mexican-Spanish words and expressions. You will be able to determine their meanings from context.

It had rained in thundering sheets every afternoon that summer. A dog-tired Sinesio returned home from his job in a mattress sweat shop. With a weary step from the *autobús,* Sinesio gathered the last of his strength and darted across the busy *avenida* into the ramshackle *colonia* where children played in the meandering pathways that would soon turn into a noisy *arroyo* of rushing water. The rain drops striking the *barrio's*[1] tin, wooden and cardboard roofs would soon become a sheet of water from heaven.

Every afternoon Sinesio's muffled knock on their two-room shack was answered by Faustina, his wife. She would unlatch the door and return to iron more shirts and dresses of people who could afford the luxury. When thunder clapped, a frightened Faustina would quickly pull the electric cord, believing it would attract lightning. Then she would occupy herself with preparing dinner. Their three children would not arrive home for another hour.

On this day Sinesio laid down his tattered lunch bag, a lottery ticket and his week's wages on the oily tablecloth. Faustina threw a glance at the lottery ticket.

Sinesio's silent arrival always angered Faustina so she glared back at the lottery ticket, "Throwing money away! Buying paper dreams! We can't afford dreams, and you buy them!"

Sinesio ignored her anger. From the table, he picked up a letter, smelled it, studied the U.S. stamp, and with the emphatic opening of the envelope sat down at the table and slowly read aloud the letter from his brother Aurelio as the rain beat against the half tin, half wooden rooftop.

Dear Sinesio,

I write to you from this country of abundance, the first letter I write from los Estados Unidos.[2] *After two weeks of nerves and frustration I finally have a job at a canning factory. It took me that long only because I did not have the necessary social security number. It's amazing how much money one can make, but just as amazing how fast it goes. I had to pay for the social security number, two weeks of rent, food, and a pair of shoes. The good pair you gave me wore out on our journey across the border. From the border we crossed*

°**La Puerta** (lä pwĕr′tä).
°**José Antonio Burciaga** (hō-sā′ än-tō′nyō būr-syä′gä).
1. *barrio* (bä′ryō): a district in a Latin American country.

2. *los Estados Unidos* (lō-sĕs-tä′*th*ō-sōō-nē′*th*ōs): the United States.

two mountains, and the desert in between.

I will get ahead because I'm a better worker than the rest of my countrymen. I can see that already and so does the "boss." Coming here will be hard for you, leaving Faustina and the children. It was hard enough for me and I'm single without a worry in life. But at least you will have me here if you come and I'm sure I can get you a job. All you've heard about the crossing is true. Even the lies are true. "Saludos" from your "compadres" Silvio and Ramiro. They are doing fine. They're already bothering me for the bet you made against the Dodgers.

Next time we get together I will relate my adventures and those of my "compañeros"...things to laugh and cry about.

Aurelio signed the letter *Saludos y abrazo.* Sinesio looked off into space and imagined himself there already. But this dreaming was interrupted by the pelting rain and Faustina's knife dicing *nopal,*[3] cactus, on the wooden board.

¿Qué crees?—"What do you think?" Faustina asked Sinesio.

¡No sé!—"I don't know," Sinesio responded with annoyance.

"But you do know, Sinesio. How could you not know? There's no choice. We have turned this over and around a thousand times. That miserable mattress factory will never pay you enough to eat with. We can't even afford the mattresses you make!"

Sinesio's heart sank as if he was being pushed out or had already left his home. She would join her *comadres*[4] as another undocumented widow. Already he missed his three children, Celso, Jenaro, and Natasia his eldest, a joy every time he saw her. "An absence in the heart is an empty pain," he thought.

Faustina reminded Sinesio of the inevitable trip with subtle statements and proverbs that went straight to the heart of the matter. "Necessity knows no frontiers," she would say. The dicing of the *nopal* and onions took on the fast clip of the rain. Faustina looked up to momentarily study a trickle of water that had begun to run on the inside of a heavily patched glass on the door. It bothered her, but unable to fix it at the moment she went back to her cooking.

Sinesio accepted the answer to a question he wished he had never asked. The decision was made. There was no turning back. "I will leave for *el norte* in two weeks," he said gruffly and with authority.

Faustina's heart sank as she continued to make dinner. After the rain, Sinesio went out to help his *compadre* widen a ditch to keep the water from flooding in front of his door. The children came home, and it became Faustina's job to inform them that *Papá* would have to leave for a while. None of them said anything. Jenaro refused to eat. They had expected and accepted the news. From their friends, they knew exactly what it meant. Many of their friends' fathers had already left and many more would follow.

Throughout the following days, Sinesio continued the same drudgery at work but as his departure date approached he began to miss even that. He secured his family and home, made all the essential home repairs he had put off and asked his creditors for patience and trust. He asked his sisters, cousins and neighbors to check on his family. Another *compadre* lent him money for the trip and the coyote.[5] Sinesio did not know when he would return but told everyone, "One year, no more. Save enough money, buy things to sell here and open up a *negocio,* a small business the family can help with."

3. *nopal* (nō-päl'): a kind of cactus found chiefly in Mexico.
4. *comadres* (kō-mä'*thr*ĕs): intimate friends; gossips.

5. **coyote:** slang for a smuggler.

Taxco (1932) by Andrew Dasburg. Watercolor, 14 x 20¾ inches.

The last trip home from work was no different except for the going-away gift, a bottle of *mezcal*,[6] and the promise of his job when he returned. As usual, the *autobús* was packed. And as usual, the only ones to talk were two loud young men, *sinvergüenzas*—without shame.

The two young men talked about the *Lotería Nacional* and a lottery prize that had gone unclaimed for a week. "*¡Cien millones de pesos!*— One hundred million pesos! *¡Caray!*" one of them kept repeating as he slapped the folded newspaper on his knees again and again. "Maybe the fool that bought it doesn't even know!"

"Or can't read!" answered the other. And they laughed with open mouths.

This caught Sinesio's attention. Two weeks earlier he had bought a lottery ticket. "Could . . . ? No!" he thought. But he felt a slight flush of blood rush to his face. Maybe this was his lucky day. The one day out of the thousands that he had lived in poverty.

The two jumped off the bus, and Sinesio reached for the newspaper they had left behind. There on the front page was the winning number. At the end of the article was the deadline to claim the prize: 8 that night.

Sinesio did not have the faintest idea if his ticket matched the winning number. So he swung from the highest of hopes and dreams to resigned despair as he wondered if he had won one hundred million pesos.

6. **mezcal** (mĕs-käl′): a liquor made from the agave plant.

Jumping off the bus, he ran home, at times slowing to a walk to catch his breath. The times he jogged, his heart pounded, the newspaper clutched in his hand, the heavy grey clouds ready to pour down.

Faustina heard his desperate knock and swung the door open.

"¿Dónde está?" Sinesio pleaded. "Where is the lottery ticket I bought?" He said it slowly and clearly so he wouldn't have to repeat himself.

Faustina was confused, "What lottery ticket?"

Sinesio searched the table, under the green, oily cloth, on top of the dresser and through his papers, all the while with the jabbing question, "What did you do with the *boleto de lotería?*"

Thunder clapped. Faustina quit searching and unplugged the iron. Sinesio sounded off about no one respecting his papers and how no one could find anything in that house. *¿Dónde está el boleto de lotería?*—Where is the lottery ticket?

They both stopped to think. The rain splashed into a downpour against the door. Faustina looked at the door to see if she had fixed the hole in the glass.

¡La puerta!—"The door!" blurted Faustina, "I put it on the door to keep the rain from coming in!"

Sinesio turned to see the ticket glued on the broken window pane. It was light blue with red numbers and the letters *"Lotería Nacional."* Sinesio brought the newspaper up to the glued lottery ticket and with his wife compared the numbers off one by one—*Seis–tres–cuatro–uno–ocho–nueve–uno–¡SIETÉ–DOS!*—Sinesio yelled.

"¡No!" trembled a disbelieving and frightened Sinesio, "One hundred million pesos!" His heart pounded, afraid this was all a mistake, a bad joke. They checked it again and again only to confirm the matching numbers.

Sinesio then tried to peel the ticket off. His fingernail slid off the cold, glued lottery ticket. Faustina looked at Sinesio's stubby fingernails and moved in. But Faustina's thinner fingernails also slid off the lottery ticket. Sinesio walked around the kitchen table looking, thinking, trying to remain calm.

Then he grew frustrated and angry. "What time is it?"

"A quarter to seven," Faustina said looking at the alarm clock above the dresser. They tried hot water and a razor blade with no success. Sinesio then lashed out at Faustina in anger, "You! I never answered your mockery! Your lack of faith in me! I played the lottery because I knew this day would come! *"¡Por Dios Santo!"* and he swore and kissed his crossed thumb and forefinger. "And now? Look what you have done to me, to us, to your children!"

"We can get something at the *farmacia!* The doctor would surely have something to unglue the ticket."

"¡Sí! ¡O sí!" mocked Sinesio. "Sure! We have time to go there."

Time runs faster when there is a deadline. The last bus downtown was due in a few minutes. They tried to take the broken glass pane off the door but he was afraid the ticket would tear more. Sinesios fear and anger mounted with each glance at the clock.

In frustration, he pushed the door out into the downpour and swung it back into the house, cracking the molding and the inside hinges. One more swing, pulling, twisting, splintering, and Sinesio broke the door completely off.

Faustina stood back with hands over her mouth as she recited a litany to all the *santos* and virgins in heaven as the rain blew into their home and splashed her face wet.

Sinesio's face was also drenched. But Faustina could not tell if it was from the rain or tears of anger, as he put the door over his head and ran down the streaming pathway to catch the *autobús.*

For Study and Discussion

Analyzing and Interpreting the Story

1. What details in the opening paragraphs of the story establish the setting?

2. Why does Sinesio feel he must leave his home even though he doesn't want to do so?

3. Describe the conflict between Sinesio and Faustina. How is their relationship affected by their living conditions?

4. What do you think will happen to Sinesio's dreams? Will he be able to claim the lottery prize?

5. How does Burciaga's use of Spanish words and phrases add to the flavor of the setting?

Literary Elements

Local Color

Burciaga's story is set in a small village in Mexico. The narrative and the conversations of the inhabitants are sprinkled with Spanish words and expressions, and the descriptions of streets and houses convey the character of the region.

All the details associated with a particular setting—speech, dress, customs, and scenery—are known as **local color.** The purpose of local color is to give readers the flavor of a specific locale.

Return to the story and find at least three details that provide local color. What would the story lose if these details were not included?

Focus on Narrative Writing

Using Vivid Verbs

Verbs are especially important in storytelling because they show actions. Make your verbs in a story as vivid and precise as you can. In the opening paragraphs of "La Puerta," for example, notice some of Burciaga's vivid verbs: *darted, meandering, clapped, glared* (see page 166).

Find a magazine article about a sports contest, a concert, or a political debate. Make a list of all the verbs in the article that you think are especially vivid. Then get together with a partner and compare lists. Save your notes.

About the Author

José Antonio Burciaga (1940–)

José Antonio Burciaga describes himself as "a bilingual and bicultural Chicano artist and writer, originally from El Paso, Texas." Burciaga is noted for his humorous approach to everyday subjects and his ability to poke fun at himself, as well as for his sharp social criticism. His books include *Restless Serpents* (1976), *Weedee Peepo: A Collection of Essays* (1988), *Undocumented Love* (1992), an anthology of poetry that received the American Book Award, and *Drink Cultura* (1993).

The Author Comments on His Story

On a trip to Mexico City, I happened to meet the director of the National Mexican Lottery, a most important Mexican government position. In my conversation with this man, I mentioned that he must have run across some very interesting real stories of lottery winners. Yes, he answered, and he told me about a man's wife with little hope of winning on a ticket her husband had bought. So she pasted it on a door window to cover a little hole. Then upon winning, he couldn't take the ticket off the door, so he went to claim his prize with the whole door. "La Puerta" comes from a real-life story. I created the characters' names and the situation, the structure on which to hang the plot and climax. I used my imagination and knowledge of the type of house they must have lived in, their economic situation, and the number of people that *have* to leave Mexico, not because they want to but because they *have* to.

Connecting Cultures

Tracing Words from Spanish

Spanish has become the second most widely spoken language in the United States. Many words from Spanish are in common use in English, including *corral, patio, rodeo, ranch,* and *sombrero.* Here are some others:

contras   nacho   taco   macho / machismo
guerrilla   burrito   salsa   flautas

Making Connections: Activities

The word *guerrilla* comes from the word *guerra,* which means "war" in Spanish. A guerrilla force is a small band that makes surprise raids. Choose three of the words listed above. Find their origins in a college or an unabridged dictionary. Share your findings with other members of the class.

Lacquered Chest. Olinalá, Guerrero (c. 1880–1920).
Courtesy of the San Antonio Museum of Art, San Antonio, Texas

The Gift of the Magi

O. HENRY

The Magi were wise men from the East who brought gifts to the infant Jesus in the manger. What is the gift referred to in the title of this story?

One dollar and eighty-seven cents. That was all. And sixty cents of it was in pennies. Pennies saved one and two at a time by bulldozing the grocer and the vegetable man and the butcher until one's cheek burned with silent imputation of parsimony[1] that such close dealing implied. Three times Della counted it. One dollar and eighty-seven cents. And the next day would be Christmas.

There was clearly nothing to do but flop down on the shabby little couch and howl. So Della did it. Which instigates the moral reflection that life is made up of sobs, sniffles, and smiles, with sniffles predominating.

While the mistress of the home is gradually subsiding from the first stage to the second, take a look at the home. A furnished flat at eight dollars per week. It did not exactly beggar description, but it certainly had that word on the lookout for the mendicancy squad.[2]

In the vestibule below was a letter box into which no letter would go, and an electric button from which no mortal finger could coax a ring. Also appertaining thereunto was a card bearing the name "Mr. James Dillingham Young."

The "Dillingham" had been flung to the breeze during a former period of prosperity when its possessor was being paid thirty dollars per week. Now, when the income was shrunk to twenty dollars, the letters of "Dillingham" looked blurred, as though they were thinking

1. **imputation** (ĭm′pyoo̅-tā′shən) **of parsimony** (pär′sə-mō′nē): accusation of stinginess.

2. **mendicancy** (mĕn′dĭ-kən-sē) **squad:** a police squad that picked up beggars.

Drawing for *The Gift of the Magi* by Lisabeth Zwerger.

seriously of contracting to a modest and unassuming *D*. But whenever Mr. James Dillingham Young came home and reached his flat above he was called "Jim" and greatly hugged by Mrs. James Dillingham Young, already introduced to you as Della. Which is all very good.

Della finished her cry and attended to her cheeks with the powder rag. She stood by the window and looked out dully at a gray cat walking a gray fence in a gray backyard. Tomorrow would be Christmas Day, and she had only one dollar and eighty-seven cents with which to buy Jim a present. She had been saving every penny she could for months, with this result. Twenty dollars a week doesn't go far. Expenses had been greater than she had calculated. They always are. Only one dollar and eighty-seven cents to buy a present for Jim. Her Jim. Many a happy hour she had spent planning for something nice for him. Something fine and rare and sterling—something just a little bit near to being worthy of the honor of being owned by Jim.

There was a pier glass[3] between the windows of the room. Perhaps you have seen a pier glass in an eight-dollar flat. A very thin and very agile person may, by observing his reflection in a rapid sequence of longitudinal strips, obtain a fairly accurate conception of his looks. Della, being slender, had mastered the art.

Suddenly she whirled from the window and stood before the glass. Her eyes were shining brilliantly, but her face had lost its color within twenty seconds. Rapidly she pulled down her hair and let it fall to its full length.

Now there were two possessions of the James Dillingham Youngs in which they both took a mighty pride. One was Jim's gold watch that had been his father's and his grandfather's. The other was Della's hair. Had the Queen of

Sheba[4] lived in the flat across the air shaft, Della would have let her hair hang out the window someday to dry, just to depreciate Her Majesty's jewels and gifts. Had King Solomon been the janitor, with all his treasures piled up in the basement, Jim would have pulled out his watch every time he passed, just to see him pluck at his beard from envy.

So now Dell's beautiful hair fell about her, rippling and shining like a cascade of brown waters. It reached below her knee and made itself almost a garment for her. And then she did it up again nervously and quickly. Once she faltered for a minute and stood still while a tear or two splashed on the worn red carpet.

On went her old brown jacket; on went her old brown hat. With a whirl of skirts and with the brilliant sparkle still in her eyes, she fluttered out the door and down the stairs to the street.

Where she stopped the sign read: "Mme. Sofronie. Hair Goods of All Kinds." One flight up Della ran—and collected herself, panting. Madame, large, too white, chilly, hardly looked the "Sofronie."

"Will you buy my hair?" asked Della.

"I buy hair," said Madame. "Take yer hat off and let's have a sight at the looks of it."

Down rippled the brown cascade.

"Twenty dollars," said Madame, lifting the mass with a practiced hand.

"Give it to me quick," said Della.

Oh, and the next two hours tripped by on rosy wings. Forget the hashed metaphor. She was ransacking the stores for Jim's present.

She found it at last. It surely had been made for Jim and no one else. There was no other like it in any of the stores, and she had turned

---

3. **pier glass:** a long, narrow mirror designed to fit between two windows.

4. **Queen of Sheba** (shē′bə): in the Bible, a queen from southern Arabia, famous for her wealth and beauty. When she heard of King Solomon's reputation for wisdom, she came to test him with hard questions.

all of them inside out. It was a platinum fob chain simple and chaste in design, properly proclaiming its value by substance alone and not by meretricious[5] ornamentation—as all good things should do. It was even worthy of The Watch. As soon as she saw it she knew that it must be Jim's. It was like him. Quietness and value—the description applied to both. Twenty-one dollars they took from her for it, and she hurried home with the eighty-seven cents. With that chain on his watch Jim might be properly anxious about the time in any company. Grand as the watch was, he sometimes looked at it on the sly on account of the old leather strap that he used in place of a chain.

When Della reached home her intoxication gave way a little to prudence and reason. She got out her curling irons and lighted the gas and went to work repairing the ravages made by generosity added to love. Which is always a tremendous task, dear friends—a mammoth task.

Within forty minutes her head was covered with tiny, close-lying curls that made her look wonderfully like a truant schoolboy. She looked at her reflection in the mirror long, carefully, and critically.

"If Jim doesn't kill me," she said to herself, "before he takes a second look at me, he'll say I look like a Coney Island chorus girl. But what could I do—oh! what could I do with a dollar and eighty-seven cents?"

At seven o'clock the coffee was made and the frying pan was on the back of the stove hot and ready to cook the chops.

Jim was never late. Della doubled the fob chain in her hand and sat on the corner of the table near the door that he always entered. Then she heard his step on the stair away down on the first flight, and she turned white

5. **meretricious** (mĕr′ə-trĭsh′əs): attractive in a cheap, flashy way.

for just a moment. She had a habit of saying little silent prayers about the simplest everyday things, and now she whispered, "Please, God, make him think I am still pretty."

The door opened and Jim stepped in and closed it. He looked thin and very serious. Poor fellow, he was only twenty-two—and to be burdened with a family! He needed a new overcoat and he was without gloves.

Jim stopped inside the door, as immovable as a setter at the scent of quail. His eyes were fixed upon Della; and there was an expression in them that she could not read, and it terrified her. It was not anger, nor surprise, nor disapproval, nor horror, nor any of the sentiments that she had been prepared for. He simply stared at her fixedly with that peculiar expression on his face.

Della wriggled off the table and went to him.

"Jim, darling," she cried, "don't look at me that way. I had my hair cut off and sold it because I couldn't have lived through Christmas without giving you a present. It'll grow out again—you won't mind, will you? I just had to do it. My hair grows awfully fast. Say 'Merry Christmas!' Jim, and let's be happy. You don't know what a nice—what a beautiful, nice gift I've got for you."

"You've cut off your hair?" asked Jim laboriously, as if he had not arrived at that patent fact yet even after the hardest mental labor.

"Cut it off and sold it," said Della. "Don't you like me just as well, anyhow? I'm me without my hair, ain't I?"

Jim looked about the room curiously.

"You say your hair is gone?" he said, with an air almost of idiocy.

"You needn't look for it," said Della. "It's sold, I tell you—sold and gone, too. It's Christmas Eve, boy. Be good to me, for it went for you. Maybe the hairs of my head were numbered," she went on with a sudden serious sweetness, "but nobody could ever count my love for you. Shall I put the chops on, Jim?"

Out of his trance Jim seemed quickly to wake. He enfolded his Della. For ten seconds let us regard with discreet scrutiny some inconsequential object in the other direction. Eight dollars a week or a million a year—what is the difference? A mathematician or a wit would give you the wrong answer. The Magi[6] brought valuable gifts, but that was not among them. This dark assertion will be illuminated later on.

Jim drew a package from his overcoat pocket and threw it upon the table.

"Don't make any mistake, Dell," he said, "about me. I don't think there's anything in the way of a haircut or a shave or a shampoo that could make me like my girl any less. But if you'll unwrap that package you may see why you had me going awhile at first."

White fingers and nimble tore at the string and paper. And then an ecstatic scream of joy; and then, alas! a quick feminine change to hysterical tears and wails, necessitating the immediate employment of all the comforting powers of the lord of the flat.

For there lay The Combs—the set of combs, side and back, that Della had worshiped for long in a Broadway window. Beautiful combs, pure tortoise shell, with jeweled rims—just the shade to wear in the beautiful vanished hair. They were expensive combs, she knew, and her heart had simply craved and yearned over them without the least hope of possession. And now they were hers, but the tresses that should have adorned the coveted adornments were gone.

But she hugged them to her bosom, and at length she was able to look up with dim eyes and a smile and say, "My hair grows so fast, Jim!"

And then Della leaped up like a little singed cat and cried, "Oh, oh!"

6. **Magi** (mā′jī′).

Jim had not yet seen his beautiful present. She held it out to him eagerly upon her open palm. The dull precious metal seemed to flash with a reflection of her bright and ardent spirit.

"Isn't it a dandy, Jim? I hunted all over town to find it. You'll have to look at the time a hundred times a day now. Give me your watch. I want to see how it looks on it."

Instead of obeying, Jim tumbled down on the couch and put his hands under the back of his head and smiled.

"Della," said he, "let's put our Christmas presents away and keep 'em awhile. They're too nice to use just at present. I sold the watch to get the money to buy your combs. And now suppose you put the chops on."

The Magi, as you know, were wise men—wonderfully wise men—who brought gifts to the Babe in the manger. They invented the art of giving Christmas presents. Being wise, their gifts were no doubt wise ones, possibly bearing the privilege of exchange in case of duplication. And here I have lamely related to you the uneventful chronicle of two foolish children in a flat who most unwisely sacrificed for each other the greatest treasures of their house. But in a last word to the wise of these days let it be said that of all who give gifts these two were the wisest. Of all who give and receive gifts, such as they are wisest. Everywhere they are wisest. They are the Magi.

Reading Check

1. What are the two prized possessions of Jim and Della?
2. How much money does Della get from Madame Sofronie?
3. What gift does Della choose for Jim?
4. What is contained in the package Jim has brought home?

For Study and Discussion

Analyzing and Interpreting Theme

1. What is the author's attitude toward Della? For example, do his humorous comments about her indicate that he thinks she is silly and impractical? Or are these comments affectionate and good-natured? Explain.

2. An ironic situation is one in which the characters' actions bring about an unexpected result. **a.** What is ironic about the outcome of "The Gift of the Magi"? **b.** Often, an ironic situation tends to belittle characters, to make them seem foolish or contemptible. Is this the case with Della and Jim? Why or why not?

3. O. Henry is famous for the surprise endings in his stories. Some of his endings have been criticized as unfair tricks. Is the end of "The Gift of the Magi" unfair? Or is it a logical ending, considering what you know about Jim and Della? Explain.

4a. What is the gift O. Henry refers to in the title and what has it to do with the Magi? **b.** Why, according to O. Henry, are people like Jim and Della "the wisest"?

Literary Elements

Theme

As you read "The Gift of the Magi," you probably realized that O. Henry was not simply telling a story about a young married couple whose plans misfire. Behind his plot and its surprise ending there is a controlling idea about what is important and unimportant in life. In the last paragraph of the story, he explicitly states his controlling idea—that love such as Della's and Jim's is far more important than any material gift. Such a controlling idea—an expression of a point of view about life—is called a **theme.** How does the story's theme give significance to Della and Jim, who otherwise might be viewed as an insignificant poor couple living in a large city?

Allusions

In expressing his theme, O. Henry compares Della's and Jim's gifts to the gifts of the Magi. He expects his readers to know the story of the three wise men who made the journey to Bethlehem to pay homage to the Christ Child. According to tradition, the Magi were three kings named Melchior, Gaspar, and Balthazar; the gifts they brought were gold, frankincense, and myrrh. Understanding the story's theme depends to some extent on recognizing this **allusion** to the Biblical story.

An allusion is an indirect reference to literature, history, art, music, or the like, which a writer expects readers to recognize. When an allusion is used effectively, it helps the reader call up certain associations that clarify or enrich the writer's meaning. At one point in his narrative, O. Henry makes an allusion to the Biblical story of Solomon and Sheba. Locate this allusion and tell how it is important to the plot and theme.

Language and Vocabulary

Learning About Word Histories

The study of the origin and development of words is called **etymology** (ĕt′ə-mŏl′ə-jē). The word *etymology* also refers to the history of a word. In a dictionary entry, information about the history of a word is usually shown in brackets. Here, for example, is the etymology, or history, of the word *Magi*, showing how it developed from earlier languages:

[Magi L., pl. of *magus* <Gr. *magos* <O Per. *magus* (or Iran. *magu-*) member of a priestly caste, magician <IE. base **magh-*, to be able, whence MIGHT, L. *machina*]

This etymology tells you that *Magi* is the Latin plural of *magus*, which comes from the Greek word *magos*, which itself was derived from an Old Persian or Iranian word meaning a "member of a priestly caste or a magician." The base of the word can be traced back to an Indo-European family of languages. The word *Magi* is related through this ancestor to *might*, which came into the English language through another Latin word, *machina*.

The abbreviations used in etymologies are generally explained in the front matter of a dictionary. Become familiar with the symbols and abbreviations used in your own dictionary.

Using an unabridged or college dictionary, answer the following questions about words used in "The Gift of the Magi."

1. What is the meaning of the Latin word *calculus,* a root for our word *calculate*?

2. To which languages can we trace the word *cascade*?

3. What is the original slang meaning of *coax*?

4. The word *dandy* is probably a playful form of what boy's name?

5. What are the meanings of *in + toxicare,* responsible for our word *intoxicate*?

6. What are the meanings of *rann + saka,* the roots of *ransack*?

7. What language can *shabby* be traced back to?

8. What is the meaning of *transe,* an Old French ancestor of *trance*?

9. To which languages can we trace the word *treasure*?

10. What is the meaning of the Old French origin of *truant*?

Writing About Literature

Evaluating a Story

"The Gift of the Magi" is one of the most famous short stories ever written. It has appeared in countless anthologies. What do you think is the reason for the story's appeal? In your estimation, how important is the surprise ending? How important is the theme?

Focus on Narrative Writing

Exploring Themes

The **theme** of a story is its main idea about life or its basic meaning. Some writers know the theme they want to express before they start to write a story. For other writers the theme may emerge or undergo transformations while a story is in the process of creation.

Select a theme for a brief story of your own. You may use one of the following suggestions, or you may choose another theme.

1. It takes time for true friendship to develop.
2. True love is forgiving.
3. Laughter is the best medicine.
4. Anything worth doing is worth doing well.

When you have chosen a theme, make some notes on the plot, setting, and characters that you might use to develop the theme into a story. Save your notes.

About the Author

O. Henry   (1862–1910)

The Granger Collection, New York

O. Henry's real name was William Sydney Porter. The son of a doctor, he grew up in Greensboro, North Carolina. When he was twenty, he moved to Texas for reasons of health. He settled in Austin, where he worked as a clerk, bookkeeper, and bank teller. To earn more money, he began contributing news items and sketches to newspapers throughout the country, and in 1895, he moved to Houston to work as a reporter for the Houston *Post*. Nine months later he was called back to Austin to stand trial for bank embezzlement. Porter was almost certainly innocent of the charge. The bank he had worked for was notoriously lax in its accounting procedures, and Porter himself had probably been no more than careless. He boarded a train to Austin, but on impulse he went to New Orleans instead, and then to Honduras in Central America. Three years later, the news that his wife was seriously ill brought him back to Texas. He stood trial, was convicted, and served five years in prison.

When he was released, he went to Pittsburgh, Pennsylvania, where he began once again to write. His editors encouraged him to move to New York. It was in New York that Porter adopted the pen name of O. Henry and became a famous writer of short stories. He was a prolific writer. In 1905 alone he wrote sixty-five short stories. In his stories, he drew on his experiences out West and in Latin America. Above all, he drew on his knowledge of and fascination with New York, whose streets he roamed in search of ideas. He called New York "Baghdad-on-the-Subway," comparing it to the fabulous city of Scheherazade's *A Thousand and One Nights*. Some of his best stories are collected in *The Four Million, The Voice of the City, Hearts of the West, The Gentle Grafter,* and *Whirligigs*.

The Balek Scales

HEINRICH BÖLL

Translated by
Leila Vennewitz

You have seen that an object used as a symbol can stand for something larger than itself. In what way do the Balek scales function as a symbol in this story?

Where my grandfather came from, most of the people lived by working in the flax sheds. For five generations they had been breathing in the dust which rose from the crushed flax stalks, letting themselves be killed off by slow degrees, a race of long-suffering, cheerful people who ate goat cheese, potatoes, and now and then a rabbit; in the evening they would sit at home spinning and knitting; they sang, drank mint tea and were happy. During the day they would carry the flax stalks to the antiquated machines, with no protection from the dust and at the mercy of the heat which came pouring out of the drying kilns. Each cottage contained only one bed, standing against the wall like a closet and reserved for the parents, while the children slept all round the room on benches. In the morning the room would be filled with the odor of thin soup; on Sundays there was stew, and on feast days the children's faces would light up with pleasure as they watched the black acorn coffee turning paler and paler from the milk their smiling mother poured into their coffee mugs.

The parents went off early to the flax sheds; the housework was left to the children: they would sweep the room, tidy up, wash the dishes and peel the potatoes, precious pale-yellow fruit whose thin peel had to be produced afterwards to dispel any suspicion of extravagance or carelessness.

As soon as the children were out of school they had to go off into the woods and, depending on the season, gather mushrooms and herbs: woodruff and thyme, caraway, mint and foxglove, and in summer, when they had brought in the hay from their meager fields, they gathered hayflowers. A kilo[1] of hayflowers was worth one pfennig,[2] and they were sold by the apothecaries in town for twenty pfennigs a kilo to highly strung ladies. The mushrooms were highly prized: they fetched twenty pfennigs a kilo and were sold in the shops in town for one mark[3] twenty. The

---

1. **kilo** (kē′lō): short for *kilogram*, a unit of weight a little over two pounds.
2. **pfennig** (fĕn′ĭg): a coin like the United States penny.
3. **mark:** at one time, the monetary unit in several European countries; now the monetary unit in Germany. There are one hundred pfennigs to a mark.

children would crawl deep into the green darkness of the forest during the autumn when dampness drove the mushrooms out of the soil, and almost every family had its own places where it gathered mushrooms, places which were handed down in whispers from generation to generation.

The woods belonged to the Baleks, as well as the flax sheds, and in my grandfather's village the Baleks had a château, and the wife of the head of the family had a little room next to the dairy where mushrooms, herbs and hayflowers were weighed and paid for. There on the table stood the great Balek scales, an old-fashioned, ornate bronze-gilt contraption, which my grandfather's grandparents had already faced when they were children, their grubby hands holding their little baskets of mushrooms, their paper bags of hayflowers, breathlessly watching the number of weights Frau Balek had to throw on the scale before the swinging pointer came to rest exactly over the black line, that thin line of justice which had to be redrawn every year. Then Frau Balek would take the big book covered in brown leather, write down the weight, and pay out the money, pfennigs or ten-pfennigs or ten-pfennig pieces and very, very occasionally, a mark. And when my grandfather was a child there was a big glass jar of lemon drops standing there, the kind that cost one mark a kilo, and when Frau Balek—whichever one happened to be presiding over the little room—was in a good mood, she would put her hand into this jar and give each child a lemon drop, and the children's faces would light up with pleasure, the way they used to when on feast days their mother poured milk into their coffee mugs, milk that made the coffee turn paler and paler until it was as pale as the flaxen pigtails of the little girls.

One of the laws imposed by the Baleks on the village was: No one was permitted to have any scales in the house. The law was so ancient that nobody gave a thought as to when and how it had arisen, and it had to be obeyed, for anyone who broke it was dismissed from the flax sheds, he could not sell his mushrooms or his thyme or his hayflowers, and the power of the Baleks was so far-reaching that no one in the neighboring villages would give him work either, or buy his forest herbs. But since the days when my grandfather's parents had gone out as small children to gather mushrooms and sell them in order that they might season the meat of the rich people of Prague[4] or be baked into game pies, it had never occurred to anyone to break this law: flour could be measured in cups, eggs could be counted, what they had spun could be measured by the yard, and besides, the old-fashioned bronze-gilt, ornate Balek scales did not look as if there was anything wrong with them, and five generations had entrusted the swinging black pointer with what they had gone out as eager children to gather from the woods.

True, there were some among these quiet people who flouted the law, poachers bent on making more money in one night than they could earn in a whole month in the flax sheds, but even these people apparently never thought of buying scales or making their own. My grandfather was the first person bold enough to test the justice of the Baleks, the family who lived in the château and drove two carriages, who always maintained one boy from the village while he studied theology at the seminary in Prague, the family with whom the priest played taroc every Wednesday, on whom the local reeve,[5] in his carriage emblazoned with the Imperial coat of arms, made an annual New Year's Day call and on whom the Emperor conferred a title on the first day of the year 1900.

4. **Prague** (präg): the capital of Czechoslovakia.
5. **reeve:** the chief officer of a district.

My grandfather was hardworking and smart: he crawled further into the woods than the children of his clan had crawled before him, he penetrated as far as the thicket where, according to legend, Bilgan the Giant was supposed to dwell, guarding a treasure. But my grandfather was not afraid of Bilgan: he worked his way deep into the thicket, even when he was quite little, and brought out great quantities of mushrooms; he even found truffles, for which Frau Balek paid thirty pfennigs a pound. Everything my grandfather took to the Baleks he entered on the back of a torn-off calendar page: every pound of mushrooms, every gram of thyme, and on the right-hand side, in his childish handwriting, he entered the amount he received for each item; he scrawled in every pfennig, from the age of seven to the age of twelve, and by the time he was twelve the year 1900 had arrived, and because the Baleks had been raised to the aristocracy by the Emperor, they gave every family in the village a quarter of a pound of real coffee, the Brazilian kind; there was also free beer and tobacco for the men, and at the château there was a great banquet; many carriages stood in the avenue of poplars leading from the entrance gates to the château.

But the day before the banquet the coffee was distributed in the little room which had housed the Balek scales for almost a hundred years, and the Balek family was now called Balek von Bilgan because, according to legend, Bilgan the Giant used to have a great castle on the site of the present Balek estate.

My grandfather often used to tell me how he went there after school to fetch the coffee for four families: the Cechs, the Weidlers, the Vohlas and his own, the Brüchers. It was the afternoon of New Year's Eve: there were the front rooms to be decorated, the baking to be done, and the families did not want to spare four boys and have each of them go all the way to the château to bring back a quarter of a pound of coffee.

And so my grandfather sat on the narrow wooden bench in the little room while Gertrud the maid counted out the wrapped four-ounce packages of coffee, four of them, and he looked at the scales and saw that the pound weight was still lying on the left-hand scale; Frau Balek von Bilgan was busy with preparations for the banquet. And when Gertrud was about to put her hand into the jar with the lemon drops to give my grandfather one, she discovered it was empty: it was refilled once a year, and held one kilo of the kind that cost a mark.

Gertrud laughed and said: "Wait here while I get the new lot," and my grandfather waited with the four four-ounce packages which had been wrapped and sealed in the factory, facing the scales on which someone had left the pound weight, and my grandfather took the four packages of coffee, put them on the empty scale, and his heart thudded as he watched the black finger of justice come to rest on the left of the black line: the scale with the pound weight stayed down, and the pound of coffee remained up in the air; his heart thudded more than if he had been lying behind a bush in the forest waiting for Bilgan the Giant, and he felt in his pocket for the pebbles he always carried with him so he could use his catapult to shoot the sparrows which pecked away at his mother's cabbage plants—he had to put three, four, five pebbles beside the packages of coffee before the scale with the pound weight rose and the pointer at last came to rest over the black line. My grandfather took the coffee from the scale, wrapped the five pebbles in his kerchief, and when Gertrud came back with the big kilo bag of lemon drops which had to last for another whole year in order to make the children's faces light up with pleasure, when Gertrud let the lemon drops rattle into the glass jar, the pale little fellow was still standing there, and nothing seemed to have changed. My grandfather only took three of the packages, then Gertrud looked in startled surprise at the white-faced child who threw the lemon drop onto the floor, ground it under his heel, and said: "I want to see Frau Balek."

"Balek von Bilgan, if you please," said Gertrud.

"All right, Frau Balek von Bilgan," but Gertrud only laughed at him, and he walked back to the village in the dark, took the Cechs, the Weidlers and the Vohlas their coffee, and said he had to go and see the priest.

Instead he went out into the dark night with his five pebbles in his kerchief. He had to walk a long way before he found someone who had scales, who was permitted to have them; no one in the villages of Blaugau and Bernau had any, he knew that, and he went straight through them till, after two hours' walking, he reached the little town of Dielheim where Honig the apothecary lived. From Honig's house came the smell of fresh pancakes, and Honig's breath, when he opened the door to the half-frozen boy, already smelled of punch, there was a moist cigar between his narrow lips, and he clasped the boy's cold hands firmly for a moment, saying: "What's the matter, has your father's lung got worse?"

"No, I haven't come for medicine, I wanted . . ." My grandfather undid his kerchief, took out the five pebbles, held them out to Honig and said: "I wanted to have these weighed." He glanced anxiously into Honig's face, but when Honig said nothing and did not get angry, or even ask him anything, my grandfather said: "It is the amount that is short of justice," and now, as he went into the warm room, my grandfather realized how wet his feet were. The snow had soaked through his cheap shoes, and in the forest the branches had showered him with snow which was now melting, and he was tired and hungry and suddenly began to cry because he thought of the quantities of mushrooms, the herbs, the flowers, which had been weighed on the scales which were short five pebbles' worth of justice. And when Honig, shaking his head and holding the five pebbles, called his wife, my grandfather thought of the generations of his parents, his grandparents, who had all had to have their mushrooms, their flowers, weighed on the scales, and he was overwhelmed by a great wave of injustice, and began to sob louder than ever, and, without waiting to be asked, he sat down on a chair, ignoring the pancakes, the cup of hot coffee which nice plump Frau Honig put in front of him, and did not stop crying till Honig himself came out from the shop at the back and, rattling the pebbles in his hand, said in a low voice to his wife: "Fifty-five grams, exactly."

My grandfather walked the two hours home through the forest, got a beating at home, said nothing, not a single word, when he was asked about the coffee, spent the whole evening doing sums on the piece of paper on which he had written down everything he had sold to Frau Balek, and when midnight struck, and the cannon could be heard from the château, and the whole village rang with shouting and laughter and the noise of rattles, when the family kissed and embraced all round, he said into the New Year silence: "The Baleks owe me eighteen marks and thirty-two pfennigs." And again he thought of all the children there were in the village, of his brother Fritz who had gathered so many mushrooms, of his sister Ludmilla; he thought of the many hundreds of children who had all gathered mushrooms for the Baleks, and herbs and flowers, and this time he did not cry but told his parents and brothers and sisters of his discovery.

When the Baleks von Bilgan went to High Mass on New Year's Day, their new coat of

Three Shepherds (1955) by Alex Colville. Tempera.

arms—a giant crouching under a fir tree—already emblazoned in blue and gold on their carriage, they saw the hard, pale faces of the people all staring at them. They had expected garlands in the village, a song in their honor, cheers and hurrahs, but the village was completely deserted as they drove through it, and in church the pale faces of the people were turned toward them, mute and hostile, and when the priest mounted the pulpit to deliver his New Year's sermon he sensed the chill in those otherwise quiet and peaceful faces, and he stumbled painfully through his sermon and went back to the altar drenched in sweat. And as the Baleks von Bilgan left the church after Mass, they walked through a lane of mute, pale faces. But young Frau Balek von Bilgan stopped in front of the children's pews, sought out my grandfather's face, pale little Franz Brücher, and asked him, right there in the church: "Why didn't you take the coffee for your mother?" And my grandfather stood up and said: "Because you owe me as much money as five kilos of coffee would cost." And

The Balek Scales **185**

he pulled the five pebbles from his pocket, held them out to the young woman and said: "This much, fifty-five grams, is short in every pound of your justice"; and before the woman could say anything the men and women in the church lifted up their voices and sang: "The justice of this earth, O Lord, hath put Thee to death. . . ."

While the Baleks were at church, Wilhelm Vohla, the poacher, had broken into the little room, stolen the scales and the big fat leather-bound book in which had been entered every kilo of mushrooms, every kilo of hayflowers, everything bought by the Baleks in the village, and all afternoon of that New Year's Day the men of the village sat in my great-grandparents' front room and calculated, calculated one tenth of everything that had been bought—but when they had calculated many thousands of talers[6] and had still not come to an end, the reeve's gendarmes[7] arrived, made their way into my great-grandfather's front room, shouting and stabbing as they came, and removed the scales and the book by force. My grandfather's little sister Ludmilla lost her life, a few men were wounded, and one of the gendarmes was stabbed to death by Wilhelm Vohla the poacher.

Our village was not the only one to rebel: Blaugau and Bernau did too, and for almost a week no work was done in the flax sheds. But a great many gendarmes appeared, and the men and women were threatened with prison, and the Baleks forced the priest to display the scales publicly in the school and demonstrate that the finger of justice swing to and fro accurately. And the men and women went back to the flax sheds—but no one went to the school to watch the priest: he stood there all alone, helpless and forlorn with his weights, scales, and packages of coffee.

6. **talers** (tä'lərz): silver coins.
7. **gendarmes** (zhän'därmz): a semimilitary police force.

And the children went back to gathering mushrooms, to gathering thyme, flowers and foxglove, but every Sunday, as soon as the Baleks entered the church, the hymn was struck up: "The justice of this earth, O Lord, hath put Thee to death," until the reeve ordered it proclaimed in every village that the singing of the hymn was forbidden.

My grandfather's parents had to leave the village, and the new grave of their little daughter; they became basket weavers, but did not stay long anywhere because it pained them to see how everywhere the finger of justice swung falsely. They walked along behind their cart, which crept slowly over the country roads, taking their thin goat with them, and passers-by could sometimes hear a voice from the cart singing: "The justice of this earth, O Lord, hath put Thee to death." And those who wanted to listen could hear the tale of the Baleks von Bilgan, whose justice lacked a tenth part. But there were few who listened.

Reading Check

1. How were the children kept employed while their parents worked in the flax sheds?
2. What law had the Baleks imposed on the village?
3. What kind of record was kept by the narrator's grandfather?
4. Why did the narrator's grandfather go to the home of Honig the apothecary?
5. How was the rebellion of the villagers suppressed?

For Study and Discussion

Analyzing and Interpreting the Story

1. The narrator is telling a story about his grandfather's boyhood in a small village in Europe. **a.** What impression do you get of these villagers and the way that they lived? **b.** How would you describe their attitude toward the laws imposed by the Baleks?

2. The Balek family becomes known as Balek von Bilgan, after the giant Bilgan. Recall what you know about wicked giants in folk stories. **a.** In what way is the Balek family like such giants? **b.** How does such a comparison make clear the narrator's attitude toward the Baleks?

3. In the central incident of the story, the narrator's grandfather, Franz Brücher, makes an important discovery. **a.** What does he learn about the Balek scales? **b.** What do you know about his character that prepares you for his subsequent actions?

4a. After the villagers learn of Franz's discovery, what happens? **b.** Do you feel that the story's ending is the logical outcome of earlier events? Give reasons for your answer.

5. As you read "The Balek Scales," you probably began to realize that it is not simply about one group of people in one village. The story also expresses a **theme,** a general idea about life. Try to state the theme of this story in a sentence or two. As you formulate the theme, keep in mind the story's ending as well as the words of the hymn that the villagers sing.

6. Throughout the story the narrator uses irony to point up the contrast between appearance and reality. Find examples of this irony in the story and tell how it serves to reinforce the theme.

Literary Elements

Expressing a Theme

If you have already read "The Gift of the Magi," you have found that O. Henry explicitly states the theme of the story in the final paragraph. Heinrich Böll makes no such explicit statement. Yet passages and details throughout the story help make readers aware that a general idea is being expressed through specific incidents. The general idea, or theme, concerns justice and injustice on earth. Notice how, near the end of the story, a reference to Bilgan the Giant emphasizes the unjust relationship between the Baleks and the people in the village.

> When the Baleks von Bilgan went to High Mass on New Year's Day, their new coat of arms—a giant crouching under a fir tree—already emblazoned in blue and gold on their carriage, they saw the hard, pale faces of the people all staring at them (pages 184–185).

The people have already learned how the Baleks have cheated them for five generations. The image of a wicked giant crouching under a tree, waiting to ambush the unwary traveler, suggests both the power and the unjust actions of the Baleks.

How do the following passages help express the story's theme?

> There on the table stood the great Balek scales . . . which my grandfather's grandparents had already faced when they were children, . . . breathlessly watching the number of weights Frau Balek had to throw on the scale before the swinging pointer came to rest exactly over the black line, that thin line of justice which had to be re-drawn every year (page 182).

> One of the laws imposed by the Baleks on the village was: No one was permitted to have any scales in the house. The law was so ancient that nobody gave a thought as to when and how it had arisen . . . (page 182).

My grandfather undid his kerchief, took out the five pebbles, held them out to Honig and said: "I wanted to have these weighed." He glanced anxiously into Honig's face, but when Honig said nothing and did not get angry, or even ask him anything, my grandfather said: "It is the amount that is short of justice" . . . (page 184).

Find other passages in "The Balek Scales" that help make readers aware of the story's theme.

Language and Vocabulary

Using Context Clues

Sometimes the meaning of a word is clear because of the context in which it appears. For example, the meanings of *ornate* and *contraption* are clear because of clues in the rest of this passage:

> There on the table stood the great Balek scales, an old-fashioned, *ornate* bronze-gilt *contraption* . . .

"Bronze-gilt" suggests decoration, so one can guess that *ornate* means "heavily decorated." The phrase "an old-fashioned, ornate bronze-gilt contraption" is another way of describing "the great Balek scales," so it is evident that a *contraption* is some kind of object, or more specifically a device or gadget.

Use context clues to determine the meaning of the italicized words in these other passages from the story. You may check your answers in the glossary or in a dictionary.

> . . . when Frau Balek—whichever one happened to be *presiding* over the little room—was in a good mood, she would put her hand into this jar and give each child a lemon drop . . .

> True, there were some among these quiet people who *flouted* the law, poachers bent on making more money in one night than they could earn in a whole month in the flax sheds . . .

> . . . the local reeve, in his carriage *emblazoned* with the Imperial coat of arms, made an annual New Year's Day call and on whom the Emperor *conferred* a title on the first day of the year 1900.

> . . . he felt in his pocket for the pebbles he always carried with him so he could use his *catapult* to shoot the sparrows . . .

> They had expected *garlands* in the village, a song in their honor, cheers and hurrahs, but the village was completely deserted as they drove through it . . .

Writing About Literature

Discussing a Symbol

Write a brief essay in which you discuss the symbolic meaning of the Balek scales. Take into account what the scales look like, how old they are, and how they are used. Show the connection between the symbol and the general idea, or theme, of the story.

Creative Writing

Writing a Sentence That Builds to a Climax

When the narrator tells about his grandfather going home on New Year's Eve and finally declaring that the Baleks are dishonest, he does it all in one sentence.

> My grandfather walked the two hours home through the forest, got a beating at home, said nothing, not a single word, when he was asked about the coffee, spent the whole evening doing some sums on the piece of paper on which he had written down everything he had sold to Frau Balek, and when midnight struck, and the cannon could be heard from the château, and the whole village rang with shouting and laughter and the noise of rattles, when the family kissed and embraced all round, he said into the New Year silence: "The Baleks owe me eighteen marks and thirty-two pfennigs."

Notice how all the details of the sentence build to a high point, the boy's outburst. You have a sense of the boy's outrage building up through the evening in dramatic contrast to the merriment of the villagers, who are still innocent of the truth.

Write your own climactic sentence, using details that build to a high point at the end. (Your sentence need not be as long as Böll's.) Choose your own subject or use one of the following:

A racer beginning slowly, gaining speed, and coming to the finish line

Two students trying to pass each other in a narrow school corridor

Paul Revere riding to warn the colonists about the British

The last few minutes of a basketball (hockey, football, tennis) game where the score is tied

Focus on Narrative Writing

Thinking About Theme and Tone

Tone is the attitude that a writer expresses or implies toward the subject, the characters, and the audience. The tone of a story can be serious or humorous, tender or ironic, dignified or informal, angry or philosophical.

The tone of a story is usually related to its **theme,** or central idea. For example, in "The Balek Scales" Böll uses a serious, ironic tone. This tone is appropriate for his theme, which deals with injustice and oppression of the weak by the strong.

Make some notes about a movie or TV episode that you have seen recently and enjoyed. Freewrite about the characters, the main events, and the setting for a few minutes. Then state the theme of the story in one or two sentences. Use another sentence or two to describe the story's tone. Save your writing.

About the Author

Heinrich Böll   (1917–1985)

Heinrich Böll (bœl) was born in Cologne, Germany. He served in the German army during World War II, mostly on the Russian front, and was wounded four times. After his release from a prisoner-of-war camp in 1945, he returned to Cologne. There he found a job with the city government and began to write. In his novels and short stories, Böll probed the nature of German society.

In 1972 Böll was awarded the Nobel Prize for Literature for his contributions "to a renewal of German literature." Critics have noted a strong vein of ironic humor that runs through his basically serious work. One German critic has called him "Germany's best as well as best-selling author whose work is both profound and eminently readable."

Literature and Symbols

The Measure of Justice

In a number of cultural traditions, scales are associated with justice. For example, in classical mythology, Astraea, the goddess of human justice, is often pictured holding scales.

Making Connections: Activities

1. Consider whether the symbol of the scales is appropriate for the concept of justice. Why is the goddess pictured with a sword and a blindfold?

2. Using a dictionary of symbols or mythology, locate cultural traditions that have used the scales as a symbol for justice.

The Necklace

GUY DE MAUPASSANT

As you read this famous short story, note the author's attitude toward his central character. Do you share his attitude or do you have a different opinion about the character?

She was one of those pretty and charming girls, born, as if by an accident of fate, into a family of clerks. With no dowry, no prospects, no way of any kind of being met, understood, loved, and married by a man both prosperous and famous, she was finally married to a minor clerk in the Ministry of Education.

She dressed plainly because she could not afford fine clothes, but was as unhappy as a woman who has come down in the world; for women have no family rank or social class. With them, beauty, grace, and charm take the place of birth and breeding. Their natural poise, their instinctive good taste, and their mental cleverness are the sole guiding principles which make daughters of the common people the equals of ladies in high society.

She grieved incessantly, feeling that she had been born for all the little niceties and luxuries of living. She grieved over the shabbiness of her apartment, the dinginess of the walls, the worn-out appearance of the chairs, the ugliness of the draperies. All these things, which another woman of her class would not even have noticed, gnawed at her and made her furious. The sight of the little Breton[1] girl who did her humble housework roused in her disconsolate regrets and wild daydreams. She would dream of silent chambers, draped with Oriental tapestries and lighted by tall bronze floor lamps, and of two handsome butlers in knee breeches, who, drowsy from the heavy warmth cast by the central stove, dozed in large overstuffed armchairs.

She would dream of great reception halls hung with old silks, of fine furniture filled with priceless curios, and of small, stylish, scented sitting rooms just right for the four o'clock chat with intimate friends, with distinguished and sought-after men whose attention every woman envies and longs to attract.

When dining at the round table, covered for the third day with the same cloth, opposite her husband, who would raise the cover of the soup tureen, declaring delightedly, "Ah! a good stew! There's nothing I like better . . ." she would dream of fashionable dinner parties, of gleaming silverware, of tapestries making the walls alive with characters out of history and strange birds in a fairyland forest; she would dream of delicious dishes served on wonderful china, of gallant compliments whispered and listened to with a sphinxlike smile as one eats the rosy flesh of a trout or nibbles at the wings of a grouse.

She had no evening clothes, no jewels, noth-

1. **Breton** (brĕt'n): a native of Brittany, a province in northwestern France.

ing. But those were the things she wanted; she felt that was the kind of life for her. She so much longed to please, be envied, be fascinating and sought after.

She had a well-to-do friend, a classmate of convent-school days whom she would no longer go to see, simply because she would feel so distressed on returning home. And she would weep for days on end from vexation, regret, despair, and anguish.

Then one evening, her husband came home proudly holding out a large envelope.

"Look," he said, "I've got something for you."

She excitedly tore open the envelope and pulled out a printed card bearing these words:

"The Minister of Education and Mme. Georges Ramponneau[2] beg M. and Mme. Loisel[3] to do them the honor of attending an evening reception at the Ministerial Mansion on Friday, January 18."

Instead of being delighted, as her husband had hoped, she scornfully tossed the invitation on the table, murmuring, "What good is that to me?"

"But, my dear, I thought you'd be thrilled to death. You never get a chance to go out, and this is a real affair, a wonderful one! I had an awful time getting a card. Everybody wants one; it's much sought after, and not many clerks have a chance at one. You'll see all the most important people there."

She gave him an irritated glance and burst out impatiently, "What do you think I have to go in?"

He hadn't given that a thought. He stammered, "Why, the dress you wear when we go to the theater. That looks quite nice, I think."

He stopped talking, dazed and distracted to see his wife burst out weeping. Two large tears slowly rolled from the corners of her eyes to the corners of her mouth; he gasped, "Why, what's the matter? What's the trouble?"

By sheer will power she overcame her outburst and answered in a calm voice while wiping the tears from her wet cheeks:

"Oh, nothing. Only I don't have an evening dress and therefore I can't go to that affair. Give the card to some friend at the office whose wife can dress better than I can."

He was stunned. He resumed, "Let's see, Mathilde.[4] How much would a suitable outfit cost—one you could wear for other affairs too—something very simple?"

She thought it over for several seconds, going over her allowance and thinking also of the amount she could ask for without bringing an immediate refusal and an exclamation of dismay from the thrifty clerk.

Finally, she answered hesitatingly, "I'm not sure exactly, but I think with four hundred francs[5] I could manage it."

He turned a bit pale, for he had set aside just that amount to buy a rifle so that, the following summer, he could join some friends who were getting up a group to shoot larks on the plain near Nanterre.[6]

However, he said, "All right. I'll give you four hundred francs. But try to get a nice dress."

As the day of the party approached, Mme. Loisel seemed sad, moody, and ill at ease. Her outfit was ready, however. Her husband said to her one evening, "What's the matter? You've been all out of sorts for three days."

And she answered, "It's embarrassing not to

2. **Mme. Georges Ramponneau** (ma-dam′ zhôrzh ram′ pə-nō).
3. **M. . . . Loisel** (mə-syûr′ . . . lwa-zĕl′).

4. **Mathilde** (ma-tēld′).
5. **four hundred francs:** at that time, about eighty dollars.
6. **Nanterre** (nȧN-târ′): a town near Paris.

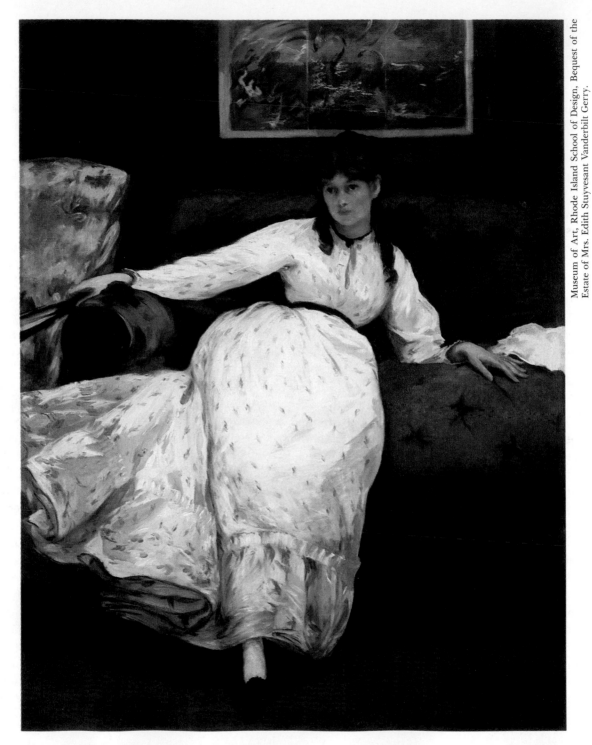

Le Repos (portrait of Berthe Morisot) by Edouard Manet (1832–1883). Oil on canvas, 58¼ x 43¾ in.

have a jewel or a gem—nothing to wear on my dress. I'll look like a pauper: I'd almost rather not go to that party."

He answered, "Why not wear some flowers? They're very fashionable this season. For ten francs you can get two or three gorgeous roses."

She wasn't at all convinced. "No. . . . There's nothing more humiliating than to look poor among a lot of rich women."

But her husband exclaimed, "My, but you're silly! Go see your friend Mme. Forestier[7] and ask her to lend you some jewelry. You and she know each other well enough for you to do that."

She gave a cry of joy, "Why, that's so! I hadn't thought of it."

The next day she paid her friend a visit and told her of her predicament.

Mme. Forestier went toward a large closet with mirrored doors, took out a large jewel box, brought it over, opened it, and said to Mme. Loisel: "Pick something out, my dear."

At first her eyes noted some bracelets, then a pearl necklace, then a Venetian cross, gold and gems, of marvelous workmanship. She tried on these adornments in front of the mirror, but hesitated, unable to decide which to part with and put back. She kept on asking, "Haven't you something else?"

"Oh, yes, keep on looking. I don't know just what you'd like."

All at once she found, in a black satin box, a superb diamond necklace; and her pulse beat faster with longing. Her hands trembled as she took it up. Clasping it around her throat, outside her high-necked dress, she stood in ecstasy looking at her reflection.

Then she asked, hesitatingly, pleading, "Could I borrow that, just that and nothing else?"

"Why, of course."

She threw her arms around her friend, kissed her warmly, and fled with her treasure.

The day of the party arrived. Mme. Loisel was a sensation. She was the prettiest one there, fashionable, gracious, smiling, and wild with joy. All the men turned to look at her, asked who she was, begged to be introduced. All the Cabinet officials wanted to waltz with her. The minister took notice of her.

She danced madly, wildly, drunk with pleasure, giving no thought to anything in the triumph of her beauty, the pride of her success, in a kind of happy cloud composed of all the adulation, of all the admiring glances, of all the awakened longings, of a sense of complete victory that is so sweet to a woman's heart.

She left around four o'clock in the morning. Her husband, since midnight, had been dozing in a small empty sitting room with three other gentlemen whose wives were having too good a time.

He threw over her shoulders the wraps he had brought for going home, modest garments of everyday life whose shabbiness clashed with the stylishness of her evening clothes. She felt this and longed to escape, unseen by the other women who were draped in expensive furs.

Loisel held her back.

"Hold on! You'll catch cold outside. I'll call a cab."

But she wouldn't listen to him and went rapidly down the stairs. When they were on the street, they didn't find a carriage; and they set out to hunt for one, hailing drivers whom they saw going by at a distance.

They walked toward the Seine,[8] disconsolate and shivering. Finally on the docks they found one of those carriages that one sees in Paris only after nightfall, as if they were ashamed to

---

7. **Forestier** (fô-rə-styā′).

8. **Seine** (sĕn): a river that runs through Paris.

show their drabness during daylight hours.

It dropped them at their door in the Rue des Martyrs, and they climbed wearily up to their apartment. For her, it was all over. For him, there was the thought that he would have to be at the Ministry at ten o'clock.

Before the mirror, she let the wraps fall from her shoulders to see herself once again in all her glory. Suddenly she gave a cry. The necklace was gone.

Her husband, already half undressed, said, "What's the trouble?"

She turned toward him despairingly, "I . . . I . . . I don't have Mme. Forestier's necklace."

"What! You can't mean it! It's impossible!"

They hunted everywhere, through the folds of the dress, through the folds of the coat, in the pockets. They found nothing.

He asked, "Are you sure you had it when leaving the dance?"

"Yes, I felt it when I was in the hall of the Ministry."

"But if you had lost it on the street we'd have heard it drop. It must be in the cab."

"Yes, Quite likely. Did you get its number?"

"No. Didn't you notice it either?"

"No."

They looked at each other aghast. Finally Loisel got dressed again.

"I'll retrace our steps on foot," he said, "to see if I can find it."

And he went out. She remained in her evening clothes, without the strength to go to bed, slumped in a chair in the unheated room, her mind a blank.

Her husband came in about seven o'clock. He had had no luck.

He went to the police station, to the newspapers to post a reward, to the cab companies, everywhere the slightest hope drove him.

That evening Loisel returned, pale, his face lined; still he had learned nothing.

"We'll have to write your friend," he said, "to tell her you have broken the catch and are having it repaired. That will give us a little time to turn around."

She wrote to his dictation.

At the end of a week, they had given up all hope.

And Loisel, looking five years older, declared, "We must take steps to replace that piece of jewelry."

The next day they took the case to the jeweler whose name they found inside. He consulted his records. "I didn't sell that necklace, madame," he said. "I only supplied the case."

Then they went from one jeweler to another hunting for a similar necklace, going over their recollections, both sick with despair and anxiety.

They found, in a shop in Palais Royal,[9] a string of diamonds which seemed exactly like the one they were seeking. It was priced at forty thousand francs. They could get it for thirty-six.

They asked the jeweler to hold it for them for three days. And they reached an agreement that he would take it back for thirty-four thousand if the lost one was found before the end of February.

Loisel had eighteen thousand francs he had inherited from his father. He would borrow the rest.

He went about raising the money, asking a thousand francs from one, four hundred from another, a hundred here, sixty there. He signed notes, made ruinous deals, did business with loan sharks, ran the whole gamut of moneylenders. He compromised the rest of his life, risked his signature without knowing if he'd be able to honor it, and then, terrified by the outlook for the future, by the blackness of despair about to close around him, by the pros-

9. **Palais Royal** (på-lā′ rwȧ-yȧl′): a section of Paris with fashionable stores.

pect of all the privations of the body and tortures of the spirit, he went to claim the new necklace with the thirty-six thousand francs which he placed on the counter of the shopkeeper.

When Mme. Loisel took the necklace back, Mme. Forestier said to her frostily, "You should have brought it back sooner; I might have needed it."

She didn't open the case, an action her friend was afraid of. If she had noticed the substitution, what would she have thought? What would she have said? Would she have thought her a thief?

Mme. Loisel experienced the horrible life the needy live. She played her part, however, with sudden heroism. That frightful debt had to be paid. She would pay it. She dismissed her maid; they rented a garret under the eaves.

She learned to do the heavy housework, to perform the hateful duties of cooking. She washed dishes, wearing down her shell-pink nails scouring the grease from pots and pans; she scrubbed dirty linen, shirts, and cleaning rags which she hung on a line to dry; she took the garbage down to the street each morning and brought up water, stopping on each landing to get her breath. And, clad like a peasant woman, basket on arm, guarding sou[10] by sou her scanty allowance, she bargained with the fruit dealers, the grocer, the butcher, and was insulted by them.

Each month notes had to be paid, and others renewed to give more time.

Her husband labored evenings to balance a tradesman's accounts, and at night, often, he copied documents at five sous a page.

And this went on for ten years.

Finally, all was paid back, everything including the exorbitant rates of the loan sharks and accumulated compound interest.

Mme. Loisel appeared an old woman, now. She became heavy, rough, harsh, like one of the poor. Her hair untended, her skirts askew, her hands red, her voice shrill, she even slopped water on her floors and scrubbed them herself. But, sometimes, while her husband was at work, she would sit near the window and think of that long-ago evening when, at the dance, she had been so beautiful and admired.

What would have happened if she had not lost that necklace? Who knows? Who can say? How strange and unpredictable life is! How little there is between happiness and misery!

Then one Sunday when she had gone for a walk on the Champs Élysées[11] to relax a bit from the week's labors, she suddenly noticed a woman strolling with a child. It was Mme. Forestier, still young-looking; still beautiful, still charming.

Mme. Loisel felt a rush of emotion. Should she speak to her? Of course. And now that everything was paid off, she would tell her the whole story. Why not?

She went toward her. "Hello, Jeanne."

The other, not recognizing her, showed astonishment at being spoken to so familiarly by this common person. She stammered, "But . . . madame . . . I don't recognize . . . You must be mistaken."

"No, I'm Mathilde Loisel."

Her friend gave a cry, "Oh, my poor Mathilde, how you've changed!"

"Yes, I've had a hard time since last seeing you. And plenty of misfortunes—and all on account of you!"

"Of me . . . How do you mean?"

10. **sou** (sō͞o): a coin then worth about one cent.

11. **Champs Élysées** (shan′ zā-lē-zā′): the main avenue of Paris.

"Do you remember that diamond necklace you loaned me to wear to the dance at the Ministry?"

"Yes, but what about it?"

"Well, I lost it."

"You lost it! But you returned it."

"I brought you another just like it. And we've been paying for it for ten years now. You can imagine that wasn't easy for us who had nothing. Well, it's over now, and I am glad of it."

Mme. Forestier stopped short. "You mean to say you bought a diamond necklace to replace mine?"

"Yes. You never noticed, then? They were quite alike."

And she smiled with proud and simple joy.

Mme. Forestier, quite overcome, clasped her by the hands. "Oh, my poor Mathilde. But mine was only paste.[12] Why, at most it was worth only five hundred francs!"

12. **paste:** a brilliant, glassy material used in imitation diamonds.

Reading Check

1. Why is Mme. Loisel unhappy when she receives an invitation to an evening reception?
2. How are Mme. Loisel's dreams realized at the party?
3. At what point does she become aware that the necklace is gone?
4. What excuse does she give her friend for not returning the necklace immediately?
5. What does she finally learn about the necklace?

For Study and Discussion

Analyzing and Interpreting the Story

1. The first six paragraphs of the story tell about the life Madame Loisel wishes to lead and the life she really leads. What details bring out this contrast?

2. Madame Loisel wishes to have an expensive dress for the reception. **a.** How does her husband react to her wish? **b.** What does this incident reveal about the values of Madame Loisel and of her husband?

3a. What reason does Madame Loisel give for needing a jewel to go with her dress? **b.** Do you think her concern is reasonable or foolish? **c.** Why does she choose the necklace rather than any of the other pieces of jewelry?

4a. At the reception, what incident shows the contrast between Madame Loisel's apparent situation in life and her true situation? **b.** What incident contrasts her values with her husband's values? **c.** After the Loisels leave to go home, what incident suggests a return to her true life?

5a. What actions do the Loisels take to replace the necklace? **b.** What qualities of character are revealed by these actions? **c.** Why do you think they do not tell Madame Forestier that they have lost the necklace?

6a. How does Madame Loisel's character change as a result of the hardships she has to endure? **b.** Do you think her values change? Give reasons for your answer.

7. "The Necklace" is famous for its surprise ending. How does the surprise drive home the story's theme—the underlying idea about true and false values?

8a. What is the author's attitude toward Mathilde Loisel? **b.** Does his attitude toward her change by the end of the story? Give reasons for your answer.

Literary Elements

Implicit Theme

The theme of "The Necklace" depends upon a contrast between true values and false values. Nowhere is the contrast directly stated, nor is the author's attitude toward Madame Loisel specifically declared. Yet readers can perceive this attitude as they learn more about Madame and Monsieur Loisel. For example, Madame Loisel's desire for an expensive evening dress shows that she values appearances and does not consider how such an extravagance will strain her husband's finances. Details such as this not only characterize Madame Loisel but also shape readers' attitudes toward her and her values.

Give at least three other details that Maupassant uses to shape your attitude toward Madame Loisel and her values. Show how these details are related to the theme of the story.

Language and Vocabulary

Using Words with Exactness

Often, looking up a word in a dictionary is only the first step to learning its exact meaning. We must also look at the way the word is used in a specific context. Look up each italicized word in the following passages from "The Necklace." Show that you understand the exact meaning of each word by using it in the same sense in a sentence of your own.

Their natural *poise,* their *instinctive* good taste . . . are the sole guiding principles which make daughters of the common people the equals of ladies in high society.

She grieved *incessantly* . . .

The sight of the little Breton girl who did her humble housework roused in her *disconsolate* regrets and wild daydreams.

She danced madly, wildly, drunk with pleasure, . . . in a kind of happy cloud composed of all the *adulation,* of all the admiring glances . . .

He threw over her shoulders the wraps he had brought for going home, modest garments of everyday life whose *shabbiness* clashed with the stylishness of her evening clothes.

Writing About Literature

Comparing Themes

If you have already read "The Gift of the Magi," write a composition comparing the theme of that story with the theme of "The Necklace." In your composition, consider the following question: How does the theme of each story depend upon a contrast between true and false values?

Creative Writing

Writing a Sequel

Write a sequel to "The Necklace." Tell how Madame Loisel reacts to the discovery that the necklace is paste. How does this discovery affect the lives of Madame Loisel and her husband?

Guy de Maupassant (1850–1893)

Guy de Maupassant (gē də mō-pä-sän′) was born in Normandy, a province of France. After he served in the French army during the Franco-Prussian War, he went to Paris and got a job as a government clerk. An aspiring writer, he made friends with a number of distinguished French writers, among them Gustave Flaubert. Maupassant became Flaubert's protégé and showed the older man many manuscripts before Flaubert decided that his young disciple was ready to publish. Maupassant's first published story, "Ball of Fat," was acclaimed a masterpiece. By 1882, he had achieved success as a writer and was able to quit his government post. He wrote prolifically, producing sixteen volumes of short stories, six novels, and several volumes of travel sketches. It is for his short stories that Maupassant is principally remembered. They are famous for their clear, smooth style, their compression, and their eye for telling detail. His stories reflect his knowledge of country life and small-town life in Normandy, and of fashionable and unfashionable life in Paris. Among his best-known stories are "The Piece of String," "The Duel," "At Sea," "Two Little Soldiers," and "The Diary of a Madman." Maupassant's most famous story is "The Necklace"; it is one of the most frequently anthologized stories of all time.

Literature and the Arts

Interpreting a Painting

Examine the painting called *Le Repos (The Rest)* on page 192. Do you think this painting suggests the character of Madame Loisel in "The Necklace"? Why or why not? What mood is captured in the painting?

Making Connections: Activities

Imagine that this painting represents a scene out of Mathilde Loisel's life. Is this Mathilde's home or another place? Are there other people in the room? What has just happened? What is about to happen? Create a narrative that accounts for all the details in the painting.

The Fifty-First Dragon

HEYWOOD BROUN

You have seen that a symbol—like the scarlet ibis in James Hurst's story—can have more than one meaning. Sometimes an entire story can be read on more than one level. As you read this famous story, can you detect a serious comment beneath the humor?

Of all the pupils at the knight school Gawaine le Cœur-Hardy[1] was among the least promising. He was tall and sturdy, but his instructors soon discovered that he lacked spirit. He would hide in the woods when the jousting class was called, although his companions and members of the faculty sought to appeal to his better nature by shouting to him to come out and break his neck like a man. Even when they told him that the lances were padded, the horses no more than ponies, and the field unusually soft for late autumn, Gawaine refused to grow enthusiastic. The Headmaster and the Assistant Professor of Pleasaunce[2] were discussing the case one spring afternoon and the Assistant Professor could see no remedy but expulsion.

1. **Gawaine le Cœur-Hardy** (gä'wĭn lə kûr'här'dē): Gawaine the Boldhearted. *Cœur* is French for "heart."
2. **Pleasaunce** (plĕz'əns): Usually this word means "pleasure." Here, it probably means "courtesy."

"No," said the Headmaster, as he looked out at the purple hills which ringed the school, "I think I'll train him to slay dragons."

"He might be killed," objected the Assistant Professor.

"So he might," replied the Headmaster brightly, but he added, more soberly, "we must consider the greater good. We are responsible for the formation of this lad's character."

"Are the dragons particularly bad this year?" interrupted the Assistant Professor. This was characteristic. He always seemed restive when the head of the school began to talk ethics and the ideals of the institution.

"I've never known them worse," replied the Headmaster. "Up in the hills to the south last week they killed a number of peasants, two cows and a prize pig. And if this dry spell holds there's no telling when they may start a forest fire simply by breathing around indiscriminately."

"Would any refund on the tuition fee be necessary in case of an accident to young Cœur-Hardy?"

"No," the principal answered, judicially, "that's all covered in the contract. But as a matter of fact he won't be killed. Before I send him up in the hills I'm going to give him a magic word."

"That's a good idea," said the Professor. "Sometimes they work wonders."

From that day on Gawaine specialized in dragons. His course included both theory and practice. In the morning there were long lectures on the history, anatomy, manners and customs of dragons. Gawaine did not distinguish himself in these studies. He had a marvelously versatile gift for forgetting things. In the afternoon he showed to better advantage, for then he would go down to the South Meadow and practice with a battle-ax. In this exercise he was truly impressive, for he had enormous strength as well as speed and grace He even developed a deceptive display of ferocity. Old alumni say that it was a thrilling sight to see Gawaine charging across the field toward the dummy paper dragon which had been set up for his practice. As he ran he would brandish his ax and shout, "A murrain[3] on thee!" or some other vivid bit of campus slang. It never took him more than one stroke to behead the dummy dragon.

Gradually his task was made more difficult. Paper gave way to papier-mâché[4] and finally to wood, but even the toughest of these dummy dragons had no terrors for Gawaine. One sweep of the ax always did the business. There were those who said that when the practice was protracted until dusk and the dragons threw long, fantastic shadows across the meadow, Gawaine did not charge so impetuously nor

3. **murrain** (mûr′ĭn): plague.
4. **papier-mâché** (pā′pər-mə-shā′): a material made of paper pulp mixed with glue or rosin. It can be molded into different shapes when wet, and then hardens as it dries.

Drawing by Wayne Anderson

shout so loudly. It is possible there was malice in this charge. At any rate, the Headmaster decided by the end of June that it was time for the test. Only the night before, a dragon had come close to the school grounds and had eaten some of the lettuce from the garden. The faculty decided that Gawaine was ready. They gave him a diploma and a new battle-ax and the Headmaster summoned him to a private conference.

"Sit down," said the Headmaster. "Have a cigarette."

Gawaine hesitated.

"Oh, I know it's against the rules," said the Headmaster. "But after all, you have received your preliminary degree. You are no longer a boy. You are a man. Tomorrow you will go out into the world, the great world of achievement."

Gawaine took a cigarette. The Headmaster offered him a match, but he produced one of his own and began to puff away with a dexterity which quite amazed the principal.

"Here you have learned the theories of life," continued the Headmaster, resuming the thread of his discourse, "but after all, life is not a matter of theories. Life is a matter of facts. It calls on the young and the old alike to face these facts, even though they are hard and sometimes unpleasant. Your problem, for example, is to slay dragons."

"They say that those dragons down in the south wood are five hundred feet long," ventured Gawaine, timorously.

"Stuff and nonsense!" said the Headmaster. "The curate saw one last week from the top of Arthur's Hill. The dragon was sunning himself down in the valley. The curate didn't have an opportunity to look at him very long because he felt it was his duty to hurry back to make a report to me. He said the monster—or shall I say, the big lizard?—wasn't an inch over two hundred feet. But the size has nothing at all to do with it. You'll find the big ones even easier than the little ones. They're far slower on their feet and less aggressive, I'm told. Besides, before you go I'm going to equip you in such fashion that you need have no fear of all the dragons in the world."

"I'd like an enchanted cap," said Gawaine.

"What's that?" asked the Headmaster, testily.

"A cap to make me disappear," explained Gawaine.

The Headmaster laughed indulgently. "You mustn't believe all those old wives' stories," he said. "There isn't any such thing. A cap to make you disappear, indeed! What would you do with it? You haven't even appeared yet. Why, my boy, you could walk from here to London, and nobody would so much as look at you. You're nobody. You couldn't be more invisible than that."

Gawaine seemed dangerously close to a relapse into his old habit of whimpering. The Headmaster reassured him: "Don't worry; I'll give you something much better than an enchanted cap. I'm going to give you a magic word. All you have to do is to repeat this magic charm once and no dragon can possibly harm a hair of your head. You can cut off his head at your leisure."

He took a heavy book from the shelf behind his desk and began to run through it. "Sometimes," he said, "the charm is a whole phrase or even a sentence. I might, for instance, give you 'To make the'—no, that might not do. I think a single word would be best for dragons."

"A short word," suggested Gawaine.

"It can't be too short or it wouldn't be potent. There isn't so much hurry as all that. Here's a splendid magic word: 'Rumplesnitz.' Do you think you can learn that?"

Gawaine tried and in an hour or so he seemed to have the word well in hand. Again and again he interrupted the lesson to inquire,

"And if I say 'Rumplesnitz' the dragon can't possibly hurt me?" And always the Headmaster replied, "If you only say 'Rumplesnitz,' you are perfectly safe."

Toward morning Gawaine seemed resigned to his career. At daybreak the Headmaster saw him to the edge of the forest and pointed him to the direction in which he should proceed. About a mile away to the southwest a cloud of steam hovered over an open meadow in the woods and the Headmaster assured Gawaine that under the steam he would find a dragon. Gawaine went forward slowly. He wondered whether it would be best to approach the dragon on the run as he did in his practice in the South Meadow or to walk slowly toward him, shouting "Rumplesnitz" all the way.

The problem was decided for him. No sooner had he come to the fringe of the meadow than the dragon spied him and began to charge. It was a large dragon and yet it seemed decidedly aggressive in spite of the Headmaster's statement to the contrary. As the dragon charged it released huge clouds of hissing steam through its nostrils. It was almost as if a gigantic teapot had gone mad. The dragon came forward so fast and Gawaine was so frightened that he had time to say "Rumplesnitz" only once. As he said it, he swung his battle-ax and off popped the head of the dragon. Gawaine had to admit that it was even easier to kill a real dragon than a wooden one if only you said "Rumplesnitz."

Gawaine brought the ears home and a small section of the tail. His schoolmates and the faculty made much of him, but the Headmaster wisely kept him from being spoiled by insisting that he go on with his work. Every clear day Gawaine rose at dawn and went out to kill dragons. The Headmaster kept him at home when it rained, because he said the woods were damp and unhealthy at such times and that he didn't want the boy to run needless risks. Few good days passed in which Gawaine failed to get a dragon. On one particularly fortunate day he killed three, a husband and a wife and a visiting relative. Gradually he developed a technique. Pupils who sometimes watched him from the hilltops a long way off said that he often allowed the dragon to come within a few feet before he said "Rumplesnitz." He came to say it with a mocking sneer. Occasionally he did stunts. Once when an excursion party from London was watching him he went into action with his right hand tied behind his back. The dragon's head came off just as easily.

As Gawaine's record of killings mounted higher the Headmaster found it impossible to keep him completely in hand. He fell into the habit of stealing out at night and engaging in long drinking bouts at the village tavern. It was after such a debauch that he rose a little before dawn one fine August morning and started out after his fiftieth dragon. His head was heavy and his mind sluggish. He was heavy in other respects as well, for he had adopted the somewhat vulgar practice of wearing his medals, ribbons and all, when he went out dragon hunting. The decorations began on his chest and ran all the way down to his abdomen. They must have weighed at least eight pounds.

Gawaine found a dragon in the same meadow where he had killed the first one. It was a fair-sized dragon, but evidently an old one. Its face was wrinkled and Gawaine thought he had never seen so hideous a countenance. Much to the lad's disgust, the monster refused to charge and Gawaine was obliged to walk toward him. He whistled as he went. The dragon regarded him hopelessly, but craftily. Of course it had heard of Gawaine. Even when the lad raised his battle-ax the dragon made no move. It knew that there was no salvation in the quickest thrust of the head, for it had been informed that this hunter was protected by an

Drawing by Wayne Anderson

enchantment. It merely waited, hoping something would turn up.

Gawaine raised the battle-ax and suddenly lowered it again. He had grown very pale and he trembled violently.

The dragon suspected a trick. "What's the matter?" it asked, with false solicitude.

"I've forgotten the magic word," stammered Gawaine.

"What a pity," said the dragon. "So that was the secret. It doesn't seem quite sporting to me, all this magic stuff, you know. Not cricket, as we used to say when I was a little dragon; but after all, that's a matter of opinion."

Gawaine was so helpless with terror that the dragon's confidence rose immeasurably and it could not resist the temptation to show off a bit.

"Could I possibly be of any assistance?" it asked. "What's the first letter of the magic word?"

"It begins with an 'r,'" said Gawaine weakly.

"Let's see," mused the dragon, "that doesn't tell us much, does it? What sort of a word is this? Is it an epithet,[5] do you think?"

Gawaine could do no more than nod.

5. **epithet** (ĕp′ə-thĕt′): a word or phrase used to describe a person, thing, or idea. An epithet is sometimes used as a substitute for a name.

"Why, of course," exclaimed the dragon, "reactionary Republican."

Gawaine shook his head.

"Well, then," said the dragon, "we'd better get down to business. Will you surrender?"

With the suggestion of a compromise Gawaine mustered up enough courage to speak.

"What will you do if I surrender?" he asked.

"Why, I'll eat you," said the dragon.

"And if I don't surrender?"

"I'll eat you just the same."

"Then it doesn't mean any difference, does it?" moaned Gawaine.

"It does to me," said the dragon with a smile. "I'd rather you didn't surrender. You'd taste much better if you didn't."

The dragon waited for a long time for Gawaine to ask "Why?" but the boy was too frightened to speak. At last the dragon had to give the explanation without his cue line. "You see," he said, "if you don't surrender you'll taste better because you'll die game."

This was an old and ancient trick of the dragon's. By means of some such quip he was accustomed to paralyze his victims with laughter and then to destroy them. Gawaine was sufficiently paralyzed as it was, but laughter had no part in his helplessness. With the last word of the joke the dragon drew back his head and struck. In that second there flashed into the mind of Gawaine the magic word "Rumplesnitz," but there was no time to say it. There was time only to strike and, without a word, Gawaine met the onrush of the dragon with a full swing. He put all his back and shoulders into it. The impact was terrific and the head of the dragon flew almost a hundred yards and landed in a thicket.

Gawaine did not remain frightened very long after the death of the dragon. His mood was one of wonder. He was enormously puzzled. He cut off the ears of the monster almost in a trance. Again and again he thought to himself, "I didn't say 'Rumplesnitz'!" He was sure of that and yet there was no question that he had killed the dragon. In fact, he had never killed one so utterly. Never before had he driven a head for anything like the same distance. Twenty-five yards was perhaps his best previous record. All the way back to the knight school he kept rumbling about in his mind seeking an explanation for what had occurred. He went to the Headmaster immediately and after closing the door told him what had happened. "I didn't say 'Rumplesnitz,'" he explained with great earnestness.

The Headmaster laughed. "I'm glad you've found out," he said. "It makes you ever so much more of a hero. Don't you see that? Now you know that it was you who killed all these dragons and not that foolish little word 'Rumplesnitz.'"

Gawaine frowned. "Then it wasn't a magic word after all?" he asked.

"Of course not," said the Headmaster, "you ought to be too old for such foolishness. There isn't any such thing as a magic word."

"But you told me it was magic," protested Gawaine. "You said it was magic and now you say it isn't."

"It wasn't magic in a literal sense," answered the Headmaster, "but it was much more wonderful than that. The word gave you confidence. It took away your fears. If I hadn't told you that, you might have been killed the very first time. It was your battle-ax did the trick."

Gawaine surprised the Headmaster by his attitude. He was obviously distressed by the explanation. He interrupted a long philosophic and ethical discourse by the Headmaster with "If I hadn't of hit 'em all mighty hard and fast any one of 'em might have crushed me like a, like a——" He fumbled for a word.

"Eggshell," suggested the Headmaster.

"Like a eggshell," assented Gawaine, and he said it many times. All through the evening meal people who sat near him heard him muttering, "Like a eggshell, like a eggshell."

The next day was clear, but Gawaine did not get up at dawn. Indeed, it was almost noon when the Headmaster found him cowering in bed, with the clothes pulled over his head. The principal called the Assistant Professor of Pleasaunce, and together they dragged the boy toward the forest.

"He'll be all right as soon as he gets a couple more dragons under his belt," explained the Headmaster.

The Assistant Professor of Pleasaunce agreed. "It would be a shame to stop such a fine run," he said. "Why, counting that one yesterday, he's killed fifty dragons."

They pushed the boy into a thicket above which hung a meager cloud of steam. It was obviously quite a small dragon. But Gawaine did not come back that night or the next. In fact, he never came back. Some weeks afterward brave spirits from the school explored the thicket, but they could find nothing to remind them of Gawaine except the metal parts of his medals. Even the ribbons had been devoured.

The Headmaster and the Assistant Professor of Pleasaunce agreed that it would be just as well not to tell the school how Gawaine had achieved his record and still less how he came to die. They held that it might have a bad effect on school spirit. Accordingly, Gawaine has lived in the memory of the school as its greatest hero. No visitor succeeds in leaving the building today without seeing a great shield which hangs on the wall of the dining hall. Fifty pairs of dragon's ears are mounted upon the shield and underneath in gilt letters is "Gawaine le Cœur-Hardy," followed by the simple inscription, "He killed fifty dragons." The record has never been equaled.

Reading Check

1. Why did Gawaine receive special training as a dragon-slayer?
2. What did the Headmaster give Gawaine to protect him from dragons?
3. Why did Gawaine have trouble when he went to kill his fiftieth dragon?
4. What caused Gawaine to lose his confidence?
5. How was Gawaine honored by his school?

For Study and Discussion

Analyzing and Interpreting the Story

1. A traditional tale about knights and dragons would not include, as one of its characters, an "Assistant Professor of Pleasaunce." Nor would the character ask "Would any refund on the tuition fee be necessary in case of an accident?" Such **anachronisms**—that is, events existing out of their proper time in history—add to the humor of the story. Cite other details in which the "knight school" is treated as if it were a school of today.

2a. Explain the Headmaster's plan to turn Gawaine into a bold knight. **b.** What attitude toward human nature is behind this plan? **c.** Would you call it a cynical attitude? Explain.

3a. Gawaine has several assets as a dragon-slaying knight: "enormous strength as well as speed and grace." But he also has a serious flaw. What is it? **b.** What other flaws in his character emerge after he becomes a famous dragon slayer?

4. The encounter with the fiftieth dragon, a key episode in the story, is both humorous and suspenseful. **a.** Point out humorous passages. **b.** What details contribute to the suspense?

5. When Gawaine tells the Headmaster about his encounter with the fiftieth dragon, the Headmaster reveals that there is no such thing as a magic word. **a.** What effect does this revelation have on Gawaine? **b.** If you were in Gawaine's place, would you have wanted to be told the truth about the magic word? Why or why not?

6. "The Fifty-First Dragon" can be understood on two levels. On the most obvious level, it is an amusing spoof of tales about knights and dragons. On a deeper level, it makes a serious comment about human beings and their need for beliefs. State the theme, using evidence from the story to support your answer.

Language and Vocabulary

Recognizing Analogies

You are familiar with vocabulary questions that ask you to identify synonyms or antonyms. These questions usually involve a pair of words. Some other vocabulary questions, called **analogies,** involve two pairs of words. You must first decide what relationship exists between the words in the first pair. The same relationship applies to the second pair.

An analogy question has a special format and uses special symbols. Let's look at one type of analogy question:

    intelligent : smart :: cold : _____
    a. high   **b.** quick   **c.** chilly   **d.** bright

The two dots (:) stand for "is to"; the four dots (::) stand for "as." The example, therefore, reads "Intelligent *is to* smart *as* cold *is to* _____." Since the first two words, *intelligent* and *smart*, are synonyms, the correct answer is **c.** The word that means the same thing as *cold* is *chilly*.

In addition to questions involving synonym and antonym relationships, analogy questions may test understanding of grammatical or verbal relationships, cause-and-effect relationships, sequential relationships, and the like.

Complete the following analogies:

Synonyms
1. wealthy : rich :: restive : _____
  a. classic   **c.** natural
  b. restless   **d.** responsible
2. think : consider :: hover : _____
  a. float   **c.** cause
  b. sell   **d.** handle
3. stop : halt :: cower : _____
  a. command   **c.** criticize
  b. complain   **d.** cringe
4. battle : fight :: solicitude : _____
  a. silence   **c.** concern
  b. difference   **d.** cause

Antonyms
5. versatile : rigid :: indiscriminate : _____
  a. picky   **c.** rival
  b. ideal   **d.** hilarious
6. preliminary : concluding :: meager : _____
  a. plentiful   **c.** timid
  b. honest   **d.** responsible
7. give : take :: protract : _____
  a. claim   **c.** promise
  b. own   **d.** end
8. winning : losing :: impetuous : _____
  a. cautious   **c.** secretive
  b. embarrassing **d.** unemployed

Grammatical Relationship
9. heroism : heroic :: ferocity : _____
  a. fierce   **c.** fortunate
  b. friendly   **d.** thankful
10. ethics : ethical :: justice : _____
  a. joyous   **c.** judicial
  b. emphatic   **d.** judge

Action and Object Relationship

11. answer : question :: muster : _____
- **a.** prayer
- **b.** troops
- **c.** camera
- **d.** skill

12. drive : automobile :: brandish : _____
- **a.** airplane
- **b.** commercial
- **c.** adventure
- **d.** sword

Degree Relationship

13. puddle : pond :: thicket : _____
- **a.** forest
- **b.** thorn
- **c.** fabric
- **d.** ticket

Cause-and-Effect Relationship

14. investigation : proof :: malice : _____
- **a.** value
- **b.** fortune
- **c.** suffering
- **d.** freedom

Focus on Narrative Writing

Creating a Story Map

A **story map** is a plan or outline that pulls together all the essential elements of a narrative. Here is a sample story map:

Story Title: _____
Point of View: _____
Characters
    1: _____
    2: _____
    3: _____
Setting
    Time: _____
    Place: _____
Plot
    Exposition: _____
    Conflict: _____
    Complications: _____
    Climax: _____
    Resolution: _____

Create a story map for a modern equivalent of "The Fifty-First Dragon." Update Broun's story by choosing some profession or trade that Gawaine might follow today. (Feel free to change Gawaine's name!) Instead of an encounter with the fiftieth dragon, choose a comparable encounter as the key episode in your story. Here are some possibilities:

1. Gawaine is an overconfident offensive football player who encounters a 330-pound tackle.
2. Gawaine is a supersalesperson who discovers that the product he sells is defective.

When you have finished your story map, get together with a small group of classmates and evaluate your updatings of Broun's story. Save your writing.

About the Author

Heywood Broun   (1888–1939)

Born in Brooklyn, New York, Heywood Broun attended the Horace Mann School in Manhattan, where he edited the school newspaper. After attending Harvard, he got a job with the New York *Telegraph* as a sports writer. In 1912 he went to work for the New York *Tribune*, where he began his column, "It Seems to Me." In time, it became one of the most popular newspaper columns in America. Although Broun published several novels, he was best known as a newspaper columnist. He had strong, controversial opinions and did not hesitate to express them. One critic has written that Broun's work at its best shows "a depth, a warmth, and a power…that were the outward expression of the man himself."

Reading and Critical Thinking

A close study of the various elements of narrative can heighten your enjoyment and understanding of short stories. Below are some criteria you can use to *evaluate,* or judge, the merits of other short stories. Use a separate sheet of paper to answer the questions marked with this symbol (■).

Plot

1. *Is the main conflict of the story handled well?* Do the episodes of the story grow logically out of the conflict? Is the resolution of the conflict believable or is it improbable?

Are the elements of suspense and foreshadowing handled skillfully? Is your interest sustained?

■ "They laughed at the unexpected eruption of apples, and clapped their hands in applause of the long shot by the man with the ginger beard" (page 44). Make some notes to evaluate the plot elements and resolution of Jack London's "War."

Character

2. *Are the characters believable and presented effectively?* Are their actions well motivated? Are they revealed through their thoughts, actions, and words or merely through direct characterization?

■ "I told maybe a story," he said. "I told them I thought you would want to see me" (page 91). What do these words suggest about Jerry's personality and situation in "A Mother in Mannville"?

Point of View

3. *What point of view is used and what is its purpose?* How does the author use point of view to control your reactions to characters and events?

■ "You, who so well know the nature of my soul, will not suppose, however, that I gave utterance to a threat" (page 95). How is the point of view significant in Poe's "The Cask of Amontillado"?

Setting

4. *What role does setting play?* Does the setting help to create atmosphere or to depict character?

■ "In the evening after supper George left the house and wandered in the neighborhood" (page 147). Make some notes on the links of setting with plot, character, and mood in Malamud's "A Summer's Reading."

Theme

5. *Does the story offer some insight into human experience?* Does the story have a theme, or does it exist chiefly for entertainment?

■ "But there were few who listened" (page 186). What is the theme of Böll's "The Balek Scales"? Test your statement by seeing if it includes all important aspects of the story.

■ What is the theme of "The Portable Phonograph" (page 139)? How does setting contribute to the theme?

Read the following story and on a separate sheet of paper, answer the questions on page 208.

What Happened During the Ice Storm
Jim Heynen

One winter there was a freezing rain. How beautiful! people said when things outside started to shine with ice. But the freezing rain kept coming. Tree branches glistened like glass. Then broke like glass. Ice thickened on the windows until everything outside blurred. Farmers moved their livestock into the barns, and most animals were safe. But not the pheasants. Their eyes froze shut.

Some farmers went ice-skating down the gravel roads with clubs to harvest the pheasants that sat helplessly in the roadside ditches. The boys went out into the freezing rain to find pheasants too. They saw dark spots along a fence. Pheasants, all right. Five or six of them. The boys slid their feet along slowly, trying not to break the ice that covered the snow. They slid up close to the pheasants. The pheasants pulled their heads down between their wings. They couldn't tell how easy it was to see them huddled there.

The boys stood still in the icy rain. Their breath came out in slow puffs of steam. The pheasants' breath came out in quick little white puffs. Some of them lifted their heads and turned them from side to side, but they were blindfolded with ice and didn't flush. The boys had not brought clubs or sacks, or anything but themselves. They stood over the pheasants, turning their own heads, looking at each other, each expecting the other to do something. To pounce on a pheasant, or to yell Bang! Things around them were shining and dripping with icy rain. The barbed-wire fence. The fence posts. The broken stems of grass. Even the grass seeds. The grass seeds looked like little yolks inside gelatin whites. And the pheasants looked like unborn birds glazed in egg white. Ice was hardening on the boys' caps and coats. Soon they would be covered with ice too.

Then one of the boys said, Shh. He was taking off his coat, the thin layer of ice splintering in flakes as he pulled his arms from the sleeves. But the inside of the coat was dry and warm. He covered two of the crouching pheasants with his coat, rounding the back of it over them like a shell. The other boys did the same. They covered all the helpless pheasants. The small gray hens and the larger brown cocks. Now, the boys felt the rain soaking through their shirts and freezing. They ran across the slippery fields, unsure of their footing, the ice clinging to their skin as they made their way toward the blurry lights of the house.

THE WRITING PROCESS AND NARRATIVE WRITING

The Writing Process

Writing is often referred to as a *process,* which consists of several key stages or phases:

- Prewriting
- Writing a First Draft
- Evaluating and Revising
- Proofreading and Publishing

In the writing process, much of the most important work precedes the actual writing of a paper. In the **prewriting** stage, you make decisions about what to say and how to say it. Prewriting activities include the following:

- choosing and limiting a topic
- identifying your purpose and audience
- gathering ideas and information
- arriving at the main or unifying idea (sometimes called the thesis) of the whole paper
- organizing your material

In the **writing** stage, you use your working plan to write a first draft of the paper. As you write, new ideas and better ways of organizing your material may often occur to you, and you should revise your working plan accordingly.

After you have finished your first draft, you polish it in the **evaluating and revising** stage. At this point you take a fresh look at the whole paper to consider how you might improve content, organization, and style. Here are some of the ways good writers typically revise their drafts:

- adding or deleting ideas
- rearranging sentences
- making words or phrases more vivid and precise
- rephrasing for clarity

The last stage of the writing process, **proofreading and publishing,** really involves two distinct activities. Good writers always proofread their semifinal drafts to correct any errors in spelling, punctuation, capitalization, grammar, and usage. Then writers produce a clean copy of the paper—and proofread this final draft, just to make sure it is free from errors.

Deciding on an audience in the prewriting stage of the writing process means that you are planning to share your ideas. The last step in the process is to consider ways to publish or share your writing. How you share it will often depend on the nature of the particular piece, on your audience, and on opportunities in your local area. Here are some helpful ideas:

- enter a writing contest
- send your writing to a newspaper
- make a class anthology
- use your writing as the basis for an illustrated presentation

Narrative Writing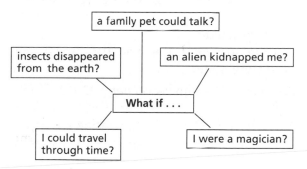

Narration, or storytelling, is probably the most fundamental kind of writing. Narratives range from book-length tales, such as novels and epics, to the length of a paragraph, as in fables and anecdotes. Other kinds of narrative include short stories, mysteries, movie scripts, television series, ballads, comic strips, histories, and journals. During this unit you have examined many of the important elements and techniques of storytelling. Now you will have the chance to write your own narrative.

Prewriting

1. One helpful strategy to explore story ideas for a narrative is to brainstorm, using a "What if?" scenario. For example, ask yourself questions like these:

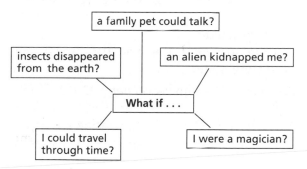

Freewrite for five or ten minutes about one or two of these ideas. You can also explore story plots by getting together with a small group of classmates and trading ideas about recent stories in the newspapers or on TV. Finally, you may want to review the notes you have made for the writing assignments in this unit.

2. After you have found a promising story idea, start to explore the **plot** of your story in more detail. Remember the key plot elements in a narrative:

- **Exposition:** background information
- **Conflict:** main struggle
- **Complications:** additional difficulties
- **Climax:** point of greatest intensity
- **Resolution:** outcome or falling action

Pay special attention to introducing a **conflict** for the main character(s) right at the beginning of your story, so that you can capture the reader's interest. Here are four types of conflict to consider. The first three types are **external conflicts.** The fourth is **internal conflict.**

- a person versus another person
- a person versus society
- a person versus a force of nature
- two forces struggling within a person

[See **Focus** assignments on pages 30 and 103.]

3. Make some notes on the other important story elements. Start with **point of view,** or the vantage point from which you will tell the narrative. There are three basic points of view from which you can choose:

- **first-person:** one of the characters tells the story in his/her own words
- **third-person limited:** the writer tells the story from the vantage point of one character
- **third-person omniscient:** an outside observer with complete knowledge of all the characters tells the story

Which point of view would best suit your story line? First-person point of view has the advantage of giving your readers an intimate impression of one character, the storyteller. This point of view has the disadvantage, though, of ruling out any event or conversation that the storyteller does not witness. Whatever point of view you choose, remember that you must stick to it consistently. [See **Focus** assignment on page 138.]

4. Now think about your **characters** in more detail. Here are some items you may want to know about each character you create:

- Name
- Age
- Habits
- Appearance
- Personality
- Reputation
- Likes and Dislikes
- Way of Speaking

Remember that it is generally more effective to **show** your characters through **indirect characterization** than to **tell** about them in **direct characterization**. Here are some methods of indirect characterization to keep in mind:

- showing the character acting and speaking
- revealing the character's thoughts
- revealing what other characters think about the character

[See **Focus** assignment on page 69.]

5. Make some notes about the **setting,** or the time and place of your narrative. Which details would contribute best to your story's **verisimilitude,** or appearance of reality? Think about how you can describe the setting with **sensory details.** [See **Focus** assignments on pages 153 and 165.]

6. Gather your notes together and make a **story map,** a plan or outline for all the essential elements of your narrative. [For an example of a story map, see the **Focus** assignment on page 207.]

Writing

1. Use **chronological** or **time order** to narrate the actions and events of your story. Remember that **transitions** can help you to make the relationship of ideas and events clear. Here are some useful transitional words for chronological order:

after	finally	suddenly
at once	first	then
before	meanwhile	when
eventually	next	

[See **Focus** assignment on page 45.]

2. Make your story come alive by using **dialogue.** As you create dialogue for your characters, remember these guidelines:

- Make the words fit the character who speaks them.
- Use conversational language.
- Use dialogue tags ("he whispered," "she called") to show *how* the words are spoken.
- Be sure that the dialogue moves the story along.

[See **Focus** assignment on page 75.]

3. Verbs are action words, so they are especially important in a narrative, which tells about actions and events. Make your narrative as exciting as you can by using **vivid, precise verbs.** [See **Focus** assignment on page 171.]

4. The **climax** of a narrative is the point of greatest emotional intensity, interest, or suspense: for example, the young man's opening one of the doors in Frank R. Stockton's "The Lady, or the Tiger?" (see page 36) or the judge's ruling in favor of Eliza in Jessamyn West's "The Pacing Goose" (see

page 135). As you write the first draft of your story, make sure that events in your plot lead up to a turning point, or climax. If there is no clear high point in your story, go back and reconsider the events and actions on your story map.

Evaluating and Revising

1. When you have finished your first draft, step back and try to evaluate your story as objectively as you can. You might want to trade papers with a classmate at this stage and give each other a review. What are the weaknesses in your story, and how can you improve them? Pay special attention to the way your story ends. Is the resolution satisfying and appropriate for your story's theme and tone? [See **Focus** assignments on pages 180 and 189.]

Below is an example of how one writer revised an opening paragraph for a narrative.

Writer's Model

They were all gone ~~because~~ the ^mystery^ virus had killed the ^last^ ~~remaining~~ insects on earth three days ago. ^Staring^ ~~Looking~~ out the dining room windows, ^across the lawn^ Hemming ^spied gaunt^ ~~saw~~ a bluejay flap its wings weakly at the top of a pine tree. "Birds will be next," he ~~said.~~ ^murmured sadly^

2. As you think about other parts of your first draft, you will find the following checklist helpful.

Checklist for Evaluation and Revision

✓ Do I capture the reader's attention with a strong conflict at the beginning?
✓ Is the point of view consistent?
✓ Is the order of events clear?
✓ Are the characters lifelike and interesting?
✓ Is the dialogue realistic? Does it suit the characters and help to move the action along?
✓ Is the setting vivid?
✓ Does the story build to a climax?
✓ Am I satisfied with the ending?

Proofreading and Publishing

1. Proofread your narrative to find and correct any errors in grammar, usage, capitalization, and punctuation. (You may find it helpful at this stage to refer to the **Handbook for Revision** on pages 884–930.) Pay special attention to the rules for punctuating and paragraphing dialogue correctly. Then prepare a final version of your narrative by making a clean copy.

2. Consider some of the following publication methods for sharing your narrative:

- read your story aloud in a story theater
- enter your story in a contest
- create an anthology of stories for younger students
- adapt your story for a puppet show

Portfolio If your teacher approves, you may wish to keep a copy of your work in your writing folder or portfolio.

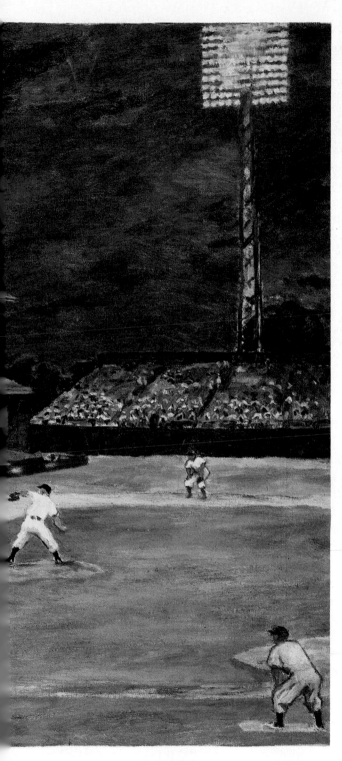

NONFICTION

Imagine yourself a sportswriter at this game of night baseball. In order to write your column for the local newspaper, you would need a special vocabulary of baseball terms, including the following:

> diamond
> home plate
> pitcher's mound
> shutout
> double play

What other terms can you add to this list?

Join with a few members of your class and write an article about this game as it might appear in the sports pages of your local or school newspaper. Then compare your column with that of an actual sportswriter. How well did you succeed in capturing the feel and the thrill of the game?

Detail from *Night Baseball* (1951) by Marjorie Phillips.
Oil on canvas.
The Phillips Collection, Washington, D.C.

The line between *fiction* and *nonfiction* is sometimes difficult to establish, but in general we can say that fiction deals with imaginary characters and events, nonfiction with real people, their experiences and ideas. Many different kinds of writing are classified as nonfiction. Two major categories—essays and true narratives—are represented in this unit.

The purpose of nonfiction may be to entertain, to inform, to explain, or to persuade. Whatever the purpose, writers make use of *description,* to give a picture of the subject and to communicate sensory impressions; *narration,* to tell about a series of events; *exposition,* to present information or to explain a subject; and *argumentation* or *persuasion,* to influence or change people's ideas or actions.

ESSAYS

It was Michel de Montaigne, the sixteenth-century French writer, who coined the word *essai* and who wrote the first modern essay. The essay for Montaigne was an attempt in prose (the French *J'essaie* means "I try") to set forth his ideas in a limited and personal manner on a wide range of topics. Although the essay has taken many forms since Montaigne, his basic definition still holds true. Today an essay can be loosely defined as a piece of prose writing that deals with its subject briefly and from a personal point of view.

It is customary to classify essays as *formal* or *informal.* The formal essay is serious in tone, tightly organized, and generally objective. The informal, or *familiar,* essay may range freely over the subject; we are interested as much in the writer's personality and point of view as in what he or she has to say. Neither Montaigne nor Francis Bacon, the English writer and statesman whose *Essays* were first published in 1597, considered the essay to be a complete or thorough discussion of the subject, though the essay did become a treatise in the hands of later writers. The topics of essays may vary widely. In this unit, for example, one essayist analyzes her feelings about eating certain foods; another deals with the subject of naming dogs; a third describes stages in the death of a tree; still another discusses the circumstances surrounding the publication of a famous book. In the hands of James Thurber, E. B. White, and other modern essayists, the essay continues to be what it was for Montaigne and Bacon. We are engaged by the writer's *style*—the way the writer uses language—as well as by the subject.

*A*lthough there is great variety in the subjects and purposes of essays, one element that all good essays share is the successful union of style and subject. As you read, you should pay close attention not only to the subject of an essay but also to its style—the choice of words and the ways in which they have been arranged. You also need to be aware of how you are responding to the essay. As an active reader you should realize that the author of an essay has had to make many decisions—deleting and substituting words, rewriting phrases and sentences, perhaps rearranging entire sections of the essay in order to inform, entertain, or persuade the reader. In reading, ask yourself how elements of style (imagery, metaphor, and the like) work together to convey the author's meaning and attitude toward a subject as well as to affect your response. Get into the habit of reading an essay more than once. In your first reading think about the main point of the essay and the evidence the author presents to support that idea. In rereading pay closer attention to elements of style and to your own response to the writing.

Guidelines for Close Reading

1. Determine the purpose of the essay. Is the object to entertain, to inform, to persuade, or some combination of purposes?

2. Determine the tone of the essay. Is it formal or informal? Is it serious or light? Does it combine approaches?

3. What impressions do you get of the writer and why?

4. Note what the writer does with language. How do you respond to the language of the essay?

5. Clarify your own response to the essay and state its main idea in your own words.

Here is a brief informal essay, "Security" by E. B. White, which originally appeared in a magazine, *Harper's Monthly*. The notes in the margin show how one reader has responded to this selection. If you wish, cover up the printed notes and take notes of your own on a separate sheet of paper. Then compare your responses with these printed comments.

ONE READER'S RESPONSE

I remember riding on a Ferris wheel at an amusement park.

White must be joking.

I noticed that some adults didn't want to go on the ride.

I remember how much fun it was to look down on the crowd.

I wonder if this is an old song.

Security

E. B. WHITE

It was a fine clear day for the Fair this year, and I went up early to see how the Ferris wheel was doing and to take a ride. It pays to check up on Ferris wheels these days: by noting the volume of business one can get some idea which side is ahead in the world—whether the airborne freemen outnumber the earth-bound slaves. It was encouraging to discover that there were still quite a few people at the Fair who preferred a feeling of high, breezy insecurity to one of solid support. My friend Healy surprised me by declining to go aloft; he is an unusually cautious man, however—even his hat is insured.

I like to watch the faces of people who are trying to get up their nerve to take to the air. You see them at the ticket booths in amusement parks, in the waiting room at the airport. Within them two irreconcilables[1] are at war—the desire for safety, the yearning for a dizzy release. My *Britannica* tells nothing about Mr. G. W. G. Ferris, but he belongs with the immortals. From the top of the wheel, seated beside a small boy, windswept and fancy free, I looked down on the Fair and for a moment was alive. Below us the old harness drivers pushed their trotters round the dirt track, old men with their legs still sticking out stiffly round the rumps of horses. And from the cluster of loud speakers atop the judges' stand came the "Indian Love Call," bathing heaven and earth in jumbo tenderness.

This silvery wheel, revolving slowly in the cause of freedom, was only just holding its own, I soon discovered; for farther along in the midway, in a sideshow tent, a tattoo artist was doing a land-office business, not with anchors, flags, and pretty mermaids, but with Social Security Numbers, neatly pricked on your forearm with the electric needle. He had plenty of customers, mild-mannered pale men, asking glumly for the sort of indelible ignominy[2] that was once reserved for prisoners and

1. **irreconcilables** (ĭ-rĕk′ən-sī′lə-bəlz): conflicting or incompatible ideas.
2. **indelible** (ĭn-dĕl′ə-bəl) **ignominy** (ĭg′nə-mĭn′ē): permanent public disgrace or dishonor.

beef cattle. Drab times these, when the bravado and the exhibitionism are gone from tattooing and it becomes simply a branding operation. I hope the art that produced the bird's eye view of Sydney will not be forever lost in the routine business of putting serial numbers on people who are worried about growing old.

The sight would have depressed me had I not soon won a cane by knocking over three cats with three balls. There is no moment when a man so surely has the world by the tail as when he strolls down the midway swinging a prize cane.

Did people really do this willingly?

White thinks that people's fear of insecurity makes them do strange things.

White must be a person who likes to enjoy himself and not brood about problems.

Looking at Yourself as a Reader

Compare your own responses with those in the notes alongside White's essay. How did you feel after reading the essay? Did you understand White's point of view about security? Did the essay make you think about the concept of security in a new way?

Imagine writing a reply to White's essay in a letter to the editor of a newspaper. Would you agree or disagree with White's position? Use examples from your own experience to support your point of view.

Growing Up Game

BRENDA PETERSON

The author grew up in the California Sierras, where her father worked for the Forest Service. In this essay she talks about her attitude toward hunting and eating wild animals. Her method is to select key incidents from her life and to analyze her feelings about each episode. As you read, determine why she considers the truth to be "not so simple."

When I went off to college my father gave me, as part of my tuition, fifty pounds of moose meat. In 1969, eating moose meat at the University of California was a contradiction in terms. Hippies[1] didn't hunt. I lived in a rambling Victorian house which boasted sweeping circular staircases, built-in lofts, and a landlady who dreamed of opening her own health food restaurant. I told my housemates that my moose meat in its nondescript white butcher paper was from a side of beef my father had bought. The carnivores[2] in the house helped me finish off such suppers as sweet and sour moose meatballs, mooseburgers (garnished with the obligatory avocado and sprouts), and mooseghctti. The same dinner guests who remarked upon the lean sweetness of the meat would have recoiled if I'd told them the not-so-simple truth: that I grew up on game, and the moose they were eating had been brought down, with one shot through his magnificent

heart, by my father—a man who had hunted all his life and all of mine.

One of my earliest memories is of crawling across the vast continent of crinkled linoleum in our Forest Service cabin kitchen, down splintered back steps, through wildflowers growing wheat-high. I was eye-level with grasshoppers who scolded me on my first solo trip outside. I made it to the shed, a cool and comfortingly square shelter that held phantasmagoric[3] metal parts; they smelled good, like dirt and grease. I had played a long time in this shed before some maternal shriek made me lift up on my haunches to listen to those urgent, possessive sounds that were my name. Rearing up, my head bumped into something hanging in the dark; gleaming white, it felt sleek and cold against my cheek. Its smell was dense and musty and not unlike the slabs of my grandmother's great arms after her cool, evening sponge baths. In that shed I looked up and saw

1. **Hippies:** a group with unconventional ideas about dress, work, and living habits.
2. **carnivores** (kär′nə-vôrz′, -vōrz′): flesh-eaters.

3. **phantasmagoric** (făn-tăz′mə-gôr′ĭk): fantastic and dreamlike.

Huntsman and Dogs (1891) by Winslow Homer (1836–1910). Oil on canvas.

the flensed[4] body of a doe; it swung gently, slapping my face. I felt then as I do even now when eating game: horror and awe and hunger.

Growing up those first years on a forest sta-

tion high in the Sierra[5] was somewhat like belonging to a white tribe. The men hiked off every day into their forest and the women stayed behind in the circle of official cabins, breeding. So far away from a store, we ate veni-

4. **flensed** (flĕnsd): stripped of its skin.

5. **Sierra** (sē-ĕr′ə): in northeastern California.

Philadelphia Museum of Art, The William L. Elkins Collection

son and squirrel, rattlesnake and duck. My brother's first rattle, in fact, was from a King Rattler my father killed as we watched, by snatching it up with a stick and winding it, whiplike, around a redwood sapling. Rattlesnake tastes just like chicken, but has many fragile bones to slither one's way through; we also ate salmon, rabbit, and geese galore. The game was accompanied by such daily garden dainties as fried okra, mustard greens, corn fritters, wilted lettuce (our favorite because of that rare, blackened bacon), new potatoes and peas, stewed tomatoes, barbecued butter beans.

I was four before I ever had a beef hamburger and I remember being disappointed by its fatty, nothing taste and the way it fell apart at the seams whenever my teeth sank into it. Smoked pork shoulder came much later in the South; and I was twenty-one, living in New York City, before I ever tasted leg of lamb. I approached that glazed rack of meat with a certain guilty self-consciousness, as if I unfairly stalked those sweet-tempered white creatures myself. But how would I explain my squeamishness to those urban sophisticates? How explain that I was shy with mutton when I had been bred on wild things?

Part of it, I suspect, had to do with the belief I'd also been bred on—we become the spirit and body of animals we eat. As a child eating venison I liked to think of myself as lean and lovely just like the deer. I would never be caught dead just grazing while some man who wasn't even a skillful hunter crept up and konked me over the head. If someone wanted to hunt me, he must be wily and outwitting. He must earn me.

My father had also taught us as children that animals were our brothers and sisters under their skin. They died so that we might live. And of this sacrifice we must be mindful. "God make us grateful for what we are about to receive," took on a new meaning when one knew the animal's struggle pitted against our own appetite. We also used *all* the animal so that an elk became elk steaks, stew, salami, and sausage. His head and horns went on the wall to watch us more earnestly than any babysitter, and every Christmas Eve we had a ceremony of making our own moccasins for the new year out of whatever Father had tanned. "Nothing wasted," my father would always say, or, as we munched on sausage cookies made from moosemeat or venison, "Think about who you're eating." We thought of ourselves as intricately linked to the food chain. We knew, for example, that a forest fire meant, at the end of the line, we'd suffer too. We'd have buck stew instead of venison steak and the meat would be stringy, withered-tasting because in the animal kingdom, as it seemed with humans, only the meanest and leanest and orneriest survived.

Once when I was in my early teens, I went along on a hunting trip as the "main cook and bottle-washer," though I don't remember any bottles; none of these hunters drank alcohol. There was something else coursing through their veins as they rose long before dawn and disappeared, returning to my little camp most often dragging a doe or pheasant or rabbit. We ate innumerable cornmeal-fried catfish, had rabbit stew seasoned only with blood and black pepper.

This hunting trip was the first time I remember eating game as a conscious act. My father and Buddy Earl shot a big doe and she lay with me in the back of the tarp-draped station wagon all the way home. It was not the smell I minded, it was the glazed great, dark eyes and the way that head flopped around crazily on what I knew was once a graceful neck. I found myself petting this doe, murmuring all those graces we'd been taught long ago as children. *Thank you for the sacrifice, thank you for letting us be like you so that we can grow up strong as game.* But there was an uneasiness in me that night as I bounced along in the back of the car with the deer.

What was uneasy is still uneasy—perhaps it always will be. It's not easy when one really starts thinking about all this: the eating game, the food chain, the sacrifice of one for the other. It's never easy when one begins to think about one's most basic actions, like eating. Like becoming what one eats: lean and lovely and mortal.

Why should it be that the purchase of meat at a butcher shop is somehow more righteous than eating something wild? Perhaps it has to do with our collective unconscious[6] that sees the animal bred for slaughter as doomed. But that wild doe or moose might make it without the hunter. Perhaps on this primitive level of archetype[7] and unconscious knowing we even believe that what's wild lives forever.

My father once told this story around a hunting campfire. His own father, who raised cattle during the Depression[8] on a dirt farm in the Ozarks,[9] once fell on such hard times that he had to butcher the pet lamb for supper. My father, bred on game or their own hogs all his life, took one look at the family pet on that meat platter and pushed his plate away from him. His siblings followed suit. To hear my grandfather tell it, it was the funniest thing he'd ever seen. "They just couldn't eat Bo-Peep," Grandfather said. And to hear my father tell it years later around that campfire, it was funny, but I saw for the first time his sadness. And I realized that eating had become a conscious act for him that day at the dinner table when Bo-Peep offered herself up.

Now when someone offers me game I will eat it with all the qualms and memories and reverence with which I grew up eating it. And I think it will always be this feeling of horror and awe and hunger. And something else— full knowledge of what I do, what I become.

6. **collective unconscious:** deeply embedded psychological experiences that all individuals share.
7. **archetype** (är′kə-tīp′): a first model or type.
8. **Depression:** the Great Depression of the 1930s.
9. **Ozarks** (ō′zärks): Ozark Mountains extending from southeast Missouri across northwest Arkansas into eastern Oklahoma.

raised on? **b.** What attitude toward nature is revealed in these beliefs?

5. During a hunting trip the author says she became aware of eating game as "a conscious act." To what does she attribute her uneasiness?

6. At the conclusion of an essay, a writer will often restate his or her main point. **a.** Pick out a sentence in the last paragraph in which Peterson answers her implied question about the "not-so-simple truth" posed in the introduction. **b.** Has she given evidence of this conflict throughout the essay?

7. Explain the title of the essay.

For Study and Discussion

Analyzing and Interpreting the Essay

1. At the opening of the essay, Peterson recalls an experience from college days that provides a point of departure for the essay. **a.** What does the episode reveal about people's attitudes toward eating game? **b.** What irony is involved in the reactions of her dinner guests to the "lean sweetness" of the moose meat?

2. In the second paragraph of the essay, Peterson recalls playing in a shed where she came in contact with the flesh of a doe. **a.** How did she feel? **b.** Where else in the essay does she experience a similar mixture of emotions?

3. Peterson says that she felt a "guilty self-consciousness" about eating leg of lamb. **a.** How do you account for her squeamishness? **b.** How does the anecdote about Bo-Peep at the end of the essay relate to this episode?

4. The author was raised on the belief that hunters "become the spirit and body of animals" they eat. **a.** What other belief was she

Language and Vocabulary

Using Context Clues

The *context* of a word can help you determine its meaning. The context may be a single sentence, a passage, or even a whole work. Consider the word *game* in the title of Peterson's essay. What different meanings of the word are suggested by the essay as a whole?

Use context clues to define the italicized words in the following excerpts from the essay. Check your answers in the glossary or in a dictionary.

I told my housemates that my moose meat in its *nondescript* white butcher paper was from a side of beef . . .

If someone wanted to hunt me, he must be *wily* and outwitting.

Why should it be that the purchase of meat at a butcher shop is somehow more *righteous* than eating something wild?

For Oral Expression

Holding an Interview

Plan to interview a relative or neighbor about some episode in the past. For example, if you know someone who lived through the Great Depression, does he or she have any stories of hardship comparable to that of Bo-Peep? Give thought to your questions so that you invite extended replies instead of *yes* and *no* answers. Give the other person time to respond to your questions. During the interview take notes or ask permission to use a tape recorder. You can make your interview the subject of an oral report or a composition.

Focus on Expository Writing

Identifying Parts of a Process

In "Growing Up Game," Brenda Peterson uses incidents to explain a **process** of growing awareness. In a similar way you can use parts, steps, or stages of a process to explain how something works or to inform your readers about a topic.

A good example of a process with stages or parts is the food chain of an ecosystem (see page 224). Here is a highly simplified outline of a food chain. The arrows connect each step in the movement of food and energy.

Solar energy →
Abiotic (nonliving) substances, like water and
　phosphorus →
Producers (trees, plants) →
Primary consumers (rabbits, squirrels: eat
　plants, grass, nuts, seeds) →
Secondary consumers (hawks, foxes: eat rab-
　bits, other small animals) →
Decomposers (bacteria, fungi: decompose
　animal and plant remains into nutrients
　needed by growing plants)

Now try your hand at expository writing. Write a paragraph about the food chain that explains the information in the diagram. When you have finished, get together with a partner and trade paragraphs. Offer each other suggestions for revision. Save your writing.

About the Author

Brenda Peterson (1950–　)

Brenda Peterson was born in Quincy, California, but considers her roots to be Southern. Her family moved wherever her father's forestry work took them. She spent the first part of her childhood in California, then moved to Virginia and later to Georgia. After graduating from the University of California at Davis, she worked in New York City for *The New Yorker*. Her first novel, *River of Light,* was published in 1978. It was followed by *Becoming the Enemy* (1988) and *Duck and Cover* (1991). She is also the author of a collection of essays, *Living by Water: Essays on Life, Land and Spirit* (1990). She lives on Puget Sound in Seattle, Washington.

How to Name a Dog

JAMES THURBER

Thurber is a master of the informal essay. One of his methods as an essayist and satirist is to focus on a subject or area of experience, and to range freely, introducing ideas and experiences not always closely related to the subject he began with. This is the method of the conversationalist. Thurber shares with the reader his amusement over human foibles—the comic oddities of character rather than its faults.

As you read, note that Thurber reveals as much about himself as he does about his subject.

Every few months somebody writes me and asks if I will give him a name for his dog. Several of these correspondents in the past year have wanted to know if I would mind the use of my own name for their spaniels. Spaniel-owners seem to have the notion that a person could sue for invasion of privacy or defamation of character if his name were applied to a cocker without written permission, and one gentleman even insisted that we conduct our correspondence in the matter through a notary public. I have a way of letting communications of this sort fall behind my roll-top desk, but it has recently occurred to me that this is an act of evasion, if not, indeed, of plain cowardice. I have therefore decided to come straight out with the simple truth that it is as hard for me to think up a name for a dog as it is for anybody else. The idea that I am an expert in the business is probably the outcome of a piece I wrote several years ago, incautiously revealing the fact that I have owned forty or more dogs in my life. This is true, but it is also deceptive.

All but five or six of my dogs were disposed of when they were puppies, and I had not gone to the trouble of giving to these impermanent residents of my house any names at all except Shut Up! and Cut That Out! and Let Go!

Names of dogs end up in 176th place in the list of things that amaze and fascinate me. Canine cognomens should be designed to impinge on the ears of dogs and not to amuse neighbors, tradespeople, and casual visitors. I remember a few dogs from the past with a faint but lingering pleasure: a farm hound named Rain, a roving Airedale named Marco Polo, a female bull terrier known as Brody[1] because she liked to jump from moving motor cars and second-story windows, and a Peke called Darien;[2] but that's all.

1. **Brody:** A man named Steven Brodie pretended to jump off the Brooklyn Bridge in 1886.
2. **Peke called Darien:** *Peke* is short for Pekingese. Thurber is punning on the phrase "a peak in Darien" from the sonnet "On First Looking into Chapman's Homer" by John Keats.

Well, there is Poker, alias *Fantôme Noir*,[3] a miniature black poodle I have come to know since I wrote the preceding paragraphs. Poker, familiarly known as Pokey, belongs to Mr. and Mrs. J. G. Gude, of White Plains, and when they registered him with the American Kennel Club they decided he needed a more dignified name. It wasn't easy to explain this to their youngest child, David, and his parents never did quite clear it up for him. When he was only eight, David thought the problem over for a long while and then asked his father solemnly, "If he belongs to that club, why doesn't he ever go there?" Since I wrote this piece originally, I have also heard about a sheepdog named Jupiter, which used to belong to Jimmy Cannon, journalist, critic, and man about dog shows. He reported in a recent column of his that Jupiter used to eat geraniums. I have heard of other dogs that ate flowers, but I refuse to be astonished by this until I learn of one that's downed a nasturtium.

The only animals whose naming demands concentration, hard work, and ingenuity are the seeing-eye dogs. They have to be given unusual names because passers-by like to call to seeing-eyers—"Here, Sport" or "Yuh, Rags" or "Don't take any wooden nickels, Rin Tin Tin." A blind man's dog with an ordinary name would continually be distracted from its work. A tyro at naming these dogs might make the mistake of picking Durocher[4] or Teeftallow.[5] The former is too much like Rover and the latter could easily sound like "Here, fellow" to a dog. Ten years ago I met a young man in his twenties who had been mysteriously blind for nearly five years and had been led about by a seeing-eye German shepherd during all of that time, which included several years of study at Yale. Then suddenly one night the dog's owner began to get his vision back, and within a few weeks was able to read the fine print of a telephone book. The effect on his dog was almost disastrous, and it went into a kind of nervous crackup, since these animals are trained to the knowledge, or belief, that their owners are permanently blind. After the owner regained his vision he kept his dog, of course, not only because they had become attached to each other but because the average seeing-eye dog cannot be transferred from one person to another.

Speaking of puppies, as I was a while back, I feel that I should warn inexperienced dog-owners who have discovered to their surprise and dismay a dozen puppies in a hall closet or under the floor of the barn, not to give them

3. *Fantôme Noir* (fàn'tôm nwár): French for "black phantom."

4. **Durocher:** Leo Durocher, a manager of the Brooklyn Dodgers.
5. **Teeftallow:** the title of a book by T. S. Stribling, published in the 1920's.

away. Sell them or keep them, but don't give them away. Sixty percent of persons who are given a dog for nothing bring him back sooner or later and plump him into the reluctant and unprepared lap of his former owner. The people say that they are going to Florida and can't take the dog, or that he doesn't want to go; or they point out that he eats first editions or lace curtains or spinets, or that he doesn't see eye to eye with them in the matter of housebreaking, or that he makes disparaging remarks under his breath about their friends. Anyway, they bring him back and you are stuck with him—and maybe six others. But if you charge ten or even five dollars for pups, the new owners don't dare return them. They are afraid to ask for their money back because they believe you might think they are hard up and need the five or ten dollars. Furthermore, when a mischievous puppy is returned to its former owner it invariably behaves beautifully, and the person who brought it back is likely to be regarded as an imbecile or a dog-hater or both.

Names of dogs, to get back to our subject, have a range almost as wide as that of the violin. They run from such plain and simple names as Spot, Sport, Rex, Brownie to fancy appellations such as Prince Rudolph Hertenberg Gratzheim of Darndorf-Putzelhorst, and Darling Mist o' Love III of Heather-Light-Holyrood—names originated by adults, all of whom in every other way, I am told, have made a normal adjustment to life. In addition to the plain and fancy categories, there are the Cynical and the Coy. Cynical names are given by people who do not like dogs too much. The most popular cynical names during the war[6] were Mussolini, Tojo, and Adolf. I never have been able to get very far in my exploration of the minds of people who call their dogs Mussolini, Tojo, and Adolf,

6. **war:** World War II.

and I suspect the reason is that I am unable to associate with them long enough to examine what goes on in their heads. I nod, and I tell them the time of day, if they ask, and that is all. I never vote for them or ask them to have a drink. The great Coy category is perhaps the largest. The Coy people call their pets Bubbles and Boggles and Sparkles and Twinkles and Doodles and Puffy and Lovums and Sweetums and Itsy-Bitsy and Betsy-Bye-Bye and Sugarkins. I pass these dog-owners at a dog-trot, wearing a horrible fixed grin.

There is a special subdivision of the Coys that is not quite so awful, but awful enough. These people, whom we will call the Wits, own two dogs, which they name Pitter and Patter, Willy and Nilly, Helter and Skelter, Namby and Pamby, Hugger and Mugger, and even Wishy and Washy, Ups and Daisy, Fitz and Startz, Fetch and Carrie, and Pro and Connie. Then there is the Cryptic category. These people select names for some private reason or for no reason at all—except perhaps to arouse a visitor's curiosity, so that he will exclaim, "Why in the world do you call your dog *that*?" The Cryptic name their dogs October, Bennett's Aunt, Three Fifteen, Doc Knows, Tuesday, Home Fried, Opus 38, Ask Leslie, and Thanks for the Home Run, Emil. I make it a point simply to pat these unfortunate dogs on the head, ask no question of their owners, and go about my business.

This article has degenerated into a piece that properly should be entitled "How Not to Name a Dog." I was afraid it would. It seems only fair to make up for this by confessing a few of the names I have given my own dogs, with the considerable help, if not, indeed, the insistence, of their mistress. Most of my dogs have been females, and they have answered, with apparent gladness, to such names as Jennie, Tessa, Julie, and Sophie. I have never owned a dog named Pamela, Jennifer,

© James Thurber, Helen Thurber

I shook hands, and he didn't seem to me any more depressed than any other spaniel I have met. He had, however, the expression of a bachelor on his way to a party he has tried in vain to get out of, and I think it must have been this cast of countenance that had reminded Mr. Stong of the dog I draw. The dog I draw is, to be sure, much larger than a spaniel and not so shaggy, but I confess, though I am not a spaniel man, that there are certain basic resemblances between my dog and all other dogs with long ears and troubled eyes.

Perhaps I should suggest at least one name for a dog, if only to justify the title of this piece. All right, then, what's the matter with Stong? It's a good name for a dog, short, firm, and effective. I recommend it to all those who have written to me for suggestions and to all those who may be at this very moment turning over in their minds the idea of asking my advice in this difficult and perplexing field of nomenclature.

Since I first set down these not too invaluable rules for naming dogs, I have heard of at least a dozen basset hounds named Thurber, a Newfoundland called Little Bears Thurber and a bloodhound named Tiffany's Thurber. This is all right with me, so long as the owners of Thurbers do not bring them to call on me at my house in Connecticut without making arrangements in advance. Christabel, my old and imperious poodle, does not like unannounced dog visitors, and tries to get them out of the house as fast as she can. Two years ago a Hartford dog got lost in my neighborhood and finally showed up at my house. He hadn't had much, if anything, to eat for several days, and we fed him twice within three hours, to the high dismay and indignation of Christabel, who only gets one big meal a day. The wanderer was returned to its owner, through a story in the Hartford *Courant*, and quiet descended on my home until a handsome young

Clarrisa, Jacqueline, Guinevere, or Shelmerdene.

About fifteen years ago, when I was looking for a house to buy in Connecticut, I knocked on the front door of an attractive home whose owner, my real-estate agent had told me, wanted to sell it and go back to Iowa to live. The lady agent who escorted me around had informed me that the owner of this place was a man named Strong, but a few minutes after arriving at the house, I was having a drink in the living room with Phil Stong,[7] for it was he. We went out into the yard after a while and I saw Mr. Stong's spaniel. I called to the dog and snapped my fingers, but he seemed curiously embarrassed, like his master. "What's his name?" I asked the latter. He was cornered and there was no way out of it. "Thurber," he said, in a small frightened voice. Thurber and

7. **Phil Stong:** American writer (1899–1957), author of *State Fair.*

male collie showed up one night. We had quite a time getting him out of the house. Christabel kept telling him how wonderful it was out-doors and trotting to the door, but the collie wasn't interested. I tried to pick him up, but I am too old to pick up a full-grown collie. In the end Christabel solved the problem herself by leading him outside on the promise of letting him chew one of the bones she had buried. He still keeps coming back to visit us from time to time, but Christabel has hidden her bones in new places. She will romp with the young visi-tor for about twenty seconds, then show her teeth and send him home. I don't do anything about the situation. After all, my home has been in charge of Christabel for a great many years now, and I never interfere with a woman's ruling a household.

Reading Check

1. According to Thurber, which dogs require unusual names?
2. Why does Thurber advise dog own-ers to sell their puppies rather than give them away?
3. What does Thurber think would be a more appropriate title for his essay?
4. What is the one name Thurber sug-gests for a dog?

For Study and Discussion

Analyzing and Interpreting the Essay

1. An informal essay may reveal as much about the personality of its author as it does about its subject. **a.** What impression do you get of Thurber from his various comments in the opening paragraph? **b.** Would you say that he is tolerant or intolerant of people's quirks and foibles? **c.** Does he have a sense of humor about himself as well as about oth-ers?

2. Thurber's essay points out that the naming of a dog reveals something of the owner's personality. **a.** What incident shows that Poker's owners are snobs? **b.** What is special about spaniel-owners? **c.** According to Thurber, what do the Cynical, Coy, and Cryp-tic categories of names tell about dog-owners?

3. An **informal essay** is often written in a con-versational style complete with digressions and humorous anecdotes. **a.** At what points in the essay does Thurber let on that he has wan-dered from the subject? **b.** How does he make a return to the subject?

4a. How does Thurber show that he credits his dogs with intelligence and with individual personalities? **b.** What do the names he chose for his own dogs tell you about him? **c.** Would you consider him a genuine dog-lover?

Literary Elements

Opening Sentences

Paragraphs usually begin with a **topic sentence**, a sentence that gives the central idea. Sometimes the central idea is not given until later in the paragraph. The opening sentence, then, states the subject of the paragraph only, and serves as a signpost to the reader.

The opening sentence of the third paragraph in Thurber's essay states the subject only:

Well, there is Poker . . . a miniature black poodle I have come to know since I wrote the preceding paragraphs.

The opening sentence of the fourth paragraph states the central idea:

The only animals whose naming demands concentration, hard work, and ingenuity are the seeing-eye dogs.

Which of Thurber's opening sentences resemble the first sentence, and which resemble the second?

Language and Vocabulary

Recognizing Words Used for Humorous Effect

Thurber uses the fancy word *cognomen* in place of the simple word *name* for humorous effect in the following sentence:

Canine cognomens should be designed to impinge on the ears of dogs and not to amuse neighbors, tradespeople, and casual visitors.

Find other examples in the essay of words and names chosen or cited for their humor.

Determining Exact Meanings

Thurber chooses words for their exact meanings. The words *impinge on* in the sentence quoted above carry the meaning of "colliding with"—and that is the exact meaning Thurber wants in his sentence. The name should catch the attention of the dog, make its ears perk up—in short, collide with the dog. Look up the italicized words in the following sentences and explain how each word or phrase is used:

I have a way of letting communications of this sort fall behind my roll-top desk, but it has recently occurred to me that this is an act of *evasion*, if not, indeed, of plain cowardice.

The only animals whose naming demands concentration, hard work, and *ingenuity* are the seeing-eye dogs.

. . . I feel that I should warn inexperienced dog-owners who have discovered to their surprise and *dismay* a dozen puppies in a hall closet or under the floor of the barn, not to give them away.

Cynical names are given by people who do not like dogs too much.

The great *Coy* category is perhaps the largest.

Then there is the *Cryptic* category.

This article has *degenerated* into a piece that properly should be entitled "How Not to Name a Dog."

. . . I think it must have been this *cast of countenance* that had reminded Mr. Stong of the dog I draw.

Creative Writing

Writing a Humorous Essay

Write a humorous essay on one of the following topics. In your opening paragraph, introduce yourself to your reader as Thurber does. Conclude your essay with a final anecdote or an observation about your experience.

Living with a family pet
The pleasures of raising and caring for a pet
Getting along with neighborhood pets

Focus on Expository Writing

Choosing a Process to Explain

Thurber's humorous explanation of a process reflects the author's interest in dogs. When you consider topics for an expository essay, you may find these strategies useful:

1. Make a list of your interests.
2. Think about the value and appeal to others of various skills and processes.
3. Consider how much your audience knows about the topic.
4. Evaluate the extent of the topic: Is it suitable for a short essay?

Choose *two* topics for informative essays. One topic should be on how to do something, whereas the other should be on how something works. For each topic make a prewriting chart like the one below:

```
Topic: _____
Value/Interest: _____
Audience: _____
Steps/Stages in process
    1: _____
    2: _____
    3: _____
    4: _____
```

When you have finished writing, get together with a small group of classmates to discuss your ideas. Save your notes.

About the Author

James Thurber (1894–1961)

The American satirist James Thurber was born and raised in Columbus, Ohio, where he later attended Ohio State University. Most of his sketches, stories, and illustrations first appeared in *The New Yorker* magazine, with which Thurber was closely associated throughout his writing career. Thurber lost the use of one eye as a boy, and by the time of his death he was almost completely blind; yet he continued to write with undiminished humor and vigor.

Thurber is famous not only as a writer but also as a cartoonist. He created a gallery of memorable dogs. His most famous dog was known as "Thurberhound." It had the body and head of a bloodhound and the short legs of a basset. Thurber's essays and cartoons about dogs were collected in the volume *Thurber's Dogs*. In that book Thurber wrote: "The dog has got more fun out of Man than Man has got out of the dog, for the clearly demonstrable reason that Man is the more laughable of the two animals."

The Death of a Tree

EDWIN WAY TEALE

Teale was raised in Joliet, Illinois, but up to the age of sixteen lived most of his summers with his grandparents on their farm in northern Indiana, close to the dunes of Lake Michigan. It is this world that Teale describes in the essay reprinted here. Teale uses an important form of analysis, that of process—here, *a natural process rather than an artificial or a historical one.*

In reading this essay, notice that each paragraph focuses on a single idea and usually states that idea in the opening sentence. At every point in the essay, the reader sees where he or she is going. Yet Teale manages his transitions skillfully: he does not clutter the essay with signposts that detract attention from ideas and details. Teale writes in simple language, in a familiar style that never calls attention to itself. We hear always the voice of the speaking man—of a human being who communicates in writing as he would converse with us, seriously, about what he has observed in his lifetime.

For a great tree death comes as a gradual transformation. Its vitality ebbs slowly. Even when life has abandoned it entirely it remains a majestic thing. On some hilltop a dead tree may dominate the landscape for miles around. Alone among living things it retains its character and dignity after death. Plants wither; animals disintegrate. But a dead tree may be as arresting, as filled with personality, in death as it is in life. Even in its final moments, when the massive trunk lies prone and it has moldered into a ridge covered with mosses and fungi, it arrives at a fitting and a noble end. It enriches and refreshes the earth. And later, as part of other green and growing things, it rises again.

The death of the great white oak which gave our Indiana homestead its name and which played such an important part in our daily lives was so gentle a transition that we never knew just when it ceased to be a living organism.

It had stood there, toward the sunset from the farmhouse, rooted in that same spot for two hundred years or more. How many generations of red squirrels had rattled up and down its gray-black bark! How many generations of robins had sung from its upper branches! How many humans, from how many lands, had paused beneath its shade!

The passing of this venerable giant made a profound impression upon my young mind. Just what caused its death was then a mystery.

Looking back, I believe the deep drainage ditches, which had been cut through the dune-country marshes a few years before, had lowered the water table just sufficiently to affect the roots of the old oak. Millions of delicate root tips were injured. As they began to wither, the whole vast underground system of nourishment broke down and the tree was no longer able to send sap to the upper branches.

Like a river flowing into a desert, the life stream of the tree dwindled and disappeared before it reached the topmost twigs. They died first. The leaf at the tip of each twig, the last to unfold, was the first to wither and fall. Then, little by little, the twig itself became dead and dry. This process of dissolution, in the manner of a movie run backward, reversed the development of growth. Just as, cell by cell, the twig had grown outward toward the tip, so now death spread, cell by cell, backward from the tip.

Sadly we watched the blight work from twig to branch, from smaller branch to larger branch, until the whole top of the tree was dead and bare. For years those dry, barkless upper branches remained intact. Their wood became gray and polished by the winds. When thunderstorms rolled over the farm from the northwest the dead branches shone like silver against the black and swollen sky. Robins and veeries sang from these lofty perches, gilded by the sunset long after the purple of advancing dusk filled the spaces below.

Then, one by one, their resiliency gone, the topmost limbs crashed to earth, carried away by the fury of stormwinds. In fragments and patches, bark from the upper trunk littered the ground below. The protecting skin of the tree was broken. In through the gaps poured a host of microscopic enemies, the organisms of decay.

Ghostly white fungus penetrated into the sapwood. It worked its way downward along the unused tubes, those vertical channels through which had flowed the lifeblood of the oak. The continued flow of this sap might have kept out the fungus. But sap rises only to branches clothed with leaves. As each limb became blighted and leafless, the sap level dropped to the next living branch below. And close on the heels of this descending fluid followed the fungus. From branch to branch its silent, deadly descent continued.

Soft and flabby, so unsubstantial it can be crushed without apparent pressure between a thumb and forefinger, this pale fungus is yet able to penetrate through the hardest of woods. This amazing and paradoxical feat is accomplished by means of digestive enzymes which the fungus secretes and which dissolve the wood as strong acids might do. These fungus enzymes, science has learned, are virtually the same as those produced by the single-celled protozoa which live in the bodies of the termites and enable those insects to digest the cellulose in wood.

Advancing in the form of thin white threads, which branch again and again, the fungus works its way from side to side as well as downward through the trunk of a dying tree. Beyond the reach of our eyes the fungus kept spreading within the body of the old oak, branching into a kind of vast, interlacing root system of its own, pale and ghostly.

Behind the fungus, along the dead upper trunk, yellow hammers drummed on the dry wood. I saw them, with their chisel-bills, hewing out nesting holes which, in turn, admitted new organisms of decay. In effect, the dissolution of a great tree is like the slow turning of an immense wheel of life. Each stage of its decline and decay brings a whole new, interdependent population of dwellers and their parasites.

Even while the lower branches of the oak were still green, insect wreckers were already at work above them. First to arrive were the bark beetles. In the earliest stages their fare was the tender inner layer of the bark, the living bond between the trunk and its covering. As death spread downward in the oak, as freezing and storms loosened the bark, the beetles descended, foot by foot. Some of them left behind elaborate patterns, branching mazes of tunnels that took on the appearance of fantastic "thousand-leggers" engraved on wood.

During the winter when I was twelve years old a gale of abnormal force swept the Great Lakes region. Gusts reached almost hurricane proportions. Weakened by the work of the fungus, bacteria, woodpeckers, and beetles, the whole top of the tree snapped off some seventy feet from the ground. After that the progress of its dissolution was rapid.

Finally the last of the lower leaves disappeared. The green badge of life returned no more. On summer days the sound of the wind sweeping through the old oak had a winter shrillness. No more was there the rustling of a multitude of leaves above our hammock; no more was there the "plump!" of falling acorns.

Leaves and acorns, life and progress, were at an end.

In the days that followed, as the bark loosened to the base, the wheel of life, which had its hub in the now-dead oak, grew larger.

I saw carpenter ants hurrying this way and that over the lower tree trunk. Ichneumon flies, trailing deadly, drill-like ovipositors,[1] hovered above the bark in search of buried larvae on which to lay their eggs. Carpenter bees, their black abdomens glistening like patent leather, bit their way into the dry wood of the dead branches. Click beetles and sow bugs and small spiders found security beneath fragments of the loosened bark. And around the base of the tree swift-legged carabid beetles hunted their insect prey under cover of darkness.

Yellowish-brown, the wood flour of the powder-post beetles began to sift about the foot of the oak. It, in turn, attracted the larvae of the darkling beetles. Thus, link by link, the chain of life expanded. To the expert eye the condition of the wood, the bark, the ground about the base of the oak—all told of the action of the interrelated forms of life attracted by the death and decay of a tree.

But below all this activity, beyond the power of human sight to detect, other changes were taking place. The underground root system, comprising almost as much wood as was visible in the tree rising above ground, was also altering.

Fungus, entering the damaged root tips or working downward from the infected trunk, followed the sap channels and hastened decay. The great main roots, spreading out as far as the widest branches of the tree itself, altered rapidly. Their fibers grew brittle; their old pliancy disappeared; their bark split and loosened. The breakdown of the upper tree found

its counterpart, within the darkness of the earth, in the dissolution of the lower roots.

I remember well the day the great oak came down. I was fourteen at the time. Gramp had measured distances and planned his cutting operations in advance. He chopped away for fully half an hour before he had a V-shaped bite cut exactly in position to bring the trunk crashing in the place desired. Hours filled with the whine of the crosscut saw followed.

Then came the great moment. A few last, quick strokes. A slow, deliberate swaying. The crack of parting fibers. Then a long "swoo-sh!" that rose in pitch as the towering trunk arced downward at increasing speed. There followed a vast tumult of crashing, crackling sound; the dance of splintered branches; a haze of dead, swirling grass. Then a slow settling of small objects and silence. All was over. Lone oak was gone.

Gram, I remember, brushed away what she remarked was dust in her eyes with a corner of her apron and went inside. She had known and loved that one great tree since she had come to the farm as a bride of sixteen. She had seen it under all conditions and through eyes colored by many moods. Her children had grown up under its shadow and I, a grandchild, had known its shade. Its passing was like the passing of an old, old friend. For all of us there seemed an empty space in our sky in the days that followed.

Gramp and I set to work, attacking the fallen giant. Great piles of cordwood, mounds of broken branches for kindling, grew around the prostrate trunk as the weeks went by. Eventually only the huge, circular table of the low stump remained—reddish-brown and slowly dissolving into dust.

For two winters wood from the old oak fed the kitchen range and the dining-room stove. It had a clean, well-seasoned smell. And it burned with a clear and leaping flame,

---

1. **Ichneumon** (ĭk-nōō'mən); **ovipositor** (ō'və-pŏz'ə-tər).

continuing—unlike the quickly consumed poplar and elm—for an admirable length of time. Like the old tree itself, the fibers of these sticks had character and endurance to the very end.

Reading Check

1. What was responsible for the death of the oak tree?
2. What was the first outward sign that the tree was dying?
3. What part of the tree is compared to a protective skin?
4. What microscopic organisms and other wreckers attacked the tree?
5. What kind of damage was done by winds?

For Study and Discussion

Analyzing and Interpreting the Essay

1. Teale states his central idea, or **thesis,** in his opening paragraph. Death comes to the tree as a "gradual transformation." **a.** How does this transformation make the death of the tree different from the death of plants and animals? **b.** What point is Teale making about the tree in the whole paragraph?

2a. How do the details of the description illustrate the point that "Each stage of its decline and decay brings a whole new, interdependent population of dwellers and their parasites"? **b.** How does this process of dissolution explain the phrase, "the slow turning of an immense wheel of life"?

3. What are the three main stages in the death of the tree, and how does Teale keep them in focus for the reader?

4a. How do the details of the final paragraphs relate the tree to the human world? **b.** How does Teale restate his thesis in the final paragraph?

Literary Elements

Figures of Speech

In discussing the possible cause of the tree's death, and the beginning of the process, Teale uses metaphor and simile. The tree is metaphorically a "venerable giant," as if it possessed human qualities. This particular kind of metaphor is called **personification.** How are these qualities suggested in the details of the living tree? What comparisons or similies does Teale use to make the process of dying concrete?

Language and Vocabulary

Determining Exact Meanings

Use your dictionary to determine the exact meaning of each of the following words:

blight	dissolution	molder
disintegrate	dwindle	wither

Write sentences of your own, using each word to show its exact meaning.

Recognizing Parallelism

Teale occasionally arranges sentences in parallel order to stress the similarity in ideas:

> How many generations of robins had sung from its upper branches!
>
> How many humans, from how many lands, had paused beneath its shade!

Phrases and clauses within a sentence can be balanced in the same way: "How many humans, from how many lands." Find examples of other phrases or clauses balanced in the same way.

Focus on Expository Writing

Outlining a Process Explanation

Teale's essay clearly describes the stages of the old tree's death. Teale also arranges the information in his essay logically; for example, he combines chronological order with spatial order (from top to bottom of the tree) to discuss the stages of the tree's decline.

Make an outline for an expository essay to describe a process with which you are very familiar. Some possible topics include repairing a bicycle tire, cooking a favorite dish, and programming a VCR. Assume that your audience has never performed this process before and therefore needs to be informed about the materials or tools needed as well as the details of each step in the process.

When you have finished writing, ask a classmate to review and comment on your outline. Save your notes.

About the Author

Edwin Way Teale   (1899–1980)

Edwin Way Teale, one of America's foremost authors of nature books, was born on a farm in the Midwest. He began his career as a naturalist by recording his observations of insects. After graduating from Columbia University, he worked as a teacher, a writer, and an editor for *Popular Science*. In his writing Teale introduced his readers to the subtle beauties of nature. *The American Seasons*, his major work, consists of four volumes: *North with the Spring, Journey into Summer, Autumn Across America,* and *Wandering*

Through Winter. The last of these volumes was awarded the Pulitzer Prize in 1966.

Literature and the Natural World

Scientific and Poetic Descriptions

Consider Teale's use of language in "The Death of a Tree." While he uses scientific terminology, such as "cellulose," "single-celled protozoa," and "ovipositors" to describe a natural process, he also uses poetic language. Note the descriptions of fungus as "ghostly" and "white" and of carpenter ants whose black abdomens glistened like "patent leather."

Making Connections: Activities

1. Read about some natural process that interests you (for example, the growth of certain plants or the behavior of certain animals). Describe the process, using some of the scientific terminology you have learned. Also use colorful, descriptive, and poetic language to express your reactions to what you observe. Ask yourself what emotions arise in your contemplation of the natural world. Study the language of Teale's essay to help you in your writing.

2. On your way to school, while in the park, or on a planned field trip with other students, discover which species of trees grow in your immediate neighborhood. Find out as much as you can about one of these species by consulting an illustrated encyclopedia or one of these books: *The Complete Trees of North America* by Thomas S. Elias; *The International Book of Trees* by Hugh Johnson; *The Audubon Society Field Guide to North American Trees* by Elbert L. Little, Jr. You may want to take photographs of some trees and include them with your report in a class presentation.

The Flight of Rachel Carson

GEOFFREY NORMAN

In this essay, Geoffrey Norman focuses on the events leading up to and following the publication of Rachel Carson's Silent Spring, *a book that gave impetus to the environmental movement. Norman's purpose is not simply to report the facts but to persuade the reader that Carson's work was a monumental achievement. As you read, consider the relationship of Norman's introduction and conclusion to the body of the essay and to his thesis.*

You did not have to be a bird watcher to notice, fifteen years after the end of the Second World War, that something was wrong. Many species were not reappearing in the spring in numbers as large as usual. Some of the larger, most majestic birds seemed on the verge of vanishing altogether. I can remember seeing fewer and fewer ospreys in the places where I had always seen them before and thinking that they were suffering from the same complaint that had eliminated the bald eagle from the rivers and bays and bayous that I prowled. We all knew that eagles did not like to share territory, not with other birds and especially not with man. So I assumed the same was true of the osprey, a raptor like the eagle, colored very much like him, but smaller and more abundant. But they were gone one year. Osprey nests that had been used, spring after spring, sat abandoned in the tall, dead pine trees. Eventually the untended nests crumbled until there were only a few forlorn twigs where they had been.

The absence of the pelicans was even more conspicuous and baffling. All along the coasts of the Gulf and the southern Atlantic, pelicans had been so abundant you felt they were everywhere. If you looked out across a stretch of water and saw a piling without a pelican perched on it, the vista was somehow incomplete. If you sat on a beach for twenty minutes, you would be sure to see a formation of pelicans fly by, pumping their wings in unison, then gliding for a few improbable beats. They looked too heavy for that, and you would never call them graceful. But they were able fliers and very determined, slightly comic and irresistible if you cared about birds.

Not everybody does, of course. And there is nothing wrong with that. But many people who do care about birds care intensely. They care almost as much as John James Audubon[1] cared. Something in the flight and song and color of birds serves for them as a window onto all the wonders and beauty of this world. Such a person was Rachel Carson. And she wrote the book that explained what was killing the birds and why we might be next.

It was the late Fifties when she first took an interest in the slow disappearance and, in some cases, massive die-offs of birds. She was then a best-selling author of a trilogy about the sea, *The Sea Around Us, Under the Sea-Wind,* and *The Edge of the Sea.* Her books were serialized by *The New Yorker* and had earned her a vast following and many correspondents, all of whom she was careful to answer. One of them wrote

1. **John James Audubon:** an American naturalist and ornithologist (1785–1851), known for his paintings of North American birds. The Audubon Society, a conservation organization, is named for him.

to ask for her help in stopping the spraying over a private bird sanctuary near Cape Cod. Carson made some inquiries, and as she learned more she became more alarmed. That was the beginning of a labor that was to result in her book *Silent Spring,* which led to action that saved the birds and energized millions to work and campaign and vote for an enduring cause that, for lack of a better name, is called "the environmental movement."

When the book was published, it was an ordinary occurrence for an airplane to fly over a community, trailing a heavy fog that settled slowly to earth and then disappeared like smoke. The fog contained poisons that had been developed during war research and were meant to kill mosquitoes, Japanese beetles, gypsy moths, and other insects lumped together under the category "pests." The poisons were, technically, chlorinated hydrocarbons. The most common was called DDT.

The spraying was done in the name of public health.

And it was done enthusiastically, almost messianically.[2] Tourist communities boasted of the number of tons of DDT sprayed over them each year to keep them "insect-free." In their advertising, chemical companies came close to suggesting that their efforts were the last line of defense against famine and plague. The spraying had the uncritical support of the government, especially the Department of Agriculture. Pesticide spraying was public policy from the local courthouse all the way to Washington, D.C. It was profitable, too, for the chemical companies, universities, food packagers, grocery chains, and farmers. But

the stakes went beyond profit. People in the pesticide programs *believed* in what they were doing. Their faith was of the same order as the faith of physicists who wanted to split the atom—back before there ever was a bomb. The physicists believed that man was destined first to understand and then to control the universe. The sprayers were more modest. They believed that man was meant to control nature. They did not believe it was necessary, however, to understand it first.

But theirs was a real faith, and it did not react kindly when challenged. Twenty-one years after the publication of *Silent Spring*, against a background of Love Canal,[3] routine alarms over contaminated drinking water, and a scandal at the Environmental Protection Agency, which did not even exist then . . . with those benchmarks to go by, it seems extraordinary today that scientists and intelligent laymen could believe that there was nothing dangerous about dumping tons of poisons on the earth to kill bugs. That the bugs would cooperatively die (rather than build resistance to the poisons) and that nothing else would be harmed. That we could, through chemistry, create an insect-free Eden. But that is exactly what people believed.

Shortly after she had begun her research into the effects of spraying, Rachel Carson was asked to testify at an upcoming trial. A group in Long Island was trying to stop spraying against gypsy moths—spraying that had also killed birds and fish and at least one horse. The group had filed for an injunction[4] and would be getting a hearing. Her testimony could be helpful. She was immediately sympathetic and began researching in preparation.

2. **messianically** (mĕs′ē-ăn′ĭk-lē): in the manner of saviors.

3. **Love Canal:** a hazardous waste site in Niagara Falls, New York.
4. **injunction:** a court order prohibiting someone or some group from doing something.

All her life she had loved birds. She was an Audubon member and, in the days before she became a best-selling author, when she was an anonymous Washington bureaucrat, Audubon outings had been perhaps her greatest source of pleasure. There never was much of it. She'd had to work hard to support her family—mother, father, sisters, and, when one of her sisters died, the small, orphaned children. Though she never married—a fact that her detractors turned into a slur—she supported dependents all of her life, much of the time on a small government salary.

So the outings and the birds must have meant a great deal to her. She loved nature, and had from the time she was a small, solitary girl growing up in Pennsylvania farm country. But more than a lover of birds, she was a scientist. She wrote out of her training. She had read the technical papers about the spraying that questioned both the effectiveness and the safety of the chemicals. She was concerned.

But in the end she was unable to testify at the Long Island trial. She was seriously ill. But she was convinced that the trial was important and could be made to stand for the question of pesticide use worldwide. Somebody, she thought, should attend the trial and write about it. She could not do it herself; she had other projects in mind, among them a book on evolution, and there was the matter of her health. Also, she probably knew that any book she wrote on the subject would become, necessarily, a book on the environment and therefore a large undertaking. An ordeal.

So she wrote E. B. White, whom she knew through *The New Yorker*. He was a writer who cared about the natural world and had the gifts to turn coverage of the trial into something larger than itself. He decided not to write the story but agreed it was important and that somebody should. He urged her to write it. She finally agreed, almost as though she had known all along that she would. But she did not cover the trial, which, as it developed, failed to stop the spraying on Long Island. Instead she started at the very beginning.

The research and writing took four years. During that time she was seriously ill. She had arthritis, developed an ulcer, and came down with staph[5] infections so severe that she could not walk. Her mother was also in poor health. Her niece died and left a very young boy, whom she adopted. Then her mother died. Finally, she was told she had cancer.

The misfortunes did not stop her. Neither did they rush her. Rather, they seemed to

deepen her resolve to write the book and make it impregnable. She knew it would be attacked. She wrote letters to her editor, explaining her intentions, and she continued to work.

Her methods were simple enough. She read the available documents and corresponded with experts. Then, she went through several drafts, revising until she was satisfied with the flow of the prose.

The book that her efforts resulted in was about the spraying and what it did to the birds and other creatures. But that does not begin to describe its scope or account for its impact. One might just as well say that Darwin[6] wrote

5. **staph:** a short form of Staphylococcus, a kind of bacteria.

6. **Darwin:** Charles Darwin (1809–1892), a naturalist who originated the theory that life forms evolve by a process of natural selection.

about turtles and the Pacific islands where they were found.

What Carson did in *Silent Spring* was to introduce to the general imagination the concept of ecology: the way the natural world fit together, the pieces so tightly and inextricably bound that you could not isolate cause and effect. The consequences of any action rippled through the whole system, affecting everything and sometimes even changing the system itself. So when we poisoned gypsy moths with massive sprayings of DDT, we were, ultimately, poisoning ourselves.

The book opened with a parable that described a landscape from which the birds and fish had vanished and where people died of mysterious ailments. It is, on rereading, the weakest portion of the book. But you can understand why it was necessary when you recall that in 1962 people needed to be shocked. They thought pesticides were safe, if they thought about them at all.

From that first chapter, she went on to explain that life on the planet had been changing for millions of years, that such change was slow and organic and inevitable. But now there was something different, a new force at work. Man had made it possible to alter the environment suddenly and drastically, with unforeseen and possibly disastrous consequences.

After sounding the alarm and stating her thesis in the first two chapters, she described the poisons that we were encountering—DDT was showing up even in the fatty tissues of Eskimo who lived in areas where the stuff had never been sprayed. She used diagrams to show the molecular structure of the chlorinated hydrocarbons and made the distinctions between these new poisons and the older ones.

The book went on to detail the effects of these poisons on the environment. Not surprisingly, the most affecting chapter was on the birds. The book's title was inspired by some lines in Keats[7] and an imagined spring when no birds returned.

There was information—data on every page. There was nothing half-baked or mystical about the book. More than fifty pages of sources were cited. But the science and information came filtered through her intelligence and shaped by her graceful writing style. On almost every page there was a gem that owed more to her vision than the research of any laboratory scientist. The best passages are, in fact, lyrical.

Some 10,000 acres of sagelands were sprayed by the [United States Forest] Service, yielding to pressure of cattlemen for more grasslands. The sage was killed, as intended. But so was the green, life-giving ribbon of willows that traced its way across these plains, following the meandering streams. Moose had lived in these willow thickets, for willow is to the moose what sage is to the antelope. Beaver had lived there, too, feeding on the willows, felling them and making a strong dam across the tiny stream. Through the labor of the beavers, a lake backed up. Trout in the mountain streams seldom were more than six inches long; in the lake they thrived so prodigiously that many grew to five pounds. Waterfowl were attracted to the lake, also. Merely because of the presence of the willows and the beavers that depended on them, the region was an attractive recreational area with excellent fishing and hunting.

But with the "improvement" instituted by the Forest Service, the willows went the way of the sagebrush, killed by the same impar-

7. **Keats:** John Keats (1795–1821), an English poet. The lines are from "La Belle Dame sans Merci":
   The sedge has withered from the lake,
      And no birds sing.

tial spray. . . . The moose were gone and so were the beaver. Their principal dam had gone out for want of attention by its skilled architects, and the lake had drained away. None of the large trout were left. None could live in the tiny creek that remained, threading its way through a bare, hot land where no shade remained. The living world was shattered. . . .

As she expected, the book was attacked almost as soon as it was serialized in *The New Yorker*. One chemical firm that was not mentioned by name (though its products were) found a lawyer on the staff who was willing to threaten a lawsuit if her publishers actually brought the book out. He was also not above a little Red-baiting.[8] Members of the chemical industry, he wrote in his letter to Houghton Mifflin, had enough trouble with the food faddists already. Now here was a book that would ". . . reduce the use of agricultural chemicals in this country and in the countries of western Europe, so that our supply of food will be reduced to east-curtain parity. Many innocent groups are financed and led into attacks on the chemical industry by these sinister parties." It was later discovered that the lawyer's client was dumping highly toxic chemicals into the Mississippi River. The poisons caused massive fish kills.

Other chemical company spokesmen and officials in the spraying programs worked tirelessly to discredit the book. They attacked it as offering the bad side of an either-or choice, which it did not; Carson said that pesticides had their uses but were dangerous and that we needed to use them with caution. But the forces attacking the book ignored distinctions she was careful to make. She would have us choose birds over people, they said. Her point was that when you kill the birds you are also

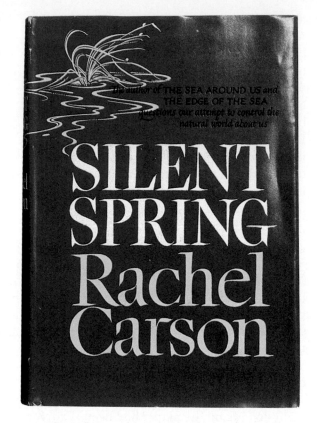

the author of THE SEA AROUND US and THE EDGE OF THE SEA questions our attempt to control the natural world about us

SILENT SPRING Rachel Carson

slowly killing people. M.D.s and heads of university departments of agriculture and presidents of chemical companies attacked the book or merely satisfied themselves with a little ad hominem:[9] ". . . not a scientist," one of them said, "but rather a fanatic defender of the cult of the balance of nature." Another cited her "disregard of the rubrics[10] of evidence, of a nice regard for scientific validity, or any feeling that what she presented should be unbiased." And so on, until it became quite clear that men of science were no more dispassionate now than in the time of Darwin.

Through it all, she kept her silence, letting the book speak for itself. And it held its own

---

8. **Red-baiting:** denouncing someone as a communist.

9. **ad hominem** (ăd hŏm′ĭ-něm): a Latin phrase used to describe an argument which appeals to prejudice or emotions rather than to reason.
10. **rubrics** (ro͞o′brĭks): established rules or directions.

very nicely. It was a best seller for almost a year. Translated all over the world. It was the subject of countless stories and editorials in the newspapers, was reviewed favorably and accepted by millions. . . .

Rachel Carson did not live to see DDT banned or to follow the successes and setbacks of the movement her book launched. She died two years after it was published, at her home in Silver Spring, Maryland. She had testified before Congress and appeared on television and been honored widely. She accepted it all with grace and good humor. (Tiring, perhaps, of the nature-loving-food-faddist charges, she once answered the question "Miss Carson, what do *you* eat?" by saying, "Chlorinated hydrocarbons, just like everyone else.") She left some of her money to the Sierra Club and The Nature Conservancy, and there is a vast wildlife preserve named for her in Maine. A small organization run by a friend continues her work and answers the occasional letter that still comes in addressed to Rachel Carson, usually from someone who has just read the book.

The fight to save the earth from our own destructive excesses will never end. Or, if it does, it will end badly. But since *Silent Spring*, the pelicans and the ospreys have returned. In the morning before I wrote these words, my daughter and I watched from our porch as a pair of ospreys flew along the beach, hunting fish. We admired them together, their graceful, purposeful flight and their heart-catching dives when they spotted prey. They flew on, returning no doubt to their nests and their young, with small fish impaled on their talons. Several large flocks of pelicans also came by, flying in echelon,[11] low to the water, on their way to a rookery. We watched with shared awe, and I recalled some lines Rachel Carson had

11. **echelon** (ĕsh′ə-lŏn): in steplike formation.

written a year or two before she began work on *Silent Spring*. Her subject was encouraging awareness in children, and it could serve as a coda:[12]

A child's world is fresh and new and beautiful, full of wonder and excitement. It is our misfortune that for most of us that clear-eyed vision, that true instinct for what is beautiful and awe-inspiring, is dimmed and even lost before we reach adulthood. If I had influence with the good fairy who is supposed to preside over the christening of all children I should ask that her gift to each child in the world be a sense of wonder so indestructible that it would last throughout life, as an unfailing antidote against the boredom and disenchantments of later years, the sterile preoccupation with things that are artificial, the alienation from the sources of our strength.

That sense of wonder never left Rachel Carson. It was her own source of strength and her legacy.

12. **coda** (kō′də): a concluding passage, usually in music.

Reading Check

1. According to Norman, which birds appeared to be vanishing in the late 1950s?
2. Before Rachel Carson began her research into the effects of spraying pesticides, what had been the subject of her published works?
3. How did Carson become involved in research on pesticides?
4. Who were the most vigorous opponents of Carson's book?
5. What were her methods of research?

For Study and Discussion

Analyzing and Interpreting the Essay

1a. According to Norman, what was the most important consequence of *Silent Spring*? **b.** Briefly restate Carson's thesis.

2. Norman includes two passages written by Carson. **a.** What does the first passage (page 245) reveal about Carson's methods as a researcher? **b.** In what way does the word *lyrical* apply to this passage? **c.** What do both passages reveal about Carson as a person?

3. The body of this essay is framed by an introduction and a conclusion, in which Norman speaks about his personal observations of birds. **a.** What connection is there between these sections and the main body of the essay? **b.** How do these sections drive home Norman's thesis—that Rachel Carson's book created awareness of the complex relationships between living organisms and their environment?

4a. What do you think the title refers to? **b.** Why is the word *flight* an appropriate word for this essay?

Language and Vocabulary

Learning Words from the Latin

The word *pesticide* is made up of the word *pest,* which goes back to a Latin word for "plague," and the suffix *-cide,* which comes from a Latin verb meaning "to kill." Etymologically, the word *pesticide* means "plague killer." We now use it to refer to any chemical that kills such "pests" as rodents, insects, or weeds.

Find these words in a dictionary and tell how they are related to the meaning of *pest:*

pestiferous   pestilence   pestilential

The suffix *-cide* appears in many English words. Find these words in a dictionary and tell what they mean:

deicide   fungicide   regicide

Focus on Expository Writing

Developing a Thesis Statement

In the **thesis statement** of an essay, you identify your topic and your main idea about it in a sentence or two. Geoffrey Norman's thesis, for example, is that Rachel Carson introduced the concept of ecology to a large audience (see page 245). Although Norman places his thesis statement halfway through the essay, many writers prefer to state their thesis early, often in the introduction.

The best thesis statements are clear and specific. Avoid vague words like *interesting* and *important.* Give your readers a definite focus.

Reread your notes for the writing assignments on pages 233 and 239, or make some notes on a new topic for an expository essay. Use your notes to develop a clear, specific thesis statement. Save your writing.

About the Author

Geoffrey Norman (1943–   )

Geoffrey Norman grew up on the Gulf Coast of Florida and Alabama. Before becoming a columnist for *Esquire,* he worked as a magazine editor. His mystery short story, "Armed and Dangerous," was awarded an Edgar Award in 1979. A novel, *Midnight Water,* was published in 1983.

BIOGRAPHY AND PERSONAL RECOLLECTION

"There is properly no history; only biography," said Ralph Waldo Emerson, the great American essayist and poet. He was echoing his British contemporary and friend, Thomas Carlyle, who wrote in his own essay on history, "History is the essence of innumerable biographies."

The interest in great men and women has brought readers to biography since ancient times. We desire to know how these people thought and felt, and what may have been the source of their success in life—and their failures. We also turn to biography to discover our "roots," to use a word Alex Haley has popularized. Perhaps more so than in any previous time, we enjoy reading about ordinary people whose lives helped shape the present world.

My Mother, Rachel West

DOROTHY WEST

Dorothy West recalls scenes of family life, anecdotes, and conversations in an effort to understand her mother. What impression do you form of Rachel West from this portrait?

When my mother died, we who had sparred with her over the years of our growth and maturity said with relief, well, we won't have her intruding herself in our lives again. Our saying it may have been a kind of swaggering, or maybe we were in shock, trying to hide what was really inside us.

My mother had often made the declaration that she was never going to die. She knew what was here, she would say with a laugh, but she didn't know what was there. Heaven was a long way from home. She was staying right here.

So we just accepted it as fact that she would be the death of us instead. When her own death came first, we didn't know what to make of it. There was a thinness in the air. There was silence where there had been sound and fury. There was no longer that beautiful and compelling voice bending us to her will against our own.

The house that I grew up in was four-storied, but we were an extended family, continuously adding new members, and the perpetual joke was, if we lived in the Boston Museum, we'd still need one more room. Surrounded by all these different personalities, each one wanting to be first among equals, I knew I wanted to be a writer. Living with them was like living inside a story.

My mother was the dominant figure by the force of her vitality, and by the indisputable fact that she had the right to rule the roof that my father provided. She was a beautiful woman, and there was that day when I was grown, eighteen or so, ready to go off on my own, sure that I knew everything, that I said to her, "Well, your beauty was certainly wasted on you. All you did with it was raise children and run your sisters' lives."

My mother had done what she felt she had to do, knowing the risks, knowing there would be no rewards, but determined to build a foundation for the generations unborn. She had gathered us together so that the weakness of one would be balanced by her strength, and the loneliness of another eased by her laughter, and someone else's fears tempered by her fierce bravado, and the children treated alike, no matter what their degree of lovability, and her eye riveting mine if I tried to draw a distinction between myself and them.

We who had been the children under her command, and then the adults, still subject to her meddling in our intimate affairs, were finally bereaved, free of the departed, and in a rush to divorce ourselves from any resemblance to her influence.

When one of us said something that Mother might have said, and an outraged chorus shouted, "You sound just like her," the speaker, stung with shame and close to tears, shouted back, "I do not!"

Then as time passed, whoever forgot to watch her language and echoed some sentiment culled from my mother responded to the catcalls with a cool, "So what?"

As time increased its pace, although there were diehards who would never relent, there were more of us shifting positions, examining our ambivalent feelings, wondering if the life force that had so overwhelmed our exercise of free will, and now no longer had to be reckoned with, was a greater loss than a relief.

When a newborn disciple recited my mother's sayings as if they were gospel, the chiding came from a scattered chorus of uninspired voices.

Then there was the day when someone said with wonder, "Have you noticed that those of us who sound just like her are the ones who laugh a lot, love children a lot, don't have any hangups about race or color, and never give up without trying?"

"Yes, I've noticed," one of us answered, with the rest of us adding softly, "Me, too."

I suppose that was the day and the hour of our acknowledgment that some part of her was forever imbedded in our psyches,[1] and we were not the worse for it.

But I still cannot put my finger on the why of her. What had she wanted, this beautiful woman? Did she get it? I would look at her face when it was shut away, and I would long to offer her a penny for her thoughts. But I knew she would laugh and say, "I was just thinking it's time to start dinner," or something equally far from her yearning heart.

I don't think she ever realized how often she made the remark, "Speech was given man to hide his thoughts." At such times I would say

1. **psyches** (sī′kēz): souls.

to myself, she will die with her secrets. I had guessed a few, but they had been only surface deep, easy to flush out. I know that the rest went with her on her flight to heaven.

Reading Check

1. Why did the author want to be a writer?
2. Why did she accuse her mother of wasting her life?
3. What was the chief cause of the children's resentment?
4. Which of their mother's characteristics did the children recognize in one another?

For Study and Discussion

Analyzing and Interpreting the Selection

1. Dorothy West describes her feelings toward her mother as *ambivalent*. What evidence can you find of her conflicting feelings about her mother?

2a. How did Rachel West show a sense of humor? **b.** How did she "build a foundation for the generations unborn"? **c.** What influence did she have on her children?

3. At the end of this biographical sketch, Dorothy West confesses that her mother remains a mystery. **a.** What questions remain unanswered about her mother's life? **b.** Why do you suppose Rachel West never revealed her deepest thoughts?

Language and Vocabulary

Distinguishing Meanings

Explain how the word or words in brackets would change the meaning of the preceding italicized word:

> There was no longer that beautiful and *compelling* [driving] voice bending us to her will against our own.

> My mother was the *dominant* [governing] figure by the force of her vitality . . .

> She had gathered us together so . . . someone else's fears [were] tempered by her fierce *bravado* [show of courage] . . .

About the Author

Dorothy West   (1910–   )

Dorothy West was born in Boston. During the 1920s she moved to New York City and became active in the Harlem Renaissance group of writers and artists. Her autobiographical novel, *The Living Is Easy,* appeared in 1948. Of Dorothy West's relationship with her mother, Mary Helen Washington has written, "Many black women writers, including West, find their own literary voices through a rediscovery of their mother's power and sensibilities." West now lives on Martha's Vineyard, where she writes a regular column for the island's newspaper. She is completing her second novel, *The Wedding*.

Straw into Gold: The Metamorphosis of the Everyday

SANDRA CISNEROS°

A metamorphosis *is a complete change from one form to another. In real life, it is the changing of a caterpillar into a butterfly. In the fairy tale of Rumpelstiltskin, it is the transformation that takes place when straw is spun into gold. As you read this essay, ask yourself why Cisneros has used the word* metamorphosis *in her title. How does "the everyday" become changed?*

When I was living in an artists' colony in the south of France, some fellow Latin-Americans who taught at the university in Aix-en-Provence[1] invited me to share a home-cooked meal with them. I had been living abroad almost a year then on an NEA grant,[2] subsisting mainly on French bread and lentils while in France so that my money could last longer. So when the invitation to dinner arrived, I accepted without hesitation. Especially since they had promised Mexican food.

What I didn't realize when they made this invitation was that I was supposed to be involved in preparing this meal. I guess they assumed I knew how to cook Mexican food because I was Mexican. They wanted specifically tortillas, though I'd never made a tortilla in my life.

It's true I had witnessed my mother rolling the little armies of dough into perfect circles, but my mother's family is from Guanajuato,[3] *provinciales,*[4] country folk. They only know how to make flour tortillas. My father's family, on the other hand, is *chilango,*[5] from Mexico City. We ate corn tortillas but we didn't make them. Someone was sent to the corner tortilleria to buy some. I'd never seen anybody make corn tortillas. Ever.

Well, somehow my Latino hosts had gotten a hold of a packet of corn flour, and this is what they tossed my way with orders to produce tortillas. *Asi como sea.*[6] Any ol' way, they said and went back to their cooking.

Why did I feel like the woman in the fairy tale who was locked in a room and ordered to spin straw into gold? I had the same sick feeling when I was required to write my critical essay

°**Cisneros** (sēs-nā′rōs).
1. **Aix-en-Provence** (ĕks′än-prô-väns′): a city in southeastern France.
2. **NEA grant:** The National Endowment for the Arts gives money to artists and writers to enable them to carry on their studies.

3. **Guanajuato** (gwä′nä-hwä′tō): a state in central Mexico.
4. *provinciales* (prō-bĕn-syäl′ĕs): plain country people.
5. *chilango* (chē-län′gō): city people.
6. *Asi como sea* (ä-sē′ kō-mō sä-ä).

for my MFA[7] exam—the only piece of noncreative writing necessary in order to get my graduate degree. How was I to start? There were rules involved here, unlike writing a poem or story, which I did intuitively. There was a step-by-step process needed and I had better know it. I felt as if making tortillas, or writing a critical paper for that matter, were tasks so impossible I wanted to break down into tears.

Somehow though, I managed to make those tortillas—crooked and burnt, but edible nonetheless. My hosts were absolutely ignorant when it came to Mexican food; they thought my tortillas were delicious. (I'm glad my mama wasn't there.) Thinking back and looking at that photograph documenting the three of us consuming those lopsided circles I am amazed. Just as I am amazed I could finish my MFA exam (lopsided and crooked, but finished all the same). Didn't think I could do it. But I did.

I've managed to do a lot of things in my life I didn't think I was capable of and which many others didn't think me capable of either. Especially because I am a woman, a Latina, an only daughter in a family of six men. My father would've liked to have seen me married long ago. In our culture, men and women don't leave their father's house except by way of marriage. I crossed my father's threshold with nothing carrying me but my own two feet. A woman whom no one came for and no one chased away.

To make matters worse, I had left before any of my six brothers had ventured away from home. I had broken a terrible taboo. Somehow, looking back at photos of myself as a child, I wonder if I was aware of having begun already my own quiet war.

I like to think that somehow my family, my Mexicanness, my poverty all had something to do with shaping me into a writer. I like to think my parents were preparing me all along for my life as an artist even though they didn't know it. From my father I inherited a love of wandering. He was born in Mexico City but as a young man he traveled into the U.S. vagabonding. He eventually was drafted and thus became a citizen. Some of the stories he has told about his first months in the U.S. with little or no English surface in my stories in *The House on Mango Street* as well as others I have in mind to write in the future. From him I inherited a sappy heart. (He still cries when he watches the Mexican soaps—especially if they deal with children who have forsaken their parents.)

My mother was born like me—in Chicago but of Mexican descent. It would be her tough, streetwise voice that would haunt all my stories and poems. An amazing woman who loves to draw and read books and can sing an opera. A smart cookie.

When I was a little girl we traveled to Mexico City so much I thought my grandparents' house on La Fortuna, Number 12, was home. It was the only constant in our nomadic ramblings from one Chicago flat to another. The house on Destiny Street, Number 12, in the colonia Tepeyac,[8] would be perhaps the only home I knew, and that nostalgia for a home would be a theme that would obsess me.

My brothers also figured greatly in my art. Especially the oldest two; I grew up in their shadows. Henry, the second oldest and my favorite, appears often in poems I have written and in stories which at times only borrow his nickname, Kiki. He played a major role in my childhood. We were bunkbed mates. We were co-conspirators. We were pals. Until my oldest brother came back from studying in Mexico and left me odd-woman-out for always.

What would my teachers say if they knew I

---

7. **MFA:** Master of Fine Arts, a degree granted for study beyond the bachelor's degree.

8. **colonia Tepeyac** (kō-lō′nē-ä tĕ-pā′yäk): a district of Mexico City.

Woman of Taos (1931)
by Selden Gile. Oil on board,
9 x 7⅜ inches.

was a writer? Who would've guessed it? I wasn't a very bright student. I didn't much like school because we moved so much and I was always new and funny-looking. In my fifth-grade report card, I have nothing but an avalanche of C's and D's, but I don't remember being that stupid. I was good at art and I read plenty of library books and Kiki laughed at all my jokes. At home I was fine, but at school I never opened my mouth except when the teacher called on me, the first time I'd speak all day.

When I think how I see myself, it would have to be at age eleven. I know I'm thirty-two on the outside, but inside I'm eleven. I'm the girl in the picture with skinny arms and a crumpled shirt and crooked hair. I didn't like school because all they saw was the outside me. School was lots of rules and sitting with your hands folded and being very afraid all the time. I liked looking out the window and thinking. I liked staring at the girl across the way writing her name over and over again in red ink. I wondered why the boy with the dirty collar in front of me didn't have a mama who took better care of him.

I think my mama and papa did the best they could to keep us warm and clean and never hungry. We had birthday and graduation parties and things like that, but there was another hunger that had to be fed. There was a hunger I didn't even have a name for. Was this when I began writing?

In 1966 we moved into a house, a real one, our first real home. This meant we didn't have to change schools and be the new kids on the block every couple of years. We could make friends and not be afraid we'd have to say good-bye to them and start all over. My brothers and the flock of boys they brought home would become important characters eventually for my stories—Louie and his cousins, Meme Ortiz and his dog with two names, one in English and one in Spanish.

My mother flourished in her own home. She took books out of the library and taught herself to garden, producing flowers so envied we had to put a lock on the gate to keep out the midnight flower thieves. My mother is still gardening to this day.

This was the period in my life, that slippery age when you are both child and woman and neither, I was to record in *The House on Mango Street*. I was still shy. I was a girl who couldn't come out of her shell.

How was I to know I would be recording and documenting the women who sat their sadness on an elbow and stared out a window? It would be the city streets of Chicago I would later record, but from a child's eyes.

I've done all kinds of things I didn't think I could do since then. I've gone to a prestigious[9] university, studied with famous writers, and taken away an MFA degree. I've taught poetry in the schools in Illinois and Texas. I've gotten an NEA grant and run away with it as far as my courage would take me. I've seen the bleached and bitter mountains of the Peloponnesus.[10] I've lived on a Greek island. I've been to Venice twice. In Rapallo, I met Ilona once and forever and took her sad heart with me across the south of France and into Spain.

I've lived in Yugoslavia. I've been to the famous Nice flower market behind the opera house. I've lived in a village in the pre-Alps[11] and witnessed the daily parade of promenaders.

I've moved since Europe to the strange and wonderful country of Texas, land of polaroid-blue skies and big bugs. I met a mayor with my last name. I met famous Chicana/o artists and writers and *políticos*.[12]

Texas is another chapter in my life. It brought with it the Dobie-Paisano Fellowship,[13] a six-month residency on a 265-acre ranch. But most important Texas brought Mexico back to me.

Sitting at my favorite people-watching spot, the snaky Woolworth's counter across the street from the Alamo,[14] I can't think of anything else I'd rather be than a writer. I've traveled and lectured from Cape Cod to San Francisco, to Spain, Yugoslavia, Greece, Mexico, France, Italy, and finally today to Seguin,[15] Texas. Along the way there is straw for the taking. With a little imagination, it can be spun into gold.

---

9. **prestigious** (prĕ-stē′jəs, stij′əs): prominent; influential.

10. **Peloponnesus** (pĕl′ə-pə-nē′səs): a peninsula forming the southern part of the Greek mainland.
11. **pre-Alps:** the foothills of the Alps, a mountain range in south central Europe.
12. *políticos* (pō-lē′tē-kōs): politicians.
13. **Dobie-Paisano Fellowship:** a grant established by Frank J. Dobie, a writer and teacher who received the Presidential Medal of Freedom in 1964. The grant allows writers to live and work at Paisano, Dobie's ranch on the outskirts of Austin, Texas.
14. **Alamo:** a mission in San Antonio, Texas, where a battle between Texans and Mexicans took place in 1836.
15. **Seguin:** Cisneros was a speaker at Texas Lutheran College in Seguin.

or your own experiences. Then jot down some notes about how you could use these anecdotes in an autobiographical essay. Also write some answers to the following questions and save your notes.

1. Does each anecdote reveal a significant personality trait?
2. Do the anecdotes have similar or different tones?
3. What would be the best order to tell your anecdotes?
4. What main idea might you use to unify your essay?

For Study and Discussion

Analyzing and Interpreting the Essay

1. Cisneros says that as a child she had already begun her "own quiet war." **a.** What forces do you think she was warring against? **b.** What strategies did she use in the "war"?

2. She says "there was a hunger I didn't even have a name for." Why do you think she turned to writing to satisfy that hunger?

3. What is the "straw" that the writer turns into gold? Give some examples of "the everyday" that the author has transformed into literature.

Focus on Expository Writing

Using Anecdotes

An **anecdote** is a brief story about an interesting or humorous incident. "Straw into Gold" contains two types of anecdotes. For example, Cisneros uses an **autobiographical** anecdote when she tells about the tortilla episode; she also tells **biographical** anecdotes about her parents.

Make a list of some favorite mini-stories that you like to tell about your family, your friends,

About the Author

Sandra Cisneros (1954–   )

Deeply committed to Mexican American affairs and culture, Cisneros finds her subject matter in the events of her own life. She experienced a major turning point at the University of Iowa Writers' Workshop in the 1970s, when she realized that her history was different from that of her classmates. They, she says, "were from the best schools in the country. They had been bred as fine hothouse flowers. I was a yellow weed among the city's cracks." After this realization, she began to find pride in her own heritage.

Cisneros has received grants from the National Endowment for the Arts to help support her writing. She has published a volume of poetry, *My Wicked Wicked Ways* (1987); a young adult novel, *The House on Mango Street* (1984); and a collection of short stories, *Woman Hollering Creek* (1991).

By Any Other Name

SANTHA RAMA RAU°

The title of this essay alludes to some famous lines in Shakespeare's Romeo and Juliet. *Having learned that Romeo is the son of her father's enemy, Juliet asks,*

> What's in a name? That which we call a rose
> By any other name would smell as sweet.
> (II, 2, 43–44; see page 511)

Santha Rama Rau recalls an incident involving a change of names. As you read, think of the influence names can have on behavior and personality. Imagine how a name change might affect you.

At the Anglo-Indian day school[1] in Zorinabad[2] to which my sister and I were sent when she was eight and I was five and a half, they changed our names. On the first day of school, a hot, windless morning of a north Indian September, we stood in the headmistress's study and she said, "Now you're the *new* girls. What are your names?"

My sister answered for us. "I am Premila, and she"—nodding in my direction—"is Santha."

The headmistress had been in India, I suppose, fifteen years or so, but she still smiled her helpless inability to cope with Indian names. Her rimless half-glasses glittered, and the precarious bun on the top of her head trembled as she shook her head. "Oh, my dears, those are much too hard for me. Suppose we give you pretty English names. Wouldn't that be more

jolly? Let's see, now—Pamela for you, I think." She shrugged in a baffled way at my sister. "That's as close as I can get. And for *you*" she said to me, "how about Cynthia? Isn't that nice?"

My sister was always less easily intimidated than I was, and while she kept a stubborn silence, I said, "Thank you," in a very tiny voice.

We had been sent to that school because my father, among his responsibilities as an officer of the civil service, had a tour of duty to perform in the villages around that steamy little provincial town, where he had his headquarters at that time. He used to make his shorter inspection tours on horseback, and a week before, in the stale heat of a typically postmonsoon[3] day, we had waved goodbye to him and a little procession—an assistant, a secretary, two bearers, and the man to look after the bedding rolls and luggage. They rode away through our large garden, still bright green from the rains,

---

°**Santha Rama Rau** (sän′thä räm′ä rou).
1. **Anglo-Indian day school:** a school headed by English officials in India. Anglo-Indian also refers to persons of English and Indian ancestry.
2. **Zorinabad:** a village in northern India.

3. **postmonsoon:** a dry period following the season of winds and heavy rain.

and we turned back into the twilight of the house and the sound of fans whispering in every room.

Up to then, my mother had refused to send Premila to school in the British-run establishments of that time, because, she used to say, "you can bury a dog's tail for seven years and it still comes out curly, and you can take a Britisher away from his home for a lifetime and he still remains insular." The examinations and degrees from entirely Indian schools were not, in those days, considered valid. In my case, the question had never come up, and probably never would have come up if Mother's extraordinary good health had not broken down. For the first time in my life, she was not able to continue the lessons she had been giving us every morning. So our Hindi[4] books were put away, the stories of the Lord Krishna[5] as a little boy were left in midair, and we were sent to the Anglo-Indian school.

That first day at school is still, when I think of it, a remarkable one. At that age, if one's name is changed, one develops a curious form of dual personality. I remember having a certain detached and disbelieving concern in the actions of "Cynthia," but certainly no responsibility. Accordingly, I followed the thin, erect back of the headmistress down the veranda to my classroom feeling, at most, a passing interest in what was going to happen to me in this strange, new atmosphere of School.

The building was Indian in design, with wide verandas opening onto a central courtyard, but Indian verandas are usually whitewashed, with stone floors. These, in the tradition of British schools, were painted dark brown and had matting on the floors. It gave a feeling of extra intensity to the heat.

I suppose there were about a dozen Indian children in the school—which contained perhaps forty children in all—and four of them were in my class. They were all sitting at the back of the room, and I went to join them. I sat next to a small, solemn girl who didn't smile at me. She had long, glossy-black braids and wore a cotton dress, but she still kept on her Indian jewelry—a gold chain around her neck, thin gold bracelets, and tiny ruby studs in her ears. Like most Indian children, she had a rim of black kohl[6] around her eyes. The cotton dress should have looked strange, but all I could think of was that I should ask my mother if I couldn't wear a dress to school, too, instead of my Indian clothes.

I can't remember too much about the proceedings in class that day, except for the beginning. The teacher pointed to me and asked me to stand up. "Now, dear, tell the class your name."

I said nothing.

"Come along," she said, frowning slightly. "What's your name, dear?"

"I don't know," I said, finally.

The English children in the front of the class—there were about eight or ten of them—giggled and twisted around in their chairs to look at me. I sat down quickly and opened my eyes very wide, hoping in that way to dry them off. The little girl with the braids put out her hand and very lightly touched my arm. She still didn't smile.

Most of that morning I was rather bored. I looked briefly at the children's drawings pinned to the wall, and then concentrated on a lizard clinging to the ledge of the high, barred window behind the teacher's head. Occasionally it would shoot out its long yellow tongue for a fly, and then it would rest, with its eyes closed and its belly palpitating, as though it were swal-

4. **Hindi** (hĭn′dē): the official language of India.
5. **Lord Krishna** (krĭsh′nə): the name of the Hindu god Vishnu when he takes human form.

6. **kohl** (kōl): a powdery substance used as eye makeup.

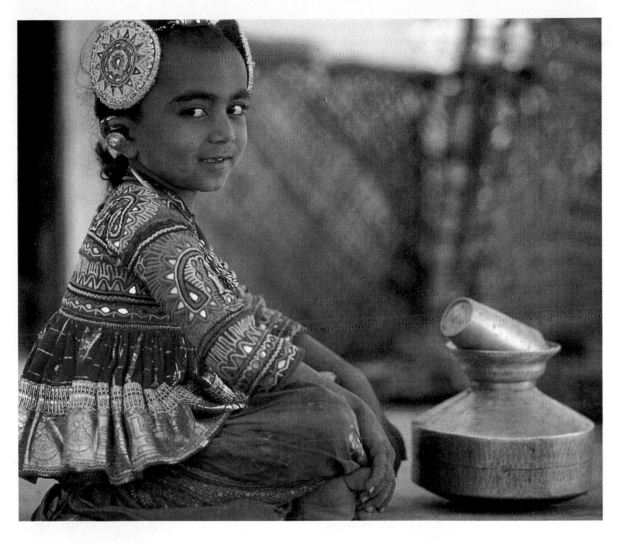

lowing several times quickly. The lessons were mostly concerned with reading and writing and simple numbers—things that my mother had already taught me—and I paid very little attention. The teacher wrote on the easel blackboard words like "bat" and "cat," which seemed babyish to me; only "apple" was new and incomprehensible.

When it was time for the lunch recess, I followed the girl with braids out onto the veranda. There the children from the other classes were assembled. I saw Premila at once and ran over to her, as she had charge of our lunchbox. The children were all opening packages and sitting down to eat sandwiches. Premila and I were the only ones who had Indian food—thin wheat chapatties,[7] some vegetable curry, and a bottle of buttermilk. Premila thrust half of it into my hand and whispered fiercely that I should go and sit with my class, because that was what the others seemed to be doing.

The enormous black eyes of the little Indian

7. **chapatties** (chä-păt′ēz): thin griddlecakes of unleavened bread, used in northern India.

girl from my class looked at my food longingly, so I offered her some. But she only shook her head and plowed her way solemnly through her sandwiches.

I was very sleepy after lunch, because at home we always took a siesta. It was usually a pleasant time of day, with the bedroom darkened against the harsh afternoon sun, the drifting off into sleep with the sound of Mother's voice reading a story in one's mind, and, finally, the shrill, fussy voice of the ayah[8] waking one for tea.

At school, we rested for a short time on low, folding cots on the veranda, and then we were expected to play games. During the hot part of the afternoon we played indoors, and after the shadows had begun to lengthen and the slight breeze of the evening had come up we moved outside to the wide courtyard.

I had never really grasped the system of competitive games. At home, whenever we played tag or guessing games, I was always allowed to "win"—"because," Mother used to tell Premila, "she is the youngest, and we have to allow for that." I had often heard her say it, and it seemed quite reasonable to me, but the result was that I had no clear idea of what "winning" meant.

When we played twos-and-threes[9] that afternoon at school, in accordance with my training, I let one of the small English boys catch me, but was naturally rather puzzled when the other children did not return the courtesy. I ran about for what seemed like hours without ever catching anyone, until it was time for school to close. Much later I learned that my attitude was called "not being a good sport," and I stopped allowing myself to be caught, but it was not for years that I really learned the spirit of the thing.

8. **ayah** (ä′yə): a native maid or nursemaid in India.
9. **twos-and-threes:** a game like tag.

When I saw our car come up to the school gate, I broke away from my classmates and rushed toward it yelling, "Ayah! Ayah!" It seemed like an eternity since I had seen her that morning—a wizened, affectionate figure in her white cotton sari,[10] giving me dozens of urgent and useless instructions on how to be a good girl at school. Premila followed more sedately, and she told me on the way home never to do that again in front of the other children.

When we got home we went straight to Mother's high, white room to have tea with her, and I immediately climbed onto the bed and bounced gently up and down on the springs. Mother asked how we had liked our first day in school. I was so pleased to be home and to have left that peculiar Cynthia behind that I had

10. **sari** (sä′rē): a garment worn by Indian women, consisting of a long piece of cloth with one end wrapped around the waist and the other draped over the shoulder.

nothing whatever to say about school, except to ask what "apple" meant. But Premila told Mother about the classes, and added that in her class they had weekly tests to see if they had learned their lessons well.

I asked, "What's a test?"

Premila said, "You're too small to have them. You won't have them in your class for donkey's years." She had learned the expression that day and was using it for the first time. We all laughed enormously at her wit. She also told Mother, in an aside, that we should take sandwiches to school the next day. Not, she said, that *she* minded. But they would be simpler for me to handle.

That whole lovely evening I didn't think about school at all. I sprinted barefoot across the lawns with my favorite playmate, the cook's son, to the stream at the end of the garden. We quarreled in our usual way, waded in the tepid water under the lime trees, and waited for the night to bring out the smell of the jasmine. I listened with fascination to his stories of ghosts and demons, until I was too frightened to cross the garden alone in the semidarkness. The ayah found me, shouted at the cook's son, scolded me, hurried me in to supper—it was an entirely usual, wonderful evening.

It was a week later, the day of Premila's first test, that our lives changed rather abruptly. I was sitting at the back of my class, in my usual inattentive way, only half listening to the teacher. I had started a rather guarded friendship with the girl with the braids, whose name turned out to be Nalini (Nancy in school). The three other Indian children were already fast friends. Even at that age it was apparent to all of us that friendship with the English or Anglo-Indian children was out of the question. Occasionally, during the class, my new friend and I would draw pictures and show them to each other secretly.

The door opened sharply and Premila marched in. At first, the teacher smiled at her in a kindly and encouraging way and said, "Now, you're little Cynthia's sister?"

Premila didn't even look at her. She stood with her feet planted firmly apart and her shoulders rigid, and addressed herself directly to me. "Get up," she said. "We're going home."

I didn't know what had happened, but I was aware that it was a crisis of some sort. I rose obediently and started to walk toward my sister.

"Bring your pencils and your notebook," she said.

I went back for them, and together we left the room. The teacher started to say something just as Premila closed the door, but we didn't wait to hear what it was.

By Any Other Name   **261**

In complete silence we left the school grounds and started to walk home. Then I asked Premila what the matter was. All she would say was "We're going home for good."

It was a very tiring walk for a child of five and a half, and I dragged along behind Premila with my pencils growing sticky in my hand. I can still remember looking at the dusty hedges, and the tangles of thorns in the ditches by the side of the road, smelling the faint fragrance from the eucalyptus trees and wondering whether we would ever reach home. Occasionally a horse-drawn tonga[11] passed us, and the women, in their pink or green silks, stared at Premila and me trudging along on the side of the road. A few coolies[12] and a line of women carrying baskets of vegetables on their heads smiled at us. But it was nearing the hottest time of day, and the road was almost deserted. I walked more and more slowly, and shouted to Premila, from time to time, "Wait for me!" with increasing peevishness. She spoke to me only once, and that was to tell me to carry my notebook on my head, because of the sun.

When we got to our house the ayah was just taking a tray of lunch into Mother's room. She immediately started a long, worried questioning about what are you children doing back here at this hour of the day.

Mother looked very startled and very concerned, and asked Premila what had happened.

Premila said, "We had our test today, and She made me and the other Indians sit at the back of the room, with a desk between each one."

Mother said, "Why was that, darling?"

"She said it was because Indians cheat," Premila added. "So I don't think we should go back to that school."

Mother looked very distant, and was silent a

long time. At last she said, "Of course not, darling." She sounded displeased.

We all shared the curry she was having for lunch, and afterward I was sent off to the beautifully familiar bedroom for my siesta. I could hear Mother and Premila talking through the open door.

Mother said, "Do you suppose she understood all that?"

Premila said, "I shouldn't think so. She's a baby."

Mother said, "Well, I hope it won't bother her."

Of course, they were both wrong. I understood it perfectly, and I remember it all very clearly. But I put it happily away, because it had all happened to a girl called Cynthia, and I never was really particularly interested in her.

Reading Check

1. Why are Premila and Santha sent to the Anglo-Indian school?
2. Why does the headmistress change her new students' names?
3. How are the Indian children separated from the other students at the school?
4. Why is Santha puzzled by the games that the children play?
5. What causes Premila and Santha to leave school abruptly?

For Study and Discussion

Analyzing and Interpreting the Essay

1. The author says that when her name was changed, she developed a form of dual personality. Explain what she means.

2a. Why was the mother reluctant to send her children to the British-run school? **b.** Do you

---

11. **tonga** (tŏng′gə): a light, horse-drawn two-wheeled carriage.
12. **coolies:** unskilled laborers.

feel that the experiences at the Anglo-Indian school confirm her fears?

3. At the end of the essay, Rama Rau observes that she was able to put the incident "happily" away because she wasn't interested in what happened to Cynthia. **a.** Why do you think she wasn't interested? **b.** Is her statement totally believable? Give reasons for your answer.

4. Consider the quotation from *Romeo and Juliet* that gives the essay its title. Do you think this is a good title for the selection? Explain.

Literary Elements

Allusions

In the title of the essay "Straw into Gold" (page 252), Sandra Cisneros alludes to the fairy tale of Rumpelstiltskin. In this essay Rama Rau uses a well-known phrase from a Shakespearean play as her title. These references to other works of literature are one kind of **allusion.** Many commonly used expressions are allusions to literature. The term "Big Brother," for example, which is used for an all-powerful government or organization that exerts power over people's actions, is an allusion to incidents in *1984,* a novel by George Orwell.

Using a dictionary, explain the allusion in each of the following statements:

Many citizens look back nostalgically at the Camelot of the Kennedy years.

We could not penetrate the iron curtain of secrecy that marked the incumbent's campaign.

Because of his tendency to sleep through roll call, the senator has been dubbed the Rip Van Winkle of Congress.

About the Author

Santha Rama Rau (1923–   )

Santha Rama Rau was born in India but was educated in England and the United States. Because her father was a diplomat who represented India in London, the United States, the former Union of South Africa, and Japan, Rama Rau's family traveled extensively. She is the author of many books and essays about her travels. Her works include *Home to India* (1945), *East of Home* (1950), *The Adventuress* (1970), and *A Princess Remembers* (1977). In 1960 she adapted E. M. Forster's famous novel *A Passage to India* for the theater. "By Any Other Name" first appeared in *The New Yorker.*

Literature and History

Cultures in Conflict

European countries often competed for control of India during the sixteenth and seventeenth centuries. In 1858 the British government became a dominant power in India. While some Indians favored British rule, there was considerable unrest, which came to a head after World War II. Finally, after years of struggle, India was declared an independent and democratic nation on January 26, 1950.

Making Connections: Activities

Rudyard Kipling's novel *Kim* is about an orphaned Irish boy's immersion in Indian culture. Examine the relationship between the Indians and the British in the novel. How do the two cultures differ in customs and values? How do they relate to one another? Consider the author's attitude toward each culture.

By Any Other Name **263**

Fragments of an Autobiography

CHARLES DICKENS

When he was twelve years old, Charles Dickens was forced to support himself by working at a blacking (shoe polish) warehouse near the Thames River. Shortly afterward his father was imprisoned for debt and the household broke up. Dickens found these experiences the most painful of his life—so painful that he never told his wife and children about them. He recorded them in an autobiography which he did not complete. These fragments of the autobiography were later revealed to his friend and trusted biographer, John Forster.

As you read this selection, note how Dickens keeps you aware of both the child's view and the adult's view of these experiences.

[It was] an evil hour for me, as I often bitterly thought. Its chief manager, James Lamert, the relative who had lived with us in Bayham Street, seeing how I was employed from day to day, and knowing what our domestic circumstances then were, proposed that I should go into the blacking warehouse, to be as useful as I could, at a salary, I think, of six shillings a week. I am not clear whether it was six or seven. I am inclined to believe, from my uncertainty on this head, that it was six at first, and seven afterwards. At any rate the offer was accepted very willingly by my father and mother, and on a Monday morning I went down to the blacking warehouse to begin my business life.

It is wonderful to me how I could have been so easily cast away at such an age. It is wonder-ful to me that, even after my descent into the poor little drudge I had been since we came to London, no one had compassion enough on me—a child of singular abilities, quick, eager, delicate, and soon hurt, bodily or mentally—to suggest that something might have been spared, as certainly it might have been, to place me at any common school. Our friends, I take it, were tired out. No one made any sign. My father and mother were quite satisfied. They could hardly have been more so, if I had been twenty years of age, distinguished at a grammar school, and going to Cambridge.

The blacking warehouse was the last house on the left-hand side of the way, at old Hungerford Stairs. It was a crazy, tumbledown old house, abutting of course on the river, and

Fleet Street, a London thoroughfare, in the nineteenth century.

literally overrun with rats. Its wainscotted rooms, and its rotten floors and staircase, and the old gray rats swarming down in the cellars, and the sound of their squeaking and scuffling coming up the stairs at all times, and the dirt and decay of the place, rise up visibly before me, as if I were there again. The counting-house was on the first floor, looking over the coal barges and the river. There was a recess in it, in which I was to sit and work. My work was to cover the pots of paste-blacking, first with a piece of oilpaper, and then with a piece of blue paper; to tie them round with a string; and then to clip the paper close and neat, all round, until it looked as smart as a pot of ointment from an apothecary's[1] shop. When a certain number of grosses of pots had attained this pitch of perfection, I was to paste on each a printed label, and then go on again with more pots. Two or three other boys were kept at similar duty downstairs on similar wages. One of them came up, in a ragged apron and a paper cap, on the first Monday morning, to show me the trick of using the string and tying the knot. His name was Bob Fagin; and I took the liberty of using his name, long afterwards, in *Oliver Twist.*

Our relative had kindly arranged to teach me something in the dinner hour, from twelve to one, I think it was, every day. But an arrangement so incompatible with counting-house business soon died away, from no fault of his or mine; and for the same reason, my small worktable, and my grosses of pots, my papers, string, scissors, pastepot, and labels, by little and little, vanished out of the recess in the countinghouse, and kept company with the other small worktables, grosses of pots, papers, string, scissors, and pastepots, downstairs. It was not long before Bob Fagin and I, and another boy whose name was Paul Green, but who was currently believed to have been christened Poll (a belief which I transferred, long afterwards again, to Mr. Sweedlepipe, in *Martin Chuzzlewit*), worked generally, side by side. Bob Fagin was an orphan, and lived with his brother-in-law, a waterman. Poll Green's father had the additional distinction of being a fireman, and was employed at Drury Lane Theater, where another relation of Poll's, I think his little sister, did imps in the pantomimes.

No words can express the secret agony of my soul as I sunk into this companionship; compared these everyday associates with those of my happier childhood; and felt my early hopes of growing up to be a learned and distinguished man, crushed in my breast. The deep remembrance of the sense I had of being utterly neglected and hopeless; of the shame I felt in my position; of the misery it was to my young heart to believe that, day by day, what I had learned, and thought, and delighted in, and raised my fancy and my emulation up by, was passing away from me, never to be brought back any more, cannot be written. My whole nature was so penetrated with the grief and humiliation of such considerations, that even now, famous and caressed and happy, I often forget in my dreams that I have a dear wife and children, even that I am a man, and wander desolately back to that time of my life.

My mother and my brothers and sisters (excepting Fanny in the Royal Academy of Music) were still encamped, with a young servant-girl from Chatham Workhouse, in the two parlors in the emptied house in Gower Street North. It was a long way to go and return within the dinner hour, and, usually, I either carried my dinner with me, or went and bought it at some neighboring shop. In the latter case, it was commonly a saveloy[2] and a penny loaf; some-

---

1. **apothecary** (ə-pŏth′ə-kĕr′ē): druggist.

2. **saveloy** (săv′ə-loi): spicy, dried sausage.

times, a fourpenny plate of beef from a cook's shop; sometimes, a plate of bread and cheese, and a glass of beer, from a miserable old public house over the way: The Swan, if I remember right, or The Swan and something else that I have forgotten. Once, I remember tucking my own bread (which I had brought from home in the morning) under my arm, wrapped up in a piece of paper like a book, and going into the best dining room in Johnson's a la mode beefhouse in Clare Court, Drury Lane, and magnificently ordering a small plate of a la mode beef to eat with it. What the waiter thought of such a strange little apparition coming in all alone, I don't know; but I can see him now, staring at me as I ate my dinner, and bringing up the other waiter to look. I gave him a halfpenny, and I wish now that he hadn't taken it.

The household broke up. Dickens' mother and the younger children went to live with John Dickens in the Marshalsea Prison.

The key of the house was sent back to the landlord, who was very glad to get it; and I (small Cain that I was, except that I had never done harm to anyone) was handed over as a lodger to a reduced old lady, long known to our family, in Little College Street, Camden Town, who took children in to board, and had once done so at Brighton; and who, with a few alterations and embellishments, unconsciously began to sit for Mrs. Pipchin in *Dombey* when she took in me.

She had a little brother and sister under her care then, somebody's natural children, who were very irregularly paid for, and a widow's little son. The two boys and I slept in the same room. My own exclusive breakfast, of a penny cottage loaf and a pennyworth of milk, I provided for myself. I kept another small loaf, and a quarter of a pound of cheese, on a particular shelf of a particular cupboard, to make my supper on when I came back at night. They made a hole in the six or seven shillings, I know well; and I was out at the blacking warehouse all day, and had to support myself upon that money all the week. I suppose my lodging was paid for, by my father. I certainly did not pay it myself; and I certainly had no other assistance whatever (the making of my clothes, I think, excepted), from Monday morning until Saturday night. No advice, no counsel, no encouragement, no consolation, no support, from anyone that I can call to mind, so help me God.

Sundays, Fanny and I passed in the prison. I was at the academy in Tenterden Street, Hanover Square, at nine o'clock in the morning, to fetch her; and we walked back there together, at night.

I was so young and childish, and so little qualified—how could I be otherwise?—to undertake the whole charge of my own existence, that, in going to Hungerford Stairs of a morning, I could not resist the stale pastry put out at half price on trays at the confectioners' doors in Tottenham Court Road; and I often spent in that, the money I should have kept for my dinner. Then I went without my dinner, or bought a roll, or a slice of pudding.

There were two pudding shops between which I was divided, according to my finances. One was in a court close to St. Martin's Church (at the back of the church) which is now removed altogether. The pudding at that shop was made with currants, and was rather a special pudding, but was dear: two penn'orth[3] not being larger than a penn'orth of more ordinary pudding. A good shop for the latter was in the Strand, somewhere near where the Lowther Arcade is now. It was a stout, hale pudding, heavy and flabby, with great raisins

3. **penn'orth:** pennyworth.

A morning scene at Covent Garden, London, in the nineteenth century.

in it, stuck in whole, at great distances apart. It came up hot, at about noon every day; and many and many a day did I dine off it.

We had half an hour, I think, for tea. When I had money enough, I used to go to a coffee shop, and have half a pint of coffee, and a slice of bread and butter. When I had no money, I took a turn in Covent Garden market, and stared at the pineapples. The coffee shops to which I most resorted were, one in Maiden Lane; one in a court (nonexistent now) close to Hungerford Market; and one in St. Martin's Lane, of which I only recollect that it stood near the church, and that in the door there was an oval glass plate, with COFFEE ROOM painted on it, addressed towards the street. If I ever find myself in a very different kind of coffee room now, but where there is such an inscription on glass, and read it backward on the wrong side MOOR EEFFOC (as I often used to do then, in a dismal reverie), a shock goes through my blood.

I know I do not exaggerate, unconsciously and unintentionally, the scantiness of my resources and the difficulties of my life. I know that if a shilling or so were given me by anyone, I spent it in a dinner or a tea. I know that I worked, from morning to night, with common men and boys, a shabby child. I know that I tried, but ineffectually, not to anticipate my money, and to make it last the week through, by putting it away in a drawer I had in the counting house, wrapped into six little parcels, each parcel containing the same amount, and labeled with a different day. I know that I have lounged about the streets, insufficiently and unsatisfactorily fed. I know that, but for the mercy of God, I might easily have been, for any care that was taken of me, a little robber or a little vagabond.

But I held some station at the blacking warehouse too. Besides that my relative at the countinghouse did what a man so occupied, and dealing with a thing so anomalous,[4] could, to treat me as one upon a different footing from the rest, I never said, to man or boy, how it was that I came to be there, or gave the least indication of being sorry that I was there. That I suffered in secret, and that I suffered exquisitely, no one ever knew but I. How much I suffered, it is, as I have said already, utterly beyond my power to tell. No man's imagination can overstep the reality. But I kept my own counsel, and I did my work. I knew from the first that if I could not do my work as well as any of the rest, I could not hold myself above slight and contempt. I soon became at least as expeditious and as skillful with my hands as either of the other boys. Though perfectly familiar with them, my conduct and manners were different enough from theirs to place a space between us. They, and the men, always spoke of me as "the young gentleman." A certain man (a soldier once) named Thomas, who was the foreman, and another named Harry, who was the carman and wore a red jacket, used to call me "Charles" sometimes, in speaking to me; but I think it was mostly when we were very confidential, and when I had made some efforts to entertain them over our work with the results of some of the old readings, which

were fast perishing out of my mind. Poll Green uprose once, and rebelled against the "young gentleman" usage; but Bob Fagin settled him speedily.

My rescue from this kind of existence I considered quite hopeless, and abandoned as such, altogether; though I am solemnly convinced that I never, for one hour, was reconciled to it, or was otherwise than miserably unhappy. I felt keenly, however, the being so cut off from my parents, my brothers, and sisters; and, when my day's work was done, going home to such a miserable blank; and *that*, I thought, might be corrected. One Sunday night I remonstrated with my father on this head, so pathetically and with so many tears that his kind nature gave way. He began to think that it was not quite right. I do believe he had never thought so before, or thought about it. It was the first remonstrance I had ever made about my lot, and perhaps it opened up a little more than I intended. A back attic was found for me at the house of an insolvent court agent, who lived in Lant Street in the borough, where Bob Sawyer lodged many years afterwards. A bed and bedding were sent over for me, and made up on the floor. The little window had a pleasant prospect of a timber yard; and when I took possession of my new abode, I thought it was a Paradise.

Bob Fagin was very good to me on the occasion of a bad attack of my old disorder. I suffered such excruciating pain that time, that they made a temporary bed of straw in my old recess in the countinghouse, and I rolled about on the floor, and Bob filled empty blacking bottles with hot water, and applied relays of them to my side, half the day. I got better, and quite easy towards evening; but Bob (who was much bigger and older than I) did not like the idea of my going home alone, and took me under his protection. I was too proud to let

4. **anomalous** (ə-nŏm′ə-ləs): irregular.

him know about the prison; and after making several efforts to get rid of him, to all of which Bob Fagin in his goodness was deaf, shook hands with him on the steps of a house near Southwark Bridge on the Surrey side, making believe that I lived there. As a finishing piece of reality in case of his looking back, I knocked at the door, I recollect, and asked, when the woman opened it, if that was Mr. Robert Fagin's house.

I am not sure that it was before this time, or after it, that the blacking warehouse was removed to Chandos Street, Covent Garden. It is no matter. Next to the shop at the corner of Bedford Street in Chandos Street, are two rather old-fashioned houses and shops adjoining one another. They were one then, or thrown into one, for the blacking business; and had been a butter shop. Opposite to them was, and is, a public house, where I got my ale, under these new circumstances. The stones in the street may be smoothed by my small feet going across to it at dinnertime and back again. The establishment was larger now, and we had one or two new boys. Bob Fagin and I had attained to great dexterity in tying up the pots. I forget how many we could do in five minutes. We worked, for the light's sake, near the second window as you come from Bedford Street; and we were so brisk at it that the people used to stop and look in. Sometimes there would be quite a little crowd there. I saw my father coming in at the door one day when we were very busy, and I wondered how he could bear it.

Now, I generally had my dinner in the warehouse. Sometimes I brought it from home, so I was better off. I see myself coming across Russell Square from Somers Town, one morning, with some cold hotchpotch[5] in a small basin

5. **hotchpotch:** a stew of meats and vegetables.

tied up in a handkerchief. I had the same wanderings about the streets as I used to have, and was just as solitary and self-dependent as before; but I had not the same difficulty in merely living. I never, however, heard a word of being taken away, or of being otherwise than quite provided for.

At last, one day, my father, and the relative so often mentioned, quarreled; quarreled by letter, for I took the letter from my father to him which caused the explosion, but quarreled very fiercely. It was about me. It may have had some backward reference, in part, for anything I know, to my employment at the window. All I am certain of is that, soon after I had given him the letter, my cousin (he was a sort of cousin, by marriage) told me he was very much insulted about me; and that it was impossible to keep me, after that. I cried very much, partly because it was so sudden, and partly because in his anger he was violent about my father, though gentle to me. Thomas, the old soldier, comforted me, and said he was sure it was for the best. With a relief so strange that it was like oppression, I went home.

My mother set herself to accommodate the quarrel, and did so next day. She brought home a request for me to return next morning, and a high character of me, which I am very sure I deserved. My father said I should go back no more, and should go to school. I do not write resentfully or angrily: for I know how all these things have worked together to make me what I am: but I never afterwards forgot, I never shall forget, I never can forget, that my mother was warm for my being sent back.

From that hour until this at which I write, no word of that part of my childhood which I have now gladly brought to a close, has passed my lips to any human being. I have no idea how long it lasted, whether for a year, or much more, or less. From that hour until this, my father and my mother have been stricken dumb upon it. I have never heard the least allusion to it, however far off and remote, from either of them. I have never until I now impart it to this paper, in any burst of confidence with anyone, my own wife not excepted, raised the curtain I then dropped, thank God.

Until old Hungerford Market was pulled down, until old Hungerford Stairs were destroyed, and the very nature of the ground changed, I never had the courage to go back to the place where my servitude began. I never saw it. I could not endure to go near it. For many years, when I came near to Robert Warren's in the Strand, I crossed over to the opposite side of the way, to avoid a certain smell of the cement they put upon the blacking corks, which reminded me of what I was once. It was a very long time before I liked to go up Chandos Street. My old home by the borough made me cry, after my eldest child could speak.

In my walks at night I have walked there often, since then, and by degrees I have come to write this. It does not seem a tithe of what I might have written, or of what I meant to write.

Reading Check

1. What was Dickens' job at the blacking warehouse?
2. How much did he earn for his work?
3. What was he expected to provide for out of his salary?
4. When did Dickens visit his parents at the prison?
5. How was he finally "rescued" from the warehouse?

For Study and Discussion

Analyzing and Interpreting the Selection

1. In this autobiographical fragment, Dickens views the most painful episode of his childhood from the vantage point of maturity. **a.** What impression do you form of Dickens as a child from his relationship with the other boys in the blacking warehouse? **b.** From the description of his meals and his lodgings? **c.** From his solitary walks through the city?

2. As a writer Dickens is well known for his evocative descriptions of settings. Where in this selection does he create vivid pictures of his surroundings?

3. In his novels Dickens created a gallery of memorable characters. Where does he show that early in his life he had keen insight into human nature?

Language and Vocabulary

Explaining Phrases from Context

Explain the following phrases and state what they reveal about Dickens' feelings about himself:

> What . . . raised my fancy and my emulation up by, was passing away from me . . .
> . . . small Cain that I was . . .
> . . . a shabby child.
> . . . as expeditious and as skillful with my hands as either of the other boys.

Rewriting a Passage in Modern English

Had Dickens been writing his autobiography in the 1990s, he would have written different sentences and used different words. Rewrite the following sentence in your own language. Make your words communicate the same feelings and ideas:

> The deep remembrance of the sense I had of being utterly neglected and hopeless; of the shame I felt in my position; of the misery it was to

my young heart to believe that, day by day, what I had learned, and thought, and delighted in, and raised my fancy and my emulation up by, was passing away from me, never to be brought back any more, cannot be written.

You might want to start your sentence, "I cannot write" or "I can't tell you," instead of delaying the verb phrase until the end of the sentence as Dickens does.

About the Author

Charles Dickens   (1812–1870)

Charles Dickens was born in a town on the south coast of England, where his father was a clerk in the Naval Pay Office. Dickens spent his boyhood in various parts of southeast England, including London and Rochester; he described this world in his novel *Great Expectations.*

The Dickens family moved to London permanently when Charles was ten, and sank quickly into poverty and debt. Charles was sent to work at a shoe polish warehouse when he was twelve years old. He lived in a small attic room close to the Marshalsea Prison, where his father was imprisoned for debt. Dickens later used these experiences in his novel *David Copperfield.*

Literature and Social Background

Child Labor and Debtors' Prisons

Charles Dickens was probably the most famous social reformer in nineteenth-century England. In his novels he condemned the evils of child labor and exposed the conditions of debtors' prisons.

Making Connections: Activities

1. During Dickens' time it was not unusual for children to work sixteen hours a day in textile mills. Some children worked in mines or around dangerous machines in factories. Read the novel *Oliver Twist,* and in a report tell how Dickens' novel exposes social problems in nineteenth-century England.

2. In *Pickwick Papers* Dickens describes life in a debtors' prison similar to the one in which his father was imprisoned. Read one or more of Chapters 41–45 in *Pickwick Papers,* and write a short essay on details that reveal to you the attitude in early nineteenth-century England toward poor people or those incapable of taking care of themselves. You might want to discuss how Dickens reveals his own attitude toward debtors' prisons or the situation of poor people in them.

A Whole Nation and a People

HARRY MARK PETRAKIS

In this excerpt from his autobiography, Petrakis creates a memorable portrait of a man who helped him to understand and appreciate his own ethnic culture.

There was one storekeeper I remember above all others in my youth. It was shortly before I became ill, spending a good portion of my time with a motley group of varied ethnic ancestry. We contended with one another to deride the customs of the old country. On our Saturday forays into neighborhoods beyond our own, to prove we were really Americans, we ate hot dogs and drank Cokes. If a boy didn't have ten cents for this repast he went hungry, for he dared not bring a sandwich from home made of the spiced meats our families ate.

One of our untamed games was to seek out the owner of a pushcart or a store, unmistakably an immigrant, and bedevil him with a chorus of insults and jeers. To prove allegiance to the gang it was necessary to reserve our fiercest malevolence for a storekeeper or peddler belonging to our own ethnic background.

For that reason I led a raid on the small, shabby grocery of old Barba Nikos, a short, sinewy Greek who walked with a slight limp and sported a flaring, handlebar mustache.

We stood outside his store and dared him to come out. When he emerged to do battle, we plucked a few plums and peaches from the baskets on the sidewalk and retreated across the street to eat them while he watched. He waved a fist and hurled epithets at us in ornamental Greek.

Aware that my mettle was being tested, I raised my arm and threw my half-eaten plum at the old man. My aim was accurate and the plum struck him on the cheek. He shuddered and put his hand to the stain. He stared at me across the street, and although I could not see his eyes, I felt them sear my flesh. He turned and walked silently back into the store. The boys slapped my shoulders in admiration, but it was a hollow victory that rested like a stone in the pit of my stomach.

At twilight, when we disbanded, I passed the grocery alone on my way home. There was a small light burning in the store and the shadow of the old man's body outlined against the glass. Goaded by remorse, I walked to the door and entered.

The old man moved from behind the narrow wooden counter and stared at me. I wanted to turn and flee, but by then it was too late. As he motioned for me to come closer, I braced myself for a curse or a blow.

"You were the one," he said, finally, in a harsh voice.

I nodded mutely.

"Why did you come back?"

I stood there unable to answer.

"What's your name?"

"Haralambos," I said, speaking to him in Greek.

He looked at me in shock. "You are Greek!" he cried. "A Greek boy attacking a Greek grocer!" He stood appalled at the immensity of my crime. "All right," he said coldly. "You are here because you wish to make amends." His great mustache bristled in concentration. "Four plums, two peaches," he said. "That makes a total of seventy-eight cents. Call it seventy-five. Do you have seventy-five cents, boy?"

I shook my head.

"Then you will work it off," he said. "Fifteen cents an hour into seventy-five cents makes"— he paused—"five hours of work. Can you come here Saturday morning?"

"Yes," I said.

"Yes, Barba Nikos," he said sternly. "Show respect."

"Yes, Barba Nikos," I said.

"Saturday morning at eight o'clock," he said. "Now go home and say thanks in your prayers that I did not loosen your impudent head with a solid smack on the ear." I needed no further urging and fled.

Saturday morning, still apprehensive, I returned to the store. I began by sweeping, raising clouds of dust in dark and hidden corners. I washed the windows, whipping the squeegee swiftly up and down the glass in a fever of fear that some member of the gang would see me. When I finished I hurried back inside.

For the balance of the morning I stacked cans, washed the counter, and dusted bottles of yellow wine. A few customers entered, and Barba Nikos served them. A little after twelve o'clock he locked the door so he could eat lunch. He cut himself a few slices of sausage, tore a large chunk from a loaf of crisp-crusted

Greek vase, early fifth century B.C., showing a red-figured musician.
The Metropolitan Museum of Art, The Fletcher Fund

bread, and filled a small cup with a dozen black shiny olives floating in brine. He offered me the cup. I could not help myself and grimaced.

"You are a stupid boy," the old man said. "You are not really Greek, are you?"

"Yes, I am."

"You might be," he admitted grudgingly. "But you do not act Greek. Wrinkling your nose at these fine olives. Look around this store for a minute. What do you see?"

"Fruits and vegetables," I said. "Cheese and olives and things like that."

He stared at me with a massive scorn. "That's what I mean," he said. "You are a bonehead. You don't understand that a whole nation and a people are in this store."

I looked uneasily toward the storeroom in the rear, almost expecting someone to emerge.

"What about olives?" he cut the air with a sweep of his arm. "There are olives of many shapes and colors. Pointed black ones from Kalamata, oval ones from Amphissa, pickled green olives and sharp tangy yellow ones. Achilles[1] carried black olives to Troy and after a day of savage battle leading his Myrmidons, he'd rest and eat cheese and ripe black olives such as these right here. You have heard of Achilles, boy, haven't you?"

"Yes," I said.

"Yes, Barba Nikos."

"Yes, Barba Nikos," I said.

He motioned at the row of jars filled with varied spices. "There is origanon there and basilikon and daphne and sesame and miantanos, all the marvelous flavorings that we have used in our food for thousands of years. The men of Marathon[2] carried small packets of these spices into battle, and the scents reminded them of their homes, their families, and their children."

He rose and tugged his napkin free from around his throat. "Cheese, you said. Cheese! Come closer, boy, and I will educate your abysmal ignorance." He motioned toward a wooden container on the counter. "That glistening white delight is feta, made from goat's milk, packed in wooden buckets to retain the flavor. Alexander the Great demanded it on his table with his casks of wine when he planned his campaigns."

He walked limping from the counter to the window where the piles of tomatoes, celery, and green peppers clustered. "I suppose all you see here are some random vegetables?" He did not wait for me to answer. "You are dumb again. These are some of the ingredients that go to make up a Greek salad. Do you know what a Greek salad really is? A meal in itself, an experience, an emotional involvement. It is created deftly and with grace. First, you place large lettuce leaves in a big, deep bowl." He spread his fingers and moved them slowly, carefully, as if he were arranging the leaves. "The remainder of the lettuce is shredded and piled in a small mound," he said. "Then comes celery, cucumbers, tomatoes sliced lengthwise, green peppers, origanon, green olives, feta, avocado, and anchovies. At the end you dress it with lemon, vinegar, and pure olive oil, glinting golden in the light."

He finished with a heartfelt sigh and for a moment closed his eyes. Then he opened one eye to mark me with a baleful intensity. "The story goes that Zeus[3] himself created the recipe and assembled and mixed the ingredients on Mount Olympus[4] one night when he had invited some of the other gods to dinner."

---

1. **Achilles** (ə-kĭl′ēz): a legendary Greek warrior, hero of the epic poem *The Iliad.*
2. **Marathon:** an ancient Greek village, site of a battle between the Greeks and the Persians in the fifth century B.C.

3. **Zeus:** in Greek mythology, the king of the gods.
4. **Mount Olympus:** the home of the ancient Greek gods and goddesses.

He turned his back on me and walked slowly again across the store, dragging one foot slightly behind him. I looked uneasily at the clock, which showed that it was a few minutes past one. He turned quickly and startled me. "And everything else in here," he said loudly. "White beans, lentils, garlic, crisp bread, kokoretsi, meatballs, mussels and clams." He paused and drew a deep, long breath. "And the wine," he went on, "wine from Samos, Santorini, and Crete, retsina and mavrodaphne, a taste almost as old as water . . . and then the fragrant melons, the pastries, yellow diples and golden loukoumades, the honey custard glatobouriko. Everything a part of our history, as much a part as the exquisite sculpture in marble, the bearded warriors, Pan[5] and the oracles at Delphi,[6] and the nymphs dancing in the shadowed groves under Homer's[7] glittering moon." He paused, out of breath again, and coughed harshly. "Do you understand now, boy?"

He watched my face for some response and then grunted. We stood silent for a moment until he cocked his head and stared at the clock. "It is time for you to leave," he motioned brusquely toward the door. "We are square now. Keep it that way."

I decided the old man was crazy and reached behind the counter for my jacket and cap and started for the door. He called me back. From a box he drew out several soft, yellow figs that he placed in a piece of paper. "A bonus because you worked well," he said. "Take them. When you taste them, maybe you will understand what I have been talking about."

I took the figs and he unlocked the door and I hurried from the store. I looked back once

and saw him standing in the doorway, watching me, the swirling tendrils of food curling like mist about his head.

I ate the figs late that night. I forgot about them until I was in bed, and then I rose and took the package from my jacket. I nibbled at one, then ate them all. They broke apart between my teeth with a tangy nectar, a thick sweetness running like honey across my tongue and in the pockets of my cheeks. In the morning when I woke, I could still taste and inhale their fragrance.

I never again entered Barba Nikos' store. My spell of illness, which began some months later, lasted two years. When I returned to the streets I had forgotten the old man and the grocery. Shortly afterwards my family moved from the neighborhood.

5. **Pan:** a god of fields and forests.
6. **oracles . . . Delphi:** The gods were consulted through oracles—priests and priestesses who uttered divine prophecies.
7. **Homer:** a Greek epic poet, author of the *Iliad* and the *Odyssey*.

Some twelve years later, after the war, I drove through the old neighborhood and passed the grocery. I stopped the car and for a moment stood before the store. The windows were stained with dust and grime, the interior bare and desolate, a store in a decrepit group of stores marked for razing so new structures could be built.

I have been in many Greek groceries since then and have often bought the feta and Kalamata olives. I have eaten countless Greek salads and have indeed found them a meal for the gods. On the holidays in our house, my wife and sons and I sit down to a dinner of steaming, buttered pilaf like my mother used to make and lemon-egg avgolemono and roast lamb richly seasoned with cloves of garlic. I drink the red and yellow wines, and for dessert I have come to relish the delicate pastries coated with honey and powdered sugar. Old Barba Nikos would have been pleased.

But I have never been able to recapture the halcyon flavor of those figs he gave me on that day so long ago, although I have bought figs many times. I have found them pleasant to my tongue, but there is something missing. And to this day I am not sure whether it was the figs or the vision and passion of the old grocer that coated the fruit so sweetly I can still recall their savor and fragrance after almost thirty years.

Reading Check

1. What type of food did Harry and his friends eat to prove they were Americans?
2. Why did Harry go to Barba Nikos' store alone?
3. Why did Harry work for Barba Nikos?
4. What was Harry's greatest fear while he worked at the store?
5. What gift did Barba Nikos give Harry as a bonus?

For Study and Discussion

Analyzing and Interpreting the Selection

1. In his opening paragraphs, Petrakis tells how he and his friends banded together to reject their own ethnic backgrounds. Why is this information important to understanding the experience he narrates?

2a. What details characterize Barba Nikos?
b. What shows his feelings about how children are raised in America?

3. Although the narrator wants the respect of his companions, he feels that the attack on the grocer is "a hollow victory." Why?

4a. What role does ancient Greek culture play in Barba Nikos' life? b. How does the culture shape his values?

5a. How does the concluding statement about the figs suggest a central point or thesis?
b. Is the appearance of the store twelve years later important to what Petrakis is saying about Barba Nikos' values and world?

Focus on Expository Writing

Outlining a Biographical Sketch

A **biographical sketch** is a much shorter version of a **biography**—an account of a person's life written by another person. Harry Mark Petrakis' description of Barba Nikos is an example of a biographical sketch. Notice that when you write a sketch you must select a small number of details on which to focus. Petrakis, for example, concentrates on Barba Nikos' moral and cultural values.

Write an outline like the one below for a three- to four-paragraph sketch of a person whom you admire—perhaps an athlete, an entertainer, or a government leader. You might get some ideas for the details of your sketch by skimming recent issues of magazines such as *People*. Save your writing.

Biographical Sketch

I. Introduction
   A. Attention grabber: _____

   _____

   B. Thesis statement: _____

   _____

II. Body
   Facts/anecdotes: _____

   _____

   _____

   _____

III. Conclusion
   A. Restatement of thesis: _____

   _____

   B. Summary of person's significance:

   _____

Language and Vocabulary

Examining Phrases from Context

Explain these phrases from the selection:

  . . . motley group . . .
  . . . our fiercest malevolence . . .
  . . . my mettle was being tested . . .
  . . . your abysmal ignorance.
  . . . created deftly and with grace.
  . . . he motioned brusquely . . .
  . . . swirling tendrils of food . . .
  . . . decrepit group of stores . . .
  . . . the halcyon flavor of these figs . . .

About the Author

Harry Mark Petrakis (1923–   )

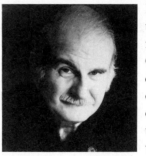

Harry Mark Petrakis is the author of short stories and novels about Greek Americans. His characters often hold onto memories of an older culture and seek to join the old ways with new customs and attitudes. Petrakis' books have twice been nominated for a National Book Award, and his stories have appeared in such magazines as *Harper's Bazaar* and *The Atlantic*.

Petrakis was born in St. Louis, Missouri, and grew up in Chicago. Before becoming a writer, he worked in steel mills and as a truck driver. Today he lives in Chesterton, Indiana, across Lake Michigan from his former home in Chicago. The selection reprinted here is from his autobiography, *Stelmark* (1983).

Life on
the Mississippi

MARK TWAIN

Before turning to a career as a writer, Samuel Langhorne Clemens worked as a Mississippi river pilot. In 1863 he chose the pen name Mark Twain— adopting the leadsman's call on Mississippi riverboats. "By the mark, twain," indicated a depth of two fathoms, or twelve feet, a safe depth for riverboats.

In this excerpt, Twain draws an analogy—an extended comparison— between reading a book and reading a river. What does the "language" of the river consist of? What does Twain feel he sacrifices for mastery of this language?

The face of the water, in time, became a wonderful book—a book that was a dead language to the uneducated passenger, but which told its mind to me without reserve, delivering its most cherished secrets as clearly as if it uttered them with a voice. And it was not a book to be read once and thrown aside, for it had a new story to tell every day. Throughout the long twelve hundred miles there was never a page that was void of interest, never one that you could leave unread without loss, never one that you would want to skip, thinking you could find higher enjoyment in some other thing. There never was so wonderful a book written by man; never one whose interest was so absorbing, so unflagging, so sparklingly renewed with every reperusal.[1] The passenger who could not read it was charmed with a peculiar sort of faint dimple on its surface (on the rare occasions when he did not overlook it altogether); but to the pilot that was an *italicized* passage; indeed, it was more than that, it was a legend of the largest capitals, with a string of shouting exclamation points at the end of it; for it meant that a wreck or a rock was buried there that could tear the life out of the strongest vessel that ever floated. It is the faintest and simplest expression the water ever makes, and the most hideous to a pilot's eye. In truth, the passenger who could not read this book saw nothing but all

1. **reperusal** (rē′pə-rōō′zəl): rereading.

Maiden Rock. A Currier and Ives lithograph.
Museum of the City of New York

manner of pretty pictures in it, painted by the sun and shaded by the clouds, whereas to the trained eye these were not pictures at all, but the grimmest and most dead-earnest of reading matter.

Now when I had mastered the language of this water and had come to know every trifling feature that bordered the great river as familiarly as I knew the letters of the alphabet, I had made a valuable acquisition. But I had lost something, too. I had lost something which could never be restored to me while I lived. All the grace, the beauty, the poetry had gone out of the majestic river! I still keep in mind a certain wonderful sunset which I witnessed when steamboating was new to me. A broad expanse of the river was turned to blood; in the middle distance the red hue brightened into gold, through which a solitary log came floating, black and conspicuous; in one place a long, slanting mark lay sparkling upon the water; in another the surface was broken by boiling, tumbling rings, that were as many-tinted as an opal; where the ruddy flush was faintest, was a smooth spot that was covered with graceful circles and radiating lines, ever so delicately traced; the shore on our left was densely wooded, and the somber shadow that fell from this forest was broken in one place by a long ruffled trail that shone like silver; and high above the forest wall a clean-stemmed dead tree waved a single leafy bough that glowed like a flame in the unobstructed splendor that was flowing from the sun. There were graceful curves, reflected images, woody heights, soft distances; and over the whole scene, far and near, the dissolving lights drifted steadily, enriching it, every passing moment, with new marvels of coloring.

I stood like one bewitched. I drank it in, in a speechless rapture. The world was new to me, and I had never seen anything like this at home. But as I have said, a day came when I began to cease from noting the glories and the charms which the moon and the sun and the twilight wrought upon the river's face; another day came when I ceased altogether to note them. Then, if that sunset scene had been repeated, I should have looked upon it without rapture, and should have commented upon it, inwardly, after this fashion: This sun means that we are going to have wind tomorrow; that floating log means that the river is rising, small thanks to it; that slanting mark on the water refers to a bluff reef which is going to kill somebody's steamboat one of these nights, if it keeps on stretching out like that; those tumbling "boils" show a dissolving bar and a changing channel there; the lines and circles in the slick water over yonder are a warning that the troublesome place is shoaling up[2] dangerously; that silver streak in the shadow of the forest is the "break" from a new snag, and he has located himself in the very best place he could have found to fish for steamboats; that tall dead tree, with a single living branch, is not going to last long, and then how is a body ever going to get through this blind place at night without the friendly old landmark?

No, the romance and the beauty were all gone from the river. All the value any feature of it had for me now was the amount of usefulness it could furnish toward compassing the safe piloting of a steamboat. Since those days, I have pitied doctors from my heart. What does the lovely flush in a beauty's cheek mean to a doctor but a "break" that ripples above some deadly disease? Are not all her visible charms sown thick with what are to him the signs and symbols of hidden decay? Does he ever see her beauty at all, or doesn't he simply view her professionally, and comment upon her unwholesome condition all to himself? And doesn't he sometimes wonder whether he has gained most or lost most by learning his trade?

2. **shoaling up:** becoming shallow.

Reading Check

1. How many miles of river did Twain learn to read?
2. What did a dimple on the surface of the water indicate to him?
3. What is Twain's most cherished memory of the river?
4. What does Twain say were lost once he acquired knowledge of the river?

For Study and Discussion

Analyzing and Interpreting the Selection

1. An **analogy** draws a point-by-point comparison between two things.   **a.** What does Twain mean by the "language" of the river? **b.** What specific examples does he give of "reading" the river?

2a. What does Twain mean by the "poetry" of the river?   **b.** What example does he give?

3. What similarity does Twain see between his own experience and that of a doctor?

Writing About Literature

Comparing Two Passages

Compare the passage in which Twain describes the wonderful sunset on the river with the passage in which he views the sunset scene from the pilot's viewpoint. What differences are there in the tone of the two passages? In your answer consider the connotations of the words Twain uses.

About the Author

Mark Twain   (1835–1910)

Samuel Langhorne Clemens was raised in Hannibal, Missouri, on the Mississippi River. At twelve he was apprenticed to a town printer. Later in his life he worked as a typesetter, a Mississippi river pilot, a Nevada prospector, and a journalist. For a short time he was an irregular soldier on the Confederate side, in the Civil War.

Twain's reputation as a writer grew with his humorous travel books. *Innocents Abroad*, published in 1869, was his first successful book in this genre. Twain enjoyed portraying innocent Americans who find themselves in the clutches of cunning European hotel owners and tour guides; his comparison of American and European customs was always to the advantage of the former. In other books like *Roughing It* (1872), *The Adventures of Tom Sawyer* (1876), *Life on the Mississippi* (1883), and *The Adventures of Huckleberry Finn* (1885), Twain drew on his Mississippi boyhood and experiences in the American West.

Connecting Cultures

Pen Names

Writers in different cultures have used pen names for a variety of reasons. Some have used different names for different kinds of books. Some have used pen names to protect themselves from punishment. Mary Ann Evans used the name George Eliot in order to hide the fact that one of Victorian England's greatest novelists was a woman.

Making Connections: Activities

Discover the identity of each of the following writers. Find the origin of their pen names.

Paul Annixter George Orwell
Lewis Carroll   Saki
Gordon Daviot   Voltaire
Elia

A Taste of Snow

JEANNE WAKATSUKI HOUSTON

When the United States declared war on Japan in December 1941, approximately 127,000 persons of Japanese ancestry were living in the United States, most of them on the West Coast. The Roosevelt administration was pressured to relocate Japanese Americans to ten internment camps located in Arizona, Arkansas, California, Colorado, Idaho, Utah, and Wyoming. More than 100,000 persons were relocated by September 1942. All the camps were closed by the end of 1945. Jeanne Wakatsuki Houston here recalls one memorable experience from her years in an internment camp.

I first saw snow one Christmas when I lived in the high desert of Owens Valley, California. I was nine years old. It was during the Second World War, the first winter my family and I spent at Manzanar.[1] When the crystal flakes floated down, like translucent coconut chips dancing in the breeze, I ran out into the clear area between the barracks, twirling and dancing and opening my mouth to catch the powdery ice. The snow reminded me of cotton candy, wispy and delicate, and gone with one whisk of the tongue.

I was surprised by the sharp coldness of the air and somehow disappointed that such beauty had its price to be paid—icy feet and hands, and uncomfortable wetness when the snow melted upon contact with my clothes and face. Still, the utter loveliness of this new phenomenon was so overpowering I soon forgot my discomfort.

Other people began coming out of the barracks into a transformed world. Some carried brightly colored Japanese parasols and wore high wooden *getas*[2] to raise their stockinged feet above the snow. It was odd not to hear the "kata-kata" clatter of wooden clogs scraping across sand and gravel. The blanket of snow muffled sound and thickened the thin planed roofs of the barracks, softening the stark landscape of white on white. It was strangely soothing to me, silent and tranquil. I found myself moved to tears.

This particular imprint in my memory is easily explained. Before being sent to Manzanar we lived in Ocean Park, on Dudley Avenue, a block from the beach. Ocean Park Pier was my playground. All the kids in the neighborhood played ball and skated along the wide cement promenade that bordered the beach from Ocean Park to Venice.

Memories of Ocean Park are warm ones of sunshine, hot days on the beach, building sand castles, playing *Tarzan* and *Jungle Girl,* jumping off lifeguard stands and spraining ankles.

---

1. **Manzanar** (măn′zə-när′): a Japanese American relocation center in Inyo County in eastern California.

2. **getas** (gā′täs): A geta is a clog held on to the foot by a thong between the first and second toes.

Fourth of July was a balmy evening of crowds milling around the pier waiting for fireworks to spray the sky with luminous explosives. Easter was as colorful as the many-hued eggs the local service club buried in the sand for the kids to uncover. And Christmas was just another version of this type of buoyant, high-spirited celebration my family enjoyed before the war.

In my memory Christmas morning seemed always sunny and clear. Strolling along the promenade in my new orange-flowered dress and white high-topped shoes, pushing the doll carriage Santa had left under the big tree in our living room, I proudly displayed myself and my gifts as did the other children of the neighborhood. My oldest brother Bill, who was then in his twenties, walked with me and helped me feed popcorn to the pigeons warbling and pecking around our feet. Then he rushed me off in his old blue roadster to visit his girl friend Molly who played the violin while he sang, and I slept.

Like a story within a story, or a memory within a memory, I cannot think of one memorable Christmas, but of these two. They are yin and yang,[3] each necessary to appreciate the other. I don't remember Christmas trees in Manzanar. But we gathered driftwood from the creeks that poured down from the nearby Sierras[4] and across the high desert. With these we improvised. In my mind's eye they co-exist: a lush, brilliantly lit fir tree; and a bare manzanita limb embellished with origami[5] cranes.

To this day, when I travel in the high country, I can cry seeing nature's exquisite winter garb and remembering my first taste of snow.

---

3. **yin and yang:** In Eastern philosophy, yin and yang are contrasting and complementary forces or principles in the universe. Yin is the passive or negative force; yang is the active or positive force.
4. **Sierras** (sē-ĕr′əz): the Sierra Nevada (Spanish for "snowy range"), a mountain range in eastern California.
5. **origami** (ôr′ĭ-gä′mē): the art of folding paper to form birds and other shapes.

Reading Check

1. Where was the narrator living when she saw snow for the first time?
2. Why does she compare the snow to cotton candy?
3. What are the narrator's memories of Christmas spent at Ocean Park?
4. How did people improvise Christmas trees in the desert?

For Study and Discussion

Analyzing and Interpreting the Selection

1. How did the snowfall transform Manzanar?

2a. Why does Houston characterize her memories of Christmas as a "yin and yang" experience? **b.** How do the Christmas trees symbolically represent the "yin and yang" philosophy?

3a. Why does Houston cry when she remembers her first taste of snow? **b.** What might be the "memory within the memory"?

Literary Elements

Tone

Tone is the attitude a writer takes toward his or her subject. A writer's tone is revealed through **diction,** or choice of words. In the first paragraph of the selection, Houston says that when she first saw the snow, she ran out into the clear air "twirling and dancing." How does the phrase "twirling and dancing" convey her attitude? Locate other words and phrases that are evidence of her attitude toward her subject.

Language and Vocabulary

Distinguishing Denotative from Connotative Meanings

In addition to their literal, or **denotative,** meanings, words have suggested, or **connotative,** meanings. The word *tiger,* for example, denotes, or names, a particular member of the cat family; we have given the **denotation** when we have stated all the ways the tiger is different from all members of the class of animals to which it belongs. The word *tiger* also **connotes,** or suggests, different feelings to people: beauty to some, terror and mystery to others. The English poet William Blake describes a tiger in the opening lines of one of his poems:

> Tiger Tiger, burning bright,
> In the forests of the night;
> What immortal hand or eye,
> Could frame thy fearful symmetry?

Beauty, terror, mystery, perfection of form—all of these **connotations** are evoked by Blake. None of them is a quality or feeling we find in the dictionary definition of the tiger.

In the following excerpts, what do the italicized words denote, and what additional feelings and qualities do they connote?

...softening the *stark* landscape of white on white.

...waiting for fireworks to spray the sky with *luminous* explosives.

a bare manzanita limb *embellished* with origami cranes.

Writing About Literature

Comparing and Contrasting Attitudes

Several authors whose work appears in this unit have experienced a conflict between two cultures: Sandra Cisneros, in "Straw into Gold" (page 252); Santha Rama Rau, in "By Any Other Name" (page 257); Harry Mark Petrakis, in "A Whole Nation and a People" (page 273); and Jeanne Wakatsuki Houston, in "A Taste of Snow."

Choose any two of these selections and compare and contrast the writers' attitudes toward the conflict of traditions and experiences. For example, do Cisneros and Petrakis express similar feelings about their ethnic backgrounds? Write a brief essay in which you develop your position. For assistance in planning and writing your paper, see the section called *Writing About Literature* on page 838.

Focus on Expository Writing

Using Transitions

Transitional words and phrases clarify the relationships of information and ideas in your writing. In the first paragraph of "A Taste of Snow," for instance, Jeanne Wakatsuki Houston uses several transitions to indicate chronological order: *first, when,* and *during* (see page 284).

The chart below lists transitions you may find useful as you write an expository essay.

Transitional Words and Phrases

Showing Time/Narration

after	eventually	first	then
before	finally	next	when

Showing Place/Description

above	before	here	over
across	behind	inside	there
around	down	into	under

Showing Importance/Evaluation

first	mainly		then
last	more important		to begin with

Showing Cause and Effect/Narration

as a result	for	so that
because	since	therefore
consequently	so	

Locate an informative magazine article about a person or topic that interests you. Read the article carefully and make a list of transitional words and phrases that the writer uses. Share your list with a small group of classmates. Save your notes.

About the Author

Jeanne Wakatsuki Houston (1934–   )

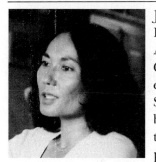

Jeanne Wakatsuki Houston, a Japanese American, was born in California. She attended the University of San Jose and the Sorbonne in Paris. She is the author of novels, plays, and an award-winning screenplay based on *Farewell to Manzanar: A True Story of Japanese American Experience During and After the World War II Internment* (1973), which she wrote with her husband, James D. Houston. "A Taste of Snow" is taken from the sequel, *Beyond Manzanar: Views of Asian-American Womanhood* (1985). Houston currently lives in Santa Cruz, California.

The Author Comments on Her Essay

"A Taste of Snow" was written in response to a magazine's request for a piece on a memorable Christmas. Experiencing snow for the first time and having to improvise our Christmas tree remained powerful images throughout my growing-up years. Thus, writing this recollection gave me the opportunity to shape those memories into "word pictures"—recording in words what a camera can capture in photographs.

Children's Experience of War

Children are often the most tragic victims of war. "A Taste of Snow" and "Our House in Hadong" (page 308) show some of the effects of war on young people.

Making Connections: Activities

1. Read Anne Frank's *Diary of a Young Girl,* a record kept by a young Jewish girl hiding from the Nazis during World War II. In an essay or in an oral report, tell how Anne Frank's youth influenced her impressions of the war.

2. *Zlata's Diary* by Zlata Filipović is an account of her life in Sarajevo between September 1991 and October 1993, during the conflict in her country. If you have read the *Diary of Anne Frank,* compare the two books.

3. Two autobiographical accounts of Japanese Americans who were children during World War II are *Farewell to Manzanar,* by Jeanne Wakatsuki Houston and James D. Houston, and *Journey to Topaz* by Yoshiko Uchida. Read these books and discuss the similarities and differences of the authors' experiences.

Reading and Critical Thinking

UNDERSTANDING CAUSE AND EFFECT

In order to develop an idea, an expository writer often depends upon cause-and-effect relationships. In the following passage from *Silent Spring,* Rachel Carson shows a cause-and-effect chain of events. A single act—the spraying of sagelands with pesticides—has an effect that in turn becomes the cause for another effect, and so on.

As you read the passage, fill out a chart like the one that follows to show the cause-and-effect chain that Carson describes.

Some 10,000 acres of sagelands were sprayed by the [United States Forest] Service, yielding to pressure of cattlemen for more grasslands. The sage was killed, as intended. But so was the green, life-giving ribbon of willows that traced its way across these plains, following the meandering streams. Moose had lived in these willow thickets, for willow is to the moose what sage is to the antelope. Beaver had lived there, too, feeding on the willows, felling them and making a strong dam across the tiny stream. Through the labor of the beavers, a lake backed up. Trout in the mountain streams seldom were more than six inches long; in the lake they thrived so prodigiously that many grew to five pounds. Waterfowl were attracted to the lake, also. Merely because of the presence of the willows and the beavers that depended on them, the region was an attractive recreational area with excellent fishing and hunting.

But with the "improvement" instituted by the Forest Service, the willows went the way of the sagebrush, killed by the same impartial spray. . . . The moose were gone and so were the beaver. Their principal dam had gone out for want of attention by its skilled architects, and the lake had drained away. None of the large trout were left. None could live in the tiny creek that remained, threading its way through a bare, hot land where no shade remained. The living world was shattered. . . .

—From *Silent Spring*

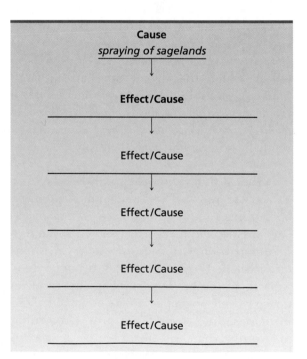

Cause
spraying of sagelands

↓

Effect/Cause

↓

Effect/Cause

↓

Effect/Cause

↓

Effect/Cause

↓

Effect/Cause

EXPOSITORY WRITING

*T*here are many ways to share information in your writing. For example, you can explain how to do something or how a process works. You can share information in an essay about your own discoveries. You can describe an interesting or notable person in a biographical sketch. You can explain in a report the causes and effects of a trend or a scientific phenomenon. Process explanations, essays, biographies, and reports are all examples of **expository writing**. During this unit, you have investigated some of the elements of this kind of writing. Now you will have the chance to write an expository essay on a topic of your choice.

Prewriting ∿

1. To find a good topic for your essay, make a list or inventory of your interests. Ask yourself questions like the following:

- What do I know how to do well?
- What celebrities or other notable persons do I admire?
- What interesting facts, trends, and events have I heard or read about recently?
- What natural processes am I curious about?

Write some notes about one or two topics on your list. Keep in mind that a suitable topic for an expository essay should

- have value or appeal to others
- be neither too broad ("how to raise children") nor too narrow ("how to dry a plate")

Also keep in mind that your essay can follow several different formats. It can be

- an explanation of how to do something or of how a process works
- a biographical sketch
- a cause-and-effect explanation

[See **Focus** assignment on page 233.]

2. The **purpose** of an expository essay is to share information. Whatever format your essay will take, you need to think about who your **audience** is and what they may already know about your topic. You also need to consider how to "hook" your audience on the value or interest of the information you have to share. Make some notes for your paper on how you will appeal to the audience. Maybe the way to show the audience "what's in it for them" is to start out with a striking fact, a quotation, a question, or a command. Notice, for example, how Geoffrey Norman directly addresses the reader in the first sentence of "The Flight of Rachel Carson" on page 240.

3. However you begin your essay, the opening paragraph or two should include a **thesis statement**. This is a statement of one or two sentences in which you identify your topic and your main idea about it. Look over your notes and write a thesis statement that will help you unify your essay. For example, if you plan to write a process explanation, you might state a thesis this way: "Cooking a special meal for the whole family can be both fun and challenging." A thesis statement for a biographical sketch might run as follows: "Aunt Sophie may not have been a celebrity in the usual sense of the word, but in our family's world she was very special." [See **Focus** assignment on page 248.]

4. Making an **outline** of your essay will help guide you. Below are some sample outlines for three different kinds of expository essay: a process explanation, a biographical sketch, and a cause-and-effect explanation.

Process Explanation
Introduction: grab reader's attention
    identify topic/state thesis
Body: list essential materials
    define unfamiliar terms
    explain each step in order
Conclusion: discuss advantages of process
    include further hints/advice

Biographical Sketch
Introduction: grab reader's attention
    identify person/state thesis
Body: present facts/anecdotes in logical order
Conclusion: restate thesis
    sum up significance of person

Cause-and-Effect Explanation
Introduction: grab reader's attention
    identify topic
    state thesis, focusing on causes, effects, or both
Body: discuss cause/effect A
    discuss cause/effect B
    discuss cause/effect C
Conclusion: summarize main points
    add a final comment or prediction

[See **Focus** assignments on pages 226 and 239.]

Writing

1. Using your outline as a guide, write the **first draft** of your essay. Focus on including all the necessary information a reader must have to understand your main idea. For example, in a process explanation, if you omit a step or part of the process, you will confuse your readers. You will also confuse them if you do not explain the stages of a process in the correct order. If you are writing a cause-and-effect explanation, remember that a single event can have more than one cause. Likewise, a single event can lead to more than one significant effect.

2. To clarify the relationship of information and ideas in your essay, be sure to use appropriate **transitions.** Transitional words and phrases can show relationships such as these:

- time
- place
- order of importance
- cause and effect

You will find a chart of many useful transitions in the **Focus** assignment on page 286.

Evaluating and Revising

After you have finished your first draft, you can use the checklist on page 291 as a guide for evaluating and revising an expository essay. You might want to trade papers with a classmate. Then you can both use the checklist to offer each other some suggestions on your writing.

Here is an example of an opening paragraph for a cause-and-effect essay. The thesis statement is underlined. Notice the writer's revisions.

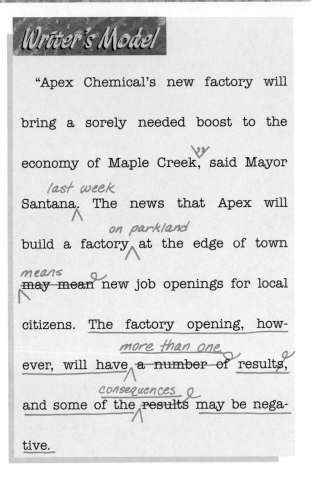

Writer's Model

"Apex Chemical's new factory will

bring a sorely needed boost to the

economy of Maple Creek, said Mayor

last week

Santana. The news that Apex will

on parkland

build a factory at the edge of town

means

~~may mean~~ new job openings for local

citizens. The factory opening, how-

more than one

ever, will have ~~a number of~~ results,

consequences

and some of the ~~results~~ may be nega-

tive.

Checklist for Evaluation and Revision

✓ Do I appeal to the reader's interest in the introduction?

✓ Do I state my thesis clearly?

✓ Do I supply any necessary background information? Do I explain what materials may be needed? Do I define any unfamiliar terms?

✓ Do I discuss the steps of a process, the facts/anecdotes about a person, or the causes and effects of an event in a clear, logical order?

✓ Does my conclusion restate the main idea and wrap up my paper in a suitable way?

Proofreading and Publishing

1. Proofread your essay to correct errors in grammar, usage, and mechanics. (You may find it helpful to refer to the **Handbook for Revision** on pages 884–930.) Focus on making sure that your facts are accurate and on spelling any unfamiliar words correctly. Then prepare a final version of your essay by making a clean copy.

2. Consider some of the following publication methods for sharing your essay:

- stage a "how-to" day in class
- send your essay to a newspaper or magazine
- use your essay as the basis for an illustrated lecture
- post your essay on the class bulletin board

Portfolio If your teacher approves, you may want to keep a copy of your work in your writing folder or portfolio.

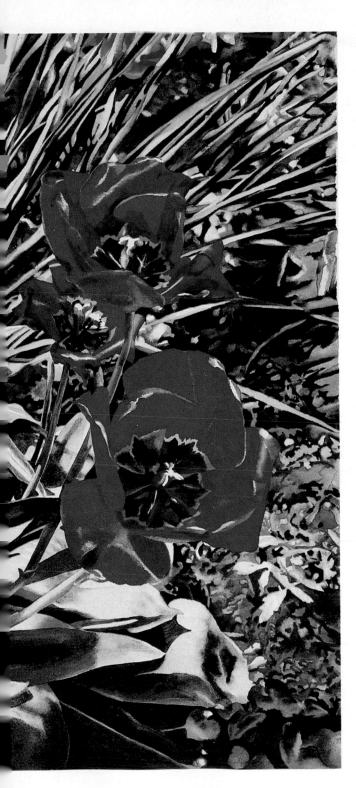

POETRY

Many poems have been inspired by art. A well-known poem by John Keats, "Ode on a Grecian Urn," was written after the poet saw ancient Greek pottery in the British Museum.

Look at the painting reproduced on these pages. Why do you think the artist called it *Last Red Tulips?* Are there any details in the work that give you a clue to the title?

Jot down your thoughts as you study the watercolor. What do you respond to most in the painting? How does it make you feel?

Write a draft of a poem based on your response to the painting. Use rhyme if you wish. If you like, share your poem with others. You may want to hold on to this draft and rework it as you study the poems in this unit.

Last Red Tulips (Baltimore Spring 1984) (1984) by Carolyn Brady (1937–). Watercolor over graphite on white wove paper, 96.4 x 140.8 cm.

Worcester Art Museum, Worcester, Massachusetts. Acquired through the National Endowment for the Arts Museum Plan, 1984. 132.

293

Close Reading OF A POEM

We live in a fast-moving age that often forces us to move fast, too. It is the age of "speed-reading," and students are frequently encouraged to read quickly so that they can take in large amounts of information in a short time. Many ads and articles are written in simple, stripped-down form so they can be read and digested swiftly. But poetry is a different kind of writing and demands a different kind of reading—reading that is more leisurely, more personal. A poem is not read like a newspaper, for quick information, but rather for an emotional and thought-provoking experience.

To experience a poem fully is to be aware of its special language and structure. Poets rely on the suggestive powers of language and choose words for their connotative as well as their denotative values. Through imagery, figurative language, and symbols, poets appeal to both the intellect and the senses. The meaning of a poem is conveyed not only through its words but also through its sounds. To intensify meaning, poets choose patterns of sound, including rhyme and rhythm. Poets achieve their effects, also, through special kinds of organization, in structures called stanzas, and in conventional forms such as sonnets and ballads.

To respond to a poem fully, you need to understand and react to its special language and structure. It is a good idea to read a poem several times and aloud at least once. Read slowly and distinctly, paying attention to meaning as well as to sound. It often helps to write a prose paraphrase of a poem, restating all its ideas in plain language. A paraphrase can help you clarify and simplify the author's text.

Guidelines for Close Reading

1. Read the poem several times and aloud at least once, trying to follow the thought. Commas, semicolons, colons, dashes, and periods tell you where to pause. You are not expected to pause automatically at the end of each line. Sometimes a complete thought runs over into a new stanza. In some lines more than one pause may be indicated.

2. Respond thoughtfully to key words and references. In poetry a word is often used in an unfamiliar or unusual way. Be alert to connotative meanings.

3. Write a paraphrase of any lines that need clarification or simplification. A paraphrase helps a reader respond more fully to the poem and to understand imagery and figurative language. It also puts inverted word order into normal word order.

4. Use your own reactions to explore the poet's meaning. Try to state the central idea or meaning of the poem in one or two sentences.

On page 296 you will find a well-known poem by Emily Dickinson. The notes in the margin represent one reader's response to the poem. If you wish, cover up these notes and make your own notes on a separate sheet of paper. At a later point you may wish to compare your own responses with the printed comments.

Grasshopper Sparrow [Yellow-winged Sparrow]
by John James Audubon (1785–1851).

Original watercolors by John James Audubon
provided by National Audubon Society

A Bird Came Down the Walk

EMILY DICKINSON

The bird doesn't know someone is watching him.

A bird came down the walk:
He did not know I saw;
He bit an angleworm° in halves
And ate the fellow, raw.

What does she mean by convenient? Whatever is there?
Hop is a good word for the way a bird moves.

And then he drank a dew   5
From a convenient grass,
And then hopped sidewise to the wall
To let a beetle pass.

I like the comparison of the bird's eyes to beads.

He glanced with rapid eyes
That hurried all abroad—   10
They looked like frightened beads, I thought.
He stirred his velvet head

I've seen birds this cautious.
Did the bird take the food? I don't think so. The poet must have frightened him off.

Like one in danger; cautious,
I offered him a crumb,
And he unrolled his feathers   15
And rowed him softer home

The movement of the bird's wings is compared to oars dividing the water.
Butterflies swim? Maybe the poet means they move through the air as if they're swimming.

Than oars divide the ocean,
Too silver for a seam,
Or butterflies, off banks of noon,
Leap, plashless,° as they swim.   20

3. **angleworm:** earthworm.   20. **plashless:** without a splash.

Looking at Yourself as a Reader

Compare your own responses with those in the notes alongside the poem. Using the Guidelines on page 295, evaluate the reader's response. Do you agree or disagree with any of the reader's comments?

Write a paragraph discussing your response and your thoughts about the poem's meaning. Share your reactions with other readers.

Field Sparrow by John James Audubon (1785–1851).

Original watercolors by John James Audubon provided by National Audubon Society

THE SPEAKER

The poet Robert Frost once said that a poem is "spoken by a person in a scene—in character, in a setting." This person, or *speaker*, is often simply the poet, but may be someone or something altogether different from the poet. Through the ages, poets have delighted in disguising their voices, like actors, and speaking as characters.

One aid to understanding a poem is to identify its speaker. Your knowledge of who or what the speaker is will help you understand other things about the poem: where and when the poem is set, what situation it describes, what story it tells.

The Face in the Mirror

ROBERT GRAVES

This poem is a self-portrait. What is the speaker's attitude toward his own face? How do you know that he regards himself ironically?

Grey haunted eyes, absent-mindedly glaring
From wide, uneven orbits; one brow drooping
Somewhat over the eye
Because of a missile fragment still inhering,°
Skin deep, as a foolish record of old-world fighting.   5

Crookedly broken nose—low tackling caused it;
Cheeks, furrowed; coarse grey hair, flying frenetic;
Forehead, wrinkled and high;
Jowls, prominent; ears, large; jaw, pugilistic;°
Teeth, few; lips, full and ruddy; mouth ascetic.°   10

I pause with razor poised, scowling derision
At the mirrored man whose beard needs my attention,
And once more ask him why
He still stands ready, with a boy's presumption,
To court the queen in her high silk pavilion.   15

4. **inhering** (ĭn-hîr′əng): remaining fixed.   9. **pugilistic** (pyo͞o′jə-lĭs′tĭk): like a fighter.
10. **ascetic** (ə-sĕt′ĭk): severe.

The Granger Collection, New York

Analyzing and Interpreting the Poem

1. In the first two stanzas of the poem, Graves gives us a detailed description of his face.
a. What do these details reveal about his past?
b. Would you call this portrait realistic or idealistic? Explain.

2. In line 12 Graves refers to his reflection as "the mirrored man." Why do you suppose he views this image with ridicule, "scowling derision"?

3. Consider the last two lines of the poem. "To court the queen in her high pavilion" suggests an episode from the age of chivalry. **a.** What do you think Graves means by "a boy's presumption"? **b.** How do you know that he has not been disillusioned by his experiences or by the ravages of time? **c.** What evidence is there that the "inner man" is different from the image in the mirror?

Language and Vocabulary

Learning Word Origins

The word *pavilion* in Graves's poem refers to a large, ornate tent such as those shown in illustrations of knights' tournaments during the Middle Ages. The word *pavilion* can be traced through French to the Latin word *papilio*, meaning "butterfly." The pavilion received its name because it resembled the wings of a butterfly.

In a dictionary find the origin of the words *ascetic* and *pugilistic*. What are their derivations? Can you see how these words came to have their present-day meanings?

FROM

The Cloud

PERCY BYSSHE SHELLEY

It is not at all unusual for poets to personify *the natural world—to describe
a natural force as though it possessed human qualities. This is Shelley's method
in "The Cloud." As you read the following stanza from the poem, determine
what kind of personality Shelley has given the speaker.*

I bring fresh showers for the thirsting flowers,
   From the seas and the streams;
I bear light shade for the leaves when laid
   In their noonday dreams.
From my wings are shaken the dews that waken   5
   The sweet buds every one,
When rocked to rest on their mother's breast,
   As she dances about the sun.
I wield the flail° of the lashing hail,
   And whiten the green plains under,   10
And then again I dissolve it in rain,
   And laugh as I pass in thunder.

9. **flail:** a tool with a free-swinging stick, used to thresh grain.

For Study and Discussion

Analyzing and Interpreting the Poem

1. The point of view of this poem is that of the cloud, which relates its different functions. How does Shelley attribute purpose and meaning to these actions?

2. Like the other great Romantic poets of the nineteenth century, Shelley loved nature and was able in his poetry to capture the tumultuous power of the wind and the sea. What characteristics does he attribute to the cloud?

Creative Writing

Creating a Speaker

Write a brief paragraph in which the speaker is something that does not really talk: an animal, a building, a school desk, or a street. Try to make your language appropriate to your speaker.

Focus on Descriptive Writing

Finding a Focus

Shelley's "The Cloud" is an example of **descriptive writing.** In his poem Shelley focuses on an aspect of nature. He uses various details—the cloud's functions and characteristics—to describe a familiar subject. Shelley adds an unusual note to the description by making the cloud the speaker.

When you choose a subject for your own descriptive writing, you will find these guidelines helpful:

1. Think of someone or something familiar.
2. Choose a subject you can observe directly.
3. Limit your subject to one you can cover in a few paragraphs.

Look around your classroom at school. List three or four familiar things that could serve as subjects for a description. When you have finished writing, exchange lists with a partner and compare notes. Save your list.

About the Authors

Robert Graves   (1895–1985)

Robert Graves was born in Wimbledon near London. During World War I he served in a regiment of the Royal Welch Fusiliers. He was wounded in action and later suffered shell shock. After the war he studied at Oxford. Graves became a prolific poet who experimented with a wide variety of verse forms. Apart from poetry, he wrote critical esays, translations, mythological studies, and historical novels.

Percy Bysshe Shelley   (1792–1822)

In his "Ode to the West Wind," Shelley describes himself as "tameless, and swift, and proud." By the standards of his own day, his life was highly unconventional. He produced his greatest poetry while he was living in Italy with his wife, Mary Shelley. Among his best-known poems are "Ode to a Skylark," "Ode to the West Wind," *Adonais,* and *Prometheus Unbound.* Shortly before his thirtieth birthday, he was drowned in a boating accident when he was swept overboard during a storm.

DICTION

In their *diction*, or choice of words, poets aim for clearness and effectiveness. They often prefer a concrete word to an abstract word. In "The Face in the Mirror," Graves's diction is precise: instead of using the word *looking* in line 1, he uses *glaring*. Note also the specific modifiers he uses for each of his features in stanza 2.

Poets also choose words that arouse particular sensations or moods. There would be a far different effect in line 2 of "The Cloud" if Shelley had written "bodies of salt water" instead of *seas*, or "small rivers" instead of *streams*.

The diction of a poem may be formal and even elegant, or it may be informal to the point of being slangy. You will find that poets choose their words carefully in order to control the reader's response.

To Satch

SAMUEL ALLEN (PAUL VESEY)

The "Satch" to whom this poem is dedicated was the phenomenal baseball pitcher Satchel Paige. Paige was one of the "iron men" of baseball. He was still pitching in the major leagues when most men his age had long retired from baseball. He was as well known for his sense of humor as for his genius with the change-up pitch.

Sometimes I feel like I will *never* stop
Just go on forever
'Til one fine mornin'
I'm gonna reach up and grab me a handfulla stars
Swing out my long lean leg
And whip three hot strikes burnin' down the heavens
And look over at God and say
How about that!

For Study and Discussion

Analyzing and Interpreting the Poem

1a. Who is the speaker of this poem?
b. How do you know?

2a. How does the speaker reveal confidence in his abilities? **b.** How does he also reveal a sense of humor?

3. This poem makes use of dialect, slang, and lively expressions. How is this language appropriate to the subject?

Cargoes

JOHN MASEFIELD

The English poet John Masefield is best known for his poems about the sea, and the following poem is one of his most famous. Do not be put off by the strange words in the opening line: a quinquireme (kwĭn′kwī-rēm′) *was a galley ship of olden times;* Nineveh (nĭ′nə-və), *the galley's home port, was a city of ancient* Assyria (ə-sîr′ē-ə); *and* Ophir (ō′fər) *was a Biblical land famed for its great stores of gold.*

Quinquireme of Nineveh from distant Ophir,
Rowing home to haven in sunny Palestine,
With a cargo of ivory,
And apes and peacocks,
Sandalwood, cedarwood, and sweet white wine.   5

Stately Spanish galleon coming from the Isthmus,°   6. **Isthmus** (is′məs): Panama.
Dipping through the Tropics by the palm-green shores,
With a cargo of diamonds,
Emeralds, amethysts,
Topazes, and cinnamon, and gold moidores.°   10   10. **moidores** (moi′dôrz′): Portuguese gold coins.

Dirty British coaster with a salt-caked smokestack,
Butting through the Channel in the mad March days,
With a cargo of Tyne coal,°   13. **Tyne coal:** coal from the British mining center of Newcastle-upon-Tyne.
Road rails, pig lead,
Firewood, ironware, and cheap tin trays.   15

For Study and Discussion

Analyzing and Interpreting the Poem

1. Each stanza of this poem describes a ship from a different period in history. The ship in stanza 1 is from Biblical times. Identify the historical periods in stanzas 2 and 3.

2. Compare the first two lines of each stanza which describe the ships' movements and locations. What differences do you find between the first two ships and the third one?

3. The cargoes of the first two ships are exotic, rich, and colorful. **a.** How do they differ from the cargo of the third ship? **b.** What is this poem implying about the differences between past times and modern times?

4. The poet's attitude toward each ship is different. **a.** How would you describe the poet's attitude toward the third ship and its cargo? **b.** Which words in the last stanza lead you to think so?

The Fleet of Pedro Alvares Cabral from a sixteenth-century
Portuguese manuscript.
© The Pierpont Morgan Library, New York, M. 525, f.17

Language and Vocabulary

Recognizing Connotative Meanings

A word can have **denotative** and **connotative**
meanings. **Denotation** is a word's literal, "dictionary" meaning. For example, the word
springtime denotes the season between winter
and summer. **Connotations** are the additional
meanings a word gains because of its associations. *Springtime* has connotations of youth, rebirth, and romance.

A poet may draw on a word's connotations to
arouse a special feeling in the reader. Each
stanza of "Cargoes" ends with a list of things
one of the ships carries. What connotations do
the words in each list have? Suppose that line 3
read: "With a cargo of dead elephants' tusks"
instead of "With a cargo of ivory." In what way
would the effect of the line be different?

Creative Writing

Describing a Modern Cargo

Imagine a modern cargo carried by modern
means, such as a truck, train, or airplane.
Write a short essay describing such a cargo,
using words whose connotations reveal your
attitude toward the cargo. For example, a truck
full of poultry might be described as "a gleaming van full of fine, fat fowls," or as "a clatter-
ing old wreck with crates of half-dead
chickens." If you like, try to write a fourth
stanza to Masefield's poem, describing the kind
of cargo a ship might carry today.

Dream Deferred

LANGSTON HUGHES

A deferred dream is one that has been delayed or put off. What do you think the poet means by the word dream?

What happens to a dream deferred?

Does it dry up
like a raisin in the sun?

Or fester like a sore—
And then run?   5

Does it stink like rotten meat?
Or crust and sugar over—
like a syrupy sweet?

Maybe it just sags
like a heavy load.   10

Or does it explode?

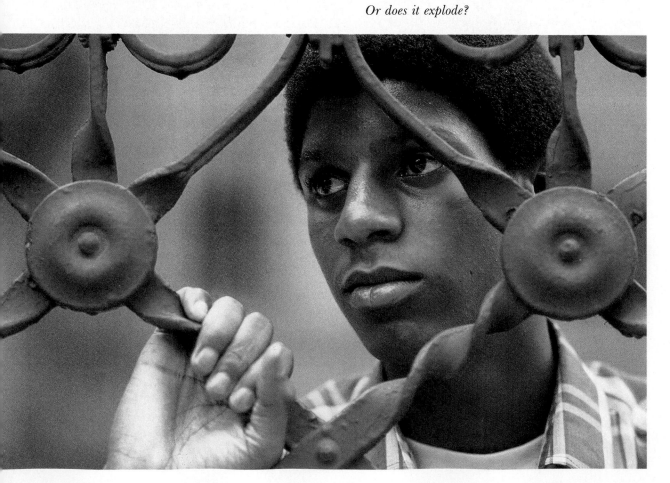

For Study and Discussion

Analyzing and Interpreting the Poem

1. Hughes's poem is organized as a series of questions. In lines 2–10 the questions are phrased as comparisons. How does this approach immediately engage your interest?

2a. What words does the poet use that have unpleasant connotations? **b.** Why is this language effective? **c.** How would you describe the speaker's emotions?

Writing About Literature

Analyzing Diction

Compare the diction in "Dream Deferred" with the diction of "Cargoes" (page 304). How would you characterize the diction in each poem? How is the diction of each poem suited to its subject? In your composition, cite examples that illustrate your point.

About the Authors

Samuel Allen (1917–   )

Samuel Allen was born in Columbus, Ohio. He attended Fisk University and Harvard, then continued his studies at the Sorbonne in Paris. Some of his early poems were published by Richard Wright, who was then living in Paris. In 1956, an edition of Allen's poems was published in Germany in both German and English. Allen's poetry has appeared in *American Negro Poetry, New Negro Poets: U.S.A.,* and other publications. He sometimes uses the pseudonym "Paul Vesey."

The Granger Collection, New York

John Masefield was born in England. At the age of fourteen he ran away to sea. Three years later, when his ship docked in New York, he decided to live for a while in America. He supported himself through a variety of jobs: working in a bakery, a livery stable, a saloon, and a carpet mill. The sights he had seen and the experiences he had undergone made him want to read and write poetry, so during his stay in America, he eagerly read all the great English poets. He returned to England and worked for a time as a journalist, and, in 1902, he published his first book of poems, *Salt Water Ballads.* In addition to poetry he wrote dramas, such as *The Tragedy of Pompey the Great,* and novels, such as *Lost Endeavor.* In 1930, John Masefield was made Poet Laureate of England.

Langston Hughes (1902–1967)

Langston Hughes began traveling at the age of fourteen. He went to Mexico and then New York City, where he attended Columbia University for a year. He signed on as a crew member of a steamer and spent two years working his way around Africa and Europe. For his poetry, Hughes drew on modern folk and jazz rhythms, the kind of speech and music he heard in the African American community. Hughes's work, down-to-earth and realistic, pointed the way to a new, distinctly American kind of poetry.

IMAGERY

Although we do a great deal of our thinking with words, many of our thoughts come to us as pictures or as imagined sensations. For instance, if you think about riding a roller coaster, you may see a picture of long tracks stretching down before you, and imagine a lurching feeling in the pit of your stomach. Such imagined pictures or sensations are called *images.*

Poets attempt to share their experiences with us by appealing to our imaginations. One way in which a poet makes an experience seem real, vivid, and fresh to us is through the skillful use of *imagery.*

Our House in Hadong

WENDY WILDER LARSEN
AND TRAN THI NGA°

The speaker is recalling cherished memories of a home in Hadong (also spelled Ha Dong), a village about 150 miles south of Hanoi in northern Vietnam. To which senses does the poem appeal? Which images tell that this house was isolated from the outside world as well as from the war?

Our best house, the house where we were happy,
was our brick house on Ha Van Street
with its two hectares° of land
lichee and mangosteen° and starfruit in the back,
the two Hoa Moc trees white as snow in the front.   5
We'd put the petals in our tea to sweeten our breath.

From far down the road
I could smell the heavy jackfruit.
Father never allowed us to eat them
said they were too rich for the climate.   10
He'd give them to the soldiers outside the walls.
When he was away, we ate until we got fevers.
My younger sister climbed the apple trees
and shook the apples down.

3. two hectares (hĕk′târz′): about five acres.
4. mangosteen (măng′gə-stēn′): a fruit with a thick, reddish-brown rind and sweet, juicy pulp.

°**Tran Thi Nga** (trăn tĭ nä).

We had everything.   15
There was a flower garden
with dark red roses, orchids and yellow mimosa.
We had our own cauliflower, tomatoes,
the artichokes my father loved,
chickens, pigs, ducks and pigeons.   20
We needed the market only for beef
and rice kept in giant brown jars in the storeroom.

We even had two ponds.
Each New Year
we'd let the water out of the big pond   25
to catch the butter fish
we'd fed all year.

On a tiny island in the middle of the smaller pond,
the cook built an imitation mountain
with caves, bamboo, porcelain angels,   30
and two old matchmakers playing chess.
When the moon came up,
we'd watch the goldfish move in the warm water
and listen to night noises
remembering the sounds of the jungle.   35

For Study and Discussion

Analyzing and Interpreting the Poem

1. The speaker is remembering a home in which she was happy as a child. What was special about the house and its garden?

2. Which images reveal that the house was isolated from the outside world?

3. Until recently, marriages in Vietnam were generally arranged. What reference does the poem make to this custom?

4. Look at the last two lines. What "sounds of the jungle" might the speaker be remembering?

The Meadow Mouse

THEODORE ROETHKE°

Poets choose their images carefully—as they choose their words—to control the reader's response. How do the images in this poem gain sympathy and affection for the baby mouse?

I

In a shoe box stuffed in an old nylon stocking
Sleeps the baby mouse I found in the meadow,
Where he trembled and shook beneath a stick
Till I caught him up by the tail and brought him in,
Cradled in my hand,   5
A little quaker, the whole body of him trembling,
His absurd whiskers sticking out like a cartoon-mouse,
His feet like small leaves,
Little lizard-feet,
Whitish and spread wide when he tried to struggle away,   10
Wriggling like a miniscule° puppy.

11. **miniscule:** tiny.

Now he's eaten his three kinds of cheese and drunk from
    his bottle-cap watering-trough—
So much he just lies in one corner,

° **Roethke** (rĕt′kē).

His tail curled under him, his belly big
As his head; his batlike ears
Twitching, tilting toward the least sound.   15

Do I imagine he no longer trembles
When I come close to him?
He seems no longer to tremble.

II

But this morning the shoe-box house on the back porch is
    empty.   20
Where has he gone, my meadow mouse,
My thumb of a child that nuzzled in my palm?—
To run under the hawk's wing,
Under the eye of the great owl watching from the elm tree,
To live by courtesy of the shrike,° the snake, the tomcat.   25   **25. shrike:** a violent, shrill-voiced bird of prey.

  26. nestling: baby bird.

I think of the nestling° fallen into the deep grass,
The turtle gasping in the dusty rubble of the highway,
The paralytic stunned in the tub, and the water rising—
All things innocent, hapless,° forsaken.   **29. hapless:** unfortunate.

For Study and Discussion

Analyzing and Interpreting the Poem

1. In line 7, the speaker describes the mouse as having whiskers "like a cartoon-mouse." What other comparisons does the speaker use to describe the mouse?

2. In the first part of the poem, the speaker describes the mouse several times as "trembling." **a.** What does he imagine in lines 17–19? **b.** How do you think the speaker feels toward the mouse?

3. The second part of the poem contrasts sharply with the first part. The images in the first part create a mood of playfulness and affection. **a.** What images in the second part create a mood of helplessness and terror? **b.** How does the speaker express compassion for all helpless creatures?

Language and Vocabulary

Analyzing Word Structure

Many words in our language are made up of separate word elements. The word *innocent*, for example, is made up of two parts. The first part, *in-*, is a **prefix** from Latin meaning "not." The main part or *root* of the word is *nocens*, also from Latin, meaning "to do wrong to." *Innocent* means "not doing wrong to" or "guiltless." The word *whitish* is also made up of two parts. The root is the word *white* and the part at the end, *-ish*, is a **suffix** meaning "somewhat."

Identify the separate elements in each of these words, using a dictionary where necessary: *absurd, batlike, forsake, hapless, nestling, twitching.*

The Fawn

EDNA ST. VINCENT MILLAY

*How do the images in the final stanza of this poem contrast with the images in
the first stanza? How does this contrast affect your feelings for the fawn?*

There it was I saw what I shall never forget
And never retrieve.
Monstrous and beautiful to human eyes, hard to believe,
He lay, yct there he lay,
Asleep on the moss, his head on his polished cleft small ebony°   5. **ebony:** black.
    hooves,   5
The child of the doe, the dappled child of the deer.

Surely his mother had never said, "Lie here
Till I return," so spotty and plain to see
On the green moss lay he.
His eyes had opened; he considered me.   10

I would have given more than I care to say
To thrifty ears, might I have had him for my friend
One moment only of that forest day:

Might I have had the acceptance, not the love
Of those clear eyes;   15
Might I have been for him the bough above
Or the root beneath his forest bed,
A part of the forest, seen without surprise.

Was it alarm, or was it the wind of my fear lest° he depart   19. **lest:** that.
That jerked him to his jointy knees,   20
And sent him crashing off, leaping and stumbling
On his new legs, between the stems of the white trees?

For Study and Discussion

Analyzing and Interpreting the Poem

1. The speaker in this poem sees a rare sight—a lone fawn. **a.** What are her feelings when she sees the fawn? **b.** What images does she use to describe the fawn? **c.** What do you think she means by the word *monstrous* in line 3?

2. In line 14, the speaker says she wished she might have "the acceptance, not the love" of the shy fawn. She knows it would be impossible for so wild a creature to love any human being. Reread lines 16–18. What do you think she means by "acceptance"?

Focus on Descriptive Writing

Identifying Your Purpose

Your **purpose** affects the kind of description you write. For example, if your purpose is to express yourself, you will normally include your thoughts and feelings in a **subjective description.** This kind of description often uses first-person point of view and an informal tone. It is common in letters, poems, and stories. Millay's poem "The Fawn" is an example of subjective description.

If your purpose is to inform, however, you will usually be writing an **objective description,** in which you limit yourself to factual details. This kind of description normally uses third-person point of view and a formal tone; it appears in reports and articles.

Choose two subjects, one for each type of description. Each subject should be a person, place, or thing that you know well. Freewrite for five minutes about each subject. Save your writing.

Without Title

for my Father who lived without ceremony

DIANE GLANCY

When a person leaves behind the "old ways," often what replaces them is shallow and meaningless. How do you think the speaker's father feels about his life after coming to the city?

It's hard you know without the buffalo,
the shaman,° the arrow,
but my father went out each day to hunt
as though he had them.
He worked in the stockyards.
All his life he brought us meat.
No one marked his first kill,
no one sang his buffalo song.
Without a vision he had migrated to the city
and went to work in the packing house.
When he brought home his horns and hides
my mother said
get rid of them.
I remember the animal tracks of his car
out the drive in snow and mud,
the aerial on his old car waving
like a bow string.
I remember the silence of his lost power,
the red buffalo painted on his chest.
Oh, I couldn't see it
but it was there, and in the night I heard
his buffalo grunts like a snore.

2. **shaman** (shä′mən, shā′-):
a priest or medicine man
in some Native American
cultures.

For Study and Discussion

Analyzing and Interpreting the Poem

1. Why do you think the speaker's father "migrated to the city" (line 9)?

2. What does the phrase "Without a vision" suggest?

3. What do you think is meant in line 18 by the "lost power"?

4. Is this merely an untitled poem or is the poem suggesting some other meaning?

The Space

GARY SOTO

How does this poem make use of imagery to give you a picture of a specific place?

West of town,
Near Hermosa's well,
I sleep sometimes—
In a hammock of course—
Among avocado trees,   5
Cane, spider-grass,
The hatchet-faced chula,°
The banana's umbrella
Of leaves.
It is here   10
In the spiny brush
Where cocks gabble,
Where the javelina°
Lies on its side
Like an overturned high-heel.   15
I say it is enough
To be where the smells
Of creatures
Braid like rope
And to know if   20
The grasses' rustle
Is only
A lizard passing.
It is enough, brother,
Listening to a bird coo   25
A leash of parables,°
Keeping an eye
On the moon,
The space
Between cork trees   30
Where the sun first appears.

7. **chula** (chōō′lə): a plant that is indigenous to northern Mexico.

13. **javelina** (hä′və-lē′nä): a piglike animal.

26. **parables** (păr′ə-bəlz): short simple stories illustrating a lesson.

Analyzing and Interpreting the Poem

1. From the details of description, what can you infer about the location of "the space"?

2a. Which senses does the poem appeal to? **b.** Locate specific examples of each kind of imagery.

3. The speaker refers to a bird cooing "A leash of parables." What kind of "lessons" might the bird teach?

4a. Why does the speaker repeat the phrase "it is enough"? **b.** How do you think he feels about this particular place?

About the Authors

Wendy Wilder Larsen
Tran Thi Nga

Wendy Wilder Larsen, a poet and teacher, was born in Boston, Massachusetts. Her husband was the Vietnam Bureau Chief for *Time* magazine, and while in Vietnam in 1970, Larsen met Tran Thi Nga, a native of Saigon and the *Time* bureau bookkeeper. Larsen returned to the United States, and Nga emigrated there with her children in 1975. Together the two women wrote a book called *Shallow Graves* (1986), from which "Our House in Hadong" is taken.

Larsen is also the author of *Literary Authority and the Modern Chinese Writer* (1991), a study of Chinese autobiography. She is Associate Professor of Chinese Language and Literature at the University of Oregon.

The Author Comments on Her Poem

In 1970 I taught Shakespeare and Romantic Poetry to Vietnamese teachers. My husband was then the *Time* magazine bureau chief and Tran Thi Nga was the bookkeeper and the only woman in the office. She helped me when I lived in her country. In 1975 when she had to flee her country because she had worked for us, I helped her. Together we wrote *Shallow Graves: Two Women and Vietnam*.

I wanted to know what the home of a Minister of Education in Vietnam was like so I asked Mrs. Nga to describe her father's house. She said that house, the one they had in the north before they were forced to move south in 1954 because of the Geneva Agreements, was her favorite. I was amazed how self-sufficient they were. They grew almost everything they needed to eat except for the rice kept in special jars. Vietnamese, like the Chinese who are on their border to the north, eat many kilos of rice. They eat the rice with chopsticks.

I loved learning the names of the trees. Hoa Moc is pronounced "wha." Later when Mrs. Nga came to the United States, she wanted to have a garden in the back just the way she had in her homeland. Instead, she got a horrible case of poison ivy trying to clear the space.

New Year, which the Vietnamese call Tet, is a very special time. They prepare dishes to offer to their ancestors, whose death days they always remember. They have a saying: "Birds have nests / People have ancestors." The matchmakers in the garden are important because in the old days and not so long ago, many marriages were arranged.

The house seemed so beautiful and peaceful. It was sad to think that very soon bombs would be falling and Mrs. Nga and her brothers and sisters would be running into the garden where the father had built bomb shelters. They would run and hide and wait for the all-clear signal, then return in the moonlight to their beds.

Theodore Roethke   (1908–1963)

Theodore Roethke was born in Saginaw, Michigan, and spent much of his youth exploring the wild countryside or observing the mysterious processes of growth and life in his father's greenhouses. His poetry is rich in observations of the natural world and covers a wide range of moods. He won many awards for poetry, including a Pulitzer Prize and two National Book Awards.

Edna St. Vincent Millay   (1892–1950)

The Granger Collection, New York

Edna St. Vincent Millay was born in Rockland, Maine. She began publishing poetry when she was still in high school, and her first long poem, "Renascence," was written when she was barely nineteen. After graduating from college, she moved to New York City, where she made her living as an actress and playwright for the Provincetown Players. In 1923, her collection of poems, *The Harp-Weaver,* was awarded the Pulitzer Prize.

Diane Glancy   (1941–   )

Although only one of her great-grandparents was Cherokee, Diane Glancy feels that her Cherokee heritage has had the strongest influence upon her. She has said, "I am part heir to the Indian culture, and even that small part has leavened the whole lump." She is the author of several books of poetry, including *Drystalks of the Moon* (1981), *Iron Woman* (1990), and *Claiming Breath* (1991), and two collections of short stories about Indian culture, *Trigger Dance* (1990) and *Firesticks* (1993). Glancy has received grants from the National Endowment for the Arts to help support her writing. She is currently an assistant professor of English at Macalester College in St. Paul, Minnesota.

Gary Soto   (1952–   )

Gary Soto was born in Fresno, California, and attended California State University. His first book of poems, *The Elements of San Joaquin* (1977), won the United States Award of International Poetry Forum. He has received a number of other awards, including the Academy of American Poets Prize. "The Space" is from *The Tale of Sunlight* (1978), which is a book-length poem about two characters, Molina and Manuel Zaragoza. Critics and reviewers have likened Soto's writing to that of Carl Sandburg. In contrast to Sandburg's figures, who are Midwestern landowners and farmers, Soto's subjects are migrant workers who know and work the land, but who have little hope of ever owning it. Soto recently edited a volume of new Chicano fiction, *Pieces of the Heart* (1993).

FIGURATIVE LANGUAGE

In our everyday speech, we often use *figurative language*—language that represents one thing in terms of another. We may describe an action or a feeling by comparing it to something else: "I felt like a worm"; "We ate like kings"; "That test was murder." Expressions that describe one thing in terms of another are called *figures of speech*.

Figures of speech help to make language richer in meaning and more imaginative. In *Macbeth,* William Shakespeare describes a storm in which the sky grows so dreary that it seems as though "dark night strangles" the sun. Emily Dickinson, describing a violent storm, uses this figure of speech to evoke the sound of a shrill wind: "There came a wind like a bugle." Through figurative language poets can express fresh, exciting, or unusual relationships between things, and so give us new insights into what we see and feel.

The Day Is Done

HENRY WADSWORTH LONGFELLOW

*Poetry is often compared to music, primarily because poetry depends on the
sounds of words for many of its effects. Note how Longfellow makes use of that
comparison here.*

The day is done, and the darkness
  Falls from the wings of night, — 2
As a feather is wafted downward
  From an eagle in his flight.

I see the lights of the village   5
  Gleam through the rain and the mist,
And a feeling of sadness comes o'er me,
  That my soul cannot resist:

A feeling of sadness and longing,
  That is not akin to pain,   10
And resembles sorrow only
  As the mist resembles the rain.

Come, read to me some poem,
  Some simple and heartfelt lay,°   **14. lay:** a ballad or story
That shall soothe this restless feeling,   15   poem.
  And banish the thoughts of day.

Not from the grand old masters,
  Not from the bards sublime,°   **18. bards sublime:** poets who
Whose distant footsteps echo   wrote lofty, exalted poems.
  Through the corridors of time.   20

For, like strains of martial music, — 21   *simile*
  Their mighty thoughts suggest
Life's endless toil and endeavor;
  And tonight I long for rest.

Read from some humbler poet,   25
  Whose songs gushed from his heart,
As showers from the clouds of summer, — 27   *simile*
  Or tears from the eyelids start;

Who, through long days of labor,
  And nights devoid of ease,
Still heard in his soul the music
  Of wonderful melodies.

30

Such songs have power to quiet
  The restless pulse of care,
And come like the benediction°
  That follows after prayer.

35   35. **benediction:** blessing.

Then read from the treasured volume
  The poem of thy choice,
And lend to the rhyme of the poet
  The beauty of thy voice.

40

And the night shall be filled with music,
  And the cares, that infest the day,
Shall fold their tents, like the Arabs,
  And as silently steal away.

For Study and Discussion

Analyzing and Interpreting the Poem

1a. What is the speaker's mood at the beginning of the poem? **b.** What does he believe has power to change his mood?

2. The speaker distinguishes between two kinds of poems. How is the "music" of these poems different?

3. The final stanza of Longfellow's poem is famous and is often quoted. **a.** How is the concluding stanza related to the opening stanzas of the poem? **b.** How does it bring the poem to a satisfying close?

Literary Elements

Similes

A **simile** is a figure of speech that compares two unlike things, using a word such as *like, as,* or *than* to suggest the similarity. Simple similes occur in our everyday speech:

  He runs *like* the wind.
  Her sunburn made her face red *as* a beet.
  Superman is faster *than* a speeding bullet.

  In "The Day Is Done," Longfellow uses several striking similes. Look, for example, at the comparison in the sixth stanza:

  For, like strains of martial music,
    Their mighty thoughts suggest
  Life's endless toil and endeavor;

The word *martial* means "military" or "warlike." What is Longfellow comparing to the sounds of martial music?

  Look at the simile in stanza 9. What two things are being compared? A famous and often-quoted comparison is found in the last stanza. What is Longfellow comparing his cares to?

  Find other similes in the poem and explain the comparison in each one.

I'll Tell You How the Sun Rose

EMILY DICKINSON

Emily Dickinson's figurative language is known for its striking originality.
How does her depiction of sunset differ figuratively from that of sunrise?

I'll tell you how the sun rose—
A ribbon at a time.
The steeples swam in amethyst,
The news like squirrels ran.

The hills untied their bonnets,   5
The bobolinks begun.
Then I said softly to myself,
"That must have been the sun!"

But how he set, I know not.
There seemed a purple stile°   10
Which little yellow boys and girls
Were climbing all the while

Till when they reached the other side,
A dominie° in gray
Put gently up the evening bars,   15
And led the flock away.

10. **stile:** steps enabling a person to climb over a fence or wall.

14. **dominie:** clergyman.

For Study and Discussion

Analyzing and Interpreting the Poem

1. The speaker describes the sun rising "a ribbon at a time." What image does this phrase give you?

2a. What is the color of amethyst? **b.** In what way might the steeples appear to *swim* "in amethyst"?

3a. What does the word *news* refer to in line 4? **b.** How might the spreading of the news look like squirrels running?

4. Notice the colors the speaker uses to describe the "stile" (line 10), the children (line 11), and the "dominie" (line 14). How do these colors and the actions described in lines 10–16 help to suggest the setting sun?

Literary Elements

Metaphors

Like a simile, a **metaphor** points out a resemblance between two unlike things. A simile makes the comparison through the use of connecting words such as *like* or *as:* Jim growled *like* a bear. A metaphor identifies the two things as one: Jim is a bear.

Emily Dickinson is famous for her unusual metaphors. In line 5 of this poem, she says that the hills "untied their bonnets." A bonnet, like any other kind of hat, hides part of the wearer's head and also keeps the head warm. What is she comparing the hills to? Why is it appropriate that the hills should "untie their bonnets" when the sun rises?

Inverted Word Order

Emily Dickinson often uses **inverted word order** in her poetry; that is, the words in a line are turned around so that they do not occur in the usual or expected position. Normally we would say "The news ran like squirrels." Dickinson, however, writes "The news like squirrels ran." What emphasis is gained when the poet changes the normal word order of this sentence?

Another example of inversion occurs in line 9. What is gained by the change in normal word order?

It Bids Pretty Fair

ROBERT FROST

*"All the world's a stage," Shakespeare's metaphor,
may help you understand the metaphor in this poem.*

The play seems out for an almost infinite run.
Don't mind a little thing like the actors fighting.
The only thing I worry about is the sun.
We'll be all right if nothing goes wrong with the lighting.

For Study and Discussion

Analyzing and Interpreting the Poem

1. This poem consists of a single metaphor.
a. What is the play referred to in the first line?
b. Why does this play have "an almost infinite run"? **c.** Who are the actors and why are they fighting?

2. The poem's title, "It Bids Pretty Fair," means "It looks pretty good." **a.** How is the title ironic? **b.** Do you think the speaker really believes that "we'll be all right"? **c.** What does the metaphor of the play tell you about the speaker's attitude?

Moon Tiger

DENISE LEVERTOV

What metaphor is expressed in the title of this poem? How is the metaphor developed in the poem?

The moon tiger.
In the room, here.
It came in, it is
prowling sleekly
under and over   5
the twin beds.
See its small head,
silver smooth,
hear the pad of its
large feet. Look,   10
its white stripes
in the light that slid
through the jalousies.°
It is sniffing our
clothes, its cold nose   15
nudges our bodies.
The beds are narrow,
but I'm coming in with you.

13. **jalousies** (jăl′ə-sēz): a type of window
or door that is made of adjustable slats.

Habitation (1939) by Marvin D. Cone (1891–1965). Oil on canvas.

For Study and Discussion

Analyzing and Interpreting the Poem

1. Like Frost's "It Bids Pretty Fair," "Moon Tiger" is based on one central metaphor. **a.** To what thing is the moon compared? **b.** What does this comparison tell you about the speaker's feelings toward the moon?

2a. What phrases and details make the comparison strong? **b.** How might moonlight seem to prowl, sniff, or nudge bodies?

Literary Elements

Implied Metaphor

Sometimes a metaphor is suggested or **implied.** It does not directly state that one thing is another, different thing. What comparisons are implied by the following metaphors?

The wind drove the galloping storm clouds across the sky.

Carefully, cleverly, the spy wove his web of deceit and waited to entrap his victim.

The windows of the old house stared out into the night, and the open door seemed to grin.

Moon Tiger   **325**

Silver

WALTER DE LA MARE

This poem is famous for its evocation of a mood. How does the repetition of the word silver *help to build that mood?*

Slowly, silently, now the moon
Walks the night in her silver shoon;°
This way, and that, she peers, and sees
Silver fruit upon silver trees;
One by one the casements° catch   5
Her beams beneath the silvery thatch;
Couched in his kennel, like a log,
With paws of silver sleeps the dog;
From their shadowy cote° the white breasts peep
Of doves in a silver-feathered sleep;   10
A harvest mouse goes scampering by,
With silver claws and a silver eye;
And moveless fish in the water gleam,
By silver reeds in a silver stream.

2. **shoon:** shoes.   5. **casements:** window frames.   9. **cote:** coop.

For Study and Discussion

Analyzing and Interpreting the Poem

1. How are objects and animals transformed by the moonlight?

2. The first line of the poem sets a still and silent mood. What images in the poem add to this mood?

3. The word *silver* is repeated throughout the poem. **a.** What is the effect of this repetition? **b.** Would the word *golden* have been equally effective? Explain.

4. Reread the poem and listen closely to its sounds. **a.** What sounds are repeated? **b.** How do these sounds help to create a quiet, still mood?

Literary Elements

Personification

Personification is a figure of speech that gives human qualities to something nonhuman. At the New Year, cartoonists depict the old year as a toothless old man and the new year as a sturdy baby. Death is often portrayed as a grim and bony figure in a hooded robe, carrying a scythe. The natural world is personified as Mother Nature. Through personification, a writer can describe a quality or idea in a concrete, yet imaginative way. In "Silver," Walter de la Mare personifies the moon. Which words and phrases in the poem suggest that the moon is human?

A Song of the Moon

CLAUDE McKAY

The moonlight breaks upon the city's domes,
And falls along cemented steel and stone,
Upon the grayness of a million homes,
Lugubrious° in unchanging monotone.

4. **lugubrious** (loo-gōō′brē-əs,
loo-gyōō′-): mournful.

Upon the clothes behind the tenement,   5
That hang like ghosts suspended from the lines,
Linking each flat,° but to each indifferent,
Incongruous° and strange the moonlight shines.

7. **flat:** apartment.

8. **incongruous** (ĭn-kŏng′
grōō-əs): unsuitable.

There is no magic from your presence here,
So moon, sad moon, tuck up your trailing robe,   10
Whose silver seems antique and too severe
Against the glow of one electric globe.

Go spill your beauty on the laughing faces
Of happy flowers that bloom a thousand hues,
Waiting on tiptoe in the wilding° spaces,   15
To drink your wine mixed with sweet draughts° of dews.

15. **wilding:** uncultivated.

16. **draughts** (drăfts).

For Study and Discussion

Analyzing and Interpreting the Poem

1. What aspects of urban life are emphasized in the first two stanzas of the poem?

2. What makes the moonlight "incongruous and strange" (line 8)?

3. In line 9 the poet says that there is no magic in the moon's presence. **a.** What does he mean by "magic"? **b.** Why is it lacking in the scene?

4. Why does the poet address the moon as "sad" in line 10?

5. Where does the poet feel the beauty of moonlight belongs?

Focus on Descriptive Writing

Thinking About Your Audience

Consider how familiar your **audience** is with your subject for description. Complete the chart below by listing a different subject for description for each audience. Then discuss in a small group any special needs that the audience for each description might have. Save your notes.

Subject	Audience
1. _____	Fourth-graders
2. _____	Friend your age
3. _____	Grandparents

Mending Wall

ROBERT FROST

This is one of Robert Frost's best-known poems, and it has been interpreted in various ways. Here are some questions to keep in mind as you read: What is the attitude of the speaker toward the wall? What is his attitude toward his neighbor? What impression do you get of the speaker from his thoughts and his actions?

Something there is that doesn't love a wall,
That sends the frozen-ground-swell under it
And spills the upper boulders in the sun,
And makes gaps even two can pass abreast.
The work of hunters is another thing: 5
I have come after them and made repair
Where they have left not one stone on a stone,
But they would have the rabbit out of hiding,
To please the yelping dogs. The gaps I mean,
No one has seen them made or heard them made, 10
But at spring mending-time we find them there.
I let my neighbor know beyond the hill;
And on a day we meet to walk the line
And set the wall between us once again.
We keep the wall between us as we go. 15
To each the boulders that have fallen to each.
And some are loaves and some so nearly balls
We have to use a spell to make them balance:
"Stay where you are until our backs are turned!"
We wear our fingers rough with handling them. 20
Oh, just another kind of outdoor game,
One on a side. It comes to little more:
There where it is we do not need the wall:
He is all pine and I am apple orchard.
My apple trees will never get across 25
And eat the cones under his pines, I tell him.
He only says, "Good fences make good neighbors."
Spring is the mischief in me, and I wonder
If I could put a notion in his head:
"*Why* do they make good neighbors? Isn't it 30
Where there are cows? But here there are no cows.

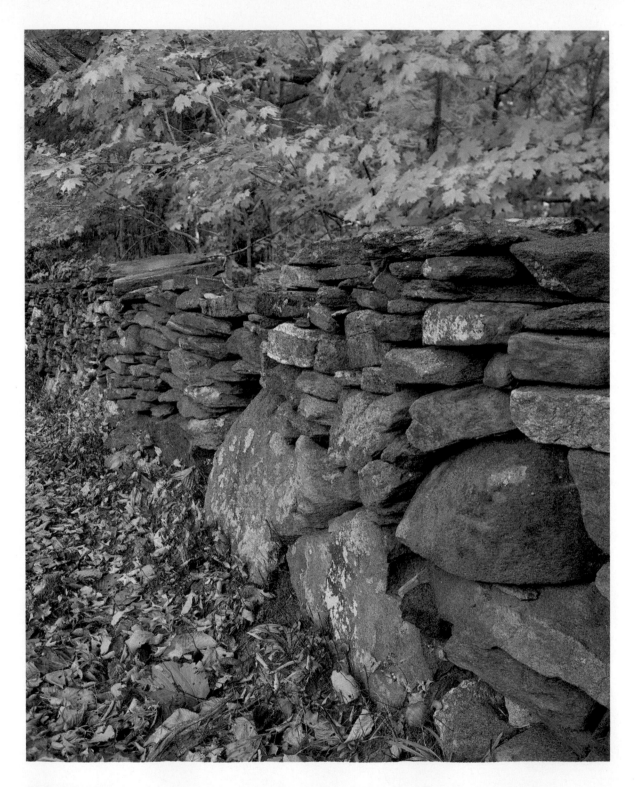

Before I built a wall I'd ask to know
What I was walling in or walling out,
And to whom I was like to give offense.
Something there is that doesn't love a wall,   35
That wants it down." I could say "Elves" to him,
But it's not elves exactly, and I'd rather
He said it for himself. I see him there,
Bringing a stone grasped firmly by the top
In each hand, like an old-stone savage armed.   40
He moves in darkness as it seems to me,
Not of woods only and the shade of trees.
He will not go behind his father's saying,
And he likes having thought of it so well
He says again, "Good fences make good neighbors."   45

For Study and Discussion

Analyzing and Interpreting the Poem

1a. Although the speaker meets with his neighbor each spring to mend the wall, he thinks that the wall is unnecessary. Why? **b.** What is his neighbor's attitude toward mending the wall? **c.** What do these attitudes reveal about the speaker and his neighbor?

2. What does the speaker think people should consider before they put up walls?

3a. What simile does the speaker use near the end of the poem to describe his neighbor? **b.** In what sense does the neighbor "move in darkness" (line 41)?

4. In the first four lines, the speaker suggests that there is "Something"—a force or drive— that insists on breaking down walls. This "Something" can make a gap so wide that "even two can pass abreast." What does this image of two people walking side by side through a broken wall suggest to you?

5a. What is your impression of the speaker? **b.** Where does he exhibit a sense of humor? **c.** Do you think he has a good grasp of human nature? Explain.

Literary Elements

Symbols

Symbols are a part of our everyday lives. The eagle is a symbol of America; the skull and crossbones on a bottle is a symbol of poison; the dove is a symbol of peace.

Symbolism is one of the most powerful devices that a writer can use. It enables a writer to compress a very complex idea or set of ideas into one image or even one word. Certain symbols occur again and again in literature. For example, the butterfly is frequently used to symbolize the human soul; night, the sea, and winter often symbolize death; a journey often symbolizes the journey through life.

Writers often create their own symbols. Robert Frost seems to be talking about a simple and familiar process—mending a wall with a neighbor in spring. Yet, by the end of the poem, the wall, the neighbor, and the act of putting up a wall become symbolic; they come to represent things larger than themselves. What does the "wall" symbolize? What is the "Something . . . that doesn't love a wall"?

About the Authors

Henry Wadsworth Longfellow (1807–1882)

Henry Wadsworth Longfellow was born in Portland, Maine. Four of his ancestors were pilgrims at Plymouth. Longfellow became the most famous American poet of his day and one of the most productive. He emphasized the values of freedom and wrote fearlessly against slavery at a time when many, less courageous, were silent. He was one of the first American writers to celebrate American events, and his historical poems are among his most famous: "Paul Revere's Ride," *Hiawatha, The Courtship of Miles Standish,* and *Evangeline.* Europeans as well as Americans were enthusiastic about his work; it was translated into twenty-four languages. Longfellow was the first American poet to have his bust placed in London's Westminster Abbey, where memorials are placed to England's greatest writers.

Emily Dickinson (1830–1886)

It was said of Emily Dickinson that her life story could be told in very few words: she was born in Amherst, a small town in Massachusetts. She had an independent and intelligent mind, but was also extremely sensitive and shy. As she grew older, she withdrew more and more from the world, seldom meeting outsiders and rarely leaving her father's house and garden. She dressed only in white, and wrote her poetry on small scraps of paper that she stitched together into little packets and kept hidden in her room. Only a handful of these poems were published in her lifetime, none with her consent, and several without her name. It was only after her death that her many packets of poems were discovered. Today, these poems are recognized as some of the most original poetry of the nineteenth century, and Emily Dickinson, who died almost totally unknown to the public, is considered one of the great poets of her time.

Robert Frost (1874–1963)

Robert Frost was born in San Francisco, California. When he was eleven years old his father died, and he moved with his mother to Lawrence, Massachusetts. Although Frost was determined to write poetry, no one seemed interested in or impressed with his work. He worked as a farmer in New England to support himself, but he did not like farming and was not successful at it. Still, Frost managed to scratch out a living, and he refused to believe he was not a good poet. His courage and determination were finally rewarded. He became one of America's best-known and most-respected poets, and the winner of four Pulitzer Prizes. His poems are distinguished for their wisdom and wit and for the different levels of meaning that lie beneath their surfaces.

Denise Levertov (1923–   )

Denise Levertov was born in Essex, England, and received her schooling entirely at home. Her early poetry was traditional, but after the publication of her first book, *The Double Image* (1946), she turned to freer and less conventional forms. During her childhood, Levertov overheard many discussions in her home about the mystical Jewish movement called Hasidism, which was part of her ancestry. She asserted in an interview that "a sense of wonder at creation" is the force behind her poetry.

Levertov has won many awards, including a Guggenheim Fellowship in 1962 and a National Institute of Arts and Letters grant in 1965. Her most recent publications are a collection of poems, *Evening Train* (1990), and *New and Selected Essays* (1992).

Walter de la Mare (1873–1956)

Walter de la Mare was born in Kent, England, and spent most of his life around London. His first volume of poetry, *Songs of Childhood*, was published under the pseudonym of "Walter Ramal." De la Mare is a master of mood. One of his most famous poems, "The Listeners," conveys an eerie sense of the supernatural.

Claude McKay (1890–1948)

Claude McKay was born in Sunny Ville, Jamaica, in the West Indies. He moved to Kingston, where he began to write poems. When he was twenty-two, he published two collections of poetry, which won an award. He immigrated to the United States and attended Tuskegee Institute and Kansas State College. He became a prominent member of the Harlem Renaissance writers. His most important volume of poetry, *Harlem Shadows*, was published in 1922. He also wrote several novels, including *Home to Harlem*.

SOUND PATTERNS

"To take sound away from poetry," said one poet, "is like tearing the wings from a bird." Poets, like musicians, are sensitive to the effects of sound. By varying rhythms, they can excite different emotions in the reader. They may use harsh or melodious sounds to convey a particular mood. Rhyme and other devices of repetition can make a poem pleasant, forceful, or comic. In combination, these devices can give a poem a rich texture of sound, which is pleasurable in itself and which also enhances the poem's meaning.

The Destruction of Sennacherib

GEORGE GORDON, LORD BYRON

Sennacherib (sĭ-năk′ər-ĭb) was king of the ancient Assyrians. His story is told in the Bible, II Kings 19:35. Sennacherib led an army against Jerusalem, in hopes of conquering that city. But the night before his troops were to attack, "the angel of the Lord went out and struck down a hundred and eighty-five thousand men in the Assyrian camp; when morning dawned, they all lay dead."

The Assyrian came down like the wolf on the fold,°
And his cohorts were gleaming in purple and gold;
And the sheen of their spears was like stars on the sea,
When the blue wave rolls nightly on deep Galilee.

1. **fold:** flock of sheep, or place where sheep are kept.

Like the leaves of the forest when Summer is green,   5
That host with their banners at sunset were seen:
Like the leaves of the forest when Autumn hath blown,
That host on the morrow lay withered and strown.°

8. **strown:** strewn, scattered.

For the Angel of Death spread his wings on the blast,°
And breathed in the face of the foe as he passed;   10
And the eyes of the sleepers waxed° deadly and chill,
And their hearts but once heaved, and forever grew still!

9. **blast:** wind.

11. **waxed:** grew.

Destruction of Sennacherib's Host by Gustave Doré (1832–1883). Etching.

And there lay the steed with his nostril all wide,
But through it there rolled not the breath of his pride;
And the foam of his gasping lay white on the turf,   15
And cold as the spray of the rock-beating surf.

And there lay the rider distorted and pale,
With the dew on his brow, and the rust on his mail:
And the tents were all silent, the banners alone,
The lances unlifted, the trumpet unblown.   20

And the widows of Ashur° are loud in their wail,
And the idols are broke in the temple of Baal;°
And the might of the Gentile,° unsmote by the sword,
Hath melted like snow in the glance of the Lord!

21. **Ashur** (ä´shŏŏr´): Assyria.
22. **Baal** (bā´ɔl): chief Assyrian god.
23. **Gentile:** non-Jew; here, the Assyrian Sennacherib.

For Study and Discussion

Analyzing and Interpreting the Poem

1a. What similes in the first stanza help you picture the power of the Assyrians? **b.** How is the change in their power described in the second stanza?

2. The destruction of the Assyrians is related in detail in stanzas 3–6. **a.** Tell in your own words what each stanza describes. **b.** How does each stanza build toward the climax of the poem?

Literary Elements

Rhythm and Meter

Rhythm occurs everywhere in nature: in the phases of the moon, in the tides, in the beating of our hearts. And rhythm has always had a profound effect on human beings. From the earliest times, people have sung, danced, chanted, and made music out of an instinctive love of rhythm.

The rhythm of a poem may be compared to a person's heartbeat. Rhythm may beat slowly, swiftly, or irregularly, but it gives movement and vitality to the poem. In English poetry, rhythm is based on a pattern of stressed and unstressed syllables. The stressed syllables are marked ´ and the unstressed syllables ˘.

When the rhythm of a poem has a regular and pronounced pattern, we call it **meter**. The metrical pattern in "The Destruction of Sennacherib" looks like this:

The Assyrian came down like the wolf on the fold,
And his cohorts were gleaming in purple and gold;

Two unstressed syllables are followed by a stressed syllable. How many stressed syllables do you find in each line? Analyze the meter of lines 5–8. What variety has Byron introduced in the pattern?

Byron has chosen a swift meter for this poem. Why is such a meter appropriate to his subject?

Jazz Fantasia

CARL SANDBURG

Read this poem aloud and listen to its sounds. What are some of its particularly effective sound devices? How does Sandburg convey the character of individual instruments?

Drum on your drums, batter on your banjoes,
sob on the long cool winding saxophones.
Go to it, O jazzmen.

Sling your knuckles on the bottoms of the happy
tin pans,° let your trombones ooze, and go husha-   5
husha-hush with the slippery sandpaper.°

Moan like an autumn wind high in the lonesome treetops, moan soft like
you wanted somebody terrible, cry like a racing car slipping away from a
motorcycle cop, bang-bang! you jazzmen, bang altogether drums, traps,°
banjoes, horns, tin cans—make two people fight on top of a stairway and   10
scratch each other's eyes in a clinch tumbling down the stairs.

Can the rough stuff . . . now a Mississippi steamboat pushes up the night
river with a hoo-hoo-hoo-oo . . . and the green lanterns calling to the
high soft stars . . . a red moon rides on the humps of the low river
hills . . . go to it, O jazzmen.   15

5. **tin pans:** In early years jazz players often improvised instruments, using tin pans, coconuts, or anything else that could make interesting sounds.   6. **slippery sandpaper:** Sandpaper, too, was used as an instrument.   9. **traps:** percussion instruments.

For Study and Discussion

Analyzing and Interpreting the Poem

1. Father of the blues and grandfather of rock music, jazz came into being in the late nineteenth and early twentieth centuries. Freer and livelier than traditional music, it created a new style and influenced modern composers. **a.** What images in the poem convey the intensity and roughness of jazz? **b.** What images indicate that jazz can be soft and serene as well?

2. The word *fantasia* in the title refers to a musical composition without a fixed form. Its structure is invented by the composer. Jazz is often created by improvisation. **a.** How does the last stanza give the impression of being improvised? **b.** In what way is the poem like a "jazz fantasia"?

3. Unlike "The Destruction of Sennacherib," this poem has an irregular rhythm. **a.** Why is irregular rhythm appropriate? **b.** At what points in the poem can you feel the rhythm change?

Eldorado

EDGAR ALLAN POE

*During the sixteenth century, many explorers came to the New World in search
of El Dorado, the legendary kingdom of fabulous wealth. The name El Dorado
has come to have another meaning—that of an unattainable ideal.*

Gaily bedight,°
  A gallant knight,
In sunshine and in shadow,
  Had journeyed long,
  Singing a song,   5
In search of Eldorado.

But he grew old—
  This knight so bold—
And o'er his heart a shadow
  Fell as he found   10
  No spot of ground.
That looked like Eldorado.

And, as his strength
  Failed him at length,
He met a pilgrim° shadow—   15
  "Shadow," said he,
  "Where can it be—
This land of Eldorado?"

"Over the Mountains
  Of the Moon,   20
Down the Valley of the Shadow,
  Ride, boldly ride,"
  The shade° replied—
"If you seek for Eldorado!"

1. **bedight:** dressed.   15. **pilgrim:** wanderer.
23. **shade:** ghost.

Detail from *The Departure* (1837) by Thomas Cole
(1801–1848). Oil on canvas, 39½ x 63 in. (100.33 x
160.02 cm.).

In the Collection of the Corcoran Gallery of Art,
Gift of William Wilson Corcoran

For Study and Discussion

Analyzing and Interpreting the Poem

1. The first two stanzas tell how the knight
grew old on his quest. What is about to happen
to the knight near the end of the poem?

2a. What pair of rhyming words is repeated in
each stanza? **b.** Does the word *shadow* mean
the same thing in each stanza? Explain.

3. The shade's reply to the knight is mysterious. What is the shade telling the knight about
his quest for Eldorado?

Next!

OGDEN NASH

Humorous poetry often relies upon pronounced rhythms and clever rhymes.
What surprising and funny rhymes can you find in this poem?

I thought that I would like to see
The early world that used to be,
That mastodonic° mausoleum,°
The Natural History Museum.
On iron seat in marble bower,   5
I slumbered through the closing hour.
At midnight in the vasty hall
The fossils gathered for a ball.
High above notices and bulletins
Loomed up the Mesozoic° skeletons.   10
Aroused by who knows what elixirs,
They ground along like concrete mixers.
They bowed and scraped in reptile pleasure,
And then began to tread the measure.
There were no drums or saxophones,   15
But just the clatter of their bones,
A rolling, rattling, carefree circus
Of mammoth polkas and mazurkas.
Pterodactyls° and brontosauruses°
Sang ghostly prehistoric choruses.   20
Amid the megalosauric° wassail°
I caught the eye of one small fossil.
Cheer up, old man, he said, and winked—
It's kind of fun to be extinct.

3. **mastodonic** (măs′tə-dŏn′ĭk): referring to certain extinct elephantlike mammals.
mausoleum (mô′sə-lē′əm): here, a large building that houses animal remains.   10.
Mesozoic (měz′ə-zō′ĭk): in prehistoric times, the age of reptiles.   19. **Pterodactyls**
(tĕr′ə-dăk′tĭlz): flying reptiles. **brontosauruses** (brŏn′tə-sôr′əs-əs): plant-eating dino-
saurs.   21. **megalosauric** (měg′ə-lə-sôr′ĭk): The megalosaur was a meat-eating
dinosaur.   **wassail** (wŏs′əl): here, a revel or festivity.

3. Nash is known for his clever and humorous rhymes. He often pairs words in unusual and unexpected combinations. For example, in lines 19–20, Nash rhymes *brontosauruses* with *choruses*. Find other examples of comic rhymes in the poem.

4. What lines in the poem suggest that the narrator is dreaming?

5. What do you think the title means?

Literary Elements

Rhyme and Rhyme Scheme

Rhyme is the correspondence of sounds in words or phrases that appear close to each other in a poem. Most rhymes are **end rhymes,** that is, the rhyme occurs on final syllables:

> Gaily be*dight*
> A gallant *knight*

Find other examples of end rhyme in Poe's poem.

Sometimes rhyme occurs within a line of poetry:

> The splendor *falls* on castle *walls.*

This is called **internal rhyme.**

One reason a poet uses rhyme is to give a poem structure. Usually rhyme words are arranged in a pattern called a **rhyme scheme.** Consider the pattern in the first stanza of "Eldorado":

Gaily bedight,	*a*
A gallant knight,	*a*
In sunshine and in shadow,	*b*
Had journeyed long,	*c*
Singing a song,	*c*
In search of Eldorado.	*b*

This stanza has an *aabccb* rhyme scheme (each new rhyme is indicated by a different letter of the alphabet). In which stanza does the rhyme scheme change? Look at "The Destruction of Sennacherib" (page 334). What is the rhyme scheme of the first two stanzas?

For Study and Discussion

Analyzing and Interpreting the Poem

1. In medieval times, people believed that there was a substance called the "elixir of life," which could give eternal life. What humorous use does Nash make of this idea in the poem?

2. Polkas and mazurkas are lively dances that require agility and lightness of movement. Why is it particularly comical to have these dances performed by "Mesozoic skeletons"?

The Shell

JAMES STEPHENS

As you read this poem aloud, can you hear the sounds of the wind and the sea?

And then I pressed the shell
Close to my ear
And listened well,
And straightway like a bell
Came low and clear   5
The slow, sad murmur of the distant seas,
Whipped by an icy breeze
Upon a shore
Wind-swept and desolate.
It was a sunless strand° that never bore   10
The footprint of a man,
Nor felt the weight
Since time began
Of any human quality or stir
Save what the dreary winds and waves incur.°   15
And in the hush of waters was the sound
Of pebbles rolling round,
Forever rolling with a hollow sound.
And bubbling seaweeds as the waters go
Swish to and fro   20
Their long, cold tentacles of slimy gray.
There was no day,
Nor ever came a night
Setting the stars alight
To wonder at the moon: 25
Was twilight only and the frightened croon,°
Smitten° to whimpers, of the dreary wind
And waves that journeyed blind—
And then I loosed° my ear . . . O, it was sweet
To hear a cart go jolting down the street.   30

10. **strand:** beach.   15. **incur:** here, cause.   26. **croon:** a murmuring sound.
27. **Smitten:** struck.   29. **loosed:** moved away.

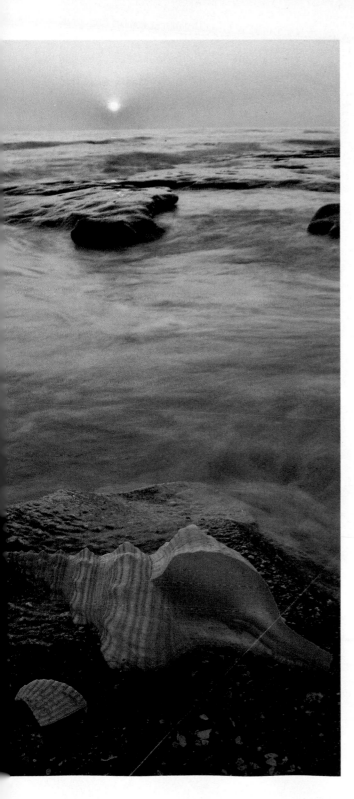

For Study and Discussion

Analyzing and Interpreting the Poem

1a. Describe the place that the speaker imagines as he holds the seashell to his ear. **b.** What is the only sound of life? **c.** What other sounds does he hear?

2a. In lines 22–28, what strange and forbidding images are we given of this place? **b.** How does the mood of the poem suddenly change in lines 29–30?

3. The speaker brings us closer to his experience by using words whose sounds suggest the whistling wind, the rush of waves, and the murmur of the sea. **a.** Find examples of words whose sounds echo the sounds of the wind and the sea. **b.** What sounds are repeated most often?

Literary Elements

Onomatopoeia, Alliteration, and Assonance

One technique that is commonly used by poets is **onomatopoeia** (ŏn′ə-măt′ə-pē′ə), in which the sound of a word imitates a natural sound. For example, the word *crack* sounds like something cracking. Which word in line 6 of "The Shell" is onomatopoetic? Which other words in the poem are onomatopoetic?

Sometimes a poet creates special sound effects by **alliteration**—the repetition of consonant sounds, usually at the beginning of words. Many familiar expressions employ alliteration: *w*ild and *w*ooly, *s*weet *s*ixteen, *th*rough *th*ick and *th*in. Find an example of alliteration in the poem and explain its effect.

The name **assonance** is sometimes used for the repetition of vowel sounds. Assonance occurs in line 27:

Sm*i*tten to wh*i*mpers, of the dreary w*i*nd

How does the assonance in lines 17–18 echo the meaning of those lines?

The Shell **343**

God Creating the Animals from an undated German manuscript.

Psalm 96
from *The King James Bible*

*In addition to such devices as rhyme and rhythm, poets make use of
parallelism—the repetition of phrases or sentences that are similar in structure or meaning. Note how this poet achieves balance and emphasis through
parallel structure.*

O sing unto the Lord a new song:
Sing unto the Lord, all the earth.
Sing unto the Lord, bless his name;
Show forth his salvation from day to day.
Declare his glory among the heathen,   5
His wonders among all people.
For the Lord is great, and greatly to be praised:
He is to be feared above all gods.
For all the gods of the nations are idols:
But the Lord made the heavens.   10
Honor and majesty are before him:
Strength and beauty are in his sanctuary.
Give unto the Lord, O ye kindreds of people,
Give unto the Lord glory and strength.
Give unto the Lord the glory due unto his name: 15
Bring an offering, and come into his courts.
O worship the Lord in the beauty of holiness:
Fear before him, all the earth.
Say among the heathen that the Lord reigneth:
The world also shall be established that it shall not be
    moved: 20
He shall judge the people righteously.
Let the heavens rejoice, and let the earth be glad;
Let the sea roar, and the fullness thereof.
Let the field be joyful, and all that is therein:
Then shall all the trees of the wood rejoice   25
Before the Lord: for he cometh,
For he cometh to judge the earth:
He shall judge the world with righteousness,
And the people with his truth.

For Study and Discussion

Analyzing and Interpreting the Poem

1a. How are the first three lines of Psalm 96 similar in meaning and in structure? **b.** How are lines 4–6 alike?

2a. What reasons does the poet give for praising the Lord? **b.** According to the poet, in what ways can people praise the Lord?

3. The ancient Hebrew poets were fond of using images from nature. **a.** According to this poet, how will nature respond to the knowledge of God? **b.** How does the poet use nature imagery to build to a joyful climax?

Literary Elements

Parallelism

One of the devices most frequently used in the poetry of the Psalms is **parallelism**—the repetition of phrases or sentences that are similar in meaning or in structure. Look, for example, at lines 22–24:

> Let the heavens rejoice, and let the earth be glad;
> Let the sea roar, and the fullness thereof.
> Let the field be joyful, and all that is therein:

The three lines are related in meaning; they call for universal rejoicing. The lines are also parallel in structure: each line is broken in the middle by a comma, and each begins with the words *let the*. The structure of the lines also gives rise to a parallel rhythm, so that the lines seem to balance and echo one another. This rhythmic parallelism gives the lines a special emphasis when they are read aloud. What other examples of parallelism can you find?

Because of its often stirring emotional impact, parallelism has been used in diverse forms of literature. You are probably familiar with this famous example of parallelism in

"The Gettysburg Address": "government of the people, by the people, for the people."

Writing About Literature

Analyzing a Psalm

Choose one of the Psalms in the Bible and analyze its musical devices. Some of the best-known Psalms are 23, 24, and 121.

Focus on Descriptive Writing

Making a Description Chart

To explore ideas for a description, skim some recent issues of illustrated magazines for articles on your favorite subjects, such as sports, hobbies, entertainment, or arts and crafts. When you have found a promising subject for descriptive writing, freewrite about it for five or ten minutes. Then use a **description chart** like the one below to organize your freewriting.

> **Subject:** _____
> **Purpose:** _____
>   (creative or informative)
> **Type of Description:** _____
>   (subjective or objective)
> **Audience:** _____
> **Point of View:** _____
>   (first or third person)
> **Tone:** _____
>   (personal or formal)

Starfish

LORNA DEE CERVANTES

*Poets often help their readers discover the world anew. How does this poem
make you aware of the beauty as well as the fragility of starfish?*

They were lovely in the quartz and jasper° sand
As if they had created terrariums with their bodies
On purpose; adding sprigs of seaweed, seashells,
White feathers, eel bones, miniature
Mussels, a fish jaw. Hundreds; no—   5
Thousands of baby stars. We touched them,
Surprised to find them soft, pliant, almost
Living in their attitudes. We would dry them, arrange them,
Form seascapes, geodesics° . . . We gathered what we could
In the approaching darkness. Then we left hundreds of   10
Thousands of flawless five-fingered specimens sprawled
Along the beach as far as we could see, all massed
Together: little martyrs, soldiers, artless° suicides
In lifelong liberation from the sea. So many
Splayed° hands, the tide shoveled in.   15

1. **jasper:** of a reddish, yellow, or brown color.

9. **geodesics** (jē′ə-dĕs′ĭks): in interlocking patterns.

13. **artless:** simple, innocent.

15. **Splayed:** spread out.

For Study and Discussion

Analyzing and Interpreting the Poem

1. A terrarium is a small enclosure where plants or animals are grown. Why does the poet associate terrariums with the starfish?

2. What characteristics of the starfish does the poet focus on in the first ten lines?

3a. What are the connotations of the word *specimens* in line 11? **b.** What is the effect of the words *sprawled* (line 11) and *shoveled in* (line 15)? **c.** How do these words signal a shift in attitude?

4a. What sound devices does the poet use? **b.** Where are these devices used for emphasis?

Focus on Descriptive Writing

Identifying Sensory Details

Sensory details are words and phrases that appeal to the five senses: sight, sound, touch, smell, and taste. They are the best resource of a descriptive writer. Notice, for example, how Lorna Dee Cervantes uses details of sight (lines 1–5, 11–15) and touch (lines 6–8), as well as sound devices, in her poem "Starfish."

Working with a partner, select *one* of the following four subjects. See how many sensory details you can think of to describe the subject you have chosen. Fill in an observation chart like the one below. Save your notes.

popcorn   lemonade   sunrise   the circus

Observation Chart				
Subject:				
Sight	Sound	Touch	Smell	Taste

About the Authors

George Gordon, Lord Byron (1788–1824)

George Gordon, Lord Byron has been called "the most interesting personality in the history of the world." He was a dashing, rebellious genius, as famous for the scandals he was involved in as for his poems. When he was a student at Cambridge, he objected to a rule prohibiting students from keeping dogs. He protested by buying a bear—an animal not prohibited—to keep as a pet. His rebelliousness alienated him from many of his peers, and he left England forever in 1816. Thereafter, he devoted himself to various international revolutionary causes. He became an officer in the Greek revolutionary army which sought independence for Greece from Turkish rule. However, he never participated in the revolution, for shortly after he arrived in Greece, at the age of thirty-six, he died of a fever. Byron created not only a body of enduring poetry but also a legend and a new kind of hero: the young rebel.

Carl Sandburg (1878–1967)

Carl Sandburg, the son of Swedish immigrant parents, had to quit school at thirteen to help support his family. He held almost every kind of job— from washing soda bottles to harvesting wheat. At the start of the Spanish-American War in 1898, he joined the army. After the war, he returned to his native Illinois where he worked as a firefighter to put himself through college. Later, he worked in politics and as a reporter. His ramblings across the country, his wide experience in working with ordinary people, and his deep interest in America's past combined to make him a poet who celebrated everyday life and average people. An author of children's books and a historian as well as a poet, Sandburg won a Pulitzer Prize in 1940 for his biography of Abraham Lincoln, and another Pulitzer Prize in 1950 for his *Complete Poems.*

Edgar Allan Poe   (1809–1849)

For a biography of Poe, see page 103.

Ogden Nash   (1902–1971)

Before Ogden Nash began writing poetry, he was a schoolteacher, a salesman, and a copywriter for a publisher. After his first poem was accepted by *The New Yorker* in 1931, he joined the staff of the magazine and turned to writing as a full-time career. Nash is generally acknowledged to be America's foremost humorous poet. He published more than twenty books of poetry and prose. He also collaborated with S. J. Perelman on the libretto for *One Touch of Venus,* a musical comedy.

James Stephens   (1882–1950)

James Stephens lacked a formal education, but through his own reading he made himself an authority on art and folk music, as well as a successful novelist and poet. His first success was a book of fairy stories, *The Crock of Gold.* All of his writing is full of fantasy and deep imagination. Stephens could hold a group spellbound for hours with Irish stories, legends, and poetry.

Lorna Dee Cervantes   (1954–   )

While growing up in California, Lorna Dee Cervantes discovered literature by reading books she found in the houses where her mother worked. She began to write poetry at age eight, her sense of rhythm strengthened by exposure to the musical talents of her brother, Steve. After her first poem was printed in *El Heraldo,* a Mexico City newspaper, in 1974, Cervantes devoted herself to writing, and founded her own literary magazine called *Mango.* Since then her poems have appeared in several periodicals, including *The Latin American Literary Review.* "Starfish" is from her first book, *Emplumada* (1981). The title is a combination of two words: *emplumado,* which means "plumage," and *plumada,* which means "pen flourish."

STRUCTURES

If a poem is to work, it must have the right kind of structure to carry it. One of the poet's most difficult tasks is to match the content of a poem to the form that is best suited for it. The basic unit of structure in most poems is the *stanza*. A stanza is any group of lines that forms a division of a poem. It may be based on the number of lines, rhyme scheme, rhythm, or other devices of repetition.

The Sound of the Sea

HENRY WADSWORTH LONGFELLOW

As you read, note how the form of this sonnet reflects the speaker's thoughts. What shift occurs at the end of line 8?

Rhyme Scheme		
a	The sea awoke at midnight from its sleep,	
b	And round the pebbly beaches far and wide	
b	I heard the first wave of the rising tide	
a	Rush onward with uninterrupted sweep;	
a	A voice out of the silence of the deep,	5
b	A sound mysteriously multiplied	
b	As of a cataract° from the mountain's side,	
a	Or roar of winds upon a wooded steep.	
c	So comes to us at times, from the unknown	
d	And inaccessible° solitudes of being,	10
e	The rushing of the sea-tides of the soul;	
c	And inspirations, that we deem° our own,	
d	Are some divine foreshadowing and foreseeing	
e	Of things beyond our reason or control.	

7. **cataract:** huge, crashing waterfall.   10. **inaccessible:** (ĭn′ăk-sĕs′ə-bəl) impossible to reach.   12. **deem:** judge.

Coast Scene, Mt. Desert (1863) by Frederic Edwin Church (1826–1900). Oil on canvas.

For Study and Discussion

Analyzing and Interpreting the Poem

1. What sounds of the sea are described in the first eight lines of the poem?

2. In lines 9–14 Longfellow draws an **analogy**—an extended comparison. Explain this analogy in your own words.

Literary Elements

The Petrarchan Sonnet

One of the most popular poetic forms is the **sonnet**—a fourteen-line poem with a traditional rhyme scheme. "The Sound of the Sea" is an example of a **Petrarchan** sonnet. It consists of two parts. The first part is eight lines long and has a rhyme scheme of *abbaabba*. It is called the **octave,** from the Latin word for "eight." The second, six-line part usually has a *cdecde* rhyme scheme, and is called a **sestet,** from the Latin word for "six." Where does the first sentence of the poem end? How does this strengthen the two-part division of the poem?

Sometimes in a Petrarchan sonnet the octave raises an idea that the sestet extends. In the octave of this poem, the speaker describes the sea tide as sounding awesome. In the sestet, what does he compare to the sea tide? What, according to the speaker, is the true source of our inspirations? How do the speaker's attitudes toward the sea and toward inspiration help to unify the sonnet?

Sonnet 55

WILLIAM SHAKESPEARE

Each of Shakespeare's sonnets presents an "argument" in verse. How do the first twelve lines develop the idea that this poem is a more permanent tribute than a stone monument? How do the last two lines summarize the argument?

Rhyme Scheme

a	Not marble, nor the gilded monuments	
b	Of princes, shall outlive this powerful rime;	
a	But you shall shine more bright in these contents°	
b	Than unswept stone, besmeared with sluttish time.	
c	When wasteful war shall statues overturn,	5
d	And broils° root out the work of masonry,	
c	Nor Mars his sword° nor war's quick fire shall burn	
d	The living record of your memory.	
e	'Gainst death and all-oblivious enmity°	
f	Shall you pace forth; your praise shall still find room	10
e	Even in the eyes of all posterity	
f	That wear this world out to the ending doom.	
g	So, till the judgment that yourself° arise,	
g	You live in this, and dwell in lovers' eyes.	

3. **these contents:** the contents of this poem.   6. **broils:** fights, brawls.   7. **Mars his sword:** Mars's sword.   9. **all-oblivious enmity:** war which sends all to oblivion.   12–13. These lines refer to the belief that the world will come to an end with a final day of judgment, when all the dead will arise.   **that yourself:** when you yourself.

For Study and Discussion

Analyzing and Interpreting the Poem

1. Each stanza of Shakespeare's sonnet is a self-contained unit of thought. **a.** What are the "marble" and "gilded monuments" referred to in line 1? **b.** How are these memorials affected by time? **c.** Why does the poet believe that his memorial is superior to stone monuments?

2. The second stanza deals with the destructiveness of "wasteful war." What is the "living record" that survives these disasters?

3. According to stanza 3, how does the poet assure his subject's immortality?

4. The word *live* is a key word in Shakespeare's sonnet. In what sense does he use the word in the last line of the poem?

Literary Elements

The Shakespearean Sonnet

A sonnet usually has fourteen iambic pentameter lines—that is, ten syllables with a stress on every other syllable.

When wásteful wár shall státues óvertúrn

The Italian, or Petrarchan, form of the sonnet, as you have seen, is divided into the **octave** and the **sestet**. The structure of the Shakespearean sonnet is different. It contains three **quatrains** —four-line stanzas—and a **couplet**—a pair of rhyming lines. The rhyme scheme is *abab cdcd efef gg.* In the Petrarchan sonnet, the last six lines usually present a comment on or a summary of the argument that has been presented in the first eight lines. In the Shakespearean sonnet, by contrast, the conclusion or resolution is generally delivered in the final two lines.

Manhole Covers

KARL SHAPIRO

This poem may appear at first to have no particular form, but after you read it, you will find that it has a special structure of its own.

The beauty of manhole covers—what of that?
Like medals struck by a great savage khan,°
Like Mayan calendar stones, unliftable, indecipherable,
Not like old electrum, chased and scored,°
Mottoed and sculptured to a turn,   5
But notched and whelked° and pocked and smashed
With the great company names:
Gentle Bethlehem, smiling United States.
This rustproof artifact of my street,
Long after roads are melted away, will lie   10
Sidewise in the grave of the iron-old world,
Bitten at the edges,
Strong with its cryptic° American,
Its dated beauty.

2. **khan:** Asian ruler, such as Genghis Khan.

4. **chased and scored:** delicately etched and marked.

6. **whelked:** twisted.

13. **cryptic:** mysterious.

Analyzing and Interpreting the Poem

1a. How do the comparisons in lines 2–3 of this poem make the manhole covers seem exotic and mysterious? **b.** According to the speaker, what will finally become of manhole covers? Why will they be *cryptic*?

2. Where in the poem do you find the devices of parallelism and simile?

3. Look carefully at the structure of the poem. The first eight lines describe the manhole covers, the last six comment on their significance. What kind of poem does this pattern resemble?

Literary Elements

Free Verse

In your reading, you have seen that not all poems are organized by stanzas, and many poems do not seem to have a fixed rhythm, rhyme scheme, or line length. This kind of poetry, called **free verse**, has become a popular form in the twentieth century. It is called free verse because no set pattern controls it. It may rhyme in some places and not in others, or not rhyme at all. Its lines may be of different lengths. It may have no dominant rhythm, or it may switch rhythms as it progresses.

Free verse enables poets to create effects that are not possible within the restrictions of a set pattern. Poets are freer to fit sounds and rhythms more closely to the meaning of a poem. They can use everyday language and natural speech rhythms. In what ways does "Manhole Covers" illustrate these characteristics?

The danger of free verse is that it looks easy to write, but it is actually very difficult to write well. Like other poetry, it must have structure. In free verse, with no traditional guidelines for direction, the poet must create and develop a special structure for each poem. As easy as it seems to be, free verse is considered by many poets to be the hardest kind of verse to write.

Although there is no fixed pattern of rhythm in free verse, it sometimes uses very strong rhythms. Listen to "Manhole Covers" being read aloud. Would you call the rhythm light and graceful, or heavy? Is the rhythm appropriate to the subject? Lines that end with a stressed syllable tend to be more forceful than lines that do not. How many lines in the poem end with a stressed syllable? Poetry, free verse or otherwise, usually contains more stressed syllables than ordinary language. What lines can you find in the poem that contain many stressed syllables?

Focus on Descriptive Writing

Identifying Factual Details

You can use **factual details** in both subjective and objective descriptions. These are details that can be measured or checked: for example, the details Karl Shapiro gives about the manufacturers and the rustproof quality of the manhole covers (lines 7–9). Factual details are especially important in scientific writing.

Find an encyclopedia article about your favorite animal, bird, or flower. Read the article carefully, and make a list of some of the factual details it includes about the subject. Then make some notes on how you could classify these details: for example, into categories such as size, color, shape, weight, and habits. Save your writing.

400-meter Freestyle

MAXINE KUMIN

Poetry is meant to be heard, but poets have experimented with how it looks on the page as well. Modern poets in particular take delight in playing with the shapes of poems, experimenting with strange arrangements of lines and print. A poem may be written so that its shape on the page resembles its subject; there are poems shaped like swans, wineglasses, Christmas trees, and sets of wings. If the appearance of the following poem puzzles you at first, just imagine the movements of a swimmer back and forth across a pool.

THE GUN full swing the swimmer catapults and cracks

s

i

x

feet away onto that perfect glass he catches at

a

n

d

throws behind him scoop after scoop cunningly moving

t

h

e

water back to move him forward. Thrift is his wonderful

s

e

c

ret; he has schooled out all extravagance. No muscle

r

i

p

ples without compensation wrist cock to heel snap to

h

i

s

mobile mouth that siphons in the air that nurtures

h

i

m

at half an inch above the sea level so to speak.

T
h
e
astonishing whites of the soles of his feet rise
                                        a
                                          n
                                            d
salute us on the turns. He flips, converts, and is gone
a
l
  l
in one. We watch him for signs. His arms are steady at
                                        t
                                          h
                                            e
catch, his cadent feet tick in the stretch, they know
t
h
  e
lesson well. Lungs know, too; he does not list for
                                        a
                                          i
                                            r

he drives along on little sips carefully expended
b
u
t
that plum red heart pumps hard cries hurt how soon
                                                    i
                                                      t
                                                        s
near one more and makes its final surge TIME: 4:25:9

For Study and Discussion

Analyzing and Interpreting the Poem

1a. What do the words in capitals at the beginning and end of the poem signify? **b.** How does the arrangement of the lines imitate the movement of the swimmer in the pool?

2a. What does the poet mean when she says of the swimmer "Thrift is his wonderful secret"? **b.** What examples does she give of this "thrift"?

3a. Show how the poet uses alliteration and assonance to make the lines move with force and strenuousness, like the swimmer. **b.** What lines do you think vividly capture the movements and feelings of the swimmer?

Creative Writing

Experimenting with Line Arrangements

Write a few lines of your own that form a recognizable shape on the page. Have the lines express some thought or idea, and be sure that the shape you create has something to do with your subject. Imagination is all you need for this kind of expression; you may write some lines in a shape that is as simple as a box or as complicated as a plate of spaghetti.

Focus on Descriptive Writing

Gathering Descriptive Details

Here are four strategies that you will find helpful when you gather sensory and factual details for a description:

Observing Use all your senses to observe your subject directly. Take notes for at least ten minutes.

Recalling Shut your eyes and brainstorm to call up a mental picture of your subject.

Reading Get ideas for details from essays, encyclopedias, and photographs.

Imagining Make up some realistic or fantastic details of your own.

Working with a partner, choose a famous person (musician, actor, government leader, or athlete) that you both admire. Using the strategies outlined above, compile a list of details for a description of this person. When you have finished writing, get together with another pair of classmates to compare lists. Save your notes.

The Time We Climbed Snake Mountain

LESLIE MARMON SILKO

How is the subject of this poem conveyed by the arrangement of lines?

seeing good places
        for my hands
I grab the warm parts of the cliff
        and I feel the mountain as I climb.

somewhere around here
    yellow spotted snake is sleeping
           on his rock
                in the sun.

so please
    I tell them,
        watch out,
don't step on yellow spotted snake,
          he lives here.
            The mountain is his.

For Study and Discussion

Analyzing and Interpreting the Poem

1. Examine the visual pattern of the poem. **a.** How do the lines suggest a winding course up a steep incline? **b.** Why do you suppose an extra space appears between the words *somewhere* and *around* in line 5?

2a. What is the speaker's attitude toward the snake? **b.** What attitude toward nature is conveyed in this poem?

About the Authors

William Shakespeare (1564–1616)

William Shakespeare is generally considered the greatest writer in the English language. He was born in an English town called Stratford-on-Avon. He left for London sometime in his early twenties and joined a company of actors. He soon became the company's chief playwright, and by the time he returned to Stratford-on-Avon, he had written thirty-seven plays—a great body of tragedies, comedies, histories, and romances. Ben Jonson, a great dramatist in his own right, said this of Shakespeare: "He was not of an age, but for all time." Jonson's prophecy has turned out to be true, for today Shakespeare's works are read and performed all over the world.

Karl Shapiro (1913–   )

Karl Jay Shapiro was born in Baltimore, Maryland, and attended the University of Virginia. When World War II broke out, he was inducted into the Army and sent to the South Pacific. He wrote poetry during his years in the service, and his fiancée had this work published while Shapiro was overseas. His volume *Person, Place, and Thing* (1942) won high praise from critics, and *V-Letter and Other Poems* (1944) was awarded the Pulitzer Prize. Shapiro's recent publications include *Reports of My Death* (1988), an autobiography, and *The Old Horsefly* (1992), a collection of poems.

Maxine Kumin (1925–   )

One reviewer has admired Maxine Kumin's gift as a poet for focusing on the ordinary and exposing what is remarkable about it. She has told an interviewer that for her, writing a poem is "to some extent a mystical process, because when a poem is . . . getting ready to be written, I know it. . . . I have what amounts to almost an aura, a real prickle at the base of my neck."

Kumin was born in Philadelphia, Pennsylvania, and attended Radcliffe College. She has been an instructor in English at Tufts University and a fellow at the Radcliffe Institute for Independent Study. In addition to collections of poetry, such as *House, Bridge, Fountain, Gate* (1975), *The Retrieval System* (1978), and *Looking for Luck* (1992), she has written books for young people. In 1973 she won a Pulitzer Prize for *Up Country: Poems of New England.*

Leslie Marmon Silko (1948–   )

Leslie Marmon Silko, who has called herself "a mixed breed Laguna Pueblo woman," was born in Albuquerque and attended the University of New Mexico. In 1977 her novel *Ceremony,* which focuses on Pueblo Indian World War II veterans, established her—in the view of one critic—as "one of the most gritty and imaginative Native American writers." In 1981 she was granted a MacArthur Foundation award, enabling her to complete her ambitious novel *Almanac of the Dead* (1991), a work about Native American life, customs, religion, and death.

TONE

People speak in many tones of voice: angry, thoughtful, joking, tired, and so on. Tone shows the speaker's mood, the emotion behind the words. Poets, too, speak in a variety of tones. The tone of a poem shows its speaker's attitude toward the subject as well as toward the audience. It results from all the different parts of the poem working together. Although there may be shifts of mood within a work, poets generally aim for uniformity of tone.

Diction, or choice of words, affects tone. The words *ladies and gentlemen* convey a tone different from that of *guys and dolls*. If an automotive mechanic says, "Your car could use some repair," the statement indicates a measure of respect for both the car and its owner. Compare the tone of that statement with the tone carried by these words: "Your clunker of a car is falling apart."

Imagery, too, can affect tone. If, for instance, you were describing the food in a cafeteria, the details you select would help convey your attitude. Images such as "the sizzle of frying chicken" and "the aroma of fresh strawberries" convey altogether different feelings from such images as "an overripe tomato slice on a wilted lettuce leaf" and "a cold hot dog on a stale bun."

Even the sounds of the words within a poem help shape its tone. Repetition, as you have seen, can have an emphatic, hypnotic, or haunting emotional effect. Such devices as alliteration, assonance, and onomatopoeia help communicate the poet's attitude toward subject and audience. Rhythm, like words, can affect tone, and so can rhyme or lack of rhyme. A poem with a tightly controlled rhythm and rhyme scheme creates a more formal tone than does a poem that imitates the rhythms of ordinary speech.

Sentence structure, too, can color the tone of a poem. The more complicated the sentence structure, usually the more formal the poem. Parallelism can help determine the tone of a poem as can stanzaic form and organization.

At Woodward's Gardens

ROBERT FROST

This poem is like a fable—a short, simple story that illustrates a moral.
Woodward's Gardens was a large estate with a zoo in San Francisco.

A boy, presuming on his intellect,
Once showed two little monkeys in a cage
A burning-glass they could not understand
And never could be made to understand.
Words are no good: to say it was a lens   5
For gathering solar rays would not have helped.
But let him show them how the weapon worked.
He made the sun a pinpoint on the nose
Of first one, then the other, till it brought
A look of puzzled dimness to their eyes   10
That blinking could not seem to blink away.
They stood arms laced together at the bars,
And exchanged troubled glances over life.
One put a thoughtful hand up to his nose
As if reminded—or as if perhaps   15

Within a million years of an idea.
He got his purple little knuckles stung.
The already known had once more been confirmed
By pyschological experiment,
And that were° all the finding to announce
Had the boy not presumed too close and long.
There was a sudden flash of arm, a snatch,
And the glass was the monkeys', not the boy's.
Precipitately° they retired back-cage
And instituted an investigation
On their part, though without the needed insight.
They bit the glass and listened for the flavor.
They broke the handle and the binding off it.
Then none the wiser, frankly gave it up,
And having hid it in their bedding straw
Against the day of prisoners' ennui,°
Came dryly forward to the bars again
To answer for themselves: Who said it mattered
What monkeys did or didn't understand?
They might not understand a burning-glass.
They might not understand the sun itself.
It's knowing what to do with things that counts.

20

25

30

35

20. **were:** This subjunctive form of *be* has the meaning here of "would have been."

24. **Precipitately:** hurriedly.

31. **ennui** (än'wē'): boredom.

For Study and Discussion

Analyzing and Interpreting the Poem

1. What is the "burning-glass"?

2a. What does Frost mean when he says the boy is "presuming on his intellect"?   **b.** How would you describe this attitude in everyday language?

3a. How would you describe the poet's attitude toward the boy's experiment?   **b.** Toward the monkeys?

4a. For what different purposes do the boy and the monkeys try to use the burning-glass? **b.** What comment does the poem make on our use of scientific discoveries?

5. How would you describe the poem's overall tone? Would you characterize it as serious, mocking, comic, ironic? Explain.

Focus on Descriptive Writing

Organizing Descriptive Details

Here are three methods for organizing details in a description:

Spatial Order   Arrange details in the order you see them (for instance, top to bottom, or left to right).
Order of Importance   Place the most important details either first or last.
Order of Impression   Start with the most notable detail and move on to other details in chronological order.

Review the list of details for the **Focus** assignment on page 358, or compile a different list on a new subject. Use one of the methods above to arrange your details in a logical order.

Art Review

KENNETH FEARING

The art that forms the subject of this poem is graffiti (grə-fē′tē), *crude drawings on walls and doors in public places. What different kinds of graffiti does the speaker itemize?*

Recently displayed at the Times Square° Station, a new
    Vandyke° on the face-cream girl.
(Artist unknown. Has promise, but lacks the brilliance shown
    by the great masters of the Elevated age°)
The latest wood carving in a Whelan° telephone booth, titled
    "O Mortal Fools WA 9-5090," shows two winged hearts
    above an ace of spades.
(His meaning is not entirely clear, but this man will go far)
A charcoal nude in the rear of Flatbush° Ahearn's Bar &
    Grill, "Forward to the Brotherhood of Man," has been
    boldly conceived in the great tradition.   5
(We need more, much more of this)
Then there is the chalk portrait, on the walls of a waterfront
    warehouse, of a gentleman wearing a derby hat:
    "Bleecker Street° Mike is a double-crossing rat."
(Morbid, but powerful. Don't miss)

Know then by these presents, know all men by these signs
    and omens, by these simple thumbprints on the throat of
    time,
Know that Pete, the people's artist, is ever watchful,   10
That Tuxedo Jim has passed among us, and was much
    displeased, as always,
That George the Ghost (no man has ever seen him) and Billy
    the Bicep boy will neither bend nor break,
That Mr. Harkness of Sunnyside still hopes for the best, and
    has not lost his human touch,
That Phantom Phil, the master of them all, has come and
    gone, but will return, and all is well.

1. **Times Square:** a colorful section of Manhattan in New York City. **Vandyke:** a pointed beard named after the Flemish painter Vandyke. 2. **Elevated age:** of elevated trains. 3. **Whelan:** the name of a chain of drugstores. 5. **Flatbush:** a community in Brooklyn, New York. 7. **Bleecker Street:** a street in downtown Manhattan.

For Study and Discussion

Analyzing and Interpreting the Poem

1. Part of the mock-serious tone of this poem comes from treating the subject of graffiti in elegant language. For instance, the beard scribbled on the "face-cream girl" is described as being "recently displayed," as if it were a work of art. The person who drew it is described as an unknown artist, as if the work were listed in a museum guide. What other examples can you find of ordinary subjects described in lofty language?

2. This poem, like a play, has a cast of characters. The characters' names help describe them and also define the poet's attitude toward them. What tone do the names create?

3a. Do you think the poet is more critical of the artists or of the world they portray in their art? Explain.   **b.** How does the title help convey the poem's tone?

Bribe

PAT MORA

The word bribe *usually has negative connotations. How does the poet use the word here?*

I hear Indian women
    chanting, chanting
I see them long ago bribing
the desert with turquoise threads.
in the silent morning coolness,   5
kneeling, digging, burying
their offering in the Land
    chanting, chanting
        Guide my hands, Mother,
        to weave singing birds   10
        flowers rocking in the wind, to trap
        them on my cloth with a web of thin threads.

Secretly I scratch a hole in the desert
by my home. I bury a ballpoint pen
and lined yellowing paper. Like the Indians   15
I ask the Land to smile on me, to croon
softly, to help me catch her music with words.

For Study and Discussion

Analyzing and Interpreting the Poem

1. A *bribe* is a gift used to influence or persuade someone to do something wrong. **a.** How is the poet using the word? **b.** What "bribe" do the Indian women offer the land? **c.** What do they ask in return?

2a. What is the speaker's offering? **b.** What does she ask in return for her bribe?

Writing About Literature

Analyzing tone

Choose one of the poems in this unit and analyze its tone. Show how the poet's use of different elements helps create the tone.

Poems for Comparison

The Charge of the Light Brigade

ALFRED, LORD TENNYSON

The charge described in the following poem took place in 1854, during the Crimean War, at Balaklava (băl'ə-klä'və) on the Black Sea. The English Light Brigade, armed only with swords, was ordered by mistake to attack well-fortified Russian gun positions.

Half a league,° half a league,
Half a league onward,
All in the valley of Death
   Rode the six hundred.
"Forward the Light Brigade!   5
Charge for the guns!" he said.
Into the valley of Death
   Rode the six hundred.

"Forward, the Light Brigade!"
Was there a man dismayed?   10
Not though the soldier knew
   Someone had blundered.
Theirs not to make reply,
Theirs not to reason why,
Theirs but to do and die,   15
Into the valley of Death
   Rode the six hundred.

Cannon to right of them,
Cannon to left of them,
Cannon in front of them   20
   Volleyed and thundered;

1. **league** (lēg): about three miles or less than five kilometers.

Scotland Forever (*Charge of the Light Brigade*) by Butler.　　　　Leeds City Art Galleries

Stormed at with shot and shell,
Boldly they rode and well,
Into the jaws of Death,
Into the mouth of hell　　　　　　　25
　　Rode the six hundred.

Flashed all their sabers bare,
Flashed as they turned in air
Sab'ring the gunners there,
Charging an army, while　　　　　　30
　　All the world wondered.
Plunged in the battery° smoke　　　　32. **battery:** heavy guns.
Right through the line they broke;
Cossack° and Russian　　　　　　　34. **Cossack** (kŏs′ăk): The Cossacks, from
Reeled from the saber-stroke　　　　southern Russia, were noted as cavalry-
　　Shattered and sundered.°　　　　men.
Then they rode back, but not,　　　　36. **sundered** (sŭn′dərd): divided.
　　Not the six hundred.

Cannon to right of them,
Cannon to left of them,   40
Cannon behind them
    Volleyed and thundered;
Stormed at with shot and shell,
While horse and hero fell,
They that had fought so well   45
Came through the jaws of Death,
Back from the mouth of hell,
All that was left of them,
    Left of six hundred.

When can their glory fade?   50
O the wild charge they made!
    All the world wondered.
Honor the charge they made!
Honor the Light Brigade,
    Noble six hundred!   55

For Study and Discussion

Analyzing and Interpreting the Poem

1a. Why did the men follow the command to "Charge for the guns"?   **b.** Which lines comment on a soldier's duty in the face of a command?

2. In lines 31 and 52 Tennyson says "All the world wondered." Does he mean that the world marvelled at the bravery of the men, or that the world wondered about the mistake that caused the men to be slaughtered? Explain your answer.

3. Why does Tennyson believe the memory of these men should be honored?

4. Which phrases and lines create the feeling of battle?

5. Some readers think that the repetitions of rhymes suggest the mechanical actions of the soldiers as they respond to the commands. Do you agree, or do you think the repetition serves another purpose in the poem?

6. How would you describe the poet's attitude toward the events described in this poem?

Eighteenth-century engraving of the Battle of Blenheim.

The Battle of Blenheim

ROBERT SOUTHEY

*In 1704, during the War of the Spanish Succession, the English-Austrian
army won a decisive victory over the French and their allies at Blenheim
(blĕn' əm), a village in Germany.*

It was a summer evening;
   Old Kaspar's work was done,
And he before his cottage door
   Was sitting in the sun,
And by him sported on the green   5
His little grandchild Wilhelmine.

She saw her brother Peterkin
   Roll something large and round,
Which he beside the rivulet
   In playing there had found;   10
He came to ask what he had found,
That was so large, and smooth, and round.

Old Kaspar took it from the boy,
    Who stood expectant by;
And then the old man shook his head,   15
    And with a natural sigh,
"'Tis some poor fellow's skull," said he,
"Who fell in the great victory.

"I find them in the garden,
    For there's many here about;   20
And often, when I go to plow,
    The plowshare turns them out!
For many thousand men," said he,
"Were slain in that great victory."

"Now tell us what 'twas all about,"   25
    Young Peterkin, he cries;
And little Wilhelmine looks up
    With wonder-waiting eyes;
"Now tell us all about the war,
And what they fought each other for."   30

"It was the English," Kaspar cried,
    "Who put the French to rout;
But what they fought each other for,
    I could not well make out;
But everybody said," quoth he,   35
"That 'twas a famous victory.

"My father lived at Blenheim then,
    Yon little stream hard by;°
They burnt his dwelling to the ground,
    And he was forced to fly;   40
So with his wife and child he fled,
Nor had he where° to rest his head.

"With fire and sword the country round
    Was wasted far and wide,
And many a childing° mother then   45
    And newborn baby died;
But things like that, you know, must be
At every famous victory.

38. **Yon . . . hard by:** near yonder little stream.   42. **where:** a place in which.   45. **childing:** with child.

"They say it was a shocking sight
   After the field was won;
For many thousand bodies here
   Lay rotting in the sun;
But things like that, you know, must be
After a famous victory.   50

"Great praise the Duke of Marlbro'° won,   55
   And our good Prince Eugene."°
"Why, 'twas a very wicked thing!"
   Said little Wilhelmine.
"Nay . . nay . . my little girl," quoth he,
"It was a famous victory.   60

"And everybody praised the Duke
   Who this great fight did win."
"But what good came of it at last?"
   Quoth little Peterkin.
"Why, that I cannot tell," said he,   65
"But 'twas a famous victory."

55. **Duke of Marlbro':** Marlborough was in command of the English forces.
56. **Prince Eugene:** He was in command of the Austrian forces.

For Study and Discussion

Analyzing and Interpreting the Poem

1. Old Kaspar cannot remember the reasons why the war was fought. **a.** What does he remember? **b.** Why do you think he cannot remember "what they fought each other for"?

2. The phrases "great victory" and "famous victory" recur throughout the poem as a refrain. How do you know that these repetitions are ironic?

3a. State the attitude of each character toward the battle. **b.** What contrast is intended between the attitude of the old man and that of the grandchildren?

Focus on Descriptive Writing

Evaluating Descriptive Details

Use the following criteria to **evaluate** descriptive details in your essay:

1. Does each detail contribute to a single, overall impression?
2. Is each detail sharp and vivid?
3. Is every detail accurate?
4. Do some details identify unique or especially notable features of the subject?

Fill out an observation chart (see page 348) for either a subjective or an objective description. Trade charts with a classmate. Use the criteria above to evaluate each other's details. Save your notes.

About the Authors

Kenneth Fearing   (1902–1961)

Kenneth Fearing was born in Oak Park, Illinois, a suburb of Chicago. After attending the University of Wisconsin, he worked at various jobs before turning to writing as a career. Much of Fearing's poetry is about life in the modern American city.

Pat Mora   (1942–   )

Pat Mora has said, "I write because I am a reader. I want to give to others what writers have given me, a chance to hear the voices of people I will never meet. . . . I write because I believe that Hispanics need to take their rightful place in American literature . . . so that the stories and ideas of our people won't quietly disappear." Many of her poems contain Spanish words and expressions. "Bribe" appears in *Chants,* a collection of poems about the desert around El Paso, where she has lived. In addition to writing poems, Mora writes fiction, essays, and children's books.

The Author Comments on Her Poem

"Bribe" is the first poem in my first book, *Chants.* When I wrote the poem, I was living on the border in El Paso, Texas, the city of my birth, the desert city in which I have spent most of my life. The Native American presence is strong in that Chihuahua desert and strong in the history of Mexico. I am a twentieth-century Mexican American woman who wants to remain connected with the land and with past traditions, to be part of them and have them be part of me. In our noisy world, the poem is a quiet chant for guidance.

Alfred, Lord Tennyson   (1809–1892)

Tennyson wrote an epic poem at the age of twelve, a blank verse drama at fourteen, and he published a book of poetry while he was still in his early twenties. He became one of England's most popular poets and for over forty years was poet laureate. He was made Lord Tennyson in honor of his achievements as a poet. His masterpiece, *In Memoriam,* was written after the death of his best friend. Among his best-known poems are the *Idylls of the King,* about the legend of King Arthur and the Round Table.

Robert Southey   (1774–1843)

Like Tennyson, Southey (sou'*th*ē, sŭ*th*'ē) was poet laureate of England. Early in his career he traveled to Spain and Portugal, gathering material on the history and legends of these countries. He used this material to write a number of narrative poems. "The Cataract of Lodore" is one of the best onomatopoetic poems in our language.

Types of Poetry

The following section covers three major types of poetry: *lyric, narrative,* and *dramatic.* Although these categories frequently overlap (a narrative poem may also be dramatic, for instance), each type has distinctive characteristics. Lyric poems are generally short poems that express an intense emotional response of the speaker to some person, place, object, or idea. Narrative poems tell a story. Dramatic poems present characters who speak to other characters or to an implied audience.

LYRIC POETRY

In ancient Greece, lyrics were sung to the music of a lyre, a sort of harp. We still call the words of a song its lyrics. Lyric poems are rich in musical devices. There are many different kinds of lyric poems, including sonnets, hymns, songs, odes, and elegies.

John Anderson My Jo

ROBERT BURNS

Robert Burns wrote many love songs in Scottish dialect. As you read this poem,
note its beauty of sound.

John Anderson my jo,° John,
  When we were first acquent,°
Your locks were like the raven,
  Your bonny brow was brent,°
But now your brow is beld,° John,   5
  Your locks are like the snow;
But blessings on your frosty pow,°
  John Anderson my jo.

John Anderson my jo, John,
  We clamb the hill thegither;   10
And mony a canty° day, John,
  We've had wi' ane anither:
Now we maun° totter down, John,
  And hand in hand we'll go,
And sleep thegither at the foot,   15
  John Anderson my jo.

1. **jo:** joy, sweetheart.
2. **acquent:** acquainted.
4. **brent:** unwrinkled.
5. **beld:** bald.
7. **pow** (pō, pou): head.
11. **canty:** happy.
13. **maun:** must.

For Study and Discussion

Analyzing and Interpreting the Poem

1a. Who is the speaker in this poem?
b. How have she and her sweetheart changed?
c. What does the speaker recall about their days together?

2a. What symbolic meaning is suggested by the phrases "clamb the hill" and "totter down"?
b. What do you think is the meaning of line 15?

3. Read the poem aloud, paying attention to the words in Scottish dialect. How do the rhyme, alliteration, and repetition of words and phrases contribute to the music of the poem?

4. Although this poem is written in Scottish dialect, it is one of the best-known love poems in our language. **a.** What do you think is the source of its wide appeal? **b.** Why would it appeal to both young and old readers?

O Mistress Mine

WILLIAM SHAKESPEARE

This is a love song sung by the clown, Feste, in Twelfth Night. *The title* mistress *was a courteous way to address a lady, and it was also a word for "sweetheart."*

O mistress mine, where are you roaming?
O, stay and hear, your true-love's coming,
   That can sing both high and low.
Trip no further, pretty sweeting;
Journeys end in lovers meeting,
   Every wise man's son doth know.   5

What is love? 'Tis not hereafter;
Present mirth hath present laughter;
   What's to come is still unsure:
In delay there lies no plenty;   10
Then come and kiss me, sweet and twenty,
   Youth's a stuff will not endure.

For Study and Discussion

Analyzing and Interpreting the Poem

1. In this poem the speaker pleads with his beloved to return his love quickly, since the time of youth is short. Which lines express this idea?

2. What is the argument of lines 7–10?

Focus on Descriptive Writing

Using Precise Words

Precise words create a sharp, clear image. Here are some examples of precise words from Shakespeare's song:

> *roaming* versus going (line 1)
> *trip* versus go (line 4)
> *mirth* versus joy (line 8)
> *endure* versus remain (line 12)

Reread a letter that you wrote or received recently. Make a list of words to revise so that they are sharper and more precise. Save your notes.

I Wandered Lonely as a Cloud

WILLIAM WORDSWORTH

I wandered lonely as a cloud
   That floats on high o'er vales° and hills,
When all at once I saw a crowd,
   A host, of golden daffodils,
Beside the lake, beneath the trees,   5
Fluttering and dancing in the breeze.

Continuous as the stars that shine
   And twinkle on the Milky Way,
They stretched in never-ending line
   Along the margin of a bay:°   10
Ten thousand saw I at a glance,
Tossing their heads in sprightly dance.

2. **vales:** valleys.

10. **margin of a bay:** edge of the water.

The waves beside them danced; but they
  Outdid the sparkling waves in glee;
A poet could not but be gay,   15
  In such a jocund° company;
I gazed—and gazed—but little thought
What wealth the show to me had brought:

For oft, when on my couch I lie
  In vacant or in pensive mood,   20
They flash upon that inward eye
  Which is the bliss of solitude;
And then my heart with pleasure fills,
And dances with the daffodils.

16. **jocund:** merry.

For Study and Discussion

Analyzing and Interpreting the Poem

1a. What was the poet's mood before he encountered the great wild garden of flowers?
b. How did his discovery change his mood?

2a. Did the poet realize, at the time he saw the flowers, how important the sight would become to him? **b.** How do the flowers continue to be a thing of beauty even when he can no longer see them? **c.** What is the "inward eye" Wordsworth refers to in line 21?

3a. Which lines in the poem contain similes and personifications? **b.** Which lines strike you as particularly melodious?

4. Notice the very regular rhyme scheme.
a. Where in the poem does the poet use inversion? **b.** How does inverted word order enable him to keep a tight rhyme scheme?

Writing About Literature

Comparing a Poem with a Prose Description

Wordsworth's sister, Dorothy, kept a journal in which she recorded observations made during walks with her brother. Here is an entry for April 15, 1802, in which she tells of seeing daffodils. Compare Wordsworth's poem with this prose description. How much agreement is there in details? What has Wordsworth added in order to create a poem out of this experience?

When we were in the woods beyond Gowbarrow Park we saw a few daffodils close to the water side. We fancied that the lake had floated the seeds ashore and that the little colony had so sprung up. But as we went along there were more and yet more and at last under the boughs of the trees, we saw that there was a long belt of them along the shore, about the breadth of a country turnpike road. I never saw daffodils so beautiful. They grew among the mossy stones about and about them, some rested their heads upon these stones as on a pillow for weariness and the rest tossed and reeled and danced and seemed as if they verily laughed. . . .

Loveliest of Trees

A. E. HOUSMAN

Loveliest of trees, the cherry now
Is hung with bloom along the bough,
And stands about the woodland ride°
Wearing white for Eastertide.

Now, of my threescore years and ten,°   5
Twenty will not come again,
And take from seventy springs a score,
It only leaves me fifty more.

And since to look at things in bloom
Fifty springs are little room,   10
About the woodlands I will go
To see the cherry hung with snow.

3. **woodland ride:** a forest path, usually for riding horses.
5. **threescore years and ten:** seventy years, a Biblical allusion to the average human life span. See Psalm 90:10.

For Study and Discussion

Analyzing and Interpreting the Poem

1a. How old does the speaker say he is in stanza 2?   **b.** What do lines 7–8 mean?

2a. What does the speaker mean by saying "Fifty springs are little room"?   **b.** Why does he go to see the trees?

3. Both this poem and "I Wandered Lonely as a Cloud" (page 377) express delight in nature. **a.** How are the speakers' attitudes toward nature similar?   **b.** Are their attitudes different in any way? If so, how?

Desert Places

ROBERT FROST

We usually think of a desert as a hot, sandy, sun-baked land. But the word also means any barren, desolate place. As this poem shows, a desert can be a state of mind as well.

Snow falling and night falling fast, oh, fast
In a field I looked into going past,
And the ground almost covered smooth in snow,
But a few weeds and stubble showing last.

The woods around it have it—it is theirs.   5
All animals are smothered° in their lairs.
I am too absent-spirited to count;
The loneliness includes me unawares.

6. **smothered:** here, asleep or hibernating.

And lonely as it is, that loneliness
Will be more lonely ere it will be less—   10
A blanker whiteness of benighted° snow
With no expression, nothing to express.

11. **benighted:** overtaken by the night or darkness.

They cannot scare me with their empty spaces
Between stars—on stars where no human race is.
I have it in me so much nearer home   15
To scare myself with my own desert places.

For Study and Discussion

Analyzing and Interpreting the Poem

1a. What mood is evoked in the first two stanzas of the poem? **b.** Which details of scene contribute to this mood?

2. What is the meaning of lines 7–8?

3. In stanza 3, the speaker looks into the future. **a.** What change does he foresee in the scene? **b.** In his mood?

4a. In stanza 4, who do you think "They" are? **b.** What does the speaker mean by his "own desert places"?

Creative Writing

Describing a Scene in Nature

"I Wandered Lonely as a Cloud" and "Loveliest of Trees" are about spring and the emotions nature evokes in the speakers. "Desert Places" is about a winter scene and the speaker's reaction to it. Write a brief essay describing a scene in summer or fall, and the emotions it stirs in you. Make your description as specific as you can, using words that communicate your feelings to the reader.

Recessional

RUDYARD KIPLING

A recessional is the hymn that is sung as the choir and clergy are leaving the church at the end of a service. Rudyard Kipling wrote this poem in 1897, the year of England's celebration of the sixtieth anniversary—the Diamond Jubilee—of the reign of Queen Victoria. In that year, England was at its height as a world power.

God of our fathers, known of old,
  Lord of our far-flung battle line,
Beneath whose awful Hand we hold
  Dominion over palm and pine—
Lord God of Hosts, be with us yet,   5
Lest we forget—lest we forget!

The tumult and the shouting dies;
  The captains and the kings depart:
Still stands Thine ancient sacrifice,
  An humble and a contrite heart.   10
Lord God of Hosts, be with us yet,
Lest we forget—lest we forget!

Far-called, our navies melt away;
  On dune and headland sinks the fire:
Lo, all our pomp of yesterday   15
  Is one with Nineveh and Tyre!°
Judge of the Nations, spare us yet,
Lest we forget—lest we forget!

If, drunk with sight of power, we loose
  Wild tongues that have not Thee in awe,   20
Such boasting as the Gentiles° use,
  Or lesser breeds without the Law°—
Lord God of Hosts, be with us yet,
Lest we forget—lest we forget!

16. **Nineveh** (nĭn'ə-və) **and Tyre** (tīr): great centers of ancient civilizations. According to the Bible, they neglected God's commandments and decayed. 21. **Gentiles** (jĕn'tīlz): here, in the Biblical sense of "outsider"—those who did not obey God's Law. 22. **the Law:** the Hebrew Law of the Old Testament.

For heathen heart that puts her trust   25
    In reeking tube and iron shard,°
All valiant dust that builds on dust,
    And guarding, calls not Thee to guard,
For frantic boast and foolish word—
Thy Mercy on Thy People, Lord!   30

26. **shard:** a hard or brittle fragment—here, a bullet from the "reeking tube" of a gun.

For Study and Discussion

Analyzing and Interpreting the Poem

1a. In what things does Kipling say his nation should not put its trust? **b.** Why should it reject these sources of power? **c.** On what would Kipling have his country rely?

2a. What examples does Kipling give to prove that success in war and conquest will not keep a nation great? **b.** Why, as an empire expands, might its power tend to "melt away"? **c.** How might a nation's puffing up with a sense of its own importance hasten this process?

3. A word, a phrase, a line, or a group of lines that reappears from stanza to stanza is called a **refrain**. **a.** What lines does Kipling use as a refrain? **b.** How does the refrain grow in effect and meaning each time it is repeated in the poem? **c.** Where does Kipling vary the refrain and what new ideas are introduced in these variations?

About the Authors

Robert Burns (1759–1796)

Robert Burns has sometimes been called the national poet of Scotland. He was born in Ayr in southwestern Scotland. His family was poor and Burns received little formal schooling. He learned old Scottish songs and stories, and while he worked as a plowboy on his family's farm, he composed many of his poems to the tunes of traditional Scottish songs. Burns is one of the greatest songwriters in English literature. Many of his poems have been set to music. Some well-known love poems are "Highland Mary," "Sweet Afton," and "The Banks o' Doon."

William Wordsworth (1770–1850)

William Wordsworth is generally considered to be the first major Romantic poet in English literature and the greatest nature poet in the language. He was a leader in the rebellion against the content and technique of eighteenth-century poetry. His idea of poetry is set forth in a famous document, the preface to the second edition of *Lyrical Ballads*, a collection of poetry that marks the beginning of the Romantic period in English literature. In this preface, Wordsworth rejected the idea that the subject matter or language of poetry need be exalted or elegant. He emphasized that the language of poetry should be natural and that its subject matter should be drawn from everyday life.

A. E. Housman (1859–1936)

Alfred Edward Housman, a renowned classical scholar, was professor of Latin at University College, London, and then at Trinity College, Cambridge. His literary reputation is largely founded on *A Shropshire Lad*, a collection of sixty-three poems he published in 1896. The speaker in these poems is a farm lad of Shropshire whom Housman described as "an imaginary figure, with something of my own temper and view of life." The poems are famous for their simple diction, their melody, and their craftsmanship.

Rudyard Kipling (1865–1936)

Rudyard Kipling was born in Bombay, India. When he was not quite six years old, he was sent to England for his education. He stayed there until he was seventeen, then returned to India where he worked as a journalist. When he was twenty-one, he published a volume of light verse called *Departmental Ditties*, and a year later he published a collection of stories, *Plain Tales from the Hills*. By the time he returned to England from India in his mid-twenties, he was famous. Kipling's work is characterized by its power and vitality. Some of his best-known novels are *The Light That Failed*, *Captains Courageous*, and *Kim*. Among his well-known poems are "If," "The Ballad of East and West," "Gunga Din," "Danny Deever," and "Mandalay." In 1907 he was awarded the Nobel Prize for literature.

NARRATIVE POETRY

Narrative poetry includes comparatively short works such as "The Charge of the Light Brigade" and long works like the *Odyssey*, an epic in twenty-four books. As you will see in the selections included here, there is often a strong dramatic element in narrative poems.

Lord Randal

This old version of a famous folk ballad tells a story through the dialogue of Lord Randal and his mother. Though the spelling may look strange, most of the words will be clear if pronounced aloud, and the lines will rhyme more closely than they appear to on the page.

"O where hae° ye been, Lord Randal my son?
O where hae ye been, my handsome young man?"
  "I hae been to the wild wood; mother, make my bed soon,
  For I'm weary wi'° hunting, and fain wald° lie down."

"Where got ye your dinner, Lord Randal my son?   5
Where got ye your dinner, my handsome young man?"
  "I dined wi' my true-love; mother, make my bed soon,
  For I'm weary wi' hunting, and fain wald lie down."

"What got ye to your dinner, Lord Randal my son?
What got ye to your dinner, my handsome young man?"   10
  "I got eels boiled in broo,° mother, make my bed soon,
  For I'm weary wi' hunting, and fain wald lie down."

"What became of your bloodhounds, Lord Randal my son?
What became of your bloodhounds, my handsome young man?"
  "O they swelled and they died; mother, make my bed soon,   15
  For I'm weary wi' hunting, and fain wald lie down."

"O I fear ye are poisoned, Lord Randal my son!
O I fear ye are poisoned, my handsome young man!"
  "O yes, I am poisoned; mother, make my bed soon,
  For I'm sick at the heart, and I fain wald lie down."   20

1. **hae:** have

4. **wi':** with. **fain wald** (wäd): gladly would.

11. **eels boiled in broo** (bro͞o): eels in broth, a soup.

Falcon Hunt. Fifteenth-century Franco-Flemish tapestry.

For Study and Discussion

Analyzing and Interpreting the Poem

1. Sometimes we must read between the lines of a poem to tell exactly what happens. This poem is like a short murder mystery. **a.** Who has poisoned Lord Randal? **b.** Which of the mother's questions indicate that she suspects, from the beginning, that something bad has happened?

2a. Why do you think Lord Randal does not immediately tell his mother that he has been poisoned? **b.** In what ways is he "sick at the heart"?

3. Like most songs, folk ballads use repetition freely. Where do you find alliteration in this poem?

4a. Which phrases and lines form refrains (see page 382)? **b.** What variations occur in these refrains? **c.** How do the refrains help to build drama and suspense in the poem?

Lord Randal   **385**

All in green went my love riding

e. e. cummings

What characteristics does this poem share with the popular ballad?

All in green went my love riding
on a great horse of gold
into the silver dawn.

four lean hounds crouched low and smiling
the merry deer ran before.   5

Fleeter be they than dappled° dreams
the swift sweet deer
the red rare° deer.

Four red roebuck° at a white water
the cruel bugle sang before.   10

Horn at hip went my love riding
riding the echo down
into the silver dawn.

four lean hounds crouched low and smiling
the level meadows ran before.   15

Softer be they than slippered sleep
the lean lithe deer
the fleet flown deer.

Four fleet does at a gold valley
the famished arrow sang before   20

Bow at belt went my love riding
riding the mountain down
into the silver dawn.

6. **dappled:** speckled.

8. **rare:** very fine.

9. **roebuck:** male roe deer, a type of small, swift deer.

four lean hounds crouched low and smiling
the sheer peaks ran before. 25

Paler be they than daunting° death
the sleek slim deer
the tall tense deer.

26. **daunting:** frightening.

Four tall stags at a green mountain
the lucky hunter sang before. 30

All in green went my love riding
on a great horse of gold
into the silver dawn.

four lean hounds crouched low and smiling
my heart fell dead before. 35

For Study and Discussion

Analyzing and Interpreting the Poem

1. This poem is a **literary ballad**. A literary ballad has a known author and is intended to be read rather than sung. It has several characteristics in common with folk ballads. Which lines and images in Cummings' poem establish the setting as far off in the past?

2. Certain images, such as those of the smiling dogs and the silver dawn, give the poem a strange, almost supernatural atmosphere. What other words and phrases give the landscape and animals an air of mystery?

3. Ballads often shift scenes rapidly, leaving gaps in the action. In this poem there are several abrupt shifts of scene as the hunter pursues different groups of deer. Where do these shifts occur?

4. In many old poems, the lover is described as a hunter pursuing the beloved. **a.** Who is the hunter's last "victim" in this poem? **b.** What is meant by the last line?

5. Like many ballads, this poem uses repetition and refrain. **a.** Which lines appear in exactly the same form from stanza to stanza? **b.** Which lines are repeated with slight variations?

Literary Elements

The Ballad

One of the most enduring types of narrative poetry is the **ballad.** The earliest ballads we have are called **folk ballads** or **popular ballads.** These poems were composed to be sung, and they survived by being passed along orally for generations. In the process, they were altered by storytellers, and over the years appeared in many different versions.

A ballad is usually composed in four-line rhymed stanzas, with strong, simple rhythm. Frequently the story is told through the dialogue of the characters. There is generally one central dramatic or tragic incident, told simply and briefly. Ballads often shift rapidly from scene to scene, or leave gaps in the story that must be filled in by the audience.

Focus on Descriptive Writing

Exploring Connotations

Connotations are the emotions or associations that a word or phrase may arouse—as opposed to a word's **denotation,** or literal, "dictionary" meaning (see page 305). Connotations can be very effective in descriptive writing.

Freewrite some notes on the associations that the phrases in italics from Cummings' poem prompt in you:

> "*red rare* deer" (line 8)
> "*cruel* bugle" (line 10)
> "*famished* arrow" (line 20)
> "*daunting* death" (line 26)

Get together with a small group and compare notes. Save your writing.

In the Collection of the Corcoran Gallery of Art, Gift of William Wilson Corcoran

Detail from *The Departure* (1837) by Thomas Cole. Oil on canvas, 39½ x 63 in. (100.33 x 160.02 cm.).

The Castle

EDWIN MUIR

All through that summer at ease we lay,
And daily from the turret° wall
We watched the mowers in the hay
And the enemy half a mile away.
They seemed no threat to us at all.   5

For what, we thought, had we to fear
With our arms and provender, load on load,
Our towering battlements, tier on tier,
And friendly allies drawing near
On every leafy summer road.   10

Our gates were strong, our walls were thick,
So smooth and high, no man could win
A foothold there, no clever trick
Could take us, have us dead or quick.°
Only a bird could have got in.   15

What could they offer us for bait?
Our captain was brave and we were true. . . .
There was a little private gate,
A little wicked wicket gate.
The wizened° warder let them through.   20

Oh then our maze of tunneled stone°
Grew thin and treacherous as air.
The cause was lost without a groan.
The famous citadel° overthrown,
And all its secret galleries° bare.   25

How can this shameful tale be told?
I will maintain until my death
We could do nothing, being sold;
Our only enemy was gold,
And we had no arms to fight it with.   30

2. **turret:** tower.

14. **quick:** alive.

20. **wizened:** (wĭz′ənd) wrinkled.

21. **maze . . . stone:** the stone castle, designed to confuse and repel enemies.

24. **citadel:** fortress.

25. **galleries:** halls.

For Study and Discussion

Analyzing and Interpreting the Poem

1a. What made the inhabitants of the castle feel safe, even though the enemy was near?
b. What deed or action caused the castle to fall into enemy hands?

2a. What does the fifth stanza mean? **b.** What "cause" was lost? **c.** In what sense was it lost "without a groan"?

3. You are never told what castle, what battle, or what war the speaker refers to. Why do you think the poet deliberately refrains from setting the narrative in a specific locale at a specific time?

4. The speaker's story has a moral. **a.** Which lines in the poem might be taken as a statement of that moral? **b.** Tell in your own words what they mean.

Creative Writing

Writing a Ballad

Ballads have been composed about various subjects: love, death, adventure, mystery, war. Many ballads deal with a famous figure from history or legend. A number of American ballads, for example, grew up around the exploits of the Western desperado Billy the Kid.

Choose a subject for a ballad. It may be based on a historical or legendary incident. You may choose some character in a television series or a cartoon strip as the hero or heroine of your ballad. If you wish, write a humorous ballad. Try to incorporate repetition and refrains in your ballad.

About the Authors

E. E. Cummings (1894–1962)

Edward Estlin Cummings was born in Cambridge, Massachusetts. He attended Harvard University. During World War I he enlisted in the French Ambulance Corps, then served in the United States Infantry. After the war he divided his time between New York and Paris. Unlike many poets, he was able to support himself entirely through the sale and reading of his poems. Cummings experimented with visual and verbal devices to communicate to his readers the beauty and freshness of what he saw around him.

Edwin Muir (1887–1959)

Edwin Muir was born in Orkney, Scotland. For many years, Muir was known as a critic, teacher, and translator. Not until he was almost sixty did he publish a book of poems, *The Voyager*. This book, and the following one, *The Labyrinth*, established him as a major poet.

DRAMATIC POETRY

In dramatic poetry there are characters who speak in their own person, just like characters in a stage play. In some dramatic poems there are two speakers and the poem consists largely of their dialogue. A special kind of dramatic poem is the *dramatic monologue,* or *dramatic lyric,* in which a speaker addresses someone whose presence is implied.

The Seven Ages of Man

WILLIAM SHAKESPEARE

The speaker of this poem is Jaques, a character in As You Like It. *What impression do you form of Jaques from his speech?*

All the world's a stage,
And all the men and women merely players.
They have their exits and their entrances,
And one man in his time plays many parts,
His acts being seven ages. At first the infant,   5
Mewling° and puking in the nurse's arms.
Then the whining schoolboy, with his satchel
And shining morning face, creeping like snail
Unwillingly to school. And then the lover,
Sighing like furnace, with a woeful ballad   10
Made to his mistress' eyebrow. Then a soldier,
Full of strange oaths and bearded like the pard,°
Jealous in honor, sudden and quick in quarrel,
Seeking the bubble reputation
Even in the cannon's mouth. And then the justice,   15
In fair round belly with good capon° lined,
With eyes severe and beard of formal cut,
Full of wise saws and modern instances,°
And so he plays his part. The sixth age shifts
Into the lean and slippered Pantaloon°   20
With spectacles on nose and pouch on side,
His youthful hose, well saved, a world too wide

6. **Mewling:** whimpering, whining.

12. **pard:** leopard.

16. **capon:** chicken.

18. **saws and modern instances:** old sayings and obvious examples.

20. **Pantaloon:** a foolish old man. Pantaloon was a stock character in Italian comedies.

For his shrunk shank,° and his big manly voice,
Turning again toward childish treble, pipes
And whistles in his sound. Last scene of all,   25
That ends this strange eventful history,
Is second childishness and mere oblivion,°
Sans° teeth, sans eyes, sans taste, sans everything.

23. **shrunk shank:** shrunken legs.

27. **oblivion:** forgetfulness.

28. **Sans:** without.

Seven Ages of Man by William Mulready (1786–1863). Oil on canvas.
Victoria and Albert Museum

Analyzing and Interpreting the Poem

1. The speaker of this poem is a character named Jaques (jā′kwēz) from one of Shakespeare's comedies, *As You Like It.* In the speech Jaques tells what life is like: a great stage on which people play a variety of roles as they age. **a.** How does Jaques' description make each age sound unpleasant, silly, or futile? **b.** What words and images create these impressions about each age?

2. Some of Jaques' descriptions are comic. **a.** Point out lines, such as that of the lover "sighing like furnace," that make fun of some of the "characters" people play. **b.** Does the last line strike you as humorous? If not, what tone does it have?

3. Shakespeare uses several vivid similes and metaphors that show us how Jaques feels about life. Jaques shows his contempt for fame by referring to reputation as a "bubble." Point out some other figures of speech and tell how they are effective in revealing Jaques' attitudes.

Literary Elements

Dramatic Poetry

Dramatic poetry is poetry that resembles a play in some way. A dramatic poem may be in the form of a dialogue between two or more people, or the speaker may be talking to someone who does not answer but whose presence is understood. Many narrative poems are also dramatic. "Lord Randal" (page 384) is a dialogue between two characters. Who are the speakers? Who is the speaker in "The Castle" (page 389)? To whom do you think he is telling his shameful tale?

Literature and the Arts

All the World's a Stage

Art throughout the centuries has inspired the creation of other art. Because of their dramatic depiction of human struggle, ancient myths, Biblical stories, and many literary masterpieces, such as Shakespeare's plays, have been interpreted in paintings, sculptures, musical compositions, and films.

Making Connections: Activities

Identify each of the seven "players" in "The Seven Ages of Man" and their characteristics. Imagine what they look like. Then study Mulready's painting on page 392. Write a review in which you evaluate the painting in terms of its faithfulness to the speech. Which details would you include or exclude? How would your depiction differ? Does Mulready's interpretation capture the tone of the poem? How does it elaborate on the speech?

Uphill

CHRISTINA ROSSETTI

Who are the questioner and answerer in this poem?

Does the road wind uphill all the way?
    Yes, to the very end.
Will the day's journey take the whole long day?
    From morn to night, my friend.

But is there for the night a resting place?   5
    A roof for when the slow dark hours begin.
May not the darkness hide it from my face?
    You cannot miss that inn.

Shall I meet other wayfarers at night?
    Those who have gone before.   10
Then must I knock, or call when just in sight?
    They will not keep you standing at that door.

Shall I find comfort, travel-sore and weak?
    Of labor you shall find the sum.
Will there be beds for me and all who seek?   15
    Yea, beds for all who come.

For Study and Discussion

Analyzing and Interpreting the Poem

1. At first this poem seems to be simply about a traveler preparing for a journey. But the poem has a symbolic level too. **a.** What might this journey stand for? **b.** What might the inn symbolize? **c.** What clues in the poem point to these symbolic meanings?

2a. How would you describe the attitude of the questioner? **b.** What is the tone of the answers? Are they optimistic, reassuring, frightening, cynical?

3a. How does the poet use line length, indentation, and punctuation to show that there are two speakers in the poem? **b.** What is the rhyme scheme of the poem? **c.** How does it help identify the speakers?

4. Explain the title of the poem.

The Erl-King

JOHANN WOLFGANG VON GOETHE

Translated by
Sir Walter Scott

*There are three characters in this dramatic poem: a father, his child, and the
Erl-King* (der Erlkönig), *a folklore spirit who does mischief and evil, especially to children.*

O who rides by night thro' the woodland so wild?
It is the fond father embracing his child;
And close the boy nestles within his loved arm.
To hold himself fast, and to keep himself warm.

"O father, see yonder! see yonder!" he says;   5
"My boy, upon what dost thou fearfully gaze?"
"O, 'tis the Erl-King with his crown and his shroud."
"No, my son, it is but a dark wreath of the cloud."

(The Erl-King speaks)
"O come and go with me, thou loveliest child;
By many a gay sport shall thy time be beguiled;   10
My mother keeps for thee full many a fair toy,
And many a fine flower shall she pluck for my boy."

"O father, my father, and did you not hear
The Erl-King whisper so low in my ear?"
"Be still, my heart's darling—my child, be at ease;   15
It was but the wild blast as it sung thro' the trees."

(Erl-King)
"O wilt thou go with me, thou loveliest boy?
My daughter shall tend thee with care and with joy;
She shall bear thee so lightly thro' wet and thro' wild,
And press thee, and kiss thee, and sing to my child."   20

"O father, my father, and saw you not plain
The Erl-King's pale daughter glide past thro' the rain?"

"O yes, my loved treasure, I knew it full soon;
It was the gray willow that danced to the moon."

(Erl-King)
"O come and go with me, no longer delay,   25
Or else, silly child, I will drag thee away."
"O father! O father! now, now, keep your hold,
The Erl-King has seized me—his grasp is so cold!"

Sore trembled the father; he spurr'd thro' the wild,
Clasping close to his bosom his shuddering child;   30
He reaches his dwelling in doubt and in dread,
But, clasp'd to his bosom, the infant was dead.

Private Collection

For Study and Discussion

Analyzing and Interpreting the Poem

1. The child is aware of the Erl-King's presence, but his father is not. **a.** Why do you think this is so? **b.** How does the father react to the child's fear? **c.** At what point does he sense danger?

2a. What does the Erl-King promise the boy? **b.** Why are these promises fearful?

3. What elements contribute to the mysterious and supernatural atmosphere of the poem?

Literature and the Arts

Musical Interpretations

The lyrics of many well-known poems have been set to music. Franz Schubert (1797–1828) wrote the music for a number of separate songs and song cycles. He was only eighteen when he wrote the music for Goethe's poem "The Erl-King."

Making Connections: Activities

Locate a recording of "The Erl-King" to share with the class. Discuss the effectiveness of Schubert's interpretation of the mood and tragic events of the poem.

About the Authors

Christina Rossetti   (1830–1894)

Christina Rossetti came from one of the most remarkable artistic families in England. Her father was an Italian poet whose political verses so angered his enemies that he had to flee to England for his life. Her brother Dante Gabriel was a leading poet and painter, and another brother, Michel, was a writer, editor, and influential art critic. Her sister Maria was a teacher and critic who later became a nun. Christina Rossetti, like her father and brothers, was artistic, and like her sister, intensely religious. She spent the last fifteen years of her life almost totally withdrawn from the world, performing devotional acts and writing. She died, as she probably would have wished, while at prayer.

Johann Wolfgang von Goethe   (1749–1832)

The Granger Collection, New York

Johann Wolfgang von Goethe was a famous German poet, dramatist, and novelist whose wide interests also extended into science, law, and philosophy. Goethe spent a happy childhood in Frankfurt and later studied and practiced law before beginning his writing career. A drama published in 1773 brought him his first recognition, and he became famous the next year with a novel, *The Sorrows of Young Werther*. Goethe was invited to the court of Charles Augustus, Duke of Saxe-Weimar, in 1775. He remained there for the rest of his life, at one time serving as the Duke's chief minister. His travels in Italy, and his friendship with Schiller, another German writer and philosopher, did much to influence his writings. His finest work, the one on which his fame rests, is his long poetic drama, *Faust*.

RELATING SOUND TO MEANING

As you have seen in this unit, the sound of words, as well as their meanings, can contribute to effective description. Sound patterns include rhythm, meter, rhyme, alliteration, assonance, onomatopoeia, and parallelism. Writers often use these sound devices in prose descriptions, as well as in poetry.

■ Read aloud the three short passages below. Then make notes on how you think the sound of the words in each passage contributes to the meaning of the description.

1. My son squats in the snow in his blue
        snowsuit.
   All around him stubble, the brown
   degraded bushes. In the morning air
   they seem to stiffen into words.
   And, between, the white steady silence.
   A wren hops on the airstrip
   under the sill, drills
   for sustenance, then spreads
   its short wings, shadows
   dropping from them.

   —Louise Glück,
   from "Illuminations"

2. Soft you day, be velvet soft,
        My true love approaches,
   Look you bright, you dusty sun,
        Array your golden coaches.

        Soft you wind, be soft as silk,
   My true love is speaking.
        Hold you birds, your silver throats,
   His golden voice I'm seeking.

   Come you death, in haste, do come
        My shroud of black be weaving,
   Quiet my heart, be deathly quiet,
        My true love is leaving.

   —Maya Angelou,
   "The Gamut"

3. The image of Zhen lingers most in my mind. I remember Zhen vividly on a day when I left Wuyipeng, when her brief appearance seemed like a parting gift. I had found her not far from camp sitting hunched on a moss-covered boulder, muzzle tucked into her folded arms. Quietly I approached to within forty-five feet and waited. She raised her head and with a disinterested gaze looked at me, then leaned forward, her back to me, and continued her rest. There was a startling self-assurance, a striking kind of freedom, in the way she ignored me. At intervals she changed position, resting on side or belly, and occasionally she sat up to scratch or paw flies off her face. Once she glanced in the direction of loud voices from camp. After two and a half hours, with the onset of a heavy rain, she raised her arms above her head, stretched, and yawned cavernously. She descended from the boulder and began to munch shoots. I left her there, her pelage[1] gleaming softly in the bamboo twilight, until like falling snow she melted gently into the forest.

   —George B. Schaller,
   from *The Last Panda*

1. **pelage** (pĕl′ĭj): the animal's coat.

DESCRIPTIVE WRITING

*W*riters use **description** for many purposes: for example, to express feelings, to persuade an audience to act or think in a certain way, or to inform an audience. This kind of writing appears in poetry, as well as in novels, short stories, biographies, news stories, letters, and ads. You will have a chance to write a description on a topic of your own choice.

Prewriting ～～✐

1. As you look for a focus for your description, you may find these hints helpful:

- Think of a familiar person, place, or thing.
- Choose a subject you can observe directly.
- Limit your subject to one that you can cover in a few paragraphs. [See **Focus** assignment on page 301.]

2. Decide if your **purpose** is to write a **subjective** or an **objective description**. The chart below lists some of the features of these two types.

	Subjective	Objective
Point of View	First-person	Third-person
Tone	Informal, personal	Formal, businesslike
Type of Writing	Letters, poems, stories, essays, journals	Reports articles, speeches
Details	Factual and sensory; writer's thoughts and feelings; figures of speech	Factual and sensory

Also consider your **audience.** How much do they already know about your subject? What background information may they need? Will you have to define any unfamiliar terms so that they can understand your description? [See **Focus** assignments on pages 313 and 328.]

3. Summarize your planning so far by filling out a **description chart** like the one below:

Subject: _____

Type of Description: _____

Purpose: _____

Audience: _____

Point of View: _____

Tone: _____

[See **Focus** assignment on page 346.]

4. At the heart of any description are the specific details it contains. Here are three types of details you can use:

- **sensory details:** appeal to sight, sound, taste, touch, smell
- **factual details:** can be measured or checked
- **figures of speech:** words or phrases that are not meant literally
  —simile: comparison with *like* or *as*
  —metaphor: direct comparison
  —personification: giving human features to something nonhuman

The diagram on page 400 shows you four ways of gathering details.

[See **Focus** assignments on pages 348, 355, and 358.]

5. Organize your details in a way that makes sense. Three ways to present your material in a description are the following:

- **spatial order:** arranging details in the order you see them
- **order of importance:** putting the most important details either first or last
- **order of impression:** starting with the most prominent detail and moving on to other details in the order that they impress you

[See **Focus** assignment on page 363.]

Writing ∿

1. Try "hooking" your audience by starting your essay with an especially vivid detail. By the end of the first paragraph, be sure that your focus is clear and that you've set the tone for your essay.

2. As you write, use the following criteria to **evaluate** the details you include in your essay:

- Are sensory details sharp and vivid?
- Are factual details accurate?
- Does every detail contribute to a single, overall impression?

[See **Focus** assignment on page 372.]

3. Use **transitions** to clarify relationships in your writing. Below is a list of useful transitional words:

above	first	most important
across	here	over
around	inside	then
before	into	there
behind	last	under
down	mainly	up

Evaluating and Revising ∿

1. Put your first draft aside for a while. Then try to look at it with fresh eyes. You may want to ask a peer reader to review your description. Pay special attention to your **diction,** or choice of words. Are all your nouns, verbs, adjectives, and adverbs as precise and vivid as you can make them? Watch out for vague, nondescriptive words like *go, move, really, some,* or *thing.* If you have included figures of speech in your description, have you been careful to avoid clichés, or overused, worn-out expressions? Have you been alert to the **connotations** or associations of the words and phrases you've used? [See **Focus** assignments on pages 376 and 388.]

Below is an example of how one writer revised an opening paragraph for a descriptive essay.

Writer's Model

Some people think that Boots ~~is not~~ *only pretends* ~~really~~ *to be* a Siamese. His habits simply aren't typical of the breed. ~~He is not~~ *Far from being* standoffish. He loves to rub his fur *creamy* and *seal-brown* muzzle against human legs. The shrilly repeated *meows* ~~sounds~~ of Siamese are not ~~made by Boots~~ *for him*. Instead, Boots is a master of gesture, expressing his feelings with a *flick* ~~movement~~ of his tail or a glance from those eyes that are ~~really~~ *as* blue *as a mountain lake in June*.

2. By yourself or with a partner, use the following checklist to evaluate and revise your writing.

Checklist for Evaluation and Revision

✓ Do I grab the attention of the audience in the introduction?
✓ Is the focus of my description clear?
✓ Do I use sensory and factual details to give a clear picture of my subject?
✓ Have I organized the details in a way that makes sense?
✓ Do all the details I've included contribute to a single, overall impression?
✓ If I have used figures of speech, are they fresh and imaginative?
✓ If the description is subjective, have I included my own thoughts and feelings?
✓ Are the tone and point of view consistent?

Proofreading and Publishing

1. Proofread your essay to correct errors in grammar, usage, capitalization, and punctuation. (You may find it helpful to refer to the **Handbook for Revision** on pages 884–930.) Then prepare a final version of your essay by making a clean copy.

2. Consider some of the following ways of publishing and sharing your essay:

- gather photographs or drawings and make your essay the centerpiece of an illustrated display on the class bulletin board
- send your essay to a magazine
- deliver your essay as an oral commentary
- submit your essay to the school paper

Portfolio If your teacher approves, you may wish to keep a copy of your work in your writing folder or portfolio.

DRAMA

Edward Hopper's painting *Two on the Aisle* shows members of an audience taking their seats in a theater. What can you conclude from the way the people are dressed? Look at the orchestra pit. What can you tell about the evening's performance?

The indoor theater is a relatively recent idea in the history of drama. The ancient Greeks held their plays in open-air amphitheaters. In Shakespeare's day plays took place in inn courtyards and on stages where there was no artificial lighting and little scenery.

1. Describe some of the different stages and theaters you have seen. Include open-air theaters, puppet theaters, and theaters-in-the-round.

2. With a partner or a group of classmates, adapt one of the short stories you have read as a play for radio or television. If necessary, create dialogue for the characters.

Two on the Aisle (1927) by Edward Hopper (1882-1967). Oil on canvas, 40⅛ x 48¼".

The Toledo Museum of Art, Toledo, Ohio; Purchased with funds from the Libbey Endowment, Gift of Edward Drummond Libbey

Drama, like poetry, is a very old literary genre that developed long before the novel and short story. Many nations have a rich dramatic tradition. The classical Indian drama *Shakuntala* (shä′kən-tä′lä) was written around the fifth century A.D. Chinese drama developed out of popular entertainment and court performances nearly a thousand years ago. Japanese *Noh* (nō) drama, first performed in the 1300s, and *Kabuki* (kä-bōō′kē), which evolved out of Noh theater, are still widely performed. The oldest dramas that have survived in Western literature—those of the Greek playwrights Aeschylus, Sophocles, and Euripides—were composed and performed twenty-five hundred years ago. Some people believe these early plays have never been surpassed.

The two major forms of drama are tragedy and comedy. The word *tragedy* comes from a Greek word meaning "goat song." No one knows what the association with goat means, but it is generally agreed that the drama had some connection with religious rituals. Perhaps a goat was sacrificed to one of the gods, or perhaps the actors wore goatskins. The word *comedy* also comes from the Greek. Roughly translated, it means "a singer in the revels," indicating that it was associated with a joyous festival of some kind.

Within each major type of drama there are subtypes, each with its own traditions. It is possible to distinguish different kinds of tragedy: Greek classical tragedy, Shakespearean tragedy, domestic tragedy, heroic tragedy, and the like. *Romeo and Juliet* (page 482) is a Shakespearean tragedy. Comedy, likewise, may be subdivided into categories: romantic comedy, comedy of humors, comedy of manners, for example. *A Marriage Proposal* by Anton Chekhov (chĕk′ôf′) (page 413) is a type of comedy known as *farce*, which depends on improbable situations and exaggerated characters.

In earlier times, plays were written almost exclusively for performance in a theater—whether that theater was outdoors or indoors. In our own time we have had plays developed for different media. *Visit to a Small Planet* by Gore Vidal (page 423) and *Thunder on Sycamore Street* by Reginald Rose (page 449) were both written for television. In reading these plays you will find special sets of directions governing the position of the television cameras.

Many of the elements that you have already studied in connection with short stories are relevant to the study of drama. Throughout this unit you will have opportunity to examine the dramatist's art.

Close Reading OF A PLAY

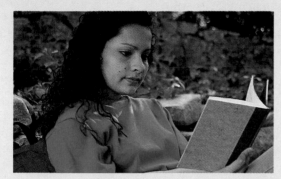

*M*any of the elements you responded to in connection with short stories and poetry are also relevant to the study of drama. In addition, drama has its own conventions, or practices, including stage directions, sound effects, soliloquies, monologues, and asides. Generally, however, dialogue is the dramatist's most important device for presenting character and for moving the action along.

Guidelines for Close Reading

1. Note any information that establishes the setting and the situation that will start the plot moving. This information may be given in stage directions, or it may emerge during the opening scenes.

2. Note clues that tell you what the players are doing or how the lines are spoken. This information is not always revealed in stage directions. You may need to infer actions, gestures, and tone from the dialogue.

3. Anticipate the action that will develop out of each scene. Try to predict what will happen next.

4. Be alert to the mood of the play and shifts in tone. A comedy may have serious scenes, and a tragedy may have scenes of comic relief. Ask yourself how these shifts in tone and mood affect your response.

5. Be aware of dramatic conventions. Most modern plays have a realistic style. Shakespearean drama uses both prose and verse and special kinds of speeches known as soliloquies and asides.

6. Using your responses to the play, write a statement of the theme or underlying meaning of the play.

The following play, *Mozart and the Gray Steward,* is a "three-minute" play by Thornton Wilder, a major American playwright. Wilder got the idea for his play from an incident in the composer's life. Shortly before his death, Mozart was visited by a stranger, who commissioned him to compose a requiem. The notes in the margin show how one reader has responded to the play. If you wish, cover up these notes and make your own notes as you read. You may wish to compare your own responses with the printed comments at a later point.

Mozart and the Gray Steward
THORNTON WILDER

Mozart *is seated at a table in a mean room in Vienna orchestrating* The Magic Flute.[1] *Leaves of ruled paper are strewn about the floor. His wife enters in great excitement.*

Constanze. There's someone come to see you, someone important. Pray God, it's a commission from Court.

Mozart (*unmoved*). Not while Salieri's[2] alive.

Constanze. Put on your slippers, dear. It's someone dressed all in gray, with a gray mask over his eyes, and he's come in a great coach with its coat of arms all covered up with gray cloth. Pray God, it's a commission from Court for a *Te Deum*[3] or something. (*She tidies up the room in six gestures.*)

Mozart. Not while Salieri's alive.

Constanze. But, now, do be nice, 'Gangl,[4] please. We must have some money, my treasure. Just listen to him and say "yes" and "thank you" and then you and I'll talk it over after he's gone. (*She holds his coat.*) Come, put this on. Step into your slippers.

Mozart (*sighing*). I'm not well. I'm at home. I'm at work. There's not a single visitor in the whole world that could interest me. Bring him in.

A facsimile of the first page of Mozart's *Requiem*.

[*She hurries out and presently reenters preceding the visitor. The visitor is dressed from head to foot in gray silk. His bright eyes look out through the*

---

1. **The Magic Flute:** an opera completed in 1791, the year of the composer's death.
2. **Salieri:** Antonio Salieri (1750–1825), an Italian composer who became prominent in Viennese musical life. He was the supposed enemy of Mozart.
3. **Te Deum** (tā'dā'əm, tē'dē'əm): a Latin hymn. The opening words are *Te Deum Laudamus*, meaning "We praise Thee, O God."
4. **'Gangl** (gän'gəl): a shortened form of Wolfgang, Mozart's given name.

holes in a narrow gray silk mask. He holds to his nose a gray perfumed handkerchief. One would say: an elegant undertaker.]

The Gray Steward. Kapellmeister[5] Mozart, *servus*.[6] Gracious lady, *servus*.

Mozart. *Servus.*

The Gray Steward. Revered and noble master, wherever music reigns, wherever genius is valued, the name of Wolfgang Amadeus Mozart is...

Mozart. Sir, I have always been confused by compliments and beg you to spare me that mortification by proceeding at once to the cause of your visit . . . the . . . the honor of your visit.

The Gray Steward. Revered master, before I lay my business before you, may I receive your promise that—whether you accept my commission or not—you both will . . .

Mozart. I promise you our secrecy, unless our silence would prove dishonorable to me or injurious to someone else. Pray continue.

5. **Kapellmeister** (kä-pĕl′mīs′tər): German for "choir master."
6. *servus* (sûr′vŭs): Latin for "your servant."

A scene from the film *Amadeus*.

This character looks sinister. Why is he wearing a mask? If Mozart was a choir master, why was he poor?

Mozart doesn't like to be flattered.

The steward must be some kind of servant.

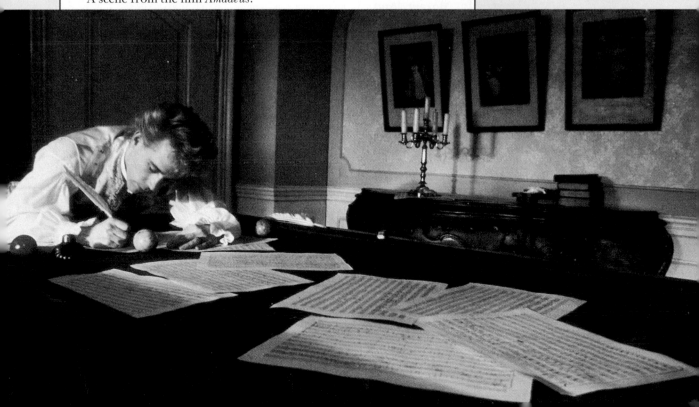

Is Mozart making fun of him?

He wants Mozart to compose a Requiem Mass. So why the disguise?

The patron wants people to believe the work is his own.

That's a good point.

I would never let anyone take credit for my work.

The Gray Steward. Know then, gracious and revered genius, that I come from a prince who combines all the qualities of birth, station, generosity, and wisdom.

Mozart. Ha! a European secret.

The Gray Steward. His Excellency moreover has just sustained a bitter misfortune. He has lately lost his wife and consort, a lady who was the admiration of her court and the sole light of her bereaved husband's life. Therefore, his Excellency, my master, commissions you to compose a Requiem Mass in honor of his lady. He asks you to pour into it the height of your invention and that wealth of melody and harmony that have made you the glory of our era. And for this music he asks leave to pay you the sum of four hundred crowns—two hundred now, and the second two hundred crowns when you deliver the first four numbers.

Mozart. Well, Constanze, I must not be proud.

The Gray Steward. There is but one proviso.[7]

Mozart. Yes, I heard it. The work must represent the height of my invention.

The Gray Steward. That was an easy assumption, master. The proviso is this: You shall let his Excellency have this music as an anonymous work, and you shall never by any sign, by so much as the nod of your head, acknowledge that the work is yours.

Mozart. And his Excellency is not aware that the pages I may compose at the height of my invention may be their own sufficient signature?

The Gray Steward. That may be. Naturally my master will see to it that no other composer will ever be able to claim the work as his.

Mozart. Quick, give me your paper and I will sign it. Leave your two hundred crowns with my wife at the foot of the stairs. Come back in August and you will have the first four numbers. *Servus. Servus.*

The Gray Steward (*backing out*). *Servus*, master. *Servus*, madame.

[Constanze *returns in a moment and looks anxiously towards her husband.*]

Constanze. A visit from Heaven, 'Gangl. Now you can go into the country. Now you can drink all the Bohemian water in the world.

7. **proviso** (prə-vī′zō): condition.

Young Mozart wearing court dress (1763). Portrait
attributed to Pietro Antonio Lorenzoni. Oil on canvas.

Mozart (*bitterly*). Good. And just at a time when I was contemplating a Requiem Mass. But for *myself*. However, I must not be proud.

Constanze (*trying to divert him*). Who can these people be? Try and think.

Mozart. Oh, there's no mystery about that. It's the Count von Walsegg. He composes himself. But for the most part he buys string quartets from us; he erases the signatures and has them played in his castle. The courtiers flatter him and pretend that they have guessed him to be the composer. He does not deny it. He tries to appear confused. And now he has succeeded in composing a Requiem. But that will reduce my pride.

Constanze. You know he will only be laughed at. The music will speak for itself. Heaven wanted to give us four hundred crowns—

Mozart. And Heaven went about it humorously.

Constanze. What was his wife like?

Mozart. Her impudences smelt to Heaven. She dressed like a page and called herself Cherubin.[8] Her red cheeks and her black teeth and her sixty years are in my mind now.

Constanze (*after a pause*). We'll give back the money. You can write the music, without writing it for them.

Mozart. No, I like this game. I like it for its very falseness. What does it matter who signs such music or to whom it is addressed? (*He flings himself upon the sofa and turns his face to the wall.*) For whom do we write music? for musicians? Salieri!—for patrons? Von Walsegg!—for the public? The Countess von Walsegg! I shall write this Requiem, but it shall be for myself, since I am dying.

Constanze. My beloved, don't talk so! Go to sleep. (*She spreads a shawl over his body.*) How can you say such things? Imagine even thinking such a thing! You will live many years and write countless beautiful pages. We will return the money and refuse the commission. Then the matter will be closed. Now go to sleep, my treasure.

[*She goes out, quietly closing the door behind her.* Mozart, *at the mercy of*

---

8. **Cherubin** (kā-rōō-bĕn′): presumably after Cherubino, a character in Mozart's opera *The Marriage of Figaro*.

Mozart knows who the patron is.

Is he being ironic?

It sounds like he's bitter and feels humiliated.

his youth, his illness, and his genius, is shaken by a violent fit of weeping. The sobs gradually subside and he falls asleep. In his dream The Gray Steward *returns.*]

A scene from the film *Amadeus*.

The Gray Steward. Mozart! Turn and look at me. You know who I am.

Mozart (*not turning*). You are the steward of the Count von Walsegg. Go tell him to write his own music. I will not stain my pen to celebrate his lady, so let the foul bury the foul.

The Gray Steward. Lie then against the wall, and learn that it is Death itself that commissions...

Mozart. Death is not so fastidious. Death carries no perfumed handkerchief.

The Gray Steward. Lie then against the wall. Know first that all the combinations of circumstance can suffer two interpretations, the apparent and the real.

Mozart. Then speak, sycophant;[9] I know the apparent one. What other reading can this humiliation bear?

---

9. **sycophant** (sĭkʹə-fənt): a servile flatterer.

In the dream the
steward answers
Mozart's question. He
writes music for
everyone.

The Gray Steward. It is Death itself that commands you this Requiem. You are to give a voice to all those millions sleeping, who have no one but you to speak for them. There lie the captains and the thieves, the queens and the drudges, while the evening of their earthly remembrance shuts in, and from that great field rises an eternal *miserere nobis.*[10] Only through the intercession[11] of great love can that despairing cry be eased. Was that not sufficient cause for this commission to be anonymous?

Mozart (*drops trembling on one knee beside the couch*). Forgive me.

The Gray Steward. And it was for this that the pretext and mover was chosen from among the weakest and vainest of humans. Death has her now, and all her folly has passed into the dignity and grandeur of her state. Where is your pride now? Here are her slippers and her trinkets. Press them against your lips. Again! Again! Know henceforth that only he who has kissed the leper[12] can enter the kingdom of art.

Mozart. I have sinned, yet grant me one thing. Grant that I may live to finish the Requiem.

The Gray Steward. No! No!

[*And it remains unfinished.*]

10. *miserere nobis* (mĭz′ə-râr′ē nō′bĭs): Latin for "Have mercy upon us."
11. **intercession** (ĭn′tər-sĕsh′ən): mediation; interceding on behalf of others.
12. **he...leper:** This may be an allusion to a story about Saint Francis of Assisi (1182–1226). In order to do God's will, he overcame his repugnance for lepers and forced himself to greet a leper with the kiss of peace.

I think I understand the
meaning. Great art is
not created for one
person but for all time.
Great art is more
important than pride.

But everyone knows it
was his work—right?

Looking at Yourself as a Reader

Did you have any unanswered questions at the end of the play? Did you need to look up the meanings of any words? Review your responses carefully. What aspects of the play had the greatest effect on you? Why? What was your reaction to the setting? the language? the characters? the action?

If you took your own notes, compare them with the notes alongside the selection. Do both sets of responses focus on the same elements of the play? Do you feel your response to the play shows a better grasp of its meaning?

Imagine how you might go about dramatizing an episode in the life of a famous person. If you wish, write a "three-minute" play and share it with your classmates.

A Marriage Proposal

ANTON CHEKHOV

People walking down the road to happiness often trip over their own feet. This is the message of A Marriage Proposal, *a wild, fast-paced farce set in nineteenth-century Russia. The play is about a landowner who decides to marry the girl next door. What could go wrong? You are about to find out.*

Characters

Stepan Stepanovitch Tschubukov (stě-pän′ stě-pä′nô-vĭch chōō-bōō-kôf′), a country farmer

Natalia Stepanovna (nä-täl′yə stě-pä′nôv-nə), his daughter, age twenty-five

Ivan Vassiliyitch Lomov (ĭ-vän′ vä-sĭl′ē-yĭch lô′môf), Tschubukov's neighbor

Scene: *Reception room in* Tschubukov's *country home, Russia.* Tschubukov *discovered as the curtain rises. Enter* Lomov, *wearing a dress suit.*

Tschubukov (*going toward him and greeting him*). Who is this I see? My dear fellow! Ivan Vassiliyitch! I'm so glad to see you! (*Shakes hands*) But this is a surprise! How are you?

Lomov. Thank you! And how are you?

Tschubukov. Oh, so-so, my friend. Please sit down. It isn't right to forget one's neighbor. But tell me, why all this ceremony? Dress clothes, white gloves and all? Are you on your way to some engagement, my good fellow?

Lomov. No, I have no engagement except with you, Stepan Stepanovitch.

Tschubukov. But why in evening clothes, my friend? This isn't New Year's!

Lomov. You see, it's simply this, that— (*composing himself*) I have come to you, Stepan Stepanovitch, to trouble you with a request. It is not the first time I have had the honor of turning to you for assistance, and you have always, that is—I beg your pardon, I am a bit excited! I'll take a drink of water first, dear Stepan Stepanovitch. (*He drinks.*)

Tschubukov (*aside*). He's come to borrow money! I won't give him any! (*To* Lomov) What is it, then, dear Lomov?

Lomov. You see—dear—Stepanovitch, pardon me, Stepan—Stepan—dearvitch—I mean—I am terribly nervous, as you will be so good as to see—! What I mean to say—you are the only one who can help me, though I don't deserve it, and—and I have no right whatever to make this request of you.

Tschubukov. Oh, don't beat about the bush, my dear fellow. Tell me!

Lomov. Immediately—in a moment. Here it is, then: I have come to ask for the hand of your daughter, Natalia Stepanovna.

Tschubukov (*joyfully*). Angel! Ivan Vassiliyitch! Say that once again! I didn't quite hear it!

Lomov. I have the honor to beg——

Tschubukov (*interrupting*). My dear, dear man! I am so happy that everything is so—everything! (*Embraces and kisses him*) I have wanted this to happen for so long. It has been my dearest wish! (*He represses a tear.*) And I have always loved you, my dear fellow, as my own son! May God give you His blessings and His grace and—I always wanted it to happen. But why am I standing here like a blockhead? I am completely dumbfounded with pleasure, completely dumbfounded. My whole being—I'll call Natalia——

Lomov. Dear Stepan Stepanovitch, what do you think? May I hope for Natalia Stepanovna's acceptance?

Tschubukov. Really! A fine boy like you—and you think she won't accept on the minute? Lovesick as a cat and all that—!(*He goes out right.*)

Lomov. I'm cold. My whole body is trembling as though I was going to take my examination! But the chief thing is to settle matters! If a person meditates too much, or hesitates, or talks about it, waits for an ideal or for true love, he never gets it. Brr! It's cold! Natalia is an excellent housekeeper, not at all bad-looking, well educated—what more could I ask? I'm so excited my ears are roaring! (*He drinks water.*) And not to marry, that won't do! In the first place, I'm thirty-five—a critical age, you might say. In the second place, I must live a well-regulated life. I have a weak heart, continual palpitation, and I am very sensitive and always getting excited. My lips begin to tremble and the pulse in my right temple throbs terribly. But the worst of all is sleep! I hardly lie down and begin to doze before something in my left side begins to pull and tug, and something begins to hammer in my left shoulder—and in my head, too! I jump up like a madman, walk about a little, lie down again, but the moment I fall asleep I have a terrible cramp in the side. And so it is all night long!

[*Enter* Natalia Stepanovna.]

Natalia. Ah! It's you. Papa said to go in: there was a dealer in there who'd come to buy something. Good afternoon, Ivan Vassiliyitch.

Lomov. Good day, my dear Natalia Stepanovna.

Natalia. You must pardon me for wearing my apron and this old dress: we are working today. Why haven't you come to see us oftener? You've not been here for so long! Sit down. (*They sit down.*) Won't you have something to eat?

Lomov. Thank you, I have just had lunch.

Natalia. Smoke, do, there are the matches. Today it is beautiful and only yesterday it rained so hard that the workmen couldn't do a stroke of work. How many bricks have you cut? Think of it! I was so anxious that I had the whole field mowed, and now I'm sorry I did it, because I'm afraid the hay will rot. It would have been better if I had waited. But what on earth is this? You are in evening clothes! The latest cut! Are you on your way to a ball? And you seem to be looking better, too—really. Why are you dressed up so gorgeously?

Lomov (*excited*). You see, my dear Natalia Stepanovna—it's simply this: I have decided to ask you to listen to me—of course it will be a surprise and indeed you'll be angry, but I—— (*Aside*) How fearfully cold it is!

Natalia. What is it? (*A pause*) Well?

Lomov. I'll try to be brief. My dear Natalia Stepanovna, as you know, for many years, since my childhood, I have had the honor to know your family. My poor aunt and her husband, from whom, as you know, I inherited the estate, always had the greatest respect for your father and your poor mother. The Lomovs and the Tschubukovs have been for decades on the friendliest, indeed the closest, terms with each other, and furthermore my property, as you know, adjoins your own. If you will be so good as to remember, my meadows touch your birchwoods.

Natalia. Pardon the interruption. You said "my meadows"—but are they yours?

Lomov. Yes, they belong to me.

Natalia. What nonsense! The meadows belong to us—not to you!

Lomov. No, to me! Now, my dear Natalia Stepanovna!

Natalia. Well, that is certainly news to me. How do they belong to you?

Lomov. How? I am speaking of the meadows lying between your birchwoods and my brick earth.

Natalia. Yes, exactly. They belong to us.

Lomov. No, you are mistaken, my dear Natalia Stepanovna, they belong to me.

Natalia. Try to remember exactly, Ivan Vassiliyitch. Is it so long ago that you inherited them?

Lomov. Long ago! As far back as I can remember they have always belonged to us.

Natalia. But that isn't true! You'll pardon my saying so.

Lomov. It is all a matter of record, my dear Natalia Stepanovna. It is true that at one time the title to the meadows was disputed, but now everyone knows they belong to me. There is no room for discussion. Be so good as to listen: my aunt's grandmother put these meadows, free from all costs, into the hands of your father's grandfather's peasants for a certain time while they were making bricks for my grandmother. These people used the meadows free of cost for about forty years, living there as they would on their own property. Later, however, when——

Natalia. There's not a word of truth in that! My grandfather, and my great-grandfather, too, knew that their estate reached back to the swamp, so that the meadows belong to us. What further discussion can there be? I can't understand it. It is really most annoying.

Lomov. I'll show you the papers, Natalia Stepanovna.

Natalia. No, either you are joking, or trying to lead me into a discussion. That's not at all nice! We have owned this property for nearly three hundred years, and now all at once we hear that it doesn't belong to us. Ivan Vassiliyitch, you will pardon me, but I really can't believe my ears. So far as I am concerned, the meadows are worth very little. In all they don't contain more than five acres and they are worth only a few hundred rubles,[1] say three hundred, but the injustice of the thing is what affects me. Say what you will, I can't bear injustice.

Lomov. Only listen until I have finished, please! The peasants of your respected father's grandfather, as I have already had the honor to tell you, baked bricks for my grandmother. My aunt's grandmother wished to do them a favor——

Natalia. Grandfather! Grandmother! Aunt! I know nothing about them. All I know is that the meadows belong to us, and that ends the matter.

Lomov. No, they belong to me!

Natalia. And if you keep on explaining it for two days, and put on five suits of evening clothes, the meadows are still ours, ours, ours! I don't want to take your property, but I refuse to give up what belongs to us!

Lomov. Natalia Stepanovna, I don't need the meadows, I am only concerned with the principle. If you are agreeable, I beg of you, accept them as a gift from me!

Natalia. But I can give them to you, because they belong to me! That is very peculiar, Ivan

---

1. **ruble:** the Russian unit of money.

Scene from a 1912 stage production of *A Marriage Proposal* in New York City.

Vassiliyitch! Until now we have considered you as a good neighbor and a good friend; only last year we lent you our threshing machine, so that we couldn't thresh until November, and now you treat us like thieves! You offer to give me my own land. Excuse me, but neighbors don't treat each other that way. In my opinion, it's a very low trick—to speak frankly——

Lomov. According to you I'm a usurper, then, am I? My dear lady, I have never appropriated other people's property, and I shall permit no one to accuse me of such a thing! (*He goes quickly to the bottle and drinks water.*) The meadows are mine!

Natalia. That's not the truth! They are mine!

Lomov. Mine!

Natalia. Eh? I'll prove it to you! This afternoon I'll send my reapers into the meadows.

Lomov. W–h–a–t?

Natalia. My reapers will be there today!

Lomov. And I'll chase them off!

Natalia. If you dare!

Lomov. The meadows are mine, you understand? Mine!

Natalia. Really, you needn't scream so! If you want to scream and snort and rage you may do it at home, but here please keep yourself within the limits of common decency.

Lomov. My dear lady, if it weren't that I were suffering from palpitation of the heart and hammering of the arteries in my temples, I would deal with you very differently! (*In a loud voice*) The meadows belong to me!

Natalia. Us!

Lomov. Me!

[*Enter* Tschubukov, *right.*]

Tschubukov. What's going on here? What is he yelling about?

Natalia. Papa, please tell this gentleman to whom the meadows belong, to us or to him?

Tschubukov (*to* Lomov). My dear fellow, the meadows are ours.

Lomov. But, merciful heavens, Stepan Stepanovitch, how do you make that out? You at least might be reasonable. My aunt's grandmother gave the use of the meadows free of cost to your grandfather's peasants; the peasants lived on the land for forty years and used it as their own, but later when——

Tschubukov. Permit me, my dear friend. You forget that your grandmother's peasants never paid, because there had been a lawsuit over the meadows, and everyone knows that the meadows belong to us. You haven't looked at the map.

Lomov. I'll prove to you that they belong to me!

Tschubukov. Don't try to prove it, my dear fellow.

Lomov. I will!

Tschubukov. My good fellow, what are you shrieking about? You can't prove anything by yelling, you know. I don't ask for anything that belongs to you, nor do I intend to give up anything of my own. Why should I? If it has gone so far, my dear man, that you really intend to claim the meadows, I'd rather give them to the peasants than you, and I certainly shall!

Lomov. I can't believe it! By what right can you give away property that doesn't belong to you?

Tschubukov. Really, you must allow me to decide what I am to do with my own land! I'm not accustomed, young man, to have people address me in that tone of voice. I, young man, am twice your age, and I beg you to address me respectfully.

Lomov. No! No! You think I'm a fool! You're making fun of me! You call my property yours and then expect me to stand quietly by and talk to you like a human being. That isn't the way a good neighbor behaves, Stepan Stepanovitch! You are no neighbor, you're no better than a land-grabber. That's what you are!

Tschubukov. Wh—at? What did he say?

Natalia. Papa, send the reapers into the meadows this minute!

Tschubukov (*to* Lomov). What was that you said, sir?

Natalia. The meadows belong to us and I won't give them up! I won't give them up! I won't give them up!

Lomov. We'll see about that! I'll prove in court that they belong to me.

Tschubukov. In court! You may sue in court, sir, if you like! Oh, I know you, you are only waiting to find an excuse to go to law! You're an intriguer, that's what you are! Your whole family were always looking for quarrels. The whole lot!

Lomov. Kindly refrain from insulting my family. The entire race of Lomov has always been honorable! And never has one been brought to trial for embezzlement, as your dear uncle was!

Tschubukov. And the whole Lomov family were insane!

Natalia. Every one of them!

Tschubukov. Your grandmother was a dipsomaniac, and the younger aunt, Nastasia Michailovna, ran off with an architect.

Lomov. And your mother limped. (*He puts his hand over his heart.*) Oh, my side pains! My temples are bursting! Water!

Tschubukov. And your dear father was a gambler—and a glutton!

Natalia. And your aunt was a gossip like few others!

Lomov. And you are an intriguer. Oh, my heart! And it's an open secret that you cheated at the elections—my eyes are blurred! Where is my hat?

Natalia. Oh, how low! Liar! Disgusting thing!

Lomov. Where's the hat—? My heart! Where shall I go? Where is the door—? Oh—it seems—as though I were dying! I can't—my legs won't hold me   (*Goes to the door*)

Tschubukov (*following him*). May you never darken my door again!

Natalia. Bring your suit to court! We'll see!

[Lomov *staggers out, center*]

Tschubukov (*angrily*). The devil!

Natalia. Such a good-for-nothing! And then they talk about being good neighbors!

Tschubukov. Loafer! Scarecrow! Monster!

Natalia. A swindler like that takes over a piece of property that doesn't belong to him and then dares to argue about it!

Tschubukov. And to think that this fool dares to make a proposal of marriage!

Natalia. What? A proposal of marriage?

Tschubukov. Why, yes! He came here to make you a proposal of marriage.

Natalia. Why didn't you tell me that before?

Tschubukov. That's why he had on his evening clothes! The poor fool!

Natalia. Proposal for me? Oh! (*Falls into an armchair and groans*) Bring him back! Bring him back!

Tschubukov. Bring whom back?

Natalia. Faster, faster, I'm sinking! Bring him back! (*She becomes hysterical.*)

Tschubukov. What is it? What's wrong with you (*His hands to his head*) I'm cursed with bad luck! I'll shoot myself! I'll hang myself!

Natalia. I'm dying! Bring him back!

Tschubukov. Bah! In a minute! Don't bawl! (*He rushes out, center.*)

Natalia (*groaning*). What have they done to me? Bring him back! Bring him back!

Tschubukov (*comes running in*). He's coming at once! The devil take him! Ugh! Talk to him yourself, I can't.

Natalia (*groaning*). Bring him back!

Tschubukov. He's coming, I tell you! What a task it is to be the father of a grown daughter! I'll cut my throat! I really will cut my throat! We've argued with the fellow, insulted him, and now we've thrown him out!—and you did it all, you!

Natalia. No, you! You haven't any manners, you are brutal! If it weren't for you, he wouldn't have gone!

Tschubukov. Oh, yes, I'm to blame! If I shoot or hang myself, remember *you'll* be to blame. You forced me to it! You! (Lomov *appears in the doorway*.) There, talk to him yourself! (*He goes out.*)

Lomov. Terrible palpitation!—My leg is lamed! My side hurts me——

Natalia. Pardon us, we were angry, Ivan Vassiliyitch. I remember now—the meadows really belong to you.

Lomov. My heart is beating terribly! My meadows—my eyelids tremble——(*They sit down.*) We were wrong. It was only the principle of the thing—the property isn't worth much to me, but the principle is worth a great deal.

Natalia. Exactly, the principle! Let us talk about something else.

Lomov. Because I have proofs that my aunt's grandmother had, with the peasants of your good father——

Natalia. Enough enough. (*Aside*) I don't know how to begin. (*To* Lomov) Are you going hunting soon?

Lomov. Yes, heath-cock shooting, respected

Natalia Stepanovna. I expect to begin after the harvest. Oh, did you hear? My dog, Ugadi,[2] you know him—limps!

Natalia. What a shame! How did that happen?

Lomov. I don't know. Perhaps it's a dislocation, or maybe he was bitten by some other dog. (*He sighs.*) The best dog I ever had—to say nothing of his price! I paid Mironov a hundred and twenty-five rubles for him.

Natalia. That was too much to pay, Ivan Vassiliyitch.

Lomov. In my opinion it was very cheap. A wonderful dog!

Natalia. Papa paid eighty-five rubles for his Otkatai,[3] and Otkatai is much better than your Ugadi.

Lomov. Really? Otkatai is better than Ugadi? What an idea! (*He laughs.*) Otkatai better than Ugadi!

Natalia. Of course he is better. It is true Otkatai is still young; he isn't full-grown yet, but in the pack or on the leash with two or three, there is no better than he, even——

Lomov. I really beg your pardon, Natalia Stepanovna, but you quite overlooked the fact that he has a short lower jaw, and a dog with a short lower jaw can't snap.

Natalia. Short lower jaw? That's the first time I ever heard that!

Lomov. I assure you, his lower jaw is shorter than the upper.

Natalia. Have you measured it?

Lomov. I have measured it. He is good at running, though.

Natalia. In the first place, our Otkatai is a purebred, a full-blooded son of Sapragavas and Stameskis,[4] and as for your mongrel, nobody could ever figure out his pedigree; he's old and ugly, and as skinny as an old hag.

Lomov. Old, certainly! I wouldn't take five of your Otkatais for him! Ugadi is a dog and Otkatai is—it is laughable to argue about it! Dogs like your Otkatai can be found by the dozens at any dog dealer's, a whole poundful!

Natalia. Ivan Vassiliyitch, you are very contrary today. First our meadows belong to you and then Ugadi is better than Otkatai. I don't like it when a person doesn't say what he really thinks. You know perfectly well that Otkatai is a hundred times better than your silly Ugadi. What makes you keep on saying he isn't?

Lomov. I can see, Natalia Stepanovna, that you consider me either a blindman or a fool. But at least you may as well admit that Otkatai has a short lower jaw!

Natalia. It isn't so!

Lomov. Yes, a short lower jaw!

Natalia (*loudly*). It's not so!

Lomov. What makes you scream, my dear lady?

Natalia. What makes you talk such nonsense? It's disgusting! It is high time that Ugadi was shot, and yet you compare him with Otkatai!

Lomov. Pardon me, but I can't carry on this argument any longer. I have palpitation of the heart!

Natalia. I have always noticed that the hunters who do the most talking know the least about hunting.

Lomov. My dear lady, I beg of you to be still. My heart is bursting! (*He shouts.*) Be still!

Natalia. I won't be still until you admit that Otkatai is better!

[*Enter* Tschubukov.]

Tschubukov. Well, has it begun again?

Natalia. Papa, say frankly, on your honor, which dog is better: Otkatai or Ugadi?

Lomov. Stepan Stepanovitch, I beg of you, just

---

2. **Ugadi** (o͞o-gä-dī′).
3. **Otkatai** (ät-kä-tī′).
4. **Sapragavas** (sä-prə-gä′vəs); **Stameskis** (stä-mĕs′kĭs).

answer this: has your dog a short lower jaw or not? Yes or no?

Tschubukov. And what if he has? Is it of such importance? There is no better dog in the whole country.

Lomov. My Ugadi is better. Tell the truth, now!

Tschubukov. Don't get so excited, my dear fellow! Permit me. Your Ugadi certainly has his good points. He is from a good breed, has a good stride, strong haunches, and so forth. But the dog, if you really want to know it, has two faults; he is old and he has a short lower jaw.

Lomov. Pardon me, I have palpitation of the heart!—Let us keep to facts—just remember in Maruskins' meadows, my Ugadi kept ear to ear with the Count Rasvachai and your dog.

Tschubukov. He was behind, because the Count struck him with his whip.

Lomov. Quite right. All the other dogs were on the fox's scent, but Otkatai found it necessary to bite a sheep.

Tschubukov. That isn't so!—I am sensitive about that and beg you to stop this argument. He struck him because everybody looks on a strange dog of good blood with envy. Even you, sir, aren't free from the sin. No sooner do you find a dog better than Ugadi than you begin to—this, that—his, mine—and so forth! I remember distinctly.

Lomov. I remember something, too!

Tschubukov (*mimicking him*). I remember something, too! What do you remember?

Lomov. Palpitation! My leg is lame—I can't——

Natalia. Palpitation! What kind of hunter are you? You ought to stay in the kitchen by the stove and wrestle with the potato peelings, and not go fox-hunting! Palpitation!

Tschubukov. And what kind of hunter are you? A man with your diseases ought to stay at home and not jolt around in the saddle. If you

were a hunter—! But you only ride around in order to find out about other people's dogs, and make trouble for everyone. I am sensitive! Let's drop the subject. Besides, you're no hunter.

Lomov. You only ride around to flatter the Count!—My heart! You intriguer! Swindler!

Tschubukov. And what of it? (*Shouting*) Be still!

Lomov. Intriguer!

Tschubukov. Baby! Puppy! Walking drugstore!

Lomov. Old rat! Oh, I know you!

Tschubukov. Be still! Or I'll shoot you—with my worst gun, like a partridge! Fool! Loafer!

Lomov. Everyone knows that—oh, my heart!—that your poor late wife beat you. My leg—my temples—Heavens—I'm dying—I——

Tschubukov. And your housekeeper wears the trousers in your house!

Lomov. Here—here—there—there—my heart has burst! My shoulder is torn apart. Where is my shoulder? I'm dying! (*He falls into a chair.*) The doctor! (*Faints*)

Tschubukov. Baby! Half-baked clam! Fool!

Natalia. Nice sort of hunter you are! You can't even sit on a horse. (*To Tschubukov*) Papa, what's the matter with him? (*She screams.*) Ivan Vassiliyitch! He is dead!

Lomov. I'm ill! I can't breathe! Air!

Natalia. He is dead! (*She shakes Lomov in the chair.*) Ivan Vassiliyitch! What have we done! He is dead! (*She sinks into a chair.*) The doctor—doctor! (*She goes into hysterics.*)

Tschubukov. Ahh! What is it? What's the matter with you?

Natalia (*groaning*). He's dead!—Dead!

Tschubukov. Who is dead? Who? (*Looking at Lomov*) Yes, he is dead! Water! The doctor! (*Holding the glass to Lomov's lips*) Drink! No, he won't drink! He's dead! What a terrible situation! Why didn't I shoot myself? Why have I never cut my throat? What am I waiting for now? Only give me a knife! Give me a pistol! (*Lomov moves.*) He's coming to! Drink some water—there!

Lomov. Sparks! Mists! Where am I?

Tschubukov. Get married! Quick, and then go to the devil! She's willing! (*He joins the hands of* Lomov *and* Natalia.) She's agreed! Only leave me in peace!

Lomov. Wh—what? (*Getting up*) Whom?

Tschubukov. She's willing! Well? Kiss each other and—the devil take you both!

Natalia (*groans*). He lives! Yes, yes, I'm willing!

Tschubukov. Kiss each other!

Lomov. Eh? Whom? (Natalia *and* Lomov *kiss.*) Very nice—! Pardon me, but what is this for? Oh, yes, I understand! My heart—sparks—I am happy, Natalia Stepanovna. (*He kisses her hand.*) My leg is lame!

Natalia. I'm happy, too!

Tschubukov. Ahh! A load off my shoulders! Ahh!

Natalia. And now at least you'll admit that Ugadi is worse than Otkatai!

Lomov. Better!

Natalia. Worse!

Tschubukov. Now the domestic joys have begun.—Champagne!

Lomov. Better!

Natalia. Worse, worse, worse!

Tschubukov (*trying to drown them out*). Champagne, champagne!

[*Curtain.*]

Reading Check

1. What is Lomov's purpose in coming to Tschubukov's home?
2. Why do Lomov and Natalia begin quarreling?
3. How much are the meadows worth?
4. What topic of conversation leads to the second quarrel?

For Study and Discussion

Analyzing and Interpreting the Play

1a. Why does Lomov want to marry Natalia?
b. What does he think her qualifications are?
c. Does he think she is his ideal love?

2. Considering the purpose of Lomov's visit, why is his argument with Natalia over the meadows particularly absurd?

3. Just when the characters seem to have patched up their quarrel, there is another disagreement. What causes this new conflict?

4. How does Lomov's state of health affect the outcome of the play?

5. What is ironic about the title of the play?

Literary Elements

Farce

Farces begin with an absurd situation: an unimportant lie gets someone into big trouble, or something crucial left unsaid causes a ruckus. The farcical basis of *A Marriage Proposal* is Lomov's inability to propose.

Other types of comedy begin with absurd situations. What makes a farce different is the element of **exaggeration.** While farce stops short of the pie-in-the-face physical humor of slapstick comedy, it can get fairly wild. Lomov's shrieking and fainting is a fair example.

In farce, characters are painted in broad, uncomplicated strokes. A character's every gesture and reaction is typical of that character. The characters do not have subtle internal contradictions.

Choose one of the episodes in the play and describe the farcical elements of character and situation.

Language and Vocabulary

Determining Precise Meanings

While they are trading insults, Lomov claims that Tschubukov's uncle was brought to trial as an *embezzler*. Shortly thereafter Natalia calls Lomov a *swindler*. The words *embezzler* and *swindler* are close in meaning, but they are not synonyms. *To embezzle* is to steal money or property that has been entrusted to one's care. *To swindle* is to use fraud or trickery to get money from someone else.

Look at the italicized words in this speech:

According to you I'm a *usurper*, then, am I? My dear lady, I have never *appropriated* other people's property . . .

Check the precise meanings of the verbs *usurp* and *appropriate* in a dictionary.

Focus on Persuasive Writing

Choosing a Topic for Persuasion

The purpose of **persuasive writing** is to get your readers to adopt a certain opinion or perform an action or do both. A suitable topic for a persuasive essay is one on which people can have conflicting or opposing opinions. For example, in *A Marriage Proposal* Lomov argues with Natalia and Tschubukov about who owns the land and about whose dog is better.

When you choose a topic for your own persuasive writing, follow these steps:

1. Be sure that the topic is an issue about which people can have opinions, rather than a matter of facts, which are either true or false →
2. Identify the audience that you want to convince →
3. State your own opinion about the topic in one or two sentences

Scan some recent issues of your school or community paper. You might want to pay special attention to the editorial section. List two issues that you care about. Write a statement of your opinion on each issue. Save your notes.

About the Author

Anton Chekhov   (1860–1904)

Chekhov was born in Taganrog (tăg'ən-räg'), a tiny Russian town he later described as "dirty and dull, with deserted streets and a lazy, ignorant population." His father was a shop-keeper who loved the arts, tyrannized his family, and neglected his business so much that Anton and his brothers and sister grew up in poverty. In 1879, Chekhov moved to Moscow to study medicine. But most of his time was spent writing short stories and sketches, which he sold to literary magazines to support his family. Gradually, Chekhov practiced medicine less and less and began writing plays. First came a series of one-act comedies. *A Marriage Proposal* was among them. *Ivanov*, his first major play, was produced in 1887. It was followed by *The Sea Gull, Uncle Vanya, The Three Sisters*, and *The Cherry Orchard*.

In Chekhov's best writing, human nature is explored with scientific precision and loving compassion simultaneously. This is no small accomplishment. His characters frequently stop listening to each other, constantly contradict themselves, and always make up excuses for their own failings. Yet Chekhov was able to use these shortcomings in human nature to make his audiences laugh, and perhaps understand themselves a little better.

Visit to a Small Planet

GORE VIDAL

Farce is one kind of comedy; satire *is another. Satire holds up to ridicule certain human weaknesses or wrongdoings. What are the targets of Vidal's satire in this science-fiction teleplay?*

Characters

Kreton	Aide
Roger Spelding	Paul Laurent
Ellen Spelding	Second Visitor
Mrs. Spelding	President of Paraguay
John Randolph	Technicians
General Powers	Soldiers

Act One

Stock Shot:[1] *The night sky, stars. Then slowly a luminous object arcs into view. As it is almost upon us,* dissolve to[2] *the living room of the Spelding house in Maryland.*

Superimpose card: "The Time: The Day After Tomorrow"

The room is comfortably balanced between the expensively decorated and the homely. Roger Spelding *is concluding his TV broadcast. He is middle aged, unctuous[3], resonant. His wife, bored and vague, knits passively while he talks at his desk. Two Technicians are on hand, operating the equipment. His daughter,* Ellen, *a lively girl of twenty, fidgets as she listens.*

Spelding (*into microphone*). . . . and so, according to General Powers . . . who should know if anyone does . . . the flying object which has given rise to so much irresponsible conjecture is nothing more than a meteor passing through the earth's orbit. It is not, as many believe, a secret weapon of this country. Nor is it a spaceship as certain lunatic elements have suggested. General Powers has assured me that it is highly doubtful there is any form of life on other planets capable of building a spaceship. "If any traveling is to be done in space, we will do it first." And those are his exact words. . . .

Which winds up another week of news. (*Crosses to pose with wife and daughter*) This is Roger Spelding, saying good night to Mother and Father America, from my old homestead in Silver Glen, Maryland, close to the warm pulsebeat of the nation.

Technician. Good show tonight, Mr. Spelding.

Spelding. Thank you.

Technician. Yes sir, you were right on time.

---

1. **Stock shot:** film footage taken from the television studio's library rather than made specifically for the project at hand.
2. **dissolve to:** to cause one image to disappear while a second image appears simultaneously.
3. **unctuous** (ŭngk′choo-əs): falsely earnest.

[Spelding *nods wearily, his mechanical smile and heartiness suddenly gone.*]

Mrs. Spelding. Very nice, dear. Very nice.
Technician. See you next week, Mr. Spelding.
Spelding. Thank you, boys.

[Technicians *go.*]

Spelding. Did you like the broadcast, Ellen?
Ellen. Of course I did, Daddy.
Spelding. Then what did I say?
Ellen. Oh, that's not fair.
Spelding. It's not very flattering when one's own daughter won't listen to what one says while millions of people . . .
Ellen. I always listen, Daddy, you know that.
Mrs. Spelding. We love your broadcasts, dear. I don't know what we'd do without them.

Spelding. Starve.
Ellen. I wonder what's keeping John?
Spelding. Certainly not work.
Ellen. Oh, Daddy, stop it! John works very hard and you know it.
Mrs. Spelding. Yes, he's a perfectly nice boy, Roger. I like him.
Spelding. I know, I know; he has every virtue except the most important one: he has no get-up-and-go.
Ellen (*precisely*). He doesn't want to get up and he doesn't want to go because he's already where he wants to be on his own farm, which is exactly where *I'm* going to be when we're married.
Spelding. More thankless than a serpent's tooth is an ungrateful child.[4]

4. **More . . . child:** The Speldings are misquoting lines from *King Lear* by William Shakespeare. The correct quotation is "How sharper than a serpent's tooth it is/To have a thankless child!" (I, 4, 312)

Ellen. I don't think that's right. Isn't it "more deadly . . ."

Spelding. Whatever the exact quotation is, I stand by the sentiment.

Mrs. Spelding. Please don't quarrel. It always gives me a headache.

Spelding. I never quarrel. I merely reason, in my simple way, with Miss Know-it-all here.

Ellen. Oh, Daddy! Next you'll tell me I should marry for money.

Spelding. There is nothing wrong with marrying a wealthy man. The horror of it has always eluded me. However, my only wish is that you marry someone hard-working, ambitious, a man who'll make his mark in the world. Not a boy who plans to sit on a farm all his life, growing peanuts.

Ellen. English walnuts.

Spelding. Will you stop correcting me?

Ellen. But, Daddy, John grows walnuts . . .

[John *enters, breathlessly.*]

John. Come out! Quickly. It's coming this way. It's going to land right here!

Spelding. *What's* going to land?

John. The spaceship. Look!

Spelding. Apparently you didn't hear my broadcast. The flying object in question is a meteor, not a spaceship.

[John *has gone out with* Ellen. Spelding *and* Mrs. Spelding *follow.*]

Mrs. Spelding. Oh, my! Look! Something *is* falling! Roger, you don't think it's going to hit the house, do you?

Spelding. The odds against being hit by a falling object that size are, I should say, roughly ten million to one.

John. Ten million to one or not, it's going to land right here and it's *not* falling.

Spelding. I'm sure it's a meteor.

Mrs. Spelding. Shouldn't we go down to the cellar?

Spelding. If it's not a meteor, it's an optical illusion . . . mass hysteria.

Ellen. Daddy, it's a real spaceship. I'm sure it is.

Spelding. Or maybe a weather balloon. Yes, that's what it is. General Powers said only yesterday . . .

John. It's landing!

Spelding. I'm going to call the police . . . the army! (*Bolts inside*)

Ellen. Oh, look how it shines!

John. Here it comes!

Mrs. Spelding. Right in my rose garden!

Ellen. Maybe it's a balloon.

John. No, it's a spaceship and right in your own backyard.

Ellen. What makes it shine so?

John. I don't know but I'm going to find out. (*Runs off toward the light*)

Ellen. Oh, darling, don't! John, please! John, John, come back!

[Spelding, *wide-eyed, returns.*]

Mrs. Spelding. Roger, it's landed right in my rose garden.

Spelding. I got General Powers. He's coming over. He said they've been watching this thing. They . . . they don't know what it is.

Ellen. You mean it's nothing of ours?

Spelding. They believe it . . . (*swallows hard*) . . . it's from outer space.

Ellen. And John's down there! Daddy, get a gun or something.

Spelding. Perhaps we'd better leave the house until the army gets here.

Ellen. We can't leave John.

Spelding. I can. (*Peers nearsightedly*) Why, it's not much larger than a car. I'm sure it's some kind of meteor.

Ellen. Meteors are blazing hot.

Spelding. This is a cold one . . .

Ellen. It's opening . . . the whole side's opening! (*Shouts*) John! Come back! Quick. . . .

Mrs. Spelding. Why, there's a man getting out of it! (*Sighs*) I feel much better already. I'm sure if we ask him, he'll move that thing for us. Roger, you ask him.

Spelding (*ominously*). If it's really a man?

Ellen. John's shaking hands with him. (*Calls*) John darling, come on up here . . .

Mrs. Spelding. And bring your friend . . .

Spelding. There's something wrong with the way that creature looks . . . if it is a man and not a . . . not a monster.

Mrs. Spelding. He looks perfectly nice to me.

[John *and the* Visitor *appear. The* Visitor *is in his forties, a mild, pleasant-looking man with side whiskers and dressed in the fashion of 1860. He pauses when he sees the three people, in silence for a moment. They stare back at him, equally interested.*]

Visitor. I seem to've made a mistake. I *am* sorry. I'd better go back and start over again.

Spelding. My dear sir, you've only just arrived. Come in, come in. I don't need to tell you what a pleasure this is . . . Mister . . . Mister . . .

Visitor. Kreton . . . This *is* the wrong costume, isn't it?

Spelding. Wrong for what?

Kreton. For the country, and the time.

Spelding. Well, it's a trifle old-fashioned.

Mrs. Spelding. But really awfully handsome.

Kreton. Thank you.

Mrs. Spelding (*to husband*). Ask him about moving that thing off my rose bed.

[Spelding *leads them all into living room.*]

Spelding. Come on in and sit down. You must be tired after your trip.

Kreton. Yes, I am a little. (*Looks around delightedly*) Oh, it's better than I'd hoped!

Spelding. Better? What's better?

Kreton. The house . . . that's what you call it? Or is this an apartment?

Spelding. This is a house in the State of Maryland, U.S.A.

Kreton. In the late twentieth century! To think this is really the twentieth century. I must sit down a moment and collect myself. The *real* thing! (*He sits down.*)

Ellen. You . . . you're not an American, are you?

Kreton. What a nice thought! No, I'm not.

John. You sound more English.

Kreton. Do I? Is my accent very bad?

John. No, it's quite good.

Spelding. Where *are* you from, Mr. Kreton?

Kreton (*evasively*). Another place.

Spelding. On this earth, of course.

Kreton. No, not on this planet.

Ellen. Are you from Mars?

Kreton. Oh dear, no, not Mars. There's nobody on Mars . . . at least no one I know.

Ellen. I'm sure you're testing us and this is all some kind of publicity stunt.

Kreton. No, I really am from another place.

Spelding. I don't suppose you'd consent to my interviewing you on television?

Kreton. I don't think your authorities will like that. They are terribly upset as it is.

Spelding. How do you know?

Kreton. Well, I . . . pick up things. For instance, I know that in a few minutes a couple of people from your army will be here to question me and they . . . like you . . . are torn by doubt.

Spelding. How extraordinary!

Ellen. Why did you come here?

Kreton. Simply a visit to your small planet. I've been studying it for years. In fact, one might say, you people are my hobby. Especially this period of your development.

Scene from a 1957 stage production of *Visit to a Small Planet*.
New York Public Library

John. Are you the first person from your . . . your planet to travel in space like this?

Kreton. Oh my, no! Everyone travels who wants to. It's just that no one wants to visit you. I can't think why. *I* always have. You'd be surprised what a thorough study I've made. (*Recites*) The planet, Earth, is divided into five continents with a number of large islands. It is mostly water. There is one moon. Civilization is only just beginning. . . .

Spelding. Just beginning! My dear sir, we have had . . .

Kreton (*blandly*). You are only in the initial stages, the most fascinating stage as far as I'm concerned . . . I do hope I don't sound patronizing.

Ellen. Well, we are very proud.

Kreton. I know, and that's one of your most endearing, primitive traits. Oh, I can't believe I'm here at last!

[General Powers, *a vigorous product of the National Guard, and his* Aide *enter.*]

Powers. All right, folks. The place is surrounded by troops. Where is the monster?

Kreton. I, my dear General, am the monster.

Powers. What are you dressed up for, a fancy-dress party?

Kreton. I'd hoped to be in the costume of the period. As you see, I am about a hundred years too late.

Powers. Roger, who is this joker?

Spelding. This is Mr. Kreton . . . General Powers. Mr. Kreton arrived in that thing outside. He is from another planet.

Powers. I don't believe it.

Ellen. It's true. We saw him get out of the flying saucer.

Powers (*to* Aide). Captain, go down and look at that ship. But be careful. Don't touch anything. And don't let anybody else near it. (Aide *goes.*) So you're from another planet.

Kreton. Yes. My, that's a very smart uniform but I prefer the ones made of metal, the ones you used to wear, you know: with the feathers on top.

Powers. That was five hundred years ago . . . Are you *sure* you're not from the Earth?

Kreton. Yes.

Powers. Well, I'm not. You've got some pretty tall explaining to do.

Kreton. Anything to oblige.

Visit to a Small Planet **427**

Powers. All right, which planet?

Kreton. None that you have ever heard of.

Powers. Where is it?

Kreton. You wouldn't know.

Powers. This solar system?

Kreton. No.

Powers. Another system?

Kreton. Yes.

Powers. Look, Buster, I don't want to play games: I just want to know where you're from. The law requires it.

Kreton. It's possible that I could explain it to a mathematician but I'm afraid I couldn't explain it to you, not for another five hundred years and by then of course *you'd* be dead because you people do die, don't you?

Powers. What?

Kreton. Poor fragile butterflies, such brief little moments in the sun . . . You see, *we* don't die.

Powers. You'll die all right if it turns out you're a spy or a hostile alien.

Kreton. I'm sure you wouldn't be so cruel.

[Aide *returns; he looks disturbed*.]

Powers. What did you find?

Aide. I'm not sure, General.

Powers (*heavily*). Then do your best to describe what the object is like.

Aide. Well, it's elliptical, with a fourteen-foot diameter. And it's made of an unknown metal which shines and inside there isn't anything.

Powers. Isn't anything?

Aide. There's nothing inside the ship: no instruments, no food, nothing.

Powers (*to Kreton*). What did you do with your instrument board?

Kreton. With my what? Oh, I don't have one.

Powers. How does the thing travel?

Kreton. I don't know.

Powers. You don't know. Now look, mister, you're in pretty serious trouble. I suggest you do a bit of cooperating. You claim you traveled here from outer space in a machine with no instruments . . .

Kreton. Well, these cars are rather common in my world and I suppose, once upon a time, I must've known the theory on which they operate but I've long since forgotten. After all, General, we're not mechanics, you and I.

Powers. Roger, do you mind if we use your study?

Spelding. Not at all. Not at all, General.

Powers. Mr. Kreton and I are going to have a chat. (*To* Aide) Put in a call to the Chief of Staff.

Aide. Yes, General.

[Spelding *rises, leads* Kreton *and* Powers *into next room, a handsomely furnished study, many books and a globe of the world.*]

Spelding. This way, gentlemen.

[Kreton *sits down comfortably beside the globe, which he twirls thoughtfully. At the door,* Spelding *speaks in a low voice to* Powers.]

I hope I'll be the one to get the story first, Tom.

Powers. There isn't any story. Complete censorship. I'm sorry but this house is under martial law. I've a hunch we're in trouble.

[*He shuts the door.* Spelding *turns and rejoins his family.*]

Ellen. I think he's wonderful, whoever he is.

Mrs. Spelding. I wonder how much damage he did to my rose garden . . .

John. It's sure hard to believe he's really from outer space. No instruments, no nothing . . . boy, they must be advanced scientifically.

Mrs. Spelding. Is he spending the night, dear?

Spelding. What?

Mrs. Spelding. Is he spending the night?

Spelding. Oh yes, yes, I suppose he will be.

Mrs. Spelding. Then I'd better go make up the bedroom. He seems perfectly nice to me. I like his whiskers. They're so very . . . comforting. Like Grandfather Spelding's. (*She goes.*)

Spelding (*bitterly*). I *know* this story will leak out before I can interview him. I just know it.

Ellen. What does it mean, we're under martial law?

Spelding. It means we have to do what General Powers tells us to do. (*He goes to the window as a* Soldier *passes by.*) See?

John. I wish I'd taken a closer look at that ship when I had the chance.

Ellen. Perhaps he'll give us a ride in it.

John. Traveling in space! Just like those stories. You know: intergalactic drive stuff.

Spelding. *If* he's not an impostor.

Ellen. I have a feeling he isn't.

John. Well, I better call the family and tell them I'm all right.

[*He crosses to telephone by the door which leads into hall*.]

Aide. I'm sorry, sir, but you can't use the phone.

Spelding. He certainly can. This is my house . . .

Aide (*mechanically*). This house is a military reservation until the crisis is over: order General Powers. I'm sorry.

John. How am I to call home to say where I am?

Aide. Only General Powers can help you. You're also forbidden to leave this house without permission.

Spelding. You can't do this!

Aide. I'm afraid, sir, we've done it.

Ellen. Isn't it exciting!

[Cut to[5] *study*.]

Powers. Are you deliberately trying to confuse me?

Kreton. Not deliberately, no.

Powers. We have gone over and over this for two hours now and all that you've told me is that you're from another planet in another solar system . . .

Kreton. In another dimension. I think that's the word you use.

Powers. In another dimension and you have come here as a tourist.

Kreton. Up to a point, yes. What did you expect?

Powers. It is my job to guard the security of this country.

Kreton. I'm sure that must be very interesting work.

Powers. For all I know, you are a spy, sent here by an alien race to study us, preparatory to invasion.

5. **Cut to:** to change the camera angle or scene abruptly, without using a dissolve.

Kreton. Oh, none of my people would *dream* of invading you.

Powers. How do I know that's true?

Kreton. You don't, so I suggest you believe me. I should also warn you: I can tell what's inside.

Powers. What's inside?

Kreton. What's inside your mind.

Powers. You're a mind reader?

Kreton. I don't really read it. I hear it.

Powers. What am I thinking?

Kreton. That I am either a lunatic from the earth or a spy from another world.

Powers. Correct. But then you could've guessed that. (*Frowns*) What am I thinking now?

Kreton. You're making a picture. Three silver stars. You're pinning them on your shoulder, instead of the two stars you now wear.

Powers (*startled*). That's right. I was thinking of my promotion.

Kreton. If there's anything I can do to hurry it along, just let me know.

Powers. You can. Tell me why you're here.

Kreton. Well, we don't travel much, my people. We used to, but since we see everything through special monitors and re-creators, there is no particular need to travel. However, *I* am a hobbyist. I love to gad about.

Powers (*taking notes*). Are you the first to visit us?

Kreton. Oh, no! We started visiting you long before there were people on the planet. However, we are seldom noticed on our trips. I'm sorry to say I slipped up, coming in the way I did . . . but then this visit was all rather impromptu. (*Laughs*) I am a creature of impulse, I fear.

[Aide *looks in*.]

Aide. Chief of Staff on the telephone, General.

Powers (*picks up phone*). Hello, yes, sir. Powers

speaking. I'm talking to him now. No, sir. No, sir. No, we can't determine what method of power was used. He won't talk. Yes, sir. I'll hold him there. I've put the house under martial law . . . belongs to a friend of mine, Roger Spelding, the TV commentator. Roger Spelding, the TV . . . What? Oh, no, I'm sure he won't say anything. Who . . . oh, yes, sir. Yes, I realize the importance of it. Yes, I will. Goodbye. (*Hangs up*) The President of the United States wants to know all about you.

Kreton. How nice of him! And I want to know all about him. But I do wish you'd let me rest a bit first. Your language is still not familiar to me. I had to learn them all, quite exhausting.

Powers. You speak *all* our languages?

Kreton. Yes, all of them. But then it's easier than you might think since I can see what's inside.

Powers. Speaking of what's inside, we're going to take your ship apart.

Kreton. Oh, I wish you wouldn't.

Powers. Security demands it.

Kreton. In that case *my* security demands you leave it alone.

Powers. You plan to stop us?

Kreton. I already have. . . . Listen.

[*Far-off shouting.* Aide *rushes into the study.*]

Aide. Something's happened to the ship, General. The door's shut and there's some kind of wall all around it, an invisible wall. We can't get near it.

Kreton (*to camera*). I hope there was no one inside.

Powers (*to Kreton*). How did you do that?

Kreton. I couldn't begin to explain. Now if you don't mind, I think we should go in and see our hosts.

[*He rises, goes into living room.* Powers *and* Aide *look at each other.*]

Powers. Don't let him out of your sight.

[Cut to *living room as* Powers *picks up phone.* Kreton *is with* John *and* Ellen.]

Kreton. I don't mind curiosity but I really can't permit them to wreck my poor ship.

Ellen. What do you plan to do, now you're here?

Kreton. Oh, keep busy. I have a project or two. . . . (*Sighs*) I can't believe you're real.

John. Then we're all in the same boat.

Kreton. Boat? Oh, yes! Well, I should have come ages ago but I . . . I couldn't get away until yesterday.

John. Yesterday? It only took you a *day* to get here?

Kreton. One of *my* days, not yours. But then you don't know about time yet.

John. Oh, you mean relativity.

Kreton. No, it's much more involved than that. You won't know about time until . . . now let me see if I remember . . . no, I don't, but it's about two thousand years.

John. What do we do between now and then?

Kreton. You simply go on the way you are, living your exciting primitive lives . . . you have no idea how much fun you're having now.

Ellen. I hope you'll stay with us while you're here.

Kreton. That's very nice of you. Perhaps I will. Though I'm sure you'll get tired of having a visitor underfoot all the time.

Ellen. Certainly not. And Daddy will be deliriously happy. He can interview you by the hour.

John. What's it like in outer space?

Kreton. Dull.

Ellen. I should think it would be divine!

[Powers *enters.*]

Kreton. No, General, it won't work.

Powers. What won't work?
Kreton. Trying to blow up my little force field.[6] You'll just plow up Mrs. Spelding's garden.

[Powers *snarls and goes into study.*]

Ellen. Can you tell what we're *all* thinking?
Kreton. Yes. As a matter of fact, it makes me a bit giddy. Your minds are not at all like ours. You see, we control our thoughts while you . . . well, it's extraordinary the things you think about!
Ellen. Oh, how awful! You can tell *everything* we think?
Kreton. Everything! It's one of the reasons I'm here, to intoxicate myself with your primitive minds . . . with the wonderful rawness of your emotions! You have no idea how it excites me! You simply seethe with unlikely emotions.
Ellen. I've never felt so sordid.
John. From now on I'm going to think about agriculture.
Spelding (*entering*). You would.
Ellen. Daddy!
Kreton. No, no. You must go right on thinking about Ellen. Such wonderfully *purple* thoughts!
Spelding. Now see here, Powers, you're carrying this martial law thing too far . . .
Powers. Unfortunately, until I have received word from Washington as to the final disposition of this problem, you must obey my orders: no telephone calls, no communication with the outside.
Spelding. This is unsupportable.
Kreton. Poor Mr. Spelding! If you like, I shall go. That would solve everything, wouldn't it?
Powers. You're not going anywhere, Mr. Kreton, until I've had my instructions.
Kreton. I sincerely doubt if you could stop me.

6. **force field:** a space inside of which electrical or magnetic energies are active.

However, I put it up to Mr. Spelding. Shall I go?
Spelding. Yes! (Powers *gestures a warning.*) Do stay, I mean, we want you to get a good impression of us . . .
Kreton. And of course you still want to be the first journalist to interview me. Fair enough. All right, I'll stay on for a while.
Powers. Thank you.
Kreton. Don't mention it.
Spelding. General, may I ask our guest a few questions?
Powers. Go right ahead, Roger. I hope you'll do better than I did.
Spelding. Since you read our minds, you probably already know what our fears are.
Kreton. I do, yes.
Spelding. We are afraid that you represent a hostile race.
Kreton. And I have assured General Powers that my people are not remotely hostile. Except for me, no one is interested in this planet's present stage.
Spelding. Does this mean you might be interested in a *later* stage?
Kreton. I'm not permitted to discuss your future. Of course my friends think me perverse to be interested in a primitive society, but there's no accounting for tastes, is there? You are my hobby. I love you. And that's all there is to it.
Powers. So you're just here to look around . . . sort of going native.
Kreton. What a nice expression! That's it exactly. I am going native.
Powers (*grimly*). Well, it is my view that you have been sent here by another civilization for the express purpose of reconnoitering prior to invasion.
Kreton. That *would* be your view! The wonderfully primitive assumption that all strangers are hostile. You're almost too good to be true, General.

Powers. You deny your people intend to make trouble for us?

Kreton. I deny it.

Powers. Then are they interested in establishing communication with us? Trade? That kind of thing?

Kreton. We have always had communication with you. As for trade, well, we do not trade . . . that is something peculiar only to your social level. (*Quickly*) Which I'm not criticizing! As you know, I approve of everything you do.

Powers. I give up.

Spelding. You have no interest then in . . . well, trying to dominate the earth.

Kreton. Oh, yes!

Powers. I thought you just said your people weren't interested in us.

Kreton. *They're* not, but *I* am.

Powers. You!

Kreton. Me . . . I mean I. You see, I've come here to take charge.

Powers. Of the United States?

Kreton. No, of the whole world. I'm sure you'll be much happier and it will be great fun for me. You'll get used to it in no time.

Powers. This is ridiculous. How can one man take over the world?

Kreton (*gaily*). Wait and see!

Powers (*to* Aide). Grab him!

[Powers *and* Aide *rush* Kreton *but within a foot of him, they stop, stunned.*]

Kreton. You can't touch me. That's part of the game. (*He yawns.*) Now, if you don't mind, I shall go up to my room for a little lie-down.

Spelding. I'll show you the way.

Kreton. That's all right, I know the way. (*Touches his brow*) Such savage thoughts! My head is vibrating like a drum. I feel quite giddy, all of you thinking away. (*He starts to the door; he pauses beside* Mrs. Spelding.) No, it's not a dream, dear lady. I shall be here in the morn-

ing when you wake up. And now, good night, dear, wicked children. . . .

[*He goes as we* fade out.]

Reading Check

1. Why does Spelding disapprove of Ellen's beau?
2. Where does the spaceship land?
3. Why does Kreton think he has made a mistake?
4. How does Kreton prevent the soldiers from taking his spaceship apart?
5. According to Kreton, why has he come to the earth?

For Study and Discussion

Analyzing and Interpreting the Play

1a. How does the setting of Spelding's newscast differ from that of a typical newscast today? **b.** What is the significance of setting the play in Maryland, close to "the warm pulsebeat of the nation"?

2. Compare the reactions of the different characters to the landing of the spaceship. Of these reactions, which do you think is the most appropriate and why?

3. "I do hope I don't sound patronizing," Kreton says at one point. **a.** List some instances in which Kreton does behave in a patronizing manner. **b.** What powers or qualities does Kreton have that make him superior to people on Earth? **c.** Why is his playfulness both amusing and sinister?

4a. What is absurd about Powers' angry, threatening attitude? **b.** What is ironic about Powers' belief that Kreton represents a hostile race?

Visit to a Small Planet **433**

5. At the end of the act, the conflict of the play becomes apparent. State the conflict in terms of who wants what.

Language and Vocabulary

Finding Meanings of Modifiers

A number of Vidal's stage directions are adverbs that tell the actors precisely how to deliver their speeches. When Spelding sees Kreton getting out of the spaceship, he speaks *ominously* (page 426). When Kreton is asked where he comes from, he responds *evasively* (page 426). In referring to the primitive state of civilization on earth, Kreton speaks *blandly* (page 427). The aide who keeps John from using the telephone answers questions *mechanically* (page 430).

Find the exact meanings of these adverbs and demonstrate how each speech would be spoken.

Act Two

Fade in on[1] *Kreton's bedroom next morning. He lies fully clothed on bed with cat in his lap.*

Kreton. Poor cat! Of course I sympathize with you. Dogs *are* distasteful. What? Oh, I can well believe they do: yes, yes, how disgusting. They don't ever groom their fur! But you do *constantly,* such a fine coat. No, no, I'm not just saying that, I really mean it: exquisite texture. Of course, I wouldn't say it was *nicer* than skin but even so . . . What? Oh, no! They *chase* you! Dogs chase you for no reason at all except pure malice? You poor creature. Ah, but you *do* fight back! That's right! Give it to them: slash, bite, scratch! Don't let them get away with a

---
1. **Fade in on:** to cause an image to appear gradually on the screen in place of darkness.

trick . . . No! Do dogs really do that? Well, I'm sure *you* don't. What . . . oh, well, yes, I completely agree about mice. They *are* delicious! (Ugh!) Pounce, snap, and there is a heavenly dinner. No, I don't know any mice yet . . . they're not very amusing? But, after all, think how you must terrify them because you are so bold, so cunning, so beautifully predatory! (*Knock at door*) Come in.

Ellen (*enters*). Good morning. I brought you your breakfast.

Kreton. How thoughtful! (*Examines bacon*) Delicious, but I'm afraid my stomach is not like yours, if you'll pardon me. I don't eat. (*Removes pill from his pocket and swallows it*) This is all I need for the day. (*Indicates cat*) Unlike this creature, who would eat her own weight every hour, given a chance.

Ellen. How do you know?

Kreton. We've had a talk.

Ellen. You can *speak* to the cat?

Kreton. Not speak exactly, but we communicate. I look inside and the cat cooperates. Bright red thoughts, very exciting, though rather on one level.

Ellen. Does kitty like us?

Kreton. No, I wouldn't say she did. But then she has very few thoughts not connected with food. Have you, my quadruped criminal? (*He strokes the cat, which jumps to the floor.*)

Ellen. You know you've really upset everyone.

Kreton. I supposed that I would.

Ellen. Can you really take over the world, just like that?

Kreton. Oh, yes.

Ellen. What do you plan to do when you *have* taken over?

Kreton. Ah, that is my secret.

Ellen. Well, I think you'll be a very nice President, *if* they let you, of course.

Kreton. What a sweet girl you are! Marry him right away.

Ellen. Marry John?

Kreton. Yes. I see it in your head *and* in his. He wants you very much.

Ellen. Well, we plan to get married this summer, if Father doesn't fuss too much.

Kreton. Do it before then. I shall arrange it all if you like.

Ellen. How?

Kreton. I can convince your father.

Ellen. That sounds awfully ominous. I think you'd better leave poor Daddy alone.

Kreton. Whatever you say. (*Sighs*) Oh, I love it so! When I woke up this morning I had to pinch myself to prove I was really here.

Ellen. We were all doing a bit of pinching too. Ever since dawn we've had nothing but visitors and phone calls and troops outside in the garden. No one has the faintest idea what to do about you.

Kreton. Well, I don't think they'll be confused much longer.

Ellen. How do you plan to conquer the world?

Kreton. I confess I'm not sure. I suppose I must make some demonstration of strength, some colorful trick that will frighten everyone . . . though I much prefer taking charge quietly. That's why I've sent for the President.

Ellen. The President? *Our* President?

Kreton. Yes, he'll be along any minute now.

Ellen. But the President just doesn't go around visiting people.

Kreton. He'll visit me. (*Chuckles*) It may come as a surprise to him, but he'll be in this house in a few minutes. I think we'd better go downstairs now. (*To cat*) No, I will not give you a mouse. You must get your own. Be self-reliant. Beast!

[*Dissolve to* the study. Powers *is reading book entitled* The Atom and You. *Muffled explosions offstage.*]

Aide (*entering*) Sir, nothing seems to be working. Do we have the General's permission to try a fission bomb on the force field?

Powers. No . . . no. We'd better give it up.

Aide. The men are beginning to talk.

Powers (*thundering*). Well, keep them quiet! (*Contritely*) I'm sorry, Captain. I'm on edge. Fortunately, the whole business will soon be in the hands of the World Council.

Aide. What will the World Council do?

Powers. It will be interesting to observe them.

Aide. You don't think this Kreton can really take over the world, do you?

Powers. Of course not. Nobody can.

[*Dissolve to* living room. *Mrs. Spelding* and Spelding *are talking.*]

Mrs. Spelding. You still haven't asked Mr. Kreton about moving that thing, have you?

Spelding. There are too many *important* things to ask him.

Mrs. Spelding. I hate to be a nag but you know the trouble I have had getting anything to grow in that part of the garden . . .

John (*enters*). Good morning.

Mrs. Spelding. Good morning, John.

John. Any sign of your guest?

Mrs. Spelding. Ellen took his breakfast up to him a few minutes ago.

John. They don't seem to be having much luck, do they? I sure hope you don't mind my staying here like this.

[*Spelding* glowers.]

Mrs. Spelding. Why, we love having you! I just hope your family aren't too anxious.

John. One of the GI's finally called them, said I was staying here for the weekend.

Spelding. The rest of our *lives*, if something isn't done soon.

John. Just how long do you think that'll be, Dad?

Spelding. Who knows?

[Kreton *and* Ellen *enter.*]

Kreton. Ah, how wonderful to see you again! Let me catch my breath. . . . Oh, your minds!

It's not easy for me, you know. So many crude thoughts blazing away! Yes, Mrs. Spelding, I will move the ship off your roses.

Mrs. Spelding. That's awfully sweet of you.

Kreton. Mr. Spelding, if any interviews are to be granted, you will be first. I promise you.

Spelding. That's very considerate, I'm sure.

Kreton. So you can stop thinking *those* particular thoughts. And now where is the President?

Spelding. The President?

Kreton. Yes, I sent for him. He should be here. (*He goes to the terrace window.*) Ah, that must be he. (*A swarthy* Man *in uniform with a sash across his chest is standing, bewildered, on the terrace.* Kreton *opens the glass doors.*) Come in, sir, come in, Your Excellency. Good of you to come on such short notice.

[Man *enters.*]

Man (*in Spanish accent*). Where am I?

Kreton. You *are* the President, aren't you?

Man. Of course I am the President. What am I doing here? I was dedicating a bridge and I find myself . . .

Kreton (*aware of his mistake*). Oh, dear! *Where* was the bridge?

Man. Where do you think, you idiot, in Paraguay!

Kreton (*to others*). I seem to've made a mistake. Wrong President. (*Gestures and the* Man *disappears.*) Seemed rather upset, didn't he?

John. You can make people come and go just like that?

Kreton. Just like that.

[Powers *looks into room from the study.*]

Powers. Good morning, Mr. Kreton. Could I see you for a moment?

Kreton. By all means. (*He crosses to the study.*)

Spelding. I believe I am going mad.

[Cut to *study. The* Aide *stands at attention while* Powers *addresses* Kreton.]

Powers. . . . and so we feel, the government of the United States feels, that this problem is too big for any one country; therefore we are turning the whole affair over to Paul Laurent, the Secretary-General of the World Council.

Kreton. Very sensible, I should've thought of that myself.

Powers. Mr. Laurent is on his way here now. And I may add, Mr. Kreton, you've made me look singularly ridiculous.

Kreton. I'm awfully sorry. (*Pause*) No, you can't kill me.

Powers. You were reading my mind again.

Kreton. I can't really help it, you know. And such *black* thoughts today, but intense, very intense.

Powers. I regard you as a menace.

Kreton. I know you do and I think it's awfully unkind. I do mean well.

Powers. Then go back where you came from and leave us alone.

Kreton. I'm afraid I can't do that just yet . . .

[*Phone rings; the* Aide *answers it.*]

Aide. He's outside? Sure, let him through. (*To* Powers) The Secretary-General of the World Council is here, sir.

Powers (*to* Kreton). I hope you'll listen to *him*.

Kreton. Oh, I shall, of course. I love listening.

[*The door opens and* Paul Laurent, *middle-aged and serene, enters.* Powers *and his* Aide *stand to attention.* Kreton *goes forward to shake hands.*]

Laurent. Mr. Kreton?

Kreton. At your service, Mr. Laurent.

Laurent. I welcome you to this planet in the name of the World Council.

Kreton. Thank you, sir, thank you.

Laurent. Could you leave us alone for a moment, General?

Powers. Yes, sir.

[Powers *and* Aide *go.* Laurent *smiles at* Kreton.]

Laurent. Shall we sit down?

Kreton. Yes, yes, I love sitting down. I'm afraid my manners are not quite suitable, yet.

[*They sit down.*]

Laurent. Now, Mr. Kreton, in violation of all the rules of diplomacy, may I come to the point?

Kreton. You may.

Laurent. Why are you here?

Kreton. Curiosity. Pleasure.

Laurent. You are a tourist then in this time and place?

Kreton. (*nods*). Yes. Very well put.

Laurent. We have been informed that you have extraordinary powers.

Kreton. By your standards, yes, they must seem extraordinary.

Laurent. We have also been informed that it is your intention to . . . to take charge of this world.

Kreton. That is correct. . . . What a remarkable mind you have! I have difficulty looking inside it.

Laurent (*laughs*). Patience. I've attended so many conferences. . . . May I say that your conquest of our world puts your status of tourist in a rather curious light?

Kreton. Oh, I said nothing about *conquest*.

Laurent. Then how else do you intend to govern? The people won't allow you to direct their lives without a struggle.

Kreton. But I'm sure they will if I ask them to.

Laurent. You believe you can do all this without, well, without violence?

Kreton. Of course I can. One or two demonstrations and I'm sure they'll do as I ask. (*Smiles*) Watch this.

[*Pause. Then shouting.* Powers *bursts into room.*]

Powers. Now what've you done?

Kreton. Look out the window, Your Excellency.

[Laurent *goes to window. A rifle floats by, followed by an alarmed* Soldier.]

Nice, isn't it? I confess I worked out a number of rather melodramatic tricks last night. Incidentally, all the rifles of the soldiers in all the world are now floating in the air. (*Gestures*) Now they have them back.

Powers (*to* Laurent). You see, sir, I didn't exaggerate in my report.

Laurent (*awed*). No, no, you certainly didn't.

Kreton. You were skeptical, weren't you?

Laurent. Naturally. But now I . . . now I think it's possible.

Powers. That this . . . this gentleman is going to run everything?

Laurent. Yes, yes I do. And it might be wonderful.

Kreton. You *are* more clever than the others. You begin to see that I mean only good.

Laurent. Yes, only good. General, do you realize what this means? We can have one government . . .

Kreton. With innumerable bureaus, and intrigue. . . .

Laurent (*excited*). And the world could be incredibly prosperous, especially if he'd help us with his superior knowledge.

Kreton (*delighted*). I will, I will. I'll teach you to look into one another's minds. You'll find it devastating but enlightening: all that self-interest, those *lurid* emotions . . .

Laurent. No more countries. No more wars . . .

Kreton (*startled*). Oh, but I like a lot of countries. Besides, at this stage of your development you're supposed to have lots of countries and lots of wars . . . innumerable wars . . .

Laurent. But you can help us change all that.

Kreton. *Change* all that! My dear sir, I am your friend.

Laurent. What do you mean?

Kreton. Why, your deepest pleasure is violence. How can you deny that? It is the whole point to you, the whole point to my hobby . . . and you are my hobby, all mine.

Laurent. But our lives are devoted to *controlling* violence, and not creating it.

Kreton. Now, don't take me for an utter fool. After all, I can see into your minds. My dear fellow, don't you *know* what you are?

Laurent. What are we?

Kreton. You are savages. I have returned to the dark ages of an insignificant planet simply because I want the glorious excitement of being among you and reveling in your savagery! There is murder in all your hearts and I love it! It intoxicates me!

Laurent (*slowly*). You hardly flatter us.

Kreton. I didn't mean to be rude but you did ask me why I am here and I've told you.

Laurent. You have no wish then to . . . to help us poor savages.

Kreton. I couldn't even if I wanted to. You won't be civilized for at least two thousand years and you won't reach the level of my people for about a million years.

Laurent (*sadly*). Then you have come here only to . . . to observe?

Kreton. No, more than that. I mean to regulate your pastimes. But don't worry: I won't upset things too much. I've decided I don't want to be known to the people. You will go right on with your countries, your squabbles, the way you always have, while I will *secretly* regulate things through you.

Laurent. The World Council does not govern. We only advise.

Kreton. Well, I shall advise you and you will advise the governments and we shall have a lovely time.

Laurent. I don't know what to say. You obviously have the power to do as you please.

Kreton. I'm glad you realize that. Poor General Powers is now wondering if a hydrogen bomb might destroy me. It won't, General.

Powers. Too bad.

Kreton. Now, Your Excellency, I shall stay in this house until you have laid the groundwork for my first project.

Laurent. And what is that to be?

Kreton. A war! I want one of your really splendid wars, with all the trimmings, all the noise and the fire . . .

Laurent. A war! You're joking. Why, at this moment we are working as hard as we know how *not* to have a war.

Kreton. But secretly you want one. After all, it's the one thing your little race does well. You'd hardly want me to deprive you of your simple pleasures, now would you?

Laurent. I think you must be mad.

Kreton. Not mad, simply a philanthropist. Of course I myself shall get a great deal of pleasure out of a war (the vibrations must be incredible!) but I'm doing it mostly for you. So, if you don't mind, I want you to arrange a few incidents, so we can get one started spontaneously.

Laurent. I refuse.

Kreton. In that event, I shall select someone else to head the World Council. Someone who *will* start a war. I suppose there exist a few people here who might like the idea.

Laurent. How can you do such a horrible thing to us? Can't you see that we don't want to be savages?

Kreton. But you have no choice. Anyway, you're just pulling my leg! I'm sure you want a war as much as the rest of them do and that's what you're going to get: the biggest war you've ever had!

Laurent (*stunned*). Heaven help us!

Kreton (*exuberant*). Heaven won't! Oh, what fun it will be! I can hardly wait! (*He strikes the globe of the world a happy blow as we fade out.*)

For Study and Discussion

Analyzing and Interpreting the Play

1. Kreton converses with the cat almost as if he were conversing with a person. What is the significance of his remarks to the cat?

2. What two things does the incident with the President of Paraguay show us about Kreton's powers?

3a. What does the remark Laurent makes as he sits down with Kreton imply about the rules of diplomacy? **b.** Why does Kreton find it difficult to look into Laurent's mind?

4a. What benefits does Laurent at first see in Kreton's plan to dominate the world? **b.** What does Kreton's first project turn out to be?

5. Kreton states that the deepest pleasure for human beings is violence. What evidence does he give for his conclusion?

Act Three

Fade in on the study, two weeks later. *Kreton* is sitting at desk on which a map is spread out. He has a pair of dividers, some models of jet aircraft. Occasionally he pretends to dive-bomb, imitating the sound of a bomb going off. *Powers* enters.

Powers. You wanted me, sir?

Kreton. Yes, I wanted those figures on radioactive fallout.

Powers. They're being made up now, sir. Anything else?

Kreton. Oh, my dear fellow, why do you dislike me so?

Powers. I am your military aide, sir: I don't have to answer that question. It is outside the sphere of my duties.

Kreton. Aren't you at least happy about your promotion?

Powers. Under the circumstances, no, sir.

Kreton. I find your attitude baffling.

Powers. Is that all, sir?

Kreton. You have never once said what you thought of my war plans. Not once have I got a single word of encouragement from you, a single compliment . . . only black thoughts.

Powers. Since you read my mind, sir, you know what I think.

Kreton. True, but I can't help but feel that deep down inside of you there is just a twinge of professional jealousy. You don't like the idea of an outsider playing your game better than you do. Now confess!

Powers. I am acting as your aide only under duress.

Kreton (*sadly*). Bitter, bitter . . . and to think I chose you especially as my aide. Think of all the other generals who would give anything to have your job.

Powers. Fortunately, they know nothing about my job.

Kreton. Yes, I do think it wise not to advertise my presence, don't you?

Powers. I can't see that it makes much difference, since you seem bent on destroying our world.

Kreton. I'm not going to destroy it. A few dozen cities, that's all, and not very nice cities either. Think of the fun you'll have building new ones when it's over.

Powers. How many millions of people do you plan to kill?

Kreton. Well, quite a few, but they love this sort of thing. You can't convince me they don't. Oh, I know what Laurent says. But he's a misfit, out of step with his time. Fortunately, my new World Council is more reasonable.

Powers. Paralyzed is the word, sir.

Kreton. You don't think they like me either?

Powers. You *know* they hate you, sir.

Kreton. But love and hate are so confused in your savage minds and the vibrations of the one are so very like those of the other that I can't always distinguish. You see, we neither love nor hate in my world. We simply have hobbies. (*He strokes the globe of the world tenderly.*) But now to work. Tonight's the big night: first, the sneak attack, then: boom! (*He claps his hands gleefully.*)

[Dissolve to *the living room, to* John *and* Ellen.]

Ellen. I've never felt so helpless in my life.

John. Here we all stand around doing nothing while he plans to blow up the world.

Ellen. Suppose we went to the newspapers.

John. He controls the press. When Laurent resigned they didn't even print his speech.

[*A gloomy pause*]

Ellen. What are you thinking about, John?

John. Walnuts.

[*They embrace.*]

Ellen. Can't we do anything?

John. No, I guess there's nothing.

Ellen (*vehemently*). Oh! I could kill him!

[Kreton *and* Powers *enter.*]

Kreton. Very good, Ellen, *very* good! I've never felt you so violent.

Ellen. You heard what I said to John?

Kreton. Not in words, but you were absolutely bathed in malevolence.

Powers. I'll get the papers you wanted, sir. (*Powers exits.*)

Kreton. I don't think he likes me very much but your father does. Only this morning he offered to handle my public relations and I said I'd let him. Wasn't that nice of him?

John. I think I'll go get some fresh air. (*He goes out through the terrace door.*)

Kreton. Oh, dear! (*Sighs*) Only your father is really entering the spirit of the game. He's a much better sport than you, my dear.

Ellen (*exploding*). Sport! That's it! You think we're sport. You think we're animals to be played with: well, we're not. We're people and we don't want to be destroyed.

Kreton (*patiently*). But *I* am not destroying you. You will be destroying one another of your own free will, as you have always done. I am simply a . . . a kibitzer.

Ellen. No, you are a vampire!

Kreton. A vampire? You mean I drink blood? Ugh!

Ellen. No, you drink emotions, our emotions. You'll sacrifice us all for the sake of your . . . your vibrations!

Kreton. Touché.[1] Yet what harm am I really doing? It's true I'll enjoy the war more than anybody; but it will be *your* destructiveness, after all, not mine.

Ellen. You could stop it.

1. **Touché** (tōō-shā′): a French fencing term meaning "touched"; that is, "You have scored a point."

Kreton. So could you.

Ellen. I?

Kreton. Your race. They could stop altogether but they won't. And I can hardly intervene in their natural development. The most I can do is help out in small, practical ways.

Ellen. We are not what you think. We're not so . . . so primitive.

Kreton. My dear girl, just take this one house-hold: your mother dislikes your father but she is too tired to do anything about it, so she knits and she gardens and she tries not to think about him. Your father, on the other hand, is bored with all of you. Don't look shocked; he doesn't like you any more than you like him . . .

Ellen. Don't say that!

Kreton. I am only telling you the truth. Your

father wants you to marry someone important; therefore he objects to John, while you, my girl . . .

Ellen (*with a fierce cry,* Ellen *grabs vase to throw*). You devil! (*Vase breaks in her hand.*)

Kreton. You see? That proves my point perfectly. (*Gently*) Poor savage, I cannot help what you are. (*Briskly*) Anyway, you will soon be distracted from your personal problems. Tonight is the night. If you're a good girl, I'll let you watch the bombing.

[Dissolve to *study. Eleven forty-five.* Powers *and the* Aide *gloomily await the war.*]

Aide. General, isn't there anything we can do?

Powers. It's out of our hands.

[Kreton, *dressed as a hussar*[2] *with shako,*[3] *enters.*]

Kreton. Everything on schedule?

Powers. Yes, sir. Planes left for their targets at twenty-two hundred.

Kreton. Good . . . good. I, myself, shall take off shortly after midnight to observe the attack firsthand.

Powers. Yes, sir.

[Kreton *goes into the living room, where the family is gloomily assembled.*]

Kreton (*enters from study*). And now the magic hour approaches! I hope you're all as thrilled as I am.

Spelding. You still won't tell us who's attacking whom?

Kreton. You'll know in exactly . . . fourteen minutes.

Ellen (*bitterly*). Are we going to be killed too?

Kreton. Certainly not! You're quite safe, at least in the early stages of the war.

Ellen. Thank you.

Mrs. Spelding. I suppose this will mean rationing again.[4]

Spelding. Will . . . will we see anything from here?

Kreton. No, but there should be a good picture on the monitor in the study. Powers is tuning in right now.

John (*at window*). Hey look, up there! Coming this way!

[Ellen *joins him.*]

Ellen. What is it?

John. Why . . . it's *another* one! And it's going to land.

Kreton (*surprised*). I'm sure you're mistaken. No one would dream of coming here. (*He has gone to the window, too.*)

Ellen. It's landing!

Spelding. Is it a friend of yours, Mr. Kreton?

Kreton (*slowly*). No, no, not a friend . . . (Kreton *retreats to the study; he inadvertently*[5] *drops a lace handkerchief beside the sofa.*)

John. Here he comes.

Ellen (*suddenly bitter*). Now we have two of them.

Mrs. Spelding. My poor roses.

[*The new* Visitor *enters in a gleam of light from his ship. He is wearing a most futuristic costume. Without a word, he walks past the awed family into the study.* Kreton *is cowering behind the globe.* Powers *and the* Aide *stare, bewildered, as the* Visitor *gestures sternly and* Kreton *reluctantly removes shako and sword. They communicate by odd sounds.*]

---

2. **hussar** (hŏŏ-zär'): a European cavalry soldier in a brightly colored uniform.
3. **shako** (shăk'ō): a fancy, cylindrical military hat with a plume on top.

4. **rationing again:** Mrs. Spelding is remembering World War II, when gasoline and food consumption were restricted in the United States.
5. **inadvertently** (in'əd-vûr'tənt-lē): through an oversight.

Visitor (*to* Powers). Please leave us alone.

[Cut to *living room as* Powers *and the* Aide *enter from the study.*]

Powers (*to* Ellen). Who on earth was that?
Ellen. It's another one, another visitor.
Powers. Now we're done for.
Ellen. I'm going in there.
Mrs. Spelding. Ellen, don't you dare!
Ellen. I'm going to talk to them. (*Starts to door*)
John. I'm coming, too.
Ellen (*grimly*). No, alone. I know what I want to say.

[Cut to *interior of the study, to* Kreton *and the other* Visitor *as* Ellen *enters.*]

Ellen. I want you both to listen to me . . .
Visitor. You don't need to speak. I know what you will say.
Ellen. That you have no right here? That you mustn't . . .
Visitor. I agree. Kreton has no right here. He is well aware that it is forbidden to interfere with the past.
Ellen. The past?
Visitor (*nods*). You are the past, the dark ages: we are from the future. In fact, we are *your* descendants on another planet. We visit you from time to time but we never interfere because it would change *us* if we did. Fortunately, I arrived in time.
Ellen. There won't be a war?
Visitor. There will be no war. And there will be no memory of any of this. When we leave here you will forget Kreton and me. Time will turn back to the moment before his arrival.
Ellen. Why did you want to hurt us?
Kreton (*heartbroken*). Oh, but I didn't! I only wanted to have . . . well, to have a little fun, to indulge my hobby . . . against the rules, of course.

Visitor (*to* Ellen). Kreton is a rarity among us. Mentally and morally he is retarded. He is a child and he regards your period as his toy.
Kreton. A child, now really!
Visitor. He escaped from his nursery and came back in time to you . . .
Kreton. And *everything* went wrong, everything! I wanted to visit 1860 . . . that's my *real* period but then something happened to the car and I ended up here, not that I don't find you nearly as interesting but . . .
Visitor. We must go, Kreton.
Kreton (*to* Ellen). You did like me just a bit, didn't you?
Ellen. Yes, yes, I did, until you let your hobby get out of hand. (*To* Visitor) What is the future like?
Visitor. Very serene, very different . . .
Kreton. Don't believe him: it is dull, dull, dull beyond belief! One simply floats through eternity: no wars, no excitement . . .
Visitor. It is forbidden to discuss these matters.
Kreton. I can't see what difference it makes, since she's going to forget all about us anyway.
Ellen. Oh, how I'd love to see the future . . .
Visitor. It is against . . .
Kreton. Against the rules: how tiresome you are. (*To* Ellen) But, alas, you can never pay us a call because you aren't born yet! I mean where we are you are not. Oh, Ellen, dear, think kindly of me, until you forget.
Ellen. I will.
Visitor. Come. Time has begun to turn back. Time is bending.

[*He starts to door.* Kreton *turns conspiratorially to* Ellen.]

Kreton. Don't be sad, my girl. I shall be back one bright day, but a bright day in 1860. I dote on the Civil War, so exciting . . .

Visitor. Kreton!

Kreton. Only next time I think it'll be more fun if the *South* wins! (*He hurries after the* Visitor.)

[Cut to *clock as the hands spin backwards*. Dissolve to *the living room, exactly the same as the first scene:* Spelding, Mrs. Spelding, Ellen.]

Spelding. There is nothing wrong with marrying a wealthy man. The horror of it has always eluded me. However, my only wish is that you marry someone hard-working, ambitious, a man who'll make his mark in the world. Not a boy who is content to sit on a farm all his life, growing peanuts . . .

Ellen. English walnuts! And he won't just sit there.

Spelding. Will you stop contradicting me?

Ellen. But, Daddy, John grows walnuts . . .

[John *enters.*]

John. Hello, everybody.

Mrs. Spelding. Good evening, John.

Ellen. What kept you, darling? You missed Daddy's broadcast.

John. I saw it before I left home. Wonderful broadcast, sir.

Spelding. Thank you, John.

[John *crosses to window.*]

John. That meteor you were talking about, well, for a while it looked almost like a spaceship or something. You can just barely see it now.

[Ellen *joins him at window. They watch, arms about one another.*]

Spelding. Spaceship! Nonsense! Remarkable what some people will believe, *want* to believe.

Besides, as I said in the broadcast; if there's any traveling to be done in space, we'll do it first.

[He notices Kreton's *handkerchief on sofa and picks it up. They all look at it, puzzled, as we* cut to stock shot *of the starry night, against which two spaceships vanish in the distance, one serene in its course, the other erratic, as we* fade out.]

Reading Check

1. What position does Powers now hold?
2. What motive does Kreton ascribe to Powers?
3. What is due to happen at midnight?
4. How are the beings of Kreton's world related to the people on earth?

For Study and Discussion

Analyzing and Interpreting the Play

1a. What difference is there in the way Laurent and General Powers react to Kreton's plans? **b.** Why does Kreton keep Paul Laurent's speech from appearing in the press?

2a. How and why does Ellen's attitude toward Kreton change? **b.** Why is it logical that Mr. Spelding wants to work for Kreton, now that Kreton is in command?

3. Kreton's speech about the Spelding household is a key speech in the play. **a.** What primitive anger does he see in each family member? **b.** Which human capacity does he dismiss?

4a. What does the Visitor mean when he says that Kreton is morally retarded? **b.** Why is it forbidden for the visitors to interfere with what happens on Earth?

5. Why is Kreton's forgotten handkerchief crucial to the ending of the play?

Language and Vocabulary

Using Combining Forms

Many words have been created by combining older words or word fragments. Often it is possible to figure out the original meaning of a word simply by separating it into parts—provided you know what the parts mean.

inter-

> **John.** Traveling in space! Just like those stories. You know: intergalactic drive stuff.

Inter- is a prefix meaning "between or among." Therefore, *intergalactic* travel means "travel between galaxies." What is an *interfaith* conference? An *intercollegiate* football game? An *interplanetary* mission? An *interdepartmental* meeting?

mal-

> **Kreton.** . . . you were absolutely bathed in malevolence.

Mal- is a combining form meaning "bad or badly, wrong or ill." The remainder of the word *malevolence* is related to the word *voluntary.* A voluntary action is something you do because you wish to do it or have a will to do it. Therefore, *malevolence* is ill will. What is *malnutrition?* What does *malodorous* mean? What is a *malfunction?* What is *malpractice?*

philo- and *anthropo-*

> **Laurent.** I think you must be mad.
> **Kreton.** Not mad, simply a philanthropist.

You probably know that a philanthropist is a giver of charity. In the quotation above, Kreton means more than that.

Philo- (*phil-* before a vowel) means "loving or liking."

Anthropo (*anthrop-* before a vowel) means "human."

A philanthropist, therefore, is a lover of human beings.

Use your dictionary to find out what the second part of each of the following words means. You will find the answers in the derivation entries for the words in question, not in the definitions. You may have to do some cross-referencing. Read the definitions after you have found the answers.

anthropocentric	philharmonic
anthropology	Philip
anthropometry	philology
anthropomorphism	philosophy

Writing About Literature

Analyzing Satirical Elements

A **satire** is a literary work that points up or attacks follies or vices in human nature. Satire can range in tone from lighthearted wit to scorching ironic bitterness. Almost all comic writers use some satirical elements in their work.

Choose one of the following aspects of Vidal's satire for analysis, and develop a short paper, using evidence from the play to support your conclusions.

What are some examples of hypocrisy that occur in the play? Why is Kreton particularly suited to expose them?

Kreton tends to emphasize the negative rather than the positive aspects of humanity. Are his observations useful, destructive, or both? Apply your answer to satire in general as you elaborate.

Gore Vidal's original plan when he was writing *Visit to a Small Planet* was to end the play with the entire world blowing up. Which ending better suits the satirical points that the author has to make? Explain.

Focus on Persuasive Writing

Thinking About Your Audience

Market researchers for television programs and commercials know that it pays to analyze the needs and tastes of the viewing audience. In the same way, when you plan a persuasive essay, you should consider your audience. What are their interests and concerns? How much do they already know about the topic? What group might strongly disagree with your opinion on the issue? What reason(s) would they have for disagreeing?

Select one of the topics identified earlier in this unit (see page 422), or choose a new topic. Fill out an audience chart like the one below. Save your writing.

Audience Chart

Topic: _____

Position/Opinion: _____

_____

Audience: _____

Interests and Concerns: _____

_____

Possible Opposing Opinions: _____

_____

Likely Reasons for Opposition: _____

_____

_____

About the Author

Gore Vidal (1926–)

Gore Vidal—novelist, dramatist, essayist—wrote his first novel, *Williwaw,* at age nineteen. The novel was based on his experiences as first mate on a ship during World War II. From 1954 to 1956 he devoted much of his time to writing plays for television. *Visit to a Small Planet* was first telecast in 1955. Later Vidal rewrote it for the Broadway stage, where it had a long and successful run.

Since 1967 Vidal has written a series of novels about American history and politics: *Washington, D.C.* (1967), *Burr* (1973), *1876* (1976), *Lincoln* (1984), *Empire* (1987), and *Hollywood* (1990). He is also the author of many essays about literature and American life. One collection of essays, *The Second American Revolution,* won the National Book Critics Award for criticism in 1982. His most recent novel is *LIVE from Golgotha* (1992), an irreverent look at what it might be like if a television crew could return to the time of Christ.

Thunder on Sycamore Street

REGINALD ROSE

Something important is about to happen on Sycamore Street. As you read this suspenseful television play, you will gradually discover what that something is and how it tests several people's courage and convictions.

Characters

Frank Morrison

Clarice Morrison

Roger Morrison

Christopher Morrison

Arthur Hayes

Phyllis Hayes

Mr. Harkness

Joseph Blake

Anna Blake

Judy Blake

Mrs. Blake

Charlie Denton

Mrs. Carson

Act One

Fade in on *a long shot of Sycamore Street in the pleasant and tidy village of Eastmont. It is 6:40* P.M. *and just getting dark. We see three houses, modest but attractive, side by side, each an exact replica of the other. Each has a tiny front lawn and a tree or two in front of it. Each has been lived in and cared for by people who take pride in their own hard-won respectability. The street is quiet. Walking toward the houses now we see* Arthur Hayes, *a quiet, bespectacled man between thirty-five and thirty-eight years of age. He lives in the second of the three houses. He walks slowly, carrying a newspaper under his arm and smoking a pipe. He stops in front of his house and, almost in a daze, knocks the dottle*[1] *out of his pipe against*

1. **dottle** (dŏt'l): tobacco ash.

his heel. As he is doing this, we see Frank Morrison *enter, also carrying a newspaper. He is a heavy man, forceful and aggressive, with a loud voice and a hearty laugh. He is about forty years of age.* Frank Morrison *lives right next door to* Arthur *in the first of the three houses. He sees* Arthur *and waves.*

Frank (*jovially*). Hey, Artie. How ya doin'?

[Arthur *is preoccupied. He doesn't register at first. He looks blankly at* Frank.]

Frank (*laughing*). Hey . . . wake up, boy. It's almost time for supper.

[Arthur *snaps out of it and forces a smile.*]

Arthur (*quietly*). Oh . . . hello, Frank. Sorry, I didn't see you.

Frank. Didn't see me? Hey, wait till I tell Clarice. That diet she's got me on must be working. You have to look twice to see me! (*Laughing hard,* Frank *reaches for his keys.*) That's a hot one! (Arthur *smiles weakly.*) Say . . . isn't

Thunder on Sycamore Street **449**

this late for you to be getting home?

Arthur. No, I don't think so. (*He looks at his watch.*) It's twenty to seven. I always get home about this time.

Frank. Yeah. Well I wouldn't want you to be late tonight. You know what tonight is, don't you?

Arthur (*slowly*). Yes, I know what tonight is.

Frank (*a little hard*). Good.

[*We hear footsteps and see a man walk by them. He is Joseph Blake, a man in his late thirties, a big, powerful, but quiet man. Joseph Blake lives in the third house on the street. As he walks by them, they both look at him silently. Arthur turns away then, but Frank continues to stare at him. Camera moves in on Frank as he stares coldly at Joseph Blake. His face is hard, full of hatred. The footsteps recede.*]

Frank (*low*). See you later, Artie.

[*Frank turns and fits the key into the lock. There is utter silence. He fumbles with the lock, then silently swings the door open. He walks into the small foyer. The living room ahead is brightly lighted, but we see no one. Frank walks slowly, silently into the living room. As he enters it, we hear a dozen pistol shots. Frank stiffens, clutches himself and falls to the floor as if dead. Then we hear a chorus of shrill screams and two small boys wearing cowboy hats and carrying pistols fling themselves upon Frank's body. Frank doesn't move as they clamber over him. One is Roger, age ten; the other is Christopher, age six. Christopher wears "Dr. Dentons."[2]*]

Christopher (*screaming*). I got him! I got him first.

Roger. You did not!

Christopher. I did so! Get offa him. I got him first. (*Calling*) Hey, Mom . . .

Roger (*superior*). Boy, are you stupid! I got him three times before you even pulled the trigger.

2. *"Dr. Dentons":* a sleeping outfit.

450 DRAMA

Christopher (*squeaking*). What d'ya mean? I got him before you even——(Roger *tries to push* Christopher *off* Frank's *motionless body.*) Before you even——(Christopher *grunts and fights back.*) Cut it out! Hey, Mom . . .

[*Clarice, Frank's wife, a pleasant-looking woman in her early thirties, comes to living-room door from kitchen. She wears an apron. She calls out before she sees them.*]

Clarice. Now you boys stop that noise. (*She sees* Roger *pushing* Christopher.) Roger!

Christopher. Cut it out, willya. I got him——

Clarice. Roger! Stop that pushing. . . .

Christopher. I'm gonna sock you. . . .

Clarice (*angrily*). Christopher, don't you dare! Frank! Will you do something . . . please!

Roger. Go ahead. Sock me. You couldn't hurt a flea!

Christopher (*winding up*). Who says so?

Roger. Boy, you must be deaf. I said so!

Clarice: Frank!

[*As* Christopher *swings at* Roger, Frank *suddenly comes to life with a tremendous roar. He rolls over, toppling both boys to the floor and with lightning swiftness he grabs both of their cap pistols. He stands up grinning. They both look at him, startled.*]

Frank (*barking*). Get up! (*They both do, slowly.*) Get your hands up! (*They look at each other.*) Make it snappy if you don't want to draw lead. (Christopher *shrugs and raises his hands.*) (*To* Roger) You too, hombre!

Roger. Aaaah, Dad . . .

Frank. Last warning.

Roger (*disgusted*). Come on . . . (Frank *shoots him with the cap pistol.*) What are you so serious about?

[*He walks away.* Frank *watches him, still not giving up the cowboy pose.*]

Clarice. All right. Now that's enough gunplay. All three of you can just settle down. (*To* Frank) Hand 'em over.

[*He grins and gives her the guns. Then he bends over and kisses her.*]

Frank. Hello, honey.

[*She kisses him dutifully, then speaks to* Roger, *handing him the guns.*]

Clarice. Put these in your room and come back with your hands washed. We're sitting down to supper right now.
Roger (*desperately*). Right now? I gotta watch "Rangebusters."
Clarice. Not tonight. I told you we were eating early.
Roger. Ah, Mom . . . please . . .
Clarice. Absolutely not. Come on, now. Inside . . .

[Roger *slumps off.* Clarice *turns to* Christopher *as* Frank *begins to take off his coat.*]

Clarice. And you're going to bed, mister.
Christopher. No! I can't go to bed!
Clarice. Christopher!
Christopher (*backing away*). I'm not tired yet. Honest!

[Frank *is hanging his coat up in the foyer.* Clarice *advances toward* Chris, *who looks for means of escape.*]

Clarice. I'm not going to argue with you.
Christopher. Mom, fifteen minutes. Come on. Please . . .
Clarice. I'm going to start counting. One, two——
Christopher (*fast*). Three four five six seven eight nine ten.

[*He runs away from her, but right into the arms of* Frank, *who picks him up.*]

Frank. Trapped! Let's go, pal.
Christopher. Aaah . . .

[Frank *carries him past* Clarice, *who kisses him on the way by. As they reach the door which leads into bedroom,* Roger *comes out.* Christopher, *in his father's arms, raps* Roger *on the head with his knuckle.*]

Roger. Hey!
Christopher (*grinning*). Good night, Rog.
Roger. Stupid!
Frank. All right, now. That's enough out of both of you. I don't want to hear another peep.

[Frank *takes* Christopher *into bedroom. Camera follows* Roger *over to a dining table set at one end of living room near a picture window. This would probably be an L-shaped living room-dining room set-up and would be exactly the same in all three houses. The only difference in the three interior sets will be the way in which they are decorated. There are dishes on the table, glassware, etc.* Roger *slumps into his chair and takes a piece of bread. He munches on it as* Clarice *comes in from kitchen carrying a steaming bowl of stew. She sets it down and sits down.*]

Clarice (*calling*). Frank.
Frank (*off*). Okay. I'll be right there.
Roger. Hey, Mom, what are we eating so early for?
Clarice (*serving*). Don't say "Hey, Mom."
Roger. Well, what are we eating so early for?
Clarice. Because we feel like eating early. (*Calling*) Frank!

[Frank *walks in, loosening his tie.*]

Frank. What's for supper?

Clarice. Beef stew.

Roger. Look, if I could see the first five minutes of "Rangebusters"——

[Clarice *ladles out the stew as* Frank *sits at the table.*]

Clarice. Roger, I'm not going to tell you again.

Roger (*anguished*). But Mom, you don't know what's happening. There's this sneaky guy

Frank. Come on, boy, dig into your dinner.

[Roger *makes a face and gives up the battle.*]

Frank (*to* Clarice). What time is the sitter coming?

Clarice. Ten after seven. Do you know that's the third time today you've asked me.

Frank. Just want to be sure.

Clarice. I don't see why they have to make it so early anyway.

[Frank *has a mouthful of food, so he shrugs.*]

Roger. Make what so early, Dad?

Clarice. Nothing. Eat your dinner.

Frank. Good stew.

Clarice. There's plenty more.

Frank (*chewing*). Mmmm. Hmmmm. Do anything special today, Rog?

Roger. Nope. Just kinda hung around.

Frank. Well, I don't know why you don't get out and do something. A boy your age . . .

Roger. Some of the kids dumped garbage on the Blakes' lawn again.

Frank (*casually*). That so? What about you?

Roger. Ah, what fun is that after you do it a couple of times?

Frank (*chewing*). Mmmm. Hey, how about eating your stew.

Roger. I'm not hungry.

Clarice. Frank, I wish you'd do something about that boy's eating. He's beginning to look like a scarecrow.

Frank. He'll be all right. What time is it?

Clarice (*looking at watch*). Five of seven.

Frank. We'd better snap it up.

Clarice. Plenty of time. I'm leaving the dishes till later.

Frank. Y'know, Clarry, this really ought to be something tonight.

[*Roger starts to get up, but stops.*]

Roger. What ought to be something?

Clarice. You just sit down and pay attention to your dinner. There's a glass of milk to be finished before you get up.

Roger (*grudgingly*). Okay. (*He sips the milk for a moment.*) Where are you going tonight, Dad?

Frank. We're going for a little walk.

Roger. Well, what d'ya have to go out so early for?

Frank. Just like that.

Roger (*aggressively*). Well, what the heck is the big secret, that's what I'd like to know. Everybody's acting so mysterious.

Frank (*sharply*). That's enough. Now I don't want to hear any more questions out of you. Your mother and I have some business to attend to, and that's it. You mind yours.

[Roger, *stunned, looks at his father, then down at his plate. There is an awkward silence.* Frank *eats stolidly. They watch him.*]

Frank (*to* Clarice). Where's that sitter?

Clarice. It's not time yet. Take it easy, Frank.

[Frank *gets up from the table, goes over to a box of cigars on top of the TV set, and lights one.* Clarice *and* Roger *watch him silently.*]

Clarice. Aren't you going to have some des-

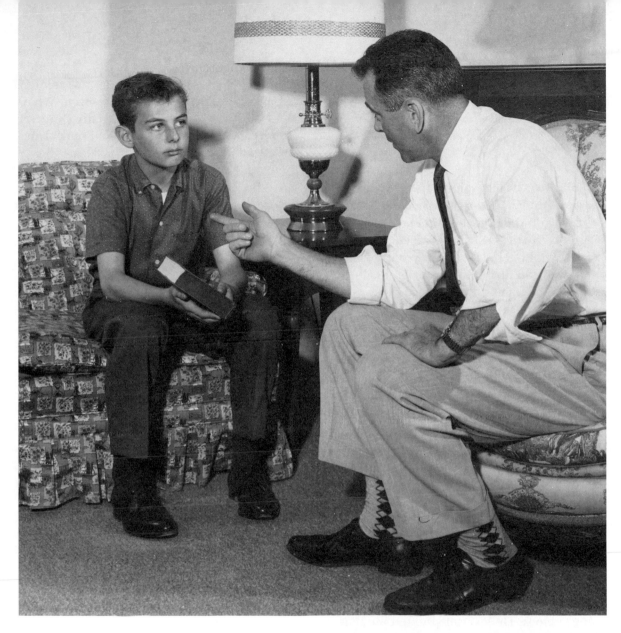

sert, Frank? There's some cherry pie left.
Frank. I'll have it later.

[*He puffs on the cigar.*]

Roger (*low*). I'm sorry, Dad.
Frank (*turning*). Well, it's about time you learned some respect, d'you hear me? If I want you to know something I'll tell it to you.
Roger (*softly*). Okay . . .

Clarice (*quickly*). Have some pie, honey. I heated it special.

[Frank *goes to the table and sits down. He puts the cigar down and* Clarice *begins to cut him some pie.*]

Clarice. How late do you think we'll be, Frank?
Frank. I don't know.
Clarice. Do you think I ought to pack a ther-

mos of hot coffee? It's going to be chilly.

Frank. Might not be a bad idea.

[Frank *now begins to show the first signs of being excited about the evening. He speaks, almost to himself*.]

Frank. Boy, I can't wait till I see his face. The nerve of him. The absolute nerve. (*Grinning*.) What d'you think he'll do when we all——

Clarice (*looking at* Roger). Frank . . .

Frank (*as* Roger *stares*) Oh, yeah, go ahead, Rog. You can turn on your program.

Roger. Gee thanks, Dad.

[*He jumps up, goes to the TV set and turns it on. Frank and Clarice watch him get settled in front of TV set. We hear dialogue from set faintly.* Roger *watches in background, enraptured*.]

Frank (*quietly*). What are they saying on the block?

Clarice. I didn't speak to anyone. I was ironing all day.

Frank. Charlie Denton called me at the office. I was right in the middle of taking an order from Martin Brothers for three A-81 tractors.

Clarice. Three? Frank, that's *wonderful!*

Frank. Not bad. Anyway, I made Mr. Martin wait while I spoke to Charlie. Charlie says it's gonna be one hundred percent. Every family on the block. He just called to tell me that.

Clarice. Well, that's good. Everyone should be in on this.

Frank (*eating*). Clarry, I'm telling you this is going to be a job well done. It's how you have to do these things. Everybody getting together first . . . and boom, it's over. I can't wait til it's started. It's been long enough.

Clarice. I saw her out the window today, hanging clothes in her yard like nothing was wrong. She didn't even look this way.

Frank. What time is it?

Clarice. Now you just asked me two minutes ago. It's about three minutes to seven. What's the matter with you? You'll be getting yourself an ulcer over this thing. Relax, Frank. Here, have some more pie.

Frank. No, No more.

[*He gets up and walks around nervously, slapping his fist into his palm.* Roger *is looking at him now. He is tense, excited, completely caught up in the impending event*.]

Frank. This is something big, you know that, Clarry? We're getting action without pussyfooting for once. That's it. That's the big part. There's too much pussyfooting going on all the time. Can't hurt anyone's feelings. Every time you turn around you're hurting some idiot's feelings. Well that's tough, I say . . .

Clarice (*indicating* Roger), Frank . . .

Frank. He can hear! He's old enough. You want something bad, you gotta go out and get it! That's how this world is. Boy, I like this, Clarry. You know what it makes me feel like? It makes me feel like a man!

[*He stalks up and down the room for a few moments as they watch him. Then he goes to the window and stands there looking out*.]

Clarice (*quietly*). I think I'll just stack the dishes.

[*She starts to do it. The doorbell rings.* Roger *jumps up*.]

Roger. I'll get it.

[*He goes to the door and opens it.* Arthur Hayes *stands there a bit apologetically. He wears no overcoat, having just come from next door. He looks extremely upset*.]

Arthur. Rog, is your dad in?

Roger. Sure. Come on in, Mr. Hayes.

[Arthur *walks in slowly.* Frank *turns around, still excited. He goes over to* Arthur.]

Frank (*loud*). Hey, Artie. Come on in.

Arthur. Hello, Frank . . .

Frank (*laughing*). What can I do for you? (Arthur *looks hesitatingly at* Roger.) Oh, sure. Rog, go help your mother.

Roger (*annoyed*). Okay . . .

[*He walks off to dining table.*]

Frank (*chuckling*). That's some kid, isn't he, Artie? How old is yours now?

Arthur. Twenty-one months.

Frank. Yeah. Well, that's still nothing but a crying machine. Wait a couple years. He'll kill you.

Arthur. I guess so.

Frank. And how! Sit down for a minute, Artie. What's on your mind?

Arthur (*sitting. Hesitantly*). Well, I don't know. . . I just . . . well . . . I just wanted . . . to talk.

Frank. No kidding. Say, y'know you look a little green around the gills? What's the matter?

[Arthur Hayes *takes off his eyeglasses and begins to polish them, a nervous habit in which he indulges when upset.*]

Arthur. Nothing. I've had an upset stomach for a couple of days. Maybe that's it.

Frank (*nodding*). Yeah, that'll get you down all right. Probably a virus.

[Arthur *nods and they look at each other awkwardly for a moment.*]

Frank. Well, what did you want to talk to me about?

[Arthur *looks at the floor, trying to frame his answer carefully, afraid to offend. Finally he blurts it out.*]

Arthur. What do you think about this thing tonight?

Frank (*surprised*). What do you mean what do I think about it?

Arthur. Well, I've been kind of going over it all day, Frank. I talked with Phyllis before.

Frank (*a little hard*). And . . .

Arthur. Well, it was just talk. We were just talking it over to get clear on it, you know.

Frank. Go ahead.

Arthur. And . . . well, look, Frank, it's a pretty hard thing. Supposing it were you?

Frank. It's not.

Arthur. Well, I know that, but supposing it were?

[Frank *stands up and goes over to* Arthur.]

Frank. Your glasses are clean. You wear 'em out, you have to buy a new pair. (Arthur *looks down at his glasses, then puts them on nervously.*) Now what about it, Artie? What if I was the guy?

Arthur. Well, you know . . . how would you feel?

Frank. How would I feel, huh? Now that's a good question, Artie. I'll answer it for you. It doesn't make any difference how I'd feel. Now let me ask you a question. Is he a life-long buddy of yours?

Arthur. Well, now, you know he's not, Frank.

Frank. Do you know him to say hello to?

Arthur. That's not the idea. He's——

Frank. Artie . . . you don't even know the guy. What are you getting yourself all hot and bothered about? We all agreed, didn't we?

Arthur. Yes . . . everybody agreed.

Frank. You. Me. The Dentons. The McAllisters. The Fredericks. The Schofields. Every family on Sycamore Street for that matter. We all agreed. That's how it is. The majority. Right?

Arthur. Well . . . I think we all ought to talk it over, maybe. Let it wait a few days.

[*He takes off his glasses again and begins to wipe them.*]

Frank. Artie . . . we talked it over. (Frank *takes the handkerchief out of* Arthur's *hand and tucks it into his pocket.*) In about ten minutes we're starting. We expect to have a solid front, you know what I mean? Everybody. You included. You're my next-door neighbor, boy. I don't want to hear people saying Artie Hayes wasn't there.

Arthur (*hesitantly*). Well, I don't know, Frank. I thought——

[*The phone rings.* Frank *goes toward it.*]

Frank. Go home, Artie. Don't worry about it. I'll see you in a few minutes. (Frank *goes to the phone and picks it up.* Arthur *stares at him.*) Hello . . . (Arthur *turns away and walks slowly to door.*) Speaking.

[Arthur *goes out, dazed and frightened.* Clarice *comes into living room and stands waiting as* Frank *listens to phone.*]

Frank (*angry*). What do you mean you can't get here? (*Pause*) Well, this is a great time to call! (*Pause*) I know. Yeah. (*He slams the phone down. To* Clarice.) Our sitter can't get here. How d'you like that?

Clarice. What's wrong with her?

Frank. I don't know. She's got a cold, or something. Nice dependable girl you pick.

Clarice (*snapping*). Well, I didn't exactly arrange for her to get a cold, you know.

Frank. Look, Clarry, we're going to this thing no matter what.

Clarice. Well, I'm not leaving Chris with Roger. They'll claw each other to pieces.

Frank. Then we'll take them with us.

Clarice. You wouldn't . . .

Frank. Who wouldn't? We're doing it for them as much as anyone else, aren't we? Well, they might as well see it.

Clarice. Maybe I'd better stay home with them.

Frank. No, sir. You've been in on this from the beginning. You're going. Come on, get Chris dressed. We haven't got much time.

Clarice. Well . . . whatever you think, Frank . . .

Frank. I'm telling you it's all right. Won't hurt 'em a bit. (*To* Roger) What d'you say, son? Want to come along?

Roger (*eagerly*). Oh, boy! Really? (Frank *nods and grins.* Roger *leaps happily.*) Gee, Dad, you're the greatest guy in all the whole world.

[*He runs over and hugs* Frank.]

Frank (*grinning*). Go on, Clarry. Make it snappy.

[Clarice *goes into the bedroom. Doorbell rings.*]

Roger. I'll get it, Dad.

[*He runs to the door and opens it. Charlie Denton, forty years old and eager as a child, stands there. He comes in fast, excited.*]

Charlie. Hiya, Rog. Frank, you all set?

Frank. Hello, Charlie. Another minute or two. How's it look?

Charlie. Great. I'm checking house to house. Everybody's ready.

Frank. Good. Any changes?

Charlie. Nope. It's gonna be fast and quiet. What time you got?

Frank (*calling*). Clarry, what time is it?

Clarice (*calling*). Twelve after.

Charlie (*looking at watch*). Make it thirteen. At fifteen we go.

Frank. Right. Hey listen, you better look in on Artie Hayes next door. He's been acting a little peculiar.

Charlie. I spoke to him a little while ago on the street. I think he was coming over to see you. Don't worry about a thing. I'll be watching him. See you, Frank. Let's make this good.

Frank. You bet we will. It looks like a beaut. Take off. (Charlie *goes out fast.*) Get on your coat, Rog. (*Calling.*) Clarry!

[Roger *goes to closet and begins to get his coat.* Frank *stalks nervously up and down.*]

Clarice (*calling*). In a minute . . .

[Frank *goes to the window and looks out. He watches and waits. We can see the excitement building within him.* Roger, *hat and coat on, joins him at window.* Frank *puts his arm on* Roger's *shoulder and talks, half to himself.*]

Frank (*low*). How do you like that Artie Hayes? Maybe we ought to think it over! I could've belted him one. How do you like that guy!

Roger. What do you mean, Dad?

Frank (*calling*). Clarry!

Clarice (*calling*). Here I am. Come on, Chris.

[Clarice *walks into living room followed by a very sleepy* Christopher. *He is in his hat and coat. He wanders over to* Frank.]

Frank. What time is it?

Clarice. Almost fourteen after.

Frank. Almost fifteen. Put on your coat.

[Clarice *goes to the closet and does so.* Frank *follows her and gets his. He puts it on.* Clarice *picks up a large thermos from the foyer table.*]

Clarice (*low*). Frank . . . I'm busting with excitement.

Frank (*low*). Yeah. So'm I, honey. (*Louder*) Come over here, boys. (*The two boys walk over to them.*) Stand here.

[They *wait now behind the closed front door, all four of them tense, quiet, hardly able to stand the suspense. They wait for several seconds, and then, in the street, we begin to hear the heavy tread of marching feet.*]

Christopher. Hey, Daddy . . . where we going?

Frank. Ssh. Be quiet, son.

[He *bends over and picks* Christopher *up. The sound of marching feet grows louder and stronger. They wait till it reaches a crescendo.* Frank *speaks quietly now.*)

Frank. Let's go.

[He *opens the front door and they walk into a mob of grimly advancing men and women. They join the mob and walk with them quietly, and the only sound we hear is the frightening noise of the tramping feet. Fade out.*]

Reading Check

1. When does the first act of the play begin?
2. What does Frank Morrison do to surprise his children?
3. Why is the family eating dinner earlier than their usual time?
4. Why does Arthur Hayes visit Frank?
5. What do Frank and his family do at the end of Act One?

Analyzing and Interpreting the Play

1a. At the beginning of Act One, how are Frank Morrison and Arthur Hayes contrasted physically?   **b.** What other contrast emerges from their conversation?

2. What is revealed about Frank when he is shown playing with his sons that is disturbing?

3a. What do the Morrisons' actions and words reveal about their attitude toward their neighbors, the Blakes?   **b.** Point out specific examples.

4. Frank tells Clarice about a conversation he had with Charlie Denton. What important information is provided?

5a. How does Arthur Hayes's visit to the Morrisons confirm and develop the contrast between Frank and Arthur?   **b.** Which character do you find less sympathetic?

6. What is ominous about the conclusion of Act One?

Act Two

Fade in on *long shot of Sycamore Street. It is once again 6:40 P.M., the same night. We have gone backward in time and we now duplicate exactly the scene which opened Act One. Arthur Hayes walks on, stops in front of his house, knocks his pipe against his heel. Frank Morrison enters. Each of the movements they make, the attitudes they strike and the inflections they use must be exact imitations of the Act One business. The audience must feel that this scene is a clip of film which we are rerunning.*

Frank (*jovially*). Hey, Artie. How ya doin'?

[Arthur *is preoccupied. He doesn't register at first. He looks blankly at* Frank.]

Frank (*laughing*). Hey . . . wake up, boy. It's almost time for supper.

[Arthur *snaps out of it and forces a smile.*]

Arthur (*quietly*). Oh . . . hello, Frank. Sorry, I didn't see you.
Frank. Didn't see me? Hey, wait till I tell Clarice. That diet she's got me on must be working. You have to look twice to see me! (*Laughing hard,* Frank *reaches for his keys.*) That's a hot one! (Arthur *smiles weakly.*) Say . . . isn't this late for you to be getting home?
Arthur. No, I don't think so. (*He looks at his watch.*) It's twenty to seven. I always get home about this time.
Frank. Yeah. Well I wouldn't want you to be late tonight. You know what tonight is, don't you?
Arthur (*slowly*). Yes, I know what tonight is.
Frank (*a little hard*). Good.

[*We hear footsteps and see a man walk by them. He is* Joseph Blake, *a man in his late thirties, a big, powerful, but quiet man.* Joseph Blake *lives in the third house on the street. As he walks by them they both look at him silently. And now, for the first time, this scene moves in a different direction than did the scene at the beginning of Act One. Instead of coming in close on* Frank, *the camera comes in close on* Arthur Hayes *as he stands nervously in front of his door, afraid to look at either* Joseph Blake *or* Frank Morrison. *We hear* Joseph's *footsteps fade out.* Arthur *reaches for his keys.*]

Frank (*low, off*). See you later, Artie.

[Arthur *winces at this. We hear* Frank's *door opening and closing softly.* Arthur *turns now and looks off at* Joseph Blake's *house for a moment. Then he turns and opens his door. As he enters his foyer we hear dance music playing softly. The living room is lighted, and looking on from the foyer, we can see*

Mr. Harkness, Arthur's *father-in-law, seated in an armchair, reading the newspaper. He is perhaps sixty-five years old, and usually does nothing more than sit reading the newspapers. He looks up as Arthur comes in.*]

Mr. Harkness. Hello, Arthur. (*Calling off*) Here he is, Phyllis. (*To Arthur*) Little bit late, aren't you?

[Arthur *is hanging up his coat. He is obviously worried. His face shows concern. His entire manner is subdued. He speaks quietly, even for* Arthur.]

Arthur. No. Usual time.

[Mr. Harkness *takes out a pocket watch, looks at it, shakes it.*]

Mr. Harkness. Mmm. Must be fast.

[*He goes back to his newspaper.* Arthur *walks into the living room tiredly.*]

Arthur (*not caring*). How's your cough?
Mr. Harkness (*reading*). Still got it. I guess I must've swigged enough cough syrup to float a rowboat today. Waste of time and money!

[Phyllis *enters from kitchen as* Arthur *goes over to phonograph from which the dance music is blasting. He is just ready to turn it off as she enters.*]

Mr. Harkness. Cough'll go away by itself like it always does.
Phyllis (*brightly*). Hello, darling. Ah . . . don't turn it off.

[*He turns as she walks over to him. She kisses him possessively and leads him away from the phonograph. The music continues.*]

Phyllis. How did it go today, dear?

Arthur. All right. Nothing special.
Phyllis. What about the Franklin closing?
Arthur. It's called off till tomorrow.
Phyllis. How come?
Arthur. I didn't ask them.
Phyllis. Well, you'd think they'd at least give you a reason. You should've asked. I don't like it when people push you around like that.

[Arthur *goes over to a chair without answering. A pipe is on an end table next to the chair. He begins to fill it.* Phyllis *goes to a small bar on which is a cocktail shaker and one glass. She picks up the shaker.*]

Arthur. What's that?
Phyllis. I made you a drink.
Arthur. No. No, thanks. I don't want a drink now.
Phyllis. Oh, Artie! I made it specially for you. You look tired. Come on, it'll do you good. (*She begins to pour the drink*) Sit down, dear. I'll bring it over to you.

[Arthur *sits down.* Phyllis *finishes pouring the drink and brings it to him. He takes it. She waits, smiling, for him to drink it.*)

Arthur. How come you made me a drink tonight?
Phyllis. Just for luck. Taste it. (*She sits on the arm of the chair. He tastes it slowly. She puts her arm around him.*) Good?
Arthur (*slowly*). It's good.
Phyllis. I thought you'd like it.
Arthur. Where's Billy?
Phyllis. Asleep.
Arthur. Isn't it kind of early?
Phyllis. He didn't get much of a nap today. The poor baby couldn't keep his eyes open. Artie, he's getting to be such a devil. You should've seen him this afternoon. He got into my bag and took my lipstick. If I only could've taken a picture of his face. He walked into the

kitchen and I swear I almost screamed. You never saw anything so red in your life. Drink your drink, darling. It took me ten minutes to scrub it off.

[*Obediently,* Arthur *sips his drink.*]

Arthur (*mildly*). I'd like to have seen him before he went to bed.
Phyllis. Now you know I had to get finished early tonight, Artie. (*She gets up and goes toward the kitchen.*) We're eating in a few minutes. I'm just making melted cheese sandwiches. We can have a snack later if you're hungry.
Arthur. Later?
Phyllis (*looking at him oddly*). Yes, later. When we get back.

[Arthur *puts his drink down. All of his movements are slow, almost mechanical, as if he has that day aged twenty years. Phyllis goes into the kitchen. He takes off his glasses and begins polishing them.*]

Mr. Harkness. Melted cheese sandwiches.
Arthur (*not hearing*). What?
Mr. Harkness. I said melted cheese sandwiches. That gluey cheese. Do you like it?
Arthur. No.
Mr. Harkness. Me neither. Never did.

[*He goes back to his paper.* Arthur *gets up and goes to phonograph. He stands over it, listening.* Phyllis *comes in carrying a tray on which are three glasses of tomato juice. She gives it to* Arthur.]

Phyllis. Put these on the table like a good boy. (*He takes it and looks at her strangely.*) What's the matter with you, Artie? You've hardly said a word since you got home . . . and you keep looking at me. Are you sick, or something?
Arthur. No. I'm not sick.
Phyllis. Here, let me feel your head. (*She does so.*) No, you feel all right. What is it?

Arthur. Nothing. I'm just tired, I guess.
Phyllis. Well, I hope you perk up a little.

[*She goes off into kitchen.* Arthur *goes slowly to dining table, which is set in the same spot as the Morrison dining table. He puts the glasses on it, and sets the tray on the end table. He takes a sip of his drink.* Phyllis *comes in from the kitchen carrying a platter of melted cheese sandwiches. She goes to the table, puts it down.*]

Phyllis. Dinner. Come on, Dad, while they're hot. Artie . . .
Arthur. You go ahead. I'm not hungry.
Phyllis. Oh, now, let's not start that. You have to eat. Try one. They're nice and runny.
Arthur. Really, I'm not hungry.
Phyllis. Well, you can at least sit with us. I haven't seen you since half past eight this morning.

[Arthur *goes slowly over to the table and sits down.* Mr. Harkness *ambles over.*]

Mr. Harkness. Well, I'm good and hungry. Tell you that. Got any pickles?
Phyllis. No pickles. You know they give you heartburn.
Mr. Harkness. Haven't had heartburn in a long time. Wouldn't mind a slight case if it came from pickles.

[*They are all seated now,* Phyllis *facing the window.* Arthur *sits quietly.* Mr. Harkness *busies himself drinking water while* Phyllis *serves the sandwiches, potato salad, etc.*]

Phyllis. Artie . . . potato salad?
Arthur. No. Look, Phyllis . . .
Phyllis. Just a little.

[*She puts a spoonful on a heavily loaded plate and passes it to him. He takes it. Now she serves her father.*]

Phyllis. Potato salad, Dad?

Mr. Harkness. I'll help myself.

[*She puts the bowl down and helps herself as does* Mr. Harkness.]

Phyllis (*brightly*). What happened at the office, dear? Anything new?

Arthur. No. It was quiet.

Phyllis. Did you hear about the Walkers wanting to sell their house?

Arthur. No.

Phyllis. You know, for a real-estate man you hear less about real estate than anyone I ever saw. I spoke to Margie Walker this morning. I just got to her in time. You're going to handle the sale. She told me she hadn't even thought of you till I called. Why is that, dear?

Arthur. I don't know why it is.

Phyllis. Well, anyway, she's expecting you to call her tomorrow. It ought to be a very nice sale for you, dear.

[Arthur *nods and looks down at his plate. There is silence for a moment.*]

Mr. Harkness (*chewing*). This stuff gets under my teeth.

Phyllis. Dad!

Mr. Harkness. Well, I can't help it, can I?

[*They eat for a moment and then* Phyllis, *looking out the window, sees movement in the house next door, the Blake house. She can no longer hold back the topic she's been trying not to discuss in front of Arthur.*]

Phyllis. Look at them. Every shade in the house is down. (*She looks at her watch.*) There isn't much more time. I wonder if they know. Do you think they do, Artie?

Arthur (*tired*). I don't know.

Phyllis. They must. You can't keep a thing like this secret. I wonder how they feel. (*She looks at* Arthur.) Artie, aren't you going to eat your dinner?

Arthur (*slowly*). How can you talk about them and my dinner in the same breath?

Phyllis. For Heaven's sakes . . . I don't know what's the matter with you tonight.

Arthur (*quietly*). You don't, do you?

[*He gets up from the table and walks over to the phonograph. He stands there holding it with both hands, listening to the slick dance music. Then abruptly, he turns it off.* Phyllis *looks as if she is about to protest, but then decides not to.*]

Mr. Harkness. What d'you suppose is gonna happen over there? Boy, wouldn't I like to go along tonight.

Phyllis (*looking at* Arthur). Dad, will you please stop?

Mr. Harkness. Well, I would! How do you think it feels to be sixty-two years old and baby-sitting when there's real action going on right under your nose? Something a man wants to get into.

Arthur (*turning*). Be quiet!

Mr. Harkness. Now listen here——

Arthur. I said be quiet! (*He takes off his glasses and walks over to the table.*)

Phyllis. Artie, stop it! There's no need for you to raise your voice like that.

[Arthur *speaks more quietly now, feeling perhaps that he has gone too far.*]

Arthur. Then tell your father to keep his ideas to himself!

Mr. Harkness (*angrily*). Wait a minute!

[Phyllis, *in the ensuing argument, is quiet, calm, convincing, never losing her temper, always trying to soothe* Arthur, *to sweeten the ugly things she says by saying them gently.*]

Phyllis. Dad, be quiet. Listen, Artie, I know you're tired, darling, but there's something we might as well face. In about fifteen or twenty minutes you and I and a group of our friends and neighbors are going to be marching on that house next door. Maybe it's not such a pleasant thing to look forward to, but something has to be done. You know that, Artie. You agreed to it with all the others.

Arthur. I didn't agree to anything. You agreed for the Hayes household. Remember?

Phyllis. All right, I agreed. I didn't hear you disagreeing. Oh, what's the difference, darling? You've been acting like there's a ten-ton weight on your back ever since you heard about it. And there's no point to it. It's all decided.

Arthur. All decided. What right have we got to decide?

Phyllis. It's not a question of right, Artie. Don't you see? It's something we have to do, right or wrong. Do you really want them to live next door to you? Do you really want them?

Arthur. I always thought a man was supposed to be able to live anywhere he chooses no matter what anyone else wants.

Phyllis. But, dear, this isn't anywhere. This is Sycamore Street. It's not some back alley in a slum! This is a respectable neighborhood. Artie, let's be realistic. That's one of the few things we can really say we have. We're respectable. Do you remember how hard we worked to get that way?

Arthur. Respectable! Phyllis, for heaven's sakes. We're talking about throwing a man out of his own home. What is the man? He's not a monster. He's a quiet guy who minds his own business. How does that destroy our respectability?

Phyllis (*hard*). He got out of prison two months ago. He's a common hoodlum.

Arthur. We don't know for sure.

Phyllis. We know. Charlie Denton doesn't lie.

He saw the man's picture in the Rockville papers just fifty miles from here the day he got out. Tell me, what does he do for a living? Where did he get the money to buy that house?

Arthur. I don't think that's any of your business.

Phyllis. But, Artie, the man was in jail for four years. That's our business! How do you know what he did? How do you know he won't do it again?

Arthur. We have police.

Phyllis. Police! Will the police stop his child from playing with Billy? What kind of a child must that be? Think about it. Her father is an ex-convict. That's a lovely thing to tell our friends. Why yes . . . you know Billy's little friend Judy. Of course you do. Her father spent a great deal of time in prison. Charming people. It's beautiful for the neighborhood, isn't it, Artie? It makes real-estate prices just skyrocket up. Tell me, who do you think'll be moving in next . . . and where'll we go?

[Arthur *doesn't answer. He sits down in a chair, troubled, trying to find an argument. Phyllis watches him closely.*]

Mr. Harkness. Listen, Artie——

[*But* Phyllis *puts her hand on his arm to shut him up.* Arthur *is thinking and she wants to see if her argument has worked.*]

Arthur. Look, Phyllis, this is a mob we're getting together. We're going to order this man out of his house . . . or we're going to throw him out. What right have we got to do it? Maybe most of us'd rather not have him as a neighbor, but, Phyllis, the man is a human being, not an old dog. This is an ugly thing we're doing . . .

Phyllis. We've got to do something to keep our

homes decent. There's no other way. Somebody's always got to lose, Artie. Why should it be all of us when there's only one of him?

Arthur. I . . . I don't know.

[Arthur *suddenly gets up and goes toward the front door as if going out. He buttons his jacket.* Phyllis *gets up, concerned.*]

Phyllis. Where are you going?

Arthur. I'm going to talk to Frank Morrison.

Phyllis. All right. Maybe Frank'll make sense to you. (*Calling*) Wear your coat.

[But Arthur *has opened the door and intends to go out without it.* Phyllis *looks at her watch.*]

Phyllis. Arthur, it's freezing out! (*He is outside the door now.*) You'll catch cold. (*The door closes. She stands watching after him, obviously upset. Her father resumes his eating. She looks at the door for a long time. Then, without looking around*) Dad . . .

Mr. Harkness. Mmmm?

Phyllis. What do you think he'll do?

Mr. Harkness. Well . . . I don't know. You got any more of these cheese businesses? I'm hungry.

Phyllis. No. (*She goes to the window and looks out.*)

Mr. Harkness. Why don't you sit down, Phyl? He'll be all right.

Phyllis. What do you mean all right? Look at him. He's standing in front of Frank's house afraid to ring the bell.

Mr. Harkness. He'll calm down. Come away from that window and sit down. Have some coffee.

[She moves away from the window and sits at table.]

Phyllis. I've never seen him like this before.

Mr. Harkness. Well, what are you worried about? Tell you what. I'll go along with you. Boy, wouldn't I like to be in on a thing like this once. Let Artie stay home and mind the baby if that's how he feels.

[Phyllis *turns to her father violently and for the first time we see how much* Arthur's *decision means to her.*]

Phyllis (*fiercely*). He's got to go! Don't you understand?

Mr. Harkness. What the dickens is eating you? No, I don't understand. (Phyllis *gets up and goes to the window. She looks out tensely.*) Would you mind telling me what you're talking about?

Phyllis (*startled*). Oh, no!

[She turns and runs to the front door. She starts to open it and run out. As she gets it half open we hear a low voice calling. Charlie Denton's voice.]

Charlie (*low*). Artie! Hey, Artie!

[She closes the door silently and stands against it, frightened. Cut to street in front of Frank's house. Arthur *stands there, having just been hailed by* Charlie. He turns, and then we see Charlie hurrying down the street toward him. Charlie gets to him, takes him by the arm.]

Charlie (*low*). What are you doing out here now?

Arthur (*guiltily*). Nothing. I was . . . well, I was getting some air, that's all.

Charlie. Look, boy, this thing has got to be timed on the button. Everybody's supposed to be in his house right now. Nobody's supposed to be wandering around the streets. What time've you got?

Arthur (*with an effort*). Listen, Charlie, I want to talk to you about tonight.

Charlie. I haven't got time to talk.

Arthur. Please. It's important.

Charlie (*tough*). What the heck's the matter with you?

Arthur. Nothing. Nothing, Charlie . . .

Charlie. What time've you got? (*He grabs* Arthur's *wrist and holds it up to the light. He holds his own wrist next to it and compares the watches.*) You're three minutes slow.

Arthur. I know. This watch . . . it runs slow, Charlie . . .

Charlie. Well, fix it, willya? The timing's the most important part

Arthur. I will. Look, about this thing tonight . . .

Charlie. Listen, if you're gonna start in with me about the plan, take it up with the committee, will ya, please? All of a sudden everybody's an expert on how to run the show. If you want the organizing job I'll be glad to give it to you.

Arthur. No, it's not that. It's organized very well. There's something else.

Charlie. Are you gonna fix that watch?

Arthur. I will. I've been meaning to set it all day. Listen . . . these people . . . the Blakes. They've got a kid . . .

Charlie. So has my mother. Here, gimme this. (*He grabs* Arthur's *wrist and sets his watch.*) There. At seven-fifteen on the nose we go. Now get back into your house. (*He walks off fast.*)

Arthur. Charlie . . .

[*But* Charlie *keeps going.* Arthur *watches him. Then he goes up to* Frank Morrison's *front door and rings the bell. From inside we hear* Roger *calling.*]

Roger (*off*). I'll get it.

[Roger *opens the front door, and now again,* Roger's *and* Arthur's *movements must be exactly as they were in the first act, except that now the camera catches them from outside the house.*]

Arthur. Rog, is your Dad in?

Roger. Sure. Come on in, Mr. Hayes.

[Arthur *walks in slowly. The door closes.*

Fade out.

Fade in on the living room of Arthur's *house.* Phyllis *sits tensely waiting for him. The dining table is cleared.* Mr. Harkness *is back in his easy chair reading the papers. We hear a key in the lock, the door opens, and* Arthur *enters. He walks slowly, despising himself for not having been stronger with* Frank *or* Charlie. Phyllis *gets up as he comes in. He doesn't look at her but walks over to the window and stands there. She comes up behind him. He doesn't turn around.*]

Phyllis. Artie . . . Artie, are you all right?

[*He turns around slowly, speaks heavily.*]

Arthur. Yeah, I'm fine.

Phyllis. What happened? What'd you say to them?

Arthur. I said nothing.

Phyllis (*hopefully*). Well, what do you mean you said nothing. Didn't you talk about it?

Arthur. No, I didn't talk about it. I didn't talk about anything. Will you leave me alone?

[*She backs away, alarmed. Then she looks at her watch.*]

Phyllis (*softly*). We only have a couple of minutes, dear.

Arthur. I'm not going out there.

Phyllis. I'd better get our coats.

Arthur. Did you hear what I just said?

Phyllis. We'll have to bundle up. It's only about twenty degrees out. Did you know that?

Arthur. I said I'm not going.

[Phyllis *backs away from him. He turns to the win-*

dow. We can see that she is hugely upset; almost desperate. She looks at him fiercely. Mr. Harkness gets up quietly with his paper and goes into the next room. We hear the door close. Arthur doesn't move.]

Phyllis (*strongly*). I want to tell you something. I'm going to get our coats now, and we're going to put them on, and we're going to stand in the doorway of our house until it's seven-fifteen.
Arthur (*turning*). Stop it.
Phyllis. And thcn we're going to walk out into the gutter, you and me, the Hayes family, and we're going to be just like everybody else on Sycamore Street!

Arthur (*shouting*). Phyllis! I've told you . . . I'm not going to be a part of this thing!

[Phyllis *studies him for a long moment.*]

Phyllis. Listen to me, Artie. Listen to me good. I didn't think you needed to hear this before. But you're going to hear it now. We're going out there. Do you want to know why? Because we're not going to be next!
Arthur. You're out of your mind!
Phyllis (*roaring*). Sure I am! I'm out of my mind all right. I'm crazy with fear because I don't want to be different. I don't want my

neighbors looking at us and wondering why we're not like them.

Arthur (*amazed*). Phyllis . . . you're making this up! They won't think that.

Phyllis. They will think that! We'll be the only ones, the odd ones who wanted to let an ex-convict live with us. They'll look the other way when we walk the streets. They'll become cold and nasty . . . and all of a sudden we won't have any neighbors. (*Pointing at the Blake house.*) We'll be like them!

[Arthur *stands looking at her and it begins to sink in. She knows it and goes after him.*]

Phyllis. We can't be different! We can't afford it! We live on the good will of these people. Your business is in this town. Your neighbors buy us the bread we eat! Do you want them to stop?

Arthur. I don't know . . . Phyllis . . . I don't know what to think . . . I . . . can't throw a stone at this man.

Phyllis (*strong*). You can! You've got to, or we're finished here.

[He stares at her, not knowing what to say next. She has almost won and knows it. She looks at her watch.]

Phyllis. Now just . . . wait . . . just stand there . . . (*She runs to the closet and takes out their overcoats. She throws hers on and brings his to him, holds it for him.*)

Phyllis. Put it on!

Arthur. I . . . can't. They're people. It's their home.

Phyllis (*shouting*). We're people too! I don't care what happens to them. I care what happens to us. We belong here. We've got to live here. Artie, for the love of God, we don't even know them. What's the difference what happens to them? What about us?

[He has no answer. She begins to put his coat on. He stands there, beaten, wrecked, moving his arms automatically, no longer knowing the woman who is putting on his coat. She talks as she helps him.]

Phyllis. There. It won't be long. I promise you. It won't be long. That's my Artie. That's my darling. Let's button up, dear. It's cold, We'll be back in an hour, and it'll be over. There. Now put on your gloves, darling.

[She takes him by the arm and he stands there letting her do as she will. He puts on his gloves without knowing he is doing it, and they wait together, there in the doorway. She looks at him, trying to read him, as we begin to hear the cold and chilling sound of the tramping feet. Mr. Harkness *comes out of the bedroom and stands there looking at them.* Phyllis *looks at her watch. The tramping grows louder. They wait in silence. Then she opens the door. We see the crowd, grimly marching, and the* Morrisons *are at the head of it. No one looks at the* Hayeses. *The dull thud of the tramping feet is sickening to hear.* Arthur *closes his eyes. Slowly now* Phyllis *pushes him forward. He steps out of the house and moves ahead to join the others, as if in a dream.* Phyllis *follows, catches up, and takes his arm as they join the marching mob. Fade out.*]

Reading Check

1. When does Act Two begin?
2. Whom does Arthur Hayes encounter when he first enters his house?
3. What kind of work does Arthur Hayes do?
4. What do people on Sycamore Street have against Hayes's neighbor?
5. What happens at the end of Act Two?

For Study and Discussion

Analyzing and Interpreting the Play

1. Act Two begins as Act One did. **a.** When does it begin to be different? **b.** What does the difference lead you to expect?

2. Phyllis tells Arthur, "I don't like it when people push you around like that." What does this statement reveal about her attitude toward him?

3. Phyllis and Arthur argue about what is planned for that evening. **a.** What do you learn that suggests Phyllis is the dominant one in the family? **b.** What reasons does she give for going through with what is about to happen?

4a. At the end of the act, why does Phyllis insist that Arthur join the march? **b.** What practical reason does she give? **c.** What general issue is raised?

5. Compare the ending of Act Two with that of Act One. How are Arthur and Frank contrasted?

Act Three

Fade in on *a long shot of Sycamore Street. It is once again 6:40 P.M., same night. We have gone backward in time, and again we duplicate the scene which opened Acts One and Two. Arthur Hayes walks on, stops in front of his house, knocks his pipe against his heel. Frank Morrison enters. Again, each of the movements must be exact imitations of the movements in Acts One and Two. It is as if we are starting the play again.*

Frank (*jovially*). Hey, Artie. How ya doin'?

[Arthur *is preoccupied. He doesn't register at first. He looks blankly at* Frank.]

Frank (*laughing*). Hey . . . wake up, boy. It's almost time for supper.

[Arthur *snaps out of it and forces a smile.*]

Arthur (*quietly*). Oh . . . hello, Frank. Sorry, I didn't see you.
Frank. Didn't see me? Hey, wait till I tell Clarice. That diet she's got me on must be working. You have to look twice to see me! (*Laughing hard,* Frank *reaches for his keys.*) That's a hot one! (Arthur *smiles weakly.*) Say . . . isn't this late for you to be getting home?
Arthur. No, I don't think so. (*He looks at his watch.*) It's twenty to seven. I always get home about this time.
Frank. Yeah. Well, I wouldn't want you to be late tonight. You know what tonight is, don't you?
Arthur (*slowly*). Yes, I know what tonight is.
Frank (*a little hard*). Good.

[*We hear footsteps and see a man walk by them. He is* Joseph Blake. *They both look at him silently. Camera now follows him as he walks silently toward his house, the third of the three houses we see. As he walks, we hear faintly in background.*]

Frank (*off*). See you later, Artie.

[*We hear* Frank's *door open and close. Then we hear* Arthur's *door open, and for an instant, we hear the same dance music coming from* Arthur's *house that we heard in Act Two. Then* Arthur's *door closes. By this time* Joseph Blake *is in front of his door. He looks off silently at the other two houses. Then he opens his front door and enters his house. As he closes the door we hear running feet, and then we see* Judy, *Joe's six-year-old daughter, in a bathrobe and slippers, running at him.*]

Judy (*calling*). Daddy Daddy Daddy Daddy.

[*She runs into his arms. He lifts her up and hugs her.*]

Joe. Mmm. You smell sweet.
Judy (*excited*). I had a hairwash with Mommy's special shampoo. It smells like gar . . . gar . . .
Joe. Gardenias. Did anyone ever tell you you smelled like gardenias even without Mommy's shampoo?
Judy (*grinning*). You're silly.

[*He tickles her and she giggles.*]

Anna (*calling*). Judy!
Judy (*importantly*). We've got company.

Joe. Oh? Who is it, darling?
Anna (*calling*). Judy!
Judy. A lady.

[Joe *puts her down. She runs inside.* Joe *takes off his coat, puts it into the closet, and walks into the living room.* Joe's *wife, Anna, stands near a chair. Anna, in her early thirties, is a quiet, small woman who has obviously been through a great deal of suffering in the past five years. She looks extremely nervous and upset now. Seated at the far end of the room in a rocking chair is* Joe's *mother, Mrs. Blake. She is quite old, quite spry for her years, and inclined to be snappish. Also seated in the room is a middle-aged woman, a neighborhood busybody named Mrs. Car-*

son. *She wears an odd, old-fashioned hat and sits stiffly, not at home, quite uncomfortable, but determined to do what she has come to do. The living room again is an exact duplicate of the Morrison and Hayes living rooms. It is furnished sparsely and not well. It is obvious that the Blakes have not been living there long. As* Joe *gets into the room,* Anna *comes toward him.*]

Anna. Joe, this is Mrs. Carson.
Joe (*politely*). Mrs. Carson.

[*He turns to her for a moment. She nods curtly. Then he turns back to* Anna *and kisses her gently.*]

Joe. Hello, darling.
Anna. Joe . . .

[*But he walks away from her and goes to his mother. He bends over and kisses her on the forehead.*]

Mrs. Blake. Your face is cold.
Joe (*smiling*). It's freezing out. How do you feel?
Mrs. Blake. Just fine, Joe.

[*He pats her cheek and turns to find* Judy *behind him, holding a piece of drawing paper and a crayon. On the paper is a childish scribble that looks vaguely like a boat.* Anna, *a tortured expression on her face, wants to say something, but* Joe *looks at the drawing, grinning.*]

Judy. Daddy . . .
Joe. The *Queen Mary*! Now that is what I call beautiful.
Judy. It is not! It's just s'posed to be a sailboat. How do you draw a sail?
Anna (*shakily*). Joe . . . Mrs. Carson . . .
Joe. Well, let's see . . . (*He takes the crayon and paper and studies it.*) I suppose you think it's easy to draw a sail.
Judy (*serious*). No. I don't.

Anna (*sharply*). Joe. (*She comes over and snatches the paper away from him. He looks at her.*) Judy, go into your room.
Joe. Wait a minute, Anna. Take it easy.
Anna (*near tears*). Judy, did you hear me?
Joe. Darling, what's the matter with you?
Anna. Joe . . .
Judy. Mommy, do I have to?
Joe (*gently*). Maybe you'd better go inside for a few minutes, baby.

[Judy *unhappily goes into her room.* Anna *waits till we hear the door close.* Joe *puts his arms around her.*]

Joe. Tell me. What's wrong, Anna?
Anna (*almost sobbing*). Joe! I don't understand it! Mrs. Carson says . . . She . . .
Joe (*gently*). Mrs. Carson says what?
Anna (*breaking down*). She says . . . Joe . . . they're going to throw us out of our house. Tonight! Right now! What are we going to do?
Joe (*softly*). Well, I don't know. Who's going to throw us out of our house?

[*But* Anna *can't answer.* Joe *grips her tightly, then releases her and walks to* Mrs. Carson, *who sits stolidly, waiting.*]

Joe. Who's going to throw us out, Mrs. Carson? Do you know?
Mrs. Carson. Well, like I told Mrs. Blake there, I suppose it's none of my business, but I'm just not the kind that thinks a thing like this ought to happen to people without them getting at least a . . . well, a warning. Know what I mean?
Joe. No, I don't know what you mean, Mrs. Carson. Did someone send you here?
Mrs. Carson (*indignantly*). Well, I should say not! If my husband knew I was here he'd drag me out by the hair. No, I sneaked in here, if you please, Mr. Blake. I felt it was my Christian duty. A man ought to have the right to run away, I say.

Joe. What do you mean run away. Mrs. Carson?

Mrs. Carson. Well, you know what I mean.

Joe. Who's going to throw us out?

Mrs. Carson. Well, everybody. The people on Sycamore Street. You know. They don't feel you ought to live here because . . . Now I don't suppose I have to go into that.

Joe (*understanding*). I see.

Anna (*breaking in*). Joe, I've been waiting and waiting for you to come home. I've been sitting here . . . and waiting. Listen . . .

Joe (*quietly*). Hold it, Anna. (*To* Mrs. Carson.) What time are they coming, Mrs. Carson?

Mrs. Carson. Quarter after seven. That's the plan. (*She looks at her watch and gets up.*) It's near seven now. They're very angry people, Mr. Blake. I don't think it'd be right for anyone to get hurt. That's why I'm here. If you take my advice, you'll just put some stuff together in a hurry and get out. I don't think there's any point in your calling the police either. There's only two of 'em in Eastmont and I don't think they'd do much good against a crowd like this.

Joe. Thank you, Mrs. Carson.

Mrs. Carson. Oh, don't thank me. It's like I said. I don't know you people, but there's no need for anyone getting hurt long as you move out like everybody wants. No sir. I don't want no part nor parcel to any violence where it's not necessary. Know what I mean?

Joe. Yes, I know what you mean.

Mrs. Carson. I don't know why a thing like this had to start up anyway. It's none of my business, but a man like you ought to know better than to come pushing in here . . . a fine old neighborhood like this! After all, right is right.

Joe (*controlled*). Get out, Mrs. Carson.

Mrs. Carson. What? Well I never! You don't seem to know what I've done for you, Mr. Blake.

Anna. Joe . . .

Joe. Get out of this house.

[*He goes to a chair in which lies* Mrs. Carson's *coat. He picks it up and thrusts it at her. She takes it, indignant and a bit frightened.* Joe *turns from her. She begins to put her coat on.*]

Mrs. Carson. Well, I should think you'd at least have the decency to thank me. I might've expected this though. People like you!

Anna. Mrs. Carson, please . . .

Joe. Anna, stop it!

[*He strides to the door and holds it open.* Mrs. Carson *walks out.*]

Mrs. Carson. I think maybe you'll be getting what you deserve, Mr. Blake. Good night.

[*She goes out.* Joe *slams the door.*]

Anna. It's true. I can't believe it! Joe! Did you hear what she said? (*She goes to* Joe, *who still stands at the door, shocked.*) Well, what are you standing there for?

Joe (*amazed*). I don't know.

Anna. Joe, I'm scared. I'm so scared, I'm sick to my stomach. What are we going to do?

[Joe *puts his arms around her as she begins to sob. He holds her close till she quiets down. Then he walks her slowly over to his mother.*]

Joe (*to his mother*). Will you read to Judy for a few minutes, Mother? It's time for her story. (*Mrs. Blake* starts to get up.) Winnie the Pooh. She'll tell you what page.

[*Mrs. Blake* nods and gets up and goes into Judy's room.]

Anna. What are you doing, Joe? We've only got fifteen minutes . . . Don't you understand?

Joe (*quietly*). What do you want me to do? I can't stop them from coming here.

[*She goes to him and looks up at him, pleading now.*]

Anna (*whispering*). Joe. Let's get out. We've got time. We can throw some things into the car. . . .

Joe. Isn't it a remarkable thing? A quiet street like this and people with thunder in their hearts.

Anna. Listen to me, Joe—please. We can get most of our clothes in the car. We can stop at a motel. I don't care where we go. Anywhere. Joe, you're not listening. (*Loud*) What's the matter with you?

Joe. We're staying.

Anna (*frightened*). No!

Joe. Anna, this is our home and we're staying in it. No one can make us get out of our home. No one. That's a guarantee I happen to have since I'm born.

Anna (*sobbing*). Joe, you can't! Do you know what a mob is like? Do you know what they're capable of doing?

Joe. It's something I've never thought of before . . . a mob. I guess they're capable of doing ugly things.

Anna. Joe, you're talking and talking and the clock is ticking so fast. Please . . . please . . .

Joe. We can run. We can go somewhere else to live. It's not so hard.

Joe. It's very hard, Anna, when it's not your own choice.

Anna (*sobbing*). What are you talking about? What else've we got to do? Stand here and fight them? We're not an army. We're one man and one woman and an old lady and a baby.

Joe. And the floor we stand on belongs to us. Not to anyone else.

Anna. They don't care about things like that. Joe, listen to me, please. You're not making sense. Listen . . . Judy's inside. She's six years old now and she's only really known you for a few weeks. We waited four years for you, and she didn't remember you when you picked her up and kissed her hello, but, Joe, she was so happy. What are you gonna tell her when they set fire to her new house?

Joe. I'm gonna tell her that her father fought like a tiger to stop them.

Anna (*crying*). Oh, no! No! No! What good will that do? Joe . . . please . . . please . . .

Joe (*thundering*). Stop it! (Anna *turns away from him and covers her face. After a long pause, quietly.*) It's this way, Anna. We have a few things we own. We have this house we've just bought with money left from before . . . money you could have used many times. We have a mortgage and a very old car and a few pieces of furniture. We have my job.

Anna (*bitterly*). Selling pots and pans at kitchen doors.

Joe (*patiently*). We have my job. And we have each other and that's what we have. Except there's one more thing. We have the right to live where we please and how we please. We're keeping all of those things, Anna. They belong to us.

[*He comes up behind her and puts his hands on her shoulders. She sinks down in a chair, turned away from him, and sobs. He stands over her. She continues to sob. He holds her and tries to quiet her. The bedroom door opens and* Judy *bounces into the room.* Joe *gets up and goes to her as* Anna *tries to dry her tears.*]

Judy. Grandma says I'm supposed to go to bed now. Do I have to, Daddy?

Joe (*smiling*). It's time, honey.

Judy (*disappointed*). Gee whiz. Some night, I'm gonna stay up until four o'clock in the morning!

Joe. Some night, you can. (*He kisses her.*) Good night, baby. Give Mommy a kiss.

[Judy *goes to* Anna *and speaks as she is kissing her.*]

Judy. Really? I really can stay up till four o'clock?
Joe. Really.
Judy. Night, Mommy.
Anna. Good night, darling.

[Judy *runs off gleefully to the bedroom.*]

Judy. Oh boy! (*Calling*) Grandma . . .

[*The door closes.* Anna *gets up and goes to window. She is still terrified, but a bit calmer now. She looks out and then turns to* Joe. *He watches her.*]

Anna. What've we done to hurt them? What've we done? I don't understand.
Joe (*softly*). Well, I guess maybe they think we've destroyed the dignity of their neighborhood, darling. That's why they've thrown garbage on our lawn.
Anna. Dignity! Throwing garbage. Getting together a mob. Those are dignified things to do. Joe, how can you want to stay? How can you want to live on the same street with them? Don't you see what they are?
Joe. They're people, Anna. And I guess they're afraid, just like we are. That's why they've become a mob. It's what people always do.

[*The bedroom door opens and* Joe's *mother enters. She goes to her rocker and sits in it and begins to rock.*]

Anna. What are they afraid of?
Joe. Living next door to someone they think is beneath them. An ex-convict. Me.

[Anna *runs to* Joe *and grips him excitedly.*]

Anna. What do they think you did? They must think you're a thief or a murderer.
Joe. Maybe they do.

Anna. Well, they can't. You'll tell them. You'll tell them, Joe.
Joe. Anna, listen . . .
Anna. It could've happened to any one of them. Tell them you're not a common criminal. You were in an accident, and that's all it was. An accident. Joe, they'll listen. I know they will.
Joe. No, Anna . . .
Anna (*eagerly*). All you have to do is tell them and they'll go away. It's not like you committed a crime or anything. You were speeding. Everybody speeds. You hit an old man, and he died. He walked right in front——
Joe. They're not asking what I did, Anna.
Anna (*pleading*). Joe, please. Look at me. I'm so frightened . . . You have to tell them.
Joe. Anna, we have our freedom. If we beg for it, then it's gone. Don't you see that?
Anna. (*shouting*). No!

[*He comes to her and grips her, and speaks to her with his face inches from hers.*]

Joe. How can I tell it to you? Listen, Anna, we're only little people, but we have certain rights. Judy's gonna learn about them in school in a couple of years . . . and they'll tell her that no one can take them away from her. She's got to be able to believe that. They include the right to be different. Well, a group of our neighbors have decided that we have to get out of here because they think we're different. They think we're not nice. (*Strongly.*) Do we have to smile in their faces and tell them we are nice? We don't have to win the right to be free! It's the same as running away, Anna. It's staying on their terms, and if we can't stay here on our terms, then there are no more places to stay anywhere. For you—for me—for Judy—for anyone, Anna.

[*She sees it now and she almost smiles, but the tears*

are running down her cheeks and it's difficult to smile. Joe *kisses her forehead.*]

Joe (*quietly*). Now we'll wait for them.

[Anna *goes slowly to a chair and sits in it.* Mrs. Blake *rocks rhythmically on her rocking chair.* Joe *stands firm at one side of the room and they wait in silence. Suddenly the ticking of the clock on the mantelpiece thunders in our ears and the monotonous beat of it is all we hear. They wait.* Anna *looks at* Joe *and then speaks softly.*]

Anna. Joe. My hands are shaking. I don't want them to shake.

[Joe *walks over to her, stands over her strongly, and clasps both her hands together. Then he holds them in his till they are still. The clock ticks on, and now we cut to it. It reads ten after seven. Dissolve to a duplicate of the clock which now reads quarter after seven. Cut to long shot of room as we begin to hear the tramping of the feet down the street. They wait. The rocker rocks. The clock ticks. The trampling grows louder.* Joe *stands in the center of the room, hard and firm. Then he turns to his mother and speaks gently and softly.*]

Joe. Go inside, Mother.
Mrs. Blake (*slowly*). No, Joe. I'm staying here. I want to watch you. I want to hear you. I want to be proud.

[*She continues to rock and now the tramping noise reaches a crescendo and then stops. For a moment there is silence, absolute silence, and then we hear a single angry voice.*]

Charlie Denton (*shouting*). Joseph Blake! (*There is a chorus of shouts and a swelling of noise.*) Joseph Blake . . . come out here!

[*The noise from outside grows in volume. Inside only the rocking chair moves.*]

First Man (*shouting*). Come out of that house!

[*The noise, the yelling of the crowd, continues to grow. Inside the room no one gives a signal that they have heard.*]

Second Man (*shouting*). We want you, Joseph Blake!
Frank Morrison (*shouting*). Come out—or we'll drag you out!

[*The yelling continues, grows louder. Still the* Blakes *do not move. Then suddenly a rock smashes through the window. Glass sprays to the floor. The pitch of the noise outside rises even more.* Joe *begins to walk firmly to the door.*]

Anna (*softly*). Joe . . .

[*But he doesn't hear her. He gets to the door and flings it open violently and steps outside. As he does, the shouting, which has reached its highest pitch, stops instantly and from deafening noise we plunge into absolute silence, broken only by the steady creaking of the rocking chair inside.* Joe *stands there in front of his house like a rock. Now for the first time we see the crowd. The camera plays over the silent faces watching him—the faces of the men and women and children. The* Morrisons *are directly in front,* Charlie Denton *is further back.* Mrs. Carson *is there. And far to the rear we see* Arthur Hayes *and* Phyllis. *Still the silence holds. Then, little by little, the people begin to speak. At first we only hear single voices from different parts of the crowd.*]

First Man (*shouting*). Look at him, standing there like he owns the block!

[*There is a chorus of ad-lib[1] approvals.*]

Second Man (*shouting*). Who do you think you are, busting in where decent people live?

1. **ad-lib** (ăd lĭb'): spontaneous; unrehearsed.

Thunder on Sycamore Street **473**

[*Another chorus of approvals.* Joe *stands like a fierce and powerful statue.*]

First Woman (*shouting*). Why don't you go live with your own kind . . . in a gutter somewhere?

[*Another chorus of approvals. The camera moves about catching the eagerness, the mounting temper of the crowd, then the shame and anguish of* Arthur Hayes, *then the giant strength of* Joe]

First Man (*shouting*). Your limousine is waiting, Mr. Blake. You're taking a one-way trip!

[*There are a few laughs at this, and now the crowd, although not moving forward, is a shouting mass again.* Joe *still waits quietly.*]

Charlie Denton (*shouting*). Well, what are we waiting for? Let's get him!

[*The intensity of the noise grows and the mob begins to move forward. Then, with a tremendous roar,* Frank Morrison *stops them.*]

Frank (*roaring*). Quiet! Everybody shut up.

[*The noise dies down gradually.*]

Frank (*to crowd*). Now listen to me! This thing is gonna be handled the way we planned at the meeting.

[Roger, *standing next to* Frank, *looks at him adoringly.* Chris *holds* Clarice's *hand and looks around calmly.*]

Clarice (*loud*). That's right! It's what we agreed on.
Frank (*shouting*). This man here is gonna be asked politely and quietly to pack his things and get his family out of here. We don't have to

tell him why. He knows that. He's gonna be given a chance to leave right now. If he's got any brains in his head he'll be out in one hour— and nobody'll touch him or his house. If he hasn't——

[*There is a low-throated, ominous murmur from the crowd.*]

Frank. Right! This thing is gonna be done fair and square. (*Turning to* Joe.) What d'ya say, Mr. Blake?

[Joe *looks at him for a long time. The crowd waits silently.* Arthur Hayes *lowers his head and clenches his fists, and looks as if he wants to be sick. The crowd waits. When* Joe *speaks, it is with a controlled fury that these people have never heard before. He speaks directly to* Frank.]

Joe. I spit on your fairness! (*The crowd gasps.* Joe *waits, then he thunders out.*) I own this house and God gave me the right to live in it. The man who tries to take it away from me is going to have to climb over a pile of bones to do it. You good people of Sycamore Street are going to have to kill me tonight! Are you ready, Mr. Morrison? Don't bother to be fair. You're the head man here. Be first!

[*The crowd, rocked back on its heels, doesn't know what to do. Behind* Joe, *in the house, we see framed in the doorway the rocking chair moving steadily, and* Anna *standing next to it.* Frank *is stunned by this outburst. He calls for action. But not with the force he displayed earlier.*]

Frank. You heard him, everybody. . . . Let's get him.
Joe. I asked for you first, Mr. Morrison!
Frank (*shouting*). Listen to me! Let's go, men!

[*But the crowd is no longer moving as a whole. Some*

of them are still strongly with Frank, including Charlie, *the first man, the second man, and several of the others. But others are not so sure of themselves now.*]

Charlie (*roaring*). Don't let him throw you, Frank! He asked for it. Let's give it to him!

[Joe *looks only at* Frank. *Waits calmly for him.*]

Frank (*roaring*). Come on!

[*He takes a step forward, but the people behind him don't follow. He turns to them.*]

Frank. What's the matter with you people?
Joe. They're waiting for you, Mr. Morrison.

[Frank *whirls and faces him and they look long and hard at each other. Cut to* Charlie Denton *at rear of crowd. He has a stone in his hand.*]

Charlie (*shouting*). Let's start it off, Frankie boy.

[*He flings the stone. We hear it hit and drop to the ground. The crowd gasps. Cut to* Joe. *There is blood running down the side of his head. He stands there firmly. Cut to* Arthur Hayes. *He looks up in horror, and then a transformation comes over him. He seems to grow taller and broader. His face sets strongly and he begins to stride forward, elbowing people aside.* Phyllis *knows. She clings to him to pull him back.*]

Phyllis (*screaming*). Artie . . . Artie . . . don't . . .

[*But he breaks loose from her and pushes forward. Whoever is in his way is knocked aside, and finally he reaches* Joe. *He looks up at* Joe. *Then he turns and stands next to him. He takes off his eyeglasses and flings them into the crowd.*]

Arthur (*strong*). Throw the next stone at me, neighbors. I live here too!

[*Now the crowd is uncertain as the two men stand together and the blood runs down* Joe's *face.* Frank *tries to rally them. During his next lines we shoot through the open door into the living room.* Mrs. Blake *gets up from her rocking chair and takes* Anna's *hand. Together they walk to the front door, come outside, and stand proudly behind* Joe *and* Arthur.]

Frank. Listen to me! Pay attention, you people. Let's remember what we came here to do . . . and why! This man is garbage! He's cluttering up our street. He's wrecking our neighborhood. We don't want him here. We agreed, every last man and woman of us . . . we agreed to throw him out! Are we gonna let him stop us? If we do—you know what'll happen.

[Mrs. Blake *and* Anna *are out of the house now. They wait, along with* Joe *and* Arthur. *The crowd listens.* Frank *shouts on, running from person to person as the crowd begins ashamedly to drift away.* Christopher *clings to* Frank's *jacket, and begins to sob.*]

Frank. You know what Sycamore Street'll be like. I don't have to tell you. How do we know who we'll be rubbing elbows with next? Listen, where are you going? We're all together in this! What about our kids? Listen to me, people. Our kids'll be playing and going to school with his. How do you like that, neighbors? Makes you a little sick, doesn't it? Come back here! I'm telling you we've got to do this! Come back here!

[*But the crowd continues to drift away. Finally only the* Morrisons *and* Phyllis Hayes *are left in the street.* Joe *and his family, and* Arthur, *watch them, proudly.* Roger *looks at his bewildered father and then he turns away, takes* Clarice's *hand, and his father is no longer the greatest guy in the world.* Frank *looks down at the sobbing* Christopher, *and picks him up and walks slowly off.* Clarice *and* Roger *follow. The* Blakes *turn to go into their house, leaving* Arthur *on the porch. And standing alone, starkly in the middle of the street, is* Phyllis. Arthur *looks at her as she stands, heartbreakingly alone, for a long time.*]

Arthur (*sadly*). Well, what are you standing there for? My neighbor's head is bleeding!

[*And then, slowly, knowing that* Arthur *is no longer a grown-up child,* Phyllis *moves forward into* Joseph Blake's *house.*]

[*Fade out.*]

Reading Check

1. Where does most of Act Three take place?
2. Who brings the news to Joe about what his neighbors intend to do?
3. What does Joe decide to do?
4. What did Joe do to get sent to prison?
5. Who joins Joe in resisting the mob?

For Study and Discussion

Analyzing and Interpreting the Play

1a. Near the beginning of the act, how is sympathy created for Joe Blake?   **b.** What do you learn from Anna's words that indicates Joe is not a dangerous criminal?

2. What reason does Joe give for resisting the mob?

3. What sounds in Act Three help create suspense?

4a. How does Arthur Hayes change in Act Three?   **b.** How have you been prepared for the change?

5a. What issue about human rights does the play explore?   **b.** What stand does the play take on the issue?   **c.** How do you know?

6. Has the play reinforced or changed your opinion about the issue? Explain.

Literary Elements

Exposition

Exposition is the part of a play that provides the audience with important information. Many plays provide a good deal of exposition at the beginning. Reginald Rose, however, deliberately controls the exposition so that only gradually does the audience arrive at a full understanding of the situation.

Find expository passages in Act One that provide hints of what is to happen at 7:15 P.M. Find passages in Act Two that provide more information.

Find passages in Acts Two and Three that provide information about Joe Blake. How does the exposition in Act Three make Joe a sympathetic character?

Why might Reginald Rose have decided to present exposition gradually rather than all at once?

Language and Vocabulary

Emotionally Loaded Language

Emotionally loaded language can be used to present a favorable or unfavorable impression of someone or something. For example, a person who liked Arthur Hayes might call him "a cautious man," but someone who had a low opinion of him might describe him as "a timid man" or even "a pipsqueak." In Act One, Frank Morrison refers to himself and his neighbors as "the majority," but in Act Three Joe Blake calls them a "mob."

Find other examples of emotionally loaded language used to present a favorable or an unfavorable impression. Rewrite each example to present the opposite impression. Then write a sentence presenting Frank Morrison in a favorable light and another sentence presenting him in an unfavorable light.

Writing About Literature

Analyzing a Play's Theme

In Act Three, Joe Blake tells his wife:

Listen, Anna, we're only little people, but we have certain rights. Judy's gonna learn about them in school in a couple of years . . . and they'll tell her that no one can take them away from her. She's got to be able to believe that. They include the right to be different. Well, a group of our neighbors have decided that we have to get out of here because they think we're different. They think we're not nice. . . . Do we have to smile in their faces and tell them we are nice? We don't have to win the right to be free! It's the same as running away, Anna. It's staying on their terms, and if we can't stay on our terms, then there are no places to stay anywhere. For you—for me—for Judy—for anyone, Anna.

Write an essay showing how this passage brings out the play's theme—its underlying idea. Then show how the theme is also brought out by other characters' words and actions.

Focus on Persuasive Writing

Supporting an Opinion: Logical Appeals

One way to support your opinion in a persuasive essay is to use **logical appeals.** The diagram below shows three useful types of logical appeal.

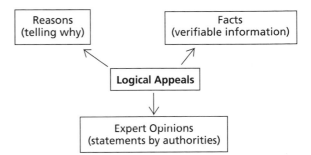

Choose a position or opinion you would like to support in a persuasive speech to your classmates. Write a statement of your opinion in one or two sentences. Then list as many reasons, facts, and expert opinions as you can to support your view. Save your writing.

About the Author

Reginald Rose   (1920–   )

The New York Times *Encyclopedia of Television* calls Reginald Rose "one of the outstanding playwrights to emerge from TV's drama era" of the 1950s. He wrote his first television play, *Bus to Nowhere,* in 1951. Rose's other television plays include *The Sacco-Vanzetti Story, A Man Is Ten Feet Tall* (which starred Sidney Poitier), and *Twelve Angry Men.* He adapted *Twelve Angry Men* (the members of a jury) into a successful motion picture starring Henry Fonda.

Rose has written scripts for a number of other films. In 1961, he created and wrote *The Defenders,* a television series about a father and son who are partners in a law practice.

Thunder on Sycamore Street   **477**

Romeo and Juliet

Romeo and Juliet is probably the most popular romantic tragedy in the English-speaking world. It has had a long and successful stage history (four hundred years), and in our own time has been produced on film and on television as well as on stage. So powerful is Shakespeare's concept of the "star-crossed lovers" that his tragedy has inspired composers, artists, and choreographers to create original works based on the play.

Shakespeare did not invent the story of Romeo and Juliet. It was already well known and popular when he came to write the play sometime around 1594. But in Shakespeare's hands the narrative was skillfully transformed into a magnificent poetic drama, the most lyrical of the tragedies Shakespeare was to write.

A scene from the 1985 BBC-TV production of *Romeo and Juliet*.

Shakespeare's Life

Comparatively little is known about Shakespeare's early life. He was born in 1564 in Stratford-on-Avon, a small English town in Warwickshire. He married Anne Hathaway when he was eighteen and she twenty-six. The couple had three children.

Sometime in his twenties Shakespeare went to London and became involved in the theater, acting in and writing plays. In 1594 he became a shareholder in a company of actors called the Lord Chamberlain's Men. Shakespeare wrote *Romeo and Juliet* for this company. When James became King of England in 1603, he renamed the Chamberlain's Men the "King's Men." About 1610 Shakespeare retired to Stratford-on-Avon, where he died on April 23, 1616.

Statue of Shakespeare in Poets' Corner, Westminster Abbey, London.

Shakespeare's Theater

In Shakespeare's day London had several theaters, all well attended. Competition among rival theaters was keen. Because literary property was not protected by law, it was common for popular plays to be pirated.

The sixteenth-century theater resembled the open courtyard of an inn. There was no roof. The stage was a large platform without a curtain or stage setting. At the back of the stage were two large doors. In the center of the platform was a recess or inner stage, which was usually concealed by a curtain. In *Romeo and Juliet* this inner stage could serve as Friar Laurence's cell or Juliet's tomb. Above the recess was a balcony. In *Romeo and Juliet* it would serve for the garden scene.

Since there was no front curtain, the actors had to make their entrances and exits in full view of the audience. There was no scenery and no artificial lighting. Plays were held in the afternoon. In order to create atmosphere, playwrights and actors had to rely on words and actions. In the great balcony scene in *Romeo and Juliet,* the feeling of a moonlit night is evoked by the language. The lack of elaborate equipment had other advantages. Because no scenery had to be changed, the action of the play could flow more quickly.

There were no actresses in Shakespeare's day. The young women's parts were played by boys. There were usually about fifteen full members in a company of players, who shared in the profits of their performances. In such a small company, certain roles became specialized, and playwrights frequently wrote parts tailored to the talents of their star actors.

The audience was made up of individuals from every walk of life. Few members of the audience could afford to buy seats. Most spectators stood in the yard around the platform stage. They were known as groundlings. The well-to-do customers sat in covered galleries around the stage.

The audience demanded action and excitement. They liked their action gory. The majority of people could not read, but they loved the music of good language. They responded to the dignity and grandeur of poetry, and they liked puns and word games. Shakespeare was able to satisfy the many different tastes of his audience. In *Romeo and Juliet* he included vigorous action, boisterous humor, and splendid poetry.

A drawing of the reconstruction of the second Globe Theater by C. Walter Hodges. Many of Shakespeare's plays were produced at the first Globe Theater, which was destroyed by fire in 1613. No playhouses from Shakespeare's time have survived.

Romeo and Juliet

WILLIAM SHAKESPEARE

Characters

The Montagues

Lord Montague
Lady Montague
Romeo, son of Montague
Benvolio, nephew of Montague
    and friend of Romeo
Balthasar, servant of Romeo
Abraham, servant of Montague

The Capulets

Lord Capulet
Lady Capulet
Juliet, daughter of Capulet
Tybalt, nephew of Lady Capulet
Nurse to Juliet
Peter, servant of the Nurse
Sampson }
Gregory } servants of Capulet
An Old Man of the Capulet family

Prince Escalus, ruler of Verona
Mercutio, kinsman of the Prince and friend of Romeo
Friar Laurence, a Franciscan priest
Friar John, another Franciscan priest
Count Paris, a young nobleman, kinsman of the Prince
Apothecary
Page to Paris
Chief Watchman
Three Musicians
An Officer

Citizens of Verona, Kinsfolk of both houses, Maskers, Guards, Watchmen, and Attendants

The Time: The fourteenth century
The Place: Verona; Mantua, in northern Italy

Prologue

[*From the back of the stage the* Chorus° *enters to introduce and explain the theme of the play.*]

Chorus. Two households, both alike in dignity,° ~~RANK~~
    In fair Verona, where we lay our scene,
      From ancient grudge break to new mutiny,° ~~Riot~~
    Where civil blood makes civil hands unclean.
    From forth the fatal loins of these two foes   5
      A pair of star-crossed° lovers take their life, ~~doomed by unlucky stars.~~
    Whose misadventured piteous overthrows
      Do with their death bury their parents' strife.
    The fearful passage of their death-marked love,
      And the continuance of their parents' rage,   10
    Which, but their children's end, naught could remove,
      Is now the two hours' traffic° of our stage; ~~business~~
    The which if you with patient ears attend,
    What here shall miss, our toil shall strive to mend.° ~~make clearer~~

Act One

Scene 1

[*Verona. A public place. Enter* Sampson *and* Gregory, *of the House of Capulet, with swords and bucklers.*°]

Sampson. Gregory, on my word, we'll not carry coals.° ~~Put up w/insults~~
Gregory. No, for then we should be colliers.° ~~coal-dealers.~~
Sampson. I mean, an° we be in choler,° we'll draw. ~~if, anger~~
Gregory. Aye, while you live, draw your neck out o' the collar.° ~~hangman's noose~~
Sampson. I strike quickly, being moved.   5
Gregory. But thou art not quickly moved to strike.
Sampson. A dog of the house of Montague moves me.
Gregory. To move is to stir, and to be valiant is to stand. Therefore if thou art moved,
    thou runn'st away.
Sampson. A dog of that house shall move me to stand. I will take the wall° of any man or   10
    maid of Montague's. ~~Go to the inside of the sidewalk, where the ground was cleaner~~

Prologue. **Chorus:** an actor who addresses the audience directly and comments on the action. 1. **dignity:** rank.
3. **mutiny:** riot. 6. **star-crossed:** doomed by unlucky stars. 12. **traffic:** business. 14. **mend:** make clearer.
    S.D. (The abbreviation S.D. stands for *stage direction*.) **bucklers:** small shields. 1. **carry coals:** put up with insults. 2.
colliers: coal-dealers. 3. **an:** if. **choler:** anger. 4. **collar:** hangman's noose. The characters are punning on the words
collier, choler, and *collar.* For a discussion of puns, see page 585. 10. **take the wall:** go to the inside of the sidewalk, where
the ground was cleaner.

Gregory. That shows thee a weak slave, for the weakest goes to the wall.°

Sampson. 'Tis true, and therefore women, being the weaker vessels, are ever thrust to the wall. Therefore I will push Montague's men from the wall and thrust his maids to the wall. 15

Gregory. The quarrel is between our masters and us their men.

Sampson. 'Tis all one, I will show myself a tyrant. When I have fought with the men, I will be cruel with the maids. I will cut off their heads.

Gregory. The heads of the maids?

Sampson. Aye, the heads of the maids, or their maidenheads—take it in what sense thou 20 wilt.

Gregory. They must take it in sense that feel it.

Sampson. Me they shall feel while I am able to stand. And 'tis known I am a pretty piece of flesh.

Gregory. 'Tis well thou art not fish. If thou hadst, thou hadst been poor John.° Draw thy 25 tool. Here comes two of the house of Montagues.

[Enter Abraham and Balthasar, servants of Montague.]

Sampson. My naked weapon is out. Quarrel—I will back thee.

Gregory. How! Turn thy back and run?

Sampson. Fear me not.

Gregory. No, marry,° I fear thee! 30

Sampson. Let us take the law of our sides.° Let them begin.

Gregory. I will frown as I pass by, and let them take it as they list.°

Sampson. Nay, as they dare. I will bite my thumb° at them, which is a disgrace to them, if they bear it.

Abraham. Do you bite your thumb at us, sir? 35

Sampson. I do bite my thumb, sir.

Abraham. Do you bite your thumb at us, sir?

Sampson. *[Aside to Gregory]* Is the law of our side, if I say aye?

Gregory. No.

Sampson. No, sir, I do not bite my thumb at you, sir; but I bite my thumb, sir. 40

Gregory. Do you quarrel, sir?

Abraham. Quarrel, sir! No, sir.

Sampson. But if you do, sir, I am for you. I serve as good a man as you.

Abraham. No better.

Sampson. Well, sir. 45

[Enter Benvolio, nephew of Montague.]

Gregory. *[Aside to Sampson]* Say "Better." Here comes one of my master's kinsmen.

Sampson. Yes, better sir.

12. **weakest . . . wall:** another proverb. 25. **poor John:** salted hake, an inexpensive food. 30. **marry:** by the Virgin Mary. 31. **take . . . sides:** be legally in the right. 32. **list:** please. 33. **bite my thumb:** an insulting gesture.

Abraham. You lie.

Sampson. Draw, if you be men. Gregory, remember thy (swashing°) blow. *slashing*

[*They fight.*]

Benvolio. Part, fools. [*Beating down their weapons.*] Put up your swords. You know not what   50
you do.

[*Enter* Tybalt, *hot-tempered nephew of* Lady Capulet, *with sword drawn.*]

Tybalt. What, art thou drawn among these (heartless hinds?°) *cowardly servants*
Turn thee, Benvolio, look upon thy death.
Benvolio. I do but keep the peace. Put up thy sword,
Or manage it to part these men with me.   55
Tybalt. What, drawn, and talk of peace! I hate the word
As I hate Hell, all Montagues, and thee.
Have at thee, coward!

[*They fight.*]

[*Enter several of both houses, who join the fray; then enter* Citizens *and* Peace Officers, *with*
clubs.]

Different kinds of spears

First Officer. Clubs, bills, and partisans!° Strike! Beat them down!
Down with the Capulets! Down with the Montagues!   60

[*Enter old* Capulet *in his gown, and* Lady Capulet.]

Capulet. What noise is this? Give me my long sword, ho!

Lady Capulet. A crutch, a crutch! Why call you for a sword?
Capulet. My sword, I say! Old Montague is come,
And flourishes his blade (in spite of°) me. *to spite*

[*Enter old* Montague *and* Lady Montague.]

Montague. Thou villain Capulet!—Hold me not, let me go.   65
Lady Montague. Thou shalt not stir one foot to seek a foe.

[*Enter* Prince Escalus, *with* Attendants. *At first no one hears him.*]

Prince. Rebellious subjects, enemies to peace,
Profaners of this (neighbor-stainèd steel°—) *swords stained w/the blood of neighbors.*

49. **swashing:** slashing. 52. **heartless hinds:** cowardly servants. 59. **bills . . . partisans:** different kinds of spears.
64. **in spite of:** to spite. 68. **neighbor-stainèd steel:** swords stained with the blood of neighbors.

Will they not hear? What ho! You men, you beasts,
That quench the fire of your pernicious rage   70
With purple fountains issuing from your veins,
On pain of torture, from those bloody hands
Throw your (mistempered°) weapons to the ground, *ill-made*
And hear the sentence of your movèd prince.
Three civil brawls, bred of an (airy°) word, *light*   75
By thee, old Capulet and Montague,
Have thrice disturbed the quiet of our streets,
And made Verona's ancient citizens
Cast by their (grave beseeming ornaments°) *Dignified ornaments of peace, suitable to aged citizens.*
To wield old partisans, in hands as old,   80
Cankered with peace, to part your (cankered°) hate. *Rusted, corroded*
If ever you disturb our streets again,
Your lives shall pay the forfeit of the peace.

---

73. **mistempered:** ill-made and ill-used.   75. **airy:** light.   79. **grave . . . ornaments:** dignified ornaments of peace, suitable to aged citizens.   81. **cankered:** rusted, corroded.

A scene from the 1985 BBC-TV production of *Romeo and Juliet*.

For this time, all the rest depart away.
You, Capulet, shall go alone with me, 85
And, Montague, come you this afternoon,
To know our further pleasure in this case,
To old Freetown, our common judgment place.
Once more, on pain of death, all men depart.

[*Exeunt*° *all but* Montague, Lady Montague, *and* Benvolio.]

Montague. Who set this ancient quarrel new abroach?° 90
Speak, Nephew, were you by when it began?

Benvolio. Here were the servants of your adversary
And yours close fighting ere I did approach.
I drew to part them. In the instant came
The fiery Tybalt, with his sword prepared, 95
Which as he breathed defiance to my ears,
He swung about his head and cut the winds,
Who, nothing hurt withal,° hissed him in scorn.
While we were interchanging thrusts and blows,
Came more and more, and fought on part and part 100
Till the Prince came, who parted either part.

Lady Montague. Oh, where is Romeo? Saw you him today?
Right glad I am he was not at this fray.

Benvolio. Madam, an hour before the worshiped sun
Peered forth the golden window of the east, 105
A troubled mind drave me to walk abroad,
Where, underneath the grove of sycamore
That westward rooteth from the city's side,
So early walking did I see your son.
Towards him I made; but he was ware° of me, 110
And stole into the covert° of the wood.
I, measuring his affections by my own,
That most are busied when they're most alone,
Being one too many by my weary self,
Pursued my humor,° not pursuing his, 115
And gladly shunned who gladly fled from me.

Montague. Many a morning hath he there been seen,
With tears augmenting the fresh morning's dew,
Adding to clouds more clouds with his deep sighs.
But all so soon as the all-cheering sun 120
Should in the farthest east begin to draw
The shady curtains from Aurora's° bed,
Away from light steals home my heavy° son,

S.D. **Exeunt:** plural form of *Exit.* 90. **abroach:** afoot, astir. 98. **withal:** by this. 110. **ware:** aware. 111. **covert:** covering. 115. **humor:** mood. 122. **Aurora:** goddess of the dawn. 123. **heavy:** melancholy.

And private in his chamber pens himself,
Shuts up his windows, locks fair daylight out,   125
And makes himself an artificial night.
Black and portentous must this humor prove
Unless good counsel may the cause remove.
Benvolio. My noble uncle, do you know the cause?
Montague. I neither know it nor can learn of him.   130
Benvolio. Have you impórtuned° him by any means? *asked insistently*
Montague. Both by myself and many other friends.
But he, his own affections' counselor,
Is to himself—I will not say how true—
But to himself so secret and so close,   135
So far from sounding and discovery,
As is the bud bit with an envious° worm *hateful*
Ere he can spread his sweet leaves to the air,
Or dedicate his beauty to the sun.
Could we but learn from whence his sorrows grow,   140
We would as willingly give cure as know.

[*Enter* Romeo *in a melancholy mood.*]

Benvolio. See where he comes. So please you, step aside.
I'll know his grievance, or be much denied.
Montague. I would thou wert so happy° by thy stay *fortunate*
To hear true shrift.° Come, madam, let's away. *confession* [*Exeunt* Montague *and* Lady.]   145
Benvolio. Good morrow,° Cousin. *GOOD MORNING* "cousin" is a name used for any
Romeo.   Is the day so young? *Relative.*
Benvolio. But new struck nine.
Romeo.   Aye me, sad hours seem long!
Was that my father that went hence so fast?
Benvolio. It was. What sadness lengthens Romeo's hours?
Romeo. Not having that which, having, makes them short.   150
Benvolio. In love?
Romeo. Out——
Benvolio. Of love?
Romeo. Out of her favor where I am in love.
Benvolio. Alas that love,° so gentle in his view,° *here, cupid, god of love.* *appearance* 155
Should be so tyrannous and rough in proof!
Romeo. Alas that love, whose view is muffled still,° *always blindfolded*
Should without eyes see pathways to his will!
Where shall we dine? Oh me! What fray was here?

131. **impórtuned:** asked insistently. 137. **envious:** hateful. 144. **happy:** fortunate. 145. **shrift:** confession. 146.
Good morrow: Good morning. "Cousin" is a name used for any relative. 155. **love:** here, Cupid, god of love. **view:**
appearance. 157. **muffled still:** always blindfolded.

Yet tell me not, for I have heard it all.   160
Here's much to do with hate, but more with love.
Why then, O brawling love! O loving hate!
O anything, of nothing first create!
O heavy lightness! Serious vanity!
Misshapen chaos of well-seeming forms!   165
Feather of lead, bright smoke, cold fire, sick health!
Still-waking sleep, that is not what it is!
This love feel I, that feel no love in this.
Dost thou not laugh?
Benvolio.   No, Coz,° I rather weep.   *couzin*
Romeo. Good heart, at what?
Benvolio.   At thy good heart's oppression.   170
Romeo. Why, such is love's transgression.
    Griefs of mine own lie heavy in my breast,
    Which thou wilt propagate,° to have it pressed°   *increase   ,burdened*
    With more of thine. This love that thou hast shown
    Doth add more grief to too much of mine own.   175
    Love is a smoke raised with the fume of sighs;
    Being purged, a fire sparkling in lovers' eyes;
    Being vexed, a sea nourished with lovers' tears.
    What is it else? A madness most discreet,
    A choking gall and a preserving sweet.   180
    Farewell, my coz.
Benvolio.   Soft!° I will go along. *an exclamation meaning "wait"*
    And if you leave me so, you do me wrong.
Romeo. Tut, I have lost myself, I am not here.
    This is not Romeo, he's some other where.
Benvolio. Tell me in sadness,° who is that you love? *seriousness*   185
Romeo. What, shall I groan and tell thee?
Benvolio.   Groan! Why, no,
    But sadly tell me who.
Romeo. Bid a sick man in sadness make his will.
    Ah, word ill urged to one that is so ill!
    In sadness, Cousin, I do love a woman.   190
Benvolio. I aimed so near when I supposed you loved.
Romeo. A right good mark-man! And she's fair I love.
Benvolio. A right fair mark, fair Coz, is soonest hit.
Romeo. Well, in that hit you miss. She'll not be hit
    With Cupid's arrow. She hath Dian's° wit, *Diana was the Roman Goddess of*   195
chastity, hunting, and the moon.

169. **Coz:** cousin.   173. **propagate** (prŏp′ə-gāt′): increase.   **pressed:** burdened   181. **Soft:** an exclamation meaning
"Wait."   185. **sadness:** seriousness.   195. **Dian:** Diana was the Roman goddess of chastity, hunting, and the moon.

And in strong proof° of chastity well armed, ~armor, power~
From love's weak childish bow she lives unharmed.
She will not stay the siege of loving terms,
Nor bide the encounter of assailing eyes,
Nor ope her lap to saint-seducing gold.   200
Oh, she is rich in beauty, only poor
That when she dies, with beauty dies her store.° ~she will leave no child to pass on her beauty.~

Benvolio. Then she hath sworn that she will still live chaste?

Romeo. She hath, and in that sparing makes huge waste;
For beauty, starved with her severity,   205
Cuts beauty off from all posterity.
She is too fair, too wise, wisely too fair,
To merit bliss by making me despair.
She hath forsworn° to love, and in that vow ~sworn not to~
Do I live dead, that live to tell it now.   210

Benvolio. Be ruled by me, forget to think of her.

Romeo. Oh, teach me how I should forget to think.

Benvolio. By giving liberty unto thine eyes.
Examine other beauties.

Romeo.   'Tis the way
To call hers exquisite, in question more.° ~by comparing her beauty more w/others.~   215
These happy masks° that kiss fair ladies' brows, ~Elizabethan women wore mask to protect~
Being black, put us in mind they hide the fair. ~their faces from the sun.~
He that is stricken blind cannot forget
The precious treasure of his eyesight lost.
Show me a mistress that is passing° fair, ~very~   220
What doth her beauty serve but as a note
Where I may read who passed that passing fair?° ~surpassed those who are very pretty~
Farewell. Thou canst not teach me to forget.

Benvolio. I'll pay that doctrine,° or else die in debt. ~pay for that teaching~   [*Exeunt.*]

Scene 2

[*A street. Enter* Capulet *with* Paris, *a kinsman of the* Prince, *and* Servant.]

Capulet. But Montague is bound° as well as I, ~pledge to keep the peace~
In penalty alike, and 'tis not hard, I think,
For men so old as we to keep the peace.

196. **proof:** armor; power.   202. **with . . . store:** She will leave no child to pass on her beauty.   209. **forsworn to:** sworn not to.   215. **in question more:** by comparing her beauty more with others.   216. **masks:** Elizabethan women wore masks to protect their faces from the sun.   220. **passing:** very.   222. **passed . . . fair:** surpassed those who are very pretty.   224. **pay that doctrine:** pay for that teaching.
  1. **bound:** pledged to keep the peace.

Paris. Of honorable (reckoning°) are you both, _Reputation_

And pity 'tis you lived at odds so long. 5

But now, my lord, what say you to my suit?

Capulet. But saying o'er what I have said before.

My child is yet a stranger in the world—

She hath not seen the change of fourteen years.

Let two more summers wither in their pride 10

Ere we may think her ripe to be a bride.

Paris. Younger than she are happy mothers made.

Capulet. And too soon marred are those so early made.

The earth hath swallowed all my hopes but she,

She is the hopeful lady of my (earth.°) _body, "flesh and blood."_ 15

But woo her, gentle Paris, get her heart.

My will to her consent is but a part;

_if_ (An°) she agree, within her (scope°) of choice _Range_

Lies my consent and fair (according°) voice. _agreeing_

This night I hold an old accustomed feast, 20

Whereto I have invited many a guest

Such as I love, and you among the store,

One more, most welcome, makes my number more.

At my poor house look to behold this night

Earth-treading stars that make dark heaven light 25

Such comfort as do lusty young men feel

When well-appareled April on the heel

Of limping winter treads, even such delight

Among fresh female buds shall you this night

have (Inherit°) at my house. Hear all, all see, 30

And like her most whose merit most shall be.

Which on more view, of many mine, being one,

May stand in number, though in (reckoning none.°) _not worth considering_

Come, go with me. [_To Servant, giving a paper_] Go, (sirrah,°) trudge about _a term used in_

Through fair Verona. Find those persons out _addressing servants._ 35

Whose names are written there, and to them say

My house and welcome on their pleasure stay. [_Exeunt_ Capulet _and_ Paris.]

Servant. [_Who cannot read_] Find them out whose names are written here! It is written that the

LEISURE shoemaker should meddle with his (yard°) and the tailor with his last, the fisher with his

pencil and the painter with his nets; but I am sent to find those persons whose names 40

are here writ, and can never find what names the writing person hath here writ. I must

to the learned. In (good time.°) _What luck! Just in time_

---

4. **reckoning:** reputation. 15. **earth:** body, "flesh and blood." 18. **An:** if. **scope:** range. 19. **according:** agreeing.
30. **Inherit:** have. 33. **reckoning none:** not worth considering. 34. **sirrah:** a term used in addressing servants. 39.
yard: measure. The servant mixes his metaphors. He means that people ought to stick to what they can do best. 42. **In
good time:** What luck! Just in time!

[*Enter* Benvolio *and* Romeo.]

Benvolio. Tut, man, one fire burns out another's burning,
　　One pain is lessened by another's anguish.
　　Turn giddy, and be holp° by backward turning,　~helped~　45
　　One desperate grief cures with another's languish.
　　Take thou some new infection to thy eye,
　　And the rank poison of the old will die.
Romeo. Your plantain° leaf is excellent for that.　~a weed used to stop bleeding~
Benvolio. For what, I pray thee?
Romeo.　　　　　　　　For your broken° shin.　~scratched~　50
Benvolio. Why, Romeo, art thou mad?
Romeo. Not mad, but bound more than a madman is,
　　Shut up in prison, kept without my food,
　　Whipped and tormented and——Godden,° good fellow.　~good evening, a greeting used in the afternoon.~
Servant. God gi' godden. I pray, sir, can you read?　55
Romeo. Aye, mine own fortune in my misery.
Servant. Perhaps you have learned it without book, but I pray, can you read anything you
　　see?
Romeo. Aye, if I know the letters and the language.
Servant. Ye say honestly. Rest you merry!°　~God keep you merry~　60
Romeo, Stay, fellow, I can read. [*Reads.*]

　　"Signior Martino and his wife and daughters; County°　~count~　Anselme and his beauteous
　　sisters; the lady widow of Vitruvio; Signior Placentio and his lovely nieces; Mercutio and
　　his brother Valentine; mine uncle Capulet, his wife, and daughters; my fair niece
　　Rosaline; Livia; Signior Valentio and his cousin Tybalt; Lucio and the lively Helena."　65

　　A fair assembly. Whither should they come?
Servant. Up.
Romeo. Whither?
Servant. To supper, to our house.
Romeo. Whose house?　70
Servant. My master's.
Romeo. Indeed I should have asked you that before.
Servant. Now I'll tell you without asking. My master is the great rich Capulet, and if you be
　　not of the House of Montagues, I pray come and crush° a cup of wine. Rest you merry!　~drink~
　　[*Exit.*]
Benvolio. At this same ancient° feast of Capulet's　~That is, established by tradition~　75
　　Sups the fair Rosaline whom thou so lovest,

---

45. **holp:** helped.　49. **plantain:** a weed used to stop bleeding.　50. **broken:** scratched.　54. **Godden:** good evening, a
greeting used in the afternoon.　60. **Rest you merry:** God keep you merry.　62. **County:** Count.　74. **crush:** drink.
75. **ancient:** that is, established by tradition.

With all the admirèd beauties of Verona.
Go thither, and with unattainted° eye *unprejudiced*
Compare her face with some that I shall show,
And I will make thee think thy swan a crow.   80

Romeo. When the devout religion of mine eye
    Maintains such falsehood, then turn tears to fires,
And these, who, often drowned, could never die,
bright Transparent° heretics, be burned for liars!
One fairer than my love! The all-seeing sun   85
Ne'er saw her match since first the world begun.

Benvolio. Tut, you saw her fair, none else being by,
Herself poised° with herself in either eye. *balanced*
But in that crystal scales° let there be weighed *Romeo's eyes*
Your lady's love against some other maid   90
That I will show you shining at this feast,
And she shall scant° show well that now seems best. *scarcely*

Romeo. I'll go along, no such sight to be shown,
But to rejoice in splendor of mine own.   [*Exeunt.*]

Scene 3

[*A room in* Capulet's house. *Enter* Lady Capulet *and* Nurse.]

Lady Capulet. Nurse, where's my daughter? Call her forth to me.
Nurse. Now, by my maidenhead at twelve year old,
    I bade her come. What, lamb! What, ladybird!°—God forbid!—*a small insect w/ bright*
Where's this girl? What, Juliet!   *red spots; a pretty little thing*

[*Enter* Juliet.]

Juliet. How now! Who calls?   5
Nurse. Your mother.
Juliet. Madam, I am here. What is your will?
Lady Capulet. This is the matter. Nurse, give leave° awhile, *leave us alone*
    We must talk in secret.—Nurse, come back again,
I have remembered me, thou'st° hear our counsel. *Thou shalt*   10
Thou know'st my daughter's of a pretty age.
Nurse. Faith, I can tell her age unto an hour.

---

78. **unattainted:** unprejudiced. 84. **Transparent:** bright. 88. **poised:** balanced. 89. **crystal scales:** Romeo's eyes.
92. **scant:** scarcely.
  3. **ladybird:** a small insect with bright red spots; a pretty little thing. 8. **give leave:** leave us alone. 10. **thou'st:** thou shalt.

Lady Capulet. She's not fourteen.

Nurse.   I'll lay fourteen of my teeth—

    And yet, to my teen° be it spoken, I have but four— *sorrow*

    She is not fourteen. How long is it now   15

    To Lammastide?° *a church festival celebrated August 1.*

Lady Capulet.   A fortnight and odd days.

Nurse. Even or odd, of all days in the year,

    Come Lammas Eve at night shall she be fourteen.

    Susan and she—God rest all Christian souls!—

    Were of an age. Well, Susan is with God.   20

    She was too good for me.—But, as I said,

    On Lammas Eve at night shall she be fourteen.

    That shall she, marry, I remember it well.

    'Tis since the earthquake now eleven years,° *An earthquake occurred in England in 1580.*

    And she was weaned—I never shall forget it—   25

    Of all the days of the year, upon that day.

    For I had then laid wormwood to my dug,

    Sitting in the sun under the dovehouse wall;

    My lord and you were then at Mantua.—

    Nay, I do bear a brain.°—But, as I said, *I have a head (memory)*   30

    When it did taste the wormwood on the nipple

    Of my dug, and felt it bitter, pretty fool,

    To see it tetchy,° and fall out with the dug! *Peevish*

    Shake, quoth the dovehouse. 'Twas no need, I trow,° *guess*

    To bid me trudge.   35

    And since that time it is eleven years;

    For then she could stand high-lone°—nay, by the rood, *unaided* → *cross, crucifix*

    She could have run and waddled all about,

    For even the day before, she broke her brow,

    And then my husband—God be with his soul!   40

    A'° was a merry man—took up the child. *he*

    "Yea," quoth he, "dost thou fall upon thy face?

    Thou wilt fall backward when thou hast more wit,

    Wilt thou not, Jule?" And, by my holidame,° *holy relic*

    The pretty wretch left crying, and said "Aye."   45

    To see now how a jest shall come about!

    I warrant an I should live a thousand years,

    I never should forget it. "Wilt thou not, Jule?" quoth he,

    And, pretty fool, it stinted,° and said "Aye." *stopped*

Lady Capulet. Enough of this. I pray thee hold thy peace.   50

---

14. **teen:** sorrow.   16. **Lammastide:** a church festival celebrated August 1.   24. **'Tis . . . years:** An earthquake occurred in England in 1580.   30. **I . . . brain:** I have a head (memory).   33. **tetchy:** peevish.   34. **trow:** guess.   37. **high-lone:** unaided.   **rood:** cross, crucifix.   41. **A':** he.   44. **holidame:** holy relic.   49. **stinted:** stopped.

Nurse. Yes, madam, yet I cannot choose but laugh
    To think it should leave crying, and say "Aye."
    And yet, I warrant, it had upon its brow
    A bump as big as a young cockerel's stone,
    A perilous° knock, and it cried bitterly.   55
    "Yea," quoth my husband, "fall'st upon thy face?
    Thou wilt fall backward when thou comest to age,
    Wilt thou not, Jule?" It stinted, and said "Aye."
Juliet. And stint thou too, I pray thee, Nurse, say I.
Nurse. Peace, I have done. God mark° thee to His grace!   60
    Thou wast the prettiest babe that e'er I nursed.
    An I might live to see thee married once,
    I have my wish.
Lady Capulet. Marry° that "marry" is the very theme
    I came to talk of. Tell me, daughter Juliet,   65
    How stands your disposition to be married?
Juliet. It is an honor that I dream not of.
Nurse. An honor! Were not I thine only nurse,
    I would say thou hadst sucked wisdom from thy teat.
Lady Capulet. Well, think of marriage now. Younger than you   70
    Here in Verona, ladies of esteem,
    Are made already mothers. By my count,
    I was your mother much upon these years°
    That you are now a maid. Thus then in brief—
    The valiant Paris seeks you for his love.   75
Nurse. A man, young lady! Lady, such a man
    As all the world—Why, he's a man of wax.°
Lady Capulet. Verona's summer hath not such a flower.
Nurse. Nay, he's a flower, in faith, a very flower.
Lady Capulet. What say you? Can you love the gentleman?   80
    This night you shall behold him at our feast.
    Read o'er the volume° of young Paris' face,
    And find delight writ there with beauty's pen.
    Examine every married lineament,°
    And see how one another lends content,   85
    And what obscured in this fair volume lies
    Find written in the margent° of his eyes.
    This precious book of love, this unbound lover,
    To beautify him, only lacks a cover.
    The fish lives in the sea, and 'tis much pride   90

55. **perilous:** severe.   60. **mark:** select, choose.   64. **Marry:** indeed.   73. **much . . . years:** at much the same age.   77.
man of wax: perfect, like a wax model.   82–93. **volume . . . story:** In these lines, Shakespeare compares Paris to a book.
84. **married lineament:** perfectly united part.   87. **margent:** margin.

For fair without the fair within to hide.
That book in many's eyes doth share the glory
That in gold clasps locks in the golden story.
So shall you share all that he doth possess,
By having him making yourself no less.   95

Nurse. No less! Nay, bigger. Women grow by men.
Lady Capulet. Speak briefly. Can you like of Paris' love?
Juliet. I'll look to like, if looking liking move.° *arose*
But no more deep will I endart mine eye
Than your consent° gives strength to make it fly. *approval*   100

[*Enter a* Servingman.]

Servant. Madam, the guests are come, supper served up, you called, my young lady asked
for, the nurse cursed in the pantry, and everything in extremity.° I must hence to wait. *confusion*
I beseech you, follow straight.° *Right away at once.*
Lady Capulet. We follow thee.   [*Exit* Servingman.]
Juliet, the County stays.° *waits for you*   105
Nurse. Go, girl, seek happy nights to happy days.   [*Exeunt.*]

Scene 4

[*A street. Enter* Romeo, Mercutio, Benvolio, *with five or six other* Maskers, *and* Torchbearers
on their way to Capulet's *house.*]

Romeo. What, shall this speech be spoke for our excuse?°
Or shall we on without apology?
Benvolio. The date is out of such prolixity°
We'll have no Cupid hoodwinked° with a scarf, *blindfolded*
Bearing a Tartar's painted bow of lath,° *short curved bow*   5
Scaring the ladies like a crow-keeper;° *scarecrow*
Nor no without-book prologue, faintly spoke
After the prompter, for our entrance.
But let them measure us by what they will,
We'll measure them a measure,° and be gone. *Dance*   10
Romeo. Give me a torch. I am not for this ambling.° *mincing*
Being but heavy,° I will bear the light. *sad*
Mercutio. Nay, gentle Romeo, we must have you dance.

98. **move:** arouse. 100. **consent:** approval. 102. **extremity:** confusion. 103. **straight:** right away, at once. 105.
stays: waits for you.
   1. **excuse:** In Elizabethan times, it was customary for uninvited maskers to send a messenger with a speech to announce
their coming. 3. **prolixity:** an elaborate device. Benvolio says that the custom of sending a messenger in costume is out
of date. 4. **hoodwinked:** blindfolded. 5. **bow of lath:** short curved bow. 6. **crow-keeper:** scarecrow. 10. **measure:**
dance. 11. **ambling:** mincing. 12. **heavy:** sad.

Romeo. Not I, believe me. You have dancing shoes

With nimble soles. I have a soul of lead   15

So stakes me to the ground I cannot move.

Mercutio. You are a lover. Borrow Cupid's wings,

And soar with them above a common bound.° [leap]

Romeo. I am too sore enpiercèd with his shaft° [pierced, wounded → arrow]

To soar with his light feathers, and so bound,   20

I cannot bound a pitch° above dull woe. [leap a flight]

Under love's heavy burden do I sink.

Mercutio. And to sink in it, should you burden love,

Too great oppression for a tender thing.

Romeo. Is love a tender thing? It is too rough,   25

Too rude, too boisterous, and it pricks like thorn.

Mercutio. If love be rough with you, be rough with love.

Prick love for pricking, and you beat love down.

Give me a case to put my visage° in.

A visor for a visor!° What care I   30

What curious eye doth quote° deformities?

Here are the beetle° brows shall blush for me.

Benvolio. Come, knock and enter, and no sooner in

But every man betake him to his legs.°

Romeo. A torch for me. Let wantons light of heart   35

Tickle the senseless rushes° with their heels,

For I am proverbed with a grandsire phrase.°

I'll be a candleholder,° and look on.

The game was ne'er so fair, and I am done.°

Mercutio. Tut, dun's the mouse, the constable's own word.   40

If thou art dun, we'll draw thee from the mire°

Of this sir-reverence love wherein thou stick'st

Up to the ears. Come, we burn daylight,° ho.

Romeo. Nay, that's not so.

Mercutio.   I mean, sir, in delay

We waste our lights in vain, like lamps by day.   45

Take our good meaning, for our judgment sits

Five times in that ere once in our five wits.°

Romeo. And we mean well in going to this mask,

But 'tis no wit to go.

---

18. **bound:** leap.   19. **enpiercèd** (pronounced as 3 syllables): pierced, wounded.   **shaft:** arrow.   21. **bound a pitch:** leap in flight.   29. **visage:** face. Mercutio covers his face with a mask.   30. **visor for a visor:** mask for an ugly face.   31. **quote:** note.   32. **beetle:** overhanging.   34. **betake him to his legs:** begin to dance.   36. **rushes:** Floors were covered with rushes, grasslike plants.   37. **grandsire phrase:** old proverb.   38. **candleholder:** onlooker.   39. **The game . . . done:** I am too tired for the game no matter how fair it is.   40–41. **dun's . . . mire:** a reference to a game, "dun is in the mire," in which a heavy log (dun) was pulled through the mud.   43. **burn daylight:** waste time   46–47. **judgment . . . wits:** People judge us five times for our reputation before they judge us for our intellect.

A scene from the Oregon Shakespeare Festival's 1982 production of *Romeo and Juliet.*

Mercutio.   Why, may one ask?
Romeo. I dreamed a dream tonight.
Mercutio.   And so did I.   50
Romeo. Well, what was yours?
Mercutio.   That dreamers often lie.
Romeo. In bed asleep, while they do dream things true.
Mercutio. Oh then, I see Queen Mab° hath been with you.
      She is the fairies' midwife, and she comes
      In shape no bigger than an agate stone°   55
      On the forefinger of an alderman,
      Drawn with a team of little atomies°
      Athwart men's noses as they lie asleep—
      Her wagon spokes made of long spinners'° legs;
      The cover, of the wings of grasshoppers;   60
      Her traces,° of the smallest spider's web;
      Her collars, of the moonshine's watery beams;
      Her whip, of cricket's bone; the lash, of film;°
      Her wagoner,° a small gray-coated gnat
      Not half so big as a round little worm   65

53. **Queen Mab:** the fairy queen.   55. **agate** (ăg′ĭt) **stone:** large seal ring.   57. **atomies:** tiny creatures.   59. **spinners:** spiders.   61. **traces:** harness.   63. **film:** spider's thread.   64. **wagoner:** coachman.

Pricked from the lazy finger of a maid.°
Her chariot is an empty hazelnut,
Made by the joiner° squirrel or old grub,
Time out o' mind the fairies' coachmakers.
And in this state° she gallops night by night   70
Through lovers' brains, and then they dream of love;
O'er courtiers' knees, that dream on curtseys straight;
O'er lawyers' fingers, who straight dream on fees;
O'er ladies' lips, who straight on kisses dream,
Which oft the angry Mab with blisters plagues   75
Because their breaths with sweetmeats° tainted are.
Sometime she gallops o'er a courtier's nose,
And then dreams he of smelling out a suit.°
And sometime comes she with a tithe pig's° tail
Tickling a parson's nose as a' lies asleep,   80
Then dreams he of another benefice.°
Sometime she driveth o'er a soldier's neck,
And then dreams he of cutting foreign throats,
Of breaches, ambuscadoes,° Spanish blades,
Of healths° five fathom deep; and then anon   85
Drums in his ear, at which he starts and wakes,
And being thus frighted swears a prayer or two,
And sleeps again. This is that very Mab
That plaits the manes of horses in the night,
And bakes the elflocks° in foul sluttish hairs,   90
Which once untangled much misfortune bodes.
This is the hag,° when maids lie on their backs.
That presses them and learns them first to bear,
Making them women of good carriage.
This is she——

Romeo.   Peace, peace, Mercutio, peace!   95
Thou talk'st of nothing.

Mercutio.   True, I talk of dreams,
Which are the children of an idle brain,
Begot of nothing but vain fantasy,°
Which is as thin of substance as the air
And more inconstant than the wind, who woos   100
Even now the frozen bosom of the North,

65–66. **worm...maid:** In Shakespeare's time, it was a popular superstition that lazy maids grew worms in their fingers.
68. **joiner:** carpenter.   70. **state:** grand style.   76. **sweetmeats:** sweets; candy, cakes.   78. **suit:** a petition for special
favor.   79. **tithe** (tīth) **pig:** the parson was often paid in goods, such as a pig, instead of money.   81. **benefice:** church
appointment, source of income.   84. **ambuscadoes:** ambushes.   85. **healths:** toasts.   90. **elflocks:** Mischievous fairies
were supposed to make knots in horses' manes and to tangle human hair.   92. **hag:** nightmare.   98. **fantasy:** fancy.

And, being angered, puffs away from thence,
Turning his face to the dew-dropping South.
Benvolio. This wind you talk of blows us from ourselves.
Supper is done, and we shall come too late.   105
Romeo. I fear, too early. For my mind misgives°
Some consequence, yet hanging in the stars,
Shall bitterly begin his fearful date°
With this night's revels, and expire the term
Of a despisèd life° closed in my breast   110
By some vile forfeit of untimely death.
But He that hath the steerage of my course
Direct my sail! On, lusty gentlemen.
Benvolio. Strike, drum.   [*Exeunt.*]

Scene 5

[*A hall in* Capulet's *house. Musicians waiting. Enter* Servingmen, *with napkins.*]

First Servant. Where's Potpan, that he helps not to take away? He shift a trencher!° He
scrape a trencher!
Second Servant. When good manners shall lie all in one or two men's hands, and they un-
washed too, 'tis a foul thing.
First Servant. Away with the joint stools,° remove the court cupboard,° look to the plate.°   5
Good thou, save me a piece of marchpane.° And, as thou lovest me, let the porter let
in Susan Grindstone and Nell. Antony, and Potpan!
Second Servant. Aye, boy, ready.
First Servant. You are looked for and called for, asked for and sought for, in the great
chamber.°   10
Third Servant. We cannot be here and there too. Cheerly, boys. Be brisk a while, and the
longer liver take all.°   [*They retire behind.*]

[*Enter* Capulet, *with* Juliet *and others of his house, meeting the* Guests *and* Maskers.]

Capulet. Welcome, gentlemen! Ladies that have their toes
Unplagued with corns will have a bout with you.
Ah ha, my mistresses! Which of you all   15
Will now deny to dance? She that makes dainty,°
She, I'll swear, hath corns—am I come near ye now?°

---

106. **misgives:** fears.   108. **date:** time, period.   109–110. **expire . . . life:** cause the lease of my life to come to an end.
   1. **trencher:** wooden platter.   5. **joint stools:** stools made by a joiner (carpenter). **cupboard:** sideboard. **plate:** silver
plate.   6. **marchpane:** marzipan, a mixture made of almond paste.   9-10. **great chamber:** used for dining and social
occasions.   12. **longer liver take all:** The last survivor takes all.   16. **makes dainty:** pretends to be shy.   17. **come near ye
now:** touching a tender spot.

Welcome, gentlemen! I have seen the day
That I have worn a visor,° and could tell
A whispering tale in a fair lady's ear   20
Such as would please. 'Tis gone, 'tis gone, 'tis gone.
You are welcome, gentlemen! Come, musicians, play.
A hall, a hall!° Give room! And foot it, girls. [*Music plays, and they dance.*]
More light, you knaves, and turn the tables up,
And quench the fire, the room is grown too hot.   25
Ah, sirrah, this unlooked-for sport° comes well.
Nay, sit, nay, sit, good Cousin Capulet,
For you and I are past our dancing days.
How long is 't now since last yourself and I
Were in a mask?
Second Capulet.   By 'r Lady, thirty years.   30
Capulet. What, man! 'Tis not so much, 'tis not so much.
'Tis since the nuptial of Lucentio,
Come Pentecost° as quickly as it will,
Some five and twenty years, and then we masked.
Second Capulet. 'Tis more, 'tis more. His son is elder, sir,   35
His son is thirty.
Capulet.   Will you tell me that?
His son was but a ward° two years ago.

[Romeo, *masked and unrecognized, sees* Juliet *and instantly falls in love with her.*]

Romeo. [*To a* Servingman] What lady's that which doth enrich the hand
Of yonder knight?
Servant. I know not, sir.   40
Romeo. Oh, she doth teach the torches to burn bright!
It seems she hangs upon the cheek of night
Like a rich jewel in an Ethiop's ear—
Beauty too rich for use, for earth too dear!°
So shows a snowy dove trooping with crows   45
As yonder lady o'er her fellows shows.
The measure° done, I'll watch her place of stand,
And, touching hers, make blessèd my rude hand.
Did my heart love till now? Forswear it, sight!
For I ne'er saw true beauty till this night.   50
Tybalt. This, by his voice, should be a Montague.
Fetch me my rapier, boy. What dares the slave

---

19. **worn a visor:** worn a mask—that is, has been a dancer.   23. **A hall, a hall:** that is, clear the hall for dancing.   26.
unlooked-for sport: Capulet had not expected the maskers.   33. **Pentecost:** the seventh Sunday after Easter.   37. **ward:**
a minor in the charge of a guardian.   44. **dear:** precious.   47. **measure:** dance.

Come hither, covered with an antic face,°
To fleer° and scorn at our solemnity?°
Now, by the stock and honor of my kin,   55
To strike him dead I hold it not a sin.

Capulet. Why, how now, kinsman! Wherefore storm you so?

Tybalt. Uncle, this is a Montague, our foe,
A villain, that is hither come in spite
To scorn at our solemnity this night.   60

Capulet. Young Romeo, is it?

Tybalt.   'Tis he, that villain Romeo.

Capulet. Content thee, gentle Coz, let him alone,
He bears him like a portly° gentleman,
And, to say truth, Verona brags of him
To be a virtuous and well-governed youth.   65
I would not for the wealth of all this town
Here in my house do him disparagement.°
Therefore be patient, take no note of him.
It is my will, the which if thou respect,
Show a fair presence and put off these frowns,   70
An ill-beseeming semblance° for a feast.

Tybalt. It fits when such a villain is a guest.
I'll not endure him.

Capulet. [*Losing his temper*] He shall be endured.
What, goodman boy° I say he shall. Go to,°
Am I the master here, or you? Go to.   75
You'll not endure him! God shall mend my soul,
You'll make a mutiny among my guests!
You will set cock-a-hoop!° You'll be the man!

Tybalt. Why Uncle, 'tis a shame.

Capulet.   Go to, go to,
You are a saucy boy. Is't so, indeed?   80
This trick° may chance to scathe° you, I know what.
You must contrary me! Marry, 'tis time.
Well said, my hearts! You are a princox,° go.
Be quiet, or——More light, more light! For shame!
I'll make you quiet. What, cheerly, my hearts!   85

Tybalt. Patience perforce° with willful choler° meeting
Makes my flesh tremble in their different greeting.

---

53. **antic face:** grotesque mask.   54. **fleer:** sneer.   **solemnity:** celebration.   63. **portly:** dignified.   67. **disparagement** (dĭs-păr′ĭj-mənt): disrespect, insult.   71. **semblance:** appearance.   74. **goodman boy:** an insulting phrase. Goodman is a man under the rank of gentleman.   **Go to:** an exclamation showing impatience.   78. **You...cock-a-hoop:** You want to start fighting.   81. **trick:** habit (of quarreling).   **scathe:** injure.   83. **princox:** conceited boy.   86. **perforce:** forced (on me).   **choler** (kŏl′ər): anger.

I will withdraw. But this intrusion shall,
Now seeming sweet, convert to bitterest gall. [*Exit.*]

Romeo. [*To* Juliet] If° I profane with my unworthiest hand 90
This holy shrine, the gentle fine° is this,
My lips, two blushing pilgrims, ready stand
To smooth that rough touch with a tender kiss.

Juliet. Good pilgrim, you do wrong your hand too much,
Which mannerly devotion° shows in this; 95
For saints have hands that pilgrims' hands do touch,
And palm to palm is holy palmers'° kiss.

Romeo. Have not saints lips, and holy palmers too?

Juliet. Aye, pilgrim, lips that they must use in prayer.

Romeo. Oh then, dear saint, let lips do what hands do. 100
They pray. Grant thou, lest faith turn to despair.

Juliet. Saints do not move, though grant for prayers' sake.

90–103. **If...take:** These fourteen lines are a Shakespearean sonnet. The dialogue is based on the metaphor that Romeo is a pilgrim and Juliet a saint. 91. **fine:** punishment. 95. **devotion:** the pilgrim's vow. 97. **palmer:** a pilgrim who carried a palm leaf to show that he or she had been to the Holy Land.

A scene from the 1985 BBC-TV production of *Romeo and Juliet.*

Romeo. Then move not while my prayer's effect I take.
Thus from my lips by thine my sin is purged.

[*Kissing her.*]

Juliet. Then have my lips the sin that they have took.   105
Romeo. Sin from my lips? Oh, trespass sweetly urged!°
Give me my sin again.
Juliet.   You kiss by the book.°
Nurse. Madam, your mother craves a word with you.
Romeo. What is her mother?
Nurse.   Marry, bachelor,
Her mother is the lady of the house,   110
And a good lady, and a wise and virtuous.
I nursed her daughter, that you talked withal.°
I tell you, he that can lay hold of her
Shall have the chinks.°
Romeo.   Is she a Capulet?
Oh, dear account! My life is my foe's debt.°   115
Benvolio. Away, be gone. The sport is at the best.
Romeo. Aye, so I fear. The more is my unrest.
Capulet. Nay, gentlemen, prepare not to be gone,
We have a trifling foolish banquet toward.°
Is it e'en so? Why then, I thank you all,   120
I thank you, honest gentlemen. Good night.
More torches here! Come on, then, let's to bed.
Ah, sirrah, by my fay,° it waxes° late.
I'll to my rest.

[*Exeunt all but* Juliet *and* Nurse. *At first* Juliet *hides her feelings for* Romeo.]

Juliet. Come hither, Nurse. What is yond gentleman?   125
Nurse. The son and heir of old Tiberio.
Juliet. What's he that now is going out of door?
Nurse. Marry, that, I think, be young Petruchio.
Juliet. What's he that follows there, that would not dance?
Nurse. I know not.   130
Juliet. Go ask his name. If he be marrièd,
My grave is like to be my wedding bed.

---

106. **urged:** argued.   107. **by the book:** according to the book; that is, you are merely being gallant.   112. **withal:** with.
114. **chinks:** cash.   115. **is my foe's debt:** belongs to my enemy.   119. **toward:** in preparation.   123. **fay:** faith.
waxes: grows.

Nurse. His name is Romeo, and a Montague,
  The only son of your great enemy.
Juliet. My only love sprung from my only hate!   135
  Too early seen unknown, and known too late!
  Prodigious° birth of love it is to me,
  That I must love a loathèd enemy.
Nurse. What's this? What's this?
Juliet.   A rhyme I learned even now
  Of one I danced withal. [*One calls within,* "Juliet."]
Nurse.   Anon, anon!   140
  Come, let's away, the strangers all are gone.   [*Exeunt.*]

137. **Prodigious:** monstrous, unnatural.

Reading Check

1. How does Sampson begin the quarrel with Montague's servants?
2. What is Benvolio's relationship to Romeo?
3. According to Romeo, what vow has Rosaline taken?
4. How old is Juliet?
5. How do Benvolio and Romeo learn about Capulet's feast?
6. Where does Juliet see Paris for the first time?
7. How are Juliet and Tybalt related?
8. According to Mercutio, what creature visits people at night and influences their dreams?
9. Why does Tybalt send for his sword during the feast?
10. How do Romeo and Juliet learn each other's identity?

For Study and Discussion

Analyzing and Interpreting the Play

1. In fourteen lines the Prologue gives the setting and background of the play and prepares the audience for what is to come. **a.** Which words in the Prologue point to the influence of fate in the deaths of Romeo and Juliet? **b.** What effect will their deaths have on their parents' quarrel?

2a. Why do you think Shakespeare never explains how the quarrel between the Montagues and the Capulets began? **b.** What does the Prince think has caused "three civil brawls"? **c.** How does he intend to punish any future outbreaks of violence?

3a. Describe Romeo's mood when he first enters. **b.** What has caused him to feel as he does?

4. Paris wishes to marry Juliet. **a.** Why is Capulet reluctant to accept the Count's offer? **b.** What do you learn about Capulet's feelings for his daughter?

5a. For what reason does Benvolio urge Romeo to attend Capulet's feast? **b.** Why does Romeo want to go?

6a. How would you characterize Juliet's behavior toward her mother? **b.** What is Juliet's feeling about marriage? **c.** Do you think her answer (Scene 3, lines 98–100) pleases her mother?

7a. What do you learn about the Nurse's character in Scene 3? **b.** How does she provide humor in the scene?

8a. How does Mercutio attempt to cheer Romeo in Scene 4? **b.** Does he really believe in Queen Mab? **c.** What is his purpose in describing Queen Mab to Romeo?

9. Reread Tybalt's lines in Scene 1. How is his behavior at Capulet's feast consistent with his behavior in the earlier scene?

10. In Scene 1, Capulet calls for a sword when he sees his enemy Montague. Yet when Tybalt wishes to attack Romeo, Capulet restrains him. Why?

11. The first fourteen lines that Romeo and Juliet speak to each other form a sonnet (see page 503) in which Romeo sees himself as a pilgrim and Juliet as the saint he worships. What does the language show about their feelings for each other?

12a. How does Shakespeare keep you aware of the bitter hatred between the Montagues and the Capulets throughout Act One? **b.** Which characters do you think will come into conflict in later scenes?

Literary Elements

Dramatic Structure: The Foil

To examine how a play has been put together, we analyze its **structure**. The most important structural device in *Romeo and Juliet* is **juxtaposition for contrast**. Shakespeare repeatedly places two people or words or actions side by side in order to heighten the differences between them.

A character who serves as a contrast for another character is called a **foil**. Originally, "foil" meant a thin sheet of metal (remember aluminum foil) that was placed under a jewel to make it appear brighter.

In the first scene of the play, Benvolio is a foil for Tybalt. Benvolio attempts to keep the peace but Tybalt insists on fighting. Each character is intensified by the other's presence.

In Scene 3, how does the Nurse serve as a foil for Lady Capulet? In Scene 4, how does Mercutio serve as a foil for Romeo? In Scene 5, Tybalt's discovery of Romeo at the Capulet party almost leads to conflict. This episode is followed by the meeting of Romeo and Juliet. Tell how these sequences make for dramatic contrast.

Personification

Personification is a figure of speech in which an animal, object, or idea is treated as if it were human. Many characters in *Romeo and Juliet* speak of love (an idea) as a person.

Alas that love, whose view is muffled still,
Should without eyes see pathways to his will!

Romeo in this speech has in mind the old saying "Love is blind," which really means that those who are in love do not see the faults of those they love. Romeo personifies love, saying it is like a person who can see how to get what he wants even though he is blindfolded.

Explain what is being personified in each of these quotations from Act One:

In the instant came
The fiery Tybalt, with his sword prepared,
Which as he breathed defiance to my ears,
He swung about his head and cut the winds,
Who, nothing hurt withal, hissed him in scorn.
(1, 94–98)

Madam, an hour before the worshiped sun
Peered forth the golden window of the east,
A troubled mind drave me to walk abroad. . . .
(1, 104–106)

Such comfort as do lusty young men feel
When well-appareled April on the heel
Of limping winter treads . . .
(2, 26–28)

One fairer than my love! The all-seeing sun
Ne'er saw her match since first the world
begun.
(2, 85-86)

Writing About Literature

Analyzing Dramatic Technique

Romeo and Juliet fall in love at first sight. How does Shakespeare convince us of this instant and mutual attraction? What do we learn about Romeo and Juliet before they meet? How does the language of their first encounter tell us that they are already deeply in love? Write a paper in which you consider these questions.

Focus on Persuasive Writing

Supporting an Opinion: Emotional Appeals

When Romeo falls in love with Juliet, he appeals to her emotions so that she will grant him a kiss. In a persuasive essay or speech, you need to use **emotional appeals** as well as logical arguments.

Some of the most effective emotional appeals are specific examples or personal experiences that help to support your opinion. For example, to convince an audience to help raise money for animal shelters, you might describe a particular dog or cat that has been abandoned.

Write one or two sentences stating your opinion on an issue you care about. Jot down notes for two emotional appeals you could make in a speech to support your opinion. Save your writing.

Act Two

Prologue

[Enter Chorus.]

Chorus. Now old desire° doth in his deathbed lie,
  And young affection gapes to be his heir.
That fair for which love groaned for and would die,
  With tender Juliet matched, is now not fair.
Now Romeo is beloved and loves again,   5
  Alike° bewitchèd by the charm of looks,
But to his foe supposed he must complain,
  And she steal love's sweet bait from fearful hooks.
Being held a foe, he may not have access
  To breathe such vows as lovers use to swear,   10
And she as much in love, her means much less
  To meet her new belovèd anywhere.
But passion lends them power, time means, to meet,
Tempering extremities° with extreme sweet.   [Exit.]

Scene 1

[A lane by the wall of Capulet's orchard. Enter Romeo, alone.]

Romeo. Can I go forward when my heart is here?
  Turn back, dull earth,° and find thy center° out.   [Exit.]

[Enter Benvolio with Mercutio.]

Benvolio. Romeo! My cousin Romeo!
Mercutio.   He is wise,
  And, on my life, hath stol'n him home to bed.
Benvolio. He ran this way, and leaped this orchard wall.   5
  Call, good Mercutio.
Mercutio.   Nay, I'll conjure° too.
  Romeo! Humors! Madman! Passion! Lover!
  Appear thou in the likeness of a sigh.
  Speak but one rhyme, and I am satisfied,
  Cry but "aye me!" pronounce but "love" and "dove."   10

---

1. **old desire:** Romeo's love for Rosaline.   6. **Alike:** equally.   14. **extremities:** great difficulties.
2. **earth:** body.   **center:** the center of the universe—that is, Juliet.   6. **conjure:** call up a spirit.

Speak to my gossip° Venus one fair word,
One nickname for her purblind° son and heir,
Young Adam Cupid, he that shot so trim
When King Cophetua° loved the beggar maid!   15
He heareth not, he stirreth not, he moveth not.
The ape is dead, and I must conjure him.
I conjure thee by Rosaline's bright eyes,
By her high forehead and her scarlet lip,
By her fine foot, straight leg, and quivering thigh,
And the demesnes that there adjacent lie,   20
That in thy likeness thou appear to us!

Benvolio. An if he hear thee, thou wilt anger him.

Mercutio. This cannot anger him. 'Twould anger him
To raise a spirit in his mistress' circle
Of some strange nature, letting it there stand   25
Till she had laid it and conjured it down.
That were some spite. My invocation
Is fair and honest, and in his mistress' name
I conjure only but to raise up him.

Benvolio. Come, he hath hid himself among these trees,   30
To be consorted° with the humorous° night.
Blind is his love, and best befits the dark.

Mercutio. If love be blind, love cannot hit the mark.
Now will he sit under a medlar° tree,
And wish his mistress were that kind of fruit   35
As maids call medlars when they laugh alone.
Oh, Romeo, that she were, Oh, that she were
An open et cetera, thou a poperin pear!
Romeo, good night. I'll to my truckle bed,°
This field bed is too cold for me to sleep.   40
Come, shall we go?

Benvolio.   Go then, for 'tis in vain
To seek him here that means not to be found.

Scene 2

[*Capulet's orchard. Enter* Romeo.]

Romeo. He jests° at scars that never felt a wound.

11. **gossip:** friend.   12. **purblind:** dim-sighted.   14. **King Cophetua:** the hero of a ballad, who married a beggar maid.
31. **consorted:** associated.   **humorous:** moody.   34. **medlar:** a tree that produces a fruit like an apple.   39. **truckle bed:**
trundle bed, a baby bed pushed under the great bed during the daytime.
   1. **jests:** laughs, jokes.

[Juliet *appears above at a window.*]

But, soft! What light through yonder window breaks?
It is the east, and Juliet is the sun!
Arise, fair sun, and kill the envious moon,
Who is already sick and pale with grief   5
That thou her maid art far more fair than she.
Be not her maid, since she is envious.
Her vestal livery° is but sick and green,
And none but fools do wear it. Cast it off.
It is my lady, oh, it is my love!   10
Oh, that she knew she were!
She speaks, yet she says nothing. What of that?
Her eye discourses,° I will answer it.
I am too bold, 'tis not to me she speaks.
Two of the fairest stars in all the heaven,   15
Having some business, do entreat her eyes
To twinkle in their spheres° till they return.
What if her eyes were there, they in her head?
The brightness of her cheek would shame those stars
As daylight doth a lamp; her eyes in heaven   20
Would through the airy region stream so bright
That birds would sing and think it were not night.
See how she leans her cheek upon her hand!
Oh, that I were a glove upon that hand,
That I might touch that cheek!

Juliet.   Aye me!
Romeo. [*Softly, to himself*]   She speaks.   25
    Oh, speak again, bright angel! For thou art
    As glorious to this night, being o'er my head,
    As is a wingèd messenger of Heaven
    Unto the white-upturnèd wondering eyes
    Of mortals that fall back to gaze on him   30
    When he bestrides the lazy-pacing clouds
    And sails upon the bosom of the air.

Juliet. O Romeo, Romeo, wherefore° art thou Romeo?
    Deny thy father and refuse thy name,
    Or, if thou wilt not, be but sworn my love   35
    And I'll no longer be a Capulet.

Romeo. [*Aside*] Shall I hear more, or shall I speak at this?
Juliet. 'Tis but thy name that is my enemy.

8. **vestal livery:** maiden's dress.   13. **discourses:** speaks.   17. **spheres:** orbits.   33. **wherefore:** why.

Thou art thyself, though not° a Montague.
What's Montague? It is nor hand, nor foot, 40
Nor arm, nor face, nor any other part
Belonging to a man. Oh, be some other name!
What's in a name? That which we call a rose
By any other name would smell as sweet.
So Romeo would, were he not Romeo called, 45
Retain that dear perfection which he owes°
Without that title. Romeo, doff° thy name,
And for thy name, which is no part of thee,
Take all myself.
Romeo. [*Aloud*]   I take thee at thy word.
Call me but love, and I'll be new baptized. 50
Henceforth I never will be Romeo.
Juliet. What man art thou that, thus bescreened in night,
So stumblest on my counsel?°
Romeo.   By a name
I know not how to tell thee who I am.
My name, dear saint, is hateful to myself 55
Because it is an enemy to thee.
Had I it written, I would tear the word.
Juliet. My ears have yet not drunk a hundred words
Of thy tongue's uttering, yet I know the sound.
Art thou not Romeo, and a Montague? 60
Romeo. Neither, fair saint, if either thee dislike.°
Juliet. How camest thou hither, tell me, and wherefore?
The orchard walls are high and hard to climb,
And the place death, considering who thou art,
If any of my kinsmen find thee here. 65
Romeo. With love's light wings did I o'erperch° these walls,
For stony limits cannot hold love out.
And what love can do, that dares love attempt,
Therefore thy kinsmen are no let° to me.
Juliet. If they do see thee, they will murder thee. 70
Romeo. Alack, there lies more peril in thine eye
Than twenty of their swords. Look thou but sweet,
And I am proof° against their enmity.
Juliet. I would not for the world they saw thee here.
Romeo. I have night's cloak to hide me from their eyes, 75
And but° thou love me, let them find me here.

39. **though not:** even if you were not. 46. **owes:** owns. 47. **doff:** remove. 53. **counsel:** innermost thoughts.
61. **dislike:** displease. 66. **o'erperch:** climb over. 69. **let:** hindrance, obstacle. 73. **proof:** armored, safe. 76. **And but:** unless:

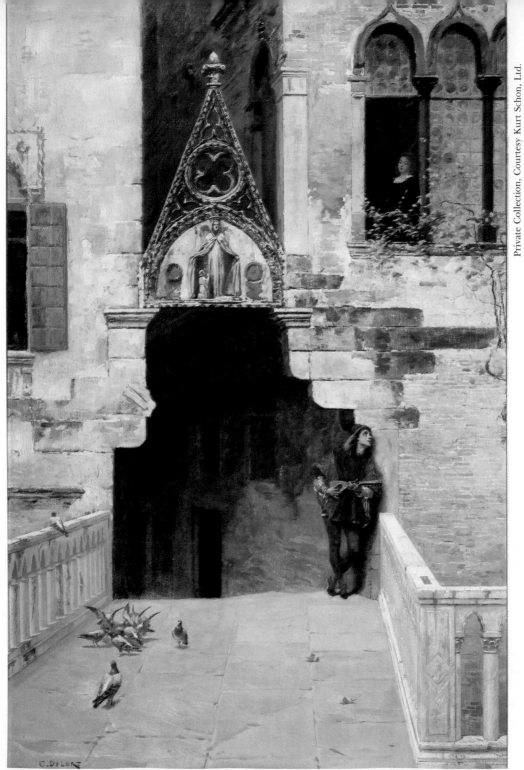

Romeo and Juliet—Capulet's Garden by Charles Edward Delort (1841–1895). Oil on panel.
Romeo is depicted with a lute, the instrument associated with courtship.

My life were better ended by their hate
Than death prorogued,° wanting of° thy love.
Juliet. By whose direction found'st thou out this place?
Romeo. By love, that first did prompt me to inquire.   80
    He lent me counsel, and I lent him eyes.
    I am no pilot, yet wert thou as far
    As that vast shore washed with the farthest sea,
    I would adventure for such merchandise.
Juliet. Thou know'st the mask of night is on my face,   85
    Else would a maiden blush bepaint my cheek
    For that which thou hast heard me speak tonight.
    Fain° would I dwell on form,° fain, fain deny
    What I have spoke. But farewell compliment!°
    Dost thou love me? I know thou wilt say "Aye,"   90
    And I will take thy word. Yet if thou swear'st,
    Thou mayst prove false. At lovers' perjuries
    They say Jove° laughs. O gentle Romeo,
    If thou dost love, pronounce it faithfully.
    Or if thou think'st I am too quickly won,   95
    I'll frown and be perverse and say thee nay,
    So° thou wilt woo; but else, not for the world.
    In truth, fair Montague, I am too fond,°
    And therefore thou mayst think my 'havior light.
    But trust me, gentleman, I'll prove more true   100
    Than those that have more cunning to be strange.°
    I should have been more strange, I must confess,
    But that thou overheard'st, ere I was ware,°
    My true love's passion. Therefore pardon me,
    And not impute this yielding to light love,   105
    Which the dark night hath so discovered.°
Romeo. Lady, by yonder blessed moon I swear,
    That tips with silver all these fruit-tree tops——
Juliet. Oh, swear not by the moon, th' inconstant moon,
    That monthly changes in her circled orb,°   110
    Lest that thy love prove likewise variable.
Romeo. What shall I swear by?
Juliet.   Do not swear at all.
    Or, if thou wilt, swear by thy gracious self,
    Which is the god of my idolatry,
    And I'll believe thee.

78. **prorogued** (prō-rōg′ əd): postponed.   **wanting of:** lacking.   88. **Fain:** gladly.   **dwell on form:** behave in the customary way.   89. **compliment:** polite manners.   93. **Jove** (jōv): in classical mythology, the ruler of the gods.   97. **So:** so long as.   98. **fond:** foolishly affectionate.   101. **strange:** cold, distant.   103. **ware:** aware.   106. **discovered:** revealed.   110. **orb:** orbit.

Romeo.   If my heart's dear love——   115
Juliet. Well, do not swear. Although I joy in thee,
    I have no joy of this contráct° tonight.
    It is too rash, too unadvised, too sudden,
    Too like the lightning, which doth cease to be
    Ere one can say "It lightens." Sweet, good night!   120
    This bud of love, by summer's ripening breath,
    May prove a beauteous flower when next we meet.
    Good night, good night! As sweet repose and rest
    Come to thy heart as that within my breast!
Romeo. Oh, wilt thou leave me so unsatisfied?   125
Juliet. What satisfaction canst thou have tonight?
Romeo. The exchange of thy love's faithful vow for mine.
Juliet. I gave thee mine before thou didst request it,
    And yet I would it were to give again.
Romeo. Wouldst thou withdraw it? For what purpose, love?   130
Juliet. But to be frank,° and give it thee again.
    And yet I wish but for the thing I have.
    My bounty° is as boundless as the sea,
    My love as deep; the more I give to thee,
    The more I have, for both are infinite.   135
    I hear some noise within. Dear love, adieu!

             [Nurse *calls within.*°]

    Anon,° good Nurse! Sweet Montague, be true.
    Stay but a little, I will come again.   *[Exit]*
Romeo. Oh, blessed, blessed night! I am afeard,
    Being in night, all this is but a dream,   140
    Too flattering-sweet to be substantial.°

           [*Reenter* Juliet, *above.*]

Juliet. Three words, dear Romeo, and good night indeed.
    If that thy bent° of love be honorable,
    Thy purpose marriage, send me word tomorrow
    By one that I'll procure to come to thee,   145
    Where and what time thou wilt perform the rite,
    And all my fortunes at thy foot I'll lay,
    And follow thee my lord throughout the world.

---

117. **contráct:** betrothal. 131. **frank:** generous. 133. **bounty:** generosity. S.D. **within:** off stage. 137. **Anon:** in a minute. 141. **substantial:** real. 143. **bent:** intention.

Nurse. [*Within*] Madam!

Juliet. I come, anon.—But if thou mean'st not well, I do beseech thee—— 150

Nurse. [*Within*] Madam!

Juliet.   By and by, I come—
  To cease thy suit, and leave me to my grief.
  Tomorrow will I send.

Romeo.   So thrive my soul——

Juliet. A thousand times good night!   [*Exit.*]

Romeo. A thousand times the worse, to want thy light. 155
  Love goes toward love as schoolboys from their books,
  But love from love toward school with heavy looks.   [*Retiring slowly.*]

[*Reenter Juliet, above.*]

Juliet. Hist! Romeo, hist!—Oh, for a falconer's° voice,
  To lure this tassel-gentle° back again!
  Bondage is hoarse,° and may not speak aloud, 160
  Else would I tear the cave where Echo° lies
  And make her airy tongue more hoarse than mine
  With repetition of my Romeo's name.

Romeo. It is my soul that calls upon my name.
  How silver-sweet sound lovers' tongues by night, 165
  Like softest music to attending° ears!

Juliet. Romeo!

Romeo.   My dear?

Juliet.   At what o'clock tomorrow
  Shall I send to thee?

Romeo.   At the hour of nine.

Juliet. I will not fail. 'Tis twenty years till then.
  I have forgot why I did call thee back. 170

Romeo. Let me stand here till thou remember it.

Juliet. I shall forget, to have thee still stand here,
  Remembering how I love thy company.

Romeo. And I'll still stay, to have thee still forget,
  Forgetting any other home but this. 175

Juliet. 'Tis almost morning. I would have thee gone,
  And yet no farther than a wanton's° bird,
  Who lets it hop a little from her hand,
  Like a poor prisoner in his twisted gyves,°

158. **falconer:** keeper of hawks. 159. **tassel-gentle:** male falcon. 160. **Bondage is hoarse:** that is, being under the control of my parents, I must whisper. 161. **Echo:** in classical mythology, a wood nymph. Rejected by the man she loved, Echo retired to a cave and pined away until all that was left of her was her voice. 166. **attending:** attentive. 177. **wanton:** spoiled child. 179. **gyves** (jīvz): fetters.

And with a silk thread plucks it back again,   180
So loving-jealous of his liberty.
Romeo. I would I were thy bird.
Juliet.   Sweet, so would I.
Yet I should kill thee with much cherishing.
Good night, good night! Parting is such sweet sorrow
That I shall say good night till it be morrow.   [*Exit.*]   185
Romeo. Sleep dwell upon thine eyes, peace in thy breast!
Would I were sleep and peace, so sweet to rest!
Hence will I to my ghostly° father's cell,
His help to crave and my dear hap° to tell.   [*Exit.*]

Scene 3

[*Friar Laurence's cell. Enter* Friar Laurence, *with a basket.*]

Friar Laurence. The gray-eyed morn smiles on the frowning night,
Checkering the eastern clouds with streaks of light,
And fleckèd° darkness like a drunkard reels
From forth day's path and Titan's° fiery wheels.
Now, ere the sun advance his burning eye,   5
The day to cheer and night's dank dew to dry,
I must upfill° this osier cage° of ours
With baleful° weeds and precious-juicèd flowers.
The earth that's Nature's mother is her tomb,
What is her burying grave, that is her womb.   10
And from her womb children of divers kind
We sucking on her natural bosom find,
Many for many virtues excellent,
None but for some, and yet all different.
Oh, mickle° is the powerful grace° that lies   15
In herbs, plants, stones, and their true qualities.
For naught so vile that on the earth doth live,
But to the earth some special good doth give;
Nor aught so good but, strained° from that fair use,
Revolts from true birth,° stumbling on abuse.°   20
Virtue itself turns vice, being misapplied,
And vice sometime's by action dignified.

---

188. **ghostly:** spiritual.   189. **hap:** luck.
  3. **fleckèd:** spotted.   4. **Titan:** the sun. In classical mythology, the sun god drove his chariot across the sky.   7. **upfill:** fill up.   **osier cage:** wicker basket.   8. **baleful:** poisonous.   15. **mickle:** great.   **grace:** goodness.   19. **strained:** turned aside.   20. **Revolts from true birth:** turns away from its true function.   **abuse:** misuse.

Within the infant rind of this small flower
Poison hath residence, and medicine power.
For this, being smelt, with that part cheers each part, 25
Being tasted, slays all senses with the heart.°
Two such opposèd kings encamp them still°
In man as well as herbs, grace and rude will;°
And where the worser is predominant,°
Full soon the canker°death eats up that plant. 30

[*Enter* Romeo.]

Romeo. Good morrow, Father.
Friar Laurence. Benedicite!
What early tongue so sweet saluteth me?
Young son, it argues a distempered° head
So soon to bid good morrow to thy bed.
Care keeps his watch in every old man's eye, 35
And where care lodges, sleep will never lie;
But where unbruisèd youth with unstuffed brain
Doth couch his limbs, there golden sleep doth reign.
Therefore thy earliness doth me assure
Thou art uproused by some distemperature.° 40
Or if not so, then here I hit it right,
Our Romeo hath not been in bed tonight.
Romeo. That last is true. The sweeter rest was mine.
Friar Laurence. God pardon sin! Wast thou with Rosaline?
Romeo. With Rosaline, my ghostly father? No. 45
I have forgot that name and that name's woe.
Friar Laurence. That's my good son. But where hast thou been, then?
Romeo. I'll tell thee ere thou ask it me again.
I have been feasting with mine enemy,
Where on a sudden one hath wounded me 50
That's by me wounded. Both our remedies
Within thy help and holy physic° lies.
I bear no hatred, blessed man, for, lo,
My intercession° likewise steads° my foe.
Friar Laurence. Be plain, good son, and homely° in thy drift.° 55
Riddling° confession finds but riddling shrift.°

24–26. **Poison . . . heart:** The plant can be used as a poison or as a restorative: if smelled, it acts as a stimulant; if tasted, it is deadly. 27. **still:** always. 28. **rude will:** the natural desire for evil. 29. **predominant:** stronger. 30. **canker:** worm. 33. **distempered:** disturbed. 40. **distemperature:** sickness. 52. **physic:** remedy. 54. **intercession:** prayer, plea. **steads:** benefits. 55. **homely:** simple, plain. **drift:** speech. 56. **Riddling:** speaking in riddles. **shrift:** forgiveness.

Romeo. Then plainly know my heart's dear love is set
    On the fair daughter of rich Capulet.
    As mine on hers, so hers is set on mine,
    And all combined° save what thou must combine   60
    By holy marriage. When, and where, and how,
    We met, we wooed and made exchange of vow,
    I'll tell thee as we pass; but this I pray,
    That thou consent to marry us today.

Friar Laurence. Holy Saint Francis, what a change is here!   65
    Is Rosaline, that thou didst love so dear,
    So soon forsaken? Young men's love then lies
    Not truly in their hearts, but in their eyes.
    Jesu Maria, what a deal of brine
    Hath washed thy sallow cheeks for Rosaline!   70
    How much salt water thrown away in waste,
    To season° love, that of it doth not taste!
    The sun not yet thy sighs from heaven clears,
    Thy old groans ring yet in mine ancient ears.
    Lo, here upon thy cheek the stain doth sit   75
    Of an old tear that is not washed off yet.
    If e'er thou wast thyself and these woes thine,
    Thou and these woes were all for Rosaline.
    And art thou changed? Pronounce this sentence° then——
    Women may fall when there's no strength in men.   80

Romeo. Thou chid'st° me oft for loving Rosaline.

Friar Laurence. For doting, not for loving, pupil mine.

Romeo. And bad'st me bury love.

Friar Laurence.   Not in a grave
    To lay one in, another out to have.

Romeo. I pray thee, chide not. She whom I love now   85
    Doth grace for grace and love for love allow.
    The other did not so.

Friar Laurence.   Oh, she knew well
    Thy love did read by rote° and could not spell.
    But come, young waverer, come, go with me,
    In one respect I'll thy assistant be;   90
    For this alliance may so happy prove,
    To turn your households' rancor° to pure love.

Romeo. Oh, let us hence. I stand on sudden haste.°

Friar Laurence. Wisely and slow. They stumble that run fast.   [*Exeunt.*]

---

60. **combined:** united.   72. **season:** keep fresh, as meat is preserved by salt.   79. **sentence:** proverb.   81. **chid'st:** scolded.   88. **by rote:** by heart.   92. **rancor:** hatred.   93. **stand on sudden haste:** am impatient.

Scene 4

[*A street. Enter* Benvolio *and* Mercutio.]

Mercutio. Where the devil should this Romeo be?
    Came he not home tonight?
Benvolio. Not to his father's, I spoke with his man.°
Mercutio. Ah, that same pale hardhearted wench, that Rosaline,
    Torments him so that he will sure run mad.   5
Benvolio. Tybalt, the kinsman of old Capulet,
    Hath sent a letter to his father's house.
Mercutio. A challenge, on my life.
Benvolio. Romeo will answer it.
Mercutio. Any man that can write may answer a letter.   10
Benvolio. Nay, he will answer the letter's master, how he dares, being dared.
Mercutio. Alas, poor Romeo, he is already dead! Stabbed with a white wench's black eye,
    shot thorough the ear with a love song, the very pin° of his heart cleft with the blind
    bowboy's butt shaft.° And is he a man to encounter Tybalt?
Benvolio. Why, what is Tybalt?   15
Mercutio. More than Prince of Cats,° I can tell you. Oh, he's the courageous captain of
    compliments.° He fights as you sing prick song,° keeps time, distance, and proportion;
    rests me his minim° rest, one, two, and the third in your bosom. The very butcher of a
    silk button, a duelist, a duelist, a gentleman of the very first house,° of the first and sec-
    ond cause.° Ah, the immortal passado! The punto reverso! The hai!°   20
Benvolio. The what?
Mercutio. The pox of such antic, lisping, affecting fantasticoes,° these new tuners of accents!
    "By Jesu, a very good blade! A very tall° man! A very good whore!" Why, is not this a
    lamentable thing, Grandsire, that we should be thus afflicted with these strange flies,
    these fashionmongers, these perdona-mi's° who stand so much on the new form that   25
    they cannot sit at ease on the old bench? Oh, their bones,° their bones!

[*Enter* Romeo *no longer melancholy*]

Benvolio. Here comes Romeo, here comes Romeo.
Mercutio. Without his roe, like a dried herring. Oh, flesh, flesh, how art thou fishified! Now
    is he for the numbers° that Petrarch flowed in. Laura to his lady was but a kitchen

---

3. **man:** servant. 13. **pin:** center of the target. 13–14. **blind bowboy's butt shaft:** Cupid's blunt arrow. A butt shaft, an unpointed arrow, was used in target practice. 16. **Prince of Cats:** In stories of Reynard the fox, Tybalt is Prince of Cats. 16–17. **captain of compliments:** expert in fashionable behavior. **prick song:** melody accompanying a song. 18. **minim rest:** the shortest rest. 19. **first house:** finest school. **first and second cause:** the reasons that caused a gentleman to issue a challenge to a duel. 20. **passado . . . hai:** dueling terms. The *passado* is a lunge; *punto reverso* is a backhand stroke; *hai* is the cry as the fencer thrusts home. 22. **fantasticoes:** fantastical fellows. 23. **tall:** brave. 25. **perdona-mi's:** Italian for "pardon me." 26. **bones:** wordplay on *bon*, the French word for "good." 29. **numbers:** verses. Petrarch wrote sonnets to a woman named Laura.

wench—marry, she had a better love to berhyme her—Dido, a dowdy;° Cleopatra, a   30
gypsy; Helen and Hero, hildings° and harlots; Thisbe, a gray eye or so, but not to the
purpose. Signior Romeo, *bon jour!*—there's a French salutation to your French slop.°
You gave us the counterfeit° fairly last night.

Romeo. Good morrow to you both. What counterfeit did I give you?

Mercutio. The slip, sir, the slip. Can you not conceive?   35

Romeo. Pardon, good Mercutio, my business was great, and in such a case as mine a man
may strain courtesy.

Mercutio. That's as much as to say, Such a case as yours constrains a man to bow in the
hams.

Romeo. Meaning, to curtsy.

Mercutio. Thou hast most kindly hit it.   40

Romeo. A most courteous exposition.

Mercutio. Nay, I am the very pink of courtesy.

Romeo. Pink for flower.

Mercutio. Right.

Romeo. Why, then is my pump well flowered.°   45

Mercutio. Well said. Follow me this jest now till thou hast worn out thy pump, that, when
the single sole of it is worn, the jest may remain, after the wearing, solely singular.

Romeo. Oh, single-soled jest, solely singular for the singleness!

Mercutio. Come between us, good Benvolio. My wits faint.

Romeo. Switch and spurs,° switch and spurs, or I'll cry a match.°   50

Mercutio. Nay, if thy wits run the wild-goose chase,° I have done; for thou hast more of the
wild goose in one of thy wits than, I am sure, I have in my whole five. Was I with you
there for the goose?°

Romeo. Thou wast never with me for anything when thou wast not there for the goose.

Mercutio. I will bite thee by the ear for that jest.   55

Romeo. Nay, good goose, bite not.

Mercutio. Thy wit is a very bitter sweeting, it is a most sharp sauce.

Romeo. And is it not well served in to a sweet goose?

Mercutio. Oh, here's a wit of cheveril,° that stretches from an inch narrow to an ell broad!

Romeo. I stretch it out for that word "broad," which, added to the goose, proves thee far   60
and wide a broad goose.

Mercutio. Why, is not this better now than groaning for love? Now art thou sociable, now
art thou Romeo; now art thou what thou art, by art as well as by nature. For this drivel-
ing love is like a great natural° that runs lolling up and down to hide his bauble° in a
hole.   65

Benvolio. Stop there, stop there.

Mercutio. Thou desirest me to stop in my tale against the hair.°

---

30. **dowdy:** a slovenly woman.   31. **hildings:** wretches.   32. **slop:** baggy breeches.   33. **counterfeit:** A counterfeit coin
was called a slip.   45. **pump . . . flowered:** My shoe is pinked, or punched, with a pattern of flowers.   50. **Switch and
spurs:** at full gallop.   **I'll . . . match:** If you can't keep up this contest of wits, I claim the bet.   51. **wild-goose chase:** In
this race the second horseman has to follow wherever the first horseman leads.   53. **Was . . . goose:** Have I proved you
to be a goose?   59. **cheveril:** kid skin.   64. **natural:** fool.   **bauble:** the fool's stick, which had a doll's head.   67. **against
the hair:** contrary to one's nature.

Benvolio. Thou wouldst else have made thy tale large.

Mercutio. Oh, thou art deceived—I would have made it short. For I was come to the whole
depth of my tale, and meant indeed to occupy the argument no longer. 70

Romeo. Here's goodly gear!°

[*Enter* Nurse *and* Peter]

Mercutio. A sail, a sail!

Benvolio. Two, two—a shirt and a smock.°

Nurse. Peter!

Peter. Anon? 75

Nurse. My fan, Peter.

Mercutio. Good Peter, to hide her face, for her fan's the fairer face.

Nurse. God ye good morrow, gentlemen.

Mercutio. God ye good-den, fair gentlewoman.

Nurse. Is it good-den?° 80

Mercutio. 'Tis no less, I tell you, for the bawdy hand of the dial is now upon the
prick° of noon.

Nurse. Out upon you! What a man are you!

Romeo. One, gentlewoman, that God hath made himself to mar.

Nurse. By my troth, it is well said. "For himself to mar," quoth a'? Gentlemen, can any 85
of you tell me where I may find the young Romeo?

Romeo. I can tell you, but young Romeo will be older when you have found him than he was
when you sought him. I am the youngest of that name, for fault of a worse.

Nurse. You say well

Mercutio. Yea, is the worst well? Very well took,° i' faith—wisely, wisely. 90

Nurse. If you be he, sir, I desire some confidence° with you.

Benvolio. She will indite° him to some supper.

Mercutio. A bawd, a bawd, a bawd! So ho!

Romeo. What hast thou found?

Mercutio. No hare,° sir, unless a hare, sir, in a lenten pie, that is something stale and 95
hoar° ere it be spent. [*Sings.*]
> "An old hare hoar,
> And an old hare hoar,
> Is very good meat in Lent.
> But a hare that is hoar, 100
> Is too much for a score
> When it hoars ere it be spent."

Romeo, will you come to your father's? We'll to dinner thither.

---

71. **gear:** stuff. 73. **shirt...smock:** a man and a woman. 80. **good-den:** afternoon. 82. **prick:** point. 90. **took:**
understood. 91. **confidence:** for "conference." The Nurse uses long words but doesn't always know their
meaning. 92. **indite:** for "invite." 95. **hare:** prostitute. 96. **hoar:** moldy.

Romeo. I will follow you.

Mercutio. Farewell, ancient lady, farewell [*Singing*], "lady, lady, lady." 105

[*Exeunt* Mercutio *and* Benvolio.]

Nurse. Marry, farewell! I pray you, sir, what saucy merchant was this, that was so full of his ropery?°

Romeo. A gentleman, Nurse, that loves to hear himself talk, and will speak more in a minute than he will stand to in a month.

Nurse. An a' speak anything against me, I'll take him down, an a' were lustier than he is, and 110
twenty such Jacks;° and if I cannot, I'll find those that shall. Scurvy knave! I am none of his flirt-gills,° I am none of his skainsmates.° [*Turning to* Peter] And thou must stand by too, and suffer every knave to use me at his pleasure?

Peter. I saw no man use you at his pleasure. If I had, my weapon should quickly have been out, I warrant you. I dare draw as soon as another man, if I see occasion in a good 115
quarrel and the law on my side.

Nurse. Now, afore God, I am so vexed that every part about me quivers. Scurvy knave! Pray you, sir, a word. And as I told you, my young lady bade me inquire you out— what she bade me say, I will keep to myself. But first let me tell ye, if ye should lead her into a fool's paradise, as they say, it were a very gross kind of behavior, as they say. 120
For the gentlewoman is young, and therefore if you should deal double with her, truly it were an ill thing to be offered to any gentlewoman, and very weak dealing.

Romeo. Nurse, commend me to thy lady and mistress. I protest° unto thee—

Nurse. Good heart, and i' faith, I will tell her as much. Lord, Lord, she will be a joyful woman. 125

Romeo. What wilt thou tell her, Nurse? Thou dost not mark° me.

Nurse. I will tell her, sir, that you do protest, which, as I take it, is a gentlemanlike offer.

Romeo. Bid her devise
Some means to come to shrift° this afternoon,
And there she shall at Friar Laurence' cell 130
Be shrived and married. Here is for thy pains.

Nurse. No, truly, sir, not a penny.

Romeo. Go to, I say you shall.

Nurse. This afternoon, sir? Well, she shall be there.

Romeo. And stay, good Nurse, behind the abbey wall. 135
Within this hour my man shall be with thee,
And bring thee cords made like a tackled stair,°
Which to the high topgallant° of my joy
Must be my convoy in the secret night.
Farewell. Be trusty, and I'll quit thy pains.° 140
Farewell, commend me to thy mistress.

---

107. **ropery:** for "roguery." 111. **Jacks:** knaves. 112. **flirt-gills:** loose women. **skainsmates:** gangsters. 123. **protest:** declare. 126. **mark:** pay attention to. 129. **shrift:** confession. 137. **tackled stair:** rope ladder. 138. **topgallant:** topmast. 140. **quit thy pains:** reward your trouble.

A scene from a 1936 film version of Romeo and Juliet.

Nurse. Now God in Heaven bless thee! Hark you, sir.

Romeo. What say'st thou, my dear nurse?

Nurse. Is your man secret? Did you ne'er hear say

Two may keep counsel, putting one away?° 145

Romeo. I warrant thee, my man's as true as steel.

Nurse. Well, sir, my mistress is the sweetest lady—Lord, Lord, when 'twas a little prating
thing—Oh, there is a nobleman in town, one Paris, that would fain lay knife aboard;°
but she, good soul, had as lieve° see a toad, a very toad, as see him. I anger her sometimes, and tell her that Paris is the properer° man. But I'll warrant you, when I say so, 150
she looks as pale as any clout° in the versal world.° Doth not rosemary and Romeo begin
both with a letter?

Romeo. Aye, Nurse, what of that? Both with an R.

Nurse. Ah, mocker! That's the dog's name.° R is for the—No, I know it begins with some
other letter—and she hath the prettiest sententious° of it, of you and rosemary, that it 155
would do you good to hear it.

Romeo. Commend me to thy lady.

Nurse. Aye, a thousand times. [*Exit* Romeo.] Peter!

Peter. Anon?

Nurse. Peter, take my fan, and go before, and apace.° [*Exeunt.*] 160

145. **Two...away:** Two can keep a secret—if only one of them knows of it.   148. **lay knife aboard:** get her for himself.   149. **lieve:** soon.   150. **properer:** more handsome.   151. **clout:** cloth.   **versal world:** universe.   154. **dog's
name:** The letter *R* because it suggests a growling sound.   155. **sententious:** for "sentence" or proverb.   160. **apace:**
quickly.

[*Capulet's orchard. Enter* Juliet, *waiting impatiently for the Nurse.*]

Juliet. The clock struck nine when I did send the nurse.
  In half an hour she promised to return.
  Perchance she cannot meet him. That's not so.
  Oh, she is lame! Love's heralds should be thoughts,
  Which ten times faster glide than the sun's beams,   5
  Driving back shadows over lowering° hills.
  Therefore do nimble-pinioned° doves draw love,
  And therefore hath the wind-swift Cupid wings.
  Now is the sun upon the highmost hill
  Of this day's journey, and from nine till twelve   10
  Is three long hours; yet she is not come.
  Had she affections and warm youthful blood,
  She would be as swift in motion as a ball,
  My words would bandy° her to my sweet love,
  And his to me.   15
  But old folks, many feign as they were dead,
  Unwieldy, slow, heavy and pale as lead.

[*Enter* Nurse, *with* Peter.]

  Oh, God, she comes! O honey Nurse, what news?
  Hast thou met with him? Send thy man away.
Nurse. Peter, stay at the gate.   [*Exit* Peter.]   20
Juliet. Now, good sweet Nurse—Oh, Lord, why look'st thou sad?
  Though news be sad, yet tell them merrily;
  If good, thou shamest the music of sweet news
  By playing it to me with so sour a face.
Nurse. I am aweary, give me leave° a while.   25
  Fie, how my bones ache! What a jaunce° have I had!
Juliet. I would thou hadst my bones and I thy news.
  Nay, come, I pray thee, speak, good, good Nurse, speak.
Nurse. Jesu, what haste? Can you not stay° a while?
  Do you not see that I am out of breath?   30
Juliet. How art thou out of breath when thou hast breath
  To say to me that thou art out of breath?
  The excuse that thou dost make in this delay
  Is longer than the tale thou dost excuse.
  Is thy news good, or bad? Answer to that.   35

---

  6. **lowering:** frowning.   7. **nimble-pointed:** swift-winged.   14. **bandy:** bat, hit (like a tennis ball).   25. **give me leave:** let me alone.   26. **jaunce:** running back and forth.   29. **stay:** wait.

Say either, and I'll stay the circumstance.°
Let me be satisfied, is't good or bad?

Nurse. Well, you have made a simple° choice. You know not how to choose a man. Romeo!
No, not he, though his face be better than any man's, yet his leg excels all men's; and
for a hand, and a foot, and a body, though they be not to be talked on, yet they are past   40
compare. He is not the flower of courtesy,° but, I'll warrant him, as gentle as a lamb. Go
thy ways, wench, serve God. What, have you dined at home?

Juliet. No, no. But all this did I know before.
What says he of our marriage? What of that?

Nurse. Lord, how my head aches! What a head have I!   45
It beats as it would fall in twenty pieces.
My back o' t' other side—ah, my back, my back!
Beshrew° your heart for sending me about
To catch my death with jauncing up and down!

Juliet. I' faith, I am sorry that thou art not well.   50
Sweet, sweet, sweet Nurse, tell me, what says my love?

Nurse. Your love says, like an honest gentleman, and a courteous, and a kind, and a handsome, and, I warrant, a virtuous—Where is your mother?

Juliet. Where is my mother! Why, she is within,
Where should she be? How oddly thou repliest!   55
"Your love says, like an honest gentleman,
Where is your mother?"

Nurse.   Oh, God's Lady dear!°
Are you so hot?° Marry, come up, I trow.°
Is this the poultice° for my aching bones?
Henceforward do your messages yourself.   60

Juliet. Here's such a coil!° Come, what says Romeo?

Nurse. Have you got leave to go to shrift today?

Juliet. I have.

Nurse. Then hie° you hence to Friar Laurence' cell,
There stays a husband to make you a wife.   65
Now comes the wanton blood up in your cheeks,
They'll be in scarlet straight at any news.
Hie you to church, I must another way,
To fetch a ladder by the which your love
Must climb a bird's nest soon when it is dark.   70
I am the drudge, and toil in your delight,
But you shall bear the burden soon at night.
Go, I'll to dinner, hie you to the cell.

Juliet. Hie to high fortune! Honest Nurse, farewell.   *[Exeunt.]*

---

36. **stay the circumstance:** wait for details. 38. **simple:** foolish. 41. **flower of courtesy:** perfect gentleman.
48. **Beshrew:** a plague on. 57. **God's Lady dear:** by God's dear Mother (the Virgin Mary). 58. **hot:** impatient.
Marry...trow: Come, come, you're too impatient, I say. 59. **poultice:** remedy. 61. **coil:** fuss. 64. **hie:** hurry.

Scene 6

[*Friar Laurence's cell. Enter* Friar Laurence *and* Romeo.]

Friar Laurence. So smile the Heavens upon this holy act
   That afterhours with sorrow chide us not!
Romeo. Amen, amen! But come what sorrow can,
   It cannot countervail° the exchange of joy
   That one short minute gives me in her sight.   5
   Do thou but close our hands with holy words,
   Then love-devouring death do what he dare,
   It is enough I may but call her mine.
Friar Laurence. These violent delights have violent ends,
   And in their triumph die, like fire and powder°   10
   Which as they kiss consume. The sweetest honey
   Is loathsome in his own deliciousness,
   And in the taste confounds the appetite.
   Therefore, love moderately, long love doth so,
   Too swift arrive as tardy as too slow.   15

[*Enter* Juliet.]

   Here comes the lady. Oh, so light a foot
   Will ne'er wear out the everlasting flint.°
   A lover may bestride the gossamer°
   That idles in the wanton° summer air,
   And not yet fall, so light is vanity.°   20
Juliet. Good even to my ghostly confessor.
Friar Laurence. Romeo shall thank thee, daughter, for us both.
Juliet. As much° to him, else is his thanks too much.
Romeo. Ah, Juliet, if the measure of thy joy
   Be heaped like mine, and that thy skill be more   25
   To blazon° it, then sweeten with thy breath
   This neighbor air, and let rich music's tongue
   Unfold the imagined happiness that both
   Receive in either by this dear encounter.
Juliet. Conceit, more rich in matter than in words,   30
   Brags of his substance, not of ornament.°
   They are but beggars that can count their worth,

---

4. **countervail:** counterbalance, outweigh.   10. **powder:** gunpowder.   17. **flint:** hard stone.   18. **gossamer:** a spider's web.   19. **wanton:** playful.   20. **vanity:** unreality.   23. **As much:** the very same greeting.   26. **blazon** (blā′zən): describe.   30–31. **Conceit . . . ornament:** True understanding (conceit) does not need words.

But my true love is grown to such excess,
I cannot sum up sum of half my wealth.
Friar Laurence. Come, come with me, and we will make short work,   35
For, by your leaves, you shall not stay alone
Till Holy Church incorporate two in one.   [*Exeunt.*]

Reading Check

1. What danger does Romeo risk in entering Capulet's orchard?
2. Before parting, what decision do the lovers come to?
3. Why has Tybalt sent a letter to the Montagues?
4. What excuse does Juliet use for going to Friar Laurence's cell?
5. How does Romeo plan to enter Juliet's house?

For Study and Discussion

Analyzing and Interpreting the Play

1a. To whom does Romeo refer in Scene 2 when he says, "He jests at scars that never felt a wound"?   **b.** What does this remark mean?

2. Scene 2 takes place in the Capulet orchard late at night after the party. In what two ways does darkness influence what happens in the scene?

3. The balcony scene is famous for its poetry. **a.** Which lover uses images of light? **b.** Which one uses images of flowers and birds?   **c.** Find lines in which they express their feelings for each other through these images.

4. In what way does Juliet exhibit more common sense and practicality than Romeo?

5a. Why is the Friar surprised at Romeo's confession of a new love?   **b.** Why does he consent to marry Romeo and Juliet?

6. Although Mercutio teases Romeo in Scene 4, he is actually worried for him. Why?

7. Look closely at the Nurse's description of Romeo in Scene 5.   **a.** Is she praising him or finding fault?   **b.** Is she really tired when she enters or is she just teasing Juliet?

8. What concern does the Friar express in Scene 6 about the relationship of Romeo and Juliet?

Literary Elements

Dramatic Structure: Conventions

Prose and Poetry

At different times in the history of the theater, dramatists have adopted certain **conventions,** or practices that become established and accepted by players and audiences. Shakespeare wrote most of his plays in verse. This was a convention of the Elizabethan theater. Prose is generally reserved for comic passages. Most of the prose passages in *Romeo and Juliet* are spoken by servants and by the Nurse but Mercutio's comic banter is written in prose too. Prose, as a rule, is used for the "lighter" moments of the play.

The most common form of verse in Shakespeare's play is **blank verse.** Blank verse is unrhymed iambic pentameter. In a line that is perfectly regular, an unstressed syllable is always followed by a stressed syllable. This pattern is called iambic.

> Bŭt sóft! / Whăt líght / thrŏugh yón/dĕr
> wín/dŏw bréaks?

The meter is called pentameter because there are five feet in each line, indicated above by slash marks.

A blank verse line is sometimes divided between two speakers:

Jul. Take all myself.
Rom. I take thee at thy word.

Not all lines are perfectly regular. Without variety in rhythm, the speeches would become monotonous.

A pair of rhymed lines in iambic pentameter is called a **heroic couplet.** Shakespeare often closes a scene with a couplet:

> Farewell. Thou canst not teach me to forget.
> I'll pay that doctrine, or else die in debt.
>
> (I, 1)

> Hence will I to my ghostly father's cell,
> His help to crave and my dear hap to tell.
>
> (II, 2)

For, by your leaves, you shall not stay alone
Till Holy Church incorporate two in one.

(II, 6)

Soliloquy, Monologue, and Aside

When the Friar stands alone on the stage at the beginning of Act Two, Scene 3, and talks to himself, we understand that he is speaking his thoughts aloud so that we can hear them. This is another convention known as **soliloquy.** A soliloquy is spoken by a character who is alone on stage.

Mercutio's famous speech on Queen Mab in Act One, Scene 4, is a **monologue.** A monologue is a long, virtually uninterrupted speech that is spoken in the presence of other characters.

An **aside** is a short remark usually directed to the audience and not intended to be heard by the other characters on stage. Sometimes, however, an aside is directed at another character. In the first scene of Act One, the servants Gregory and Sampson speak to each other in asides that are not intended to be overheard by Abraham and Balthasar.

Writing About Literature

Discussing Contrasts in Character

Shakespeare's play provides a balanced view of young people and their elders. In the first act Benvolio clearly serves as a contrast to Tybalt, and the Nurse as a contrast to Lady Capulet. In Act Two we meet Friar Laurence, who might be considered a **foil**, or contrast, to the Montagues, the Capulets, and the Nurse. What qualities does he show that are not apparent in the other characters? Write a paper in which you discuss these contrasts.

Act Three

Scene 1

[*A public place. Enter* Mercutio, Benvolio, Page, *and* Servants.]

Benvolio. I pray thee, good Mercutio, let's retire.
　　The day is hot, the Capulets abroad,
　　And if we meet, we shall not 'scape a brawl;
　　For now these hot days is the mad blood stirring.

Mercutio. Thou art like one of those fellows that when he enters the confines of a tavern   5
　　claps me his sword upon the table and says, "God send me no need of thee!" and by
　　the operation of the second cup draws it on the drawer,° when indeed there is no
　　need.

Benvolio. Am I like such a fellow?

Mercutio. Come, come, thou art as hot a Jack in thy mood as any in Italy, and as soon ✗   10
　　moved to be moody,° and as soon moody to be moved.

Benvolio. And what to?

Mercutio. Nay, an there were two such, we should have none shortly, for one would kill
　　the other. Thou! Why, thou wilt quarrel with a man that hath a hair more, or a hair
　　less, in his beard than thou hast. Thou wilt quarrel with a man for cracking nuts, hav-   15
　　ing no other reason but because thou hast hazel eyes. What eye but such an eye would
　　spy out such a quarrel? Thy head is as full of quarrels as an egg is full of meat, and
　　yet thy head hath been beaten as addle as an egg for quarreling. Thou hast quarreled
　　with a man for coughing in the street, because he hath wakened thy dog that hath lain
　　asleep in the sun. Didst thou not fall out with a tailor for wearing his new doublet° be-   20
　　fore Easter? With another for tying his new shoes with old ribbon? And yet thou wilt
　　tutor me from quarreling!°

Benvolio. An I were so apt to quarrel as thou art, any man should buy the fee simple° of
　　my life for an hour and a quarter.

Mercutio. The fee simple! Oh, simple!   25

[Enter Tybalt *and others*.]

Benvolio. By my head, here come the Capulets. ✗

Mercutio. By my heel, I care not.

Tybalt. Follow me close, for I will speak to them.
　　Gentlemen, good-den—a word with one of you.

Mercutio. And but one word with one of us? Couple it with something—make it a word   30
　　and a blow.

---

7. **drawer:** waiter. 11. **moody:** angry. 20. **doublet:** short, close-fitting jacket. 22. **tutor me from quarreling:** teach
me how to avoid quarreling. 23. **fee simple:** absolute possession.

Tybalt. You shall find me apt enough to that, sir, an you will give me occasion.

Mercutio. Could you not take some occasion without giving?

Tybalt. Mercutio, thou consort'st° with Romeo——

Mercutio. Consort! What, dost thou make us minstrels?° An thou make minstrels of us,   35
look to hear nothing but discords. Here's my fiddlestick,° here's that shall make you
dance. 'Zounds,° consort!

Benvolio. We talk here in the public haunt of men.
Either withdraw unto some private place,
And reason coldly of your grievances,   40
Or else depart. Here all eyes gaze on us.

Mercutio. Men's eyes were made to look, and let them gaze.
I will not budge for no man's pleasure, I.

[Enter Romeo, *now kinsman by marriage to the* Capulets.]

Tybalt. Well, peace be with you sir. Here comes my man.°

Mercutio. But I'll be hanged, sir, if he wear your livery.°   45
Marry, go before to field,° he'll be your follower.
Your worship in that sense may call him man.

Tybalt. Romeo, the hate I bear thee can afford
No better term than this—thou art a villain.

Romeo. Tybalt, the reason that I have to love thee   50
Doth much excuse the appertaining rage°
To such a greeting. Villain am I none,
Therefore farewell. I see thou know'st me not.°

Tybalt. Boy, this shall not excuse the injuries
That thou hast done me, therefore turn and draw.   55

Romeo. I do protest I never injured thee,
But love thee better than thou canst devise°
Till thou shalt know the reason of my love.
And so, good Capulet—which name I tender°
As dearly as mine own—be satisfied.   60

Mercutio. Oh, calm, dishonorable, vile submission!
Alla stoccata° carries it away. [*Draws his sword.*]
Tybalt, you ratcatcher, will you walk?

Tybalt. What wouldst thou have with me?

Mercutio. Good King of Cats,° nothing but one of your nine lives, that I mean to make   65

---

34. **consort'st:** are friendly with.   35. **minstrels:** Mercutio puns on another meaning of consort—a party of musicians.
36. **fiddlestick:** rapier, his sword.   37. **'Zounds:** by God's wounds.   44. **my man:** the man I want.   45. **your livery:**
servant's uniform. Mercutio interprets *man* in its other sense of "servant."   46. **field:** dueling place.   51. **appertaining
rage:** the anger with which I would otherwise respond.   53. **know'st me not:** Tybalt does not know they are now kinsmen
because Romeo has married Juliet.   57. **devise:** guess, imagine.   59. **tender:** regard, care for.   62. **Alla stoccata:** a
thrust in fencing. Mercutio uses this term as a name for Tybalt.   65. **King of Cats:** See note 16 on page 519.

bold withal, and, as you shall use me hereafter, dry-beat° the rest of the eight. Will you pluck your sword out of his pilcher° by the ears? Make haste, lest mine be about your ears ere it be out.

Tybalt. I am for you. [*Drawing*]

Romeo. Gentle Mercutio, put thy rapier up.   70

Mercutio. Come, sir, your passado.°

[*They fight.*]

Romeo. Draw, Benvolio, beat down their weapons.
Gentlemen, for shame, forbear this outrage!
Tybalt, Mercutio, the Prince expressly hath
Forbid this bandying° in Verona streets.   75
Hold, Tybalt, good Mercutio!

[Tybalt *under* Romeo's *arm stabs* Mercutio *and flies with his followers.*]

Mercutio.   I am hurt.
A plague o' both your houses! I am sped.°
Is he gone, and hath nothing?

Benvolio.   What, art thou hurt?

Mercutio. Aye, aye, a scratch, a scratch—marry, 'tis enough.
Where is my page? Go, villain,° fetch a surgeon.   [*Exit* Page.]   80

Romeo. Courage, man, the hurt cannot be much.

Mercutio. No, 'tis not so deep as a well nor so wide as a church door, but 'tis enough, 'twill serve. Ask for me tomorrow and you shall find me a grave man.° I am peppered,° I warrant, for this world. A plague o' both your houses! 'Zounds, a dog, a rat, a mouse, a cat, to scratch a man to death! A braggart, a rogue, a villain, that fights by the book   85
of arithmetic!° Why the devil came you between us! I was hurt under your arm.

Romeo. I thought all for the best.

Mercutio. Help me into some house, Benvolio,
Or I shall faint. A plague o' both your houses!
They have made worms' meat of me. I have it,   90
And soundly too—your houses!   [*Exeunt* Mercutio *and* Benvolio.]

Romeo. This gentleman, the Prince's near ally,
My very friend, hath got his mortal hurt
In my behalf, my reputation stained
With Tybalt's slander—Tybalt, that an hour   95
Hath been my kinsman. O sweet Juliet,

66. **dry-beat:** bruise.   67. **pilcher:** scabbard, a case for a sword.   71. **passado:** lunge.   75. **bandying:** quarreling.   77. **sped:** done for.   80. **villain:** term used in addressing a servant.   83. **grave man:** Mercutio's last pun. The two meanings of grave are "serious" and "dead."   **peppered:** shot, wounded.   85–86. **book of arithmetic:** textbook on fencing; by exact rules.

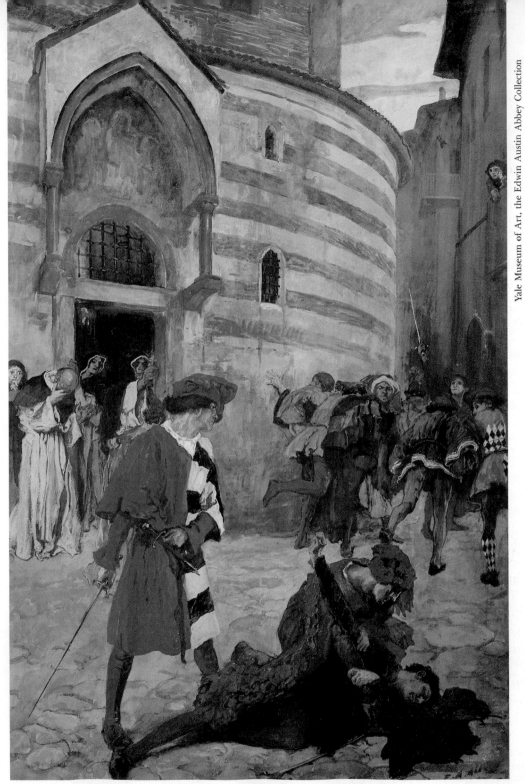

Death of Mercutio (1902) by Edwin Austin Abbey. Watercolor.

Thy beauty hath made me effeminate,°
And in my temper softened valor's steel!

[*Reenter* Benvolio.]

Benvolio. O Romeo, Romeo, brave Mercutio's dead!
    That gallant spirit hath aspired° the clouds,   100
    Which too untimely here did scorn the earth.
Romeo. This day's black fate on more days doth depend,°
    This but begins the woe others must end.

[*Reenter* Tybalt.]

Benvolio. Here comes the furious Tybalt back again.
Romeo. Alive, in triumph! And Mercutio slain!   105
    Away to Heaven, respective lenity,°
    And fire-eyed fury be my conduct° now!
    Now, Tybalt, take the "villain" back again
    That late thou gavest me; for Mercutio's soul
    Is but a little way above our heads,   110
    Staying for thine to keep him company.
    Either thou, or I, or both, must go with him.
Tybalt. Thou, wretched boy, that didst consort him here,
    Shalt with him hence.
Romeo.   This shall determine that.

[*They fight;* Tybalt *falls dead.*]

Benvolio. Romeo, away, be gone!   115
    The citizens are up, and Tybalt slain.
    Stand not amazed. The Prince will doom thee death
    If thou art taken. Hence, be gone, away!
Romeo. Oh, I am fortune's fool!°
Benvolio.   Why dost thou stay!   [*Exit* Romeo.]

[*Enter* Citizens.]

First Citizen. Which way ran he that killed Mercutio?   120
    Tybalt, that murderer, which way ran he?
Benvolio. There lies that Tybalt.

97. **effeminate:** womanly.   100. **aspired:** soared to.   102. **on more days doth depend:** will be followed by more fatal
days.   106. **respective lenity:** considerate mercy (which Romeo has shown to Tybalt).   107. **conduct:** guide.   119.
fortune's fool: fooled by fortune.

First Citizen.   Up, sir, go with me.
   I charge thee in the Prince's name, obey.

   [*Enter* Prince, *attended;* Montague, Capulet, *their* Wives, *and others.*]

Prince. Where are the vile beginners of this fray?
Benvolio. O noble Prince, I can discover° all   125
   The unlucky manage° of this fatal brawl.
   There lies the man, slain by young Romeo,
   That slew thy kinsman, brave Mercutio.
Lady Capulet. Tybalt, my cousin! Oh, my brother's child!
   O Prince! O Cousin! Husband! Oh, the blood is spilt   130
   Of my dear kinsman! Prince, as thou art true,
   For blood of ours shed blood of Montague.
   O Cousin, Cousin!
Prince. Benvolio, who began this bloody fray?
Benvolio. Tybalt, here slain, whom Romeo's hand did slay—   135
   Romeo that spoke him fair, bade him bethink
   How nice° the quarrel was, and urged withal
   Your high displeasure. All this uttered
   With gentle breath, calm look, knees humbly bowed,
   Could not take truce with the unruly spleen°   140
   Of Tybalt deaf to peace, but that he tilts
   With piercing steel at bold Mercutio's breast,
   Who, all as hot, turns deadly point to point,
   And, with a martial scorn, with one hand beats
   Cold death aside and with the other sends   145
   It back to Tybalt, whose dexterity
   Retorts it. Romeo, he cries aloud,
   "Hold, friends! Friends, part!" and, swifter than his tongue,
   His agile arm beats down their fatal points,
   And 'twixt them rushes. Underneath whose arm   150
   An envious° thrust from Tybalt hit the life
   Of stout Mercutio, and then Tybalt fled,
   But by and by comes back to Romeo,
   Who had but newly entertained revenge,
   And to 't they go like lightning. For ere I   155
   Could draw to part them was stout Tybalt slain,
   And as he fell, did Romeo turn and fly.
   This is the truth, or let Benvolio die.

125. **discover:** reveal. 126. **manage:** circumstances. 137. **nice:** trifling, trivial. 140. **spleen:** fiery temper. 151.
envious: hateful.

Lady Capulet. He is a kinsman to the Montague,
    Affection makes him false, he speaks not true.   160
    Some twenty of them fought in this black strife,
    And all those twenty could but kill one life.
    I beg for justice, which thou, Prince, must give.
    Romeo slew Tybalt, Romeo must not live.
Prince. Romeo slew him, he slew Mercutio.   165
    Who now the price of his dear blood doth owe?
Montague. [*Pleading*] Not Romeo, Prince, he was Mercutio's friend.
    His fault concludes but what the law should end,
    The life of Tybalt.
Prince. [*His anger roused*] And for that offense
    Immediately we do exile him hence.   170
    I have an interest° in your hate's proceeding,
    My blood for your rude brawls doth lie a-bleeding.
    But I'll amerce° you with so strong a fine
    That you shall all repent the loss of mine.
    I will be deaf to pleading and excuses,   175
    Nor tears nor prayers shall purchase out° abuses.
    Therefore use none. Let Romeo hence in haste,
    Else, when he's found, that hour is his last.
    Bear hence this body, and attend our will.°
    Mercy but murders, pardoning those that kill.   [*Exeunt.*]   180

Scene 2

[Capulet's *orchard. Enter* Juliet.]

Juliet. Gallop apace, you fiery-footed steeds,
    Toward Phoebus'° lodging. Such a wagoner
    And Phaëton° would whip you to the west,
    And bring in cloudy night immediately.
    Spread thy close curtain, love-performing night,   5
    That runaways' eyes may wink, and Romeo
    Leap to these arms, untalked of and unseen.
    Lovers can see to do their amorous rites
    By their own beauties; or, if love be blind,
    It best agrees with night. Come, civil night,   10

---

171. **interest:** concern. Mercutio was the Prince's kinsman.   173. **amerce:** punish.   176. **purchase out:** pay for.   179.
attend our will: come to receive my judgment.
    2. **Phoebus** (fē′bəs): the sun god, Phoebus Apollo, who according to mythology was drawn across the sky in his chariot
every day.   3. **Phaëton** (fā′ə-tən): the son of Phoebus. He tried to drive his father's chariot, but was unable to control the
horses.

Thou sober-suited matron, all in black,
And learn me how to lose a winning match
Played for a pair of stainless maidenhoods.
Hood my unmanned blood bating in my cheeks
With thy black mantle, till strange love grown bold   15
Think true love acted simple modesty.
Come, night, come, Romeo, come, thou day in night,
For thou wilt lie upon the wings of night
Whiter than new snow on a raven's back.
Come, gentle night, come, loving, black-browed night,   20
Give me my Romeo; and when he shall die,
Take him and cut him out in little stars,
And he will make the face of heaven so fine
That all the world will be in love with night,
And pay no worship to the garish° sun.   25
Oh, I have bought the mansion of a love,
But not possessed it, and though I am sold,
Not yet enjoyed. So tedious is this day
As is the night before some festival
To an impatient child that hath new robes   30
And may not wear them. Oh, here comes my nurse,
And she brings news, and every tongue that speaks
But Romeo's name speaks heavenly eloquence.

[*Enter* Nurse, *with ladder of cords.*]

Now, Nurse, what news? What hast thou there? The cords
That Romeo bid thee fetch?   35
Nurse. Aye, aye, the cords. [*Throws them down.*]
Juliet. Aye me! What news? Why dost thou wring thy hands?
Nurse. Ah, welladay! He's dead, he's dead, he's dead.
    We are undone, lady, we are undone.
    Alack the day! He's gone, he's killed, he's dead.   40
Juliet. Can Heaven be so envious?
Nurse.   Romeo can,
    Though Heaven cannot. O Romeo, Romeo!
    Who ever would have thought it? Romeo!
Juliet. What devil art thou that dost torment me thus?
    This torture should be roared in dismal Hell.   45
    Hath Romeo slain himself? Say thou but "I,"°
    And that bare vowel "I" shall poison more

---

25. **garish:** gaudy.   46. **"I":** Juliet puns on "aye" and "I."

Than the death-darting eye of cockatrice.°
I am not I, if there be such an I,
Or those eyes shut, that make thee answer "I."   50
If he be slain, say "I," or if not, no.
Brief sounds determine of my weal or woe.

Nurse. I saw the wound, I saw it with mine eyes—
God save the mark!—here on his manly breast.
A piteous corse,° a bloody piteous corse,   55
Pale, pale as ashes, all bedaubed in blood,
All in gore blood. I swounded° at the sight.

Juliet. Oh, break, my heart! Poor bankrupt, break at once!
To prison, eyes, ne'er look on liberty!
Vile earth° to earth resign, end motion here,   60
And thou and Romeo press one heavy bier!

Nurse. O Tybalt, Tybalt, the best friend I had!
O courteous Tybalt! Honest gentleman!
That ever I should live to see thee dead!

Juliet. What storm is this that blows so contrary?   65
Is Romeo slaughtered, and is Tybalt dead?
My dear-loved cousin, and my dearer lord?
Then, dreadful trumpet,° sound the general doom!
For who is living if those two are gone?

Nurse. Tybalt is gone, and Romeo banishèd—   70
Romeo that killed him, he is banishèd.

Juliet. Oh, God! Did Romeo's hand shed Tybalt's blood?

Nurse. It did, it did. Alas the day, it did!

Juliet. Oh, serpent heart, hid with a flowering face!
Did ever dragon keep so fair a cave?   75
Beautiful tyrant! Fiend angelical!
Dove-feathered raven! Wolvish-ravening lamb!°
Despisèd substance of divinest show!
Just opposite to what thou justly seem'st,
A damnèd saint, an honorable villain!   80
O Nature, what hadst thou to do in Hell
When thou didst bower° the spirit of a fiend
In mortal paradise of such sweet flesh?
Was ever book containing such vile matter
So fairly bound? Oh, that deceit should dwell   85
In such a gorgeous palace!

---

48. **cockatrice:** a fabulous serpent that could kill with a glance. 55. **corse:** corpse. 57. **swounded:** swooned, fainted.
60. **Vile earth:** Juliet refers to herself. 68. **dreadful trumpet:** the trumpet that is supposed to announce the end of the
world. 74–77. **Oh . . . lamb:** This series of images combining opposite or contradictory ideas is typical in early Elizabethan poetry. 82. **bower:** embower.

A scene from the 1985 BBC-TV production of *Romeo and Juliet*.

Nurse.   There's no trust,
    No faith, no honesty in men—all perjured,
    All forsworn, all naught, all dissemblers.°
    Ah, where's my man? Give me some aqua vitae.°
    These griefs, these woes, these sorrows, make me old.   90
    Shame come to Romeo!
Juliet.   Blistered be thy tongue
    For such a wish! He was not born to shame.
    Upon his brow shame is ashamed to sit,
    For 'tis a throne where honor may be crowned
    Sole monarch of the universal earth.   95
    Oh, what a beast was I to chide at him!
Nurse. Will you speak well of him that killed your cousin?
Juliet. Shall I speak ill of him that is my husband?
    Ah, poor my lord, what tongue shall smooth thy name

88. **dissemblers:** pretenders, hypocrites.   89. **aqua vitae** (vī′tē): spirits.

When I, thy three-hours wife, have mangled it? 100
But wherefore, villain, didst thou kill my cousin?
That villain cousin would have killed my husband.
Back, foolish tears, back to your native spring,
Your tributary drops belong to woe
Which you mistaking offer up to joy. 105
My husband lives, that Tybalt would have slain,
And Tybalt's dead, that would have slain my husband.
All this is comfort, wherefore weep I, then?
Some word there was, worser than Tybalt's death,
That murdered me. I would forget it fain,° 110
But, oh, it presses to my memory
Like damnèd guilty deeds to sinners' minds.
"Tybalt is dead, and Romeo banishèd."
That "banishèd," that one word "banishèd,"
Hath slain ten thousand Tybalts. Tybalt's death 115
Was woe enough if it had ended there.
Or, if sour woe delights in fellowship,
And needly° will be ranked with other griefs,
Why followed not, when she said "Tybalt's dead,"
Thy father, or thy mother, nay, or both, 120
Which modern° lamentation might have moved?
But with a rearward following Tybalt's death,
"Romeo is banishèd." To speak that word
Is father, mother, Tybalt, Romeo, Juliet,
All slain, all dead. "Romeo is banishèd." 125
There is no end, no limit, measure, bound,
In that word's death; no words can that woe sound.
Where is my father, and my mother, Nurse?

Nurse. Weeping and wailing over Tybalt's corse.
Will you go to them? I will bring you thither. 130

Juliet. Wash they his wounds with tears. Mine shall be spent,
When theirs are dry, for Romeo's banishment.
Take up those cords. Poor ropes, you are beguiled,
Both you and I, for Romeo is exiled.
He made you for a highway to my bed, 135
But I, a maid, die maiden-widowèd.
Come, cords, come, Nurse, I'll to my wedding bed,
And death, not Romeo, take my maidenhead!

Nurse. Hie to your chamber. I'll find Romeo
To comfort you. I wot° well where he is. 140

110. **fain:** willingly.   118. **needly:** necessarily.   121. **modern:** ordinary.   140. **wot:** know.

Hark ye, your Romeo will be here at night.
I'll to him—he is hid at Laurence' cell.
Juliet. Oh, find him! Give this ring to my true knight,
And bid him come to take his last farewell.   [*Exeunt.*]

Scene 3

[Friar Laurence*'s cell. Enter* Friar Laurence.]

Friar Laurence. Romeo, come forth, come forth, thou fearful° man.
Affliction is enamored of thy parts,°
And thou art wedded to calamity.

[*Enter* Romeo.]

Romeo. Father, what news? What is the Prince's doom?°
What sorrow craves acquaintance at my hand   5
That I yet know not?
Friar Laurence.   Too familiar
Is my dear son with such sour company.
I bring thee tidings of the Prince's doom.
Romeo. What less than Doomsday is the Prince's doom?
Friar Laurence. A gentler judgment vanished° from his lips,   10
Not body's death, but body's banishment.
Romeo. Ha, banishment! Be merciful, say "death,"
For exile hath more terror in his look,
Much more, than death. Do not say "banishment."
Friar Laurence. Hence from Verona art thou banishèd.   15
Be patient, for the world is broad and wide.
Romeo. There is no world without° Verona walls,
But Purgatory, torture, Hell itself.
Hence banishèd is banished from the world.
And world's exile is death. Then "banishèd,"   20
Is death mistermed. Calling death "banishèd,"
Thou cut'st my head off with a golden ax,
And smilest upon the stroke that murders me.
Friar Laurence. Oh, deadly sin! Oh, rude unthankfulness!
Thy fault our law calls death, but the kind Prince,   25
Taking thy part, hath rushed° aside the law,

---

1. **fearful:** full of fear.   2. **Affliction . . . parts:** Misfortune has fallen in love with your good qualities (and so follows wherever you go).   4. **doom:** sentence.   10. **vanished:** escaped.   17. **without:** outside.   26. **rushed:** brushed.

A scene from the Oregon Shakespeare Festival's 1982 production of *Romeo and Juliet*.

And turned that black word "death" to "banishment."
This is dear° mercy, and thou seest it not.
Romeo. 'Tis torture, and not mercy. Heaven is here,
　　Where Juliet lives, and every cat and dog　　　　　　　　　　30
　　And little mouse, every unworthy thing,
　　Live here in Heaven and may look on her,
　　But Romeo may not. More validity,
　　More honorable state, more courtship, lives
　　In carrion flies than Romeo. They may seize　　　　　　　　　35
　　On the white wonder of dear Juliet's hand,
　　And steal immortal blessing from her lips,
　　Who, even in pure and vestal modesty,
　　Still blush, as thinking their own kisses sin.
　　But Romeo may not, he is banishèd.　　　　　　　　　　　40
　　This may flies do, but I from this must fly.
　　They are free men, but I am banishèd.
　　And say'st thou yet that exile is not death?
　　Hadst thou no poison mixed, no sharp-ground knife,
　　No sudden mean of death, though ne'er so mean　　　　　　45
　　But "banishèd" to kill me?—"Banishèd"?
　　O Friar, the damnèd use that word in Hell,

28. **dear:** precious.

Howling attends it. How hast thou the heart,
Being a divine, a ghostly confessor,
A sin-absolver, and my friend professed,   50
To mangle me with that word "banishèd"?

Friar Laurence. Thou fond° madman, hear me but speak a word.

Romeo. Oh, thou wilt speak again of banishment.

Friar Laurence. I'll give thee armor to keep off that word,
Adversity's sweet milk, philosophy,   55
To comfort thee, though thou art banishèd.

Romeo. Yet "banishèd"? Hang up philosophy!
Unless philosophy can make a Juliet,
Displant° a town, reverse a Prince's doom,
It helps not, it prevails not. Talk no more.   60

Friar Laurence. Oh, then I see that madmen have no ears.

Romeo. How should they when that wise men have no eyes?

Friar Laurence. Let me dispute° with thee of thy estate.°

Romeo. Thou canst not speak of that thou dost not feel.
Wert thou as young as I, Juliet thy love,   65
An hour but married, Tybalt murderèd,
Doting like me, and like me banishèd,
Then mightst thou speak, then mightst thou tear thy hair
And fall upon the ground, as I do now,
Taking the measure of an unmade grave.   70

[*As he falls to the ground, someone knocks within.*]

Friar Laurence. Arise, one knocks. Good Romeo, hide thyself.

Romeo. Not I, unless the breath of heartsick groans
Mistlike enfold me from the search of eyes. [*Knocking.*]

Friar Laurence. Hark how they knock! Who's there? Romeo, arise,
Thou wilt be taken.—Stay awhile!—Stand up, [*Knocking.*]   75
Run to my study.—By and by!°—God's will,
What simpleness is this!—I come, I come! [*Knocking.*]
Who knocks so hard? Whence come you? What's your will?

Nurse. [*Within*] Let me come in, and you shall know my errand.
I come from Lady Juliet.

Friar Laurence.   Welcome, then.   80

[*Enter* Nurse.]

Nurse. O holy Friar, oh, tell me, holy Friar,
Where is my lady's lord, where's Romeo?

52. **fond:** foolish. 59. **Displant:** uproot. 63. **dispute:** discuss. **estate:** circumstances. 76. **By and by:** Wait a moment.

Friar Laurence. There on the ground, with his own tears made drunk.

Nurse. Oh, he is even in my mistress' case,
 Just in her case!

Friar Laurence.   Oh, woeful sympathy!   85
 Piteous predicament!

Nurse.   Even so lies she,
 Blubbering and weeping, weeping and blubbering.
 Stand up, stand up, stand, an you be a man.
 For Juliet's sake, for her sake, rise and stand.
 Why should you fall into so deep an O?°   90

Romeo. Nurse!

Nurse. Ah sir, ah sir! Well, death's the end of all.

Romeo. Spakest thou of Juliet? How is it with her?
 Doth she not think me an old° murderer,
 Now I have stained the childhood of our joy   95
 With blood removed but little from her own?
 Where is she? And how doth she? And what says
 My concealed lady° to our canceled love?

Nurse. Oh, she says nothing, sir, but weeps and weeps,
 And now falls on her bed, and then starts up   100
 And Tybalt calls, and then on Romeo cries,
 And then down falls again.

Romeo.   As if that name,
 Shot from the deadly level° of a gun,
 Did murder her, as that name's cursèd hand
 Murdered her kinsman. Oh, tell me, Friar, tell me,   105
 In what vile part of this anatomy°
 Doth my name lodge? Tell me, that I may sack°
 The hateful mansion. [*Drawing his dagger.*]

Friar Laurence.   Hold thy desperate hand.
 Art thou a man? Thy form cries out thou art.
 Thy tears are womanish, thy wild acts denote   110
 The unreasonable fury of a beast.
 Unseemly woman in a seeming man!
 Or ill-beseeming beast in seeming both!°
 Thou hast amazed me. By my holy order,
 I thought thy disposition better tempered.°   115
 Hast thou slain Tybalt? Wilt thou slay thyself?
 And slay thy lady too that lives in thee,
 By doing damnèd hate upon thyself?
 Why rail'st thou on thy birth, the Heaven and earth?

90. **O:** cry of grief.   94. **old:** experienced.   98. **concealed lady:** secret bride.   103. **level:** aim.   106. **anatomy:** body. 107. **sack:** destroy.   113. **Or . . . both:** a shameful beast for you are neither man nor woman.   115. **tempered:** mixed.

Since birth and Heaven and earth all three do meet   120
In thee at once, which thou at once wouldst lose.
Fie, fie, thou shamest thy shape, thy love, thy wit,
Which, like a usurer,° abound'st in all,
And usest none in that true use indeed
Which should bedeck thy shape, thy love, thy wit.   125
Thy noble shape is but a form of wax,
Digressing from the valor of a man;
Thy dear love sworn, but hollow perjury,
Killing that love which thou hast vowed to cherish;
Thy wit, that ornament to shape and love,   130
Misshapen in the conduct of them both,
Like powder in a skill-less soldier's flask,
Is set afire by thine own ignorance,
And thou dismembered with thine own defense.°
What, rouse thee, man! Thy Juliet is alive,   135
For whose dear sake thou wast but lately dead.
There art thou happy. Tybalt would kill thee,
But thou slew'st Tybalt. There art thou happy too.
The law, that threatened death, becomes thy friend
And turns it to exile. There art thou happy.   140
A pack of blessings lights upon thy back,
Happiness courts thee in her best array;
But, like a misbehaved and sullen wench,
Thou pout'st upon thy fortune and thy love.
Take heed, take heed, for such die miserable.   145
Go, get thee to thy love, as was decreed,
Ascend her chamber—hence and comfort her.
But look thou stay not till the watch be set,°
For then thou canst not pass to Mantua,
Where thou shalt live till we can find a time   150
To blaze° your marriage, reconcile your friends,
Beg pardon of the Prince, and call thee back
With twenty hundred thousand times more joy
Than thou went'st forth in lamentation.
Go before, Nurse. Commend me to thy lady,   155
And bid her hasten all the house to bed,
Which heavy sorrow makes them apt unto.
Romeo is coming.
Nurse. Oh Lord, I could have stayed here all the night

---

123. **usurer:** miser.   134. **dismembered . . . defense:** blown to pieces by your own weapon.   148. **watch be set:** watchmen go on duty at the gates.   151. **blaze:** make public.

To hear good counsel. Oh, what learning is!   160
  My lord, I'll tell my lady you will come.
Romeo. Do so, and bid my sweet prepare to chide.
Nurse. Here, sir, a ring she bid me give you, sir.
  Hie you, make haste, for it grows very late.   [*Exit.*]
Romeo. How well my comfort is revived by this!   165
Friar Laurence. Go hence, good night, and here stands all your state.°
  Either be gone before the watch be set,
  Or by the break of day disguised from hence.
  Sojourn° in Mantua. I'll find out your man,
  And he shall signify from time to time   170
  Every good hap° to you that chances here.
  Give me thy hand, 'tis late. Farewell, good night.
Romeo. But that a joy past joy calls out to me,
  It were a grief so brief to part with thee.
  Farewell.   [*Exeunt.*] 175

Scene 4

[*A room in* Capulet's *house.*]

Capulet. Things have fall'n out, sir, so unluckily,
  That we have had no time to move° our daughter.
  Look you, she loved her kinsman Tybalt dearly,
  And so did I. Well, we were born to die.
  'Tis very late, she'll not come down tonight.   5
  I promise you, but for your company
  I would have been abed an hour ago.
Paris. These times of woe afford no time to woo.
  Madam, good night. Commend me to your daughter.
Lady Capulet. I will, and know her mind early tomorrow;   10
  Tonight she's mewed up to her heaviness.°
Capulet. Sir Paris, I will make a desperate tender°
  Of my child's love. I think she will be ruled
  In all respects by me——nay, more, I doubt it not.
  Wife, go you to her ere you go to bed,   15
  Acquaint her here of my son° Paris' love,
  And bid her, mark you me, on Wednesday next——
  But, soft! what day is this?

166. **here . . . state:** on this depends all your good fortune.   169. **Sojourn:** remain.   171. **hap:** happening.
  2. **move:** make your proposal to.   11. **mewed . . . heaviness:** shut up in seclusion with her sorrow.   12. **desperate tender:** bold offer.   16. **son:** future son-in-law.

Paris.   Monday, my lord.

Capulet. Monday! Ha, ha! Well, Wednesday is too soon.
    O' Thursday let it be. O' Thursday, tell her,   20
    She shall be married to this noble Earl.
    Will you be ready? Do you like this haste?
    We'll keep no great ado, a friend or two;
    For, hark you, Tybalt being slain so late,°
    It may be thought we held him carelessly,°   25
    Being our kinsman, if we revel much.
    Therefore we'll have some half a dozen friends,
    And there an end. But what say you to Thursday?

Paris. My lord, I would that Thursday were tomorrow.

Capulet. Well, get you gone. O' Thursday be it, then   30
    Go you to Juliet ere you go to bed,
    Prepare her, wife, against° this wedding day.
    Farewell, my lord. Light to my chamber, ho!
    Afore me,° it is so very very late
    That we may call it early by and by.   35
    Good night.   [*Exeunt.*]

Scene 5

[*Capulet's orchard. Enter* Romeo *and* Juliet, *above, at the window.*]

Juliet. Wilt thou be gone? It is not yet near day.
    It was the nightingale, and not the lark,°
    That pierced the fearful hollow of thine ear.
    Nightly she sings on yond pomegranate tree.
    Believe me, love, it was the nightingale.   5

Romeo. It was the lark, the herald of the morn,
    No nightingale. Look, love, what envious streaks
    Do lace° the severing clouds in yonder east.
    Night's candles° are burnt out, and jocund day
    Stands tiptoe on the misty mountaintops.   10
    I must be gone and live, or stay and die.

Juliet. Yond light is not daylight, I know it, I.
    It is some meteor that the sun exhales,°
    To be to thee this night a torchbearer

---

24. **late:** lately, recently. 25. **held him carelessly:** did not care about him. 32. **against:** in readiness for. 34. **Afore me:** an oath meaning "before God."

  2. **nightingale . . . lark:** The nightingale sings at night; the lark sings in the early morning. 8. **lace:** stripe. 9. **Night's candles:** the stars. 13. **exhales:** gives out.

A scene from a 1936 film version of *Romeo and Juliet*.

And light thee on thy way to Mantua.   15
Therefore stay yet—thou need'st not to be gone.
Romeo. Let me be ta'en, let me be put to death,
I am content, so thou wilt have it so.
I'll say yon gray is not the morning's eye,
'Tis but the pale reflex° of Cynthia's° brow;   20
Nor that is not the lark whose notes do beat
The vaulty heaven so high above our heads.

20. **reflex:** reflection. **Cynthia's:** the moon's.

I have more care to stay than will to go.
Come, death, and welcome! Juliet wills it so.
How is 't, my soul? Let's talk. It is not day.   25
Juliet. It is, it is. Hie hence, be gone, away!
It is the lark that sings so out of tune,
Straining harsh discords and unpleasing sharps.
Some say the lark makes sweet division.°
This doth not so, for she divideth us.   30
Some say the lark and loathèd toad change eyes.°
Oh, now I would they had changed voices too!
Since arm from arm that voice doth us affray,°
Hunting thee hence with hunt's-up° to the day
Oh, now be gone, more light and light it grows.   35
Romeo. More light and light. More dark and dark our woes!

[*Enter* Nurse, *to the chamber.*]

Nurse. Madam!
Juliet. Nurse?
Nurse. Your lady mother is coming to your chamber.
The day is broke, be wary, look about.   [*Exit.*]   40
Juliet. Then, window, let day in, and let life out.
Romeo. Farewell, farewell! One kiss, and I'll descend.
[*He climbs down by the ladder of cords.*]
Juliet. Art thou gone so? Love, lord, aye, husband, friend!
I must hear from thee every day in the hour,
For in a minute there are many days.   45
Oh, by this count I shall be much in years
Ere I again behold my Romeo!
Romeo. Farewell!
I will omit no opportunity
That may convey my greetings, love, to thee.   50
Juliet. Oh, think'st thou we shall ever meet again?
Romeo. I doubt it not, and all these woes shall serve
For sweet discourses in our time to come.
Juliet. Oh God! I have an ill-divining° soul.
Methinks I see thee, now thou art below,   55
As one dead in the bottom of a tomb.
Either my eyesight fails or thou look'st pale.

---

29. **division:** melody.   31. **change eyes:** People believed that the toad and lark had once exchanged eyes. This belief would explain why larks are beautiful but have ugly eyes while toads are ugly but have beautiful eyes.   33. **affray:** frighten.   34. **hunt's-up:** hunters' morning song.   54. **ill-divining:** fearful, foreseeing evil.

Romeo. And trust me, love, in my eye so do you.
    Dry sorrow drinks° our blood. Adieu, adieu!   [*Exit.*]   60
Juliet. O Fortune, Fortune, all men call thee fickle.
    If thou art fickle, what dost thou with him
    That is renowned for faith? Be fickle, Fortune,
    For then, I hope, thou wilt not keep him long,
    But send him back.
Lady Capulet. [*Within*] Ho, daughter! Are you up?   65
Juliet. Who is 't that calls? It is my lady mother!
    Is she not down so late, or up so early?
    What unaccustomed cause procures her hither?

                [*Enter* Lady Capulet.]

Lady Capulet. Why, how now, Juliet!
Juliet.   Madam, I am not well.
Lady Capulet. Evermore weeping for your cousin's death?   70
    What, wilt thou wash him from his grave with tears?
    And if thou couldst, thou couldst not make him live,
    Therefore have done. Some grief shows much of love,
    But much of grief shows still some want of wit.
Juliet. Yet let me weep for such a feeling° loss.   75
Lady Capulet. So shall you feel the loss, but not the friend
    Which you weep for.
Juliet.   Feeling so the loss,
    I cannot choose but ever weep the friend.
Lady Capulet. Well, girl, thou weep'st not so much for his death
    As that the villain lives which slaughtered him.   80
Juliet. What villain, madam?
Lady Capulet.   That same villain, Romeo.
Juliet. (*Aside*) Villain and he be many miles asunder.
    God pardon him! I do, with all my heart,
    And yet no man like° he doth grieve my heart.
Lady Capulet. That is because the traitor murderer lives.   85
Juliet. Aye, madam, from the reach of these my hands.
    Would none but I might venge my cousin's death!
Lady Capulet. We will have vengeance for it, fear thou not.
    Then weep no more. I'll send to one in Mantua,
    Where that same banished runagate° doth live,   90
    Shall give such an unaccustomed dram°

---

59. **drinks:** drains. Sorrow was believed to drain the blood. 75. **feeling:** deeply felt. 84. **like:** as much as. 90. **runagate:** runaway. 91. **unaccustomed dram:** unexpected dose.

That he shall soon keep Tybalt company.
And then I hope thou wilt be satisfied.
Juliet. Indeed I never shall be satisfied
With Romeo till I behold him—dead—   95
Is my poor heart so for a kinsman vexed.
Madam, if you could find out but a man
To bear a poison, I would temper° it,
That Romeo should, upon receipt thereof,
Soon sleep in quiet. Oh, how my heart abhors   100
To hear him named and cannot come to him,
To wreak° the love I bore my cousin
Upon his body that hath slaughtered him!
Lady Capulet. Find thou the means, and I'll find such a man.
But now I'll tell thee joyful tidings, girl.   105
Juliet. And joy comes well in such a needy time.
What are they, I beseech your ladyship?
Lady Capulet. Well, well, thou hast a careful° father, child,
One who, to put thee from thy heaviness,
Hath sorted° out a sudden day of joy,   110
That thou expect'st not, nor I looked not for.
Juliet. Madam, in happy time,° what day is that?
Lady Capulet. Marry, my child, early next Thursday morn,
The gallant, young, and noble gentleman,
The County Paris, at Saint Peter's Church,   115
Shall happily make thee there a joyful bride.
Juliet. Now, by Saint Peter's Church, and Peter too,
He shall not make me there a joyful bride.
I wonder at this haste, that I must wed
Ere he that should be husband comes to woo.   120
I pray you tell my lord and father, madam,
I will not marry yet. And when I do, I swear
It shall be Romeo, whom you know I hate,
Rather than Paris. These are news indeed!
Lady Capulet. Here comes your father, tell him so yourself   125
And see how he will take it at your hands.

[*Enter* Capulet *and* Nurse.]

Capulet. When the sun sets, the air doth drizzle dew,
But for the sunset of my brother's son
It rains downright.

98. **temper:** mix.   102. **wreak:** revenge.   108. **careful:** considerate.   110. **sorted:** chosen.   112. **in happy time:** indeed.

How now! A conduit,° girl? What, still in tears? 130
Evermore showering? In one little body
Thou counterfeit'st° a bark,° a sea, a wind.
For still thy eyes, which I may call the sea,
Do ebb and flow with tears; the bark thy body is,
Sailing in this salt flood; the winds, thy sighs, 135
Who raging with thy tears, and they with them,
Without a sudden calm will overset
Thy tempest-tossed body. How now, wife!
Have you delivered to her our decree?

Lady Capulet. Aye, sir, but she will none, she gives you thanks. 140
I would the fool were married to her grave!

Capulet. Soft! Take me with you, take me with you,° wife.
How! Will she none? Doth she not give us thanks?
Is she not proud? Doth she not count her blest,
Unworthy as she is, that we have wrought 145
So worthy a gentleman to be her bridegroom?

Juliet. Not proud you have, but thankful that you have.
Proud can I never be of what I hate,
But thankful even for hate that is meant love.

Capulet. How, how! How, how! Chop-logic!° What is this? 150
"Proud," and "I thank you," and "I thank you not,"
And yet "not proud." Mistress minion,° you,
Thank me no thankings, nor proud me no prouds,
But fettle° your fine joints 'gainst Thursday next,
To go with Paris to Saint Peter's Church, 155
Or I will drag thee on a hurdle° thither.
Out, you green-sickness carrion!° Out, you baggage!
You tallow-face!

Lady Capulet. [*To* Capulet] Fie, fie! What, are you mad?

Juliet. Good Father, I beseech you on my knees,
Hear me with patience but to speak a word. 160

Capulet. Hang thee, young baggage! Disobedient wretch!
I tell thee what. Get thee to church o' Thursday
Or never after look me in the face.
Speak not, reply not, do not answer me.
My fingers itch. Wife, we scarce thought us blest 165
That God had lent us but this only child,
But now I see this one is one too much,

130. **conduit:** fountain. 132. **Thou counterfeit'st:** You imitate. **bark:** boat. 142. **Take me with you:** What do you mean? 150. **Chop-logic:** hair-splitting. 152. **Mistress minion:** saucy miss. 154. **fettle:** make ready. 156. **hurdle:** a frame used to carry condemned criminals to execution. 157. **green-sickness carrion:** anemic lump of flesh.

And that we have a curse in having her.
Out on her, hilding!°
Nurse: God in Heaven bless her!
You are to blame, my lord, to rate° her so.   170
Capulet. And why, my lady wisdom? Hold your tongue,
Good prudence. Smatter° with your gossips,° go.
Nurse. I speak no treason.
Capulet.   Oh, God ye godden.
Nurse. May not one speak?
Capulet.   Peace, you mumbling fool!
Utter your gravity° o'er a gossip's bowl,   175
For here we need it not.
Lady Capulet.   You are too hot.
Capulet. [*To* Juliet] God's bread!° It makes me mad.
Day, night, hour, tide, time, work, play,
Alone, in company, still° my care hath been
To have her matched. And having now provided   180
A gentleman of noble parentage,
Of fair demesnes,° youthful, and nobly trained,
Stuffed,° as they say, with honorable parts,°
Proportioned as one's thought would wish a man—
And then to have a wretched puling° fool,   185
A whining mammet,° in her fortune's tender,°
To answer "I'll not wed, I cannot love,
I am too young, I pray you, pardon me."
But an you will not wed, I'll pardon you.
Graze where you will, you shall not house with me.   190
Look to 't, think on't, I do not use to° jest.
Thursday is near. Lay hand on heart, advise.°
An you be mine, I'll give you to my friend.
An you be not, hang, beg, starve, die in the streets,
For, by my soul, I'll ne'er acknowledge thee,   195
Nor what is mine shall never do thee good—
Trust to't, bethink you, I'll not be forsworn.°   [*Exit.*]
Juliet. Is there no pity sitting in the clouds
That sees into the bottom of my grief?
O sweet my mother, cast me not away!   200
Delay this marriage for a month, a week;

---

169. **hilding:** worthless girl.   170. **rate:** scold.   172. **Smatter:** chatter.   **gossips:** cronies.   175. **gravity:** wise words.
177. **God's bread:** by the sacred host.   179. **still:** always.   182. **demesnes** (dĭ-mānz´): estates, wealth.   183. **stuffed:**
full. **parts:** qualities.   185. **puling:** whining.   186. **mammet:** doll.   **in her fortune's tender:** when good fortune is offered to her.   191. **use to:** usually.   192. **advise:** be careful.   197. **be forsworn:** break my vow.

Or, if you do not, make the bridal bed
In that dim monument where Tybalt lies.

Lady Capulet. Talk not to me, for I'll not speak a word.
Do as thou wilt, for I have done with thee.   [*Exit.*]   205

Juliet. Oh, God!—O Nurse, how shall this be prevented?
My husband is on earth, my faith in Heaven.
How shall that faith return again to earth
Unless that husband send it me from Heaven
By leaving earth? Comfort me, counsel me.   210
Alack, alack, that Heaven should practice stratagems°
Upon so soft a subject as myself!
What say'st thou? Hast thou not a word of joy?
Some comfort, Nurse.

Nurse.   Faith, here it is.
Romeo is banished, and all the world to nothing°   215
That he dares ne'er come back to challenge° you;
Or if he do, it needs must be by stealth.
Then, since the case so stands as now it doth,
I think it best you married with the County.
Oh, he's a lovely gentleman!   220
Romeo's a dishclout to him.° An eagle, madam,
Hath not so green, so quick, so fair an eye
As Paris hath. Beshrew° my very heart,
I think you are happy in this second match,
For it excels your first. Or if it did not,   225
Your first is dead, or 'twere as good he were
As living here and you no use of him.

Juliet. Speakest thou from thy heart?

Nurse. And from my soul too, else beshrew them both.

Juliet. Amen!

Nurse.   What?

Juliet.   Well, thou hast comforted me marvelous much.   230
Go in, and tell my lady I am gone,
Having displeased my father, to Laurence' cell,
To make confession and to be absolved.

Nurse: Marry, I will, and this is wisely done.   [*Exit.*]

Juliet. Ancient damnation!° Oh, most wicked fiend!   235
Is it more sin to wish me thus forsworn,°
Or to dispraise my lord with that same tongue

---

211. **stratagems:** violent deeds.   215. **all the world to nothing:** the odds are overwhelming.   216. **challenge:** claim.
221. **to him:** compared to him.   223. **Beshrew:** curse.   235. **Ancient damnation:** old devil.   236. **forsworn:** per-
jured.

Which she hath praised him with above compare
So many thousand times? Go, counselor.
Thou and my bosom° henceforth shall be twain.   240
I'll to the Friar, to know his remedy.
If all else fail, myself have power to die.   [*Exit.*]

240. **bosom:** inner thoughts.

Reading Check

1. At the opening of the act, why does Benvolio advise Mercutio to leave the streets of Verona?
2. How is Romeo punished for Tybalt's death?
3. How does Friar Laurence help Romeo?
4. What does Capulet threaten to do if Juliet refuses to marry Paris?
5. To whom does Juliet decide to go for help?

For Study and Discussion

Analyzing and Interpreting the Play

1a. How has the audience been prepared for the dueling scene at the opening of Act Three? **b.** What have you learned about Tybalt and Mercutio that makes their actions in this scene consistent with their characters?

2a. Why does Romeo refuse to accept Tybalt's challenge? **b.** How does Mercutio interpret Romeo's action? **c.** Why does he decide to fight Tybalt?

3a. How does Juliet first react when she learns that Romeo has killed Tybalt? **b.** Why does she then change her mind? **c.** What do these reactions show about her?

4. At the opening of Scene 3, Romeo is in despair. **a.** What happens to raise his spirits? **b.** Where else in the play has Romeo shown a sudden change in spirits?

5. In Act One Capulet was not eager to see Juliet married. Why has he suddenly decided to accept Paris' offer?

6a. Why are Capulet and his wife surprised by Juliet's refusal to marry? **b.** How do they react? **c.** How has Shakespeare prepared you for Capulet's reaction in earlier scenes of the play?

7a. What is the Nurse's advice to Juliet? **b.** Why do you suppose Juliet pretends to be comforted by the Nurse? **c.** What has she realized she must do?

Literary Elements

Dramatic Structure: Plot

Most plays begin with an **exposition**, an introduction to the situation and setting of the action. The first act of *Romeo and Juliet* presents the conflict between the Montagues and Capulets. Out of the enmity between these two houses will grow misfortune for all the major characters in the play. When the lovers meet at the Capulet party, the main action is set into motion.

The exposition of a play is followed by the **rising action**, a sequence of events that lead to a **turning point**, or **crisis**. During the second act, Romeo and Juliet declare their love and get married. They have not yet been struck by tragedy. There is even a possibility, nursed by Friar Laurence, that the marriage of the lovers will serve to unite the warring factions. But in Act Three, Tybalt kills Mercutio, and Romeo kills Tybalt. This is the turning point of the play; it determines how the action will come out.

Following the turning point is the **falling action**, which ends with the **resolution**, or conclusion of the play. The fortunes of the lovers steadily decline. Romeo is banished. The lovers must separate. Juliet finds herself alone, without the support of her parents or the Nurse. The action from this point on will lead directly to the final catastrophe. The **climax**, the point of greatest emotional intensity, usually comes at the end of a Shakespearean play.

Language and Vocabulary

Recognizing Classical Allusions

The heroes and gods of ancient Greek and Roman mythology, largely forgotten during Medieval times, were of great interest during the Renaissance, when Shakespeare lived. References to these ancient heroes and gods are known as **classical allusions**.

Here is a classical allusion from Act Three, Scene 2:

> Gallop apace, you fiery-footed steeds,
> Toward Phoebus' lodging.

The allusion, as the footnote tells, is to the horses of Phoebus (Apollo) the sun god, who, as the myth would have it, drove his chariot (the sun) across the sky each day. Juliet is urging the sun to hurry across the sky and set.

Using a dictionary or a book of mythology, explain the allusion in each of these quotations:

> But all so soon as the all-cheering sun
> Should be in the farthest east begin to draw
> The shady curtains from *Aurora's* bed . . .
>
> (I, 1, 120–122)
>
> She'll not be hit
> With *Cupid's* arrow.
>
> (I, 1, 194–195)
>
> Bondage is hoarse, and may not speak aloud,
> Else would I tear the cave where *Echo* lies
> And make her airy tongue more hoarse than mine
> With repetition of my Romeo's name.
>
> (II, 2, 160–163)
>
> I'll say yon gray is not the morning's eye,
> 'Tis but the pale reflex of *Cynthia's* brow . . .
>
> (III, 5, 19–20)

Focus on Persuasive Writing

Evaluating Your Reasoning

When you **evaluate** your own reasoning in a persuasive essay or speech, be on the alert for statements that look like reasons but aren't. Here are four types of errors:

1. **Circular reasoning:** merely using different words to restate your opinion, rather than giving a reason
2. **False cause and effect:** assuming that one event caused another just because the first one came before the second in time order
3. **Attacking the person:** trying to discredit your opponent(s) rather than dealing with the issue
4. **Hasty generalization:** basing a sweeping claim on a small or insufficient number of examples

Look through some magazine ads and see if you can come up with a few examples of these reasoning errors. Jot down a few notes about each example you find. Save your writing.

Act Four

Scene 1

[Friar Laurence's *cell. Enter* Friar Laurence *and* Paris.]

Friar Laurence. On Thursday, sir? The time is very short.
Paris. My father° Capulet will have it so,
    And I am nothing slow to slack his haste.°
Friar Laurence. You say you do not know the lady's mind
    Uneven is the course,° I like it not.   5
Paris. Immoderately she weeps for Tybalt's death,
    And therefore have I little talked of love,
    For Venus smiles not in a house of tears.
    Now, sir, her father counts it dangerous
    That she doth give her sorrow so much sway,   10
    And in his wisdom hastes our marriage,
    To stop the inundation° of her tears,
    Which, too much minded° by herself alone,
    May be put from her by society.°
    Now do you know the reason of this haste.   15
Friar Laurence. [*Aside*] I would I knew not why it should be slowed.
    Look, sir, here comes the lady toward my cell.

[*Enter* Juliet.]

Paris. Happily met, my lady and my wife!
Juliet. That may be, sir, when I may be a wife.
Paris. That may be must be, love, on Thursday next.   20
Juliet. What must be shall be.
Friar Laurence.   That's a certain text.
Paris. Come you to make confession to this Father?
Juliet. To answer that, I should confess to you.
Paris. Do not deny to him that you love me.
Juliet. I will confess to you that I love him.   25
Paris. So will ye, I am sure, that you love me.
Juliet. If I do so, it will be of more price
    Being spoke behind your back than to your face.
Paris. Poor soul, thy face is much abused with tears.

---

2. **father:** future father-in-law. 3. **And . . . haste:** I am as eager as he to hasten the marriage. 5. **Uneven is the course:** a rough proceeding. 12. **inundation:** flood. 13. **minded:** brooded over. 14. **society:** the company of others.

Juliet. The tears have got small victory by that, 30
   For it was bad enough before their spite.°
Paris. Thou wrong'st it more than tears with that report.
Juliet. That is no slander, sir, which is a truth,
   And what I spake, I spake it to my face.
Paris. Thy face is mine, and thou hast slandered it. 35
Juliet. It may be so, for it is not mine own.
   Are you at leisure, holy Father, now,
   Or shall I come to you at evening mass?
Friar Laurence. My leisure serves me, pensive° daughter, now.
   My lord, we must entreat the time alone. 40
Paris. God shield° I should disturb devotion!
   Juliet, on Thursday early will I rouse ye.
   Till then, adieu, and keep this holy kiss.   [*Exit.*]
Juliet. Oh, shut the door, and when thou hast done so,
   Come weep with me—past hope, past cure, past help! 45
Friar Laurence. Ah, Juliet, I already know thy grief.
   It strains me past the compass° of my wits.
   I hear thou must, and nothing may prorogue° it,
   On Thursday next be married to this County.
Juliet. Tell me not, Friar, that thou hear'st of this, 50
   Unless thou tell me how I may prevent it.
   If in thy wisdom thou canst give no help,
   Do thou but call my resolution wise, [*Draws a dagger*]
   And with this knife I'll help it presently.°
   God joined my heart and Romeo's, thou our hands, 55
   And ere this hand, by thee to Romeo's sealed,
   Shall be the label to another deed,°
   Or my true heart with treacherous revolt
   Turn to another, this shall slay them both.
   Therefore, out of thy long-experienced time, 60
   Give me some present counsel; or, behold,
   'Twixt my extremes° and me this bloody knife
   Shall play the umpire, arbitrating that
   Which the commission° of thy years and art
   Could to no issue of true honor bring. 65
   Be not so long to speak, I long to die
   If what thou speak'st speak not of remedy.
Friar Laurence. Hold, daughter. I do spy a kind of hope,
   Which craves as desperate an execution

31. **spite:** injury. 39. **pensive:** thoughtful, solemn. 41. **shield:** forbid. 47. **compass:** reach. 48. **prorogue:** postpone. 54. **presently:** immediately. 56–57. **ere . . . deed:** before my hand agrees to another contract. 62. **extremes:** misfortunes. 64. **commission:** authority.

As that is desperate which we would prevent.   70
If, rather than to marry County Paris,
Thou hast the strength of will to slay thyself,
Then is it likely thou wilt undertake
A thing like death to chide away this shame,
That copest° with death himself to 'scape from it.   75
And, if thou darest, I'll give thee remedy.

Juliet. Oh, bid me leap, rather than marry Paris,
From off the battlements of yonder tower;
Or walk in thievish ways; or bid me lurk
Where serpents are; chain me with roaring bears;   80
Or shut me nightly in a charnel house,°
O'ercover'd quite with dead men's rattling bones,
With reeky° shanks and yellow chapless° skulls;
Or bid me go into a new-made grave,
And hide me with a dead man in his shroud—   85
Things that to hear them told have made me tremble—
And I will do it without fear or doubt,
To live an unstained wife to my sweet love.

Friar Laurence. Hold, then, go home, be merry, give consent
To marry Paris. Wednesday is tomorrow.   90
Tomorrow night look that thou lie alone,
Let not thy nurse lie with thee in thy chamber.
Take thou this vial, being then in bed,
And this distillèd liquor drink thou off,
When presently through all thy veins shall run   95
A cold and drowsy humor;° for no pulse
Shall keep his native° progress, but surcease.°
No warmth, no breath, shall testify thou livest.
The roses in thy lips and cheeks shall fade
To paly ashes, thy eyes' windows fall,   100
Like death when he shuts up the day of life.
Each part, deprived of supple government,°
Shall, stiff and stark and cold, appear like death.
And in this borrowed likeness of shrunk death
Thou shalt continue two and forty hours,   105
And then awake as from a pleasant sleep.
Now, when the bridegroom in the morning comes
To rouse thee from thy bed, there art thou dead.
Then, as the manner of our country is,

---

75. **copest:** deals.   81. **charnel house:** shed for bones from old graves.   83. **reeky:** stinking.   **chapless:** without jaws.
96. **humor:** moisture, fluid.   97. **native:** natural.   **surcease:** cease.   102. **supple government:** ability to move.

A scene from a 1968 film version of *Romeo and Juliet*.

In thy best robes uncovered on the bier 110
Thou shalt be borne to that same ancient vault
Where all the kindred of the Capulets lie.
In the meantime, against° thou shalt awake,
Shall Romeo by my letters know our drift,°
And hither shall he come, and he and I 115
Will watch thy waking, and that very night
Shall Romeo bear thee hence to Mantua.
And this shall free thee from this present shame,
If no inconstant toy° nor womanish fear
Abate thy valor in the acting it. 120

Juliet. [*Taking the vial*] Give me, give me! Oh, tell not me of fear!

113. **against:** before.   114. **drift:** purpose, intention.   119. **inconstant toy:** fickle fancy, foolish whim.

Friar Laurence. Hold, get you gone, be strong and prosperous
　　In this resolve. I'll send a friar with speed
　　To Mantua, with my letters to thy lord.
Juliet. Love give me strength! And strength shall help afford.　　　　　125
　　Farewell, dear Father!　　　　　　　　　　　　　　*[Exeunt.]*

Scene 2

　　[Hall in Capulet's house. Enter Capulet, Lady Capulet, Nurse, and two Servingmen.]

Capulet. So many guests invite as here are writ.　　　*[Exit First Servant.]*
　　Sirrah, go hire me twenty cunning cooks.
Second Servant. You shall have none ill, sir, for I'll try if they can lick their fingers.
Capulet. How can'st thou try them so?
Second Servant. Marry, sir, 'tis an ill cook that cannot lick his own fingers. Therefore, he　　5
　　that cannot lick his fingers goes not with me.
Capulet. Go, be gone.　　　　　　　　　　　　　*[Exit Second Servant.]*
　　We shall be much unfurnished° for this time.
　　What, is my daughter gone to Friar Laurence?
Nurse. Aye, forsooth.　　　　　　　　　　　　　　　　　　　　　　10
Capulet. Well, he may chance to do some good on her.
　　A peevish self-willed harlotry° it is.

　　　　　　　　　　　[Enter Juliet.]

Nurse. See where she comes from shrift with merry look.
Capulet. How now, my headstrong! Where have you been gadding?
Juliet. Where I have learned me to repent the sin　　　　　　　　15
　　Of disobedient opposition
　　To you and your behests, and am enjoined
　　By holy Laurence to fall prostrate here,
　　To beg your pardon. *[Kneeling]* Pardon, I beseech you!
　　Henceforward I am ever ruled by you.　　　　　　　　　　　　20
Capulet. Send for the County, go tell him of this.
　　I'll have this knot knit up tomorrow morning.
Juliet. I met the youthful lord at Laurence' cell,
　　And gave him what becomèd° love I might,
　　Not stepping o'er the bounds of modesty.　　　　　　　　　　25
Capulet. Why, I am glad on 't, this is well. Stand up.
　　This is as' t should be. Let me see the County.

8. **unfurnished:** unprepared.　12. **harlotry:** hussy.　24. **becomèd:** suitable, proper.

Aye, marry, go. I say, and fetch him hither.
Now, afore God, this reverend holy Friar,
All our whole city is much bound° to him.   30
Juliet. Nurse, will you go with me into my closet,°
 To help me sort° such needful ornaments
 As you think fit to furnish me tomorrow?
Lady Capulet. No, not till Thursday, there is time enough.
Capulet. Go, Nurse, go with her. We'll to church tomorrow. [*Exeunt* Juliet *and* Nurse.] 35
Lady Capulet. We shall be short in our provision.
 'Tis now near night.
Capulet.   Tush, I will stir about,
 And all things shall be well, I warrant thee, wife.
 Go thou to Juliet, help to deck up her.
 I'll not to bed tonight, let me alone,   40
 I'll play the housewife for this once. What ho!°
 They are all forth. Well, I will walk myself
 To County Paris, to prepare him up
 Against tomorrow. My heart is wondrous light
 Since this same wayward girl is so reclaimed.   [*Exeunt.*] 45

Scene 3

     [Juliet'*s chamber. Enter* Juliet *and* Nurse.]

Juliet. Aye, those attires are best. But, gentle Nurse,
 I pray thee leave me to myself tonight;
 For I have need of many orisons°
 To move the Heavens to smile upon my state,°
 Which well thou know'st, is cross° and full of sin.   5

     [*Enter* Lady Capulet.]

Lady Capulet. What, are you busy, ho? Need you my help?
Juliet. No, madam, we have culled° such necessaries
 As are behooveful° for our state tomorrow.
 So please you, let me now be left alone,
 And let the nurse this night sit up with you,   10
 For I am sure you have your hands full all
 In this so sudden business.

---

30. **bound:** in debt 31. **closet:** small private room. 32. **sort:** select. 41. **What ho!:** Capulet calls for a servant.
 3. **orisons:** prayers. 4. **state:** condition. 5. **cross:** amiss. 7. **culled:** selected. 8. **behooveful:** fit.

Lady Capulet.   Goodnight.
    Get thee to bed and rest, for thou hast need.   [*Exeunt* Lady Capulet *and* Nurse.]
Juliet. Farewell! God knows when we shall meet again.
    I have a faint cold fear thrills through my veins   15
    That almost freezes up the heat of life.
    I'll call them back again to comfort me.
    Nurse!—What should she do here?
    My dismal scene I needs must act alone.
    Come, vial.   20
    What if this mixture do not work at all?
    Shall I be married then tomorrow morning?
    No, no, this shall forbid it. Lie thou there.

                      [*Laying down a dagger.*]

    What if it be a poison which the Friar
    Subtly hath ministered° to have me dead,   25
    Lest in this marriage he should be dishonored
    Because he married me before to Romeo?
    I fear it is. And yet methinks it should not,
    For he hath still been tried° a holy man.
    How if, when I am laid into the tomb,   30
    I wake before the time that Romeo
    Come to redeem me? There's a fearful point.
    Shall I not then be stifled in the vault,
    To whose foul mouth no healthsome air breathes in,
    And there die strangled ere my Romeo comes?   35
    Or if I live, is it not very like,
    The horrible conceit° of death and night,
    Together with the terror of the place,
    As in a vault, an ancient receptacle,
    Where for this many hundred years the bones   40
    Of all my buried ancestors are packed;
    Where bloody Tybalt, yet but green in earth,°
    Lies festering in his shroud; where, as they say,
    At some hours in the night spirits resort—
    Alack, alack, is it not like that I   45
    So early waking, what with loathsome smells
    And shrieks like mandrakes'° torn out of the earth,
    That living mortals hearing them run mad?
    Oh, if I wake, shall I not be distraught,

25. **ministered:** provided. 29. **tried:** found to be. 37. **conceit:** idea. 42. **green in earth:** newly buried. 47. **mandrakes:** plants with forked roots, which, according to superstition, screamed when dug up.

Environèd with all these hideous fears,   50
And madly play with my forefathers' joints,
And pluck the mangled Tybalt from his shroud,
And in this rage, with some great kinsman's bone,
As with a club, dash out my desperate brains?
Oh, look! Methinks I see my cousin's ghost   55
Seeking out Romeo, that did spit his body
Upon a rapier's point. Stay, Tybalt, stay!
Romeo, I come! This do I drink to thee.

                                [She falls upon her bed, within the curtains.]

Scene 4

        [Hall in Capulet's *house. Enter* Lady Capulet *and* Nurse.]

Lady Capulet. Hold, take these keys, and fetch more spices, Nurse.
Nurse. They call for dates and quinces in the pastry.°

                  [Enter Capulet.]

Capulet. Come, stir, stir, stir! The second cock hath crowed,
   The curfew bell hath rung, 'tis three o'clock.
   Look to the baked meats, good Angelica.   5
   Spare not for cost.
Nurse.   Go, you cotquean,° go,
   Get you to bed. Faith, you'll be sick tomorrow
   For this night's watching.
Capulet. No, not a whit. What! I have watched ere now
   All night for lesser cause, and ne'er been sick.   10
Lady Capulet. Aye, you have been a mousehunt° in your time,
   But I will watch you from such watching now.   *[Exeunt* Lady Capulet *and* Nurse.]
Capulet. A jealoushood,° a jealoushood!

     [Enter three or four Servingmen, *with spits, and logs, and baskets.]*

                      Now, fellow, what's there?
First Servingman. Things for the cook, sir, but I know not what.
Capulet. Make haste, make haste. *[Exit* First Servingman.] Sirrah, fetch drier logs.   15
   Call Peter, he will show thee where they are.

---

2. **pastry:** the room where baking was done. 6. **cotquean** (kŏt′kwēn): a man who meddles with women's affairs. 11.
mousehunt: in today's slang, "a wolf." 13. **jealoushood:** jealousy.

Second Servingman. I have a head, sir, that will find out logs
    And never trouble Peter for the matter.
Capulet. Mass,° and well said, a merry whoreson, ha!
    Thou shalt be loggerhead.° [*Exit* Second Servingman.] Good faith, 'tis day.   20
    The County will be here with music straight,
    For so he said he would. [*Music within.*] I hear him near.
    Nurse! Wife! What ho! What, Nurse, I say!

[Reenter Nurse.]

    Go waken Juliet, go and trim her up.
    I'll go and chat with Paris. Hie, make haste,   25
    Make haste. The bridegroom he is come already.
    Make haste, I say.   [*Exeunt.*]

Scene 5

[Juliet's chamber. Curtains drawn around her bed. Enter Nurse.]

Nurse. Mistress! What, mistress! Juliet! Fast,° I warrant her, she.
    Why, lamb! Why, lady! Fie, you slugabed!
    Why, love, I say! Madam! Sweetheart! Why, bride!
    What, not a word? You take your pennyworths now,
    Sleep for a week; for the next night, I warrant,   5
    The County Paris hath set up his rest
    That you shall rest but little. God forgive me,
    Marry and amen, how sound is she asleep!
    I needs must wake her. Madam, madam, madam!
    Aye, let the County take you in your bed,   10
    He'll fright you up, i'faith. Will it not be?   [*Undraws the curtains.*]
    What, dressed! And in your clothes! And down again!
    I must needs wake you. Lady, lady, lady!
    Alas, alas! Help, help! My lady's dead!
    Oh, welladay that ever I was born!   15
    Some aqua vitae, ho! My lord! My lady!

[Enter Lady Capulet.]

Lady Capulet. What noise is here?
Nurse.   Oh, lamentable day!

---

19. **Mass:** by the mass.   20. **loggerhead:** blockhead.
 1. **Fast:** fast asleep.

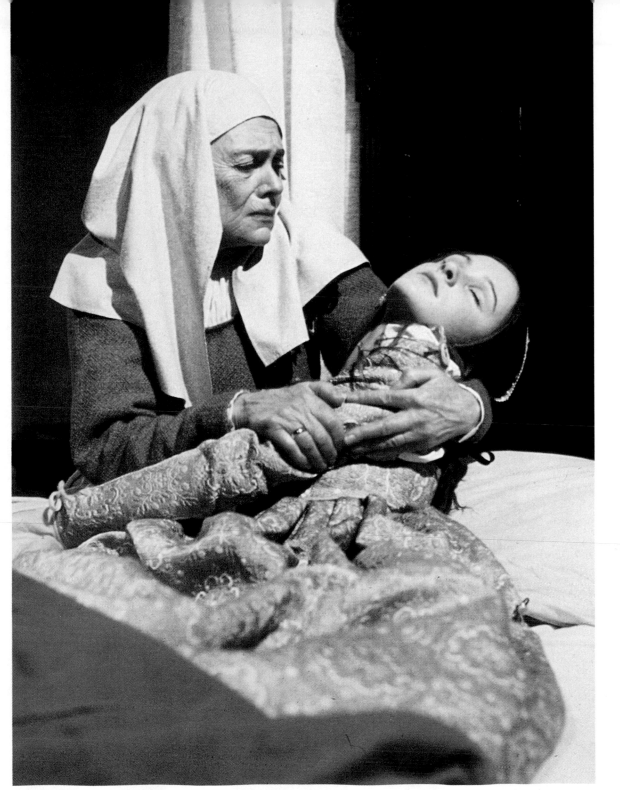

A scene from the 1985 BBC-TV production of *Romeo and Juliet*.

Lady Capulet. What is the matter?

Nurse.   Look, look! Oh, heavy day!

Lady Capulet. Oh me, oh me! My child, my only life,
    Revive, look up, or I will die with thee.   20
    Help! help! Call help.

[*Enter* Capulet.]

Capulet. For shame, bring Juliet forth, her lord is come.

Nurse. She's dead, deceased, she's dead, alack the day!

Lady Capulet. Alack the day, she's dead, she's dead, she's dead!

Capulet. Ha! Let me see her. Out, alas! She's cold.   25
    Her blood is settled and her joints are stiff.
    Life and these lips have long been separated.
    Death lies on her like an untimely frost
    Upon the sweetest flower of all the field.

Nurse. Oh, lamentable day!

Lady Capulet.   Oh, woeful time!   30

Capulet. Death, that hath ta'en her hence to make me wail,
    Ties up my tongue and will not let me speak.

[*Enter* Friar Laurence *and* Paris *with* Musicians.]

Friar Laurence. Come, is the bride ready to go to church?

Capulet. Ready to go, but never to return.
    O son, the night before thy wedding day   35
    Hath death lain with thy wife. See, there she lies,
    Flower as she was, deflowerèd by him.
    Death is my son-in-law, Death is my heir,
    My daughter he hath wedded. I will die,
    And leave him all—life, living, all is Death's.   40

Paris. Have I thought long to see this morning's face
    And doth it give me such a sight as this?

Lady Capulet. Accurst, unhappy, wretched, hateful day!
    Most miserable hour that e'er time saw
    In lasting labor of his pilgrimage!   45
    But one, poor one, one poor and loving child,
    But one thing to rejoice and solace° in,
    And cruel death hath catched it from my sight!

Nurse. Oh, woe! Oh, woeful, woeful, woeful day!
    Most lamentable day, most woeful day,   50

47. **solace:** take comfort.

That ever, ever, I did yet behold!
Oh, day, oh, day, oh, day! Oh, hateful day!
Never was seen so black a day as this.
Oh, woeful day, oh, woeful day!

Paris. Beguiled, divorced, wronged, spited, slain!   55
Most detestable death, by thee beguiled,
By cruel cruel thee quite overthrown!
Oh, love! Oh, life! Not life, but love in death!

Capulet. Despised, distressed, hated, martyred, killed!
Uncomfortable° time, why camest thou now   60
To murder, murder our solemnity?
O child! O child! My soul, and not my child!
Dead art thou! Alack, my child is dead,
And with my child my joys are burièd!

Friar Laurence. Peace ho, for shame! Confusion's cure lives not   65
In these confusions. Heaven and yourself
Had part in this fair maid, now Heaven hath all,
And all the better is it for the maid.
Your part in her you could not keep from death,
But Heaven keeps his part in eternal life.   70
The most you sought was her promotion,
For 'twas your heaven she should be advanced.
And weep ye now, seeing she is advanced
Above the clouds, as high as Heaven itself?
Oh, in this love, you love your child so ill   75
That you run mad, seeing that she is well.°
She's not well married that lives married long,
But she's best married that dies married young.
Dry up your tears, and stick your rosemary°
On this fair corse, and, as the custom is,   80
In all her best array bear her to church.
For though fond nature° bids us all lament,
Yet nature's tears are reason's merriment.°

Capulet. All things that we ordainèd° festival
Turn from their office to black funeral.   85
Our instruments to melancholy bells,
Our wedding cheer to a sad burial feast,
Our solemn hymns to sullen dirges change,
Our bridal flowers serve for a buried corse,
And all things change them to the contrary.   90

60. **Uncomfortable:** distressing. 76. **well:** that is, in heaven. 79. **rosemary:** Rosemary was used for weddings and funerals. 82. **nature:** human nature. 83. **nature's tears . . . merriment:** though natural to weep, there is also reason to rejoice (because Juliet is in heaven). 84. **ordainèd:** intended for.

Friar Laurence. Sir, go you in, and, madam, go with him.
And go, Sir Paris, everyone prepare
To follow this fair corse unto her grave.
The Heavens do lour° upon you for some ill;
Move them no more by crossing their high will.   95

[*Exeunt* Capulet, Lady Capulet, Paris, *and* Friar.]

First Musician. Faith, we may put up our pipes, and be gone.
Nurse. Honest good fellows, ah, put up, put up,
For well you know this is a pitiful case.   [*Exit.*]
Second Musician. Aye, by my troth, the case° may be amended.

[*Enter* Peter.]

Peter. Musicians, oh, musicians, "Heart's ease,° heart's ease." Oh, an you will have me live,   100
play "Heart's ease."
First Musician. Why "Heart's ease"?
Peter. Oh, musicians, because my heart itself plays "My heart is full of woe." Oh, play me
some merry dump,° to comfort me.
First Musician. Not a dump we, 'tis no time to play now.   105
Peter. You will not, then?
First Musician. No.
Peter. I will then give it you soundly.
First Musician. What will you give us?
Peter. No money, on my faith, but the gleek.° I will give you the minstrel.°   110
First Musician. Then will I give you the serving creature.
Peter. Then will I lay the serving creature's dagger on your pate. I will carry no crotchets.°
I'll re you, I'll fa you, do you note me?
First Musician. An you re us and fa us, you note us.
Second Musician. Pray you put up your dagger and put out your wit.   115
Peter. Then have at you with my wit! I will dry-beat you with an iron wit, and put up my
iron dagger. Answer me like men:
       "When griping grief the heart doth wound
          And doleful dumps the mind oppress,
          Then music with her silver sound——"   120
Why "silver sound"? Why "music with her silver sound"?—What say you, Simon
Catling?°
First Musician. Marry, sir, because silver hath a sweet sound.
Peter. Pretty! What say you, Hugh Rebeck?°

---

94. **lour:** frown, scowl.   99. **case:** Two meanings are intended: **case** meaning "instrument box" and **case** meaning "affair."
100. **"Heart's ease":** a song.   104. **dump:** sad little song.   110. **gleek:** mock.   **give you the minstrel:** beat you.   113.
carry no crotchets: not put up with your whims.   122. **Catling:** catgut string.   124. **Rebeck:** a type of fiddle.

Second Musician. I say "silver sound" because musicians sound for silver. 125
Peter. Pretty too! What say you, James Soundpost?°
Third Musician. Faith, I know not what to say.
Peter. Oh, I cry you mercy, you are the singer. I will say for you. It is "music with her silver sound" because musicians have no gold for sounding.

"Then music with her silver sound 130
With speedy help doth lend redress."   [*Exit.*]

First Musician. What a pestilent knave is this same!
Second Musician. Hang him, Jack! Come, we'll in here. Tarry for the mourners, and stay° dinner.   [*Exeunt.*]

126. **Soundpost:** part of a violin.   134. **stay:** wait for.

Reading Check

1. What pretext does Juliet use in order to see Friar Laurence?
2. According to Paris, why has Capulet moved up the date for the wedding?
3. How is Juliet reconciled with her father?
4. What does Juliet plan to do if the potion does not work?
5. Where is Juliet to be buried?

For Study and Discussion

Analyzing and Interpreting the Play

1. Why do you think the Friar doesn't tell Paris or the Capulets that Juliet is already married to Romeo?

2a. How does Juliet respond to Paris' gallantries when she meets him at Friar Laurence's cell?   **b.** Is Paris aware of her true feelings for him?   **c.** How do you know?

3a. What is the Friar's scheme for reuniting Romeo and Juliet?   **b.** How is Romeo to be told of this plan?

4a. How and why does Capulet's mood change during Scene 2?   **b.** What important change does he make in the wedding plans?   **c.** How will this change affect the timing of the Friar's plan?

5a. What doubts does Juliet have before drinking the Friar's potion?   **b.** What are her fears?   **c.** What finally causes her to drink the potion?

6. How does the mood of Scene 4 differ from that of Scenes 3 and 5?

7a. What argument does the Friar use to comfort Paris, Juliet's parents, and the Nurse?   **b.** What "ill" is he probably referring to in line 94 in Scene 5?

8. From the point of view of her parents, the Nurse, and Paris, what must have been the cause of Juliet's death?

9. In Shakespeare's tragedies there are frequently scenes of comic relief provided by clowns or servants like Peter. The foolery at the end of Act Four depends largely on wordplay. What are the two meanings intended for the word **note** in line 113?

Literary Elements

Dramatic Structure: Dramatic Irony

In Scene 4 we watch Capulet happily making preparations for Juliet's wedding. We know that at any moment he will discover that Juliet is dead. We know something that he does not.

This is an example of **dramatic irony.** We are outside the play, yet we possess special knowledge that would affect the characters if they were aware of it. But, of course there is no way we can affect the action on stage.

Dramatic irony is one of the most powerful tools playwrights have at their disposal. Dramatic irony heightens suspense. It involves us in the action and increases our sympathy for the characters.

Look back through the first four acts of the play and locate some moments of dramatic irony. Jot down what piece of information you had that the characters lacked.

Language and Vocabulary

Noting Obsolete and Archaic Meanings

Look at the word *and* in this quotation:

> Nay, and there were two such, we should have none shortly, for one would kill the other.

Nowadays we would say *if* rather than *and*. But in Shakespeare's time, *if* was one of the meanings of *and*. The dictionary tells us that *if* is an **obsolete** meaning of *and*. Obsolete means "out of date, no longer used." The word **archaic** also means "out of date." However, there is this difference: an archaic meaning might still be used, but rarely, and only for special purposes.

Try to define the italicized words in the following passages without looking back at the footnotes. Then consult the notes to check your answers.

And then my husband—God be with his soul!
'A was a merry man—took up the child.

(I, 3, 40–41)

Therefore pardon me,
And not impute this yielding to light love,
Which the dark night hath so *discovered*.

(II, 2, 104–106)

Tybalt would kill thee,
But thou slew'st Tybalt. There art thou *happy* too.

(III, 3, 137–138)

Take thou this vial, being then in bed,
And this distillèd liquor drink thou off,
When presently through all thy veins shall run
A cold and drowsy *humor* . . .

(IV, 1, 93–96)

What if it be a poison which the Friar
Subtly hath ministered to have me dead . . .
I fear it is; and yet methinks it should not,
For he hath *still* been tried a holy man.

(IV, 3, 24–25, 28–29)

Focus on Persuasive Writing

Organizing a Persuasive Essay

Use the sample **outline** below to organize a persuasive essay on a topic of your choice. When you have finished, ask a peer reader to review your outline and offer comments. Save your writing.

I. Introduction
   A. Attention grabber
   B. Statement of opinion on issue
II. Body
   A. Most important reason + emotional appeal
   B. Second reason + emotional appeal
   C. Additional reasons (if needed)
III. Conclusion
   A. Restatement of opinion
   B. Call to action (if needed)

Act Five

Scene 1

[*Mantua. A street. Enter* Romeo.]

Romeo. If I may trust the flattering truth of sleep,°
My dreams presage° some joyful news at hand.
My bosom's lord° sits lightly in his throne,
And all this day an unaccustomed spirit
Lifts me above the ground with cheerful thoughts.   5
I dreamed my lady came and found me dead—
Strange dream, that gives a dead man leave to think!—
And breathed such life with kisses in my lips
That I revived and was an emperor.
Ah me, how sweet is love itself possessed   10
When but love's shadows are so rich in joy!

[*Enter Balthasar, Romeo's servant, booted.*°]

News from Verona! How now, Balthasar!
Dost thou not bring me letters from the Friar?
How doth my lady? Is my father well?
How fares my Juliet? That I ask again;   15
For nothing can be ill if she be well.
Balthasar. Then she is well, and nothing can be ill.
Her body sleeps in Capels' monument,°
And her immortal part with angels lives.
I saw her laid low in her kindred's vault,   20
And presently took post° to tell it you.
Oh, pardon me for bringing these ill news,
Since you did leave it for my office,° sir.
Romeo. Is it e'en so? Then I defy you, stars!
Thou know'st my lodging. Get me ink and paper,   25
And hire post horses. I will hence tonight.
Balthasar. I do beseech you, sir, have patience.
Your looks are pale and wild, and do import°
Some misadventure.°
Romeo.   Tush, thou art deceived.

---

1. **flattering truth of sleep:** happy dreams that seemed true.   2. **presage** (prĭ-sāj′): foretell.   3. **bosom's lord:** heart.
S.D. **booted:** in riding boots.   18. **monument:** tomb.   21. **took post:** rode fast.   23. **office:** duty.   28. **import:** suggest,
imply.   29. **misadventure:** misfortune.

Leave me, and do the thing I bid thee do.   30
Hast thou no letters to me from the Friar?
Balthasar. No, my good lord.
Romeo.   No matter. Get thee gone,
    And hire those horses. I'll be with thee straight.   [*Exit* Balthasar.]
    Well, Juliet, I will lie with thee tonight.
    Let's see for means—O mischief, thou art swift   35
    To enter in the thoughts of desperate men!
    I do remember an apothecary,
    And hereabouts he dwells, which late I noted
    In tattered weeds,° with overwhelming° brows,
    Culling of simples.° Meager were his looks,   40
    Sharp misery had worn him to the bones.
    And in his needy shop a tortoise hung,
    An alligator stuffed and other skins
    Of ill-shaped fishes; and about his shelves
    A beggarly account° of empty boxes,   45
    Green earthen pots, bladders, and musty seeds,
    Remnants of packthread and old cakes of roses,°
    Were thinly scattered, to make up a show.
    Noting this penury, to myself I said,
    "An if a man did need a poison now,   50
    Whose sale is present death in Mantua,
    Here lives a caitiff° wretch would sell it him."
    Oh, this same thought did but forerun my need,
    And this same needy man must sell it me.
    As I remember, this should be the house.   55
    Being holiday, the beggar's shop is shut.
    What ho! Apothecary!

[*Enter* Apothecary.]

Apothecary.   Who calls so loud?
Romeo. Come hither, man. I see that thou art poor.
    Hold, there is forty ducats. Let me have
    A dram of poison, such soon-speeding gear°   60
    As will disperse itself through all the veins,
    That the life-weary taker may fall dead,
    And that the trunk° may be discharged of breath

---

39. **weeds:** clothes. **overwhelming:** overhanging. 40. **simples:** herbs. 45. **account:** number. 47. **cakes of roses:** dried rose leaves compressed into cakes, used for perfume. 52. **caitiff** (kā′tĭf): miserable. 60. **gear:** stuff. 63. **trunk:** body.

As violently as hasty powder fired
Doth hurry from the fatal cannon's womb.   65
Apothecary. Such mortal drugs I have, but Mantua's law
Is death to any he that utters° them.
Romeo. Art thou so bare and full of wretchedness,
And fear'st to die? Famine is in thy cheeks,
Need and oppression starveth in thy eyes,   70
Contempt and beggary hangs upon thy back,
The world is not thy friend, nor the world's law.
The world affords no law to make thee rich,
Then be not poor, but break it, and take this.
Apothecary. My poverty, but not my will, consents.   75
Romeo. I pay thy poverty and not thy will.
Apothecary. Put this in any liquid thing you will,
And drink it off, and if you had the strength
Of twenty men, it would dispatch you straight.
Romeo. There is thy gold, worse poison to men's souls,   80
Doing more murder in this loathsome world
Than these poor compounds that thou mayst not sell.
I sell thee poison, thou hast sold me none.
Farewell. Buy food, and get thyself in flesh.
Come, cordial° and not poison, go with me   85
To Juliet's grave, for there must I use thee.   [*Exeunt.*]

Scene 2

[Friar Laurence's *cell. Enter* Friar John.]

Friar John. Holy Franciscan friar! Brother, ho!

[*Enter* Friar Laurence.]

Friar Laurence. This same should be the voice of Friar John.
Welcome from Mantua. What says Romeo?
Or if his mind be writ, give me his letter.
Friar John. Going to find a barefoot brother out,   5
One of our order, to associate° me
Here in this city visiting the sick,
And finding him, the searchers° of the town,
Suspecting that we both were in a house

67. **utters:** sells.   85. **cordial:** restorative medicine.
  6. **associate:** accompany.   8. **searchers:** health officers.

Where the infectious pestilence° did reign, 10
Sealed up the doors and would not let us forth,
So that my speed to Mantua there was stayed.
Friar Laurence. Who bare my letter, then, to Romeo?
Friar John. I could not send it—here it is again—
Nor get a messenger to bring it thee, 15
So fearful were they of infection.
Friar Laurence. Unhappy fortune! By my brotherhood,
The letter was not nice,° but full of charge°
Of dear import,° and the neglecting it
May do much danger. Friar John, go hence. 20
Get me an iron crow° and bring it straight
Unto my cell.
Friar John. Brother, I'll go and bring it thee. [*Exit.*]
Friar Laurence. Now must I to the monument alone.
Within this three hours will fair Juliet wake. 25
She will beshrew° me much that Romeo
Hath had no notice of these accidents.
But I will write again to Mantua,
And keep her at my cell till Romeo come.
Poor living corse, closed in a dead man's tomb! [*Exit.*] 30

Scene 3

[*A churchyard; in it a monument belonging to the* Capulets. *Enter* Paris *and his* Page, *bearing flowers and a torch.*]

Paris. Give me thy torch, boy. Hence, and stand aloof.
Yet put it out, for I would not be seen.
Under yond yew trees lay thee all along,°
Holding thine ear close to the hollow ground.
So shall no foot upon the churchyard tread, 5
Being loose, unfirm, with digging up of graves,
But thou shalt hear it. Whistle then to me,
As signal that thou hear'st something approach.
Give me those flowers. Do as I bid thee, go.
Page. [*Aside*] I am almost afraid to stand alone 10
Here in the churchyard, yet I will adventure. [*Retires.*]

10. **pestilence:** plague. When a case of plague was discovered, all persons in the house were locked in to prevent the disease from spreading. 18. **nice:** trivial. **full of charge:** weighty, important. 19. **dear import:** great importance. 21. **crow:** crowbar. 26. **beshrew:** blame.
3. **all along:** at full length.

Paris. Sweet flower, with flowers thy bridal bed I strew—
    Oh, woe! Thy canopy is dust and stones—
  Which with sweet water nightly I will dew,
    Or, wanting that, with tears distilled by moans.   15
  The obsequies° that I for thee will keep
  Nightly shall be to strew thy grave and weep.

[The Page whistles.]

  The boy gives warning something doth approach.
  What cursèd foot wanders this way tonight,
  To cross° my obsequies and true love's rite?   20
  What, with a torch! Muffle° me, night, awhile.   [Retires.]

[Enter Romeo and Balthasar, with a torch, mattock,° etc.]

Romeo. Give me that mattock and the wrenching iron.
  Hold, take this letter. Early in the morning
  See thou deliver it to my lord and father.
  Give me the light. Upon thy life, I charge thee,   25
  Whate'er thou hear'st or seest, stand all aloof,
  And do not interrupt me in my course.
  Why I descend into this bed of death
  Is partly to behold my lady's face,
  But chiefly to take thence from her dead finger   30
  A precious ring, a ring that I must use
  In dear employment.° Therefore hence, be gone.
  But if thou, jealous,° dost return to pry
  In what I farther shall intend to do,
  By Heaven, I will tear thee joint by joint   35
  And strew this hungry churchyard with thy limbs.
  The time and my intents are savage-wild,
  More fierce and more inexorable far
  Than empty° tigers or the roaring sea.
Balthasar. I will be gone, sir, and not trouble you.   40
Romeo. So shalt thou show me friendship. Take thou that. [Giving money]
  Live, and be prosperous, and farewell, good fellow.
Balthasar. [Aside] For all this same, I'll hide me hereabout.
  His looks I fear, and his intents I doubt.°   [Retires.]
Romeo. Thou detestable maw,° thou womb of death,   45
  Gorged with the dearest morsel of the earth,

---

16. **obsequies** (ob′sə-kwēz): funeral rites.   20. **cross:** thwart, interrupt.   21. **Muffle:** hide.   S.D. **mattock:** a tool like a pick, with a broad end.   32. **in dear employment:** for an important purpose.   33. **jealous:** curious.   39. **empty:** hungry.   44. **doubt:** suspect.   45. **maw:** stomach.

Thus, I enforce thy rotten jaws to open,
And in despite° I'll cram thee with more food.

[*Opens the tomb.*]

Paris. This is that banished haughty Montague
That murdered my love's cousin, with which grief   50
It is supposèd the fair creature died,
And here is come to do some villainous shame
To the dead bodies. I will apprehend° him.

[*Comes forward.*]

Stop thy unhallowed toil, vile Montague!
Can vengeance be pursued further than death?   55
Condemnèd villain, I do apprehend thee.
Obey, and go with me, for thou must die.
Romeo. I must indeed, and therefore came I hither.
Good gentle youth, tempt not a desperate man.
Fly hence and leave me. Think upon these gone,   60
Let them affright thee. I beseech thee, youth,
Put not another sin upon my head,
By urging me to fury. Oh, be gone!
By Heaven, I love thee better than myself,
But I come hither armed against myself.   65
Stay not, be gone. Live, and hereafter say
A madman's mercy bid thee run away.
Paris. I do defy thy conjurations°
And apprehend thee for a felon here.
Romeo. Wilt thou provoke me? Then have at thee, boy!   70
Page. Oh, Lord, they fight! I will go call the watch.   [*Exit.*]
Paris. Oh, I am slain! [*Falls.*] If thou be merciful,
Open the tomb, lay me with Juliet.   [*Dies.*]
Romeo. In faith, I will. Let me peruse this face.
Mercutio's kinsman, noble County Paris!   75
What said my man, when my betossèd° soul
Did not attend° him as we rode? I think
He told me Paris should have married Juliet.
Said he not so? Or did I dream it so?
Or am I mad, hearing him talk of Juliet,   80
To think it was so? Oh, give me thy hand,

---

48. **despite:** scorn, defiance. 53. **apprehend:** arrest. 68. **conjurations:** spells. 76. **betossèd:** upset. 77. **attend:** listen to.

One writ with me in sour misfortune's book!
I'll bury thee in a triumphant grave—
A grave? Oh, no, a lantern,° slaughtered youth;
For here lies Juliet, and her beauty makes   85
This vault a feasting presence° full of light.
Death, lie thou there, by a dead man interred.

[*Laying* Paris *in the monument.*]

How oft when men are at the point of death
Have they been merry! Which their keepers call
A lightning° before death. Oh, how may I   90
Call this a lightning? [*Sees* Juliet.] O my love! My wife!
Death, that hath sucked the honey of thy breath,
Hath had no power yet upon thy beauty.
Thou art not conquered; beauty's ensign° yet
Is crimson in thy lips and in thy cheeks,   95
And death's pale flag is not advancèd there.
Tybalt, liest thou there in thy bloody sheet?
Oh, what more favor can I do to thee
Than with that hand that cut thy youth in twain
To sunder° his that was thine enemy?   100
Forgive me, Cousin! Ah, dear Juliet,
Why art thou yet so fair? Shall I believe
That unsubstantial death is amorous,
And that the lean abhorrèd monster keeps
Thee here in the dark to be his paramour?   105
For fear of that, I still will stay with thee,
And never from this palace of dim night
Depart again. Here, here will I remain
With worms that are thy chambermaids. Oh, here
Will I set up my everlasting rest,   110
And shake the yoke of inauspicious° stars
From this world-wearied flesh. Eyes, look your last!
Arms, take your last embrace! And lips, O you
The doors of breath, seal with a righteous kiss
A dateless° bargain to engrossing° death!   115
Come, bitter conduct,° come unsavory guide!
Thou desperate pilot,° now at once run on
The dashing rocks thy seasick weary bark.°

---

84. **lantern:** dome with windows that gives additional light to a hall. 86. **a feasting presence:** a hall lit brightly for a feast.
90. **lightning:** brightening. 94. **ensign:** flag. 100. **sunder:** cut off. 111. **inauspicious:** unlucky. 115. **dateless:**
unending. **engrossing:** self-encompassing. 116. **conduct:** guide. 117. **desperate pilot:** Romeo. 118. **bark:** ship.

Here's to my love! [*Drinks the poison.*] O true apothecary!
Thy drugs are quick. Thus with a kiss I die.   [*Dies.*]   120

[*Enter, at the other end of the churchyard,* Friar Laurence, *with a lantern, crowbar, and spade.*]

Friar Laurence. Saint Francis be my speed!° How oft tonight
    Have my old feet stumbled° at graves! Who's there?
Balthasar. Here's one a friend, and one that knows you well.
Friar Laurence. Bliss be upon you! Tell me, good my friend.
    What torch is yond that vainly lends his light   125
    To grubs and eyeless skulls? As I discern,
    It burneth in the Capels' monument.
Balthasar. It doth so, holy sir, and there's my master,
    One that you love.
Friar Laurence.   Who is it?
Balthasar.   Romeo.
Friar Laurence. How long hath he been there?
Balthasar.   Full half an hour.   130
Friar Laurence. Go with me to the vault.
Balthasar.   I dare not, sir.
    My master knows not but I am gone hence,
    And fearfully did menace me with death
    If I did stay to look on his intents.
Friar Laurence. Stay, then, I'll go alone. Fear comes upon me—   135
    Oh, much I fear some ill unlucky thing.
Balthasar. As I did sleep under this yew tree here,
    I dreamed my master and another fought,
    And that my master slew him.
Friar Laurence.   Romeo! [*Advances.*]
    Alack, alack, what blood is this which stains   140
    The stony entrance of this sepulcher?
    What mean these masterless and gory swords
    To lie discolored by this place of peace?
    [*Enters the tomb.*] Romeo! Oh, pale! Who else? What, Paris too?
    And steeped in blood? Ah, what an unkind hour   145
    Is guilty of this lamentable chance!
    The lady stirs.

[Juliet *wakes.*]

Juliet. O comfortable° Friar! Where is my lord?

121. **speed:** help.   122. **stumbled:** Stumbling was considered an evil omen.   148. **comfortable:** comforting.

I do remember well where I should be,
And there I am. Where is my Romeo? 150

[*Noise within.*]

Friar Laurence. I hear some noise. Lady, come from that nest
Of death, contagion, and unnatural sleep.
A greater power than we can contradict
Hath thwarted our intents. Come, come away.
Thy husband in thy bosom there lies dead, 155
And Paris too. Come, I'll dispose of thee
Among a sisterhood of holy nuns.
Stay not to question, for the watch is coming.
Come, go, good Juliet, I dare no longer stay.
Juliet. Go, get thee hence, for I will not away. [*Exit Friar Laurence.*] 160
What's here? A cup, closed in my true love's hand?
Poison, I see, hath been his timeless° end.
O churl! Drunk all, and left no friendly drop
To help me after? I will kiss thy lips—
Haply° some poison yet doth hang on them 165
To make me die with a restorative. [*Kisses him.*]
Thy lips are warm.
First Watchman. [*Within*] Lead, boy. Which way?
Juliet. Yea, noise? Then I'll be brief. O happy dagger!

[*Snatching* Romeo's *dagger.*]

This is thy sheath. [*Stabs herself.*] There rust, and let me die. 170

[*Falls on* Romeo's *body, and dies.*]

[*Enter* Watch, *with the* Page *of* Paris.]

Page. This is the place—there, where the torch doth burn.
First Watchman. The ground is bloody. Search about the churchyard.
Go, some of you, whoe'er you find attach.°
Pitiful sight! Here lies the County slain,
And Juliet bleeding, warm, and newly dead. 175
Who here hath lain this two days burièd.
Go tell the Prince. Run to the Capulets,
Raise up the Montagues. Some others search.
We see the ground whereon these woes do lie,

162. **timeless:** untimely. 165. **Haply:** perhaps. 173. **attach:** arrest.

But the true ground of all these piteous woes   180
We cannot without circumstance° descry.°

[Reenter some of the Watch, with Balthasar.]

Second Watchman. Here's Romeo's man. We found him in the churchyard.
First Watchman. Hold him in safety till the Prince come hither.

[Reenter Friar Laurence, and another Watchman.]

Third Watchman. Here is a friar that trembles, sighs, and weeps.
  We took this mattock and this spade from him   185
  As he was coming from this churchyard's side.
First Watchman. A great suspicion. Stay the friar too.

[Enter the Prince and Attendants.]

Prince. What misadventure is so early up
  That calls our person from our morning rest?

[Enter Capulet, Lady Capulet, and others.]

Capulet. What should it be that they so shriek abroad?   190
Lady Capulet. The people in the street cry Romeo,
  Some Juliet, and some Paris, and all run
  With open outcry toward our monument.
Prince. What fear is this which startles in our ears?
First Watchman. Sovereign, here lies the County Paris slain,   195
  And Romeo dead, and Juliet, dead before,
  Warm and new-killed.
Prince. Search, seek, and know how this foul murder comes.
First Watchman. Here is a friar, and slaughtered Romeo's man,
  With instruments upon them fit to open   200
  These dead men's tombs.
Capulet. Oh, heavens! O wife, look how our daughter bleeds!
  This dagger hath mista'en, for, lo, his house°
  Is empty on the back of Montague,
  And it missheathèd in my daughter's bosom!   205
Lady Capulet. Oh me! This sight of death is as a bell°
  That warns my old age to a sepulcher.

---

181. **circumstance:** knowledge of the facts. **descry:** understand. 203. **house:** here, sheath. 206. **bell:** Church bells tolled for the dead.

Prince. Come, Montague, for thou art early up,
    To see thy son and heir more early down.
Montague. Alas, my liege, my wife is dead tonight,   210
    Grief of my son's exile hath stopped her breath.
    What further woe conspires against mine age?
Prince. Look, and thou shalt see.
Montague. O thou untaught! What manners is in this,
    To press before thy father to a grave?   215
Prince. Seal up the mouth of outrage° for a while
    Till we can clear these ambiguities
    And know their spring,° their head, their true descent.
    And then will I be general of your woes,
    And lead you even to death. Meantime forbear,   220
    And let mischance be slave to patience.
    Bring forth the parties of suspicion.°
Friar Laurence. I am the greatest, able to do least,
    Yet most suspected, as the time and place
    Doth make against me, of this direful murder.   225
    And here I stand, both to impeach° and purge°
    Myself condemnèd and myself excused.
Prince. Then say at once what thou dost know in this.
Friar Laurence. I will be brief, for my short date of breath°
    Is not so long as is a tedious tale.   230
    Romeo, there dead, was husband to that Juliet,
    And she, there dead, that Romeo's faithful wife.
    I married them, and their stol'n marriage day
    Was Tybalt's doomsday, whose untimely death
    Banished the new-made bridegroom from this city,   235
    For whom, and not for Tybalt, Juliet pined.
    You, to remove that siege of grief from her,
    Betrothed and would have married her perforce
    To County Paris. Then comes she to me,
    And with wild looks bid me devise some mean   240
    To rid her from this second marriage,
    Or in my cell there would she kill herself.
    Then gave I her, so tutored by my art,
    A sleeping potion, which so took effect
    As I intended, for it wrought on her   245

---

216. **mouth of outrage:** the tomb where violent deeds were done. At this point the curtains at the back of the stage would be closed to hide the bodies. 218. **spring:** source. 222. **parties of suspicion:** suspected persons. 226. **impeach:** accuse. **purge:** clear (of guilt). 229. **my short date of breath:** the little life left me.

The form of death. Meantime I writ to Romeo
That he should hither come as this° dire night,
To help to take her from her borrowed° grave,
Being the time the potion's force should cease.
But he which bore my letter, Friar John,   250
Was stayed by accident, and yesternight
Returned my letter back. Then all alone
At the prefixèd hour of her waking
Came I to take her from her kindred's vault,
Meaning to keep her closely° at my cell   255
Till I conveniently could send to Romeo.
But when I came, some minute ere the time
Of her awaking, here untimely lay
The noble Paris and true Romeo dead.
She wakes, and I entreated her come forth,   260
And bear this work of Heaven with patience.
But then a noise did scare me from the tomb,
And she too desperate would not go with me,
But, as it seems, did violence on herself.
All this I know, and to the marriage   265
Her nurse is privy.° And if aught in this
Miscarried by my fault, let my old life
Be sacrificed some hour before his time
Unto the rigor of severest law.
Prince. We still° have known thee for a holy man.   270
   Where's Romeo's man? What can he say in this?
Balthasar. I brought my master news of Juliet's death,
   And then in post he came from Mantua
   To this same place, to this same monument.
   This letter he early bid me give his father,   275
   And threatened me with death, going in the vault,
   If I departed not and left him there.
Prince. Give me the letter, I will look on it.
   Where is the County's page, that raised the watch?
   Sirrah, what made° your master in this place?   280
Page. He came with flowers to strew his lady's grave,
   And bid me stand aloof, and so I did.
   Anon comes one with light to ope the tomb,
   And by and by my master drew on him,
   And then I ran away to call the watch.   285
Prince. This letter doth make good the Friar's words,

247. **as this:** this same. 248. **borrowed:** temporary. 255. **closely:** secretly. 266. **is privy:** shares the secret. 270. **still:** always. 280. **made:** did.

A scene from a 1968 film version of *Romeo and Juliet*.

Their course of love, the tidings of her death.
And here he writes that he did buy a poison
Of a poor 'pothecary, and therewithal
Came to this vault to die and lie with Juliet. 290
Where be these enemies? Capulet! Montague!
See what a scourge° is laid upon your hate
That Heaven finds means to kill your joys with love!
And I, for winking° at your discords too,
Have lost a brace° of kinsmen. All are punished. 295
Capulet. O Brother Montague, give me thy hand.
This is my daughter's jointure,° for no more
Can I demand.
Montague.   But I can give thee more.
For I will raise her statue in pure gold,
That whiles Verona by that name is known 300
There shall no figure at such rate° be set
As that of true and faithful Juliet.
Capulet. As rich shall Romeo's by his lady's lie,
Poor sacrifices of our enmity!
Prince. A glooming° peace this morning with it brings, 305
The sun for sorrow will not show his head.
Go hence, to have more talk of these sad things.
Some shall be pardoned and some punishèd.
For never was a story of more woe
Than this of Juliet and her Romeo.   [*Exeunt.*] 310

---

292. **scourge:** punishment.   294. **winking:** shutting my eyes.   295. **brace:** pair.   297. **jointure:** wedding gift.   301.
rate: value.   305. **glooming:** cloudy, overcast.

Reading Check

1. Who brings Romeo the news of Juliet's death?
2. Why does Romeo have to bribe the Apothecary?
3. What messenger fails to deliver Friar Laurence's letter to Romeo?
4. What reason does Romeo give Balthasar for entering the Capulets' tomb?
5. What does Romeo ask Balthasar to deliver to his father?
6. When Paris sees Romeo in the tomb, what does he assume?
7. Whose forgiveness does Romeo ask before he kills himself?
8. What suspects do the watchmen bring before Prince Escalus?
9. Which of the Prince's kinsmen have died?
10. How does Montague plan to honor Juliet?

For Study and Discussion

Analyzing and interpreting the Play

1. When Romeo says "I defy you, stars!" he challenges fate to do its worst. How is his reaction at this point similar to some of his reactions earlier in the play?

2a. Why does Romeo think he will be able to convince the Apothecary to break the law of Mantua? **b.** What substances does Romeo consider to be more harmful than poison and why?

3. What circumstances kept Friar John from delivering the letter to Romeo?

4a. Why does Paris come to Juliet's tomb? **b.** What effect does Paris' last request have on Romeo?

5. Why does the Friar run away?

6a. How are Juliet's last actions in the play typical of her? **b.** Where else has she acted with such decisiveness?

7a. What does the Prince mean when he says "all are punished"? **b.** What does he see as his own mistake?

8. What good has come from the deaths of Romeo and Juliet?

Language and Vocabulary

Understanding Puns

A **pun** is a play on words. Shakespeare was fond of puns and his plays are full of them, even in serious moments.

Sometimes a pun plays on different meanings of a single word. When Mercutio refers to himself as a "grave man," he puns on two meanings of *grave*: "serious" and "ready for the grave." Sometimes a pun plays on different words that sound alike but that have different meanings. *Romeo and Juliet* begins with a triple pun on *collier* (coal vendor), which sounds like *choler* (anger) and *collar* (hangman's noose).

Identify the puns in the following quotations and state what different meanings are intended for each one.

Give me a torch. I am not for this ambling.
Being but heavy, I will bear the light.

(I, 4, 11–12)

Not I, believe me. You have dancing shoes
With nimble soles. I have a soul of lead
So stakes me to the ground I cannot move.

(I, 4, 14–16)

. . . What, dost thou make us minstrels? An thou make minstrels of us, look to hear nothing but discords.

(III, 1, 35–36)

We see the ground whereon these woes do lie,
But the true ground of all these piteous woes
We cannot without circumstance descry.

(V, 3, 179–181)

Writing About Literature

Noting Shakespeare's Use of Irony

Irony contrasts what is real and what appears to be real. In dramatic irony, the contrast depends upon the difference between what a character believes and what the audience knows to be true. Find instances of irony in the final act of *Romeo and Juliet*. How do the ironic events affect the outcome of the play?

For Further Discussion

1. From 1660 to 1845, *Romeo and Juliet* was most often performed with an altered ending in which the young lovers did not die, but lived happily ever after. **a.** Would you have preferred the play to end happily? **b.** How does a happy ending alter the meaning of the play?

2a. Is Romeo's love for Rosaline different from his love for Juliet? **b.** Does Romeo's character change during the play? Cite specific evidence to defend your answer.

3. Does Juliet develop a will of her own during the play, or does she merely shift her obedience from her parents to Romeo? Support your answer with quotations.

4. As the play is presented, do you think that Romeo and Juliet are responsible for what happens, or are they just the playthings of fate?

5. At the end of the play, Prince Escalus announces that "all are punished." **a.** Does everyone deserve to be punished? **b.** Does anyone get off too easily? Discuss.

Literature and the Arts

Shakespeare and the Modern Musical

The story of Romeo and Juliet existed even before Shakespeare wrote his play in the sixteenth century, but without Shakespeare's powerful drama and glorious language, it is not likely that so many composers, playwrights, and artists would continue to find dramatic potential in this love story. *Romeo and Juliet* has inspired operas, movies, ballets, paintings, and orchestral scores. The musical drama *West Side Story*, a contemporary version of the story set in New York City, is perhaps the most famous adaptation of the story in our own day.

Making Connections: Activities

Locate a copy of *West Side Story* at your local video store or film library and organize a screening with some other students. After watching the film, compare the characters with those in Shakespeare's play. What elements of the sixteenth-century play were successfully adapted to a twentieth-century urban setting? Were any important elements missing? Write a review and circulate it among members of the class.

DISTINGUISHING FACT FROM OPINION

*W*hether you are reading or writing persuasion, it is important to distinguish fact from opinion. Facts are statements that can be checked and declared to be either true or false. Opinions are beliefs or attitudes that vary from person to person.

Persuasive writers often state their opinions explicitly. For example, editorials, campaign speeches, and advertisements openly argue for certain beliefs or actions. Sometimes, however, persuasive writers influence their readers more subtly. Indirect persuasion is especially common in essays, opinion columns, and reviews.

Read the following excerpts from a newspaper column by Ellen Goodman. After you have finished reading, make a chart of facts and opinions in the column. Then sum up in a sentence or two the outlook toward life that Goodman favors in her column.

The Cove and the Tide

CASCO BAY, Maine—The huge blue heron glides over our cottage roof and settles down gently, taking up his post at the mouth of the tidal cove. Standing guard on elegant long legs, he picks off trespassers who swim too close to the border. When he is through and the water begins to intrude again, he takes off, arcing out over the bay. . . . Watching him at my own porch post, I cannot imagine anything more different than tides and clocks, any way of life more different than one in tune with tides and another regimented by numbers. . . .

The most basic of human rhythms disappears in our workaday lives, the way the sound of a cricket disappears in the city. Whatever is natural in our biological patterns gets knocked out of sequence by the metronome of our social existence. From the time we're small, we learn to wake up to alarms and work to somebody else's schedule. We have lunch when it's lunchtime, go to bed when it's bedtime. Sunrise and sunset are less relevant to our lives than 9 to 5. Hot and cold are less significant than thermostats. . . .

I suppose it's something of a miracle that, given time and environment, any modern urban dweller can still drift into his or her own nature. It's as if there is some center waiting to be rediscovered, one that we can touch when we are at rest. Maybe simplicity is a secular miracle today the way that Willa Cather's archbishop[1] once described religious miracles: something that comes when our perceptions are made finer "so that for a moment our eyes can see and our ears can hear what is there about us always."

I don't know if I can take simplicity home with me tomorrow. Like multicolored sand carefully layered in a glass jar, it doesn't travel well. By the time I return to the city, the subtlety may be jostled away. But during this list-making, schedule-hopping, clock-abiding fall, I can retreat—at least in memory—to the cove and the tide.

1. **Cather's archbishop:** a reference to *Death Comes for the Archbishop*, a novel by Willa Cather.

PERSUASIVE WRITING

*P*ersuasive writing is all around us, in ads, political speeches, and editorials. What are some of the topics or issues you feel deeply about? You'll have a chance now to express your opinion on one of these subjects in a persuasive essay.

Prewriting

1. Explore possible topics for your essay by listing some issues about which you have an opinion. Make sure that these issues really are arguable—namely, that people can have conflicting or opposing opinions about them.

2. Write a statement of your position on an issue in one or two sentences. This statement will serve as the **main idea** for your essay. [See **Focus** assignment on page 422.]

3. Decide on the **audience** you want to convince. Make an **audience chart** like the one shown on page 447.

4. Develop support for your opinion. In a persuasive essay, you need to appeal to both the head and the heart. Use these two methods:

- **logical appeals:** reasons, facts, expert opinions
- **emotional appeals:** examples and/or personal experiences that arouse specific feelings in the audience

[See **Focus** assignments on pages 477 and 507.]

5. Evaluate your reasoning for logical soundness. Avoid statements that look like reasons but aren't. Here are four specific examples:

- **circular reasoning:** merely restating your opinion in different words
- **false cause and effect:** claiming that one event caused another just because the first happened before the second
- **attacking the person:** rather than confronting the issue
- **hasty generalization:** basing a sweeping claim on a small number of examples

[See **Focus** assignment on page 555.]

Writing

1. Follow an **outline** like the one below as you write your first draft:

I. Introduction
   A. Attention-grabbing statement
   B. Background (if needed)
   C. Statement of opinion

II. Body
   A. Most important reason, with evidence + emotional appeal (if appropriate)
   B. Next reason, with evidence + emotional appeal (if appropriate)
   C. Additional reasons, with evidence + emotional appeals (if appropriate)

III. Conclusion
   A. Restatement of opinion
   B. Call to action (if appropriate)

[See **Focus** assignment on page 570.]

2. Remember that the most effective persuasion maintains a balance between logical and emotional appeals. Refer to your audience chart as you write. See if you can counter some of the audience's reasons for holding a different opinion on the issue.

Evaluating and Revising

1. When you revise your essay, pay special attention to the language you have used. Here are some points to consider:

- **Active-voice verbs** help your writing sound strong.
- **Connotations,** or associations, of words are useful in emotional appeals.

2. You may find the following checklist helpful as you revise your essay:

Checklist for Evaluation and Revision

✓ Do I grab the audience's attention?
✓ Do I state my opinion clearly?
✓ Do I use logical and emotional appeals?
✓ Is my reasoning sound?
✓ Have I organized my support logically?
✓ Is the tone of my essay suitable?
✓ Do I end with a strong conclusion?

Proofreading and Publishing

1. Proofread your persuasive essay and correct any errors you find in grammar, usage, and mechanics. (Here you may find it helpful to refer to the **Handbook for Revision** on pages 884–930.) Then prepare a final version of your essay by making a clean copy.

2. Consider some of the following ways to publish and share your essay:

- send your essay to a newspaper in the form of a letter to the editor
- deliver your essay as a speech in class

Below is an example of a persuasive paragraph that combines a logical approach with an emotional appeal. Notice the writer's revisions.

Writer's Model

The most important reason ⁀we need a traffic signal ~~is needed~~ at the corner next to the high school is that it is a ⁀heavily used ~~busy~~ intersection. Each weekday, ~~many~~ ⁀250 vehicles and ~~numerous~~ ⁀350 pedestrians pass this corner from 7:00 to 8:00 A.M. and from 2:00 to 3:00 P.M. Many ~~peo-ple~~ ⁀of you, ⁀I'm sure, have ⁀been ~~unhappy~~ ⁀grumbled at the long lines of cars backed up at the STOP signs because ~~they've~~ ⁀you've been nervous about getting to work on time or making an afternoon appointment.

Portfolio If your teacher approves, you may wish to keep a copy of your work in your writing folder or portfolio.

AN EPIC POEM: THE ODYSSEY

If you look closely at the upper right-hand corner of the painting, you will see the first four Greek letters that spell Homer's name. Homer is believed to be the author of the *Iliad* and the *Odyssey*, two poems that are generally considered to be among the greatest epics ever composed.

Judging from details in the painting, who do you think the different figures are? What can you infer from the scrolls and the musical instruments? What can you tell about the setting? Does the painting tell a story?

Freewrite for a few minutes, focusing on some aspect of the painting that interests you. Share your responses with others and compare interpretations.

A Reading from Homer by Sir Lawrence Alma-Tadema (1836–1912). Oil on canvas.
Philadelphia Museum of Art, George W. Elkins Collection

591

An *epic* is a long narrative poem about a national or legendary hero. Ancient Greece produced two epics—the *Iliad* and the *Odyssey*—which are considered the first great works of Western literature. The *Odyssey* is named for its hero, Odysseus, who is also known as Ulysses. The *Iliad* is not named for its hero, Achilles, but for Ilium, or Troy, the setting of the action.

Since classical times, both epics have been attributed to a poet named Homer. We know almost nothing about him. Seven different cities claimed to be his birthplace, but none could prove the claim. There is a tradition that Homer was blind, and an ancient bust shows him to be so. If he was blind, he must have had his sight at one time, for the poems are so rich in visual imagery that they are clearly the creation of someone who had observed the world carefully.

Scholars have established that the *Iliad* was composed sometime between 900 and 700 B.C. and that it preceded the *Odyssey* by some years. The raw material of both epics was a well-known body of legend about the most famous event in Greek history, the Trojan War, which had occurred several centuries earlier, about 1200 B.C. The probable cause of the Trojan War was economic. Troy's location enabled it to control all trade and shipping through the Dardanelles: once Troy was destroyed, the Greeks could expand their trade routes as much as they pleased. According to legend, however, the war began when Helen, the most beautiful woman in the world and wife of King Menelaus of Sparta, was kidnapped by Paris, a young Trojan prince. It took several years for the outraged Menelaus to assemble an army, for Greece was not a unified nation at that time. Kings and soldiers from all over Greece—Achilles and Odysseus among them—sailed to Troy to bring back Helen. The war went on for ten years, and finally the Trojans were defeated.

Homer used this legendary material as the basis for his poems. He added an original plot structure, realistic characters, dialogue and detail, and tales of fabulous monsters. Against the drama on earth he set the drama of the Olympian gods and goddesses, who were interested in human affairs and who often intervened to protect or punish mortals. Homer's portrayal of the gods made them seem human. They quarreled and loved and were jealous of one another. Although Homer occasionally treats the gods lightly, he is always respectful. A pervasive theme throughout these epics is that respect for the gods is essential to survival.

When the poems were first composed, they were not written down. They were passed orally from one generation to the next. They were memorized by traveling poets called *rhapsodes* (răp′sōdz′), who recited the epics in the banquet halls of kings and nobles. Both poems were re-

Corinthian bronze helmet, early fifth century B.C.
The Granger Collection, New York

Dionysiac mask.
Bronze with traces
of silver and copper,
first century A.D.
In Greek mythology,
Dionysos was the god
of revelry.
The Metropolitan Museum
of Art, gift of
Mrs. Gerald van der Kemp

cited in public every four years in Athens at the festival of Athena, goddess of wisdom and patron of the city. In time, the study of Homer's epics became the basis of Greek education. From Homer, Greek youths learned how to tell a story, to portray character, to give a speech, and to express the Greek ideals of thought and action. The *Iliad* and the *Odyssey* became models for later writers, notably the Roman poet Virgil, author of the *Aeneid* (ĭ-nē′ĭd).

The *Iliad* opens in the tenth—and last—year of the Trojan War. The war is at a stalemate, and in the Greek camp there is much dissension. Achilles, the greatest warrior among the Greeks, and Agamemnon, the leader of the Greeks, have had a bitter quarrel over a captive slave girl. Achilles has withdrawn from the war and is sulking in his tent. His absence from the field gives the Trojans an advantage in the war. Only after Hector, the great Trojan hero, kills Achilles' friend Patroclus (pə-trō′kləs) does Achilles return to combat. He kills Hector, and his victory demoralizes the Trojans. The *Iliad* ends with a twelve-day truce in which both sides bury and mourn their dead.

Homer tells about the last days of the Trojan War in his second epic. The man responsible for the fall of Troy is Odysseus, the shrewdest of the Greeks. He conceives a plan to leave a huge wooden horse filled with Greek warriors outside the gates of Troy. Believing that the Greek ships have sailed for home and that this wooden horse is an offering to the gods, the Trojans bring the horse within their gates. When the Trojans are off guard, the Greeks slip out of the horse and open the city gates to their own army.

Because Odysseus is instrumental in the destruction of Troy, he angers the gods who are sympathetic to Troy. They vow that he will have a long and difficult journey home. This homeward journey—which takes ten years—is the subject of the *Odyssey*.

The *Odyssey* is a very long poem—11,300 lines divided into twenty-four books. The poem has three major plot strands. First, there is the story of what happens in Ithaca to Odysseus' wife and son as they await his return. The second story is the tale of Odysseus' wanderings during the ten years following the Trojan War. These two strands come together when Odysseus returns to Ithaca and joins forces with his son, Telemachus, to destroy their enemies.

You will be reading some of the best-known excerpts from the poem. In Part 1 of the unit, you will read about the adventures of Odysseus and his crew as they attempt to return to Ithaca. In Part 2, you will read how Odysseus takes his place as rightful king of Ithaca. The text is a translation from the Greek by the American poet Robert Fitzgerald.

Close Reading OF AN EPIC

Even though you will be reading parts of the Odyssey *in an English translation, you will find that many characteristics of the original epic are preserved. Homer was probably a professional bard, a poet who recited his poetry orally and who accompanied his words with music. Oral poetry tends to use repetition as an aid to memory. In the* Odyssey, *speeches, images, and descriptions are often repeated.*

Guidelines for Close Reading

1. Become familiar with the names of characters and places. There are many characters, often referred to by different descriptive phrases. Refer to the list provided on pages 597–598 as often as necessary. The individual entries identify the people and places mentioned in the *Odyssey* and will give you assistance in pronouncing each name.

2. Take note of the heroic characteristics of the central figure or figures. Expect that actions will be extraordinary and that adventures will be on a grand scale.

3. Determine the role played by gods, goddesses, and other supernatural agents. Consider their responsibility for the destiny of human beings. Odysseus has friends and enemies among the gods and goddesses of Olympus. Note how they intervene to help or hinder him.

4. Note the conventional elements of the epic. The conventions of the Homeric epic include an invocation to the Muse, lengthy speeches, repetitions of passages, and digressions. Two conventions deserve special attention: the *epithet* and the *epic simile*. An *epithet* is a word or phrase used to characterize a person or thing. Homer uses many epithets for the gods and goddesses as well as for the human characters in his poem. Some epithets for Zeus are "the father of gods and men," "the master of heaven and high thunder," "Hera's consort," "the lord of cloud," and "the son of Cronus." An *epic simile* is an extended comparison, often running several lines. Here is an epic simile from the *Odyssey*:

Just as a farmer's hunger grows, behind
the bolted plow and share, all day afield,
drawn by his team of winedark oxen; sundown
is benison for him, sending him homeward
stiff in the knees from weariness, to dine;
just so, the light on the sea rim gladdened Odysseus....

5. Look for the underlying beliefs and values of the culture that produced the epic. The qualities attributed to the heroic figures of the epic generally reflect the ideals of its society.

The following invocation, which opens the *Odyssey,* is an appeal for help. The poet asks for inspiration in telling the story of his hero, "the great song." The lofty tone and the dignified style of the epic are evident in its opening lines. Note that these lines also give a brief summation of the hero's adventures. After the Trojan War Odysseus becomes a "wanderer." He attempts to bring his shipmates home but fails. His men are all destroyed by "their own recklessness" in killing the cattle of Helios, the god of the sun. Odysseus is left to wander alone. For a time he is held captive by a beautiful goddess, Calypso. Finally he is allowed to return home to his family in Ithaca, where he faces other dangers.

Sing in me, Muse,° and through me tell the story
of that man skilled in all ways of contending,
the wanderer, harried for years on end,
after he plundered the stronghold
on the proud height of Troy.
                He saw the townlands
and learned the minds of many distant men,
and weathered many bitter nights and days
in his deep heart at sea, while he fought only
to save his life, to bring his shipmates home.
But not by will nor valor could he save them,
for their own recklessness destroyed them all—
children and fools, they killed and feasted on
the cattle of Lord Helios, the Sun,
and he who moves all day through heaven
took from their eyes the dawn of their return.

°**Muse:** one of the goddesses who preside over the arts.

Of these adventures, Muse, daughter of Zeus,
tell us in our time, lift the great song again.
Begin when all the rest who left behind them
headlong death in battle or at sea
had long ago returned, while he alone still hungered
for home and wife. Her ladyship Calypso
clung to him in her sea-hollowed caves—
a nymph, immortal and most beautiful,
who craved him for her own.
                              And when long years and seasons
wheeling brought around that point of time
ordained for him to make his passage homeward,
trials and dangers, even so, attended him
even in Ithaca, near those he loved.

Looking at Yourself as a Reader

What strategies did you use in reading these lines? Did you read them aloud, following the writer's clues for phrasing? Did you find that reading aloud helped you understand the flow of ideas? Did you have questions about specific words or phrases? Did you use a dictionary or other reference work to check the meanings of unfamiliar words?

Summarize your response to this passage in a few lines. If you wish, write a paraphrase of several lines, restating the content in simple form.

The Granger Collection, New York

Ulysses and Calypso. Detail from Attic red-figured vase, fifth century B.C. Ulysses is the Roman name for Odysseus. In the *Odyssey*, he spends seven years on the island of Calypso, a sea nymph.

People and Places in
The *Odyssey*

Achaeans (ə-kē′ənz): Greeks; specifically, the people of Achaea in northeastern Greece.

Aeaea (ē-ē′ə): island home of Circe, the enchantress.

Agamemnon (ăg′ə-mĕm′nŏn′): commander of the Greeks during the Trojan War.

Alcinous (ăl-sĭn′ō-əs): King of Phaeacia.

Antinous (ăn-tĭn′ō-əs): an Ithacan noble, most arrogant of the suitors.

Apollo (ə-pŏl′ō): in Greek mythology, god of poetry, music, and prophecy.

Argo (är′gō): the ship manned by Jason and his crew of Greek heroes on their quest for the Golden Fleece.

Athena (ə-thē′nə): Greek goddess of wisdom, crafts, and war; also called Pallas (păl′əs) Athena.

Calypso (kə-lĭp′sō): beautiful sea nymph, who kept Odysseus on her island for seven years.

Charybdis (kə-rĭb′dĭs): a whirlpool in the Straits of Messina, personified as a female monster.

Cicones (sĭ-kō′nēz): a people living on the southwestern coast of Thrace, who were attacked by Odysseus' men on their way home from Troy.

Circe (sûr′sē): beautiful witch-goddess who transformed Odysseus' men into beasts.

Cronus (krō′nəs): in Greek mythology, a Titan and ruler of the universe until he was overthrown by his son, Zeus.

Cyclops (sī′klŏps): member of a race of one-eyed giants. The Cyclopes (sī-klō′pēz) were said to have lived as shepherds on the island of Sicily.

Eumaeus (yōō-mē′əs): a swineherd, an old and loyal servant to Odysseus.

Eurycleia (yōō-rĭ-klē′yə): Penelope's servant and Odysseus' old nurse.

Eurylochus (yōō-rĭl′ə-kəs): one of Odysseus' crew.

Eurymachus (yōō-rĭm′ə-kəs): one of Penelope's suitors, an Ithacan noble.

Eurynome (yōō-rĭn′ə-mē): Penelope's housekeeper.

Helios (hē′lē-ŏs′): in early Greek mythology, the sun god.

Ithaca (ĭth′ə-kə): Odysseus' home, an island off the western coast of Greece.

Laertes (lā-ûr′tēz): Odysseus' father.

Laestrygonians (lĕs′trĭ-gō′nē-ənz): race of man-eating giants.

Odysseus (ō-dĭs′yo͞os′, ōdĭs′ē-əs): King of Ithaca and hero of the *Odyssey*. The Latin version of his name is Ulysses.

Penelope (pə-nĕl′ə-pē): Odysseus' wife.

Phaeacia (fē-ā′shə): an island kingdom inhabited by seafarers and traders.

Polyphemus (pŏl′ə-fē′məs): a Cyclops, son of Poseidon.

Poseidon (pō-sī′dən): Greek god of the sea; identified with the Roman god Neptune.

Scylla (sĭl′ə): a dangerous rock in the Straits of Messina, personified as a female monster with six heads who devoured passing sailors.

Sirens (sī′rənz): sea nymphs who lured sailors to destruction with their songs.

Telemachus (tə-lĕm′ə-kəs): son of Odysseus and Penelope.

Zeus (zo͞os): ruler of the gods and goddesses on Mount Olympus. He is sometimes called Zeus Cronion, meaning the "son of Cronus" (see page 597).

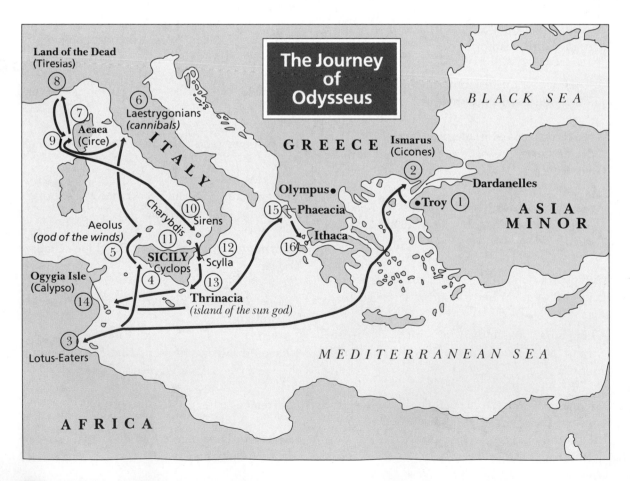

The Journey of Odysseus

FROM
The Odyssey

HOMER

Translated by
Robert Fitzgerald

PART 1 FAR FROM HOME

"I Am Odysseus"

Odysseus is in the banquet hall of Alcinous (ăl-sĭn'ō-əs), King of Phaeacia (fē-ā'shə), who helps him on his way after all his comrades have been killed and his last vessel destroyed. Odysseus tells the story of his adventures thus far.

"I am Lacrtes° son, Odysseus.
             Men hold me
formidable for guile in peace and war:
this fame has gone abroad to the sky's rim.
My home is on the peaked sea-mark of Ithaca°
under Mount Neion's° wind-blown robe of leaves,   5
in sight of other islands—Dulichium,°
Same, wooded Zacynthus°—Ithaca
being most lofty in that coastal sea,
and northwest, while the rest lie east and south.
A rocky isle, but good for a boy's training;   10
I shall not see on earth a place more dear,
though I have been detained long by Calypso,°
loveliest among goddesses, who held me
in her smooth caves, to be her heart's delight,
as Circe of Aeaea,° the enchantress,   15
desired me, and detained me in her hall.
But in my heart I never gave consent.
Where shall a man find sweetness to surpass
his own home and his parents? In far lands
he shall not, though he find a house of gold.   20

1. **Laertes** (lā-ûr'tēz).

4. **Ithaca** (ĭth'ə-kə): an island off the west coast of Greece.
5. **Neion** (nē-ī'ən).
6. **Dulichium** (doo-lĭk'ē-əm).
7. **Zacynthus** (zə-sĭn'thəs).

12. **Calypso** (kə-lĭp'sō).

15. **Circe** (sûr'sē) of **Aeaea** (ē-ē'ə).

A re-creation of Odysseus' ship. The voyage of Odysseus from the site of Troy (in present-day Turkey) to Ithaca was re-created in 1985 in a trip led by British navigator Tim Severin.

What of my sailing, then, from Troy?
>   What of those years
of rough adventure, weathered under Zeus?°
The wind that carried west from Ilion°
brought me to Ismarus, on the far shore,
a strongpoint on the coast of the Cicones.°   25
I stormed that place and killed the men who fought.
Plunder we took, and we enslaved the women,
to make division, equal shares to all—
but on the spot I told them: 'Back, and quickly!
Out to sea again!' My men were mutinous,   30
fools, on stores of wine. Sheep after sheep
they butchered by the surf, and shambling cattle,
feasting—while fugitives went inland, running
to call to arms the main force of Cicones.
This was an army, trained to fight on horseback   35
or, where the ground required, on foot. They came

22. **Zeus** (zo͞os): king of the gods.
23. **Ilion** (ĭl′ē-ŏn): Troy.

25. **Cicones** (sĭ-kō′nēz).

with dawn over that terrain like the leaves
and blades of spring. So doom appeared to us,
dark word of Zeus for us, our evil days.
My men stood up and made a fight of it—   40
backed on the ships, with lances kept in play,
from bright morning through the blaze of noon
holding our beach, although so far outnumbered;
but when the sun passed toward unyoking time,
then the Achaeans,° one by one, gave way.   45
Six benches were left empty in every ship
that evening when we pulled away from death.
And this new grief we bore with us to sea:
our precious lives we had, but not our friends.
No ship made sail next day until some shipmate   50
had raised a cry, three times, for each poor ghost
unfleshed by the Cicones on that field.

45. **Achaeans** (ə-kē′ənz): Greeks (Odysseus' men).

The Lotus-Eaters

Now Zeus the lord of cloud roused in the north
a storm against the ships, and driving veils
of squall moved down like night on land and sea.   55
The bows went plunging at the gust; sails
cracked and lashed out strips in the big wind.
We saw death in that fury, dropped the yards,
unshipped the oars, and pulled for the nearest lee:°
Then two long days and nights we lay offshore   60
worn out and sick at heart, tasting our grief,
until a third Dawn came with ringlets shining.
Then we put up our masts, hauled sail, and rested,
letting the steersmen and the breeze take over.

59. **lee:** place sheltered from the wind.

I might have made it safely home, that time,   65
but as I came round Malea° the current
took me out to sea, and from the north
a fresh gale drove me on, past Cythera.°
Nine days I drifted on the teeming sea
before dangerous high winds. Upon the tenth   70
we came to the coastline of the Lotus-Eaters,
who live upon that flower. We landed there
to take on water. All ships' companies
mustered alongside for the midday meal.

66. **Malea** (mə′lē-ə).

68. **Cythera** (sĭ-thĭr′ə).

Then I sent out two picked men and a runner   75
to learn what race of men that land sustained.
They fell in, soon enough, with Lotus-Eaters,
who showed no will to do us harm, only
offering the sweet Lotus to our friends—
but those who ate this honeyed plant, the Lotus,   80
never cared to report, nor to return:
they longed to stay forever, browsing on
that native bloom, forgetful of their homeland.
I drove them, all three wailing, to the ships,
tied them down under their rowing benches,   85
and called the rest: 'All hands aboard;
come, clear the beach and no one taste
the Lotus, or you lose your hope of home.'
Filing in to their places by the rowlocks
my oarsmen dipped their long oars in the surf,   90
and we moved out again on our seafaring.

The Cyclops

In the next land we found were Cyclopes,°

giants, louts, without a law to bless them.
In ignorance leaving the fruitage of the earth in mystery
to the immortal gods, they neither plow   95
nor sow by hand, nor till the ground, though grain—
wild wheat and barley—grows untended, and
wine grapes, in clusters, ripen in heaven's rain.
Cyclopes have no muster and no meeting,
no consultation or old tribal ways,   100
but each one dwells in his own mountain cave
dealing out rough justice to wife and child,
indifferent to what the others do. . . .

As we rowed on, and nearer to the mainland,
at one end of the bay, we saw a cavern   105
yawning above the water, screened with laurel,
and many rams and goats about the place
inside a sheepfold—made from slabs of stone
earthfast between tall trunks of pine and rugged
towering oak trees.

       A prodigious° man   110
slept in this cave alone, and took his flocks

92. **Cyclopes** (sī-klō′pēz), plural form of Cyclops (sī-klŏps); a race of one-eyed giants.

110. **prodigious** (prə-dĭj′əs): gigantic.

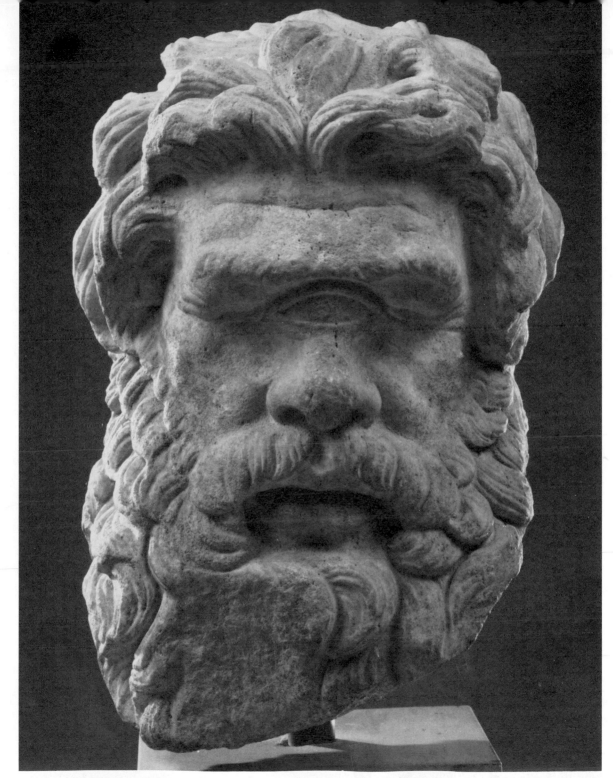

Head of the Cyclops (Polyphemus). Marble, c. 150 B.C. or later, 0.383m.

Gift in Honor of Edward W. Forbes from his friends, Courtesy, Museum of Fine Arts, Boston

to graze afield—remote from all companions,
knowing none but savage ways, a brute
so huge, he seemed no man at all of those
who eat good wheaten bread; but he seemed rather   115
a shaggy mountain reared in solitude.
We beached there, and I told the crew
to stand by and keep watch over the ship;
as for myself I took my twelve best fighters
and went ahead. I had a goatskin full   120
of that sweet liquor that Euanthes'° son,
Maron, had given me. He kept Apollo's°
holy grove at Ismarus; for kindness
we showed him there, and showed his wife and child,
he gave me seven shining golden talents°   125
perfectly formed, a solid silver winebowl,
and then this liquor—twelve two-handled jars
of brandy, pure and fiery. Not a slave
in Maron's household knew this drink; only
he, his wife and the storeroom mistress knew;   130
and they would put one cupful—ruby-colored,
honey-smooth—in twenty more of water,
but still the sweet scent hovered like a fume
over the winebowl. No man turned away
when cups of this came round.

                A wineskin full   135
I brought along, and victuals in a bag,
for in my bones I knew some towering brute
would be upon us soon—all outward power,
a wild man, ignorant of civility.

We climbed, then, briskly to the cave. But Cyclops   140
had gone afield, to pasture his fat sheep,
so we looked round at everything inside:
a drying rack that sagged with cheeses, pens
crowded with lambs and kids, each in its class:
firstlings apart from middlings, and the 'dewdrops,'   145
or newborn lambkins, penned apart from both.
And vessels full of whey were brimming there—
bowls of earthenware and pails for milking.
My men came pressing round me, pleading:

                            'Why not
take these cheeses, get them stowed, come back,   150
throw open all the pens, and make a run for it?

121. **Euanthes** (yōō-ăn′thēz).

122. **Apollo** (ə-pŏl′ō): god of music, prophecy, and medicine.

125. **talent:** a unit of money in ancient Greece.

We'll drive the kids and lambs aboard. We say
put out again on good salt water!'
                    Ah,
how sound that was! Yet I refused, I wished
to see the cave man, what he had to offer—   155
no pretty sight, it turned out, for my friends.

We lit a fire, burnt an offering,
and took some cheese to eat; then sat in silence
around the embers, waiting. When he came
he had a load of dry boughs on his shoulder   160
to stoke his fire at suppertime. He dumped it
with a great crash into that hollow cave,
and we all scattered fast to the far wall.
Then over the broad cavern floor he ushered
the ewes he meant to milk. He left his rams   165
and he-goats in the yard outside, and swung
high overhead a slab of solid rock
to close the cave. Two dozen four-wheeled wagons,
with heaving wagon teams, could not have stirred
the tonnage of that rock from where he wedged it   170
over the doorsill. Next he took his seat
and milked his bleating ewes. A practiced job
he made of it, giving each ewe her suckling;
thickened his milk, then, into curds and whey,
sieved out the curds to drip in withy° baskets,   175   175. **withy** (wĭ*th*′ē): made of
and poured the whey to stand in bowls   slender twigs.
cooling until he drank it for his supper.
When all these chores were done, he poked the fire,
heaping on brushwood. In the glare he saw us.

'Strangers,' he said, 'who are you? And where from?   180
What brings you here by seaways—a fair traffic?
Or are you wandering rogues, who cast your lives
like dice, and ravage other folk by sea?'

We felt pressure on our hearts, in dread
of that deep rumble and that mighty man   185
But all the same I spoke up in reply:

'We are from Troy, Achaeans, blown off course
by shifting gales on the Great South Sea;
homeward bound, but taking routes and ways

uncommon; so the will of Zeus would have it.
We served under Agamemnon,° son of Atreus—
the whole world knows what city
he laid waste, what armies he destroyed.
It was our luck to come here; here we stand,
beholden for your help, or any gifts
you give—as custom is to honor strangers.
We would entreat you, great Sir, have a care
for the gods' courtesy; Zeus will avenge
the unoffending guest.'
             He answered this
from his brute chest, unmoved:
                        'You are a ninny,
or else you come from the other end of nowhere,
telling me, mind the gods! We Cyclopes
care not a whistle for your thundering Zeus
or all the gods in bliss; we have more force by far.
I would not let you go for fear of Zeus—
you or your friends—unless I had a whim to.
Tell me, where was it, now, you left your ship—
around the point, or down the shore, I wonder?'

He thought he'd find out, but I saw through this,
and answered with a ready lie:
                          'My ship?
Poseidon° Lord, who sets the earth a-tremble,
broke it up on the rocks at your land's end.
A wind from seaward served him, drove us there.
We are survivors, these good men and I.'

Neither reply nor pity came from him,
but in one stride he clutched at my companions
and caught two in his hands like squirming puppies
to beat their brains out, spattering the floor.
Then he dismembered them and made his meal,
gaping and crunching like a mountain lion—
everything: innards, flesh, and marrowbones.
We cried aloud, lifting our hands to Zeus,
powerless, looking on at this, appalled;
but Cyclops went on filling up his belly
with manflesh and great gulps of whey,
then lay down like a mast among his sheep.
My heart beat high now at the chance of action,

190

195

200

205

210

215

220

225

191. **Agamemnon** (ăg'ə-mĕm'
nŏn'): Greek king who led the
Greeks against the Trojans.

211. **Poseidon** (pō-sī'dən): god
of the sea and of earthquakes.

and drawing the sharp sword from my hip I went
along his flank to stab him where the midriff
holds the liver. I had touched the spot   230
when sudden fear stayed me: if I killed him
we perished there as well, for we could never
move his ponderous doorway slab aside.
So we were left to groan and wait for morning.

When the young Dawn with fingertips of rose   235
lit up the world, the Cyclops built a fire
and milked his handsome ewes, all in due order,
putting the sucklings to the mothers. Then,
his chores being all dispatched, he caught
another brace° of men to make his breakfast,   240   240. **brace:** pair.
and whisked away his great door slab
to let his sheep go through—but he, behind,
reset the stone as one would cap a quiver.
There was a din of whistling as the Cyclops
rounded his flock to higher ground, then stillness.   245
And now I pondered how to hurt him worst,
if but Athena° granted what I prayed for.   247. **Athena** (ə-thē′nə): god-
Here are the means I thought would serve my turn: dess of wisdom.

A club, or staff, lay there along the fold—
an olive tree, felled green and left to season   250
for Cyclops' hand. And it was like a mast
a lugger of twenty oars, broad in the beam—
a deep-sea-going craft—might carry:
so long, so big around, it seemed. Now I
chopped out a six-foot section of this pole   255
and set it down before my men, who scraped it;
and when they had it smooth, I hewed again
to make a stake with pointed end. I held this
in the fire's heart and turned it, toughening it,
then hid it, well back in the cavern, under   260
one of the dung piles in profusion there.
Now came the time to toss for it: who ventured
along with me? whose hand could bear to thrust
and grind that spike in Cyclops' eye, when mild
sleep had mastered him? As luck would have it,   265
the men I would have chosen won the toss—
four strong men, and I made five as captain.

At evening came the shepherd with his flock,
his woolly flock. The rams as well, this time,
entered the cave: by some sheepherding whim—   270
or a god's bidding—none were left outside.
He hefted his great boulder into place
and sat him down to milk the bleating ewes
in proper order, put the lambs to suck,
and swiftly ran through all his evening chores.   275
Then he caught two more men and feasted on them.
My moment was at hand, and I went forward
holding an ivy bowl of my dark drink,
looking up, saying:
                'Cyclops, try some wine.
Here's liquor to wash down your scraps of men.   280
Taste it, and see the kind of drink we carried
under our planks. I meant it for an offering
if you would help us home. But you are mad,
unbearable, a bloody monster! After this,
will any other traveler come to see you?'   285

He seized and drained the bowl, and it went down
so fiery and smooth he called for more:

'Give me another, thank you kindly. Tell me,
how are you called? I'll make a gift will please you.
Even Cyclopes know the wine grapes grow   290
out of grassland and <u>loam</u> in heaven's rain,
but here's a bit of nectar and ambrosia!°

Three bowls I brought him, and he poured them down.
I saw the fuddle and flush come over him,
then I sang out in cordial tones:
                    'Cyclops,   295
you ask my honorable name? Remember
the gift you promised me, and I shall tell you.
My name is Nohbdy: mother, father, and friends,
everyone calls me Nohbdy.'
             And he said:
'Nohbdy's my meat, then, after I eat his friends.   300
Others come first. There's a noble gift, now.'

Even as he spoke, he reeled and tumbled backward,
his great head lolling to one side; and sleep

292. **nectar and ambrosia** (ăm-brō′zhə): drink and food of the Olympian gods.

The Blinding of Cyclops. Detail from Attic black-figured vase, sixth century B.C. The Granger Collection, New York

took him like any creature. Drunk, hiccuping,
he dribbled streams of liquor and bits of men.   305

Now, by the gods, I drove my big hand spike
deep in the embers, charring it again,
and cheered my men along with battle talk
to keep their courage up: no quitting now.
The pike of olive, green though it had been,   310
reddened and glowed as if about to catch.
I drew it from the coals and my four fellows
gave me a hand, lugging it near the Cyclops
as more than natural force nerved them; straight
forward they sprinted, lifted it, and rammed it   315
deep in his crater eye, and I leaned on it
turning it as a shipwright turns a drill

in planking, having men below to swing
the two-handled strap that spins it in the groove.
So with our brand we bored that great eye socket   320
while blood ran out around the red-hot bar.
Eyelid and lash were seared; the pierced ball
hissed broiling, and the roots popped.

                  In a smithy
one sees a white-hot axhead or an adz
plunged and wrung in a coldtub, screeching steam—   325
the way they make soft iron hale and hard:
just so that eyeball hissed around the spike.
The Cyclops bellowed and the rock roared round him,
and we fell back in fear. Clawing his face
he tugged the bloody spike out of his eye,   330
threw it away, and his wild hands went groping;
then he set up a howl for Cyclopes
who lived in caves on windy peaks nearby.
Some heard him; and they came by divers° ways
to clump around outside and call: 335

                        'What ails you,
Polyphemus?° Why do you cry so sore
in the starry night? You will not let us sleep.
Sure no man's driving off your flock? No man
has tricked you, ruined you?'

                  Out of the cave
the mammoth Polyphemus roared in answer: 340

'Nohbdy, Nohbdy's tricked me, Nohbdy's ruined me!'

To this rough shout they made a sage reply:

'Ah well, if nobody has played you foul
there in your lonely bed, we are no use in pain
given by great Zeus. Let it be your father,   345
Poseidon Lord, to whom you pray.'

                   So saying
they trailed away. And I was filled with laughter
to see how like a charm the name deceived them.
Now Cyclops, wheezing as the pain came on him,
fumbled to wrench away the great doorstone   350
and squatted in the breach with arms thrown wide
for any silly beast or man who bolted—
hoping somehow I might be such a fool.

334. divers (dī′vərz): various.

336. Polyphemus (pŏl′ə-fē′məs).

But I kept thinking how to win the game:
death sat there huge; how could we slip away? 355
I drew on all my wits, and ran through tactics,
reasoning as a man will for dear life,
until a trick came—and it pleased me well.
The Cyclops' rams were handsome, fat, with heavy
fleeces, a dark violet.
         Three abreast 360
I tied them silently together, twining
cords of willow from the ogre's bed;
then slung a man under each middle one
to ride there safely, shielded left and right.
So three sheep could convey each man. I took 365
the woolliest ram, the choicest of the flock
and hung myself under his kinky belly,
pulled up tight, with fingers twisted deep
in sheepskin ringlets for an iron grip.
So, breathing hard, we waited until morning. 370

When Dawn spread out her fingertips of rose
the rams began to stir, moving for pasture,
and peals of bleating echoed round the pens
where dams with udders full called for a milking.
Blinded, and sick with pain from his head wound, 375
the master stroked each ram, then let it pass,
but my men riding on the pectoral° fleece
the giant's blind hands blundering never found.
Last of them all my ram, the leader, came,
weighted by wool and me with my meditations. 380
The Cyclops patted him, and then he said:

'Sweet cousin ram, why lag behind the rest
in the night cave? You never linger so,
but graze before them all, and go afar
to crop sweet grass, and take your stately way 385
leading along the streams, until at evening
you run to be the first one in the fold.
Why, now, so far behind? Can you be grieving
over your Master's eye? That carrion rogue°
and his accurst companions burnt it out 390
when he had conquered all my wits with wine.
Nohbdy will not get out alive, I swear.
Oh, had you brain and voice to tell

377. **pectoral** (pĕk′tər-əl): on the chest.

389. **carrion** (kăr′ē-ən) **rogue:** rotten scoundrel.

Odysseus Bound Beneath the Belly of a Ram, detail from Attic Red Figure Pelike, near the Goettingen Painter, 490–480 B.C., 0.30m.

where he may be now, dodging all my fury!
Bashed by this hand and bashed on this rock wall   395
his brains would strew the floor, and I should have
rest from the outrage Nohbdy worked upon me.'

He sent us into the open, then. Close by,
I dropped and rolled clear of the ram's belly,
going this way and that to untie the men.   400
With many glances back, we rounded up
his fat, stiff-legged sheep to take aboard,
and drove them down to where the good ship lay.
We saw, as we came near, our fellows' faces
shining; then we saw them turn to grief   405
tallying those who had not fled from death.
I hushed them, jerking head and eyebrows up,
and in a low voice told them: 'Load this herd;
move fast, and put the ship's head toward the breakers.'
They all pitched in at loading, then embarked   410
and struck their oars into the sea. Far out,
as far offshore as shouted words would carry,
I sent a few back to the adversary:

'O Cyclops! Would you feast on my companions?
Puny, am I, in a cave man's hands?   415
How do you like the beating that we gave you,
you damned cannibal? Eater of guests
under your roof! Zeus and the gods have paid you!'

The blind thing in his doubled fury broke
a hilltop in his hands and heaved it after us,   420
Ahead of our black prow it struck and sank
whelmed in a spuming geyser, a giant wave
that washed the ship stern foremost back to shore.
I got the longest boathook out and stood
fending us off, with furious nods to all   425
to put their backs into a racing stroke—
row, row, or perish. So the long oars bent
kicking the foam sternward, making head
until we drew away, and twice as far.
Now when I cupped my hands I heard the crew   430
in low voices protesting:
                    'Godsake, Captain!
Why bait the beast again? Let him alone!'

'That tidal wave he made on the first throw
all but beached us.'

              'All but stove us in!'
'Give him our bearing with your trumpeting,   435

he'll get the range and lob a boulder.'
                               'Aye!
He'll smash our timbers and our heads together!'

I would not heed them in my glorying spirit,
but let my anger flare and yelled:
                           'Cyclops,
if ever mortal man inquire   440
how you were put to shame and blinded, tell him
Odysseus, raider of cities, took your eye:
Laertes' son, whose home's on Ithaca!'

At this he gave a mighty sob and rumbled:

'Now comes the weird° upon me, spoken of old.   445   **445. weird:** fate or destiny.
A wizard, grand and wondrous, lived here—Telemus,
a son of Eurymus; great length of days
he had in wizardry among the Cyclopes,
and these things he foretold for time to come:
my great eye lost, and at Odysseus' hands.   450
Always I had in mind some giant, armed
in giant force, would come against me here.
But this, but you—small, pitiful and twiggy—
you put me down with wine, you blinded me.
Come back, Odysseus, and I'll treat you well,   455
praying the god of earthquake° to befriend you—   **456. god of earthquake:** Posei-
his son I am, for he by his avowal   don.
fathered me, and, if he will, he may
heal me of this black wound—he and no other
of all the happy gods or mortal men.'   460

Few words I shouted in reply to him:

'If I could take your life I would and take
your time away, and hurl you down to hell!
The god of earthquake could not heal you there!'

At this he stretched his hands out in his darkness   465
toward the sky of stars, and prayed Poseidon:

'O hear me, lord, blue girdler of the islands,
if I am thine indeed, and thou art father:

grant that Odysseus, raider of cities, never
see his home: Laertes' son, I mean,   470
who kept his hall on Ithaca. Should destiny
intend that he shall see his roof again
among his family in his fatherland,
far be that day, and dark the years between.
Let him lose all companions, and return   475
under strange sail to bitter days at home.'

In these words he prayed, and the god heard him.
Now he laid hands upon a bigger stone
and wheeled around, titanic for the cast,
to let it fly in the black-prowed vessel's track.   480
But it fell short, just aft the steering oar,
and whelming seas rose giant above the stone
to bear us onward toward the island.
                                   There
as we ran in we saw the squadron waiting,
the trim ships drawn up side by side, and all   485
our troubled friends who waited, looking seaward.
We beached her, grinding keel in the soft sand,
and waded in, ourselves, on the sandy beach.
Then we unloaded all the Cyclops' flock
to make division, share and share alike,   490
only my fighters voted that my ram,
the prize of all, should go to me. I slew him
by the seaside and burnt his long thighbones
to Zeus beyond the stormcloud, Cronus' son,°
who rules the world. But Zeus disdained my offering: 495
destruction for my ships he had in store
and death for those who sailed them, my companions.
Now all day long until the sun went down
we made our feast on mutton and sweet wine,
till after sunset in the gathering dark   500
we went to sleep above the wash of ripples.

When the young Dawn with fingertips of rose
touched the world, I roused the men, gave orders
to man the ships, cast off the mooring lines;
and filing in to sit beside the rowlocks   505
oarsmen in line dipped oars in the gray sea.
So we moved out, sad in the vast offing,
having our precious lives, but not our friends.

494. **Cronus' son:** Cronus
(krō′nəs) was a Titan who ruled
the universe before Zeus.

Reading Check

1. Why are Odysscus' men vulnerable when the Cicones attack?
2. What happens to the men who eat the Lotus plant?
3. When the Cyclops asks about his ship, what does Odysseus tell him?
4. Why does Odysseus refrain from killing the Cyclops?
5. Why do none of the other Cyclopes come when Polyphemus cries for help?

by ignoring their advice. Identify both instances and tell why Odysseus acts as he does.

7. Odysseus devises a plan that enables him and his men to escape from the Cyclops' cave and to prevent anyone coming to the Cyclops' aid. What is each stage of the plan?

8. What aspects of Odysseus' character are revealed in the incident with the Cyclops?

9. Reread the Cyclops' prayer to Poseidon (lines 467–476). **a.** What lines suggest that Odysseus will have to face other trials? **b.** How does this foreshadowing add to the suspense of the poem?

For Study and Discussion

Analyzing and Interpreting the Epic

1. Odysseus begins his narrative when he and his men set sail from Troy. What does the episode of the Cicones reveal about Odysseus and his men?

2. Almost all of the adventures in the *Odyssey* illustrate some aspect of Odysseus' character. What specific characteristics are revealed in the episode of the Lotus-Eaters?

3. The land of the Lotus-Eaters has been said to symbolize *escapism*—that is, withdrawal from reality into a dream world. Do you agree? If you do, point out lines that support your view. If you do not, give reasons for your opinion.

4. Why does Odysseus consider the Cyclopes barbarians?

5. Hospitality to strangers is a theme that recurs throughout the *Odyssey*. The ancient Greeks believed that the gods themselves sometimes came to earth disguised as humble strangers. How does the Cyclops respond to Odysseus' plea for hospitality?

6. Twice in the Cyclops episode Odysseus brings misfortune upon himself and his men

Focus on Personal Narrative

Choosing a Topic

Part 1 of these selections from Homer's *Odyssey* is an extended personal narrative, in which the hero Odysseus tells the story of his adventures to the Phaeacians.

A **personal narrative** tells about an experience that happened to you and explores the meaning of that experience. When you select a topic for a personal narrative, use the following guidelines:

1. Choose an experience that was meaningful and important.
2. Choose an experience that you remember well.
3. Choose an experience that you are willing to share.

Freewrite for ten minutes about *one* of the following topics or about a topic of your own choice. Save your notes.

an unforgettable meeting
a holiday at home
an argument with a friend
a personal victory

The Sirens

Odysseus and his crew arrive next at the island of Aeolus (ēo'ə-ləs), god of the winds, who helps them homeward by bottling up unfavorable winds and sending them a fair breeze. After nine days' sail, with Ithaca in sight, the men untie the bag of winds, and their ships are blown straight back to Aeolus' island. Realizing that their voyage is cursed by the gods, Aeolus drives them away.

In the land of the Laestrygonians (lĕs'trĭ-gō'nē-ənz), a race of cannibals, all the ships but one are destroyed and their crews devoured. Odysseus' own ship escapes and proceeds to the island of Aeaea, where the goddess Circe transforms Odysseus' men into swine. After Circe releases his men from the spell, Odysseus spends a year with her. He longs however, to return to Ithaca. Odysseus sails to the land of the dead, where the ghost of the blind prophet Tiresias (tĭ-rē'sē-)s) tells him what he must do to reach home. Before setting sail for Ithaca, Odysseus returns briefly to Circe's island. She warns him of the dangers that lie ahead, and Odysseus tells his men what Circe has predicted.

Detail from *Ulysses at the Palace of Circe* (1667) by Willem Schubert van Ehrenberg. Oil on canvas. The painting shows Odysseus' men being transformed into animals.
The J. Paul Getty Museum

As Circe spoke, Dawn mounted her golden throne,
and on the first rays Circe left me, taking   510
her way like a great goddess up the island.
I made straight for the ship, roused up the men
to get aboard and cast off at the stern.
They scrambled to their places by the rowlocks
and all in line dipped oars in the gray sea.   515
But soon an offshore breeze blew to our liking—
a canvas-bellying breeze, a lusty shipmate
sent by the singing nymph with sunbright hair.°   518. **nymph . . . hair:** Circe.
So we made fast the braces, and we rested,
letting the wind and steersman work the ship.   520
The crew being now silent before me, I
addressed them, sore at heart:
                         'Dear friends,
more than one man, or two, should know those things
Circe foresaw for us and shared with me,
so let me tell her forecast: then we die   525
with our eyes open, if we are going to die,
or know what death we baffle if we can. Sirens
weaving a haunting song over the sea
we are to shun, she said, and their green shore
all sweet with clover; yet she urged that I   530
alone should listen to their song. Therefore
you are to tie me up, tight as a splint,
erect along the mast, lashed to the mast,
and if I shout and beg to be untied,
take more turns of the rope to muffle me.'   535

I rather dwelt on this part of the forecast,
while our good ship made time, bound outward down
the wind for the strange island of Sirens.
Then all at once the wind fell, and a calm
came over all the sea, as though some power   540
lulled the swell.
                  The crew were on their feet
briskly, to furl the sail, and stow it; then,
each in place, they poised the smooth oar blades
and sent the white foam scudding by. I carved
a massive cake of beeswax into bits   545
and rolled them in my hands until they softened—
no long task, for a burning heat came down   548. **Helios** (hē′lē-ŏs′): the sun
from Helios,° lord of high noon. Going forward   god.

Ulysses and his companions passing the island of the Sirens.
Roman mosaic, third century A.D.

I carried wax along the line, and laid it
thick on their ears. They tied me up, then, plumb   550
amidships, back to the mast, lashed to the mast,
and took themselves again to rowing. Soon,
as we came smartly within hailing distance,
the two Sirens, noting our fast ship
off their point, made ready, and they sang: 555

     'This way, oh turn your bows,
        Achaea's glory,
   As all the world allows—
       Moor and be merry.

   Sweet coupled airs we sing.   560
       No lonely seafarer
   Holds clear of entering
       Our green mirror.

Pleased by each purling note
    Like honey twining   565
From her throat and my throat,
    Who lies a-pining?

Sea rovers here take joy
    Voyaging onward,
As from our song of Troy   570
Graybeard and rower-boy
    Goeth more learnèd.

All feats on that great field
    In the long warfare,
Dark days the bright gods willed,   575
    Wounds you bore there,

Argos' old soldiery°
    On Troy beach teeming,
Charmed out of time we see.
No life on earth can be   580
    Hid from our dreaming.'

The lovely voices in ardor appealing over the water
made me crave to listen, and I tried to say
'Untie me!' to the crew, jerking my brows;
but they bent steady to the oars. Then Perimedes°   585
got to his feet, he and Eurylochus,°
and passed more line about, to hold me still.
So all rowed on, until the Sirens
dropped under the sea rim, and their singing
dwindled away.
        My faithful company   590
rested on their oars now, peeling off
the wax that I had laid thick on their ears;
then set me free.

577. Argos' old soldiery: the soldiers from Argos, a city in ancient Greece, who fought in the Trojan War.

585. Perimedes(pĕr′ə-mē′dēz).

586. Eurylochus(yo͞o-rĭl′ə-kəs).

Scylla and Charybdis

*Circe has warned Odysseus of another sea peril. He and his crew must pass be-
tween Scylla (sĭl'ə) and Charybdis (kə-rĭb'dĭs). Scylla is a terrifying monster
with six heads. She dwells in a high rocky cave, devouring sailors in ships that
pass close by. Charybdis is a whirlpool. Three times a day she swallows the sea,
then vomits it up fiery hot. Circe has advised Odysseus to sail toward Scylla's
crag, for it is better to lose six of his men—one to each of her heads—than for
all to perish in the whirlpool.*

But scarcely had that island
faded in blue air than I saw smoke
and white water, with sound of waves in tumult—   595
a sound the men heard, and it terrified them.
Oars flew from their hands; the blades went knocking
wild alongside till the ship lost way,
with no oarblades to drive her through the water.

Well, I walked up and down from bow to stern,   600
trying to put heart into them, standing over
every oarsman, saying gently,
                                'Friends,
have we never been in danger before this?
More fearsome is it now, than when the Cyclops
penned us in his cave? What power he had!   605
Did I not keep my nerve, and use my wits
to find a way out for us?
                                Now I say
by hook or crook this peril too shall be
something that we remember.
                                Heads up, lads!
We must obey the orders as I give them,   610
Get the oarshafts in your hands, and lay back
hard on your benches; hit these breaking seas.
Zeus help us pull away before we founder.
You at the tiller, listen, and take in
all that I say—the rudders are your duty;   615
keep her out of the combers and the smoke;
steer for that headland; watch the drift, or we
fetch up in the smother, and you drown us.'

That was all, and it brought them round to action.
But as I sent them on toward Scylla, I   620

The Monster Scylla. Ceramic vase, early Hellenistic ̶ ̶ ̶ ̶, third century B.C
Museum of Fine Arts, Boston, H. L. Pierce Fund

told them nothing, as they could do nothing.
They would have dropped their oars again, in panic,
to roll for cover under the decking. Circe's
bidding against arms had slipped my mind,
so I tied on my cuirass° and took up   625   625. **cuirass** (kwĭ-răs′): armor
two heavy spears, then made my way along   for the chest and back.
to the foredeck—thinking to see her first from there,
the monster of the gray rock, harboring
torment for my friends. I strained my eyes
upon that cliffside veiled in cloud, but nowhere   630
could I catch sight of her.
               And all this time,
in travail, sobbing, gaining on the current,
we rowed into the strait—Scylla to port
and on our starboard beam Charybdis, dire
gorge° of the salt-sea tide. By heaven! when she   635   635. **gorge:** devouring mouth.
vomited, all the sea was like a caldron
seething over intense fire, when the mixture
suddenly heaves and rises.
               The shot spume
soared to the landside heights, and fell like rain.

But when she swallowed the sea water down   640
we saw the funnel of the maelstrom,° heard   641. **maelstrom**   (māl′strəm):
the rock bellowing all around, and dark   violent whirlpool.
sand raged on the bottom far below.
My men all blanched against the gloom, our eyes
were fixed upon that yawning mouth in fear   645
of being devoured.
             Then Scylla made her strike,
whisking six of my best men from the ship.
I happened to glance aft at ship and oarsmen
and caught sight of their arms and legs, dangling
high overhead. Voices came down to me   650
in anguish, calling my name for the last time.

A man surf-casting on a point of rock
for bass or mackerel, whipping his long rod
to drop the sinker and the bait far out,
will hook a fish and rip it from the surface   655
to dangle wriggling through the air:
                     so these
were borne aloft in spasms toward the cliff.

She ate them as they shrieked there, in her den,
in the dire grapple, reaching still for me—
and deathly pity ran me through   660
at that sight—far the worst I ever suffered,
questing the passes of the strange sea.
                                    We rowed on.
The Rocks were now behind; Charybdis, too,
and Scylla dropped astern. . . .

The Cattle of the Sun God

*Odysseus urges his exhausted crew to bypass Thrinacia (thrĭn-ā'sh‚), the island
of the sun god. The men, however, insist on landing. Odysseus makes them
swear not to touch the god's cattle, for both Circe and Tiresias have warned him
of disaster if the cattle are harmed.*

In the small hours of the third watch, when stars   665
that shone out in the first dusk of evening
had gone down to their setting, a giant wind
blew from heaven, and clouds driven by Zeus
shrouded land and sea in a night of storm;
so, just as Dawn with fingertips of rose   670
touched the windy world, we dragged our ship
to cover in a grotto, a sea cave
where nymphs had chairs of rock and sanded floors.
I mustered all the crew and said:
                                    'Old shipmates,
our stores are in the ship's hold, food and drink;   675
the cattle here are not for our provision,
or we pay dearly for it.
                        Fierce the god is
who cherishes these heifers and these sheep:
Helios; and no man avoids his eye.'

To this my fighters nodded. Yes. But now   680
we had a month of onshore gales, blowing
day in, day out—south winds, or south by east.
As long as bread and good red wine remained
to keep the men up, and appease their craving,
they would not touch the cattle. But in the end,   685
when all the barley in the ship was gone,
hunger drove them to scour the wild shore

with angling hooks, for fishes and seafowl,
whatever fell into their hands; and lean days
wore their bellies thin.

     The storms continued   690
So one day I withdrew to the interior
to pray the gods in solitude, for hope
that one might show me some way of salvation.
Slipping away, I struck across the island
to a sheltered spot, out of the driving gale.   695
I washed my hands there, and made supplication
to the gods who own Olympus,° all the gods—
but they, for answer, only closed my eyes
under slow drops of sleep.

     Now on the shore Eurylochus
made his insidious plea:

     'Comrades,' he said,   700
'You've gone through everything; listen to what I say.
All deaths are hateful to us, mortal wretches,
but famine is the most pitiful, the worst
end that a man can come to.

     Will you fight it?
Come, we'll cut out the noblest of these cattle 705
for sacrifice to the gods who own the sky;
and once at home, in the old country of Ithaca,
if ever that day comes—
we'll build a costly temple and adorn it
with every beauty for the Lord of Noon.°   710
But if he flares up over his heifers lost,
wishing our ship destroyed, and if the gods
make cause with him, why, then I say: Better
open your lungs to a big sea once for all
than waste to skin and bones on a lonely island!' 715

Thus Eurylochus; and they murmured 'Aye!'
trooping away at once to round up heifers.
Now, that day tranquil cattle with broad brows
were grazing near, and soon the men drew up
around their chosen beasts in ceremony.   720
They plucked the leaves that shone on a tall oak—
having no barley meal—to strew the victims,
performed the prayers and ritual, knifed the kine°
and flayed each carcass, cutting thighbones free
to wrap in double folds of fat. These offerings, 725

697. Olympus (ō-lĭm′pəs): Mount Olympus, believed to be the home of the gods.

710. Lord of Noon: Helios.

723. kine: cattle.

Companions of Ulysses Slaying the Cattle of the Sun. Sixteenth-century
mural by Tibaldi.
Academy of Science, Bologna, Italy

with strips of meat, were laid upon the fire.
Then, as they had no wine, they made libation°
with clear spring water, broiling the entrails first;
and when the bones were burnt and tripes shared,
they spitted the carved meat.

                     Just then my slumber   730
left me in a rush, my eyes opened,
and I went down the seaward path. No sooner
had I caught sight of our black hull, than savory
odors of burnt fat eddied around me;
grief took hold of me, and I cried aloud: 735

727. **libation:** ritual pouring of
wine or other liquid.

'O Father Zeus and gods in bliss forever,
you made me sleep away this day of mischief!
O cruel drowsing, in the evil hour!
Here they sat, and a great work they contrived.'

Lampetia° in her long gown meanwhile
had borne swift word to the Overlord of Noon:

'They have killed your kine.'
                          And the Lord Helios
burst in angry speech amid the immortals:

'O Father Zeus and gods in bliss forever,
punish Odysseus' men! So overweening,
now they have killed my peaceful kine, my joy
at morning when I climbed the sky of stars,
and evening, when I bore westward from heaven.
Restitution or penalty they shall pay—
and pay in full—or I go down forever
to light the dead men in the underworld.'

Then Zeus who drives the stormcloud made reply:

'Peace, Helios: shine on among the gods,
shine over mortals in the fields of grain.
Let me throw down one white-hot bolt, and make
splinters of their ship in the winedark sea.'

—Calypso later told me of this exchange,
as she declared that Hermes° had told her.
Well, when I reached the sea cave and the ship,
I faced each man, and had it out; but where
could any remedy be found? There was none.
The silken beeves of Helios were dead.
The gods, moreover, made queer signs appear:
cowhides began to crawl, and beef, both raw
and roasted, lowed like kine upon the spits.

Now six full days my gallant crew could feast
upon the prime beef they had marked for slaughter
from Helios' herd; and Zeus, the son of Cronus,
added one fine morning.
                          All the gales

740

745

750

755

760

765

740. **Lampetia** (lămp-pē′shə):
a nymph.

758. **Hermes** (hûr′mēz′): the
messenger of the gods.

had ceased, blown out, and with an offshore breeze   770
we launched again, stepping the mast and sail,
to make for the open sea. Astern of us
the island coastline faded, and no land
showed anywhere, but only sea and heaven,
when Zeus Cronion piled a thunderhead   775
above the ship, while gloom spread on the ocean.
We held our course, but briefly. Then the squall
struck whining from the west, with gale force, breaking
both forestays, and the mast came toppling aft
along the ship's length, so the running rigging   780
showered into the bilge.
                    On the afterdeck
the mast had hit the steersman a slant blow
bashing the skull in, knocking him overside,
as the brave soul fled the body, like a diver.
With crack on crack of thunder, Zeus let fly   785
a bolt against the ship, a direct hit,
so that she bucked, in reeking fumes of sulfur,
and all the men were flung into the sea.
They came up round the wreck, bobbing awhile
like petrels° on the waves.

790. **petrels** (pĕt′rəlz): small sea birds.

                    No more seafaring   790
homeward for these, no sweet day of return;
the god had turned his face from them.
                              I clambered
fore and aft my hulk until a comber
split her, keel from ribs, and the big timber
floated free; the mast, too, broke away.   795
A backstay floated dangling from it, stout
rawhide rope, and I used this for lashing
mast and keel together. These I straddled,
riding the frightful storm.
                    Nor had I yet
seen the worst of it: for now the west wind   800
dropped, and a southeast gale came on—one more
twist of the knife—taking me north again,
straight for Charybdis. All that night I drifted,
and in the sunrise, sure enough, I lay
off Scylla mountain and Charybdis deep.   805
There, as the whirlpool drank the tide, a billow
tossed me, and I sprang for the great fig tree,
catching on like a bat under a bough.

Nowhere had I to stand, no way of climbing,
the root and bole° being far below, and far   810   810. **bole:** tree trunk.
above my head the branches and their leaves,
massed, overshadowing Charybdis pool.
But I clung grimly, thinking my mast and keel
would come back to the surface when she spouted.
And ah! how long, with what desire, I waited!   815
till, at the twilight hour, when one who hears
and judges pleas in the marketplace all day
between contentious men, goes home to supper,
the long poles at last reared from the sea.

Now I let go with hands and feet, plunging   820
straight into the foam beside the timbers,
pulled astride, and rowed hard with my hands
to pass by Scylla. Never could I have passed her
had not the Father of gods and men,° this time,   824. **Father of gods and men:**
kept me from her eyes. Once through the strait,   825   Zeus.
nine days I drifted in the open sea
before I made shore, buoyed up by the gods
upon Ogygia° Isle The dangerous nymph   828. **Ogygia** (ō-jĭj′ē-ə).
Calypso lives and sings there, in her beauty,
and she received me, loved me.
                              But why tell   830
the same tale that I told last night in hall
to you and to your lady? Those adventures
made a long evening, and I do not hold
with tiresome repetition of a story."

Reading Check

1. How does Odysseus keep his men from hearing the voices of the Sirens?
2. Identify Scylla and Charybdis.
3. Why do the men disobey Odysseus on the island of the sun god?
4. What offerings are made to the gods?
5. Where does Odysseus come ashore after drifting in the sea for nine days?

For Study and Discussion

Analyzing and Interpreting the Epic

1. How do the Sirens tempt Odysseus?

2. Faced with a choice between Scylla and Charybdis, Odysseus chooses Scylla. He knows that six of his men will die, yet he withholds this information from his crew. Is this a strength or weakness in his character? Explain.

3. Consider each of the episodes you have read so far. **a.** How well does Odysseus control his men in each episode? **b.** How effective and responsible is he as a leader? Cite specific lines to support your answer.

4. Before Odysseus' men feast on the cattle of the sun god, they perform a ritual of sacrifice. **a.** Why does the ritual fail to please the gods? **b.** How are the men punished?

5. How is Odysseus aided by Zeus?

Language and Vocabulary

Learning Words from the Epic

A number of words from the *Odyssey* have become part of our language. The word *odyssey,* for example, is used for any extended journey.

The Cyclopes are the origin for the word *Cyclopean.* What can you infer about the meaning of this word?

Circe is the enchantress who changes Odysseus' men into beasts. What do you think the word *Circean* means?

In his famous speech in the Virginia Convention, Patrick Henry warns Americans not to listen to the "song of that siren." Locate the speech and find out what he means.

Odysseus has to steer a course between two dangers, Scylla and Charybdis. What do you think the expression "to pass between Scylla and Charybdis" has come to mean?

Check your answers in a dictionary.

Focus on Personal Narrative

Thinking About Purpose and Audience

In a personal narrative, your **purpose** is to express yourself. You should include details to suggest your own thoughts and feelings about the experience you describe. As you plan a personal narrative, also give some thought to your **audience.** Ask yourself what your readers will need to know about your topic. If your audience did not witness the experience, for example, they will almost certainly need some background information.

Develop the topic for a personal narrative chosen earlier in this unit (see page 616) or select a new topic. Focus on your audience by filling out a chart like the one below.

```
Audience: _____
Age: _____
Interests: _____
Special Needs: _____
Familiarity with Topic: _____
_____
```

Father and Son

After hearing the story of Odysseus' wanderings, the king of Phaeacia offers him a boat and crew to take him home to Ithaca. Thus Odysseus returns to his own land after an absence of twenty years.

The goddess Athena appears to Odysseus and tells him to proceed cautiously. Believing that he is dead, many suitors have besieged his palace, eager to marry his beautiful wife, Penelope. Penelope does not believe that Odysseus is dead, but she is unable to make the suitors leave. They remain in Ithaca, eating and drinking at her expense. They are even plotting to murder her son, Telemachus (tə-lĕm'ə-kəs), before he is old enough to inherit his father's lands. Telemachus, who hopes for his father's return, has gone to Sparta to ask for news of him.

Athena disguises Odysseus as a ragged old beggar and sends him to the hut of Eumaeus (yōo-mē'əs), an old and loyal swineherd. She then directs Telemachus to return to Ithaca and tells Odysseus that it is time to reveal his identity to his son.

Head of Greek warrior (detail). Bronze, c. fifth century B.C.
Museum of Archaeology, Calabria, Italy

    . . . From the air   835
she walked, taking the form of a tall woman,
handsome and clever at her craft, and stood
beyond the gate in plain sight of Odysseus,
unseen, though, by Telemachus, unguessed,
for not to everyone will gods appear.   840
Odysseus noticed her; so did the dogs,
who cowered whimpering away from her. She only
nodded, signing to him with her brows,
a sign he recognized. Crossing the yard,
he passed out through the gate in the stockade   845
to face the goddess. There she said to him·

"Son of Laertes and the gods of old,
Odysseus, master of landways and seaways,
dissemble to your son no longer now.
The time has come: tell him how you together   850
will bring doom on the suitors in the town.
I shall not be far distant then, for I
myself desire battle."
      Saying no more,
she tipped her golden wand upon the man,
making his cloak pure white, and the knit tunic   855
fresh around him. Lithe and young she made him,
ruddy with sun, his jawline clean, the beard
no longer gray upon his chin. And she
withdrew when she had done.
       Then Lord Odysseus
reappeared—and his son was thunderstruck.   860
Fear in his eyes, he looked down and away
as though it were a god, and whispered:
          "Stranger,
you are no longer what you were just now!
Your cloak is new; even your skin! You are
one of the gods who rule the sweep of heaven!   865
Be kind to us, we'll make you fair oblation°
and gifts of hammered gold. Have mercy on us!"

The noble and enduring man replied:

"No god. Why take me for a god? No, no.
I am that father whom your boyhood lacked   870
and suffered pain for lack of. I am he."

866. **oblation:** an offering to a god.

Held back too long, the tears ran down his cheeks
as he embraced his son.
                              Only Telemachus,
uncomprehending, wild
with incredulity, cried out:
                              "You cannot   875
be my father Odysseus! Meddling spirits
conceived this trick to twist the knife in me!
No man of woman born could work these wonders
by his own craft, unless a god came into it
with ease to turn him young or old at will.   880
I swear you were in rags and old,
and here you stand like one of the immortals!"

Odysseus brought his ranging mind to bear
and said:
          "This is not princely, to be swept
away by wonder at your father's presence.   885
No other Odysseus will ever come,
for he and I are one, the same; his bitter
fortune and his wanderings are mine.
Twenty years gone, and I am back again
on my own island.
                    As for my change of skin,   890
that is a charm Athena, Hope of Soldiers,
uses as she will; she has the knack
to make me seem a beggar man sometimes
and sometimes young, with finer clothes about me.
It is no hard thing for the gods of heaven   895
to glorify a man or bring him low."

When he had spoken, down he sat.
                              Then, throwing
his arms around this marvel of a father
Telemachus began to weep. Salt tears
rose from the wells of longing in both men,   900
and cries burst from both as keen and fluttering
as those of the great taloned hawk,
whose nestlings farmers take before they fly.
So helplessly they cried, pouring out tears,
and might have gone on weeping so till sundown,   905
had not Telemachus said:
                              "Dear father! Tell me

what kind of vessel put you here ashore
on Ithaca? Your sailors, who were they?
I doubt you made it, walking on the sea!"

Then said Odysseus, who had borne the barren sea: 910

"Only plain truth shall I tell you, child.
Great seafarers, the Phaeacians, gave me passage
as they give other wanderers. By night
over the open ocean, while I slept,
they brought me in their cutter, set me down   915
on Ithaca, with gifts of bronze and gold
and stores of woven things. By the gods' will
these lie all hidden in a cave. I came
to this wild place, directed by Athena,
so that we might lay plans to kill our enemies.   920
Count up the suitors for me, let me know
what men at arms are there, how many men.
I must put all my mind to it, to see
if we two by ourselves can take them on
or if we should look round for help."

                    Telemachus   925
replied:
        "O, Father, all my life your fame
as a fighting man has echoed in my ears—
your skill with weapons and the tricks of war—
but what you speak of is a staggering thing,
beyond imagining, for me. How can two men   930
do battle with a houseful in their prime?
For I must tell you this is no affair
of ten or even twice ten men, but scores,
throngs of them. You shall see, here and now.
The number from Dulichium alone   935
is fifty-two, picked men, with armorers,
a half-dozen; twenty-four came from Same,°   937. **Same** (sā′mē).
twenty from Zacynthus; our own island
accounts for twelve, high-ranked, and their retainers,
Medon° the crier, and the Master Harper,   940   940. **Medon** (mē′dŏn).
besides a pair of handymen at feasts.
If we go in against all these
I fear we pay in salt blood for your vengeance.
You must think hard if you would conjure up
the fighting strength to take us through."

who had endured the long war and the sea
answered:
          "I'll tell you now.
Suppose Athena's arm is over us, and Zeus
her father's, must I rack my brains for more?"

Clearheaded Telemachus looked hard and said: 950

"Those two are great defenders, no one doubts it,
but throned in the serene clouds overhead;
other affairs of men and gods they have
to rule over."
          And the hero answered:
"Before long they will stand to right and left of us   955
in combat, in the shouting, when the test comes—
our nerve against the suitors' in my hall.
Here is your part: At break of day tomorrow
home with you, go mingle with our princes.
The swineherd later on will take me down   960
the port-side trail—a beggar, by my looks,
hangdog and old. If they make fun of me
in my own courtyard, let your ribs cage up
your springing heart, no matter what I suffer,
no matter if they pull me by the heels   965
or practice shots at me, to drive me out.
Look on, hold down your anger. You may even
plead with them, by heaven! in gentle terms
to quit their horseplay—not that they will heed you,
rash as they are, facing their day of wrath.   970
Now fix the next step in your mind.
          Athena,
counseling me, will give me word, and I
shall signal to you, nodding: at that point
round up all armor, lances, gear of war
left in our hall, and stow the lot away   975
back in the vaulted storeroom. When the suitors
miss those arms and question you, be soft
in what you say—answer:
                    'I thought I'd move them
out of the smoke. They seemed no longer those
bright arms Odysseus left us years ago   980
when he went off to Troy. Here where the fire's

hot breath came, they had grown black and drear.
One better reason, too, I had from Zeus:
Suppose a brawl starts up when you are drunk,
you might be crazed and bloody one another,   985
and that would stain your feast, your courtship. Tempered
iron can magnetize a man.'
                Say that.
But put aside two broadswords and two spears
for our own use, two oxhide shields nearby
when we go into action. Pallas Athena   990
and Zeus All-Provident will see you through,
bemusing our young friends.
                Now one thing more.
If son of mine you are and blood of mine,
let no one hear Odysseus is about.
Neither Laertes, nor the swineherd here,   995
nor any slave, nor even Penelope.
But you and I alone must learn how far
the women are corrupted; we should know
how to locate good men among our hands,
the loyal and respectful, and the shirkers   1000
who take you lightly, as alone and young."

Reading Check

1. How does Athena transform Odysseus?
2. What trick does Telemachus suspect?
3. Which two Olympians does Odysseus depend on to help him fight the suitors?
4. What disguise will Odysseus assume when he comes to the palace?
5. What weapons does Odysseus ask his son to put aside?

For Study and Discussion

Analyzing and Interpreting the Epic

1a. What makes Telemachus think that Odysseus must be a god? **b.** How does Odysseus convince Telemachus that he is his father?

2. Telemachus warns Odysseus that there are far too many suitors for the two of them to fight. How does Odysseus persuade Telemachus that they can win?

3. Odysseus outlines his plan in lines 958–990. What is Telemachus' part in the plan?

4. Why does Odysseus want to keep his return a secret?

Argos

The next day Odysseus appears at the manor disguised as a beggar. He is ac-companied by the swineherd Eumaeus, to whom he has been confiding his plans.

          While he spoke
an old hound, lying near, pricked up his ears
and lifted up his muzzle. This was Argos,
trained as a puppy by Odysseus,   1005
but never taken on a hunt before
his master sailed for Troy. The young men, afterward,
hunted wild goats with him, and hare, and deer,
but he had grown old in his master's absence.
Treated as rubbish now, he lay at last   1010
upon a mass of dung before the gates—
manure of mules and cows, piled there until
fieldhands could spread it on the king's estate.
Abandoned there, and half destroyed with flies,
old Argos lay.   But when he knew he heard   1015
Odysseus' voice nearby, he did his best
to wag his tail, nose down, with flattened ears,
having no strength to move nearer his master.
And the man looked away,
wiping a salt tear from his cheek, but he   1020
hid this from Eumaeus. Then he said:

"I marvel that they leave this hound to lie
here on the dung pile;
he would have been a fine dog, from the look of him,
though I can't say as to his power and speed   1025
when he was young. You find the same good build
in house dogs, table dogs landowners keep
all for style."

         And you replied, Eumaeus:
"A hunter owned him—but the man is dead
in some far place. If this old hound could show   1030
the form he had when Lord Odysseus left him,
going to Troy, you'd see him swift and strong.
He never shrank from any savage thing
he'd brought to bay in the deep woods; on the scent

no other dog kept up with him. Now misery   1035
has him in leash. His owner died abroad,
and here the women slaves will take no care of him.
You know how servants are: without a master
they have no will to labor, or excel.
For Zeus who views the wide world takes away   1040
half the manhood of a man, that day
he goes into captivity and slavery."

Eumaeus crossed the court and went straight forward
into the mégaron° among the suitors;
but death and darkness in that instant closed   1045
the eyes of Argos, who had seen his master,
Odysseus, after twenty years.

The Suitors

*Odysseus enters the hall of his home and passes among the suitors to beg. Antin-
ous (ăn-tĭn'ō-əs), the most arrogant and outspoken of the suitors, breaks into a
rage.*

But here Antinous broke in, shouting:
                              "God!
What evil wind blew in this pest?
                         Get over,
stand in the passage! Nudge my table, will you?   1050
Egyptian whips are sweet
to what you'll come to here, you nosing rat,
making your pitch to everyone!
These men have bread to throw away on you
because it is not theirs. Who cares? Who spares   1055
another's food, when he has more than plenty?"

With guile Odysseus drew away, then said:

"A pity that you have more looks than heart.
You'd grudge a pinch of salt from your own larder
to your own handyman. You sit here, fat   1060
on others' meat, and cannot bring yourself
to rummage out a crust of bread for me!"

Then anger made Antinous' heart beat hard,

and, glowering under his brows, he answered:

                                            "Now!
You think you'll shuffle off and get away   1065
after that impudence? Oh, no you don't!"

The stool he let fly hit the man's right shoulder
on the packed muscle under the shoulder blade—
like solid rock, for all the effect one saw.
Odysseus only shook his head, containing   1070
thoughts of bloody work, as he walked on,
then sat, and dropped his loaded bag again
upon the doorsill. Facing the whole crowd
he said, and eyed them all:
                          "One word only,
my lords, and suitors of the famous queen.   1075
One thing I have to say.
There is no pain, no burden for the heart
when blows come to a man, and he defending
his own cattle—his own cows and lambs.
Here it was otherwise. Antinous   1080
hit me for being driven on by hunger—
how many bitter seas men cross for hunger!
If beggars interest the gods, if there are Furies°
pent in the dark to avenge a poor man's wrong, then may
Antinous meet his death before his wedding day!"   1085

Then said Eupeithes'° son, Antinous:
                          "Enough.
Eat and be quiet where you are, or shamble elsewhere,
unless you want these lads to stop your mouth
pulling you by the heels, or hands and feet,
over the whole floor, till your back is peeled!"   1090

But now the rest were mortified, and someone
spoke from the crowd of young bucks to rebuke him:

"A poor show, that—hitting this famished tramp—
bad business, if he happened to be a god.
You know they go in foreign guise, the gods do,   1095
looking like strangers, turning up
in towns and settlements to keep an eye
on manners, good or bad."
                      But at this notion

1083. Furies: three goddesses who punished those crimes that went unavenged.

1086. Eupeithes (yōō-pī′thēz).

Antinous only shrugged.

               Telemachus,
after the blow his father bore, sat still   1100
without a tear, though his heart felt the blow.
Slowly he shook his head from side to side,
containing murderous thoughts.

               Penelope
on the higher level of her room had heard
the blow, and knew who gave it. Now she murmured: 1105

"Would god you could be hit yourself, Antinous—
hit by Apollo's bowshot!"

               And Eurynome,°
her housekeeper, put in:

               "He and no other?
If all we pray for came to pass, not one
would live till dawn!"

               Her gentle mistress said: 1110

"Oh, Nan, they are a bad lot; they intend
ruin for all of us; but Antinous
appears a blacker-hearted hound than any.
Here is a poor man come, a wanderer,
driven by want to beg his bread, and everyone   1115
in hall gave bits, to cram his bag—only
Antinous threw a stool, and banged his shoulder!"

So she described it, sitting in her chamber
among her maids—while her true lord was eating.
Then she called in the forester and said: 1120

"Go to that man on my behalf, Eumaeus,
and send him here, so I can greet and question him.
Abroad in the great world, he may have heard
rumors about Odysseus—may have known him!"

1107. **Eurynome** (yōō-rĭn′ə-mē).

Penelope

*Later that night Penelope meets secretly with the old beggar. She asks him if he
has heard any news of her husband.*

"Friend, let me ask you first of all: 1125
who are you, where do you come from, of what nation
and parents were you born?"
      And he replied:

"My lady, never a man in the wide world
should have a fault to find with you. Your name
has gone out under heaven like the sweet   1130
honor of some god-fearing king, who rules
in equity over the strong: his black lands bear
both wheat and barley, fruit trees laden bright,
new lambs at lambing time—and the deep sea
gives great hauls of fish by his good strategy,   1135
so that his folk fare well.
      O my dear lady,
this being so, let it suffice to ask me
of other matters—not my blood, my homeland.
Do not enforce me to recall my pain.
My heart is sore; but I must not be found   1140
sitting in tears here, in another's house:
it is not well forever to be grieving.
One of the maids might say—or you might think—
I had got maudlin over cups of wine."

And Penelope replied:
      "Stranger, my looks,   1145
my face, my carriage, were soon lost or faded
when the Achaeans crossed the sea to Troy,
Odysseus my lord among the rest.
If he returned, if he were here to care for me,
I might be happily renowned!   1150
But grief instead heaven sent me—years of pain.
Sons of the noblest families on the islands,
Dulichium, Same, wooded Zacynthus,
with native Ithacans, are here to court me,
against my wish; and they consume this house.   1155
Can I give proper heed to guest or suppliant
or herald on the realm's affairs?

Penelope Seated. Roman copy of Greek original. Stone, c. first century A.D.

Museo Pio Clementino, Vatican Museums

How could I?

wasted with longing for Odysseus, while here
they press for marriage.

Ruses served my turn

to draw the time out—first a close-grained web 1160
I had the happy thought to set up weaving
on my big loom in hall. I said, that day:
'Young men—my suitors, now my lord is dead,
let me finish my weaving before I marry,
or else my thread will have been spun in vain. 1165
It is a shroud I weave for Lord Laertes
when cold Death comes to lay him on his bier.
The country wives would hold me in dishonor
if he, with all his fortune, lay unshrouded.'
I reached their hearts that way, and they agreed. 1170
So every day I wove on the great loom,
but every night by torchlight I unwove it;
and so for three years I deceived the Achaeans.
But when the seasons brought a fourth year on,
as long months waned, and the long days were spent, 1175
through imprudent folly in the slinking maids
they caught me—clamored up to me at night;
I had no choice then but to finish it.
And now, as matters stand at last,
I have no strength left to evade a marriage, 1180
cannot find any further way; my parents
urge it upon me, and my son
will not stand by while they eat up his property.
He comprehends it, being a man full-grown,
able to oversee the kind of house 1185
Zeus would endow with honor.

But you too

confide in me, tell me your ancestry.
Your were not born of mythic oak or stone."

The beggar invents a tale of how he had seen Odysseus twenty years ago in
Crete, when Odysseus was bound for Troy. He convinces Penelope that the story
is true by describing Odysseus' clothes in detail. Then he tells her he has heard
that Odysseus is about to set sail for Ithaca.

"You see, then, he is alive and well, and headed
homeward now, no more to be abroad 1190
far from his island, his dear wife and son.

Here is my sworn word for it. Witness this,
god of the zenith,° noblest of the gods,
and Lord Odysseus' hearthfire, now before me:
I swear these things shall turn out as I say.
Between this present dark and one day's ebb,
after the wane, before the crescent moon,
Odysseus will come."

1193. **god of the zenith:** Zeus.

1195

Reading Check

1. How does Argos recognize Odysseus?
2. Why does Antinous strike Odysseus?
3. Why does Penelope send for the beggar?
4. What does the beggar predict will happen?

For Study and Discussion

Analyzing and Interpreting the Epic

1. Odysseus' encounter with his dog Argos is one of the most moving episodes in the *Odyssey*. **a.** Which details are particularly effective in arousing your sympathy for the animal? **b.** What truths about people and life in general are suggested by the story of Argos?

2. A number of years have passed since Odysseus' adventure with the Cyclops. How has Odysseus changed?

3. Penelope represents characteristics that the Greeks admired in women. **a.** What qualities does she reveal about herself in her discussion with her housekeeper (lines 1111–1117)? **b.** In her interview with the beggar? **c.** How was Penelope able to trick the suitors for three years? **d.** What does this ruse show about her?

4. The scene in which Penelope meets her husband Odysseus disguised as a beggar is an example of **dramatic irony,** for the reader knows something that Penelope does not know. Why do you think Odysseus keeps his identity a secret from his wife?

Focus on Personal Narrative

Gathering Details

Traditional singers of oral epic poetry like Homer had remarkable memories for detail. Because we depend so much on writing in modern times, we often have to jog our memories. For a personal narrative about an experience, you must try to remember **details** from your past. Here are some helpful techniques:

> freewriting
> brainstorming
> interviewing others who shared or witnessed
>   the experience
> visualizing

Fill in a chart like the one below to gather as many specific details as you can for a personal narrative. Save your notes.

Topic of Narrative: _____
Events: _____
People: _____
Places: _____
Thoughts / Feelings: _____

The Challenge

The suitors summon Penelope to the hall and demand that she choose one of them at once. Penelope announces a challenge: she will marry whoever can string Odysseus' great bow and shoot an arrow through a row of twelve ax-handle sockets, as Odysseus used to do. One by one the suitors try but fail to even bend the bow. The old beggar then asks for a turn. The suitors protest until both Penelope and Telemachus insist that he be given the bow.

. . . And Odysseus took his time,
turning the bow, tapping it, every inch,   1200
for borings that termites might have made
while the master of the weapon was abroad.
The suitors were now watching him, and some
jested among themselves:
        "A bow lover!"

"Dealer in old bows!"
        "Maybe he has one like it   1205
at home!"
      "Or has an itch to make one for himself."

"See how he handles it, the sly old buzzard!"

And one disdainful suitor added this:

"May his fortune grow an inch for every inch he bends it!"

But the man skilled in all ways of contending,   1210
satisfied by the great bow's look and heft,
like a musician, like a harper, when
with quiet hand upon his instrument
he draws between his thumb and forefinger
a sweet new string upon a peg: so effortlessly   1215
Odysseus in one motion strung the bow.
Then slid his right hand down the cord and plucked it,
so the taut gut vibrating hummed and sang
a swallow's note.
        In the hushed hall it smote the suitors
and all their faces changed. Then Zeus thundered   1220
overhead, one loud crack for a sign.
And Odysseus laughed within him that the son
of crooked-minded Cronus had flung that omen down.

He picked one ready arrow from his table
where it lay bare: the rest were waiting still   1225
in the quiver for the young men's turn to come.
He nocked° it, let it rest across the handgrip,
and drew the string and grooved butt of the arrow,
aiming from where he sat upon the stool.

1227. **nocked:** placed an arrow against the string of the bow.

                               Now flashed
arrow from twanging bow clean as a whistle   1230
through every socket ring, and grazed not one,
to thud with heavy brazen head beyond.
                             Then quietly
Odysseus said.
                  "Telemachus, the stranger
you welcomed in your hall has not disgraced you.
I did not miss, neither did I take all day   1235
stringing the bow. My hand and eye are sound,
not so contemptible as the young men say.
The hour has come to cook their lordships' mutton—
supper by daylight. Other amusements later,
with song and harping that adorn a feast."   1240

He dropped his eyes and nodded, and the prince
Telemachus, true son of King Odysseus,
belted his sword on, clapped hand to his spear,
and with a clink and glitter of keen bronze
stood by his chair, in the forefront near his father.   1245

Odysseus' Revenge

Now shrugging off his rags the wiliest fighter of the islands
leapt and stood on the broad doorsill, his own bow in his hand.
He poured out at his feet a rain of arrows from the quiver
and spoke to the crowd:
        "So much for that. Your clean-cut game is over.
Now watch me hit a target that no man has hit before,   1250
if I can make this shot. Help me, Apollo."

He drew to his fist the cruel head of an arrow for Antinoüs
just as the young man leaned to lift his beautiful drinking
      cup,
embossed, two-handled, golden: the cup was in his fingers:
the wine was even at his lips: and did he dream of death?   1255

How could he? In that revelry amid his throng of friends
who would imagine a single foe—though a strong foe indeed—
could dare to bring death's pain on him and darkness on his
    eyes?
Odysseus' arrow hit him under the chin
and punched up to the feathers through his throat.   1260

Backward and down he went, letting the winecup fall
from his shocked hand. Like pipes his nostrils jetted
crimson runnels, a river of mortal red,
and one last kick upset his table
knocking the bread and meat to soak in dusty blood.   1265
Now as they craned to see their champion where he lay
the suitors jostled in uproar down the hall,
everyone on his feet. Wildly they turned and scanned
the walls in the long room for arms; but not a shield,
not a good ashen spear was there for a man to take and
    throw.   1270
All they could do was yell in outrage at Odysseus:

"Foul! to shoot at a man! That was your last shot!"
"Your own throat will be slit for this!"
                            "Our finest lad is down!
You killed the best on Ithaca."
                        "Buzzards will tear your eyes out!"

For they imagined as they wished—that it was a wild shot,   1275
an unintended killing—fools, not to comprehend
they were already in the grip of death.
But glaring under his brows Odysseus answered:

"You yellow dogs, you thought I'd never make it
home from the land of Troy. You took my house to plunder.   1280

                ... You dared
bid for my wife while I was still alive.
Contempt was all you had for the gods who rule wide heaven,
contempt for what men say of you hereafter.
Your last hour has come. You die in blood."   1285

As they all took this in, sickly green fear
pulled at their entrails, and their eyes flickered
looking for some hatch or hideaway from death.

Eurymachus° alone could speak. He said:

1289. **Eurymachus** (yōō-rĭ′mə-kəs).

"If you are Odysseus of Ithaca come back,   1290
all that you say these men have done is true.
Rash actions, many here, more in the countryside.
But here he lies, the man who caused them all.
Antinous was the ringleader, he whipped us on
to do these things. He cared less for a marriage   1295
than for the power Cronion has denied him
as king of Ithaca. For that
he tried to trap your son and would have killed him.
He is dead now and has his portion. Spare
your own people. As for ourselves, we'll make   1300
restitution of wine and meat consumed,
and add, each one, a tithe of twenty oxen
with gifts of bronze and gold to warm your heart.
Meanwhile we cannot blame you for your anger."

Odysseus glowered under his black brows   1305
and said:
            "Not for the whole treasure of your fathers,
all you enjoy, lands, flocks, or any gold
put up by others, would I hold my hand.
There will be killing till the score is paid.
You forced yourselves upon this house. Fight your way out,   1310
or run for it, if you think you'll escape death.
I doubt one man of you skins by."

They felt their knees fail, and their hearts—but heard
Eurymachus for the last time rallying them.

"Friends," he said, "the man is implacable.   1315
Now that he's got his hands on bow and quiver
he'll shoot from the big doorstone there
until he kills us to the last man.
                        Fight, I say,
let's remember the joy of it. Swords out!
Hold up your tables to deflect his arrows.   1320
After me, everyone: rush him where he stands.
If we can budge him from the door, if we can pass
into the town, we'll call out men to chase him.
This fellow with his bow will shoot no more."

He drew his own sword as he spoke, a broadsword of fine
    bronze, 1325
honed like a razor on either edge. Then crying hoarse and
    loud
he hurled himself at Odysseus. But the kingly man let fly
an arrow at that instant, and the quivering feathered butt
sprang to the nipple of his breast as the barb stuck in his
    liver.
The bright broadsword clanged down. He lurched and fell
    aside, 1330
pitching across his table. His cup, his bread and meat,
were spilt and scattered far and wide, and his head slammed
    on the ground.
Revulsion, anguish in his heart, with both feet kicking out,
he downed his chair, while the shrouding wave of mist closed
    on his eyes.

Amphinomus now came running at Odysseus, 1335
broadsword naked in his hand. He thought to make
the great soldier give way at the door.
But with a spear throw from behind Telemachus hit him
between the shoulders, and the lancehead drove
clear through his chest. He left his feet and fell 1340
forward, thudding, forehead against the ground.
Telemachus swerved around him, leaving the long dark
    spear
planted in Amphinomus. If he paused to yank it out
someone might jump him from behind or cut him down
    with a sword
at the moment he bent over. So he ran—ran from the tables 1345
to his father's side and halted, panting, saying:

"Father let me bring you a shield and spear,
a pair of spears, a helmet.
I can arm on the run myself; I'll give
outfits to Eumaeus and this cowherd. 1350
Better to have equipment."
          Said Odysseus:

"Run then, while I hold them off with arrows
as long as the arrows last. When all are gone
if I'm alone they can dislodge me."
          Quick

upon his father's word Telemachus   1355
ran to the room where spears and armor lay.
He caught up four light shields, four pairs of spears,
four helms of war high-plumed with flowing manes,
and ran back, loaded down, to his father's side.
He was the first to pull a helmet on   1360
and slide his bare arm in a buckler strap.
The servants armed themselves, and all three took their
    stand
beside the master of battle.
                While he had arrows
he aimed and shot, and every shot brought down
one of his huddling enemies.   1365
But when all barbs had flown from the bowman's fist,
he leaned his bow in the bright entryway
beside the door, and armed: a four-ply shield
hard on his shoulder, and a crested helm,
horsetailed, nodding stormy upon his head.   1370
then took his tough and bronze-shod spears. . . .

Odysseus, Telemachus, and the two faithful servants kill every suitor. Several times Athena saves Odysseus' life by turning aside the suitors' deadly blows.

And Odysseus looked around him, narrow-eyed,
for any others who had lain hidden
while death's black fury passed.
                   In blood and dust
he saw that crowd all fallen, many and many slain.   1375

Think of a catch that fishermen haul in to a half-moon bay
in a fine-meshed net from the whitecaps of the sea:
how all are poured out on the sand, in throes for the salt sea,
twitching their cold lives away in Helios' fiery air:
so lay the suitors heaped on one another.   1380

Reading Check

1. What sign does Zeus send as an omen?
2. Who is the first suitor to be slain?
3. How does Eurymachus try to bargain for his life?
4. How does Odysseus hold off the suitors when they attempt to rush him?

For Study and Discussion

Analyzing and Interpreting the Epic

1. At what point in this episode does Odysseus reveal his identity to the suitors?

2. Eurymachus tries to convince Odysseus to spare the suitors' lives. Restate his arguments in your own words. What reason does Odysseus give for refusing?

3. Do you think Odysseus' revenge is excessive? Give reasons for your opinion.

4. Why are the stringing of Odysseus' bow and the slaying of the suitors considered the climax of the *Odyssey*?

Penelope Tests Odysseus

After twenty years of waiting for Odysseus, Penelope hesitates to acknowledge the stranger as her husband. She tests him with a secret only Odysseus could know.

Greathearted Odysseus, home at last,
was being bathed now by Eurynome
and rubbed with golden oil, and clothed again
in a fresh tunic and a cloak. Athena
lent him beauty, head to foot. She made him   1385
taller, and massive, too, with crisping hair
in curls like petals of wild hyacinth
but all red-golden. Think of gold infused
on silver by a craftsman, whose fine art
Hephaestus° taught him, or Athena—one   1390   1390. **Hephaestus** (hĭ-fĕs′təs):
whose work moves to delight: just so she lavished   god of metalworking.
beauty over Odysseus' head and shoulders.
He sat then in the same chair by the pillar,
facing his silent wife, and said:
                              "Strange woman,
the immortals of Olympus made you hard,   1395
harder than any. Who else in the world
would keep aloof as you do from her husband
if he returned to her from years of trouble,
cast on his own land in the twentieth year?

Nurse, make up a bed for me to sleep on.   1400
Her heart is iron in her breast."
                              Penelope
spoke to Odysseus now. She said:
                                "Strange man,
if man you are . . . This is no pride on my part
nor scorn for you—not even wonder, merely.
I know so well how you—how he—appeared   1405
boarding the ship for Troy. But all the same . . .

Make up his bed for him, Eurycleia.
Place it outside the bedchamber my lord
built with his own hands. Pile the big bed
with fleeces, rugs, and sheets of purest linen."   1410

With this she tried him to the breaking point,
and he turned on her in a flash raging:

"Woman, by heaven you've stung me now!
Who dared to move my bed?
No builder had the skill for that—unless   1415
a god came down to turn the trick. No mortal
in his best days could budge it with a crowbar.
There is our pact and pledge, our secret sign,
built into that bed—my handiwork
and no one else's!   1420
                      An old trunk of olive
grew like a pillar on the building plot,
and I laid out our bedroom round that tree,
lined up the stone walls, built the walls and roof,
gave it a doorway and smooth-fitting doors.
Then I lopped off the silvery leaves and branches,   1425
hewed and shaped that stump from the roots up
into a bedpost, drilled it, let it serve
as model for the rest. I planed them all,
inlaid them all with silver, gold and ivory,
and stretched a bed between—a pliant web   1430
of oxhide thongs dyed crimson.
                            There's our sign!
I know no more. Could someone else's hand
have sawn that trunk and dragged the frame away?"

Their secret! as she heard it told, her knees
grew tremulous and weak, her heart failed her.   1435

With eyes brimming tears she ran to him,
throwing her arms around his neck, and kissed him,
murmuring:
        "Do not rage at me, Odysseus!
No one ever matched your caution! Think
what difficulty the gods gave: they denied us   1440
life together in our prime and flowering years,
kept us from crossing into age together.
Forgive me, don't be angry. I could not
welcome you with love on sight! I armed myself
long ago against the frauds of men,   1445
impostors who might come—and all those many
whose underhanded ways bring evil on! . . .
But here and now, what sign could be so clear
as this of our own bed?
No other man has ever laid eyes on it—   1450
only my own slave, Actoris,° that my father   1451. **Actoris** (ăk′tôr-ĭs).
sent with me as a gift—she kept our door.
You make my stiff heart know that I am yours."

Now from his breast into his eyes the ache
of longing mounted, and he wept at last,   1455
his dear wife, clear and faithful, in his arms,
longed for as the sunwarmed earth is longed for by a
    swimmer
spent in rough water where his ship went down
under Poseidon's blows, gale winds and tons of sea.
Few men can keep alive through a big surf   1460
to crawl, clotted with brine, on kindly beaches
in joy, in joy, knowing the abyss behind:
and so she too rejoiced, her gaze upon her husband,
her white arms round him pressed as though forever.

Postscript

*The following morning Odysseus and Telemachus set out for the country estate
of Laertes, Odysseus' father. Their happy reunion is interrupted by the arrival
of angry relatives of the slain suitors, armed for battle. Athena appears and
commands them to make peace. So ends the* Odyssey, *with Odysseus restored
to his family and to his kingdom.*

Reading Check

1. How does Athena once again transform Odysseus?
2. Why does Odysseus accuse Penelope of being hardhearted?
3. Why is Penelope so cautious?
4. What convinces her that the stranger is Odysseus?

For Study and Discussion

Analyzing and Interpreting the Epic

1. What does Penelope imply by the phrase "if man you are" in line 1403?

2. What test does Penelope devise to tell whether the stranger is really Odysseus?

3. How does Penelope show that she and Odysseus are well-matched?

Literary Elements

Characteristics of the Epic

Homeric Simile

As you know, a simile is a comparison of two dissimilar actions or objects that are usually linked by *like*, *as*, or some other connecting word. A **Homeric simile** is an extended comparison of two actions or objects that develops mounting excitement and usually ends in a climax. In the following passage, Scylla seizing Odysseus' men is compared to a fisherman landing a fish:

> A man surf-casting on a point of rock
> for bass or mackerel, whipping his long rod
> to drop the sinker and the bait far out,
> will hook a fish and rip it from the surface
> to dangle wriggling through the air:
> >   so these
> were borne aloft in spasms toward the cliff.

Notice how the simile is extended by describing the actions of a fisherman and the parallel actions of the monster. How does Homer's choice of details make the action rise in excitement?

Look at the simile Homer uses to describe Odysseus' stringing of the bow (lines 1212–1216). Why is this simile strikingly effective?

Find other examples of Homeric similes and tell how the comparisons make the actions more vivid and gripping.

The Epithet

Like the extended simile, the **epithet** is a favorite device of the ancient epic poets. An epithet is a word or phrase used to characterize someone or something, as in "the *winedark* sea." Homer refers to Odysseus as "raider of cities," "the wiliest fighter of the islands," and "Laertes' son." The gods and goddesses are often identified by epithets. Zeus, for example, is called "Father of gods and men," "god of the zenith," "the lord of cloud," and "All Provident." Find other epithets Homer uses in the *Odyssey*.

Writing About Literature

Analyzing Odysseus as Epic Hero

In the opening lines of this translation of the *Odyssey,* Odysseus describes himself as "formidable for guile in peace and war." Do you think Odysseus characterizes himself accurately? Why or why not?

The hero of an epic is generally larger than life. He is stronger, braver, and more clever than the other characters. Sometimes his powers are superhuman. Write a brief composition in which you analyze Odysseus as an epic hero. Use evidence from the poem to support your analysis.

Analyzing the Role of the Olympians

In Homer's epics the Olympian gods and goddesses frequently intervene in human affairs. In the *Iliad,* they join the battle of the Greeks and the Trojans on the plains outside Troy. They take sides: Athena and Hera fight for the Greeks, Apollo and Aphrodite for the Trojans. The gods intervene in several ways—by starting arguments, by shielding warriors, or by changing the course of an arrow.

How do the gods and goddesses affect the action of the *Odyssey*? Choose several episodes that illustrate *divine intervention* and tell in a brief composition the motives for these interventions and their consequences.

Focus on Personal Narrative

Using Dialogue

Dialogue is the direct speech of characters in a narrative or play. When Homer narrates the episode of Odysseus' revenge, he uses dialogue to make the scene vivid and dramatic.

In the same way, you can use dialogue to make your personal narrative more lifelike. Here are some guidelines to follow when you put words into the mouths of your characters. Your dialogue should

- sound natural—the way people speak in real life
- be appropriate for the character(s)
- move your story along

Make some notes for adding dialogue to your personal narrative. Try to remember what you and others actually said during the experience that you are narrating. If you can't remember exact words, jot down a paraphrase of what was said and then convert your paraphrase into dialogue. Save your notes.

About the Translator

Robert Fitzgerald (1910–1985)

Fitzgerald began writing when he was in high school and while at college had several poems published in *Poetry* magazine. He was well known as a poet, critic, and translator. He collaborated with Dudley Fitts on translations of several classical Greek plays. He worked on his translation of the *Odyssey* while he was living in Italy. In 1961 his version of the poem received the first Bollingen Award for translation of poetry. In 1983 he brought out a translation of a classical Latin epic, the *Aeneid* by Virgil, the last major work before his death.

Literature and Archeology

Trojan Ruins

The excavation of Troy is an exciting story. Heinrich Schliemann, a German businessman, found the remains of an ancient city at a place called Hissarlik, in Asia Minor. After digging under layers of ruins, he discovered what is believed to be the ancient city of Troy. More recent excavations have uncovered evidence of a large Bronze Age city of the thirteenth century B.C. (see *New York Times,* February 23, 1993). In 1992 archeologists discovered a thick clay wall that may be the wall described in Homer's *Iliad.*

Making Connections: Activities

For information on Schliemann's work, consult encyclopedia entries on Troy and Heinrich Schliemann. Other sources are *The Walls of Windy Troy,* by Marjorie Braymer, and *The Gold of Troy,* by Robert Payne. To evaluate the evidence that there was a war that destroyed the city of Troy in the thirteenth century B.C., read Appendix II in *The World of Odysseus,* by M. I. Finley, or other books in your school and local libraries.

The Lotus-Eaters

ALFRED, LORD TENNYSON

You have read the episode of the Lotus-Eaters (lines 65–91). After Odysseus'
men eat the lotus plant, they have no desire to go home and must be forced back
to the ships.

Alfred, Lord Tennyson expanded the incident into a famous poem. In the
first section of the poem, which follows, Odysseus speaks to his men as they first
sight the shore. How does Tennyson suggest a mood of indolence?

"Courage!" he said, and pointed toward the land,
"This mounting wave will roll us shoreward soon."
In the afternoon they came unto a land
In which it seemèd always afternoon.
All round the coast the languid air did swoon,   5
Breathing like one that hath a weary dream.
Full-faced above the valley stood the moon;
And, like a downward smoke, the slender stream
Along the cliff to fall and pause and fall did seem.

A land of streams! some, like a downward smoke,   10
Slow-dropping veils of thinnest lawn,° did go;   11. **lawn:** a thin, sheer fabric.
And some through wavering lights and shadows broke,
Rolling a slumbrous sheet of foam below.
They saw the gleaming river seaward flow.
From the inner land; far off, three mountaintops,   15
Three silent pinnacles of aged snow,
Stood sunset-flushed; and, dewed with showery drops,
Up-clomb° the shadowy pine above the woven copse.°   18. **clomb:** climbed. **copse:** a thick growth of small trees.

The charmèd sunset lingered low adown
In the red West; through mountain clefts the dale   20
Was seen far inland, and the yellow down°   21. **down:** rolling, upland countryside.
Bordered with palm, and many a winding vale
And meadow, set with slender galingale,°   23. **galingale** (găl′ĭn-gāl′): an aromatic plant of the ginger family.
A land where all things always seemed the same!
And round about the keel with faces pale,   25
Dark faces pale against that rosy flame,
The mild-eyed melancholy Lotus-eaters came.

Branches they bore of that enchanted stem,
Laden with flower and fruit, whereof they gave
To each, but whoso did receive of them   30
And taste, to him the gushing of the wave
Far, far away did seem to mourn and rave
On alien shores; and if his fellow spake,
His voice was thin, as voices from the grave;
And deep asleep he seemed, yet all awake,   35
And music in his ears his beating heart did make.

They sat them down upon the yellow sand,
Between the sun and moon upon the shore;
And sweet it was to dream of fatherland,
Of child, and wife, and slave; but evermore   40
Most weary seemed the sea, weary the oar,
Weary the wandering fields of barren foam.
Then someone said, "We will return no more";
And all at once they sang, "Our island home
Is far beyond the wave; we will no longer roam."   45

Focus on Personal Narrative

Reflecting on the Meaning of the Experience

What was the meaning of Odysseus' adventure with the Lotus-Eaters? In Tennyson's version, as in Homer's, the experience of ease and forgetfulness was so pleasant that it nearly put an end to the return of Odysseus and his men to their homeland.

When you write a personal narrative, you want your audience to understand the meaning that your experience has for you. As you reflect on the meaning of your experience, here are some questions to ask yourself:

1. What was I like before the experience?
2. How did the experience change me?
3. What did I learn about myself and others?
4. How did I feel after the experience?

To explore the meaning of an experience, fill out a chart like the one below. Save your notes.

	Before	After
Feelings:	_____	_____
	_____	_____
Opinions:	_____	_____
	_____	_____
Views of Self:	_____	_____
	_____	_____

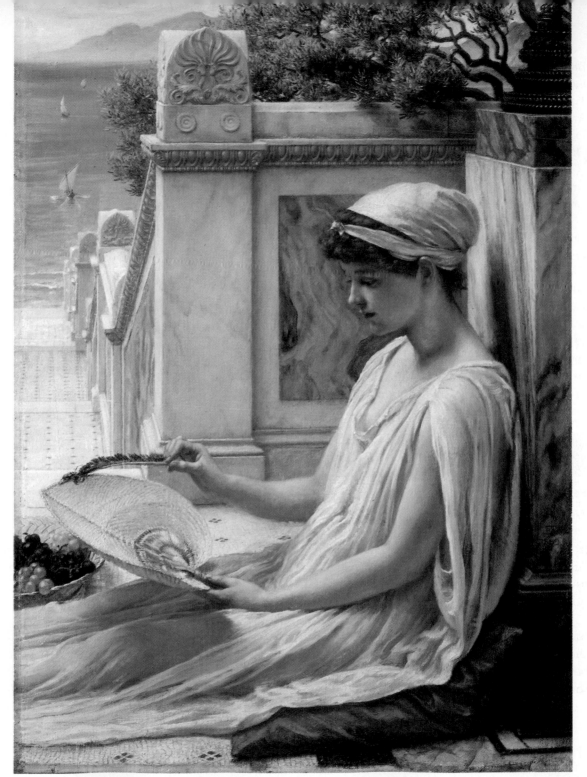

On the Terrace by Sir Edward Poynter (1836–1919). Oil on panel.
Walker Art Gallery, Liverpool

Learning to Walk Alone
FROM Penelope's Journal

JUDITH ORTIZ COFER

In this poem Judith Ortiz Cofer draws on the emotions Penelope experiences in Odysseus' absence. What contrast is drawn between Penelope and her servant, Hestia?

Today I followed my servant, Hestia, down the dusty path
that leads away from the sea. Trudging towards
the barren hills that separate my house from her world,
her stiff back told me
that a woman walking home after a day of laboring   5
over someone else's hearth
had nothing to share with a fortunate fool
strolling in the heat of late afternoon
for pleasure.
         As we approached the last clump of trees
huddled together like beggars at the edge of the village,   10
I gave up the contest of wills. I followed Hestia's brown form
with my eyes, as she descended into a marketplace
filled with hagglers, stray dogs, and flies, until
she became part of the crowd.
         I stood there with my arms around a thin old tree
for a long time, listening to the sounds of words   15
I could not decipher, the empty cadences of far-away voices
rising and falling.
         Without you, Odysseus,
I have come to hate living on this island—the constant whine
of the sea licking its own wounds. If I could, I would follow
the vagrant gulls to crowded places and feast on crumbs.   20
I would wait with the winning patience of birds
for someone to extend an open hand.

For Study and Discussion

Analyzing and Interpreting the Poem

1. Why does Penelope follow Hestia?

2. What do you think is the "contest of wills" referred to in line 12?

3. How does Cofer's view of Penelope differ from the view presented in Homer's *Odyssey*?

Focus on Personal Narrative

Organizing a Personal Narrative

Begin your personal narrative with an attention grabber, such as a provocative quotation or a striking fact or statement. Next, give the background information that your readers need to understand the experience that you tell about. Then follow **chronological** or **time order.** Occasionally, you may want to use a **flashback,** a scene in which you interrupt the action to tell about an earlier action or event. Use **transitional words and phrases** to help your audience follow the order of events.

Write an **outline** to organize events in a personal narrative.

   I. Introduction
      A. Capture readers' interest
      B. Give background information
  II. Body
      A. Describe event 1: give details about people, places, thoughts, feelings
      B. Describe event 2: give details about people, places, thoughts, feelings
      C. Describe additional events
 III. Conclusion
      A. Sum up meaning of experience
      B. End with thought-provoking comment or prediction

About the Author

Judith Ortiz Cofer (1952–   )

Judith Ortiz Cofer was born in Puerto Rico and spent her childhood partly on the island and partly in Paterson, New Jersey. Her bicultural heritage has been a strong influence on her work. She is the author of a novel, *The Line of the Sun* (1989); a collection of essays and poetry, *Silent Dancing* (1990); and two books of poetry, *Terms of Survival* (1987) and *Reaching for the Mainland* (1987). Cofer has won many awards, including a grant from the National Endowment for the Arts and a Bread Loaf Fellowship.

The Author Comments on Her Poetry

I wrote *Penelope's Journal* for both literary and personal reasons. Having taught world literature, I found that many of the women in these stories did not have a voice of their own. I wanted to re-create the lives of these women, give them voice, and complete their stories. I have done the same for Helen of Troy, Salome, Hagar, and others.

In teaching the *Odyssey*, I was aware that Penelope did not have a voice. I gave her a voice by having her keep a journal of her own evolution as a thinking person. Penelope and many women in literature spent much of their time at home waiting for the return of their men, but their lives had value too.

From a personal view, I saw my own mother spending much of her life at home waiting for my father's return. My father was in the navy and was away on duty often. My mother was left in the age-old, typical woman's role of waiting; however, that did not keep her from learning, thinking, and living.

WRITING A PERSONAL NARRATIVE

*E*xploring your thoughts, feelings, and dreams can help you discover more about yourself. In a **personal narrative** you focus on an experience that happened to you and explore the meaning of that experience. A personal narrative is longer than an autobiographical anecdote, because in a narrative you take the time to reflect on your experience in a more leisurely way. On the other hand, a personal narrative is much shorter than an autobiography, because in a narrative you focus on a single experience.

Prewriting

1. Explore and evaluate possible topics for a personal narrative, using these criteria:

- significance of the experience to you
- your vivid memory of the experience
- your willingness to share the experience

You might want to use a chart such as the one below to identify possible topics. Do the words at the top of each column prompt any associations in your mind? Feel free to use different triggers for your memories if you wish.

Family	Friend	Holiday	Success	Failure
_____	_____	_____	_____	_____
_____	_____	_____	_____	_____
_____	_____	_____	_____	_____

[See **Focus** assignment on page 616.]

2. After you have identified a promising topic for a narrative, think about your purpose and audience. Your **purpose** in a personal narrative is to express yourself. You should use the first-person pronouns *I, me, my,* and *mine.* Your tone should be personal and informal, and you should include details to suggest your own thoughts and feelings about the experience. Your **audience** may be your classmates, your friends, or a group of adults. If your audience did not witness or share your experience, you will probably need to supply some background information. Jot down some notes about your audience's familiarity with your subject and about their interests and special needs. [See **Focus** assignment on page 630.]

3. Use one or more of the methods listed below to gather details for your narrative:

- freewriting
- brainstorming
- interviewing
- visualizing

Make a chart like the one that follows, and fill in as many details as you can recall about your experience. Try especially hard to remember **sensory details** that appeal to sight, hearing, taste, smell, and touch.

Details Chart			
Events _____		Places _____	
_____		_____	
_____		_____	
People _____		Thoughts / _____	
_____		Feelings _____	
_____		_____	

[See **Focus** assignment on page 644.]

4. Jot down some notes on the overall meaning of the experience for you. Ask yourself questions like the following:

- What was I like before the experience?
- How have I changed as a result of the experience?
- What have I learned about myself and others?

[See **Focus** assignment on page 657.]

5. Organize the most vivid and significant details for your narrative. A personal narrative usually has a three-part structure:

  I. Introduction
     A. Capture reader's interest
     B. Provide background information
  II. Body
     A. Describe events
     B. Give your thoughts and emotions
  III. Conclusion: Tell meaning of experience

Most personal narratives use **chronological** or **time order** to tell about the events or actions that happened. [See **Focus** assignment on page 660.]

Writing

1. Because your narrative is *personal,* you should try to use your own "voice" as you write. Your narrative should sound friendly and informal. As you write your first draft, use the first-person point of view to tell about the events that happened and the feelings you had. If you imagine that you are holding a conversation with your readers, you will probably succeed in the objective of sounding like *you.*

2. Use **dialogue** to make your narrative more vivid and lifelike. Dialogue can help you *show* events and characters, rather than merely *tell* about them. Here are some guidelines to use when you create dialogue:

  a. Be sure that your dialogue sounds natural—the way people talk in real life.
  b. Make your dialogue fit the personality of the character who speaks.
  c. Use your dialogue to move the story forward.

[See **Focus** assignment on page 655.]

Evaluating and Revising

1. When you have finished your narrative, put it aside for a while. Then reread it as objectively as you can. (You may want to ask a peer reader to read your narrative and give you comments on it.) Make sure your details are organized in a logical way and that you have included comments about the meaning of the experience. Check to see that you have used **transitions** to help your readers follow the order of events. Some useful transitional words and phrases include the following:

after	finally	soon
at first	later	then
at last	next	to begin with

Below is an example of how one writer revised the opening paragraph of a personal narrative.

I was determined not to give up. ~~I reasoned,~~ Years of experience should be worth something in the baby-sitting ~~field~~ arena. There was also my ~~personality, which~~ charming bedside manner, so ~~was~~ very effective with the younger members of my own family. ~~But~~ I when found little Tobias Stanton, age four, calmly chatting on the long-distance phone with a "friend" ~~mate~~ in Sydney, Australia (he had dialed direct), I almost despaired.

2. You may find the following checklist helpful as you revise your narrative:

Checklist for Evaluation and Revision

✓ Do I capture the reader's attention in the introduction?

✓ Do I supply any necessary background?

✓ Do I use first-person point of view and a friendly, informal tone?

✓ Do I provide a sufficient number of vivid details so that the audience can "see" and understand the experience?

✓ Do I include details about my own thoughts and feelings?

✓ Do I tell events in a logical order?

✓ Do I include a discussion of the meaning of the experience?

Proofreading and Publishing

1. Proofread your personal narrative and correct any errors you find in grammar, usage, and mechanics. (Here you may find it helpful to refer to the **Handbook for Revision** on pages 884–930.) Then prepare a final version of your narrative by making a clean copy.

2. Consider some of the following publication methods for your narrative:

- adapt your narrative into a skit, and act it out with the help of some classmates
- give an oral presentation of your narrative in a story theater
- contribute your narrative to a school or community magazine

Portfolio If your teacher approves, you may wish to keep a copy of your work in your writing folder or portfolio.

THE NOVEL

A novel is a story with many threads. The action may cover a long period and there may be a number of characters who affect the main action.

Imagine that the scene pictured here is the opening scene of a novel set in nineteenth-century England. Find someone in the painting who could become your main character. What is he or she doing at this seaside resort? What other characters shown in the painting are going to become involved in the main character's story?

Write the first paragraph of your novel. Try to catch the reader's interest. Share your paragraph with another writer and compare ideas.

Ramsgate Sands (1854) by
William Powell Frith (1819–1909). Oil on canvas.
The Royal Collection © 1994 Her Majesty, Queen Elizabeth II

Novels are so familiar to us that we might easily assume that they have been in existence for as long as, for example, the drama, which dates back for centuries. However, the novel is one of the most recent forms of literature. It came into being only about three hundred years ago. Essentially a novel is a long story, often with many characters and more than one story line.

The novel and the short story, both of which are classified as fiction, make use of the same basic elements: plot, character, setting, point of view, and theme. Because of its greater length and scope, a novel makes more extensive use of these elements. The plot is frequently more complicated than in a short story, and there may be one or more subplots related to the main action. In a novel there are generally more characters than in a short story, and the characters are portrayed in greater depth. The setting of a novel can reflect the background, ideas, and customs of a historical period, and since the novel is a long work, there is time and space to explore and develop important themes.

Guidelines for Close Reading

1. Respond actively as you read, asking questions and drawing inferences. Try to predict how some character will act or how some incident will turn out. Try to determine the author's purpose as you read.

2. Note information that establishes the setting or background of the novel. Determine the role that setting plays in the novel.

3. Look for clues that reveal what characters are like: key speeches, important actions, descriptive details. Discover how characters develop and change as the novel progresses. Try to understand relationships between characters.

4. Be aware of what forms the major action of the novel. Dickens' novels usually contain several *subplots* in addition to a *main plot.* As you read, consider how individual episodes are connected to the main plot or subplot(s) of the novel.

5. Note the point of view of the novel. Ask yourself the author's reason for choosing this point of view.

6. Consider how all the elements of the novel contribute to its theme. Take into account your own responses and try to clarify your understanding of the author's underlying idea by stating this idea in your own words.

About the Author

Charles Dickens (1812–1870)

Charles Dickens by William Powell Frith.
Oil on canvas.
Victoria and Albert Museum

Dickens was born in Portsmouth, England, on February 7, 1812. In 1823 his family moved to London. John Dickens, his father, was arrested for debt. In order to support himself, Charles, who was twelve, went to work in a blacking warehouse, labeling bottles for six shillings a week. This experience was to haunt him for the rest of his life. After his father was released from Marshalsea Debtors' Prison, Dickens was able to leave his job and return to school.

At fifteen Dickens took a job as a law clerk. He taught himself shorthand and began working as a free-lance newspaper reporter. Dickens' first literary work, *Sketches by Boz*, appeared in 1833 ("Boz" was a pseudonym Dickens used to sign his prose sketches). His first novel, *The Pickwick Papers* (1836–1837), like his subsequent novels, appeared in serial form. Shortly after the first installment of the book was published, Dickens married Catherine Hogarth, the daughter of a journalist.

During the next thirty years, Dickens produced an extraordinary series of books: *Oliver Twist* (1837); *Nicholas Nickleby* (1838–1839); *The Old Curiosity Shop* (1840–1841); *Barnaby Rudge* (1841); *A Christmas Carol* (1843); *Martin Chuzzlewit* (1843–1844); *Dombey and Son* (1846–1848); *David Copperfield* (1849–1850); *Bleak House* (1852–1853); *Hard Times* (1854); *Little Dorrit* (1855–1857); *A Tale of Two Cities* (1859); *Great Expectations* (1860–1861); and *Our Mutual Friend* (1864–1865). When he died in 1870, Dickens was working on another novel, *Edwin Drood.*

Dickens' books have been consistently popular for more than a hundred years. Dickens is one of the greatest storytellers who ever lived, and, with the single exception of Shakespeare, no writer of the English-speaking world has had a greater gift for creating sharply individualized characters.

Great Expectations is the last of Dickens' great novels. In the book we follow the development of Pip, the central character (and narrator), from childhood to manhood. When we first meet Pip, he is a frightened, sensitive boy who aspires to a world outside his reach. Through a strange twist of fate, he is allowed to fulfill his early dreams, and he learns what kind of life he truly wishes to lead.

Great Expectations

CHARLES DICKENS

Chapter 1

In this chapter we meet Pip, who meets a convict in a graveyard.

My father's family name being Pirrip, and my Christian name Philip, my infant tongue could make of both names nothing more explicit than Pip. So I called myself Pip, and came to be called Pip.

I gave Pirrip as my father's family name, on the authority of his tombstone and my sister—Mrs. Joe Gargery, who married the blacksmith. I never saw my father or my mother, and never saw a picture of either of them.

Ours was the marsh country, down by the river, within twenty miles of the sea. My first vivid impression of things seems to me to have been gained on a memorable raw afternoon toward evening. At such a time I found out for certain that this bleak place was the churchyard; and that Philip Pirrip, late of this parish, and Georgiana, wife of the above, were dead and buried. I knew that the dark flat wilderness beyond was the marshes; and that the low leaden line beyond was the river; and that the distant savage lair from which the wind was rushing was the sea; and that the small bundle of shivers growing afraid of it all and beginning to cry was Pip.

"Hold your noise!" cried a terrible voice, as a man started up from among the graves. "Keep still, you little devil, or I'll cut your throat!"

A fearful man, all in coarse gray, with a great iron on his leg. A man with no hat, and with broken shoes, and with an old rag tied around his head. A man who had been soaked in water, and smothered in mud, and lamed by stones, and cut by flints, and stung by nettles, and torn by briars; who limped and shivered, and glared and growled; and whose teeth chattered in his head as he seized me by the chin.

"Oh! Don't cut my throat, sir," I pleaded in terror. "Pray don't do it, sir."

"Tell us your name!" said the man. "Quick!"

"Pip, sir."

"Once more," said the man, staring at me. "Give it mouth!"

"Pip. Pip, sir."

"Show us where you live," said the man. "Pint out the place!"

I pointed to where our village lay, a mile or more from the church.

The man, after looking at me for a moment, turned me upside down and emptied my pockets. There was nothing in them but a piece of bread. He ate the bread ravenously.

"You young dog," said the man, licking his lips. "What fat cheeks you ha' got. Darn me if I couldn't eat 'em, and if I han't half a mind to't!"

I held tighter to the tombstone on which he had put me; partly, to keep myself upon it; partly, to keep myself from crying.

"Now lookee here!" said the man. "Where's your mother?"

All movie stills are from a 1946 production of *Great Expectations*.

"There, sir!" said I.

He started, made a short run, and stopped and I looked over his shoulder.

"There, sir!" I timidly explained. "Also Georgiana. That's my mother."

"Oh!" said he, coming back. "And is that your father alonger your mother?"

"Yes, sir," said I; "him too."

"Ha!" he muttered. "Who d'ye live with—supposin' you're kindly let to live, which I han't made up my mind about?"

Quest. one

← "My sister, sir—Mrs. Joe Gargery wife of Joe Gargery, the blacksmith, sir."

"Blacksmith, eh?" said he. And looked down at his leg.

After darkly looking at his leg and at me several times, he came closer, took me by both arms, and tilted me back as far as he could hold me.

"Now lookee here," he said, "the question being whether you're to be let to live. You know what a file is?"

"Yes, sir."

"And you know what wittles[1] is?"

"Yes, sir."

After each question he tilted me over a little more, so as to give me a greater sense of helplessness and danger.

"You get me a file." He tilted me again. "And you get me wittles." He tilted me again. "You bring 'em both to me." He tilted me again. "Or I'll have your heart and liver out."

I was dreadfully frightened, and so giddy that I clung to him with both hands and said, "If you would kindly please to let me keep upright, sir, perhaps I shouldn't be sick, and perhaps I could attend more."

He gave me a tremendous dip and roll. Then he held me by the arms in an upright position and went on in these fearful terms:

"You bring me, tomorrow morning early,

that file and them wittles to that old Battery[2] over yonder. You do it, and you never dare to say a word or dare to make a sign concerning your having seen such a person as me, or any person sumever, and you shall be let to live. You fail, or you go from my words in any partickler, no matter how small it is, and your heart and your liver shall be tore out, roasted, and ate. Now, I ain't alone, as you may think I am. There's a young man hid with me. That young man hears the words I speak. That young man has a secret way of getting at a body, and at his heart, and at his liver. It is in wain for a boy to attempt to hide himself from that young man. A boy may lock his door, may be warm in bed, may tuck himself up, may draw the clothes over his head, may think himself comfortable and safe, but that young man will creep his way to him and tear him open. I am a-keeping that young man from harming of you at the present moment, with great difficulty. I find it wery hard to hold that young man off of your inside. Now, what do you say?"

I said that I would get him the file, and I would get him what broken bits of food I could, and I would come to him at the Battery early in the morning.

"Say, Lord strike you dead if you don't!" said the man.

I said so, and he took me down.

"Now," he pursued, "you remember what you've undertook, and you remember that young man, and you get home."

He hugged his shuddering body in both his arms and limped toward the low church wall. He got over it, like a man whose legs were numbed and stiff, and then turned round to look for me. I looked all around for the horrible young man, and could see no signs of him. But now I was frightened again, and ran home without stopping.

---

1. **wittles:** victuals (vĭt′lz), food. The convict and other characters pronounce *v* like *w*.

2. **Battery:** a bank of earth on which large guns are mounted.

Chapter 2

We now meet Mrs. Joe Gargery, Pip's sister, and Joe Gargery the blacksmith, his brother-in-law.

My sister, Mrs. Joe Gargery, was more than twenty years older than I, and had established a great reputation with herself and the neighbors because she had brought me up "by hand." Knowing her to have a hard and heavy hand, and to be much in the habit of laying it upon her husband as well as upon me, I supposed that Joe Gargery and I were both brought up by hand.

She was not a good-looking woman, my sister; and I had a general impression that she must have made Joe Gargery marry her by hand. Joe was a fair man, with curls of flaxen hair on each side of his smooth face, and with eyes of a very undecided blue. He was a mild, good-natured, sweet-tempered, easygoing, foolish, dear fellow—a sort of Hercules in strength, and also in weakness. My sister, Mrs. Joe, with black hair and eyes, was tall and bony, and almost always wore a coarse apron, fastened over her figure behind with two loops.

Joe's forge adjoined our house, which was a wooden house, as many of the dwellings in our country were. When I ran home from the churchyard, the forge was shut up, and Joe was sitting alone in the kitchen. Joe and I being fellow sufferers, Joe imparted a confidence to me the moment I raised the latch of the door and peeped in at him.

"Mrs. Joe has been out a dozen times looking for you, Pip. And she's out now making it a baker's dozen."

"Is she?"

"Yes, Pip," said Joe, "and what's worse, she's got Tickler with her."

At this dismal intelligence,[1] I twisted the only button on my waistcoat round and round, and looked in great depression at the fire. Tickler was a wax-ended piece of cane, worn smooth by collision with my tickled frame.

"She sot down," said Joe, "and she got up, and she made a grab at Tickler, and she Ram-paged[2] out. That's what she did," said Joe, "she Ram-paged out, Pip."

"Has she been gone long, Joe?" I always treated him as a larger child, and as no more than my equal.

"Well," said Joe, "she's been on the Rampage, this last spell, about five minutes, Pip. She's a-coming! Get behind the door, old chap."

I took the advice. My sister, Mrs. Joe, throwing the door wide open, and finding an obstruction behind it, immediately divined the cause, and applied Tickler. She concluded by throwing me at Joe, who passed me on into the chimney and quietly fenced me up there with his great leg.

"Where have you been, you young monkey?" said Mrs. Joe, stamping her foot. "Tell me directly what you've been doing to wear me away with fret and fright and worrit, or I'd have you out of that corner if you was fifty Pips, and he was five hundred Gargerys."

"I have only been to the churchyard," said I, from my stool, crying and rubbing myself.

"Churchyard!" repeated my sister. "If it warn't for me you'd have been to the churchyard long ago, and stayed there. Who brought you up by hand?"

"You did," said I.

"And why did I do it, I should like to know?" exclaimed my sister.

I whimpered, "I don't know."

"*I* don't!" said my sister. "I'd never do it again! I know that. It's bad enough to be a

1. **intelligence:** here, news.

2. **Ram-paged:** Joe is giving emphasis to the word *rampage,* to storm about in a fit of anger.

blacksmith's wife, and him a Gargery, without being your mother."

My thoughts strayed from that question as I looked disconsolately at the fire. For, the fugitive out on the marshes with the ironed leg, the mysterious young man, the file, the food, and the dreadful pledge I was under to commit a larceny on those sheltering premises, rose before me in the avenging coals.

My sister had a way of cutting our bread and butter for us that never varied. First, with her left hand she jammed the loaf hard against her bib. Then she took some butter (not too much) and spread it on the loaf, then sawed a very thick round off the loaf and hewed it into two halves, of which Joe got one, and I the other. Though I was hungry, I dared not eat my slice. I felt that I must have something in reserve for my dreadful acquaintance and his ally, the still more dreadful young man. I resolved to put my hunk of bread and butter down the leg of my trousers.

Joe was about to take a bite when his eye fell on me, and he saw that my bread and butter was gone.

The wonder and consternation with which Joe stopped and stared at me were too evident to escape my sister's observation.

"What's the matter now?" she said.

"I say, you know!" muttered Joe, shaking his head at me in a very serious remonstrance. "Pip, old chap! You'll do yourself a mischief. It'll stick somewhere. You can't have chawed it, Pip."

"What's the matter *now*?" repeated my sister, more sharply than before.

"If you can cough any trifle of it up, Pip, I'd recommend you to do it," said Joe, all aghast. "Manners is manners, but still your 'elth's your 'elth."

By this time, my sister was quite desperate, so she pounced on Joe, and, taking him by the two whiskers, knocked his head for a little

while against the wall behind him while I sat in the corner looking guiltily on.

"Now, perhaps you'll mention what's the matter," said my sister, out of breath, "you staring great stuck pig."

Joe looked at her in a helpless way; then took a helpless bite and looked at me again.

"Been bolting his food, has he?" cried my sister.

"You know, old chap," said Joe, "I bolted, myself, when I was your age, but I never see your bolting equal yet, Pip."

My sister made a dive at me, and fished me up by the hair, saying nothing more than the awful words, "You come along and be dosed."

Some medical beast had revived tar-water[3] in those days as a fine medicine, and Mrs. Joe always kept a supply of it in the cupboard. The urgency of my case demanded a pint of this mixture, which was poured down my throat while Mrs. Joe held my head under her arm.

Conscience is a dreadful thing. The guilty knowledge that I was going to rob Mrs. Joe—I never thought I was going to rob Joe, for I never thought of any of the housekeeping property as his—united to the necessity of always keeping one hand on my bread and butter as I sat, or when I was ordered about the kitchen on any small errand, almost drove me out of my mind.

It was Christmas Eve, and I had to stir the pudding for the next day with a copper stick. I tried it with the load upon my leg (and that made me think afresh of the man with the load on *his* leg), and found the tendency of exercise to bring the bread and butter out at my ankle quite unmanageable. Happily I slipped away and deposited that part of my conscience in my garret bedroom.

"Hark!" said I, when I had done my stirring,

---

3. **tar-water:** a solution of tar and water regarded as a cure-all and also used as a tonic.

and was taking a final warm in the chimney corner before being sent up to bed. "Was that great guns, Joe?"

"Ah," said Joe. "There's another conwict off."

"What does that mean, Joe?" said I.

"There was a conwict off last night," said Joe, "after sunset gun. And they fired warning of him. And now it appears they're firing warning of another."

"*Who's* firing?" said I.

"Drat that boy," interposed my sister, frowning at me over her work; "what a questioner he is. Ask no questions, and you'll be told no lies."

"Mrs. Joe," said I, "I should like to know—if you wouldn't much mind—where the firing comes from?"

"Lord bless the boy!" exclaimed my sister, as if she didn't quite mean that but rather the contrary. "From the Hulks!"

"And please what's Hulks?" said I.

"That's the way with this boy!" exclaimed my sister, pointing me out with her needle and thread, and shaking her head at me. "Answer him one question, and he'll ask you a dozen directly. Hulks are prison ships, right 'cross th' meshes." We always used that name for marshes in our country.

"I wonder who's put into prison ships, and why they're put there?" said I, in a general way, and with quiet desperation.

It was too much for Mrs. Joe, who immediately rose. "I tell you what, young fellow," said she; "I didn't bring you up by hand to badger people's lives out. People are put in the Hulks because they murder, and because they rob, and forge, and do all sorts of bad; and they always begin by asking questions. Now, you get along to bed!"

I was never allowed a candle to light me to bed, and, as I went upstairs in the dark, I was in mortal terror of the young man who wanted my heart and liver; I was in mortal terror of the man with the iron leg; I was in mortal terror of myself, from whom an awful promise had been extracted.

As soon as the great black velvet pall outside my little window was shot with gray, I got up and went downstairs, every board upon the way, and every crack in every board, calling after me, "Stop thief!" and "Get up, Mrs. Joe!" I had no time to spare. I stole some bread, some rind of cheese, and about half a jar of mincemeat (which I tied up in my pocket handkerchief with my last night's slice), some brandy from a stone bottle, diluting the stone bottle from a jug in the kitchen cupboard, a meat bone with very little on it, and a beautiful round compact pork pie.

There was a door in the kitchen communicating with the forge; I unlocked and unbolted that door and got a file from among Joe's tools. Then I put the fastenings as I had found them, opened the door at which I had entered when I ran home last night, shut it, and ran for the misty marshes.

Chapter 3

A second convict appears.

It was a rimy morning and very damp. On every rail and gate, wet lay clammy, and the marsh mist was thick. However fast I went, I couldn't warm my feet, to which the damp cold seemed riveted as the iron was riveted to the leg of the man I was running to meet. I knew my way to the Battery, for I had been down there with Joe, and Joe had told me that, when I was apprenticed[1] to him, we would have such

1. **apprenticed:** In former times, apprenticeship was the most common way to learn a trade. A boy (with his parents or guardian) signed a contract, called "indentures," by which he was bound to serve a master workman without pay for five to seven years. In return for this service, he was taught the workman's trade.

larks[2] there! I had just crossed a ditch which I knew to be very near the Battery, and had just scrambled up the mound beyond, when I saw the man sitting before me. His back was toward me, and he had his arms folded and was nodding forward, heavy with sleep, so I went forward softly and touched him on the shoulder. He instantly jumped up, and it was not the same man, but another man!

And yet this man was dressed in coarse gray, too, and had a great iron on his leg, and was lame, and hoarse, and cold, and everything that the other man was except that he had not the same face, and had a flat, broad-brimmed, low-crowned felt hat on. He swore an oath at me and then he ran into the mist, stumbling twice as he went.

"It's the young man!" I thought, feeling my heart shoot as I identified him. I dare say I should have felt a pain in my liver, too, if I had known where it was.

I was soon at the Battery, and there was the right man—hugging himself and limping to and fro, as if he had never all night left off hugging and limping—waiting for me. He was awfully cold, to be sure. His eyes looked awfully hungry, too. He did not turn me upside down this time, but left me right side upward while I opened the bundle and emptied my pockets.

"What's in the bottle, boy?" said he.

"Brandy," said I.

He was already handing mincemeat down his throat in the most curious manner—more like a man who was putting it away somewhere in a violent hurry, than a man who was eating it—but he left off to take some of the liquor. He shivered all the while so violently that it was quite as much as he could do to keep the neck of the bottle between his teeth without biting it off.

"I think you have got the ague,"[3] said I.

"I'm much of your opinion, boy," said he.

"It's bad about here," I told him. "You've been lying out on the meshes."

"I'll eat my breakfast afore they're the death of me," said he. "I'd do that if I was going to be strung up to that there gallows over there, directly arterward. I'll beat the shivers so far, *I'll* bet you."

He was gobbling mincemeat, meat bone, bread, cheese, and pork pie, all at once; staring distrustfully while he did so at the mist all around us, and often stopping to listen. Some real or fancied sound, some clink upon the river or breathing of beast upon the marsh, now gave him a start, and he said, suddenly:

"You're not a deceiving imp? You brought no one with you?"

"No, sir! No!"

"Well," said he, "I believe you. You'd be but a fierce young hound indeed, if at your time of life you could help to hunt a wretched warmint, hunted as near death as this poor wretched warmint is!"

Something clicked in his throat as if he had works in him like a clock, and was going to strike. And he smeared his ragged rough sleeve over his eyes.

Pitying his desolation, and watching him as he gradually settled down upon the pie, I made bold to say, "I am glad you enjoy it."

"Thankee, my boy. I do."

"I am afraid you won't leave any of it for him," said I, timidly. "There's no more to be got where that came from."

"Leave any for him? Who's him?" said my friend, stopping in his crunching of piecrust.

"The young man that you spoke of. That was hid with you."

"Oh, ah!" he returned, with something like a gruff laugh. "Him? Yes, Yes! *He* don't want no wittles."

2. **larks:** fun.

3. **ague** (ā'gyōo): chills and fever.

"I thought he looked as if he did," said I.

The man stopped eating and regarded me with the keenest scrutiny and the greatest surprise.

"Looked? When?"

"Just now."

"Where?"

"Yonder," said I, pointing: "over there, where I found him nodding asleep, and thought it was you."

He held me by the collar and stared at me so that I began to think his first idea about cutting my throat had revived.

"Dressed like you, you know, only with a hat," I explained, trembling; "and—and—" I was very anxious to put this delicately—"and with—the same reason for wanting to borrow a file. Didn't you hear the cannon last night?"

"When a man's alone on these flats, with a light head and a light stomach, perishing of cold and want, he hears nothin' all night but guns firing and voices calling. But this man— did you notice anything in him?"

"He had a badly bruised face," said I.

"Not here?" exclaimed the man, striking his left cheek.

"Yes, there!"

"Where is he?" He crammed what little food was left into the breast of his gray jacket. "Show me the way he went. I'll pull him down, like a bloodhound. Curse this iron on my sore leg! Give us hold of the file, boy."

He was down on the rank wet grass, filing at his iron like a madman, and not minding me or minding his own leg, which had an old chafe upon it and was bloody, but which he handled as roughly as if it had no more feeling in it than the file.

I was very much afraid of him again, now that he had worked himself into this fierce hurry, and I was likewise very much afraid of keeping away from home any longer. I told him I must go, but he took no notice, so I thought the best thing I could do was to slip off. The last I saw of him, his head was bent over his knee and he was working hard at his fetter, muttering impatient imprecations at it and his leg. The last I heard of him, I stopped in the mist to listen, and the file was still going.

Chapter 4

We meet the Christmas dinner guests: Mr. Wopsle, the parish clerk; Mr. and Mrs. Hubble, a wheelwright and his wife; and Mr. Pumblechook, Joe's uncle, a corn merchant.

I fully expected to find a constable in the kitchen, waiting to take me up. But not only was there no constable there, but no discovery had yet been made of the robbery. Mrs. Joe was prodigiously busy in getting the house ready for the festivities of the day.

"And where the deuce ha' *you* been?" was Mrs. Joe's Christmas salutation, when I and my conscience showed ourselves.

I said I had been down to hear the carols. "Ah, well!" observed Mrs. Joe. "You might ha' done worse." Joe secretly crossed his two forefingers and exhibited them to me as our token that Mrs. Joe was in a cross temper.

We were to have a superb dinner, consisting of a leg of pickled pork and greens, and a pair of roast stuffed fowls. A handsome mince pie had been made yesterday morning (which accounted for the mincemeat not being missed), and the pudding was already on the boil. My sister, having so much to do, was going to church vicariously; that is to say, Joe and I were going. In his working clothes, Joe was a well-knit, characteristic-looking blacksmith; in his holiday clothes, he was more like a scarecrow in good circumstances than anything else.

Nothing that he wore then fitted him or seemed to belong to him. As to me, when I was taken to have a new suit of clothes, the tailor had orders to make them like a kind of reformatory, and on no account to let me have the free use of my limbs. Joe and I going to church, therefore, must have been a moving spectacle for compassionate minds. Yet what I suffered outside was nothing to what I underwent within. The terrors that had assailed me whenever Mrs. Joe had gone near the pantry were only to be equaled by the remorse with which my mind dwelt on what my hands had done.

Mr. Wopsle, the clerk[1] at church, was to dine with us; and Mr. Hubble, the wheelwright, and Mrs. Hubble; and Uncle Pumblechook, who was a well-to-do corn chandler[2] in the nearest town, and drove his own chaise-cart.[3] The dinner hour was half past one. When Joe and I got home, we found the table laid, and Mrs. Joe dressed, and the dinner dressing, and the front door unlocked (it never was at any other time) for the company to enter by, and everything most splendid. And still, not a word of the robbery.

The time came, without bringing with it any relief to my feelings, and the company came. Mr. Wopsle, united to a Roman nose and a large, shining, bald forehead, had a deep voice which he was uncommonly proud of. He punished the *amens* tremendously; and when he gave out the psalm, he looked all round the congregation first, as much as to say, "You have heard our friend overhead; oblige me with your opinion of this style!"

I opened the door to the company, first to Mr. Wopsle, next to Mr. and Mrs. Hubble, and last of all to Uncle Pumblechook. (*I* was not allowed to call him "uncle," under the severest penalties.)

"Mrs. Joe," said Uncle Pumblechook—a large, hard-breathing, middle-aged, slow man, with a mouth like a fish, dull staring eyes, and sandy hair standing upright on his head, so that he looked as if he had just been all but choked, and had that moment come to—"I have brought you as the compliments of the season—I have brought you, mum, a bottle of sherry wine—and I have brought you, mum, a bottle of port wine." Every Christmas Day he presented himself, as a profound novelty, with exactly the same words, and carrying the two bottles like dumbbells.

We dined on these occasions in the kitchen, and adjourned, for the nuts and oranges and apples, to the parlor. Among this good company I should have felt myself, even if I hadn't robbed the pantry, in a false position. I should not have minded that if they would only have left me alone. But they wouldn't leave me alone. They seemed to think the opportunity lost if they failed to point the conversation at me, every now and then, and stick the point into me.

It began the moment we sat down to dinner. Mr. Wopsle said grace with theatrical declamation and ended with the very proper aspiration that we might be truly grateful. Upon which my sister fixed me with her eyes and said in a low reproaching voice. "Do you hear that? Be grateful."

"Especially," said Mr. Pumblechook, "be grateful, boy, to them which brought you up by hand."

Joe always aided and comforted me when he could, in some way of his own, and he always did so at dinnertime by giving me gravy, if there were any. There being plenty of gravy today, Joe spooned into my plate, at this point, about half a pint.

---

1. **clerk:** an official who assists the minister at church services and who teaches in the local school.
2. **corn chandler:** a person who buys and sells corn.
3. **chaise-cart** (shāz-kärt): a two-wheeled, one-horse carriage with a folding top.

"He was a world of trouble to you, ma'am," said Mrs. Hubble, commiserating my sister.

"Trouble?" echoed my sister. "Trouble?" And then entered on a fearful catalogue of all the illnesses I had been guilty of, and all the acts of sleeplessness I had committed, and all the high places I had tumbled from, and all the low places I had tumbled into, and all the injuries I had done myself, and all the times she had wished me in my grave, and I had contumaciously[4] refused to go there. Everybody looked at me with indignation and abhorrence.

"Have a little brandy, uncle," said my sister.

O Heavens, it had come at last! He would find it was weak, he would say it was weak, and I was lost! I held tight to the leg of the table with both hands and awaited my fate.

My sister went for the stone bottle, came back with the stone bottle, and poured his brandy out; no one else taking any. The wretched man trifled with his glass—took it up, looked at it through the light, put it down—prolonged my misery. All this time Mrs. Joe and Joe were briskly clearing the table for the pie and pudding.

I couldn't keep my eyes off him. I saw the miserable creature finger his glass playfully, take it up, smile, throw his head back, and drink the brandy off. Instantly, the company was seized with unspeakable consternation, owing to his springing to his feet, turning round several times in an appalling, spasmodic whooping-cough dance, and rushing out at the door; he then became visible through the window, making the most hideous faces and apparently out of his mind.

I held on tight, while Mrs. Joe and Joe ran to him. I didn't know how I had done it, but I had no doubt I had murdered him somehow. In my dreadful situation, it was a relief when he was brought back, and surveying the company all round as if *they* had disagreed with him, sank down into his chair with the one significant gasp, "Tar!"

I had filled up the bottle from the tar-water jug!

"Tar!" cried my sister, in amazement. "Why, how ever could tar come there?"

But Uncle Pumblechook, who was omnipotent in that kitchen, wouldn't hear the word, wouldn't hear of the subject, imperiously waved it all away with his hand, and asked for hot gin-and-water. My sister, who had begun to be alarmingly meditative, had to employ herself actively in getting the gin, the hot water, the sugar, and the lemon peel, and mixing them. For the time at least, I was saved. I still held on to the leg of the table, but clutched it now with the fervor of gratitude.

By degrees, I became calm enough to release my grasp and partake of pudding. Mr. Pumblechook partook of pudding. All partook of pudding. I began to think I should get over the day, when my sister said to Joe, "Clean plates—cold."

I clutched the leg of the table again immediately. I foresaw what was coming, and I felt that this time I really was gone.

"You must taste," said my sister, addressing the guests with her best grace, "you must taste, to finish with, a pie; a savory pork pie."

My sister went out to get it. I heard her steps proceed to the pantry. I saw Mr. Pumblechook balance his knife. I heard Joe say, "You shall have some, Pip." I felt that I could bear no more, and that I must run away. I released the leg of the table and ran for my life.

But I ran no farther than the house door, for there I ran head foremost into a party of soldiers with their muskets, one of whom held out a pair of handcuffs to me, saying: "Here you are, look sharp, come on!"

4. **contumaciously** (kŏn′tōō-mā′shəs-lē): stubbornly, disobediently.

Chapter 5

The sergeant finds the two convicts.

The apparition of a file of soldiers ringing down the butt ends of their loaded muskets on our doorstep caused the dinner party to rise from table in confusion, and caused Mrs. Joe, reentering the kitchen empty-handed, to stop short and stare in her wondering lament of "Gracious goodness, gracious me, what's gone—with the—pie!"

The sergeant and I were in the kitchen when Mrs. Joe stood staring. It was the sergeant who had spoken to me, and he was now looking round at the company, with his handcuffs invitingly extended toward them in his right hand, and his left on my shoulder.

"Excuse me, ladies and gentlemen," said the sergeant, "but I want the blacksmith. You see, blacksmith," said the sergeant, who had by this time picked out Joe with his eye, "we have had an accident with these, and I find the lock of one of 'em goes wrong. As they are wanted for immediate service, will you throw your eye over them?"

Joe threw his eye over them and pronounced that the job would necessitate the lighting of his forge fire, and would take nearer two hours than one. "Will it? Then will you set about it at once, blacksmith?" said the offhand sergeant, "as it's on His Majesty's service." With that he called to his men, who came trooping into the kitchen one after another and piled their arms in a corner.

I was in an agony of apprehension. But, beginning to perceive that the handcuffs were not for me, and that the military had so far got the better of the pie as to put it in the background, I collected a little more of my scattered wits.

"How far might you call yourselves from the

marshes, hereabouts? Not above a mile, I reckon?"

"Just a mile," said Mrs. Joe.

"That'll do. We begin to close in upon 'em about dusk. That'll do."

"Convicts, sergeant?" asked Mr. Wopsle, in a matter-of-course way.

"Aye!" returned the sergeant. "Two. They're pretty well known to be out on the marshes still, and they won't try to get clear of 'em before dusk. Anybody here seen anything of any such game?"

Everybody, myself excepted, said no, with confidence. Nobody thought of me.

"Well," said the sergeant, "they'll find themselves trapped in a circle. Now, blacksmith! If you're ready, His Majesty the King is."

Joe had got his coat and waistcoat and cravat[1] off, and his leather apron on, and passed into the forge. One of the soldiers opened its wooden windows, another lighted the fire, another turned to at the bellows, the rest stood round the blaze, which was soon roaring. Then Joe began to hammer and clink, hammer and clink, and we all looked on.

At last Joe's job was done, and the ringing and roaring stopped. As Joe got on his coat, he mustered courage to propose that some of us should go down with the soldiers and see what came of the hunt. Mr. Wopsle said he would go, if Joe would. Joe said he was agreeable and would take me.

The sergeant took a polite leave of the ladies, and his men resumed their muskets and fell in. Mr. Wopsle, Joe, and I received strict charge to keep in the rear and to speak no word after we reached the marshes. When we were all out in the raw air and were steadily moving toward our business, I treasonably whispered to Joe, "I hope, Joe, we shan't find them." And Joe whispered to me, "I'd give a

shilling if they had cut and run, Pip."

We were joined by no stragglers from the village, for the weather was cold and threatening, the way dreary, the footing bad, darkness coming on, and the people had good fires indoors, and were keeping the day.[2] We struck out on the open marshes, through the gate at the side of the churchyard. A bitter sleet came rattling against us here on the east wind, and Joe took me on his back.

Now that we were out upon the dismal wilderness where they little thought I had been within eight or nine hours, and had seen both men hiding, I considered for the first time, with great dread, if we should come upon them, would my particular convict suppose that it was I who had brought the soldiers there? He had asked me if I was a deceiving imp, and he said I should be a fierce young hound if I joined the hunt against him. Would he believe that I was both imp and hound in treacherous earnest, and had betrayed him?

It was of no use asking this question now. There I was, on Joe's back, and there was Joe beneath me, charging at the ditches like a hunter. The soldiers were in front of us, extending into a pretty wide line with an interval between man and man.

With my heart thumping like a blacksmith at Joe's broad shoulder, I looked all about for any sign of the convicts. I could see none, I could hear none. The soldiers were moving on in the direction of the old Battery, and we were moving on a little way behind them, when, all of a sudden, we all stopped. For there had reached us, on the wings of the wind and rain, a long shout. It was repeated. The sergeant, a decisive man, ordered that the sound should not be answered, but that the course should be changed, and that his men should make toward it "at the double."

---

1. **cravat** (krə-văt): necktie.

2. **keeping the day:** observing Christmas Day.

It was a run indeed now. Down banks and up banks, and over gates, and splashing into dikes, and breaking among coarse rushes, no man cared where he went. As we came nearer to the shouting, it became more and more apparent that it was made by more than one voice. After a while, we could hear one voice calling "Murder!" and another voice, "Convicts! Runaways! Guard! This way for the runaway convicts!" Then both voices would seem to be stifled in a struggle, and then would break out again. And when it had come to this, the soldiers ran like deer, and Joe too.

The sergeant ran in first, and two of his men ran in close upon him. Their pieces[3] were cocked and leveled when we all ran in.

"Here are both men!" panted the sergeant, struggling at the bottom of a ditch. "Surrender, you two! and confound you for two wild beasts! Come asunder!"

Water was splashing, and mud was flying, and oaths were being sworn, and blows were being struck, when some more men went down into the ditch to help the sergeant, and dragged out, separately, my convict and the other one. Both were bleeding and panting and execrating and struggling; but of course I knew them both directly.

"Mind," said my convict, wiping blood from his face with his ragged sleeves, and shaking torn hair from his fingers, "I took him! I give him up to you! Mind that!"

"It's not much to be particular about," said the sergeant. "It'll do you small good, my man, being in the same plight yourself. Handcuffs there!"

"I don't expect it to do me any good. I don't want it to do me more good than it does now," said my convict, with a greedy laugh. "I took him. He knows it. That's enough for me."

The other convict, in addition to the old bruised left side of his face, seemed to be bruised and torn all over. He could not so much as get his breath to speak, until they were both separately handcuffed, but leaned upon a soldier to keep himself from falling.

"Take notice, guard—he tried to murder me," were his first words.

"Tried to murder him?" said my convict disdainfully. "Try, and not do it? I took him, and giv' him up, that's what I done. I not only prevented him getting off the marshes, but I dragged him here. He's a gentleman if you please, this villain. Now the Hulks has got its gentleman again, through me. Murder him? When I could do worse and drag him back!"

The other one still gasped, "He tried—he tried—to—murder me. Bear—bear witness."

"Lookee here!" said my convict to the sergeant. "Singlehanded I got clear of the prison ship; I made a dash and I done it. I could ha' got clear of these death-cold flats likewise—look at my leg; you won't find much iron on it—if I hadn't made discovery that *he* was here. Let *him* go free? Let *him* profit by means as I found out? Let *him* make a tool of me afresh and again? Once more? No, no, no. If I had died at the bottom there," and he made an emphatic swing at the ditch with his manacled hands, "I'd have held to him with that grip, that you should have been safe to find him in my hold."

The other fugitive, who was evidently in extreme horror of his companion, repeated, "He tried to murder me. I should have been a dead man if you had not come up."

"He lies!" said my convict, with fierce energy. "He's a liar born, and he'll die a liar. Look at his face: ain't it written there? Let him turn those eyes of his on me. I defy him to do it."

The other looked at the soldiers, and looked about at the marshes and at the sky, but certainly did not look at the speaker.

---

3. **pieces:** muskets.

"Do you see him?" pursued my convict. "Do you see what a villain he is? Do you see those groveling and wandering eyes? That's how he looked when we were tried together. He never looked at me."

The other, turning his eyes restlessly about him far and near, did at last turn them for a moment on the speaker, with the words, "You are not much to look at," and with a half-taunting glance at the bound hands. At that point, my convict became so frantically exasperated that he would have rushed upon him but for the interposition of the soldiers. "Didn't I tell you," said the other convict then, "that he would murder me, if he could?" And anyone could see that he shook with fear, and that there broke out upon his lips curious white flakes, like thin snow.

"Enough of this parley," said the sergeant. "Light those torches."

As one of the soldiers, who carried a basket, went down on his knee to open it, my convict looked round him for the first time and saw me. I had alighted from Joe's back on the brink of the ditch when we came up, and had not moved since. I looked at him eagerly when he looked at me, and slightly moved my hands and shook my head. I had been waiting for him to see me, that I might try to assure him of my innocence. He gave me a look that I did not understand, and it all passed in a moment. But if he had looked at me for an hour or for a day, I could not have remembered his face ever afterwards, as having been more attentive.

The soldier with the basket soon lighted three or four torches. Before we departed from that spot, four soldiers, standing in a ring, fired twice into the air. Presently we saw other torches kindled at some distance behind us, and others on the marshes on the opposite bank of the river. "All right," said the sergeant. "March."

We had not gone far when three cannon were fired ahead of us with a sound that seemed to burst something inside my ear. "You are expected on board," said the sergeant to my convict. "They know you are coming. Don't straggle, my man. Close up here."

The two were kept apart, and each walked surrounded by a separate guard. I had hold of Joe's hand now, and Joe carried one of the torches. Mr. Wopsle had been for going back, but Joe was resolved to see it out, so we went on with the party. The two prisoners limped along in the midst of the muskets. We could not go fast, because of their lameness; and they were so spent, that two or three times we had to halt while they rested.

After an hour or so, we came to a rough wooden hut and a landing place. Then we went into the hut, where there was a smell of tobacco and whitewash, and a bright fire, and a lamp.

My convict never looked at me, except that once. While we stood in the hut, he turned to the sergeant and remarked:

"I wish to say something respecting this escape. It may prevent some persons laying under suspicion alonger me."

"You can say what you like," returned the sergeant, standing coolly looking at him with his arms folded, "but you have no call to say it here. You'll have opportunity enough to say about it, and hear about it, before it's done with, you know."

"I know, but this is another matter. A man can't starve; at least *I* can't. I took some wittles, up at the village over yonder."

"You mean stole," said the sergeant.

"And I'll tell you where from. From the blacksmith's."

"Halloa!" said the sergeant, staring at Joe.

"Halloa, Pip!" said Joe, staring at me.

"It was some broken wittles—that's what it was—and a dram of liquor, and a pie."

"Have you happened to miss such an article

as a pie, blacksmith?" asked the sergeant confidentially.

"My wife did, at the very moment when you came in. Don't you know, Pip?"

"So," said my convict, turning his eyes on Joe in a moody manner, and without the least glance at me; "so you're the blacksmith, are you? Then I'm sorry to say, I've eat your pie."

"God knows you're welcome to it—so far as it was ever mine," returned Joe, with a saving remembrance of Mrs. Joe. "We don't know what you have done, but we wouldn't have you starved to death for it, poor miserable fellow creature. Would us, Pip?"

The something that I had noticed before clicked in the man's throat again, and he turned his back. The boat had returned, and his guard were ready, so we followed him to the landing place, and saw him put into the boat, which was rowed by a crew of convicts like himself. No one seemed surprised to see him, or interested in seeing him, or glad to see him, or sorry to see him, or spoke a word except that somebody in the boat growled as if to dogs, "Give way, you!" which was the signal for the dip of the oars. By the light of the torches, we saw the black Hulk lying out a little way from the mud of the shore, like a wicked Noah's ark. Cribbed and barred and moored by massive rusty chains, the prison ship seemed in my young eyes to be ironed like the prisoners. We saw the boat go alongside, and we saw him taken up the side and disappear. Then, the ends of the torches were flung hissing into the water, and went out, as if it were all over with him.

I do not recall that I felt any tenderness of conscience in reference to Mrs. Joe, when the fear of being found out was lifted off me. But I loved Joe—perhaps for no better reason in those days than because the dear fellow let me love him—and it was much on my mind that I ought to tell Joe the whole truth. Yet I did not, and for the reason that I mistrusted that if I did, he would think me worse than I was. The fear of losing Joe's confidence tied up my tongue. In a word, I was too cowardly to do what I knew to be right, as I had been too cowardly to avoid doing what I knew to be wrong.

Chapter 6

We meet Mr. Wopsle's great-aunt and Biddy, her granddaughter.

When I was old enough, I was to be apprenticed to Joe, and until I could assume that dignity I was not to be what Mrs. Joe called "Pompeyed," or (as I render it) pampered. Therefore, I was not only odd boy about the forge, but if any neighbor happened to want an extra boy to frighten birds, or pick up stones, or do any such job, I was favored with the employment. A money box was kept on the kitchen mantel shelf, into which it was publicly made known that all my earnings were dropped, but I had no hope of any personal participation in the treasure.

Mr. Wopsle's great-aunt kept an evening school in the village. She was a ridiculous old woman who used to go to sleep from six to seven every evening, in the society of youth who paid twopence[1] per week each for the improving opportunity of seeing her do it. She rented a small cottage, and Mr. Wopsle had the room upstairs, where we students used to overhear him reading aloud in a most dignified and terrific manner, and occasionally bumping on the ceiling. There was a fiction that Mr. Wopsle "examined" the scholars once a quarter. What he did on those occasions was to turn up his cuffs, stick up his hair, and give us Mark

1. **twopence** (tŭp′əns): about four cents in American money in Dickens' time.

Antony's oration over the body of Caesar.[2]

Mr. Wopsle's great-aunt, besides keeping this educational institution, kept—in the same room—a little general shop. She had no idea what stock she had, or what the price of anything in it was; but there was a little greasy memorandum book kept in a drawer, which served as a catalogue of prices, and by this oracle Biddy arranged all the shop transactions. Biddy was Mr. Wopsle's great-aunt's granddaughter. She was an orphan like myself; like me, too, had been brought up by hand. Her hair always wanted brushing, her hands always wanted washing, and her shoes always wanted mending and pulling up at heel.

More by the help of Biddy than of Mr. Wopsle's great-aunt, I struggled through the alphabet as if it had been a bramblebush, getting considerably worried and scratched by every letter. After that, I fell among those thieves, the nine figures,[3] who seemed every evening to do something new to disguise themselves and baffle recognition. But at last I began, in a groping way, to read, write, and cipher,[4] on the very smallest scale.

One night, I was sitting in the chimney corner with my slate, expending great efforts on the production of a letter to Joe. I think it must have been a full year after our hunt upon the marshes, for it was a long time after, and it was winter and a hard frost. With an alphabet on the hearth at my feet for reference, I contrived in an hour or two to print and smear this epistle:

MI DeEr JO i opE U r krWitE wEll i opE i sHAl soN B haBeLL 4 2 teeDge U JO an theN wE sHOrl b sO gLOdd aN wEn i M preNgtD 2 u JO woT larX an bLEvE ME inF xn PiP.

2. **Mark . . . Caesar:** a famous speech from William Shakespeare's play *Julius Caesar*.
3. **the nine figures:** the numbers one through nine.
4. **cipher:** to do arithmetic.

There was no necessity for my communicating with Joe by letter, inasmuch as he sat beside me and we were alone. But I delivered this written communication (slate and all) with my own hand, and Joe received it as a miracle of erudition.

"I say, Pip, old chap!" cried Joe, opening his blue eyes wide. "What a scholar you are! Ain't you?"

"I should like to be," said I, glancing at the slate as he held it, with a misgiving that the writing was rather hilly.

"Why, here's a J," said Joe, "and a O equal to anythink! Here's a J and a O, Pip, and a J-O, Joe."

I had never heard Joe read aloud to any greater extent than this monosyllable, and I had observed at church last Sunday, when I accidentally held our prayer book upside down, that it seemed to suit his convenience quite as well as if it had been all right. Wishing to embrace the present occasion of finding out whether, in teaching Joe, I should have to begin quite at the beginning, I said, "Ah! But read the rest, Joe."

"The rest, eh, Pip?" said Joe, looking at it with a slowly searching eye. "One, two, three. Why, here's three J's, and three O's, and three J-O, Joe's, in it, Pip!"

I leaned over Joe, and, with the aid of my forefinger, read him the whole letter.

"Astonishing!" said Joe, when I had finished. "You *are* a scholar."

"How do you spell Gargery, Joe?" I asked.

"I don't spell it at all," said Joe.

"But supposing you did?"

"It *can't* be supposed," said Joe. "Tho' I'm oncommon fond of reading, too."

"Are you, Joe?"

"Oncommon. Give me," said Joe, "a good book, or a good newspaper, and sit me down afore a good fire, and I ask no better. Lord!" he continued, after rubbing his knees a little, "when you *do* come to a J and a O, and says you, 'Here, at last, is a J-O, Joe,' how interesting reading is!"

I derived from this last, that Joe's education, like steam, was yet in its infancy. Pursuing the subject, I inquired:

"Didn't you ever go to school, Joe, when you were as little as me?"

"No, Pip."

"Why didn't you ever go to school, Joe, when you were as little as me?"

"Well, Pip," said Joe, taking up the poker, and settling himself to his usual occupation, when he was thoughtful, of slowly raking the fire between the lower bars, "I'll tell you. My father, Pip, he were given to drink, and when he were overtook with drink, he hammered away at my mother most onmerciful. My mother and me we ran away from my father several times; and then my mother she'd go out to work, and she'd say, 'Joe,' she'd say, 'now, please God, you shall have some schooling, child,' and she'd put me to school. But my father were that good in his heart that he couldn't a-bear to be without us. So, he took us home and hammered us. Which, you see, Pip" said Joe, "were a drawback on my learning."

"Certainly, poor Joe!"

"Though mind you, Pip," said Joe, "rendering unto all their doo, and maintaining equal justice betwixt man and man, my father were that good in his heart, don't you see?"

I didn't see; but I didn't say so.

"'Consequence, my father didn't make objections to my going to work; so I went to work at my present calling, and I worked tolerable hard, I assure *you*, Pip. In time I were able to keep him, and I kep him till he went off in a purple leptic fit.[5] My mother, she were in poor 'elth, and quite broke. She waren't long of following, poor soul, and her share of peace come round at last."

Joe's blue eyes turned a little watery. "It were but lonesome then," said Joe, "living here alone, and I got acquainted with your sister. Now, Pip," Joe looked firmly at me, as if he knew I was not going to agree with him, "your sister is a fine figure of a woman."

I could not help looking at the fire, in an obvious state of doubt.

"Whatever family opinions, or whatever the world's opinions, on that subject may be, Pip, your sister is," Joe tapped the top bar with the poker after every word following, "a—fine—figure—of—a—woman!"

I could think of nothing better to say than "I am glad you think so, Joe."

"So am I," returned Joe. "When I offered to your sister to keep company, and to be asked in church, at such times as she was willing and ready to come to the forge, I said to her, 'And bring the poor little child. God bless the poor little child,' I said to your sister, 'there's room for *him* at the forge!'"

I broke out crying and hugged Joe round the neck, who dropped the poker to hug me, and to say, "Ever the best of friends; ain't us, Pip? Don't cry, old chap!"

When this little interruption was over, Joe resumed:

"Well, you see, Pip, and here we are! Now, when you take me in hand in my learning, Pip (and I tell you beforehand I am awful dull, most awful dull), Mrs. Joe mustn't see too much of what we're up to. It must be done, as I may say, on the sly. I'll tell you why, Pip.

"Your sister is given to government," said Joe. "Which I meantersay the government of you and myself."

"Oh!"

"And she ain't overpartial to having scholars on the premises," Joe continued, "and in partickler would not be overpartial to my

---

5. **purple leptic fit:** Joe means an *apoplectic* (ăp′ə-plĕk′tĭk) *fit. Apoplexy* (ăp′ə-plĕk′sē) is a sudden paralysis or loss of consciousness, sometimes called a *stroke*.

being a scholar, for fear as I might rise. Like a sort of rebel, don't you see?"

Young as I was, I believe that I dated a new admiration of Joe from that night. We were equals afterward, as we had been before; but afterward, at quiet times when I sat looking at Joe and thinking about him, I had a new sensation of feeling conscious that I was looking up to Joe in my heart.

"However," said Joe, rising to replenish the fire, "here's the Dutch clock a-working himself up to being equal to strike eight of 'em, and she's not home yet!"

Mrs. Joe made occasional trips with Uncle Pumblechook on market days to assist him in buying such household stuffs and goods as required a woman's judgment, Uncle Pumblechook being a bachelor. This was market day, and Mrs. Joe was out on one of these expeditions.

Joe made the fire and swept the hearth, and then we went to the door to listen for the chaise-cart. It was a dry, cold night.

"Here comes the mare," said Joe, "ringing like a peal of bells!"

Mrs. Joe was soon landed, and Uncle Pumblechook was soon down too, and we were soon all in the kitchen, carrying so much cold air with us that it seemed to drive all the heat out of the fire.

"Now," said Mrs. Joe, unwrapping herself with haste and excitement, and throwing her bonnet back on her shoulders, where it hung by the strings, "if this boy ain't grateful this night, he never will be!"

I looked as grateful as any boy possibly could who was wholly uninformed why he ought to assume that expression.

"It's only to be hoped," said my sister, "that he won't be Pompeyed. But I have my fears."

"She ain't in that line, mum," said Mr. Pumblechook. "She knows better."

She? I looked at Joe, making the motion with my lips and eyebrows. "She?" Joe looked at me, making the motion with *his* lips and eyebrows. "She?" My sister catching him in the act, he drew the back of his hand across his nose with his usual conciliatory air on such occasions, and looked at her.

"Well?" said my sister, in her snappish way. "What are you staring at? Is the house afire?"

"Which some individual," Joe politely hinted, "mentioned she."

"And she is a she, I suppose?" said my sister. "Unless you call Miss Havisham a he. And I doubt if even you'll go so far as that."

"Miss Havisham uptown?" said Joe.

"Is there any Miss Havisham downtown?" returned my sister. "She wants this boy to go and play there. And of course he's going. And he had better play there," said my sister, shaking her head at me as an encouragement to be extremely light and sportive, "or I'll work him."

I had heard of Miss Havisham uptown—everybody for miles round had heard of Miss Havisham uptown—as an immensely rich and grim lady who lived in a large and dismal house barricaded against robbers, and who led a life of seclusion.

"Well, to be sure!" said Joe, astounded. "I wonder how she comes to know Pip!"

"Noodle!" cried my sister. "Who said she knew him?"

"Which some individual," Joe again politely hinted, "mentioned that she wanted him to go and play there."

"And couldn't she ask Uncle Pumblechook if he knew of a boy to go and play there? Isn't it just barely possible that Uncle Pumblechook may be a tenant of hers, and that he may sometimes go there to pay his rent? And couldn't she then ask Uncle Pumblechook if he knew of a boy to go and play there? And couldn't Uncle Pumblechook—being always considerate and thoughtful for us, though you may not think it,

Joseph, then mention this boy that I have forever been a willing slave to?"

"Good again!" cried Uncle Pumblechook. "Well put! Good indeed! Now, Joseph, you know the case."

"No, Joseph," said my sister, in a reproachful manner, "you do not yet—though you may not think it—know the case. Uncle Pumblechook, being sensible that this boy's fortune may be made by his going to Miss Havisham's, has offered to take him into town tonight in his own chaise-cart and to keep him tonight and to take him with his own hands to Miss Havisham's tomorrow morning. And Lor-a-mussy[6] me!" cried my sister, casting off her bonnet in sudden desperation, "here I stand talking to mere mooncalfs, with Uncle Pumblechook waiting, and the mare catching cold at the door, and the boy grimed with crock and dirt from the hair of his head to the sole of his foot!"

With that she pounced on me, like an eagle on a lamb, and my face was squeezed into wooden bowls in sinks, and my head was put under taps of water butts, and I was soaped, and kneaded, and toweled, and thumped, and harrowed, and rasped, until I really was quite beside myself.

When my ablutions were completed, I was put into clean linen of the stiffest character, and was trussed up in my tightest and fearfulest suit. I was then delivered over to Mr. Pumblechook, who formally received me as if he were the sheriff, and who let off upon me the speech that I knew he had been dying to make all along: "Boy, be forever grateful to all friends, but especially unto them which brought you up by hand!"

"Goodbye, Joe!"

"God bless you, Pip, old chap!"

I had never parted from him before, and what with my feelings and what with soapsuds,

6. **Lor-a-mussy:** Lord have mercy (on).

I could at first see no stars from the chaise-cart. But they twinkled out one by one, without throwing any light on the questions why on earth I was going to play at Miss Havisham's, and what on earth I was expected to play at.

Chapter 7

We are introduced to Miss Havisham and her ward Estella.

Mr. Pumblechook's premises in the High Street of the market town were of a peppercorny character, as the premises of a corn chandler and seedsman should be. It was in the early morning after my arrival that I entertained this speculation. On the previous night, I had been sent straight to bed in an attic with a sloping roof, which was so low in the corner where the bedstead was that I calculated the tiles as being within a foot of my eyebrows.

Mr. Pumblechook and I breakfasted at eight o'clock in the parlor behind the shop while his shopman took his mug of tea and hunch of bread and butter on a sack of peas in the front premises. I considered Mr. Pumblechook wretched company. Besides giving me as much crumb as possible in combination with as little butter, and putting a great quantity of warm water in my milk, his conversation consisted of nothing but arithmetic. On my politely bidding him good morning, he said pompously, "Seven times nine, boy?" And how should *I* be able to answer, dodged in that way, in a strange place, on an empty stomach! I was hungry, but before I had swallowed a morsel, he began a running sum that lasted all through the breakfast. "Seven?" "And four?" "And eight?" "And six?" "And two?" "And ten?" And so on.

I was very glad when ten o'clock came and we started for Miss Havisham's. Within a quarter of an hour we came to Miss Havisham's house, which was of old brick, and dismal, and had a great many iron bars to it. Some of the windows had been walled up; of those that remained, all the lower were rustily barred. There was a courtyard in front, and that was barred; so we had to wait, after ringing the bell, until someone should come to open it. While we waited at the gate, I saw that at the side of the house there was a large brewery. No brewing was going on in it, and none seemed to have gone on for a long time.

A window was raised, and a clear voice demanded, "What name?" To which my conductor replied, "Pumblechook." The voice returned, "Quite right," and the window was shut again, and a young lady came across the courtyard, with keys in her hand.

"This," said Mr. Pumblechook, "is Pip."

"This is Pip, is it?" returned the young lady, who was very pretty, and seemed very proud. "Come in, Pip."

Mr. Pumblechook was coming in also, when she stopped him with the gate.

"Oh!" she said. "Did you wish to see Miss Havisham?"

"If Miss Havisham wished to see me," returned Mr. Pumblechook, discomfited.

"Ah!" said the girl. "But you see she don't."

She said it so finally, that Mr. Pumblechook could not protest. But he eyed me severely—as if *I* had done anything to him!—and departed with the words reproachfully delivered: "Boy! Let your behavior here be a credit unto them which brought you up by hand!"

My young conductress locked the gate, and we went across the courtyard. It was paved and clean, but grass was growing in every crevice. The brewery beyond stood open, and all was empty and disused. The cold wind seemed to blow colder there than outside the gate; and it made a shrill noise in howling in and out at the open sides of the brewery, like the noise of the wind in the rigging of a ship at sea.

"What is the name of this house, miss?"

"Its name was Satis; which is Greek, or Latin, or Hebrew, or all three—or all one to me—for enough."

"Enough House!" said I. "That's a curious name, miss."

"Yes," she replied, "but it meant more than it said. It meant, when it was given, that whoever had this house, could want nothing else. They must have been easily satisfied in those days, I should think. But don't loiter, boy."

Though she called me "boy" so often, and with a carelessness that was far from complimentary, she was of about my own age. She seemed much older than I, of course, being a girl, and beautiful and self-possessed; and she was as scornful of me as if she had been one-and-twenty, and a queen.

We went into the house by a side door—the great front entrance had two chains across it outside—and the first thing I noticed was that the passages were all dark, and that she had left a candle burning there. She took it up, and we went through more passages and up a staircase, and still it was all dark, and only the candle lighted us.

At last we came to the door of a room, and she said, "Go in."

I answered, more in shyness than politeness, "After you, miss."

To this she returned. "Don't be ridiculous, boy; I am not going in." And scornfully walked away, and—what was worse—took the candle with her.

This was very uncomfortable, and I was half afraid. However, the only thing to be done being to knock at the door, I knocked, and was told from within to enter. I entered, therefore, and found myself in a pretty large room, well lighted with wax candles. No glimpse of daylight was to be seen in it. It was a dressing room, as I supposed from the furniture. But prominent in it was a draped table with a gilded looking glass, and that I made out at first sight to be a fine lady's dressing table.

In an armchair, with an elbow resting on the table and her head leaning on that hand, sat the strangest lady I have ever seen, or shall ever see.

She was dressed in rich materials—satins, and lace, and silks—all of white. Her shoes were white. And she had a long white veil dependent from her hair, and she had bridal flowers in her hair, but her hair was white. Some bright jewels sparkled on her neck and on her hands, and some other jewels lay sparkling on the table. Dresses and half-packed trunks were scattered about. She had not quite finished dressing, for she had but one shoe on—the other was on the table near her hand—her veil was but half arranged, her watch and chain were not put on, and some lace for her bosom lay with those trinkets, and with her handkerchief, and gloves, and some flowers, and a prayer book, all confusedly heaped about the looking glass.

But I saw that everything within my view which ought to be white had lost its luster, and was faded and yellow. I saw that the bride within the bridal dress had withered like the dress, and like the flowers, and had no brightness left but the brightness of her sunken eyes. I saw that the dress had been put upon the rounded figure of a young woman, and that the figure upon which it now hung loose had shrunk to skin and bone.

"Who is it?" said the lady at the table.

"Pip, ma'am."

"Pip?"

"Mr. Pumblechook's boy, ma'am. Come—to play."

"Come nearer; let me look at you. Come closer."

It was when I stood before her, avoiding her eyes, that I took note of the surrounding objects in detail, and saw that her watch had stopped at twenty minutes to nine, and that a clock in the room had stopped at twenty minutes to nine.

"Look at me," said Miss Havisham. "You are not afraid of a woman who has never seen the sun since you were born?"

I regret to state that I was not afraid of telling the enormous lie comprehended in the answer, "No."

"Do you know what I touch here?" she said, laying her hands, one upon the other, on her left side.

"Yes, ma'am."

"What do I touch?"

"Your heart."

"Broken!"

She uttered the word with an eager look, and with strong emphasis, and with a weird smile that had a kind of boast in it.

"I am tired," said Miss Havisham. "I sometimes have sick fancies, and I have a sick fancy that I want to see some play. There, there!" with an impatient movement of the fingers of her right hand, "play, play, play!"

I stood looking at Miss Havisham in what I suppose she took for a stubborn manner, inasmuch as she said, when we had taken a good look at each other:

"Are you sullen and obstinate?"

"No, ma'am, I am very sorry for you, and very sorry I can't play just now. If you complain of me, I shall get into trouble with my sister, so I would do it if I could; but it's so new here, and so strange, and so fine—and melancholy—" I stopped, fearing I might say too much, or had already said it, and we took another look at each other.

Before she spoke again, she turned her eyes from me, and looked at the dress she wore, and at the dressing table, and finally at herself in the looking glass.

"So new to him," she muttered, "so old to me; so strange to him, so familiar to me; so melancholy to both of us! Call Estella."

As she was still looking at the reflection of herself, I thought she was still talking to herself, and kept quiet.

"Call Estella," she repeated, flashing a look at me. "You can do that. Call Estella. At the door."

To stand in the dark in a mysterious passage of an unknown house, bawling Estella to a scornful young lady neither visible nor responsive, and feeling it a dreadful liberty so to roar out her name, was almost as bad as playing to order. But, she answered at last, and her light came along the dark passage like a star.

Miss Havisham beckoned her to come close, and took up a jewel from the table, and tried its effect against her pretty brown hair. "Your own, one day, my dear, and you will use it well. Let me see you play cards with this boy."

"With this boy! Why, he is a common laboring boy!"

I thought I overheard Miss Havisham answer—only it seemed so unlikely—"Well? You can break his heart."

"What do you play, boy?" asked Estella of me, with the greatest disdain.

"Nothing but beggar my neighbor, miss."

"Beggar him," said Miss Havisham to Estella. So we sat down to cards.

It was then I began to understand that everything in the room had stopped, like the watch and the clock, a long time ago. I noticed that Miss Havisham put down the jewel exactly on the spot from which she had taken it up. As Estella dealt the cards, I glanced at the dressing table again, and saw that the shoe upon it, once white, now yellow, had never been worn. I glanced down at the foot from which the shoe was absent, and saw that the silk stocking on it, once white, now yellow, had been trodden ragged.

Miss Havisham sat, corpselike, as we played at cards.

"He calls the knaves jacks, this boy!" said Estella with disdain, before our first game was out. "And what coarse hands he has! And what thick boots!"

I had never thought of being ashamed of my

hands before; but her contempt for me was so strong that it became infectious, and I caught it.

She won the game, and I dealt. I misdealt, as was only natural when I knew she was lying in wait for me to do wrong; and she denounced me for a stupid, clumsy, laboring boy.

"You say nothing of her," remarked Miss Havisham to me, as she looked on. "She says many hard things of you, yet you say nothing of her. What do you think of her?"

"I don't like to say," I stammered.

"Tell me in my ear," said Miss Havisham, bending down.

"I think she is very proud," I replied, in a whisper.

"Anything else?"

"I think she is very pretty."

"Anything else?"

"I think she is very insulting." (She was looking at me then with a look of supreme aversion.)

"Anything else?"

"I think I should like to go home."

"And never see her again, though she is so pretty?"

"I am not sure that I shouldn't like to see her again, but I should like to go home now."

"You shall go soon," said Miss Havisham aloud. "Play the game out."

I played the game to an end with Estella, and she beggared me. She threw the cards down on the table when she had won them all, as if she despised them for having been won of me.

"When shall I have you here again?" said Miss Havisham. "Let me think. Come again after six days. You hear?"

"Yes, ma'am."

"Estella, take him down. Let him have something to eat, and let him roam and look about him while he eats. Go, Pip."

I followed the candle down, as I had followed the candle up, and she stood it in the place where we had found it.

"You are to wait here, you boy," said Estella. She disappeared and closed the door.

I took the opportunity of being alone to look at my coarse hands and my common boots. They had never troubled me before, but they troubled me now. I determined to ask Joe why he had ever taught me to call those picture cards jacks, which ought to be called knaves. I wished Joe had been rather more genteelly brought up, and then I should have been so too.

She came back, with some bread and meat and a little mug of beer. She put the mug down on the stones of the yard, and gave me the bread and meat without looking at me, as insolently as if I were a dog in disgrace. I was so humiliated, hurt, spurned, offended, angry, sorry, that tears started to my eyes. The moment they sprang there, the girl looked at me with a quick delight in having been the cause of them. This gave me power to keep them back and to look at her; so she gave a contemptuous toss—but with a sense, I thought, of having made too sure that I was so wounded—and left me.

But, when she was gone, I got behind one of the gates in the brewery lane, and leaned my sleeve against the wall there, and leaned my forehead on it, and cried. As I cried, I kicked the wall, and took a hard twist at my hair, so bitter were my feelings.

I got rid of my injured feelings for the time, by kicking them into the brewery wall, and twisting them out of my hair, and then I smoothed my face with my sleeve, and came from behind the gate. The bread and meat were acceptable, and the beer was warming and tingling.

Even with those aids, I might not have come to myself as soon as I did, but that I saw Estella approaching with the keys to let me out. She gave me a triumphant glance in passing me, as if she rejoiced that my hands were so coarse and my boots were so thick, and she opened the gate and stood holding it. I was passing out without looking at her when she touched me with a taunting hand.

"Why don't you cry?"

"Because I don't want to."

"You do," said she. "You have been crying till you are half blind, and you are near crying again now."

She laughed contemptuously, pushed me out, and locked the gate upon me. I went straight to Mr. Pumblechook's, and was immensely relieved to find him not at home. So, leaving word with the shopman on what day I was wanted at Miss Havisham's again, I set off on the four-mile walk to our forge, pondering, as I went along, on all I had seen, and that I was a common laboring boy; that my hands were coarse; that my boots were thick; that I was much more ignorant than I had considered myself last night; and generally that I was in a low-lived, bad way.

Chapter 8

Pip tells some tall tales.

When I reached home, my sister was very curious to know all about Miss Havisham's, and asked a number of questions. And I soon found myself getting heavily bumped from behind in the nape of the neck and the small of the back, and having my face ignominiously shoved against the kitchen wall, because I did not answer those questions at sufficient length.

I felt convinced that if I described Miss Havisham's as my eyes had seen it, I should not be understood. Not only that, but I felt convinced that Miss Havisham too would not be understood; and although she was perfectly incomprehensible to me, I entertained an impression that there would be something coarse and treacherous in my dragging her as she really was (to say nothing of Miss Estella) before the contemplation of Mrs. Joe. Consequently, I said as little as I could, and had my face shoved against the kitchen wall.

The worst of it was that bullying old Pumblechook, preyed upon by a devouring curiosity to be informed of all I had seen and heard, came gaping over in his chaise-cart at teatime, to have the details divulged to him.

"Well, boy," Uncle Pumblechook began, as soon as he was seated in the chair of honor by the fire. "How did you get on uptown?"

I answered, "Pretty well, sir," and my sister shook her fist at me.

"Pretty well?" Mr. Pumblechook repeated. "Pretty well is no answer. Tell us what you mean by pretty well, boy."

My sister with an exclamation of impatience was going to fly at me—I had no shadow of defense, for Joe was busy in the forge—when Mr. Pumblechook interposed with "No! Don't lose your temper. Leave this lad to me, ma'am; leave this lad to me." Mr. Pumblechook then turned me toward him, as if he were going to cut my hair. "Boy! What like is Miss Havisham?" Mr. Pumblechook began, folding his arms tight on his chest.

"Very tall and dark," I told him.

"Is she, uncle?" asked my sister.

Mr. Pumblechook winked assent, from which I at once inferred that he had never seen Miss Havisham, for she was nothing of the kind.

"Good!" said Mr. Pumblechook, conceitedly. "This is the way to have him! We are beginning to hold our own, I think, mum?"

"I am sure, uncle," returned Mrs. Joe; "I wish you had him always; you know so well how to deal with him."

"Now, boy! What was she a-doing of, when you went in today?" asked Mr. Pumblechook.

"She was sitting," I answered, "in a black velvet coach."

Mr. Pumblechook and Mrs. Joe stared at one another—as they well might—and both repeated, "In a black velvet coach?"

"Yes," said I. "And Miss Estella—that's her niece, I think—handed her in cake and wine at the coach window, on a gold plate. And we all had cake and wine on gold plates. And I got up behind the coach to eat mine, because she told me to."

Mr. Pumblechook and Mrs. Joe stared at one another again, in utter amazement. I was perfectly frantic—a reckless witness under the torture—and would have told them anything.

"Did you ever see her in it, uncle?" asked Mrs. Joe.

"How could I," he returned, forced to the admission, "when I never see her in my life? Never clapped eyes upon her!"

"Goodness, uncle! And yet you have spoken to her?"

"Why, don't you know," said Mr. Pumblechook testily, "that when I have been there, I have been took up to the outside of her door, and the door has stood ajar, and she has spoken to me that way. What did you play at, boy?"

"We played with flags," I said. (I beg to observe that I think of myself with amazement, when I recall the lies I told on this occasion.)

"Flags!" echoed my sister.

"Yes," said I. "Estella waved a blue flag, and I waved a red one, and Miss Havisham waved one sprinkled all over with little gold stars, out at the coach window. And then we all waved our swords and hurrahed."

If they had asked me any more questions, I should undoubtedly have betrayed myself. The subject still held them when Joe came in from his work to have a cup of tea. To whom my sister, more for the relief of her own mind than for the gratification of his, related my pretended experiences.

Now, when I saw Joe open his blue eyes and roll them all round the kitchen in helpless amazement, I was overtaken by penitence. Toward Joe, and Joe only, I considered myself a young monster, while they sat debating what results would come to me from Miss Havisham's acquaintance and favor. They had no doubt that Miss Havisham would "do something" for me. My sister stood out for "property." Mr. Pumblechook was in favor of a handsome premium[1] for binding me apprentice to some genteel trade—say, the corn and seed trade, for instance.

After Mr. Pumblechook had driven off, and when my sister was washing up, I stole into the forge to Joe, and remained by him until he had done for the night. Then I said, "Before the fire goes out, Joe, I should like to tell you something."

"Should you, Pip?" said Joe, drawing his shoeing stool near the forge. "Then tell us. What is it, Pip?"

"Joe," said I, taking hold of his rolled-up shirt sleeve, and twisting it between my finger and thumb, "you remember all that about Miss Havisham's?"

"Remember?" said Joe. "I believe you! Wonderful!"

"It's a terrible thing, Joe; it ain't true."

"What are you telling of, Pip?" cried Joe, falling back in the greatest amazement. "You don't mean to say it's——"

"Yes, I do; it's lies, Joe."

As I fixed my eyes hopelessly on Joe, Joe contemplated me in dismay. "Pip, old chap! This won't do, old fellow! I say! Where do you expect to go to?"

"It's terrible, Joe; ain't it?"

"Terrible?" cried Joe. "Awful! What possessed you?"

"I don't know what possessed me, Joe," I replied, letting his shirt sleeve go, and sitting down in the ashes at his feet, hanging my head; "but I wish you hadn't taught me to call knaves at cards jacks, and I wish my boots weren't so thick nor my hands so coarse."

And then I told Joe that I felt very miserable, and that I hadn't been able to explain myself to Mrs. Joe and Pumblechook, who were so rude to me, and that there had been a beautiful young lady at Miss Havisham's who

1. **premium:** a fee paid to a master workman by a prospective apprentice.

was dreadfully proud, and that she had said I was common, and that I knew I was common, and that I wished I was not common, and that the lies had come of it somehow, though I didn't know how.

"There's one thing you may be sure of, Pip," said Joe, "namely, that lies is lies. Howsever they come, they didn't ought to come, and they come from the father of lies, and work round to the same. Don't you tell me no more of 'em, Pip. *That* ain't the way to get out of being common, old chap. And as to being common, I don't make it out at all clear. You are oncommon in some things. You're oncommon small. Likewise you're a oncommon scholar."

"No, I am ignorant and backward, Joe."

"Why, see what a letter you wrote last night! Wrote in print even! I've seen letters—ah! and from gentlefolks!—that I'll swear weren't wrote in print," said Joe.

"I have learned next to nothing, Joe. You think much of me. It's only that."

"Well, Pip," said Joe, "you must be a common scholar afore you can be a oncommon one, I should hope!"

"You are not angry with me, Joe?"

"No, old chap. That's all, old chap, and don't never do it no more."

When I got up to my little room and said my prayers, my young mind was in that disturbed and unthankful state that I thought long after I laid me down, how common Estella would consider Joe, a mere blacksmith, how thick his boots, and how coarse his hands. I thought how Joe and my sister were then sitting in the kitchen, and how I had come up to bed from the kitchen, and how Miss Havisham and Estella never sat in a kitchen, but were far above the level of such common doings. I fell asleep recalling what I "used to do" when I was at Miss Havisham's; as though I had been there weeks or months, instead of hours.

That was a memorable day to me, for it made great changes in me. But it is the same with any life. Imagine one selected day struck out of it, and think how different its course would have been. Pause, you who read this, and think for a moment of the long chain of iron or gold, of thorns or flowers, that would never have bound you, but for the formation of the first link on one memorable day.

Chapter 9

A mysterious stranger appears with a surprise for Pip.

The felicitous idea occurred to me a morning or two later when I woke, that the best step I could take toward making myself uncommon was to get out of Biddy everything she knew. I mentioned to Biddy when I went to Mr. Wopsle's great-aunt's at night, that I had a particular reason for wishing to get on in life, and that I should feel very much obliged to her if she would impart all her learning to me. Biddy, who was the most obliging of girls, immediately said she would, and indeed began to carry out her promise within five minutes.

The educational scheme or course established by Mr. Wopsle's great-aunt may be resolved into the following synopsis. The pupils ate apples and put straws down one another's backs until Mr. Wopsle's great-aunt collected her energies and made an indiscriminate totter at them with a birch rod. After receiving the charge with every mark of derision, the pupils formed in line and buzzingly passed a ragged book from hand to hand. The book had an alphabet in it, some figures and tables, and a little spelling. Biddy gave out the number of the page, and then we all read aloud in a frightful chorus, Biddy leading with a high, shrill, monotonous voice, and none of us having the least notion of, or reverence for, what we were reading about.

It appeared to me that it would take time to become uncommon under these circumstances; nevertheless, I resolved to try it, and that very evening Biddy entered on our special agreement by lending me, to copy at home, a large Old English *D* which she had imitated from the heading of some newspaper, and which I supposed, until she told me what it was, to be a design for a buckle.

Of course there was a public house[1] in the village, and of course Joe liked sometimes to smoke his pipe there. I had received strict orders from my sister to call for him at the Three Jolly Bargemen that evening, on my way from school, and bring him home at my peril. To the Three Jolly Bargemen, therefore, I directed my steps.

Joe was smoking his pipe in company with Mr. Wopsle and a stranger. Joe greeted me as usual with "Halloa, Pip, old chap!" and the moment he said that, the stranger turned his head and looked at me.

He was a secret-looking man whom I had never seen before. His head was all on one side, and one of his eyes was half shut up, as if he were taking aim at something with an invisible gun. He had a pipe in his mouth, and he took it out, and, after slowly blowing all his smoke away and looking hard at me all the time, nodded. So I nodded, and then he nodded again, and made room on the settle[2] beside him that I might sit down there.

But, as I was used to sit beside Joe whenever I entered that place of resort, I said, "No, thank you, sir," and fell into the space Joe made for me on the opposite settle. The strange man, after glancing at Joe, and seeing that his attention was otherwise engaged, nodded to me again when I had taken my seat, and then rubbed his leg—in a very odd way, as it struck me.

"You were saying," said the strange man, turning to Joe, "that you was a blacksmith. What'll you drink, Mr. Gargery? At my expense? To top up with?"

"Well," said Joe, "to tell you the truth, I ain't much in the habit of drinking at anybody's expense but my own."

"Habit? No," returned the stranger, "but once and away, and on a Saturday night, too. Come! Put a name to it, Mr. Gargery."

"I wouldn't wish to be stiff company," said Joe. "Rum."

"Rum," repeated the stranger. "And will the other gentleman originate a sentiment?"

"Rum," said Mr. Wopsle.

"Three rums!" cried the stranger, calling to the landlord. "Glasses round!"

The stranger put his legs up on the settle that he had to himself. He wore a flapping broad-brimmed traveler's hat and under it a handkerchief tied over his head in the manner of a cap, so that he showed no hair.

"I am not acquainted with this country, gentlemen, but it seems a solitary country toward the river."

"Most marshes is solitary," said Joe.

"No doubt, no doubt. Do you find any gypsies, now, or tramps, or vagrants of any sort, out there?"

"No," said Joe; "none but a runaway convict now and then. And we don't find *them* easy."

"Seems you have been out after such?" asked the stranger.

"Once," returned Joe. "Not that we wanted to take them, you understand; we went out as lookers-on, me and Mr. Wopsle and Pip. Didn't us, Pip?"

"Yes, Joe."

The stranger looked at me again and said,

---

1. **public house:** in England, a bar or tavern, often called a *pub*.
2. **settle:** bench.

"He's a likely young parcel of bones, that. What is it you call him?"

"Pip," said Joe.

"Christened Pip?"

"No, not christened Pip."

"Surname Pip?"

"No," said Joe; "it's a kind of a family name what he gave himself when a infant, and is called by."

"Son of yours?"

"Well—" said Joe meditatively, "well—no. No, he ain't."

"Nevvy?"[3] said the strange man.

"Well," said Joe, "he is not—no, not to deceive you, he is *not*—my nevvy."

"What the blue blazes is he?" asked the stranger.

Mr. Wopsle expounded the ties between me and Joe. All this while the strange man looked at nobody but me, and looked at me as if he were determined to have a shot at me at last, and bring me down. But he said nothing until the glasses were brought: and then he made his shot, and a most extraordinary shot it was.

He stirred his rum-and-water pointedly at me, and he tasted his rum-and-water pointedly at me—not with a spoon that was brought to him, but *with a file.*

He did this so that nobody but I saw the file; and when he had done it, he wiped the file and put it in a breast pocket. I knew it to be Joe's file, and I knew that he knew my convict, the moment I saw the instrument. I sat gazing at him, spellbound. Joe got up to go, and took me by the hand.

"Stop half a moment, Mr. Gargery," said the strange man. "I think I've got a bright new shilling somewhere in my pocket, and if I have, the boy shall have it."

He looked it out from a handful of small change, folded it in some crumpled paper, and gave it to me. "Yours!" said he. "Mind! Your own."

I thanked him, staring at him far beyond the bounds of good manners, and holding tight to Joe. On the way home I was in a manner stupefied by this turning up of my old misdeed and old acquaintance, and could think of nothing else.

My sister was not in a very bad temper when we presented ourselves in the kitchen, and Joe was encouraged by that unusual circumstance to tell her about the bright shilling. "A bad un, I'll be bound," said Mrs. Joe triumphantly, "or he wouldn't have given it to the boy. Let's look at it."

I took it out of the paper, and it proved to be a good one. "But what's this?" said Mrs. Joe, throwing down the shilling and catching up the paper. "Two one-pound notes?"[4]

Joe caught up his hat again, and ran with them to the Jolly Bargemen to restore them to their owner. While he was gone I sat down on my usual stool and looked vacantly at my sister, feeling pretty sure that the man would not be there.

Presently Joe came back, saying that the man was gone, but that he, Joe, had left word at the Three Jolly Bargemen concerning the notes. Then my sister sealed them up in a piece of paper, and put them under some dried rose leaves in an ornamental teapot on the top of a press in the parlor. There they remained a nightmare to me many and many a night and day.

I had sadly broken sleep when I got to bed, through thinking of the strange man and of the guiltily coarse and common thing it was to be on secret terms of conspiracy with convicts—a feature in my low career that I had previously forgotten. I was haunted by the file

3. **Nevvy:** nephew.

4. **Two one-pound notes:** forty shillings, or almost ten dollars in American money, which was a considerable sum of money in Dickens' time.

too. A dread possessed me that when I least expected it, the file would reappear. I coaxed myself to sleep by thinking of Miss Havisham's next Wednesday; and in my sleep I saw the file coming at me out of a door, without seeing who held it, and I screamed myself awake.

Chapter 10

We meet Camilla and her husband, Miss Sarah Pocket, Georgiana, and a pale young gentleman.

At the appointed time I returned to Miss Havisham's, and my hesitating ring at the gate brought out Estella. She locked it after admitting me, as she had done before, and took me to quite another part of the house, a small paved courtyard, the opposite side of which was formed by a detached dwelling house. There was a clock in the outer wall of this house. Like the clock in Miss Havisham's room, and like Miss Havisham's watch, it had stopped at twenty minutes to nine.

We went in at the door, which stood open, and into a gloomy room with a low ceiling, on the ground floor at the back. There was some company in the room, and Estella said, "You are to go and stand there, boy, till you are wanted." "There" being the window, I crossed to it and stood "there," in a very uncomfortable state of mind, looking out.

I divined that my coming had stopped conversation in the room, and that its other occupants were looking at me. There were three ladies in the room and one gentleman. Before I had been standing at the window five minutes, they somehow conveyed to me that they were all toadies and humbugs.[1]

They all had a listless and dreary air of wait-

ing somebody's pleasure. The most talkative of the ladies, whose name was Camilla, very much reminded me of my sister, with the difference that she was older and of a blunter cast of features.

"Poor dear soul!" said this lady. "Nobody's enemy but his own!"

"It would be much more commendable to be somebody else's enemy," said the gentleman; "far more natural."

"Cousin Raymond," observed another lady, "we are to love our neighbor."

"Sarah Pocket," returned Cousin Raymond, "if a man is not his own neighbor, who is?"

"Poor soul!" Camilla presently went on (I knew they had all been looking at me in the meantime), "he is so very strange! Would anyone believe that when Tom's wife died, he actually could not be induced to see the importance of the children's having the deepest of trimmings to their mourning? 'Good Lord!' says he, 'Camilla, what can it signify so long as the poor bereaved little things are in black?' So like Matthew! The idea!"

"Good points in him, good points in him," said Cousin Raymond, "but he never had and he never will have any sense of the proprieties."

The ringing of a distant bell, combined with the echoing of some cry or call along the passage by which I had come, interrupted the conversation and caused Estella to say to me, "Now, boy!"

As we were going with our candle along the dark passage, Estella stopped all of a sudden and, facing round, said in her taunting manner, with her face quite close to mine:

"Well?"

"Well, miss," I answered, almost falling over her and checking myself.

She stood looking at me, and of course I stood looking at her.

"Am I pretty?"

---

1. **toadies and humbugs:** flatterers and people who are not what they pretend to be.

"Yes, I think you are very pretty."

"Am I insulting?"

"Not as much as you were last time," said I.

"Not so much so?"

"No."

She slapped my face with such force as she had.

"Now?" said she. "You little coarse monster, what do you think of me now?"

"I shall not tell you."

"Because you are going to tell upstairs. Is that it?"

"No," said I, "that's not it."

"Why don't you cry again, you little wretch?"

"Because I'll never cry for you again," said I. Which was, I suppose, as false a declaration as ever was made; for I was inwardly crying for her then, and I know what I know of the pain she cost me afterward.

We went on our way upstairs after this episode; and, as we were going up, we met a gentleman groping his way down.

"Whom have we here?" asked the gentleman, stopping and looking at me.

"A boy," said Estella.

He was a burly man of an exceedingly dark complexion, with an exceedingly large head. He took my chin in his large hand and turned up my face to have a look at me by the light of the candle. He was prematurely bald on the top of his head, and had bushy black eyebrows that wouldn't lie down, but stood up bristling. His eyes were set very deep in his head, and were disagreeably sharp and suspicious. He had a large watch chain, and strong black dots where his beard and whiskers would have been if he had let them. He was nothing to me, and I could have had no foresight then that he ever would be anything to me, but it happened that I had this opportunity of observing him well.

"Boy of the neighborhood? Hey?" said he.

"Yes, sir," said I.

"How do you come here?"

"Miss Havisham sent for me, sir," I explained.

"Well! Behave yourself. I have a pretty large experience of boys, and you're a bad set of fellows. Now mind!" said he, biting the side of his great forefinger, as he frowned at me, "you behave yourself!"

With these words he released me—which I was glad of, for his hand smelt of scented soap—and went his way downstairs. We were soon in Miss Havisham's room. Estella left me standing near the door, and I stood there until Miss Havisham cast her eyes upon me from the dressing table.

"So!" she said. "The days have worn away, have they?"

"Yes, ma'am. Today is——"

"There, there, there!" with the impatient movement of her fingers. "I don't want to know. Are you ready to play?"

I was obliged to answer in some confusion, "I don't think I am, ma'am."

"Not at cards again?" she demanded with a searching look.

"Yes, ma'am; I could do that, if I was wanted."

"Since this house strikes you old and grave, boy," said Miss Havisham impatiently, "and you are unwilling to play, are you willing to work?"

I could answer this inquiry with a better heart than I had been able to find for the other question, and I said I was quite willing.

"Then go into that opposite room," said she, pointing at the door behind me with her withered hand, "and wait there till I come."

I crossed the staircase landing and entered the room she indicated. From that room, too, the daylight was completely excluded, and it had an airless smell that was oppressive. Every discernible thing in it was covered with dust and mold, and dropping to pieces. The most prominent object was a long table with a table-cloth spread on it, as if a feast had been in preparation when the house and the clocks all stopped together. A centerpiece of some kind was in the middle of this cloth; it was so heavily overhung with cobwebs that its form was quite undistinguishable. I saw speckled-legged spiders with blotchy bodies running home to it, and running out from it.

I heard the mice, too, rattling behind the panels.

These crawling things had fascinated my attention, and I was watching them from a distance when Miss Havisham laid a hand upon my shoulder. In her other hand she had a crutch-headed stick on which she leaned, and she looked like the witch of the place.

"This," said she, pointing to the long table with her stick, "is where I will be laid when I am dead. They shall come and look at me here."

"What do you think that is," she asked me, again pointing with her stick; "that, where those cobwebs are?"

"I can't guess, ma'am."

"It's a great cake. A bride cake. Mine!"

She looked all round the room in a glaring manner, and then said, leaning on me while her hand twitched my shoulder, "Come, come, come! Walk me, walk me!"

I made out from this that the work I had to do was to walk Miss Havisham round and round the room. Accordingly, she leaned on my shoulder and we went away at a pace.

After a while she said, "Call Estella," so I went out on the landing and roared that name as I had done on the previous occasion. When her light appeared, I returned to Miss Havisham, and we started away again round and round the room.

If only Estella had come to be a spectator of our proceedings, I should have felt sufficiently discontented; but, as she brought with her the three ladies and the gentleman whom I had seen below, I didn't know what to do. I would have stopped; but Miss Havisham twitched my shoulder and we posted on.

"Dear Miss Havisham," said Miss Sarah Pocket. "How well you look!"

"I do not," returned Miss Havisham. "I am yellow skin and bone."

Camilla brightened when Miss Pocket met with this rebuff; and she murmured, as she plaintively contemplated Miss Havisham, "Poor dear soul! Certainly not to be expected to look well, poor thing. The idea!"

"And how are *you*?" said Miss Havisham to Camilla. As we were close to Camilla then, I would have stopped as a matter of course, only Miss Havisham wouldn't stop. We swept on, and I felt that I was highly obnoxious to Camilla.

"Thank you, Miss Havisham," she returned. "I am as well as can be expected."

"Why, what's the matter with you?" asked Miss Havisham, with exceeding sharpness.

"Nothing worth mentioning," replied Camilla. "I don't wish to make a display of my feelings, but I have habitually thought of you more in the night than I am quite equal to."

"Then don't think of me," retorted Miss Havisham.

"Oh!" cried Camilla. "It's a weakness to be so affectionate, but I can't help it."

Miss Havisham and I kept going round and round the room; now brushing against the skirts of the visitors; now giving them the whole length of the dismal chamber.

"There's Matthew!" said Camilla. "Never mixing with any natural ties, never coming here to see how Miss Havisham is!"

When this same Matthew was mentioned, Miss Havisham stopped me and herself, and stood looking at the speaker. This change had a great influence in bringing Camilla's chemistry to a sudden end.

"Matthew will come and see me at last," said Miss Havisham sternly, "when I am laid on that table. That will be his place—there," striking the table with her stick, "at my head! And yours will be there! And your husband's there! And Sarah Pocket's there! And Georgiana's there! Now you all know where to take your stations when you come to feast upon me.[2] And now go!"

At the mention of each name, she had struck the table with her stick in a new place. She now said, "Walk me, walk me!" and we went on again.

While Estella was away lighting them down, Miss Havisham still walked with her hand on my shoulder, but more and more slowly. At last she stopped before the fire and said, after muttering and looking at it some seconds:

"This is my birthday, Pip."

I was going to wish her many happy returns, when she lifted her stick.

"I don't suffer it to be spoken of. I don't suffer those who were here just now, or anyone, to speak of it. They come here on the day, but they dare not refer to it."

Of course I made no further effort to refer to it.

"On this day of the year, long before you were born, this heap of decay," stabbing with her crutched stick at the pile of cobwebs on the table, but not touching it, "was brought here. It and I have worn away together. The mice have gnawed at it, and sharper teeth than teeth of mice have gnawed at me."

She held the head of her stick against her heart as she stood looking at the table; she in her once white dress, all yellow and withered; the once white cloth all yellow and withered; everything around in a state to crumble under a touch.

2. **feast . . . me:** that is, to collect their shares of her will after her death.

"When the ruin is complete," said she, with a ghastly look, "and when they lay me dead, in my bride's dress on the bride's table—which shall be done, and which will be the finished curse upon him—so much the better if it is done on this day!"

I remained quiet. Estella returned, and she too remained quiet. At length, Miss Havisham said, "Let me see you two play at cards; why have you not begun?" With that, we returned to her room, and sat down as before; I was beggared as before, and again, as before, Miss Havisham watched us all the time, directed my attention to Estella's beauty, and made me notice it the more by trying her jewels on Estella's breast and hair.

Estella, for her part, likewise treated me as before, except that she did not condescend to speak. When we had played some half-dozen games, a day was appointed for my return, and I was taken down into the yard to be fed in the former doglike manner. There, too, I was again left to wander about as I liked.

I strolled into the garden and found myself in the dismal corner upon which I had looked out of a window. Never questioning for a moment that the house was now empty, I looked in at another window, and found myself, to my great surprise, exchanging a broad stare with a pale young gentleman with red eyelids and light hair.

This pale young gentleman quickly disappeared and reappeared beside me. He had been at his books when I had found myself staring at him, and I now saw that he was inky.

"Who let *you* in?" said he.

"Miss Estella."

"Who gave you leave to prowl about?"

"Miss Estella."

"Come and fight," said the pale young gentleman.

What could I do but follow him? I have often asked myself the question since; but, what else could I do? His manner was so final and I was so astonished that I followed where he led, as if I had been under a spell.

"Stop a minute, though," he said, wheeling round before we had gone many paces. "I ought to give you a reason for fighting, too. There it is!" In a most irritating manner he instantly slapped his hands against one another, daintily flung one of his legs up behind him, pulled my hair, slapped his hands again, dipped his head, and butted it into my stomach.

I hit out at him, and was going to hit out again, when he said, "Aha! Would you?" and began dancing backward and forward in a manner quite unparalleled within my limited experience.

"Laws of the game" said he. Here, he skipped from his left leg on to his right. "Regular rules!" Here, he skipped from his right leg on to his left. "Come to the ground, and go through the preliminaries!" Here, he dodged backward and forward, and did all sorts of things while I looked helplessly at him.

I was secretly afraid of him when I saw him so dexterous; but I followed him without a word to a retired nook of the garden. On his asking me if I was satisfied with the ground, and on my replying "Yes," he begged my leave to absent himself for a moment, and quickly returned with a bottle of water and a sponge dipped in vinegar. "Available for both," he said, and fell to pulling off, not only his jacket and waistcoat, but his shirt, too, in a manner at once lighthearted, businesslike, and bloodthirsty. Although he did not look very healthy, these dreadful preparations quite appalled me. I judged him to be about my own age, but he was much taller.

My heart failed me when I saw him squaring at me with every demonstration of mechanical nicety, and eyeing my anatomy as if he were minutely choosing his bone. I never have been so surprised in my life as I was when I let out the first blow and saw him lying on his back, looking up at me with a bloody nose.

But he was on his feet directly, and after sponging himself began squaring again. The second greatest surprise I have ever had in my life was seeing him on his back again, looking up at me out of a black eye.

His spirit inspired me with great respect. He seemed to have no strength, and he never once hit me hard, and he was always knocked down. He got heavily bruised, but he came up again and again until at last he got a bad fall with the back of his head against the wall. Even after that, he got up and turned round confusedly a few times; but finally went on his knees to his sponge and threw it up, panting out, "That means you have won."

He seemed so brave and innocent that although I had not proposed the contest, I felt but a gloomy satisfaction in my victory. However, I got dressed and said, "Can I help you?" and he said, "No, thankee," and I said, "Good afternoon," and *he* said, "Same to you."

When I got into the courtyard, I found Estella waiting with the keys. But she neither asked me where I had been, nor why I had kept her waiting; and there was a bright flush upon her face, as though something had happened to delight her. Instead of going straight to the gate, too, she stepped back into the passage and beckoned me.

"Come here! You may kiss me if you like."

I kissed her cheek as she turned it to me. I think I would have gone through a great deal to kiss her cheek. But I felt that the kiss was given to the coarse common boy as a piece of money might have been, and that it was worth nothing.

What with the birthday visitors, and what with the cards, and what with the fight, my stay had lasted so long that when I neared home, the light off the point on the marshes was gleaming against a black night sky, and Joe's furnace was flinging a path of fire across the road.

Chapter 11

Pip becomes Joe's apprentice.

My mind grew very uneasy on the subject of the pale young gentleman. The more I thought of the fight, and recalled the pale young gentleman on his back, the more certain it appeared that something would be done to me. When the day came round for my return to the scene of the deed of violence, my terrors reached their height. However, go to Miss Havisham's I must, and go I did. And behold! nothing came of the late struggle. It was not alluded to in any way, and no pale young gentleman was to be discovered on the premises.

On the broad landing between Miss Havisham's own room and that other room in which the long table was laid out, I saw a garden-chair—a light chair on wheels, that you pushed from behind. I entered, that same day, on a regular occupation of pushing Miss Havisham in this chair (when she was tired of walking with her hand upon my shoulder) round her own room, and across the landing, and round the other room. Over and over and over again, we would make these journeys, and sometimes they would last as long as three hours at a stretch. I fall into a general mention of these journeys as numerous, because it was at once settled that I should return every alternate day at noon, and because I am now going to sum up a period of at least eight or ten months.

As we began to be more used to one another, Miss Havisham talked more to me, and asked me such questions as what had I learned and what was I going to be? I told her I was going to be apprenticed to Joe, I believed; and I enlarged upon my knowing nothing and wanting to know everything, in the hope that she might offer some help toward that desirable end. But she did not; on the contrary, she seemed to prefer my being ignorant. Neither did she ever give me any money or anything but my daily dinner—nor even stipulate that I should be paid for my services.

Estella was always about, and always let me in and out, but never told me I might kiss her again. Sometimes, she would be quite familiar with me; sometimes, she would tell me energetically that she hated me. Miss Havisham would often ask me in a whisper, or when we were alone, "Does she grow prettier and prettier, Pip?" And when I said "Yes" (for indeed she did), would seem to enjoy it greedily. Also, when we played at cards, Miss Havisham would look on, with a miserly relish of Estella's moods, whatever they were. And sometimes, when her moods were so many and so contradictory that I was puzzled what to say or do, Miss Havisham would embrace her with lavish fondness, murmuring something in her ear that sounded like "Break their hearts, my pride and hope, break their hearts and have no mercy!"

Perhaps I might have told Joe about the pale young gentleman if I had not previously been betrayed into those enormous inventions to which I had confessed. I reposed complete confidence in no one but Biddy; but I told poor Biddy everything. Why it came natural for me to do so, and why Biddy had a deep concern in everything I told her, I did not know then, though I think I know now.

Meanwhile, councils went on in the kitchen at home. Pumblechook and my sister would pair off in nonsensical speculations about Miss Havisham, and about what she would do with me and for me. In these discussions, Joe bore no part. But he was often talked at, while they

were in progress, by reason of Mrs. Joe's perceiving that he was not favorable to my being taken from the forge.

We went on in this way for a long time, when, one day, Miss Havisham stopped short as she and I were walking and said with some displeasure:

"You are growing tall, Pip!"

She said no more at the time, but she presently stopped and looked at me again; and after that looked frowning and moody. On the next day of my attendance, she stayed me with a movement of her impatient fingers:

"Tell me the name of that blacksmith of yours."

"Joe Gargery, ma'am."

"Meaning the master you were to be apprenticed to?"

"Yes, Miss Havisham."

"You had better be apprenticed at once. Would Gargery come here with you, and bring your indentures,[1] do you think?"

"At any particular time, Miss Havisham?"

"There, there! I know nothing about times. Let him come soon, and come along with you."

When I delivered this message at home, my sister "went on the Ram-page," threw a candlestick at Joe, got out the dustpan—which was always a very bad sign—and cleaned us out of house and home so that we stood shivering in the backyard. It was ten o'clock at night before we ventured to creep in again.

It was a trial to my feelings, on the next day but one, to see Joe arraying himself in his Sunday clothes to accompany me to Miss Havisham's. At breakfast time, my sister declared her intention of going to town with us, and being left at Uncle Pumblechook's and called for "when we had done with our fine ladies."

---

1. **indentures:** a contract binding an apprentice to a master. See footnote on page 673.

The forge was shut up for the day, and Joe inscribed in chalk upon the door (as it was his custom to do on the very rare occasions when he was not at work) the monosyllable HOUT,[2] accompanied by a sketch of an arrow supposed to be flying in the direction he had taken. When we came to Pumblechook's, my sister bounced in and left us. As it was almost noon, Joe and I held straight on to Miss Havisham's house. Estella opened the gate as usual, and led us the way that I knew so well.

Estella told me we were both to go in, so I took Joe by the coat cuff and conducted him into Miss Havisham's presence. She was seated at her dressing table, and looked round at us immediately.

"Oh!" said she to Joe. "You are the husband of the sister of this boy?"

I could barely have imagined dear old Joe looking so unlike himself or so like some extraordinary bird, standing, as he did, speechless, with his tuft of feathers ruffled, and his mouth open as if he wanted a worm.

"You are the husband," repeated Miss Havisham, "of the sister of this boy?"

It was very aggravating; but, throughout the interview, Joe persisted in addressing me instead of Miss Havisham. It was quite in vain for me to make him sensible that he ought to speak to Miss Havisham. The more I made faces and gestures to him to do it, the more confidential, argumentative, and polite he persisted in being to me.

"Have you brought his indentures with you?" asked Miss Havisham.

"Well, Pip, you know," replied Joe, as if that were a little unreasonable, "you yourself see me put 'em in my 'at, and therefore you know as they are here." With which he took them out, and gave them, not to Miss Havisham, but to me. I am afraid I was ashamed of the dear good fellow—I *know I* was ashamed of him—when I saw that Estella stood at the back of Miss Havisham's chair, and that her eyes laughed mischievously. I took the indentures out of his hand and gave them to Miss Havisham.

"You expected," said Miss Havisham, as she looked them over, "no premium with the boy?"

"Joe!" I remonstrated; for he made no reply at all. "Why don't you answer——"

"Pip," returned Joe, cutting me short as if he were hurt, "which I meantersay that were not a question requiring a answer betwixt yourself and me, and which you know the answer to be full well 'No.' You know it to be 'No,' Pip, and wherefore should I say it?"

Miss Havisham glanced at him as if she understood what he really was, better than I had thought possible; and took up a little bag from the table beside her.

"Pip has earned a premium here," she said, "and here it is. There are five-and-twenty guineas[3] in this bag. Give it to your master, Pip."

Joe, even at this pass, persisted in addressing me. "This is very liberal on your part, Pip," said Joe, "and it is as such received and grateful welcome, though never looked for. And now, old chap," said Joe, "may you and me do our duty, both on us by one and another."

"Goodbye, Pip!" said Miss Havisham. "Let them out, Estella."

"Am I to come again, Miss Havisham?" I asked.

"No. Gargery is your master now. Gargery! One word!"

Thus calling him back as I went out of the door, I heard her say to Joe, in a distinct emphatic voice. "The boy has been a good boy here, and that is his reward. Of course, as an

---

2. **Hout:** out.

3. **guinea** (gĭn′ē): a gold coin worth twenty-one shillings, a little more than five dollars in American money at that time.

honest man, you will expect no other and no more."

In another minute we were outside the gate, and it was locked, and Estella was gone. When we stood in the daylight alone again, Joe backed up against a wall and said to me, "Astonishing!" And there he remained so long, saying "Astonishing" at intervals so often that I began to think his senses were never coming back. At length he prolonged his remark into, "Pip, I do assure you this is as-TON-ish-ing!" and so, by degrees, became conversational and able to walk away.

"Well!" cried my sister, addressing us both at once, when we arrived at Pumblechook's. "I wonder you condescend to come back to such poor society as this, I am sure I do! And, what did she give young Rantipole[4] here?"

"She giv' him," said Joe, handing the bag to my sister, "five-and-twenty pound."

"It's five-and-twenty pound, mum," echoed that basest of swindlers, Pumblechook, rising to shake hands with her; "and it's no more than your merits (as I said when my opinion was asked), and I wish you joy of the money!"

"Goodness knows, Uncle Pumblechook," said my sister (grasping the money), "we're deeply beholden to you."

"Never mind me, mum," returned that diabolical corn chandler. "A pleasure's a pleasure all the world over. But this boy, you know; we must have him bound. I said I'd see to it—to tell you the truth."

The justices were sitting in the town hall near at hand, and we at once went over to have me bound apprentice to Joe. I say we went over, but I was pushed over by Pumblechook, exactly as if I had that moment picked a pocket or fired a rick.[5] Indeed, it was the general impression in court that I had been taken red-handed; for, as Pumblechook shoved me before him through the crowd, I heard some people say, "What's he done?" and others, "He's a young 'un, too, but looks bad, don't he?" One person of mild and benevolent aspect even gave me a tract entitled, TO BE READ IN MY CELL.

When we had come out again, we went back to Pumblechook's. And there my sister became so excited by the twenty-five guineas that nothing would serve her but we must have a dinner at the Blue Boar, and that Mr. Pumblechook must go over in his chaise-cart and bring the Hubbles and Mr. Wopsle.

My only remembrances of the great festival are that they wouldn't let me go to sleep, but whenever they saw me dropping off, woke me up and told me to enjoy myself and that when I got into my little bedroom, I was truly wretched, and had a strong conviction on me that I should never like Joe's trade. I had liked it once, but once was not now.

It is a most miserable thing to feel ashamed of home. Home had never been a very pleasant place to me, because of my sister's temper. But Joe had sanctified it, and I believed in it. I had believed in the best parlor as a most elegant saloon;[6] I had believed in the kitchen as a chaste though not magnificent apartment; I had believed in the forge as the glowing road to manhood and independence. Within a single year all this was changed. Now, it was all coarse and common, and I would not have had Miss Havisham and Estella see it on any account.

How much of my ungracious condition of mind may have been my own fault, how much Miss Havisham's, how much my sister's, is now of no moment to me or anyone. The change was made in me; the thing was done. Well or ill done, it was done.

Once it had seemed to me that when I

4. **Rantipole:** a wild and unruly person.
5. **fired a rick:** set fire to a haystack.

6. **saloon:** large room.

should at last roll up my shirt sleeves and go into the forge, Joe's 'prentice, I should be distinguished and happy. Now I only felt that I was dusty with the dust of the small coal, and that I had a weight upon my daily remembrance to which the anvil was a feather. There have been occasions in my later life when I have felt for a time as if a thick curtain had fallen on all its interest and romance, to shut me out from anything save dull endurance any more. Never has that curtain dropped so heavy and blank, as when my way in life lay stretched out straight before me through the newly entered road of apprenticeship to Joe.

But I am glad to know that I never breathed a murmur to Joe while my indentures lasted. It is about the only thing I *am* glad to know of myself in that connection. It was not because I was faithful, but because Joe was faithful, that I never ran away and went for a soldier or a sailor. It was not because I had a strong sense of the virtue of industry, but because Joe had a strong sense of virtue of industry, that I worked with tolerable zeal against the grain. It is not possible to know how far the influence of any amiable, honest-hearted, duty-doing man flies out into the world, but I know right well that any good that intermixed itself with my apprenticeship came of plain, contented Joe, and not of restless, aspiring, discontented me.

What I dreaded was that in some unlucky hour I, being at my grimiest and commonest, should lift up my eyes and see Estella looking in at one of the wooden windows of the forge. I was haunted by the fear that she would, sooner or later, find me out, with a black face and hands, doing the coarsest part of my work, and would exult over me and despise me. Often after dark, when I was pulling the bellows for Joe, I would fancy that I saw her just drawing her face away, and would believe that she had come at last.

After that, when we went in to supper, the place would have a more homely look than ever, and I would feel more ashamed of home than ever, in my own ungracious breast.

Chapter 12

Introducing Orlick.

As I was getting too big for Mr. Wopsle's great-aunt's room, my education under that preposterous female terminated; not, however, until Biddy had imparted to me everything she knew, from the little catalogue of prices to a comic song she had once bought for a half-penny. Although the only coherent part of the latter piece of literature was the opening lines,

> When I went to Lunnon town, sirs,
>> Too rul loo rul!
>> Too rul loo rul!
> Wasn't I done very brown, sirs?
>> Too rul loo rul!
>> Too rul loo rul!

—still, in my desire to be wiser, I got this composition by heart with the utmost gravity. In my hunger for information, I made proposals to Mr. Wopsle to bestow some intellectual crumbs upon me; with which he kindly complied. As it turned out, however, that he only wanted me for a dramatic lay figure,[1] to be contradicted and embraced and wept over and bullied and clutched and stabbed and knocked about in a variety of ways, I soon declined that course of instruction, though not until Mr. Wopsle in his poetic fury had severely mauled me.

Whatever I acquired, I tried to impart to Joe. This statement sounds so well that I can-

---

1. **lay figure:** a puppet or dummy; here used in its secondary meaning of an unimportant or servile person.

not in my conscience let it pass unexplained. I wanted to make Joe less ignorant and common, that he might be worthier of my society and less open to Estella's reproach.

The old Battery out on the marshes was our place of study, and a broken slate and a short piece of slate pencil were our educational implements, to which Joe always added a pipe of tobacco. I never knew Joe to remember anything from one Sunday to another, or to acquire, under my tuition, any piece of information whatever. Yet he would smoke his pipe at the Battery with a far more sagacious air than anywhere else—even with a learned air—as if he considered himself to be advancing immensely. Dear fellow, I hope he did.

It was pleasant and quiet out there with the sails on the river. Whenever I watched the vessels standing out to sea with their white sails spread, I somehow thought of Miss Havisham and Estella. One Sunday I resolved to mention a thought concerning them that had been much in my head.

"Joe," said I, "don't you think I ought to pay Miss Havisham a visit?"

"Well, Pip," returned Joe, slowly considering. "What for?"

"What for, Joe? What is any visit made for?"

"There is some wisits p'r'aps," said Joe, "as forever remains open to the question, Pip. But in regard of wisiting Miss Havisham. She might think you wanted something—expected something of her."

I had thought of that too, and it was very far from comforting to me to find that he had thought of it; for it seemed to render it more probable.

"But, Joe."

"Yes, old chap."

"Here am I, getting on in the first year of my time, and since the day of my being bound I have never thanked Miss Havisham, or asked after her, or shown that I remember her."

"Well," said Joe, "if I was yourself, Pip, I wouldn't. No, I would *not.*"

"But, Joe; what I wanted to say was, that as we are rather slack just now, if you would give me a half holiday tomorrow, I think I would go uptown and make a call on Miss Est— Havisham."

"Which her name," said Joe gravely, "ain't Eastavisham, Pip, unless she has been rechris'ened."

"I know, Joe. It was a slip. What do you think of it, Joe?"

In brief, Joe thought that if I thought well of it, he thought well of it. But he was particular in stipulating that if I were not received with cordiality, or if I were not encouraged to repeat my visit, as a visit which had no ulterior object, but was simply one of gratitude for a favor received, then this experimental trip should have no successor. By these conditions I promised to abide.

Now, Joe kept a journeyman[2] at weekly wages whose name was Orlick. He was a broad-shouldered, loose-limbed, swarthy fellow of great strength, never in a hurry, and always slouching. He never even seemed to come to his work on purpose, but would slouch in as if by mere accident. He lodged at a sluice keeper's[3] out on the marshes, and on working days would come slouching from his hermitage, with his hands in his pockets and his dinner loosely tied in a bundle round his neck and dangling on his back.

This morose journeyman had no liking for me. When I was very small and timid, he gave me to understand that the Devil lived in a black corner of the forge, and that he knew the fiend

---

2. **journeyman** (jûr'nē-mən): a person who has learned a trade and is no longer an apprentice, but who still works for a master craftsman.
3. **sluice** (sloos) **keeper:** a person in charge of a gate that regulates the flow of water in a sluice, an artificial stream used for drainage and irrigation.

very well; also that it was necessary to make up the fire, once in seven years, with a live boy, and that I might consider myself fuel. When I became Joe's 'prentice, Orlick was perhaps confirmed in some suspicion that I should displace him; howbeit he liked me still less.

Orlick was at work and present, next day, when I reminded Joe of my half holiday. He said nothing at the moment, for he and Joe had just got a piece of hot iron between them, and I was at the bellows; but by and by he said, leaning on his hammer:

"Now, master! Sure you're not a-going to favor only one of us. If Young Pip has a half holiday, do as much for Old Orlick." I suppose he was about five-and-twenty, but he usually spoke of himself as an ancient person.

"Why, what'll you do with a half holiday if you get it?" said Joe.

"What'll *I* do with it? What'll *he* do with it? I'll do as much with it as *him*." said Orlick.

"As to Pip, he's going uptown," said Joe.

"Well, then, as to Old Orlick, *he's* a-going uptown," retorted that worthy. "Two can go uptown. 'Tain't only one wot can go uptown."

"Don't lose your temper," said Joe.

"Shall if I like," growled Orlick. "Now, master! Come. No favoring in this shop. Be a man!"

"Then, as in general you stick to your work as well as most men," said Joe, "let it be a half holiday for all."

My sister had been standing silent in the yard, within hearing—she was a most unscrupulous spy and listener—and she instantly looked in at one of the windows.

"Like you, you fool!" said she to Joe, "giving holidays to great idle hulkers like that. You are a rich man, upon my life, to waste wages in that way. I wish *I* was his master!"

"You'd be everybody's master if you durst," retorted Orlick, with an ill-favored grin.

"Let her alone," said Joe.

"I'd be a match for all noodles and all rogues," returned my sister, beginning to work herself into a mighty rage. "And I couldn't be a match for the noodles without being a match for your master, who's the dunderheaded king of the noodles. And I couldn't be a match for the rogues without being a match for you, who are the meanest-looking and the worst rogue between this and France. Now!"

"You're a foul shrew, Mother Gargery," growled the journeyman. "If that makes a judge of rogues, you ought to be a good 'un."

"Let her alone, will you?" said Joe.

"What did you say?" cried my sister, beginning to scream. "What did you say? What did that fellow Orlick say to me, Pip? What did he call me, with my husband standing by? Oh! Oh! Oh!" Each of these exclamations was a shriek. "Oh! Hold me! Oh!"

"Ah-h-h!" growled the journeyman, between his teeth. "I'd hold you, if you was my wife. I'd hold you under the pump and choke it out of you."

"I tell you, let her alone," said Joe.

"Oh! To hear him!" cried my sister, with a clap of her hands and a scream together. "To hear the names he's giving me! That Orlick! In my own house! Me, a married woman! With my husband standing by! Oh! Oh!"

What could the wretched Joe do now but stand up to his journeyman? They went at one another like two giants. But if any man in that neighborhood could stand up long against Joe, I never saw the man. Orlick was very soon among the coal dust, and in no hurry to come out of it. Then Joe picked up my sister, who had dropped insensible at the window, and carried her into the house. Afterward came that calm and silence which succeed all uproars—and I went upstairs to dress.

When I came down again, I found Joe and Orlick sweeping up, without any other traces of discomposure than a slit in one of Orlick's nostrils. A pot of beer had appeared from the Jolly Bargemen, and they were sharing it by turns in a peaceable manner. Joe followed me out into the road to say, as a parting observation that might do me good, "On the Rampage, Pip, and off the Ram-page, Pip—such is life!"

With what absurd emotions (for, we think the feelings that are very serious in a man quite comical in a boy) I found myself again going to Miss Havisham's, matters little here. Nor, how I passed and repassed the gate many times before I could make up my mind to ring.

Miss Sarah Pocket came to the gate. No Estella.

"How, then? You here again?" said Miss Pocket. "What do you want?"

When I said that I only came to see how Miss Havisham was, Sarah let me in, and presently brought the sharp message that I was to "come up."

Everything was unchanged, and Miss Havisham was alone.

"Well!" said she, fixing her eyes upon me. "I hope you want nothing? You'll get nothing."

"No indeed, Miss Havisham. I only wanted you to know that I am doing very well in my apprenticeship, and am always much obliged to you."

"There, there!" with the old restless fingers. "Come now and then; come on your birthday. —Aye!" she cried suddenly, turning herself and her chair toward me. "You are looking round for Estella? Hey?"

I had been looking round—in fact, for Estella—and I stammered that I hoped she was well.

"Abroad," said Miss Havisham; "educating for a lady; far out of reach; prettier than ever; admired by all who see her. Do you feel that you have lost her?"

There was such a malignant enjoyment in her utterance of the last words, and she broke into such a disagreeable laugh, that I was at a loss what to say. She spared me the trouble of considering, by dismissing me. When the gate was closed upon me, I felt more than ever dissatisfied with my home and with my trade and with everything.

As I was loitering along the High Street, looking at the shop windows and thinking what I would buy if I were a gentleman, who should come out of the bookshop but Mr. Wopsle. He insisted on my accompanying him to the Pumblechookian parlor. I made no great resistance; consequently, we turned into Pumblechook's just as the street and shops were lighting up.

It was a very dark night when I set out with Mr. Wopsle on the walk home. Beyond town we found a heavy mist out, and it fell wet and thick. The turnpike lamp was a blur, and its rays looked solid substance on the fog. We were noticing this when we came upon a man, slouching under the lee of the turnpike house.

"Halloa!" we said, stopping. "Orlick there?"

"Ah!" he answered, slouching out. "I was standing by a minute on the chance of company."

"You are late," I remarked.

Orlick not unnaturally answered, "Well? And *you're* late."

"We have been," said Mr. Wopsle, "indulging, Mr. Orlick, in an intellectual evening."

Old Orlick growled, as if he had nothing to say about that, and we all went on together. I asked him presently whether he had been spending his half holiday up and down town?

"Yes," said he, "all of it. I come in behind yourself. I didn't see you, but I must have been pretty close behind you. By the bye, the guns is going again."

"At the Hulks?" said I.

"Aye! There's some of the birds flown from the cages. The guns have been going since dark, about. You'll hear one presently."

In effect, we had not walked many yards further when the well-remembered boom came toward us, deadened by the mist.

"A good night for cutting off in," said Orlick. "We'd be puzzled how to bring down a jailbird on the wing tonight." Orlick, with his hands in his pockets, slouched heavily at my side. I thought he had been drinking, but he was not drunk.

Thus we came to the village. The way by which we approached it took us past the Three Jolly Bargemen, which we were surprised to find—it being eleven o'clock—in a state of commotion, with the door wide open, and lights scattered about. Mr. Wopsle dropped in to ask what was the matter (surmising that a convict had been taken), but came running out in a great hurry.

"There's something wrong," said he, without stopping, "up at your place, Pip. Run all!"

"What is it?" I asked, keeping up with him. So did Orlick, at my side.

"I can't quite understand. The house seems to have been violently entered when Joe Gargery was out. Supposed by convicts. Somebody has been attacked and hurt."

We were running too fast to admit of more being said, and we made no stop until we got into our kitchen. It was full of people; the whole village was there or in the yard, and there was a surgeon, and there was Joe, and there was a group of women, all on the floor in the midst of the kitchen. The unemployed bystanders drew back when they saw me, and so I became aware of my sister—lying without sense or movement on the bare boards where she had been knocked down by a tremendous blow on the back of the head, dealt by some unknown hand when her face was turned toward the fire—destined never to be on the Ram-page again, while she was the wife of Joe.

Joe had been at the Three Jolly Bargemen, smoking his pipe, from a quarter after eight o'clock to a quarter before ten. While he was there, my sister had been seen standing at the kitchen door and had exchanged good night with a farm laborer going home. When Joe went home at five minutes before ten, he found her struck down on the floor, and promptly called in assistance.

Nothing had been taken away from any part of the house. But there was one remarkable piece of evidence on the spot. She had been struck with something blunt and heavy, on the head and spine; after the blows were dealt, something heavy had been thrown down at her with considerable violence, as she lay on her face. And on the ground beside her, when Joe picked her up, was a convict's leg iron which had been filed asunder.

Now, Joe, examining this iron with a smith's eye, declared it to have been filed asunder some time ago. The hue and cry going off to the Hulks, and people coming thence to examine the iron, Joe's opinion was corroborated. They claimed to know for certain that that particular manacle had not been worn by either of two convicts who had escaped last night. Further, one of those two was already retaken, and had not freed himself of his iron.

Knowing what I knew, I believed the iron to be my convict's iron—the iron I had seen and heard him filing at, on the marshes—but my mind did not accuse him of having put it to its latest use. For I believed one of two other persons to have become possessed of it, and to have turned it to this cruel account. Either Orlick, or the strange man who had shown me the file.

Now, as to Orlick; he had gone to town exactly as he told us when we picked him up at the turnpike, he had been seen about town all the evening, he had been in several public houses, and he had come back with myself and Mr. Wopsle. There was nothing against him, save the quarrel; and my sister had quarreled with him, and with everybody else about her, ten thousand times. As to the strange man: if he had come back for his two bank notes, there could have been no dispute about them, because my sister was fully prepared to restore them. Besides, there had been no altercation; the assailant had come in so silently and suddenly that she had been felled before she could look round.

The constables were about the house for a week or two. They took up several obviously wrong people, and they ran their heads very hard against wrong ideas, and persisted in trying to fit the circumstances to the ideas, instead of trying to extract the ideas from the circumstances.

Long after these constitutional powers had dispersed, my sister lay ill in bed. Her sight was disturbed, so that she saw objects multiplied; her hearing was greatly impaired; her memory also; and her speech was unintelligible. It was necessary to keep my slate always by her, that she might indicate in writing what she could not indicate in speech.

However, her temper was greatly improved, and she was patient. We were at a loss to find a suitable attendant for her, until a circumstance happened conveniently to relieve us. Mr. Wopsle's great-aunt conquered a confirmed habit of living into which she had fallen,[4] and Biddy became part of our establishment. Biddy came to us with a small speckled box containing the whole of her worldly effects and became a blessing to the household. Above all she was a blessing to Joe, for the dear old fellow was sadly cut up by the constant contemplation of the wreck of his wife. Biddy instantly taking the cleverest charge of her, Joe became able in some sort to appreciate the greater quiet of his life, and to get down to the Jolly

4. **conquered . . . fallen:** died.

Bargemen now and then for a change that did him good.

Biddy's first triumph in her new office was to solve a difficulty that had completely vanquished me. Again and again and again, my sister had traced upon the slate a character that looked like a curious *T*, and then with the utmost eagerness had called our attention to it as something she particularly wanted. I had in vain tried everything producible that began with a *T*, from tar to toast and tub. At length it had come into my head that the sign looked like a hammer, and on my lustily calling that word in my sister's ear, she had begun to hammer on the table and had expressed a qualified assent. Thereupon, I had brought in all our hammers, one after another, but without avail.

When my sister found that Biddy was very quick to understand her, this mysterious sign reappeared on the slate. Biddy looked thoughtfully at it, heard my explanation, looked thoughtfully at Joe (who was always represented on the slate by his initial letter), and ran into the forge, followed by Joe and me.

"Why, of course!" cried Biddy with an exultant face. "Don't you see? It's *him*!"

Orlick, without a doubt! She had lost his name, and could only signify him by his hammer. We told him why we wanted him to come into the kitchen, and he slowly laid down his hammer, wiped his brow with his arm, took another wipe at it with his apron, and came slouching out.

I confess that I expected to see my sister denounce him, and that I was disappointed by the different result. She manifested the greatest anxiety to be on good terms with him, was evidently much pleased by his being at length produced, and motioned that she would have him given something to drink. She watched his countenance as if she were particularly wishful to be assured that he took kindly to his reception. After that, a day rarely passed without her drawing the hammer on her slate, and without Orlick's slouching in and standing doggedly before her, as if he knew no more than I did what to make of it.

Chapter 13

Pip opens his heart to Biddy.

I now fell into a regular routine of apprenticeship life, which was varied, beyond the limits of the village and the marshes, by no more remarkable circumstance than the arrival of my birthday and my paying another visit to Miss Havisham. The interview lasted but a few minutes, and she gave me a guinea when I was going, and told me to come again on my next birthday. I may mention at once that this became an annual custom. I tried to decline taking the guinea on the first occasion, causing her to ask me angrily if I expected more. Then, and after that, I took it. So unchanging was the dull old house, it bewildered me, and under its influence I continued at heart to hate my trade and to be ashamed of home.

Imperceptibly I became conscious of a change in Biddy, however. Her shoes came up at the heel, her hair grew bright and neat, her hands were always clean. She was not beautiful—she was common, and could not be like Estella—but she was pleasant and wholesome and sweet-tempered. I observed to myself one evening that she had curiously thoughtful and attentive eyes; eyes that were very pretty and very good. I laid down my pen, and Biddy stopped in her needlework without laying it down.

"Biddy," said I, "how do you manage it? Either I am very stupid, or you are very clever."

"What is it that I manage? I don't know," returned Biddy, smiling.

She managed her whole domestic life, and wonderfully too; but I did not mean that, though that made what I did mean more surprising.

"How do you manage, Biddy," said I, "to learn everything that I learn, and always to keep up with me?" I was beginning to be rather vain of my knowledge, for I spent my birthday guineas on it and the greater part of my pocket money.

"I suppose I must catch it—like a cough," said Biddy quietly, and went on with her sewing.

"You are one of those, Biddy," said I, "who make the most of every chance. You never had a chance before you came here, and see how improved you are!"

Biddy looked at me for an instant, and went on with her sewing. "I was your first teacher, though, wasn't I?" said she, as she sewed.

"Yes, Biddy," I observed, "you were my first teacher, and that at a time when we little thought of ever being together like this in this kitchen. I must consult you a little more, as I used to do. Let us have a quiet walk on the marshes next Sunday, Biddy, and a long chat."

My sister was never left alone now; and Joe more than readily undertook the care of her on that Sunday afternoon, and Biddy and I went out together. It was summertime and lovely weather. When we came to the riverside and sat down on the bank, I resolved that it was a good time and place for the admission of Biddy into my inner confidence.

"Biddy," said I, after binding her to secrecy, "I want to be a gentleman."

"Oh, I wouldn't, if I was you!" she returned.

"I don't think it would be right."

"Biddy," said I, with some severity, "I have particular reasons for wanting to be a gentleman."

"You know best, Pip; but don't you think you are happier as you are?"

"Biddy," I exclaimed impatiently, "I am not at all happy as I am. I am disgusted with my calling and with my life. Don't be absurd."

"Was I absurd?" said Biddy, quietly raising her eyebrows. "I am sorry for that; I didn't mean to be. I only want you to do well and be comfortable."

"Well, then, understand once for all that I never shall or can be comfortable—or anything but miserable—there, Biddy!—unless I can lead a very different sort of life from the life I lead now."

"That's a pity!" said Biddy, shaking her head with a sorrowful air.

"If I could have settled down," I said to Biddy, "I know it would have been much better for me. You and I and Joe would have wanted nothing then, and Joe and I would perhaps have gone partners when I was out of my time, and I might even have grown up to keep company with you. I should have been good enough for *you*; shouldn't I, Biddy?"

Biddy sighed and returned for an answer, "Yes; I am not overparticular." It scarcely sounded flattering, but I knew she meant well.

"Instead of that, see how I am going on. Dissatisfied and uncomfortable, and—what would it signify to me, being coarse and common, if nobody had told me so!"

Biddy turned her face suddenly toward mine and looked attentively at me.

"It was neither a very true nor a very polite thing to say," she remarked. "Who said it?"

"The beautiful young lady at Miss Havisham's, and she's more beautiful than anybody ever was, and I admire her dread-fully, and I want to be a gentleman on her account."

"Do you want to be a gentleman to spite her or to gain her over?" Biddy quietly asked me, after a pause.

"I don't know," I moodily answered.

"Because if it is to spite her," Biddy pursued, "I should think—but you know best—that might be better and more independently done by caring nothing for her words. And if it is to gain her over, I should think—but you know best—she was not worth gaining over."

"It may be all quite true," said I to Biddy, "but I admire her dreadfully."

I turned over on my face when I came to that, and got a good grasp on the hair on each side of my head, and wrenched it well. Biddy was the wisest of girls, and she tried to reason no more with me. She put her hand, which was a comfortable hand though roughened by work, upon my hands and gently took them out of my hair. Then she softly patted my shoulder in a soothing way, while with my face upon my sleeve I cried a little—exactly as I had done in the brewery yard—and felt vaguely convinced that I was very much ill-used by somebody, or by everybody; I can't say which.

"I am glad of one thing," said Biddy, "and that is, that you have felt you could give me your confidence, Pip." So, with a quiet sigh for me, Biddy rose from the bank and said, with a fresh and pleasant change of voice, "Shall we walk a little farther or go home?"

"Biddy," I cried, getting up, putting my arm around her neck, and giving her a kiss, "I shall always tell you everything."

"Till you're a gentleman," said Biddy.

"You know I never shall be, so that's always. Not that I have any occasion to tell you anything, for you know everything I know—as I told you at home the other night."

"Ah!" said Biddy, quite in a whisper, and

then repeated, with her former pleasant change, "shall we walk a little farther or go home?"

We talked a good deal as we walked, and all that Biddy said seemed right. Biddy was never insulting, or capricious, or Biddy today and somebody else tomorrow; she would have derived only pain, and no pleasure, from giving me pain.

I began to consider whether I was not more naturally and wholesomely situated, after all, in these circumstances, than playing beggar my neighbor by candlelight in the room with the stopped clocks, and being despised by Estella. How could it be, then, that I did not like her much the better of the two?

"Biddy," said I, when we were walking homeward, "I wish you could put me right."

"I wish I could!" said Biddy.

"If I could only get myself to fall in love with you—you don't mind my speaking so openly to such an old acquaintance?"

"Oh, dear, not at all!" said Biddy. "Don't mind me."

"If I could only get myself to do it, *that* would be the thing for me."

"But you never will, you see," said Biddy.

When we came near the churchyard, we had to cross an embankment and get over a stile near a sluice gate. There started up, from the rushes, Old Orlick.

"Halloa!" he growled. "Where are you two going?"

"Where should we be going, but home?"

"Well, then," said he, "I'm jiggered if I don't see you home!"

Biddy said to me in a whisper, "Don't let him come; I don't like him." As I did not like him either, I took the liberty of saying that we thanked him, but we didn't want seeing home. He dropped back, but came slouching after us at a little distance.

Curious to know whether Biddy suspected him of having had a hand in that murderous attack of which my sister had never been able to give any account, I asked her why she did not like him.

"Oh," she replied, glancing over her shoulder as he slouched after us, "because I—I am afraid he likes me!"

"Did he ever tell you he liked you?" I asked indignantly.

"No," said Biddy, glancing over her shoulder again, "he never told me so; but he dances at me whenever he can catch my eye."

I kept an eye on Orlick after that night. He had struck root in Joe's establishment, by reason of my sister's sudden fancy for him, or I should have tried to get him dismissed. He quite understood and reciprocated my good intentions, as I had reason to know thereafter.

And now my mind was confused. At times, I would decide that my disaffection to dear old Joe and the forge was gone, and that I was growing up in a fair way to be partners with Joe and to keep company with Biddy—when all in a moment some remembrance of the Havisham days would fall upon me and scatter my wits again. Scattered wits take a long time picking up; and often they would be dispersed in all directions by one stray thought, that perhaps after all Miss Havisham was going to make my fortune when my time was out.

If my time had run out, it would have left me still at the height of my perplexities, I dare say. It never did run out, however, but was brought to a premature end, as I proceed to relate.

Chapter 14

Mr. Jaggers, a lawyer, brings astonishing news.

It was in the fourth year of my apprenticeship to Joe, and it was a Saturday night. There was a group assembled round the fire at the Three

Jolly Bargemen, attentive to Mr. Wopsle as he read the newspaper aloud. Of that group I was one.

I became aware of a strange gentleman leaning over the back of the settle opposite me, looking on. There was an expression of contempt on his face, and he bit the side of a great forefinger as he watched the group of faces.

"Well!" said the stranger to Mr. Wopsle, when the reading was done. "You have settled it all to your own satisfaction, I have no doubt?"

The strange gentleman, with an air of authority not to be disputed, and a manner expressive of knowing something secret about every one of us came into the space between the two settles, in front of the fire.

"From information I have received," said he, looking round at us as we all quailed before him, "I have reason to believe there is a blacksmith among you, by name Joseph—or Joe—Gargery. Which is the man?"

"Here is the man," said Joe.

The strange gentleman beckoned him out of his place, and Joe went.

"You have an apprentice," pursued the stranger, "commonly known as Pip? Is he here?"

"I am here!" I cried.

The stranger did not recognize me, but I recognized him as the gentleman I had met on the stairs on the occasion of my second visit to Miss Havisham. I had known him the moment I saw him looking over the settle. I checked off again in detail his large head, his dark complexion, his deep-set eyes, his bushy black eyebrows, his large watch chain, his strong black dots of beard and whisker, and even the smell of scented soap on his great hand.

"I wish to have a private conference with you two," said he, when he had surveyed me at his leisure. "It will take a little time. Perhaps we had better go to your place of residence."

Amidst a wondering silence, we three walked out of the Jolly Bargemen and in a wondering silence walked home. Joe went on ahead to open the front door. Our conference was held in the parlor, which was feebly lighted by one candle.

It began with the strange gentleman's sitting down at the table, drawing the candle to him, and looking over some entries in his pocketbook.

"My name," he said, "is Jaggers, and I am a lawyer in London. I am pretty well known. I have unusual business to transact with you, and I commence by explaining that it is not of my originating. If my advice had been asked, I should not have been here. It was not asked, and you see me here. What I have to do as the confidential agent of another, I do. No less, no more.

"Now, Joseph Gargery, I am the bearer of an offer to relieve you of this young fellow, your apprentice. You would not object to cancel his indentures at his request and for his good? You would want nothing for so doing?"

"Lord forbid that I should want anything for not standing in Pip's way," said Joe, staring.

"Lord forbidding is pious, but not to the purpose," returned Mr. Jaggers. "The question is, would you want anything? Do you want anything?"

"The answer is," returned Joe sternly, "no."

I thought Mr. Jaggers glanced at Joe, as if he considered him a fool for his disinterestedness. But I was too much bewildered between breathless curiosity and surprise to be sure of it.

"Very well," said Mr. Jaggers. "Now, I return to this young fellow. And the communication I have got to make is that he has Great Expectations."

Joe and I gasped and looked at one another.

"I am instructed to communicate to him," said Mr. Jaggers, throwing his finger at me sideways, "that he will come into a handsome property. Further, that it is the desire of the present possessor of that property that he be immediately removed from his present sphere of life and from this place and brought up as a gentleman—in a word, as a young fellow of great expectations."

My dream was out; my wild fancy was surpassed by sober reality; Miss Havisham was going to make my fortune on a grand scale.

"Now, Mr. Pip," pursued the lawyer, "I address the rest of what I have to say to you. You are to understand, first, that it is the request of the person from whom I take my instructions that you always bear the name of Pip. You will have no objection, I dare say, but if you have any objection, this is the time to mention it."

My heart was beating so fast, and there was such a singing in my ears, that I could scarcely stammer I had no objection.

"I should think not! Now you are to understand, secondly, Mr. Pip, that the name of the person who is your liberal benefactor remains a profound secret until the person chooses to reveal it at firsthand by word of mouth to yourself. When or where that intention may be carried out, no one can say. It may be years hence. It is not the least to the purpose what the reasons of this prohibition are; they may be the strongest and gravest reasons, or they may be a mere whim. This is not for you to inquire into. The condition is laid down. Your acceptance of it, and your observance of it as binding, is the only remaining condition that I am charged with by the person from whom I take my instructions. That person is the person from whom you derive your expectations, and the secret is solely held by that person and by me. If you have any objection to it, this is the time to mention it. Speak out."

Once more, I stammered that I had no objection.

"I should think not! Now, Mr. Pip, I have done with stipulations. We come next to mere details of arrangement. You must know that although I have used the term 'expectations' more than once, you are not endowed with expectations only. There is already lodged in my hands a sum of money amply sufficient for your suitable education and maintenance. You will please consider me your guardian.

"Oh!" for I was going to thank him. "I tell you at once, I am paid for my services, or I shouldn't render them. It is considered that you must be better educated, in accordance with your altered position."

I said I had always longed for it.

"Never mind what you have always longed for, Mr. Pip," he retorted. "Keep to the record. If you long for it now, that's enough. Am I answered that you are ready to be placed at once under some proper tutor? Is that it?"

I stammered yes, that was it.

"There is a certain tutor who I think might suit the purpose," said Mr. Jaggers. "The gentleman I speak of is one Mr. Matthew Pocket."

Ah! I caught at the name directly. Miss Havisham's relation. The Matthew whom Mr. and Mrs. Camilla had spoken of. The Matthew whose place was to be at Miss Havisham's head when she lay dead in her bride's dress on the bride's table.

"You know the name?" said Mr. Jaggers, looking shrewdly at me. "What do you say of it?"

I said that I was much obliged to him for his mention of Mr. Matthew Pocket, and that I would gladly try that gentleman.

"Good. You had better try him in his own house. The way shall be prepared for you, and you can see his son first, who is in London. When will you come to London?"

I said (glancing at Joe, who stood looking on, motionless) that I supposed I could come directly.

"First," said Mr. Jaggers, "you should have some new clothes to come in, and they should not be working clothes. Say this day week.[1] You'll want some money. Shall I leave you twenty guineas?"

He produced a long purse, with the greatest coolness, and counted them out on the table and pushed them over to me, and sat swinging his purse and eyeing Joe.

"Well, Joseph Gargery? You look dumfoundered?"

"I *am*!" said Joe, in a very decided manner.

"It was understood that you wanted nothing for yourself, remember?"

"It were understood," said Joe. "And it are understood. And it ever will be similar according."

"But what," said Mr. Jaggers, swinging his purse, "what if it was in my instructions to make you a present, as compensation?"

"As compensation what for?" Joe demanded.

"For the loss of his services."

Joe laid his hand upon my shoulder with the touch of a woman. "Pip is that hearty welcome," said Joe, "to go free with his services, to honor and fortun', as no words can tell him. But if you think as money can make compensation to me for the loss of the little child—what come to the forge—and ever the best of friends!——"

Oh, dear good Joe, whom I was so ready to leave and so unthankful to, I see you again, with your muscular blacksmith's arm before your eyes, and your broad chest heaving, and your voice dying away.

But I encouraged Joe at the time. I begged Joe to be comforted, for (as he said) we had ever been the best of friends, and (as I said) we ever would be so, Joe scooped his eyes with his wrist, but said not another word.

Mr. Jaggers had looked on at this, as one who recognized in Joe the village idiot, and in me his keeper. When it was over, he said, "Now, Joseph Gargery, I warn you this is your last chance. If you mean to take a present that I have in charge to make you, speak out, and you shall have it. If on the contrary you mean to say——" Here, to his great amazement, he was stopped by Joe's suddenly working round him with every demonstration of a pugilistic purpose.[2]

"Which I meantersay," cried Joe, "that if you come into my place bull-baiting and badgering me, come out! Which I meantersay as sech if you're a man, come on!"

I drew Joe away, and he immediately became placable. Mr. Jaggers backed near the door and there delivered his valedictory remarks:

"Well, Mr. Pip, I think the sooner you leave here, the better. Let it stand for this day week, and you shall receive my printed address in the meantime. You can take a hackney coach at the stagecoach office in London, and come straight to me."

Something came into my head which induced me to run after him.

"I beg your pardon, Mr. Jaggers."

"Halloa!" said he. "What's the matter?"

"I wish to be quite right, Mr. Jaggers. Would there be any objection to my taking leave of anyone I know about here, before I go away?"

"No," said he, looking as if he hardly understood me.

"I don't mean the village only, but uptown?"

"No," said he. "No objection."

---

1. **this day week:** a week from today.

2. **pugilistic** (pyo͞o′jə-lĭs′tĭk) **purpose:** intention of fighting.

I thanked him and ran home again, and there I found that Joe had already locked the front door and was seated by the kitchen fire with a hand on each knee, gazing intently at the burning coals. I too sat down before the fire and gazed at the coals, and nothing was said for a long time.

My sister was in her cushioned chair in her corner, and Biddy sat at her needlework before the fire, and Joe sat next to Biddy.

At length I got out, "Joe, have you told Biddy?"

"No, Pip," returned Joe, "I left it to yourself, Pip."

"I would rather you told, Joe."

"Pip's a gentleman of fortun', then," said Joe, "and God bless him in it!"

Biddy dropped her work and looked at me. Joe held his knees and looked at me. I looked at both of them. After a pause they both heartily congratulated me; but there was a certain touch of sadness in their congratulations that I rather resented.

I took it upon myself to impress Biddy (and through Biddy, Joe) with the grave obligation I considered my friends under, to know nothing and say nothing about the maker of my fortune. Biddy nodded her head thoughtfully at the fire and said she would be very particular; and Joe said, "Aye, aye, I'll be ekervally partickler, Pip," and then they congratulated me again, and went on to express so much wonder at the notion of my being a gentleman that I didn't half like it.

"Saturday night," said I, when we sat at our supper of bread-and-cheese and beer. "Five more days, and then the day before *the* day! They'll soon go."

"Yes, Pip," observed Joe, whose voice sounded hollow in his beer mug. "They'll soon go."

"I have been thinking, Joe, that when I go downtown on Monday and order my new clothes, I shall tell the tailor that I'll come and put them on there, or that I'll have them sent to Mr. Pumblechook's. It would be very disagreeable to be stared at by all the people here."

"Mr. and Mrs. Hubble might like to see you in your new genteel figure, too, Pip," said Joe. "So might Wopsle. And the Jolly Bargemen might take it as a compliment."

"That's just what I don't want, Joe. They would make such a business of it—such a coarse and common business—that I couldn't bear myself."

Biddy asked me here, "Have you thought about when you'll show yourself to Mr. Gargery, and your sister, and me? You will show yourself to us, won't you?"

"Biddy," I returned with some resentment, "you are so exceedingly quick that it's difficult to keep up with you. I shall bring my clothes here in a bundle one evening—most likely on the evening before I go away."

Biddy said no more. Handsomely forgiving her, I soon exchanged an affectionate good night with her and Joe, and went up to bed. When I got into my little room, I sat down and took a long look at it, as a mean little room that I should soon be parted from and raised above forever.

As I put the window open and stood looking out, I saw Joe come slowly forth at the dark door below and take a turn or two in the air; and then I saw Biddy come and bring him a pipe and light it for him. He never smoked so late, and it seemed to hint to me that he wanted comforting, for some reason or other. I drew away from the window and sat down in my one chair by the bedside, feeling it very sorrowful and strange that this first night of my bright fortunes should be the loneliest I had ever known.

I put my light out and crept into bed; and it was an uneasy bed now, and I never slept the old sound sleep in it any more.

Chapter 15

Pip visits Trabb, the tailor, and has a brief encounter with Trabb's boy.

Morning made a considerable difference in my general prospect of life. After breakfast, Joe brought out my indentures from the press in the best parlor, and we put them in the fire, and I felt that I was free.

After our early dinner, I strolled out alone. As I passed the church, I thought—with something akin to shame—of my companionship with the fugitive whom I had once seen limping among those graves. My comfort was that he had doubtless been transported a long way off, and that he was dead to me, and might be veritably[1] dead into the bargain. I made my way to the old Battery, and, lying down there to consider the question whether Miss Havisham intended me for Estella, fell asleep.

When I awoke, I was much surprised to find Joe sitting beside me, smoking his pipe. He greeted me with a cheerful smile on my opening my eyes, and said:

"As being the last time, Pip, I thought I'd foller."

"And, Joe, I am very glad you did so."

"Thankee, Pip."

"You may be sure, dear Joe," I went on, after we had shaken hands, "that I shall never forget you."

"No, no, Pip!" said Joe, in a comfortable tone. "*I'm* sure of that. Aye, aye, old chap!"

"It's a pity now, Joe," said I, "that you did not get on a little more when we had our lessons here, isn't it?"

"Well, I don't know," returned Joe. "I'm so awful dull. I'm only master of my own trade. It were always a pity as I was so awful dull; but it's

no more of a pity now than it was—this day twelvemonth[2]—don't you see!"

What I had meant was that when I came into my property and was able to do something for Joe, it would have been much more agreeable if he had been better qualified for a rise in station. He was so perfectly innocent of my meaning, however, that I thought I would mention it to Biddy in preference.

So, when we had walked home and had had tea, I took Biddy into our little garden and said I had a favor to ask of her.

"And it is, Biddy," said I, "that you will not omit any opportunity of helping Joe on a little."

"How helping him on?" asked Biddy, with a steady sort of glance.

"Well! Joe is a dear good fellow—in fact, I think he is the dearest fellow that ever lived—but he is rather backward in some things. For instance, Biddy, in his learning and his manners."

"Oh, his manners! Won't his manners do, then?" asked Biddy, plucking a black-currant leaf.

"My dear Biddy, they do very well here——"

"Oh! they *do* very well here?" interrupted Biddy, looking closely at the leaf in her hand.

"Hear me out—but if I were to remove Joe into a higher sphere, as I shall hope to remove him when I fully come into my property, they would hardly do him justice."

"And don't you think he knows that?" asked Biddy.

It was such a provoking question (for it had never in the most distant manner occurred to me) that I said, snappishly, "Biddy, what do you mean?"

"Have you never considered that he may be proud?"

---

1. **veritably** (vĕr′ə-tə-blē): actually.

2. **this day twelvemonth:** a year ago today.

"Proud?" I repeated, with disdainful emphasis.

"Oh! there are many kinds of pride," said Biddy, looking full at me and shaking her head; "pride is not all of one kind——"

"Well? What are you stopping for?" said I.

"Not all of one kind," resumed Biddy. "He may be too proud to let anyone take him out of a place that he is competent to fill, and fills well and with respect."

"Now, Biddy," said I, "I am very sorry to see this in you. You are envious, Biddy, and grudging. You are dissatisfied on account of my rise in fortune, and you can't help showing it."

"If you have the heart to think so," returned Biddy, "say so. Say so over and over again, if you have the heart to think so."

"If you have the heart to be so, you mean, Biddy," said I, in a virtuous and superior tone. "Don't put it off upon me. I am extremely sorry to see this in you, Biddy. It's a—it's a bad side of human nature."

I walked away from Biddy, and Biddy went into the house, and I went out at the garden gate and took a dejected stroll until suppertime, again feeling it very sorrowful and strange that this, the second night of my bright fortunes, should be as lonely and unsatisfactory as the first.

But morning once more brightened my view, and I extended my clemency to Biddy, and we dropped the subject. Putting on the best clothes I had, I went into town as early as I could hope to find the shops open, and presented myself before Mr. Trabb, the tailor, who was having his breakfast in the parlor behind his shop, and who did not think it worth his while to come out to me, but called me in to him.

"Well!" said Mr. Trabb, in a hail-fellow-well-met kind of way. "How are you, and what can I do for you?"

"Mr. Trabb," said I, "it's an unpleasant thing to have to mention, because it looks like boasting, but I have come into a handsome property."

A change passed over Mr. Trabb. He got up from the bedside and wiped his fingers on the tablecloth, exclaiming, "Lord bless my soul!"

"I am going up to my guardian in London," said I, casually drawing some guineas out of my pocket and looking at them, "and I want a fashionable suit of clothes to go in. I wish to pay for them," I added, "with ready money."

"My dear sir," said Mr. Trabb, "may I venture to congratulate you? Would you do me the favor of stepping into the shop?"

Mr. Trabb's boy was the most audacious boy in all that countryside. When I had entered, he was sweeping the shop, and he had sweetened his labors by sweeping over me. He was still sweeping when I came out into the shop with Mr. Trabb, and he knocked the broom against all possible corners and obstacles, to express equality with any blacksmith, alive or dead.

"Hold that noise," said Mr. Trabb with the greatest sternness, "or I'll knock your head off! Do me the favor to be seated, sir. Now," said Mr. Trabb, taking down a roll of cloth.

I selected the materials for a suit, and reentered the parlor to be measured. When he had at last done and had appointed to send the articles to Mr. Pumblechook's, he said, "I know, sir, that London gentlemen cannot be expected to patronize local work, as a rule; but if you would give me a turn now and then, I should greatly esteem it. Good morning, sir, much obliged.—Door!"

The last word was flung at the boy, who had not the least notion what it meant. But I saw him collapse as his master rubbed me out with his hands, and my first decided experience of the stupendous power of money was that it had morally laid upon his back Trabb's boy.

After this memorable event I went to the hatter's, and the bootmaker's, and the hosier's, and felt rather like Mother Hubbard's dog whose outfit required the services of so many trades. I also went to the coach office and took my place for seven o'clock on Saturday morning. When I had ordered everything I wanted, I directed my steps toward Pumblechook's, and, as I approached that gentleman's place of business, I saw him standing at his door.

He was waiting for me with great impatience. He had been out early with the chaise-cart, and had called at the forge and heard the news. He had prepared a collation[3] for me in the parlor, and he too ordered his shopman to "come out of the gangway" as my sacred person passed.

"To think," said Mr. Pumblechook, after snorting admiration at me for some moments, "that I should have been the humble instrument of leading up to this, is a proud reward."

I begged Mr. Pumblechook to remember that nothing was to be ever said or hinted on that point. I mentioned that I wished to have my new clothes sent to his house, and he was ecstatic on my so distinguishing him. I mentioned my reason for desiring to avoid observation in the village, and he lauded it to the skies. There was nobody but himself, he intimated, worthy of my confidence. Then he asked me tenderly if I remembered our boyish games at sums, and how we had gone together to have me bound apprentice, and, in effect, how he had ever been my favorite fancy and my chosen friend. If I had taken ten times as many glasses of wine, I should have known that he never stood in that relation to me, and should in my heart of hearts have repudiated the idea. Yet for all that, I remember feeling convinced that I had been much mistaken in him, and that he was a sensible, practical, good-hearted, prime fellow.

3. **collation** (kə-lā′shən): a light meal, usually served cold.

Tuesday, Wednesday, and Thursday passed, and on Friday morning I went to Mr. Pumblechook's to put on my new clothes and pay my visit to Miss Havisham. My clothes were rather a disappointment, of course. Probably every new and eagerly expected garment ever put on fell a trifle short of the wearer's expectation. But after I had had my new suit on some half an hour, it seemed to fit me better.

I went to Miss Havisham's by all the back ways, and rang at the bell. Sarah Pocket came to the gate and positively reeled back when she saw me so changed.

"You?" said she. "You? Good gracious! What do you want?"

"I am going to London, Miss Pocket," said I, "and want to say goodbye to Miss Havisham."

I was not expected, for she left me locked in the yard while she went to ask if I were to be admitted. After a very short delay, she returned and took me up, staring at me all the way.

Miss Havisham was taking exercise in the room with the long spread table, leaning on her crutch stick. The room was lighted as of yore, and at the sound of our entrance, she stopped and turned. She was then just abreast of the rotted bride cake.

"Don't go, Sarah," she said. "Well, Pip?"

"I start for London, Miss Havisham, tomorrow." I was exceedingly careful what I said. "And I thought you would kindly not mind my taking leave of you."

"This is a gay figure, Pip," said she, making her crutch stick play round me, as if she, the fairy godmother who had changed me, were bestowing the finishing gift.

"I have come into such good fortune since I saw you last, Miss Havisham," I murmured. "And I am so grateful for it, Miss Havisham!"

"Aye, aye!" said she, looking at the envious

Sarah with delight. "I have seen Mr. Jaggers. *I* have heard about it, Pip. So you go tomorrow?"

"Yes, Miss Havisham."

"And are you adopted by a rich person?"

"Yes, Miss Havisham."

"Not named?"

"No, Miss Havisham."

"And Mr. Jaggers is made your guardian?"

"Yes, Miss Havisham."

She quite gloated on these questions and answers, so keen was her enjoyment of Sarah Pocket's jealous dismay. "Well!" she went on, "You have a promising career before you. Be good—deserve it—and abide by Mr. Jaggers' instructions." She looked at me, and looked at Sarah, and Sarah's countenance wrung out of her watchful face a cruel smile. "Goodbye, Pip! —you will always keep the name of Pip, you know."

"Yes, Miss Havisham."

"Goodbye, Pip!"

She stretched out her hand, and I went down on my knee and put it to my lips. I had not considered how I should take leave of her; it came naturally to me at the moment to do this. She looked at Sarah Pocket with triumph in her weird eyes, and so I left my fairy godmother, with both her hands on her crutch stick, standing in the midst of the dimly lighted room beside the rotten bride cake that was hidden in cobwebs.

And now, those six days which were to have run out so slowly had run out fast and were gone, and tomorrow looked me in the face more steadily than I could look at it. As the six evenings had dwindled away, I had become more and more appreciative of the society of Joe and Biddy. On this last evening, I dressed myself out in my new clothes for their delight and sat in my splendor until bedtime. We had a hot supper on the occasion, graced by the inevitable roast fowl. We were all very low, and

none the higher for pretending to be in spirits.

I was to leave our village at five in the morning, and I had told Joe that I wished to walk away all alone. I am afraid that this purpose originated in my sense of the contrast there would be between me and Joe if we went to the coach together. I had pretended with myself that there was nothing of this taint in the arrangement; but when I went up to my little room on this last night, I felt compelled to admit that it might be so, and had an impulse upon me to go down again and entreat Joe to walk with me in the morning. I did not.

It was a hurried breakfast with no taste in it. I got up from the meal, saying with a sort of briskness, as if it had only just occurred to me, "Well! I suppose I must be off!" and then I kissed my sister, who was nodding and shaking in her usual chair, and kissed Biddy, and threw my arms around Joe's neck. The last I saw of them was when dear old Joe waved his strong right arm above his head, crying huskily, "Hoo-roar!" and Biddy put her apron to her face.

I walked away at a good pace, thinking it was easier to go than I had supposed it would be. The village was very peaceful and quiet, and all beyond was so unknown and great that in a moment with a strong heave and sob I broke into tears. I was better after I had cried than before—more sorry, more aware of my own ingratitude, more gentle. If I had cried before, I should have had Joe with me then.

When I was on the coach, and it was clear of the town, I deliberated with an aching heart whether I would not get down when we changed horses and walk back, and have another evening at home, and a better parting. We changed, and I had not made up my mind, and still reflected for my comfort that it would be quite practicable to get down and walk back, when we changed again. We changed again, and yet again, and it was now too late, and too far to go back, and I went on. And the mists had all solemnly risen now, and the world lay spread before me.

This Is the End of the First Stage of Pip's Expectations.

Reading Check

1. What two things does the convict make Pip promise to bring to the Battery?
2. What signal is used to indicate that convicts have escaped from prison ships?
3. Why do soldiers come to the Gargery home?
4. How does Miss Havisham hear of Pip?
5. What is Satis House?
6. Who assists Pip in his lessons?
7. What happens to Pip at the Three Jolly Bargemen?
8. Why does Estella allow Pip to kiss her?
9. What two reasons does Orlick have for disliking Pip?
10. What are the two conditions Pip must agree to when Mr. Jaggers brings news of his great expectations?

For Study and Discussion

Analyzing and Interpreting the Novel

Characters

1. In the first stage of his expectations, Pip is involved in events in three very different "worlds": the forge, the marsh, and the strange mansion of Miss Havisham. Make a list of the main characters in each of these "worlds" and identify each one in a sentence or two.

2. What do you learn about Pip from his encounters with the convict on the marsh? Is Pip generous? Is he honest? Does he feel sympathy for those who are less fortunate than he is? Explain.

3a. When Pip encounters each of the two convicts, the first one frightens him, and the second is frightened by him. Despite this, Pip likes the first convict better. Why? **b.** Why does the first convict tell the sergeant he stole the food Pip brought him? **c.** What does this show about his feelings toward Pip?

4a. What impression do you receive of "Mrs. Joe" from Pip's description of her? **b.** Why do you think she treats Pip so harshly?

5. Pip's opinion of himself, his home, and his family changes after his first visit to Miss Havisham's mansion. What is the inner conflict that results from Pip's exposure to Miss Havisham and Estella?

6. Miss Havisham is one of Dickens' great eccentric characters. **a.** From the objects in her rooms and the things she says about them, what can you infer about her past? **b.** What do you think is her purpose in sending for Pip? **c.** What kind of feelings does she seem to enjoy arousing in other people? **d.** Why do you think she takes pleasure in doing this?

7a. What are Joe's feelings toward Pip? **b.** When Mr. Jaggers offers Joe money for releasing Pip from his apprenticeship, how does Joe react? **c.** What does his reaction show about his attitude toward life?

8. The nature of Pip's relationship with Joe is one of the important threads in the novel. Consider this relationship during the first part of the novel. **a.** How does Pip's attitude toward Joe change? **b.** What does this change reveal about Pip's character?

9. Compare Biddy and Estella. **a.** How are they different? **b.** How does each one influence Pip? **c.** Why does Pip choose Estella over Biddy?

10a. What do Mrs. Joe and Mr. Pumblechook expect that Miss Havisham will do for Pip? **b.** From what you know of Miss Havisham and her attitude toward people, do you think these expectations are realistic and reasonable or foolish and unfounded? Why?

11. Compare the Pip of the first few chapters with the Pip who leaves for London. How has he developed and changed?

Plot

12. The plot of the novel is built around Pip's "great expectations." **a.** What is the meaning of this phrase? **b.** Who first uses it in the novel? **c.** What facts and circumstances lead Pip to believe that the source of his "great expectations" is Miss Havisham?

13. *Great Expectations* was first published in weekly installments in a magazine, which was edited by Dickens, called *All the Year Round.* To keep people interested in the story—and eager to buy the next issue of the magazine—Dickens made skillful use of mystery and suspense. Look back at the chapter endings in Stage 1 and note how often many of them arouse your curiosity about what will happen next. At the end of Stage 1, several questions have been left unanswered, such as "Who was the pale young gentleman?" and "Who attacked Mrs. Joe?" What are some other unanswered questions?

14. In *Great Expectations,* as in many novels, there is a main plot and several subplots. The main plot focuses on how Pip grows and changes. The subplots are skillfully interwoven with this main plot. The story of the convicts in the marsh is one of the subplots. At first, the convicts seem to be only a passing episode in Pip's life. But the appearance of the man with the file, who gives Pip two one-pound notes, suggests that we will hear more about the convicts. What other subplots has Dickens connected with Pip's story in the first part of the novel?

15. Throughout the novel, Dickens deliberately introduces some comic scenes to lighten the tone of the narrative. What makes the Christmas dinner with Uncle Pumblechook such a funny scene?

Setting

16. The action of the story begins very dramatically with Pip's encounter with the convict in the graveyard. **a.** How does the setting in the graveyard add to the excitement and suspense of this scene? **b.** Which details of the setting and of the convict's appearance are especially effective in creating an atmosphere of mystery and terror?

17. Throughout the novel, the atmosphere of the marshes suggests loneliness and gloom. **a.** What might Dickens have intended the atmosphere of the marshes to symbolize? **b.** What other settings are associated with a specific mood? **c.** What influence on Pip do you think is symbolized by each?

Point of View

18. *Great Expectations* is told from the first-person point of view. We are able to share Pip's reactions to the other characters and everything they do. We also have Pip's insights into his own actions and thoughts from the vantage point of an adult looking back at his early life. **a.** How does Pip judge his own behavior toward Joe? **b.** Toward Biddy? **c.** Toward Estella?

Theme

19. Pip is quick to notice that some people treat him differently the minute they learn he has come into money. Mr. Pumblechook, Trabb the tailor, and Trabb's foolish boy—who seems to be the village clown—are among the first to alter their manner toward Pip. That money has power to change people's attitudes toward one another was a favorite subject of Dickens'. Tell how he develops this theme in the early part of *Great Expectations*. Choose several episodes from Stage 1 that illustrate different characters' attitudes toward money. Or, if you wish, focus on two characters whose attitudes are strikingly different.

Language and Vocabulary

Learning Word Histories

As a blacksmith, Joe has two helpers, Pip and Orlick. They are his *apprentice* and his *journeyman*, respectively, and Joe is their *master*. In the England of Pip's day, a boy's apprenticeship (or period of training) had to be paid for. A legal contract called his *indentures* provided that his master be paid a certain sum, in return for which the boy received his room and board and training in the master's craft or trade.

Then, as now, a journeyman was a worker who had completed the term of apprenticeship. A master was an experienced worker who was capable of doing superior work.

We still use these old terms and titles. A *master* plumber is the person you would want to install a new sink, and you would probably not choose an *apprentice* carpenter to build your furniture. We also use such expressions as "journeyman playwright" and "master architect." What do these expressions mean?

Writing About Literature

Analyzing Methods of Characterization

Although the characters in a novel are more fully developed than those in a short story, the techniques for revealing character are the same in both forms of fiction. The author may comment directly on a character or use several means of indirect characterization: through description; through words, actions, and thoughts; through the reactions of other characters. Authors frequently use both direct and indirect characterization.

In direct characterization, the author summarizes a character's traits. In the following passage, Dickens tells us directly the kind of person Joe is:

He was a mild, good-natured, sweet-tempered, easygoing, foolish, dear fellow—a sort of Hercules in strength, and also in weakness.

In indirect characterization, the author implies what a character is like. Dickens gives us insight into Mr. Pumblechook's character when he tells us that at breakfast, Mr. Pumblechook gave Pip "as much crumb as possible in combination with as little butter." Dickens does not say directly that Mr. Pumblechook is stingy, but we can infer this trait from his actions.

Choose one of the characters introduced in Stage 1 of the novel and write a composition showing how Dickens reveals that character through direct and indirect characterization.

Focus on Literary Analysis

Analyzing Story Elements

A **literary analysis** examines a literary work's separate elements, presents a main idea about the work, and provides support for that idea in the form of quotations and other details.

There are five basic elements of a story or novel:

Plot: the events
Setting: the time and place
Characters: the people
Point of view: the vantage point from which the story is told
Theme: the chief idea about life or human nature

When you analyze the elements of a literary work, here are some questions you can use:

1. What important conflicts do the characters face?
2. What is the story's climax?
3. Is the setting related to the characters and events?
4. Does the setting contribute to a mood?
5. What are the characters like?
6. How does the point of view affect what you know or feel about the characters?
7. What point about life or human nature does the author seem to make?

In a literary analysis you can either examine individual elements or compare and contrast elements. If you focus on comparison and contrast, make sure that the elements you choose share one or more important features.

Choose one of your favorite short stories. Reread the story slowly and carefully, and use the questions above to make prewriting notes for a literary analysis. Save your notes.

Looking Ahead to Stage 2

In many ways the problems that Pip faces are much like those a young man or woman might face today. In Stage 1 he has already begun to change under the pressures of the world around him. Do you think Pip is satisfied with the change in his life and his new expectations? Will he become a "gentleman" and win Estella as his love? Will he renew his bonds with Joe and Biddy? What do you think lies ahead for Pip in London?

The Second Stage of Pip's Expectations

Chapter 16

Pip meets Wemmick, Mr. Jaggers' clerk, and Herbert Pocket.

The journey from our town to the metropolis was a journey of about five hours. It was a little past midday when the four-horse stagecoach by which I was a passenger got into the ravel of traffic frayed out about the Cross Keys, Wood Street, Cheapside, London. We Britons had at that time particularly settled that it was treasonable to doubt our having and our being the best of everything; otherwise, while I was scared by the immensity of London, I think I might have had some faint doubts whether it was not rather ugly, crooked, narrow, and dirty.

Mr. Jaggers had duly sent me his address: it was Little Britain. A hackney coachman packed me up in his coach and hemmed me in with a folding and jingling barrier of steps, as if he were going to take me fifty miles. I had scarcely had time to enjoy the coach when I observed the coachman beginning to get down, as if we were going to stop presently. And stop we presently did, in a gloomy street, at certain offices with an open door, whereon was painted MR. JAGGERS.

I went into the front office and asked was Mr. Jaggers at home?

"He is not," returned the clerk. "He is in court at present. Am I addressing Mr. Pip?"

I signified that he was addressing Mr. Pip.

"Mr. Jaggers left word would you wait in his room. He couldn't say how long he might be, having a case on. But it stands to reason, his time being valuable, that he won't be longer than he can help."

With those words, the clerk opened a door and ushered me into an inner chamber at the back. Mr. Jaggers' room was lighted by a skylight only, and was a most dismal place. I sat wondering and waiting in Mr. Jaggers' close room, until I really could not bear it and got up and went out.

I told the clerk that I would take a turn in the air while I waited, and turned into a street where I saw the great black dome of Saint Paul's[1] bulging at me from behind a grim stone building which a bystander said was Newgate Prison. Following the wall of the jail, I found the roadway covered with straw to deaden the noise of passing vehicles; and from this and from the quantity of people standing about smelling strongly of spirits and beer, I inferred that the trials were on.

I dropped into the office to ask if Mr. Jaggers had come in yet, and I found he had not, and I strolled out again. I became aware that other people were waiting about for Mr. Jaggers, as well as I. There were two men of secret appearance lounging in Bartholemew Close, one of whom said to the other when they first passed me that "Jaggers would do it if it was to be done." There was a knot of three men and two women standing at a corner, and one of the women was crying on her dirty shawl, and the other comforted her by saying as she pulled her own shawl over her shoulders, "Jaggers is for him, 'Melia, and what more *could* you have?" These testimonies to the popularity of my guardian made a deep impression on me, and I admired and wondered more than ever.

At length I saw Mr. Jaggers coming across the road toward me. All the others who were waiting saw him at the same time, and there was quite a rush at him. Mr. Jaggers addressed himself to his followers.

First, he took the two secret men.

1. **Saint Paul's:** a famous church designed by the English architect Christopher Wren (1632–1723).

"Now, I have nothing to say to *you*," said Mr. Jaggers. "I told you from the first it was a tossup. Have you paid Wemmick?"

"Yes, sir," said both the men together.

"Very well; then you may go. If you say a word to me, I'll throw up the case."

"We thought, Mr. Jaggers—" one of the men began, pulling off his hat.

"That's what I told you not to do," said Mr. Jaggers. "*You* thought! I think for you; that's enough for you.

"And now *you*!" said Mr. Jagger, suddenly stopping and turning on the two women with the shawls. "Once for all; if you come here, bothering about your Bill, I'll make an example of both your Bill and you, and let him slip through my fingers. Have you paid Wemmick?"

"Oh, yes, sir! Every farthing."

"Very well. Say another word—one single word—and Wemmick shall give you your money back." This terrible threat caused the two women to fall off immediately.

Without further interruption we reached the front office. My guardian then took me into his own room, and while he lunched, informed me what arrangements he had made for me. I was to go to Barnard's Inn, to young Mr. Pocket's rooms, where a bed had been sent in for my accommodation; I was to remain with young Mr. Pocket until Monday; on Monday I was to go with him to his father's house on a visit. Also, I was told what my allowance was to be—it was a very liberal one—and had handed to me the cards of certain tradesmen with whom I was to deal for all kinds of clothes and such other things as I could in reason want. "You will find your credit good, Mr. Pip," said my guardian, "but I shall by this means be able to check your bills, and to pull you up if I find you outrunning the constable. Of course you'll go wrong somehow, but that's no fault of mine."

After I had pondered a little over this encouraging sentiment, I asked Mr. Jaggers if I could send for a coach. He said it was not worthwhile, I was so near my destination; Wemmick should walk round with me, if I pleased.

I then found that Wemmick was the clerk in the next room. I accompanied him into the street, after shaking hands with my guardian. We found a new set of people lingering outside, but Wemmick made a way among them by saying coolly yet decisively, "I tell you it's no use; he won't have a word to say to one of you"; and we soon got clear of them and went on side by side.

Casting my eyes on Mr. Wemmick as we went along, to see what he was like in the light of day, I found him to be a dry man, rather short in stature, with a square wooden face. He wore his hat on the back of his head, and looked straight before him, walking in a self-contained way as if there were nothing in the streets to claim his attention. His mouth was such a post office of a mouth that he had a mechanical appearance of smiling.

"Do you know where Mr. Matthew Pocket lives?" I asked Mr. Wemmick.

"Yes," said he, nodding in the direction. "At Hammersmith, west of London."

"Is that far?"

"Well! Say five miles."

"Do you know him?"

"Why, you are a regular cross-examiner!" said Mr. Wemmick, looking at me with an approving air. "Yes, I know him. *I* know him!"

There was an air of toleration about these words that rather depressed me; and I was still looking sideways at his block of a face in search of any encouraging note when he said here we were at Barnard's Inn. I had supposed that establishment to be a hotel kept by Mr. Barnard, to which the Blue Boar in our town was a mere public house. Whereas I now found Barnard to be a fiction and his inn the dingiest collection of shabby buildings ever squeezed together in a rank corner as a club for tomcats. We entered a melancholy little square that looked to me like a flat burying ground. I thought it had the most dismal trees in it, and the most dismal sparrows, and the most dismal cats, and the most dismal houses that I had ever seen. The windows of the houses were in every stage of dilapidated blind and curtain, crippled flowerpot, cracked glass, dusty decay, and miserable makeshift.

So imperfect was this realization of the first of my great expectations that I looked in dismay at Mr. Wemmick. He led me up a flight of stairs, which appeared to be slowly collapsing into sawdust, to a set of chambers on the top floor. MR POCKET, JUN., was printed on the door, and there was a label on the letter box, "Return shortly."

"He hardly thought you'd come so soon," Mr. Wemmick explained. "You don't want me any more?"

"No, thank you," said I.

"As I keep the cash," Mr. Wemmick observed, "we shall most likely meet pretty often. Good day."

When he was gone, I opened the staircase window and had nearly beheaded myself, for the lines had rotted away, and it came down like the guillotine.[2] After this escape, I was content to stand dolefully looking out, saying to myself that London was decidedly overrated.

Mr. Pocket, Junior's, idea of "shortly" was not mine, for I had nearly maddened myself with looking out for half an hour, and had written my name with my finger several times in the dirt of every pane in the window, before I heard footsteps on the stairs. Gradually there arose before me the hat, head, waistcoat, trousers, boots, of a member of society of about my own standing. He had a paper bag under each arm and a pottle[3] of strawberries in one hand, and was out of breath.

"Mr. Pip?" said he.

"Mr. Pocket?" said I.

"Dear me!" he exclaimed, "I am extremely sorry; but I knew there was a coach from your part of the country at midday, and I thought you would come by that one. The fact is, I have been out on your account—not that that is any excuse—for I thought, coming from the country, you might like a little fruit after dinner, and I went to Covent Garden Market to get it."

For a reason that I had, I felt as if my eyes would start out of my head. I began to think this was a dream.

"Pray come in," said Mr. Pocket, Junior. "Allow me to lead the way. I am rather bare here, but I hope you'll be able to make out tolerably well till Monday. My father thought you would get on more agreeably through tomorrow with me than with him, and might like to take a walk about London. I am sure I shall be very happy to show London to you. As to our table, it will be supplied from our coffeehouse here, and (it is only right I should add) at your expense, such being Mr. Jaggers' directions. As to our lodging, it's not by any means splendid, because I have my own bread to earn, and my father hasn't anything to give me, and I shouldn't be willing to take it if he had. This is our sitting room—just such chairs and tables and carpet and so forth, you see, as they could spare from home. This is my little bedroom; rather musty, but Barnard's *is* musty. This is your bedroom; the furniture's hired for the occasion, but I trust it will answer the purpose; if you should want anything, I'll go and fetch

---

2. **guillotine** (gĭl'ə-tēn): a machine with a heavy blade, used to cut off a person's head.

3. **pottle** (pŏt'l): a small basket used for holding fruit (British).

it. The chambers are retired,[4] and we shall be alone together, but we shan't fight, I dare say."

As I stood opposite to Mr. Pocket, Junior, I saw the starting appearance come into his own eyes that I knew to be in mine, and he said, falling back:

"Lord bless me, you're the prowling boy!"

"And you," said I, "are the pale young gentleman!"

Chapter 17

Pip gets a new name.

The pale young gentleman and I stood contemplating one another in Barnard's Inn, until we both burst out laughing.

"The idea of its being you!" said he. "The idea of its being *you*!" said I. And then we contemplated one another afresh, and laughed again. "Well!" said the pale young gentleman, reaching out his hand good-humoredly, "it's all over now, I hope, and it will be magnanimous in you if you'll forgive me for having knocked you about so."

I derived from this speech that Mr. Herbert Pocket (for Herbert was the pale young gentleman's name) still rather confounded his intention with his execution. But I made a modest reply, and we shook hands warmly.

"You hadn't come into your good fortune at that time?" said Herbert Pocket.

"No," said I.

"No," he acquiesced. "I heard it had happened very lately. *I* was rather on the lookout for good fortune then."

"Indeed?"

"Yes. Miss Havisham had sent for me, to see if she could take a fancy to me. But she couldn't—at all events, she didn't."

I thought it polite to remark that I was surprised to hear that.

"Bad taste," said Herbert, laughing, "but a fact. Yes, she had sent for me on a trial visit, and if I had come out of it successfully, I suppose I should have been provided for; perhaps I should have been what-you-may-call-it to Estella."

"What's that?" I asked, with sudden anxiety.

He was arranging his fruit in plates while we talked, which divided his attention, and was the cause of his having made this lapse of a word. "Affianced," he explained, still busy with the fruit. "Engaged. Betrothed."

"How did you bear your disappointment?" I asked.

"Pooh!" said he. "I didn't care much for it. *She's* a tartar."[1]

"Miss Havisham?"

"I don't say no to that, but I meant Estella. That girl's hard and haughty and capricious to the last degree, and has been brought up by Miss Havisham to wreak revenge on all the male sex."

"What relation is she to Miss Havisham?"

"None," said he. "Only adopted."

"Why should she wreak revenge on all the male sex? What revenge?"

"Lord, Mr. Pip!" said he. "Don't you know?"

"No," said I.

"Dear me! It's quite a story, and shall be saved till dinnertime. Mr. Jaggers is your guardian, I understand?" he went on.

"Yes."

"You know he is Miss Havisham's man of business and solicitor,[2] and has her confidence when nobody else has?"

This was bringing me (I felt) toward dangerous ground. I answered with a constraint I made no attempt to disguise that I had seen Mr. Jaggers in Miss Havisham's house on the very day of our combat, but never at any other time, and that I believed he had no recollection of having ever seen me there.

"He was so obliging as to suggest my father for your tutor, and he called on my father to propose it. Of course he knew about my father from his connection with Miss Havisham. My father is Miss Havisham's cousin; not that that implies familiar intercourse between them, for he is a bad courtier and will not propitiate[3] her."

Herbert Pocket had a frank and easy way with him that was very taking. I have never seen anyone who more strongly expressed to me, in every look and tone, a natural incapacity to do anything secret and mean. There was something wonderfully hopeful about his general air, and something that at the same time whispered to me he would never be very successful or rich. He was still a pale young gentleman, without much strength. He had not a handsome face, but it was better than handsome, being extremely amiable and cheerful.

As he was so communicative, I told him my small story, and laid stress on my being forbidden to inquire who my benefactor was. I further mentioned that as I had been brought up a blacksmith in a country place, and knew very little of the ways of politeness, I would take it as a great kindness in him if he would give me a hint whenever he saw me at a loss or going wrong.

"With pleasure," said he, "though I venture to prophesy that you'll want very few hints. Will you begin at once to call me by my Christian name, Herbert?"

I thanked him and said I would. I informed him in exchange that my Christian name was Philip.

"I don't take to Philip," said he, smiling, "for it sounds like a moral boy out of the spelling book. Would you mind Handel for a familiar name? There's a charming piece of music by Handel[4] called the Harmonious Blacksmith."

"I should like it very much."

"Then, my dear Handel," said he, turning round as the door opened, "here is the dinner."

We had made some progress in the dinner, when I reminded Herbert of his promise to tell me about Miss Havisham.

"True," he replied. "Let me introduce the topic, Handel, by mentioning that in London it is not the custom to put the knife in the mouth—for fear of accidents—and that while the fork is reserved for that use, it is not put farther in than necessary. It is scarcely worth mentioning, only it's as well to do as other people do. Also, the spoon is not generally used overhand, but under. This has two advantages. You get at your mouth better (which after all is the object), and you save a good deal of the attitude of opening oysters on the part of the right elbow."

He offered these friendly suggestions in such a lively way that we both laughed.

"Now," he pursued, "Miss Havisham was a spoiled child. Her mother died when she was a baby, and her father denied her nothing. He was very rich and very proud. So was his daughter."

"Miss Havisham was an only child?" I hazarded.

"Stop a moment, I am coming to that. No, she was not an only child; she had a half brother. Her father privately married again— his cook, I rather think."

3. **propitiate** (prō-pĭsh′ē-āt): court the favor of.

4. **Handel** (hănd′l): George Frederick Handel (1685–1759).

"I thought he was proud," said I.

"My good Handel, so he was. He married his second wife privately, because he *was* proud, and in the course of time *she* died. When she was dead, I apprehend he first told his daughter what he had done, and then the son became a part of the family, residing in the house you are acquainted with. As the son became a young man, he turned out riotous, extravagant, undutiful—altogether bad. At last his father disinherited him; but he softened when he was dying and left him well off, though not nearly so well off as Miss Havisham.

"Miss Havisham was now an heiress, and was looked after as a great match. Her half brother had now ample means again, but wasted them most fearfully. There were strong differences between him and her, and it is suspected that he cherished a deep and mortal grudge against her. Now, I come to the cruel part of the story.

"There appeared upon the scene a certain man, who made love to Miss Havisham. I have heard my father mention that he was a showy man, and the kind of man for the purpose. But he was not to be mistaken for a gentleman. Well! This man pursued Miss Havisham closely and professed to be devoted to her. There is no doubt that she perfectly idolized him. He got great sums of money from her, and he induced her to buy her brother out of a share in the brewery (which had been weakly left him by his father) at an immense price, on the plea that when he was her husband he must hold and manage it all. Your guardian was not at that time in Miss Havisham's councils, and she was too haughty and too much in love to be advised by anyone. Her relations were poor and scheming, with the exception of my father; he was poor enough, but not time-serving or jealous. The only independent one among them, he warned her that she was doing too much for this man, and was placing herself too unreservedly in his power. She took the first opportunity of angrily ordering my father out of the house, in his presence, and my father has never seen her since."

I thought of her having said, "Matthew will come and see me at last when I am laid dead upon that table."

"To return to the man and make an end of him. The marriage day was fixed, the wedding dresses were bought, the wedding guests were invited. The day came, but not the bridegroom. He wrote a letter——"

"Which she received," I struck in, "when she was dressing for her marriage? At twenty minutes to nine?"

"At the hour and minute," said Herbert, nodding, "at which she afterward stopped all the clocks. What was in it, further than that it most heartlessly broke the marriage off, I can't tell you, because I don't know. When she recovered from a bad illness, she laid the whole place waste, as you have seen it, and she has never since looked upon the light of day."

"Is that all the story?" I asked, after considering it.

"All that I know of it. But I have forgotten one thing. It has been supposed that the man to whom she gave her misplaced confidence acted throughout in concert with her half brother; that it was a conspiracy between them; and that they shared the profits."

"What became of the two men? Are they alive now?"

"I don't know."

"You said just now that Estella was not related to Miss Havisham, but adopted. When adopted?"

Herbert shrugged his shoulders. "There has always been an Estella, since I have heard of a Miss Havisham. I know no more."

"And all I know," I replied, "you know."

"I fully believe it. And as to the condition on which you hold your advancement in life—

namely, that you are not to inquire or discuss to whom you owe it—you may be very sure that it will never be even approached by me."

He said this with so much delicacy that I felt he as perfectly understood Miss Havisham to be my benefactress as I understood the fact myself.

We were very gay and sociable, and I asked him in the course of conversation what he was. He replied, "An insurer of ships. I shall not rest satisfied with merely insuring ships. I think I shall trade," said he, leaning back in his chair, "to the East Indies for shawls, spices, dyes, drugs, and precious woods. It's an interesting trade."

Quite overpowered by the magnificence of these transactions, I asked him where the ships he insured mostly traded to at present.

"I haven't begun insuring yet," he replied. "I am looking about me."

Somehow, that pursuit seemed more in keeping with Barnard's Inn. I said (in a tone of conviction), "Ah-h!"

"Yes, I am in a countinghouse,[5] and looking about me."

"Is a countinghouse profitable?" I asked.

"Why, n-no; not to me. Not directly profitable. That is, it doesn't pay me anything, and I have to—keep myself. But the thing is, that you look about you. *That's* the grand thing. You are in a countinghouse, you know, and you look about you."

This was very like his way of conducting that encounter in the garden; very like. His manner of bearing his poverty, too, exactly corresponded to his manner of bearing that defeat. It seemed to me that he took all blows and buffets now, with just the same air as he had taken mine then. It was evident that he had nothing around him but the simplest necessaries, for

5. **countinghouse:** an office or building where a company handles accounts and correspondence.

everything that I remarked upon turned out to have been sent in on my account from the coffeehouse or somewhere else. Yet, having already made his fortune in his own mind, he was so unassuming that I felt quite grateful to him for not being puffed up. It was a pleasant addition to his naturally pleasant ways, and we got on famously.

Chapter 18

Pip meets Mr. Matthew Pocket.

On Monday morning at a quarter before nine, Herbert went to the countinghouse to report himself—to look around him, too, I suppose— and I bore him company. He was to come away in an hour or two to attend me to Hammersmith, and I was to wait about for him. When Herbert came, we went and had lunch and then took coach for Hammersmith. We arrived at two or three o'clock in the afternoon. Lifting the latch of a gate, we passed into a garden overlooking the river, where Mr. Pocket's children were playing about.

Mr. Pocket came out to make my acquaintance. He was a gentleman with a rather perplexed expression of face, and with his very gray hair disordered on his head, as if he didn't quite see his way to putting anything straight. Mr. Pocket said he was glad to see me, and he hoped I was not sorry to see him. "For I am really not," he added, with his son's smile, "an alarming personage." He was a young-looking man, in spite of his perplexities and his very gray hair, and his manner seemed quite natural.

Mr. Pocket took me into the house and showed me my room, which was a pleasant one. He then knocked at the doors of two other similar rooms and introduced me to their occupants, by name Drummle and

Startop. Drummle, an old-looking young man of a heavy order of architecture,[1] was whistling. Startop, younger in years and appearance, was reading and holding his head, as if he thought himself in danger of exploding it with too strong a charge of knowledge.

By degrees I learned, chiefly from Herbert, that Mr. Pocket had been educated at Harrow and Cambridge,[2] where he had distinguished himself. He had come to London and here, after gradually failing in loftier hopes, he had turned his acquirements to the account of literary compilation[3] and correction.

In the evening there was rowing on the river. As Drummle and Startop had each a boat, I resolved to set up mine, and to cut them both out. I was pretty good at most exercises in which country boys are adepts, but as I was conscious of wanting elegance of style for the Thames,[4] I at once engaged to place myself under the tuition of the winner of a prize wherry[5] who plied at our stairs, and to whom I was introduced by my new allies.

After two or three days, when I had established myself in my room and had gone backward and forward to London several times, Mr. Pocket and I had a long talk together. He knew more of my intended career than I knew myself, for his having been told by Mr. Jaggers that I was not designed for any profession, and that I should be well enough educated for my destiny if I could "hold my own" with the average of young men in prosperous circumstances.

When I had begun to work in earnest, it oc-curred to me that if I could retain my bedroom in Barnard's Inn, my life would be agreeably varied, while my manners would be none the worse for Herbert's society; so I went off to Little Britain and imparted my wish to Mr. Jaggers.

"If I could buy the furniture now hired for me," said I, "and one or two other little things, I should be quite at home there."

"Go it!" said Mr. Jaggers, with a short laugh. "I told you you'd get on. Well! How much do you want?"

I said I didn't know how much.

"Come!" retorted Mr. Jaggers. "How much? Fifty pounds?"

"Oh, not nearly so much."

"Five pounds?" said Mr. Jagger.

This was such a great fall, that I said in discomfiture, "Oh! more than that."

"More than that, eh!" retorted Mr. Jaggers. "How much more?"

"It is so difficult to fix a sum," said I, hesitating.

"Wemmick!" said Mr. Jaggers, opening his office door. "Take Mr. Pip's written order, and pay him twenty pounds."

This strongly marked way of doing business made a strongly marked impression on me, and that not of an agreeable kind. As he happened to go out now, and as Wemmick was brisk and talkative, I said to Wemmick that I hardly knew what to make of Mr. Jaggers' manner.

"Tell him that, and he'll take it as a compliment," answered Wemmick. "He don't mean that you *should* know what to make of it.—Oh!" for I looked surprised, "it's not personal; it's professional, only professional."

He went on to say in a friendly manner:

"If at any odd time when you have nothing better to do, you wouldn't mind coming over to see me at Walworth, I could offer you a bed, and I should consider it an honor. I have not

1. **heavy . . . architecture:** a large and heavyset physique.
2. **Harrow and Cambridge:** Harrow is a preparatory school, and Cambridge a famous university in England.
3. **compilation:** the gathering of materials from different sources for a book such as an anthology.
4. **Thames** (tĕmz): a river that passes through London.
5. **wherry** (hwĕr′ē): a light, fast rowboat, sometimes used for racing.

much to show you but such two or three curiosities as I have and a bit of garden and a summerhouse."

I said I should be delighted to accept his hospitality.

"Thankee," said he. "Then we'll consider that it's to come off, when convenient to you. Have you dined with Mr. Jaggers yet?"

"Not yet."

"Well," said Wemmick, "he'll give you wine, and good wine. I'll give you punch, and not bad punch. And now I'll tell you something. When you go to dine with Mr. Jaggers, look at his housekeeper."

"Shall I see something very uncommon?"

"Well," said Wemmick, "you'll see a wild beast tamed. It won't lower your opinion of Mr. Jaggers' powers. Keep your eye on it."

I told him I would do so, with all the interest and curiosity that his preparation awakened.

Chapter 19

Pip's friendships increase.

Bentley Drummle, who was so sulky a fellow that he even took up a book as if its writer had done him an injury, did not take up an acquaintance in a more agreeable spirit. Heavy in figure, movement, and comprehension, he was idle, proud, niggardly, reserved, and suspicious. He came of rich people who had nursed this combination of qualities until they made the discovery that it was just of age and a blockhead. Thus, Bentley Drummle had come to Mr. Pocket when he was a head taller than that gentleman, and half a dozen heads thicker than most gentlemen.

Startop had been spoiled by a weak mother and kept at home when he ought to have been at school, but he was devotedly attached to her and admired her beyond measure. He had a woman's delicacy of feature. It was but natural that I should take to him much more kindly than to Drummle, and that even in the earliest evenings of our boating, he and I should pull homeward abreast of one another, conversing from boat to boat, while Bentley Drummle came up in our wake alone.

Herbert was my intimate companion and friend. I presented him with a half share in my boat, which was the occasion of his often coming down to Hammersmith; and my possession of a half share in his chambers often took me up to London. We used to walk between the two places at all hours.

These were the surroundings among which I settled down and applied myself to my education. I soon contracted expensive habits and began to spend an amount of money that within a few short months I should have thought almost fabulous; but through good and evil I stuck to my books. Between Mr. Pocket and Herbert I got on fast.

I had not seen Mr. Wemmick for some weeks when I thought I would write him a note and propose to go home with him on a certain evening. He replied that it would give him much pleasure, and that he would expect me at the office at six o'clock. Thither I went, and found him, putting the key of his safe down his back as the clock struck.

"Did you think of walking down to Walworth?" said he.

"Certainly," said I, "if you approve."

"Very much," was Wemmick's reply, "for I have had my legs under the desk all day, and shall be glad to stretch them. Now I'll tell you what I've got for supper—a cold roast fowl. You don't object to an aged parent, I hope?"

I really thought he was still speaking of the fowl, until he added, "Because I have got an aged parent at my place." I then said what politeness required.

"So you haven't dined with Mr. Jaggers yet?" he pursued, as we walked along.

"Not yet."

"He told me so this afternoon. I expect you'll have an invitation tomorrow. He's going to ask your pals, too. Three of 'em, ain't there? Well, he's going to ask the whole gang."

Mr. Wemmick and I beguiled the time talking, until he gave me to understand that we had arrived in the district of Walworth. It appeared to be a collection of black lanes, ditches, and little gardens. Wemmick's house was a little wooden cottage in the midst of plots of garden, and the top of it was cut out and painted like a battery mounted with guns.

"My own doing," said Wemmick. "Looks pretty, don't it?"

I highly commended it. I think it was the smallest house I ever saw.

"That's a real flagstaff, you see," said Wemmick, "and on Sundays I run up a real flag. Then look here. After I have crossed this bridge, I hoist it up—so—and cut off the communication."

The bridge was a plank, and it crossed a chasm about four feet wide and two deep. But it was very pleasant to see the pride with which he hoisted it up and made it fast, smiling as he did so, with a relish and not merely mechanically.

"At nine o'clock every night, Greenwich time,"[1] said Wemmick, "the gun fires. There he is, you see! And when you hear him go, I think you'll say he's a Stinger."

That piece of ordnance referred to was mounted in a separate fortress, constructed of latticework. It was protected from the weather by an ingenious little tarpaulin umbrella.

"Then, at the back," said Wemmick, "there's a pig, and there are fowls and rabbits; and I grow cucumbers. So, sir," said Wemmick, smiling again, but seriously, too, as he shook his head, "if you can suppose the little place besieged, it would hold out a devil of a time in point of provisions."

Then he conducted me to a bower about a dozen yards off, and in this retreat our glasses were already set forth.

"I am my own engineer, and my own carpenter, and my own plumber, and my own gardener, and my own Jack-of-all-trades," said Wemmick, in acknowledging my compliments. "Well, it's a good thing, you know. It brushes the Newgate[2] cobwebs away, and pleases the Aged. You wouldn't mind being at once introduced to the Aged, would you? It wouldn't put you out?"

I expressed the readiness I felt, and we went into the castle. There we found, sitting by a fire, a very old man in a flannel coat; clean, cheerful, comfortable, and well cared for, but intensely deaf.

"Well, Aged Parent," said Wemmick, shaking hands with him in a cordial way, "how am you?"

"All right, John; all right!" replied the old man.

"Here's Mr. Pip, Aged Parent," said Wemmick, "and I wish you could hear his name. Nod away at him, Mr. Pip; that's what he likes. Nod away at him, if you please."

"This is a fine place of my son's, sir," cried the old man, while I nodded as hard as I possibly could.

"You're as proud of it as Punch; ain't you, Aged?" said Wemmick, contemplating the old man, with his hard face really softened; "there's a nod for you," giving him a tremendous one; "there's another for you," giving him a still more tremendous one; "you like that, don't you? If you're not tired, Mr. Pip—though I

---

1. **Greenwich** (grĭn′ĭj) **time:** the official basis of standard time throughout the world.

2. **Newgate:** Newgate Prison. Wemmick's dealings as Mr. Jaggers' clerk were largely with persons who were trying to get out or keep out of Newgate.

know it's tiring to strangers—will you tip him one more? You can't think how it pleases him."

I tipped him several more, and he was in great spirits. We left him bestirring himself to feed the fowls, and we sat down to our punch in the arbor, where Wemmick told me, as he smoked a pipe, that it had taken him a good many years to bring the property up to its present pitch of perfection.

"I hope Mr. Jaggers admires it," I said.

"Never seen it," said Wemmick. "Never heard of it. Never seen the Aged. Never heard of him. No; the office is one thing, and private life is another. When I go into the office, I leave the Castle behind me, and when I come into the Castle, I leave the office behind me. If it's not in any way disagreeable to you, you'll oblige me by doing the same. I don't wish it professionally spoken about."

Of course I felt my good faith involved in the observance of his request. The punch being very nice, we sat there drinking it and talking until it was almost nine o'clock. "Getting near gunfire," said Wemmick then, as he laid down his pipe. "It's the Aged's treat."

Proceeding into the Castle again, we found the Aged heating the poker, with expectant eyes, as a preliminary to the performance of this great nightly ceremony. Wemmick stood with his watch in his hand until the moment was come for him to take the red-hot poker from the Aged, and repair[3] to the Battery. He took it, and went out, and presently the Stinger went off with a bang that shook the crazy little box of a cottage as if it must fall to pieces, and made every glass and teacup in it ring. Upon this the Aged—who I believe would have been blown out of his armchair but for holding on by the elbows—cried out exultingly, "He's fired! I heared him!" and I nodded at the old gentleman until I absolutely could not see him.

3. **repair:** go.

The supper was excellent. I was heartily pleased with my whole entertainment. Nor was there any drawback to my little turret bedroom.

Our breakfast was as good as the supper, and at half past eight we started for Little Britain. By degrees, Wemmick seemed to get drier and harder as we went along. At last when we got to his place of business and he pulled out his key, he looked as unconscious of his Walworth property as if the Castle and the drawbridge and the arbor and the Aged had all been blown into space together by the last discharge of the Stinger.

Chapter 20

Pip has dinner at Mr. Jaggers' and observes his housekeeper.

It fell out, as Wemmick had told me it would, that my guardian gave me the invitation for myself and my friends. "No ceremony," he stipulated, "and no dinner dress, and say tomorrow."

When I and my friends repaired to him at six o'clock next day, he conducted us to Gerard Street, Soho, to a house on the south side of that street, rather a stately house of its kind, but dolefully in want of painting, and with dirty windows. We went up a dark brown staircase into a series of three dark brown rooms on the first floor.

Dinner was laid in the best of these rooms. The table was comfortably laid and at the side of his chair was a dumbwaiter,[1] with a variety of bottles and decanters on it and four dishes of fruit for dessert. I noticed throughout that he kept everything under his own hand, and distributed everything himself.

1. **dumbwaiter:** small, movable table used for serving food.

As he had scarcely seen my three companions until now—for he and I had walked together—he stood on the hearthrug, after ringing the bell, and took a searching look at them. To my surprise, he seemed at once to be principally, if not solely, interested in Drummle.

"Pip," said he, putting his large hand on my shoulder and moving me to the window, "I don't know one from the other. Who's the Spider?"

"The Spider?" said I.

"The blotchy, sprawly, sulky fellow."

"That's Bentley Drummle," I replied. "The one with the delicate face is Startop."

Not taking the least account of "the one with the delicate face," he returned, "Bentley Drummle is his name, is it? I like the look of that fellow."

He immediately began to talk to Drummle. I was looking at the two when there came between me and them the housekeeper, with the first dish for the table.

She was a woman of about forty, tall, of a lithe, nimble figure, extremely pale, with large faded eyes and a quantity of streaming hair. She set the dish on, touched my guardian quietly on the arm with a finger to notify that dinner was ready, and vanished. No other attendant appeared.

Induced to take particular notice of the housekeeper, both by her own striking appearance and by Wemmick's preparation, I observed that whenever she was in the room, she kept her eyes attentively on my guardian. I fancied that I could detect in his manner a purpose of always holding her in suspense.

Dinner went off gaily, and although my guardian seemed to follow rather than originate subjects, I knew that he wrenched the weakest part of our dispositions out of us. I found that I was expressing my tendency to lavish expenditure, and to patronize Herbert, and to boast of my great prospects. It was so with all of us, but with no one more than Drummle. He informed our host that he much preferred our room to our company, and that as to skill he was more than our master, and that as to strength he could scatter us like chaff. He fell to baring and spanning his arm to show how muscular it was, and we all fell to baring and spanning our arms in a ridiculous manner.

Now the housekeeper was at that time clearing the table, my guardian taking no heed of her. Suddenly, he clapped his large hand on the housekeeper's like a trap, as she stretched it across the table.

"If you talk of strength," said Mr. Jaggers, "*I'll* show you a wrist. Molly, let me see your wrist."

Her entrapped hand was on the table, but she had already put her other hand behind her waist. "Master," she said, in a low voice, with her eyes attentively and entreatingly fixed upon him. "Don't."

"*I'll* show you a wrist," repeated Mr. Jaggers, with an immovable determination to show it. "Molly, let them see your wrist."

"Master," she again murmured. "Please!"

"Molly," said Mr. Jaggers, not looking at her, "let them see *both* your wrists. Show them. Come!"

He took his hand from hers, and turned that wrist up on the table. She brought her other hand from behind her, and held the two out side by side. The last wrist was much disfigured—deeply scarred and scarred across and across. When she held her hands out, she took her eyes from Mr. Jaggers, and turned them watchfully on every one of the rest of us in succession.

"There's power here," said Mr. Jaggers, coolly tracing out the sinews with his forefinger. "Very few men have the power of wrist that this woman has. It's remarkable what mere force of grip there is in these hands. I have had occasion to notice many hands; but I never saw stronger in that respect, man's or woman's, than these. That'll do, Molly. You have been admired, and can go." She withdrew her hands and went out of the room, and Mr. Jaggers filled his glass and passed round the wine.

"At half past nine, gentlemen," said he, "we must break up. Pray make the best use of your time. I am glad to see you all. Mr. Drummle, I drink to you."

If his object in singling out Drummle were to bring him out still more, it perfectly succeeded. In a sulky triumph Drummle showed his morose depreciation of the rest of us in a more and more offensive degree, until he became downright intolerable. Through all his states, Mr. Jaggers followed him with the same strange interest.

In our boyish want of discretion I dare say we took too much to drink, and I know we talked too much. We became particularly hot upon some boorish sneer of Drummle's to the effect that we were too free with our money. Startop tried to turn the discussion aside with some small pleasantry that made us all laugh. Resenting this little success more than anything, Drummle, without any threat or warning, pulled his hands out of his pockets, dropped his round shoulders, swore, took up a large glass, and would have flung it at his adversary's head, but for our entertainer's dexterously seizing it at the instant it was raised.

"Gentlemen," said Mr. Jaggers, deliberately putting down the glass, "I am exceedingly sorry to announce that it's half past nine."

On this hint we all rose to depart. Before we got to the street door, Startop was cheerily calling Drummle "old boy," as if nothing had happened. But the old boy would not even walk to Hammersmith on the same side of the way; so Herbert and I, who remained in town, saw them going down the street on opposite sides, Startop leading, and Drummle lagging behind in the shadow of the houses.

In about a month after that, the Spider's time with Mr. Pocket was up for good, and, to the great relief of all the house, he went home to the family hole.

Chapter 21

Pip has a visitor.

MY DEAR MR. PIP:

I write this by request of Mr. Gargery, for to let you know that he is going to London in company with Mr. Wopsle and would be glad if agreeable to be allowed to see you. He would call at Barnard's Hotel Tuesday morning at nine o'clock, when if not agreeable please leave word. Your poor sister is much the same as when you left. We talk of you in the kitchen every night, and wonder what you are saying and doing. If now considered in the light of a liberty, excuse it for the love of poor old days. No more, dear Mr. Pip, from

Your ever obliged,
and affectionate servant,
Biddy.

P.S. He wishes me most particular to write *what larks*. He says you will understand. I hope and do not doubt it will be agreeable to see him even though a gentleman, for you had ever a good heart, and he is a worthy man. I have read him all excepting only the last little sentence, and he wishes me most particular to write again *what larks*.

I received this letter by post on Monday morning, and therefore its appointment was for next day. Let me confess exactly with what feelings I looked forward to Joe's coming.

Not with pleasure, though I was bound to him by so many ties; no, with considerable disturbance and some mortification. If I could have kept him away by paying money, I certainly would have paid money. My greatest reassurance was that he was coming to Barnard's Inn, not to Hammersmith. I had little objection to his being seen by Herbert or his father, for both of whom I had respect; but I had the sharpest sensitiveness as to his being seen by Drummle, whom I held in contempt. So throughout life, our worst weaknesses and meannesses are usually committed for the sake of the people whom we most despise.

I had got on so fast of late that I had even started a boy in boots[1]—top boots—and had clothed him with a blue coat, canary waistcoat, white cravat, creamy breeches, and the boots already mentioned. I had to find him a little to do and a great deal to eat; and with both of these horrible requirements he haunted my existence.

I came into town on Monday night to be ready for Joe, and I got up early in the morning, and caused the sitting room and breakfast table to assume their most splendid appearance.

Presently I heard Joe on the staircase. I knew it was Joe by his clumsy manner of coming upstairs. When at last he stopped outside our door, I could hear his finger tracing over the painted letters of my name. Finally he gave a faint single rap, and Pepper[2] announced, "Mr. Gargery!"

"Joe, how are you, Joe?"

"Pip, how AIR you, Pip?"

With his good honest face all glowing and shining, and his hat put down on the floor between us, he caught both my hands and worked them straight up and down.

1. **started . . . boots:** hired a serving boy.
2. **Pepper:** the servant.

"I am glad to see you, Joe. Give me your hat."

But Joe, taking it up carefully with both hands, like a bird's nest with eggs in it, wouldn't hear of parting with that piece of property.

"Which you have that growed," said Joe, "and that gentlefolked," Joe considered a little before he discovered this word; "as to be a honor to your king and country."

"And you, Joe, look wonderfully well."

"Thank God," said Joe, "I'm ekerval to most. And your sister, she's no worse than she were. And Biddy, she's ever right and ready."

Herbert had entered the room, so I presented Joe to Herbert. Joe, being invited to sit down to table, looked all round the room for a suitable spot on which to deposit his hat and ultimately stood it on an extreme corner of the chimney piece, from which it ever afterward fell off at intervals.

"Do you take tea or coffee, Mr. Gargery?" asked Herbert, who always presided of a morning.

"Thankee, sir," said Joe, stiff from head to foot, "I'll take whichever is most agreeable to yourself."

"What do you say to coffee?"

"Thankee, sir," said Joe, evidently dispirited by the proposal, "since you *are* so kind as to make chice of coffee, I will not run contrairy to your own opinions. But don't you never find it a little 'eating?"

"Say tea, then," said Herbert, pouring it out.

Here Joe's hat tumbled off the mantelpiece, and he started out of his chair and picked it up, and fitted it to the same exact spot.

"When did you come to town, Mr. Gargery?"

"Were it yesterday afternoon?" said Joe, after coughing behind his hand. "No it were not. Yes it were. Yes. It were yesterday afternoon" (with an appearance of mingled wisdom, relief, and strict impartiality).

"Have you seen anything of London, yet?"

"Why, yes, sir," said Joe, but his attention was attracted by his hat, which was toppling. Indeed, it demanded from him a constant attention. He made extraordinary play with it, and showed the greatest skill, now rushing at it and catching it neatly as it dropped; now merely stopping it midway, beating it up, finally splashing it into the slop basin, where I took the liberty of laying hands upon it.

Then he fell into such unaccountable fits of meditation, with his fork midway between his plate and his mouth; had his eyes attracted in such strange directions; was afflicted with such remarkable coughs; sat so far from the table; and dropped so much more than he ate, and pretended that he hadn't dropped it; that I was heartily glad when Herbert left us for the city.

I had neither the good sense nor the good feeling to know that this was all my fault, and that if I had been easier with Joe, Joe would have been easier with me. I felt impatient of him and out of temper with him.

"Us two being now alone, sir—" began Joe.

"Joe," I interrupted pettishly, "How can you call me sir?"

Joe looked at me for a single instant with something faintly like reproach. I was conscious of a sort of dignity in the look.

"Us two being now alone," resumed Joe, "and me having the intentions and abilities to stay not many minutes more, I will now conclude—leastways begin—to mention what have led to my having had the present honor.

"Well, sir, this is how it were. I were at the Bargemen t'other night, Pip" (whenever he subsided into affection, he called me Pip, and whenever he relapsed into politeness he called me sir), "when there come up in his shay-cart Pumblechook. Well, Pip; this same identical come to me at the Bargemen and his word were, 'Joseph, Miss Havisham she wish to speak to you'!"

"Miss Havisham, Joe?"

"'She wished,' were Pumblechook's word, 'to speak to you.'" Joe sat and rolled his eyes at the ceiling.

"Yes, Joe? Go on, please."

"Next day, sir," said Joe, looking at me as if I were a long way off, "having cleaned myself, I go and I see Miss A."[3]

"Miss A., Joe? Miss Havisham?"

"Which I say, sir," replied Joe, with an air of legal formality, as if he were making his will, "Miss A., or otherways Havisham. Her expression air then as follering: 'Mr. Gargery. You air in correspondence with Mr. Pip?' Having had a letter from you, I were able to say 'I am.' 'Would you tell him, then' said she, 'that which Estella has come home, and would be glad to see him.'"

I felt my face fire up as I looked at Joe.

"Biddy," pursued Joe, "when I got home and asked her fur to write the message to you, a little hung back. Biddy says, 'I know he will be very glad to have it by word of mouth; it is holiday time, you want to see him, go!' I have now concluded, sir," said Joe, rising from his chair, "and, Pip, I wish you ever well and ever prospering to a greater and greater height."

"But you are not going now, Joe?"

"Yes I am," said Joe.

"But you are coming back to dinner, Joe?"

"No I am not," said Joe.

Our eyes met, and all the "sir" melted out of that manly heart as he gave me his hand.

"Pip, dear old chap, life is made of ever so many partings welded together, as I may say, and one man's a blacksmith, and one's a whitesmith,[4] and one's a goldsmith, and one's a cop-

---

3. **Miss A.:** Joe pronounces Havisham as "avisham."
4. **whitesmith:** a tinsmith.

persmith. Diwisions among such must come, and must be met as they come. If there's been any fault at all today, it's mine. You and me is not two figures to be together in London; nor yet anywheres else but what is private, and beknown, and understood among friends. It ain't that I am proud, but that I want to be right, as you shall never see me no more in these clothes. I am wrong in these clothes. I'm wrong out of the forge, the kitchen, or off th' meshes. You won't find half so much fault in me if you think of me in my forge dress, with my hammer in my hand, or even my pipe. You won't find half so much fault in me if, supposing as you should ever wish to see me, you come and put your head in at the forge window and see Joe the blacksmith, there at the old anvil, in the old burned apron, sticking to the old work. I'm awful dull, but I hope I've beat out something nigh the rights of this at lest. And so God bless you, dear old Pip, old chap, God bless you!"

I had not been mistaken in my fancy that there was a simple dignity in him. The fashion of his dress could no more come in its way when he spoke these words than it could come in its way in Heaven. He touched me gently on the forehead, and went out. As soon as I could recover myself sufficiently, I hurried out after him and looked for him in the neighboring streets; but he was gone.

Chapter 22

The mysterious stranger returns, and so does Orlick.

It was clear that I must repair to our town next day, and in the first flow of my repentance it was equally clear that I must stay at Joe's. But when I secured my box-place by tomorrow's coach, I began to invent reasons for putting up

at the Blue Boar. All other swindlers upon earth are nothing to the self-swindlers, and with such pretenses did I cheat myself. I settled that I must go to the Blue Boar.

At that time it was customary to carry convicts down to the dockyards by stagecoach. As I had often seen them on the highroad dangling their ironed legs over the coach roof, I had no cause to be surprised when Herbert came up and told me there were two convicts going down with me. But I had a reason that was an old reason now for faltering whenever I heard the word convict.

"You don't mind them, Handel?" said Herbert.

"Oh, no!"

"I thought you seemed as if you didn't like them?"

"I can't pretend that I do like them, and I suppose you don't particularly. But I don't mind them."

"See! There they are," said Herbert, "and what a degraded and vile sight it is!"

The two convicts were handcuffed together, and had irons on their legs—irons of a pattern that I knew well. They wore the dress that I likewise knew well. One was a taller and stouter man than the other, and his attire disguised him, but I knew his half-closed eye at one glance. There stood the man whom I had seen on the settle at the Three Jolly Bargemen on a Saturday night!

But this was not the worst of it. It came out that the whole of the back of the coach had been taken by a family, and that there were no places for the two prisoners but on the seat in front, behind the coachman. The convict I had recognized sat behind me with his breath on the hair of my head.

"Goodbye, Handel!" Herbert called out as we started. I thought what a blessed fortune it was that he had found another name for me than Pip.

The weather was miserably raw. I dozed off myself in considering the question whether I ought to restore a couple of pounds sterling to this creature before losing sight of him, and how it could best be done. In the act of dipping forward, I woke in a fright and took the question up again. Cowering forward for warmth and to make me a screen against the wind, the convicts were closer to me than before. The very first words I heard them interchange, as I became conscious, were the words of my own thought, "Two one-pound notes."

"How did he get 'em?" said the convict I had never seen.

"How should I know?" returned the other. "He had 'em stowed away somehows. Give him by friends, I expect."

"I wish," said the other, with a bitter curse upon the cold, "that I had 'em here."

"Two one-pound notes, or friends?"

"Two one-pound notes. I'd sell all the friends I ever had, for one, and think it a blessed good bargain. Well? So he says—?"

"So he says," resumed the convict I had recognized "—it was all said and done in half a minute, behind a pile of timber in the dockyards—'You're a-going to be discharged!' Yes, I was. Would I find out that boy that had fed him and kep' his secret, and give him them two one-pound notes? Yes, I would. And I did."

"More fool you," growled the other. "I'd have spent 'em on wittles and drink. He must have been a green one. Mean to say he knowed nothing of you?"

"Not a ha'porth.[1] Different gangs and different ships. He was tried again for prison breaking, and got made a lifer."[2]

"And was that the only time you worked out, in this part of the country?"

"The only time."

"What might have been your opinion of the place?"

"A most beastly place. Mudbank, mist, swamp, and work; work, swamp, mist, and mudbank."

They both execrated the place in very strong language, and gradually growled themselves out, and had nothing left to say.

After overhearing this dialogue, I resolved to alight as soon as we touched the town and put myself out of his hearing. This device I executed successfully. As to the convicts, they went their way with the coach, and I knew at what point they would be spirited off to the river. In my fancy, I saw the boat with its convict crew waiting for them at the slime-washed stairs—again heard the gruff "Give way, you!" like an order to dogs—again saw the wicked Noah's Ark[3] lying out on the black water. I could not have said what I was afraid of, but there was great fear upon me.

Betimes in the morning I was up and out. It was too early yet to go to Miss Havisham's, so I loitered into the country on Miss Havisham's side of town—which was not Joe's side; I could go there tomorrow—thinking about my patroness, and painting brilliant pictures of her plans for me.

She had adopted Estella, she had as good as adopted me, and it could not fail to be her intention to bring us together. I loved Estella with the love of a man; I loved her simply because I found her irresistible. I knew to my sorrow, often and often, if not always, that I loved her against reason, against promise, against peace, against hope, against happiness, against all discouragement that could be. I loved her none the less because I knew it, and it had no more influence in restraining me than if I had devoutly believed her to be human perfection.

1. **ha'porth:** ha'penny worth; in other words, very little.
2. **got made a lifer:** was sentenced to life imprisonment.

3. **Noah's Ark:** the Hulks, the prison boat.

I so shaped out my walk as to arrive at the gate at my old time. I heard the side door open, and steps come across the courtyard, and started to find myself confronted by a man in a sober gray dress—the last man I should have expected to see in that place of porter at Miss Havisham's door.

"Orlick!"

"Ah, young master, there's more changes than yours. But come in, come in. It's opposed to my orders to hold the gate open."

I entered and he swung it, and locked it, and took the key out. "Yes!" said he, facing round. "Here I am!"

"How did you come here?"

"I come here," he retorted, "on my legs."

"Are you here for good?"

"I ain't here for harm, young master, I suppose."

I was not so sure of that. "Then you have left the forge?" I said.

"Do this look like a forge?" replied Orlick.

I had gone up the staircase in the dark, many a time. I ascended it now and tapped in my old way at the door of Miss Havisham's room. "Pip's rap," I heard her say, immediately; "come in, Pip."

She was in her chair near the old table, in the old dress, with her two hands crossed on her stick, her chin resting on them. Sitting near her was an elegant lady whom I had never seen.

"Come in, Pip," Miss Havisham continued. "Come in, Pip. How do you do, Pip? So you kiss my hand as if I were a queen, eh?— Well?"

"I heard, Miss Havisham," said I, rather at a loss, "that you were so kind as to wish me to come and see you, and I came directly."

"Well?"

The lady whom I had never seen before lifted up her eyes and looked archly at me, and then I saw that the eyes were Estella's eyes. But she was so much changed, was so much more beautiful, so much more womanly, that I slipped hopelessly back into the coarse and common boy again. Oh, the sense of distance and disparity that came upon me, and the inaccessibility that came about her!

"Do you find her much changed, Pip?" asked Miss Havisham, with her greedy look, and striking her stick upon a chair that stood between them as a sign for me to sit down there.

"When I came in, Miss Havisham, I thought there was nothing of Estella in the face or figure; but now it all settles down so curiously into the old——"

"What? You are not going to say into the old Estella?" Miss Havisham interrupted. "She was proud and insulting, and you wanted to go away from her. Don't you remember?"

I said confusedly that that was long ago, and that I knew no better then. Estella smiled with perfect composure and said she had no doubt of my having been quite right, and of her having been very disagreeable.

"Is *he* changed?" Miss Havisham asked her.

"Very much," said Estella, looking at me.

"Less coarse and common?" said Miss Havisham, playing with Estella's hair.

Estella laughed. She treated me as a boy still, but she lured me on.

It was settled that I should stay there all the rest of the day, and return to the hotel at night, and to London tomorrow. When we had conversed for a while, Miss Havisham sent us two out to walk. Estella and I went into the garden, I trembling in spirit and worshiping the very hem of her dress; she quite composed and decidedly not worshiping the hem of mine.

As the garden was too overgrown and rank for walking, we came out again into the brewery yard. I showed her where I had seen her walking that first old day, and she said with a cold and careless look in that direction, "Did I?" I reminded her where she had come out of the house and given me my meat and drink,

and she said, "I don't remember." "Not remember that you made me cry?" said I. "No," said she, and shook her head and looked about her. I verily believe that her not remembering and not minding in the least made me cry again, inwardly—and that is the sharpest crying of all.

"You must know," said Estella, condescending to me as a brilliant and beautiful woman might, "that I have no heart—if that has anything to do with my memory. I have no softness there, no—sympathy—sentiment—nonsense. If we are to be thrown much together, you had better believe it at once."

Her handsome dress had trailed upon the ground. She held it in one hand now, and with the other lightly touched my shoulder as we walked. We walked round the ruined garden twice or thrice more. At last we went back into the house, and there I heard with surprise that my guardian had come down to see Miss Havisham on business, and would come back to dinner. Estella left us to prepare herself, and Miss Havisham turned to me and said in a whisper.

"Is she beautiful, graceful, well grown? Do you admire her?"

"Everybody must who sees her, Miss Havisham."

She put an arm around my neck and drew my head close down to hers as she sat in the chair. "Love her, love her, love her! How does she use you?"

Before I could answer (if I could have answered so difficult a question at all), she repeated, "Love her, love her, love her! If she favors you, love her. If she wounds you, love her. If she tears your heart to pieces—and as it gets older and stronger it will tear deeper—love her, love her, love her! Hear me, Pip! I adopted her to be loved. I bred her and educated her to be loved. I developed her into what she is, that she might be loved. Love her!"

"I'll tell you," said she in the same hurried passionate whisper, "what real love is. It is blind devotion, unquestioning self-humiliation, utter submission, trust and belief against yourself and against the whole world, giving up your whole heart and soul to the smiter—as I did!"

She rose up in the chair, in her shroud of a dress, and struck at the air as if she would as soon have struck herself against the wall and fallen dead. All this passed in a few seconds. As I drew her down into her chair, I turned and saw my guardian in the room.

Miss Havisham had seen him as soon as I, and was (like everybody else) afraid of him. She made a strong attempt to compose herself, and stammered that he was as punctual as ever.

"As punctual as ever," he repeated. "And so you are here, Pip?"

I told him when I had arrived, and how Miss Havisham wished me to come and see Estella.

"Well, Pip! How often have you seen Miss Estella before?" said he.

"How often?"

"Jaggers," interposed Miss Havisham, much to my relief; "leave my Pip alone, and go with him to your dinner."

He complied, and we groped our way down the dark stairs together.

"Pray, sir," said I, "may I ask you a question?"

"You may," said he, "and I may decline to answer it. Put your question."

"Estella's name, is it Havisham or—?" I had nothing to add.

"Or what?" said he.

"Is it Havisham?"

"It is Havisham."

This brought us to the dinner table, where she and Sarah Pocket awaited us. Mr. Jaggers scarcely directed his eyes to Estella's face once during dinner. When she spoke to him, he listened, and in due course answered, but never looked at her that I could see. On the other hand, she often looked at him, with interest and curiosity, if not distrust, but his face never showed the least consciousness.

Afterward we went up to Miss Havisham's room, and we four played at whist.[4] We played until nine o'clock, and then it was arranged that when Estella came to London I should be forewarned of her coming and should meet her at the coach; and then I took leave of her, and touched her and left her.

My guardian slept at the Boar in the next room to mine. Far into the night, Miss Havisham's words, "Love her, love her, love her!" sounded in my ears. I said to my pillow, "I love her, I love her, I love her!" hundreds of times.

Ah me! I thought those were high and great emotions. But I never thought there was anything low and small in my keeping away from Joe, because I knew she would be contemptuous of him. It was but a day gone, and Joe had brought the tears into my eyes; they had soon dried, God forgive me! soon dried.

Chapter 23

Trabb's boy has some fun with Pip.

After well considering the matter while I was dressing at the Blue Boar in the morning, I resolved to tell my guardian that I doubted Orlick's being the right sort of man to fill a post of trust at Miss Havisham's. He listened in a satisfied manner while I told him what knowledge I had of Orlick. "Very good, Pip," he observed, when I had concluded. "I'll go round presently and pay our friend off."

4. **whist** (hwĭst): a card game, the forerunner of bridge.

Rather alarmed by this summary action, I was for a little delay, and even hinted that our friend himself might be difficult to deal with. "Oh, no, he won't," said my guardian. "I should like to see him argue the question with *me*."

As we were going back together to London by the midday coach, and as I breakfasted under such terrors of Pumblechook that I could scarcely hold my cup, this gave me an opportunity of saying that I wanted a walk, and that I would go on along the London road while Mr. Jaggers was occupied, if he would let the coachman know that I would get into my place when overtaken. I was thus enabled to fly from the Blue Boar immediately after breakfast. By then making a loop of about a couple of miles into the open country at the back of Pumblechook's premises, I got round into the High Street again, a little beyond that pitfall, and felt myself in comparative security.

It was interesting to be in the quiet old town once more, and it was not disagreeable to be here and there suddenly recognized and stared after. My position was a distinguished one, and I was not at all dissatisfied with it, until Fate threw me in the way of that unlimited miscreant, Trabb's boy.

Casting my eyes along the street at a certain point of my progress, I beheld Trabb's boy approaching. Suddenly the knees of Trabb's boy smote together, his hair uprose, his cap fell off, he staggered out into the road, and crying to the populace, "Hold me! I'm so frightened!" feigned to be in a paroxysm of terror occasioned by the dignity of my appearance. As I passed him, his teeth loudly chattered in his head, and with every mark of extreme humiliation, he prostrated himself in the dust.

This was a hard thing to bear, but this was nothing. I had not advanced another two hundred yards, when, to my inexpressible amazement and indignation, I again beheld Trabb's boy approaching. He was coming round a narrow corner. He staggered round and round me with knees more afflicted, and with uplifted hands as if beseeching for mercy. His sufferings were hailed with the greatest joy by a knot of spectators, and I felt utterly confounded.

I had not got as much farther down the street as the post office when I again beheld Trabb's boy shooting round by a back way attended by a company of delighted young friends to whom he exclaimed, with a wave of his hand, "Don't know yah!" The disgrace attendant on his immediately afterwards taking to crowing and pursuing me across the bridge, culminated the disgrace with which I left town.

The coach, with Mr. Jaggers inside, came up in due time, and I took my box-seat again, and arrived in London safe—but not sound, for my heart was gone. As soon as I arrived, I sent a penitential codfish and a barrel of oysters to Joe (as reparation for not having gone myself), and then went on to Barnard's Inn.

I found Herbert dining on cold meat, and delighted to welcome me back, and I felt that I must open my breast that very evening to my friend and chum. Dinner done and we sitting with our feet upon the fender, I said to Herbert, "My dear Herbert, I have something very particular to tell you."

"My dear Handel," he returned, "I shall respect your confidence."

"It concerns myself, Herbert," said I, "and one other person."

Herbert looked at the fire with his head on one side, and looked at me because I didn't go on.

"Herbert," said I, laying my hand upon his knee. "I love—I adore—Estella. I have never left off adoring her. And she has come back, a most beautiful and most elegant creature. And I saw her yesterday. And if I adored her before, I now doubly adore her."

"Lucky for you then, Handel," said Herbert, "that you are picked out for her and allotted to her. Have you any idea yet of Estella's views on the adoration question?"

I shook my head gloomily. "Oh! She is thousands of miles away from me," said I.

"Patience, my dear Handel; time enough, time enough. But you have something more to say?"

"I am ashamed to say it," I returned, "and yet it's no worse to say it than to think it. You call me a lucky fellow. Of course, I am. I was a blacksmith's boy but yesterday, I am what shall I say I am—today?"

"Say a good fellow, if you want a phrase," returned Herbert, smiling, "a good fellow, with impetuosity and hesitation, boldness and diffidence, action and dreaming, curiously mixed in him."

"Herbert," I went on, "you say I am lucky, and yet, when I think of Estella, I cannot tell you how dependent and uncertain I feel. I may say that on the constancy of one person (naming no person) all my expectations depend. And at the best, how indefinite and unsatisfactory, only to know so vaguely what they are!"

"Now, Handel," Herbert replied, in his gay, hopeful way, "it seems to me that we are looking into our gift horse's mouth with a magnifying glass. Didn't you tell me that your guardian, Mr. Jaggers, told you in the beginning that you were not endowed with expectations only? And even if he had not told you so, could you believe that of all men in London, Mr. Jaggers is the man to hold his present relations toward you unless he was sure of his ground?"

"What a hopeful disposition you have!" said I, gratefully admiring his cheery ways.

"I ought to have," said Herbert, "for I have not much else. And now, I want to make myself seriously disagreeable to you for a moment—

positively repulsive."

"You won't succeed," said I.

"Oh, yes, I shall!" said he. "I have been thinking that Estella cannot surely be a condition of your inheritance, if she was never referred to by your guardian. Am I right in so understanding what you have told me, as that he never referred to her, directly or indirectly, in any way? Never even hinted, for instance, that your patron might have views as to your marriage ultimately?"

"Never."

"Now, Handel, I am quite free from the flavor of sour grapes, upon my soul and honor! Not being bound to her, can you not detach yourself from her?—I told you I should be disagreeable."

I turned my head aside, for, with a rush and a sweep, a feeling like that which had subdued me on the morning when I left the forge, smote upon my heart again. There was silence between us for a little while.

"My dear Handel," Herbert went on, "think of her bringing-up, and think of Miss Havisham. Think of what she is herself. This may lead to miserable things."

"I know it, Herbert," said I, with my head still turned away, "but I can't help it."

"Well!" said Herbert, getting up with a lively shake as if he had been asleep, and stirring the fire. "Now I'll endeavor to make myself agreeable again! I was going to say a word or two, Handel, concerning my father and my father's son. May I ask you if you have ever had an opportunity of remarking that the children of not exactly suitable marriages are always most particularly anxious to be married? Indeed, I think we are all engaged, except the baby."

"Then you are?" said I.

"I am," said Herbert; "but it's a secret."

"May I ask the name?" I said.

"Name of Clara," said Herbert.

"Live in London?"

"Yes. Her father had to do with the victualing[1] of passenger ships. I think he was a species of purser."

"Where is he now?" said I.

"He's an invalid now," replied Herbert. "I have never seen him, for he has always kept his room overhead since I have known Clara. But I have heard him constantly. He makes tremendous rows—roars, and pegs at the floor with some frightful instrument." In looking at me and then laughing heartily, Herbert for the time recovered his usual hearty manner.

"Don't you expect to see him?" said I.

"Oh, yes, I constantly expect to see him," returned Herbert, "because I never hear him, without expecting him to come tumbling through the ceiling. But I don't know how long the rafters may hold."

When he had once more laughed heartily, he became meek and told me that the moment he began to realize Capital,[2] it was his intention to marry this young lady. He added, "But you *can't* marry, you know, while you're looking about you."

Chapter 24

Estella arrives in London.

One day when I was busy with my books and Mr. Pocket, I received a note by the post. It had no set beginning, as Dear Mr. Pip, or Dear Pip, or Dear Sir, or Dear Anything, but ran thus:

I am to come to London the day after tomorrow by the midday coach. I believe it was settled you should meet me? At all events Miss Havisham has that impression, and I write in obedience to it. She sends you her regard.

—Yours, ESTELLA.

1. **victualing:** supplying of food (victuals).
2. **realize Capital:** obtain some money.

My appetite vanished instantly, and I knew no peace or rest until the day arrived. Then I was worse than ever, and began haunting the coach offices in Wood Street, Cheapside, before the coach had left the Blue Boar in our town. I felt as if it were not safe to let the coach office be out of my sight longer than five minutes at a time, and in this condition of unreason I performed the first half-hour of a watch of four or five hours.

In her furred traveling dress, Estella seemed more delicately beautiful than she had ever seemed yet, even in my eyes. Her manner was more winning than before, and I thought I saw Miss Havisham's influence in the change.

"I am going to Richmond," she told me. "The distance is ten miles. I am to have a carriage, and you are to take me. This is my purse, and you are to pay my charges out of it. Oh, you must take the purse! We have no choice, you and I, but to obey our instructions. We are not free to follow our own devices, you and I."

As she looked at me in giving me the purse, I hoped there was an inner meaning in her words. She said them slightingly, but not with displeasure.

"A carriage will have to be sent for, Estella. Will you rest here a little?"

"Yes, I am to rest here a little, and I am to drink some tea, and you are to take care of me the while."

She drew her arm through mine, as if it must be done, and I requested a waiter to show us a private sitting room. Upon that, he pulled out a napkin, as if it were a magic clue without which he couldn't find the way upstairs, and led us to the black hole of the establishment. On my objecting to this retreat, he took us into another room with a dinner table for thirty. I was sensible that the air of this chamber, in its strong combination of stable with soup stock, might have led one to infer that the coaching department was not doing well, and that the enterprising proprietor was boiling down the horses for the refreshment department. Yet the room was all in all to me, Estella being in it. I thought that with her I could have been happy there for life. (I was not at all happy there at the time, observe, and I knew it well.)

"Where are you going to, at Richmond?" I asked Estella.

"I am going to live," said she, "at a great expense, with a lady there, who has the power—or says she has—of taking me about and introducing me and showing people to me and showing me to people. How do you thrive with Mr. Pocket?"

"I live quite pleasantly there; at least——" It appeared to me that I was losing a chance.

"At least?" repeated Estella.

"As pleasantly as I could anywhere, away from you."

"You silly boy," said Estella, quite composedly, "how can you talk such nonsense? Your friend Mr. Matthew, I believe, is superior to the rest of his family?"

"Very superior indeed."

"He really is disinterested, and above small jealousy and spite I have heard?"

"I am sure I have every reason to say so."

"You have not every reason to say so of the rest of his people," said Estella, "for they beset Miss Havisham with reports to your disadvantage. They watch you, misrepresent you, write letters about you (anonymous sometimes), and you are the torment and occupation of their lives. You can scarcely realize the hatred those people feel for you."

"They do me no harm, I hope?"

"No, no, you may be sure of that," said Estella. "Oh, what satisfaction it gives me to see those people thwarted! Two things I can tell you. First, these people never will impair your ground with Miss Havisham, in any particular, great or small. Second, I am beholden to you as the cause of their being so busy and so mean in vain, and there is my hand upon it."

As she gave it me playfully, I held it and put it to my lips. "You ridiculous boy," said Estella, "will you never take warning? Or do you kiss my hand in the same spirit in which I once let you kiss my cheek?"

"If I say yes, may I kiss the cheek again?"

"You should have asked before you touched the hand. But, yes, if you like."

I leaned down, and her calm face was like a statue's. "Now," said Estella, gliding away the instant I touched her cheek, "you are to take care that I have some tea, and you are to take me to Richmond."

Her reverting to this tone as if our association were forced upon us and we were mere puppets, gave me pain; but everything in our intercourse did give me pain. Whatever her tone with me happened to be, I could put no trust in it, and build no hope on it; and yet I went on against trust and against hope. Why repeat it a thousand times? So it always was.

I rang for the tea, and the waiter brought in by degrees some fifty adjuncts to that refreshment, but of tea not a glimpse. A teaboard, cups and saucers, plates, knives and forks, spoons, saltcellars, a meek little muffin confined with the utmost precaution under a strong iron cover, a fat family urn. After a prolonged absence he came in with a casket of precious appearance containing twigs. These I steeped in hot water and extracted one cup of I don't know what, for Estella.

The bill paid, and the waiter remembered, and the chambermaid taken into consideration—in a word, the whole house bribed into a state of contempt and animosity, and Estella's purse much lightened—we got into our post coach and drove away. Turning into Cheapside and rattling up Newgate Street, we were soon under the walls of which I was so ashamed.[1]

1. **the walls . . . ashamed:** Newgate Prison.

"Mr. Jaggers," said I, "has the reputation of being more in the secrets of that dismal place than any man in London."

"He is more in the secrets of every place, I think," said Estella, in a low voice.

"You have been accustomed to see him often, I suppose?"

"I have been accustomed to see him at uncertain intervals ever since I can remember. But I know him no better now than I did before I could speak plainly. What is your own experience of him?"

"Once habituated to his distrustful manner," said I, "I have done very well."

"Are you intimate?"

"I have dined with him at his private house."

"I fancy," said Estella, shrinking, "that must be a curious place."

"It is a curious place."

I should have been chary[2] of discussing my guardian too freely even with her; but I should have gone on with the subject so far as to describe the dinner in Gerrard Street, if we had not then come into a sudden glare of gas.[3] When we were out of it, we fell into other talk, principally about the way by which we were traveling and about London.

It was impossible for me to avoid seeing that she cared to attract me; that she made herself winning; and would have won me even if the task had needed pains. Yet this made me none the happier, for I felt that she held my heart in her hand because she willfully chose to do it, and not because it would have wrung any tenderness in her to crush it and throw it away.

When we passed through Hammersmith, I showed her where Mr. Matthew Pocket lived, and said it was no great way from Richmond, and that I hoped I should see her sometimes.

2. **chary** (châr′ē): hesitant, cautious.
3. **gas:** gaslight.

"Oh, yes, you are to see me; you are to come when you think proper; you are to be mentioned to the family; indeed you are already mentioned."

I inquired was it a large household she was going to be a member of?

"No, there are only two, mother and daughter. The mother is a lady of some station, though not averse to increasing her income."

"I wonder Miss Havisham could part with you again so soon."

"It is a part of Miss Havisham's plans for me, Pip," said Estella, with a sigh, as if she were tired. "I am to write to her constantly and see her regularly, and report how I go on—I and the jewels—for they are nearly all mine now."

It was the first time she had ever called me by name. Of course she did so purposely, and knew that I should treasure it up.

We came to Richmond all too soon, and at our destination two cherry-colored maids came fluttering out to receive Estella. The doorway soon absorbed her boxes, and she gave me her hand and a smile, and said good night, and was absorbed likewise. And still I stood looking at the house, thinking how happy I should be if I lived there with her, and knowing that I never was happy with her, but always miserable.

Chapter 25

Pip and Herbert examine their affairs.

As I had grown accustomed to my expectations, I had insensibly begun to notice their effect upon myself and those around me. Their influence on my own character I disguised from my recognition as much as possible, but I knew very well that it was not all good. I lived in a state of chronic uneasiness respecting my behavior to Joe. My conscience was not by any means comfortable about Biddy. When I woke up in the night I used to think, with a weariness in my spirits, that I should have been happier and better if I had never seen Miss Havisham's face, and had risen to manhood content to be partners with Joe in the honest old forge. Many a time of an evening, when I sat alone looking at the fire, I thought, after all, there was no fire like the forge fire and the kitchen fire at home.

Now, concerning the influence of my position on others, I perceived it was not beneficial to anybody, and above all, that it was not beneficial to Herbert. My lavish habits led his easy nature into expenses that he could not afford, corrupted the simplicity of his life, and disturbed his peace with anxieties and regrets. I began to contract a quantity of debt. I could hardly begin but Herbert must begin too, so he soon followed.

In my confidence in my own resources, I would willingly have taken Herbert's expenses on myself; but Herbert was proud, and I could make no such proposal to him. So he got into difficulties in every direction, and continued to look about him. When we gradually fell into keeping late hours and late company, I noticed that he looked about him with a desponding eye at breakfast time; that he began to look about him more hopefully about midday; that he drooped when he came in to dinner; that he seemed to descry[1] Capital in the distance rather clearly after dinner; that he all but realized Capital toward midnight; and that about two o'clock in the morning he became so deeply despondent again as to talk of buying a rifle and going to America, with a general purpose of compelling buffaloes to make his fortune.

We spent as much money as we could, and got as little for it as people could make up their

1. **descry** (dĭ-skrī′): see.

minds to give us. We were always more or less miserable, and most of our acquaintance were in the same condition. There was a gay fiction among us that we were constantly enjoying ourselves, and a skeleton truth that we never did. To the best of my belief, our case was in the last aspect a rather common one.

At certain times I would say to Herbert, as if it were a remarkable discovery:

"My dear Herbert, we are getting on badly."

"My dear Handel," Herbert would say to me, in all sincerity, "if you will believe me, those very words were on my lips, by a strange coincidence."

"Then, Herbert," I would respond, "let us look into our affairs."

We always derived profound satisfaction from making an appointment for this purpose. Dinner over, we produced a bundle of pens, a copious supply of ink, and a goodly show of writing and blotting paper. For there was something very comfortable in having plenty of stationery.

I would then take a sheet of paper, and write across the top of it, in a neat hand, the heading, "Memorandum of Pip's debts." Herbert would also take a sheet of paper, and write across it, "Memorandum of Herbert's debts."

Each of us would then refer to a confused heap of papers at his side. The sound of our pens going refreshed us exceedingly, insomuch that I sometimes found it difficult to distinguish between this edifying business proceeding and actually paying the money.

When we had written a little while, I would ask Herbert how he got on.

"They are mounting up, Handel," Herbert would say; "upon my life they are mounting up."

"Be firm, Herbert," I would retort. "Look the thing in the face. Look into your affairs. Stare them out of countenance."

"So I would, Handel, only they are staring *me* out of countenance."

However, my determined manner would have its effect, and Herbert would fall to work again. After a time he would give up once more, on the plea that he had not got Cobbs's bill, or Lobbs's, or Nobbs's, as the case might be.

"Then, Herbert, estimate; estimate it in round numbers, and put it down."

"What a fellow of resource you are!" my friend would reply, with admiration. "Really, your business powers are very remarkable."

I thought so too. I established with myself, on these occasions, the reputation of a first-rate man of business—prompt, decisive, energetic, clear, cool-headed. When I had got all my responsibilities down upon my list, I compared each with the bill, and ticked it off. My self-approval when I ticked an entry was quite a luxurious sensation. When I had no more ticks to make, I folded all my bills up uniformly, docketed[2] each on the back, and tied the whole into a symmetrical bundle. Then I did the same for Herbert (who modestly said he had not my administrative genius), and felt that I had brought his affairs into focus for him.

But there was a calm, a rest, a virtuous hush, consequent on these examinations of our affairs, that gave me, for the time, an admirable opinion of myself. Soothed by my exertions, my method, and Herbert's compliments, I would sit with his symmetrical bundle and my own on the table before me among the stationery, and feel like a bank of some sort, rather than a private individual.

We shut our outer door on these solemn occasions in order that we might not be interrupted. I had fallen into my serene state one evening, when we heard a letter drop through

2. **docketed:** labeled.

the slit in the said door and fall on the ground. "It's for you, Handel," said Herbert, going out and coming back with it, "and I hope there is nothing the matter." This was in allusion to its heavy black seal and border.

The letter was signed TRABB & CO., and its contents were to inform me that Mrs. J. Gargery had departed this life on Monday last at twenty minutes past six in the evening, and that my attendance was requested at the interment on Monday next at three o'clock in the afternoon.

Chapter 26

Pip returns to the forge.

It was the first time that a grave had opened in my road of life, and the figure of my sister in her chair by the kitchen fire haunted me night and day. Whatever my fortunes might have been, I could scarcely have recalled my sister with much tenderness. But I suppose there is a shock of regret which may exist without much tenderness. I went down early in the morning and alighted at the Blue Boar, in good time to walk over to the forge. At last I came within sight of the house, and saw that Trabb and Co. had taken possession. Poor dear Joe, entangled in a little black cloak tied in a large bow under his chin, was seated apart at the upper end of the room, where, as chief mourner, he had evidently been stationed by Trabb. When I bent down and said to him, "Dear Joe, how are you?" he said, "Pip, old chap, you know'd her when she were a fine figure of a—" and clasped my hand and said no more.

Biddy, looking very neat and modest in her black dress, went quietly here and there, and was very helpful. When I had spoken to Biddy, as I thought it not a time for talking, I went and sat down near Joe.

"Pocket handkerchiefs out, all!" cried Mr.

Trabb at this point, in a depressed businesslike voice—"Pocket handkerchiefs out! We are ready!"

So, we all put our pocket handkerchiefs to our faces and filed out two and two; Joe and I, Biddy and Pumblechook, Mr. and Mrs. Hubble, the remains of my poor sister being carried by six bearers.

We went through the village, and now the range of marshes lay clear before us, and we went into the churchyard, close to the graves of my unknown parents, Philip Pirrip, late of this parish, and Also Georgiana, Wife of the Above. And there my sister was laid quietly in the earth while the larks sang high above it, and the light wind strewed it with beautiful shadows of clouds and trees.

When we got back and when they were all gone, Biddy, Joe, and I had a cold dinner together; but we dined in the best parlor, not in the old kitchen, and Joe was so exceedingly particular what he did with his knife and fork and the saltcellar and what not, that there was great restraint upon us. But after dinner, when I made him take his pipe, and when I had loitered with him about the forge, and when we sat down together on the great block of stone outside it, we got on better.

He was very much pleased by my asking if I might sleep in my own little room, and I was pleased too; for I felt that I had done rather a great thing in making the request.

When the shadows of evening were closing in, I took an opportunity of getting into the garden with Biddy for a little talk.

"Biddy," said I, "I think you might have written to me about these sad matters."

"Do you, Mr. Pip?" said Biddy. "I should have written if I had thought that."

She was so quiet, and had such an orderly, good, and pretty way with her that I did not like the thought of making her cry again. After looking a little at her downcast eyes as she walked beside me, I gave up that point.

"I suppose it will be difficult for you to remain here now, Biddy, dear?"

"Oh! I can't do so, Mr. Pip," said Biddy, in a tone of regret, but still of quiet conviction. "I have been speaking to Mrs. Hubble, and I am going to her tomorrow. I hope we shall be able to take some care of Mr. Gargery together until he settles down."

"How are you going to live, Biddy? If you want any mo——"

"How am I going to live?" repeated Biddy, striking in, with a momentary flush upon her face. "I'll tell you, Mr. Pip. I am going to try to get the place of mistress in the new school nearly finished here. I can be well recommended by all the neighbors, and I hope I can be industrious and patient, and teach myself while I teach others. The new schools are not like the old, but I learned a good deal from you after that time, and have had time since then to improve."

"I think you would always improve, Biddy, under any circumstances." I walked a little farther with Biddy, looking silently at her downcast eyes. "I have not heard the particulars of my sister's death, Biddy."

"They are very slight, poor thing. She had been in one of her bad states for four days, when she came out of it in the evening, just at teatime, and said quite plainly, 'Joe.' As she had never said any word for a long while, I ran and fetched in Mr. Gargery from the forge. She made signs to me that she wanted him to sit down close to her, and wanted me to put her arms around his neck. So I put them round his neck, and she laid her head down on his shoulder quite content and satisfied. And so she presently said 'Joe' again, and once 'Pardon,' and once 'Pip.' And so she never lifted her head up any more, and it was just an hour later when we laid it down on her own bed, because we found she was gone."

Biddy cried; the darkening garden, and the lane, and the stars that were coming out, were blurred in my own sight.

"Nothing was ever discovered, Biddy?"

"Nothing."

"Do you know what is become of Orlick?"

"I should think from the color of his clothes that he is working in the quarries."

"Of course you have seen him then? Why are you looking at that dark tree in the lane?"

"I saw him there on the night she died."

"That was not the last time either, Biddy?"

"No; I have seen him there since we have been walking here. It is of no use," said Biddy, laying her hand upon my arm, as I was for running out. "You know I would not deceive you; he was not there a minute, and he is gone."

It revived my utmost indignation to find that she was still pursued by this fellow, and I told her that I would spend any money or take any pains to drive him out of that country. By degrees she led me into more temperate talk, and she told me how Joe loved me, and how Joe never complained of anything—she didn't say, of me; she had no need; I knew what she meant—but ever did his duty in his way of life, and with a strong hand, a quiet tongue, and a gentle heart.

"Indeed, it would be hard to say too much for him," said I, "and of course I shall be often down here now. I am not going to leave poor Joe alone."

"Are you quite sure, then, that you *will* come to see him often?" asked Biddy, stopping in the narrow garden walk, and looking at me with a clear and honest eye.

"Oh, dear me!" said I as I found myself compelled to give up Biddy in despair. "This really is a very bad side of human nature! Don't say any more, if you please, Biddy. This shocks me very much."

For which cogent reason I kept Biddy at a distance during supper, and when I went up to my own little room, took as stately a leave of her as I could. As often as I was restless in the night, and that was every quarter of an hour, I reflected what an unkindness, what an injury, what an injustice, Biddy had done me.

Early in the morning I was to go. Early in the morning I was out, and looking in, unseen, at one of the wooden windows of the forge. There I stood, for minutes, looking at Joe, already at work with a glow of health and strength upon his face that made it show as if the bright sun of the life in store for him were shining on it.

"Goodbye, dear Joe! No, don't wipe it off— give me your blackened hand! I shall be down soon and often."

"Never too soon, sir," said Joe, "and never too often, Pip!"

Biddy was waiting for me at the kitchen door, with a mug of new milk and a crust of bread. "Biddy," said I, when I gave her my hand at parting, "I am not angry, but I am hurt."

"No, don't be hurt," she pleaded quite pathetically, "let only me be hurt, if I have been ungenerous."

Once more, the mists were rising as I walked away. If they disclosed to me, as I suspect they did, that I should *not* come back, and that Biddy was quite right, all I can say is—they were quite right too.

Chapter 27

Miss Skiffins helps serve tea.

Herbert and I went on from bad to worse, in the way of increasing our debts; and time went on; and I came of age. Herbert himself had come of age, eight months before me. As he had nothing else than his majority[1] to come into, the event did not make a profound sensation in Barnard's Inn. But we had looked forward to my one-and-twentieth birthday with a crowd of speculations and anticipations, for we had both considered that my guardian could hardly help saying something definite on that occasion.

I had taken care to have it well understood in Little Britain when my birthday was. On the day before it, I received an official note from Wemmick, informing me that Mr. Jaggers would be glad if I would call upon him at five in the afternoon of the auspicious day. This convinced us that something great was to happen, and threw me into an unusual flutter when I repaired to my guardian's office, a model of punctuality.

Wemmick offered me his congratulations, and incidentally rubbed the side of his nose with a folded piece of tissue paper that I liked the look of. It was November, and my guardian was standing before his fire with his hands under his coattails.

"Well, Pip," said he, "I must call you Mr. Pip today. Congratulations, Mr. Pip."

We shook hands and I thanked him.

"Take a chair, Mr. Pip," said my guardian.

As I sat down, I felt at a disadvantage which reminded me of that old time when I had been put upon a tombstone.

"Now, my young friend," my guardian began, as if I were a witness in the box, "I am going to have a word or two with you."

"If you please, sir."

"What do you suppose," said Mr. Jaggers, "you are living at the rate of?"

"At the rate of, sir?"

"At," repeated Mr. Jaggers, "the—rate— of?"

Reluctantly, I confessed myself quite unable

---

1. **majority:** here, legal age.

to answer the question. This reply seemed agreeable to Mr. Jaggers, who said, "I thought so! Now, I have asked *you* a question, my friend. Have you anything to ask *me*?"

"Of course it would be a great relief to me to ask you several questions, sir."

"Ask one," said Mr. Jaggers.

"Is my benefactor to be made known to me today?"

"No. Ask another."

"Is that confidence to be imparted to me soon?"

"Waive that a moment," said Mr. Jaggers, "and ask another."

"Have—I—anything to receive, sir?" On that, Mr. Jaggers said, triumphantly, "I thought we should come to it!" and called to Wemmick to give him that piece of paper. Wemmick appeared, handed it in, and disappeared.

"Now, Mr. Pip," said Mr. Jaggers, "attend if you please. You have been drawing pretty freely here; your name occurs pretty often in Wemmick's cashbook; but you are in debt, of course?"

"I am afraid I must say yes, sir."

"You know you must say yes, don't you?" said Mr. Jaggers.

"Yes, sir."

"I don't ask you what you owe, because you don't know; and if you did know, you wouldn't tell me; you would say less. Yes, yes, my friend," cried Mr. Jaggers, waving his forefinger to stop me, as I made a show of protesting; "it's likely enough that you think you wouldn't, but you would. Now, take this piece of paper in your hand. Now, unfold it and tell me what it is."

"This is a bank note," said I, "for five hundred pounds."

"You consider it, undoubtedly, a handsome sum of money. Now, that handsome sum of money, Pip, is your own. It is a present to you on this day, in earnest of your expectations. And at the rate of that handsome sum of money per annum,[2] and at no higher rate, you are to live until the donor of the whole appears. That is to say, you will now take your money affairs entirely into your own hands, and you will draw from Wemmick one hundred and twenty-five pounds per quarter until you are in communication with the fountainhead[3] and no longer with the mere agent. As I have told you before, I am the mere agent. I execute my instructions, and I am paid for doing so. I think them injudicious, but I am not paid for giving my opinion on their merits."

After a pause, I hinted:

"There was a question just now, Mr. Jaggers, which you desired me to waive for a moment. I hope I am doing nothing wrong in asking it again?"

"What is it?" said he.

"Is it likely," I said, after hesitating, "that my patron, Mr. Jaggers, will soon come to London," said I, "or summon me anywhere else?"

"Now here," replied Mr. Jaggers, fixing me for the first time with his dark deep-set eyes, "we must revert to the evening when we first encountered one another in your village. What did I tell you then, Pip?"

"You told me, Mr. Jaggers, that it might be years hence when that person appeared."

"Just so," said Mr. Jaggers. "That's my answer."

"Do you suppose it will still be some years hence, Mr. Jaggers?"

"Come!" said Mr. Jaggers. "I'll be plain with you, my friend Pip. That's a question I must not be asked. When that person discloses, you and that person will settle your own affairs. My

2. **per annum** (ăn′əm): by the year (Latin).
3. **fountainhead:** source.

part in this business will cease. And that's all I have got to say."

"If that is all you have to say, sir," I remarked, "there can be nothing left for me to say."

He nodded assent and asked me where I was going to dine. I replied at my own chambers, with Herbert. As a necessary sequence, I asked him if he would favor us with his company, and he promptly accepted the invitation. But first he had a letter or two to write, and I said I would go into the outer office and talk to Wemmick.

The fact was that when the five hundred pounds had come into my pocket, a thought had come into my head which had been often there before; and it appeared to me that Wemmick was a good person to advise with.

"Mr. Wemmick," said I, "I want to ask your opinion. I am very desirous to serve a friend. This friend is trying to get on in commercial life, but has no money and finds it difficult and disheartening to make a beginning. Now, I want somehow to help him to a beginning."

"With money down?" said Wemmick, in a tone drier than any sawdust.

"With *some* money down," I replied, for an uneasy remembrance shot across me of that symmetrical bundle of papers at home; "with *some* money down, and perhaps some anticipation of my expectations."

"Mr. Pip," said Wemmick, "pitch your money into the Thames and you know the end of it. Serve a friend with it, and you may know the end of it too—but it's a less pleasant and profitable end."

"And that," said I, "is your deliberate opinion, Mr. Wemmick?"

"That," he returned, "is my deliberate opinion in this office."

"Ah!" said I, pressing him, for I thought I saw him near a loophole here; "but would that be your opinion at Walworth?"

"Mr. Pip," he replied with gravity, "Walworth is one place, and this office is another. Much as the Aged is one person, and Mr. Jaggers is another. They must not be confounded together. My Walworth sentiments must be taken at Walworth; none but my official sentiments can be taken in this office."

"Very well," said I, much relieved, "then I shall look you up at Walworth, you may depend upon it."

"Mr. Pip," he returned, "you will be welcome there, in a private and personal capacity."

We had held this conversation in a low voice, well knowing my guardian's ears to be the sharpest of the sharp. As he now appeared in his doorway, we all three went into the street together, and from the doorstep Wemmick turned his way, and Mr. Jaggers and I turned ours.

I devoted the next Sunday afternoon to a pilgrimage to the Castle. On arriving before the battlements, I found the Union Jack flying and the drawbridge up, but undeterred by this show of defiance and resistance, I rang at the gate, and was admitted by the Aged.

"My son, sir," said the old man, after securing the drawbridge, "left word that he would soon be home from his afternoon's walk. He is very regular in his walks, is my son. Very regular in everything, is my son."

I nodded at the old gentleman, and we went in and sat down by the fireside.

"You made acquaintance with my son, sir," said the old man, in his chirping way, while he warmed his hands at the blaze, "at his office, I expect?" I nodded. "Hah! I have heered that my son is a wonderful hand at his business."

I was startled by a sudden click in the wall on one side of the chimney, and the ghostly tumbling open of a little wooden flap with "JOHN" upon it. The old man, following my eyes, cried with great triumph, "My son's come home!" and we both went out to the drawbridge. The

Aged was so delighted to work the drawbridge that I made no offer to assist him, but stood quiet until Wemmick had come across, and had presented me to Miss Skiffins, a lady by whom he was accompanied.

Miss Skiffins was of a wooden appearance, like her escort. The cut of her dress from the waist upward, both before and behind, made her figure very like a boy's kite, and I might have pronounced her gown a little too decidedly orange and her gloves a little too intensely green; but she seemed to be a good sort of fellow, and showed a high regard for the Aged. I was not long in discovering that she was a frequent visitor at the Castle.

While Miss Skiffins was taking off her bonnet (she retained her green gloves during the evening as an outward and visible sign that there was company), Wemmick invited me to take a walk with him round the property and see how the island looked in wintertime. Thinking that he did this to give me an opportunity of taking his Walworth sentiments, I seized the opportunity as soon as we were out of the Castle.

I informed Wemmick that I was anxious in behalf of Herbert Pocket, and I told him how we had first met, and how we had fought. I alluded to the advantages I had derived in my first ignorance from his society, and I confessed that I feared I had but ill repaid them, and that he might have done better without me and my expectations. For all these reasons (I told Wemmick), and because he was my young companion and friend, I sought advice how I could best help Herbert to some present income—say of a hundred a year, to keep him in good hope and heart—and gradually to buy him onto some small partnership. I begged Wemmick to understand that my help must always be rendered without Herbert's knowledge or suspicion, and that there was no one else in the world with whom I could advise. I wound up by laying my hand upon his shoulder and saying, "I can't help confiding in you, though I know it must be troublesome to you; but that is your fault in having ever brought me here."

Wemmick was silent for a little while, and then said, "Mr. Pip, I'll put on my considering cap, and I think all you want to do may be done by degrees. Skiffins (that's her brother) is an accountant and agent. I'll look him up and go to work for you."

After a little further conversation to the same effect, we returned into the Castle, where we found Miss Skiffins preparing tea. The responsible duty of making the toast was delegated to the Aged, and that excellent old gentleman prepared such a haystack of buttered toast that I could scarcely see him over it. We ate the whole of the toast and drank tea in proportion, and it was delightful to see how warm and greasy we all got after it. The Aged especially might have passed for some clean old chief of a savage tribe, just oiled. Then we drew round the fire, and Wemmick said, "Now, Aged Parent, read us the paper."

Wemmick explained to me while the Aged got his spectacles out that this was according to custom, and that it gave the old gentleman infinite satisfaction to read the news aloud. "I won't offer an apology,' said Wemmick, "for he isn't capable of many pleasures—are you, Aged P.?"

"All right, John, all right," returned the old man, seeing himself spoken to.

"Only tip him a nod every now and then when he looks off his paper," said Wemmick, "and he'll be as happy as a king. We are all attention, Aged One."

As Wemmick and Miss Skiffins sat side by side, I observed him slowly and gradually stealing his arm round Miss Skiffins' waist. In course of time I saw his hand appear on the other side of Miss Skiffins; but at that moment

Miss Skiffins neatly stopped him with the green glove, unwound his arm again as if it were an article of dress, and with the greatest deliberation laid it on the table before her. Miss Skiffins' composure while she did this was one of the most remarkable sights I have ever seen.

At last the Aged read himself into a light slumber. Of course I knew better than to offer to see Miss Skiffins home, and under the circumstances I thought I had best go first; which I did, taking a cordial leave of the Aged, and having passed a pleasant evening.

Before a week was out, I received a note from Wemmick, dated Walworth, stating that he hoped he had made some advance in that matter appertaining to our private and personal capacities. The upshot was that we found a worthy young merchant, not long established in business, who wanted intelligent help, and who wanted capital, and who in due course of time would want a partner. Between him and me secret articles were signed of which Herbert was the subject, and I paid him half of my five hundred pounds down, and engaged for other payments; some to fall due at certain dates out of my income; some contingent on my coming into my property. Miss Skiffins' brother conducted the negotiation.

The whole business was so cleverly managed that Herbert had not the least suspicion of my hand being in it. I never shall forget the radiant face with which he came home one afternoon, and told me, as a mighty piece of news, of his having fallen in with one Clarriker (the young merchant's name), and of his belief that the opening had come at last. Day by day as his hopes grew stronger and his face brighter, he must have thought me a more and more affectionate friend, for I had the greatest difficulty in restraining my tears of triumph when I saw him so happy.

At length, the thing being done, and he hav-ing that day entered Clarriker's House, and he having talked to me for a whole evening in a flush of pleasure and success, I did really cry in good earnest when I went to bed, to think that my expectations had done some good to somebody.

A great event in my life, the turning point of my life, now opens on my view. But, before I proceed to narrate it, and before I pass on to all the changes it involved, I must give one chapter to Estella. It is not much to give to the theme that so long filled my heart.

Chapter 28

Estella warns Pip.

The lady with whom Estella was placed, Mrs. Brandley by name, was a widow, with one daughter several years older than Estella. They were in what is called a good position, and they visited, and were visited by, numbers of people.

In Mrs. Brandley's house and out of Mrs. Brandley's house, I suffered every kind and degree of torture that Estella could cause me. She made use of me to tease other admirers; and she turned the very familiarity between herself and me to the account of putting a constant slight on my devotion to her. And while I think it likely that it almost maddened her other lovers, I knew too certainly that it almost maddened me. She had admirers without end. No doubt my jealousy made an admirer of everyone who went near her; but there were more than enough of them without that.

I saw her often at Richmond, I heard of her often in town, and I used often to take her and the Brandleys on all sorts of pleasures—and they were all miseries to me. I never had one hour's happiness in her society, and yet my mind all round the four-and-twenty hours was harping on the happiness of having her with me unto death. She habitually reverted to that tone which expressed that our association was forced upon us. There were other times when she would come to a sudden check in this tone and in all her many tones and would seem to pity me.

"Pip, Pip," she said one evening, when we sat apart at a darkening window of the house in Richmond; "will you never take warning?"

"Of what?"

"Of me."

"Warning not to be attracted by you, do you mean, Estella?"

"Do I mean! If you don't know what I mean, you are blind."

"At any rate," said I, "I have no warning given me just now, for you wrote to me to come to you this time."

"That's true," said Estella, with a cold careless smile that always chilled me. "The time has come round when Miss Havisham wishes to have me for a day at Satis. You are to take me there, and bring me back, if you will. She would rather I did not travel alone, and objects to receiving my maid, for she has a sensitive horror of being talked of by such people. Can you take me?"

"Can I take you, Estella!"

"You can then? The day after tomorrow, if you please. You are to pay all charges out of my purse. You hear the condition of your going?"

"And must obey," said I.

We went down on the next day but one, and we found Miss Havisham in the room where I had first beheld her. She hung upon Estella's beauty, hung upon her words, hung upon her gestures, and looked at her, as though she were devouring the beautiful creature she had reared.

From Estella she looked at me, with a searching glance that seemed to pry into my heart and probe its wounds. "How does she use you, Pip, how does she use you?" she asked me again, with her witchlike eagerness, even in Estella's hearing. But when we sat by the flickering fire at night, she was most weird, for then, keeping Estella's hand drawn through her arm and clutched in her own hand, she extorted from her by dint of referring back to what Estella had told her in her regular letters the names and conditions of the men she had fascinated, I saw in this that Estella was set to wreak Miss Havisham's revenge on men. I, too, was tormented even while the prize was reserved for me. I saw in this the reason for my being staved off so long, and the reason for my late guardian's declining to commit himself to the formal knowledge of such a scheme.

The candles that lighted that room were placed in sconces on the wall.

They were high from the ground, and they burned with the steady dullness of artificial light in air that is seldom renewed. As I looked round at them, and at the pale gloom they made, and at the stopped clock, and at the withered articles of bridal dress upon the table and the ground, and at her own awful figure with its ghostly reflection thrown large by the fire upon the ceiling and the wall, I saw in everything the construction that my mind had come to, repeated and thrown back to me.

It happened on the occasion of this visit that some sharp words arose between Estella and Miss Havisham. It was the first time I had ever seen them opposed.

Miss Havisham still clutched Estella's hand in hers, when Estella gradually began to detach herself. She had shown a proud impatience more than once before, and had rather endured that fierce affection than accepted or returned it.

"What!" said Miss Havisham, flashing her

eyes upon her. "Are you tired of me?"

"Only a little tired of myself," replied Estella, disengaging her arm.

"Speak the truth, you ingrate!" cried Miss Havisham, passionately striking her stick upon the floor. "You are tired of me."

Estella looked at her with perfect composure, and again looked down at the fire. Her graceful figure and her beautiful face expressed a self-possessed indifference to the wild heat of the other that was almost cruel.

"You stock and stone!" exclaimed Miss Havisham. "You cold, cold heart!"

"What!" said Estella. "Do you reproach me for being cold? You?"

"Are you not?" was the fierce retort.

"You should know," said Estella. "I am what you have made me."

"So proud, so proud!" moaned Miss Havisham, pushing away her gray hair with both her hands.

"Who taught me to be proud?" returned Estella. "Who praised me when I learned my lesson?"

"So hard, so hard!" moaned Miss Havisham, with her former action.

"Who taught me to be hard?" returned Estella. "Who praised me when I learned my lesson?"

"But to be proud and hard to *me*!" Miss Havisham quite shrieked, as she stretched out her arms. "Estella, Estella, Estella, to be proud and hard to *me*!"

"So," said Estella, "I must be taken as I have been made. The success is not mine, the failure is not mine, but the two together make me."

Miss Havisham had settled down, upon the floor, among the faded bridal relics with which it was strewn. I took advantage of the moment—I had sought one from the first—to leave the room, after beseeching Estella's attention to her with a movement of my hand. When I left, Estella was yet standing by the great chimney piece, just as she had stood throughout. Miss Havisham's gray hair was all adrift upon the ground, among the other bridal wrecks, and was a miserable sight to see.

It was with a depressed heart that I walked in the starlight for an hour and more, about the courtyard, and about the brewery, and about the ruined garden. When I at last took courage to return to the room, I found Estella sitting at Miss Havisham's knee. Afterward Estella and I played cards, as of yore—only we were skillful now, and played French games—and so the evening wore away, and I went to bed.

I lay in that separate building across the courtyard. It was the first time I had ever lain down to rest in Satis House, and sleep refused to come near me. At last I felt that I absolutely must get up. I put on my clothes and went out across the yard into the long stone passage. But I was no sooner in the passage than I extinguished my candle, for I saw Miss Havisham going along it in a ghostly manner, making a low cry. I followed her at a distance and saw her go up the staircase. She carried a bare candle in her hand and was a most unearthly object by its light. Standing at the bottom of the staircase, I heard her walking across into her own room, never ceasing the low cry. After a time, I tried in the dark both to get out and to go back, but I could do neither until some streaks of day strayed in and showed me where to lay my hands. During the whole interval, I heard her footstep, saw her candle pass above, and heard her ceaseless low cry.

Before we left next day, there was no revival of the difference between her and Estella, nor was it ever revived on any similar occasions; and there were four similar occasions, to the best of my remembrance.

It is impossible to turn this leaf of my life without putting Bentley Drummle's name upon it, or I would, very gladly.

On a certain occasion when the Finches[1] were assembled, the presiding Finch called the Grove to order, forasmuch as Mr. Drummle had not yet toasted a lady, it was the brute's turn to do so that day. What was my indignant surprise when he called upon the company to pledge him to "Estella!"

I tell this lightly, but it was no light thing to me. For I cannot express what pain it gave me to think that Estella should show any favor to a contemptible, clumsy, sulky booby, so very far below the average.

It was easy for me to find out, and I did soon find out, that Drummle had begun to follow her closely, and that she allowed him to do it. A little while, and he was always in pursuit of her, and Estella held him on; now with encouragement, now with discouragement, now almost flattering him, now openly despising him. The Spider, as Mr. Jaggers had called him, was used to lying in wait, however, and had the patience of his tribe.

At a certain Assembly Ball at Richmond, I resolved to speak to her concerning him. I took the opportunity when she was waiting for Mrs. Brandley to take her home.

"Are you tired, Estella?"

"Rather, Pip."

"You should be."

"Say, rather, I should not be; for I have my letter to Satis House to write before I go to sleep."

"Recounting tonight's triumph?" said I. "Surely a very poor one, Estella."

"What do you mean?"

"Estella," said I, "do look at that fellow in the corner yonder who is looking over here at us."

"Why should I look at him?" returned Estella. "What is there in that fellow in the corner that I need look at?"

1. **Finches:** a social club to which Pip, Herbert, and Drummle belonged.

"Indeed, that is the very question I want to ask you," said I. "For he has been hovering about you all night."

"Moths and all sorts of ugly creatures," replied Estella with a glance toward him, "hover about a lighted candle. Can the candle help it?"

"But, Estella, do hear me speak. It makes me wretched that you should encourage a man so generally despised as Drummle. You know he is despised."

"Well?" said she.

"You know he is an ill-tempered, lowering, stupid fellow."

"Well?" said she.

"You know he has nothing to recommend him but money, don't you?"

"Pip," said Estella, casting her glance over the room, "don't be foolish about its effect on you. It may have its effect on others, and may be meant to have. It's not worth discussing."

"Yes, it is," said I, "because I cannot bear that people should say, 'she throws away her graces and attractions on a mere boor, the lowest in the crowd.'"

"I can bear it," said Estella.

"Oh! don't be so proud, Estella, and so inflexible."

"Calls me proud and inflexible in this breath!" said Estella, opening her hands. "And in his last breath reproached me for stooping to a boor!"

"There is no doubt you do," said I, "for I have seen you give him looks and smiles this very night, such as you never gave to —me."

"Do you want me then," said Estella, turning suddenly with a fixed and serious look, "to deceive and entrap you?"

"Do you deceive and entrap him, Estella?"

"Yes, and many others—all of them but you. Here is Mrs. Brandley. I'll say no more."

And now that I have given the one chapter to the theme that so filled my heart, and so often made it ache and ache again, I pass on

unhindered to the event that had impended over me longer yet; the event that had begun to be prepared for before I knew that the world held Estella.

All the work, near and afar, that tended to the end, had been accomplished; and in an instant the blow was struck, and the roof of my stronghold dropped upon me.

Chapter 29

Pip has a midnight caller.

I was three-and-twenty years of age. Not another word had I heard to enlighten me on the subject of my expectations. We had left Barnard's Inn a year before, and lived in the Temple.[1] Our chambers were in Garden Court, down by the river. Mr. Pocket and I had for some time parted company as to our original relations, though we continued on the best terms.

Business had taken Herbert on a journey to Marseilles. I was alone, and had a dull sense of being alone. I sadly missed the cheerful face and ready response of my friend. It was wretched weather; stormy and wet, stormy and wet; mud, mud, mud, deep in all the streets. We lived at the top of the last house, and the wind rushing up the river shook the house that night, like discharges of cannon or breakings of a sea. I saw that the lamps in the court were blown out, and that the lamps on the bridges and the shore were shuddering, and that the coal fires in barges on the river were being carried away before the wind like red-hot splashes in the rain.

I read with my watch upon the table, purposing to close my book at eleven o'clock. As I shut it, all the church clocks in the city struck that hour. The sound was curiously flawed by the wind; and I was listening, when I heard a footstep on the stair.

What nervous folly made me start, and awfully connect it with the footstep of my dead sister, matters not. It was past in a moment, and I listened again, and heard the footstep stumble in coming on. Remembering then that the staircase lights were blown out, I took up my reading lamp and went out to the stairhead. Whoever was below had stopped on seeing my lamp, for all was quiet.

"There is someone down there, is there not?" I called out, looking down.

"Yes," said a voice from the darkness beneath.

"What floor do you want?"

"The top, Mr. Pip."

"That is my name. There is nothing the matter?"

"Nothing the matter," returned the voice. And the man came on.

I stood with my lamp held out over the stair rail, and he came slowly within its light. I saw a face that was strange to me, looking up with an incomprehensible air of being touched and pleased by the sight of me.

Moving the lamp as the man moved, I made out that he was substantially dressed, but roughly, like a voyager by sea. That he had long iron-gray hair. That his age was about sixty. That he was a muscular man, strong on his legs, and that he was browned and hardened by exposure to weather. As he ascended the last stair or two, I saw, with a stupid kind of amazement, that he was holding out both his hands to me.

"Pray what is your business?" I asked him.

"My business?" he repeated, pausing. "Ah! Yes, I will explain my business, by your leave."

---

1. **Temple:** group of buildings near the Thames River, which were occupied by lawyers, court officials, and clerks.

"Do you wish to come in?"

"Yes," he replied. "I wish to come in, master."

I took him into the room I had just left and, having set the lamp on the table, asked him as civilly as I could to explain himself.

He looked about him with the strangest air—an air of wondering pleasure, as if he had some part in the things he admired—and he pulled off a rough outer coat, and his hat. Then I saw that his head was furrowed and bald, and that the long iron-gray hair grew only on its sides. But I saw nothing that in the least explained him. On the contrary, I saw him next moment once more holding out both his hands to me.

"What do you mean?" said I, half-suspecting him to be mad.

He stopped in his looking at me and slowly rubbed his right hand over his head. "It's disappointing to a man," he said, in a coarse broken voice, "arter having looked for'ard so distant, and come so fur; but you're not to blame for that—neither on us is to blame for that. I'll speak in half a minute. Give me half a minute, please."

He sat down on a chair that stood before the fire, and covered his forehead with his large brown hands. I looked at him attentively then, and recoiled a little from him; but I did not know him.

"There's no one nigh," said he, looking over his shoulder, "is there?"

"Why do you, a stranger coming into my rooms at this time of the night, ask that question?" said I.

"You're a game one," he returned. "I'm glad you've grow'd up a game one! But don't catch hold of me. You'd be sorry afterwards to have done it."

I relinquished the intention he had detected, for I knew him! Even yet I could not recall a single feature, but I knew him! If the wind and the rain had driven away the intervening years, had swept us to the churchyard where we first stood face to face on such different levels, I could not have known my convict more distinctly than I knew him now, as he sat in the chair before the fire. No need to take a file from his pocket and show it to me; no need to take the handkerchief from his neck and twist it round his head; no need to hug himself with both his arms, and take a shivering turn across the room, looking back at me for recognition. I knew him before he gave me one of those aids, though a moment before I had not been conscious of remotely suspecting his identity.

He came back to where I stood and again held out both his hands. Not knowing what to do—for in my astonishment I had lost my self-possession—I reluctantly gave him my hands. He grasped them heartily, raised them to his lips, kissed them, and still held them.

"You acted nobly, my boy," said he. "Noble Pip! And I have never forgot it!"

At a change in his manners as if he were even going to embrace me, I laid a hand upon his breast and put him away.

"Stay!" said I. "Keep off! If you are grateful to me for what I did when I was a little child, I hope you have shown your gratitude by mending your way of life. If you have come here to thank me, it was not necessary. There must be something good in the feeling that has brought you here, and I will not repulse you; but surely you must understand—I——"

My attention was so attracted by the singularity of his fixed look at me that the words died away on my tongue.

"You was a-saying," he observed, when we had confronted one another in silence, "that surely I must understand. What surely must I understand?"

"That I cannot wish to renew that chance intercourse with you of long ago, under these different circumstances. I am glad to believe you have repented and recovered yourself. I

am glad to tell you so. I am glad that, thinking I deserve to be thanked, you have come to thank me. But our ways are different ways, none the less. You are wet, and you look weary. Will you drink something before you go?"

He had replaced his neckerchief loosely, and had stood, keenly observant of me, biting a long end of it. "I think," he answered, still observant of me, "that I *will* drink (I thank you) afore I go."

I made him some hot rum-and-water. I tried to keep my hand steady while I did so. When at last I put the glass to him, I saw with amazement that his eyes were full of tears. I was softened by the softened aspect of the man, and felt a touch of reproach. "I hope," said I, "that you will not think I spoke harshly to you just now. I had no intention of doing it, and I am sorry for it if I did. I wish you well and happy!"

As I put my glass to my lips, he stretched out his hand. I gave him mine, and then he drank, and drew his sleeve across his eyes and forehead.

"How are you living?" I asked him.

"I've been a sheep farmer, stockbreeder, and other trades besides, away in the new world," said he; "many a thousand mile of stormy water off from this."

"I hope you have done well?"

"I've done wonderful well. No man has done nigh as well as me. I'm famous for it."

"I'm glad to hear it."

"I hope to hear you say so, my dear boy."

Without stopping to try to understand those words or the tone in which they were spoken, I turned off to a point that had just come into my mind.

"Have you ever seen a messenger you once sent to me," I inquired, "since he undertook that trust?"

"Never set eyes upon him. I warn't likely to."

"He came faithfully, and he brought me the two one-pound notes. I was a poor boy, then, as you know, and to a poor boy they were a little fortune. But, like you, I have done well since, and you must let me pay them back. You can put them to some other poor boy's use." I took out my purse.

He watched me as I laid my purse upon the table and opened it, and he watched me as I separated two one-pound notes from its contents. They were clean and new, and I spread them out and handed them over to him. Still watching me, he laid them one upon the other, folded them longwise, gave them a twist, set fire to them at the lamp, and dropped the ashes into the tray.

"May I make so bold," he said then, with a smile that was like a frown, and with a frown that was like a smile, "as to ask you *how* you have done well, since you and me was out on them lone shivering marshes?"

He emptied his glass, got up, and stood at the side of the fire, with his heavy brown hand on the mantelshelf. He put a foot up to the bars to dry and warm it, and the wet boot began to steam; but he neither looked at it nor at the fire, but steadily looked at me. It was only now that I began to tremble.

When my lips had parted, I forced myself to tell him that I had been chosen to succeed to some property.

"Might a mere warmint ask what property?" said he.

I faltered, "I don't know."

"Might a mere warmint ask whose property?" said he.

I faltered again, "I don't know."

"Could I make a guess, I wonder," said the convict, "at your income since you come of age? As to the first figure, now. Five?"

With my heart beating like a heavy hammer of disordered action, I rose out of my chair, and stood with my hand upon the back of it, looking wildly at him.

"Concerning a guardian," he went on.

"There ought to have been some guardian or such-like, whiles you was a minor. Some lawyer, maybe. As to the first letter of that lawyer's name, now. Would it be J?"

All the truth of my position came flashing on me; and its disappointments, dangers, disgraces, consequences of all kinds, rushed in in such a multitude that I was borne down by them and had to struggle for every breath I drew. "Put it," he resumed, "as the employer of that lawyer whose name begun with a J, and might be Jaggers—put it as he had come over sea to Portsmouth, and had landed there, and had wanted to come on to you. Well! however did I find you out? Why, I wrote from Portsmouth to a person in London for particulars of your address. That person's name? Why, Wemmick."

I could not have spoken one word, though it had been to save my life. I stood, with a hand on the chair back and a hand on my breast, where I seemed to be suffocating—I stood so, looking wildly at him, until I grasped at the chair, when the room began to surge and turn. He caught me, drew me to the sofa, put me up against the cushions, and bent on one knee before me: bringing the face that I now well remembered, and that I shuddered at, very near to mine.

"Yes, Pip, dear boy, I've made a gentleman on you! It's me wot has done it! I swore that time, sure as ever I earned a guinea, that guinea should go to you. I swore arterwards, such as ever I spec'lated and got rich, you should get rich. I lived rough, that you should live smooth; I worked hard that you should be above work. What odds, dear boy? Do I tell it fur you to feel a obligation? Not a bit. I tell it fur you to know as that there hunted dog wot you kept life in got his head so high that he could make a gentleman—and, Pip, you're him!"

The abhorrence in which I held the man, the dread I had of him, the repugnance with which I shrank from him, could not have been exceeded if he had been some terrible beast.

"Look'ee here, Pip. I'm your second father. You're my son—more to me nor any son. I've put away money, only for you to spend. When I was a hired-out shepherd in a solitary hut, not seeing no faces but faces of sheep till I half forgot wot men's and women's faces wos like, I see yourn. I drops my knife many a time in that hut when I was a-eating my dinner or my supper, and I says, 'Here's the boy again, a-looking at me whiles I eats and drinks!' I see you there a many times as plain as ever I see you on them misty marshes. I says each time, 'If I gets liberty and money, I'll make that boy a gentleman!' And I done it. Why, look at you, dear boy! Look at these here lodgings of yourn, fit for a lord! A lord? Ah! You shall show money with lords for wagers, and beat 'em!"

In his heat and triumph, and in his knowledge that I had been nearly fainting, he did not remark on my reception of all this. It was the one grain of relief I had. Again he took both my hands and put them to his lips, while my blood ran cold within me.

"Don't you mind talking, Pip," said he. "You ain't looked slowly forward to this as I have; you wosn't prepared for this, as I wos. But didn't you never think it might be me?"

"Oh no, no, no," I returned. "Never, never!"

"Well, you see it *wos* me, and single-handed. Never a soul in it but my own self and Mr. Jaggers."

"Was there no one else?" I asked.

"No," said he, with a glance of surprise. "Who else should there be? And, dear boy, how good-looking you have growed! There's bright eyes somewheres—eh? Isn't there bright eyes somewheres, wot you love the thoughts on?"

O Estella, Estella!

"They shall be yourn, dear boy, if money can buy 'em. Let me finish wot I was a-telling you, dear boy. From that there hut and that there hiring-out, I got money left me by my master (which died, and had been the same as me), and got my liberty and went for myself. It all prospered wonderful. As I giv' you to understand just now, I'm famous for it. It was the money left me and gains of the first few years wot I sent home to Mr. Jaggers—all for you—when he first come arter you, agreeable to my letter."

Oh, that he had never come! That he had left me at the forge—far from contented, yet, by comparison, happy!

"And, then, dear boy, I held steady afore my mind that I would for certain come one day and see my boy, and make myself known to him, on his own ground."

He laid his hand on my shoulder. I shuddered at the thought that for anything I knew his hand might be stained with blood.

"Where will you put me?" he asked presently. "I must be put somewheres, dear boy."

"To sleep?" said I.

"Yes. And to sleep long and sound," he answered, "for I've been sea-tossed and sea-washed, months and months."

"My friend and companion," said I, rising from the sofa, "is absent; you must have his room."

"He won't come back tomorrow, will he?"

"No," said I, answering almost mechanically, "not tomorrow."

"Because, look'ee here, dear boy," he said, dropping his voice, and laying a long finger on my breast in an impressive manner, "caution is necessary."

"How do you mean? Caution?"

"It's death!"

"What's death?"

"I was sent for life. It's death to come back.

There's been overmuch coming back of late years, and I should of a certainty be hanged if took."

Nothing was needed but this; the wretched man, after loading me with his wretched gold and silver chains for years, had risked his life to come to me, and I held it there in my keeping!

My first care was to close the shutters so that no light might be seen from without, and then to close and make fast the doors. He asked me for some of my "gentleman's linen" to put on in the morning. I brought it out, and laid it ready for him, and my blood again ran cold when he again took me by both hands to give me good night.

I got away from him, without knowing how I did it, and for an hour or more I remained too stunned to think. It was not until I began to think that I began fully to know how wrecked I was, and how the ship in which I had sailed was gone to pieces.

Miss Havisham's intentions toward me, all a mere dream; Estella not designed for me; I only suffered in Satis House as a convenience, a sting for the greedy relations, a model with a mechanical heart to practice on when no other practice was at hand. But sharpest and deepest pain of all—it was for the convict, guilty of I knew not what crimes, that I had deserted Joe.

In every rage of wind and rush of rain, I heard pursuers. Twice I could have sworn there was a knocking and whispering at the outer door. With these fears upon me, I began to either imagine or recall that I had had mysterious warnings of this man's approach. Crowding up with these reflections came the reflection that I had seen him with my childish eyes to be a desperately violent man; that I had heard that other convict reiterate that he had tried to murder him; that I had seen him down in the ditch, tearing and fighting like a wild beast. Out of such remembrances, I brought into the light of the fire a half-formed terror that it might not be safe to be shut up there with him in the dead of the wild, solitary night. This impelled me to take a candle and go in and look at my dreadful burden.

He had rolled a handkerchief round his head, his face was set and lowering in his sleep. But he was asleep, and quietly, too, though he had a pistol lying on the pillow. I softly removed the key to the outside of his door, and turned it on him before I again sat down by the fire. Gradually I slipped from the chair and lay on the floor. When I awoke, the clocks were striking five, the candles were wasted out, the fire was dead, and the wind and rain intensified the thick black darkness.

This Is the End of the Second Stage of Pip's Expectations.

Reading Check

1. Who is Pip's guardian?
2. What is Estella's relation to Miss Havisham?
3. What name does Herbert give Pip?
4. Where does Herbert work when Pip meets him in London?
5. What is the Castle?
6. What is Joe's purpose in coming to London to see Pip?
7. Why is Estella sent to live with a woman in Richmond?
8. What is Pip's reason for returning to the forge?
9. What does Pip receive when he comes of age?
10. Why must the convict keep his whereabouts a secret?

For Study and Discussion

Analyzing and Interpreting the Novel

Characters

1. Dickens introduces several new characters in Stage 2 of the novel. One of the most interesting is Bentley Drummle. **a.** How does Dickens' description of Drummle make you immediately dislike him? **b.** What character from Pip's past does Bentley Drummle remind you of in physical appearance and personality?

2. Another character prominent in Stage 2 is Mr. Jaggers. **a.** What is intriguing about his behavior when Pip first sees him in London? **b.** What new facts does Pip later learn that make Jaggers seem even more mysterious?

3a. Where had Pip encountered Herbert Pocket in Stage 1 of the novel? **b.** What characteristics shown by Herbert in that encounter are still evident in him? **c.** Which of his qualities are a good influence on Pip? **d.** Which of his weaknesses does Pip pick up too easily?

4. The novels of Charles Dickens are filled with memorable portraits of characters, many of whom are eccentric, like Wemmick. Wemmick, his Aged Parent, and Miss Skiffins provide much of the humor in *Great Expectations*. **a.** What is amusing about the Aged? **b.** About Miss Skiffins? **c.** About Wemmick's "Castle" and its customs?

5. When Pip first arrives in London, Mr. Jaggers predicts, "Of course you'll go wrong somehow, but that's no fault of mine." **a.** What mistakes does Pip make in London? **b.** Do you think Pip is happy with his life there? Explain why or why not.

6. When they meet in London, Estella says to Pip: "We have no choice, you and I, but to obey our instructions. We are not free to follow our own devices, you and I." **a.** Is this true?

b. Is Pip becoming a gentleman because he enjoys being one or because his benefactor expects him to become one?

7a. Has Estella changed? If so, how? **b.** How do you think she really feels about Pip?

8. Describe Pip's relationship with Estella in this part of the novel. How are the hopes he has of being happy with her different from the way he actually feels when he is with her?

9a. How does Miss Havisham's relationship to Estella change in Stage 2 of the novel? **b.** What does Miss Havisham realize about Estella? **c.** How does she react to this realization? **d.** How does this incident gain sympathy for her?

10. Pip has become a snob. **a.** How is this shown in his treatment of Joe? **b.** After visiting Miss Havisham at Satis House, why does Pip decide to return immediately to London? **c.** What is the real reason he wants to stay at the Blue Boar instead of at the forge?

11a. When Pip learns that it is the convict who has been his benefactor, how does he react? **b.** Do you find his reaction one of weakness or strength? Explain.

12a. Where in the novel does Pip for the first time make up his own mind to do something for someone else? **b.** What does this act show about Pip's character?

Plot

13. By the end of Stage 1, most of the subplots have been revealed. In Stage 2, each of the subplots is expanded—Pip and the convict, the injury to Mrs. Joe, Pip's love for Estella. **a.** How are these subplots brought farther along in the second part of the novel? **b.** What new subplots are introduced?

Setting

14. Compare Dickens' description of the weather on the night Pip's convict arrives at his London lodgings with the description of the marshes on the day of their first meeting. **a.** How are the two descriptions similar? **b.** What words are used in both descriptions? **c.** How does setting help to connect the two episodes?

Theme

15. In *Great Expectations*, Dickens explores different kinds of love. Miss Havisham tells Pip that real love is "blind devotion, unquestioning self-humiliation, utter submission, trust… giving up your whole heart and soul to the smiter—as I did!" **a.** Would you say that Pip's love for Estella is of the same kind? **b.** What other examples of love relationships are illustrated in the novel? **c.** What statement does Dickens seem to be making about love through the different relationships he presents?

Language and Vocabulary

Differentiating Meanings

Herbert Pocket says about his father's relationship to Miss Havisham, "He is a bad courtier and will not *propitiate* her." What is the meaning of *propitiate*? Some words that Dickens might have used instead are *appease*, *conciliate*, *mollify*, *pacify*, or *placate*. In your dictionary, check the exact meaning of each of these words. Why does *propitiate* best suggest the exact relationship between Matthew Pocket and Miss Havisham? If you had to replace *propitiate* in this sentence with a synonym, which of the other five words would you choose?

Although the English language has many synonyms, few words have exactly the same meaning. Nearly every word has a unique shade of meaning that makes it more suitable in a given context than any other word. In your speaking and writing, always try to use the word that most exactly fits your meaning.

Use a dictionary to find at least two synonyms for each of the italicized words in the following passages. Then explain the different shades of meaning in each group of synonyms.

> I should have been *chary* of discussing my guardian too freely even with her...

> I lived in a state of *chronic* uneasiness respecting my behavior to Joe.

> ...I noticed that he looked about him with a *desponding* eye at breakfast time...

At one point Pip speaks of "the *hypocritical* Pumblechook." Earlier in the novel he refers to Miss Havisham's greedy relatives as "toadies and humbugs." The word *hypocritical* is from the Greek word *hypokritēs,* and refers to someone who tries to give the impression of being better (kinder or perhaps more honest) than he or she really is.

A *toady* plays up to people who are influential or rich. (Some dictionaries define a *toady* as a "toadeater.") A *humbug* is someone whose actions are deliberately deceptive and misleading.

Today we would be more likely to use the word *snob* than either *toady* or *humbug* to describe the Havisham relatives. A snob is someone who seeks to associate with those regarded as his or her superiors and who is quite cool toward those considered inferior in social position and wealth.

Which of these four words do you think most exactly describes Mr. Pumblechook?

Focus on Literary Analysis

Identifying a Main Idea

As you develop a literary analysis, focus on one or two elements to examine closely. Identify a main idea that will help you make the focus of your analysis specific. For example, if you were examining the element of setting in Stage 2 of *Great Expectations*, your main idea might be: "The vivid, realistic descriptions of London in Stage 2 are closely related to Pip's character development and expectations."

In order to identify and develop a main idea for your analysis, you may find it helpful to fill out a chart of close reading notes like the one below. List possible ideas in the left-hand column. In the right-hand column, list plot events, dialogue, and other details from the work that support each idea.

Idea	Support

Choose a short story that you would like to analyze. Make a chart of reading notes to explore ideas for an analysis. Save your notes.

Looking Ahead to Stage 3

At the end of Stage 2, Pip faces the dilemma of what to do with his benefactor, who is a condemned criminal. He also has two shattering realizations that will change the course of his life: he has deserted Joe and the life at the forge for expectations that have vanished; and Miss Havisham has never intended for him and Estella to marry. How do you think Pip's life will change as a result of these realizations?

The Third Stage of Pip's Expectations

Chapter 30

Pip confronts Jaggers.

It was fortunate for me that I had to take precautions to insure (so far as I could) the safety of my dreaded visitor; for, this thought pressing on me when I awoke held other thoughts at a distance. The impossibility of keeping him concealed in the chambers was self-evident. I was looked after by an inflammatory old female, assisted by an animated rag-bag whom she called her niece; and to keep a room secret from them would be to invite curiosity. I resolved to announce in the morning that my uncle had unexpectedly come from the country.

This course I decided on while I was yet groping about in the darkness for the means of getting a light. Not stumbling on the means after all, I was fain to go out to get the watchman to come with his lantern. Now, in groping my way down the black staircase, I fell over something, and that something was a man crouching in a corner. As the man made no answer when I asked him what he did there, I ran to the lodge and urged the watchman to come quickly. We examined the staircase from the bottom to the top and found no one there.

It troubled me that there should have been a lurker on the stairs on that night of all nights in the year, and I asked the watchman whether he had admitted at his gate any gentleman who had been dining out.

"The night being so bad, sir," said the watchman, "uncommon few have come in at my gate. Besides them three gentlemen that I know, I don't call to mind another since about eleven o'clock, when a stranger asked for you."

"My uncle," I muttered. "Yes."

"You saw him, sir?"

"Yes. Oh, yes."

"Likewise the person with him?"

"Person with him!" I repeated. "What sort of person?"

The watchman had not particularly noticed; he should say a working person; to the best of his belief, he had a dust-colored kind of clothes on, under a dark coat.

My mind was much troubled by these two circumstances taken together. I lighted my fire, which burned with a raw pale flare at that time of the morning, and fell into a doze before it. I was not able to consider my own situation, nor could I do so yet. At last the old woman and the niece came in. I imparted how my uncle had come in the night and was then asleep, and how the breakfast preparations were to be modified accordingly.

By and by, his door opened and he came out. I could not bring myself to bear the sight of him, and I thought he had a worse look by daylight.

"I do not even know," said I, speaking low as he took his seat at the table, "by what name to call you. I have given out that you are my uncle."

"That's it, dear boy! Call me uncle."

"You assumed some name, I suppose, on board ship?"

"Yes, dear boy. I took the name of Provis."

"Do you mean to keep that name?"

"Why, yes, dear boy, it's as good as another—unless you'd like another."

"What is your real name?" I asked him in a whisper.

"Magwitch," he answered in the same tone; "chrisen'd Abel."

"When you came into the Temple last night," said I, "and asked the watchman the way here, had you anyone with you?"

"With me? No, dear boy."

But there was someone there?"

"I didn't take particular notice," he said dubiously, "not knowing the ways of the place. But I think there *was* a person, too, come in alonger me."

"Are you known in London?"

"I hope not," said he, giving his neck a jerk with his forefinger that made me turn hot and sick.

"Were you known in London once?"

"Not over and above, dear boy. I was in the provinces mostly."

"Were you—tried—in London?"

"Which time?" said he, with a sharp look.

"The last time."

He nodded. "First knowed Mr. Jaggers that way. Jaggers was for me. And what I done is worked out and paid for!"

He ate in a ravenous way that was very disagreeable, and all his actions were uncouth, noisy, and greedy. Some of his teeth had failed him since I saw him eat on the marshes, and as he turned his food in his mouth, and turned his head sideways to bring his strongest fangs to bear upon it, he looked terribly like a hungry old dog. "I'm a heavy grubber, dear boy," he said, as a polite kind of apology when he had made an end of his meal. "Similarly, I must have my smoke." He got up and brought out a short black pipe and a handful of loose tobacco. Having filled his pipe, he took a live coal from the fire with the tongs and lighted his pipe at it, and turned round on the hearthrug with his back to the fire. He took out of his pocket a great thick pocketbook, bursting with papers, and tossed it on the table.

"There's something worth spending in that there book, dear boy. It's yourn. All I've got ain't mine; it's yourn. Don't you be afeerd on it. There's more where that come from. I've come to the old country fur to see my gentleman spend his money *like* a gentleman. That'll be *my* pleasure. *My* pleasure'ull be fur to see

him do it. And blast you all!" he wound up. "Blast you every one, from the judge in his wig to the colonist a-stirring up the dust, I'll show a better gentleman than the whole kit on you put together!"

"Stop!" said I, almost in a frenzy of fear and dislike. "I want to speak to you. I want to know what is to be done. I want to know how you are to be kept out of danger, how long you are going to stay, what projects you have."

"Look'ee here, Pip," said he, laying his hand on my arm in a suddenly altered and subdued manner. "I forgot myself half a minute ago. What I said was low; that's what it was; low. Look'ee here, Pip. Look over it. I ain't a-going to be low."

"First," I resumed, half groaning, "what precautions can be taken against your being recognized and seized?"

"Well, dear boy, the danger ain't so great. Without I was informed agen, the danger ain't so much to signify. There's Jaggers, and there's Wemmick, and there's you. Who else is there to inform?"

"Is there no chance person who might identify you in the street?" said I.

"Well," he returned, "there ain't many. Still, look'ee here, Pip. If the danger had been fifty times as great, I should ha' come to see you, mind you, just the same."

"And how long do you remain?"

"How long?" said he, taking his black pipe from his mouth and dropping his jaw as he stared at me. "I'm not a-going back. I've come for good."

"Where are you to live?" said I. "What is to be done with you? Where will you be safe?"

"Dear boy," he returned, "there's disguising wigs can be bought for money, and there's hair powder, and spectacles, and black clothes— and what not. As to the where and how of living, dear boy, give me your own opinions on it."

It appeared to me that I could do no better than secure him some quiet lodging hard by. That the secret must be confided to Herbert was plain to me. But it was by no means so plain to Mr. Provis (I resolved to call him by that name), who reserved his consent to Herbert's participation until he should have seen him. "And even then, dear boy," said he, pulling a greasy little clasped black Testament out of his pocket, "we'll have him on his oath." The book had the appearance of having been stolen from some court of justice.

There being a respectable lodging house in Essex Street, almost within hail of my windows, I repaired to that house and was so fortunate as to secure the second floor for my uncle, Mr. Provis. I then went from shop to shop, making such purchases as were necessary to change his appearance. This business transacted, I turned my face, on my own account, to Little Britain. Mr. Jaggers was at his desk, but seeing me enter, got up immediately and stood before his fire.

"Now, Pip," said he, "be careful."

"I will, sir," I returned.

"Don't commit yourself," said Mr. Jaggers, "and don't commit anyone. You understand—anyone."

Of course I saw that he knew the man was come.

"I merely want, Mr. Jaggers," said I, "to assure myself what I have been told is true. I have been informed by a person named Abel Magwitch that he is the benefactor so long unknown to me."

"That is the man," said Mr. Jaggers, "—in New South Wales."[1]

"And only he?" said I.

"And only he," said Mr. Jaggers.

"I am not so unreasonable, sir, as to think

you at all responsible for my wrong conclusions; but I always supposed it was Miss Havisham."

"As you say, Pip," returned Mr. Jaggers, "I am not at all responsible for that."

"And yet it looked so like it, sir," I pleaded with a downcast heart.

"Not a particle of evidence, Pip," said Mr. Jaggers. "Take nothing on its looks; take everything on evidence. There's no better rule."

"I have no more to say," said I, with a sigh, after standing silent for a little while. "I have verified my information, and there's an end."

"I communicated to Magwitch—in New South Wales—when he first wrote to me—from New South Wales—the caution that he was not at all likely to obtain a pardon, that he was expatriated for the term of his natural life, and that his presenting himself in this country would be an act of felony, rendering him liable to the extreme penalty of the law. I gave Magwitch that caution," said Mr. Jaggers, looking hard at me. "I wrote it to New South Wales. He guided himself by it, no doubt."

"No doubt," said I.

"I have been informed by Wemmick," pursued Mr. Jaggers, still looking hard at me, "that he has received a letter, from a colonist of the name of Purvis, or——"

"Or Provis," I suggested.

"Or Provis—thank you, Pip. Perhaps it is Provis? Perhaps you know it's Provis?"

"Yes," said I.

"You know it's Provis. A letter from a colonist of the name of Provis, asking for the particulars of your address, on behalf of Magwitch. Wemmick sent him the particulars, I understand, by return of post. Probably it is through Provis that you have received the explanation of Magwitch—in New South Wales?"

"It came through Provis," I replied.

"Good day, Pip," said Mr. Jaggers, offering

---

1. **New South Wales:** a state in Australia; formerly a territory to which many convicts were transported, or exiled. Magwitch had been sentenced there for life.

his hand. "Glad to have seen you. In writing by post to Magwitch—in New South Wales—or in communicating with him through Provis, have the goodness to mention that the particulars and vouchers of our long account shall be sent to you, together with the balance; for there is still a balance remaining. Good day, Pip!"

Next day the clothes I had ordered all came home, and he put them on. To my thinking there was something in him that made it hopeless to attempt to disguise him. The more I dressed him, and the better I dressed him, the more he looked like the slouching fugitive on the marshes. He dragged one of his legs as if there were still a weight of iron on it, and from head to foot there was convict in the very grain of the man.

For five days, expecting Herbert all the time, I dared not go out except when I took Provis for an airing after dark. At length, one evening when dinner was over and I had dropped into a slumber quite worn out, I was roused by the welcome footstep on the staircase. Provis, who had been asleep too, staggered up at the noise I made, and in an instant I saw his jackknife shining in his hand.

"Quiet! It's Herbert!" I said.

"Handel, my dear fellow, how are you, and again how are you, and again how are you? I seem to have been gone a twelvemonth! Why, so I must have been, for you have grown quite thin and pale! Handel, my——Halloa! I beg your pardon."

He was stopped in his running on and in his shaking hands with me, by seeing Provis. Provis, regarding him with a fixed attention, was slowly putting up his jackknife and groping in another pocket for something else.

"Herbert, my dear friend," said I, shutting the double doors, while Herbert stood staring and wondering, "something very strange has happened. This is—a visitor of mine."

"It's all right, dear boy!" said Provis, coming forward, with his little clasped black book, and then addressing himself to Herbert. "Take it in your right hand. Lord strike you dead on the spot if ever you split[2] in any way sumever. Kiss it!"

"Do so, as he wishes it," I said to Herbert. So Herbert, looking at me with a friendly uneasiness and amazement, complied, and Provis immediately shaking hands with him, said, "Now you're on your oath, you know. And never believe me on mine, if Pip shan't make a gentleman on you!"

Chapter 31

Two men, named Compeyson and Arthur, step out of the past.

In vain should I attempt to describe the astonishment and disquiet of Herbert, when he and I and Provis sat down before the fire, and I recounted the whole of the secret. Enough that I saw my own feelings reflected in Herbert's face, and, not least among them, my repugnance toward the man who had done so much for me.

"Look'ee here, Pip's comrade," he said to Herbert, after having discoursed for some time, "I know very well that once since I come back I've been low. But don't you fret yourself on that score. I ain't made Pip a gentleman, and Pip ain't a-goin' to make you a gentleman, not fur me not to know what's due to ye both."

Herbert said, "Certainly," but remained perplexed and dismayed. We were anxious for the time when he would go to his lodging and leave us together, but it was midnight before I saw him safely in at his own dark door. When

---

2. **split:** slang for "inform."

it closed upon him, I experienced the first moment of relief I had known since the night of his arrival.

Herbert received me with open arms, and I had never felt before so blessedly what it is to have a friend. When he had spoken some sound words of sympathy and encouragement, we sat down to consider the question, What was to be done?

"What," said I to Herbert, "what is to be done? He is intent upon various new expenses—horses, and carriages, and lavish appearances of all kinds. He must be stopped somehow."

"You mean that you can't accept——"

"How can I?" I interposed, as Herbert paused. "Think of him! Look at him!"

An involuntary shudder passed over both of us.

"Then," said I, "after all, stopping short here, never taking another penny from him, think what I owe him already! Then again, I am heavily in debt—very heavily for me, who have now no expectations—and I have been bred to no calling, and I am fit for nothing."

"Well, well, well!" Herbert remonstrated, "Don't say fit for nothing."

"What am I fit for? I know only one thing that I am fit for, and that is to go for a soldier."

"You would be infinitely better in Clarriker's house, small as it is. I am working up toward a partnership, you know."

Poor fellow! He little suspected with whose money.

"But there is another question," said Herbert. "This is an ignorant determined man, who has long had one fixed idea. More than that, he seems to me (I may misjudge him) to be a man of a desperate and fierce character. Think of this! He comes here at the peril of his life, for the realization of his fixed idea. After all his toil and waiting, you destroy his idea, and make his gains worthless to him. Do you

see nothing that he might do under the disappointment?"

"I have seen it, Herbert. Nothing has been in my thoughts so distinctly as his putting himself in the way of being taken."

"Then you may rely upon it," said Herbert. "That would be his reckless course if you forsook him. The first and the main thing to be done is to get him out of England. You will have to go with him, and then he may be induced to go. That done, extricate yourself, in Heaven's name, and we'll see it out together, dear old boy."

Provis came round at the appointed time, took out his jackknife, and sat down to his meal. He was full of plans "for his gentleman's coming out strong and like a gentleman" and urged me to begin speedily upon the pocket-book, which he had left in my possession. When he had made an end of his breakfast, and was wiping his knife on his leg, I said to him, without a word of preface:

"After you were gone last night, I told my friend of the struggle that the soldiers found you engaged in on the marshes. You remember?"

"Remember!" said he. "I think so!"

"We want to know something about that man—and about you. It is strange to know no more about either, and particularly you, than I was able to tell last night. Is not this as good a time as another for our knowing more?"

"Well," he said, after consideration. "You're on your oath, you know, Pip's comrade?"

"Assuredly," replied Herbert.

"And look'ee here! Wotever I done, is worked out and paid for," he insisted again.

He stuck his pipe in a buttonhole of his coat, spread a hand on each knee, and, after turning an angry eye on the fire for a few silent moments, looked around at us and said what follows:

"Dear boy and Pip's comrade, I am not

a-going fur to tell you my life, like a song or a storybook. But to give it you short and handy, I'll put it at once into a mouthful of English. In jail and out of jail, in jail and out of jail, in jail and out of jail. There, you've got it. That's *my* life pretty much, down to such times as I got shipped off, arter Pip stood my friend.

"I've done everything to, pretty well—except hanged. I've been locked up, and stuck in the stocks, and whipped and worried and drove. I've no more notion where I was born than you have. I first became aware of myself down in Essex, a-thieving turnips for my living. Summun had run away from me—a man—a tinker—and he'd took the fire with him, and left me wery cold. I knowed my name to be Magwitch, christened Abel. So fur as I could find, there warn't a soul that see young Abel Magwitch, with as little on him as in him, but wot caught fright at him, and either drove him off or took him up.[1] When I was a ragged little creetur as much to be pitied as ever I see, I got the name of being hardened. 'This is a terrible hardened one,' they says to prison visitors, picking out me. 'May be said to live in jails, this boy.' They always went on agen me about the Devil. But what the devil was I to do? I must put something into my stomach, mustn't I?

"Tramping, begging, thieving, working sometimes when I could—though that warn't as often as you may think, till you put the question whether you would ha' been over-ready to give me work yourselves—a bit of a poacher, a bit of a laborer, a bit of a wagoner, a bit of a haymaker, a bit of a hawker, a bit of most things that don't pay and lead to trouble, I got to be a man.

"At Epsom races, a matter of over twenty years ago, I got acquainted wi' a man whose skull I'd crack wi' this poker, like the claw of a lobster, if I'd got it on this hob. His right name

was Compeyson; and that's the man, dear boy, what you see me a-pounding in the ditch. He set up fur a gentleman, this Compeyson, and had learning. He was a smooth one to talk and was a dab at the ways of gentlefolks. He was good-looking too.

"Compeyson took me on to be his man and pardner. And what was Compeyson's business in which we was to go pardners? Compeyson's business was the swindling, handwriting forging, stolen bank note passing, and suchlike. All sorts of traps as Compeyson could set with his head, and let another man in for, was Compeyson's business. He'd no more heart than a iron file, he was as cold as death, and he had the head of the Devil.

"There was another in with Compeyson, as was called Arthur. Him and Compeyson had been in a bad thing with a rich lady some years afore, and they made a pot of money by it; but Compeyson betted and gamed, and he'd have run through the king's taxes. So, Arthur was a-dying and a-dying poor and with the horrors on him, and Compeyson's wife was a-having pity on him when she could and Compeyson was a-having pity on nothing and nobody.

"I might a-took warning by Arthur, but I didn't. I begun wi' Compeyson, and a poor tool I was in his hands. Arthur lived at the top of Compeyson's house. The second or third time as ever I see him, he came a-tearing down into Compeyson's parlor late at night, in only a flannel gown, with his hair all in a sweat, and he says to Compeyson's wife, 'Sally, she really is upstairs alonger me, now, and I can't get rid of her. She's all in white,' he says, 'wi' white flowers in her hair, and she's awful mad, and she's got a shroud hanging over her arm, and she says she'll put it on me at five in the morning.'

"Says Compeyson: 'Why, you fool, don't you know she's got a living body? And how should she be up there, without coming through the

1. **took him up:** put him under arrest.

door, or in at the window, and up the stairs?'

" 'I don't know how she's there,' says Arthur, shivering dreadful with the horrors, 'but she's standing in the corner at the foot of the bed. And over where her heart's broke—*you* broke it!—there's drops of blood.'

"Compeyson's wife and me took him up to bed agen, and he raved most dreadful. 'Why, look at her!' he cries out. 'She's a-shaking the shroud at me! She'll put it on me, and then I'm done for! Take it away from her, take it away!' And then he kep on a-talking to her, and answering of her, till I half believed I see her myself.

"He rested pretty quiet till it might want a few minutes of five, and then he screams out, 'Here she is! She's got the shroud again. She's unfolding it. She's coming out of the corner. She's coming to the bed. Hold me, both of you—one on each side—don't let her touch me with it.' Then he lifted himself up hard, and was dead.

"Compeyson took it easy as a good riddance for both sides. Him and me was soon busy, and I'll simply say to you, dear boy, and Pip's comrade, that that man got me into such nets as made me his slave. I was always in debt to him, always under his thumb, always a-working, always a-getting into danger. My missis as I had the hard time wi'——Stop though! I ain't brought *her* in——"

He looked about him in a confused way, turned his face to the fire, and spread his hands broader on his knees. "There ain't no need to go into it," he said, looking round once more. "At last, me and Compeyson was both committed for felony—on a charge of putting stolen notes in circulation. Compeyson says to me, 'Separate defenses, no communication,'[2] and that was all. And I was so miserable poor

that I sold all the clothes I had, except what hung on my back, afore I could get Jaggers.

"When he was put in the dock,[3] I noticed first of all what a gentleman Compeyson looked, wi' his curly hair and his black clothes and his white pocket handkercher, and what a common sort of a wretch I looked. When the prosecution opened, I noticed how heavy it all bore on me, and how light on him. When the evidence was giv in the box,[4] I noticed how it was always me that had come for'ard, and could be swore to, how it was always me that the money had been paid to, how it was always me that seemed to work the thing and get the profit. But when the defense come on, then I see the plan plainer; for, says the counselor for Compeyson, 'My lord and gentlemen, here you have afore you, side by side, two persons as your eyes can separate wide; one well brought up, one ill brought up.'

"And when the verdict come, warn't it Compeyson as was recommended to mercy on account of good character and bad company, and giving up all the information he could agen me, and warn't it me as got never a word but guilty? And when I says to Compeyson, 'Once out of this court, I'll smash that face of yourn!' ain't it Compeyson as prays the judge to be protected, and gets two turnkeys stood betwixt us? And when we're sentenced, ain't it him as gets seven year, and me fourteen, and ain't it him as the judge is sorry for, because he might a-done so well, and ain't it me as the judge perceives to be a old offender of wiolent passion, likely to come to worse?"

He had worked himself into a state of great excitement, but he checked it, and stretching out his hand toward me, said, "I ain't a-going to be low, dear boy!

"We was in the same prison ship, but I

2. **Separate . . . communication:** Each man would handle his own case, and there would be no communication between them while defending themselves.

3. **dock:** the place where prisoners stand before the court.
4. **box:** the witness chair.

couldn't get at him for long, though I tried. At last I come behind him and hit him on the cheek to turn him round and get a smashing one at him, when I was seen and seized. The black hole of that ship warn't a strong one. I escaped to the shore, and I was a-hiding among the graves there, envying them as was in 'em and all over, when I first see my boy!"

He regarded me with a look of affection that made him almost abhorrent to me again, though I had felt great pity for him.

"By my boy, I was giv to understand as Compeyson was out on them marshes too. Upon my soul, I half believed he escaped in his terror to get quit of me, not knowing it was me as had got ashore. I hunted him down. I smashed his face. 'And now,' says I, 'as the worst thing I can do, caring nothing for myself, I'll drag you back.' And I'd have swum off, towing him by the hair, if it had come to that, and I'd a got him aboard without the soldiers.

"Of course he'd much the best of it to the last and his punishment was light. I was put in irons, brought to trial again, and sent for life. I didn't stop for life, dear boy and Pip's comrade, being here."

He slowly took his tangle of tobacco from his pocket, plucked his pipe from his buttonhole, slowly filled it, and began to smoke.

"Is he dead?" I asked after a silence.

"Is who dead, dear boy?"

"Compeyson."

"He hopes *I* am, if he's alive, you may be sure," with a fierce look. "I never heard no more of him."

Herbert had been writing with his pencil in the cover of a book. He softly pushed the book over to me, as Provis stood smoking with his eyes on the fire, and I read in it:

"Young Havisham's name was Arthur. Compeyson is the man who professed to be Miss Havisham's lover."

I shut the book and nodded slightly to Herbert, and put the book by; but we neither of us said anything, and both looked at Provis as he stood smoking by the fire.

Chapter 32

Pip and Drummle exchange sharp words.

A new fear had entered in my mind by his narrative. If Compeyson were alive and should discover his return, I could hardly doubt the consequence. That Compeyson would hesitate to release himself for good from a dreaded enemy by the safe means of becoming an informer, was scarcely to be imagined.

Never had I breathed, and never would I breathe—or so I resolved—a word of Estella to Provis. But I said to Herbert that before I could go abroad, I must see both Estella and Miss Havisham. On my presenting myself at Mrs. Brandley's, Estella's maid was called to tell me that Estella had gone into the country. Where? To Satis House. She had never gone there before without me, and I went home again in complete discomfiture.

Next day, I had the meanness to feign that I was under a binding promise to go down to Joe. Provis was to be strictly careful while I was gone, and Herbert was to take the charge of him that I had taken.

Having thus cleared the way for my expedition to Miss Havisham's, I set off by the early morning coach. When we drove up to the Blue Boar, whom should I see come out under the gateway, toothpick in hand, to look at the coach, but Bentley Drummle!

As he pretended not to see me, I pretended not to see him. It was a very lame pretense on both sides; the lamer because we both went into the coffee room. I sat at my table while he stood before the fire. By degrees it became an enormous injury to me that he stood before the fire, and I got up, determined to have my share of it. I had to put my hands behind his legs for the poker when I went up to the fireplace to stir the fire, but still pretended not to know him.

"Is this a cut?"[1] said Mr. Drummle.

"Oh?" said I, poker in hand. "It's you, is it? How do you do? I was wondering who it was who kept the fire off."

With that I poked tremendously, and having done so, planted myself side by side with Mr. Drummle, my shoulders squared, and my back to the fire.

"Large tract of marshes about here, I believe?" said Drummle.

"Yes. What of that?" said I.

Mr. Drummle looked at me and laughed.

"Are you amused, Mr. Drummle?"

"No," said he, "not particularly. I am going out for a ride in the saddle. I mean to explore those marshes for amusement. Out-of-the-way villages there, they tell me. Curious little public houses—and smithies—and that. Waiter!"

"Yes, sir."

"Is that horse of mine ready?"

"Brought round to the door, sir."

"I say. Look here. The lady won't ride today; the weather won't do."

"Very good, sir."

"And I don't dine, because I am going to dine at the lady's."

"Very good, sir."

Then Drummle glanced at me with an insolent triumph. One thing was manifest to both of us, and that was that until relief came, neither of us could relinquish the fire. There we stood, well squared up before it, shoulder to shoulder and foot to foot, with our hands behind us, not budging an inch.

1. **cut:** a deliberate refusal to recognize someone.

After glancing at him once or twice, in an increased state of smoldering ferocity, I said:

"Mr. Drummle, I did not seek this conversation, and I don't think it's an agreeable one."

"I'm sure it's not," said he superciliously, over his shoulder.

"And therefore," I went on, "with your leave, I will suggest that we hold no kind of communication in future."

"Quite my opinion," said Drummle. "But don't lose your temper. Haven't you lost enough without that?"

"What do you mean, sir?"

"Waiter," said Drummle, by way of answering me.

The waiter reappeared.

"Look here, you sir. You quite understand that the young lady don't ride today, and that I dine at the young lady's?"

"Quite so, sir!"

How long we might have remained in this ridiculous position it is impossible to say, but for the incursion of three thriving farmers, who came into the coffee room unbuttoning their greatcoats and rubbing their hands, and before whom, as they charged at the fire, we were obliged to give way. I saw him through the window, seizing his horse's mane, and mounting in his blundering brutal manner, and calling for a light for the cigar in his mouth. A man in a dust-colored dress appeared, and as Drummle leaned down from the saddle and lighted his cigar and laughed, with a jerk of his head toward the coffee-room windows, the slouching shoulders and ragged hair of this man, whose back was toward me, reminded me of Orlick.

Too heavily out of sorts to care, I washed the weather and the journey from my face and hands and went out to the memorable old house that it would have been so much the better for me never to have entered, never to have seen.

In the room where the dressing table stood,

and where the wax candles burned on the wall, I found Miss Havisham and Estella; Miss Havisham seated on a settee near the fire, and Estella on a cushion at her feet. Estella was knitting and Miss Havisham was looking on. They both raised their eyes as I went in, and both saw an alteration in me. I derived that from the look they interchanged.

"And what wind," said Miss Havisham, "blows you here, Pip?"

Though she looked steadily at me, I saw that she was rather confused. Estella paused a moment in her knitting with her eyes upon me.

"Miss Havisham," said I, "I went to Richmond yesterday to speak to Estella; and finding that some wind had blown *her* here, I followed. What I had to say to Estella, Miss Havisham, I will say before you presently—in a few moments. It will not surprise you; it will not displease you. I am as unhappy as you can ever have meant me to be."

Miss Havisham continued to look steadily at me. I could see in the action of Estella's fingers as they worked that she attended to what I said, but she did not look up.

"I have found out who my patron is. It is not a fortunate discovery, and is not likely ever to enrich me in reputation, station, fortune, anything. There are reasons why I must say no more of that. It is not my secret, but another's. When you first caused me to be brought here, Miss Havisham; when I belonged to the village over yonder, that I wish I had never left; I suppose I did really come here, as any other chance boy might have come—as a kind of servant, to gratify a want or a whim, and to be paid for it?"

"Aye, Pip," replied Miss Havisham, steadily nodding her head, "you did."

"And that Mr. Jaggers——"

"Mr. Jaggers," said Miss Havisham, taking me up in a firm tone, "had nothing to do with it, and knew nothing of it. His being my lawyer, and his being the lawyer of your patron is a coincidence."

"But when I fell into the mistake I have so long remained in, at least you led me on?" said I.

"Yes," she returned, again nodding steadily, "I let you go on."

"Was that kind?"

"Who am I," cried Miss Havisham, striking her stick upon the floor and flashing into wrath so suddenly that Estella glanced up at her in surprise, "who am I that I should be kind?"

"I was liberally paid for my old attendance here," I said, to soothe her, "in being apprenticed, and I have asked these questions only for my own information. What follows has another purpose. In humoring my mistake, Miss Havisham, you punished your self-seeking relations?"

"I did. Why, they would have it so! So would you. You made your own snares. *I* never made them."

Waiting until she was quiet again—for this, too, flashed out of her in a wild and sudden way—I went on.

"I have been thrown among one family of your relations, Miss Havisham, since I went to London. And I should be false and base if I did not tell you that you deeply wrong both Mr. Matthew Pocket and his son Herbert, if you suppose them to be otherwise than generous, upright, open, and incapable of anything designing or mean."

"They are your friends," said Miss Havisham.

"They made themselves my friends," said I, "when Sarah Pocket, Miss Georgiana, and Mistress Camilla were not my friends, I think."

This contrasting of them with the rest seemed, I was glad to see, to do them good with her. She looked at me keenly for a little while, and then said quietly:

"What do you want for them?"

"I do want something, Miss Havisham. If you could spare the money to do my friend Herbert a lasting service in life, but which from the nature of the case must be done without his knowledge, I could show you how."

"Why must it be done without his knowledge?" she asked, settling her hands upon her stick that she might regard me the more attentively.

"Because," said I, "I began the service myself, more than two years ago, without his knowledge, and I don't want to be betrayed. Why I fail in my ability to finish it, I cannot explain. It is a part of the secret which is another person's and not mine."

"What else?"

"Estella," said I, turning to her now, and trying to command my trembling voice, "you know I love you. You know that I have loved you long and dearly."

She raised her eyes to my face on being thus addressed, and her fingers plied their work, and she looked at me with an unmoved countenance. I saw that Miss Havisham glanced from me to her, and from her to me.

"I should have said this sooner, but for my long mistake. It induced me to hope that Miss Havisham meant us for one another. But I must say it now."

Preserving her unmoved countenance, and with her fingers still going, Estella shook her head.

"I know," said I, in answer to that action; "I know. I have no hope that I shall ever call you mine, Estella. I am ignorant what may become of me very soon, how poor I may be, or where I may go. Still, I love you. I have loved you ever since I first saw you in this house."

Looking at me perfectly unmoved and with her fingers busy, she shook her head again.

"It would have been cruel in Miss Havisham to torture me through all these years with a vain hope and an idle pursuit, if she had reflected on the gravity of what she did. But I think she did not. I think that in the endurance of her own trial, she forgot mine, Estella."

I saw Miss Havisham put her hand to her heart and hold it there, as she sat looking by turns at Estella and at me.

"It seems," said Estella very calmly, "that there are sentiments, fancies—I don't know how to call them—which I am not able to comprehend. When you say you love me, I know what you mean, as a form of words, but nothing more. You address nothing in my breast, you touch nothing there."

"Is it not true," said I, "that Bentley Drummle is in town here, and pursuing you?"

"It is quite true," she replied, referring to him with the indifference of utter contempt.

"That you encourage him, and ride out with him, and that he dines with you this very day?"

She seemed a little surprised that I should know it, but again replied, "Quite true."

"You cannot love him, Estella?"

Her fingers stopped for the first time, as she retorted rather angrily, "What have I told you? Do you still think, in spite of it, that I do not mean what I say?"

"You would never marry him, Estella?"

She looked toward Miss Havisham. Then she said, "Why not tell you the truth? I am going to be married to him."

I dropped my face into my hands, but was able to control myself better than I could have expected, considering what agony it gave me to hear her say those words.

"Estella, dearest, dearest Estella, do not let Miss Havisham lead you into this fatal step. Put me aside forever—you have done so, I well know—but bestow yourself on some worthier person than Drummle. Miss Havisham gives you to him, as the greatest slight and injury that could be done to the many far better men who admire you, and to the few who truly love you. Among those few, there may be one who loves you even as dearly, though he has not loved you as long, as I. Take him, and I can bear it better for your sake!"

My earnestness awoke a wonder in her.

"I am going," she said again, in a gentler voice, "to be married to him. The preparations for my marriage are making, and I shall be married soon. Why do you injuriously introduce the name of my mother by adoption? It is my own act."

"Your own act, Estella, to fling yourself away upon a brute?"

"On whom should I fling myself away?" she retorted, with a smile. "Should I fling myself away upon the man who would the soonest feel that I took nothing to him? I shall do well enough, and so will my husband. As to leading me into what you call this fatal step, Miss Havisham would have had me wait, and not marry yet; but I am tired of the life I have led, which has very few charms for me, and I am willing enough to change it. Say no more. We shall never understand each other."

"Such a mean brute, such a stupid brute!" I urged in despair.

"Don't be afraid of my being a blessing to him," said Estella. "I shall not be that. Come! Here is my hand."

"Oh, Estella!" I answered, as my bitter tears fell fast on her hand, do what I would to restrain them. "Even if I remained in England and could hold my head up with the rest, how could I see you Drummle's wife?"

"Nonsense," she returned, "nonsense. This will pass in no time."

"Never, Estella!"

"You will get me out of your thoughts in a week."

"Out of my thoughts! You are part of my existence, part of myself. You have been in every line I have ever read, since I first came here,
the rough common boy whose poor heart you wounded even then. Estella, to the last hour of my life, you cannot choose but remain part of my character, part of the little good in me, part of the evil. But I associate you only with the good, for you must have done me far more good than harm. Oh, God bless you, God forgive you!"

I held her hand to my lips some lingering moments, and so I left her. But ever afterward, I remembered that the spectral figure of Miss Havisham, her hand still covering her heart, seemed all resolved into a ghastly stare of pity and remorse.

It was past midnight when I crossed London Bridge. I was not expected till tomorrow, but I had my keys, and, if Herbert were gone to bed, could get to bed myself without disturbing him.

The night porter examined me with much attention as he held the gate a little way open for me to pass in. To help his memory I mentioned my name.

"I was not quite sure, sir, but I thought so. Here's a note, sir. The messenger that brought it said would you be so good as to read it by my lantern?"

Much surprised by the request, I took the note. It was directed to Philip Pip, Esquire, and on the top of the superscription were the words, "PLEASE READ THIS HERE." I opened it, the watchman holding up his light, and read inside, in Wemmick's writing:

"DON'T GO HOME."

Chapter 33

Pip meets Clara, Herbert's fiancée.

Turning from the Temple gate as soon as I had read the warning, I made the best of the way to Fleet Street, and there got a late hackney chariot[1] and drove to the Hummums in Covent Garden. In those times a bed was always to be got there at any hour of the night, and the chamberlain, letting me in at his ready wicket, lighted the candle next in order on his shelf, and showed me straight into the bedroom next on his list.

What a doleful night! How anxious, how dismal, how long! The closet whispered, the fireplace sighed, the little washing-stand ticked, and one guitar string played occasionally in the chest of drawers. Why I was not to go home, and what had happened at home, and when I should go home, and whether Provis was safe at home, were questions occupying my mind so busily that one might have supposed there could be no more room in it for any other theme. Even when I thought of Estella, and how we had parted that day forever, I was pursuing here and there and everywhere the caution DON'T GO HOME. At last I dozed, in sheer exhaustion of mind and body.

I had left directions that I was to be called at seven; for it was plain that I must see Wemmick before seeing anyone else, and equally plain that this was a case in which his Walworth sentiments only could be taken.

The Castle battlements arose upon my view at eight o'clock. The little servant happening to be entering the fortress with two hot rolls, I crossed the drawbridge in her company and so came without announcement into the presence of Wemmick as he was making tea for himself and the Aged.

"Halloa, Mr. Pip!" said Wemmick. "You did come home, then?"

"Yes," I returned, "but I didn't go home."

"That's all right," said he, rubbing his hands. "I left a note for you at each of the Temple gates, on the chance. Which gate did you come to?"

---

1. **hackney chariot:** a horse-drawn cab.

I told him.

"I'll go round to the others in the course of the day and destroy the notes," said Wemmick. "It's a good rule never to leave documentary evidence if you can help it. Now, Mr. Pip, you and I understand one another. I accidentally heard, yesterday morning, that a certain person not altogether of uncolonial pursuits, and not unpossessed of portable property—we won't name this person—"

"Not necessary," said I.

"—had made some little stir in a certain part of the world where a good many people go, not always in gratification of their own inclination, by disappearing from such place and being no more heard of thereabouts. I also have heard that you at your chambers in Garden Court, Temple had been watched, and might be watched again."

"By whom?" said I.

"I wouldn't go into that," said Wemmick evasively. "It might clash with official responsibilities. I heard it."

As I saw that he was restrained by fealty to Little Britain from saying as much as he could, I could not press him. But I told him, after a little meditation over the fire, that I would like to ask him a question, subject to his answering or not answering, as he deemed right.

"You have heard of a man of bad character, whose true name is Compeyson?"

He answered with one nod.

"Is he living?"

One other nod.

"Is he in London?"

He gave me one last nod and went on with his breakfast.

"Now," said Wemmick, "questioning being over," which he emphasized and repeated for my guidance; "I come to what I did, after hearing what I heard. I went to Garden Court to find you; not finding you, I went to Clarriker's to find Mr. Herbert."

"And him you found?" said I, with great anxiety.

"And I found him. Without mentioning any names or going into any details, I gave him to understand that if he was aware of anybody— Tom, Jack, or Richard—being about the chambers, or about the immediate neighborhood, he had better get Tom, Jack, or Richard out of the way while you were out of the way."

"He would be greatly puzzled what to do?"

"He *was* puzzled what to do; not the less because I gave him my opinion that it was not safe to try to get Tom, Jack, or Richard too far out of the way at present. Mr. Pip, I'll tell you something. Under existing circumstances there is no place like a great city when you are once in it. Don't break cover too soon. Lie close. Wait till things slacken before you try the open, even for foreign air."

I thanked him for his valuable advice, and asked him what Herbert had done.

"Mr. Herbert," said Wemmick, "after being all of a heap for half an hour, struck out a plan. He mentioned to me as a secret that he is courting a young lady who has, as no doubt you are aware, a bedridden pa. Which pa, having been in the purser line of life, lies a-bed in a bow window where he can see the ships sail up and down the river. You are acquainted with the young lady, most probably?"

"Not personally," said I.

"The house with the bow window," said Wemmick, "being kept, it seems, by a very respectable widow, who has a furnished upper floor to let, Mr. Herbert put it to me, what did I think of that as a temporary tenement for Tom, Jack, or Richard? Now, I thought very well of it, for three reasons. Firstly. It is well away from the usual heap of streets. Secondly. Without going near it yourself, you could always hear of the safety of Tom, Jack, or Richard, through Mr. Herbert. Thirdly. After a while, and when it might be prudent, if you should want to slip Tom, Jack, or Richard on board a foreign packet boat,[2] there he is— ready."

Much comforted by these considerations, I thanked Wemmick again and again, and begged him to proceed.

"Well, sir! Mr. Herbert threw himself into the business with a will, and by nine o'clock last night he housed Tom, Jack, or Richard— whichever it may be—you and I don't want to know—quite successfully. At the old lodgings it was understood that he was summoned to Dover. Now, another advantage of all this is that it was done without you. This diverts suspicion and confuses it, and you want confusion."

Wemmick, having finished his breakfast, here looked at his watch, and began to get his coat on.

"And now, Mr. Pip," said he, with his hands still in the sleeves, "I have probably done the most I can do. Here's the address. There can be no harm in your going here tonight and seeing for yourself that all is well with Tom, Jack, or Richard, before you go home. I must be off. If you had nothing more pressing to do than to keep here till dark that's what I should advise."

I soon fell asleep before Wemmick's fire, and the Aged and I enjoyed one another's society by falling asleep before it more or less all day. Eight o'clock had struck before I got into the air that was scented, not disagreeably, by the chips and shavings of the longshore boatbuilders, and mast, oar, and blockmakers. All that waterside region of the upper and lower Pool below London Bridge was unknown ground to me, and when I struck down by the river, I found that the spot I wanted was anything but easy to find. It was called Mill Pond

2. **packet boat:** a steamship that carries mail, freight, and passengers along a regular route, in this case, from England to the Continent.

Bank, Chinks's Basin; and I had no other guide to Chinks's Basin than the Old Green Copper Rope-Walk.

Selecting from the few queer houses upon Mill Pond Bank a house with a wooden front and three stories of bow window, I looked at the plate upon the door, and read there Mrs. Whimple. That being the name I wanted, I knocked, and an elderly woman of a pleasant and thriving appearance responded. She was immediately deposed, however, by Herbert, who silently led me into the parlor and shut the door.

"All is well, Handel," said Herbert, "and he is quite satisfied, though eager to see you. My dear girl is with her father, and if you'll wait till she comes down, I'll make you known to her, and then we'll go upstairs.—*That's* her father."

I had become aware of an alarming growling overhead, and had probably expressed the fact in my countenance.

"I am afraid he is a sad old rascal," said Herbert, smiling, "but I have never seen him. Don't you smell rum? He is always at it." While he thus spoke, the growling noise became a prolonged roar, and died away.

"To have Provis for an upper lodger is quite a godsend to Mrs. Whimple," said Herbert, "for of course people in general won't stand that noise."

As we were thus conversing, a very pretty, slight, dark-eyed girl of twenty or so came in with a basket in her hand, whom Herbert tenderly relieved of the basket, and presented, blushing, as "Clara." There was something confiding, loving, and innocent in her modest manner of yielding herself to Herbert's embracing arm. I was looking at her with pleasure and admiration when suddenly the growl swelled into a roar again, and a frightful bumping noise was heard above, as if a giant with a wooden leg were trying to bore it

through the ceiling to come at us. Upon this, Clara said to Herbert, "Papa wants me, darling!" and ran away.

Clara returned soon afterward, and Herbert accompanied me upstairs to see our charge. I found Provis comfortably settled. He expressed no alarm, and seemed to feel none that was worth mentioning; but it struck me that he was softened—indefinably, for I could not have said how.

The opportunity that the day's rest had given me for reflection had resulted in my fully determining to say nothing to him respecting Compeyson. For anything I knew, his animosity toward the man might otherwise lead to his seeking him out and rushing on his own destruction. Therefore, when Herbert and I sat down with him by his fire, I asked him first of all whether he relied on Wemmick's judgment and sources of information.

"Aye, aye, dear boy!" he answered with a grave nod. "Jaggers knows."

"Then I have talked with Wemmick," said I, "and have come to tell you what caution he gave me and what advice."

I told him how Wemmick had heard in Newgate Prison that he was under some suspicion, and that my chambers had been watched; how Wemmick had recommended his keeping close for a time, and my keeping away from him; and what Wemmick had said about getting him abroad. I added that of course I should go with him. What was to follow that, I did not touch upon; neither indeed was I at all clear or comfortable about it in my own mind, now that I saw him in that softer condition, and in declared peril for my sake.

He was very reasonable throughout. His coming back was a venture, he said, and he had always known it to be a venture, and he had very little fear of his safety with such good help.

Herbert, who had been looking at the fire

and pondering, here said, "We are both good watermen, Handel, and could take him down the river ourselves when the right time comes. No boat would then be hired for the purpose, and no boatmen; that would save at least a chance of suspicion, and any chance is worth saving. Don't you think it might be a good thing if you began at once to keep a boat at the Temple stairs, and were in the habit of rowing up and down the river? You fall into that habit, and then who notices or minds? Do it twenty or fifty times, and there is nothing special in your doing it the twenty-first or fifty-first."

I liked this scheme, and Provis was quite elated by it. We agreed that it should be carried into execution, and that Provis should never recognize us if we came below Bridge and rowed past Mill Pond Bank. But we further agreed that he should pull down the blind in that part of his window which faced upon the east whenever he saw us and all was right.

Our conference being now ended, and everything arranged, I rose to go, remarking to Herbert that he and I had better not go home together, and that I would take half an hour's start of him. "I don't like to leave you here," I said to Provis, "though I cannot doubt your being safer here than near me. Good-bye!"

"Dear boy," he answered, clasping my hands, "I don't know when we may meet again, and I don't like goodbye. Say good night!"

"Good night! Herbert will go regularly between us, and when the time comes, you may be certain I shall be ready. Good night, good night!" Looking back at him, I thought of the first night of his return, when our positions were reversed, and when I little supposed my heart could ever be as heavy and anxious at parting from him as it was now.

Next day, I set myself to get the boat. It was soon done, and the boat was brought round to the Temple stairs, and lay where I could reach

her within a minute or two. Then I began to go out as for training and practice, sometimes alone, sometimes with Herbert. I was often out in cold, rain, and sleet, but nobody took much note of me after I had been out a few times. At first, I kept above Blackfriars Bridge; but as the hours of the tide changed, I took toward London Bridge. The first time I passed Mill Pond Bank, Herbert and I were pulling a pair of oars; and, both in going and returning, we saw the blind toward the east come down. Herbert was rarely there less frequently than three times in a week, and he never brought me a single word of intelligence that was at all alarming.

Still, I was always full of fears for the rash man who was in hiding. Herbert had sometimes said to me that he found it pleasant to stand at one of our windows after dark, when the tide was running down, and to think that it was flowing, with everything it bore, toward Clara. But I thought with dread that it was flowing toward Magwitch, and that any black mark on its surface might be his pursuers, going swiftly, silently, and surely to take him.

Chapter 34

Wemmick tells Pip the story of Molly.

Some weeks passed without bringing any change. We waited for Wemmick, and he made no sign. My worldly affairs began to wear a gloomy appearance, and I was pressed for money by more than one creditor. Even I myself began to know the want of ready money in my own pocket, and to relieve it by converting some easily spared articles of jewelry into cash. But I had quite determined that it would be a heartless fraud to take more money from my patron in the existing state of my uncertain thoughts and plans. Therefore, I had sent him the unopened pocketbook by Herbert, to hold in his own keeping, and I felt a kind of satisfaction in not having profited by his generosity since his revelation of himself.

It was an unhappy life that I lived. Condemned to inaction and a state of constant restlessness and suspense, I rowed about in my boat, and waited, waited, waited, as I best could.

One afternoon, late in <u>February</u>, I came ashore at the wharf at dusk. I had pulled down as far as Greenwich with the ebb tide and had turned with the tide. It had been a fine bright day, but had become foggy as the sun dropped, and I had had to feel my way back among the shipping pretty carefully. Both in going and returning, I had had seen the signal in his window, all well.

I had strolled up into Cheapside when a large hand was laid upon my shoulder, by someone overtaking me. It was Mr. Jaggers' hand, and he passed it through my arm.

"As we are going in the same direction, Pip, we may walk together. Come and dine with me."

I was going to excuse myself, when he added, "Wemmick's coming." So I changed my excuse into an acceptance.

We went to Gerrard Street, all three together, and as soon as we got there, dinner was served.

"Did you send that note of Miss Havisham's to Mr. Pip, Wemmick?" Mr. Jaggers asked, soon after we began dinner.

"No, sir," returned Wemmick; "it was going by post, when you brought Mr. Pip into the office. Here it is." He handed it to his principal, instead of to me.

"It's a note of two lines, Pip," said Mr. Jaggers, handing it on, "sent up to me by Miss Havisham, on account of her not being sure of

your address. She tells me that she wants to see you on a little matter of business you mentioned to her. You'll go down?"

"Yes," said I, casting my eyes on the note, which was exactly in those terms.

"When do you think of going down?"

"I have an impending engagement," said I, glancing at Wemmick, "that renders me rather uncertain of my time. At once, I think."

"If Mr. Pip has the intention of going at once," said Wemmick to Mr. Jaggers, "he needn't write an answer, you know."

Receiving this as an intimation that it was best not to delay, I settled that I would go tomorrow, and said so. Wemmick drank a glass of wine and looked with a grimly satisfied air at Mr. Jaggers, but not at me.

"So, Pip! Our friend the Spider," said Mr. Jaggers, "has played his cards. He has won the pool."

It was as much as I could do to assent.

"So, here's to Mrs. Bentley Drummle," said Mr. Jaggers, taking a decanter of choicer wine from his dumbwaiter, and filling for each of us and for himself. "Now, Molly, Molly, Molly, Molly, how slow you are today!"

She was at his elbow when he addressed her, putting a dish upon the table. As she withdrew her hands from it, she fell back a step or two, nervously muttering some excuse. And a certain action of her fingers as she spoke arrested my attention.

"What's the matter?" said Mr. Jaggers.

"Nothing. Only the subject we were speaking of," said I, "was rather painful to me."

The action of her fingers was like the action of knitting. She stood looking at her master, not understanding whether she was free to go, or whether he had more to say to her and would call her back if she did go. Her look was very intent. Surely, I had seen exactly such eyes and such hands on a memorable occasion very lately!

He dismissed her, and she glided out of the room. But she remained before me, as plainly as if she were still there. I looked at those hands, I looked at those eyes, I looked at that flowing hair; and I compared them with other hands, other eyes, other hair, that I knew of, and with what those might be after twenty years of a brutal husband and a stormy life. I looked again at those hands and eyes of the housekeeper. And I felt absolutely certain that this woman was Estella's mother. Only twice more did the housekeeper reappear, and then her stay in the room was very short, and Mr. Jaggers was sharp with her. But her hands were Estella's hands, and her eyes were Estella's eyes, and if she had reappeared a hundred times I could have been neither more sure nor less sure that my conviction was the truth.

Wemmick and I took our leave early, and left together. I asked him if he had ever seen Miss Havisham's adopted daughter, Mrs. Bentley Drummle? He said no. To avoid being too abrupt, I then spoke of the Aged, and of Miss Skiffins. He looked rather sly when I mentioned Miss Skiffins.

"Wemmick," said I, "do you remember telling me, before I first went to Mr. Jaggers' private house, to notice that housekeeper?"

"Did I?" he replied. "Ah, I dare say I did."

"I wish you would tell me her story. I feel a particular interest in being acquainted with it. You know that what is said between you and me goes no further."

"Well!" Wemmick replied. "I don't know her story—that is, I don't know all of it. But what I do know, I'll tell you. We are in our private and personal capacities, of course."

"Of course."

"A score or so of years ago that woman was tried at the Old Bailey for murder and was acquitted. She was a very handsome young woman, and I believe had some gypsy blood in

her. Anyhow, it was hot enough when it was up, as you may suppose."

"But she was acquitted."

"Mr. Jaggers was for her," pursued Wemmick, with a look full of meaning, "and worked the case in a way quite astonishing. It was a desperate case. The murdered person was a woman, a good ten years older, very much larger, and very much stronger. It was a case of jealousy. They both led tramping lives, and this woman in Gerrard Street here had been married very young to a tramping man, and was a perfect fury in point of jealousy. The murdered woman—more a match for the man, certainly, in point of years—was found dead in a barn. There had been a violent struggle, perhaps a fight. She was bruised and scratched and torn, and had been held by the throat at last and choked. Now, there was no reasonable evidence to implicate any person but this woman, and on the physical improbabilities of her having been able to do it, Mr. Jaggers principally rested his case. You may be sure," said Wemmick, touching me on the sleeve, "that he never dwelt upon the strength of her hands then, though he sometimes does now."

I had told Wemmick of his showing us her wrists that day at the dinner party.

"Well, sir!" Wemmick went on. "This woman was so artfully dressed from the time of her apprehension that she looked much slighter than she really was; her sleeves are always remembered to have been so skillfully contrived that her arms had a delicate look. But the backs of her hands were lacerated, and the question was, was it with fingernails? Now, Mr. Jaggers showed that she had struggled through a great lot of brambles which she could not have got through and kept her hands out of; and bits of those brambles were actually found in her skin and put in evidence. But the boldest point he made was this. It was attempted to be set up in proof of her jealousy that she was under strong suspicion of having, at about the time of the murder, frantically destroyed her child by this man—some three years old—to revenge herself upon him. Mr. Jaggers worked that in this way. 'We say these are not marks of fingernails, but marks of brambles, and we show you the brambles. You say they are marks of fingernails, and you set up the hypothesis that she destroyed her child. You must accept all consequences of that hypothesis. For anything we know, she may have destroyed her child, and the child in clinging to her may have scratched her hands. What then? You are not trying her for the murder of her child; why don't you? As to this case, if you *will* have scratches, we say that, for anything we know, you may have accounted for them, assuming for the sake of argument that you have not invented them.' To sum up, sir," added Wemmick, "Mr. Jaggers was altogether too many for the jury, and they gave in."

"Has she been in his service ever since?"

"Yes," said Wemmick, "she went into his service immediately after her acquittal, tamed as she is now."

"Do you remember the sex of the child?"

"Said to have been a girl."

"You have nothing more to say to me tonight?"

"Nothing."

We exchanged a cordial good night, and went home, with new matter for my thoughts, though with no relief from the old.

Chapter 35

Pip visits Miss Havisham for the last time.

Putting Miss Havisham's note in my pocket, I went down by coach next day. The best light of the day had gone when I passed the High Street. The cathedral chimes had at once a sadder and more remote sound to me; they seemed to call to me that the place was changed, and that Estella was gone out of it forever.

Miss Havisham was not in her own room, but was in the larger room across the landing. Looking in at the door, after knocking in vain, I saw her sitting on the hearth in a ragged chair, close before the ashy fire. I went in and stood where she could see me when she raised her eyes. There was an air of utter loneliness upon her. As I stood compassionating her,[1] and thinking how in the progress of time I too had come to be a part of the wrecked fortunes of that house, her eyes rested on me. She stared and said in a low voice, "Is it real?"

"It is I, Pip. Mr. Jaggers gave me your note yesterday, and I have lost no time."

"Thank you. Thank you.

"I want," she said, "to pursue that subject you mentioned to me when you were last here, and to show you that I am not all stone. You said, speaking for your friend, that you could tell me how to do something useful and good. Something that you would like done, is it not?"

"Something that I would like done very, very much."

"What is it?"

I began explaining to her that secret history of the partnership. I told her how I had hoped to complete the transaction out of my means, but how in this I was disappointed.

"So!" said she, assenting with her head, but not looking at me. "And how much money is wanting to complete the purchase?"

I was rather afraid of stating it, for it sounded a large sum. "Nine hundred pounds."

---

1. **compassionating her:** sympathizing deeply with her; being compassionate.

"If I give you the money for this purpose, will you keep my secret as you have kept your own?"

"Quite as faithfully."

"And your mind will be more at rest?"

"Much more at rest."

"Are you very unhappy now?"

"I am far from happy, Miss Havisham; but I have other causes of disquiet than any you know of. They are the secrets I have mentioned."

After a little while, she raised her head and looked at the fire again.

"Can I only serve you, Pip, by serving your friend? Regarding that as done, is there nothing I can do for you yourself?"

"Nothing. I thank you for the question. I thank you even more for the tone of the question. But, there is nothing."

She presently rose from her seat and looked about for the means of writing. There were none there, and she took from her pocket a yellow set of ivory tablets, mounted in tarnished gold, and wrote upon them with a pencil in a case of tarnished gold that hung from her neck.

"You are still on friendly terms with Mr. Jaggers?"

"Quite. I dined with him yesterday."

"This is an authority to him to pay you that money, to lay out at your discretion for your friend. I keep no money here; but if you would rather Mr. Jaggers knew nothing of the matter, I will send it to you."

"Thank you, Miss Havisham; I have not the least objection to receiving it from him."

She read me what she had written, and it was direct and clear, and evidently intended to absolve me from any suspicion of profiting by the receipt of the money. I took the tablets from her hand and it trembled as she took off the chain to which the pencil was attached, and put it in mine.

"My name is on the first leaf. If you can ever write under my name, 'I forgive her,' though ever so long after my broken heart is dust—pray do it!"

"Oh, Miss Havisham," said I, "I can do it now. I want forgiveness and direction far too much to be bitter with you."

She turned her face to me for the first time since she had averted it, and to my amazement, I may even add to my terror, dropped on her knees at my feet with her folded hands raised. To see her with her white hair and her worn face, kneeling at my feet, gave me a shock through all my frame.

"Oh!" she cried despairingly. "What have I done! What have I done!"

"If you mean, Miss Havisham, what have you done to injure me, let me answer. Very little. I should have loved her under any circumstances. Is she married?"

"Yes!"

It was a needless question, for a new desolation in the desolate house had told me so.

"What have I done! What have I done!" She wrung her hands, and crushed her white hair, and returned to this cry over and over again. "What have I done! Until you spoke to her the other day, and until I saw in you a looking glass that showed me what I once felt myself, I did not know what I had done. What have I done! What have I done!"

"Miss Havisham," I said, when her cry had died away, "you may dismiss me from your mind and conscience. But Estella is a different case, and if you can ever undo any scrap of what you have done amiss in keeping a part of her right nature away from her, it will be better to do that than to bemoan the past through a hundred years."

"Yes, yes, I know it. But, Pip—my dear!" There was an earnest womanly compassion for me in her new affection. "My dear! Believe this: when she first came to me, I meant to save her from misery like my own. At first I meant no more. But as she grew, and promised to be very beautiful, I gradually did worse, and with my praises, and with my jewels, and with my teachings, I stole her heart away and put ice in its place."

"Better," I could not help saying, "to have left her a natural heart, even to be bruised or broken."

"If you knew all my story," she pleaded, "you would have some compassion for me and a better understanding of me."

"Miss Havisham," I answered, as delicately as I could, "I believe I may say that I do know your story, and have known it ever since I first left this neighborhood. Does what has passed between us give me any excuse for asking you a question relative to Estella?"

She was seated on the ground, with her arms on the ragged chair, and her head leaning on them. She looked full at me and replied, "Go on."

"Whose child was Estella?"

She shook her head.

"You don't know?"

She shook her head again.

"But Mr. Jaggers brought her here, or sent her here?"

"Brought her here."

"Will you tell me how that came about?"

She answered in a low whisper and with caution, "I had been shut up in these rooms a long time when I told him that I wanted a little girl to rear and love, and save from my fate. He told me that he would look about him for such an orphan child. One night he brought her here asleep, and I called her Estella."

"Might I ask her age then?"

"Two or three. She herself knows nothing, but that she was left an orphan and I adopted her."

So convinced I was of that woman's being her mother that I wanted no evidence to estab-lish the fact in my mind. But, to any mind, the connection here was clear and straight.

What more could I hope to do by prolonging the interview? I had succeeded on behalf of Herbert, Miss Havisham had told me all she knew of Estella, I had said and done what I could to ease her mind.

Twilight was closing in when I went down-stairs into the natural air. I called to the woman who had opened the gate when I en-tered that I would not trouble her just yet, but would walk round the place before leaving. For I had a presentiment that I should never be there again, and I felt that the dying light was suited to my last view of it.

I made my way to the ruined garden. I went all round it; round by the corner where Her-bert and I had fought our battle; round by the paths where Estella and I had walked. So cold, so lonely, so dreary all!

Passing on into the front courtyard, I hesi-tated whether to call the woman to let me out at the locked gate, of which she had the key, or first to go upstairs and assure myself that Miss Havisham was as safe and well as I had left her. I took the latter course and went up.

I looked into the room where I had left her, and I saw her seated in the ragged chair upon the hearth close to the fire, with her back to-ward me. In the moment when I was with-drawing my head to go quietly away, I saw a great flaming light spring up. In the same mo-ment I saw her running at me, shrieking, with a whirl of fire blazing all about her, and soar-ing at least as many feet about her head as she was high.

I had a double-caped greatcoat on, and over my arm another thick coat. I got them off, closed with her, threw her down, and got them over her; I dragged the great cloth from the table for the same purpose, and with it dragged down the heap of rottenness in the midst and all the ugly things that sheltered

there. The closer I covered her, the more wildly she shrieked and tried to free herself. I knew that we were on the floor by the great table, and that patches of tinder yet alight were floating in the smoky air, which a moment ago had been her faded bridal dress.

Then I looked round and saw the disturbed beetles and spiders running away over the floor, and the servants coming in with breathless cries at the door. She was insensible, and I was afraid to have her moved, or even touched. Assistance was sent for, and I held her until it came, as if I unreasonably fancied that if I let her go, the fire would break out again and consume her. When I got up, on the surgeon's coming to her with other aid, I was astonished to see that both my hands were burned; for I had no knowledge of it through the sense of feeling.

On examination it was pronounced that she had received serious hurts, but that the danger lay mainly in the nervous shock. By the surgeon's directions, her bed was carried into that room and laid upon the great table, which happened to be well suited to the dressing of her injuries. When I saw her again, an hour afterward, she lay indeed where I had seen her strike her stick, and had heard her say she would lie one day.

Toward midnight she began to wander in her speech and said innumerable times, in a low solemn voice, "What have I done!" And then, "When she first came, I meant to save her from misery like mine." And then, "Take the pencil and write under my name, 'I forgive her'!" She never changed the order of these three sentences.

As I could do no service there, and as I had, nearer home, that pressing reason for anxiety and fear, I decided that I would return by the early morning coach. At about six o'clock of the morning, therefore, I leaned over her and touched her lips with mine, just as they said,

"Take the pencil and write under my name, 'I forgive her.'"

Chapter 36

Pip hears more about Provis.

My hands had been dressed twice or thrice in the night, and again in the morning. My left arm was a good deal burned to the elbow, and less severely as high as the shoulder; it was very painful, but I felt thankful it was no worse. My right hand was not so badly burned but that I could move the fingers. My left hand and arm I carried in a sling; and I could only wear my coat like a cloak, loose over my shoulders and fastened at the neck.

Herbert devoted the day to attending on me. He was the kindest of nurses, and at stated times took off the bandages and steeped them in the cooling liquid that was kept ready, and put them on again, with a patient tenderness that I was deeply grateful for.

Neither of us spoke of the boat, but we thought of it. That was made apparent by our avoidance of the subject and by our agreeing—without agreement—to make my recovery of the use of my hands a question of so many hours, not of so many weeks.

My first question when I saw Herbert had been, of course, whether all was well down the river.

"I sat with Provis last night, Handel, two good hours. Do you know, Handel, he improves?"

"I said to you I thought he was softened when I last saw him."

"So you did. And so he is. He was very communicative last night, and told me more of his life. You remember his breaking off here about some woman that he had had great trouble with? He went into that part of his life, and a dark wild part it is. Shall I tell you?"

"Tell me by all means!"

"It seems, that the woman was a young woman, and a jealous woman, and a revengeful woman; revengeful, Handel, to the last degree."

"To what last degree?"

"Murder! She was tried for it, and Mr. Jaggers defended her, and the reputation of that defense first made his name known to Provis. It was another and a stronger woman who was the victim, and there had been a struggle—in a barn."

"Was the woman brought in guilty?"

"No; she was acquitted. This acquitted young woman and Provis had a little child, a little child of whom Provis was exceedingly fond. On the evening of the very night when the object of her jealousy was strangled, the young woman presented herself before Provis for one moment, and swore that she would destroy the child (which was in her possession), and he should never see it again; then she vanished. You don't think your breathing is affected, my dear boy? You seem to breathe quickly."

"Perhaps I do, Herbert. Did the woman keep her oath?"

"There comes the darkest part of Provis' life. She did."

"That is, he says she did."

"Why, of course, my dear boy," returned Herbert, in a tone of surprise, and again bending forward to get a nearer look at me. "He says it all. I have no other information."

"No, to be sure."

"Now, whether," pursued Herbert, "he had used the child's mother ill or well, Provis doesn't say; but she had shared some four or five years of the wretched life he described to us at this fireside, and he seems to have felt pity for her. Therefore, fearing he should be called upon to depose[1] about this destroyed child, and so be the cause of her death, he hid himself (much as he grieved for the child), kept himself dark, as he says, out of the way and out of the trial, and was only vaguely talked of as a certain man called Abel, out of whom the jealousy arose. After the acquittal she disappeared, and thus he lost the child and the child's mother."

"I want to ask——"

"A moment, my dear boy, and I have done. That evil genius, Compeyson, the worst of scoundrels, knowing of his keeping out of the way at that time, of course afterward held the knowledge over his head as a means of keeping him poorer and working him harder."

"I want to know," said I, "and particularly, Herbert, whether he told you when this happened?"

"Particularly? Let me remember, then, what he said as to that. His expression was, 'a round score o' year ago, and a'most directly after I took up wi' Compeyson.' How old were you when you came upon him in the little churchyard?"

"I think in my seventh year."

"Aye. It had happened some three or four years then, he said, and you brought into his mind the little girl so tragically lost, who would have been about your age."

"Herbert," said I, after a short silence, "the man we have hiding down the river is Estella's father."

Chapter 37

Pip receives a mysterious letter.

Early next morning I took my way to Little Britain. Although I had sent Mr. Jaggers a

---

1. **depose** (dĭ-pōz'): here used in the legal sense, to testify under oath.

brief account of the accident as soon as I had arrived in town, yet I had to give him all the details now. My narrative finished, I then produced Miss Havisham's authority to receive the nine hundred pounds for Herbert. Mr. Jaggers' eyes retired a little deeper into his head when I handed him the tablets, but he presently handed them over to Wemmick with instructions to draw the check for his signature. From Little Britain I went, with my check in my pocket, to Miss Skiffins' brother, the accountant; and he going straight to Clarriker's and bringing Clarriker to me, I had the great satisfaction of concluding that arrangement. It was the only good thing I had done, and the only completed thing I had done, since I was first apprised of my great expectations.

Clarriker informed me that he would now be able to establish a small branch house in the East and that Herbert in his new partnership capacity would go out and take charge of it. And now indeed I felt as if my last anchor were loosening its hold, and I should soon be driving with the winds and waves.

We had now got into the month of March. My left arm took in the natural course so long to heal that I was still unable to get a coat on. My right arm was tolerably restored—disfigured, but fairly serviceable.

On a Monday morning, when Herbert and I were at breakfast, I received the following letter from Wemmick by the post.

Walworth. Burn this as soon as read. Early in the week, or say Wednesday, you might do what you know of, if you felt disposed to try it. Now burn.

When I had shown this to Herbert and had put it in the fire—but not before we had both got it by heart—we considered what to do. For, of course, my being disabled could now be no longer kept out of view.

"I have thought it over again and again," said Herbert, "and I think I know a better course than taking a Thames waterman. Take Startop. A good fellow, a skilled hand, fond of us, and enthusiastic and honorable."

I had thought of him more than once.

"But how much would you tell him, Herbert?"

"It is necessary to tell him very little. Let him suppose it a mere freak, but a secret one, until the morning comes; then let him know that there is urgent reason for your getting Provis aboard and away. You go with him?"

"No doubt."

"Where?"

It seemed to me almost indifferent what port we made for—Hamburg, Rotterdam, Antwerp—the place signified little, so that he was out of England. Any foreign steamer that fell in our way and would take us up would do. I had always proposed to myself to get him well down the river in the boat; certainly well beyond Gravesend, which was a critical place for search or inquiry if suspicion were afoot. As foreign steamers would leave London at about the time of high water, our plan would be to get down the river by a previous ebb tide, and lie by in some quiet spot until we could pull off to one. The time when one would be due where we lay, wherever that might be, could be calculated pretty nearly, if we made inquiries beforehand.

Herbert assented to all this, and we went out immediately after breakfast to pursue our investigations. We found that a steamer for Hamburg was likely to suit our purpose best, and we directed our thoughts chiefly to that vessel. But we noted down what other foreign steamers would leave London with the same tide, and we satisfied ourselves that we knew the build and color of each. We then separated for a few hours; I to get at once such passports as were necessary; Herbert, to see Startop at his lodgings. When we met again at one o'clock I, for my part, was prepared with passports; Herbert had seen Startop, and he was more than ready to join.

Those two would pull a pair of oars, we settled, and I would steer; our charge would be sitter, and keep quiet. We arranged that Herbert should prepare Provis to come down to some stairs hard by the house, on Wednesday, when he saw us approach, and not sooner; that all arrangements with him should be concluded that Monday night. These precautions well understood by both of us, I went home.

On opening the outer door of our chambers with my key, I found a letter in the box, directed to me—a very dirty letter, though not ill written. It had been delivered by hand and its contents were these:

> If you are not afraid to come to the old marshes tonight or tomorrow night at nine, and to come to the little sluice house by the limekiln, you had better come. If you want information regarding *your uncle Provis*, you had better come and tell no one and lose no time. *You must come alone.* Bring this with you.

What to do now, I could not tell. And the worst was that I must decide quickly, or I should miss the afternoon coach, which would take me down in time for tonight. Tomorrow night I could not think of going, for it would be too close upon the time of the flight. For anything I knew, the information might have some important bearing on the flight itself. I resolved to go.

I had to read this mysterious epistle again, twice, before its injunction to me to be secret got into my mind. Yielding to it, I left a note in pencil to Herbert, telling him that I had decided to hurry down and back to ascertain for myself how Miss Havisham was faring. I caught the coach just as it came out of the yard. I was the only inside passenger, jolting away knee-deep in straw. And now I began to wonder at myself for being in the coach, and to doubt whether I had sufficient reason for being there, and to consider whether I should get out presently and go back, and to argue against ever heeding an anonymous communication, and, in short, to pass through all those phases of contradiction and indecision to which I suppose very few hurried people are strangers. Still, the reference to Provis by name mastered everything. I reasoned that in case any harm should befall him through my not going, how could I ever forgive myself!

It was dark before we got down. Avoiding the Blue Boar, I put up at an inn of minor reputation down the town and ordered some dinner. While it was preparing, I went to Satis House and inquired for Miss Havisham; she was still very ill, though considered something better.

As I was not able to cut my dinner, the old landlord with a shining bald head did it for me. This bringing us into conversation, he was so good as to entertain me with my own story—of course with the popular feature that Pumblechook was my earliest benefactor and the founder of my fortunes.

"Do you know the young man?" said I.

"Know him?" repeated the landlord. "Ever since he was—no height at all."

"Does he ever come back to this neighborhood?"

"Aye, he comes back," said the landlord, "to his great friends, now and again, and gives the cold shoulder to the man that made him."

"What man is that?"

"Him that I speak of," said the landlord. "Mr. Pumblechook."

"Is he ungrateful to no one else?"

"No doubt he would be, if he could," returned the landlord, "but he can't. And why?

Because Pumblechook done everything for him."

"Does Pumblechook say so?"

"Say so!" replied the landlord. "He han't no call to say so."

"But does he say so?"

"It would turn a man's blood to white wine winegar to hear him tell of it, sir," said the landlord.

I thought, "Yet Joe, dear Joe, *you* never tell of it. Long-suffering and loving Joe, *you* never complain. Nor you, sweet-tempered Biddy!"

I had never been struck at so keenly for my thanklessness to Joe, as through the brazen imposter Pumblechook. The falser he, the truer Joe; the meaner he, the nobler Joe.

My heart was deeply and most deservedly humbled as I mused over the fire for an hour or more. The striking of the clock aroused me, and I got up and had my coat fastened round my neck, and went out. I had previously sought in my pockets for the letter, that I might refer to it again, but I could not find it, and was uneasy to think that it must have been dropped in the straw of the coach. I knew very well, however, that the appointed place was the little sluice house by the limekiln on the marshes, and the hour nine. Toward the marshes I now went straight, having no time to spare.

Chapter 38

Trabb's boy leads a rescue party.

It was a dark night, there was a melancholy wind, and the marshes were very dismal. A stranger would have found them insupportable, and even to me they were so oppressive that I hesitated, half inclined to go back. It was a half hour before I drew near to the kiln. The lime was burning with a sluggish, stifling smell, but the fires were made up and left, and no workmen were visible. Hard by was a small stone quarry.

Coming up to the marsh level out of this excavation, I saw a light in the old sluice house. I quickened my pace and knocked at the door. There was no answer, and I knocked again. No answer still, and I tried the latch.

The door yielded. Looking in, I saw a lighted candle on a table, a bench, and a mattress on a truckle bedstead.[1] As there was a loft above, I called, "Is there anyone here?" but no voice answered. Then I looked at my watch, and finding that it was past nine, called again, "Is there anyone here?" There being still no answer, I went out at the door, irresolute what to do.

It was beginning to rain fast. Seeing nothing, I turned back into the house. While I was considering that someone must have been there lately and must soon be coming back, or the candle would not be burning, it came into my head to look if the wick were long. I had taken up the candle in my hand, when it was extinguished by some violent shock, and the next thing I comprehended was that I had been caught in a strong running noose, thrown over my head from behind.

"Now," said a suppressed voice with an oath, "I've got you!"

"What is this?" I cried, struggling. "Who is it? Help, help, help!"

Not only were my arms pulled close to my sides, but the pressure on my bad arm caused me exquisite pain. A strong man's hand was set against my mouth to deaden my cries, and with a hot breath always close to me, I struggled ineffectually in the dark until I was fastened tight to the wall. "And now," said the suppressed voice with another oath, "call out

---

1. **truckle bedstead:** low bed on wheels, usually rolled underneath another bed.

again, and I'll make short work of you!"

Faint and sick with pain, I tried to ease my arm, but I was bound too tight. After groping about for a little, he began to strike a light. Presently I saw his lips breathing on the tinder, and then a flare of light flashed up and showed me Orlick.

Whom I had looked for, I don't know. I had not looked for him. Seeing him, I felt that I was in a dangerous strait indeed, and I kept my eyes upon him.

He lighted the candle from the flaring match with great deliberation, and dropped the match, and trod it out. Then he put the candle away from him on the table, so that he could see me, and sat with his arms folded on the table, and looked at me. I made out that I was fastened to a stout perpendicular ladder a few inches from the wall—a fixture there—the means of ascent to the loft above.

"Now," said he, when we had surveyed one another for some time, "I've got you."

"Why have you lured me here?"

"Don't you know?" said he, with a deadly look.

"Why have you set upon me in the dark?"

"Because I mean to do it all myself. One keeps a secret better than two. Oh, you enemy, you enemy!"

His enjoyment of the spectacle I furnished, as he sat with his arms folded on the table, shaking his head at me, made me tremble. As I watched him in silence, he put his hand into the corner at his side, and took up a gun with a brass-bound stock.

"Do you know this?" said he, making as if he would take aim at me. "Do you know where you saw it afore? Speak, wolf!"

"Yes," I answered.

"You cost me that place.[2] You did. Speak!"

2. **that place:** Orlick's position at Miss Havisham's house.

"What else could I do?"

"You did that, and that would be enough, without more. How dared you come betwixt me and a young woman I liked?"

"When did I?"

"When didn't you? It was you as always give Old Orlick a bad name to her."

"You gave it to yourself; you gained it for yourself. I could have done you no harm, if you had done yourself none."

"You're a liar. And you'll take any pains, and spend any money, to drive me out of this country, will you?" said he, repeating my words to Biddy in the last interview I had with her. "Now, I'll tell you a piece of information. It was never so worth your while to get me out of this country as it is tonight." As he shook his heavy hand at me, with his mouth snarling like a tiger's, I felt that it was true.

"What are you going to do to me?"

"I'm a-going," said he, bringing his fist down upon the table with a heavy blow, and rising as the blow fell, to give it greater force, "I'm a-going to have your life!"

He leaned forward staring at me, slowly unclenched his hand and drew it across his mouth as if his mouth watered for me, and sat down again.

"You was always in Old Orlick's way since ever you was a child. You goes out of his way this present night. He'll have no more on you. You're dead."

I felt that I had come to the brink of my grave. For a moment I looked wildly round my trap for any chance of escape; but there was none.

"More than that," said he, "I won't have a rag of you, I won't have a bone of you, left on earth. I'll put your body in the kiln—I'd carry two such to it, on my shoulders—and, let people suppose what they may of you, they shall never know nothing."

My mind with inconceivable rapidity followed out all the consequences of such a death. Estella's father would believe I had deserted him, would be taken, would die accusing me; even Herbert would doubt me when he compared the letter I had left for him with the fact that I had called at Miss Havisham's gate for only a moment; Joe and Biddy would never know how sorry I had been that night.

Orlick had been drinking, and his eyes were red and bloodshot. Around his neck was slung a tin bottle. He brought the bottle to his lips and took a fiery drink from it.

"Wolf!" said he, folding his arms again. "Old Orlick's a-going to tell you somethink. It was you as did for your shrew sister."

"It was you, villain," said I.

"I tell you it was your doing—I tell you it was done through you," he retorted, catching up the gun, and making a blow with the stock at the vacant air between us. "I come upon her from behind, as I come upon you tonight. I giv' it her! I left her for dead, and if there had been a limekiln as nigh her as there is now nigh you, she shouldn't have come to life again. But it warn't Old Orlick as did it; it was you. You was favored, and he was bullied and beat. Old Orlick bullied and beat, eh? Now you pays for it. You done it; now you pays for it."

He drank again, and became more ferocious. He took up the candle, and shading it with his murderous hand so as to throw its light on me, stood before me, looking at me and enjoying the sight.

"Wolf, I'll tell you something more. It was Old Orlick as you tumbled over on your stairs that night. And why was Old Orlick there? I'll tell you something more, wolf. You and her *have* pretty well hunted me out of this country, so far as getting a easy living in it goes, and I've took up with new companions and new masters. Some of 'em writes my letters when I wants 'em wrote. They writes fifty hands; they're not like sneaking you as writes but one.

I've had a firm mind and a firm will to have your life, since you was down here at your sister's burying. I han't seen a way to get you safe, and I've looked arter you to know your ins and outs. For, says Old Orlick to himself, 'Somehow or another I'll have him!' What! When I looks for you, I finds your Uncle Provis, eh?

"*You* with a uncle, too! But when Old Orlick come for to hear that your Uncle Provis had mostlike wore the leg iron wot Old Orlick had picked up on these meshes ever so many year ago, and wot he kept by him till he dropped your sister with it—when he comes to hear that—hey?—"

In his savage taunting, he flared the candle so close at me that I turned my face aside to save it from the flame.

"Ah!" he cried, laughing, after doing it again. "The burned child dreads the fire! Old Orlick knowed you was burned, Old Orlick knowed you was a-smuggling your Uncle Provis away, Old Orlick's a match for you and knowed you'd come tonight! Now I'll tell you something more, wolf, and this ends it. There's them that's as good a match for your Uncle Provis as Old Orlick has been for you. There's them that can't and that won't have Magwitch—yes, *I* know the name!—alive in the same land with them, and that's had sure information of him when he was alive in another land, as that he shouldn't leave it unbeknown and put them in danger. P'raps it's them that writes fifty hands, and that's not like sneaking you as writes but one. 'Ware Compeyson, Magwitch, and the gallows!"

There was a clear space of a few feet between the table and the opposite wall. Within this space he now slouched backward and forward with his hands hanging loose and heavy at his sides, and with his eyes scowling at me. I had no grain of hope left.

Of a sudden he stopped, took the cork out of his bottle, and tossed it away. Light as it was, I heard it fall like a plummet.[3] He swallowed slowly, tilting up the bottle by little and little, and now he looked at me no more. The last few drops of liquor he poured into the palm of his hand and licked up. Then with a sudden hurry of violence and swearing horribly, he threw the bottle from him, and stooped; and I saw in his hand a stone hammer with a long heavy handle.

I shouted out with all my might, and struggled with all my might. It was only my head and my legs that I could move, but to that extent I struggled with all the force that was within me. In the same instant I heard responsive shouts, saw figures and a gleam of light dash in at the door, heard voices and tumult, and saw Orlick emerge from a struggle of men, clear the table at a leap, and fly out into the night!

After a blank, I found that I was lying unbound on the floor, in the same place, with my head on someone's knee. My eyes were fixed on the ladder against the wall when there came between me and it, a face. The face of Trabb's boy!

"I think he's all right!" said Trabb's boy, in a sober voice. "But ain't he just pale, though!"

At these words, the face of him who supported me looked over into mine, and I saw my supporter to be——

"Herbert! Great Heaven!"

"Softly," said Herbert. "Gently, Handel. Don't be too eager."

"And our old comrade, Startop!" I cried, as he too bent over me.

"Remember what he is going to assist us in," said Herbert, "and be calm."

The allusion made me spring up, though I dropped again from the pain in my arm. "The time has not gone by, Herbert, has it? What

night is tonight? How long have I been here?"

"The time has not gone by. It is still Monday night."

"Thank God!"

"And you have all tomorrow, Tuesday, to rest in," said Herbert. "Can you stand?"

"Yes, yes," said I, "I can walk, I have no hurt but in this throbbing arm."

They did what they could until we could get to the town and obtain some cooling lotion to put upon it. Trabb's boy—Trabb's overgrown young man now—went before us with a lantern. But the moon was a good two hours higher than when I had last seen the sky, and the night though rainy was much lighter.

Entreating Herbert to tell me how he had come to my rescue, I learned that I had in my hurry dropped the letter, open, in our chambers, where he, coming home to bring with him Startop, found it very soon after I was gone. Its tone made him uneasy, and he set off for the coach office with Startop. Finding that the afternoon coach was gone, he resolved to follow in a post chaise. So he and Startop arrived at the Blue Boar, fully expecting there to find me, or tidings of me; but, finding neither, went on to Miss Havisham's, where they lost me. Hereupon they went back to the hotel to refresh themselves and to get someone to guide them upon the marshes. Among the loungers under the Boar's archway happened to be Trabb's boy. Thus Trabb's boy became their guide, and with him they went out to the sluice house. Herbert left his guide and Startop on the edge of the quarry, and went on by himself, and stole round the house two or three times. As he could hear nothing but indistinct sounds of one deep rough voice, he began to doubt whether I was there, when suddenly I cried out loudly, and he answered the cries, and rushed in, closely followed by the other two.

---

3. **plummet:** a lead weight attached to a string, used by carpenters to test the straightness of a wall.

We relinquished all thoughts of pursuing Orlick at that time. For the present, under the circumstances, we deemed it prudent to make rather light of the matter to Trabb's boy. When we parted, I presented him with two guineas (which seemed to meet his views), and told him that I was sorry ever to have had an ill opinion of him (which made no impression on him at all).

It was daylight when we reached the Temple, and I went at once to bed, and lay in bed all day.

My terror, as I lay there, of falling ill and being unfitted for tomorrow, was so besetting that I wonder it did not disable me of itself. I started at every footstep and every sound, believing that he was discovered and taken, and this was the messenger to tell me so. I persuaded myself that I knew he was taken. It happened sometimes that in the mere escape of a fatigued mind, I dozed for some moments or forgot; then I would say to myself with a start, "Now it has come, and I am turning delirious!"

They kept me very quiet all day, and kept my arm constantly dressed, and gave me cooling drinks. Whenever I fell asleep, I awoke with the notion I had had in the sluice house, that a long time had elapsed, and the opportunity to save him was gone. About midnight I got out of bed and went to Herbert with the conviction that I had been asleep for four-and-twenty hours, and that Wednesday was past. It was the last self-exhausting effort of my fretfulness, for after that, I slept soundly.

Wednesday morning was dawning when I looked out of the window. Herbert lay asleep in his bed, and our old fellow student lay asleep on the sofa. I could not dress myself without help, but I made up the fire, which was still burning, and got some coffee ready for them. In good time they too started up strong and well, and we admitted the sharp morning air at the windows, and looked at the tide that was still flowing toward us.

"When it turns at nine o'clock," said Herbert cheerfully, "look out for us, and stand ready, you over there at Mill Pond Bank!"

Chapter 39

An informer goes to his death.

It was one of those March days when the sun shines hot and the wind blows cold: when it is summer in the light, and winter in the shade. We had our peacoats[1] with us, and I took a bag. Of all my worldly possessions, I took no more than the few necessaries that filled the bag. Where I might go, what I might do, or when I might return, were questions utterly unknown to me; nor did I vex my mind with them, for it was wholly set on Provis' safety. We loitered down to the Temple stairs, and stood loitering there, as if we were not quite decided to go upon the water at all. Of course I had taken care that the boat should be ready, and everything in order. After a little show of indecision, we went on board and cast off; Herbert in the bow, I steering. It was then about high water—half-past eight.

Our plan was this. The tide, beginning to run down at nine, and being with us until three, we intended still to creep on after it had turned, and row against it until dark. We should then be well in those long reaches below Gravesend, between Kent and Essex, where the river is broad and solitary, where the waterside inhabitants are very few, and where lone public houses are scattered here and

---

1. **peacoats:** thick, woolen jackets, often worn by seamen.

there, of which we could choose one for a resting place. There, we meant to lie by all night. The steamer for Hamburg and the steamer for Rotterdam would start from London at about nine on Thursday morning. We should know at what time to expect them and would hail the first; so that if by any accident we were not taken aboard, we should have another chance. We knew the distinguishing marks of each vessel.

Old London Bridge was soon passed, and old Billingsgate market with its oyster boats and Dutchmen, and we were in among the tiers of shipping. Here were steamers, loading and unloading goods, and here, at her moorings, was tomorrow's steamer for Rotterdam, of which we took good notice; and here tomorrow's for Hamburg, under whose bowsprit[2] we crossed. And now I, sitting in the stern, could see, with a faster beating heart, Mill Pond Bank and Mill Pond stairs.

"Is he there?" said Herbert.

"Not yet."

"Right! He was not to come down till he saw us. Can you see his signal!"

"Not well from here; but I think I see it. Now I see him! Pull both. Easy, Herbert. Oars!"

We touched the stairs lightly for a single moment, and he was on board and we were off again. He had a boat cloak with him, and a black canvas bag, and he looked as like a river pilot as my heart could have wished.

"Dear boy!" he said, putting his arm on my shoulder, as he took his seat. "Faithful dear boy, well done. Thank'ee, thank'ee!"

Again among the tiers of shipping, in and out, avoiding rusty chain cables, frayed hempen hawsers,[3] and bobbing buoys, sinking for the moment, floating broken baskets, scattering floating chips of wood and shaving, cleaving floating scum of coal in and out— upon the clearer river, where the ships' boys might take their fenders[4] in, no longer fishing in troubled waters with them over the side, and where the festooned sails might fly out to the wind.

At the stairs where we had taken him aboard, and ever since, I had looked warily for any token of our being suspected. I had seen none. He had his boat cloak on him, and looked, as I have said, a natural part of the scene. It was remarkable that he was the least anxious of any of us.

"If you knowed, dear boy," he said to me, "what it is to sit here alonger my dear boy and have my smoke, arter having been day by day betwixt four walls, you'd envy me. But you don't know what it is."

"I think I know the delights of freedom," I answered.

"Ah," said he, shaking his head gravely. "But you don't know it equal to me. You must have been under lock and key, dear boy, to know it equal to me—but I ain't a-going to be low."

"If all goes well," said I, "you will be perfectly free and safe again, within a few hours."

"Well," he returned, drawing a long breath, "I hope so."

We made what way we could until the sun went down. At length we descried a light and a roof, and presently afterward ran alongside a little causeway made of stones. I stepped ashore, and found the light to be in the window of a public house. It was a dirty place enough, and I dare say not unknown to smuggling adventurers; but there was a good fire in the kitchen, and there were eggs and bacon to eat. Also, there were two double-bedded

---

2. **bowsprit** (bou′sprīt′): a pole or spar projecting from the bow (front) of a ship.
3. **hawsers** (hô′zərz): ropes.

4. **fenders:** anything used as padding against the sides of ships, to protect them from damage in bumping against wharves or other ships.

rooms—"such as they were," the landlord said. No other company was in the house than the landlord, his wife, and a grizzled male creature, the "Jack"[5] of the little causeway.

With this assistant, I went down to the boat again, and we all came ashore, and brought out the oars, and rudder, and boathook, and all else, and hauled her up for the night. We made a very good meal by the kitchen fire, and then apportioned the bedrooms; Herbert and Startop were to occupy one; I and our charge the other. We considered ourselves well off, for a more solitary place we could not have found.

While we were comforting ourselves by the fire after our meal, the Jack asked me if we had seen a four-oared galley going up with the tide. When I told him no, he said she must have gone down then, and yet she "took up too," when she left there.

"They must ha' thought better on't for some reason or another," said the Jack, "and gone down."

"A four-oared galley did you say?" said I.

"A four," said the Jack, "and two sitters."

"Did they come ashore here?"

"They put in with a stone two-gallon jar for some beer."

This dialogue made us all uneasy, and me very uneasy. The dismal wind was muttering round the house, the tide was flapping at the shore, and I had a feeling that we were caged and threatened. A four-oared galley hovering about in so unusual a way as to attract this notice was an ugly circumstance that I could not get rid of. When I had induced Provis to go up to bed, I went outside with my two companions (Startop by this time knew the state of the case) and held council. On the whole we deemed it the better course to lie where we were, until within an hour or so of the steamer's time, and

then to get out in her track, and drift easily with the tide. Having settled to do this, we returned into the house and went to bed.

I lay down with the greater part of my clothes on, and slept well for a few hours. When I awoke, the wind had risen. I looked out of the window. It commanded the causeway where we had hauled up our boat, and I saw two men looking into her. They passed by under the window, looking at nothing else, and they did not go down to the landing places but struck across the marshes. In that light, however, I soon lost them, and feeling very cold, lay down to think of the matter and fell asleep again.

We were up early. As we walked to and fro, all four together, I deemed it right to recount what I had seen. Again our charge was the least anxious of the party. However, I proposed that he and I should walk away together to a distant point, and that the boat should take us aboard there. This being considered a good precaution, soon after breakfast he and I set forth, without saying anything at the tavern.

He smoked his pipe as we went along, and sometimes stopped to clap me on the shoulder. One would have supposed that it was I who was in danger, not he, and that he was reassuring me. We spoke very little.

We waited until we saw our boat coming round. We got aboard easily and rowed out into the track of the steamer. By that time it wanted but ten minutes of one o'clock, and we began to look out for her smoke.

But it was half past one before we saw her smoke, and soon after we saw behind it the smoke of another steamer. As they were coming on at full speed, we got the two bags ready, and took that opportunity of saying goodbye to Herbert and Startop. We had all shaken hands cordially, and neither Herbert's eyes nor mine were quite dry, when I saw a four-oared galley shoot out from under the bank

---

5. **Jack:** a sailor.

but a little way ahead of us, and row out into the same track.

I called to Herbert and Startop to keep before the tide, that the steamer might see us lying by for her, and adjured Provis to sit quite still, wrapped in his cloak. He answered cheerily, "Trust to me, dear boy," and sat like a statue. Meanwhile the galley, which was skillfully handled, had crossed us, let us come up with her, and fallen alongside. Leaving just room enough for the play of the oars, she kept alongside, drifting when we drifted, and pulling a stroke or two when we pulled. Of the two sitters, one held the rudder lines, and looked at us attentively—as did all the rowers; the other sitter was wrapped up, much as Provis was, and seemed to shrink and whisper some instruction to the steerer as he looked at us. Not a word was spoken in either boat.

Startop could make out, after a few minutes, which steamer was first, and gave me the word "Hamburg," in a low voice as we sat face to face. She was nearing us very fast, and the beating of her paddles grew louder and louder. I felt as if her shadow were absolutely upon us, when the galley hailed us. I answered.

"You have a returned transport there," said the man who held the lines. "That's the man, wrapped in the cloak. His name is Abel Magwitch, otherwise Provis. I apprehend that man, and call upon him to surrender, and you to assist."

At the same moment, without giving any audible direction to his crew, he ran the galley aboard of us. They had pulled one sudden stroke ahead, had got their oars in, had run athwart us, and were holding on to our gunwale before we knew what they were doing. This caused great confusion on board of the steamer, and I heard them calling to us, and heard the order given to stop the paddles, and heard them stop, but felt her driving down upon us irresistibly. In the same moment, I saw the steersman of the galley lay his hand on his prisoner's shoulder, and saw that both boats were swinging round with the force of the tide, and saw that all hands on board the steamer were running forward frantically. Still in the same moment, I saw the prisoner start up, lean across his captor, and pull the cloak from the neck of the shrinking sitter in the galley. Still in the same moment, I saw that the face disclosed was the face of the other convict of long ago. Still in the same moment, I saw the face tilt backward with a white terror on it that I shall never forget, and heard a great cry on board the steamer and a loud splash in the water, and felt the boat sink from under me.

It was but for an instant that I seemed to struggle; that instant past I was taken on board the galley. Herbert was there, and Startop was there; but our boat was gone, and the two convicts were gone.

What with the cries aboard the steamer, and the furious blowing off of her steam, and her driving on, and our driving on, I could not at first distinguish sky from water or shore from shore; but the crew of the galley righted her with great speed, and, pulling certain swift strong strokes ahead, lay upon their oars, every man looking silently and eagerly at the water astern. Presently a dark object was seen in it, bearing toward us on the tide. No man spoke, but the steersman kept the boat straight and true before it. As it came nearer, I saw it to be Magwitch, swimming, but not freely. He was taken on board, and instantly manacled at the wrists and ankles.

The galley was kept steady, and the silent eager lookout at the water was resumed. But the Rotterdam steamer now came up, and apparently not understanding what had happened, came on at speed. By the time she had been hailed and stopped, both steamers were drifting away from us, and we were rising and falling in a troubled wake of water. The lookout was kept long after all was still again, and the two steamers were gone; but everybody knew that it was hopeless now.

At length we gave it up, and pulled under the shore toward the tavern we had lately left. Here, I was able to get some comforts for Magwitch—Provis no longer—who had received some very severe injury in the chest and a deep cut in the head.

He told me that he believed himself to have gone under the keel of the steamer, and to have been struck on the head in rising. The injury to his chest (which rendered his breathing extremely painful) he thought he had received against the side of the galley. He added that he did not pretend to say what he might have done to Compeyson, but that in the moment of his laying his hand on his cloak to identify him, that villain had staggered up and back, and they had both gone overboard together; when the sudden wrenching of Magwitch out of our boat had capsized us. He told me in a whisper that they had gone down, fiercely locked in each other's arms, and that there had been a struggle underwater, and that he had disengaged himself, struck out, and swum away.

I never had any reason to doubt the exact truth of what he had told me. The officer who steered the galley gave the same account of their going overboard.

When I asked this officer's permission to change the prisoner's wet clothes by purchasing any spare garments I could get at the public house, he gave it readily, merely observing that he must take charge of everything his prisoner had about him. So the pocketbook which had once been in my hands passed into the officer's. He further gave me leave to accompany the prisoner to London, but declined to accord that grace to my two friends.

We remained at the public house until the

tide turned, and then Magwitch was carried down to the galley and put on board. Herbert and Startop were to get to London by land, as soon as they could. We had a doleful parting, and when I took my place by Magwitch's side, I felt that that was my place henceforth while he lived.

For now my repugnance to him had all melted away, and in the hunted, wounded, shackled creature who held my hand in his, I only saw a man who had meant to be my benefactor, and who had felt affectionately, gratefully, and generously toward me with great constancy through a series of years. I only saw in him a much better man than I had been to Joe.

His breathing became more difficult and painful as the night drew on, and often he could not repress a groan. I tried to rest him on the arm I could use, in any easy position; but it was dreadful to think that I could not be sorry at heart for his being badly hurt, since it was unquestionably best that he should die. That there were, still living, people enough who were able and willing to identify him, I could not doubt. That he would be leniently treated, I could not hope—he who had been presented in the worst light at his trial, who had since broken prison and been tried again, who had returned from transportation under a life sentence, and who had occasioned the death of the man who was the cause of his arrest.

As we returned toward the setting sun we had yesterday left behind us, and as the stream of our hopes seemed all running back, I told him how grieved I was to think he had come home for my sake.

"Dear boy," he answered, "I'm quite content to take my chance. I've seen my boy, and he can be a gentleman without me."

No. I had thought about that while we had been there side by side. I foresaw that, being convicted, his possessions would be forfeited to the Crown.[6]

"Look'ee here, dear boy," said he. "It's best as a gentleman should not be knowed to belong to me now. Only come to see me as if you come by chance alonger Wemmick. Sit where I can see you when I am swore to, for the last o' many times, and I don't ask no more."

"I will never stir from your side," said I, "when I am suffered to be near you. Please God, I will be as true to you as you have been to me!"

I felt his hand tremble as it held mine, and he turned his face away as he lay in the bottom of the boat, and I heard that old sound in his throat—softened now, like all the rest of him. It was a good thing that he had touched this point, for it put into my mind what I might not otherwise have thought of until too late: that he need never know how his hopes of enriching me had perished.

Chapter 40

Mr. Wemmick takes a walk.

He was taken to the Police court next day, and would have been immediately committed for trial, but that it was necessary to send down for an old officer of the prison ship from which he had once escaped, to speak to his identity. Nobody doubted it; but Compeyson, who had meant to depose to it, was dead. I had gone direct to Mr. Jaggers at his private house, on my arrival overnight, to retain his assistance, but he told me that no power on earth could prevent its going against us. I imparted to Mr. Jaggers my design of

6. **forfeited** (fôr′fĭt-əd) **to the Crown:** taken by the government, which had the legal right to the possessions of a prisoner in Magwitch's position.

keeping him in ignorance of the fate of his wealth. Mr. Jaggers was angry with me for having "let it slip through my fingers," and said we must try at all events for some of it. But he did not conceal from me that although there might be many cases in which forfeiture would not be exacted, there were no circumstances in this case to make it one of them. I understood that very well. I was not related to the outlaw, or connected with him by any recognizable tie. I had no claim, and I resolved that my heart should never be sickened with the hopeless task of attempting to establish one.

There appeared to be reason for supposing that the drowned informer had hoped for a reward, and had obtained some accurate knowledge of Magwitch's affairs. When his body was found, many miles from the scene of his death, notes were still legible, folded in a case he carried. Among these were the name of a banking house in New South Wales where a sum of money was, and the designation of certain lands of considerable value. Both those heads of information were in a list that Magwitch, while in prison, gave to Mr. Jaggers, of the possessions he supposed I should inherit. His ignorance, poor fellow, at last served him; he never mistrusted but that my inheritance was quite safe, with Mr. Jaggers' aid.

After three days' delay, he was committed to take his trial at the next session, which would come on in a month.

It was at this dark time of my life that Herbert returned home one evening, a good deal cast down, and said:

"My dear Handel, I fear I shall soon have to leave you."

His partner having prepared me for that, I was less surprised than he thought.

"We shall lose a fine opportunity if I put off going to Cairo, and I am very much afraid I must go, Handel, when you most need me."

"Herbert, I shall always need you, because I shall always love you; but my need is no greater now than at another time."

"You will be so lonely."

"I have not leisure to think of that," said I. "You know that I am always with him to the full extent of the time allowed, and that I should be with him all day long, if I could. And when I come away from him, you know that my thoughts are with him."

"My dear fellow," said Herbert, "let the near prospect of our separation be my justification for troubling you about yourself. Have you thought of your future? In this branch house of ours, Handel, we must have a——"

I saw that his delicacy was avoiding the right word, so I said, "A clerk."

"A clerk. And I hope it is not at all unlikely that he may expand into a partner. Now, Handel—in short, my dear boy, will you come to me? Clara and I have talked about it again and again," Herbert pursued, "and the dear little thing begged me only this evening to say that if you will live with us when we come together, she will do her best to make you happy."

I thanked her heartily, and I thanked him heartily, but said I could not yet make sure of joining him.

"But if you thought, Herbert, that you could, without doing any injury to your business, leave the question open for a little while——"

"For any while," cried Herbert. "Six months, a year!"

"Not so long as that," said I. "Two or three months at most."

Herbert was highly delighted when we shook hands on this arrangement, and said he could now take courage to tell me that he believed he must go away at the end of the week.

On the Saturday in that same week, I took my leave of Herbert as he sat on one of the seaport mail coaches. I then went to my lonely home—if it deserved the name, for it was now no home to me, and I had no home anywhere.

On the stairs I encountered Wemmick. I had not seen him alone since the disastrous issue of the attempted flight; and he had come, in his private and personal capacity, to say a few words in reference to that failure.

"The late Compeyson," said Wemmick, "had by little and little got at the bottom of half of the regular business now transacted, and it was from the talk of some of his people in trouble that I heard what I did. I kept my ears open until I heard that he was absent, and I thought that would be the best time for making the attempt. I can only suppose now that it was a part of his policy, as a very clever man, habitually to deceive his own instruments. You don't blame me, I hope, Mr. Pip? I'm sure I tried to serve you, with all my heart."

"I am as sure of that, Wemmick, as you can be, and I thank you most earnestly for all your interest and friendship."

I invited Wemmick to come upstairs and refresh himself with a glass of grog before walking to Walworth. He accepted but appeared rather fidgety.

"What do you think of my meaning to take a holiday on Monday, Mr. Pip?"

"Why, I suppose you have not done such a thing these twelve months."

"These twelve years, more likely," said Wemmick. "Yes. I'm going to take a holiday. More than that; I'm going to take a walk. More than that; I'm going to ask you to take a walk with me. It ain't a long walk, and it's an early one. Say it might occupy you (including breakfast on the walk), from eight to twelve. Couldn't you stretch a point and manage it?"

He had done so much for me that this was very little to do for him. I said I could manage it—would manage it—and he was so very much pleased that I was pleased too.

Punctual to my appointment, I rang at the Castle gate on the Monday morning, and was received by Wemmick himself, who struck me as looking tighter[1] than usual, and having a sleeker hat on.

When we had fortified ourselves with biscuits and were going out for the walk, I was considerably surprised to see Wemmick take up a fishing rod and put it over his shoulder. "Why, we are not going fishing!" said I. "No," returned Wemmick, "but I like to walk with one."

I thought this odd; however, I said nothing, and we set off. We went toward Camberwell Green, and when we were thereabouts, Wemmick said suddenly:

"Halloa! Here's a church!"

There was nothing very surprising in that; but again, I was rather surprised when he said, as if he were animated by a brilliant idea:

"Let's go in!"

We went in, Wemmick leaving his fishing rod in the porch, and looked all round. In the meantime, Wemmick was diving into his coat pockets and getting something out of paper there.

"Halloa!" said he. "Here's a couple of pair of gloves! Let's put 'em on!"

As the gloves were white kid gloves, I now began to have my strong suspicions. They were strengthened into certainty when I beheld the Aged enter at a side door, escorting a lady.

"Halloa!" said Wemmick. "Here's Miss Skiffins! Let's have a wedding."

The clerk and clergyman then appeared, and true to his notion of seeming to do it all without preparation, I heard Wemmick say to himself as he took something out of his waistcoat pocket before the service began, "Halloa! Here's a ring!"

I acted in the capacity of best man to the

1. **tighter:** neater.

bridegroom, while the responsibility of giving the lady away devolved upon the Aged.

"*Now*, Mr. Pip," said Wemmick, triumphantly shouldering the fishing rod as we came out, "let me ask you whether anybody would suppose this to be a wedding party!"

Breakfast had been ordered at a pleasant little tavern a mile or so away. We had an excellent breakfast, and when anyone declined anything on the table, Wemmick said, "Provided by contract, you know; don't be afraid of it!" I drank to the new couple, drank to the Aged, drank to the Castle, saluted the bride at parting, and made myself as agreeable as I could.

Chapter 41

Pip takes final leave of Magwitch.

He lay in prison very ill during the whole interval between his committal for trial and the coming round of the sessions. He had broken two ribs, they had wounded one of his lungs, and he breathed with great pain and difficulty, which increased daily. Being far too ill to remain in the common prison, he was removed, after the first day or so, into the infirmary. This gave me opportunities of being with him that I could not otherwise have had. And but for his illness he would have been put into irons, for he was regarded as a determined prison breaker, and I know not what else.

Although I saw him every day, it was for only a short time. I do not recollect that I once saw any change in him for the better; he wasted and became slowly weaker and worse day by day from the day when the prison door closed upon him.

When the sessions came round, Mr. Jaggers caused an application to be made for the postponement of his trial and was refused. The trial came on at once, and when he was put to the bar, he was seated in a chair. No objection was made to my getting close to the dock and holding the hand that he stretched out to me.

The trial was very short and very clear. Such things as could be said for him were said—how he had taken to industrious habits, and had thriven[1] lawfully and reputably. But nothing could unsay the fact that he had returned, and was there in presence of the judge and jury. It was impossible not to try him for that, and do otherwise than find him guilty.

At that time it was the custom (as I learned from my terrible experience of that sessions) to devote a concluding day to the passing of sentences, and to make a finishing effect with the sentence of death. I saw two-and-thirty men and women put before the judge to receive that sentence together. Foremost among the two-and-thirty was he; seated, that he might get breath enough to keep life in him.

Penned in the dock, as I again stood outside it at the corner with his hand in mine, were the two-and-thirty men and women; some defiant, some stricken with terror, some sobbing and weeping, some covering their faces, some staring gloomily about. There had been shrieks from among the women convicts, but they had been stilled, and a hush had succeeded.

Then, the judge addressed them. Among the wretched creatures before him whom he must single out for special address, was one who almost from his infancy had been an offender against the laws; who, after repeated imprisonments and punishments, had been at length sentenced to exile for a term of years; and who, under circumstances of great violence and daring, had made his escape and been resentenced to exile for life. That miserable man would seem for a time to have become convinced of his errors, when far removed

---

1. **thriven** (thrĭv′ən): thrived; succeeded; prospered.

from the scenes of his old offenses, and to have lived a peaceable and honest life. But in a fatal moment, he had quitted his haven of rest and repentance, and had come back to the country where he was proscribed.[2] Being here presently denounced, he had for a time succeeded in·evading the officers of justice, but being at length seized while in the act of flight, he had resisted them, and had—he best knew whether by express design, or in the blindness of his hardihood—caused the death of his denouncer, to whom his whole career was known. The appointed punishment for his return to the land that had cast him out being death, he must prepare himself to die.

The sun was striking in at the great windows of the court, through the glittering drops of rain upon the glass, and it made a broad shaft of light between the two-and-thirty and the judge. Rising for a moment, a distinct speck of face in this way of light, the prisoner said, "My Lord, I have received my sentence of death from the Almighty, but I bow to yours," and sat down again.

I began that night to write out a petition to the Home Secretary of State, setting forth my knowledge of him and how it was that he had come back for my sake. I wrote as fervently and pathetically as I could, and when I had finished it and sent it in, I wrote out other petitions to such men in authority as I hoped were the most merciful, and drew up one to the Crown itself. For several days and nights after he was sentenced I took no rest, except when I fell asleep in my chair, but was wholly absorbed in these appeals. The daily visits I could make him were shortened now, and he was more strictly kept. Nobody was hard with him or with me. There was duty to be done, and it was done, but not harshly. Sometimes he was almost unable to speak; then, he would answer

2. **proscribed:** banished.

me with slight pressures on my hand, and I grew to understand his meaning very well.

The number of days had risen to ten, when I saw a greater change in him than I had seen yet. His eyes were turned toward the door, and lighted up as I entered.

"Dear boy," he said, as I sat down by his bed, "I thought you was late. But I knowed you couldn't be that."

"It is just the time," said I. "I waited for it at the gate."

"You always waits at the gate; don't you, dear boy?"

"Yes. Not to lose a moment of the time."

"Thank'ee dear boy, thank'ee. God bless you! You've never deserted me, dear boy."

I pressed his hand in silence, for I could not forget that I had once meant to desert him.

"And what's the best of all," he said, "you've been more comfortable alonger me since I was under a dark cloud, than when the sun shone. That's best of all."

He lay on his back, breathing with great difficulty. Do what he would, and love me though he did, the light left his face ever and again, and a film came over the placid look at the white ceiling.

"Are you in much pain today?"

"I don't complain of none, dear boy."

"You never do complain."

He had spoken his last words. He smiled, and I understood his touch to mean that he wished to lift my hand, and lay it on his breast. I laid it there, and he smiled again, and put both his hands upon it.

The allotted time ran out while we were thus; but, looking round, I found the governor of the prison standing near me, and he whispered, "You needn't go yet." I thanked him gratefully, and asked, "Might I speak to him, if he can hear me?"

The governor stepped aside and beckoned the officer away. The change, though it was made without noise, drew back the film from the placid look at the white ceiling, and he looked most affectionately at me.

"Dear Magwitch, I must tell you, now, at last. You understand what I say?"

A gentle pressure on my hand.

"You had a child once, whom you loved and lost."

A stronger pressure on my hand.

"She lived and found powerful friends. She is living now. She is a lady and very beautiful. And I love her!"

With a last faint effort, which would have been powerless but for my yielding to it, and assisting it, he raised my hands to his lips. Then he gently let it sink upon his breast again, with his own hands lying on it. The placid look at the white ceiling came back, and passed away, and his head dropped quietly on his breast.

I thought of the two men who went up into the Temple to pray, and I knew there were no better words that I could say beside his bed than, "O Lord, be merciful to him, a sinner!"[3]

Chapter 42

An old friend comes to Pip's rescue.

Now that I was left wholly to myself, I gave notice of my intention to quit the chambers in the Temple as soon as my tenancy could legally determine, and in the meanwhile to underlet them.[1] I was in debt, and had scarcely any money, and I began to be seriously alarmed by the state of my affairs. Moreover, I was falling very ill. The late stress upon me had enabled me to put off illness, but not to put it away; I knew that it was coming on me now.

For a day or two I lay on the sofa, or on the floor—anywhere, according as I happened to sink down—with a heavy head and aching limbs, and no purpose, and no power. Then there came one night which appeared of great duration, and which teemed with anxiety and horror; and when in the morning I tried to sit up in my bed and think of it, I found I could not do so. Then I saw two men looking at me.

"What do you want?" I asked, starting. "I don't know you."

"Well, sir," returned one of them, bending down and touching me on the shoulder, "you're arrested."

"What is the debt?"

"Hundred and twenty-three pound, fifteen, six. Jeweler's account, I think."

I made some attempt to get up and dress myself. When I next attended to them, they were standing a little off from the bed, looking at me. I still lay there.

"You see my state," said I. "I would come with you if I could; but indeed I am quite unable. If you take me from here, I think I shall die by the way."

As they hang in my memory by only this one slender thread, I don't know what they did, except that they forbore to[2] remove me.

That I had a fever and was avoided, that I suffered greatly, I know of my own remembrance, and did in some sort know at the time. I was delirious and sometimes struggled with real people, in the belief that they were murderers, but above all, I knew that there was a constant tendency in all these people to settle down into the likeness of Joe.

After I had turned the worst point of my illness, I opened my eyes in the night, and I saw in the great chair at the bedside, Joe. I opened

3. **"O Lord, . . . sinner!":** From Luke 18:10.
1. **I gave . . . them:** Pip gave notice that he would leave his apartment as soon as his lease could be terminated and in the meantime would sublet the rooms.

2. **forbore to:** refrained from; did not.

my eyes in the day, and, sitting on the window seat, smoking his pipe in the shaded open window, still I saw Joe. I asked for cooling drink, and the dear hand that gave it me was Joe's. I sank back on my pillow after drinking, and the face that looked so hopefully and tenderly upon me was the face of Joe.

At last one day I took courage, and said. "*Is it Joe?*"

And the dear old home voice answered, "Which it air, old chap."

"Oh, Joe, you break my heart! Look angry at me, Joe. Strike me, Joe. Tell me of my ingratitude. Don't be so good to me!"

For Joe had actually laid his head down on the pillow at my side and put his arm round my neck, in his joy that I knew him.

"Which dear old Pip, old chap," said Joe, "you and me was ever friends. And when you're well enough to go out for a ride—what larks!"

After which, Joe withdrew to the window and stood with his back toward me, wiping his eyes. And as my extreme weakness prevented me from getting up and going to him, I lay there, penitently whispering, "O God, bless him! O God, bless this gentle Christian man!"

Joe's eyes were red when I next found him beside me, but I was holding his hand and we both felt happy.

"Have you been here all the time, dear Joe?"

"Pretty nigh, old chap. For, as I says to Biddy when the news of your being ill were brought by letter, you might be amongst strangers, and you and me having been ever friends, a wisit at such a moment might not prove unacceptabobble. And Biddy, her word were, 'Go to him, without loss of time.'" There Joe cut himself off short, and informed me I was to be talked to in great moderation. So I lay quiet while he proceeded to indite a note to Biddy, with my love in it.

Evidently Biddy had taught Joe to write. As I lay in bed looking at him, it made me, in my weak state, cry with pleasure to see the pride with which he set about his letter. He got on very well indeed, and when he had signed his name, he got up and hovered about the table, trying the effect of his performance from various points of view, with unbounded satisfaction.

Not to make Joe uneasy by talking too much, even if I had been able to talk much, I deferred asking him about Miss Havisham until next day. He shook his head when I then asked him if she had recovered.

"Is she dead, Joe?"

"Why, you see, old chap," said Joe, by way of getting at it by degrees, "I wouldn't go so far as to say that, for that's a deal to say; but she ain't living."

"Did she linger long, Joe?"

"Arter you was took ill, pretty much about what you might call a week," said Joe, still determined, on my account, to come at everything by degrees.

"Dear Joe, have you heard what becomes of her property?"

"Well, old chap," said Joe, "it do appear that she had settled the most of it on Miss Estella. But she had wrote out a little coddleshell[3] in her own hand a day or two afore the accident, leaving a cool four thousand to Mr. Matthew Pocket. And why do you suppose, above all things, Pip, she left that cool four thousand unto him? 'Because of Pip's account of him, the said Matthew.' I am told by Biddy, that air the writing," said Joe.

This account gave me great joy, as it perfected the only good thing I had done. I asked Joe whether any of the other relations had any legacies.

"Miss Sarah," said Joe, "she has twenty-five

---

3. **coddleshell:** Joe means *codicil* (kŏd′ə-sĭl), an item of instruction added to a will.

pound perannium fur to buy pills. Miss Georgiana, she has twenty, Mrs.—what's the name of them wild beasts with humps?"

"Camels?" said I, wondering why he could want to know.

Joe nodded. "Mrs. Camels," by which I understood he meant Camilla, "she have five pounds fur to buy rushlights to put her in spirits when she wake up in the night. And now," said Joe, "you can take in one more shovelful today. Old Orlick he's been a-bustin' open a dwelling 'ouse."

"Whose?" said I.

"Not, I grant you, but what his manners is given to blusterous. Still, an Englishman's 'ouse is his castle, and castles must not be busted 'cept when done in wartime. And wotsume'er the failings on his part, he were a corn and seedsman in his heart."

"Is it Pumblechook's house that has been broken into, then?"

"That's it, Pip," said Joe, "and they took his till, and they took his cashbox, and they drinked his wine, and they partook of his wittles, and they slapped his face, and they pulled his nose, and they tied him up to his bedpust, and they stuffed his mouth full of flowering annuals to perwent his crying out. But he knowed Orlick, and Orlick's in the county jail."

By these approaches we arrived at unrestricted conversation. I was slow to gain strength, but I did slowly and surely become less weak, and Joe stayed with me, and I fancied I was little Pip again.

For the tenderness of Joe was so beautifully proportioned to my need that I was like a child in his hands. He would sit and talk to me in the old confidence, and with the old simplicity, and in the old unassertive protecting way, so that I would half believe that all my life since the days of the old kitchen was one of the mental troubles of the fever that was gone.

We looked forward to the day when I should go out for a ride. And when the day came and an open carriage was got into the lane, Joe wrapped me up, took me in his arms, and carried me down to it, as if I were still the small helpless creature to whom he had so abundantly given of the wealth of his great nature. When we got back again and he carried me across the court and up the stairs, I thought of that eventful Christmas Day when he had carried me over the marshes. We had not yet made any allusion to my change of fortune, nor did I know how much of my late history he was acquainted with.

"Have you heard, Joe," I asked him that evening, as he smoked his pipe at the window, "who my patron was?"

"I heered," returned Joe, "as it were not Miss Havisham, old chap."

"Did you hear who it was, Joe?"

"Well! I heered as it were a person what sent the person what give you the bank notes at the Jolly Bargemen, Pip."

"So it was."

"Astonishing!" said Joe, in the placidest way.

"Did you hear that he was dead, Joe?"

"Which? Him as sent the bank notes, Pip?"

"Yes."

"I think," said Joe, after meditating a long time, and looking rather evasively at the window seat, "as I *did* hear tell that how he were something or another in a general way in that direction."

"Did you hear anything of his circumstances, Joe?"

"Not partickler, Pip."

"If you would like to hear, Joe—" I was beginning, when Joe got up and came to my sofa.

"Look'ee here, old chap," said Joe, bending over me. "Ever the best of friends; ain't us, Pip?"

I was ashamed to answer him.

"Wery good, then," said Joe, as if I *had* answered, "that's all right; that's agreed upon. Then why go into subjects, old chap, which as betwixt two sech must be forever onnecessary?"

The delicacy with which Joe dismissed this theme made a deep impression on my mind. But whether Joe knew how poor I was, and how my great expectations had all dissolved, like our own marsh mists before the sun, I could not understand.

Another thing in Joe that I could not understand when it first began to develop itself, was this. As I became stronger and better, Joe became a little less easy with me. In my weakness and entire dependence on him, the dear fellow had fallen into the old tone, and called me by the old names, the dear "old Pip, old chap," that now were music in my ears. I too had fallen into the old ways, only happy and thankful that he let me. But imperceptibly, though I held by them fast, Joe's hold upon them began to slacken; and I soon began to understand that the fault of it was all mine.

It was on the third or fourth occasion of my going out walking that I saw this change in him very plainly. We had been sitting in the bright warm sunlight, looking at the river, and I chanced to say as we got up:

"See, Joe! I can walk quite strongly. Now, you shall see me walk back by myself."

"Do not overdo it, Pip," said Joe; "but I shall be happy fur to see you able, sir."

The last word grated on me; but how could I remonstrate! I walked no farther than the gate of the gardens, and then pretended to be weaker than I was, and asked Joe for his arm. Joe gave it me, but was thoughtful.

I, for my part, was thoughtful too. I was ashamed to tell him exactly how I was placed. He would want to help me out of his little savings, I knew, and I knew that he ought not to help me, and that I must not suffer him to do it.

It was a thoughtful evening with both of us. Before we went to bed, I had resolved that I would wait over tomorrow, tomorrow being Sunday, and would begin my new course with the new week. On Monday morning I would speak to Joe and tell him what I had in my thoughts.

We had a quiet day on the Sunday, and we rode out into the country, and then walked in the fields. At night, when I had gone to bed, Joe came into my room as he had done all through my recovery. He asked me if I felt sure that I was as well as in the morning.

"Yes, dear Joe, quite."

"And are always a-getting stronger, old chap?"

"Yes, dear Joe, steadily."

Joe patted the coverlet on my shoulder with his great good hand and said, in what I thought a husky voice, "Good night!"

When I got up in the morning, refreshed and stronger yet, I was full of my resolution to tell Joe all, without delay. I went to his room, and he was not there. Not only was he not there, but his box was gone.

I hurried then to the breakfast table and on it found a letter. These were its brief contents.

Not wishful to intrude I have departed fur you are well again dear Pip and will do better without

                                        Jo.

P.S. Ever the best of friends.

Enclosed in the letter was a receipt for the debt and costs on which I had been arrested. Down to that moment I had vainly supposed that my creditor had withdrawn until I should be quite recovered. I had never dreamed of Joe's having paid the money; but Joe had paid it, and the receipt was in his name.

What remained for me now, but to follow him to the dear old forge and there to have out my disclosure to him, and my penitent remonstrance with him, and there to relieve my mind and heart of another idea, which had begun as a vague something lingering in my thoughts and had formed into a settled purpose.

The purpose was that I would go to Biddy, that I would show her how humbled and repentant I came back, that I would tell her how I had lost all I once hoped for. Then I would say to her, "Biddy, I think you once liked me very well, when my errant heart, even while it strayed away from you, was quieter and better with you than it ever has been since. If you can like me only half as well once more, if you can take me with all my faults and disappointments on my head, if you can receive me like a forgiven child, I hope I am a little worthier of you than I was—not much, but a little. And Biddy, it shall rest with you to say whether I shall work at the forge with Joe, or whether I shall try for any different occupation down in this country, or whether we shall go away to a distant place where an opportunity awaits me which I set aside when it was offered, until I knew your answer. And now, dear Biddy, if you can tell me that you will go through the world with me, you will surely make it a better world for me, and me a better man for it, and I will try hard to make it a better world for you."

Such was my purpose. After three days more of recovery, I went down to the old place, to put it in execution. And how I sped in it is all I have left to tell.

Chapter 43

Biddy and Joe have news for Pip.

The tidings of my high fortunes having had a heavy fall had got down to my native place and its neighborhood before I got there. I found the Blue Boar in possession of the intelligence, and I found that it made a great change in the Boar's demeanor.

It was evening when I arrived, much fatigued by the journey. The Boar could not put me into my usual bedroom, which was engaged (probably by someone who had expectations), and could only assign me a very indifferent chamber among the pigeons. But I had as sound a sleep and the quality of my dreams was about the same as in the best bedroom.

Early in the morning I strolled round by Satis House. There were printed bills on the gate announcing a sale by auction of the household furniture and effects next week. The house itself was to be sold as old building materials, and pulled down. The ivy had been torn down, and much of it trailed low in the dust and was withered already. Stepping in for a moment at the open gate and looking around me with the uncomfortable air of a stranger who had no business there, I saw the auctioneer's clerk walking on the casks and telling them off for the information of a catalogue compiler, pen in hand, who made a temporary desk of the wheeled chair I had so often pushed along.

It was the pleasanter to turn to Biddy and to Joe. I went toward them slowly, for my limbs were weak, but with a sense of increasing relief as I drew nearer to them, and a sense of leaving arrogance and untruthfulness farther and farther behind.

The June weather was delicious. The sky was blue, the larks were soaring high over the green corn. I thought all that countryside more beautiful and peaceful by far than I had ever known it to be yet. Many pleasant pictures of the life that I would lead there, and of the change for the better that would come over my character when I had a guiding spirit at my side whose simple faith and clear home wisdom I had proved, beguiled my way. They awakened a tender emotion in me, for my heart was softened by my return, and such a change had come to pass that I felt like one who was toiling home barefoot from distant travel, and whose wanderings had lasted many years.

The schoolhouse where Biddy was mistress, I had never seen, but the little round-about lane by which I entered the village for quietness' sake took me past it. I was disappointed to find that the day was a holiday, no children were there, and Biddy's house was closed. Some hopeful notion of seeing her, busily engaged in her daily duties, before she saw me, had been in my mind and was defeated.

But the forge was a very short distance off, and I went toward it under the sweet green limes, listening for the clink of Joe's hammer. But the clink of Joe's hammer was not in the midsummer wind.

Almost fearing without knowing why to come in view of the forge, I saw it at last, and saw that it was closed. No gleam of fire, no glittering shower of sparks, no roar of bellows; all shut up, and still.

But the house was not deserted, and the best parlor seemed to be in use, for there were white curtains fluttering in its window, and the window was open and gay with flowers. I went softly toward it, meaning to peek over the flowers, when Joe and Biddy stood before me, arm in arm.

At first Biddy gave a cry, as if she thought it was my apparition, but in another moment she was in my embrace. I wept to see her, and she wept to see me; I, because she looked so fresh and pleasant; she, because I looked so worn and white.

"But, dear Biddy, how smart you look!"

"Yes, dear Pip."

"And Joe, how smart *you* look!"

"Yes, dear old Pip, old chap."

I looked at both of them, from one to the other, and then——

"It's my wedding day," cried Biddy, in a burst of happiness, "and I am married to Joe!"

They had taken me into the kitchen, and I had laid my head down on the old deal table. Biddy held one of my hands to her lips, and Joe's restoring touch was on my shoulder. "Which he warn't strong enough, my dear, to be surprised," said Joe. And Biddy said, "I ought to have thought of it, dear Joe, but I was too happy." They were both so overjoyed to see me, so proud to see me, so touched by my coming to them, so delighted that I should have come by accident to make their day complete!

My first thought was one of great thankfulness that I had never breathed this last baffled hope to Joe. How often, while he was with me in my illness, had it risen to my lips.

"Dear Biddy," said I, "you have the best husband in the whole world, and if you could have seen him by my bed you would have——But no, you couldn't love him better than you do."

"No, I couldn't indeed," said Biddy.

"And, dear Joe, you have the best wife in the whole world, and she will make you as happy as even you deserve to be, you dear, good, noble Joe!"

Joe looked at me with a quivering lip, and fairly put his sleeve before his eyes.

"And Joe and Biddy both, receive my humble thanks for all you have done for me, and all I have so ill repaid! And when I say that I am going away within the hour, for I am soon going abroad, and I shall never rest until I have worked for the money with which you have kept me out of prison, and have sent it to you, don't think, dear Joe and Biddy, that if I could repay it a thousand times over, I suppose I could cancel a farthing of the debt I owe you, or that I would do so if I could!"

They were both melted by these words, and both entreated me to say no more.

"But I must say more. Dear Joe, I hope you will have children to love, and that some little fellow will sit in this chimney corner of a winter night who may remind you of another little fellow gone out of it forever. Don't tell him, Joe, that I was thankless; don't tell him, Biddy, that I was ungenerous and unjust; only tell him that I honored you both, because you were both so good and true, and that, as your child, I said it would be natural to him to grow up a much better man than I did."

"I ain't a-going," said Joe, from behind his sleeve, "to tell him nothink o' that natur, Pip. Nor Biddy ain't."

"And now, though I know you have already done it in your own kind hearts, pray tell me, both, that you forgive me! Pray let me hear you say the words, that I may carry the sound of them away with me, and then I shall be able to believe that you can trust me, and think better of me, in the time to come!"

"Oh, dear old Pip, old chap," said Joe. "God knows as I forgive you, if I have anythink to forgive!"

"Amen! And God knows I do!" echoed Biddy.

"Now let me go up and look at my old little room and rest there a few minutes by myself. And then when I have eaten and drunk with you, go with me as far as the fingerpost,[1] dear Joe and Biddy, before we say goodbye!"

I sold all I had, and put aside as much as I could for my creditors—who gave me ample time to pay them in full—and I went out and joined Herbert. Within a month, I had quitted England, and within two months I was clerk to Clarriker and Co., and within four months I assumed my first undivided responsibility. For the beam across the parlor ceiling at Mill Pond Bank had then ceased to tremble under the old purser's growls and was at peace, and Herbert had gone away to marry Clara, and I was left in sole charge of the Eastern Branch until he brought her back.

Many a year went round before I was a partner in the house; but I lived happily with Herbert and his wife, and lived frugally, and paid my debts, and maintained a constant correspondence with Biddy and Joe. It was not until I became third in the firm that Clarriker betrayed me to Herbert; but he then declared

1. **fingerpost:** a signpost, often shaped like a pointing hand or finger.

that the secret of Herbert's partnership had been long enough upon his conscience, and he must tell it. So he told it, and Herbert was as much moved as amazed, and the dear fellow and I were not the worse friends for the long concealment. I must not leave it to be supposed that we were ever a great house, or that we made mints of money. We were not in a grand way of business, but we had a good name, and worked for our profits, and did very well. We owed so much to Herbert's ever cheerful industry and readiness that I often wondered how I had conceived that old idea of his inaptitude, until I was one day enlightened by the reflection that perhaps the inaptitude had never been in him at all, but had been in me.

Chapter 44

Pip and Estella meet again.

For eleven years I had not seen Joe nor Biddy when, upon an evening in December, an hour or two after dark, I laid my hand softly on the latch of the old kitchen door. I touched it so softly that I was not heard, and I looked in unseen. There, smoking his pipe in the old place by the kitchen firelight, as hale and as strong as ever, though a little gray, sat Joe; and there, fenced into the corner with Joe's leg, and sitting on my own little stool looking at the fire, was—I again!

"We giv' him the name of Pip for your sake, dear old chap," said Joe, delighted when I took another stool by the child's side, "and we hoped he might grow a little bit like you, and we think he do."

I thought so too, and I took him out for a walk next morning, and we talked immensely, understanding one another to perfection. And I took him down to the churchyard, and set him on a certain tombstone there, and he showed me from that elevation which stone was sacred to the memory of Philip Pirrip, late of this parish, and Also Georgiana, Wife of the Above.

"Biddy," said I, when I talked with her after dinner, as her little girl lay sleeping in her lap, "you must give Pip to me, one of these days; or lend him, at all events."

"No, no," said Biddy gently. "You must marry."

"So Herbert and Clara say, but I don't think I shall, Biddy. I have so settled down in their home that it's not at all likely. I am already quite an old bachelor."

Biddy looked down at her child, and put its little hand to her lips, and then put the good matronly hand with which she had touched it into mine. There was something in the action and in the light pressure of Biddy's wedding ring that had a very pretty eloquence in it.

"Dear Pip," said Biddy, "you are sure you don't fret for her?"

"Oh, no—I think not, Biddy."

"Tell me as an old friend. Have you quite forgotten her?"

"My dear Biddy, I have forgotten nothing in my life that ever had a foremost place there, and little that ever had any place there. But that poor dream, as I once used to call it, has all gone by, Biddy, all gone by!"

Dickens originally wrote only two more paragraphs to end the story, but because so many of his friends were dissatisfied with the conclusion, he rewrote the final paragraphs of the novel to read as follows. You will find the original ending on page 830.

Nevertheless, I knew while I said those words that I secretly intended to revisit the site of the old house that evening, alone, for her sake. Yes, even so. For Estella's sake.

I had heard of her as leading a most un-happy life, and as being separated from her husband, who had used her with great cruelty, and who had become quite renowned as a compound of pride, avarice, brutality, and meanness. And I had heard of the death of her husband, from an accident consequent on his ill treatment of a horse. This release had befallen her some two years before; for anything I knew she was married again.

The early dinner hour at Joe's left me time to walk over to the old spot before dark. There was no house now, no brewery, no building whatever left, but the wall of the old garden. The cleared space had been enclosed with a rough fence, and looking over it, I saw that some of the old ivy had struck root anew and was growing green on low quiet mounds of ruin. A gate in the fence standing ajar, I pushed it open and went in.

A cold silvery mist had veiled the afternoon, and the moon was not yet up to scatter it. But the stars were shining beyond the mist, and the moon was coming, and the evening was not dark. I could trace out where every part of the old house had been and was looking along the desolate garden walk, when I beheld a solitary figure in it.

The figure showed itself aware of me as I advanced. It had been moving toward me, but it stood still. As I drew nearer, I saw it to be the figure of a woman. Then, it faltered as if much surprised, and uttered my name, and I cried out:

"Estella!"

"I am greatly changed. I wonder you know me."

The freshness of her beauty was indeed gone, but its majesty and its charm remained. Those attractions in it, I had seen before; what I had never seen before was the saddened softened light of the once proud eyes; what I had never felt before was the friendly touch of the once insensible hand.

We sat down on a bench that was near, and I said, "After so many years, it is strange that we should thus meet again, Estella, here where our first meeting was! Do you often come back?"

"I have never been here since."

"Nor I."

The moon began to rise, and I thought of the prisoner's placid look at the white ceiling, which had passed away. The moon began to rise, and I thought of the pressure on my hand when I had spoken the last words he had heard on earth.

Estella was the next to break the silence.

"I have very often hoped and intended to come back, but have been prevented by many circumstances. Poor, poor old place!"

The silvery mist was touched with the first rays of the moonlight, and the same rays touched the tears that dropped from her eyes. Not knowing that I saw them, and setting herself to get the better of them, she said quietly:

"Were you wondering, as you walked along, how it came to be left in this condition?"

"Yes, Estella."

"The ground belongs to me. It is the only possession I have not relinquished. Everything else has gone from me, little by little, but I have kept this. It was the subject of the only determined resistance I made in all the wretched years."

"Is it to be built on?"

"At last it is. I came here to take leave of it before its change. And you," she said, in a voice of touching interest to a wanderer, "you live abroad still."

"Still."

"And do well, I am sure?"

"I work pretty hard for a sufficient living, and therefore—yes, I do well!"

"I have often thought of you," said Estella.

"Have you?"

"Of late, very often."

"You have always held your place in *my* heart," I answered.

And we were silent again until she spoke.

"I little thought," said Estella, "that I should take leave of you in taking leave of this spot. I am very glad to do so."

"Glad to part again, Estella? To me, parting is a painful thing. To me, the remembrance of our last parting has been ever mournful and painful."

"But you said to me," returned Estella, very earnestly, "'God bless you, God forgive you!' And if you could say that to me then, you will not hesitate to say that to me now —now, when suffering has been stronger than all other teaching, and has taught me to understand what your heart used to be. I have been bent and broken, but—I hope—into a better shape. Be as considerate and good to me as you were, and tell me we are friends."

"We are friends," said I, rising and bending over her, as she rose from the bench.

"And will continue friends apart," said Estella.

I took her hand in mine, and we went out of the ruined place; and as the morning mists had risen long ago when I first left the forge, so the evening mists were rising now, and in all the broad expanse of tranquil light they showed to me, I saw no shadow of another parting from her.

Great Expectations *originally ended with the following two paragraphs. In the original version, the final chapter was the same as the present one, up to the point where Pip tells Biddy, "that poor dream, as I once used to call it, has all gone by, Biddy, all gone by!" (See page 829.) From that point on, the original ending was as follows:*

It was two years more before I saw Estella. I had heard of her as leading a most unhappy life, and as being separated from her husband, who had used her with great cruelty, and who had become quite renowned as a compound of pride, brutality, and meanness. I had heard of the death of her husband from an accident consequent on ill treating a horse, and of her being married again to a Shropshire doctor who, against his interest, had once very manfully interposed on an occasion when he was in professional attendance on Mr. Drummle, and had witnessed some outrageous treatment of her. I had heard that the Shropshire doctor was not rich, and that they lived on her own personal fortune. I was in England again—in London, and walking along Piccadilly with little Pip—when a servant came running after me to ask would I step back to a lady in a carriage who wished to speak to me. It was a little pony carriage which the lady was driving, and the lady and I looked sadly enough on one another.

"I am greatly changed, I know; but I thought you would like to shake hands with Estella, too, Pip. Lift up that pretty child and let me kiss it!" (She supposed the child, I think, to be my child.) I was very glad afterward to have had the interview; for in her face and in her voice, and in her touch, she gave me the assurance that suffering had been stronger than Miss Havisham's teaching, and had given her a heart to understand what my heart used to be.

Reading Check

1. What are the two names the convict goes by?
2. What plan does Herbert propose for the convict's safety?
3. Who is Compeyson?
4. What does Pip ask Miss Havisham to do for Herbert?
5. What warning does Pip receive from Wemmick when he returns from Satis House?
6. Why does Pip begin to practice rowing?
7. What conclusion does Pip come to about Jaggers' housekeeper?
8. How is Pip injured?
9. What crime does Orlick reveal to Pip?
10. What happens to Pip's inheritance?

For Study and Discussion

Analyzing and Interpreting the Novel

Characters

1. In the first two stages of the novel, Pip does what other people tell him to do. Which of his actions in Stage 3 show a new independence of spirit?

2a. How has Pip changed from the snob he had become? b. What is his new attitude toward those who had been kind to him in the past? c. How is this change shown in Pip's actions toward Magwitch during and after his trial?

3a. In the third stage, which of Pip's experiences teach him the value of real friendship and affection? b. In particular, what does he learn from each of the following: meeting

Clara, Herbert's fiancée; hearing the story Pumblechook has told about him; being held prisoner by Orlick; being cared for by Joe?

4. During his last visit to Satis House, Pip says to Estella, ". . . you cannot choose but remain part of my character, part of the little good in me, part of the evil. But I associate you only with the good, for you must have done me far more good than harm." Do you agree with Pip that Estella has been the source of more good than harm? Explain.

5. Although Magwitch is a criminal, Dickens treats him with compassion, and he emerges as a character of great dignity. **a.** In what way has Magwitch been the victim of injustice? **b.** How does Dickens show the good as well as the evil in Magwitch's nature?

6. In *Great Expectations*, there are a number of characters who are **foils**—that is, these characters set each other off by contrast. Biddy and Estella are foils; clearly, the reader is intended to compare their natures and their influence on Pip. **a.** In what way are Magwitch and Miss Havisham foils? **b.** Pip and Herbert? **c.** Estella and Clara? **d.** Estella and Pip?

7. Characters who do not change in the course of a literary work are **static** characters. Characters who grow and develop are **dynamic** characters. How would you classify the following characters: Estella, Miss Havisham, Jaggers, Orlick, Herbert, Magwitch?

Plot

8. Dickens' masterful handling of plot and suspense is especially evident in his treatment of Molly. **a.** What clues does he provide to Molly's real identity? **b.** How does Molly's behavior, as observed by Pip, help to make Wemmick's story of the past convincing?

9. In this last stage of the novel, the threads of the plot come together as a logical design. **a.** Whom does Magwitch turn out to be related to? **b.** How did the other convict, Compeyson, swindle Miss Havisham? **c.** Who is Estella's mother?

10. The **climax** of a novel is usually the most exciting or dramatic part of the plot, the point at which the conflict is resolved and the outcome of the action decided. **a.** Which incident would you identify as the climax of *Great Expectations*? **b.** How does Dickens build suspense as he leads up to the climax?

11a. Which of Dickens' two endings do you prefer? Why? **b.** Which do you think is most faithful to the nature of the characters involved? **c.** Does Pip, by the end of the novel, still want to marry Estella? **d.** Does Estella, because of what she has experienced, deserve to be forgiven by Pip? **e.** Is it believable that she could have come to love him? **f.** Do you think these two can still care for each other?

Setting

12. In a way, Satis House is a symbol of Miss Havisham. **a.** How has she made it reflect her own state of mind? **b.** What is suggested by the stopped clocks? **c.** The dark passageways? **d.** The yellowed bridal gown? **e.** When Pip pulls the tablecloth off the table, spiders and beetles run out of the wedding cake. What does this suggest about Miss Havisham's lost love?

Theme

13. Throughout the novel Dickens deals with the contrast between appearance and reality, illusion and substance. After Pip learns who his benefactor is, Mr. Jaggers tells him: "Take nothing on its looks; take everything on evidence. There's no better rule" (page 780). Where in the novel has Pip been influenced by "looks" rather than by "evidence"?

14. While ill with fever, Pip realizes that his "great expectations had all dissolved, like our own marsh mists before the sun" (page 824). **a.** How is this statement, in a way, a summing-up of all that Pip has learned? **b.** In your own words, state what you think is the overall theme of *Great Expectations*.

Language and Vocabulary

Analyzing Words from Latin Roots

Pip's first feeling toward Magwitch is one of *repugnance*—a strong dislike. The word comes from the Latin prefix *re-*, which means "back," and the verb *pugnare*, which means "to fight." From the same root come the words *pugnacious*, *pugilism*, and *impugn*. What does each of these words have to do with the original meaning "to fight"? Use a dictionary to find the answer.

Compeyson had meant to *depose* to the real identity of Magwitch. *Depose* in this sense means "to testify under oath"; a *deposition* is a person's testimony. Both words come from the Latin word *deponere*, which itself is composed of the prefix *de-*, meaning "down" and the verb *ponere*, meaning "to place or put." *Deponere* means "to put down." Tell what meaning the word *depose* has in this sentence: "Richard II was *deposed* by his cousin, Henry Bolingbroke." How are both meanings of *depose* related to the Latin meaning "to put down"?

In English the root word *ponere* often appears as *pos-*, *pose-*, *pon-*, or *pone-*. Find the meanings of each of the following words by analyzing its structure. Use a dictionary if necessary.

| composure | impose | postponement |
| depository | interpose | purpose |

Focus on Literary Analysis

Organizing a Literary Analysis

In the **introduction** of a literary analysis, you state your main idea and give your audience any background they may need about the work. In the **body** of an analysis, you present the supporting evidence for your main idea. In the **conclusion,** you restate your main idea and summarize your major points.

You can use several methods to organize the details of a literary analysis. For example, if you discuss plot, you may use **chronological order.** If you focus on character, you may want to use **order of importance.** If you compare and contrast elements in one or two stories, you can use either of the frameworks outlined below:

Block Method	Point-by-Point Method
Discuss Subject 1	Discuss Feature A
Feature A	Subject 1
Feature B	Subject 2
Feature C	Discuss Feature B
Discuss Subject 2	Subject 1
Feature A	Subject 2
Feature B	Discuss Feature C
Feature C	Subject 1
	Subject 2

Write a detailed **outline** for an analysis of a literary work. Save your notes.

ANALYZING LITERATURE

*W*riters who analyze and evaluate literary works use specific evidence to support their ideas and arguments. This evidence may consist of quotations or inferences from the work itself, references to other works by the same author, facts about the author and his or her times, expert opinions, and material from a variety of other sources.

Read the following excerpt from a book of literary criticism about Charles Dickens. Write a sentence or two to sum up the author's main idea. Then make notes on how he supports that idea.

Dickens's portrayal of the clerk Wemmick in *Great Expectations* is meant to be humorous, yet nowhere in literature is the modern segregation of hearth and city, of personal life and business, so sharply and consciously drawn. Wemmick's tiny home in Walworth is a castle defended against the city. The eccentricity of its owner, his moat and drawbridge and secret communication with the outside, his livestock and cucumber frame, express the peril and safety of urban life: "if you can suppose the little place besieged, it would hold out a devil of a time in point of provisions." The whole conception of Wemmick's castle looks forward to that moment in the twentieth century when the advent of the hydrogen bomb caused a wave of shelter-building and stockpiling of powdered milk in the cities of the West. More obviously, the home life of John Wemmick uncannily resembles that of today's suburbanite: "I am my own engineer, and my own carpenter, and my own plumber, and my own gardener, and my own Jack-of-all-trades." The flash of Dickens's imagination in 1861 suddenly illuminates, in the midst of the division of labor on which the modern city is founded, that curious domestic and defensive regression to a past in which individuals performed all such tasks for themselves. This surge of independence in one aspect of the worker's life merely accentuates, and probably responds to, the increasing separation of his home from his economic function in the city. Wemmick, with his two personalities, is the very symbol of this separation: "No; the office is one thing, and private life is another. When I go into the office, I leave the Castle behind me, and when I come into the Castle, I leave the office behind me." That Wemmick adheres to this divided life with such conscious solemnity makes the point that much more universal and prophetic. For the joke is that he regards his radically divided life as perfectly natural.

—Alexander Welsh,
The City of Dickens

WRITING A LITERARY ANALYSIS

*T*he purpose of writing about literature may be to share your responses, provide information about a literary work, or evaluate a work in a review. In a **literary analysis,** you examine a literary work's separate elements, present a main idea, and support that idea with quotations and other details from the work. You have seen some of the elements of a literary analysis in the course of this unit. Now you will have the chance to write a literary analysis of a work of your own choice.

Prewriting ~~~

1. Start your prewriting with your own personal responses to a story, novel, play, or poem. What makes the work tick? How do you react to it? Jot down some notes on your feelings about the work you have chosen.

2. Move on now to a critical analysis. If you have selected a short story or novel, think about the major elements below:

- plot
- characters
- setting
- theme
- point of view

If you have chosen a play, think about these elements:

- plot
- dialogue
- theme
- stage directions

Here are some elements of poetry to consider:

- speaker
- imagery
- sound patterns
- figurative language
- tone
- structure
- theme

Use **questioning** to analyze the elements of a story. Here are some questions to ask yourself:

- What are the major conflicts, external and/or internal?
- What is the climax of the plot?
- What are the characters like? What are their motivations? Do they change?
- In what ways is the setting important? Does it contribute to the mood?
- How does point of view affect the story?
- What is the author's tone, or attitude toward the characters and events?
- What theme does the story suggest?

[See **Focus** assignment on page 729.]

3. Reread the work you have chosen to analyze slowly and carefully. This time, focus on one or two literary elements for closer analysis. As you read, jot down notes to identify a **main idea,** or overall thesis, for your essay. For example, if the work is a detective story, you might want to focus on the ways the author creates and maintains suspense. If the work features an especially interesting and complex main character, you might focus on how the author uses different methods of characterization.

4. Give some thought to your purpose, audience, and tone. In a literary analysis, your **purpose** is to give your readers a richer understanding of a literary work by sharing your ideas about it. Your **audience** is usually your teacher and your classmates. Assume that your audience has read the work that you have chosen. You will need to include details from the work to support your main idea, but you should not make your analysis a detailed summary of the plot. Use a fairly formal **tone**—one that shows that you've given the literature some careful thought.

5. State your main idea in one or two sentences. Then start gathering **details** to support your idea. You can use details of all kinds, including the following:

- plot events
- dialogue
- details of setting
- choice of words
- plot structure
- poetic devices

There is no specific number of details that you must include in an analysis to support your idea. At this stage, though, try to gather as many details as you can. Your goal is to make your main idea clear and convincing. [See **Focus** assignment on page 777.]

Writing ~~~

1. A literary analysis often consists of three parts, as follows:

I. Introduction: State main idea

II. Body: Support main idea with details

III. Conclusion: Restate main idea and summarize major points

In the **body** of your essay, organize your supporting details in a logical way. For example, if you focus on plot in your analysis, you may want to use **chronological order.** If you focus on character or theme, you may want to use **order of importance.**

2. If you use details to **compare and contrast** literary elements, you may find the frameworks outlined below especially helpful:

Block Method	Point-by-Point Method
Discuss Subject 1	Discuss Feature A
Feature A	Subject 1
Feature B	Subject 2
Feature C	Discuss Feature B
Discuss Subject 2	Subject 1
Feature A	Subject 2
Feature B	Discuss Feature C
Feature C	Subject 1
	Subject 2

[See **Focus** assignment on page 833.]

3. As you write the first draft of your analysis, be careful not to go off the track in two common ways:

a. writing just a summary of the plot

b. writing only your personal reaction

Your analysis should share ideas about the work, not just give information about what happens. Your personal responses, of course, were your starting point for the analysis. However, while your essay may include your reactions, it should go beyond these to offer objective support for your ideas about the work.

Evaluating and Revising ~~~

1. When you have finished your first draft, trade papers with a peer reader and share comments about each other's work. As you revise your essay, make sure that you have presented your material in a clear, logical fashion. Check to see that your supporting details really do back up your major points. Be sure that you have used **transitions** to help your readers understand the relationship of things and ideas. Also check that you have included evidence from the literary work in the proper form. For example, if you have quoted the author's exact words, be sure you have used quotation marks correctly. If you have paraphrased or summarized events or descriptions, be sure you have done so accurately.

Below is an example of an opening paragraph of a literary analysis. The sentence containing the main idea for the essay is underlined. Notice the writer's revisions.

> "Within a quarter of an hour we came to Miss Havisham's house, which was of old brick, ~and dismal~ and had a great many iron bars to it." In ~Chapter 7 of~ Great Expectations, Dickens introduces ~both~ Pip and the reader to Miss Havisham. ~ironically named~ Satis House~,~ the residence ~and home~ of this old lady, is a fitting symbol that reflects the character's ~state of~ mind.

2. You may find it helpful to consult the checklist below as you revise your analysis.

Checklist for Evaluation and Revision

✓ Have I carefully analyzed the elements of the literary work?

✓ Do I clearly present my main idea about the work?

✓ Do I support my main idea with specific examples, quotations, and other evidence?

✓ Do I organize my analysis consistently and clearly?

✓ Do I use an appropriate tone?

✓ Does my conclusion bring the essay to a definite close?

Proofreading and Publishing

1. Proofread your literary analysis and correct any errors you have made in grammar, usage, and mechanics. Pay special attention to the correct form for quoted passages and to the proper use of quotation marks and other punctuation. (Here you may find it helpful to refer to the **Handbook for Revision** on pages 884–930.) Then prepare a final copy of your essay.

2. Consider some of the following ways of sharing your literary analysis:

- submit your essay to the school magazine
- present your essay as a review for TV or radio
- join with students who analyzed the same or similar literary elements to discuss each other's work

Portfolio If your teacher approves, you may wish to keep a copy of your work in your writing folder or portfolio.

WRITING ABOUT LITERATURE

Developing Skills
in Critical Thinking

Many of the compositions you will be asked to write in English class will be about the literature you read. The writing may be in response to an examination question, a homework assignment, or a research project. At times you may be assigned a topic to work on; at other times you may be instructed to choose your own subject.

In writing about literature, you make an effort to understand and respond to some aspect of a literary work or group of works. For example, you may discuss the conflict that is developed in a short story; you may give your impression of a character in a play or novel; you may compare the images in two poems; you may state the main idea of an essay. Such writing assignments are an important part of literary study, which aims at greater understanding and appreciation of the works you read.

Writing about a literary work is a way of getting to know it better. Before you write a composition about a story, a poem, a play, or a group of works, you must read and reread the material carefully. You must sort out your thoughts, consider the evidence, and reach conclusions. In putting your thoughts down on paper, you become more fully involved with the literature.

Throughout your studies you will become familiar with many elements that are useful in analyzing literary works. You can assume that your readers will understand what you mean when you refer to such elements as *plot, conflict, symbol,* or *irony*. These words are part of a common vocabulary used in writing about literature. (See *Literary Terms and Techniques,* page 860.)

The material on the following pages offers help in planning and writing papers about literature. Here you will find suggestions for answering examination questions, choosing topics, gathering evidence, organizing essays, and writing, evaluating, and revising papers. Also included are several model essays.

The Writing Process

We often refer to writing an essay as a *process*, which consists of several key stages or phases: **prewriting, writing a first draft, evaluating and revising,** and **proofreading and publishing.** In this process, much of the critical work—the thinking and planning—precedes the actual writing of the paper.

In the **prewriting** stage, the writer makes decisions about what to say and how to say it. Prewriting activities include choosing a topic; considering purpose, audience, and tone; gathering ideas and organizing them; and developing a *thesis*—the controlling idea for the paper. In **writing a first draft,** the writer uses the working plan to get ideas down on paper. In the **evaluating and revising** stage, the writer judges the first draft to identify strengths and weaknesses in content, organization, and style. The writer then makes changes to eliminate the weaknesses identified through evaluating. The writer can revise by adding, cutting, reordering, or replacing ideas and details. In the **proofreading and publishing** stage, the writer checks the revised draft to correct errors in grammar, usage, and mechanics. The writer then prepares a clean copy and proofreads it to catch any omissions or errors. Finally, the completed paper is shared with others.

The stages of the writing process depend upon one another, which results in a "back and forth" movement among the stages. Few writers complete one stage entirely before moving to another, nor do they progress in a straight line from one stage to the next. For example, new ideas may emerge as the first draft is written, requiring a restatement of the thesis or additional supporting evidence. This interplay among stages is a natural part of writing—for all writers.

The amount of time devoted to each stage will vary with individual assignments. During a classroom examination, you may have limited time to plan your essay and to proofread your paper. For a term paper, you may have weeks or months to prepare your essay.

On the following pages the steps in this process are illustrated through the development of several model papers.

Answering Examination Questions

From time to time you will be asked to demonstrate your understanding of a literary work or topic by writing a short essay in class. Usually, your teacher will select the subject of the essay. How well you do will depend not only on how carefully you have prepared for the examination but on how carefully you read and interpret the essay question.

Before you begin to answer an examination question, be sure you understand what the question calls for. If a question requires that you discuss the *theme* of a story, you will not fulfill the requirements of the question if you give a summary of the story's plot. If you are asked to compare two *humorous* essays, your answer will be unacceptable if you mistakenly write about two *serious* essays. No matter how good your essay is, it will be unsatisfactory if you do not respond to the question accurately. Always take some time to read the essay question carefully in order to determine how it should be answered.

Remember that you are expected to demonstrate specific knowledge of the literature. Any general statement should be supported by evidence. If you wish to show a character's internal conflict, for example, refer to specific actions, dialogue, thoughts and feelings, or direct comments by the author in order to illustrate your point. If you are allowed to use your textbook during the examination, you may occasionally quote short passages or refer to a specific page in order to provide supporting evidence.

At the start, it may be helpful to jot down some notes to guide you in writing the essay. If you have several points to make, decide what the most effective order of presentation will be. You might build up to your strongest point, or you might present your points to develop a striking contrast. Aim for a logical organization.

Also remember that length alone is not satisfactory. Your answer must be relevant, and it must be presented in acceptable, correct English. Always take time to proofread your paper.

The key word in examination questions is the *verb*. Let us look briefly at some common instructions used in examinations.

ANALYSIS   A question may ask you to *analyze* some aspect of a literary work or topic. When you analyze something, you take it apart to see how each part works. On an examination, you will generally be directed to focus on some limited but essential aspect of a work in order to demonstrate your knowledge and understanding. A common type of exercise is *character analysis,* in which you draw on the most significant details of characterization in order to reach conclusions about a specific figure. For example, you might be asked to analyze the character of Odysseus as an epic hero, taking into account the traditional elements of characterization in classical epics (page 599). You might be asked to analyze the diction in the poem "Dream Deferred" (page 306). You might be asked to analyze the satirical elements in the play *Visit to a Small Planet* (page 423). Analysis may be applied to form, technique, or ideas.

COMPARISON CONTRAST

A question may ask that you *compare* (or *contrast*) two things, such as techniques, ideas, characters, or works. When you *compare,* you point out likenesses; when you *contrast,* you point out differences. At times you will be asked to *compare and contrast.* In that event, you will be expected to deal with similarities and differences. You might be asked to compare the themes of O. Henry's "The Gift of the Magi" (page 173) and De Maupassant's "The Necklace" (page 190). You might be asked to contrast Walter Mitty's fantasy life with his real life (page 63). You might compare and contrast the characteristics of the short story and the novel. Sometimes the instruction to *compare* implies both comparison and contrast. Always check with your teacher to make sure how inclusive the term *compare* is intended to be.

DEFINITION

A question may ask you to *define* a literary term—to answer the question "What is it?" To define a term, first classify it, or assign it to a larger class or group. Then discuss the specific features that make it different from other members of the same class. You should also provide specific examples that illustrate the term. For example, if asked to define the term *personification,* you would first identify it as a figure of speech (general class) and then indicate that it gives human qualities to something nonhuman (specific feature). You might then use "Silver," the poem by Walter de la Mare on page 326, as a specific example of personification.

DESCRIPTION

If a question asks you to *describe* a setting or a character, you are expected to give a picture in words. In describing a setting, include not only features that establish the historical period and locale, but those features that help to evoke a mood. In describing a character, deal with both direct and indirect methods of characterization (see page 67). You might be asked to describe the setting in the opening scene of *Great Expectations* (page 668) in order to demonstrate how Dickens creates an atmosphere of mystery and terror. You might be asked to describe the eccentric character of Miss Havisham in that novel.

DISCUSSION   The word *discuss* in a question is much more general than the other words we've looked at. When you are asked to discuss a subject, you are expected to examine it in detail. A question might direct you to discuss the characteristics of the informal essay that apply to James Thurber's "How to Name a Dog" (page 227). You might be asked to discuss the tone of Dickens' "Fragments of an Autobiography" (page 264). You might be asked to discuss the use of dramatic irony in Shakespeare's *Romeo and Juliet* (page 482).

EVALUATION   If a question asks you to *evaluate* a literary work or some aspect of one or more works, you are expected to determine if a writer has successfully achieved his or her purpose, and how important that purpose is. To evaluate, you must apply criteria, or standards of judgment, which may relate to both literary content and form. You must also supply evidence from the literary work or works to support your judgment. You might be asked to evaluate Tennyson's effectiveness in conveying a mood of indolence in "The Lotus-Eaters" (page 656).

EXPLANATION   A question may ask you to *explain* something. When you explain, you give reasons for something being the way it is. You make clear a character's actions, or you show how something has come about. You might, for example, be asked to explain the relation between Mitty's daydreams and actual events in "The Secret Life of Walter Mitty" (page 63.) You might be asked to explain Kreton's plan for world domination in *Visit to a Small Planet* (page 423). You might be asked to explain the concept of vengeance in the *Odyssey* (page 599) or how the subplots are connected to the main plot of *Great Expectations* (page 668).

ILLUSTRATION   The word *illustrate, demonstrate,* or *show* asks that you provide examples to support a point. You might be asked to give examples of anachronisms in Heyward Broun's "The Fifty-First Dragon" (page 199). You might be asked to illustrate Emily Dickinson's use of startling and original diction to present fresh images in her poetry (pages 295, 321). You might be asked to demonstrate musical effects in James Stephens' "The Shell" (page 342). Or you might be asked to show that in the *Odyssey* Homer mixes real and fabulous elements (page 599).

INTERPRETATION   The word *interpret* in a question asks that you give the meaning or significance of something. For example, you might be asked to provide an interpretation for a symbol, such as the journey in Christina Rossetti's "Uphill" (page 394). You might be asked to interpret the meaning of a work such as Edwin Muir's "The Castle" (page 389).

Sometimes you will be asked to agree or disagree with a stated interpretation of a work, giving specific evidence to support your position. For example, see the essay topics on page 851.

You will find that there is frequent overlapping of approaches. In discussing a subject, you may draw upon illustration, explanation, analysis, or any other approach that is useful. In comparing or contrasting two works, you may rely on description or interpretation. However, an examination question generally will have a central purpose, and it is important that you focus on this purpose in preparing your answer.

Using the Writing Process to Answer an Essay Question

Even if you are well prepared for an examination, you may not develop your essay effectively unless you manage your time well. Although you may have to work quickly, you should nevertheless devote some time to each stage of the writing process. The following suggestions indicate how you can use the writing process to develop an answer to an essay question. Once you become familiar with this pattern, you will have a plan that enables you to work quickly and efficiently.

PREWRITING   The examination question itself often establishes the topic and, through its key verb (*analyze, compare, interpret,* etc.) suggests an approach for developing an answer. Several prewriting steps remain:

1. *Write a thesis statement.* A *thesis statement* is a sentence that represents the main point of your paper. It generally appears at the beginning of an essay and establishes the position you are going to support.
2. *Develop points that support the thesis statement.* There should always be at least two supporting points. In a short essay all the points may be presented in a single paragraph. In a longer paper each point may be stated as the topic sentence of a separate paragraph. Each point should clearly support the idea expressed in the thesis.
3. *Locate supporting evidence in the literary work(s).* Evidence can include specific details, direct quotations, incidents, or images that support each point.
4. *Organize the major points and evidence.* Arrange your ideas and details logically so that your plan includes an introduction, a body, and a conclusion.

WRITING A FIRST DRAFT	Using your prewriting plan as a guide, write your essay. In the **introduction,** identify the work(s) under study and state your thesis. In the **body** present your major points with supporting evidence. In the **conclusion** restate your thesis and summarize what you have demonstrated. As you write, adopt a tone appropriate for your purpose (to convey ideas) and for your audience (your teacher, in most cases). Use straightforward language that is serious without being affected, and include transitional expressions (connecting words or phrases, such as *nevertheless, finally,* and *by contrast*) to make clear the relationships among ideas.
EVALUATING AND REVISING	Quickly evaluate, or judge, your answer by asking the following questions:

Purpose	1. Have I answered the specific assignment or questions?
Introduction	2. Have I included a thesis statement that specifies what the answer will discuss?
Body	3. Have I developed at least two major points that support the thesis statement?
	4. Have I included enough evidence from the literary work to support each major point?
	5. Is the order of ideas in the essay clear and logical?
Conclusion	6. Have I included a conclusion that summarizes findings or restates the main idea?

Using your evaluation, improve your essay by *adding, cutting, reordering,* or *replacing* ideas and details.

PROOFREADING AND PUBLISHING	Review your answer to locate and correct errors in grammar, usage, and mechanics. If your teacher indicates you have time to do so, prepare a clean copy of your answer and proofread it again to catch any errors or omissions.

Sample Examination Questions and Answers

On the following pages you will find some sample examination questions and answers for study and discussion. Note that the questions or assignments (shown in italics) may be phrased as essay topics.

QUESTION   *Poe uses irony in "The Cask of Amontillado" (page 95) to heighten the effect of horror. In a paragraph give specific examples of Poe's method.*

DEVELOPING AN ANSWER

This is an exercise in *illustration.* Your aim is to select examples of irony that intensify the terror of the narrative. How will you proceed?

One approach is to consider the kinds of irony Poe uses. You have learned that one common kind of irony is *dramatic irony,* in which the reader knows something that the character is ignorant of (see page 68). Another kind of irony, called *verbal irony,* is a way of saying one thing and meaning the opposite (see page 37). You might decide to focus on examples of these two kinds of irony. You would then need to identify effective examples of each kind in the story.

Once you have chosen an approach, jot down some prewriting notes to guide you in writing. These notes can be arranged under two heads:

Dramatic Irony

The reader knows that Montresor is plotting revenge against Fortunato, but Fortunato has no inkling of this. When the two men meet during the carnival, Fortunato is greeted as a friend.

Fortunato is wearing a clown costume. He doesn't realize what the reader knows—that he is being taken for a fool.

These examples reveal Montresor's diabolic character to the reader while hiding the truth from the intended victim.

Verbal Irony

In the vaults the dampness causes Fortunato to cough. He says that a cough will not kill him. Montresor agrees, saying that he will not die of a cough. The statement seems innocent, but the reader knows that the words are menacing.

Montresor drinks to Fortunato's long life, knowing that his hours are numbered.

These examples show Montresor toying with Fortunato before he kills him.

WRITING AN ANSWER

Here is a model paragraph developed from the prewriting notes.

Topic sentence restates question.

Subordinate Idea

Supporting Statements

In "The Cask of Amontillado," Poe uses dramatic and verbal irony to heighten the effect of horror. *His use of dramatic irony reveals Montresor's diabolic character to the reader while hiding the truth from the intended victim, Fortunato.* The reader knows from the outset that Montresor has been plotting revenge against Fortunato, but Fortunato is completely ignorant of his intention. When the two meet during the

Answering Examination Questions   **845**

carnival, Montresor greets Fortunato with pretended pleasure. Fortunato is wearing a clown suit. He does not realize what the reader knows—that he is in fact going to play the fool. *Poe makes use of verbal irony to show Montresor toying with Fortunato before he kills him.* In the vaults the dampness causes Fortunato to cough. He says in jest that the cough will not kill him, and Montresor agrees. His comment, that Fortunato will not die of a cough, appears innocent on the surface, but Montresor really means that Fortunato is going to die in some other way. When they drink a toast, Montresor drinks to Fortunato's long life, knowing full well that his hours are numbered. *The irony in the story heightens the horror because it emphasizes the cruelty of the murderer.*

Length: 200 words

In this example, the question provides you with a *thesis statement*—that irony in "The Cask of Amontillado" heightens the effect of horror. A thesis statement is a sentence that expresses the *thesis,* or the central idea that gives focus to your paper. The thesis statement indicates what the paper will be about. Although the statement of the thesis appears at the opening of the essay, it represents the end product of thinking. Generally, you will be required to formulate your own thesis statement about a subject.

II

QUESTION *Analyze the character of the speaker in Frost's "Mending Wall" (page 329).*

DEVELOPING AN ANSWER

This is an exercise in *character analysis.* This assignment is more demanding than the first assignment because you have to exercise your own judgment in setting limits to your answer. The question also requires that you supply your own thesis statement. Your thesis statement should be formulated *after* you have examined the evidence and come to a conclusion about the subject.

Assuming that you have the text of the poem to work from, you might go through it line by line, noting explicit and implicit clues to the speaker's character. You might jot down line references alongside your notes to guide you in writing your paper. As you work, look for major characteristics that will provide a focus for your essay.

This is one way to approach the assignment:

The labels in the left margin of the first paragraph read:

Subordinate Idea

Supporting Statements

Concluding Sentence

Character of Speaker

<table>
<tr><td rowspan="5">OPEN MIND</td><td>Attitude of speaker throughout poem is reflective. He likes to question things.</td></tr>
<tr><td>Speaker seems to have a strong feeling against barriers. He believes "something" in nature rebels against walls (1–4; 9–11).</td></tr>
<tr><td>He qualifies this: Some walls are useful—those that keep hunters out (5–9); those that control livestock (30–31).</td></tr>
<tr><td>He wants to reason with his neighbor about the function of walls (28–34).</td></tr>
<tr><td>He respects the ideas of others. Despite his own beliefs, at spring mending-time, he informs his neighbor of the gaps (11–12).</td></tr>
<tr><td rowspan="2">SENSE OF HUMOR</td><td>Speaker thinks of the mending as an "outdoor game" (21). He considers business silly and teases his neighbor (25–26).</td></tr>
<tr><td>He feels mischievous and plays with the idea of saying that "elves" are responsible for the pranks (36).</td></tr>
<tr><td rowspan="3">REALISTIC</td><td>He would like his neighbor to think for himself (28–34).</td></tr>
<tr><td>He suppresses the impulse to impose his own ideas (36–38).</td></tr>
<tr><td>Although he views his neighbor as a "stone savage," blindly following tradition, he does not try to change his mind (38–42).</td></tr>
</table>

WRITING AN ANSWER

What you might conclude from this set of prewriting notes is that the speaker is a mature, thoughtful man who has learned to accept and live with the shortcomings of others. Each of the overall characteristics shown in the notes can become the subject of a paragraph.

This is what the final essay might look like.

INTRODUCTION
Thesis Statement

The speaker in Frost's "Mending Wall" is a mature, thoughtful man who has learned to accept and live with the shortcomings of others. It is clear that he has a strong feeling against barriers in nature and barriers in human relationships, yet recognizes that he must be resigned to the existence of such barriers.

BODY
Topic Sentence

The first thing we learn about the speaker is that he admits he doesn't know all the answers and keeps an open mind. There is "something" in nature, he tells us, that rebels against walls. He doesn't know what this something is, but he is sympathetic to it. Not that he is inflexible on the subject of walls: he recognizes that some walls, like those that keep hunters and livestock out, are useful and necessary.

Supporting Evidence

Unlike his neighbor who clings uncritically to tradition and keeps on repeating "Good fences make good neighbors," the speaker questions the purpose of walls. Yet, he respects the ideas and rights of others. Despite his own beliefs, he feels obligated to respect his neighbor's wishes, and at spring mending-time, the men meet to repair the wall between their properties.

Topic Sentence	**The speaker shows himself to be a good-natured man with a sense of humor.** He refers to the mending of the wall as "just another kind of outdoor game." In a playful mood he teases his neighbor, telling
Supporting Evidence	him that the apple trees will never get across to eat the cones under the pine trees. He admits to feeling mischievous and considers putting the blame for the pranks on elves.
Topic Sentence	**The speaker is realistic enough to realize that he cannot change his neighbor's thinking by reasoning with him.** He knows that the wall is more than a barrier between their lands; it represents a barrier
Supporting Evidence	between their habits of thinking. He suppresses the impulse to put a notion in his neighbor's head: "I'd rather/He said it for himself." Although he views his neighbor as "an old-stone savage armed," blindly following tradition, he does not attempt to impose his own ideas. He knows his neighbor has an unquestioning mind and that it is futile to argue with him.
CONCLUSION	Even though he disagrees with his neighbor's philosophy, we know that the speaker will remain on good terms with him. Undoubtedly he will continue to meet with him at spring mending-time and keep the wall between them as they go.

Length: 396 words

III

QUESTION	*The young lovers in Shakespeare's* Romeo and Juliet *(page 482) seem ideally suited to each other because they have so many characteristics in common. Yet Shakespeare has been careful to differentiate them. Write an essay pointing out significant differences in these characters.*
DEVELOPING AN ANSWER	This is an exercise in *contrast*. Since you are to write a brief essay, you will not be able to deal with every significant aspect of the characters; you will have to select a few key aspects to focus on.
	Again, begin by taking notes:

Differences

Romeo	*Juliet*
Seems to be ruled by his emotions. In first act he is melancholy, moody, lovesick over Rosaline. After he meets Juliet he becomes ecstatic.	Juliet appears thoughtful and mature. In her first scene, she is dignified and composed. She reserves judgment until she can see for herself.

He is rash—he kills Tybalt in fury.

In Friar's cell, when he hears the Prince's edict of banishment, he loses control of himself.

He depends on others to make decisions for him. He relies on his friends and the Friar to help him resolve his difficulties.

In balcony scene she exhibits common sense and practicality. She takes lead in making the arrangements for their marriage.

She is resourceful. She pretends to accept the Nurse's counsel to avoid suspicion.

She manages to keep her head under stress. While she and the Friar plot a stratagem to avert the marriage to Paris, she pretends to be ruled by her parents' wishes.

Thesis Statement: Romeo is more emotional and excitable; Juliet is more level-headed and resourceful.

WRITING AN ANSWER

Here is a model essay developed from the prewriting notes.

INTRODUCTION
Restate Question.
Thesis Statement

The young lovers in Shakespeare's *Romeo and Juliet* have many characteristics in common. Yet Shakespeare has been careful to differentiate them. *Romeo is more emotional and impulsive; Juliet more levelheaded and resourceful.*

BODY   **Topic Sentence**

Romeo seems to be ruled by emotions rather than by reason. When we first meet him in the play, he is lovesick, moody, and restless. He spends his time daydreaming and sighing over Rosaline.

Supporting Evidence

Within a short while, he is blissfully ecstatic in declaring his love for Juliet. When he is provoked into a duel by Tybalt, he loses his head and kills him. Then, in the Friar's cell, when he learns that the Prince has banished him, he loses control of himself. He seems dependent upon others to think for him. His friends Benvolio and Mercutio have to help him get over his infatuation with Rosaline. Later, he relies on the Friar's counsel to cope with his grief. He yields easily to despair. When he hears that Juliet is dead, he immediately decides to buy poison and end his own life.

Topic Sentence

While Juliet is every bit as ardent as Romeo and shares his youthful impulsiveness, she exhibits greater thoughtfulness and common sense. When we first meet her, she appears dignified and composed.

Supporting Evidence

She does not become excited at having received a proposal of marriage, but reserves judgment until she meets Paris. After she and Romeo declare their love for one another, she takes the lead in arranging for their marriage. When she hears of her cousin Tybalt's death, Juliet is quick to condemn Romeo, then catches herself and checks her outburst. She realizes that Romeo has acted in self-defense. As circumstances threaten to overwhelm her, she shows skill in handling people. When the Nurse, her trusted confidant, suggests that she commit bigamy, Juliet pretends to accept her counsel to avoid suspicion. She manages to keep her head and not alert her family to the stratagem that she and the Friar have plotted to avert her marriage to Paris.

CONCLUSION
Topic Sentence   **By means of these differences, Shakespeare makes individuals of his characters.** Romeo and Juliet are not mere stereotypes of young people in love. Because of Shakespeare's skillful characterization, we find their actions and distinct natures true to life.

Length: 368 words

Writing on a Topic of Your Own

Prewriting: Choosing a Topic

At times you may be asked to write an essay on a topic of your own choosing. Often it will be necessary to read a work or group of works more than once before a suitable topic presents itself.

Although any literary subject that interests you is usually acceptable as a topic for study, it is a good idea to steer away from broad subjects that invite generalizations and sweeping statements. You may be fascinated by the language of *Romeo and Juliet,* but in a 350–500 word essay, you would be forced to cover the subject too superficially to demonstrate any real mastery of the material. It might be better to restrict yourself to one aspect of the language—for example, images of light—in one scene—the balcony scene of Act Two.

What the writer must often do is limit a broad subject to a narrow topic—one that can be discussed thoughtfully in the time and space available. You might have to divide a subject into several parts and select only one part as the focus of your essay.

Students sometimes worry that if they choose a narrow topic, they won't have enough to say. This will seldom present a problem if you have developed the habit of digging into a selection and examining it in depth.

A topic may focus on one element or technique in a work. If you are writing about fiction, you might concentrate on some aspect of plot, such as conflict. Or you might concentrate on character, setting, or theme. If you are writing about poetry, you might choose to analyze imagery or figurative language. In writing about drama, you might focus on dramatic irony or stage conventions. A topic may deal with more than one aspect of a work. You might, for example, discuss several elements of a short story in order to show how an idea or theme is developed. Keep the key verbs, such as *analyze, compare, illustrate,* in mind (see pages 840–843) as guides in limiting a topic.

Once you have a topic in mind, your object is to form it into a *thesis,* a controlling idea that represents the conclusion of your findings. This thesis, of course, will appear at the opening of your paper. It may be necessary to read a work several times before you can formulate a thesis. You would then need to present the evidence supporting your position. Here are some examples showing how a thesis differs from a topic.

Topic The Central Conflict in "Rules of the Game" (page 76)
Thesis The central conflict in the story is Waverly's struggle to assert her independence from her mother.

Topic John Masefield's Diction in "Cargoes" (page 304)
Thesis Masefield has chosen words with pleasant and unpleasant associations to suggest a contrast between the exotic romance of the old ships and the unromantic utility of modern vessels.

Topic The Epic Hero in the *Odyssey* (page 599)
Thesis Odysseus surpasses the other characters in intelligence, courage, and prowess, and appears at times to be superhuman, but he also has all-too-human failings that lead to misfortune for himself and his men.

Gathering Evidence/Formulating Major Points

It is a good idea to take notes as you read, even if you do not yet have a topic in mind. Later on, when you have settled on a topic, you can discard any notes that are not relevant. Some people prefer a worksheet, others index cards. In the beginning, you should record all your reactions. A topic may emerge during this early stage. As you continue to read, you will shape your topic into a rough thesis.

When you take notes, make an effort to state ideas in your own words. If a specific phrase or line is so important that it deserves to be quoted directly, be sure to enclose the words in quotation marks.

When you transfer your notes to your final paper, be sure to copy quotations exactly.

If you cite lines in a poem, you should enclose the line numbers in parentheses following the quotation. The following note, which is for the *Odyssey* (page 599), shows you how to incorporate two lines of a poem into your own paper:

> Odysseus notes that the Cyclopes are barbarians without laws and traditions when he says "Cyclopes have no muster and no meeting,/no consultation or old tribal ways" (lines 99–100).

The slash(/) shows the reader where line 99 ends and line 100 begins. If you cite three or more lines, you should separate the quotation from your own text in this way:

> Upon his return to Ithaca, the goddess Athena appears to Odysseus and transforms him so that he is seen in his former magnificence:
>
> > Lithe and young she made him,
> > ruddy with sun, his jawline clean, the beard
> > no longer gray upon his chin.
> >
> > (lines 856–858)

Sometimes a direct quotation from a literary work can be the springboard to a topic. Consider, for example, a paper based on Odysseus' characterization of himself as "formidable for guile in peace and war."

Let us suppose that you have just concluded the unit on *Great Expectations* (page 668). You are instructed to write an essay of approximately 500 words on a topic of your own choosing.

You haven't any ideas at the outset so you skim through the unit, refreshing your memory of characters and events. You reread notes and questions, sifting through this material for approaches and ideas. You become aware that one of Dickens' important themes in the novel has to do with the need for compassion in human relationships. You believe that exploring this theme will help to clarify Dickens' point of view.

The subject is too broad, however, for an essay of 500 words, so you consider ways to narrow its scope. Should you confine yourself to a chapter or to one of the stages of the novel? Should you focus on a key incident? Each approach is possible. In choosing an approach, be guided by the nature of the problem and by your own interests.

You decide to restrict your study to Pip's relationship with the convict, Abel Magwitch. At this point you begin taking notes.

Do not be concerned about taking too many notes. Until you settle on a clear focus for your paper, you should record all your reactions.

Notes

When the convict returns many years after their meeting on the marshes, Pip thinks of him as a wild animal: "The abhorrence in which I held the man, the dread I had of him, the repugnance with which I shrank from him, could not have been exceeded if he had been some terrible beast" (page 773).

Pip is terrified to be alone with him and locks him in the bedroom.

Pip is disgusted by his manners. He eats "like a hungry old dog" (page 779).

Pip learns that the convict has risked his life in coming back to England. He feels a concern for the convict's safety and plans to get him out of England.

He learns about Magwitch's miserable life and the injustice he has suffered.

He finds out that the convict is Estella's father.

After the accident with the steamer, Pip refuses to abandon Magwitch. He provides him with dry clothes and looks after him. He accompanies him to London. He feels that his place is at Magwitch's side.

Pip recognizes that a change has taken place in his feelings: "For now my repugnance to him had all melted away, and in the hunted, wounded, shackled creature who held my hand in his, I only saw a man who had meant to be my benefactor, and who had felt affectionately, gratefully, and generously toward me with great constancy through a series of years" (page 815).

Pip has nothing to gain, but he does not desert Magwitch. He does not reveal that Magwitch's possessions will be forfeited to the Crown and that all his hopes of making Pip's fortune are gone.

While Magwitch is in the prison infirmary, Pip visits him every day. During the trial Pip holds his hand and comforts him.

After Magwitch is sentenced to death, Pip petitions the Home Secretary of State and others in authority.

When the old man is dying, Pip comforts him by telling him that his child is alive, that she has become a lady, and that he loves her.

From this set of notes we can conclude that Dickens emphasizes the change in Pip's attitude toward the convict Abel Magwitch. We can also derive a thesis statement: *As Pip develops compassion for Magwitch, we witness a reformation in his character.*

Organizing Ideas

Before you begin writing, organize your main ideas to provide for an introduction, a body, and a conclusion. The introduction should identify the author(s) and work(s). It should contain a statement of your thesis as well. The body of your paper should present the evidence supporting your thesis. The conclusion should bring together your main ideas.

Your plan will grow out of the notes you have compiled. Remember that you need not use *all* the evidence you have collected. You should include material that has bearing on your topic.

This is one kind of plan. It indicates the main idea of each paragraph.

INTRODUCTION

Paragraph 1   *Thesis*   As Pip develops compassion for Magwitch, we witness a reformation in his character.

BODY

Paragraph 2   Pip is terrified and repelled when the convict reenters his life many years after their meeting on the marshes.

Paragraph 3   As he learns more about Magwitch, Pip loses his fear and strong aversion to the man.

Paragraph 4   After the accident in which Magwitch is fatally injured, Pip acts out of deep sympathy rather than a sense of obligation.

Paragraph 5   Through his compassion for Magwitch, Pip becomes a more admirable and appealing character.

CONCLUSION

Paragraph 6   Dickens seems to be saying that compassion brings out the best in human nature.

Writing the Essay

Use your prewriting plan as a guide in writing your paper. Focus on expressing clearly the major points and evidence supporting your thesis statement. Include a topic sentence and supporting sentences in each paragraph. As you write, use language that is appropriate in tone. Include transitional expressions to make clear the relationships among your ideas.

Here is a model essay developing the thesis statement. For an earlier draft of this essay, see pages 857–859.

<table>
<tr><td>TITLE</td><td></td></tr>
</table>

TITLE	THE THEME OF COMPASSION IN *GREAT EXPECTATIONS*
INTRODUCTION	An important theme in *Great Expectations* is the power of compassion to transform human nature. Dickens make this clear when Pip undergoes a change in attitude toward his benefactor, the convict Abel Magwitch.
Thesis Statement	*As Pip develops compassion for Magwitch, we witness a reformation in his character.*
BODY	
Topic Sentence	**Pip is terrified and repelled when the convict reenters his life many years after their meeting on the marshes.** Pip thinks of him as a wild animal: "The abhorrence in which I held the man, the dread I had of him, the repugnance with which I shrank from him, could not have been exceeded if he had been some terrible beast" (page 773).
Supporting Evidence	He is afraid to be alone with him, and after Magwitch goes to bed, Pip locks him in the bedroom. Pip finds his manners disgusting and watches him eat "like a hungry old dog" (page 779).
Topic Sentence	**As he learns more about Magwitch, Pip loses his fear and strong aversion to the man.** He finds out that Magwitch has suffered great wretchedness and injustice. He also discovers that the convict is Estella's father.
Supporting Evidence	Realizing that the convict has risked his life in returning to England, Pip feels it is his duty to get the man out of the country.
Topic Sentence	**After the accident in which Magwitch is fatally injured, Pip acts out of deep sympathy rather than a sense of obligation.** He treats the old man with great kindness, providing him with dry clothing and obtaining comforts for him. He refuses to abandon him and accompanies him to prison in London.
Supporting Evidence	Pip recognizes the change in himself: "For now my repugnance to him had all melted away, and in the hunted, wounded, shackled creature who held my hand in his, I only saw a man who had meant to be my benefactor, and who had felt affectionately, gratefully, and generously toward me with great constancy through a series of years" (page 815).
Topic Sentence	**Through his compassion for Magwitch, Pip becomes a more admirable and appealing character.** His final scenes with Magwitch are the most moving passages in the book. While Magwitch is in the prison infirmary, Pip visits him every day. During the trial, Pip holds his hand and comforts him.
Supporting Evidence	Out of kindness he does not reveal that Magwitch's possessions will be forfeited to the Crown and that his hopes of making Pip's fortune are gone. After Magwitch receives his death sentence, Pip petitions the Home Secretary for mercy. He sends out appeals to those in authority. Finally, to ease the old man's death, he tells

him that his little girl (Estella) is alive, that she has become a lady, and that he loves her.

CONCLUSION
Topic Sentence

Dickens seems to be saying that compassion brings out the best in human nature. Pip outgrows the snobbery that leads him to value appearance rather than substance. In recognizing the good in Magwitch's character, he becomes capable of gratitude and generosity of spirit.

Length: 485 words

Evaluating and Revising Papers

When you plan to write an essay in class, you have a limited amount of time to plan and develop your essay. Nevertheless, you should save a few minutes to read over your work and make necessary improvements. When an essay is assigned as homework, you have more time to prepare it carefully. Get into the habit of evaluating and revising your work. A first draft of an essay should be treated as a rough copy of your manuscript. Chances are that thinking about and reworking your first draft will result in a clearer and stronger paper.

To evaluate an essay, you judge its content, organization, and style by applying a set of criteria, or standards. Your goal in evaluating is to identify the strengths and weaknesses of the paper. Knowing this, you will be able to make the changes that will improve the essay. To evaluate an essay about literature, ask yourself the following questions:

Guidelines for Evaluating an Essay

Introduction

1. Have I included an introduction that identifies the subject of the paper? Have I identified the author(s) and literary work(s) the paper will deal with?

Thesis Statement

2. Have I included a thesis statement that clearly expresses the controlling idea for the paper?

Thesis Development

3. Have I included convincing main points that develop the thesis in the body of the paper?

4. Have I included sufficient evidence from the work to support each main point?

Conclusion

5. Have I included a conclusion that synthesizes the main ideas or that suggests additional ideas for study?

Coherence

6. Have I arranged ideas logically and related them clearly to one another?

Style

7. Have I varied sentence beginnings and sentence structure? Have I defined any unfamiliar words or unusual terms? Have I used vivid and specific words?

Tone

8. Have I used language that is appropriate for my purpose and audience?

Writers usually revise by using any one of four basic techniques: *adding, cutting, reordering,* and *replacing.* For example, if the relationship of ideas is unclear, you can *add* transitional expressions (such as *first, finally,* and *by contrast*). If your language is not appropriate, you can *replace* slang, contractions, and informal expressions with more formal language. You can *cut* unrelated evidence, and you can *reorder,* or rearrange, ideas that are difficult to follow.

On the following pages you will find a revised draft of the essay that appears on pages 855–856. The annotations in the margins indicate which revising techniques were used to make the changes. Compare the two versions of this paper, noting where the writer has made vague or general statements more specific, clear, and concise.

replace; cut; cut	~~One of the most~~ ^{An} important theme~~s~~ in ~~the novel~~ <u>Great Expectations</u> is the
replace; add	power of compassion to transform human nature. ~~We see this~~ *Dickens makes clear* when Pip under-
reorder; reorder; cut	goes a change in attitude toward Abel Magwitch, the convict ~~who is~~ his benefactor,
	~~tor.~~ As Pip develops compassion for Magwitch, we witness a reformation in his
	character.
replace	Pip ~~has not seen the convict since his boyhood on the marshes. When Pip~~ *is terrified and repelled when the convict reenters his life many years after their meeting on the marshes.*
replace	~~recognizes him, he is terrified.~~ Pip thinks of him as a wild animal: "The abhor-
	rence in which I held the man, the dread I had of him, the repugnance with
	which I shrank from him, could not have been exceeded if he had been some ter-
cut	rible beast" (page 773). ~~Physically he is repelled.~~ He is afraid to be alone with
	him, and after Magwitch goes to bed, Pip locks him in the bedroom. Pip finds his
	manners disgusting and watches him eat "like a hungry old dog" (page 779).

cut; add; replace; replace ~~Pip begins to change~~ [Pip loses his fear and strong aversion to the man.] as he learns [more] about Magwitch's ~~life~~. He finds out ~~how~~ [that]

add Magwitch has suffered. He also discovers that the convict is Estella's father.

replace; add [Realizing that the convict] ~~Magwitch~~ has risked his life in returning to England, Pip feels it is his duty to

get the man out of the country.

replace After the accident ~~with the steamer,~~ [in which Magwitch is fatally injured,] ~~Pip treats the old man more sympa-~~ [Pip acts out of deep sympathy rather than a sense of]

replace; add; [obligation.]

replace; replace ~~thetically.~~ He ~~provided~~ [providing] him with dry clothing and ~~looks after him.~~ [treats the old man with great kindness, obtaining comforts for him.] ~~When the old~~

replace; reorder; replace ~~man is taken~~ [He refuses to abandon him and] to prison in London, Pip accompanies him. Pip recognizes ~~that a~~ [the]

replace change ~~has taken place in his feelings:~~ [in himself:] "For now my repugnance to him had all

melted away, and in the hunted, wounded, shackled creature who held my hand

in his, I only saw a man who had meant to be my benefactor, and who had felt af-

fectionately, gratefully, and generously toward me with great constancy through

a series of years" (page 815).

reorder His final scenes with Magwitch are the most moving passages in the book.

add; cut [While Magwitch is in the prison infirmary,] Pip visits him ~~in the infirmary~~ every day. During the trial, Pip holds his hand

and comforts him. Through his compassion for Magwitch, Pip becomes a more

add ; replace; replace admirable and appealing character. He does not ~~tell Magwitch~~ [Out of kindness reveal Magwitch's] that his posses-

sions will be forfeited to the Crown and that his hopes of making Pip's fortune

replace are gone. After Magwitch receives his death sentence, Pip ~~does not give up hope~~ [petitions the Home Secretary] replace; replace   ~~of saving him.~~   ~~When the old man is dying,~~ he tells him that his ~~child~~ is alive,

for mercy. He sends out appeals to those in authority. Finally, to ease the old man's death,

little girl (Estella)

that she has become a lady, and that he loves her.

Dickens seems to be saying that compassion brings out the best in human

Pip outgrows the snobbery that leads him to value appearance rather than substance.

replace   nature.   ~~At the end of the book, Pip is no longer a snob.~~   In recognizing the good

add   in Magwitch's character, he becomes capable of gratitude and generosity.

of spirit

Proofreading and Publishing

After you have revised your draft, proofread your essay to locate and correct any errors in grammar, usage, and mechanics. Pay particular attention to the correct capitalization and punctuation of any direct quotations you cite as evidence. Then prepare a final version of your essay by following correct manuscript form or your teacher's instructions for the assignment. After writing this clean copy, proofread once more to catch any errors or omissions made in copying. Share your essay with others.

Literary Terms AND Techniques

ALLITERATION *The repetition of similar sounds, usually consonants or consonant clusters, in a group of words.* Common examples are "safe and sound," "brown as a berry," and "the more the merrier." Although most alliteration occurs at the beginning of words, it may occur within words as well. When alliteration occurs at the beginning of words, it is called **initial alliteration;** when it occurs within words, it is called **internal** or **hidden alliteration.**

Alliteration has a wide and persistent appeal. It is frequently used in clichés, such as "a dime a dozen," "bigger and better," and "jump for joy." Because alliteration adds emphasis to a group of words, it is often used in advertising jingles and in political slogans.

In poetry, alliteration can be an effective musical device as in these lines from Henry Wadsworth Longfellow's "The Day Is Done":

> The *d*ay is *d*one, and the *d*arkness
> Falls *f*rom the *w*ings of night,
> As a *f*eather is *w*afted *d*own*w*ard
> *F*rom an eagle in his *f*light.

Alliteration is often combined with **rhyme** and other musical devices, as in this stanza from Edgar Allan Poe's "Eldorado":

> *G*aily bedight,
> A *g*all*a*nt knight,
> In sun*s*hine and in *s*hadow,
> Had journeyed *l*ong,
> Singing a *s*ong
> In *s*earch of E*l*dorado.

See **Repetition.**
See also page 343.

ALLUSION *A reference in one work of literature to a person, place, or event in another work of literature or in history, art, or music.* Allusion can be used equally well in prose or poetry. As it is usually an appeal to the reader to share some experience with the writer, allusion is used to best effect when it refers to something familiar.

Allusions to the Bible are common in literature. In *Great Expectations,* Pip, the narrator, alludes to the Book of Genesis when he describes the Hulks, the prison boat, as a "wicked Noah's ark." Literature is also filled with allusions to the plays of William Shakespeare. In *Great Expectations,* Dickens expects his readers to recognize the allusion to Shakespeare's *Julius Caesar* when he describes Mr. Wopsle as a "ham" actor performing one of the noblest speeches ever written for the theater: "What he did on those occasions was to turn up his cuffs, stick up his hair, and give us Mark Antony's oration over the body of Caesar."

Allusions to ancient Greek and Roman literature are also common. The following poem alludes to a Greek myth. Medusa was one of the Gorgons, three horrible sisters with serpents for hair. Whoever looked at any of them instantly turned to stone. The allusion to Medusa here suggests that something, perhaps death, has brought the speaker's life to a halt, that it no longer has any meaning:

Medusa
Louise Bogan

> I had come to the house, in a cave of trees,
> Facing a sheer sky.
> Everything moved,—a bell hung ready to strike,
> Sun and reflection wheeled by.
>
> When the bare eyes were before me
> And the hissing hair,
> Held up at a window, seen through a door.
> The stiff bald eyes, the serpents on the forehead
> Formed in the air.
>
> This is a dead scene forever now.
> Nothing will ever stir.
> The end will never brighten it more than this,
> Nor the rain blur.
>
> The water will always fall, and will not fall,
> And the tipped bell make no sound.
> The grass will always be growing for hay
> Deep on the ground.
>
> And I shall stand here like a shadow
> Under the great balanced day,
> My eyes on the yellow dust, that was lifting in the
>   wind,
> And does not drift away.

See pages 178, 555.

ANACHRONISM   *An event or detail existing out of its proper time in history.* William Shakespeare often uses anachronisms. A classic example is the reference to the game of billiards ("Let us to billiards") in *Antony and Cleopatra*, a play set in ancient times. The game of billiards was not invented until the sixteenth century. The clock that strikes in Shakespeare's *Julius Caesar* is also an anachronism, as there were no striking clocks in ancient Rome. Writers sometimes use anachronisms deliberately, to add humor to a piece of literature or to lend a sense of timelessness—that is, to prevent something from being "dated." In "The Fifty-First Dragon," Heywood Broun uses a number of modern references in a medieval setting. Examples include the character of the Headmaster and the references to faculty members, to campus slang, and to school spirit.

See page 205.

ANALOGY   *An extended comparison showing the similarities between two things.* Analogies are often used for illustration (to explain something unfamiliar by comparing it to something familiar) or for argument (to persuade that what holds true for one thing holds true for the thing to which it is compared).

In "The Sound of the Sea," Henry Wadsworth Longfellow describes the sounds of the rising sea-tide in the first eight lines of the poem. In the last six lines, he draws an analogy between the sounds of the sea and inspiration:

So comes to us at times, from the unknown
  And inaccessible solitudes of being,
  The rushing of the sea-tides of the soul;
And inspirations, that we deem our own,
  Are some divine foreshadowing and foreseeing
  Of things beyond our reason or control.

See page 282.

ARGUMENT   *A form of discourse in which reason is used to influence or change people's ideas or actions.* Writers practice argument most often when writing nonfiction, particularly essays or speeches. In his famous speech delivered to the House of Burgesses on March 23, 1775, Patrick Henry advances the argument that only by armed resistance can the colonies defend themselves against England and gain their liberty. He concludes: "I know not what course others may take; but as for me, give me liberty or give me death!"

See **Persuasion**.
See also page 216.

ASIDE   *Words spoken by a character in a play, usually in an undertone, not intended to be heard by other characters on stage.* The aside is used in the theater to let the audience know what a character is really thinking or feeling as opposed to what he or she pretends to be thinking or feeling to the other characters in the play. Sometimes asides are exchanged between two characters whose dialogue is not meant to be heard by the other characters present. Many examples of this device may be found in the plays of William Shakespeare.

See **Conventions, Monologue, Soliloquy**.
See also page 528.

ASSONANCE   *The repetition of similar vowel sounds, usually close together, in a group of words.* Familiar examples are "*free* and *easy*," "*mad as a hatter*," and so on. Assonance is used to please the ear and to emphasize certain sounds. Like other forms of sound repetition, it is mainly a poetic device. Henry Wadsworth Longfellow uses "r*i*sing t*i*de" in "The Sound of the Sea." Another example is found in "Mending Wall," where Robert Frost writes: "*a*nd I *a*m *a*pple orchard."

See **Alliteration, Onomatopoeia, Repetition**.
See also page 343.

AUTOBIOGRAPHY   *A person's account of his or her own life.* An autobiography is generally written in narrative form and includes some introspection. Autobiographies are distinct from diaries, journals, and letters, which are not unified life stories written for publication. Autobiographies are also different from memoirs, which often deal, at least in part, with public events and important persons other than the author. It is not uncommon for anyone who has achieved distinction in life to write an account of his or her experiences. Autobiographies are frequently written by politicians, entertainers, high-ranking members of the services, and literary figures. For example, Winston Churchill's *My Early Life* is a famous autobiography by a political figure.

See **Biography, Nonfiction**.

BALLAD   *A story told in verse and usually meant to be sung.* The earliest ballads, known as **folk ballads** or **popular ballads,** were composed anonymously and transmitted orally for generations. The main ballad tradition began in Europe in the late Middle Ages. The material was taken from local and national life, from legend and folklore. The most popular themes, often tragic ones, are disappointed love, jealousy, revenge, sudden disaster, and deeds of adventure and daring. Generally, the language is simple, the rhythm pronounced, and the story told through dialogue and action. A **refrain,** or chorus, is also a common element.

The traditional **ballad stanza** consists of four lines. The first and third lines have four stressed words or syllables; the second and fourth lines have three stresses. The number of unstressed syllables in each line may vary. The second and fourth lines usually rhyme. Here is a ballad stanza from an American folk ballad, "The Lover's Lament":

> My dearest dear, the time draws near
> When you and I must part;
> But little do you know the grief or woe
> Of my poor troubled heart.

The folk ballad is still a living tradition in Sicily, Iceland, and many other parts of the world. In America, this tradition has flourished in the Appalachian Mountains, among cowhands, and within labor movements.

Another kind of ballad is the **literary ballad,** in which a known writer imitates the folk ballad. E. E. Cummings' "All in green went my love riding" is a literary ballad. Other distinguished examples include Samuel Taylor Coleridge's *The Rime of the Ancient Mariner,* John Keats's "La Belle Dame sans Merci," and Alfred Noyes's "The Highwayman."

> See **Narrative Poetry.**
> See also pages 384, 387, 388.

BIOGRAPHY   *An account of a person's life written by another person.* Biography is one of the most popular forms of nonfiction. Biographies in English have taken many different forms since they were first written in medieval times to praise the virtues of saints and to celebrate the feats of heroes. The modern biographer aims at accuracy and usually makes an attempt to interpret the personality of the subject. Details of the social and historical circumstances in which the subject lived are often included. A fine example of a detailed biography is James Boswell's *The Life of Samuel Johnson,* written in the eighteenth century and considered by many to have set the tone for modern biography.

> See **Autobiography, Nonfiction.**
> See also page 249.

BLANK VERSE   *Verse written in unrhymed iambic pentameter, where each line usually contains ten syllables and every other syllable is stressed.* Blank verse is the principal English meter, the pattern used in some of the greatest English poetry, including the tragedies of William Shakespeare and the epics of John Milton. Unrhymed iambic lines prove particularly appropriate in treating serious themes. The following lines from Shakespeare's *Romeo and Juliet* are written in blank verse:

> But soft!/What light/through yon/der win/dow
>   breaks?
> It is/the east,/ and Jul/iet is/the sun!
> > See **Iambic Pentameter, Meter.**
> > See also page 528.

CATASTROPHE   *The tragic denouement, or unknotting, of a play or story.* The deaths of Romeo and Juliet represent the final catastrophe of William Shakespeare's play.

> See **Plot.**
> See also page 555.

CHARACTERIZATION   *The personality a character displays; also, the means by which an author reveals that personality.* Generally, a writer develops a character in one or more of the following ways: (1) by showing the character acting and speaking; (2) by giving a physical description of the character; (3) by revealing the character's thoughts; (4) by revealing what other characters think about the character; (5) by commenting directly on the character. The first four methods are **indirect methods of characterization.** The writer shows or dramatizes the character and allows you to draw your own conclusions. The last method is **direct characterization.** The writer tells you directly what a character is like.

Direct characterization is always supported by indirect techniques, as characters must act or speak if the writer is developing a story. Also, if characters are to be believable, the reader must hear or see, rather than simply be told, what the characters think or feel or do.

See **Characters, Point of View.**
See also pages 67, 75, 86.

CHARACTERS *Persons—or animals, things, or natural forces presented as persons—appearing in a short story, novel, play, or narrative poem.* Characters are sometimes described as dynamic or static. **Dynamic characters** experience some change in personality or attitude. This change is an essential one and usually involves more than a mere change in surroundings or condition. In Bernard Malamud's story "A Summer's Reading," George is an example of a character who undergoes an important change. **Static characters** remain the same throughout a narrative. They do not develop or change beyond the way in which they are first presented. Mitty in James Thurber's "The Secret Life of Walter Mitty" is an example of a static character.

Characters in a **novel** are generally more fully developed than those in a short story, for example. Not only does the novelist have room to develop perhaps more than one dynamic character, but he or she may reveal a main character in many different stages of change. Pip, in Charles Dickens' novel *Great Expectations,* is a character who, in the course of growing up, undergoes important and basic changes in personality and outlook.

Characters are sometimes classified as **flat** or **round.** Flat characters have only one or two "sides," representing one or two traits. They are often stereotypes that can be summed up in a few words, for example, an "anxious miser" or a "strong, silent type." Round characters are complex and have many "sides" or traits. Their behavior is unpredictable because they are individuals, and their personalities are fully developed and require lengthy analysis. Flat characters, when developed by a skillful writer, may be as impressive as round characters.

See **Characterization.**
See also pages 75, 86.

CLIMAX *That point of greatest emotional intensity, interest, or suspense in a narrative.* In drama, the climax is often identified with the **crisis,** or **turning point.**

See **Drama.**
See also pages 37, 555.

COMEDY *In general, a literary work that is amusing and ends happily.* Comedy is distinct from **tragedy,** which is generally concerned with a central character who meets an unhappy or disastrous end. The comic hero or heroine may be a person of ordinary character and ability who does not usually achieve the heroic stature of the tragic figure.

Comedies are often concerned, at least in part, with poking fun at romantic attitudes and exposing human folly. They frequently depict a hero or heroine overthrowing rigid social fashions and customs. Wit, humor, and a sense of festivity are found in many comedies.

The term comedy is usually applied to a drama. Dramatic comedy is generally divided into two main sorts: romantic comedy—where there exist joyous situations and where the two chief figures are lovers; and satirical comedy—where the chief characters are held up to ridicule and often come between a pair of young lovers.

Anton Chekhov's *A Marriage Proposal* is an example of another type of comedy known as **farce.** It reveals through exaggerated situations the foolishness in which people can entangle themselves.

See **Drama, Farce, Satire.**
See also page 404.

COMPLICATION *A series of difficulties forming the central action in a narrative.* Complications in a story, for example, make a conflict difficult to resolve and add interest and suspense. In Frank R. Stockton's "The Lady, or the Tiger?" complications include the search for the tiger, the princess' inquiry, and her discovery of the identity of the young woman.

See **Conflict, Plot.**
See also page 37.

CONFLICT *A struggle between two opposing forces or characters in a short story, novel, play, or narrative poem.* Conflict can be **external** or **internal,** and it can take one of these forms: (1) a person against another person; (2) a person against society; (3) a person against nature; (4) two elements or ideas struggling for mastery within a person.

In a narrative there may be a single conflict that is uncomplicated and easy to recognize or there may be several, more subtle conflicts involved. In Amy Tan's story "Rules of the Game," there is conflict between Waverly and her brothers, between Waverly and her chess opponents, and between Waverly and her mother. There is also a larger conflict in the story between the values of two cultures.

See **Plot.**
See also pages 29, 37.

CONNOTATION *The emotion or association that a word or phrase may arouse.* Connotation is distinct from **denotation,** which is the literal or "dictionary" meaning of a word or phrase.

Words acquire their connotations by the way they've been used in the past and by the circumstances in which they've been used. For example, the word *springtime* literally means that season of the year between the vernal equinox and the summer solstice, but the word usually makes most people think of such things as youth, rebirth, and romance. The word *shroud* literally means a cloth used for burial purposes, or anything that covers or protects. However, most people associate the word *shroud* with death, gloom, darkness, and other unpleasant things. Advertisers are especially sensitive to the connotations of words. For example, a department of a store probably would not be called "Cheap Clothes"; it would more likely be called "Budget Sportswear."

See **Denotation, Diction.**
See also pages 305, 388.

CONVENTIONS *Unrealistic devices or procedures that the reader (or audience) agrees to accept.* In poetry, for example, the use of rhyme is a convention. In drama, the playwright is free to have characters speak aloud without other characters hearing (the aside) or speak aloud while alone on stage (the soliloquy). These are dramatic conventions. The more realistic playwrights wish to be, the fewer dramatic conventions they will use; that is, they will ask the audience to suspend their disbelief as little as possible.

Familiarity with conventions of all forms enables us to know just what is taking place. Through the convention of the "fade in" and "fade out" in film, for example, we know that there has been a shift in time and place.

See **Aside, Monologue, Soliloquy.**
See also pages 405, 528.

COUPLET *Two consecutive lines of poetry that rhyme.* Here is the concluding couplet from William

Shakespeare's Sonnet 55:

> So, till the judgment that yourself arise,
> You live in this, and dwell in lovers' eyes.

This couplet is from Lord Byron's "The Destruction of Sennacherib":

> And the might of the Gentile, unsmote by the sword,
> Hath melted like snow in the glance of the Lord!

See **Heroic Couplet.**
See page 353.

CRISIS or **TURNING POINT** *A point of great tension in a narrative that determines how the action will come out.* In Act Three of William Shakespeare's *Romeo and Juliet,* Tybalt kills Mercutio, and Romeo kills Tybalt. These events mark the turning point of the play's action.

See **Plot.**
See also page 555.

DENOTATION *The literal or "dictionary" meaning of a word.* Denotation is distinct from **connotation,** which is what is suggested by a word beyond its literal meaning. For example, the denotation, or dictionary definition, of the word *star* (as in "movie star") is "a prominent actor or actress," but the connotation of the word *star* is that of an actor or actress who is adored by fans and who leads a fascinating and glamorous life.

See **Connotation, Diction.**
See also page 305.

DESCRIPTION *Any careful detailing of a person, place, thing, or event.* We associate the term with prose, both fiction and nonfiction, but poems also use description, if a bit more economically.

Descriptions re-create sensory impressions: sights, sounds, smells, textures, tastes. Some description is direct and factual, but more often, description helps to establish a mood or stir an emotion. Here is part of the famous description of Miss Havisham in her bridal dress from Charles Dickens' novel *Great Expectations:*

> But I saw that everything within my view which ought to be white had lost its luster, and was faded and yellow. I saw that the bride within the

bridal dress had withered like the dress, and like the flowers, and had no brightness left but the brightness of her sunken eyes. I saw that the dress had been put upon the rounded figure of a young woman, and that the figure upon which it now hung loose had shrunk to skin and bone.

See **Exposition, Narration, Persuasion.** See also page 216.

DIALECT *A representation of the speech patterns of a particular region or social group.* Dialect differs from the standard speech of a country in sentence pattern, vocabulary, and pronunciation. Writers often use the distinctive patterns of dialect to establish local color. Among American writers noted for their use of regional speech are James Russell Lowell, for the dialect of rustic New England; James Whitcomb Riley, for the Hoosier dialect of Indiana; Mark Twain, for the dialect of the Mississippi Valley; and Bret Harte, for the dialect of the West.

See pages 137, 375.

DICTION *A writer's choice of words, particularly for clarity, effectiveness, and precision.* A writer's diction can be formal or informal, abstract or concrete. In choosing "the right word," writers must think of their subject and their audience. Words that are appropriate in informal dialogue would not always be appropriate in a formal essay. A writer might have a character use "tubby" in an insulting remark, but the word would not do in a medical article.

The impact that diction can have on a piece of writing is illustrated by the following versions of a nursery rhyme. The story is the same; the diction is different.

Three blind mice,
See how they run.
They all ran after the farmer's wife,
Who cut off their tails with a carving knife.
Have you ever seen such a sight in your life
As three blind mice?

Three rodents with defective vision,
Observe their rate of motion.
They all pursued an agriculturalist's spouse,
Who severed their spinal extremities with a
    common kitchen utensil.
Have you ever observed such a phenomenon in
    the span of your existence
As three rodents with defective vision?

The following poem contains no words or phrases one would consider elegant, yet the poem is eloquent. Note the impact of simple, earthy words like *soap, onions,* and *wet clay,* and their appropriateness in the poem.

Lineage
Margaret Walker

My grandmothers were strong.
They followed plows and bent to toil.
They moved through fields sowing seed.
They touched earth and grain grew.
They were full of sturdiness and singing.
My grandmothers were strong.

My grandmothers are full of memories
Smelling of soap and onions and wet clay
With veins rolling roughly over quick hands
They have many clean words to say.
My grandmothers were strong.
Why am I not as they?

See **Connotation, Denotation.** See also page 302.

DRAMA *A story acted out, usually on a stage, by actors and actresses who take the parts of specific characters.* Drama is generally divided into two types: **tragedies,** serious plays in which the central characters meet an unhappy or disastrous end, like William Shakespeare's *Romeo and Juliet;* and **comedies,** humorous plays that end happily, like Shakespeare's *A Midsummer Night's Dream.* **Plot,** the sequence of events, is an important element of drama, as is **dialogue,** the conversations held by the characters, which serve to advance the story's action. **Stage directions** are also essential to drama, as they tell actors and actresses how to move or how they should deliver certain lines. The director of a play makes particular use of stage directions.

Exposition, the presentation of important background information, usually occurs at the opening of a drama (but it may occur at any point that the audience needs information about past events). A drama then introduces the **conflict,** or opposition against which the characters must struggle. In most dramas there is a **climax,** a point of great emotional intensity or suspense. Sometimes, the term *climax* is identified with the **crisis,** a decisive **turning point** that determines the outcome of the action. The end of a drama involves the **resolution,** or outcome, usually by death in a tragedy or by marriage in a comedy.

See **Plot.**
See also page 404.

DRAMATIC IRONY *A device whereby the audience (or reader) understands more of a situation or of what is being said than the character is aware of.* Such speech or action has great significance to the audience or reader and little significance to the character speaking or performing it. The character remains unaware of the real state of affairs. Dramatic irony is a common device for involving the reader in the story's action.

See **Irony**
See also pages 68, 570.

DRAMATIC POETRY *Poetry in which one or more characters speak.* Each speaker always addresses a specific listener. This listener may be silent (but identifiable), or the listener may be another character who speaks in reply.

In "Lord Randal," there are two speakers, Lord Randal and his mother:

"O where hae ye been, Lord Randal my son?
O where hae ye been, my handsome young
    man?"
"I hae been to the wild wood; mother, make my
    bed soon,
For I'm weary wi' hunting, and fain wald lie
    down."

See **Narrative Poetry, Poetry.**
See also page 391.

DYNAMIC CHARACTER *A character who undergoes an important and basic change in personality or outlook.*

See **Characters.**
See also page 75.

EPIC *A long narrative poem that relates the deeds of a hero.* Epics incorporate myth, legend, folk tale, and history, and usually reflect the values of the societies from which they originate. The tone is generally grand, and the heroes and their adventures appear larger than life.

Many epics were drawn from an oral tradition and are known as **primary epics.** These were transmitted by song and recitation before they were written down. Two of the most famous primary epics of Western civilization are Homer's *Iliad* and *Odyssey.* Another primary epic is one of the earliest works in history, the *Epic of Gilgamesh,* from ancient Mesopotamia.

A second type of epic is the **literary** or **secondary epic.** These were written down from the start. Examples include the *Aeneid,* Rome's national epic written by the poet Virgil to give the ancient Romans a sense of their own destiny; the *Divine Comedy,* the great epic of the Middle Ages written by the Italian poet Dante; and *Paradise Lost* and *Paradise Regained,* two great epics written by the seventeenth-century English poet John Milton.

See **Narrative Poetry.**
See also page 592.

EPITHET *A descriptive adjective or phrase used to characterize someone or something.* Examples are "yellow-bellied coward," "Catherine the Great," and "Richard the Lion-Hearted." Homer's *Odyssey* is filled with epithets, such as "raider of cities" (a reference to Odysseus) and "father of gods and men" (a reference to Zeus).

See page 654

ESSAY *A piece of prose writing, usually short, that deals with a subject in a limited way and expresses a particular point of view.* An essay is never a comprehensive treatment of a subject (the word comes from a French word for "attempt" or "try"). An essay may be serious or humorous, tightly organized or rambling, restrained or emotional.

The two general classifications of essay are the **informal essay** (also called the **familiar** or **personal essay**) and the **formal essay.** The informal essay is conversational and personal, often revealing a great deal of the writer's personality. The formal essay is more serious in tone and usually objective. Its topics are often drawn from philosophy, literature, or history. However, many essays cannot be easily pigeonholed. For instance, even where the style is formal and seemingly impersonal, the writer may reveal much of his or her personality and point of view.

See **Exposition, Nonfiction.**
See also pages 216, 231.

EXPOSITION *The kind of writing that is intended primarily to present information.* Although exposition is used in fiction as well as nonfiction, the most familiar form it takes is in essays. The commentaries which introduce the major sections in this book are exposition.

Exposition is also that part of a play in which important background information is revealed to the audience. In *Romeo and Juliet,* for example, William Shakespeare begins by giving us essential information about the Montagues and the Capulets. He presents the conflict between these two houses before introducing the love story.

> See **Description, Essay, Narration, Persuasion, Plot.**
> See also pages 37, 216, 476, 554.

FABLE   *A brief story or poem that is told to present a moral, or practical lesson.* The characters in fables are often animals who speak or act like human beings. The best-known fables are those attributed to Aesop, who is said to have lived around the sixth century B.C. The following fable of the tortoise and the hare is characteristic of Aesop's terse style and clearly stated moral:

> The tortoise and the hare argued about who was swifter, and they agreed to run a race. The hare sprinted out well ahead of the tortoise. Seeing how slow his adversary was, the hare became so confident that he relaxed and even lay down for a nap by the roadside. Meanwhile, the tortoise plodded on without stopping, passed the hare asleep on the road, and got to the finish line first.
> MORAL: *Slow and steady wins the race.*

Another master of this form is the seventeenth-century French writer Jean de la Fontaine. La Fontaine took many of his stories from Aesop but translated them into verse. "The Fox and the Crow" is a fable that La Fontaine adapted from Aesop. Here a modern poet has translated the fable into English, preserving the wit and charm of La Fontaine's version:

The Fox and the Crow
Marianne Moore

On his airy perch among the branches
  Master Crow was holding cheese in his beak.
Master Fox, whose pose suggested fragrances,
  Said in language which of course I cannot
    speak,

"Aha, superb Sir Ebony, well met.
How black! who else boasts your metallic jet!
  If your warbling were unique,
  Rest assured, as you are sleek,
One would say that our wood had hatched
    nightingales."
All aglow, Master Crow tried to run a few scales,
  Risking trills and intervals,
Dropping the prize as his huge beak sang false.
The fox pounced on the cheese and remarked,
  "My dear sir,
  Learn that every flatterer
Lives at the flattered listener's cost:
A lesson worth more than the cheese that you lost."
  The tardy learner, smarting under ridicule,
Swore he'd learned his last lesson as somebody's
    fool.

Essayists and humorists such as James Thurber and E. B. White have added new twists to the fable.

FALLING ACTION   *All of the action in a play that follows the turning point.* The falling action leads to the **resolution** or conclusion of the play. In William Shakespeare's *Romeo and Juliet,* the fortunes of the two lovers steadily decline following the deaths of Mercutio and of Tybalt in Act Three. The action "falls" until the final catastrophe.

> See **Plot.**
> See also page 555.

FARCE   *A type of comedy based on a farfetched humorous situation, often with ridiculous or stereotyped characters.* The humor in a farce is often slapstick—that is, the clowning frequently involves crude physical action. The characters in a farce are often the butts of practical jokes: pies are thrown at their faces or beds cave in on them.

These elements of exaggeration and absurdity set farce apart from other forms of comedy. Anton Chekhov wrote a number of farces, including *A Marriage Proposal, The Bear,* and *The Anniversary.*

> See **Comedy.**
> See also pages 404, 421.

FICTION   *Anything that is invented or imagined, especially a prose narrative.* Although fiction may be based on actual events or personal experiences, its characters and settings are invented. Even if a story is set in an actual place and involves recognizable characters or details, we understand the story itself to be fictitious. In literature, fiction generally refers to the **novel** or the **short story.**

See page 216.

FIGURATIVE LANGUAGE *Language that is not intended to be interpreted in a literal sense.* Figurative language always makes use of a comparison between different things. By appealing to the imagination, figurative language provides new ways of looking at the world.

The interpretation of a poem often depends upon recognizing its figurative meaning. In the following poem, for example, the "poor chap" has not drowned in water, but in loneliness. He is the "I" who speaks in the first and last stanzas.

Not Waving but Drowning
Stevie Smith

Nobody heard him, the dead man,
But still he lay moaning:
I was much further out than you thought
And not waving but drowning.

Poor chap, he always loved larking
And now he's dead
It must have been too cold for him his heart gave
    way,
They said.

Oh, no no no, it was too cold always
(Still the dead one lay moaning)
I was much too far out all my life
And not waving but drowning.

Figurative language consists of **figures of speech.** The main figure of speech used in literature is **metaphor.** Metaphor draws a comparison between two unlike things without the use of any special language.

Another frequently used figure of speech is **simile.** A simile draws a comparison between two unlike things through the use of the words *like, as, as if, than, such as,* and other specific words of comparison. Similes in everyday speech are common. "His voice sounds *like* a foghorn" is a simile in which the sound of a person's voice is compared to the sound of a foghorn. Other examples are "He eats *like* a bird" and "She was *as* cool *as* a cucumber." A well-known simile from literature is William Wordsworth's line, "I wandered lonely *as* a cloud."

Another form of figurative language is **personification.** Personification invests something nonhuman with human qualities. In "The Day Is Done," Henry Wadsworth Longfellow personifies "cares" by describing them as people who can gather up their belongings and walk away:

And the cares, that infest the day,
Shall fold their tents, like the Arabs,
    And as silently steal away.

See pages 163, 300, 318, 507.

FIGURE OF SPEECH *A term applied to a specific kind of figurative language, such as metaphor or simile.* Everyday language abounds with many different figures of speech, in which we say one thing and mean another.

Frequently figures of speech compare some action or feeling to something else, as in, "He eats like a bird." Or they may express exaggeration, as in, "I'll die if I don't go to the dance." They may substitute a part of a thing for a whole, as in using "the stage" to mean the entire theatrical profession. Or they may assign personality to an animal or something that is inanimate, as in "the sea is angry." There are more than two hundred different kinds of figures of speech.

See **Figurative Language.**
See also page 318.

FLASHBACK *A scene in a short story, novel, play, or narrative poem that interrupts the action to show an event that happened at an earlier time.* Many narratives present events as they occur in time—that is, in chronological order. Sometimes, however, a writer interrupts this natural sequence of events and "flashes back" to a past event to tell the reader or audience what happened earlier in the story or in a character's life.

Homer uses flashback in the *Odyssey.* Odysseus, before making his return home, recounts to the King of Phaeacia "those years of rough adventure," his journey of ten years.

FOIL *A character who sets off another character by contrast.* By heightening the differences between two characters, a writer dramatizes the significance of both characters. For example, in the opening scene of William Shakespeare's *Romeo and Juliet,* Benvolio, who attempts to keep peace, is a foil for Tybalt, who wants to continue fighting.

See pages 506, 528.

FOLK BALLAD *A story told in verse that is by an unknown author and meant to be sung.* "Lord Randal" is a famous folk ballad.

See **Ballad.**
See also pages 384, 386, 388.

FOLK TALE *An account, legend, or story that is passed along orally from generation to generation.* Folk tales are of unknown authorship. They may be legends connected to historical figures, as is the story of George Washington and the cherry tree, or they may be fanciful accounts of the supernatural. In this last category fall stories of ghosts, of devils and spirits, of witches, of talking animals, and of legendary heroes, such as Paul Bunyan.

FORESHADOWING *The use of hints or clues in a narrative to suggest what action is to come.* Foreshadowing helps to build suspense in a story because it suggests what is about to happen. It also helps the reader savor all the details of the buildup. Foreshadowing is common in short stories, novels, and drama.

In "The Most Dangerous Game," Richard Connell foreshadows the major action of the story in the conversation between Rainsford and Whitney. Their talk of fear, death, superstition, and evil builds suspense at the outset.

See **Plot, Suspense.**
See also page 29.

FRAMEWORK STORY *A narrative that contains another narrative.* Both the framework story and the inner story add meaning to one another, and one is usually important to the outcome of the other. *The Canterbury Tales,* written by the fourteenth-century English poet Geoffrey Chaucer, is a famous example of several stories within a story.

See page 61.

FREE VERSE *Poetry that has no fixed meter or pattern and that depends on natural speech rhythms.* Free verse may rhyme or not rhyme; its lines may be of different lengths; and like natural speech, it may switch suddenly from one rhythm to another.

When used by a skillful poet, free verse displays special rhythms and melodies unlike any traditional forms. Other than the fact that it is arranged by lines, free verse is very much like rhythmical prose. The following lines are from "The Dismantled Ship," a poem by Walt Whitman, who was the first poet to use free verse extensively.

> In some unused lagoon, some nameless bay,
> On sluggish, lonesome waters, anchored near
>   the shore,
> An old, dismasted, gray and battered ship,
>   disabled, done,
> After free voyages to all the seas of earth,
>   hauled up at last and hawsered tight,
> Lies rusting, moldering.

See **Meter, Poetry.**
See also page 355.

HEROIC COUPLET *Two consecutive lines of rhyming poetry that are written in iambic pentameter and that contain a complete thought.* In a heroic couplet, there is usually one pause at the end of the first line, and another heavier pause at the end of the second line. The form was often used in England for heroic or epic poetry.

William Shakespeare frequently uses the heroic couplet. Here is an example from Act Two of *Romeo and Juliet:*

> Hence will I to my ghostly father's cell,
> His help to crave and my dear hap to tell.

See **Couplet.**
See also page 528.

HOMERIC SIMILE *An extended comparison that mounts in excitement and usually ends in a climax.* The Homeric simile is also known as the epic simile.

See **Epic, Simile.**
See also page 654.

IAMBIC PENTAMETER *The most common verse line in English poetry.* It consists of five verse **feet** (*penta-* is from a Greek word meaning "five"), with each foot an **iamb**—that is, an unstressed syllable followed by a stressed syllable. William Shakespeare's plays are written almost entirely in iambic pentameter. Here is an example from *Romeo and Juliet:*

Alack / the day! / He's gone, / he's killed, / he's dead.

See **Meter, Rhythm.**
See also page 528.

IMAGERY *Language that appeals to any sense or any combination of senses.* Most imagery tends to be visual in nature, but imagery may also suggest the way things sound, smell, taste, or feel to the touch. Imagery is put to particularly effective use in poetry. A skillful poet will carefully choose words that convey the most vivid images. The following poem conveys an experience entirely through images—those of touch, sight, and sound:

The Pond
Amy Lowell

Cold, wet leaves
Floating on moss-colored water,
And the croaking of frogs—
Cracked bell-notes in the twilight.

Writers who use imagery extensively make an experience more intense for us. Good images involve our sensory awareness and help us to be more responsive readers.

See page 308.

INVERSION *A reversal of the usual order of words to achieve some kind of emphasis.* In "The Lotus-Eaters" Tennyson writes:

And, like a downward smoke, the slender stream
Along the cliff to fall and pause and fall did seem.

It would be more common to write: "And, like a downward smoke, the slender stream seemed to fall and pause and fall along the cliff."

Inversion usually appears in poetry, but it occurs in prose and in speech as well. The effect of its slightly unexpected quality is to give special importance to a phrase or thought. It may also be used to produce effective rhyme.

See page 322.

IRONY *A contrast or an incongruity between what is stated and what is really meant, or between what is expected to happen and what actually does happen.* Two kinds of irony are (1) **verbal irony,** in which a writer or speaker says one thing and means something en-

tirely different; and (2) **dramatic irony,** in which a reader or an audience perceives something that a character in the story or play does not know.

Mark Twain's tongue-in-cheek statement below is an example of verbal irony. Twain's actual meaning is quite different from his surface meaning:

When I was a boy of fourteen, my father was so ignorant I could hardly stand to have the old man around. But when I got to be twenty-one, I was astonished at how much the old man had learned in seven years.

An example of dramatic irony is found in William Shakespeare's *Romeo and Juliet.* The audience of the play knows that Juliet is not dead but is merely drugged and appears lifeless. Romeo, however, does not know this. Presuming that his young wife is dead, Romeo kills himself.

See pages 37, 44, 68, 586.

LITERAL LANGUAGE *A fact or idea stated directly.* When a writer intends something to be understood exactly as it is written, he or she is using literal, or nonfigurative, language.

See **Figurative Language.**
See also page 163.

LITERARY BALLAD *A story told in verse in which a known writer imitates a folk ballad.* "All in green went my love riding" by E. E. Cummings is a literary ballad.

See **Ballad.**
See also pages 387, 388.

LYRIC POETRY *Poetry that expresses a speaker's personal thoughts or feelings.* The elegy, ode, and sonnet are forms of the lyric. As its Greek name indicates, a lyric was originally a poem sung to the accompaniment of a lyre, and lyrics to this day have retained a melodic quality. Lyrics may express a range of emotions and reflections: Robert Burns's "John Anderson My Jo" expresses emotions of deep love, while Robert Frost's lyric "Desert Places" expresses the loneliness and fright the speaker feels when looking at a winter landscape.

See **Poetry, Sonnet.**
See also page 374.

METAPHOR *A comparison between two unlike things with the intent of giving added meaning to one of them.*

Literary Terms and Techniques

Metaphor is one of the most important forms of **figurative language.** It is used in virtually all forms of literature. "Life is a dream," "Life is a vale of tears," "Life is a bowl of cherries" are all examples of metaphor. Unlike a **simile,** a metaphor does not use a connective word such as *like, as, than,* or *resembles* to state a comparison.

In the following poem, Eve Merriam does not say that morning is like a new sheet of paper, but rather that morning *is* a new sheet of paper. Her comparison is intended to point out that in every morning we can find a fresh, clean beginning.

Metaphor
Eve Merriam

Morning is
a new sheet of paper
for you to write on.

Whatever you want to say,
all day,
until night
folds it up
and files it away.

The bright words and the dark words
are gone
until dawn
and a new day
to write on.

Many metaphors are implied, or suggested. An **implied metaphor** does not directly state that one thing is another, different thing. Homer uses an implied metaphor in the *Odyssey* when he describes the dawn as having "fingertips of rose." This implies that dawn is a woman with rose-tipped fingers that stretch across the morning sky.

See **Figurative Language, Simile.**
See also pages 322, 325.

METER *A generally regular pattern of stressed and unstressed syllables in poetry.* In these lines from Edgar Allan Poe's "Eldorado," the stressed syllables are marked (ˊ) and the unstressed (˘):

Gáily bĕdíght,
Ă gállănt kníght,
Ĭn súnshĭne ănd ĭn shádŏw

Meter is measured in units called **feet.** A foot consists of one stressed syllable and, usually, of one or more unstressed syllables. A line of poetry has as many feet as it has stressed syllables. Standard poetic feet include: **iamb,** one unstressed syllable followed by one stressed syllable (Bŭt sóft!); **trochee,** one stressed syllable followed by one unstressed syllable (gállănt); **dactyl,** one stressed syllable followed by two unstressed syllables (híckŏrў); and **anapest,** two unstressed syllables followed by a stressed syllable (ŭndĕrstánd).

A metrical line is named for its pattern and number of feet: **iambic pentameter** (5 iambs); **trochaic tetrameter** (4 trochees); **dactylic hexameter** (6 dactyls); **anapestic trimeter** (3 anapests), and so on.

See **Rhythm.**
See also page 336.

MONOLOGUE *A long, uninterrupted speech (in a narrative or drama) that is spoken in the presence of other characters.* Unlike a soliloquy and most asides, a monologue is heard by the other characters present. The characters in William Shakespeare's plays often deliver monologues. Mercutio's speech on Queen Mab in Act One, Scene 4, of *Romeo and Juliet* is an example.

See **Aside, Conventions, Soliloquy.**
See also page 528.

NARRATION *The kind of writing or speaking that tells a story (a narrative).* Any narrative must be delivered by a narrator, whether it is the author or a character created by the author. Narration may take the form of prose or poetry. A narrative may be book length, such as a novel or an epic, or it may be paragraph length, such as a fable or an anecdote. The short stories, the ballads and other narrative poems, the epic, and the novel in this book are all examples of narration.

See **Description, Exposition, Persuasion.**
See also page 216.

NARRATIVE POETRY *Poetry that tells a story.* One kind of narrative poem is the **epic,** a long poem which sets forth the heroic ideals of a particular society. Homer's *Odyssey* is an epic. The **ballad** is another kind of narrative poem. "Lord Randal" is an example of a ballad.

See **Ballad, Epic, Poetry.**
See also page 384.

NARRATOR   *One who narrates, or tells, a story.* A writer may choose to have a story told by a **first-person narrator,** someone who is either a major or minor character. Or, a writer may choose to use a **third-person narrator,** someone who is not in the story at all. Third-person narrators are often **omniscient,** or "all-knowing"—that is, they are able to enter into the minds of all the characters in the story.

James Hurst's short story "The Scarlet Ibis" is told by an "I" who is one of the characters in the story. This narrator can reveal his own thoughts, of course, but he can report only what he thinks goes on in the minds of the other characters. Thus, we know only what the narrator tells us. Frank R. Stockton's short story "The Lady, or the Tiger?" is told by a third-person narrator. The author serves as an omniscient observer who steps outside the action of the story to address the reader.

See **Point of View.**
See also pages 101, 124, 137.

NONFICTION   *Any prose narrative that tells about things as they actually happened or that presents factual information about something.* **Autobiography** and **biography** are among the major forms of nonfiction. The purpose of this kind of writing is to give a presumably accurate accounting of a person's life. **Essays** are also common forms of nonfiction. They are generally personal observations on some subject. Other kinds of nonfiction include the stories, editorials, and letters to the editor found in newspapers, as well as diaries, journals, and travel literature.

Writers of nonfiction use the major forms of discourse: description (an impression of the subject); narration (the telling of the story); exposition (explanatory information); and persuasion (an argument to influence people's thinking).

See page 216.

NOVEL   *A fictional narrative in prose, generally longer than a short story.* The author is not restricted by historical facts but rather is free to create fictional personalities in a fictional world. The characters may be recognizable and disguised with fictitious names, or the real names of actual historical figures may be used. The setting and action of the story, no matter how detailed, are also invented, but may be based on actual places and drawn from little-known or well-known facts.

The subject matter of the novel is virtually unrestricted, and the forms the novel may take cover a wide range. For example, there are the **historical novel,** in which historical figures appear or in which characters, settings, and periods are drawn in such detail, one feels they are real; the **picaresque novel,** a kind of travel story, often satiric and usually presenting the exploits of a rogue; and the **psychological novel,** in which the characters' complex emotional and intellectual states are the focus. These are but a few of the traditional forms of the novel. Some of the many modern forms include the **detective story,** the **spy thriller,** and the **science-fiction novel.** Classifications constantly overlap, and new forms develop. Perhaps no other form of literature has undergone so much change.

See **Fiction, Short Story.**
See also page 666.

OCTAVE   *The first eight lines of a Petrarchan (or Italian) sonnet.* The octave, from the Latin word for "eight," often has the rhyme scheme *abbaabba.* A thought or idea is often introduced in the octave and further developed in the last six lines, or **sestet,** of the poem.

See **Sestet, Sonnet.**
See also page 351.

ONOMATOPOEIA   *The use of a word whose sound in some degree imitates or suggests its meaning.* The names of some birds are onomatopoetic, imitating the cry of the bird named: *cuckoo, whippoorwill, owl, crow, towhee, bobwhite.* Some onomatopoetic words are *hiss, clang, rustle,* and *snap.*

See **Alliteration, Assonance.**
See also page 343.

PARALLELISM   *The use of phrases, clauses, or sentences that are similar or complementary in structure or in meaning.* In "The Destruction of Sennacherib," Lord Byron constructs the second stanza so that the first line is parallel to the third, and the second line parallel to the fourth:

> Like the leaves of the forest when Summer is
>   green,
> That host with their banners at sunset were
>   seen:
> Like the leaves of the forest when Autumn hath
>   blown,

That host on the morrow lay withered and
strown.

The technique of parallelism is used extensively in
the Psalms in the Bible, where the idea of one line is
repeated in the next. These lines from Psalm 96 are
examples:

Give unto the Lord glory and strength.
Give unto the Lord the glory due his name.

See page 346.

PARAPHRASE   *A summary or recapitulation of a
piece of literature.* A paraphrase does not enhance a
literary work. It merely tells in the simplest form
what happened. A paraphrase of Christina
Rossetti's poem "Uphill" might go this way:

A traveler about to make a journey (the journey
of life) inquires about the direction of the road
and the length of the trip. The answer reveals that
the road winds uphill (through life's struggles)
and the journey takes "the whole long day" (a lifetime). The traveler next asks if there will be a
place to spend the night and is told there will certainly be an inn. Inquiring if there will be others
who have made the same trip (through life to
death) and what welcome to expect, the traveler is
assured of company and a ready greeting. And, in
response to questions regarding comfort and the
available supply of beds (graves), the traveler is
informed that both may be expected by all those
who need them.

This summary gives us some essential information
and is useful for checking to see just what did happen. But it is also clear that such a paraphrase is not
memorable, nor does it produce the powerful symbolic effect of the original poem.

PERSONIFICATION   *A figure of speech in which an
animal, an object, a natural force, or an idea is given personality, or described as if it were human.* In the following line from "Dirge," Percy Bysshe Shelley
personifies a storm. He addresses it as if it were a
person who could feel sadness and shed tears: "Sad
storm, whose tears are vain."

See **Figurative Language, Figure of Speech.**
See also pages 238, 300, 327, 507.

PERSUASION   *The type of speaking or writing that is
intended to make its audience adopt a certain opinion or
perform an action or do both.* Modern examples of
persuasion include political speeches, television
commercials, and newspaper editorials.

See **Argument, Description,
Exposition, Narration.**
See also page 216.

PETRARCHAN SONNET   *A fourteen-line lyric
poem consisting of two parts: the octave (or first eight lines)
and the sestet (or last six lines).* The Petrarchan, or Italian, sonnet originated in Italy in the thirteenth century and was much used by the Italian poet
Francesco Petrarch. Its rhyme scheme is *abbaabba
cdecde.*

The following poem is a Petrarchan sonnet. Note
the variation in the sestet, where the rhyme scheme
is *cddccd.*

I Wish I Could Remember That First Day
Christina Rossetti

a	I wish I could remember that first day,
b	First hour, first moment of your meeting me,
b	If bright or dim the season, it might be
a	Summer or Winter for aught I can say;
a	So unrecorded did it slip away,
b	So blind was I to see and to foresee,
b	So dull to mark the budding of my tree
a	That would not blossom yet for many a May.
c	If only I could recollect it, such
d	A day of days! I let it come and go
d	As traceless as a thaw of bygone snow;
c	It seemed to mean so little, meant so much;
c	If only now I could recall that touch,
d	First touch of hand in hand—Did one but know!

See **Sonnet.**
See also page 351.

PLOT   *The sequence of events or happenings in a literary work.* Plots may be simple or complex, loosely
constructed or close-knit. But every plot is made up
of a series of incidents that are related to one another.

Conflict, a struggle of some kind, is the most important element of plot. Conflict may be **external** or **internal.** External conflict is a clash between two or more characters, between characters and society, or between characters and nature. Internal conflict is a struggle within the mind of a character. There may be more than one form of conflict in a work. All the elements of the conflict are incorporated into the plot. As the plot advances, we learn how the conflict is resolved, either through the action or through major changes in the attitudes or personalities of the characters.

Action is generally introduced by a section of **exposition,** information essential to understanding the work. The exposition is part of the **rising action,** during which there is often a **complication,** a point where the central character meets some opposition. The action rises to a **crisis,** or **turning point.**

The falling action follows the turning point. The end of the action is the **denouement** (literally "unknotting") or **resolution,** the moment in the plot when the conflict ends. Not all plots have a resolution as such. In older stories, there generally is a resolution. But many modern stories end without a resolution. They provide us with enough information so that we may draw our own inferences as to how the conflict will be resolved.

One or several **subplots** may be interwoven with the main action. Several subsidiary plots are common in a novel.

> See the terms noted above.
> See also pages 2, 37, 554.

POETRY *Traditional poetry is language arranged in lines, with a regular rhythm and often a definite rhyme scheme. Nontraditional poetry does away with regular rhythm and rhyme, although it usually is set up in lines.* The richness of its suggestions, the sounds of its words, and the strong feelings evoked by its lines are often said to be what distinguish poetry from other forms of literature. Poetry is difficult to define, but most people know when they read it.

Lines of poetry are often arranged in **stanzas.** Through the use of **rhyme** and strong **rhythms,** poetry establishes certain feelings and effects; through the use of **imagery,** poetry suggests things we can know through our senses; and through the use of **figurative language,** poetry adds special meanings by comparison. Techniques used to build musicality

or to emphasize meaning include **alliteration, assonance, onomatopoeia, repetition,** and **inversion.**

> See the terms noted above.
> See also page 294.

POINT OF VIEW *The vantage point from which a narrative is told.* There are two basic points of view. In the **first-person point of view,** the story is told by one of the characters in his or her own words, that is, from the "I" vantage point. First-person point of view is a limited point of view, since the reader is told only what this character knows and observes. The author's use of this vantage point adds a sense of immediacy to a work. Here is an example of first-person point of view from Charles Dickens' novel *Great Expectations.*

> My father's family name being Pirrip, and my Christian name Philip, my infant tongue could make of both names nothing more explicit than Pip. So I called myself Pip, and came to be called Pip.

In the **third-person point of view,** the narrator tells the story from the vantage point of "he" or "she." The third-person narrator might be an **omniscient,** or all-knowing, observer who can describe all the characters and actions in the story as well as comment on what the characters think and feel. O. Henry's story "The Gift of the Magi" is written from an omniscient point of view:

> Now there were two possessions of the James Dillingham Youngs in which they both took a mighty pride. One was Jim's gold watch that had been his father's and his grandfather's. The other was Della's hair. Had the Queen of Sheba lived in the flat across the air shaft, Della would have let her hair hang out the window someday to dry, just to depreciate Her Majesty's jewels and gifts. Had King Solomon been the janitor, with all his treasures piled up in the basement, Jim would have pulled out his watch every time he passed, just to see him pluck at his beard from envy.

An author might also tell a story in the third person from the point of view of only one character. A **limited third-person point of view** is used in "Before the End of Summer," in which everything is told from Bennie's vantage point.

> See **Narrator.**
> See also pages 2, 101, 124, 137.

PUN *Usually, the humorous use of a word or phrase to suggest two or more meanings at the same time.* William Shakespeare's play *Richard III* opens with a famous pun:

> Now is the winter of our discontent
> Made glorious summer by this sun of York.

The "sun of York" is a reference to Edward IV, son of the Duke of York, who also had as his emblem the sun.

Sometimes puns are used seriously. The poet John Donne, in his "Hymn to God the Father," puns on the word *Son* (which has the double meaning of *Christ* and *the sun*) and on the word *done* (which is also the poet's name):

> But swear by Thy self, that at my death Thy Son
> Shall shine as he shines now, and heretofore;
> And having done that, Thou hast done.

See page 585.

QUATRAIN *Usually, a stanza or poem of four lines.* However, a quatrain may also be any group of four lines unified by a rhyme scheme. Quatrains usually follow an *abab*, *abba*, or *abcb* rhyme scheme. Here is a quatrain from Henry Wadsworth Longfellow's "The Day Is Done":

> *a* And the night shall be filled with music,
> *b* And the cares, that infest the day,
> *c* Shall fold their tents, like the Arabs,
> *b* And as silently steal away.

Shakespeare's sonnets are always divided into three quatrains and a couplet, or two rhyming lines.

See **Stanza.**
See also page 353.

REFRAIN *A word, phrase, line, or group of lines repeated regularly in a poem, usually at the end of each stanza.* Refrains are often used in ballads and other narrative poems to create a songlike rhythm and to help build suspense. Refrains can also serve to emphasize a particular idea. This refrain is used in "Lord Randal":

> ". . . For I'm weary wi' hunting;
>   and fain wald lie down."

See **Repetition.**
See also page 382.

REPETITION *The return of a word, phrase, stanza form, or effect in any form of literature.* Repetition is an effective literary device that may bring comfort, suggest order, or add special meaning to a piece of literature. Common forms of repetition are **alliteration,** repeating sounds at the beginning, middle, or end of words; **rhyme;** and **refrain.**

One of the great masters of repetition is Edgar Allan Poe, who worked out theories of how poetry affects a reader. He concluded that simple repetition was one of the most important and functional devices a poet could use. In his poem "Eldorado," which is filled with ghostly images, Poe repeats the word *shadow* in every stanza. Such repetitions build emotional tension.

In the following poem, note how the repetition of words and phrases builds tension:

If something should happen
Lucille Clifton

> for instance
> if the sea should break
> and crash against the decks
> and below decks break the cargo
> against the sides of the sea
> or
> if the chains should break
> and crash against the decks
> and below decks break the sides
> of the sea
> or
> if the seas of cities
> should crash against each other
> and break the chains
> and break the walls holding down the cargo
> and break the sides of the seas
> and all the waters of the earth wash together
> in a rush of breaking
> where will the captains run and
> to what harbor?

Sometimes a poet will repeat a phrase or part of a line, as in these lines from Robert Burns's "Sweet Afton," written after the death of his sweetheart:

> Flow gently, sweet Afton, among thy green
>   braes!
> Flow gently, I'll sing thee a song in thy praise!
> My Mary's asleep by thy murmuring stream —

Flow gently, sweet Afton, disturb not her dream!

See **Alliteration, Assonance, Refrain, Rhyme.**

RESOLUTION   *The outcome of the conflict in a play or story.* The resolution concludes the falling action.

See **Plot.**
See also pages 37, 555.

RHYME   *The repetition of sound in two or more words or phrases that usually appear close to each other in a poem.* For example: *river/shiver, song/long, leap/deep.* If the rhyme occurs at the ends of lines, it is called **end rhyme.** Here is an example of end rhyme from Ralph Waldo Emerson's "Music":

It is not only in the *rose,*
It is not only in the *bird,*
Not only where the rainbow *glows,*
Nor in the song of woman *heard,*
But in the darkest, meanest *things*
There always, always something *sings.*

If the rhyme occurs within a line, it is called **internal rhyme.** Here is an example of internal rhyme from Alfred, Lord Tennyson's "Bugle Song":

The splendor *falls* on castle *walls*

Approximate rhyme (or **near rhyme** or **partial rhyme**) is rhyme in which the final sounds of the words are similar, but not identical (as opposed to **exact rhyme**). *Cook/look* is an exact rhyme; *cook/lack* is an approximate rhyme. Rudyard Kipling uses approximate rhyme in these lines from "Recessional":

For frantic boast and foolish *word*—
Thy Mercy on Thy People, *Lord!*

Rhymes in the work of any careful poet serve many purposes: one is to increase the musicality of the poem; another is to give delight by fulfilling our expectation of a recurring sound; a third purpose is humor. Clever rhymes, for example, those in this limerick, produce a comic effect:

There was a young lady of Lynn
Who was so uncommonly thin
 That when she essayed
 To drink lemonade
She slipped through the straw and fell in.

See **Poetry, Repetition, Rhyme Scheme.**
See also page 341.

RHYME SCHEME   *The pattern of rhymes in a poem.* The rhyme scheme (indicated by a different letter of the alphabet for each new rhyme) of the first stanza of William Wordsworth's "I Wandered Lonely as a Cloud" is repeated in each succeeding stanza and gives structure to the poem:

a   I wandered lonely as a cloud
b   That floats on high o'er vales and hills,
a   When all at once I saw a crowd,
b   A host, of golden daffodils.
c   Beside the lake, beneath the trees,
c   Fluttering and dancing in the breeze.

See **Poetry, Rhyme.**
See also page 341.

RHYTHM   *The arrangement of stressed and unstressed syllables into a pattern.* Rhythm is most apparent in poetry, though it is part of all good writing. Rhythm often gives a poem a certain musical quality. Rhythm may be used to imitate the action being described and thus help to communicate the writer's meaning. In Lord Byron's "The Destruction of Sennacherib," the lines actually imitate the swooping and blowing of a swift, cold wind:

For the Angel of Death spread his wings on the
   blast,
And breathed in the face of the foe as he
   passed;
And the eyes of the sleepers waxed deadly and
   chill,
And their hearts but once heaved, and forever
   grew still!

When the rhythm of a poem has a regular (instead of an irregular) pattern of stressed (′) and unstressed (◡) syllables, this pattern is called **meter.** Good poets usually put stress on the most important words in the line. Stressed words may be accented by having them also alliterate: *face/foe; hearts/heaved.*

In addition to meter, poets use other techniques to intensify rhythm. **Rhyme** contributes to rhythm by causing us to feel that a passage has come to an end. When rhymes fall close together, we have the feeling that we must pause in our reading of the lines.

Another powerful means of building rhythm is through **repetition.** In these lines from Sidney Lanier's "Song of the Chattahoochee," the repetition of the word *abide* echoes the plants' and trees' coaxing of the river to stay:

> The rushes cried *Abide, abide,*
> The willful waterweeds held me thrall,
> The laving laurel turned my tide,
> The ferns and the fondling grass said
> 　*Stay,*
> The dewberry dipped for to work delay,
> And the little reeds sighed *Abide, abide,*
> 　*Here in the hills of Habersham,*
> 　*Here in the valleys of Hall.*

See **Meter, Repetition, Rhyme.**
See also page 336.

RISING ACTION　*Those events in a play that lead to a turning point in the action.* In William Shakespeare's *Romeo and Juliet,* the rising action begins when Romeo and Juliet declare their love and concludes with the deaths of Mercutio and Tybalt.

See **Plot.**
See also page 554.

SATIRE　*A kind of writing that holds up to ridicule or contempt the weaknesses and wrongdoings of individuals, groups, institutions, or humanity in general.* The aim of most satirists is to set a moral standard for society, and they often attempt to persuade the reader to see their point of view through the force of laughter. The laughter may be achieved by a light and witty tone or through bitter irony. In "The Secret Life of Walter Mitty," James Thurber satirizes the modern individual, who daydreams of being a romantic hero while living a humdrum existence. In *Visit to a Small Planet,* Gore Vidal satirizes hypocrisy in human nature.

See **Comedy, Irony.**
See also pages 423, 446.

SESTET　*The last six lines of a Petrarchan (or Italian) sonnet.* The sestet, from the Latin word for "six," usually has a rhyme scheme of *cdecde.* A thought or idea that is introduced in the first eight lines, or **octave,** of the poem is sometimes further developed in the sestet.

See **Octave, Sonnet.**
See also page 351.

SETTING　*The time and place of action in a narrative.* In short stories, novels, poetry, and nonfiction, setting is generally created by description. In drama, setting is usually established by stage directions and dialogue.

Setting can be of great importance in establishing not only physical background but also mood or emotional intensity. In turn, the mood contributes to the plot and theme of the narrative. For example, in the opening chapter of *Great Expectations,* Charles Dickens uses the setting to create a mood of bleakness:

> Ours was the marsh country, down by the river, within twenty miles of the sea. My first vivid impression of things seems to me to have been gained on a memorable raw afternoon toward evening. At such a time I found out for certain that this bleak place was the churchyard; and that Philip Pirrip, late of this parish, and Georgiana, wife of the above, were dead and buried. I knew that the dark flat wilderness beyond was the marshes; and that the low leaden line beyond was the river; and that the distant savage lair from which the wind was rushing was the sea; and that the small bundle of shivers growing afraid of it all and beginning to cry was Pip.

See **Plot, Theme.**
See also pages 2, 144.

SHAKESPEAREAN SONNET　*A fourteen-line lyric poem consisting of three quatrains (four-line stanzas) and a concluding couplet (two rhyming lines).* The Shakespearean, or English, sonnet was not invented by William Shakespeare, but is named for him because he is its most famous practitioner. Its rhyme scheme is *abab cdcd efef gg.* Here is one of Shakespeare's best-known sonnets:

Sonnet 18

a　Shall I compare thee to a summer's day?
b　Thou art more lovely and more temperate:
a　Rough winds do shake the darling buds of
　　May,
b　And summer's lease hath all too short a date;

c　Sometimes too hot the eye of heaven shines,
d　And often is his gold complexion dimmed;
c　And every fair from fair sometimes declines,
d　By chance, or nature's changing course, untrimmed.

e But thy eternal summer shall not fade
f Nor lose possession of that fair thou owest;
e Nor shall Death brag thou wanderest in his
     shade,
f When in eternal lines to time thou growest —

g So long as men can breathe, or eyes can see,
g So long lives this, and this gives life to thee.

> See **Sonnet.**
> See also page 353.

SHORT STORY *Narrative prose fiction that is shorter than a novel.* Biblical stories, Greek myths, legends, and fables are the ancestors of the short story, but the name itself was not used until the nineteenth century. Edgar Allan Poe is regarded by many as the originator of this form as it is known today.

Short stories vary in length. Some are no longer than five hundred words; others run to forty or fifty thousand words. An extended short story is sometimes referred to as a **novelette,** or, when slightly longer, as a **novella.**

The major difference between a short story and longer fictional forms, such as the **novel,** is that the main literary elements — **plot, setting, characterization** — are used with greater compression in the short story than in the longer forms.

> See **Fiction, Novel.**
> See also page 2.

SIMILE *A comparison made between two dissimilar things through the use of a specific word of comparison, such as* like, as, than, *or* resembles. The comparison must be between two essentially unlike things. To say "Dorothy is like her grandmother" is not to use a simile. But to say "Dorothy is like a golden flower" is to use a simile. Like all **figures of speech,** similes help us to see things in vivid, new ways.

Note how similes are used in the following poem to emphasize visions of beauty, purity, and tranquility.

Velvet Shoes
Elinor Wylie

Let us walk in the white snow
   In a soundless space;
With footsteps quiet and slow,
   At a tranquil pace,
   Under veils of white lace.

I shall go shod in silk,
   And you in wool,
White *as* a white cow's milk,
   More beautiful
   Than the breast of a gull.

We shall walk through the still town
   In a windless peace;
We shall step upon white down,
   Upon silver fleece,
   Upon softer than these.

We shall walk in velvet shoes:
   Wherever we go
Silence will fall *like* dews
   On white silence below.
   We shall walk in the snow.

> See **Figurative Language,
> Homeric Simile, Metaphor.**
> See also pages 320, 654.

SOLILOQUY *A speech, usually lengthy, in which a character, alone on stage, expresses his or her thoughts aloud.* The soliloquy is a very useful dramatic device, as it allows the dramatist to convey a character's most intimate thoughts and feelings directly to the audience. In Shakespeare's *Romeo and Juliet,* we are introduced to the Friar in Act Two through a soliloquy in which he reveals his knowledge of herbs, thus foreshadowing the plan of the sleeping potion later in the play. One of Shakespeare's masterful uses of soliloquy occurs in Act Four, Scene 3, in Juliet's speech before taking the potion. She reveals her innermost conflicts: first her fear of being poisoned by the Friar, then her terror of awaking in the tomb, and finally her desperate courage, braving death in order to be reunited with Romeo.

> See **Aside, Conventions, Monologue.**
> See also page 528.

SONNET *A fourteen-line lyric poem, usually written in rhymed iambic pentameter (in lines of ten syllables with a stress on every other syllable).* Sonnets vary in structure and rhyme scheme, but are generally of two types: the **Petrarchan,** or **Italian, sonnet** and the **Shakespearean,** or **English, sonnet.** Sonnets usually express a single theme or idea.

The Italian sonnet is a form that originated in Italy in the thirteenth century. The Italian sonnet has two parts, an **octave** (eight lines) and a **sestet** (six lines).

It is usually rhymed *abbaabba cdecde*. The two parts of the Italian sonnet play off each other in a variety of ways. Sometimes the octave raises a question which the sestet answers. Sometimes the sestet opposes what the octave says or extends it.

The Italian sonnet is often called the Petrarchan sonnet because the Italian poet Francesco Petrarch used it so extensively. Petrarch dedicated more than three hundred sonnets to a woman named Laura.

The Shakespearean sonnet, a form made famous by William Shakespeare, consists of three quatrains (four-line stanzas) and a concluding couplet (two rhyming lines), with the rhyme scheme *abab cdcd efef gg*.

The sonnet form lends itself to variations. Many modern poets have experimented with the sonnet form, combining features of the Petrarchan and Shakespearean modes or inventing new patterns.

Here the poet is working with a traditional subject — the intensity of feeling stirred by beautiful music. Note, however, how she has modified the traditional form of the sonnet.

Girl with 'Cello
May Sarton

a There had been no such music here until
b A girl came in from falling dark and snow
b To bring into this house her glowing 'cello
a As if some silent, magic animal.

a She sat, head bent, her long hair all a-spill
b Over the breathing wood, and drew the bow.
a There had been no such music here until
b A girl came in from falling dark and snow.

a And she drew out that sound so like a wail,
b A rich dark suffering joy, as if to show
b All that a wrist holds and that fingers know
a When they caress a magic animal.
a There had been no such music here until
b A girl came in from falling dark and snow.

The poet makes use of only two rhymes, including approximate rhyme (or partial rhyme); *until/animal; wail/animal*. The poet also repeats certain lines as refrains in each stanza. The first quatrain, which rhymes *abba*, is Petrarchan, but the second quatrain, which rhymes *abab*, is Shakespearean. The sestet departs from these traditional forms altogether: *abbaab*.

See pages 351, 353.

SPEAKER *The voice in a poem.* The speaker may be the poet or a character created by the poet. The speaker may also be a thing or an animal. For example, the "I" or speaker of Ralph Waldo Emerson's poem "Fable" is a squirrel arguing with a mountain:

> And I think it no disgrace
> To occupy my place.
> If I'm not so large as you,
> You are not so small as I,
> And not half so spry.
> I'll not deny you make
> A very pretty squirrel track;
> Talents differ; all is well and wisely put;
> If I cannot carry forests on my back,
> Neither can you crack a nut.

Identifying the speaker in a poem is a key to understanding the poem's meaning.

See page 298.

STAGING (or STAGECRAFT) *All the devices except dialogue which a dramatist uses to communicate to an audience.* Important elements of staging include **scenery, costume, gesture** and **movement,** and **lighting.** Use the diagram of The Globe Playhouse on page 880 to answer these questions about aspects of staging for *Romeo and Juliet.* Where might the famous balcony scene have taken place? What part of the stage could have been used for Friar Lawrence's cell or Juliet's tomb? Where would props or wardrobes have been stored? Find where the groundlings stood and the galleries for the wealthy spectators.

STANZA *A group of lines forming a unit in a poem.* Many stanzas have a fixed pattern—that is, the same number of lines and the same rhyme scheme. "I Wandered Lonely as a Cloud" by William Wordsworth has a regular pattern. Each of the four stanzas has six lines composed of a quatrain and a couplet, with the rhyme scheme *ababcc*. Some poems do not repeat the same pattern in each stanza, yet each group of lines is still referred to as a stanza. "The Fawn" by Edna St. Vincent Millay has five stanzas, but there is no regular pattern of line length or rhyme scheme.

A stanza may be as short as the **couplet,** two rhyming lines. A favorite form of many English poets has been the **heroic couplet,** two rhyming lines of iamfrom *The Globe Restored* by C. Walter Hodges. Reprinted by permission of the author.

bic pentameter. The **tercet,** or **triplet,** is a stanza of three lines, often with one rhyme. The **quatrain** is a four-line stanza with many patterns of rhyme and rhythm. In ballads, the second and fourth lines are usually rhymed while the first and third lines are unrhymed.

Some stanza forms are named for the poets who devised them. The **Spenserian stanza,** for example, a complex nine-line stanza, with the rhyme scheme *ababbcbcc,* is named for the sixteenth-century English poet Edmund Spenser.

See page 350.

STATIC CHARACTER   *A character who remains the same throughout a narrative.* Static characters do not develop or change beyond the way in which they are first presented.

See **Characters.**
See also page 75.

SUBPLOT   *Secondary action that is interwoven with the main action in a play or story.* Several subplots are not uncommon in a novel. The effect of one or more subplots may be to provide some comic relief from a more serious main plot, or to create a certain atmosphere or mood, such as suspense or intrigue. *Great Expectations* by Charles Dickens is an example of a novel with several subplots, all related to the main action of Pip's story. For instance, there is the story of Mr. Wemmick's life outside the office, a life that we find surprisingly full and warm. His story is revealed to us through his devotion to his deaf father, the Aged Parent; through his relationship with Miss Skiffins; and through his concern for his small, private home.

See **Plot.**
See also page 666.

SUSPENSE *That quality of a literary work that makes the reader or audience uncertain or tense about the outcome of events.* Suspense makes readers ask, "What will happen next?" or "How will this work out?" and impels them to read on. Suspense is greatest when it focuses attention on a sympathetic character. Thus, the most familiar kind of suspense involves a character hanging from the ledge of a tall building, or tied to railroad tracks as a train approaches, or ascending a staircase to open a suspicious door. But suspense may also arise simply from curiosity, as when a character must make an important decision, or seek an explanation for something. One of the reasons for the popularity of "The Lady, or the Tiger?" is that the author does *not* relieve our suspense. When that story is over, we are still wondering, "What happened?"

Often a writer hints at what is to come. This method of building suspense is known as **foreshadowing.** Foreshadowing helps to establish interest early in a narrative and also prepares the reader for the outcome.

See **Foreshadowing, Plot.**
See also page 29.

SYMBOL *Any object, person, place, or action that has a meaning in itself and that also stands for something larger than itself, such as a quality, an attitude, a belief, or a value.* A rose is often a symbol of love and beauty; a skull is often a symbol of death; spring and winter often symbolize youth and old age; a dove usually symbolizes peace. In "Uphill," Christina Rossetti uses the climb up a hill to symbolize life's journey.

In this poem a game of football is used to symbolize the cycle of life:

In the beginning was the
Lillian Morrison

Kickoff.
The ball flew
spiralling true
into the end zone
where it was snagged,

neatly hugged
by a swivel-hipped back
who ran up the field
and was smeared.

The game has begun.
The game has been won.
The game goes on.
Long live the game.
Gather and lock
tackle and block
move, move,
around the arena
and always the beautiful
trajectories.

See pages 163, 331.

THEME *The main idea or the basic meaning of a literary work.* The theme of a work is not the same thing as its subject. In the following poem, for example, the subject is toy bears, but the underlying idea—the theme—is that as the playthings of childhood vanish, youthful innocence is lost forever.

Bears
Adrienne Rich

Wonderful bears that walked my room all night,
Where are you gone, your sleek and fairy fur,
Your eyes' veiled imperious light?

Brown bears as rich as mocha or as musk,
White opalescent bears whose fur stood out
Electric in the deepening dusk,

And great black bears who seemed more blue than black,
More violet than blue against the dark—
Where are you now? upon what track

Mutter your muffled paws, that used to tread
So softly, surely, up the creakless stair
While I lay listening in bed?

When did I lose you? whose have you become?
Why do I wait and wait and never hear
Your thick nocturnal pacing in my room?
My bears, who keeps you now, in pride and fear?

Not all literary works can be said to express a theme. Theme generally is not a concern in those works that are told primarily for entertainment; it is of importance in those literary works that comment on or present some insight about the meaning of life.

Literary Terms and Techniques **881**

In some literary works the theme is expressed directly, but more often, theme is *implicit*—that is, it must be dug out and thought about. A simple theme can often be stated in a single sentence. But sometimes a literary work is rich and complex, and a paragraph or even an essay is needed to state the theme.

See pages 178, 187, 197.

TONE *The attitude a writer takes toward his or her subject, characters, and readers.* Through tone, a writer can amuse, anger, or shock the reader. Tone is created through the choice of words and details. William Shakespeare in *Romeo and Juliet* and Anton Chekhov in *A Marriage Proposal* deal with courtship and marriage, but from entirely different perspectives. Shakespeare treats his young lovers as tragic figures. They have nobility and dignity, and their declarations of love are among the most eloquent passages in the play. Chekhov's play presents a comic misalliance of two completely unromantic characters who seem constitutionally incompatible. Shakespeare's tone might be described as compassionate and tender; Chekhov's as wry and genially mocking.

See pages 285, 361.

TRAGEDY *In general, a literary work in which the central character meets an unhappy or disastrous end.* Unlike **comedy,** which often portrays a central character of weak nature, tragedy often depicts the problems of a central character of dignified or heroic stature. Through a related series of events, this main character, the tragic hero or heroine, is brought to a final downfall. The causes of the character's downfall vary. In traditional dramas, the cause is often an error in judgment or a combination of inexplicable outside forces that overwhelm the character. In modern dramas, the causes range from moral or psychological weakness to the evils of society. The tragic hero or heroine, though defeated, usually gains a measure of wisdom or self-awareness. There may be more than one central character in a tragedy. William Shakespeare's *Romeo and Juliet,* for example, has a tragic hero and heroine.

See **Drama.**
See also page 404.

TURNING POINT

See **Crisis, Plot.**
See also page 555.

VERSE DRAMA or **VERSE PLAY** *A play written mostly or entirely in verse.* Verse plays are often written in **blank verse** (unrhymed iambic pentameter). William Shakespeare's *Romeo and Juliet* is an example of verse drama.

See **Blank Verse.**

HANDBOOK FOR Revision

Contents

Part 1: Model Essays

■ Persuasive Essay   ■ Expository Essay

The essays on the following pages are shown in two versions: a rough draft and a final copy. In the draft, the writer has evaluated and revised the essay for logic, clarity, style, and specific support. The writer has also proofread the essay for errors in grammar, usage, punctuation, spelling, and capitalization. The corrections are shown on the draft. The reasons for many of the revisions and corrections are shown in the margin. Marginal notes in the final copy identify important parts of each essay.

Symbols for Revising and Proofreading

Symbol	Example	Meaning of Symbol
≡	Main street	Capitalize a lowercase letter.
/	Pedro's Uncle	Lowercase a capital letter.
/	sensative	Change a letter.
∧	the winnig team	Insert a missing word, letter, or punctuation mark.
ℓ	Are we we safe?	Delete a word, letter, or punctuation mark.
ℐ	Where is my key?	Leave out and close up.
(tr)	Try to make the final draft look neat (of an essay).	Transfer the circled material.
(¶)	¶ "Hi," she cried.	Begin a new paragraph.
⊙	Drive safely⊙	Add a period.
∧	Well you may be right.	Add a comma.
∨	Sams bike	Add an apostrophe.
:	as follows:	Add a colon.
∧;	Ray Leon, Jr. Wen Tan, M.F.A.	Add a semicolon.

MODEL 1: A PERSUASIVE ESSAY
Rough Draft

LUNCH BREAK

Spelling/Close quotes

"What kids are getting on those plastic trays is a shortcut to heart disese, claimed a <u>Newsweek</u> article in late 1993. The

U.S. Department of Agriculture is now leading a major effort to

improve nutrition in our nation's school lunch rooms. This project

Wordy/Comma needed

may be hard and difficult to accomplish however because of poor

nutrition education, official foot-dragging, and established

Spelling

goverment subsidies to schools. Whatever happens on a national

Comma after introductory element

level our school administration should act without delay to bring

our lunch menus into line with good nutrition standards.

Transition needed/ Usage

most serious   *young people*
The problem is that school lunches do not offer us kids a

healthful diet. While lunches usually contain suitable amounts of

vitamins, minerals, and protein, they are often loaded with too

about 40 percent
Spelling/Specific details needed

much fat, cholestrol, sugar, and salt. For example, many of the

Subject-verb agreement

calories in the average school lunch comes from fat—as opposed

30 percent
More specific details needed

to the maximum of fat recommended by most guidelines for good

nutrition. Saturated fat is especially high in such fast-food menu

MODEL 1: A PERSUASIVE ESSAY
Final Copy

LUNCH BREAK

Title

"What kids are getting on those plastic trays is a shortcut to heart disease," claimed a <u>Newsweek</u> article in late 1993. The U.S. Department of Agriculture is now leading a major effort to improve nutrition in our nation's school lunch rooms. This project may be hard to accomplish, however, because of poor nutrition education, official foot-dragging, and established government subsidies to schools. Whatever happens on a national level, our school administration should act without delay to bring our lunch menus into line with good nutrition standards.

Introduction

Position statement

The most serious problem is that school lunches do not offer young people a healthful diet. While lunches usually contain suitable amounts of vitamins, minerals, and protein, they are often loaded with too much fat, cholesterol, sugar, and salt. For example, about 40 percent of the calories in the average school lunch come from fat—as opposed to the maximum of 30 percent recommended by most guidelines for good nutrition. Saturated fat

Body

Logical appeal

Supporting evidence

	At present∧
	items as hamburgers, hot dogs, pizza, and fried potatoes. ~~T~~hese
Sentence frag-ments	very foods are regular offerings / in our school lunch room.
	are
	Butter, cheese, ice cream, and whole milk ∧ also significant sources
	of fat in school lunch menus. Potato and other snack chips are
Comma needed/ Spelling	loaded with salt , and rich desserts and cho∧clate carry high doses
	of sugar.
	Many of these foods are popular with students. Our school
	though∧
Transition needed	would be doing us a long-term favor , if there were some changes
	in the lunch menu to encourage healthier eating habits. Studies
	have shown that fat begins to clog arteries in children as young
	form
Wrong word	as five. Experts have also established that most people ∧ ~~from~~ their
	eating habits early in life. This pattern means that habits in the
	school-age years may have a lasting influence into adulthood. Too
	much saturated fat, cholesterol, and sodium in the diet of an
	adult can result in premature death from such causes as heart
New paragraph Double comparison Punctuation	attack and stroke. Some of the new, ~~more~~ healthier items that
	our school should offer for lunch include the following , fresh

is especially high in such fast-food menu items as hamburgers, hot dogs, pizza, and fried potatoes. At present, these very foods are regular offerings in our school lunch room. Butter, cheese, ice cream, and whole milk are also significant sources of fat in school lunch menus. Potato and other snack chips are loaded with salt, and rich desserts and chocolate carry high doses of sugar.

Many of these foods are popular with students. Our school **Emotional appeal** would be doing us a long-term favor, though, if there were some changes in the lunch menu to encourage healthier eating habits. Studies have shown that fat begins to clog arteries in children as **Supporting evidence** young as five. Experts have also established that most people form their eating habits early in life. This pattern means that habits in the school-age years may have a lasting influence into adulthood. Too much saturated fat, cholesterol, and sodium in the diet of an adult can result in premature death from such causes as heart attack and stroke.

Some of the new, healthier items that our school should **Additional details** offer for lunch include the following: fresh fruits and vegetables, fruits and vegetables, pasta, fish, low-fat dairy products, and

rice. Our school cafeteria might also consider setting up a salad

**Subject/verb
agreement**

bar. If these foods ~~was~~ *were* attractively prepared and presented,

students would accept them enthusiastically.

**Stronger
conclusion
needed**

If you like the idea of a "healthier you," write to the

school board now in favor of a new, healthier lunch menu policy. You might even want to quote Assistant Secretary of Agriculture Ellen Haas in your letter: "We can't make these changes alone."

pasta, fish, low-fat dairy products, and rice. Our school cafeteria might also consider setting up a salad bar. If these foods were attractively prepared and presented, students would accept them enthusiastically.

If you like the idea of a "healthier you," write to the school board now in favor of a new, healthier lunch menu policy. You might even want to quote Assistant Secretary of Agriculture Ellen Haas in your letter: "We can't make these changes alone."

Conclusion

MODEL 2: AN EXPOSITORY ESSAY
Rough Draft

MARVELOUS MIGRATIONS

Commas in series

Many creatures migrate, including antelope salmon bats

Spelling

and butterflies. The most spectacalar migrants however, are

birds. Among the 8,500 species of birds, in fact, migration is the

Word needed

rule, rather than ^the^ exception. Some species, such as the barn

Comma needed

swallow and the rare endangered Siberian crane, fly many

thousands of miles twice a year. Perhaps the champion migrant

Spelling

is the ^c^ artic tern, whose semiannual trips cover 18,000 miles,

virtually from pole to pole and back again.

The most important

^A cause for north-south migration is probably their need

Transpose

for food. Why do birds migrate? In harsh, northern winters, food

becomes scarce for many species, especially for insect-eating

birds. One cause for south-north migration is probably that birds

have more space in the far North to establish summertime

Sentence fragment

nesting territories. Even though food may be easier to obtain in

the tropics, Birds can spread out more if they nest and breed in

Change words

northern regions, thus ~~in order to reduce~~ ^reducing^ the chances that a

MODEL 2: AN EXPOSITORY ESSAY
Final Copy

MARVELOUS MIGRATIONS

Title

Many creatures migrate, including antelope, salmon, bats, and butterflies. The most spectacular migrants, however, are birds. Among the 8,500 species of birds, in fact, migration is the rule, rather than the exception. Some species, such as the barn swallow and the rare, endangered Siberian crane, fly many thousands of miles twice a year. Perhaps the champion migrant is the arctic tern, whose semiannual trips cover 18,000 miles, virtually from pole to pole and back again.

Introduction

Why do birds migrate? The most important cause for north-south migration is probably their need for food. In harsh, northern winters, food becomes scarce for many species, especially for insect-eating birds. One cause for south-north migration is probably that birds have more space in the far North to establish summertime nesting territories. Even though food may be easier to obtain in the tropics, birds can spread out more if they nest and breed in northern regions, thus reducing

Body

Explanation of process: cause and effect

Spelling

a
pred*e*tor will discover and raid their nests. A second advantage

of northward summertime migration is the increased length of

**Combine
sentences**

Since
daylight. Most birds are active only by day. The longer periods of

Spelling

daylight in summer give them more time for for*r*aging and for

raising their young. Migration in both directions thus seems to

offer birds several advantages that make up for the risks and

energy costs of long, difficult journeys.

Punctuation

How do birds navigate on these journeys? Scientists are

far less sure about the "how" of bird migration than about the

"why." Birds have excellent vision, but this feature may be of

limited importance for migration, since many birds either

migrate at night or travel across the open ocean. Experts have

**Sentence
fragment**

gathered evidence. To show that birds use certain stars and

such as the Big Dipper
constellations as navigation guides. Scientists also believe that

**Spelling
Sentence
fragment**

i
birds are sens*a*tive to the earth's magnetic field. And to the

yet another
natural polarization of daylight. According to a theory, birds may

however
use a built-in response to the earth's rotation. This method would

**Pronoun-
antecedent
agreement**

its
require a bird to have some instinctive notions about their own

the chances that a predator will discover and raid their nests. A second advantage of northward summertime migration is the increased length of daylight. Since most birds are active only by day, the longer periods of daylight in summer give them more time for foraging and for raising their young. Migration in both directions thus seems to offer birds several advantages that make up for the risks and energy costs of long, difficult journeys.

How do birds navigate on these journeys? Scientists are far less sure about the "how" of bird migration than about the "why." Birds have excellent vision, but this feature may be of limited importance for migration, since many birds either migrate at night or travel across the open ocean. Experts have gathered evidence to show that birds use certain stars and constellations, such as the Big Dipper, as navigation guides. Scientists also believe that birds are sensitive to the earth's magnetic field and to the natural polarization of daylight. According to yet another theory, birds may use a built-in response to the earth's rotation. This method, however, would require a bird to have some instinctive notions about its own

Explanation of process: additional details

weight and its speed of flight. The bird would also need an internal "computer" to examine this data and reach conclusions about compass points and flight direction.

Subject-verb agreement

The mechanisms ~~and methods~~ that birds uses to navigate ~~and find their direction~~ on their migrations are still not fully

Commas with interrupter

understood. It is becoming increasingly clear, though, that these long-range movements are among the true wonders of the natural world.

weight and its speed of flight. The bird would also need an

internal "computer" to examine this data and reach conclusions

about compass points and flight direction.

The mechanisms that birds use to navigate on their

migrations are still not fully understood. It is becoming

increasingly clear, though, that these long-range movements are

among the true wonders of the natural world.

Conclusion

For definitions of grammatical terms, see the **Grammar Reference Guide** on pages 919–930.

Part 2: Sentence Structure

- Sentence Fragments
- Run-on Sentences
- Parallel Structure
- Comparisons

SENTENCE FRAGMENTS

A **sentence** is a group of words that expresses a complete thought. A group of words that looks like a sentence but that doesn't make sense by itself is a **sentence fragment**.

1. Correct a fragment by adding the necessary sentence parts. Usually you will need to add a verb, a subject, or both.

Fragment

The poor peasants in a small German village. [verb missing: what about the peasants?]

Sentence

The poor peasants in a small German village **worked** for the Balek family.

Fragment

Discovers what is behind each door. [subject missing: who or what discovers?]

Sentence

The **princess** discovers what is behind each door.

Fragment

In one of these crude cells, heated by peat and wood fragments. [subject and verb missing]

Sentence

In one of these crude cells, heated by peat and wood fragments, three **men visit** Doctor Jenkins.

2. Correct a subordinate-clause fragment by connecting it to an independent clause.

Fragment

Even though Anton Chekhov had moved to Moscow to study medicine. He spent most of his time there writing short stories.

Sentence

Even though Anton Chekhov had moved to Moscow to study medicine, he spent most of his time there writing short stories.

RUN-ON SENTENCES

A **run-on sentence** consists of two complete sentences run together as if they were one sentence. Most run-ons are *comma splices*—or two complete thoughts separated only by a comma. Other run-ons are *fused sentences*—two complete thoughts separated by no punctuation.

1. Correct a run-on sentence by using a period to form two complete sentences.

Run-on

Harry Mark Petrakis was born in St. Louis, before becoming a writer, he took jobs as a steel mill worker and as a truck driver.

Corrected

Harry Mark Petrakis was born in St. Louis**. Before** becoming a writer, he took jobs as a steel mill worker and as a truck driver.

2. Correct a run-on by using a comma and a coordinating conjunction (such as *and*, *but*, or *yet*) to create a compound sentence.

Run-on

We may possess all the facts, most of us do not possess Sherlock Holmes's brilliant powers of reasoning.

Corrected

We may possess all the facts**, but** most of us do not possess Sherlock Holmes's brilliant powers of reasoning.

3. Correct a run-on by using a semicolon to form a compound sentence.

Run-on
A flashback shows an earlier event, foreshadowing hints at future action.

Corrected
A flashback shows an earlier event; foreshadowing hints at future action.

4. Correct a run-on by using a semicolon plus a conjunctive adverb (such as *however, moreover,* or *nevertheless*) to form a compound sentence.

Run-on
Richard Connell wrote hundreds of short stories only one of his tales, "The Most Dangerous Game," is now widely read.

Corrected
Richard Connell wrote hundreds of short stories; **however,** only one of his tales, "The Most Dangerous Game," is now widely read.

PARALLEL STRUCTURE

Parallel structure is the use of the same grammatical form or part of speech for equal ideas.

1. Balance a noun with a noun, a phrase with a phrase, and a clause with a clause.

Not Parallel
Jack London was a **hobo,** a **sailor,** and **prospected for gold.** [two nouns and a verb phrase]

Parallel
Jack London was a **hobo,** a **sailor,** and a gold **prospector.** [three nouns]

Not Parallel
The Loisels have no money for **dressing fashionably, going to balls,** and **society.** [two phrases and a noun]

Parallel
The Loisels have no money for **dressing fashionably, going to balls,** and **mingling in society.** [three phrases]

Not Parallel
Bennie knows **that his grandmother is ill** and **her death before the end of summer.** [clause and phrase]

Parallel
Bennie knows **that his grandmother is ill** and **that she will die before the end of summer.** [two clauses]

2. Repeat articles, prepositions, or pronouns if they are necessary to make your meaning clear in a parallel construction.

Unclear
James Thurber achieved fame as **an** essayist and also as cartoonist.

Clear
James Thurber achieved fame as **an** essayist and also as **a** cartoonist.

COMPARISONS

1. Be sure that a comparison contains items of the same or a similar kind. Add any words that may be necessary to clarify your meaning.

Nonstandard
The effect of first-person point of view in a story is different from third-person point of view.

Standard
The effect of first-person point of view in a story is different from **that** of third-person point of view.

2. Include the word *other* or *else* when comparing one member of a group with the rest of the members.

Nonstandard
Cesar liked the Cyclops episode more than any part of the *Odyssey.*

Standard
Cesar liked the Cyclops episode more than any **other** part of the *Odyssey.*

Nonstandard

More than anyone in her English class, Myrna loved reading poetry aloud.

Standard

More than anyone **else** in her English class, Myrna loved reading poetry aloud.

3. Avoid double comparisons.

Nonstandard

Grandfather feels that people now are **more tamer** than they used to be.

Standard

Grandfather feels that people now are **tamer** than they used to be.

Nonstandard

At the end of the story, O. Henry says that Della and Jim were the **most wisest** givers of gifts.

Standard

At the end of the story, O. Henry says that Della and Jim were the **wisest** givers of gifts.

4. Avoid using absolute modifiers in illogical comparisons. Common absolute modifiers include *entirely, final, identical, never, perfect,* and *unique.*

Nonstandard

No two versions of folk ballads are **completely identical.**

Standard

No two versions of folk ballads are **identical.**

Nonstandard

Mark Twain's descriptions of the Mississippi River are **very unique.**

Standard

Mark Twain's descriptions of the Mississippi River are **unique.**

Part 3: Pronouns

- Pronoun-Antecedent Agreement
- Case Forms of Personal Pronouns

PRONOUN-ANTECEDENT AGREEMENT

The noun or pronoun to which a pronoun refers is called its **antecedent.**

1. A pronoun must agree with its antecedent in number and in gender.

Nonstandard

On the island of Thrinacia, the followers of **Odysseus** disobey **their** warning with disastrous results.

Standard

On the island of Thrinacia, the followers of **Odysseus** disobey **his** warning with disastrous results.

2. Use a singular pronoun to refer to an antecedent that is a singular indefinite pronoun. Use a plural pronoun to refer to an antecedent that is a plural indefinite pronoun.

Nonstandard

Each of these women writers has **their** own favorite themes.

Standard

Each of these women writers has **her** own favorite themes.

Nonstandard

Many of the authors that we read use foreshadowing in **his** short stories.

Standard

Many of the authors that we read use foreshadowing in **their** short stories.

3. When the antecedent may be either masculine or feminine, rephrase the sentence to avoid an awkward construction, or use both the masculine and the feminine forms.

Standard

All the characters in *Romeo and Juliet* have **their** characteristic styles of speaking.

Standard

Each of the characters in *Romeo and Juliet* has **his** or **her** characteristic style of speaking.

4. Use a plural pronoun to refer to two or more antecedents joined by *and*.

Nonstandard

Shelley and **Wordsworth** wrote **his** poems in the nineteenth century.

Standard

Shelley and **Wordsworth** wrote **their** poems in the nineteenth century.

5. Use a singular pronoun to refer to two or more singular antecedents joined by *or* or *nor*.

Nonstandard

Neither **Bernard Malamud** nor **O. Henry** set most of **their** stories in rural America.

Standard

Neither **Bernard Malamud** nor **O. Henry** set most of **his** stories in rural America.

Sentences of this type can sound awkward if the antecedents are of different genders. If a sentence sounds awkward, revise it to avoid the problem.

Awkward

Each of these poets composed **his or her** verses carefully.

Revised

All these poets composed **their** verses carefully.

CASE FORMS OF PERSONAL PRONOUNS

1. Be sure to use the correct case for personal pronouns that are part of compound constructions. To choose the right form, try each pronoun of the compound construction separately.

Nonstandard

Brunton, the butler, conspired with another servant. When the maid and **him** opened the heavy door, however, she took her revenge.

Standard

Brunton, the butler, conspired with another servant. When the maid and **he** opened the heavy door, however, she took her revenge.

Nonstandard

Did Ms. Sanchez give you and **he** a copy of the magazine?

Standard

Did Ms. Sanchez give you and **him** a copy of the magazine?

Nonstandard

Between you and **I,** did you find *Great Expectations* easy to read?

Standard

Between you and **me,** did you find *Great Expectations* easy to read?

2. A pronoun following *than* or *as* in an incomplete (or elliptical) construction is in the same case as it would be if the construction were completed.

Nonstandard

Holmes was a master detective; few sleuths have solved their cases as ingeniously as **him.**

Standard

Holmes was a master detective; few sleuths have solved their cases as ingeniously as **he** [solved them].

3. Use the possessive case of a personal pronoun before a gerund. Use the objective case of a personal pronoun before a participle.

Nonstandard

Teale gives a vivid picture of the oak tree and describes every stage of **it dying.**

Standard

Teale gives a vivid picture of the oak tree and describes every stage of **its dying.** [gerund]

Nonstandard

At the end of Hurst's "The Scarlet Ibis," after the narrator cries out Doodle's name, he weeps when he sees **his lying** motionless on the ground.

Standard

At the end of Hurst's "The Scarlet Ibis," after the narrator cries out Doodle's name, he weeps when he sees **him lying** motionless on the ground. [participle]

Part 4: Verbs

- Missing or Incorrect Verb Endings
- Subject-Verb Agreement
- Sequence of Tenses

MISSING OR INCORRECT VERB ENDINGS

1. A *regular verb* forms the past and past participle by adding *-d* or *-ed* to the infinitive form. Don't make the mistake of leaving off or doubling the *-d* or *-ed* ending.

Nonstandard

Jody was **suppose** to finish his chores before supper.

Standard

Jody was **supposed** to finish his chores before supper.

Nonstandard

The poet Shelley was **drownded** in a boating accident.

Standard

The poet Shelley was **drowned** in a boating accident.

2. An *irregular verb* forms the past and past participle in some other way than by adding *-d* or *-ed* to the infinitive form. Irregular verbs form their past and past participle by

- changing a vowel
- changing consonants
- adding *-en*
- making no change at all

Examples

Infinitive	Past	Past Participle
begin	began	(have) begun
bring	brought	(have) brought
ride	rode	(have) ridden
put	put	(have) put

When you proofread your writing, check your sentences to determine which form—past or past participle—is called for. Remember that many nonstandard verb forms sound quite natural. Keep a dictionary handy to check any verb forms you're not sure about.

Nonstandard

In "The Cask of Amontillado," do you think Fortunato should have **saw** he was being tricked?

Standard

In "The Cask of Amontillado," do you think Fortunato should have **seen** he was being tricked?

Nonstandard

Romeo doesn't know that Juliet has **drank** a sleeping potion.

Standard

Romeo doesn't know that Juliet has **drunk** a sleeping potion.

SUBJECT-VERB AGREEMENT

1. **A verb must agree with its subject in number—either singular or plural. The number of a subject is not changed by a phrase or clause intervening between the subject and the verb.**

Nonstandard

Two **parts** of the story **contains** foreshadowing.

Standard

Two **parts** of the story **contain** foreshadowing.

2. **The number of the subject remains unchanged even when the subject is followed by a phrase beginning with expressions like** *along with, as well as, in addition to,* **and** *together with.*

Nonstandard

Mme. Loisel, along with her husband, **attend** the ball.

Standard

Mme. Loisel, along with her husband, **attends** the ball.

3. **Use a singular verb to agree with the following singular indefinite pronouns:** *anybody, anyone, anything, each, either, everybody, everyone, everything, neither, nobody, no one, nothing, one, somebody, someone,* **and** *something.*

Nonstandard

Everyone in the Spelding household **are** intrigued by the visitor whose spaceship has landed in the rose garden.

Standard

Everyone in the Spelding household **is** intrigued by the visitor whose spaceship has landed in the rose garden.

Nonstandard

These poems by Sandburg and Poe are more effective when read aloud, since **each** of them **use** striking sound patterns.

Standard

These poems by Sandburg and Poe are more effective when read aloud, since **each** of them **uses** striking sound patterns.

4. **Use a plural verb to agree with the following plural indefinite pronouns:** *both, few, many,* **and** *several.*

Nonstandard

Many of Rachel Carson's works **deals** with the environment.

Standard

Many of Rachel Carson's works **deal** with the environment.

Nonstandard

Few of my friends **has** read Longfellow's poetry.

Standard

Few of my friends **have** read Longfellow's poetry.

5. **The following indefinite pronouns are singular when they refer to singular words and plural when they refer to plural words:** *all, any, most, none,* **and** *some.*

Nonstandard

All of the information **are** given in the program.

Standard

All of the information **is** given in the program.

Nonstandard

All of the students **is** taking part in the class play.

Standard

All of the students **are** taking part in the class play.

6. Compound subjects joined by *and* usually take a plural verb.

Nonstandard

Athena and **Odysseus** almost **seems** like partners in Homer's epic.

Standard

Athena and **Odysseus** almost **seem** like partners in Homer's epic.

When the elements of a compound subject joined by *and* may be considered a single item or refer to the same thing, the compound subject takes a singular verb.

Nonstandard

Sherlock Holmes's best **friend** and **confidant were** Dr. Watson.

Standard

Sherlock Holmes's best **friend** and **confidant was** Dr. Watson.

7. Singular subjects joined by *or* or *nor* take a singular verb.

Nonstandard

Neither **Burns** nor **Housman were** an American poet.

Standard

Neither **Burns** nor **Housman was** an American poet.

When a singular subject and a plural subject are joined by *or* or *nor,* the verb agrees with the subject nearer the verb.

Nonstandard

Neither **Harriet** nor the other **campers seems** to like George.

Standard

Neither **Harriet** nor the other **campers seem** to like George.

8. When the subject follows the verb, as in questions and in sentences beginning with *here* and *there,* identify the subject and make sure that the verb agrees with it.

Nonstandard

Here **are** a **list** of some important figures of speech.

Standard

Here **is** a **list** of some important figures of speech.

Nonstandard

Where **is Verona** and **Mantua** on this map of Italy?

Standard

Where **are Verona** and **Mantua** on this map of Italy?

9. A collective noun takes a singular verb when the noun refers to the group as a unit. A collective noun takes a plural verb when the noun refers to the parts or members of the group.

Examples

At the end of Böll's story, the **family was** forced to leave the village.

The **jury were** undecided, and members continued to debate the case among themselves.

10. The title of a creative work (such as a book, song, film, or painting) and the name of a country (even if it is plural in form) take a singular verb.

Examples

"Cargoes" **is** a poem by John Masefield.

The **Commonwealth of Independent States consists** of parts of the former Soviet Union.

11. A verb should always agree with its subject, not with its predicate nominative.

Nonstandard

Walter Mitty's **daydreams is** a reaction to his experiences in real life.

Standard

Walter Mitty's **daydreams are** a reaction to his experiences in real life.

12. Subjects preceded by *every* **or** *many a(n)* **take singular verbs.**

Examples

Practically **every story** and **poem** by Poe **displays** his distinctive style.

Many a young **actress is** eager to play the role of Juliet on stage.

SEQUENCE OF TENSES

1. Changing verb tense in mid-sentence or from sentence to sentence without good reason creates awkwardness and confusion. Be sure that the verb tenses in a single sentence or in a group of related sentences are consistent.

Awkward

George **tells** Mr. Cattanzara that he **was reading** a hundred books.

Better

George **tells** Mr. Cattanzara that he **is reading** a hundred books.

George **told** Mr. Cattanzara that he **was reading** a hundred books.

2. The past perfect tense with *had* **is used to express an action that was completed before another action in the past.**

Nonstandard

The narrator **found** that Jerry **lied** to her about his mother.

Standard

The narrator **found** that Jerry **had lied** to her about his mother.

Part 5: Word Order

■ Misplaced Modifiers   ■ Dangling Modifiers

MISPLACED MODIFIERS

Avoid a *misplaced modifier,* which is a modifying phrase or clause that is placed too far from the word it sensibly modifies.

Misplaced

I read about the dragon that Gawaine had killed **in the school paper.**

Clear

I read **in the school paper** about the dragon that Gawaine had killed.

Misplaced

The Loisels work hard for ten years to pay off the debt, **crushed by their bad luck.**

Clear

The Loisels, **crushed by their bad luck,** work hard for ten years to pay off the debt.

DANGLING MODIFIERS

Avoid *dangling modifiers,* which are phrases or clauses that do not sensibly modify any word or group of words in the sentence.

Dangling

To become a professional writer, a lively imagination and a capacity for hard work are required.

Clear

To become a professional writer, a person needs a lively imagination and a capacity for hard work.

Part 6: Comma Usage

- Compound Structure
- Items in a Series
- Two or More Adjectives
- Nonessential Elements
- Introductory Elements
- Interrupters

COMPOUND STRUCTURE

Use a comma before a coordinating conjunction (*and, but, or, nor, for, so,* and *yet*) that joins two independent clauses. If the clauses are very short, you may omit the comma.

Examples

The sun had not come up yet**, but** the morning lay clear and soft and quiet as far as his eyes could see.

—Moss, "Before the End of Summer" (p. 121)

He could not deny the justice of my request**, so** with a rather rueful face he went off to his bedroom, from which he returned presently pulling a large tin box behind him.

—Conan Doyle, "The Musgrave Ritual" (p. 47)

We searched the house **but** it was empty.

ITEMS IN A SERIES

Use commas to separate words, phrases, and clauses in a series.

Examples

Canine cognomens should be designed to impinge on the ears of dogs and not to a-muse **neighbors, tradespeople, and casual visitors.**

—Thurber, "How to Name a Dog" (p. 227)

My lies were **scary, involved, and usually pointless,** but Doodle's were twice as crazy.

—Hurst, "The Scarlet Ibis" (p. 159)

Mme. Forestier **went toward a large closet with mirrored doors, took out a large jewel box, brought it over, opened it, and said to Mme. Loisel:** "Pick something out, my dear."

—Maupassant, "The Necklace" (p. 193)

Fog hides the mountain peaks, the snow swirls down the valleys, and a wind blows so bitterly that the orphanage boys who take the milk twice daily to the baby cottage reach the door with fingers stiff in an agony of numbness.

—Rawlings, "A Mother in Mannville" (p. 88)

TWO OR MORE ADJECTIVES

Use a comma to separate two or more adjectives preceding a noun. However, do not use a comma before the final adjective in a series if the adjective is thought of as being part of a noun. Determine if the adjective and noun form a unit by inserting the word *and* between the adjectives. If *and* fits sensibly, use a comma.

Examples

Eliza, Jess, and Enoch rode to the trial through a fall of **light, fresh** snow.

—West, "The Pacing Goose" (p. 132)

The moment that the case of the criminal was thus decided, **doleful iron** bells were clanged. . . .

—Stockton, "The Lady, or the Tiger?" (p. 33)

NONESSENTIAL ELEMENTS

A *nonessential* (or *nonrestrictive*) clause or participial phrase contains information that is not necessary to the meaning of the sentence. Use commas to set off nonessential clauses and nonessential participial phrases. An *essential* (or *restrictive*) clause or participial phrase is not set off by commas, because it contains information that is necessary to the meaning of the sentence.

Nonessential Clause

He gave us an assignment, **which we were to do in class,** and then he sat on the radiator and watched us work. "Don't forget to use commas," he told us.

—Troy, "Secrets" (p. 72)

Essential Clause

Among the borrowed notions **by which his barbarism had become semified** was that of the public arena, in which, by exhibitions of manly and beastly valor, the minds of his subjects were refined and cultured.

—Stockton, "The Lady, or the Tiger?" (p. 31)

Nonessential Phrase

Sally Rodriguez, **hoping to write her report on Brenda Peterson,** took notes on "Growing Up Game."

Essential Phrase

The book **lying on that desk** is mine.

INTRODUCTORY ELEMENTS

Use a comma after *yes, no,* or any mild exclamation such as *well* or *why* at the beginning of a sentence. Also use a comma after an introductory participial phrase, after two or more introductory prepositional phrases, and after an introductory adverb clause.

Examples

"**Oh,** you can trust me," said the Cossack.

—Connell, "The Most Dangerous Game" (p. 22)

"**Yes,** I do; it's lies, Joe."

—Dickens, *Great Expectations* (p. 694)

Thus speaking, Fortunato possessed himself of my arm.

—Poe, "The Cask of Amontillado" (p. 96)

On the way to the Mathises', Bennie sat on the back of the buggy.

—Moss, "Before the End of Summer" (p. 117)

As he was about to mount his horse, the animal suddenly pricked up its ears.

—London, "War" (p. 43)

INTERRUPTERS

1. Appositives and appositive phrases are usually set off by commas.

I sprinted barefoot across the lawns with my favorite playmate, **the cook's son,** to the stream at the end of the garden.

—Rama Rau, "By Any Other Name" (p. 260)

Every afternoon Sinesio's muffled knock on their two-room shack was answered by Faustina, **his wife.**

—Burciaga, "La Puerta" (p. 166)

Mr. Wopsle, **the clerk at church,** was to dine with us. . . .

—Dickens, *Great Expectations* (p. 676)

2. Words used in direct address are set off by commas.

Examples

I said to him, "You have been my friend, **Jerry.**"

—Rawlings, "A Mother in Mannville" (p. 93)

"But, **my dear,** I thought you'd be thrilled to death."

—Maupassant, "The Necklace" (p. 191)

"**Cyclops,**
if ever mortal man inquire
how you were put to shame and blinded, tell him
Odysseus, raider of cities, took your eye:
Laertes' son, whose home's on Ithaca!"

—Homer, The *Odyssey* (p. 614)

3. Use commas to set off parenthetical expressions.

Examples

Gram, **I remember,** brushed away what she remarked was dust in her eyes with a corner of her apron and went inside.

—Teale, "The Death of a Tree" (p. 237)

He became intimate, **of course,** with my pointer Pat.

—Rawlings, "A Mother in Mannville" (p. 90)

My father's family, **on the other hand,** is *chilango,* from Mexico City.

—Cisneros, "Straw into Gold" (p. 252)

Part 7: Style

- Sentence Variety
- Stringy Sentences
- Active and Passive Voice
- Overwriting
- Creative Use of Synonyms
- Vivid Words
- Clichés
- Levels of Language

SENTENCE VARIETY

1. Create sentence variety in length and rhythm by using compound, complex, and compound-complex sentences, as well as simple sentences.

Little Variation

Sherlock Holmes tells how he once solved a riddle. This riddle concerned the Musgrave family ritual. The case also concerned the fact that a butler and a maid had disappeared at the Musgrave estate. Holmes questioned Reginald Musgrave. Musgrave told Holmes that he had dismissed the butler. The butler's name was Brunton. Musgrave had caught the butler looking at a copy of a verse about the ritual.

More Variation

Sherlock Holmes tells how he once solved the riddle of the Musgrave family ritual. After the mysterious disappearance of a butler and a maid at the Musgrave estate, Holmes questioned Reginald Musgrave. Musgrave told Holmes that he had dismissed Brunton, the butler, after Musgrave had caught him looking at a copy of a verse about the ritual.

2. Expand short, choppy sentences by adding details.

Choppy

Maxine Kumin was born in Philadelphia. She graduated from college. She taught at Tufts University. She has written poetry. She has also written novels and other books. She won the Pulitzer Prize.

More Detailed

Maxine Kumin was born in Philadelphia, Pennsylvania. After graduating from Radcliffe College in Cambridge, Massachusetts, she taught English at Tufts University. In addition to several volumes of poetry, she has published novels and children's books. Her collection entitled *Up Country: Poems of New England* won the Pulitzer Prize in 1973.

3. Vary sentence openers by using appositives, single-word modifiers, phrase modifiers, and clause modifiers.

Little Variation

Lomov returns. He and Natalia argue again. The argument this time is about hunting dogs. Natalia claims that her family dog, Otkatai, is better than Lomov's dog. Lomov's dog is named Ugadi. Lomov cries that his heart is bursting with palpitations. He falls into a chair and faints.

More Variation

After Lomov returns, he and Natalia argue again. **This time,** the argument is about hunting dogs. Natalia claims that her family dog, Otkatai, is better than Lomov's dog, **Ugadi. Crying that his heart is bursting with palpitations,** Lomov falls into a chair and faints.

4. Simplify long, rambling sentences by breaking them up and regrouping ideas.

Rambling

The most important incident in Brenda Peterson's essay "Growing Up Game" is the moment of revelation she experiences in the car with the dead doe as she sits beside the animal, when she realizes that eating meat means becoming connected to an animal's actual death, and this insight also causes Peterson to realize that she too is mortal, so the moment in the car marks the end of the writer's childhood innocence.

Better

The most important incident in Brenda Peterson's essay "Growing Up Game" is the moment of revelation she experiences in the car with the dead doe. As she sits beside the animal, she realizes that eating meat means becoming connected to an animal's actual death. This insight also causes Peterson to realize that she too is mortal. The moment in the car thus marks the end of the writer's childhood innocence.

STRINGY SENTENCES

Simplify stringy sentences by writing concisely. Pare down your use of prepositional phrases. Reduce clauses to phrases, if possible. If you can, reduce clauses and phrases to single words.

Stringy

Homer used the material of legend as the basis for his poems. The main legend on which Homer drew for the *Iliad* and the *Odyssey* was the tale of the war between the Greeks and the Trojans. To this material he added original elements of plot structure, and he created characters and dialogue for his epics. Homer also drew on tales from folklore, especially in his epic story *The Odyssey*.

Better

Homer used legendary material as the basis for his poems. The main legend he drew on was the tale of the Trojan War. He added original plot elements, characters, and dialogue. He also drew on folk tales, especially in the *Odyssey*.

ACTIVE AND PASSIVE VOICE

Voice is the form a transitive verb takes to indicate whether the subject of the verb performs or receives the action. In general, the passive voice is less direct, less forceful, and less concise than the active voice. Whenever possible, revise passive verbs so that they are active.

Passive

The speaker **is told** by his neighbor that good fences have their uses.

Active

The speaker's neighbor **tells** him that good fences have their uses.

Passive

According to II Kings 19:35, Jerusalem **was attacked** by the ancient Assyrian king Sennacherib.

Active

According to II Kings 19:35, the ancient Assyrian king Sennacherib **attacked** Jerusalem.

OVERWRITING

1. Eliminate unnecessary words.

Wordy

Anton Chekhov explores **the human condition and situation** with scientific precision.

Better

Anton Chekhov explores **the human condition** with scientific precision.

Wordy

Memories and reminiscences of another culture haunt many characters in Harry Mark Petrakis' fiction.

Better

Memories of another culture haunt many characters in Harry Mark Petrakis' fiction.

2. Avoid pretentious, complicated words where plain, simple ones will do.

Pretentious

In "How to Name a Dog," Thurber **utilizes** satire to **deride the foolishness** of various **categories** of dog owners.

Simpler

In "How to Name a Dog," Thurber **uses** satire to **poke fun at** various **kinds** of dog owners.

3. Avoid unnecessary repetition and unnecessary intensifiers.

Repetitious

Sherlock Holmes was a brilliant **detective and sleuth** who solved seemingly insoluble mysteries.

Better

Sherlock Holmes was a brilliant **detective** who solved seemingly insoluble mysteries.

Repetitious

Harriet, the narrator of Toni Cade Bambara's "My Delicate Heart Condition," is the **truly central** character in the story.

Better

Harriet, the narrator of Toni Cade Bambara's "My Delicate Heart Condition," is the **central** character in the story.

CREATIVE USE OF SYNONYMS

Avoid awkward repetition by using synonyms creatively.

Awkward

Walter Van Tilburg Clark creates an ominous **atmosphere** at the outset of his **story** "The Portable Phonograph," and this **atmosphere** continues to darken during the **story**.

Better

Walter Van Tilburg Clark creates an ominous **atmosphere** at the outset of his **story** "The Portable Phonograph," and this **mood** continues to darken during the **tale**.

VIVID WORDS

1. **Whenever possible, replace vague words with specific ones.**

Vague

Mr. Pumblechook and I ate in a back room while his shopman had a snack elsewhere.

Specific

Mr. Pumblechook and I breakfasted at eight o'clock in the parlor behind the shop while his shopman took his mug of tea and hunch of bread and butter on a sack of peas in the front premises.

—Dickens, *Great Expectations* (p. 687)

2. Replace abstract words with vivid, concrete words that appeal to the senses.

Abstract

When I sat next to the dead doe, I did not mind the inconvenience. I did experience guilt, sympathy, and appreciation.

Concrete/Sensory

It was not the smell I minded, it was the glazed great, dark eyes and the way that head flopped around crazily on what I knew was once a graceful neck. I found myself petting this doe, murmuring all those graces we'd been taught long ago as children.

—Peterson, "Growing Up Game" (p. 224)

CLICHÉS

A *cliché* is a tired expression. Replace clichés in your writing with fresh, vivid expressions.

Cliché

She was **as pretty as a picture,** but she'd **had a bad break.**

Vivid

She was one of those pretty and charming girls, born, as if by an accident of fate, into a family of clerks.

—Maupassant, "The Necklace" (p. 190)

LEVELS OF LANGUAGE

Depending on your purpose, audience, and form of writing, you should use an appropriate level of language. For example, *formal English* is appropriate for serious essays, reports, and speeches on solemn occasions. *Informal English* is suitable for personal letters, journal entries, and many articles. The following chart gives an outline of formal and informal levels of language.

	Formal	Informal
WORDS	longer, rare, specialized	shorter, colloquial
SPELLING	in full	contractions
GRAMMAR	complex, complete	compound, fragmentary

Formal English usually creates a serious tone. Informal English tends to have a friendlier, more personal tone.

Formal

And here I have lamely related to you the uneventful chronicle of two foolish children in a flat who most unwisely sacrificed for each other the greatest treasures of their house. But in a last word to the wise of these days let it be said that of all who give gifts these two were the wisest.

—O. Henry, "The Gift of the Magi" (p. 177)

Informal

And everyone's standing on their feet clutching at their faces. Everyone but me. Cause I know from the getgo that Mr. and Mrs. are going to leave the bar to give Jr. room and fly over to the other side. Which is exactly what they do.

—Bambara, "My Delicate Heart Condition" (p. 107)

Part 8: Glossary of Usage

a, an Use the indefinite article *a* before words beginning with a consonant sound. Use the indefinite article *an* before words beginning with a vowel sound.

Examples

At the end of Rawlings's story, the narrator learns that Jerry does not have *a* mother in Mannville.

In Connell's "The Most Dangerous Game," General Zaroff lives and hunts on *an* island.

accept, except *Accept* is a verb meaning "to receive." *Except* may be either a verb or a preposition. As a verb, *except* means "to leave out." As a preposition, *except* means "excluding."

Examples

M. Loisel *accepts* the invitation to the ball.

The hatred of the Capulets *excepts* none of the Montagues. [verb]

Luann read all the nonfiction writers *except* James Thurber. [preposition]

adapt, adopt *Adapt* means "to change or adjust something in order to make it fit or to make it suitable." *Adopt* means "to take something and make it one's own."

Examples

Shakespeare's *Romeo and Juliet* has been *adapted* for film several times.

When he returned to his native island of Ithaca, Odysseus *adopted* a disguise as a beggar.

affect, effect *Affect* is a verb meaning "to influence." As a verb, *effect* means "to bring about" or "to accomplish." As a noun, *effect* means "the result of an action."

Examples

When you read Jack London's story "War," how did the death of the young cavalryman *affect* you?

Brenda Peterson's new experiences gradually *effect* changes in her attitudes toward eating game. [verb]

According to O. Henry, gifts from the heart have a marvelous *effect*. [noun]

all, all of The word *of* can usually be omitted, except before some pronouns.

Examples

All of us went to see the production of *Romeo and Juliet*.

Do *all* your friends love movies about ancient Greece and Rome?

Glossary of Usage **911**

allusion, illusion An *allusion* is an indirect reference to something. An *illusion* is a mistaken idea or a misleading appearance.

Examples

The title of Santha Rama Rau's essay "By Any Other Name" is an *allusion* to *Romeo and Juliet.*

In Shakespeare's play, Romeo is the victim of an *illusion* when he thinks that Juliet is dead.

among, between Use *between* when you are referring to two things at a time, or to more than two when each item is being compared individually to each of the others.

Examples

Shawna could not decide *between* Edna St. Vincent Millay and Diane Glancy as the subject for her report.

Yitzak's report explored differences *between* lyric poetry, dramatic poetry, and narrative poetry.

Use *among* when you are referring to more than two items.

Example

Among the novels of Dickens, which was Sheel's favorite?

amount, number Use *amount* to refer to a singular word. Use *number* to refer to a plural word.

Examples

Holmes's solutions to his cases always display a considerable *amount* of ingenuity.

George told Mr. Cattanzara that he was reading a large *number* of books.

as, like *Like* is a preposition. In formal situations, do not use *like* for the conjunction *as* to introduce a subordinate clause.

Examples

Nature was a favorite subject for nineteenth-century English poets *like* William Wordsworth and Percy Bysshe Shelley.

After he returned to Ithaca, did Odysseus behave toward the suitors *as* you expected he would?

awhile, a while *Awhile* is an adverb meaning "for a short time." *A while* is made up of an article and a noun and means "a period or space of time."

Examples

Jaime and I talked *awhile* at the library after school.

When he was young, Mark Twain worked for *a while* as a steamboat pilot on the Mississippi River.

bad, badly *Bad* is an adjective. *Badly* is an adverb. In standard English, only the adjective form should follow a sense verb, such as *feel, see, hear, taste, look,* or other linking verb.

Examples

Is Mme. Loisel a victim of *bad* luck, or does she deserve her fate?

The narrator of "The Scarlet Ibis" feels guilty because he thinks he behaved *badly* toward his brother Doodle.

The narrator in Amy Tan's "Rules of the Game" felt *bad* whenever her mother boasted about her.

because In formal situations, do not use the construction *reason . . . because.* Instead, use *reason . . . that.*

Informal

In Poe's "The Cask of Amontillado," the *reason* for Montresor's cruel revenge was *because* he thought Fortunato had insulted him.

Formal

In Poe's "The Cask of Amontillado," the *reason* for Montresor's cruel revenge was *that* he thought Fortunato had insulted him.

between See **among, between.**

bring, take *Bring* means "to come carrying something." *Take* means "to go carrying something."

Examples

Please *bring* copies of *Romeo and Juliet* to rehearsal after school.

Please *take* this issue of *Newsweek* to Mr. Chen in Room 136.

compare to, compare with Use *compare to* when you want to stress either the similarities or the differences between two things. Use *compare with* when you wish to stress both similarities and differences.

Examples

In his poem, Langston Hughes *compares* a postponed dream *to* a dried-up raisin in the sun.

Russell presented a report that *compared* Frost's "Mending Wall" *with* "At Woodward's Gardens."

comprise, compose *Comprise* means "to include," "to contain," or "to consist of." *Compose* means "to make up" or "constitute." *Compose* in the passive voice + *of* may be synonymous with *comprise.*

Examples

A sonnet *comprises* fourteen lines in iambic pentameter.

Housman's "Loveliest of Trees" *is composed of* (or *comprises*) three quatrains.

connote, denote *Connote* means "to suggest or imply." *Denote* means "to indicate or signify explicitly."

Examples

In Shakespeare's "The Seven Ages of Man," the word "pantaloon" in line 20 *connotes* foolishness.

The word *recessional* in the title of Kipling's poem *denotes* a closing hymn.

continual, continuous *Continual* means "happening over and over again," "repeated often." *Continuous* means "going on without interruption," "unbroken."

Examples

The Baleks' *continual* cheating of the villagers was outrageously unjust.

When the speaker in Stephens's poem presses the shell to his ear, he hears the *continuous* murmur of distant seas.

convince, persuade *Convince* means "to win someone over through argument." *Convince* is usually followed by *that* and a subordinate clause. *Persuade* means to move someone to act in a certain way. *Persuade* is often followed by *to.*

Examples

E. B. White *convinced* Rachel Carson *that* she ought to write the book herself, and the result was *Silent Spring.*

Mme. Loisel *persuades* her husband *to* give her the money for a new dress.

could of Do not write *of* with the helping verb *could.* Write *could have.* Also avoid *had of, ought to of, should of, would of, might of,* and *must of.*

Example

The nurses think that no one besides Dr. Mitty *could have* [not *of*] saved the millionaire banker.

different from, different than Use *different from,* not *different than.*

Example

Similes are *different from* metaphors because similes use the words *like, as, than,* or *resembles.*

disinterested, uninterested *Disinterested* means "impartial." *Uninterested* means "unconcerned," "inattentive."

Examples

Scientific reports are usually written in an objective, *disinterested* style.

At the start of Bernard Malamud's "A Summer's Reading," George seems bored and *uninterested* in the future.

due to the fact that Replace this wordy phrase with *because.*

Wordy

Due to the fact that Jess thought that the geese were pests, he ordered Enoch to get rid of the eggs.

Better

Because Jess thought that the geese were pests, he ordered Enoch to get rid of the eggs.

effect See **affect, effect.**

emigrate, immigrate *Emigrate* means "to leave a country or a region to settle elsewhere." *Immigrate* means "to come into a country or region to settle there." *Emigrate* is used with *from; immigrate* is used with *to.*

Examples

In several of her novels, Amy Tan has given a vivid picture of Chinese families who *immigrated to* the United States.

In Burciaga's "La Puerta," some of the characters decide to *emigrate from* their native Mexico.

everyday, every day *Everyday* is an adjective meaning "daily" or "common." *Every day* is an adverbial phrase meaning "each day."

Examples

Many of Bernard Malamud's stories are about *everyday* life in New York neighborhoods.

Every day during that summer, Bennie must have thought about his grandmother's approaching death.

everyone, every one *Everyone* is an indefinite pronoun. *Every one* consists of an adjective and a pronoun and means "every person or thing of those named."

Examples

Practically *everyone* enjoys a suspenseful detective story.

In our class discussion, Jaret had an interesting comment about *every one* of Odysseus' adventures.

except See **accept, except.**

farther, further *Farther* refers to geographical distance. *Further* means "in addition to" or "to a greater degree."

Examples

In Poe's "Eldorado," the pilgrim shadow urges the knight to ride *farther* to reach his goal.

Toward the end of "The Portable Phonograph," Doctor Jenkins' preparations for the night *further* develop the ominous mood.

fewer, less Use *fewer,* which tells "how many," to modify a plural noun. Use *less,* which tells "how much," to modify a singular noun.

Examples

Thurber shows that Walter Mitty has *fewer* heroic qualities in real life than he does in his daydreams.

Most readers of Toni Cade Bambara's "My Delicate Heart Condition" have *less* sympathy for George than for Harriet or for Willie.

good, well *Good* is an adjective. *Well* may be used as an adjective or an adverb. The expressions *feel good* and *feel well* mean different things. *Feel good* means "to feel happy or pleased." *Feel well* means "to feel healthy."

Examples

In Harry Mark Petrakis' "A Whole Nation and a People," Barba Nikos teaches the narrator to feel *good* about his cultural heritage.

Bonnie's grandmother did not feel *well,* so she called the doctor.

Avoid using *good* to modify an action verb. Instead, use *well* as an adverb meaning "capably" or "satisfactorily."

Nonstandard
Few writers have used the surprise ending as *good* as O. Henry did in his stories.

Standard
Few writers have used the surprise ending as *well* as O. Henry did in his stories.

had of See **could of.**

hanged, hung Use *hanged* to refer to an execution by hanging. Use *hung* to refer to pictures and other things that can be suspended.

Examples
In Dickens' time, many people were *hanged* for minor offenses such as petty theft.

In "The Cask of Amontillado," lighted torches called flambeaux burned in sconces that *hung* on the walls.

he, she, they Do not use an unnecessary pronoun after the subject of a clause or a sentence. This error is called the *double subject.*

Nonstandard
In Maupassant's story, Mme. Loisel *she* loses the necklace on the way home from the ball.

Standard
In Maupassant's story, Mme. Loisel loses the necklace on the way home from the ball.

historic, historical *Historic* means "crucial" or "especially important." *Historical* means "concerned or connected with history."

Examples
Rachel Carson's *Silent Spring* had *historic* significance, because the book made a large number of people aware of dangers to the environment.

Homer's epics combined memories of *historical* events with folk tales and mythology.

hopefully Be sure that this adverb modifies a specific verb. Do not use this word loosely as a modifier for the entire sentence.

Vague
Hopefully, the nuclear disaster that Clark imagines in "The Portable Phonograph" will never come to pass.

Specific
Perhaps we can now predict *hopefully* that the nuclear disaster Clark imagines in "The Portable Phonograph" will never come to pass.

illusion See **allusion, illusion.**

imply, infer *Imply* means "to suggest something indirectly." *Infer* means "to interpret" or "to get a certain meaning from a remark or an action."

Examples
At several points, Thurber *implies* that the relationship between Mitty and his wife may be strained.

Can we *infer* from Montresor's words and actions that he is really insane?

in, into, in to *In* means "within." *Into* means "from the outside to the inside." *In to* refers to motion with a purpose.

Examples
O. Henry set many of his stories *in* New York City.

The title of Sandra Cisneros' essay refers to the writer's ability to transform everyday materials *into* literature of lasting value.

During third period, Mr. Matsushita came *in to* give our class some pointers on doing library research.

its, it's *Its* is a possessive pronoun. *It's* is the contraction for *it is* or *it has.*

Examples

Lauren's favorite story was Jack London's "War"; she especially liked *its* ironic ending.

It's clear from Dorothy West's essay that Rachel West set a good example for her children.

kind(s), sort(s), type(s) With the singular form of each of these nouns, use *this* or *that*. With the plural form, use *these* or *those*.

Examples

This type of story is nearly always popular.

Those kinds of poems are dramatic or narrative, rather than lyric.

lay, lie The verb *lay* means "to put (something) in a place." *Lay* usually takes an object. The past tense of *lay* is *laid*. The verb *lie* means "to rest" or "to stay, to recline, or to remain in a certain state or position." *Lie* never takes an object. The past tense of *lie* is *lay*.

Examples

Please *lay* those magazines on the table. [present tense of *lay*]

Juliet *lies* in a deep sleep, which makes her appear to be dead. [present tense of *lie*]

leave, let *Leave* means "to go away." *Let* means "to permit" or "to allow." Avoid using *leave* for *let*.

Nonstandard

Leave us play one more game!

Standard

Let us play one more game!

Standard

The train was scheduled to *leave* at 9:10.

less See **fewer, less.**

might of, must of See **could of.**

number See **amount, number.**

on, onto, on to *On* refers to position and means "upon," "in contact with," or "supported by." *Onto* implies motion and means "to a position on." Do not confuse *onto* with *on to*.

Examples

The Baleks would weigh the vegetables and herbs *on* a bronze-gilt pair of scales.

Rainsford climbed *onto* the ship's rail, lost his balance, and fell into the water.

Anton Chekhov trained to become a doctor; he went *on to* write many famous plays and short stories.

or, nor Use *or* with *either*. Use *nor* with *neither*.

Examples

Juanita will write her report *either* on Pat Mora *or* on Claude McKay.

Neither Carl Sandburg *nor* Ogden Nash was a British poet.

oral, verbal *Oral* refers to that which is spoken, as distinguished from that which is written. *Verbal* refers to anything using words, either oral or written.

Examples

Sound effects are an important element in the *oral* interpretation of poetry.

Shakespeare's frequent puns show that he must have loved *verbal* playfulness.

ought to of See **could of.**

principal, principle *Principal* is an adjective meaning "first" or "main." It can also be a noun meaning the head of a school. *Principle* is a noun meaning "rule of conduct" or "a fact or general truth."

Examples

The *principal* character in *Great Expectations* is Pip.

The only *principle* that General Zaroff seems to respect is the law of the jungle.

relation, relationship *Relation* refers to a person connected to another by kinship. *Relationship* refers to a connection between thoughts or meanings.

Examples

Among your friends and *relations,* is there anyone who resembles Dickens' character Miss Havisham?

In *Great Expectations* Dickens explores the *relationship* between appearance and reality.

respectfully, respectively *Respectfully* means "with respect" or "full of respect." *Respectively* means "each in the order indicated."

Examples

In "A Mother in Mannville," the boy Jerry treats the narrator *respectfully.*

Brenda Peterson and Edwin Way Teale are the authors of "Growing Up Game" and "The Death of a Tree," *respectively.*

rise, raise *Rise* means "to go up" or "to get up." *Rise* never takes an object. The past tense of *rise* is *rose. Raise* means "to cause (something) to rise" or "to lift up." *Raise* usually takes an object. The past tense of *raise* is *raised.*

Examples

Dr. Watson says that in Sherlock Holmes's periods of lethargy, he would seldom *rise* from the sofa, except to move occasionally to the table.

Raise your hand if you have a question.

should of See **could of.**

sit, set *Sit* means "to rest in an upright, seated position." *Sit* seldom takes an object. The past tense of *sit* is *sat. Set* means "to put (something) in a place." *Set* usually takes an object. The past tense of *set* is *set.*

Examples

In one of his daydreams, Walter Mitty *sits* on the witness stand in a courtroom.

Eliza *set* the peach pies on the edge of her kitchen cabinet to cool.

some, somewhat In writing, do not use *some* for *somewhat* as an adverb.

Nonstandard

By the end of "A Summer's Reading," George's attitude improves *some.*

Standard

By the end of "A Summer's Reading," George's attitude improves *somewhat.*

than, then *Than* is a conjunction used in comparisons. *Then* is an adverb telling *when.*

Examples

It is difficult to imagine a detective smarter *than* Sherlock Holmes.

When he returned to Ithaca, Odysseus first visited his son Telemachus; *then* he went to the palace in disguise to take his revenge on the suitors.

that See **who, which, that.**

this here, that there The words *here* and *there* are unnecessary after *this* and *that.*

Example

This [not *this here*] poem is a sonnet, but *that* [not *that there*] poem is a ballad.

verbal See **oral, verbal.**

well See **good, well.**

when, where Do not use *when* or *where* to begin a definition.

Nonstandard

Foreshadowing is *when* the author includes a clue or hint about future action in a story.

Standard

Foreshadowing is a clue or hint about future action in a story.

Nonstandard

A simile is *where* a comparison between unlike things uses the words *like* or *as.*

Standard

A simile is a comparison between unlike things that uses the words *like* or *as.*

where   Do not use *where* for *that.*

Nonstandard

Rennie noticed *where* Gary Soto has written short stories, as well as poetry.

Standard

Rennie noticed *that* Gary Soto has written short stories, as well as poetry.

who, which, that   *Who* refers to persons only. *Which* refers to things only. *That* may refer to either persons or things.

Examples

The poet *who* wrote "The Meadow Mouse" was Theodore Roethke.

An incident at the battle of Balaklava, *which* occurred in 1854, was the basis for Tennyson's poem "The Charge of the Light Brigade."

A writer *that* I liked a lot was Grant Moss, Jr.

One episode from the *Odyssey that* most readers remember vividly is Odysseus' adventure with the Cyclops.

who, whom   *Who* is used as the subject of a verb or as a predicate nominative. *Whom* is used as an object of a verb or as an object of a preposition. The use of *who* or *whom* in a subordinate clause depends on how the pronoun functions within the clause.

Examples

In *Romeo and Juliet, who* kills Mercutio?

Odysseus is a hero *who* is as clever with words as he is courageous in action.

The poet *whom* Francine most enjoyed was Robert Frost.

To *whom* does Juliet turn for help and advice?

whose, who's   *Whose* is the possessive form of *who. Who's* is a contraction for *who is* or *who has.*

Examples

Heinrich Böll, *whose* novels won him the Nobel Prize, was one of Germany's most popular authors.

Who's seen the Franco Zeffirelli film of *Romeo and Juliet?*

without, unless   Do not use the preposition *without* in place of the conjunction *unless.*

Example

Odysseus realizes that he has little chance to take his revenge *unless* [not *without*] he manages to get his hands on the bow.

would of   See **could of.**

NOUNS

A **noun** is a word used to name a person, place, thing, or idea. Nouns can function in sentences as subjects, direct objects, indirect objects, objects of prepositions, predicate nominatives, and appositives.

> **Jess** sat in the **kitchen** at the long **table** by the west **window** where in **winter** he kept his grafting **tools.**
>
> —West, "The Pacing Goose" (p. 125)

> **Doodle** was just about the craziest **brother** a **boy** ever had.
>
> —Hurst, "The Scarlet Ibis" (p. 154)

> **Mme. Forestier,** a rich **woman,** lent her **friend** a **necklace.**

PRONOUNS

A **pronoun** is a word used in place of a noun or of more than one noun. **Personal pronouns** refer to the person speaking (first person), the person spoken to (second person), or the person, place, or thing spoken about (third person).

	Singular	Plural
First Person	I, my, mine, me	we, our, ours, us
Second Person	you, your, yours	you, your, yours
Third Person	he, his, him she, her, hers it, its	they, their, theirs, them

> "'**You** must know,' said **he,** 'that though **I** am a bachelor, **I** have to keep up a considerable staff of servants at Hurlstone, for **it** is a rambling old place and takes a good deal of looking after.' "
>
> —Conan Doyle, "The Musgrave Ritual" (p. 49)

A **reflexive pronoun** ends in *-self* or *-selves* and refers back to the subject of a verb.

> "That man said 'Puppy biscuit' to **himself.**"
>
> —Thurber, "The Secret Life of Walter Mitty" (p. 66)

An **intensive pronoun** ends in *-self* or *-selves* and adds emphasis to a noun or pronoun in the same sentence.

> Did Shakespeare **himself** act in his own plays?

A **relative pronoun** is used to introduce adjective and noun clauses.

> The Magi, as you know, were wise men—wonderfully wise men—**who** brought gifts to the babe in the manger.
>
> —O. Henry, "The Gift of the Magi" (p. 177)

> In the very olden time there lived a semibarbaric king, **whose** ideas, though somewhat polished and sharpened by the progressiveness of distant Latin neighbors, were still large, florid, and untrammeled . . .
>
> —Stockton, "The Lady, or the Tiger?" (p. 31)

> The book opened with a parable **that** described a landscape from **which** the birds and fish had vanished . . . .
>
> —Norman, "The Flight of Rachel Carson" (p. 245)

> My cousin Joanne has not been allowed to hang out with me for some time because she went and told Aunt Hazel **that** I scare her to death whenever she sleeps over at our house or I spend the weekend at hers.
>
> —Bambara, "My Delicate Heart Condition" (p. 104)

An **interrogative pronoun** is used to begin questions.

> "**What** are you doing with yourself this summer, George?"
>
> —Malamud, "A Summer's Reading" (p. 147)

A **demonstrative pronoun** is used to point out a specific person or thing.

> She had known and loved **that** one great tree since she had come to the farm as a bride of sixteen.
>
> —Teale, "The Death of a Tree" (p. 237)

Handbook for Revision

An **indefinite pronoun** is used to refer to people or things in general.

> **Something** was coming through the bush, coming slowly, carefully, coming by the same winding way Rainsford had come.
>
> —Connell, "The Most Dangerous Game" (p. 23)

VERBS

A **verb** is a word that expresses action or a state of being. An **action verb** tells what action someone or something is performing.

> The waves beside them **danced**; but they **Outdid** the sparkling waves in glee.
>
> —Wordsworth, "I Wandered Lonely as a Cloud" (p. 378)

A **linking verb** helps to make a statement by serving as a link between two words. The most commonly used linking verbs are forms of the verb *be*.

> The blacking warehouse **was** the last house on the left-hand side of the way, at old Hungerford Stairs.
>
> —Dickens, "Fragments of an Autobiography" (p. 264)

A **helping verb** is a verb that can be added to another verb to make a verb phrase.

> The same dinner guests who remarked upon the lean sweetness of the meat **would have** recoiled if **I'd** told them the not-so-simple truth: that I grew up on game, and the moose they **were** eating **had been** brought down, with one shot through his magnificent heart, by my father—a man who **had** hunted all his life and all of mine.
>
> —Peterson, "Growing Up Game" (p. 221)

ADJECTIVES

An **adjective** is a word used to modify a noun or pronoun. Adjectives tell *what kind, which one,* or *how many.*

> **four lean** hounds crouched **low** and **smiling** the **merry** deer ran before.
>
> —Cummings, "All in green went my love riding" (p. 386)

A noun may sometimes be used as an adjective. The articles *the, a,* and *an* are adjectives. *An* is used before a word beginning with a vowel sound or with an unsounded *h.*

ADVERBS

An **adverb** is a word used to modify a verb, an adjective, or another adverb. Adverbs tell *how, when, where,* and *to what extent.*

> I am **completely** dumbfounded with pleasure.
>
> —Chekhov, *A Marriage Proposal* (p. 414)

> **Anyway,** you're **just** pulling my leg. I'm sure you want a war as **much** as the rest of them do and that's what you're going to get: the biggest war you've **ever** had!
>
> —Vidal, *Visit to a Small Planet* (p. 439)

PREPOSITIONS

A **preposition** is a word that shows the relationship of a noun or a pronoun to some other word in the sentence. Prepositions are almost always followed by nouns or pronouns. A group of words that begins with a preposition and ends with a noun or pronoun is called a **prepositional phrase.**

> He would hide **in the woods** when the jousting class was called, although his companions and members **of the faculty** sought to appeal **to his better nature by shouting to him** to come out and break his neck **like a man.**
>
> —Broun, "The Fifty-First Dragon" (p. 199)

> Jumping **off the bus,** he ran home, **at times** slowing **to a walk** to catch his breath.
>
> —Burciaga, "La Puerta" (p. 170)

CONJUNCTIONS

A **conjunction** is a word used to join words or groups of words. **Coordinating conjunctions** join equal parts of a sentence or similar groups of words.

People said that Bennie's grandmother had Indian blood in her veins, **for** she had high cheekbones **and** her nose was long and straight, **but** her mouth was big.

> —Moss, "Before the End of Summer" (p. 114)

Correlative conjunctions are used in pairs to join similar words or groups of words.

> **Both** Jack London **and** O. Henry used some of their real-life adventures in their fiction.

A **subordinating conjunction** is used to introduce a clause that has less importance than the main clause in a sentence.

> "I don't know **where** he is," she said.
> —Rawlings, "A Mother in Mannville" (p. 93)

A **conjunctive adverb** is an adverb used as a conjunction to connect ideas.

> Petrakis says that he has been in many Greek groceries since the time he met Barba Nikos; **however,** he has never recaptured the flavor of the figs that Barba Nikos gave him long ago.

INTERJECTIONS

An **interjection** is a word that expresses emotion and has no grammatical relation to other words in the sentence.

> **O** sing unto the Lord a new song.
> —Psalm 96 (p. 345)

> **"By sugar,"** said Jess, "Eliza's right."
> —West, "The Pacing Goose" (p. 135)

SUBJECT-VERB AGREEMENT

A verb should agree with its subject in number—singular or plural.

> I became aware that other **people were** waiting about for Mr. Jaggers, as well as I.
> —Dickens, *Great Expectations* (p. 730)

PHRASES

A **phrase** is a group of words that does not contain a subject and a verb.

A **prepositional phrase** is a group of words that begins with a preposition and ends with a noun or pronoun.

> **between** the rocks   **near** them
> **over** the bridge   **according to** a report

An **appositive** is a noun or pronoun placed beside another noun or pronoun to identify or explain it. An **appositive phrase** is made up of an appositive and its modifiers.

> Ogden Nash, **America's foremost humorous poet,** died in 1971.

A **participial phrase** consists of a participle and its complements or modifiers. The entire participial phrase acts as an adjective.

> Its walls had been lined with human remains, **piled to the vault overhead,** in the fashion of the great catacombs of Paris.
> —Poe, "The Cask of Amontillado" (p. 98)

An **infinitive phrase** consists of an infinitive together with its modifiers and complements. The entire phrase can be used as a noun, an adjective, or an adverb.

> As Gawaine's record of killings mounted higher the Headmaster found it impossible **to keep him completely in hand.**
> —Broun, "The Fifty-First Dragon" (p. 202)

CLAUSES

A **clause** is a group of words that has a subject and a verb. An **independent clause** expresses a complete thought and can stand by itself as a sentence.

> The orphanage is high in the Carolina mountains.
> —Rawlings, "A Mother in Mannville" (p. 88)

A **subordinate clause** does not express a complete thought and cannot stand alone.

> Mama and Daddy could come and live with us **if they wanted to.**
> —Hurst, "The Scarlet Ibis" (p. 159)

Handbook for Revision

CAPITALIZATION

1. FIRST WORDS

■ **Capitalize the first word of every sentence.**

Example

Other people began coming out of the barracks into a transformed world.

— Houston, "A Taste of Snow" (p. 284)

■ **Capitalize the first word of a direct quotation when the word begins with a capital letter in the original. If the original writer has not used a capital letter, do not capitalize the first word of the quotation.**

Examples

"**I**'ve never known them worse," replied the Headmaster. "**U**p in the hills to the south last week they killed a number of peasants, two cows, and a prize pig."

— Broun, "The Fifty-First Dragon" (p. 199)

"**O**nly tip him a nod every now and then when he looks off his paper," said Wemmick, "**a**nd he'll be happy as a king."

— Dickens, *Great Expectations* (p. 763)

■ **Traditionally, the first word in a line of poetry is capitalized, although some writers do not follow this rule for reasons of style.**

Examples

Not marble, nor the gilded monuments
Of princes, shall outlive this powerful rime; . . .

— Shakespeare, "Sonnet 55" (p. 352)

Sling your knuckles on the bottoms of the happy
tin pans, let your trombones ooze, and go husha-
husha-hush with the slippery sandpaper.

— Sandburg, "Jazz Fantasia" (p. 337)

2. THE PRONOUN *I* AND THE INTERJECTION *O*

■ **Capitalize the pronoun *I* and the interjection *O*.**

Examples

Today **I** followed my servant, Hestia, down the dusty path

— Cofer, "Learning to Walk Alone" (p. 659)

And then **I** loosed my ear . . . **O**, it was sweet
To hear a cart go jolting down the street.

— Stephens, "The Shell" (p. 342)

3. PROPER NOUNS AND PROPER ADJECTIVES

■ **A *proper noun* names a particular person, place, or thing. A *proper adjective* is formed from a proper noun. Capitalize proper nouns and proper adjectives.**

Examples

Mexico	Africa	Japan	Greece
Mexican	African	Japanese	Greek

■ **In proper nouns consisting of two or more words, do *not* capitalize articles (*a, an, the*), short prepositions (those with fewer than five letters, such as *at, of, for, with*), and coordinating conjunctions (*and, but, for, nor, or, so, yet*).**

Examples

Pulitzer Prize	Mayor Lopez
San Francisco	President Taft

■ **Some proper nouns and proper adjectives have lost their capitals after long usage. Others may be written with or without capitals.**

Examples

| titanic | 60-watt bulb | ham sandwich |

If you are not sure whether to capitalize a word, check in an up-to-date dictionary.

4. NAMES OF PEOPLE

▌ **Capitalize the names of people. Note that some names may contain more than one capital letter.**

Examples
O. Henry	Toni Cade Bambara
Judith Ortiz Cofer	Tran Thi Nga
Sir Arthur Conan Doyle	Langston Hughes

5. GEOGRAPHICAL NAMES

▌ **Capitalize geographical names, such as towns, cities, counties, townships, states, regions, countries, continents, islands, mountains, bodies of water, parks, roads, highways, and streets.**

Examples
Atlanta	Key West	Lake Erie
Antarctica	Liberty Island	Park Street
Lincoln Park	Route 128	Baja California
Telegraph Hill	the Rockies	Interstate 5

▌ **Note that words such as *south, east*, and *northwest* are *not* capitalized when they indicate direction.**

Examples
east of the Mississippi   south of town

▌ **These words are capitalized, however, when they name a particular place.**

Examples
Jack London often wrote about the far North.
Leslie Marmon Silko grew up in the Southwest.

▌ **A word such as *city, island, river, park*, or *street* is capitalized only when it is part of a proper noun.**

Examples
We loved visiting Balboa Park in San Diego.
Did you meet them for a picnic in the park?

We especially enjoyed the zoo.
Mr. Diaz headed for State Street, just north of the city center.

6. ORGANIZATIONS

▌ **Capitalize the names of organizations, teams, businesses, institutions, buildings, and government bodies.**

Examples
Boy Scouts of America	New Jersey Nets
High Museum of Art	Chrysler Building
Beverly Hills Hotel	Southern Bell
Ohio State University	State Department

▌ **A word such as *hotel, theater, college, post office*, or *high school* is *not* capitalized unless it is part of a proper noun.**

Examples
Is the Hilton an expensive hotel?
Where is the theater located?
Sal is going to college in September.
Julie is a sophomore at Wells College.

7. HISTORICAL EVENTS

▌ **Capitalize the names of historical events and periods, special events, and calendar items.**

Examples
American Revolution	Labor Day
World War II	Middle Ages
Parents' Day	Martin Luther King Day
Thursday	Special Olympics

8. NATIONALITIES, RACES, AND RELIGIONS

▌ **Capitalize the names of nationalities, races, and peoples.**

Examples
Tagalog	African American	West Indian
Maya	Korean	Sioux

■ Capitalize the names of religions and their followers, holy days and celebrations, holy writings, and specific deities.

Examples

Hinduism	Yom Kippur	Mormonism
Unitarian	Easter	the Holy Ghost
Islam	Upanishads	Allah
Passover	Exodus	God
Ramadan	Taoist	Dead Sea Scrolls

9. BRAND NAMES

■ Capitalize the brand names of business products. Do *not* capitalize the noun that often follows a brand name.

Examples

GM trucks	Zenith radio
Teflon pan	Premium crackers

10. PARTICULAR PLACES, THINGS, AND EVENTS

■ Capitalize the names of ships, trains, aircraft, spacecraft, monuments, buildings, awards, planets, and any other particular places, things, or events.

Examples

Mayflower	Saturn
Silver Star	*The Spirit of St. Louis*
Washington Monument	Academy Award
Big Dipper	Inauguration Day

11. SPECIFIC COURSES, LANGUAGES

■ Do *not* capitalize the names of school subjects, except for languages and for course names followed by a number.

Examples

physics	politics	anthropology
French	Spanish	Computer Science 102

■ Do *not* capitalize the class name *senior, junior, sophomore,* or *freshman* unless it is part of a proper noun.

Examples

The sophomores will hold their class election next week.
Will you attend the Freshman Spaghetti Supper?

12. TITLES OF PEOPLE

■ Capitalize a title belonging to a particular person when it comes before a person's name.

Examples

President Reagan	Miss Clark
General Zaroff	Principal Sacks
Professor Nakamura	Dr. Watson

■ Do *not* capitalize a title used alone or following a person's name, especially if the title is preceded by *a* or *the.*

Examples

Paul Morales, mayor of Santa Fe
the judge's chambers
a king's throne

■ Capitalize a word showing a family relationship when the word is used with a person's name but *not* when it is preceded by a possessive.

Examples

Aunt Hazel	Uncle Errigo	my cousin Joanne

13. TITLES OF LITERARY AND OTHER CREATIVE WORKS

■ Capitalize the first and last words and all important words in titles of books, periodicals, poems, stories, plays, historical documents, movies, radio and television programs, works of art, and musical compositions.

Unimportant words within titles are articles (*a, an, the*), short prepositions (fewer than five letters, such as *of, to, for, from,*) and coordinating conjunctions (*and, but, for, nor, or, so, yet*).

Examples

Great Expectations	"It Bids Pretty Fair"
"My Delicate Heart Condition"	*Harper's*
	Visit to a Small Planet
Emancipation Proclamation	*Return of the Jedi*
Sixty Minutes	"The Flight of the Bumblebee"
Maiden Rock	

▪ The words *a, an,* and *the* written before a title are capitalized only when they are the first word of a title.

Examples

"The Musgrave Ritual"
The New Yorker
"A Song of the Moon"

PUNCTUATION

1. END MARKS

▪ End marks—*periods, question marks,* and *exclamation points*—are used to indicate the purpose of a sentence. (A period is also used at the end of many abbreviations.)

  Use a period to end a statement (or declarative sentence).

Example

Next morning after breakfast Jess and Enoch left the kitchen together.

—West, "The Pacing Goose" (p. 127)

▪ A question (or interrogative sentence) is followed by a question mark. Note that a direct question may have the same word order as a declarative sentence. Since it is a question, however, it is followed by a question mark.

Examples

"May I pour you another glass of port, Mr. Rainsford?"

—Connell, "The Most Dangerous Game" (p. 17)

"The train leaves at 9:00?" she inquired hastily.

▪ Do *not* use a question mark after a declarative sentence containing an indirect question.

Example

When he came out into the street again, with the overshoes in a box under his arm, Walter Mitty began to wonder what the other thing was his wife had told him to get.

—Thurber, "The Secret Life of Walter Mitty" (p. 65)

▪ Use an exclamation point to end an exclamation.

Examples

And then Della leaped up like a little singed cat and cried, "Oh, oh!"

—O. Henry, "The Gift of the Magi" (p. 177)

Her friend gave a cry, "Oh, my poor Mathilde, how you've changed!"

—Maupassant, "The Necklace" (p. 195)

And yet, that awful tiger, those shrieks, that blood!

—Stockton, "The Lady, or the Tiger?" (p. 36)

"Doodle!" I screamed above the pounding storm and threw my body to the earth above his.

—Hurst, "The Scarlet Ibis" (p. 163)

▪ An imperative sentence may be followed by either a period or an exclamation point.

Examples

"Get ready, General Zaroff."

—Connell, "The Most Dangerous Game" (p. 27)

"Look—look, Grannie!"

—Moss, "Before the End of Summer" (p. 120)

▪ Use a period after an abbreviation.

Examples

Personal Names: E. B. White
Titles Used with Names: Gen., Dr., Ms., Mrs., Mr.

States and Counties: N.J., Minn.

Time of Day: A.M., P.M.

Years: B.C., A.D.

Addresses: St., Ave.

Organizations and Companies: Inc., Corp.

Units of Measure: lb., oz., in., ft., yd., mi.

▪ No periods are used in abbreviations with states when the zip code is included: NY 10010.

▪ Abbreviations in the metric system are often written without periods: for example, km for kilometer, kg for kilogram, ml for milliliter. Abbreviations for government agencies and international organizations and some other frequently used abbreviations are written without periods: for example, USAF and IQ.

2. COMMAS: CONVENTIONAL USES

▪ Use a comma to separate items in dates and addresses.

Examples

I wrote to Tamara on November 9, 1995.

I sent the letter to 40 Williams St., Portsmouth, RI 02871.

▪ Notice that a comma also separates the final item in a date and in an address from the words that follow it. A comma does *not* separate the month from the day, the house number from the street name, or the state name from the ZIP code.

▪ Use a comma after the salutation of a friendly letter and after the closing of any letter.

Examples

Dear Ms. Tan,   My dear Pamela,

Sincerely yours,   Best regards,

▪ A comma often appears after a name followed by an abbreviation such as *Jr.*, *Sr.*, and *M.D.*

Examples

Grant Moss, Jr.   Ahmet Yalcin, M.A.

Sanjay Kothari, Ph.D.   Pedro Gonzales, M.D.

For other uses of commas, see **Part 6** (pp. 906–907).

3. SEMICOLONS

▪ Use a semicolon between independent clauses that are closely related in thought and that are not joined by *and, but, or, nor, for, so,* or *yet.*

Example

▪ **My hosts were absolutely ignorant when it came to Mexican food;** they thought my tortillas were delicious.

—Cisneros, "Straw into Gold" (p. 253)

▪ Use a semicolon between independent clauses joined by a conjunctive adverb or a transitional expression.

Example

Robert Frost did not particularly like farming; **nevertheless,** he managed to make a living at it.

▪ Use a semicolon (rather than a comma) before a coordinating conjunction to join independent clauses that contain commas.

Example

But if the accused person opened the other door, there came forth from it a lady, the most suitable to his years and station that his Majesty could select among his fair subjects; and to this lady he was immediately married, as a reward of his innocence.

—Stockton, "The Lady, or the Tiger?" (p. 33)

▪ Use a semicolon between items in a series if the items contain commas.

Example

They visited Cairo, Egypt; Tel Aviv, Israel; and Istanbul, Turkey.

4. COLONS

■ **Use a colon before a list of items, especially after expressions like *as follows* and *the following*.**

Example

Kara's favorite poets were the following: Langston Hughes, James Stephens, Pat Mora, and Leslie Marmon Silko.

■ **Use a colon before a long, formal statement or quotation.**

Example

The opening lines of Theodore Roethke's "The Meadow Mouse" are as follows:

"In a shoe box stuffed in an old nylon stocking

Sleeps the baby mouse I found in the meadow. . . ."

■ **Use a colon in certain conventional situations: between the hour and the minute, between chapter and verse in a Biblical citation, and after the salutation of a business letter.**

Examples

9:30 A.M.   Genesis 2:1   Dear Prof. Ortiz:

5. ITALICS

■ **When writing or typing, indicate italics by underlining. Use italics for titles of books, plays, periodicals, works of art, films, television series, ships, aircraft, and spacecraft.**

Examples

BOOK: *Silent Spring*
PLAY: *The Leader of the People*
PERIODICAL: *Newsweek*
WORK OF ART: *Coast Scene, Mt. Desert*
FILM: *Jurassic Park*
TELEVISION SERIES: *Murder, She Wrote*
SHIP: *Queen Elizabeth II*
AIRCRAFT: *Enola Gay*
SPACECRAFT: *Discovery*

■ **Use italics for words, letters, and figures referred to as such and for foreign words not yet adopted into English.**

Examples

Except may be a verb or a preposition.
The number *3* is symbolic in many cultures.

Now, when the income was shrunk to twenty dollars, the letters of "Dillingham" looked blurred, as though they were thinking seriously of contracting to a modest and unassuming *D.*
—O. Henry, "The Gift of the Magi" (p. 173)

After the rain, Sinesio went out to help his *compadre* widen a ditch to keep the water from flooding in front of his door.
—Burciaga, "La Puerta" (p. 168)

6. QUOTATION MARKS

■ **Use quotation marks to enclose a direct quotation—a person's exact words.**

Example

"Please, the music," said the young man.
—Clark, "The Portable Phonograph" (p. 142)

■ **Do *not* use quotation marks to enclose an indirect quotation—a rewording of a direct quotation.**

Example

My grandfather often used to tell me how he went there after school to fetch the coffee for four families.
—Böll, "The Balek Scales" (p. 183)

■ **Begin a direct quotation with a capital letter. If the direct quotation is obviously a fragment of the original quotation, it may begin with a small letter.**

Example

"Why is the sky blue? Why must you always ask stupid questions?" asked Vincent. "This is a game. These are the rules. I didn't make them up."
—Tan, "Rules of the Game" (p. 80)

■ **When an expression identifying the speaker interrupts a quoted sentence, the second part of the quotation begins with a small letter.**

Example

"Waive that a moment," said Mr. Jaggers, **"and ask another."**

——Dickens, *Great Expectations* (p. 761)

■ **A direct quotation is set off from the rest of the sentence by commas or by a question mark or an exclamation point.**

Examples

"Sometimes people try to hurt you just to see if they can do it**,**" said Nancy.

——Troy, "Secrets" (p. 73)

"How's I to know the eighth'd turn out to be Samantha**?**" Enoch asked.

——West, "The Pacing Goose" (p. 136)

"Rainsford**!**" screamed the general.

——Connell, "The Most Dangerous Game" (p. 27)

■ **Commas and periods are always placed inside closing quotation marks.**

Examples

"Then you may rely on it**,**" said Herbert.

——Dickens, *Great Expectations* (p. 783)

George felt embarrassed. "I like to walk**.**"

——Malamud, "A Summer's Reading" (p. 147)

■ **Semicolons and colons are always placed outside closing quotation marks.**

Examples

Edgar Allan Poe is the author of "The Cask of Amontillado**;**" he also wrote "The Masque of the Red Death" and "The Pit and the Pendulum."

"For never was a story of more woe"**:** this is how the Prince sums up the action of *Romeo and Juliet*.

■ **Question marks and exclamation points are placed inside closing quotation marks if the quotation is a question or an exclamation. Otherwise, they are placed outside.**

Examples

Then it was that his quick and anxious glance asked the question, "Which**?**"

——Stockton, "The Lady, or the Tiger?" (p. 36)

"Give me a fountain pen**!**" he snapped.

——Thurber, "The Secret Life of Walter Mitty" (p. 65)

Did you know that Alfred, Lord Tennyson wrote "The Charge of the Light Brigade"**?**

Say "Rumplesnitz"**!**

■ **When you write dialogue, begin a new paragraph every time the speaker changes, and enclose each speaker's words in quotation marks.**

Example

"Come in, Jerry," I said, "if you're allowed to be away this late**.**"

"I told maybe a story," he said. "I told them I thought you would want to see me**.**"

——Rawlings, "A Mother in Mannville" (p. 91)

■ **When a quoted passage consists of more than one paragraph, place quotation marks at the beginning of each paragraph and at the end of only the last paragraph in the passage.**

■ **Use single quotation marks to enclose a quotation within a quotation.**

Example

" **'**How has all gone with you, Musgrave**?'** I asked after we had cordially shaken hands."

——Conan Doyle, "The Musgrave Ritual" (p. 49)

■ **Use quotation marks to enclose titles of short works, such as short stories, short poems, essays, articles, songs, episodes of television series, and chapters and other parts of books.**

Examples

SHORT STORY: "War"
SHORT POEM: "400-meter Freestyle"
ESSAY: "The Death of a Tree"
ARTICLE: "District Attorney Will Reopen Cases"
SONG: "Jingle Bells"
TV EPISODE: "Who Shot J.R.?"
CHAPTER: "Frost's Later Poems"

7. APOSTROPHES

POSSESSIVE CASE

■ To form the possessive of a singular noun, add an apostrophe and an *s*. Add only the apostrophe to a proper name ending in an *s* sound if the name has two or more syllables or if the addition of *'s* would make the name awkward to pronounce.

Examples

a **tree's** leaves   Ms. **Martinez'** coat
the **people's** choice   **Socrates'** philosophy

■ To form the possessive of a plural noun ending in *s*, add only the apostrophe.

Examples

the **singers'** voices   the **players'** strategy

■ Do *not* use an apostrophe with possessive personal pronouns or with the possessive pronoun *whose*.

Incorrect

I thought that this scarf was **your's.**

Correct

I thought that this scarf was **yours.**

Incorrect

Who's books are on the floor?

Correct

Whose books are on the floor?

■ To form the possessive of an indefinite pronoun, add an apostrophe and an *s*.

Examples

Everyone's opinion is welcome.
Someone's lights are on.

■ Form the possessive of only the last word in a compound word, in the name of an organization or a business firm, or in a word group showing joint possession.

Examples

my **mother-in-law's** visit
the **Attorney General's** office
Pia and Jorge's wedding

■ When a possessive pronoun is part of a word group showing joint possession, each noun in the word group is also possessive.

Example

Wally's, Pablo's, and **her** skit

■ When two or more persons possess something individually, make each of their names possessive in form.

Example

Rudi's and **Winona's** math grades

CONTRACTIONS

■ Use an apostrophe to show where letters, numbers, or words have been omitted in a contraction.

Examples

You're late.   **I've** found a job.
  (You are)   (I have)

It's a great show.   **Where'll** we meet?
  (It is)   (Where will)

in the **'80s**   five **o'clock**
  (1980s)   (of the clock)

PLURALS

■ Use an apostrophe and an *s* to form the plurals of all lowercase letters, some capital letters, and some words referred to as words.

Examples

Mississippi has four *s***'s**, four *i***'s**, and two *p***'s**.
Do you know many words that start with *Z***'s**?
Did you revise some of the *while***'s** and *after***'s** in that paragraph?

8. HYPHENS

■ Use a hyphen in some compound words.

Examples

great-grandson   four-year-old
red-hot   half-gallon jug

■ Use a hyphen to divide a word at the end of a line.

Example

The poet Leslie Marmon Silko was born in Albuquerque, New Mexico, in 1948.

■ **Do not divide a one-syllable word.**

Incorrect

A character who contrasts with or sets off another character in a narrative is called a foil.

Correct

A character who contrasts with or sets off another character in a narrative is **called** a foil.

■ **Divide an already hyphenated word only at a hyphen.**

Incorrect

The Visitor, who enters in Act One, is a pleasant-looking man in his forties.

Correct

The Visitor, who enters in Act One, is a **pleasant**-looking man in his forties.

■ **Do *not* divide a word so that one letter stands alone.**

Incorrect

Persuasive writers often cast their arguments in e-motionally loaded language.

Correct

Persuasive writers often cast their arguments in **emotionally** loaded language.

■ **Use a hyphen with compound numbers from *twenty-one* to *ninety-nine* and with fractions used as modifiers.**

Examples

twenty-two players   a **three-fourths** vote

■ Use a hyphen with the prefixes *ex-*, *self-*, *all-*, with the suffix *-elect*, and with all prefixes before a proper noun or proper adjective.

Examples

our **ex-chairperson**   a **self-centered** attitude

the **all-important**   the **mayor-elect**
  game

pre-Revolutionary   **anti-American**
  Russia   propaganda

9. DASHES

■ **Use a dash to indicate an abrupt break in thought or speech or an unfinished statement or question.**

Examples

What was uneasy is still uneasy—perhaps it always will be.

—Peterson, "Growing Up Game" (p. 224)

"But you can't mean—" gasped Rainsford.

—Connell, "The Most Dangerous Game" (p. 19)

10. PARENTHESES

■ **Use parentheses to enclose informative or explanatory material of minor importance.**

Examples

A certain man (a soldier once) named Thomas, who was the foreman, and another named Harry, who was the carman and wore a red jacket, used to call me "Charles" sometimes, in speaking to me.

—Dickens, "Fragments of an Autobiography" (p. 269)

One chemical firm that was not mentioned by name (though its products were) found a lawyer on the staff who was willing to threaten a lawsuit if her publishers actually brought the book out.

—Norman, "The Flight of Rachel Carson" (p. 246)

Glossary

The words listed in the glossary in the following pages are found in the selections in this textbook. You can use this glossary as you would a dictionary—to look up words that are unfamiliar to you. Strictly speaking, the word *glossary* means a collection of technical, obscure, or foreign words found in a certain field of work. Of course, the words in this glossary are not "technical, obscure, or foreign," but are those that might present difficulty as you read the selections in this textbook.

Many words in the English language have several meanings. In this glossary, the meanings given are the ones that apply to the words as they are used in the selections in the textbook. Words closely related in form and meaning are generally listed together in one entry (**commend** and **commendable**), and the definition is given for the first form. Related words that appear as separate entries in dictionaries are listed separately (**allude** and **allusion**). Regular adverbs (ending in *-ly*) are defined in their adjective form, with the adverb form shown at the end of the definition.

The following abbreviations are used:

adj., adjective	*n.,* noun	*v.,* verb
adv., adverb	*prep.,* preposition	

For more information about the words in this glossary, consult a dictionary.

A

abash (ə-băsh′) *v.* To make ashamed or ill at ease.

abate (ə-bāt′) *v.* To reduce in amount or intensity.

abhor (ăb-hôr′) *v.* **1.** To look at with horror. **2.** To hate intensely.

abhorrence (ăb-hôr′əns) *n.* Hatred; disgust.

abhorrent (ăb-hôr′ənt) *adj.* Hateful; disgusting.

abiding (ə-bī′dĭng) *adj.* Lasting.

ablution (ə-blōō′shən) *n.* A washing of the body or part of it.

abominable (ə-bŏm′ə-nə-bəl) *adj.* Hateful; detestable.

abscond (ăb-skŏnd′) *v.* To go away quickly and secretly.

abstract (ăb-străkt′, ăb′străkt′) *adj.* Having a geometric pattern or design that does not represent any particular figure.

abstracted (ăb-străk′tĭd) *adj.* Lost in thought.

absurd (ăb-sûrd′, -zûrd′) *adj.* Ridiculous; laughable.

abundant (ə-bŭn′dənt) *adj.* Plentiful.

abut (ə-bŭt′) *v.* To border on; be next to.

abysmal (ə-bĭz′məl) *adj.* Extreme; bottomless.

abyss (ə-bĭs′) *n.* Any bottomless depth or empty space.

accommodate (ə-kŏm′ə-dāt) *v.* To settle differences; reconcile.

accomplice (ə-kŏm′plĭs) *n.* A partner in an undertaking, particularly of an illegal or secret nature.

accost (ə-kôst′, ə-kŏst′) *v.* To approach and speak to in a bold way.

accouterments (ə-kōō′tər-mənts) *n. pl.* Special clothing or equipment.

acquiesce (ăk′wē-ĕs′) *v.* To agree readily.

acquisition (ăk′wə-zĭsh′ən) *n.* Something obtained or acquired.

acrid (ăk′rĭd) *adj.* Harsh or bitter to the taste or smell.

adept (ə-dĕpt′) *adj.* Skilled; proficient.—**adeptly** *adv.*

adjoin (ə-join′) *v.* To be next to.

adjunct (ăj′ŭngkt′) *n.* Something connected to another thing in a helpful, but not necessary, way.

adjure (ə-jōōr′) *v.* To command or appeal to solemnly.

adobe (ə-dō′bē) *n.* Sun-dried brick.

adorn (ə-dôrn′) *v.* To decorate.

adulation (ăj′ōō-lā′shən) *n.* Overflowing flattery or praise.

advent (ăd′vĕnt) *n.* Arrival.

ă pat/ā pay/âr care/ä father/b bib/ch church/d deed/ē pet/ē be/f fife/g gag/h hat/hw which/ĭ pit/ī pie/îr pier/j judge/k kick/ l lid, needle/m mum/n no, sudden/ng thing/ŏ pot/ō toe/ô paw, for/oi noise/ou out/ōō took/ōō boot/p pop/r roar/s sauce/ sh ship, dish/t tight/th thin, path/*th* this, bathe/ŭ cut/ûr urge/v valve/w with/y yes/z zebra, size/zh vision/ə about, item, edi- ble, gallop, circus/à *Fr.* ami/œ *Fr.* feu, *Ger.* schön/ü *Fr.* tu, *Ger.* über/KH *Ger.* ich, *Scot.* loch/N *Fr.* bon.

adversary (ăd′vər-sĕr′ē) *n.* An opponent or enemy.

adz (ădz) *n.* An axlike tool.

affable (ăf′ə-bəl) *adj.* Friendly; pleasant.

affect (ə-fĕkt′) *v.* To assume.

affirm (ə-fûrm′) *v.* To make a solemn and formal declaration to speak the truth without taking an oath.

affluent (ăf′lōō-ənt) *adj.* Wealthy.—*n. pl.* Rich people.

aghast (ə-găst′) *adj.* Terrified; shocked.

agile (ăj′əl, ăj′īl) *adj.* Active; able to move easily and quickly.

agility (ə-jĭl′ə-tē) *n.* The ability to move quickly and easily.

alacrity (ə-lăk′rə-tē) *n.* Eagerness.

alderman (ôl′dər-mən) *n.* A member of the city government.

alienation (āl-yə-nā′shən, ā′lē-ə-) *n.* Estrangement; isolation.

allot (ə-lŏt′) *v.* To assign, distribute.

allude (ə-lōōd′) *v.* To make a casual or indirect reference.

allusion (ə-lōō′zhən) *n.* An indirect but meaningful reference.

altercation (ôl′tər-kā′shən) *n.* A noisy quarrel.

ambiguity (ăm′bĭ-gyōō′ə-tē) *n.* **1.** Something that has two or more meanings. **2.** Mystery.

ambivalent (ăm-bĭv′ə-lənt) *adj.* Showing conflicting thoughts or emotions.

amble (ăm′bəl) *v.* To walk in a slow, relaxed way.

amend (ə-mĕnd′) *v.* To change in order to correct.

amends (ə-mĕndz′) *n. pl.* Anything done or given to make up for an injury or loss.

amenity (ə-mĕn′ə-tē, ə-mē′nə-tē) *n.* Something that makes life more comfortable or convenient.

amicable (ăm′ĭ-kə-bəl) *adj.* Friendly.

amiss (ə-mĭs′) *adv.* In the wrong manner.

amorous (ăm′ər-əs) *adj.* **1.** Loving. **2.** In love.

analogy (ə-năl′ə-jē) *n.* **1.** Some similarity between otherwise different things. **2.** An explanation of one thing by comparing it to another thing.

anguish (ăng′gwĭsh) *n.* Great mental or physical suffering.

animate (ăn′ə-māt′) *v.* To make lively or energetic.

animosity (ăn′ə-mŏs′ə-tē) *n.* Extreme hatred.

annals (ăn′əlz) *n.* A record of events year by year.

antagonistic (ăn-tăg′ə-nĭs′tĭk) *adj.* Opposing; hostile.

anticipate (ăn-tĭs′ə-pāt′) *v.* To use in advance, as an allowance of money or a legacy.

antimony (ăn′tə-mō′nē) *n.* A metallic chemical element used in combination with other metals in order to harden them.

antiquated (ăn′tə-kwā′tĭd) *adj.* Very old; out-of-date.

aperture (ăp′ər-choor, -chər) *n.* An opening.

apothecary (ə-pŏth′ə-kĕr′ē) *n.* A person who prepares and sells medicines.

appall (ə-pôl′) *v.* To horrify; shock.

apparition (ăp′ə-rĭsh′ən) *n.* **1.** A ghost. **2.** A strange sight. **3.** A sudden appearance.

appease (ə-pēz′) *v.* To satisfy; relieve.

appellation (ăp′ə-lā′shən) *n.* A name.

appertain (ăp′ər-tān′) *v.* To relate to; belong to.

apportion (ə-pôr′shən, ə-pōr′-) *v.* To assign; divide.

appraise (ə-prāz′) *v.* To evaluate; judge.

apprehend (ăp′rĭ-hĕnd′) *v.* **1.** To capture. **2.** To understand.

apprehension (ăp′rĭ-hĕn′shən) *n.* Anxiety; fear.

apprehensive (ăp′rĭ-hĕn′sĭv) *adj.* Fearful.

apprise (ə-prīz′) *v.* To notify.

appropriate (ə-prō′prē-āt′) *v.* To take possession of something, frequently without permission.

aptitude (ăp′tə-tōōd′, -tyōōd) *n.* A natural ability or tendency.

ardor (är′dər) *n.* Great passion; emotional warmth.

armada (är-mä′də, -mā′də) *n.* A fleet.

array (ə-rā′) *n.* **1.** An orderly display. **2.** Fine clothes and accessories.

arrogant (ăr′ə-gənt) *adj.* Excessively self-important and proud.

arroyo (ə-roi′ō) *n.* A river or stream.

artisan (är′tə-zən, -sən) *n.* Someone with an occupation or craft that requires special skill.

ascend (ə-sĕnd′) *v.* Rise.

ascertain (ăs′ər-tān′) *v.* To make sure through examination.

aspire (ə-spīr′) *v.* To have a grand ambition.

assail (ə-sāl′) *v.* To attack violently.

assent (ə-sĕnt′) *n.* Agreement.

assert (ə-sûrt′) *v.* To declare; express.

assertion (ə-sûr′shən) *n.* A declaration without proof.

assiduous (ə-sĭj′ōō-əs) *adj.* Carefully attentive.

assumption (ə-sump′shən) *n.* Something taken for granted without proof.

astound (ə-stound′) *v.* To amaze.

asunder (ə-sŭn′dər) *adv.* Apart.

athwart (ə-thwôrt′) *prep.* Across.

attain (ə-tān′) *v.* To arrive at through effort.

audacious (ô-dā′shəs) *adj.* Fearless; rudely bold.

audacity (ô-dăs′ə-tē) *n.* Boldness; daring.

aura (ôr′ə) *n.* Distinctive or special quality.

auspicious (ô-spĭsh′əs) *adj.* Lucky; predicting a good future.

austere (ô-stîr′) *adj.* Simple; plain.

automaton (ô-tŏm′ə-tən, -tŏn′) *n.* A person or thing acting in a mechanical way.

aversion (ə-vûr′zhən) *n.* An extreme dislike.

avowal (ə-vou′əl) *n.* An open declaration.

awful (ô′fəl) *adj.* Inspiring a feeling of reverence and wonder.

azure (ăzh′ər) *adj.* Sky-blue.

B

babouche (bə-bŭsh′) *n.* A flat, backless slipper worn in North Africa.

baffle (băf′əl) *v.* To puzzle.

baleful (bāl′fəl) *adj.* Threatening; evil.

balmy (bä′mē) *adj.* Mild; pleasant.

bandy (băn′dē) *v.* To converse casually.

banish (băn′ĭsh) *v.* To exile.—**banishment** *n.*

bankrupt (băngk′rŭpt′, -rəpt) *adj.* Having no money; destitute.—*v.* To go bankrupt.

barbaric (bär-băr′ĭk) *adj.* Wild; uncivilized.

barbarous (bär′bər-əs) *adj.* Uncivilized; cruel.

barricade (băr′ə-kād′, băr′ə-kād′) *n.* A structure set up to block a passageway, usually for protection.

battlement (băt′l-mənt) *n.* A wall with open spaces to shoot through, usually on top of a tower.

bedeck (bĭ-dĕk′) *v.* To adorn.

beguile (bĭ-gīl′) *v.* **1.** To deceive; trick. **2.** To spend time pleasantly.

behest (bĭ-hĕst′) *n.* An order.

belated (bĭ-lā′tĭd) *adj.* Late.—**belatedly** *adv.*

bellow (bĕl′ō) *v.* To roar.

bemuse (bĭ-myōōz′) *v.* To stupefy.

benefactor (bĕn′ə-făk′tər) *n.* Someone who helps another person, especially financially.

benevolent (bə-nĕv′ə-lənt) *adj.* Gentle; kind.—**benevolently** *adv.*

benign (bĭ-nīn′) *adj.* Favorable.

berate (bĭ-rāt′) *v.* To scold harshly.

bereave (bĭ-rēv′) *v.* To leave sad or forlorn, as by death.—**bereaved** *adj.*

beseech (bĭ-sēch′) *v.* To ask seriously.

bestow (bĭ-stō′) *v.* To give; grant.

bevy (bĕv′ē) *n.* A group.

bier (bîr) *n.* A structure upon which a corpse, or a coffin, is placed.

bilge (bĭlj) *n.* The water around the lower part of a ship.

billow (bĭl′ō) *v.* To swell or rise.

bizarre (bĭ-zär′) *adj.* Odd; queer.

blanch (blănch, blänch) *v.* To become pale or white.

bland (blănd) *adj.* Mild; pleasant.—**blandly** *adv.*

blight (blīt) *n.* A plant disease.

blotch (blŏtch) *n.* A spot or mark differing in color from the surrounding area.

blunt (blŭnt) *adj.* Abrupt; insensitive.

bluster (blŭs′tər) *v.* To express oneself in a boastful or bullying way.

boggy (bô′gē, bog′ē) *adj.* Swampy.

boisterous (boi′stər-əs, -strəs) *adj.* Stormy; violent.

bole (bōl) *n.* The trunk of a tree.

borough (bûr′ō, bûr′ə) *n.* **1.** A self-governing town. **2.** A unit of a larger city.

boutique (bōō-tēk′) *n.* A small shop.

brace (brās) *n.* A rope used to swing or secure the sails of a ship.

brandish (brăn′dĭsh) *v.* To wave or flourish in a menacing way.

bravado (brə-vä′dō) *n.* **1.** A show of false courage. **2.** Defiant behavior.

brazen (brā′zən) *adj.* **1.** Made of or resembling brass in color and hardness. **2.** Shameless; bold.

breach (brēch) *n.* An opening or gap in a wall.

bristle (brĭs′əl) *v.* To rise and stand erect as a result of anger or fear.

broach (brōch) *v.* To bring up a topic for discussion.

brusque (brŭsk) *adj.* Abrupt in behavior or speech; discourteous.—**brusquely** *adv.*

buckler (bŭk-lər) *n.* A small round shield held or worn on the arm.

buffet (bŭf′ĭt) *n.* A punch with the fist.

bulldoze (bōōl′dōz′) *v. Slang* To bully.

buoyant (boi′ənt, bōō′yənt) *adj.* Lighthearted; cheerful.

burgeon (bûr′jən) *v.* To grow rapidly; flourish.

burnish (bûr′nĭsh) *v.* To polish; make smooth and shiny.

butt (bŭt) *n.* The thicker and larger end of an object.

Glossary

ă pat/ā pay/âr care/ä father/b bib/ch church/d deed/ĕ pet/ē be/f fife/g gag/h hat/hw which/ĭ pit/ī pie/îr pier/j judge/k kick/ l lid, needle/m mum/n no, sudden/ng thing/ŏ pot/ō toe/ô paw, for/oi noise/ou out/ōō took/ōō boot/p pop/r roar/s sauce/ sh ship, dish/t tight/th thin, path/th this, bathe/ŭ cut/ûr urge/v valve/w with/y yes/z zebra, size/zh vision/ə about, item, edi- ble, gallop, circus/à *Fr.* ami/œ *Fr.* feu, *Ger.* schön/ü *Fr.* tu, *Ger.* über/кн *Ger.* ich, *Scot.* loch/N *Fr.* bon.

C

cadence (kād′ns) *n.* Beat; rhythm.

cadent (kād′ənt) *adj.* Moving in a rhythmic, measured way.

cajole (kə-jōl′) *v.* To coax.

calamity (kə-lăm′ə-tē) *n.* A disaster; misfortune.

candelabra (kăn′də-lä′brə, -lä′brə, lä′brə) *n.* A large, branched candleholder.

canopy (kăn′ə-pē) *n.* A rooflike covering held or fastened above a person or thing for protection or decoration.

capitalize (kăp′ə-təl-īz′) *v.* To profit by.

caprice (kə-prēs′) *n.* A sudden, impulsive change of mind or way of thinking

capricious (kə-prĭsh′əs, -prē′shəs) *adj.* Tending to change one's mind suddenly; flighty.

carbine (kär′bīn′,-bēn′) *n.* A light shoulder rifle of limited range.

careen (kə-rēn′) *v.* To move from side to side in an uncontrolled manner.

carriage (kăr′ĭj) *n.* The manner of bearing the body; posture.

cascade (kăs-kād′) *n.* A waterfall.

catacombs (kăt′ə-kōmz′) *n.* A series of grave sites in an underground burial place.

catalepsy (kăt′l-ĕp′sē) *n.* A condition in which there is a sudden and temporary loss of consciousness and rigidity of the body.—**cataleptic** *adj.*

catapult (kăt′ə-pŭlt′) *n.* Slingshot.—*v.* To leap or spring up suddenly.

causeway (kôz′wā′) *n.* A raised road across water or swampland.

cavalier (kăv′ə-lîr′) *n.* A courteous, well-dressed gentleman.

cessation (sĕ-sā′shən) *n.* A stopping, either permanent or temporary.

chafe (chāf) *v.* To make sore; irritate.

char (chär) *v.* To scorch.

chide (chīd) *v.* To scold in a mild way.

chipyard (chĭp′yärd′) *n.* A place where wood is cut for fuel.

chivalry (shĭv′əl-rē) *n.* The noble qualities of courage and honor associated with medieval knights.

chorister (kôr′ĭs-tər. kōr′-, kŏr′-) *n.* A choir singer.

chronic (krŏn′ĭk) *adj.* Continuing; recurrent.

chronicle (krŏn′ĭ-kəl) *n.* A record of events in the order in which they happened.

chronological (krŏn′ə-lŏj′ĭ-kəl, krō′nə-) *adj.* Arranged in the order that the events took place.

churn (chûrn) *v.* To shake or stir forcefully.

ciphering (sī′fər-ĭng) *n.* Arithmetic.

circumscribe (sûr′kəm-skrīb′) *v.* To encircle.

civility (sə-vĭl′ə-tē) *n.* Politeness.

clamor (klăm′ər) *v.* To demand or complain noisily; to make a loud, continuous noise.—*n.* noise.—**clamorer** *n.*

cleave (klēv) *v.* To stick to; cling.

cleft (klĕft) *n.* A gap; opening.—*adj.* split.

clemency (klĕm′ən-sē) *n.* Mercy.

cogent (kō′jənt) *adj.* Forceful.

cognomen (kŏg-nō′mən) *n.* A name; nickname.

coherent (kō-hîr′ənt, kō-hĕr′-) *adj.* Logical; consistent in thought.

cohort (kō′hôrt′) *n.* A companion; associate.

collision (kə-lĭzh′ən) *n.* A violent coming together; forceful clash.

combatant (kəm-băt′ənt, kŏm′bə-tənt) *n.* Someone taking part in an armed conflict; fighter.

comber (kō′mər) *n.* A large ocean wave.

commence (kə-mĕns′) *v.* To begin.

commend (kə-mĕnd′) *v.* To give regards, or good wishes, to someone.—**commendable** *adj.*

commiserate (kə-mĭz′ə-rāt′) *v.* To sympathize with.

communal (kə-myōōn′əl, kŏm′yə-nəl) *adj.* Belonging to the community; shared.

communion (kə-myōōn′yən) *n.* Sharing of thoughts or feelings.

compass (kŭm′pəs, kŏm′) *v.* To understand.

compassion (kəm-păsh′ən) *n.* Pity.

compassionate (kĕm-păsh′ən-ĭt) *adj.* Sympathetic.

compensation (kŏm′pən-sā′shən) *n.* Something of equal worth given to make up for a loss or damage.

compilation (kŏm′pə-lā′shən) *n.* The act of gathering and putting together literary works, statistics, etc.

comply (kəm-plī′) *v.* To behave in accordance with some request or rule.

compose (kəm-pōz′) *v.* To calm or quiet oneself.

composure (kəm-pō′zhər) *n.* Calmness.

compound (kŏm′pound) *n.* An enclosed area or group of buildings where people live.

comprise (kəm-prīz′) *v.* To consist of.

compromise (kŏm′prə-mīz′) *n.* A settlement.—*v.* **1.** To place one's reputation and character in danger. **2.** To settle by having each side give up some demands.

compulsory (kəm-pŭl′sə-rē) *adj.* Required.

conceive (kən-sēv′) *v.* To think up.

concentration (kŏn′sən-trā′shən) *n.* **1.** Extreme thoughtfulness. **2.** Focused attention.

conception (kən-sĕp'shən) *n.* A mental picture; idea.

concession (kĕn-sĕsh'ən) *n.* Something yielded or granted.

conciliatory (kən-sĭl'ē-ə-tôr'ē, -tôr'ē) *adj.* Soothing; friendly.

condescend (kŏn'dĭ-sĕnd') *v.* To come down to the level of someone regarded as inferior.

condone (kən-dōn') *v.* To excuse; overlook.

confectioner (kən-fĕk'shən-ər) *n.* A person who makes or sells sweet foods.

confer (kən-fûr') *v.* To give; grant.

configuration (kən-fĭg'yə-rā'shən) *n.* The form or shape of.

confound (kən-found', kŏn-) *v.* To mix up; confuse.

confront (kən-frŭnt') *v.* To come face to face with.

congregate (kŏng'grə-gāt) *v.* To gather in a crowd.

conical (kŏn'ĭ-kəl) *adj.* In the shape of a cone.

conjecture (kən-jĕk'chər) *n.* A conclusion based on insufficient evidence.

conjure (kŏn'jər, kən-joor') *v.* To appeal to earnestly.—**conjure up 1.** To bring to mind. **2.** To cause something to happen as by magic.

connoisseurship (kŏn'ə-sûr'shĭp') *n.* Expert knowledge in some particular field, often in matters of art or fine foods.

consequence (kŏn'sə-kwĕns) *n.* Effect; result.

conspicuous (kən-spĭk'yoo-əs) *adj.* Attracting attention.

conspire (kən-spīr') *v.* **1.** To act together secretly, usually to commit a crime. **2.** To plot or plan something.

constable (kŏn'stə-bəl, kŭn'-) *n.* A peace officer in a village or a town.

consternation (kŏn'stər-nā'shən) *n.* Amazement; bewilderment.

constraint (kən-strānt') *n.* Emotional repression.

contemplate (kŏn'təm-plāt') *v.* To think about carefully; look at intently.

contemptible (kən-tĕmp'tə-bəl) *adj.* Deserving of scorn; worthless.

contemptuous (kən-tĕmp'choo-əs) *adj.* Scornful. —**contemptuously** *adv.*

contend (kən-tĕnd) *v.* To struggle against in combat or competition.

contentious (kən-tĕn'shəs) *adj.* Quarrelsome; ready to argue.

contingent (kən-tĭn'-jənt) *adj.* Dependent upon something that has not yet happened.

contraption (kən-trăp'shən) *n.* A device; gadget.

contrite (kən-trīt', kŏn'trīt') *adj.* Feeling very guilty for having done something wrong.—**contritely** *adv.*

contrive (kən-trīv') *v.* To plan cleverly; scheme.

convention (kən-vĕn'shən) *n.* A thing, behavior, or procedure established by custom and widely used throughout society.

convert (kən-vûrt') *v.* To change into another form or thing.

copious (kō'pē-əs) *adj.* Plentiful.

cordial (kôr'jəl) *adj.* Friendly; hearty.

cordwood (kôrd'wood') *n.* Wood cut in short lengths to be used for fuel.

corroborate (kə-rŏb'ə-rāt') *v.* To confirm.

corrode (kə-rōd') *v.* To wear away gradually.

corrupt (kə-rŭpt') *v.* To cause to become morally unsound.

cosmopolite (kŏz-mŏp'ə-līt') *n.* A person at home anywhere in the world.

council (koun'səl) *n.* A serious discussion among a group of people.

counsel (koun'səl) *n.* **1.** Advice. **2.** Legal representation in court. **3.** Ideas; opinions. **4.** Private, unexpressed thoughts.—*v.* To advise.

countenance (koun'tə-nəns) *n.* **1.** The face. **2.** The look on a person's face.

counterpart (koun'tər-pärt') *n.* A person or thing that closely resembles another.

countinghouse (koun'tĭng-hous') *n.* A place in which a business carries out its clerical and financial functions.

course (kôrs, kōrs, koors) *v.* To move swiftly.

courtier (kôr'tē-ər, kôr'-, -tyər) *n.* **1.** A person who serves at a royal court. **2.** A person who seeks favor through flattery.

couscous (koos'koos) *n.* A North African food made of steamed, crushed grain.

cove (kōv) *n.* A small inlet or bay.

covet (kŭv'ĭt) *v.* To have strong desire for something.

cower (kou'ər) *v.* To shrink away or hide oneself in fear.

ă pat/ā pay/âr care/ä father/b **bib**/ch **church**/d **deed**/ĕ **pet**/ē be/f **fife**/g **gag**/h **hat**/hw **which**/ĭ **pit**/ī **pie**/îr **pier**/j **judge**/k **kick**/
l **lid, needle**/m **mum**/n **no, sudden**/ng **thing**/ŏ **pot**/ō **toe**/ô **paw, for**/oi **noise**/ou **out**/oo **took**/oo **boot**/p **pop**/r **roar**/s **sauce**/
sh **ship, dish**/t **tight**/th **thin, path**/th **this, bathe**/ŭ **cut**/ûr **urge**/v **valve**/w **with**/y **yes**/z **zebra, size**/zh **vision**/ə **about, item, edi-**
ble, **gallop, circus**/à *Fr.* **ami**/œ *Fr.* **feu,** *Ger.* **schön**/ü *Fr.* **tu,** *Ger.* **über**/κн *Ger.* **ich,** *Scot.* **loch**/ɴ *Fr.* **bon.**

coy (koi) *adj.* Affectedly cute or playful.

cranny (krăn′ē) *n.* An opening or crack.

craven (krā′vən) *adj.* Very fearful; cowardly.

credulity (krĭ-dōō′lə-tē, -dyōō′lə-tē) *n.* A tendency to believe something too quickly.

credulous (krĕj′ōō-ləs) *adj.* Too easily convinced.

crescendo (krə-shĕn′-dō) *n.* An increase in volume or intensity.

crest (krĕst) *n.* A cluster of feathers or an emblem decorating the top of a helmet.

crux (krŭks) *n.* Cross.

crypt (krĭpt) *n.* An underground chamber used as a burial place.

cryptic (krĭp′tĭk) *adj.* Having an unclear meaning; mysterious.

cubicle (kyōō′bĭ-kəl) *n.* A small enclosed space or room.

cull (kŭl) *v.* To select; gather.

culminate (kŭl′mə-nāt′) *v.* To come to the highest degree or effect.

cunning (kŭn′ĭng) *adj.* Clever.—**cunningly** *adv.*

curfew (kûr′fyōō) *n.* **1.** A specified time when inhabitants of a town are required to be off the streets. **2.** A bell or other signal announcing this time.

curio (kyōōr′ē-ō′) *n.* An unusual or curious object.

currant (kûr′ənt) *n.* A seedless raisin.

cutter (kŭt′ər) *n.* A small boat that moves quickly.

cynical (sĭn′ĭ-kəl) *adj.* Of the belief that there is no true goodness in anyone; scornful.

D

damask (dăm′əsk) *n.* A heavy fabric with a woven-in-pattern used for table linen and furniture covers.

dandy (dăn′dē) *n.* An elegant dresser.

dank (dăngk) *adj.* Miserably damp and chilly.

daub (dôb) *v.* To smear or cover with paint, mud, or plaster.

deal (dēl) *n.* Pine wood.

debacle (dĭ-bä′kəl, -băk′əl) *n.* A sudden collapse or break-up.

debauch (dĭ-bôch′) *n.* An orgy.

débris (dā′brē′) *n.* Fragments.

decal (dē′kăl) *n.* A picture or design transferred onto wood, material, etc., from specially prepared paper.

decanter (dĭ-kăn′tər) *n.* An ornamental glass bottle used for serving liquids.

deceptive (dĭ-sĕp′tĭv) *adj.* Deceiving.

declaim (dĭ-klām′) *v.* To speak loudly; recite dramatically.

declamation (dĕk′lə-mā′shən) *n.* A speech delivered in a dramatic manner.

decline (dĭ-klīn′) *v.* To refuse.

decorous (dĕk′ər-əs, dĭ-kôr′əs) *adj.* Proper; in good taste.

decrepit (dĭ-krĕp′ĭt) *adj.* Worn out; broken down.

deface (dĭ-fās′) *v.* To disfigure.

defamation (dĕf′ə-mā′shən) *n.* The damaging of someone's reputation or character.

deflect (dĭ-flĕkt′) *v.* To bend; cause to go off to one side.

deft (dĕft) *adj.* Skillful in a quick and sure way.—**deftly** *adv.*

degenerate (dĭ-jĕn′ə-rāt′) *v.* To lower in quality or value; worsen.

dejected (dĭ-jĕk′tĭd) *adj.* Depressed.

delectable (dĭ-lĕk′tə-bəl) *adj.* Delightful; enjoyable.

deliberation (dĭ′lĭb′ə-rā′shən) *n.* Careful and lengthy consideration.

delirious (dĭ-lîr′ē-əs) *adj.* In a state of wild excitement.—**deliriously** *adv.*

deliverance (dĭ-lĭv′ər-əns) *n.* The state or act of being freed.

demeanor (dĭ-mē′nər) *n.* Behavior; conduct.

demented (dĭ-mĕn′tĭd) *adj.* Insane.

dependent (dĭ-pĕn′dənt) *adj.* Hanging down.

deplorable (dĭp-plôr′ə-bəl, dĭ-plôr′ə-) *adj.* Regrettable.

depreciate (dĭ-prē′shē-āt′) *v.* To belittle; make seem less valuable.

depreciation (dĭ-prē-shē-ā′shən) *n.* Belittlement.

depression (dĭ-prĕsh′ən) *n.* A hollow.

deprive (dĭ-prīv′) *v.* To deny someone the enjoyment or use of something.

deride (dĭ-rīd′) *v.* To make fun of.

derision (dĭ-rĭzh′ən) *n.* Ridicule.

derisive (dĭ-rī′sĭv) *adj.* Mocking.

desolate (dĕs′ə-lĭt) *adj.* Deserted; forlorn; lonely.—**desolately** *adv.*

desolation (dĕs′ə-lā′shən) *n.* Misery; loneliness.

despond (dĭ-spŏnd′) *v.* To become discouraged.

detestable (dĭ-tĕs′tə-bəl) *adj.* Hateful.

detractor (dĭ-trăk′tər) *n.* One who belittles or speaks ill of another.

devastate (dĕv′ə-stāt) *v.* To destroy; overwhelm.

devise (dĭ-vīz′) *v.* To plan or create something.

devious (dē′vē-əs) *adj.* Roundabout; not straightforward.

devoid (dǐ-void') *adj.* Without.

devolve (dǐ-vǒlv') *v.* To be passed on to another person, as a responsibility.

dexterity (děk-stěr'ə-tē) *n.* Skill; cleverness.

dexterous (děk'strəs) *adj.* Skillful.

diabolical (dī'ə-bŏl'ǐ-kəl) *adj.* devilish.

diadem (dī'ə-děm') *n.* Crown.

diffidence (dĭf'ə-dəns) *n.* Shyness.

diffuse (dĭ-fyōōz') *v.* To spread out in all directions.

dilapidated (dĭ-lăp'-ə-dā'tĭd) *adj.* In a state of disrepair.

diplomacy (dĭ-plō'mə-sē) *n.* The skillful handling of relationships among nations.

dipsomaniac (dĭp'sə-mā'nē-ăk) *n.* A person who craves alcoholic beverages.

dire (dīr) *adj.* Dreadful.

direful (dīr'fəl) *adj.* Frightful.

dirge (dûrj) *n.* A funeral hymn.

disaffection (dĭs'ə-fěk'shən) *n.* The loss of affection or loyalty.

disapprobation (dĭs-ăp'rə-bā'shən) *n.* Disapproval.

disband (dĭs-bănd') *v.* To break up, as a group.

discern (dĭ-sûrn', -zûrn') *v.* To see clearly.

discernible (dĭ-sûr'nə-bəl) *adj.* Distinguishable.

discomfit (dis-kŭm'fĭt) *v.* To make uneasy; embarrass.

discomfiture (dĭs-kum'fĭ chōōr') *n.* Embarrassment; uneasiness.

discomposure (dis'kəm-pō'zhər) *n.* The lack of calmness.

disconsolate (dĭs-kŏn'sə-lĭt) *adj.* Unable to be comforted; dejected.—**disconsolately** *adv.*

discord (dĭs'kôrd') *n.* **1.** A conflict or disagreement. **2.** A combination of harsh tones sounded together.

discordant (dĭs-kôr'dənt) *adj.* **1.** Harsh in sound. **2.** Not in agreement; conflicting.

discourse (dĭs'kôrs, -kors') *n.* A long speech or written piece about a particular subject.

discreet (dĭs-krēt') *adj.* Careful.—**discreetly** *adv.*

discretion (dis-krěsh'ən) *n.* Caution.

disdain (dĭs-dān') *v.* **1.** To reject scornfully. **2.** To have an attitude of contempt toward something or someone.

disdainful (dĭs-dān'fəl) *adj.* Scornful.

disintegrate (dĭs-ĭn'tə-grāt') *v.* To decay.

disinterested (dĭs-ĭn'trĭ-stĭd, -ĭn'tə-rěs'tĭd) *adj.* Having no selfish interest or motive.—**disinterestedness** *n.*

dislocate (dĭs'lō-kāt', dĭs-lō'kāt') *n.* To displace a limb or organ from its normal place in the body. —**dislocation** *n.*

dismay (dĭs-mā') *n.* Discouragement; alarm.

dismember (dĭs-měm'bər) *v.* To remove the limbs from the body.

disparage (dĭs-păr'ĭj) *v.* To belittle.

disparity (dĭs-păr'ə-tē) *n.* Inequality or difference in rank, quality, or age.

dispassionate (dĭs-păsh'ə-nĭt) *adj.* Not emotional; objective.

disperse (dĭs-pûrs') *v.* To scatter in various directions.

dispirited (dĭs-pîr'ĭt-ĭd) *adj.* Sad.

dispose (dĭs-pōz') *v.* To arrange or settle some important business.

disposition (dĭs'pə-zĭsh'ən) *n.* **1.** A settlement. **2.** A person's temperament. **3.** Inclination.

dissemble (dĭ-sěm'bəl) *v.* To hide behind a disguise.

dissolution (dĭs'ə-lōō'shən) *n.* **1.** Disintegration. **2.** Death.

dissonance (dĭs'ə-nəns) *n.* In music, a combination of sounds that create tension or discord.

distill (dĭs-tĭl') *v.* **1.** To purify or refine. **2.** To increase the strength of a substance.

distort (dĭs-tôrt') *v.* To twist out of proper shape.

distracted (dĭs-trăk'tĭd) *adj.* **1.** Having one's attention diverted. **2.** Confused or bewildered.

distraction (dĭs-trăk'shən) *n.* Mental disturbance.

distraught (dĭs-trôt') *adj.* Troubled; anxious.

divan (dĭ-văn', dī'văn') *n.* A long, low couch.

divert (dĭ-vûrt', dī-) *v.* To entertain.

divine (dĭ-vīn') *v.* To guess.

docket (dŏk'ĭt) *v.* To label or identify.

doddering (dŏd'ər-ĭng) *adj.* Feeble from age; senile.

dogged (dô'gĭd), dŏg'ĭd) *adj.* Stubborn; persistent. —**doggedly** *adv.*—**doggedness** *n.*

dolt (dōlt) *n.* A stupid person.

domestic (də-měs'tĭk) *adj.* Having to do with the family or house.

dote (dōt) *v.* To be extremely fond of.

ä pat/ā pay/âr care/ä father/b **bib**/ch **church**/d **deed**/ĕ pet/ē be/f **fife**/g **gag**/h **hat**/hw **which**/ĭ pit/ī pie/îr **pier**/j **judge**/k **kick**/ l **lid**, **needle**/m **mum**/n **no**, **sudden**/ng **thing**/ŏ pot/ō toe/ô paw, for/oi noise/ou out/ōō took/ōō boot/p **pop**/r **roar**/s **sauce**/ sh **ship**, dish/t tight/th thin, path/*th* this, bathe/ŭ cut/ûr urge/v **valve**/w **with**/y **yes**/z **zebra**, size/zh vision/ə about, item, edible, gallop, circus/à *Fr.* **ami**/œ *Fr.* **feu**, *Ger.* schön/ü *Fr.* **tu**, *Ger.* über/KH *Ger.* ich, *Scot.* loch/N *Fr.* bon.

dowry (dour′ē) *n.* The money or property a woman brings to her husband at marriage.

drawn (drôn) *adj.* Tense.

droll (drōl) *adj.* Comical in a strange way.

drudge (drŭj) *n.* Someone who does hard, tedious work.

drudgery (drŭj′ə-rē) *n.* Dull, monotonous, tiresome work.

dubious (dōō′bē-əs, dyōō′-) *adj.* Vague; doubtful. —**dubiously** *adv.*

duct (dŭkt) *n.* A tubular structure in the body through which a substance passes.—**ductal** *adj.*

dullard (dŭl′ərd) *n.* A stupid person.

duly (dōō′lē, dyōō′-) *adv.* Rightfully.

dumbwaiter (dŭm′wā′tər) *n.* A portable serving table.

dune (dōōn, dyōōn) *n.* A small hill of windblown sand.

duplication (dōō′plĭ-kā′shən, dyōō′-) *n.* An exact copy of something.

duress (dōō-rĕs′, dyōō-, dōōr′ĭs, dyōōr′-) *n.* The threat of the use of force.

dynamic (dī-năm′ĭk) *adj.* Energetic; forceful.

E

ebb (ĕb) *n.* A fading away.—*v.* To lessen.

eccentric (ĕk-sĕn′trĭk, ĭk-) *adj.* Unusual in behavior.

ecology (ĭ-kŏl′ə-jē) *n.* A biological science dealing with the relationship between living organisms and their environment.

ecstasy (ĕk′stə-sē) *n.* Intense delight.

ecstatic (ĕk-stăt′ĭk) *adj.* In a state of intense delight.

eddy (ĕd′ē) *v.* A current of air or water moving in a circular motion.

edifice (ĕd′ə-fĭs) *n.* A building.

edify (ĕd′ə-fī) *v.* To teach; enlighten.

efficacious (ĕf′ə-kā′shəs) *adj.* Having the ability to accomplish a desired effect or result.

ejaculate (ĭ-jăk′yə-lāte′) *v.* To exclaim suddenly.

elate (ĭ-lāt′) *v.* To make very happy or proud.

elation (ĭ-lā′shən) *n.* A feeling of great joy.

electrum (ĭ-lĕk′trəm) *n.* A light-yellow metal made from combining gold and silver.

elixir (ĭ-lĭk′sər) *n.* A substance that is supposed to extend life indefinitely.

elliptical (ĭ-lĭp′tĭ-kəl) *adj.* Not a perfect circle.

elude (ĭ-lōōd′) *v.* To avoid being caught; escape understanding.

elusive (ĭ-lōō′sĭv) *adj.* Hard to retain or understand.

emanate (ĕm′ə-nāt′) *v.* To come from; flow forth.

embalm (ĕm-bäm′, ĭm-) *v.* To preserve.

embellish (ĕm-bĕl′ĭsh, ĭm-) *v.* To improve by adding detail to.

embellishment (ĕm-bĕl′ĭsh-mənt) *n.* Ornamentation.

embezzle (ĕm-bĕz′əl) *v.* To steal money that has been put in one's care.—**embezzlement** *n.*

emblazon (ĕm-blā′zən, ĭm-) *v.* To decorate brightly.

embodiment (ĕm-bŏd′ĭ-mənt, ĭm-) *n.* The bodily or visible form of something.

emboss (ĕm-bôs′, -bŏs′, ĭm-) *v.* To decorate with raised designs or patterns.

emphatic (ĕm-făt′ĭk) *adj.* Forceful.

emulation (ĕm′yə-lā′shən) *n.* The imitation of another with the idea of equalling or going beyond.

encamp (ĕn-kămp′, ĭn-) *v.* To share living accommodations temporarily.

encompass (ĕn-kŭm′pəs, ĭn-) *v.* To include; enclose.

encrust (ĕn-krŭst′, ĭn-) *v.* To cover with elaborate decoration.—**encrustation.** *n.*

endeavor (ĕn-dĕv′ər, ĭn-) *n.* An earnest effort.

endow (ĕn-dou′, ĭn-) *v.* To give money or property.

endurance (ĕn-dōōr′əns, -dyōōr′əns, ĭn-) *n.* The capacity to bear up under hardship or prolonged stress.

endure (ĕn-dōōr′, -dyōōr′, ĭn-) *v.* **1.** To last. **2.** To tolerate.

enervating (ĕn′-ər-vāt′ĭng) *adj.* Depriving of strength; weakening.

enjoin (ĕn-join′, ĭn-) *v.* To order someone to do something; urge.

enmity (ĕn′mə-tē) *n.* Hostility.

ennui (än′wē) *n.* Boredom.

ensue (ĕn-sōō′, ĭn-) *v.* To follow immediately.

entrails (ĕn′trālz′, -trəlz) *n. pl.* The internal organs of humans or animals.

entrance (ĕn-trăns′, -ĭn-) *v.* To fill with delight; enchant.

environ (ĕn-vī′rən, ĭn-) *v.* To surround.

enzymes (ĕn′zīmz) *n. pl.* Substances in plant and animal cells that help bring about certain chemical processes.

ephemeral (ĭ-fĕm′-ər-əl) *adj.* Lasting only a short time.

epistle (ĭ-pĭs′əl) *n.* A letter; message.

epithet (ĕp′ə-thĕt′) *n.* A word or phrase, often insulting, used to describe someone.

equity (ĕk′wə-tē) *n.* Fairness; justice.

erode (ĭ-rōd′) *v.* To wear away.

Glossary

errant (ĕr-ənt) *adj.* Wandering.

erratic (ĭ-răt′ĭk) *adj.* **1.** Wandering. **2.** Irregular.

erudition (ĕr′yoo-dĭsh′ən, ĕr′oo-) *n.* Extensive knowledge obtained through reading and study.

eruption (ĭ-rŭp′shən) *n.* A sudden bursting out.

essence (ĕs-əns) *n.* A solution containing the fragrance of the plant from which it is taken.

esteem (ĕ-stēm′, ĭ-stēm′) *n.* High rank; renown.

ethical (ĕth′ĭ-kəl) *adj.* Having to do with what is considered to be right or wrong behavior.

ethics (ĕth′ĭks) *n. pl.* **1.** The study of standards of behavior. **2.** Rules governing the conduct of people within certain groups.

ethnic (ĕth′nĭk) *adj.* Characteristic of a particular national, racial, cultural, or religious group.

evasive (ĭ-vās′ĭv) *adj.* Vague; not straightforward. **—evasively** *adv.*

evoke (ĭ-vōk) *v.* To call forth.

ewe (yoo) *n.* A female sheep.

exact (ĕg-zăkt′, ĭg-) *v.* To force payment or the giving up of something.

exalted (ĕg-zôl′tĭd, ĭg-) *adj.* Of elevated rank or status.

exasperate (ĕg-zăs′pə-rāt′, ĭg-) *v.* To irritate; annoy.

exceeding (ĕk-sē′dĭng, ĭk-) *adj.* Extreme.

excess (ĕk-sĕs′, ĭk-, ĕk′sĕs′) *n.* A quantity that is more than required or desirable.

exclusive (ĕks-kloo′sĭv, ĭks-) *adj.* Not shared with another person.

excruciating (ĕk-skroo′shē-ā′tĭng, ĭk-) *adj.* Intense.

excursion (ĕk-skûr′zhən, ĭk-) *n.* A round trip, usually very short and taken for pleasure.

execrate (ĕk-sĭ-krāt′) *v.* To curse; denounce.

exhilaration (ĕg-zĭl ə-rā′shən, ĭg-) *n.* Excitement.

exigency (ĕk′sə-jən-sē) *n.* An emergency.

exorbitant (ĕg-zôr′bə-tənt, ĭg-) *adj.* Unreasonably high.

exotic (ĕg-zŏt′ĭk, ĭg-) *adj.* From a faraway and fantastic place.

expatriate (ĕks-pā′trē-āt′) *v.* To exile.

expeditious (ĕk′spə-dĭsh′əs) *adj.* Fast and efficient.

expend (ĕk-spĕnd′, ĭk-) *v.* To use up.

explicit (ĕk-splĭs′ĭt, ĭk-) *adj.* Definite.

expound (ĕk-spound′, ĭk-) *v.* To explain in detail.

expulsion (ĕk-spŭl′shən, ĭk-) *n.* A forcing out of someone from a group or organization.

exquisite (ĕks′kwĭ-zĭt) *adj.* Intense.—**exquisitely** *adv.*

extract (ĕk′străkt) *n.* An excerpt; passage.

extravagance (ĕk-străv′ə-gəns, ĭk-) *n.* Wastefulness.

extricate (ĕk′strĭ-kăt) *v.* To get out of an entanglement.

exuberant (ĕg-zoo′bər-ənt) *adj.* Lively.

exude (ĕg-zood′, ĭg-, ĕk-sood′, ĭk-) *v.* To give off or emit.

exultant (ĕg-zŭl′tənt, ĭg-) *adj.* Joyful.

exultation (ĕg′zŭl-tā′shən) *n.* Rejoicing or triumph.

F

fabulous (făb′yə-ləs) *adj.* Unbelievable.

factor (făc′tər) *n.* Element.

fain (fān) *adv.* Gladly.

famished (făm′ĭsht) *adj.* Starving.

fanatic (fə-năt′-ĭk) *n.* A person whose devotion to a cause is excessive or unreasonable.

fancy (făn′sē) *n.* Imagination; creativeness.

fastidious (fă-stĭd′ē-əs, fə-) *adj.* Extremely fussy about personal cleanliness and appearance.

fealty (fē-əl-tē) *n.* Loyalty.

feasible (fē′zə-bəl) *adj.* Capable of being done.—**feasibility** *n.*

felicitous (fĭ-lĭs′ə-təs) *adj.* Suitable to a specific purpose.

felon (fĕl′ən) *n.* Criminal.

ferocity (fə-rŏs′-ə-te) *n.* Fierceness.

fervent (fûr′vənt) *adj.* Having or showing intense feeling.

fervid (fûr′vĭd) *adj.* Full of emotion.

fester (fĕs′tər) *v.* To develop pus; rot.

festive (fĕs′tĭv) *adj.* Suitable for a celebration or festival.

fetter (fĕt′ər) *v.* To chain.

filament (fĭl′ə-mənt) *n.* The fine metal wire in an electric light bulb.

finicky (fĭn′ĭ-kē) *adj.* Extremely fussy. **—finickiness** *n.*

flagon (flăg′ən) *n.* A large container for liquids, as wine or liquor.

flail (flāl) *v.* To strike.

flamboyance (flăm-boi′əns) *n.* Showy behavior.

ă pat/ā **pay**/âr **care**/ä **father**/b **bib**/ch **church**/d **deed**/ĕ **pet**/ē **be**/f **fife**/g **gag**/h **hat**/hw **which**/ĭ **pit**/ī **pie**/îr **pier**/j **judge**/k **kick**/ l **lid**, needle/m **mum**/n **no**, sudden/ng **thing**/ŏ **pot**/ō **toe**/ô **paw**, for/oi **noise**/ou **out**/oo **took**/oo **boot**/p **pop**/r **roar**/s **sauce**/ sh **ship**, dish/t **tight**/th **thin**, path/*th* **this**, bathe/ŭ **cut**/ûr **urge**/v **valve**/w **with**/y **yes**/z **zebra**, size/zh **vision**/ə **about**, item, edible, gallop, circus/à *Fr.* **ami**/œ *Fr.* **feu,** *Ger.* **schön**/ü *Fr.* **tu,** *Ger.* **über**/KH *Ger.* **ich,** *Scot.* **loch**/N *Fr.* **bon**.

flare (flâr) *n.* To curve outward.

flawless (flô′ləs) *adj.* Perfect.

flax (flăks) *n.* Plants whose seeds produce linseed oil and whose fibers are spun into linen cloth.

florid (flôr′ĭd, flōr′-) *adj.* **1.** Rosy. **2.** Flowery.

flounder (floun′dər) *v.* To move with difficulty, as in mud or water.

flout (flout) *v.* To be scornful of.

folly (fŏl′ē) *n.* Foolishness.

foray (fôr′ā′) *n.* A raid.

forestay (fôr′stā′, fōr′-) *n.* A rope supporting the front mast of a ship.

forfeit (fôr′fĭt) *n.* Something a person must give up as punishment for breaking the law or rules of a game.

forfeiture (fôr′fĭ-chŏŏr′) *n.* The act of giving up something as a penalty or fine.

formidable (fôr′mə-də-bəl) *adj.* **1.** Causing fear. **2.** Very impressive because of skill or strength.

formulate (fôr′myə-lāt′) *v.* To express or state.

fortitude (fôr′tə-tōōd′, -tyōōd′) *n.* Ability to bear pain and misfortune.

founder (foun′dər) *v.* To sink.

frantic (frăn′tĭk) *adj.* Excessively emotional.

fraternal (frə-tûr′nəl) *adj.* Brotherly.

fray (frā) *n.* A fight.

frenetic (frə-nĕt′ĭk) *adj.* Wild; frantic.

fuddle (fŭd′l) *n.* Confusion.

furtive (fûr′tĭv) *adj.* Done in a sly or secret way.

fusillade (fyōō′sə-lād, -läd′, fyōō′zə-) *n.* A firing of many firearms, either at the same time or rapidly and continuously.

futile (fyōōt′l, fyōō′til′) *adj.* Useless.

G

gad (găd) *v.* To wander about seeking amusement.

gait (gāt) *n.* **1.** A particular way of walking or running. **2.** The usual speed at which certain movements are performed.

galore (gə-lôr′, -lōr′) *adj.* In abundance.

game (gām) *adj.* **1.** Spirited. **2.** Ready and willing.

gamut (găm′ət) *n.* The complete range of something.

garland (gär′lənd) *n.* A circlet or string of flowers.

garnish (gär′nĭsh) *v.* To give food some decoration to improve its taste or its appearance.

garret (găr′ĭt) *n.* The attic.

gauge (gāj) *v.* To evaluate; estimate.

gavel (găv′əl) *n.* A small, wooden hammer used to signal for silence.

genial (jēn′yəl, jē′nē-əl) *adj.* Pleasant; friendly.

gesticulation (jĕ-stĭk′yə-lā′shən) *n.* A movement of a part of the body to express something.

geyser (gī′zər) *n.* A spring that periodically gushes columns of hot water and steam into the air.

gingerly (jĭn′jər-lē) *adv.* With great care or caution.

girdler (gûrd′lər) *n.* One that encircles something.

girth (gûrth) *n.* Circumference.

glade (glād) *n.* An open area in a forest.

glint (glĭnt) *n.* To sparkle.

gloat (glōt) *v.* To feel great pleasure over another's loss or suffering.

gnarled (närld) *adj.* Lumpy and twisted.

gnaw (nô) *v.* To eat away at; torment.

goad (gōd) *v.* To urge on.

gorge (gôrj) *v.* To eat greedily.

gosling (gŏz′lĭng) *n.* A young goose.

graft (grăft, gräft) *v.* To join a part of one plant to another in order to produce a certain kind of fruit or flower.

granite (grăn′ĭt) *n.* A hard, gray rock.

grapple (grăp′əl) *n.* A grip or clutch.

gravity (grăv′ə-tē) *n.* Seriousness.

grimace (grĭ-mās′, grĭm′ĭs) *v.* To twist the face in pain or disgust.

grist (grĭst) *n.* **1.** Grain that has been ground. **2.** Something produced by grinding.

groin (groin) *n.* The fold in the body where the trunk meets the thigh.

grotesque (grŏ-tĕsk′) *adj.* Odd; fantastic.

grotto (grŏt′ō) *n.* A dark, hollow, cavelike opening.

grovel (grŭv′əl, grŏv′-) *v.* To cringe.

guile (gīl) *n.* Cunning; slyness.

guise (gīz) *n.* Style of dress.

gullible (gŭl′ə-bəl) *adj.* Easily fooled or convinced.

gyrate (jī′rāt) *v.* To rotate; whirl.

H

habituate (hə-bĭch′ōō-āt′) *v.* To get used to something through frequent and repeated exposure.

haggard (hăg′ərd) *adj.* Having a very exhausted appearance.

halcyon (hăl′sē-ən) *adj.* From an earlier, happier time.

hale (hāl) *adj.* Strong.

haunch (hônch, hänch) *n.* The hip, buttock, and thigh.

haversack (hăv′ər-săk′) *n.* A canvas bag used to carry supplies.

hearken (här′kən) v. To listen to.

heathen (hē′thən) n. pl. People who worship many gods and idols.

heed (hēd) n. Careful consideration.

henna (hĕn′ə) n. A plant of North Africa and Asia that yields a red dye.

herald (hĕr′əld) n. A person or thing that announces important news or events to come.

heresy (hĕr′ə-sē) n. Controversial belief.

hermitage (hûr′mə-tĭj) n. A place to live that is away from other people.

hew (hyōō) v. To make or shape by cutting with an ax.

hideous (hĭd′ē-əs) adj. Ugly.

hie (hī) v. To hurry.

hoist (hoist) v. To lift.

hone (hōn) v. To sharpen on a hard stone.

hover (hŭv′ər, hŏv′-) v. To float in the air or move back and forth near a particular place.

humidor (hyōō′mə-dôr) n. A case provided with a moisturizing device to keep tobacco products fresh.

humiliate (hyōō-mĭl′ē-āt′) n. To hurt someone's pride or feelings; degrade.

humiliation (hyōō-mĭl′ē-ā′shən) n. Disgrace; shame.

hurtle (hûrt′l) v. To throw with great force.

I

idol (īd′l) n. A false god.

idolatry (ī-dŏl′ə-trē) n. Extreme devotion to a person or thing.

ignominious (ĭg′nō-mĭn′ē-əs) adj. Disgraceful.—**ignominiously** adv.

ignoramus (ĭg′nə-rā′məs) n. A stupid person.

illuminate (ĭ-lōō′mə-nāt′) v. 1. To explain. 2. To decorate a handwritten book with colorful designs or pictures.

imbecile (ĭm′bə-sĭl, -səl) n. A very stupid or foolish person.

imminent (ĭm′ə-nənt) adj. About to happen.

immobile (ĭ-mō′bəl, -bēl′) adj. Not moving.

immortals (ĭ-môrt′lz) n. pl. The gods of ancient Greece and Rome.

immune (ĭ-myōōn′) adj. Not affected by something.

impact (ĭm′păkt′) n. A forceful coming together.

impale (ĭm-pāl′) v. To pierce with something pointed.—**impaled** adj.

impart (ĭm-pärt′) v. 1. To give. 2. To make known.

impartial (ĭm-pär′shəl) adj. Showing no favoritism. —**impartiality** (ĭm′pär-shē-ăl′ə-tē) n.

impel (ĭm-pĕl′) v. To drive or urge.

impend (ĭm-pĕnd′) v. To be about to happen; threaten.

impenetrable (ĭm-pĕn′ə-trə-bəl) adj. Unable to be passed through.

imperative (ĭm-pĕr′ə-tĭv) adj. Urgent.

imperceptible (ĭm′pər-sĕp′tə-bəl) adj. Hardly noticeable; gradual.—**imperceptibly** adv.

imperial (ĭm-pîr′ē-əl) adj. Outstanding; majestic.

imperious (ĭm-pîr′ē-əs) adj. Domineering; arrogant.

impetuosity (ĭm-pĕch′ōō-ŏs′ə-tē) n. An impulsive act.

impetuous (ĭm-pĕch′ōō-əs) adj. Acting suddenly without much thought.—**impetuously** adv.

impinge (ĭm-pĭnj′) v. To make an impression on.

implacable (ĭm-plāk′ə-bəl, -plak′ə-bəl) adj. 1. Incapable of being calmed. 2. Unforgiving.

imply (ĭm-plī′) v. To suggest.

import (ĭm′pôrt′, -pōrt′) n. Significance.

impose (ĭm-pōz′) v. To establish with authority.

impostor (ĭm-pŏs′tər) n. A person who pretends to be something he or she is not.

imprecation (ĭm′prə-ka′shən) n. A curse.

impregnable (ĭm-prĕg′nə-bəl) adj. Unshakable; above question or criticism.

impromptu (ĭm-prŏmp′tōō, -tyōō) adj. Done on the spur of the moment.

improvise (ĭm′prə-vīz′) v. To do or make something with the materials at hand, without prior preparation.

imprudent (ĭm-prōō′dənt) adj. Unwise.

impudence (ĭm′-pyə-dəns) n. Bold, shameless behavior.

impudent (ĭm′-pyə-dənt) adj. Disrespectful.

impulse (ĭm′pŭls′) n. A sudden desire to do something.

impunity (ĭm-pyōō′nə-tē) n. Protection against punishment.

inaccessible (ĭn′ăk-sĕs′ə-bəl) adj. Unapproachable. —**inaccessibility** n.

ă pat/ā pay/âr care/ä father/b bib/ch church/d deed/ĕ pet/ē be/f fife/g gag/h hat/hw which/ĭ pit/ī pie/îr pier/j judge/k kick/ l lid, needle/m mum/n no, sudden/ng thing/ŏ pot/ō toe/ô paw, for/oi noise/ou out/ōō took/ōō boot/p pop/r roar/s sauce/ sh ship, dish/t tight/th thin, path/th this, bathe/ŭ cut/ûr urge/v valve/w with/y yes/z zebra, size/zh vision/ə about, item, edible, gallop, circus/à Fr. ami/œ Fr. feu, Ger. schön/ü Fr. tu, Ger. über/KH Ger. ich, Scot. loch/N Fr. bon.

inadvertent (ĭn′əd-vûr′tənt) *adj.* Unintentional. —**inadvertently** *adv.*

inaptitude (ĭn-ăp′tə-tōod′, -tyōod′) *n.* Lack of ability.

incantation (ĭn′kăn-tā′shən) *n.* The chanting of magical words to cast a spell.—**incantatory** (ĭn′kăn′tə-tôr′e) *adj.*

incautious (ĭn-kô′shəs) *adj.* Not careful.—**incautiously** *adv.*

inception (ĭn-sĕp′shən) *n.* The origin of something.

incessant (ĭn-sĕs′ənt) *adj.* Continuous.—**incessantly** *adv.*

incoherent (ĭn′kō-hîr′ənt) *adj.* Unconnected; rambling.

incompatible (ĭn′kəm-păt′ə-bəl) *adj.* Conflicting.

incomprehensible (ĭn′kŏm-prĭ-hĕn′sə-bəl, ĭn-kŏm′-) *adj.* Not understandable.

inconceivable (ĭn′kən-sē′və-bəl) *adj.* Unbelievable.

inconsequential (ĭn-kŏn′sə-kwĕn′shəl) *adj.* Unimportant.

inconsolable (ĭn′kən-sō′lə-bəl) *adj.* Unable to be comforted.

incorruptible (ĭn′kə-rŭp′tə-bəl) *adj.* Not subject to becoming immoral or dishonest.

incredulity (ĭn′krə-dōo′lə-tē, -dyōo′lə-tē) *n.* Disbelief.

incubation (ĭn′kyə-bā′shən, ĭng′-) *n.* The period during which eggs are developed and hatched.

incursion (ĭn′kûr′zhən, -shən) *n.* A sudden entering into.

indecipherable (ĭn′dĭ-sī′fər-ə-bəl) *adj.* That cannot be made understandable.

indifference (ĭn-dĭf′ər-əns) *n.* A lack of interest.

indifferent (ĭn-dĭf′ər-ənt) *adj.* **1.** Without interest in. **2.** Uninvolved.

indignation (ĭn′dĭg-nā′shən) *n.* Anger.

indiscriminate (ĭn′dĭs-krĭm′ə-nĭt) *adj.* **1.** Haphazard. **2.** Unrestrained.—**indiscriminately** *adv.*

indisputable (ĭn′dĭs-pyōo′tə-bəl) *adj.* Undeniable.

indolent (ĭn′də-lənt) *adj.* Lazy.—**indolently** *adv.*

ineffectual (ĭn′ĭ-fĕk′chōo-əl) *adj.* Not producing a desired result.—**ineffectually** *adv.*

inequity (ĭn-ĕk′wə-tē) *n.* Unfairness.

inevitable (ĭn-ĕv′ə-tə-bəl) *adj.* Unavoidable.—**inevitably** *adv.*

inexplicable (ĭn-ĕk′splĭ-kə-bəl, ĭn′-ĭk-splĭk′-ə-bəl) *adj.* Not possible to explain.

inextricable (ĭn-ĕk′strĭ′kə-bəl) *adj.* Too intricate to be disentangled.—**inextricably** *adv.*

infallible (ĭn-făl′ə-bəl) *adj.* Not capable of error. —**infallibility** *n.*

infamous (ĭn′fə-məs) *adj.* Outrageous.

infer (ĭn-fûr′) *v.* To conclude from available facts.

infernal (ĭn-fûr′nəl) *adj.* Hellish; fiendish.

infest (ĭn-fĕst′) *v.* To swarm over in a destructive way.

inflammatory (ĭn-flăm′ə-tôr′ē, tôr′ē) *adj.* Fiery.

inflexible (ĭn-flĕk′sə-bəl) *adj.* Stubborn.

infuse (ĭn-fyōoz′) *v.* To put into as by pouring.

ingenuity (ĭn′jə-nōo′ə-tē, -nyōo′ə-tē) *n.* Cleverness.

ingrate (ĭn′grāt) *n.* An ungrateful person.

injudicious (ĭn′jōo-dĭsh′əs) *adj.* Unwise.

injunction (ĭn-jŭngk′shən) *n.* A command.

innards (ĭn′ərdz) *n. pl.* The intestines and other internal organs of the body.

innovation (ĭn′ə-vā′shən) *n.* A change.

insatiable (ĭn-sā′shə-bəl, -shē-ə-bəl) *adj.* Not capable of being satisfied.

inscription (ĭn-skrĭp′shən) *n.* A short message written on or carved into a hard surface.

inscrutable (ĭn-skrōo′tə-bəl) *adj.* Mysterious.

insidious (ĭn-sĭd′ē-əs) *adj.* **1.** Treacherous. **2.** Stealthy.

insinuating (ĭn-sĭn′yōo-ā′tĭng) *adj.* Arousing doubts and suspicions.—**insinuatingly** *adv.*

insolent (ĭn′sə-lənt) *adj.* Bold in a reckless way.

insolvent (ĭn-sŏl′vənt) *adj.* Not able to pay debts.

instigate (ĭn′stĭ-gāt′) *v.* To stir up.

institute (ĭn-stə-tōot′, -tyōot′) *v.* To start.

insufferable (ĭn-sŭf′ər-ə-bəl) *adj.* Unbearable.—**insufferably** *adv.*

insular (ĭn′sə-lər, ĭns′yə-) *adj.* **1.** Isolated, as if living on an island. **2.** Provincial; narrow-minded.

insupportable (ĭn′sə-pôr′tə-bəl, -pōr′tə-bəl) *adj.* Unbearable.

intact (ĭn-tăkt′) *adj.* Whole; undamaged.

integrity (ĭn-tĕg′rə-tē) *n.* Honesty; sincerity and strength of character.

inter (ĭn-tûr′) *v.* To bury.

interlope (ĭn′tər-lōp′) *v.* To intrude; meddle.—**interloper** *n.*

interment (ĭn-tûr′mənt) *n.* Burial.

interpose (ĭn′tər-pōz′) *v.* **1.** To introduce an interrupting remark in a conversation. **2.** To come between as a settling force. —**interposition** (ĭn′tər-pə-zĭsh′ən) *n.*

interstice (ĭn-tûr′stĭs) *n.* A small, narrow space between parts of a thing.

intervene (ĭn′tər-vēn′) *v.* To come in as an influencing force.

intimacy (ĭn′tə-mə-sē) *n.* A close and familiar relationship.

intimidate (ĭn′tĭm′ĭ-dāt′) *v.* To frighten.

intimate (ĭn′tə-mĭt) *adj.* Close and familiar.

intimate (ĭn′tə-māt′) *v.* To hint.

intolerable (ĭn-tŏl′ər-ə-bəl) *adj.* Unbearable.

intoxicate (ĭn-tŏk′sĭ-kāt′) *v.* To make drunk. **2.** To excite.

intricate (ĭn′trĭ-kĭt) *adj.* Full of detail; complicated.

intrigue (ĭn′trēg′, ĭn-trēg′) *v.* To scheme secretly. —**intriguer** *n.*

intrinsic (ĭn-trĭn′sĭk) *adj.* Essential.

intrusion (ĭn-trōō′zhən) *n.* An uninvited or illegal entry.

intuitive (ĭn-tōō′ĭ-tĭv, -tyōō′-) *adj.* Known without the use of conscious learning or reasoning.—**intuitively** *adv.*

invariable (ĭn′vâr′ē-ə-bəl) *adj.* Constant—**invariably** *adv.*

inveterate (ĭn′vêt′ər-ĭt) *adj.* By custom or habit.

invocation (ĭn′və-kā′shən) *n.* **1.** A serious request. **2.** A prayer asking for help.

iridescent (îr′ə-dĕs′ənt) *adj.* Bright and shifting in color.

irrational (ĭ-răsh′ən-əl) *adj.* Senseless.—**irrationally** *adv.*

irresolute (ĭ-rĕz′ə-lōōt) *adj.* Undecided.

irrevocable (ĭ-rĕv′ə-kə-bəl) *adj.* Incapable of being undone.

J

jar (jär) *v.* To make an irritating sound.

jostle (jŏs′əl) *v.* To push and shove in a crowd.

joust (jŭst, joust, jōōst) *n.* A fight with lances between two people on horseback.

jowl (joul) *n.* The flesh under the jaw.

jubilant (jōō′bə-lənt) *adj.* Joyful.—**jubilantly** *adv.*

judicial (jōō-dĭsh′əl) *adj.* Showing careful consideration of all sides of a problem when making a decision.

K

kibitzer (kĭb′ĭt-sər) *n. Informal.* A meddler who gives unwanted advice.

L

labyrinth (lab′ə-rĭnth′) *n.* A structure with winding passages.

lacerated (lăs′ə-rā′tĭd) *adj.* Wounded; torn.

lair (lâr) *n.* The home of a wild animal.

lament (lə-mĕnt′) *v.* To grieve for.

lamentable (lăm′ən-tə-bəl, lə-mĕn′-) *adj.* Distressing.

lance (lăns, läns) *n.* A thrusting weapon having a wooden shaft and a pointed metal tip.

languid (lăng′gwĭd) *adj.* Lacking energy.

languish (lăng′gwĭsh) *v.* **1.** To become weak. **2.** To long or pine for something.—*n. Obsolete.* Weakness.

lapse (lăps) *n.* A minor fault or error.

larceny (lär′sə-nē) *n.* Theft.

larder (lär′dər) *n.* A storage room for household food supplies.

lascar (lăs′kər) *n.* A sailor from India.

lateral (lăt′ər-əl) *adj.* Situated at the side.—*n.* In football, a pass thrown sidewise.—**laterally** *adv.*

lax (lăks) *adj.* Careless.

legacy (lĕg′ə-sē) *n.* Something handed down from the past.

lenient (lē′nē-ənt, lēn′yənt) *adj.* Generous.—**leniently** *adv.*

lethargy (lĕth′ər-jē) *n.* Sluggishness; lack of energy.

litany (lĭt′n-ē) *n.* A repetitive prayer.

literal (lĭt′ər-əl) *adj.* Real.—**literally** *adv.*

lithe (līth) *adj.* Limber.

livid (lĭv′ĭd) *adj.* Extremely pale.

loam (lōm) *n.* Rich, dark soil.

loath (lōth, lōth) *adj.* Unwilling.

loathsome (lōth′səm, lōth′-) *adj.* Disgusting.

loll (lŏl) *v.* To lounge; recline in a relaxed way.

longitudinal (lŏn′jə-tōōd′n-əl, -tyōōd′n-əl) *adj.* Lengthwise.

lop (lŏp) *v.* To cut off.

lope (lōp) *v.* To move with a steady, easy stride.

lore (lôr, lōr) *n.* The accumulated information on a particular subject.

lounge (lounj) *v.* **1.** To spend time idly. **2.** To move in a relaxed way.

lout (lout) *n.* A stupid person.

lucrative (lōō′krə-tĭv) *adj.* Profitable.

lugger (lŭg′ər) *n.* A small sailing vessel.

ă pat/ā pay/âr care/ä father/b bib/ch church/d deed/ĕ pet/ē be/f fife/g gag/h hat/hw which/ĭ pit/ī pie/îr pier/j judge/k kick/ l lid, needle/m mum/n no, sudden/ng thing/ŏ pot/ō toe/ô paw, for/oi noise/ou out/ōō took/ōō boot/p pop/r roar/s sauce/ sh ship, dish/t tight/th thin, path/th this, bathe/ŭ cut/ûr urge/v valve/w with/y yes/z zebra, size/zh vision/ə about, item, edi- ble, gallop, circus/å *Fr.* ami/œ *Fr.* feu, *Ger.* schön/ü *Fr.* tu, *Ger.* über/KH *Ger.* ich, *Scot.* loch/N *Fr.* bon.

luminous (loo'mə-nəs) *adj.* Giving off light.

lunacy (loo'nə-sē) *n.* **1.** Insanity. **2.** Very foolish behavior.

lunatic (loo'nə tĭk) *adj.* **1.** Insane. **2.** Exceedingly foolish.

lurch (lûrch) *v.* To fall and rise abruptly.

lurid (loor'ĭd) *adj.* Passionate; vivid.

lusterless (lŭs'tər-ləs) *adj.* Dull.

M

magnanimity (măg'nə-nĭm'ĭ-tē) *n.* Nobility and generosity of spirit.

magnanimous (măg năn'ə məs) *adj.* Noble in mind and heart.

magnetize (măg'nə-tīz') *v.* **1.** To attract. **2.** To have a strong influence upon.

malevolence (mə-lĕv'ə-ləns) *n.* A feeling of extreme ill will toward others.

malice (măl'ĭs) *n.* A desire to be hurtful to others.

malignant (mə-lĭg'nənt) *adj.* Very harmful.

malodorous (măl-ō'dər-əs) *adj.* Having an unpleasant odor.

mammoth (măm'əth) *adj.* Gigantic.

manacle (măn'ə-kəl) *v.* To handcuff.

maneuver (mə-noo'vər) *v.* To move in a purposeful and skilled way for a particular reason.

martial (mär'shəl) *adj.* Military.

martinet (mär'tə-nĕt') *n.* Someone who demands very strict observance of rules.

martyr (mär'tər) *v.* To torture.

masonry (mā'sən-rē) *n.* Brickwork or stonework.

massive (măs'ĭv) *adj.* **1.** Very large. **2.** Of such an extent to make a deep impression.

mattock (măt'ək) *n.* A digging tool similar to a pickax.

maudlin (môd'lĭn) *adj.* Tearfully sentimental.

meager (mē'gər) *adj.* A small amount.

meandering (mē-ăn'dər-ĭng) *adj.* Winding; changing course.

medieval (mē'dē-ē'vəl, mēd'ē-'vəl) *adj.* Pertaining to the Middle Ages.

meditate (mĕd'ə-tāt') *v.* To think deeply.

meditation (mĕd'ə-tā'shən) *n.* Deep thoughtfulness.

meditative (mĕd'ə-tā'tĭv) *adj.* In deep thoughtfulness; pensive.

melodramatic (mĕl'ə-drə-măt'ĭk) *adj.* Highly exciting or emotional.

menace (mĕn'ĭs) *n.* A harmful person or thing.

mentality (mĕn-tăl'ə-tē) *n.* Cast of mind.

merit (mĕr'ĭt) *v.* To deserve.

meteorite (mē'tē-ə-rīt') *n.* The part of a larger body from outer space that falls to the earth's surface.

methodical (mə thŏd'ĭ kəl) *adj.* Orderly; systematic.

meticulous (mə-tĭk'yə-ləs) *adj.* Extremely precise.

mettle (mĕt'l) *n.* Courage.

mime (mīm) *n.* A form of drama that uses movements of the body instead of words to put across ideas.

minaret (mĭn'ə-rĕt') *n.* A tall, slender tower attached to a mosque.

miscreant (mĭs'krē-ənt) *n.* A wicked person.

moderate (mŏd'ə-rāt') *v.* To become mild.

modulate (mŏj'oo lāt', mŏd'yə) *v.* **1.** To regulate or vary the pitch of the voice or a musical instrument. **2.** To change pitch within a musical composition.

momentum (mō-mĕn'təm) *n.* The force that keeps an object moving.

monitor (mŏn'ə-tər) *n.* A device used to record or regulate the performance of some machine or process.

mooch (mooch) *v.* To loaf.

moral (môr'l, mŏr'-) *adj.* Concerned with what is right or wrong behavior.

morbid (môr'bĭd) *adj.* Gruesome.

morose (mə-rōs', mô-) *adj.* Gloomy.

morsel (môr'səl) *n.* A small amount.

mortification (môr'tə-fĭ-kā'shən) *n.* Humiliation.

mortify (môr'tə-fī') *v.* **1.** To humiliate. **2.** To decay because of injury or disease.

mosaic (mō-zā'ĭk) *n.* A picture or design made by setting small pieces of colored glass or clay in mortar.

mosque (mŏsk) *n.* A Moslem house of worship.

motley (mŏt'lē) *adj.* Composed of many different and unrelated elements or colors. *n.* A clown costume.

mottle (mŏt'l) *v.* To streak or spot with many colors.

muffle (mŭf'əl) *v.* To repress or deaden a sound.

multitude (mŭl'tə-tood', -tyood') *n.* A large number of individuals.

muster (mŭs'tər) *v.* To gather together.—*n.* An assembly.

mute (myoot) *adj.* Unable to speak.—**mutely** *adv.*

mutilate (myoot'l-āt') *v.* To cut off or make useless a part of the body.—**mutilation** *n.*

mutinous (myoot'n-əs) *adj.* Rebellious.

myriad (mĭr'ē-əd) *adj.* A great number.

mythic (mĭth'ĭk) *adj.* Imaginary.

N

naive (nă-ēv′) *adj.* Not worldly-wise.

niche (nĭch) *n.* A hollow place in a wall.

niggardly (nĭg′ərd-lē) *adj.* Stingy.

ninny (nĭn′ē) *n.* A fool.

niter (nī′tər) *n.* A white or gray hardened form of potassium nitrate.

nocturne (nŏk′tûrn′) *n.* A dreamy or romantic composition, often for the piano.

nomadic (nō-măd′ĭk) *adj.* Wandering; having no permanent home.

nomenclature (nō′mən-klā′chər, nō-měn′klə-chər) *n.* A set of names for a particular group of things.

nonchalant (nŏn′shə-länt′) *adj.* Casual; unconcerned.

nondescript (nŏn′dĭ-skrĭpt′) *adj.* Lacking individual character.

nostalgia (nŏ-stăl′jə, nə-) *n.* **1.** A longing for something from long ago. **2.** Homesickness.

nucleus (nōō′klē-əs, nyōō-) *n.* Center or core.

nuptial (nŭp′shəl) *n.* A wedding.

nurture (nûr-chər) *v.* To nourish.

nuzzle (nŭz′əl) *v.* To snuggle.

nymph (nĭmf) *n.* A nature goddess.

O

obituary (ō-bĭch′ōō-ĕr′-ē) *n.* A death notice that includes a short description of the dead person's life.

obligatory (ə-blĭg′ə-tôr′ē) *adj.* Compulsory.

oblivious (ə-blĭv′ē-əs) *adj.* Unaware.

obnoxious (ŏb-nŏk′shəs, əb-) *adj.* Hateful.

obscure (ŏb-skyōōr′, əb-) *v.* To make unclear; hide.

obsess (əb-sĕs′, ŏb-) *v.* To preoccupy the mind.

obsidian (ŏb-sĭd′ē-ən) *n.* Hard volcanic glass.

ocher (ō-kər) *n.* A yellow or reddish-brown color.

ointment (oint′mənt) *n.* A salve.

ominous (ŏm′ə-nəs) *adj.* Threatening.—**ominously** *adv.*

omnipotent (ŏm-nĭp′ə-tənt) *adj.* All-powerful.

opaque (ō-pāk′) *adj.* Not letting light through.

opiate (ō′pē-ĭt, -āt′) *n.* Something that soothes.

oppression (ə-prĕsh′ən) *n.* Something that weighs heavily on the mind, body, or senses.

oppressive (ə-prĕs′ĭv) *adj.* Hard to bear.

option (ŏp′shən) *n.* A choice.

oracle (ôr′ə-kəl, ŏr′-) *n.* Something or someone believed to be a source of wisdom.

oration (ô-rā′shən, ō-ra′) *n.* A formal speech given at a formal ceremony.

orator (ôr′ə-tər, ŏr′) *n.* A skilled public speaker.

orb (ôrb) *n.* An eye.

orbit (ôr′bĭt) *n.* Eye socket.

ordnance (ôrd′nəns) *n.* Military weaponry.

ornamental (ôr′nə-měn′təl) *adj.* Made fancy with decorations.

ornate (ôr-nāt′) *adj.* Heavily decorated.

orthodox (ôr′thə-dŏks′) *adj.* Conventional; accepted.—**orthodoxy** *n.*

overweening (ō′vər-wē′nĭng) *adj.* Overbearing.

P

padre (pä′drā, -drē) *n.* A title used in addressing a priest.

palate (păl′ĭt) *n.* The sense of taste.

palatial (pə-lā′shəl) *adj.* Magnificent, like a palace.

pall (pôl) *n.* Anything dark and gloomy that covers or wraps around something.

palpable (păl′pə-bəl) *adj.* Capable of being touched.

palpitate (păl′pĭ-tāt′) *v.* To quiver or throb.

palpitation (păl′pə-tā′shən) *n.* An irregular and rapid beating of the heart.

palter (pôl′tər) *v.* To argue about terms, prices, etc.

pandemonium (păn′də-mō′nē-əm) *n.* Wild noise and disorder.

pantomime (păn′tə-mīm′) *n.* A drama performed solely with actions and gestures.

parable (păr′ə-bəl) *n.* A short, simple story teaching a moral or religious lesson.

paradox (păr′ə dŏks′) *n.* A situation or statement that has contradictory qualities.—**paradoxical** *adj.*

paragon (păr′ə-gŏn′, -gən) *n.* Model of excellence.

paramour (păr′-ə-mōōr′) *n.* A lover.

parapet (păr′ə-pĭt, pĕt′) *n.* A low wall or railing around the edge of a roof or bridge.

parasol (păr′ə-sōl′, -sŏl′) *n.* A small, light umbrella used as a sunshade.

parity (păr'ĭ-tē) *n.* Equal price or quality of farm products.

parley (pär'lē) *n.* A discussion held to settle a dispute.

paroxysm (păr'ək-sĭz'm) *n.* A sudden fit or spasm.

partridge (pär'trĭj) *adj.* A wild bird hunted for sport or food.

pathetic (pə-thĕt'ĭk) *adj.* Arousing pity.—**pathetically** *adv.*

patronize (pā'trə-nīz', păt'rə-) *v.* To treat others with an air of superiority.

pavilion (pə-vĭl'yən) *n.* A large, elegant tent such as those used during the Middle Ages.

pedigree (pĕd'ə-grē') *n.* Ancestry.

peeve (pēv) *v.* To annoy.—**peevishness** *n.*

pelt (pĕlt) *v.* To pound steadily and heavily.

penitent (pĕn'ə-tənt) *adj.* Feeling and expressing shame for having done something wrong.—**penitently** *adv.*

penitential (pĕn'ə-tĕn'shəl) *adj.* Expressing remorse for one's wrongs.

pennant (pĕn'ənt) *n.* A flag.

pensive (pen'sĭv) *adj.* Thoughtful.

penury (pĕn'yə-rē) *n.* Poverty.

perceive (pər-sēv') *v.* To become aware of something.

perceptible (pər-sĕp'tə-bəl) *adj.* Noticeable; recognizable.

perception (pər-sĕp'shən) *n.* **1.** Awareness. **2.** Insight or understanding.

perdition (pər-dĭsh'ən) *n.* Hell.

perjury (pûr'jə-rē) *n.* The telling of a lie while swearing to tell the truth.

pernicious (pər-nĭsh'əs) *adj.* Destructive; deadly.

perplex (pər-plĕks') *v.* To confuse.

persistent (pər-sĭs'tənt, zĭs'tənt) *adj.* Stubborn.—**persistently** *adv.*

pert (pûrt) *adj.* Saucy.

peruse (pə-rōōz') *v.* To read; study.

perverse (pər-vûrs') *adj.* Contrary to what is considered to be correct thinking or behavior.

perverted (pər-vûr'tĭd) *adj.* Evil.

petition (pə-tĭsh'n) *n.* A formal request to a person or group in authority.

pettish (pĕt'ĭsh) *adj.* Irritable.—**pettishly** *adv.*

pewter (pyōō'tər) *n.* A dull, grayish alloy that has tin as its major metal.

phenomenon (fĭ-nŏm'ə-nŏn) *n.* **1.** Something that can be seen but is difficult to understand. **2.** An unusual occurrence.

philanthropist (fĭ-lăn'thrə-pĭst) *n.* A person of means who helps less fortunate people.

pilgrimage (pĭl'grə-mĭj) *n.* Any long journey for a particular purpose.

pillage (pĭl'ĭj) *v.* To loot; damage.

pinion (pĭn'yən) *n.* A bird's wing.

pinnacle (pĭn'ə-kəl) *n.* A peak.

pious (pī'əs) *adj.* Showing religious devotion.

pique (pēk) *v.* To cause a feeling of resentment.

placable (plăk'ə-bəl, plā'kə-) *adj.* Capable of being calmed or soothed.

placard (plăk'ärd', -ərd) *n.* A poster used to make a public announcement.

placid (plăs'ĭd) *adj.* Calm.—**placidly** *adv.*

plaintiff (plān'tĭf) *n.* The party that brings suit in court.

plaintive (plān'tĭv) *adj.* Sad.—**plaintively** *adv.*

pliancy (plī'ən-sē) *n.* The quality of being supple or flexible.

pliant (plī'ənt) *adj.* Flexible.

ploy (ploi) *n.* A trick or stratagem.

plumb (plŭm) *adv.* Exactly.

plunder (plŭn'dər) *n.* Property taken by force.

poacher (pō'chər) *n.* Someone who hunts or fishes unlawfully on the property of another.

poise (poiz) *n.* Dignified and serene behavior.

pommel (pŭm'əl, pŏm'-) *n.* The rounded, front part of a saddle.

ponder (pŏn'dər) *v.* To consider carefully; deliberate.

ponderous (pŏn'dər-əs) *adj.* Extremely heavy—**ponderously** *adv.*

portentous (pôr-tĕn'təs, pōr-) *adj.* Threatening.

posture (pŏs'chər) *v.* To take on a bodily or mental attitude to produce a desired effect.

pounce (pouns) *v.* To spring.

prate (prāt) *v.* To chatter.

precarious (prĭ-kâr'ē-əs) *adj.* **1.** Insecure. **2.** Based on unproved statements or conclusions.—**precariously** *adv.*

preclude (prĭ-klōōd') *v.* To make impossible.

predatory (prĕd'ə-tôr'ē) *adj.* Living by catching and eating other animals.

predominate (prĭ-dŏm'ə-nāt) *v.* To be greater in quantity.

prejudice (prĕj'ə-dĭs) *n.* An opinion, usually unfavorable, formed before knowing all the facts about a person or thing.

preliminary (prĭ-lĭm'ə-nĕr'ē) *adj.* Happening before or leading up to a main action.—**preliminaries** *n. pl.*

premature ⟨prē′mə-choŏr,- toŏr, tyoŏr′⟩ *adj.* Too early or too soon.—**prematurely** *adv.*

premises ⟨prĕm′ĭs-əz⟩ *n. pl.* A building and the area surrounding it.

presentiment ⟨prĭ-zĕn′tə-mənt⟩ *n.* A feeling that a particular thing will happen.

preserve ⟨prĭ-zûrv′⟩ *n.* An area set aside for the protection of wildlife.

preside ⟨prĭ-zīd′⟩ *v.* To hold the position of authority.

presumably ⟨prĭ-zoō′ mə-blē⟩ *adv.* Probably.

presume ⟨prĭ-zoōm′⟩ *v.* To take for granted.

presumption ⟨prĭ-zŭmp′shən⟩ *n.* Boldness; forwardness.

prevail ⟨prĭ-vāl′⟩ *v.* **1.** To succeed. **2.** To be effective. **3.** To remain in force.

prevalent ⟨prĕv′ə-lənt⟩ *adj.* Common or widespread.

prim ⟨prĭm⟩ *adj.* Neat and trim.

primness ⟨prĭm′nəs⟩ *n.* Neatness.

privation ⟨prī-vā′shən⟩ *n.* The lack of the basic needs or comforts of life.

probe ⟨prōb⟩ *n.* An instrument used to explore a wound or body cavity.

procession ⟨prə-sĕsh′ən⟩ *n.* A group of people moving forward as in a parade.

proclaim ⟨prō-klām′, prə-⟩ *v.* To declare publicly.

procure ⟨prō-kyoōr′, prə-⟩ *v.* To get.

prodigious ⟨prə-dĭj′əs⟩ *adj.* Enormous; impressive in size or extent.—**prodigiously** *adv.*

prodigy ⟨prŏd′ə-jē⟩ *n.* A child with unusual talent.

profane ⟨prō-fān′, prə-⟩ *v.* To treat sacred things with contempt.—**profaner** *n.*

profanity ⟨prō-făn′ə-tē, prə-⟩ *n.* Disrespectful or irreverent language.

profess ⟨prə-fĕs′, prō-⟩ *v.* To declare openly.

profound ⟨prə-found′, prō-⟩ *adj.* Complete; deep.

profusion ⟨prə-fyoō′zhən, prō-⟩ *n.* An abundance.

proliferate ⟨prō-lĭf′ə-rāt′⟩ *v.* To increase quickly and in great quantity.

promenader ⟨prŏm′ə-nād′ûr⟩ *n.* A person who takes a walk for pleasure.

prominent ⟨prŏm′ə-nənt⟩ *adj.* Very noticeable.

promiscuous ⟨prə-mĭs′kyoō-əs⟩ *adj.* In a haphazard way.—**promiscuously** *adv.*

prone ⟨prōn⟩ *adj.* Lying flat.

proposition ⟨prŏp′ə-zĭsh′ən⟩ *n.* **1.** A plan or idea offered for consideration. **2.** In math, a problem to be solved.

proprietor ⟨prə-prī′ə-ter⟩ *n.* An owner.

proprieties ⟨prə-prī′ə-tēz⟩ *n. pl.* Accepted behavior in polite society.

prosperity ⟨prŏs-pĕr′ə-tē⟩ *n.* Wealth; success.

prostrate ⟨prŏs′trāt′⟩ *v.* **1.** To be flat; **2.** To kneel or fall to the ground in humility or surrender.—*adj.* lying flat.

protozoa ⟨prō′tə-zō′ə⟩ *n. pl.* Microscopic organisms.

protract ⟨prō-trăkt′⟩ *v.* To prolong.

protrude ⟨prō-troōd′⟩ *v.* To jut out.

provender ⟨prŏv′ən-dər⟩ *n.* Food.

Providence ⟨prŏv′ə-dəns, -dĕns′⟩ *n.* God.

provincial ⟨prə-vĭn′shəl⟩ *adj.* Rural; countrified.

provision ⟨prə-vĭzh′ən⟩ *n.* A stock of food in store for future use.

provoke ⟨prə-vōk′⟩ *v.* To anger.

prow ⟨prou⟩ *n.* The front part of a ship.

prudence ⟨proōd′əns⟩ *n.* Cautious behavior.

prune ⟨proōn⟩ *v.* To cut off dead or live parts of a plant in order to improve growth or shape.

psychological ⟨sī′kə-lŏj′ĭ-kəl⟩ *adj.* Pertaining to the mind.

puke ⟨pyoōk⟩ *v.* To vomit.

pungent ⟨pŭn′jənt⟩ *adj.* Sharp or bitter taste or smell.

Q

quack ⟨kwăk⟩ *n.* Someone who pretends to have a great deal of knowledge and skill in a certain field.

quadruped ⟨kwŏd′roō-pĕd′⟩ *adj.* Four-footed.

qualm ⟨kwäm, kwôm⟩ *n.* Uneasiness or misgiving.

quarry ⟨kwôr′ē, kwŏr′ē⟩ *n.* **1.** An animal that is being hunted. **2.** A place where building stone is taken from the ground.

quench ⟨kwĕnch⟩ *v.* To put an end to.

querulous ⟨kwĕr′ə-ləs, kwĕr′yə-⟩ *adj.* Complaining.

quest ⟨kwĕst⟩ *n.* A search.

quibble ⟨kwĭb′əl⟩ *v.* To argue at length the minor details of a topic.

quirk ⟨kwûrk⟩ *n.* A strange character trait or mannerism.

quiver (kwĭv′ər) *n.* A container for arrows.

quizzical (kwĭz′ĭ-kəl) *adj.* In a questioning way. —**quizzically** *adv.*

R

radical (răd′i-kəl) *adj.* **1.** Basic. **2.** Extreme.

rakish (rā′kĭsh) *adj.* Having a carefree, dashing appearance.—**rakishly** *adv.*

rambling (răm′blĭng) *adj.* Aimless wandering.

rampart (răm′pärt) *n.* A protective wall encircling a city or fort.

ramshackle (răm′shăk′əl) *adj.* Rickety; poorly constructed, falling to pieces.

random (răn′dəm) *adj.* Purposeless; haphazard.

ransack (răn′săk′) *v.* To search thoroughly.

rapier (rā′pē-ər) *n.* A long, slender, two-edged sword.

raptor (răp′tər) *n.* A predatory bird.

rapture (răp′chər) *n.* Ecstatic feeling.

rapturous (răp′chər-əs) *adj.* Feeling great joy.

rash (răsh) *adj.* Reckless.

ravage (răv′ĭj) *v.* To destroy; lay waste.—*n.* Destruction.

ravenous (răv′ən-əs) *adj.* Very hungry.—**ravenously** *adv.*

raze (rāz) *v.* To tear down, as a building.

rebuke (rĭ-byo͞ok′) *v.* to scold sharply.

recalcitrant (rĭ-kăl′sə-trənt) *adj.* Difficult to control.—**recalcitrance** *n.*

receptacle (rĭ-sĕp′tə-kəl) *n.* A container.

recess (rē′sĕs, rĭ-sĕs′) *n.* A hollow place or indentation in a wall.

recline (rĭ-klīn′) *v.* To lie down or lean back.

recoil (rĭ-koil′) *v.* To draw or fall back.

recompense (rĕk′əm-pĕns′) *n.* Payment; reward.

reconcile (rĕk′ən-sīl′) *v.* **1.** To accept or agree to something. **2.** To become friendly again.

reconnoiter (rē′kə-noi′tər, rĕk′ə-) *v.* To explore or inspect in order to seek out information.

recourse (rē-kôrs′) *n.* A turning to someone or something for help.

rectory (rĕk′tə-rē) *n.* The house in which the minister of a church lives.

redress (rĭ-drĕs′) *v.* To set right; make amends —**redresser** *n.*

reek (rēk) *v.* To give off smoke or steam or odors.

reeve (rēv) *n.* The chief officer of a town.

reflect (rĭ-flĕkt′) *v.* **1.** To think seriously. **2.** To give back a likeness.

reflection (rĭ-flĕk′shən) *n.* **1.** Careful thought. **2.** An image of something.

refute (rĭ-fyo͞ot′) *v.* To prove to be wrong or false.

regalia (rĭ-gāl′yə, -gā′lē-ə) *n.* Magnificent clothes.

regulation (rĕg′yə-lā′shən) *adj.* Required by rule or law.

reiterate (rē-ĭt′ə-rāt′) *v.* To say over and over again.

relay (rē′lā, rĭ-lā′) *n.* A fresh supply of something.

relent (rĭ-lĕnt′) *v.* To soften in attitude.

relentless (rĭ-lĕnt′lĭs) *adj.* Unyielding.

relevant (rĕl′ə-vənt) *adj.* Important to the matter under consideration.—**relevancy** *n.*

relic (rĕl′ĭk) *n.* An object from the past that is a keepsake or souvenir.

relinquish (rĭ-lĭng′kwĭsh) *v.* To give up.

relish (rĕl′ĭsh) *v.* To enjoy the taste of; like.

reluctance (rĭ-lŭk′təns) *n.* Nonwillingness.

reluctant (rĭ-luk′tənt) *adj.* Unwilling.

remonstrance (rĭ-mŏn′strəns) *n.* Protest.

remonstrate (rĭ-mŏn′strāt′) *v.* To protest.

remorse (rĭ-môrs′) *n.* A feeling of guilt for having done something wrong.

remote (rĭ-mōt′) *adj.* Distant; slight.—**remotely** *adv.*

render (rĕn′dər) *v.* To express in one's own way.

renowned (rĭ-nound′) *adj.* Famous.

reparation (rĕp′ə-rā′shən) *n.* Something paid or given to make up for an injury or loss.

repast (rĭ-păst′, -päst′) *n.* A meal.

repertoire (rĕp′ər-twär, -tôr) *n.* The range of techniques or skills of a particular person or group.

replenish (rĭ-plĕn′ĭsh) *v.* To resupply with fuel or goods.

replica (rĕp′lĭ-kə) *n.* A copy or reproduction of something.

repose (rĭ-pōz′) *v.* To lie at rest.—*n.* Calmness.

reprimand (rĕp′rə-mănd′, -mänd′) *n.* A severe scolding.

reproach (rĭ-prōch′) *v.* To blame or criticize.

repugnance (rĭ-pŭg′nəns) *n.* A feeling of intense dislike.

reserve (rē-zûrv′) *n.* Self-restraint.

resiliency (rĭ-zĭl′yən-sē) *n.* The ability to return quickly to good health and spirits after an illness or tragedy.

resolute (rĕz′ə-lo͞ot′) *adj.* Determined.

resolve (rĭ-zŏlv′) *n.* Firm decision; determination.

resonant (rĕz′ə-nənt) *adj.* Having a full, rich sound.

resort (rĭ-zôrt′) *v.* To go often.

resources (rē′sôrs′əz, -zôrs′əz) *n. pl.* Available money or property.

restitution (rĕs'tə-too'shən, -tyoo'shən.) *n.* The making good or paying for damage or loss.

restive (rĕs'tĭv) *adj.* Nervous; restless.

restorative (rĭ-stôr'ə-tĭv, rĭ-stōr'-) *n.* Something that brings back life or strength.

retainer (rĭ-tā'nər) *n.* Someone in the service of another.

retort (rĭ-tôrt') *v.* To answer in a sharp, quick way. *n.* A counterargument.

retribution (rĕt'rə-byoo'shən) *n.* Something given or done as a repayment or reward.

retrieve (rĭ-trēv') *v.* **1.** To bring back. **2.** To regain.

rev (rĕv) *v.* *Informal.* To cause an engine or motor to go faster.

revel (rĕv'əl) *v.* To take great pleasure in.

revelation (rĕv'ə-lā'shən) *n.* The act of making something known.

revelry (rĕv'əl-rē) *n.* Very loud merrymaking.

reverberate (rĭ-vûr'bə-rāt') *v.* To make a loud, reechoing sound.

revere (rĭ-vîr') *v.* To regard with great respect and awe.

reverence (rĕv'ər-əns) *n.* Profound respect.

reverie (rĕv'ər-ē) *n.* A daydream.

revulsion (rĭ-vŭl'shən) *n.* A feeling of disgust.

rheum (room) *n.* A watery discharge from the eyes, mouth, or nose.

ricochet (rĭk'ə-shā', -shĕt') *v.* To skip off a surface after striking it at an angle.

righteous (rī'chəs) *adj.* Morally right; fair—**righteously** *adv.*—**righteousness** *n.*

rimy (rīm'ē) *adj.* Frosty.

rite (rīt) A religious or other formal ceremony.

ritual (rĭch'oo-əl) *n.* A set of actions regularly followed in performing a ceremony.

ritualistic (rĭch'oo-əl-ĭs'tĭk) *adj.* Ceremonial; following a set ritual.

rivet (rĭv'ĭt) *v.* To hold or fix (the attention of).

roan (rōn) *adj.* Reddish-brown.

roister (rois'tər) *v.* To behave in a lively and noisy way.

romp (rŏmp) *v.* To play in a carefree, lively way.

rowel (rou'əl) *n.* A small wheel with sharp teeth on the back of a spur.

ruddy (rŭd'ē) *adj.* Reddish.

rueful (roo'fəl) *adj.* **1.** Sorrowful; mournful. **2.** Showing regret.

ruminate (roo'mə-nāt) *v.* To think about something over and over again.

rumination (roo'mə-nā'shən) *n.* **1.** The chewing of cud. **2.** Lengthy thought.

rummage (rŭm'ĭj) *v.* To search through.

runnel (rŭn'əl) *n.* A little stream.

ruse (rooz) *n.* A trick.

S

saddlebow (săd'l-bō') *n.* The arched front part of a saddle.

sagacious (sə-gā'shəs) *adj.* Knowledgeable.

sage (sāj) *adj.* Wise.

sallow (săl'ō) *adj.* Having a sickly, pale-yellow color.

salvation (săl-vā'shən) *n.* **1.** A rescue from evil or danger. **2.** The person or thing that makes rescue possible **3.** Redemption.

samovar (săm'ə-vär', săm'ə-vär') *n.* A metal urn with a spigot, used in making tea.

sanctuary (săngk'choo-ĕr'ē) *n.* A sacred place.

sandalwood (săn'dəl-wood') *n.* A wood from an Asian tree, used for woodcarving and furniture.

satchel (săch'əl) *n.* A small suitcase or bag.

savor (sā'vər) *n.* A special taste or smell.

scamper (skăm'pər) *v.* To run quickly.

scion (sī'ən) *n.* Descendant.

sconce (skŏns) *n.* A wall bracket for candles or light.

scour (skour) *v.* To search through.

screech (skrēch) To scream in a high-pitched, harsh voice.

scruple (skroo'pəl) *n.* A feeling of uneasiness about doing things that one thinks are wrong.

scrutiny (skroot'n-ē) *n.* A close, careful inspection.

securities (sĭ-kyoor'ə-tēz) *n. pl.* Stocks and bonds.

sedate (sĭ-dāt') *adj.* Quiet; calm.—**sedately** *adv.*

seethe (sē*th*) *v.* To boil.

seminary (sĕm'ə-nĕr'e) *n.* A school where priests, ministers, or rabbis are trained.

sensuous (sĕn'shoo-əs) *adj.* Pleasing to the senses; pleasurable.

sentiment (sĕn'tə-mənt) *n.* The thought or feeling behind a statement or action.

Glossary

ă pat/ā pay/âr care/ä father/b bib/ch church/d deed/ĕ pet/ē be/f fife/g gag/h hat/hw which/ĭ pit/ī pie/îr pier/j judge/k kick/
l lid, needle/m mum/n no, sudden/ng thing/ŏ pot/ō toe/ô paw, for/oi noise/ou out/oo took/oo boot/p pop/r roar/s sauce/
sh ship, dish/t tight/th thin, path/*th* this, bathe/ŭ cut/ûr urge/v valve/w with/y yes/z zebra, size/zh vision/ə about, item, edible, gallop, circus/ä *Fr.* ami/œ *Fr.* feu, *Ger.* schön/ü *Fr.* tu, *Ger.* über/KH *Ger.* ich, *Scot.* loch/N *Fr.* bon.

sepulcher (sĕp′əl-kər) *n.* A burial chamber; tomb.

sequin (sē′kwĭn) *n.* A small, shiny metal disk sewn in fabric as decoration.

serene (sĭ-rēn′) *adj.* Calm.

serge (sûrj) *n.* A heavy, smooth fabric, usually of wool.

serpentine (sûr′pən-tēn′, -tīn′) *adj.* Winding.

serrated (sĕ′rā′tĭd) *adj.* Having sawlike edges or surfaces.

shackle (shăk′əl) *n.* A device used to prevent freedom of movement.—*v.* To restrict or confine as with chains or manacles.

shamble (shăm′bəl) *v.* To walk in an awkward, shuffling way.

sheer (shîr) *adj.* Very steep.

shipwright (shĭp′rīt′) *n.* A carpenter who builds or repairs ships.

shirk (shûrk) *v.* To put off or avoid doing something that should be done.—**shirker** *n.*

shrift (shrĭft) *n. Archaic.* Confession to a priest.

shroud (shroud) *n.* A burial cloth.

sibling (sĭb′lĭng) *n.* A brother or sister.

sinewy (sĭn′yoo-ē) *adj.* Muscular.

singular (sĭng′gyə-lər) *adj.* Extraordinary; strange. —**singularly** *adv.*

singularity (sĭng′gyə-lăr′ə-tē) *n.* Distinctness; individuality.

sinister (sĭn′ĭ-stər) *adj.* Appearing evil or wicked.

sinuosity (sĭn′yoo-ŏs′ə-tē) *n.* A winding and twisting in shape or movement.

skeptical (skĕp′tĭ-kəl) *adj.* Doubting; questioning.

slaughter (slô′tər) *v.* To kill violently.—*n.* Massacre.

slither (slĭth′ər) *v.* A sliding and gliding movement.

slouch (slouch) *v.* To walk, sit, or stand in a drooping way.

slumbrous (slŭm′brəs) *adj.* Causing one to be sleepy or relaxed.

smite (smīt) *v.* **1.** To afflict. **2.** To strike forcefully. —**smiter** *n.*

smithy (smĭth′ē, smĭ*th*′ē) *n.* A workshop where metal is heated and hammered into particular objects.

smolder (smōl′dər) *v.* To burn without flame.

sniper (snī′pər) *n.* A person who shoots at others from a hidden position.

solar (sō′lər) *adj.* Coming from the sun.

solemnity (sə-lĕm′nĭ-tē) *n.* Seriousness; gravity.

solemnize (sŏl′əm-nīz′) *v.* To perform a formal ceremony.

solicitous (sə-lĭs′ə-təs) *adj.* Showing concern.

solicitude (sə-lĭs′ə-tood′, tyood′) *n.* Concern.

solitary (sŏl′ə-tĕr′ē) *adj.* Alone.

solitude (sŏl′ə-tood, -tyood) *n.* **1.** Aloneness. **2.** A lonely out-of-the-way place.

sordid (sôr′dĭd) *adj.* Dirty.

spar (spär) *v.* To exchange words in argument; dispute.

spasmodic (spăz-mŏd′ĭk) *adj.* Characterized by irregular and excitable movements.

spectral (spĕc′trəl) *adj.* Ghostly.

speculation (spĕk′yə-lā′shən) *n.* A theory or conclusion based on guesswork.

spherical (sfîr′ĭ-kəl) *adj.* Round.

spinet (spĭn′ĭt) *n.* A small, upright piano.

spontaneous (spŏn-tā′nē-əs) *adj.* Happening so naturally that there appears to be no outside influence.—**spontaneously** *adv.*

sprint (sprĭnt) *v.* To run a short distance at top speed.

spruce (sproos) *adj.* Neat in appearance.

spume (spyoom) *n.* Foam or froth.—*v.* To foam or froth.

squat (skwŏt) *adj.* Thick; low and broad.

squeamish (skwē′mĭsh) *adj.* Oversensitive—**squeamishness** *n.*

squeegee (skwē′jē′) *n.* A T-shaped tool with a rubber blade used to wipe water from a surface.

squirt (skwûrt) *n. Informal.* A small or young person.

staccato (stə-kä′tō) *adj.* Made up of separate, short, distinct sounds.

stagnant (stăg′nənt) *adj.* Not moving.

stamina (stăm′ə-nə) *n.* The ability to resist fatigue, illness, or hardship.

stance (stăns) *n.* The standing posture of a person or animal.

staple (stā′pəl) *n.* A U-shaped piece of metal driven into a surface to keep a hook, bolt, or wiring in place.

stark (stärk) *adj.* Bleak; unadorned.

statistic (stə-tĭs′-tĭk) *n.* A numerical item of information about a specific subject.—**statistically** *adv.*

stave (stāv) *v.* To break or smash.

steep (stēp) *v.* To immerse; involve.

sterile (stĕr-əl, -īl) *adj.* Without vitality or imagination.

stipulation (stĭp′yə-lā′shən) *n.* An agreed-upon condition or term, as in a contract.

stockade (stŏk′ād′) *n.* A fort or enclosed area used for protection or imprisonment.

strait (strāt) *n.* A narrow waterway connecting two larger bodies of water.

strategy (străt′ə-jē) *n.* A plan of action or scheme to achieve a specific purpose.

strew (strōō) *v.* To cover by scattering.

suave (swäv, swāv) *adj.* Refined; sophisticated.

sublime (sə-blīm′) *adj.* Inspiring awe; impressive. —**sublimity** (sə-blĭm′ə-tē) *n.*

subordinate (sə-bôr′də-nĭt) *adj.* **1.** Of inferior rank or position. **2.** Under the control or authority of another.

subside (səb-sīd′) *v.* To become less active or intense.

suffice (sə-fīs′) *v.* To be enough.

suffuse (sə-fyōōz′) *v.* To spread through or fill.

sullen (sŭl′ən) *adj.* Gloomy; slow.—**sullenly** *adv.*

sultry (sŭl′trē) *adj.* Very hot.

sumptuous (sŭmp′chōō-əs) *adj.* Magnificent; having the appearance of being costly.

supercilious (sōō′pər-sĭl′ē-əs) *adj.* Haughty; scornful.—**superciliously** *adv.*

superscription (sōō′pər-skrĭp′shən) *n.* Something written above or outside another thing.

supple (sŭp′əl) *adj.* Able to move and bend easily.

suppliant (sŭp′lī-ənt) *n.* A beggar.

supplication (sŭp′lĭ-kā′-shən) *n.* A humble prayer or request.

surmise (sər-mīz′) *v.* To guess.

surmount (sər-mount′) *v.* To be at the top of.

surpassing (sər-păs′ĭng, -päs′ĭng) *adj.* Exceptional. —**surpassingly** *adv.*

sustain (sə-stān′) *v.* To support; encourage.

swagger (swăg′ər) *v.* To boast; brag.—**swaggering** *n.*

swarthy (swôr′thē) *adj.* Having a dark complexion.

swirl (swûrl) *v.* To move with a twisting motion.

symmetrical (sĭ-mĕt′rĭ-kəl) *adj.* **1.** Showing exact correspondence in shape, size, and arrangement of elements. **2.** Harmonious in arrangement.

synopsis (sĭ-nŏp′sĭs) *n.* A brief summary.

T

tactics (tăk′tĭks) *n. pl.* Skillful methods used to achieve a specific goal.

taint (tānt) *v.* To infect; spoil.

tally (tăl′ē) *v.* To count.

tamper (tăm′pər) *v.* To interfere with in order to damage.

tangible (tan′jə-bəl) *adj.* Capable of being touched or seen; real.

taper (tā′pər) *n.* A small candle.

taroc (tăr′ək) *n.* A card game.

tarp (tärp) *n.* Waterproof canvas, short for *tarpaulin.*

tawny (tô′nē) *adj.* Light brown.

tedious (tē′dē-əs) *adj.* Tiresome.

temper (tĕm′pər) *v.* To moderate; calm.

tempered (tĕm′pərd) *adj.* Having the proper degree of hardness or elasticity (metal).

tendril (tĕn′drəl) *n.* A long slender part of a climbing plant, used for clinging to some object.

tentative (tĕn′tə-tĭv) *adj.* Uncertain.—**tentatively** *adv.*

tepid (tĕp′ĭd) *adj.* Lukewarm.

termination (tûr′mə-nā′shən) *n.* The end of something.

terrain (tə-rān′, tĕ-) *n.* **1.** A particular stretch of land. **2.** Ground.

terrarium (tə-râr′ē-əm) *n.* A small container enclosing small plants or animals.

terse (tûrs) *adj.* Free of unnecessary words.

testy (tĕs′tē) *adj.* Touchy.—**testily** *adv.*

tether (tĕth′ər) *v.* To confine an animal to a certain area by tying or chaining it.

texture (tĕks′chər) *n.* Appearance.

theoretical (thē′ə-rĕt′ĭ-kəl) *adj.* Based on a general plan or idea.—**theoretically** *adv.*

thicket (thĭck′ĭt) *n.* A thick growth of small trees.

thong (thông, thŏng) *n.* A narrow strip of leather or other material used for tying.

thresh (thrĕsh) *v.* To beat grain out of its thick outside covering.

thrive (thrīv) *v.* To prosper.

throes (thrōz) *n. pl.* A condition of painful struggle.

throng (thrŏng) *n.* A very large group of people or things.

throttle (thrŏt′l) *n.* A device that controls the amount of fuel entering an engine.

thwart (thwôrt) *v.* To frustrate; defeat.

tidings (tī′dĭngz) *n. pl.* News.

tier (tîr) *n.* One of a series of rows or layers placed one on top of the other.

ă pat/ā pay/âr care/ä father/b bib/ch church/d deed/ĕ pet/ē be/f fife/g gag/h hat/hw which/ĭ pit/ī pie/îr pier/j judge/k kick/ l lid, needle/m mum/n no, sudden/ng thing/ŏ pot/ō toe/ô paw, for/oi noise/ou out/ŏŏ took/ōō boot/p pop/r roar/s sauce/ sh ship, dish/t tight/th thin, path/*th* this, bathe/ŭ cut/ûr urge/v valve/w with/y yes/z zebra, size/zh vision/ə about, item, edible, gallop, circus/à *Fr.* ami/œ *Fr.* feu, *Ger.* schön/ü *Fr.* tu, *Ger.* über/KH *Ger.* ich, *Scot.* loch/N *Fr.* bon.

timorous (tĭm′ər-əs) *adj.* Timid.—**timorously** *adv.*

titanic (tī-tăn′ĭk) *adj.* Huge.

tithe (tīth) *n.* **1.** A tax or contribution. **2.** One tenth or any small amount.

tortilleria (tôr′tē-yər-ē′ə) *n.* A shop which sells **tortillas** (tôr-tē′yəs), a kind of flat, unleavened bread baked on a griddle.

tout (tout) *v.* To praise highly; publicize.

traipse (trāps) *v. Informal.* To walk.

tranquil (trăn′kwəl) *adj.* Calm; motionless.

transgression (trăns-grĕsh′ən, trănz-) *n.* **1.** The breaking of a law. **2.** The act of going beyond certain limits.

translation (trăn-slăsh′ən, -zlăsh′ən) *n.* The passing from one condition or form to another.

translucent (trăns-loo′sənt, tranz-) *adj.* Clear enough to let light through.

travail (trə-vāl′, trăv′āl′) *n.* Agony.

traversed (trə-vûrsd′) *adj.* Crossed; traveled over.

treacherous (trĕch′ər-əs) *adj.* **1.** Unreliable; dangerous. **2.** Disloyal.

treachery (trĕch′ə-rē) *n.* Betrayal.

treble (trĕb′əl) *n.* A high-pitched voice.

trellis (trĕl′ĭs) *n.* A frame made of strips of wood crossing each other to form square or diamond patterns.

trespass (trĕs′pəs) *v.* **1.** To enter another's property or land without permission. **2.** To intrude upon another's privacy or time.

tributary (trĭb′yə-tĕr′ē) *n.* A stream flowing into a river.

trilogy (trĭl′ə-jē) *n.* A group of three works on a related theme.

tripe (trīp) *n.* The stomach lining of cattle, used as food.

trowel (trou′əl) *n.* A flat-bladed tool used for applying plaster.

truculence (trŭk′yə-ləns) *n.* Eagerness to fight.

truffle (trŭf′əl) *n.* A potato-shaped, edible, mushroomlike plant.

tucker (tŭk′ər) *v. Informal.* To tire.—*To tucker out.*

tumult (too′məlt, tyoo′-) *n.* **1.** Great noise and confusion. **2.** Emotional disturbance.

tumultous (tə-mŭl′choo-əs) *adj.* Confused and excited.

tundra (tŭn′drə) *n.* Treeless land in an arctic region.

turnkey (tûrn′kē) *n.* A person in charge of the keys in a jail.

tyro (tī′rō) *n.* A person with no experience in a particular field.

U

ulterior (ŭl′tîr′ē-ər) *adj.* Remote; beyond what is immediately evident.

uncanny (ŭn′kăn′ē) *adj.* Weird, mysterious.

uncouth (ŭn′kooth′) *adj.* **1.** Crude. **2.** Clumsy.

undulation (un′joo-lā′shən, ŭn′dyə-, ŭn′də-) *n.* **1.** A wavy shape. **2.** Rising and falling with regularity, like waves.

unflagging (ŭn-flăg′ĭng) *adj.* Not weakening.

uniform (yoo′nə-fôrm′) *adj.* Unchanging; consistent.—**uniformly** *adv.*

uninhibited (ŭn′ĭn-hĭb′ə-tĭd) *adj.* Unrestrained.—**uninhibitedly** *adv.*

unobstructed (ŭn′əb-strŭkt′əd) *adj.* Unhindered.

unobtrusive (ŭn′əb-troo′sĭv) *adj.* Unnoticeable.—**unobtrusively** *adv.*

unorthodox (ŭn-ôr′thə-dŏks′) *adj.* Unconventional; breaking tradition.

unparalleled (ŭn′păr′ə-lĕld′) *adj.* Unequaled.

unsavory (ŭn′sā′və-rē) *adj.* Offensive; disagreeable.

unscathed (ŭn′skāthd′) *adj.* Unharmed.

unscrupulous (ŭn′skroo′pyə-ləs) *adj.* Not caring about what is right or wrong.

urbane (ûr′bān′) *adj.* Polite; refined.

usurp (yoo-sûrp′, -zûrp′) *v.* To seize power or possessions illegally.—**usurper** *n.*

V

vagabond (văg′ə-bŏnd′) *n.* A wanderer.

vague (vāg) *adj.* Unclear in thought or expression.

valedictory (văl′ə-dĭk′tə-rē) *adj.* Pertaining to a parting or farewell.

valiant (văl′yənt) *adj.* Brave.

valor (văl′ər) *n.* Bravery.

variable (vâr′ē-ə-bəl) *adj.* Changeable.

varmint (vär′mənt) *n.* A troublesome person or animal.

vault (vôlt) *v.* To leap.—*n.* **1.** An underground room or cave with an arched ceiling. **2.** A burial chamber.

veery (vîr′ē) *n.* A reddish-brown thrush.

vehement (vē′ə-mənt) *adj.* Expressing intense emotion.—**vehemently** *adv.*

vendor (vĕn′dər) *n.* A person who sells.

venerable (vĕn′ər-ə-bəl) *adj.* Deserving respect because of age and dignity.

vengeance (vĕn′jəns) *n.* The act of punishing another (or desire to do so) in return for an injury or wrong.

venison (vĕn′ə-sən, -zən) *n.* Flesh of deer.

venture (vĕn′chər) *v.* To risk; undertake.

verdict (vûr-dĭkt) *n.* A decision.

verily (vĕr′ə-lē) *adv. Archaic.* Truly.

veritable (vĕr′ə-tə-bəl) *adj.* Actual; true.—**veritably** *adv.*

vermilion (vər-mĭl′yən) *n.* Bright red.

versatile (vûr′sə-təl) *adj.* Having many uses or serving many purposes.

vertical (vûr′tĭ-kəl) *adj.* Going straight up and down.

vestibule (vĕs′tə-byool′) *n.* A small entrance room.

vex (vĕks) *v.* To irritate.

vexation (vĕk-sā′shən) *n.* Annoyance.

vial (vī′əl) *n.* A small bottle for liquids.

vicarious (vī-kâr′ē-əs, vĭ-) *adj.* Experienced through imagined sharing in another's activities.—**vicariously** *adv.*

vicious (vĭsh′əs) *adj.* Evil; dangerous.

victual (vĭt′l) *n.* Food.

vile (vīl) *adj.* Disgusting.

vintage (vĭn′tĭj) *n.* Wine of a particular year and place.

virtually (vûr′choo-ə-lē) *adv.* Practically; nearly.

virtuous (vûr′choo-əs) *adj.* Righteous; moral.

vista (vĭs′tə) *n.* A view.

vizier (vĭ-zîr′, vĭz′yər) *n.* A high officer in the government of a Moslem country.

void (void) *adj.* Empty.

vulnerable (vŭl′nər-ə-bəl) *adj.* Open to attack; susceptible.

W

waddle (wŏd′l) *v.* To walk with short steps that cause the body to sway from side to side.

waft (wăft, wäft) *v.* To carry gently through the air.

wainscot (wān′skət, -skăt′) *v.* To line a room or a wall with fabric or wood paneling.

waive (wāv) *v.* To put off for another time.

wane (wān) *n.* A gradual dimming or lessening.

wanton (wŏn′tən) *adj.* Unrestrained.

warrant (wôr′ənt, wŏr′-) *n.* An official order authorizing an arrest, search, or seizure.

waver (wā′vər) *v.* To be unsure or unsteady.

wheedle (hwēd′l) *v.* To coax and flatter to get something.

whelm (hwĕlm) *v.* To plunge in water.

whet (hwĕt) *v.* To stimulate. Also **whetten.**

whey (hwā) *n.* The watery part of milk that remains after cheese has been made from it.

whimper (hwĭm′pər) *v.* To cry and sob quietly.

wicket (wĭk′ĭt) *n.* A small gate.

wily (wī′lē) *adj.* Tricky; sly.

wizened (wĭz′ənd) *adj.* Wrinkled; dried up.

wreak (rēk) *v.* **1.** To cause harm to. **2.** To express rage or hostility.

Z

zealous (zĕl′əs) *adj.* Enthusiastically devoted to a particular interest.

zenith (zē′nĭth) *n.* The highest point in the heavens.

ă pat/ā pay/âr care/ä father/b bib/ch church/d deed/ĕ pet/ē be/f fife/g gag/h hat/hw which/ĭ pit/ī pie/îr pier/j judge/k kick/ l lid, needle/m mum/n no, sudden/ng thing/ŏ pot/ō toe/ô paw, for/oi noise/ou out/oo took/oo boot/p pop/r roar/s sauce/ sh ship, dish/t tight/th thin, path/*th* this, bathe/ŭ cut/ûr urge/v valve/w with/y yes/z zebra, size/zh vision/ə about, item, edible, gallop, circus/à *Fr.* ami/œ *Fr.* feu, *Ger.* schön/ü *Fr.* tu, *Ger.* über/KH *Ger.* ich, *Scot.* loch/N *Fr.* bon.

Outline OF *Concepts* AND *Skills*

Page numbers in italics refer to entries in Literary Terms and Techniques.

Outline of Concepts and Skills (side text)

Outline of Concepts and Skills

Outline of Concepts and Skills

Index of *Titles* by *Themes*

Index OF Fine Art AND Illustrations

Photo Credits

Abbreviations: AR—Art Resource, Inc.; BA—The Bettmann Archive; BCI—Bruce Coleman, Inc.; BS—Black Star; CP—Culver Pictures, Inc.; GC—The Granger Collection, New York; HAR—H. Armstrong Roberts; MOMA—Museum of Modern Art; MP—Magnum Photos, Inc.; NPG—National Portrait Gallery, London; NYPL—New York Public Libraries; PR—Photo Researchers, Inc; SM—The Stock Market; TIB—The Image Bank; TSI—Tony Stone Images; WW—AP/Wide World Photos.

Title page and back cover, William S. Nawrocki/Nawrocki Stock Photos; Page vi, Tom Bean/SM; vii, Private Collection, Oklahoma City, courtesy of Gerald P. Peters, Santa Fe, New Mexico; viii, CP; x, James Carmichael/BCI; xiii, Academy of Science, Bologna, Italy/AR; xiv, Museum of Modern Arts, Film Stills Archive; 2, HRW photo by Sam Dudgeon; 5, NASA, Lyndon B. Johnson Space Center; 6, Scala/AR; 16, 23, 26, Film Still Archive/MOMA; 38, CP; 45, Robert Lebeck/BS;

Photo Credits

Index OF *Authors* AND *Titles*

The page numbers in italics indicate where a brief biography of the author is located.